BUSINESS ETHICS

Readings and Cases in Corporate Morality

THIRD EDITION

W. Michael Hoffman
Bentley College
Center for Business Ethics

Robert E. Frederick
Bentley College
Center for Business Ethics

McGraw-Hill, Inc.

New York St. Louis San Francisco Auckland Bogotá
Caracas Lisbon London Madrid Mexico City Milan Montreal
New Delhi San Juan Singapore Sydney Tokyo Toronto

This book was set in Times Roman by ComCom, Inc.
The editors were Judith R. Cornwell, Cynthia Ward, and Tom Holton;
the production supervisor was Denise L. Puryear.
The cover was designed by Jo Jones.
R. R. Donnelley & Sons Company was printer and binder.

BUSINESS ETHICS
Readings and Cases in Corporate Morality

This book is printed on acid-free paper.

4 5 6 7 8 9 0 DOC/DOC 9 9 8 7 6

ISBN 0-07-029349-X

Library of Congress Cataloging-in-Publication Data

Business ethics: readings and cases in corporate morality / [edited by] W. Michael Hoffman, Robert E. Frederick.—3d ed.
p. cm.
Previous editions edited by W. Michael Hoffman and Jennifer Mills Moore.
Includes bibliographical references (p.).
ISBN 0-07-029349-X
1. Business ethics. 2. Business ethics—Case studies.
I. Hoffman, W. Michael. II. Frederick, Robert.
HF5387.B873 1995
174'.4—dc20 94-31960

ABOUT THE AUTHORS

W. MICHAEL HOFFMAN is the founding director of the Center for Business Ethics at Bentley College in Waltham, Massachusetts, a research and consulting institute and educational forum for the exchange of ideas and information in business ethics. Dr. Hoffman received his Ph.D. in philosophy at the University of Massachusetts in 1972 and is professor of philosophy at Bentley College. Dr. Hoffman has authored or edited thirteen books and has published over forty articles in professional and scholarly journals. Dr. Hoffman also serves as a consultant on business ethics for corporations and institutions of higher learning and as an expert witness on business ethics for law firms. He is a past National Endowment for the Humanities Fellow and Consultant, a lecturer at universities and conferences, and he sits on the boards of editors of several journals, including the *Journal of Business Ethics* and *Business Ethics Quarterly.*

ROBERT E. FREDERICK is associate professor and chair of the department of philosophy at Bentley College and research scholar at the Center for Business Ethics. In the past he served as assistant director of the Center. Dr. Frederick received his Ph.D. in philosophy from Brown University. He has published articles in business and environmental ethics and in other fields of philosophy.

In addition to this anthology, Professors Hoffman and Frederick have jointly co-authored articles in business ethics and have co-consulted on business ethics for various corporations.

CONTENTS

PREFACE

The preface to the first edition of *Business Ethics: Readings and Cases in Corporate Morality* began with advice from Cicero's *De Officiis:* "To everyone who proposes to have a good career, moral philosophy is indispensable." Cicero's words are as true and as timely as ever, and the third edition of this text represents our continuing commitment to the union of ethics and business.

The field of business ethics has grown tremendously since 1984, when the first edition was released. At that time, business ethics had just begun to gain momentum. Today it is a mature field. In a 1988 report, the Business Roundtable referred to corporate ethics as "a prime business asset," and corporations have begun to take significant steps toward integrating ethical values into their corporate cultures. In fact, the Center for Business Ethics at Bentley College, where we teach, is now the facilitating institution for a newly formed organization made up of practicing ethics officers of major corporations. The American Assembly of Collegiate Schools of Business has strengthened its call for grounding in ethics as one of the essential elements of sound business education. Literature in business ethics continues to grow and deepen.

In the third edition of *Business Ethics,* we have attempted to include both the best new thinking on ethical issues in business and the first and second edition's time-tested favorites. The goals of the text remain the same. We have tried to be comprehensive. In our coverage of the issues, we have selected what we believe to be the most important currently debated moral concerns in the field. We have retained many of the topics from the second edition and have added new material on issues such as sexual harassment and diversity in the workplace. The sections on ethics and business decision making, the environment, and international business have been extensively revised, and the final section on the moral corporation is entirely new. The case material has also been dramatically updated. Many cases from the second edition remain, but we have included timely new cases such as those on AIDS, executive pay, and pollution on the Rio Grande.

As with the first and second editions, we have tried to be impartial. The format of the text, for the most part, is point/counterpoint, and we have included the strongest statements we could find of different perspectives on the issues. We have made an effort to include articles by thinkers from a wide range of constituencies—not just academics, but representatives from a variety of other professions.

Finally, we have tried to be systematic. We have retained the basic organization of the first and second editions. We begin with theoretical, structural, or more widely focused issues such as economic justice, the justice of economic systems, and the nature and responsibility of business. These give a framework for discussion and understanding of more specific, concrete issues, such as employee rights, the ethics of marketing and production, environmental ethics, and multinational issues. We conclude with a chapter on the development of the moral corporation of the future. Of course, the book may be used in many different ways. Some instructors may prefer to save the more abstract topics for the end of their course. We believe that the book lends itself readily to organizational variations.

In addition to having an expanded general introduction on ethical theory, the third edition continues to include an introduction to each part that sets out the major themes of the articles and cases and places them in context. An updated general bibliography can be found at the end of the text, and a set of questions follow each chapter. These can be used as a focus for student discussion, for review, or for tests, quizzes, or student assignments.

We very much regret that Jennifer Moore was unable to participate in preparing this edition of *Business Ethics.* We hope that she will join us in future editions.

We would like to express our appreciation to Bentley College for its support of this and other projects in business ethics. We give special thanks to Josephine Letton, Dr. Hoffman's mother, who proofread the entire text with the care and thoroughness that characterized her career as one of the best school teachers in Paris, Kentucky. Thanks also go to Mary Chiasson, executive secretary of the Center for Business Ethics, and Sheryl Morrissette of the Center, for their help in preparing the manuscript and for their tireless efforts in obtaining permissions for the articles, especially from the more recalcitrant holders of copyrights. Thanks also to Sally Lydon, administrative secretary of the department of philosophy, for help with the manuscript and her uncanny ability to track down wayward authors.

Finally, we are grateful to the following scholars for their reviews of earlier versions of this book: William C. Gentry, Henderson State University; Charles T. Hughes, Chapman University; William L. Langenfus, John Carroll University; Christopher P. Mooney, Nassau Community College; Jon W. Nelson, University of Nebraska at Kearney; and Richard Srb, Middlesex Community Technical College.

W. Michael Hoffman
Robert E. Frederick

INTRODUCTION

THE NATURE OF BUSINESS ETHICS

Business is a complex web of human relationships—relationships between manufacturers and consumers, employers and employees, managers and stockholders, members of corporations and members of communities in which those corporations operate. These are economic relationships, created by the exchange of goods and services. But they are also *moral* relationships. Questions concerning profit, growth, and technological advance have ethical dimensions. These include the effects of pollution and depletion of natural resources on society at large, the quality and character of the work environment, and the safety of consumers. As an anthology in business ethics, this text proposes to explore the moral dimension of business.

Ethics may be defined as the study of what is good or right for human beings. It asks what goals people ought to pursue and what actions they ought to perform. Business ethics is a branch of applied ethics; it studies the relationship of what is good and right for business.[1]

It is sometimes said that business and ethics do not mix. In business, some argue, profit takes precedence. Business has its own rules and objectives, and ethical concepts, standards, and judgments are inappropriate in the context of business. But this view is fundamentally mistaken. Business is an economic institution, but like our economy as a whole, it has a moral foundation. The free market system reflects our convictions about the nature of the good life and the good society, about the fair distribution of goods and services, and about what kinds of goods and services to distribute. It is true that the goal of business has been profit, but profit making is not a morally neutral activity. Traditionally, we have encouraged business to pursue profits because we believed, rightly or wrongly, that profit seeking violates no rights and is best for society as a whole. This conviction has been the source of business' legitimacy, our belief in its right to exist. In the past two decades, however, the belief that business makes an entirely positive contribution to the general welfare has been challenged. For many, the connection of business to the moral foundation that justified it no longer seems clear. Mistrust of business has increased; recent polls, for example, indicate that Americans believe that the ethical standards of business are lower than those of society as a whole. Many thinkers contend that business faces a crisis of legitimacy. In such a climate, an investigation of business values, of the moral dimension of business, and of the role of business in society becomes urgent. To undertake such an investigation is the task of business ethics. This anthology approaches this task on four levels:

1. An ethical investigation of the context in which American business is conducted—that is, capitalism or the free market system. Does the system truly contribute to a good society and reflect our most important social values? In particular, is it a just system, one that reflects our beliefs about the fair distribution of goods and services? The selections included in Part One of this text explore the meaning of justice in a modern economy and the question of whether capitalism embodies that ideal. It also suggests some specific ways in which ethical values have operated or should operate in business decision making.
2. An inquiry, within this broad economic context, into the nature and role of business organizations. Is the function of business activity simply to make a profit? Do businesses have other obligations because of their vast power or relationship to other elements of society? How might corporate structures best reflect the nature and responsibilities of corporations? Such questions are taken up in Part Two of this text.
3. An examination of particular ethical issues that arise in the course of business activity, such as employee rights and duties, relationships in working life, hiring practices, advertising and product safety, obligations to the environment, and operating in foreign countries. A range of such issues is covered in Parts Three and Four.
4. An examination and ethical assessment of the values that reside implicitly in business organizations and business activity in general, such as freedom of opportunity, economic growth, and material well-being. We pursue this endeavor throughout the text, and in Part Five we examine the development of the corporate ethos and reflect on the future of the moral corporation.

Engaging in ethical reflection on business at each of these levels requires using ethical concepts, theories, and standards of judgment. The remainder of this introduction presents some of the most important principles of ethical theory. To provide a context for discussion of these principles, we begin with an example of the kind of ethical decision individuals sometimes face in business.

TYPES OF BUSINESS DECISIONS

The Amalgamated Machinery Dilemma

Ted Brown is worried. A salesman for Amalgamated Machinery, he is in charge of negotiating an important sale of construction equipment to the government of a small but rapidly developing nation. Deeply in debt, Amalgamated has staked its future on penetrating foreign markets. Ted's potential contract not only is a very large one, but it could open the door to even bigger sales in the future. If he lands the contract, Ted's future in the firm is bright, and he was convinced he would get the contract until he spoke with a powerful government official who is involved in the negotiations. Ted's bid, the official explained, is regarded very favorably. In fact, it is the lowest. All that is needed to clinch the deal is a $100,000 "commission fee" payable in cash to the official. If Ted does not pay the fee, the official regrets that the contract will go to a competitor.

Ted knows that the sale is crucial for his company. He believes that his customers would get the best possible deal by buying Amalgamated's equipment. And he knows that $100,000 is a relatively small sum compared with the potential profits represented by the contract. Yet, although he is aware that such payments are not unusual in many countries, he has always felt that they are wrong and has never before used them to secure a deal.

Ted Brown's dilemma is fictitious, but it is not farfetched. It illustrates a problem businesspeople often face: Should the interests of the firm override personal convictions about the right thing to do, or should one always act on one's personal convictions despite the consequences for the firm? Clearly, Ted's decision will not be easy. How should he go about deciding what to do? If Ted were to ask you for advice, what would you say?

One thing you might point out is that Ted needs to understand the kind of decision he is making. Although he can do only one of two things—either pay the $100,000 or not—he can formulate his decision from at least three distinct points of view:

1. Which is the better decision from a *business* point of view?
2. Which is the better decision from a *legal* point of view?
3. Which is the better decision from a *moral* point of view?

A second point is that in most cases, when someone decides to do something that he or she regards as important, the decision to act comes at the end of a process of deliberation. And to deliberate about an action is roughly to weigh the reasons for doing it according to some standard or principle. Such standards or principles have two important features. First, they are supposed to apply to all decisions of a certain kind regardless of who makes the decision. Second, they purport to differentiate between better and worse decisions of that kind. For example, if Ted were to decide from a business point of view, he would weigh the reasons for paying or not paying according to a principle that differentiates between better and worse business decisions. Often that principle is assumed to be this: In every business undertaking, one ought to do whatever maximizes long-term profits. So if Ted believes that the decision should be made from a business point of view, and if he were to judge that paying the bribe would maximize long-term profits, he would pay up.

Suppose, however, Ted believes that the decision should be made from a legal point of view. Now the principle might be this: For any action to which the law applies, one ought not do that act if it is illegal. As anyone familiar with the law knows, determining whether a specific act is legal or not can be difficult. But assume Ted decides that it is illegal to make the payment. Then the principle instructs him not to pay. On the other hand, suppose he decides it is legal. Should he pay? Not necessarily. The standard only says, "If something is illegal, don't do it." It doesn't say, "If it is legal, do it." So, in a sense, the legal principle is incomplete. Once Ted decides that the act is legal, it has nothing further to tell him about what is best to do.

The third way that Ted could make his decision—the one we are most concerned with in this introduction—is from a moral point of view. What is it to decide from a moral point of view? If we follow the model just presented, it is to evaluate the reasons, to deliberate, about doing one thing rather than another according to some moral standard or principle that differentiates between better and worse moral decisions. So to decide from a moral point of view we need, first, to know what kind of moral principles there are; second, what kind of reasons are relevant to moral action; and third, how to evaluate those reasons in light of the principle. For example, suppose the moral principle Ted accepts is this: One always ought to do what is in one's own self-interest. Then he would consider the reasons for believing that paying the bribe, or not paying, is in his best interest. Suppose, for example, that after analyzing the business aspects of paying the bribe, he finds that paying would maximize profit. This could be to his advantage because a firm that places a high value on profit is also likely to place high value on employees who contribute to profit. However, if the bribe is illegal, and if it is discovered that Ted paid the bribe, he would be in trouble. The authorities would probably impose a heavy fine on the firm, and this would not endear Ted to upper management. Furthermore, Ted might face legal sanctions himself. It seems, then, that if Ted wants to do what is in his own best interest, he has a lot of thinking to do. Making the correct decision from a moral point of view will not be easy.

In fact, it is characteristic of moral decisions that they are not easy. There are three main reasons for this. First, much more often than not, moral decisions are important. They affect our lives and the lives of others in significant ways. Second, moral decisions are complex. Frequently, no obvious or easy solution presents itself, and it is not unusual for there to be several alternatives that seem equally reasonable. Finally, there is often deep disagreement about which moral principle should be applied to the decision. Different people may have very different ideas about which standard is appropriate. To take a slightly modified famous example, suppose Paul faces the problem of either leaving home and joining the forces defending his country from invasion by an evil empire, or staying home and comforting his mother through the last stages of a debilitating and fatal illness. Should he go or stay?

Suppose Paul accepts Ted's moral standard: One always ought to do what is in one's own self-interest. And suppose Paul decides that it is in his self-interest, all things considered, to avoid the problem altogether. So he decides to relieve his mother of what small savings she has accumulated and purchase a ticket on the next plane leaving for a more peaceful and prosperous kingdom. Surely, he reasons, this would be better for him than risking his life in a war or dawdling about waiting for an old woman to die.

Most people would probably be outraged by Paul's decision. Some might argue that he has duties to his mother that override his self-interest. Others might say that he should promote the common good of his fellow citizens by defending his homeland. And still others would say that his decision shows character flaws such as cowardice and ingratitude. Each of these responses makes implicit appeal to a different ethical viewpoint—a different way of understanding what Paul ought to do. In the pages to come, we will discuss each of these viewpoints. But before we do so, we will return briefly to the three different ways that Ted can understand his decision.

THE PROBLEM OF CONFLICTING DECISION-MAKING RULES

We said that Ted can understand his decision from a business, legal, or ethical point of view. The question naturally arises: Which should he choose? The question would not be hard to answer were there never any possibility of conflict between them—that is, if the best business decision were always the best legal and ethical decision. But there is a possibility of conflict. For example, it might maximize profits to pay the bribe even if it is illegal and immoral. And bribery might be immoral even if not illegal. So the best thing to do from a moral point of view need not be the best thing to do from a business or legal point of view. On the other hand, conflict is not always present. In many cases—perhaps in most cases—the best business decision will also be legally and morally acceptable. But when conflict is present, we need some way to decide what to do.

Consider the following rules:

1. Whenever there is a conflict between ethics and the law, one should always do what the law requires.
2. Whenever there is a conflict between ethics and business principles, one should always do what business principles require.

These rules tell us what to do in situations in which ethical and legal or business principles give different instructions. Thus they resolve cases of conflict between ethics and law, and ethics and business. But should we follow them? Might there be circumstances in which it would be wrong to follow them?

There are many examples that seem to show that ethical obligations can outweigh legal obligations, and that in certain circumstances it is morally permissible to break the law. For instance, in the American civil rights movement laws were deliberately broken when it appeared that no other alternative was available to change an intolerable situation. These laws, such as the laws preventing blacks from voting, were clearly unjust. They perpetuated and enforced social arrangements that were deliberately intended to deprive blacks and other minorities of the opportunity to participate meaningfully in the economic, educational, and political system. Since many legislatures were controlled by persons unwilling to change the laws, civil disobedience was, in our view, both justified and necessary.

Two things follow from this example. First, in some circumstances, breaking the law is justified. Such circumstances may be rare, but they do occur. Second, the justification for such acts derives from ethical principles, such as principles of justice. Thus rule number 1 is not acceptable as a general rule for resolving conflicts between the law and ethics. Sometimes we ought to follow ethical principles even though what we do is against the law.

There are also many cases, a number of them in this book, that show that ethical principles sometimes take precedence over the business principle of maximizing profit. For instance, suppose a paper company were to move to a country that has few laws protecting the environment. To minimize costs, and thus enhance profits, the company legally dumps the toxic waste it produces into a nearby river. Eventually this causes health problems for the local inhabitants. The company's actions may be both legal and warranted by considerations of profit. In our view, however, they are ethically unacceptable. Corporate profit does not justify causing harm to persons, particularly when such harm is both foreseeable and preventable.

If this is correct, then profit maximization in business is not always justified. And on occasion, the justification for not doing so derives from ethical principles, such as the principle that one should not cause preventable harm. Thus, rule number 2 is not acceptable as a general principle for resolving conflicts between ethical and business principles. Sometimes we should follow ethical principles even when profit suffers.

The above examples show that legal and business principles do not always take precedence over ethical principles. But the examples do not show that ethics always comes first. That is, they do not show that

3. Whenever there is a conflict between ethical principles and business or legal principles, one should always do what ethical principles require.

Should we accept rule number 3? If someone were to do so, then for that person obeying the law and maximizing profits would always be secondary to ethics. As we will see, many philosophers have defended ethical principles that imply rule number 3 or something very close to it. The content of these principles, and the arguments for them, is our next topic.

ETHICAL SUBJECTIVISM

Understanding Subjectivism

Ethical subjectivism is a viewpoint that is sometimes expressed as "what is right for me may not be right for you." This statement is open to various interpretations. For instance, it could mean: Given our different circumstances, it would be morally right for me to do X, but it would not be morally right for you to do X. Suppose, for example, that Smith is very wealthy and Brown is very poor. Then it might be morally right for Smith annually to donate a considerable sum to charity, but wrong for Brown to do so because it would deprive her children of basic necessities. Understood this way, the statement highlights an important truth—namely, that the morally correct decision often depends on the circumstances of the person making it. If the circumstances of different persons are very different, then the right decision for them may be different, even though they accept the same moral standards.

The statement might also mean: What I think is right may not be what you think is right. Once again this expresses a truth, for, as the debate over abortion abundantly shows, there are many disagreements about what is ethically right.

Neither interpretation mentioned so far is objectionable. But there is a third interpretation that is much more controversial. It is this: The correct ethical principle for me may not be the correct ethical principle for you. Unlike the other two interpretations, this one is not obviously true. One reason it is not true, many people would argue, is that ethical principles such as "Do unto others as you would have them do unto you" apply to everyone. Whether all ethical principles apply to everyone is a difficult issue that we will discuss briefly later. However, we will try to show that subjectivism is not an acceptable account of ethics even if ethical principles do not apply universally. To explain why, we must examine it in more detail. We begin with a basic statement of the subjectivist position:

> Ethical Subjectivism: What is ethically right or wrong is strictly a matter for individuals to decide based on ethical principles they have chosen. This is because (1) each individual is the sole judge of whether the principle he or she has chosen is the right one for him or her, and (2) each individual is the sole judge of whether his or her action is ethically permissible according to his or her principle.

If ethical subjectivism is true, then what is ethically right or wrong is entirely a personal matter. Each person is the single source and only authority concerning the selection and applicability of his or her own moral standards. There are no valid public standards of moral accountability, no standards that apply to more than one person except insofar as different people choose the same principle by chance. For example, suppose Green and Robinson are thinking about whether some action X is morally permissible. Based on standards he has chosen, Green decides it is permissible and does X. Based on standards she has chosen, Robinson decides X is not morally permissible and does not do it. If Robinson accepts the argument given above, she is in no position to say to Green, "What you did is ethically wrong." Since she acknowledges that each person is sovereign in his or her choice of ethical principles, and that each person is the exclusive judge of whether his or her action conforms to the principle, the best she can do is say, "What you did is wrong according to my standards." But this is simply a statement of fact. It makes no moral evaluation of Green's action.

Subjectivism has great appeal in our diverse society where all persons are expected to think seriously about ethical issues and to come to their own conclusions. Furthermore, within limits, they have a right to express and to act on those conclusions. We expect that even when citizens very seriously disagree with each other, each will treat the other with respect. Ethical subjectivism seems to capture this attitude of tolerance and respect for diversity.

First Objection to Subjectivism

An objection to ethical subjectivism is that it has unacceptable consequences. For example, in the Smith and Brown example given above, it was said to be ethically permissible for Smith to give a large sum to charity, but not ethically permissible for Brown because it would deprive her children of basic necessities. This judgment rests on the ethical standard "It is wrong for parents voluntarily to deprive their children of basic necessities." But suppose Brown is an ethical subjectivist and that she accepts quite a different standard, one such as "I should give to charity regardless of how it affects the welfare of my relations." Then, from her point of view, it would be ethically right for her to give to charity; indeed, it would be wrong of her to choose not to give on the grounds that her children would suffer.

One would think that Brown should have moral commitments to the welfare of her children that place reasonable restrictions on her choice of other ethical principles. She should accept principles that confirm those commitments and reject those that ignore them. However, since Brown is an ethical subjectivist, there are in principle no constraints on her choice of ethical principles other than the ones she accepts. If she chooses principles compatible with the welfare of her children, well and good. If not, then, if one is an ethical subjectivist, there is no moral reason to complain of her choice.

The main point of the Brown example is this: Ethical subjectivism places no limitations on the *content* of the principles individuals choose. It is consistent with subjectivism that individuals choose principles that allow behavior detrimental to the interests and welfare of people, that ignore their rights, and that abjure personal responsibility. So Brown can choose to ignore the welfare of her children, or accept other principles such as "It is permissible for me to lie when I want to" and violate no stricture of ethical subjectivism. In short, as far as subjectivism is concerned, *any* behavior by an individual is ethically permissible as long as the behavior is permitted by a principle that individual has chosen.

But this cannot be correct. It is an unacceptable consequence of subjectivism that it places no restrictions on the kind of ethical principle an individual might select. Principles of the sort mentioned above, that is—ones that permit harm to others—are not ethical principles; rather, they are antiethical principles. They are the antithesis of ethics. It may be true that the ethical principles a person lives by are ultimately chosen by that individual, but it does not follow from this that any principle an individual might choose is rendered ethically acceptable by the mere fact that it was chosen. Persons can choose principles of evil as well as good. Since ethical subjectivism does not distinguish between such choices, it is not an acceptable account of ethics.

Second Objection to Subjectivism

Suppose a subjectivist were to respond to our argument as follows: You may be right that choosing evil principles is compatible with subjectivism, but that has nothing to do with me. My principles are good, not evil, so your argument is not relevant to the choices I have made. I have no qualms about being a subjectivist. It is people who have chosen evil principles that you need to worry about.

This response points to a second and equally important reason to reject subjectivism. To see what it is, suppose we were to ask Brown why she follows a principle that obligates her to give to charity at the expense of her children's welfare. She could give one of two answers. The first is that the choice was arbitrary. There is no reason why she chose that principle instead of another one.

Since Brown chooses arbitrarily, she cannot claim that she chooses the principle because it is good, for that is to give a reason for choosing. Moreover, it is not clear she can claim that the principle she chooses just happens to be good, for to say something is good usually implies there is reason to choose it. But most important for our purposes is to see that Brown's choice is not rational in any ordinary sense. It is rational to take the interests and welfare of oneself and others as reason for choosing one thing rather than another. It is irrational to ignore or belittle such interests. But that is exactly what Brown does. She chooses her ethical principles arbitrarily, with no regard for how the choice will affect her interests or the interests of others. Surely that is irrational, if anything is.

Brown might reply that *of course* the choice was not made arbitrarily. It was based on reasons, which is the second of the two possible answers mentioned above. And the reasons cannot be arbitrary. Otherwise, the same kind of problem would occur. They must be good reasons. But what is a good reason?

A complete answer would take us far beyond the bounds of this introduction. At least we know, however, that a good reason is not an arbitrary reason. So it would help if we knew more about the difference between good reasons and arbitrary reasons. Let us try this. The mark of a good reason—one that is not arbitrary—is that it withstands scrutiny and criticism by other reasonable people. Put another way, the goodness, so to speak, of a good reason is public in the sense that it is open to inspection and evaluation by more than one person. Thus, if a subjectivist claims she has good reasons for choosing an ethical principle, those reasons are available for other people to judge. If they judge that the reasons offered are not good, then a subjectivist can do one of three things. First, she might try to convince people that the reasons are good after all. Second, she might try to find different reasons that support her choice and are judged good. Finally, she might abandon her choice of ethical principles. What she cannot do, and still maintain that her choice is based on good reasons, is refuse to defend or modify her position. Were she to do so, she would be selecting her principles arbitrarily, which is something she is committed not to do.

Is engaging in a public process of evaluating reasons for choosing ethical standards compatible with ethical subjectivism? The answer is clearly no. For subjectivists the choice of ethical standards is supposed to be entirely personal. No person, other than the one making the choice, has any legitimate say in the matter. But subjectivists are committed to having good reasons for their choice. Since what counts as a good reason is a public matter, other people have a role in judging the worth of reasons. If the reasons offered are not good, subjectivists cannot refuse to modify their position without violating their own intellectual commitments. Hence, the choice is not entirely private. Other people are involved in the process.

This is the second problem with subjectivism. It is unacceptable because it is inconsistent. On the one hand, subjectivists claim that the choice of ethical standards is completely personal. On the other, if they claim that their choice of principles is based on good reasons, they acknowledge that other people have a role to play in the choice. They cannot have it both ways—at least, not if they claim that subjectivism is a rational ethical viewpoint.

There are two ways that subjectivists could try to avoid this conclusion. The first is to say that the choice of principles is arbitrary and not based on good reasons. But, as we argued earlier, this position is also irrational. The second is to provide a plausible account of good reasons that does not make the reasons for choosing ethical principles open to public evaluation. No subjectivist has attempted this, nor, we suggest, would they be likely to succeed were they to try. We conclude, then, that subjectivism is not a defensible ethical view.

Recall for a moment the subjectivist's complaint that she has chosen good principles, so the argument that subjectivism has unacceptable consequences does not apply to her. We can now see where her complaint goes wrong. A good ethical principle, whatever else it might be, is one that is acceptable for good reasons. And what counts as a good reason is in large part determined by public standards. The public nature of ethics is inescapable. It cannot be, as subjectivists would have it, an entirely private matter.

CHARACTERISTICS OF DISCUSSIONS ABOUT ETHICS

Let us stop for a moment and review the discussion of ethical subjectivism. We began by trying to give a clear statement of subjectivism. We then tried to show that subjectivism has implausible consequences. To avoid these consequences we attempted to modify the original statement of subjectivism. But this failed because the modification led to an inconsistency: the inconsistency that for a subjectivist the choice of ethical principles both is and is not an entirely personal matter. Thus, we claimed, subjectivism should be rejected.

In the pages to come, the general pattern of this discussion will be repeated, sometimes with slight alterations, in the analysis of other ethical principles and viewpoints. The reason is that underlying the pattern are several common assumptions and shared ideas about how to judge the validity and adequacy of ethical principles or viewpoints. These assumptions and ideas provide a context for the debate about ethics. They are the "rules of the game" that prevent it from degenerating into a pointless shouting match. It is important to know something about them for two reasons. First, it is much easier to follow the debate when one understands the rules. In the context of the rules, the pattern of the discussion makes sense. And it makes sense of why some points for or against a certain ethical principle are thought to be more telling than others. Second, not everyone who tries to be a part of the discussion accepts all the rules. They are playing a different game, which explains why the things they say about ethics may seem so peculiar.

We have divided the assumptions and ideas into three categories. The first category is essential for any discussion, regardless of the topic.

1. All parties to the debate are rational in the minimal sense that (a) they believe that it is relevant and appropriate to give reasons for what one believes, (b) if given good reasons for believing something, reasons that withstand public scrutiny, then, other things being equal, they will believe it, and (c) they are able to see that statements have logical consequences—they recognize that if some statements are true (or false), other statements are true (or false).

2. No logically inconsistent position is rationally acceptable. To have a logically inconsistent belief amounts to believing that some statement both is and is not true. Logically inconsistent ethical principles are not rationally acceptable because they will entail, for every action, both that it is ethically right or good and that it is not ethically right or good.

The second category relates more directly to ethics. It has to do with the nature of ethical judgments and with the kinds of reasons relevant to ethical judgments.

3. Ethical judgments apply primarily to the actions of moral agents. The main example of a moral agent is a person who is rational and who has enough intelligence and background information about the world to recognize that (a) persons have interests and welfare that can be enhanced or harmed, and (b) certain actions are likely to have consequences affecting the interests and welfare of persons. If someone, such as a child, does not fit this characterization of a moral agent, then his or her actions are not properly subject to ethical judgments.
4. Ethical judgments are a part of a public system for evaluating actions of moral agents that affect themselves or other persons. Actions are evaluated as ethically right or wrong, good or bad, or praiseworthy or blameworthy. These evaluations are made according to reasons and principles subject to public appraisal. Thus, whether an evaluation is fitting or not is also open to public inspection and appraisal. Just as one's choice of ethical principles is an appropriate topic of public debate, so one's evaluation of an act is an appropriate topic of public debate.
5. Since ethical judgments are about actions of moral agents that affect the interests and welfare of persons, statements that describe the interests and welfare of persons, or describe or anticipate the effects of acts on interests and welfare, are relevant to ethical judgments. These statements (if true) are morally relevant facts. In conjunction with ethical principles, these facts give us reasons for acting one way rather than another. In addition, statements describing the intentions, motives, and character of moral agents are relevant to ethical judgments. Such statements are vital for understanding the reasons for an action, and understanding the reasons for an action is germane to making ethical judgments about it. Since intentions, motives, and character are in part the cause or source of action, they are also subject to moral evaluation.

The third set of ideas and assumptions directly relates to methods for evaluating ethical principles.

6. Ethical principles are impartial in the sense that they do not allow special exceptions that benefit or harm a specific person or group. This does not necessarily imply that ethical principles are invariably neutral between the interests and welfare of persons. It may be morally permissible, for instance, to be partial to the interests and welfare of one's children. However, an ethical principle that allows partiality of this kind must allow each person to be partial to the interests of his or her children. It must not allow, say, Jones to be partial to his children, but prohibit Smith from being partial to hers.
7. Ethical principles (a) are rules for deciding between alternative courses of action involving the interests and welfare of moral agents; (b) do not require conflicting acts; (c) prescribe no act or course of action that in considered belief systematically worsens the long-term welfare of persons or is clearly detrimental to reasonable individual or group interests.

The third provision of the last assumption requires some comment. It is unavoidable, in our opinion, that one test of an ethical principle is how well it fits with considered beliefs about what is right and wrong. It cannot help but count against an ethical principle if it prescribes acts that seem plainly wrong. But one must be cautious here, for even the most carefully considered beliefs about right and wrong are not always reliable. Prejudice and bias are common human failings, as is the ability to rationalize unacceptable behavior or simply to refuse to see that a moral issue is at stake. Given all of this, often it is our considered beliefs that need to be changed, not the principle in question. Still, our beliefs about right and wrong undoubtedly carry weight in our selection of ethical principles. The difficulty is in deciding how much weight they should carry.

ETHICAL RELATIVISM

Relativism Explained

The next ethical viewpoint we will discuss is ethical relativism. This is the position that there is no universal ethical principle or set of principles by which to judge the morality of an action. Instead, each society or culture has its own set of moral rules. Furthermore, since a particular society's rules are justified by internal procedures and standards specific to and distinctive of that society, it is inappropriate, relativists argue, to evaluate one society's rules using the procedures and standards of other societies. Thus, relativists claim, ethics cannot be reduced to some master list of rules applicable to everyone. There are no ethical principles that everyone should follow. There are only local ethical principles that apply locally.

Ethical relativism, if true, implies that no society's ethical code has the special status of being "better" or "truer" than another. Each society's code is on a par with every other society's code. For example, in Ted's situation, a colleague who is an ethical relativist might argue that although bribery is immoral in the United States, it is an acceptable practice in the country in which Ted is trying to sell machinery. Different countries have different ethical principles and different ways in which those principles are justified and agreed upon. Since Ted is not a member of the culture in which he is trying to do business, he is in no position to pass judgment, either favorably or unfavorably, on their ethical views.

In the bribery example, the relativist's argument may seem reasonable. After all, if the members of a certain society believe bribery is ethically permissible, who are we to tell them otherwise? But in other cases this attitude of "ethical neutrality" is much less plausible. For instance, if a society were to practice slavery, then, if ethical relativism is correct, it would be inappropriate for us to say, "What you are doing is ethically wrong," because we would be applying our standards to the practices of a society with a different ethical code. The best we could do is say, "What you are doing is wrong according to our standards." This is not an ethical judgment, but a statement of fact. In this respect, ethical subjectivists and ethical relativists are similar. Just as subjectivists cannot legitimately make ethical judgments about the practices of other individuals, so ethical relativists cannot legitimately make ethical judgments about the practices of societies other than their own.

This is a disturbing consequence of relativism. Although we may be reluctant to make judgments about things like bribery, most of us are convinced that slavery and other acts that unjustifiably harm people are plainly wrong regardless of where they occur or who does them. And most of us feel that we are justified in condemning such practices when they occur. Since ethical relativism seems to prevent us from making judgments about these practices in other societies, there need to be powerful reasons for us to put aside our convictions and accept relativism. Are there such reasons?

The Evidence for Relativism

It is undeniable that different societies have different ethical practices,—that is, that acts permissible in some societies are impermissible in others. And, in many cases, differences in practice seem to derive from differences in ethical principles. This is often taken to be conclusive evidence in favor of ethical relativism. However, the evidence is not unequivocal. Differences in ethical practices may turn not on differences in ethical principles, but on a variety of other things, such as different physical environments, levels of social wealth, or beliefs about morally relevant facts. In one society, for instance, the practice was to kill one's parents as they began to grow old. This was morally permissible because it was thought that one would spend the afterlife in the physical state in which one died. If one were to die in a body racked by pain and disability, one would suffer torment for eternity. It was a kindness, a mark of concern for the welfare of one's parents, to ensure that they did not live to experience the infirmities of old age. Thus, despite very different practices in that culture and ours, there are underlying similarities of principle, such as the principle that one ought to honor one's parents. We can understand and appreciate the motives for their acts while at the same time we may disagree about the facts of existence in the hereafter, assuming there is a hereafter.

Let us suppose, however, that a society S_1 has an ethical standard permitting acts of type A; society S_2 has an ethical standard prohibiting acts of type A; and that the difference cannot be explained by differences in environment, wealth, or beliefs about morally relevant facts. Does this show that ethical relativism is true?

Not unless several other possibilities can be eliminated. One of them is that neither S_1 nor S_2 has made an error in logic. For example, suppose the members of S_1 falsely believe that a statement logically entails (or does not entail) some other statement, and that this belief plays an important role in their justification of the principle permitting the acts in question. If they were to find or be convinced that they were wrong about the entailment, they might also abandon the principle since it no longer is justified for them. In this case, the difference between S_1 and S_2 is more a matter of logic than ethics.

Another possibility is that the error is epistemic rather than logical. For instance, suppose that according to their own canons of evidence, the members of S_1 have incorrectly evaluated their reasons for holding the principle. They have either made a mistake in judging the weight of the various reasons, or they omitted reasons that should have been taken into account, or included in the justification reasons that should not have been included. The error here is one that, by S_1's own standards, they would admit were they to become aware of it.

A third possibility is that they are not aware that certain practices should be ethically evaluated. For example, in the recent past, many societies, our own among them, were not concerned with environmental problems caused by pollution, disposal of toxic wastes, and so on. It was not that they had carefully thought about these issues and decided that they were unimportant, but rather that they had not thought about them at all. It was only when they became aware that ethical issues were involved that they began to see environmental practices from an ethical point of view.

A final possibility is that S_1 and S_2 attach different meanings to ethical words we might try to translate as *good, justice,* or *rights.* If they do not realize that they are using these or similar words in different senses, then what may look like a difference in ethical principles could turn out to be a difference in the use of key ethical words. The possibility of misunderstanding or miscommunication should never be overlooked. Subtle differences in meaning can have important consequences for how one culture interprets the principles and justifications another culture gives for its ethical practices.

If any of these possibilities is realized, the fundamental disagreement may not be about ethical principles. There is a prior point of contention or confusion—logical, epistemic, or semantic—that needs to be resolved before the discussion about ethics can begin. If it cannot be resolved, then the ethical differences may be a consequence of disagreement about a nonethical matter. If it can be resolved, then S_1 and S_2 might come to agree about the basic principles of ethics.

Relativism and the Possibility of Error

Some ethical relativists seem to claim that if members of a society *believe* that acts of a certain type are ethically correct, then they *are* correct for that society. Thus, in ethics, unlike, say, in science, there is no difference between what is believed to be true and what is true. However, this claim is not convincing because it overlooks the possibility that social groups, like individuals, can make errors. A social group might have incorrect factual beliefs, make invalid inferences, mistakenly weigh evidence, or make some other error. In their own discussions about ethics or in conversation with other groups, they may come to realize that their ethical beliefs are unacceptable on their own standards of logic and evidence. Were this to happen, it is likely that their ethical beliefs would change. People certainly have the capacity to make errors. Happily, they also have the capacity to recognize their errors and eliminate them by changing their beliefs.

It is not hard to find examples of this. At one time, for instance, blatant racial and sexual discrimination were common in this country. Much of this discrimination, though not all of it, was based on the false belief that blacks and women are intellectually inferior to white men. As these false beliefs are replaced by true ones, we can reasonably hope and expect that discrimination will gradually disappear, for once this belief is gone, a major obstacle to living up to our own ideal of equal opportunity for all will be gone as well.

Ethical relativists who deny or ignore the possibility that social groups can make errors also counsel us to be tolerant of the beliefs of other societies. This is good advice. Our experience with discrimination shows that our society is as vulnerable to error as any other. It is a mistake to assume that our way of doing things is the only ethically acceptable way. But the reason relativists advise us to be tolerant is that they believe there is little basis for rational discussion between societies with different ethical viewpoints. After all, if a society cannot be mistaken about something it believes, there is no reason for it to subject its beliefs to critical evaluation by outsiders. Thus, relativists seem to think, since rational discussion is impossible, the only alternative modes of ethical interaction available, given the close proximity of different societies in the modern world, are tolerance and conflict. Since tolerance is much the better of the two choices, we should be tolerant. For the reasons given above, however, the fact that different societies have different ethical beliefs does not show that there is no basis for rational discussion between them. Nor does tolerance warrant indifference or inattention to the practices of other societies. If there is good reason to believe that an ethical practice is based on false beliefs about the facts, incorrect reasoning, or some other error, we may have a duty to speak out, or even take action in extreme cases, regardless of where the practice occurs. As history amply shows, the consequences of not doing so can be horrendous.

Bedrock Ethical Differences

But what if, after all the possible nonethical areas of disagreement are eliminated, S_1 and S_2 still have different ethical principles? Now should we accept ethical relativism?

As far as we know, there are no noncontroversial examples of this kind of disagreement. But let us imagine that S_1 and S_2 have completely different principles. Every principle S_1 accepts is rejected by S_2 and vice versa. And suppose S_2 is a culture very much like our own, with ethical values and principles we can understand and appreciate. What would S_1 be like?

In S_1 lying, cheating, and random violence would be the norm. There would be no strictures against murder, robbery, rape, or other acts of violence. In business, there could be no contracts, since there would be no trust or expectation of fair dealing. There would be little or no family life, since no one would be committed to the welfare of others. There would be no religion, law, or social institutions of any kind, for if such institutions are to work, people must have basic respect for themselves and others. Nor could S_1 have traditions, shared ideals, social organization, or even a history that is anything other than a series of random events. In short, S_1 would not be a culture at all. It would not have, and could not sustain, the minimum social structure needed to support a viable culture.

We mentioned earlier that relativists cite diversity of ethical practice as evidence for diversity of ethical standards. However, if the above argument is correct, there could not be a complete diversity of principles. And, as it turns out, it does seem that all societies have certain ethical rules in common, such as rules that promote reciprocity and fair play, and prohibit wanton violence. The reason is that were there no such rules, there would be no human societies. Many rules that societies have in common are essential for cultural survival. They establish the necessary conditions that make social life possible. Thus, there could not be a society that has ethical rules completely different from our own.

If this is correct, then the more extreme claims made on behalf of ethical relativism are implausible. The main evidence cited in favor of ethical relativism—that different societies have different ethical practices—does not support the claim that there is a radical and unbridgeable gap between the ethics of different societies. For one thing, all functioning societies have rules intended to help preserve social order. The evidence suggests that these rules are similar in different societies, which is not surprising since people have the same basic needs regardless of where they live. Furthermore, for all the reasons listed earlier, a difference in practice need not amount to a difference in principle. In fact, we suggest that a genuine difference in ethical principles not attributable to a different understanding of facts, different circumstances, errors of logic and evidence, and so forth, is likely to be rare.[2]

There still remains the possibility that different societies have different principles not attributable to any of the sources mentioned above. It may be very difficult to decide in any particular instance whether an apparent difference is a genuine one, but they might occur. What should we say about such differences, assuming one could be found?

Since such a difference would be a bedrock ethical difference not attributable to any nonethical source, it might seem as if a modified relativism must be true. Maybe not all rules can differ, a relativist might say, but some can, and about these rules and the practices they permit, no rational intercultural discussion can take place and no intercultural judgments can be made. Every society, at least potentially, differs ethically in some respect from other societies. This difference signifies a kind of ethical autonomy, an area of ethical freedom into which it would be disrespectful for other societies to intrude.

Although there is some truth to the above argument, it is important to see what it does and does not establish. It does not show that there are genuine differences in ethical principles, but only that there might be. It does not show that apparent differences are genuine. And it does not show that different practices are grounded in different principles. Moreover, if genuine differences are to be found, rational discussion between societies must take place. Arguments must be evaluated, circumstances assessed, mistakes discovered and corrected, and agreements reached about what is and is not a real difference. But this, of course, is a paradigm of rational ethical debate and analysis. It is precisely the process by which we discuss and analyze ethical practices in our own culture as well as others. Thus, far from showing that ethical discussion between societies is impossible, ethical relativism, if true, would seem to require that it take place. Only in this way can genuine differences be found if they are present.

Finally, note that respect for the ethical autonomy of other cultures is proposed as a universal value, one that does not have merely local application. All of us, the relativist would say, should respect the views of other societies, and one way to do this is to be tolerant of differences when we find them. But there are other ways to be respectful of ethical autonomy. One of them, even more important than tolerance in our judgment, is to respect the rationality of others. We should not assume that apparent ethical differences are irrational or founded in reasons that we cannot comprehend. If we suppose that our society has good reasons for accepting certain ethical values, principles, and judgments, then it would be impertinent and contemptuous not to attribute the same to other societies. Tolerance, unless grounded in respect for rationality, is no more than a version of paternalism. It is an attitude taken toward those inferior in intellect and ability, those with whom it is fruitless to engage in meaningful debate. If relativists are to avoid this highly unattractive attitude, if they are to grant others the full measure of respect they are due, they cannot in good conscience advise us simply to be tolerant of diversity. They must instead concede that diversity marks the beginning of rational debate about ethics, not the end.

We hope by now to have shown that ethical relativism is a fairly innocuous ethical viewpoint. It cannot support the more radical claims sometimes made on its behalf. At best it shows that some diversity of ethical principles is possible. It does not show that differences are necessary, nor that they are extensive, nor even that when real diversity is found it cannot be rationally discussed. Relativism can serve as a reminder of the complexity of ethical views, and of how arduous it may be to understand and appreciate ethical differences. But beyond this its implications for ethical theory and practice are minimal.

The Question of Relevance

In our discussion thus far there is a question, or series of questions, that we have not addressed but that some readers may have wondered about. Suppose someone responded to our analysis of ethical relativism as follows: You may be right that ethical relativism does not imply that one should not make ethical judgments about practices in other cultures, nor does it imply that rational discussion about ethics cannot take place between different societies. But nothing in your argument shows that I should make such judgments. Why should I care about what happens in other cultures? Granted that brutality, corruption, aggression, and injustice are common in the world, what does that have to do with me? Why should I be concerned?

In one sense, these questions are unanswerable. If people have no concern about the fate of anyone other than themselves, if they resolutely refuse to consider the possibility that they have ethical obligations that extend beyond the circle of their immediate acquaintance, then little we can say will change their mind. Argument is futile with those who will not listen. In another sense, however, there is an answer. To see what it is, we need to suppose that the questions implicitly contain an argument of the following sort: I should be concerned only about those things that affect my self-interest. What happens to people in distant lands has little or no effect on my self-interest. Hence, I need not be concerned about them.

The second premise of this argument is highly questionable. It is no longer true, if it ever was, that what happens in the rest of the world is of little consequence to individuals in the United States. The global economy has effectively put an end to economic and political isolationism, and with it an end to the idea that distant events are irrelevant to individual self-interest. Thus, the argument as given does not justify lack of concern about those in distant lands.

A response to the objection is that one should be concerned about distant events only to the extent that one's self-interest is involved. If there is no reasonable connection between a particular individual's self-interest and the lives of those in other lands, then that individual need not be concerned with them.

This response brings us to the first premise, the thesis that self-interest is all that matters. As we will see in the next section, this view comes in several different guises. So we can better respond to it and better give our final answer to the argument that one need not be concerned with the fate of others, we will first place it in the context of what are usually called consequentialist ethical theories.

CONSEQUENTIALISM

Essentials of Consequentialism

Consequentialism is a family of ethical viewpoints based on two central ideas. The first is a claim about what is of value for human beings. The second is that whether an act is ethically permissible or not is solely a matter of whether the act maximizes the value. For example, suppose the value is happiness. Then an act is ethically permissible if and only if it maximizes happiness—that is, if and only if it is a consequence of the act that it produces at least as much happiness as any other act. Acts that do not maximize happiness are not ethically permissible. For example, suppose the only acts available to Jones are A, B, and C, and that she can do exactly one of A, B, or C. And suppose A and B both maximize happiness, and C does not. Then it is ethically permissible for Jones to do A or to do B, and not permissible for her to do C. Since no acts are available to her except A, B, and C, and since no acts are ethically permissible for her except A and B, she is ethically obligated to do either A or B. No other ethically permissible choices are available to her.

Consequentialist theories can be subdivided according to (1) for whom the value is to be maximized and (2) the kind of value to be maximized. For instance, the version of consequentialism called *ethical egoism* claims that an act is morally permissible for a person P if and only if the act maximizes the value for P. Nonegoistic versions of consequentialism say that an act is morally permissible for P if and only if the value is maximized for some larger group of people that includes P. To distinguish this theory from ethical egoism, it is commonly called *utilitarianism.*

Values to be maximized include both intrinsic and instrumental goods. Intrinsic goods are valuable in themselves, and not valuable merely as means to something else. Examples are truth, beauty, love, friendship, pleasure, and happiness. Instrumental goods are not valuable in themselves, but are valuable because they are means to some other end. An example of an instrumental good is money. In this introduction we have space to discuss only one of these possible intrinsic goods. We will give examples of how egoism and utilitarianism propose that this good be maximized, and we will review some of the objections that have been raised against these versions of consequentialism. But before we do this, there is another position that needs discussion. It is an empirical relation of ethical egoism called *psychological egoism.* Since modern business and economic theory rely heavily on psychological egoism, we will examine it in some detail.

Psychological Egoism Explained

There is an important difference between what *is* and what *ought to be.* For example, through no fault of their own many people suffer from hunger and malnutrition. This is a fact about the world, a report of what is. But this fact about the world does not imply that things ought to be this way. Were the world a more accommodating place, there would be no hunger. No one would suffer from malnutrition. That is the way the world ought to be.

Psychological egoists make a claim about what is. It is a fact about human beings, they say, that individual human beings act only to advance their self-interest. It is not merely that human beings act from self-interest in limited but extreme circumstances, such as when their lives are at stake, or that they act from self-interest in certain social conditions, as in market economies, but rather that each person acts from self-interest in every situation. Self-interest is and can be the only human motivation. That is the way human beings are. Thus, it is useless to suggest that persons should be concerned about the welfare of others. People are incapable of concern for others except insofar as it enhances their own interests.

If psychological egoism is true, then ethics is pointless. Nothing is to be gained by exhorting people to do what they are incapable of doing, nor can they be blamed for failing to take the interests and welfare of others into account. So, for example, it would be pointless to argue that Ted Brown should consider the effects bribery would have on anyone other than himself, or to blame him for failing to do so. According to psychological egoists, it is a psychological fact that he cannot be concerned with the interests of others unless their interests are directly related to his.

Problems with Psychological Egoism

An immediate problem with psychological egoism is that apparent counterexamples are easy to find. We all know or have heard of cases in which people have sacrificed their fortunes or even their lives for the sake of others. And it is likely that many of us, when we reflect on our own experience, can recall occasions when we acted primarily from concern for others. Yet if psychological egoism is true, such acts are impossible. How do egoists explain this?[3]

One explanation egoists give is that acts apparently motivated by concern for others are, if examined closely, really motivated by self-interest. This explanation may be true in many cases. Acts that appear altruistic—that is, motivated by concern for others—may be consciously or unconsciously self-interested. However, the fact that *some* apparently altruistic acts are self-interested does not show, as psychological egoism requires, that *all* apparently altruistic acts are really self-interested. To show that egoists need to provide a lot more detail about why they think their view is true.

One argument egoists sometimes use is that people invariably do what they most want to do, assuming their action is voluntary.[4] The idea here is that people act to satisfy their desires. If they desire several things, they always pick the one that, other things being equal, they most desire. Furthermore, people always most desire to do what is in their self-interest. Thus, if one person intentionally acts in a way that benefits another person, it is because that act is what the person most wanted to do, and he or she most wanted to do it because benefitting the other person contributes to his or her self-interest.

There are three difficulties with this argument. We will mention the first two and discuss the third in more detail. The first is that it is not clear that people always do what they most desire. Sometimes they do things they would very much prefer not to, such as pay taxes or keep a promise. Second, it certainly seems as if people often desire things and do things they know are not in their self-interest. For instance, many people smoke even though they acknowledge that smoking is not in their self-interest. Finally, it could be that what someone most desires to do is intended solely to benefit someone else. For instance, in war, soldiers sometimes sacrifice their lives to save their comrades. Doesn't this show that psychological egoism is false?

Psychological egoists would claim it does not. People cannot most desire to act solely for the benefit of someone other than themselves. It is not psychologically possible. If A acts to benefit B, it must be because A believes, consciously or unconsciously, that the benefit to B helps A in some way. Otherwise, A would not act to benefit B. Thus, when soldiers give their lives to save their comrades, they must somehow believe that it is to their benefit. For example, they might believe that to witness their friends die would be a worse fate than their own death.

However, this response begs the question. It assumes the very point at issue. The alleged reason that one person cannot act solely for the benefit of another is that psychological egoism is true. But the argument is supposed to show that psychological egoism is true, and nothing is accomplished if one must assume something is true to show that it is true. So we are still left with the question: Exactly why isn't it possible for one person to act solely for the benefit of another?

The Argument for Self-Satisfaction

There are two kinds of benefits one person can derive from helping another. The first is what we might call an external benefit. For example, Jones saves Smith from the burning building to ensure that Smith is around to repay the considerable sum he owes Jones. But another kind of benefit is internal. People never act solely for the benefit of others, egoists argue, because they always get an internal feeling of self-satisfaction from helping others. Indeed, if the purpose of helping others is not to ensure some external gain, then the only reason people try to benefit others is to get this feeling of self-satisfaction. And since feeling good about ourselves is pleasurable, and feeling pleasure is in a person's self-interest, psychological egoism is true after all.

This argument is not persuasive for two reasons. The first is that self-satisfaction is not the same as self-interest. Things in our self-interest may not give us self-satisfaction, and things that give us self-satisfaction may not be in our self-interest. For example, it might be very much in Smith's self-interest to pay his debt to his bookie even though he gets no self-satisfaction from it. And many people get self-satisfaction from donating supplies to victims of natural disasters even though it is not remotely in their self-interest to help. Self-interested behavior and behavior that gives self-satisfaction are just not the same.

The second problem with the argument is that it assumes that if, say, Jones, helps another person, then her *reason* for helping must be to feel good about herself. Yet suppose Jones were to say, "Although it is true that I feel good as a result of helping others, that is not the reason I do it. I help others because I am ethically obligated to do so, and I would continue to help them even if I stopped getting self-satisfaction from it." How might psychological egoists respond?

The only response they could make is that Jones is mistaken about her motivation. She thinks she is motivated by ethical obligation, they would say, but were we to analyze her act carefully, we would find that she is actually motivated by self-interest. The reason we can be assured she is so motivated is that psychological egoism is true. People are motivated only by self-interest. Moreover, despite what Jones says, if she were to stop getting satisfaction from helping others, she would stop helping them. The reason is the same: psychological egoism is true. But by now this type of response should be familiar. It assumes the point at issue and thus begs the question.

Psychological Egoism: A Proposal

At this point, it might be helpful to review the discussion. We have posed a series of counterexamples to psychological egoism in which an individual reports that he or she performs an act for the benefit of someone else. Benefit to the other person is alleged to be the reason the act was performed, not external or internal benefit to the person performing the act. Psychological egoists then claim that the report must be mistaken because all behavior is self-interested. However, they offer no evidence that the act was self-interested other than appeal to the theory of psychological egoism. But this is unacceptable because it begs the question. Is there any way for egoists to avoid this problem?

The only way is for egoists to *show* that the acts are self-interested, and not *assert* that they are because psychological egoism is true. To do this, they must insist that showing that an act has a certain *effect* does not automatically show that it has a certain *motivation*. Otherwise, acts clearly detrimental to a person's self-interest would immediately prove that psychological egoism is false. But then, by parity of reasoning, egoists cannot claim that acts beneficial to the person performing them provide strong evidence for egoism, for such benefits could be incidental rather than intentional. Thus, the effect of acts is relatively weak evidence either for or against egoism. What egoists need is psychological evidence—that is, truthful reports of motivation from the person performing the act. And since many people report altruistic motivation, egoists must show that these reports are mistaken. Furthermore, egoists cannot take reports of self-interested motivation at face value. If they claim that reports of altruism can be mistaken, they must allow that reports of self-interest can be mistaken. If they do not, if they assert that reports of self-interested motivation cannot be wrong, they again run the risk of begging the question.

If all of this is correct, psychological egoists have an enormous research project ahead of them. To make a case for egoism, they must conduct an in-depth psychological examination of individual persons to uncover or confirm the genuine motivation of particular acts done on specific occasions. Since the theoretical and practical obstacles to this project are immense, at best it will be difficult to complete, and it may be impossible. It is not surprising, then, that it remains largely undone, and that the evidence to date is not encouraging for egoism.[5]

The question remains of what to do until empirical research settles the issue. We suggest that in the meantime, it is reasonable to believe that some acts are genuinely altruistic. There simply is no good evidence that psychological egoism is true, nor are there any convincing philosophical arguments in its favor. Moreover, there is a great deal of evidence, both anecdotal and experimental, in favor of altruism, and psychological egoists have given no compelling reason to think that this evidence is wrong. Until that happens, altruism remains a possibility, and, in our opinion, a strong probability. If this is right, then psychological egoism poses no significant threat for ethics.

Ethical Egoism

Unlike psychological egoists, ethical egoists make a claim about what ought to be. They argue that each person ought to maximize his or her own self-interest. The principle they advocate is this:

> Ethical Egoism: An act A is ethically permissible for a person P if and only if A maximizes P's self-interest. Acts that do not maximize P's self-interest are not ethically permissible for P.

Ethical egoism is the ethical principle Ted Brown tried to follow when deciding whether he should offer a bribe. In our discussion of Ted's dilemma, we pointed out that his decision is not easy because it is often difficult to anticipate the consequences of one's actions. But we said little about what Ted believes his self-interest to be, nor were we very precise about self-interest in our discussion of psychological egoism. However, to examine ethical egoism, we need to be more precise about self-interest. Note that any analysis of self-interest we might give is constrained by ethical egoism's requirement that self-interest be maximized. Because to maximize something comparisons of more and less must be made, to apply the principle of ethical egoism it must be possible to make comparisons of self-interest. So what is this comparative concept of self-interest?

An answer favored by many people is to equate self-interest with happiness. Surely, they claim, it is in our self-interest to be happy. Furthermore, we often compare present states of happiness with those of the past and future—for example, "I'm much happier now than I used to be and I expect to be happier still in the future." And there is a rough intuitive sense to the notion that happiness can be maximized. On the other hand, the concept of happiness may not be precise enough to give clear guidance for all choices that fall under the principle of ethical egoism. Consider, for example, an ethical egoist contemplating how he should lead his life. Assuming happiness is the same as self-interest, the principle of ethical egoism instructs him to do what will make him happiest. But we can imagine him asking "Exactly what will make me happiest? Is it fame, fortune, knowledge, reputation? How can I know in advance which acts will maximize my happiness? And if I cannot know, how can I make an ethical choice?

Hedonistic Egoism

These are not easy questions. It looks as if the only way an individual could answer them is to have complete knowledge of his or her future. But this is impossible. And since individuals cannot be ethically required to do what is impossible, ethical egoism is unacceptable unless there is some way to show that it imposes no such requirement. But how might it be shown?

One method sometimes attempted is to further analyze the concept of happiness. Granted that we all want to be happy, just what is it to be happy anyway? A traditional answer is that people are happy when they experience pleasure, and unhappy when they experience pain. That is all there is to it. Happiness just is experiencing pleasure and avoiding pain. The nineteenth-century philosopher John Stuart Mill puts it like this:

> the ultimate end, with reference to and for the sake of which all other things are desirable (whether we are considering our own good or that of other people), is an existence exempt as far as possible from pain, and as rich as possible in enjoyments.

Mill is here advocating a view sometimes called *hedonism*—that is, that the only thing of intrinsic value for humans is pleasure and the avoidance of pain. Everything else is and ought to be a means to that end.

Ethical egoists who accept Mills' outlook equate maximizing self-interest with maximizing pleasure and minimizing pain. This view, which we will call *hedonistic egoism,* requires that *all* acts available to a person be evaluated solely on their potential to cause pleasure or pain to that specific person. Acts that maximize pleasure or minimize pain are ethically permissible. Otherwise, they are ethically impermissible. For example, suppose Jones can do only A or B but not both, and suppose both A and B are pleasurable for Jones but A is more pleasurable. Then, hedonistic egoists argue, Jones should do A. If A and B cause the same amount of pleasure, then it does not matter which Jones does. If A is pleasurable for Jones and B is not, then Jones should do A. Finally, if both A and B cause Jones pain, but A causes less pain than B, then Jones should do A. If A and B cause the same amount of pain, then it does not matter which Jones does. Let us say that acts that conform to these examples create the greatest balance of pleasure over pain. Now we can give a more exact statement of hedonistic egoism:

> Hedonistic Egoism: An act A is ethically permissible for a person P if and only if A creates the greatest balance of pleasure over pain for P. Acts that do not create the greatest balance of pleasure over pain for P are not ethically permissible for P.

The advantage of using pleasure and pain as a measure of self-interest instead of happiness is that pleasure and pain seem much more concrete and immediate than vague feelings of happiness. Moreover, it is easier to figure out what will cause pleasure and pain than what will lead to happiness, and easier to compare degrees of pain and pleasure than degrees of happiness. Perhaps the reason for this is that pleasure and pain have a basis in human physiology that happiness seems not to have, or not to have to the same degree. However, there are two misconceptions about hedonism that should be cleared up before we consider the arguments for hedonistic egoism. First, the hedonist's concept of pleasure should not be narrowly understood. In addition to ordinary physical pleasure, it can include a variety of other things, such as intellectual and aesthetic pleasure and the pleasures of friendship. Second, it is sometimes thought that hedonists care only about immediate pleasure and give no thought to the possibility that what causes them great pleasure now may lead to even greater pain in the future. But this need not be true. Rational hedonists will strive to create the greatest balance of pleasure over pain for themselves over the long term. Thus, they will forego a short-term pleasure that leads to long-term pain and will undergo short-term pain to gain long-term pleasure. A more serious objection to hedonism is this: Happiness is too complex an idea to be captured by something as one dimensional as experiencing pleasure and avoiding pain, even if pleasure and pain are understood in the broadest sense. There is more to happiness than hedonists admit. It is possible that a life filled with little pleasure is happy for other reasons, or that a life of great pleasure is ethically repugnant. Consider, for example, a powerful dictator who receives great pleasure from tormenting others. Consequently, it is a serious error to think that happiness can be understood solely in terms of pleasure and pain.

The Case for Hedonistic Egoism

We will not speculate about how hedonistic egoists might respond to the above objection. Instead, we will suppose for the present that hedonism gives an adequate account of happiness and that self-interest is best understood in terms of happiness. The next task is to examine the arguments for hedonistic egoism. It is important to see that hedonistic egoists believe that everyone should always follow the principle of hedonistic egoism. Thus, they are unlike ethical subjectivists and ethical relativists, and unlike those who believe that business or legal principles should sometimes take precedence over ethics. But since hedonistic egoists believe that everyone should accept their position, they need to give good reasons for it. Are there such reasons?

Here is one argument. Suppose there is a God who rewards each person with the pleasures of heaven or the pains of hell based on how well the person lives up to some set of God's commands while living on this earth. The pleasures of heaven and the pains of hell are both intense and everlasting, so it maximizes long-term pleasure to attain heaven and avoid hell. Thus, it is in each person's interests to follow the commands while he or she is alive. And since persons are judged as individuals, each person is well advised to look after his or her own interests. Given the existence of such a God, ethical egoism is the only reasonable ethical viewpoint.

There are two main problems with this argument. First, it works only if there is a God who metes out rewards and punishments as described. Not everyone is convinced of this. However, granting there is such a God, say, the God of the New Testament, the second problem concerns the commands God issues. One of them is to "love thy neighbor as thyself." This in part implies that one should place the interests and welfare of one's neighbors on a par with one's own. It further implies that one should be motivated by genuine altruism, and not see protecting the interests of one's neighbors merely as a means of gaining a reward in heaven. But this is inconsistent with hedonistic egoism, since it dictates that persons should be concerned only with their own interests. Thus, the argument does not give good reasons for everyone to be a hedonistic egoist. If anything, it shows that hedonistic egoism is an unacceptable ethical viewpoint.

A second argument is that individuals best know their own interests and are best able to look after their interests. Intervening in the lives of others usually causes more problems than it solves. In addition, many people do not want anyone meddling in their affairs, even when well intended. They think of it as an invasion of privacy. Thus, were we all to look out only for ourselves, it is likely we would all be better off in the long term.

The main idea in the second argument is that one should be a hedonistic egoist because it enhances the common good: everyone would be better off. But if so, then enhancing the common good is the ultimate goal of ethical action. Hedonistic egoism is no more than the alleged best means to that end. This puts hedonistic egoists in a very bad position for two reasons. The first is that if the generalization is false and hedonistic egoism is not in fact the best means to the common good, then hedonistic egoists would be obliged to abandon their position and search for a better means. And there are grounds for thinking it false. People are often helped rather than hurt by intervention in their lives. No doubt such intervention sometimes goes awry, but it does not follow from this that were it to cease entirely, everyone would be better off. The second reason is that the notion of valuing the common good is quite foreign to hedonistic egoism. The main point of the theory is that, ethically speaking, it is the good of the individual that counts, not the good of the group. So for hedonistic egoists to appeal to the common good to justify their position is peculiar, to say the least. If hedonistic egoists are to persuade others to accept their view, they must find better reasons than the ones we have examined so far.

Hedonistic Egoism Reconsidered

So far the arguments for hedonistic egoism are not very convincing. And there are some reasons to reject it altogether. Here is one of them. Recall that if Jones has a choice of doing A or B, and if A and B cause her the same amount of pleasure, then from the point of view of hedonistic egoism it does not matter which she does. But suppose Jones knows that if she does A, then Smith will suffer a great deal of unprovoked and unnecessary harm. Yet if Jones does B, Smith will experience harmless pleasure. Can it be correct, as hedonistic egoism implies, that it is ethically indifferent which Jones does? It certainly seems not. Smith's well-being must count for something. If Jones's actions can either harm or benefit Smith at no cost to Jones, then it would seem an ethical imperative that she choose to benefit Smith. To be indifferent to Smith's well-being is ethically reprehensible. Since hedonistic egoism implies that it is not reprehensible but a matter of unconcern, hedonistic egoism is unacceptable.

Another reason to reject hedonistic egoism is this. Suppose Jones and Smith are suffering from a disease that is rapidly fatal if left untreated. There is a pill that will cure the disease, but only one. According to hedonistic egoism, Jones is ethically required to take the pill, and so is Smith. Thus, if Jones tries to take it, Smith is ethically bound to prevent her. And if Smith tries to take it, Jones is ethically bound to prevent him. Thus Jones can act ethically only by preventing Smith from doing so, and vice versa. But can any ethical viewpoint be acceptable that implies that on some occasions one person can act ethically only by *preventing* another person from acting ethically?

Let us make the case a little more concrete. Suppose Jones and Smith are siblings, and Jones knows that even if she takes the pill she will die within a few months from some other painless but fatal ailment. If Smith takes the pill, however, he will be completely restored to health and will likely lead a long and happy life. Now suppose Jones decides to let Smith take the pill. How should Jones's action be evaluated? Most of us would probably think that she made the right decision and that she should be praised and respected. At the very least, she should not be condemned for acting unethically. But if hedonistic egoism is true, it is possible that Jones acts unethically. It does not matter that she has only a few months to live as long as taking the pill will maximize benefit to her. If it does, hedonistic egoism requires that she take it. Not to do so is ethically impermissible.

In our judgment, these consequences of hedonistic egoism show that it is an unacceptable ethical viewpoint. They illustrate two deep flaws. The first is that hedonistic egoism has no method of resolving ethical conflict. When it appears that one person can act ethically only by preventing another person from doing so, the conflict between them needs to be resolved in an ethically acceptable manner. But hedonistic egoism provides no such mechanism. The second flaw is that hedonistic egoism censures acts of self-sacrifice. Sometimes it is wrong to sacrifice one's interests for the sake of others, but it is not, as hedonistic egoism implies, *always* ethically impermissible. Were it so, the world would be a poor place indeed.

Although the case for hedonistic egoism is weak and the reasons for rejecting it are compelling, we concede that it has an intuitive appeal that is hard to dismiss. We suggest that its appeal is grounded in two insights that any realistic ethical viewpoint needs to capture. The first is that mature and competent persons generally best know their own interests and are best able to look out after them. The conviction that this is true is one reason most people find paternalism so unattractive. Moreover, there is no need to appeal to the common good to justify persons looking out for their own interests. The fact that something is beneficial to someone is prima facie justification enough for him or her to do it. The second reason is that, as a practical matter, it is extremely difficult or even impossible for most persons consistently to renounce their interests for the sake of others. But if ethics is to be relevant to our lives, it must be compatible with what it is possible for human beings to do. It cannot constantly require of individuals that they heroically sacrifice their own interests.

Hedonistic egoism incorporates these insights, but it omits others that are equally important. The main one is that ethics is about relationships between people—relationships in which the interests of all parties must be considered. For hedonistic egoists, only self-interest matters, and this is a fatal flaw.

Utilitarianism

In its traditional forms, utilitarianism does not permit an individual to place special weight on his or her self-interest. Instead, the interests of all persons affected by an individual's action are given the same weight. So, for example, if Jones performs an action that affects the interests of Smith and Brown, then if she is a utilitarian she will give the interests of Smith and Brown the same weight she gives her own. For utilitarians, no one deserves or is granted special consideration. Everyone is treated alike.

But in what respect do utilitarians believe that everyone should be treated alike? To understand this, we need to make some assumptions. The first is that self-interest is equivalent to experiencing pleasure and avoiding pain. In this, utilitarians are like hedonistic egoists. The second is that the pleasures and pains of any one person are similar to those of any other person. Thus, Jones's pleasures and pains are like Smith's and Brown's. The third is that the duration and intensity of pleasure and pains can be quantified and measured. So, for example, it can be determined in any particular case whether Jones is experiencing more or less pleasure than Smith or Brown, and how much more or less. Finally, utilitarians assume that individuals are able to canvass the acts available to them and make reliable judgments about the amount of pleasure and pain distinct acts will cause each individual affected by the act. Given these assumptions, Jeremy Bentham, who founded modern utilitarianism in the eighteenth century, writes that we should

> Sum up all the values of all the pleasures on the one side, and those of all the pains on the other.

> The balance, if it be on the side of pleasure, will give the *good* tendency of the act . . . , with respect to the interests of that *individual* person; if on the side of pain, the bad tendency. . . . [then] Take an account of the *number* of persons whose interests appear to be concerned; and repeat the above process with respect to each. . . . Take the *balance;* which, if on the side of *pleasure,* will give the general *good tendency* of the act, with respect to the total number of the community of individuals concerned; if on the side of pain, the general *evil tendency,* with respect to the same community.

Bentham's idea is to take the balance of pleasure over pain for each individual affected by an act and add them all up. Acts are then ranked according to how much total pleasure or pain they cause. Bentham then supposes that the act that causes the greatest total amount of pleasure, or the least amount of pain, is the morally best act. Let us say that an act that causes the greatest total amount of pleasure for everyone affected by the act, or the least amount of pain, *maximizes utility.* This gives us the following utilitarian principle:

> Hedonistic Utilitarianism: An act is ethically permissible if and only if it maximizes utility. Acts that do not maximize utility are not ethically permissible.

For example, suppose Jones can do either A or B, but not both, and that Jones, Smith, and Brown are the only people affected by A and B. To make calculation of utility easier, also suppose pleasure is measured in positive units and pain in negative units. Now, to decide which act maximizes utility, Jones first estimates the units of pleasure A causes Smith and adds the units of pain. For instance, suppose A causes Smith six units of pleasure and two units of pain, for a sum of four units of pleasure. She does the same thing for Brown and finds that A causes her five units of pleasure. Finally, she anticipates the amount of pleasure and pain A will cause herself. Assume it is one unit of pain. Then she adds all three together and determines that A causes a total of eight units of pleasure. She repeats the same process for B and calculates that B causes a total of seven units of pleasure. Since the amount of total pleasure A causes is greater than the amount B causes, A maximizes utility.

Utilitarianism: For and Against

All forms of consequentialism claim that the morally right thing to do is to promote the good of persons. This view has great appeal. Surely it is right to do good for people. No ethical view that denied this would be remotely plausible. In addition, consequentialism has the virtue of simplicity—all actions are ethically measured against the single standard of promoting good. And consequentialism is compatible with commonsense ideas about the kinds of acts that ought to be praised or condemned. Everyone agrees that promoting the good of persons deserves praise, and inhibiting it deserves condemnation. For these reasons, consequentialism is a powerful ethical view, one that cannot be dismissed lightly.

Consequentialism begins to lose its attractions, however, when we start to think about how to implement it. For instance, particular versions of consequentialism, such as hedonistic utilitarianism, are only as plausible as the theory of human good they advocate. So hedonistic utilitarianism is only as good as the hedonistic psychology on which it rests. And hedonism is neither a very convincing theory of actual human motivation, nor of what human motivation ought to be.

But leaving that problem aside, there remain practical difficulties that may be insurmountable. For example, hedonistic utilitarianism supposes that individuals can compare their own pleasures and pains; for example, Jones can say with certainty that this act causes her twice as much pleasure as that act, or that the pleasure of this is three times as much as the pain of that. But can we make such comparisons? You may like chocolate ice cream more than vanilla, but can you say that it gives you exactly twice as much pleasure? Or that eating chocolate causes you three times more pleasure than getting a paper cut causes you pain? No doubt some pleasures are greater than others, as are some pains, but it seems unlikely that we can say exactly how much greater. And it is not clear that pleasures can at all be quantitatively compared with pains. Furthermore, how can the pleasures and pains of one individual be compared with those of another? How can one person determine that his pleasure from eating chocolate is more, less, or the same as another person's? The only way, it would seem, is for the first person to experience the pleasure of the second and compare it with his own. But this is impossible. One person cannot experience the pleasures and pains of another. And if a person cannot know exactly how much pleasure or pain an act will cause others, there is no way to calculate utility. So there is no way to decide which act is ethically permissible. And nothing could be more useless than an ethical view which exhorts one to act ethically and at the same time is so constructed as to ensure that one never knows whether one is acting ethically or not.

To implement hedonistic utilitarianism, persons must make calculations that cannot be made. Thus, as it stands, hedonistic egoism is not acceptable. Nor can it be made acceptable by substituting an alternative account of human good as long as the good for human beings is tied to subjective experience. For example, one might try, as Mill did, to distinguish between the kinds of pleasures that persons experience. Some pleasures, Mill argued, are qualitatively better than others; for instance, intellectual pleasures are better than the pleasure one gets from food. He proposed that "competent judges," who had experienced a variety of pleasures, establish a hierarchy of different kinds of pleasure. Then, when making utilitarian calculations, "better" pleasures would count more heavily than "worse" pleasures. However, what standard of measurement do these judges use to decide that some pleasures are *better* than others instead of just *different* from others? Why should their standard be used instead of some other? And how do they know that what they experience as "better" is not experienced as "worse" by some other person? Mill has no convincing answer to these questions. Regardless of the kind or quality of the subjective experience said to constitute the good for persons, it seems impossible to establish an objective measure of that experience that can be used to calculate utility.[6]

Hedonistic utilitarians could respond to these objections by pointing out that, despite the difficulties mentioned, judgments about the relative amount of pain and pleasure an act will cause are often made. For example, think of the judgments made by parents, teachers, judges, and government officials. Making judgments about the subjective experience an act will cause is an inescapable part of the responsible exercise of legal and administrative power. And it is not as chancy an enterprise as the objection portrays. Mature and thoughtful people generally have a good idea of what will cause others pleasure and pain, and of how much it will cause. So there is no need to abandon hedonistic utilitarianism so quickly. Perhaps measurement of pains and pleasures cannot be precise, but it can be good enough to permit reliable judgments about the relative ethical worth of actions.

Hedonistic utilitarians who make this reply are advocating an important revision in the theory. They are abandoning the idea that *maximizing* utility is the sole criterion of the ethical worth of an action, and are substituting in its place the criterion of *"doing the best one can"* to maximize utility. For example, suppose Jones can do either A or B, but not both.

She estimates as best she can the amount of utility A will cause and the amount B will cause. She decides that A will cause more utility and so does A. As things turn out, her estimate is wrong and A causes less utility than B would have. According to the original principle of hedonistic utilitarianism, Jones's act is ethically impermissible. But since she did the best she could to estimate the utilities of A and B, on the revised theory it can no longer be said that what she did was wrong.

How can one judge whether an act is permissible or not according to the new criterion? Formerly, it was alleged to be a relatively objective matter. If an act maximized utility it was ethically permissible; otherwise, it was not. Judgments about the intentions and abilities of the person performing the act were not relevant. But now such judgments are relevant because one must decide whether a person really did do the best he or she could. One must decide, for example, whether the person diligently looked for all the available data and made a rational judgment based on the data. The outcome of the act—the utility it causes—becomes less important than the effort and skill the person put into deciding what to do. Consequences become subordinate to good faith effort by individuals. Thus, judgments about the ethical worth of individuals, not actions, become of primary importance.

This change has far-reaching implications for hedonistic utilitarianism. So much so that it is questionable whether it is accurate to continue to classify the theory as consequentialist. But we will leave this issue and discuss another problem with implementing hedonistic utilitarianism.

Suppose Jones can do either A or B, but not both, and that A and B affect only Jones, Smith, and Brown. Jones determines that A causes twelve units of pleasure for Smith, and one unit of pain each for Jones and Brown. Thus A causes a total of ten units of pleasure. B causes three units of pleasure each for Jones, Smith, and Brown, for a total of nine units of pleasure. The principle of hedonistic utilitarianism instructs Jones to maximize utility, so she should do A. But suppose she does B instead. Has she acted unethically?

Imagine that Jones defends her action as follows: I know that A maximizes utility but I choose to do B because A *unfairly distributes* pain and pleasure. Smith gets all the pleasure and Brown and I get all the pain. B, on the other hand, gives each of us some pleasure and no one suffers pain. That seems much more fair. After all, why should Brown and I agree to suffer pain just so Smith can get all that pleasure? Why should we bear all the burdens and he get all the benefits?

Jones's defense highlights what many consider the most serious defect in hedonistic utilitarianism. It is completely insensitive to the distribution of pain and pleasure. It does not matter who gets how much pain or how much pleasure as long as utility is maximized. This makes it easy to construct examples in which hedonistic utilitarianism requires action that seems clearly wrong. For instance, suppose utility is maximized in the United States by ensuring that an ethnic minority gets all the pain and the white majority gets all the pleasure. That is unfair, but nothing in hedonistic utilitarianism prohibits it. Thus, if one believes that some distributions are more fair or just than others, and that being fair or just takes precedence over maximizing utility, then one will reject hedonistic utilitarianism.

One might suppose that utilitarianism can be repaired by adding some principle of distribution to the theory. Many attempts have been made to do this.[7] Some have argued, for instance, that individuals are justified in attaching greater weight to their own utility, thus enabling them to avoid sacrificing their personal good for the sake of the community except in rare circumstances. Others have argued that some distributions are unacceptable because they violate individual rights. These strategies assume that there is something about persons that insulates them from certain kinds of treatment, that make it unfair or unjust to treat them in certain ways. We will discuss several of these views in the pages to come. But before we do, we would like to emphasize again the importance and appeal of utilitarianism. Although many objections can be raised against it, in our opinion there is something undeniably right about utilitarianism. The basic idea—that it is morally right to contribute to the common welfare—is intuitively unassailable. The problem is to figure out exactly what one is obligated to contribute under different conditions. Sophisticated forms of utilitarianism make valiant efforts to address this problem, and not without success. Unfortunately, we are unable to discuss these theories in this introduction, but we commend them to you. Some of them are listed in the suggested readings.

DEONTOLOGICAL ETHICS

Kant and the Good Will

The ethical view developed by the eighteenth-century philosopher Immanuel Kant stands in sharp contrast to consequentialism, relativism, and subjectivism. Kant's ethic does not depend on some prior concept of human good, it does not judge the ethical worth of actions based on their consequences, and it does not appeal to the desires of individuals or the common opinion of groups as a basis for ethical rules. Instead, Kant attempts to derive certain special ethical rules from the concept of reason. And because Kant believed that all mature persons have the capacity to reason, he thought that these rules applied to everyone. His arguments are subtle and complex. They are also among the most important and influential ethical arguments ever devised.

One place to begin Kant's ethics is to ask: What gives an action moral worth? What is it about a morally praiseworthy action that makes it praiseworthy? Consequentialists think that morally praiseworthy acts are those that have the best overall consequences. Results are what count; nothing else is relevant. Kant disagrees. He argues that we cannot judge the ethical worth of an action by its consequences because we cannot guarantee that what we intend to do actually occurs. Things can, and often do, go wrong. We may will to do good and inadvertently cause evil, or will to do evil and cause good. So the moral worth of an action cannot be defined by its consequences. Rather, Kant argues, it is defined by the act of willing itself. To see how this happens, we need to make two preliminary points.

The first is that, according to Kant, the will is an internal faculty common to all persons. The will issues commands such as "Let me now do X." But it only issues commands at the end of a process of reasoning. Hence, to will to do something is to rationally choose to do that thing. Kant says that the commands issued by the will can be formulated in statements he calls *maxims.* He believes that every act of will is associated with a maxim that expresses the intention of the agent. For example, if Jones wills to pay money she owes, the maxim that expresses her intention is "Let me now pay my debt."

The second point is that Kant thinks of morality as the performance of duty. To perform a moral duty, for Kant, is to fulfill a requirement that is binding on all persons. We determine our duties by using a special rule of ethics which Kant calls the moral law. But there are at least two motivations for following a law. One is because we desire something—specifically, to gain the approval of our peers or to avoid a fine or other penalty. The other is respect for the law itself. One can choose to obey the law, not from desire or fear or calculated self-interest, but solely because one honors the law, because following the law is the right thing to do. When a person respects the moral law and does what is right because it is right and for no other reason, Kant says that he or she is acting from a *good will.*

Kant believes that a good will is good without qualification. It is the only good thing that cannot be put to a bad use. When we act from a good will—when we do our duty out of respect for the moral law—then and only then do our actions have moral worth. Thus, we have Kant's answer to the question asked above: an action has moral worth just in case it is done from a good will. However, it leads naturally to another question, namely, what is the moral law?

Kant and the Categorical Imperative

To answer this question, it is helpful to understand Kant's ethical view as an attempt to find a rule for sorting maxims into those that are ethically acceptable and those that are not. For example, suppose Jones borrowed $5 from Smith and promised to pay it back the next day. When Jones sees Smith, she could choose the maxim "Let me now pay my debt" or "Let me now avoid paying my debt." Kant believes that the former maxim is ethically correct and the latter is not. What he wants to do is find an ethical rule that always directs us to choose the former. It is this rule that he calls the moral law.

Kant argues that the rule, or moral law, will be expressed in the form of a command or imperative. He points out that there are two kinds of imperatives: hypothetical imperatives, which have the form "If you desire A, do B"; and categorical imperatives, which have the form "Do A." However, the imperative Kant is looking for cannot be hypothetical. The reason is that the moral law is both *universal* and *necessary.* It is universal in that it applies to all persons, and necessary in that it does not depend on human sense experience; that is, it does not refer to desires. But hypothetical imperatives make reference to our desires. Desires are discovered in sense experience; they are neither universal nor necessary. Thus, hypothetical imperatives are neither universal nor necessary. Thus, the rule for choosing maxims is a categorical imperative.

A categorical imperative, Kant argues, derives strictly from human reason. It makes no reference to consequences and is independent of desire. And since it arises from reason, it is acceptable to and binding upon all rational agents simply in virtue of their rationality.

It is important to see that a command like "Shut the door!" is not a categorical imperative even though it seems to have the form "Do A." The reason is that it makes implicit reference to desire, the desire to have the door shut. A true categorical imperative makes neither explicit nor implicit reference to desire. It applies to persons regardless of their desires.

To summarize thus far, Kant argues that the moral law is a categorical imperative. This imperative has the following characteristics: (1) it applies to all persons, (2) it makes no reference to desire, (3) it is a product of human reason, and (4) it can be used to sort maxims into those that are morally acceptable and those that are not. After much complex argument, Kant proposes the following as the categorical imperative:

> First Categorical Imperative: Act only according to that maxim whereby you can at the same time will that it should become a universal law.

This is the moral law. It meets all of Kant's requirements. It is a categorical imperative. It is expressed in a universal form that applies to everyone. It makes no reference to desire or consequences. And, Kant tries to show, it arises from pure reason. This is why it is appropriate to call it a law. It is a law, not in the sense that it is passed by a legislature, but because it is a product of our own reason. Since each person has the faculty of reason, each person is (or could be) the author of the moral law. So in a sense we legislate the law to ourselves. We are not bound to obey it by some external force; rather, we are motivated to follow it by respect for ourselves and our own rationality. We follow the moral law because doing so expresses our nature as rational beings. To refuse to follow it is, therefore, irrational and against our nature.

How is one supposed to use the moral law to choose maxims? The idea is something like this. When a person is faced with a moral choice he or she formulates the maxim of his or her choice as a categorical "do this." Then the person asks whether the maxim can be *universalized,* i.e, whether it can be willed that everyone, in similar circumstances, choose the same maxim and follow it. If it can be willed as a universal law, one that everyone should always follow, let us say it is *compatible with* the moral law. Maxims that are compatible with the moral law are morally acceptable. If a maxim is not compatible with the moral law, it is not morally acceptable.

But why does compatibility matter? What difference does it make whether a maxim is compatible with the moral law or not? One reason it matters, Kant says, is because the moral law is a principle of reason, and maxims incompatible with the moral law are rationally inconsistent. They require us both to will a certain act at a certain time, and not to will the same act at the same time. But we cannot rationally consent both to do something and not to do it, and anything to which we cannot rationally consent cannot imply moral duties. Thus, maxims incompatible with the moral law are not ethically acceptable guides for action.

An example of how this is supposed to work might help. Recall Ted Brown's dilemma about whether or not to pay a bribe to get a big contract. To offer a bribe is to try to ensure that one secretly receives special treatment, treatment that puts others at a clear disadvantage. Can Ted consistently will that everyone in his circumstances pay the bribe? He cannot, for if it were to be a universal law that everyone offered a bribe to get a big contract, Ted would no longer be able to use bribery to get special treatment. Everyone would know about it, and his advantage would disappear. Thus, Ted cannot universalize his action. His maxim is not compatible with the moral law and so is not morally acceptable.

Here is another example. Suppose Jones promises Smith to do something although she has no intention of keeping her promise. The maxim of her act is "Make promises when it is to your advantage even when you have no intention of keeping them." Can this be universalized? No, because if everyone were to do this, the practice of promising would be undermined. No one would accept a promise at face value. As Kant says, "No one would believe what was promised to him but would only laugh at any such assertion as vain pretense." Since the maxim cannot be universalized, it is incompatible with the moral law and is not morally acceptable.

Criticisms of Kant

One of the main features of universalizable maxims is that they prevent persons who follow them from regarding themselves as special cases deserving of treatment that others are denied. That is one of the strengths of Kant's theory. It is not ethically acceptable to make exceptions for oneself. As it turns out, however, the feature of allowing no exceptions can be turned against Kant. Here is one of Kant's own examples.

Suppose Brown, who is innocent of any wrongdoing, is fleeing from someone who intends to murder him. Brown sees you and tells you where he is going to hide. Then the murderer comes along and asks you where Brown went. Should you tell the truth?

Since a general policy of lying is incompatible with the moral law, Kant argues that you should. As he puts it, "To be truthful in all deliberations, therefore, is a sacred and absolutely commanding decree of reason, limited by no expediency." Thus, Kant seems to believe there can be no exceptions to telling the truth.

But this cannot be the whole story. It cannot be right that one's only duty is to tell the truth. Surely one also has a duty to protect Brown. However, Kant permits no exceptions for Brown. What has gone wrong?

The main problem is that in the circumstances in which you find yourself, it is unclear which maxim you should universalize. One possibility is "Always lie when asked a question." This is obviously incompatible with the moral law and should be rejected. But Kant seems to assume that rejecting this maxim implies accepting "Never lie when asked a question," which he believes is compatible with the moral law. However, there are other maxims one might follow—for example, "Lie when no other alternative is available to protect the innocent from serious harm." This seems compatible with the moral law. If it were universalized, murderers would no longer ask for directions, but that is no loss. Yet both maxims, the one Kant accepts and the one about protecting the innocent, apply in the present situation. How do you decide which to follow? And does it make a *moral* difference which decision you make?

The root of the difficulty is this. Any action can be described in a number of ways. These descriptions can be formulated into maxims, some of which will be universalizable and some not. However, Kant provides no method to decide which of the universalizable maxims should be chosen. Without this method, his theory cannot be used to make an exact determination of our moral duty. Thus, Kant's theory is incomplete. It does not give clear-cut guidance in situations in which moral choices must be made.

Someone (not Kant) might respond that it makes no moral difference which maxim one chooses as long as it is universalizable and one acts from respect for the moral law. But this is wrong. It does make a difference. Based on the maxim you choose, Brown either lives or dies. And that is certainly a moral difference. Universalizability is not sufficient to tell us our moral duty. Something else is needed, something that tells us which universalizable maxim to follow.

If universalizability is not a sufficient test for moral duty, then perhaps universalizable maxims give us only prima facie duties—that is, duties that hold unless overridden by other moral considerations. For example, the duty not to lie may be overridden by our obligation to protect the innocent. So to know our moral duty, we need to know when one obligation is overridden by another. Since Kant believes that duties are absolute rather than prima facie, he has nothing to say about this. However, here is a suggestion that might work: a duty D_1 is overridden by another duty D_2 in circumstances C just in case there is a reason for doing D_2 rather than D_1 in C that every rational person would accept. The danger here is that there may be no such reason—no reason for doing one thing rather than another that everyone would accept. If so, then there could be cases of conflict of duty that cannot be resolved. No matter what one does, one acts immorally. That would be a moral tragedy.

The Second Version of the Categorical Imperative

Kant gives a second version of the categorical imperative which he rather mysteriously claims is equivalent to the first:

> Second Categorical Imperative: Act so that you treat humanity, whether in your own person or that of another, always as an end and never as a means only.

This imperative includes two of the main ideas of ethics in the western tradition. The first is that persons should be treated as ends in themselves—that is, as beings that are intrinsically valuable in themselves. The reason, for Kant, is that persons are centers of moral goodness. He believes that moral goodness can exist in the world only in beings that can apprehend the moral law and freely choose to act from a sense of duty. The second idea is that persons are never to be treated merely as means to an end. Although we often use people as a means to gain something we want, we should at the same time acknowledge that they have value independent of their usefulness to us. They are not to be manipulated or exploited and then cast aside as one would a broken tool. For example, in relationships between teachers and students, doctors and patients, parents and children, and legislators and citizens, each party uses the other as a means to some end. But, Kant argues, each party should also regard the other as ends in themselves, and should treat them with the dignity and respect they deserve. Surely he is right about this.

Although the second imperative undeniably captures an important part of our ethical intuitions, it suffers from the same defect as the first. It does not give specific guidance in situations involving a moral choice. For example, suppose Ted Brown tries to follow the second imperative when deciding whether to offer a bribe. Does bribery treat others as ends in themselves or merely as means to an end? On one hand, it might be said that bribery does use others as mere means since it is a deceptive attempt to gain an unfair advantage. On the other, exactly which "others" are being so used? The other people who submitted a bid on the contract? But these people presumably did not submit the bid for themselves; rather, they were acting for a corporation. Corporations are not the sorts of things that apprehend the moral law and act from a sense of duty; that is something that only people can do. Thus, corporations are not intrinsically valuable in themselves. Thus, there is nothing wrong with using them as mere means.

In many business situations relations between persons, corporations, governments, unions, public interest groups, and so on, are very complex. What does it mean, what could it mean, to treat persons as ends in themselves in these circumstances? Without doubt, the sentiment is admirable, but sentiment is next to useless when one needs to know *precisely* what to do *now*. About this, the second imperative has little to say of practical use.

In response, it could be argued that the objection raised against the second imperative is unfair. Kant never envisioned Ted Brown's dilemma, nor would he claim that the second imperative gives specific instructions in all circumstances. It is most useful in personal relationships in which people know each other and can judge more accurately when a specific behavior inappropriately uses others as means. That is its real application, and it is an important one.

We concede the point. The second imperative does not comfortably fit cases like Ted Brown's, so in a sense the objection is unfair. However, even in more personal relationships it does not do much better. For example, if you tell Brown's murderer where Brown is hidden, are you treating Brown with respect as an end in himself? Or if you lie to his murderer, are you treating the murderer as a mere means? The answers are not clear; arguments could be given either way. So the second imperative, like the first, needs something else, something that permits more precise answers to the questions raised.

One possible way to supplement Kant's theory is with the idea that people have moral rights that proscribe or compel certain behaviors. We will discuss rights in the next section. But before we do, recall that at the end of the section on relativism, the question was posed: Why should I care about the interests of others as long as my interests are not involved? Kant's answer, and it is a good one, is that individuals should care about other people because they are centers of moral goodness and bearers of intrinsic value. Therefore, all people deserve to be treated with respect and dignity. To ignore the interests of other people, to shrug off the value they possess and pretend they do not matter, is to deny them what they are due. Furthermore, unless one is willing to be treated with disrespect and contempt oneself, it is to universalize a maxim that is plainly incompatible with the moral law. It is to say, "I need not consider the interests of others provided they cannot harm or help me, but when I cannot harm or help them, I want them to consider my interests nevertheless." In other words, one makes an exception for oneself for no good reason, indeed, for no reason at all other than "that is what I want."

Before we leave this section on Kant, we should emphasize that we have given only the briefest introduction to many important facets of Kant's ethical philosophy, and we have left others out entirely. At best we have provided an interpretation of Kant's ethics, one that we think fairly represents some of the things he had to say, but no doubt one that some scholars will disagree with. We encourage everyone interested in ethical questions to read Kant and make up their own minds about his views. Kant's works are sometimes difficult, but they are invariably rewarding.

RIGHTS

The Nature of Rights

Over the last several centuries the language of rights has become commonplace in moral discourse. The conviction that people have rights has motivated the writing of documents from the U.S. Declaration of Independence and the Bill of Rights to the United Nations' Universal Declaration of Human Rights. Everyone thinks he or she has rights, and everyone thinks rights are important. Among these rights are said to be rights to freedom of speech and assembly, property rights, rights to equal treatment, rights to equal pay for equal work, rights to education and basic medical care, rights to privacy, a right to know, and even a right to periodic vacation with pay. It is standard practice to invoke these and other rights in a throng of heated disputes about social and legal issues such as abortion, affirmative action, workplace privacy, the treatment of children, and environmental protection. But what are rights? Which rights do we have? And how important are they?

In many cases, to say that someone has a right is to say that he or she has a justified claim against some person or group of persons. Rights of this kind are called *claim rights.* If a person has a claim right, then he or she is justly due something from others, something that can be demanded without appealing to their kindness, gratitude, pity, or good will. No favor, permission, or grant is needed to exact anything that one has as a matter of right. A person can insist that his or her rights be respected regardless of the wishes or inclinations of others, and, should those rights be denied without sufficient justification, properly raise indignant complaint. Thus, to have a claim right to something puts it beyond the reach of others to deny or withhold except in the most extreme circumstances. It is to have the most compelling and powerful claim of all.

One reason claim rights are so powerful is that they are correlative with duties—with what is due the holder of the right. If someone has a claim right of a certain kind, others have duties toward that person. These duties require either that other people not behave in certain ways toward the person, or that he or she be provided with certain goods or benefits. For example, if someone has a right to not be tortured, then others have a duty to not torture him or her; if he or she has a right to medical care, then others are required to provide him or her with medical care. Let us say that claim rights of the former kind are *barrier rights.* If someone has a barrier right, then others are barred from acting in certain ways toward that person. Claim rights of the latter kind are *welfare rights.* If someone has a welfare right, then others are required to provide the person with some good or make the good available to the person.

Although claim rights are an important class of rights, not all rights are claim rights because not all rights imply that other people have specific duties. For example, in the United States, a woman has a right to get an abortion, but no individual has a duty to perform abortions. In business, companies have a right to sell their products, but no one has a duty to buy them. We will not discuss these other rights in this introduction. However, several detailed analyses of rights are listed in the suggested readings.

Legal and Moral Rights

Claim rights ("rights" for brevity) can be further classified as either legal or moral rights. In the United States, legal rights derive from the Constitution, laws passed by legislatures and common law. Moral rights differ from legal rights in three important ways. First, they do not originate in nor are they justified by the actions of judges or legislative bodies. Second, they are held equally by all persons at all places and times. Third, unless they are codified in law, moral rights are not legally enforceable. To assert one's moral rights is to make a moral rather than a legal claim.[8] But all of this presents a puzzle. If moral rights are had by everyone but do not derive from legislative or judicial action, then evidently one does not have to do anything to possess them. Where, then, do they come from? In virtue of what do persons possess them? And if in many cases they cannot be legally enforced, why value them? In fact, why suppose there are moral rights at all?[9]

A Case for Rights

One reason to think there are moral rights is that they seem to be both the source of many legal rights and the ground or basis from which legitimate criticisms can be made of legal rights. For example, the authors of the Declaration of Independence appealed to "unalienable rights" as a basis from which to criticize the rule of Great Britain and declare it invalid. These rights, for instance, the "Right of the People" to form a new government with new laws, were not legal rights. Indeed, they were used to justify actions that were decidedly illegal.

Moral rights can also be used to justify maintaining as well as changing law. For example, suppose that, using legal means provided for in the Constitution, an attempt is made to repeal the Bill of Rights. If you believe that this is not only a bad idea, but that persons would be wronged unless government is prevented from taking actions prohibited in the Bill of Rights, then you are assuming and appealing to moral rights that are independent of the law.[10]

There are many other examples of moral rights being used to criticize the law, or as a justification for passing laws. Social movements, such as the civil rights movement, have been organized to gain rights not codified in law. Wars have been fought to maintain them, and revolutions begun to achieve them. This reiterates a point made earlier: most people have the concept of a moral right and believe it has meaningful application in human affairs. Perhaps this pragmatic justification of moral rights is all that is needed. However, in our view, there is another and more compelling justification. To see what it is, we need to return to Kant.

Kant argues that persons are intrinsically valuable. By this he means, in part, that they have value that is independent of their being valued. Thus, persons have value independent of their value as means to some end. As Kant says, they are ends in themselves. Moreover, all persons have value regardless of whether it is acknowledged or recognized. And all persons have the same degree of intrinsic value. Individuals differ in ability, achievement, and moral and personal virtue, but their intrinsic value is the same.

Now, to say that something is intrinsically valuable or valuable in itself sometimes implies that it is *worth seeking* for itself, and not only worth seeking because it is useful. Pleasure and happiness are intrinsically valuable in this sense. But pleasure and happiness are *psychological states.* They are experiences worth seeking for themselves, and seeking to experience such states is how humans acknowledge their value. But humans are not experiences; they are things that have experiences. Thus, they are not worth seeking in the sense that pleasure and happiness are worth seeking. Thus, to acknowledge the value of persons is not to seek a certain kind of experience. If we are to acknowledge the value of persons, if we are to see them as things that are worthwhile in themselves, something else must be done. But what?

To begin with, note that Kant and the utilitarians share an important belief, which is, roughly, that persons have a moral obligation to promote, protect, or enhance whatever is intrinsically valuable. For utilitarians, intrinsic value is located, so to speak, in experience, such as the experience of pleasure. So utilitarians take it to be their moral obligation to maximize experiences of pleasure. Kant, on the other hand, locates intrinsic value in persons, and only derivatively in human experience. Thus, he believes there is a moral obligation to promote, protect, or enhance persons *qua* persons. This he proposes to do by treating persons as ends in themselves. But exactly how should we acknowledge the intrinsic value that all persons equally possess?

Here is a possibility. All normal persons have the capacity to exercise free choice in service of their interests. We suggest, then, that one way to promote, protect, and enhance the intrinsic value of persons is to grant that they have a valid claim, a *right,* to use this capacity. To respect this right is one way to acknowledge the value of persons. It is to grant that, in an important sense, to freely choose for oneself what one will do, believe, or become, is part of what it means to be a human. It need not be the only way that human value is acknowledged, but it is the only way that gives persons the "moral space" to fashion their own lives according to their own lights. It is one way to respect our common humanity, to grant us our due as beings who can apprehend the moral law and freely choose to follow it.

Barrier Rights and Welfare Rights

So far we have argued that everyone has a right to exercise free choice in service of their interests. This right can be used to discover other rights. For example, if one has a right to free choice, then it seems reasonable that one has a right to whatever is needed to exercise free choice, for without these other rights the right to free choice would be empty. Among the things needed to exercise free choice is physical security. If the security of one's person or property can be denied or abridged without penalty by arbitrary government edicts or the caprice of individuals, then free choice means little. The right to physical security in turn implies that persons have a right to not be unjustifiably harmed—that is, the right not to be murdered or tortured. These are what we earlier called barrier rights.

A number of other barrier rights have been proposed. Whether these can be derived from the right to free choice is controversial. However, it is generally supposed that barrier rights of all kinds protect vital human interests. Two important examples are the interests persons have in participating in the life of the community, and having a reasonable expectation of accomplishing personal goals. Barrier rights that protect the first interest might be, for example, rights to free speech and assembly, a right to equal treatment under law, and the right to vote and seek political office.

Barrier rights also protect the second interest. Without physical security, for example, no one could have reasonable expectations about the future. A number of people have argued, however, that barrier rights are not enough to protect the second interest. Welfare rights are needed as well. Rights to basic education, health care, and a guaranteed minimum standard of living are all needed, it has been argued, if one is to have any prospects for the future or any hope of undertaking a life plan. Whether there are welfare rights, and if there are, what specific obligations they impose, are issues we will not try to settle. We only note that if persons have a vital interest in living a fulfilling life, then it is difficult to see how one could not claim, as a matter of right, the basic goods needed to make a fulfilling life possible.[11]

Conflict of Rights

In political, social, and personal interactions there are many cases in which rights seem to conflict. For example, one person's right to free speech may conflict with another's right to privacy, or one person's right to nondiscriminatory treatment may conflict with another's right to associate with whomever he or she pleases. These cases can be handled in one of two ways. First, a conflict of rights is often only apparent and not actual. Frequently rights are stated in simple and unqualified language that encourages bold assertions based on modest reasons. Unless properly qualified, one person's "I have a right to say what I please" will inevitably conflict with another's "I have a right not to be offended by language I find distasteful." In these cases, the specific content of the right and the circumstances under which it holds need to be carefully analyzed. Not all rights hold in all situations without exception. An assertion of right, such as the right to free speech, should always be given due consideration, but it does not entitle one to shout "Fire!" in a crowded theater.

Sometimes, however, the conflict is real. It then should be recognized that rights, like duties, are prima facie: one right can be overridden by another in special cases. For example, the right to peaceful enjoyment of one's property may be overridden by concerns for public safety. The general rule is that, since rights protect interests, when one person's interests are stronger or more compelling than another's then rights to the latter can be justifiably overridden by rights to the former. Some interests are so strong, however, that it is difficult to imagine cases in which rights protecting those interests can be justifiably overridden. An example is the right to not be tortured.

Although rights can be overridden, the reasons for doing so must be very strong. One person's rights cannot be overridden by the whims of others or by marginal gains for the good of the community. Recognizing rights demonstrates our belief in the value and dignity of persons. To override a right for less than overwhelming reasons belittles the value of persons and denies their dignity. It is not something to be undertaken lightly.

THE ETHICS OF VIRTUE

The Issue of Character

At the beginning of this introduction we defined ethics as the study of what is good or right for persons, of the goals they ought to pursue, and the actions they ought to perform. We understood this definition to imply that the main task of ethics is to discover what responsible moral agents should do when confronted with decisions about right and wrong. One way to approach this task is to carefully formulate ethical or moral principles that distinguish between ethically permissible and ethically impermissible behavior. The principles are then used as guides for making ethical decisions. Utilitarianism and Kantianism are rival accounts of what those principles should be.

There is, however, quite a different way to understand the main task of ethics. Instead of focusing on moral principles, which are used to help answer the question "what should I do?", it focuses primarily on moral character, and asks "what kind of person should I be or become?" This approach to ethics is based on the concept of *virtue.* It emphasizes moral education and the development of moral character rather than a strict adherence to moral principles. The advantage of this approach, its proponents believe, is that it gives a much more complete and useful account of human life as it is actually lived by real persons in the historical and cultural circumstances in which they find themselves. It does not suppose that persons are, as one writer put it, "faceless ethical agents" striving to follow some abstract utilitarian or Kantian principle. Rather, it tries to describe and understand the traits that enable a person to lead a full and satisfying ethical life.

Virtues are traits of character that both help individuals achieve their goals and are beneficial to the larger community. Examples of virtues are courage, temperance, compassion, generosity, kindness, honesty, and concern for justice. Virtues should be distinguished from other personal traits, such as good health or innate intelligence, because virtues are components of one's character that engage the will. Virtuous acts do not happen by chance. They are chosen by someone who is fully aware of what he or she is doing. And they are chosen because they are virtuous, and not because they satisfy self-interest or are pleasurable. However, the Greek philosopher Aristotle, whose analysis of virtue is justly famous and influential, claimed that if one were trained or trained oneself to be, say, charitable, then charitable acts would become pleasurable and miserly acts painful. The charitable person does not begrudge giving money, nor does he or she resent those who receive it. For the charitable person, giving is enjoyable. But, once again, the reason one gives is not because it is enjoyable, but because it is virtuous.

The value of virtues for the individual and the community seems evident. Persons without some measure of the virtues mentioned above are not widely admired, nor, despite certain media images to the contrary, do they generally succeed in life. And a community composed of persons with few virtues is not likely to do well in the long run. Liars, cheats, cowards, and scofflaws are not valuable citizens. An important question, then, is how do persons become virtuous? According to Aristotle, it begins with moral education. Through education one learns the appropriate way to act in different circumstances. One acquires the virtue of honesty, for example, by being taught to act honestly and acting honestly in a variety of situations. Eventually these acts are chosen for their own sake, and honesty becomes a part of one's character. Other virtues are acquired in the same way.

Can one teach oneself to be virtuous? For example, can one teach oneself to be courageous? It would seem so, provided three conditions are met. First, one needs a model to follow, someone who actually is courageous. Second, one needs the willpower to act as that person would act if he or she were in a situation that calls for courage. Third, one needs real opportunities to act courageously. Courage (and all other virtues) is a behavior that is learned by doing. For instance, suppose you are a soldier about to enter a battle. You know you are not particularly courageous, but your friend Jones is. When you are in danger, you could ask yourself, "What would Jones do now?" Since Jones is courageous, she would act courageously as a matter of course. If you model your behavior after what she would do, then eventually you will become courageous as well.

If one becomes virtuous by being taught to be virtuous or modeling one's behavior after virtuous persons, then moral education is of the highest importance for a society that values virtuous people. To coin a phrase, virtuous people are made, not born. The social structure in which people live—family, religion, school, and other legal and social institutions—are of central importance in teaching virtue and making it possible for the virtues to be taught. If, through failure of will or lack of conviction, society does not ensure that people have the opportunity to learn to be virtuous, then it should come as no surprise when they are not. This does not imply that people should be brainwashed or indoctrinated with the beliefs of the cultural elite. But it does imply that stands must be taken about the kinds of behaviors that are and are not socially acceptable. Tolerance of the behavior of others is a virtue, but tolerance can be taken to extremes. To tolerate all behavior is to abandon any hope that personal and social relations can be useful, satisfying, or conducive to the general good.

Virtues and Ethical Principles

Philosophers have discussed many issues about virtues that we will be unable to cover in this introduction. They have wondered, for example, whether all virtues have something in common, whether one can have some but not all of the virtues, whether one can be virtuous some but not all of the time, and whether one can exemplify virtues in the service of evil goals. There is, however, one issue we will mention briefly. It is the issue of the relation between virtue ethics and ethical principles of the kind advocated by utilitarians and Kantians. Some virtue theorists claim that one can dispense with ethical principles altogether and construct a complete ethical viewpoint based solely on virtue. Is this possible?

We believe that ethical principles must play an important role in any ethical viewpoint. For example, consider the virtue of honesty in the context of Kant's example of the man fleeing the murderer. Suppose you are an honest person. When the murderer asks you where the man went, what is the honest thing to do? Do you tell the murderer or not?

In this case, simply being honest is of no use unless you know which act is honest. And knowing which act is honest depends in part on which ethical principles you hold. For example, suppose you believe that the man fleeing the murderer has a right to life, and that this right cannot be overridden by the murderer's request. Then you would not tell the murderer where the man went. On the other hand, suppose you are a member of a slave-owning society, and that in your society a slave owner can do with his slaves as he will. And suppose that the man fleeing is a slave owned by the murderer. Do you tell the murderer where he went? Yes, because you believe it is the honest thing to do. The rights of the slave are not a consideration, either because you believe that slaves have no rights or because you believe that property rights override the slave's right to life.[12]

The difference between these two societies is not that one has honest men and women and the other does not. The difference is that they hold very different principles about the rights of persons. The slave-owning society has the wrong ethical principles. They may be honest, but it is honesty tainted by service to a mistaken ethical viewpoint.

If our argument is correct, then a complete ethical viewpoint cannot be based solely on virtue. Ethical principles also have an important part to play. However, the role of the virtues should not be underestimated. If we were to ignore them in our account of ethics, then we would omit any understanding of what it means to be a person who actually leads an ethical life. And if we were to ignore them in our practice, then we would lack the continuity, coherence, and content that give our lives meaning. To modify one of Kant's famous phrases, virtuous people who lack ethical principles are ethically blind, but ethical principles without virtuous people are empty.

CONCLUSION

Those first beginning the study of ethics often find it confusing and even disheartening. There seem to be so many different ethical views, each apparently vulnerable to criticism, that it is very difficult to sort it all out and discover a reasonable ethical position that is applicable to everyday concerns. One might be tempted to throw up one's hands and say, "When they have it all figured out, then I will listen. Until then, I will just muddle through somehow."

But there is no need to give up so easily. Things are not as bad as they may seem. What follows is a suggestion about how one might proceed.

Suppose we try to combine some of the insights of utilitarianism and Kantianism. Suppose, for example, that we take as basic principles the two parts of Kant's second version of the categorical imperative. In other words, we adopt as a basic principle, first, that no one be treated as a means, and second, that as far as possible, everyone be treated as an end in themselves. And suppose we take the first to imply that persons have, at a minimum, barrier rights that can justifiably be overridden only in extreme circumstances. And we take the second to imply that we should enhance the well-being of others—their happiness—to the extent we are able. Thus, by accepting barrier rights we ensure that persons are not treated as means, and by promoting happiness we treat them as ends in themselves.

This gives us two practical principles of ethics: respect the rights of others, and promote their happiness. However, it is possible that enhancing the happiness of some unjustifiably violates the rights of others. So we need to state our "Kantian utilitarian" principle as follows:

> An act is ethically permissible if and only if (1) it does not unjustifiably violate any barrier rights, and (2) it brings about as much overall happiness as is consistent with (1). Acts that do not meet conditions (1) and (2) are not ethically permissible.

This principle clearly needs elaboration, analysis, and defense. For instance, it might be said that welfare rights should be included in addition to barrier rights. The number and strength of barrier rights needs to be discussed, as do the conditions under which those rights can be overridden. There remain problems about measuring the amount of happiness that one's actions bring about, and even about whether happiness is the appropriate value to use. And one could object that the principle is too stringent, that it requires too much of persons for them to use it in their ordinary lives. Still, it is, we suggest, a plausible and defensible step in the right direction. It attempts to combine the Kantian insight that it is ethically unacceptable to treat people in certain ways with the utilitarian insight that one should contribute to the general welfare. Whether it proves successful from both a philosophical and practical viewpoint is something that, for the present, we must leave for others to judge.[13]

In this introduction, lengthy though it is, we have omitted many topics in ethics and barely touched on others. This is not because they are unimportant or unworthy of extended comment, but only because choices had to be made. For good or ill, the choices we made reflect what we believe to be the minimum necessary for understanding ethical issues in the world of business. We hope that we have given the reader some of the flavor of ethics, a taste of its richness and complexity. And we hope that the reader will be motivated to continue the study of ethics. Some things, we have tried to argue, are not only useful, they are worthwhile in themselves. We believe the study of ethics is one of them.

NOTES

1. In this introduction we will use the words *moral* and *ethical* interchangeably.
2. Someone might object here that even assuming that all societies have a common set of ethical rules does not show that those rules are ethically acceptable. It might be that all societies make a similar error about the rules, or that they simply follow a rule that is ethically unacceptable.
3. We will sometimes use "egoist" as an abbreviation for "psychological egoist." It is important to see that an egoist, as we will use the term, is an advocate of a theory of human motivation, not someone who has the personality trait of being self centered.
4. By "act," we mean to include both acts and omissions.
5. For an excellent discussion of this issue, see Amitai Etzioni, *The Moral Dimension: Toward a New Economics* (New York: Free Press, 1988), and Robert H. Frank, *Passions Within Reason: The Strategic Role of the Emotions* (New York: Norton, 1988).
6. Contemporary theories try to avoid this problem by using the notion of preference instead of pleasure. What is maximized is not pleasure, but the choices available to someone. Note that distribution problems could still occur. It might happen that total preferences for a group be maximized by severely restricting the choices available to a minority.
7. Bentham made such an attempt by using the notion of "extent" in his analysis of pleasure.
8. Many moral rights are codified in law. An example is the right to not be murdered. Other moral rights are not a part of law. For instance, a legal right that many people say is not a moral right is the right to an abortion. And an example of what some allege to be a moral right that is not a legal right in the United States is the right to be guaranteed a job.
9. See Jeremy Bentham, "Anarchial Fallacies," in A.I. Melden, ed., *Human Rights* (Belmont, Calif.: Wadsworth, 1970): 28–39.
10. This example is taken from David Lyons' introduction to *Rights* (Belmont, Calif.: Wadsworth, 1979): 3–4.
11. For a defense of welfare rights, see James Sterba, "The Welfare Rights of Distant Peoples and Future Generations: Moral Side Constraints on Social Policy," Social Theory and Practice 7 (Spring 1981).
12. For an excellent discussion of slave societies of this kind, and of many other issues concerning

slavery, see Orlando Patterson, *Slavery and Social Death* (Cambridge, Mass.: Harvard University Press, 1982): 190–193.

13. This argument is taken from James W. Cornman and Keith Lehrer, *Philosophical Problems and Arguments: An Introduction* (New York: The Macmillan Company, 1968): 432–434.

SUGGESTED READINGS

There are many fine books on ethics and ethical theory. We include only a very brief selection of those that the reader may find of use should he or she wish to continue the study of ethics.

Utilitarianism

The classic source for utilitarian ethics is John Stuart Mill's *Utilitarianism,* which is in many editions. An excellent collection that includes Mill's work is *Mill: Utilitarianism,* ed. Samuel Gorovitz (Indianapolis: Bobbs-Merrill, 1971). Also see J. J. C. Smart and Bernard Williams, *Utilitarianism: For and Against* (Cambridge: Cambridge University Press, 1980), and Samuel Scheffler, *The Rejection of Consequentialism* (Oxford: Oxford University Press, 1984). A sophisticated utilitarian theory is developed by Richard B. Brandt in his *A Theory of the Good and Right* (Oxford: Clarendon Press, 1979).

Deontological Ethics

Immanuel Kant's writings about ethics extend over several volumes. Perhaps the best place to begin is his *Groundwork of the Metaphysic of Morals,* many editions. An excellent secondary source is Bruce Aune's *Kant's Theory of Morals* (Princeton: Princeton University Press, 1979).

Rights

Among the many books on rights are Ronald Dworkin, *Taking Rights Seriously* (Cambridge: Harvard University Press, 1977), James W. Nickel, *Making Sense of Human Rights* (Berkeley: University of California Press, 1987), Henry Shue, *Basic Rights* (Princeton: Princeton University Press, 1980). For a view of rights that has consequentialist underpinnings, see L. W. Sumner, *The Moral Foundation of Rights* (Oxford: Clarendon Press, 1989).

Virtue

Any investigation of the virtues should probably begin with Aristotle's *Nicomachean Ethics,* many editions. For a contemporary view see Alasdair MacIntyre, *After Virtue* (Notre Dame: University of Notre Dame Press, 1981), and *Whose Justice? Which Rationality?* (Notre Dame: University of Notre Dame Press, 1988). An anthology that has many useful readings on virtue is Christina Sommers and Fred Sommers, eds., *Vice and Virtue in Everyday Life* (New York: Harcourt Brace, 1993).

Ethics and Economics

In addition to the volumes by Etzioni and Frank listed in the endnotes to the introduction, an excellent book about ethics and its relation to economics is Allen Buchanan's, *Ethics, Efficiency and the Market* (Totowa, NJ: Rowman and Allanheld, 1985). Also see David

Gauthier's, *Morals by Agreement* (Oxford: Clarendon Press, 1986), for his insightful development of a theory of morals as a part of the theory of rational choice.

Ethical Skepticism

Finally, for a skeptical view of ethics, nothing is better than J. L. Mackie's book, *Ethics: Inventing Right and Wrong* (New York: Penguin Books, 1977), and Bernard William's *Ethics and the Limits of Philosophy* (Cambridge: Harvard University Press, 1985).

PART ONE

ETHICS AND BUSINESS: FROM THEORY TO PRACTICE

In exploring the ethical dimensions of business activity, it is not always enough to focus attention on specific ethical problems. Such issues as rights and duties of employees, product liability, and the responsibility of business to the environment arise in the context of a comprehensive economic system which deeply influences our values and structures the range of choices available to us. Often we will find that the most important ethical question is not "What is right or wrong in this particular situation?" but rather "What is the ethical status of a situation which forces such a choice on the agent?" or "How can it be restructured to provide a more satisfactory climate for ethical decision making?" Some ethical problems are not isolated, but systemic; for this reason Chapter 1 of this part examines the free market system itself from an ethical perspective. What we seek when we evaluate economic systems ethically, at least in part, is a framework for business transactions and decisions, a set of procedures which, if followed, will generally bring about just results. Justice of this kind—called procedural justice—can be illustrated by the familiar method of dividing a piece of cake between two children. Assuming that the two should receive equal slices, if one child cuts the cake and the other chooses the first slice, justice should be served. Not all just procedures produce results as just as this one does. But in choosing an economic system, we look for one that provides as much justice as possible. Traditionally, it has been held in America that capitalism is such a system; critics challenge this claim. An examination of this controversy requires a clear conception of what justice is, and the first three articles in Chapter 1 provide the groundwork for such a conception by presenting important theories of economic justice.

Even if the free market system is just, it may not mean that every event that occurs according to the rules of the system is just. Just procedures are not always sufficient to ensure just results. Suppose, for example, that a person owns one of the five waterholes on an island and that the other four unexpectedly dry up, leaving the owner with a monopoly over the water supply and the opportunity to charge exorbitantly high prices for water. It might be argued that, even if the owner of the waterhole acquired it legally, did not conspire to monopolize, and allowed his prices to be determined by the fluctuations of the market, this situation is unjust. Although procedural justice may be necessary to bring about ethical outcomes, it may not be sufficient by itself to do so. Thus, although a just economic system is essential for an ethical business climate, we may also find it necessary to examine the relationships and transactions that take place within the system and to make ethical reasoning a part of business decision making at a more specific, less general level. Chapter 2 suggests some ways in which this might be done.

DISTRIBUTIVE JUSTICE

Questions of economic justice arise when people find themselves in competition for scarce resources—wealth, income, jobs, food, housing. If there are not enough of society's benefits—and too many of society's burdens—to satisfy everyone, we must ask how to distribute these benefits and burdens fairly. One of the most important problems of economic justice, then, is that of the fair distribution of limited commodities.

What does it mean to distribute things justly or fairly? To do justice is to give each person what he or she deserves or is owed. If those who have the most in a society deserve the most and those who have the least deserve the least, that society is a just one. If not, it is unjust. But what makes one person more, another less, deserving?

Philosophers have offered a wide range of criteria for determining who deserves what. One suggestion is that everyone deserves an equal share. Others hold that benefits and burdens should be distributed on the basis of need, merit, effort or hard work, or contribution to society. John Rawls, Robert Nozick, and J.J.C. Smart each emphasize one or more of these criteria in constructing a theory of economic justice.

The theory of economic justice underlying American capitalism has tended to emphasize contribution to society, along with merit and hard work, as the basis of distribution. We do not expect everyone to end up with an equal share of benefits and burdens under a capitalist system. But supporters of capitalism hold that those who receive more do so because of their greater contribution, and that for this reason the inequalities are just. Recalling the Kantian ethical principles examined in the general introduction to the text, however, it might be argued that rewarding people on the basis of what they contribute to the general welfare implies treating them as means to an end rather than as ends in themselves and overlooks the intrinsic value of persons. Each person's contribution, furthermore, depends largely on inborn skills and qualities and circumstances which permit the development of these traits. Ought people to be rewarded in proportion to accidents of birth over which they have no control? Some philosophers, like John Rawls, think not.

As an egalitarian, Rawls believes that there are no characteristics which make one person more deserving than another; there are no differences between people that justify inequalities in the distribution of social benefits and burdens. Everyone deserves an equal share. That this is true does not mean that Rawls finds all inequalities unjust; but his theory permits only inequalities that benefit everyone and to which everyone has equal opportunity.

Rawls' principles of distribution are just, he claims, because they are the principles that would be chosen by a group of rational persons designing a society—providing they are ignorant of their own abilities, preferences, and eventual social position. We ought to choose our principles of justice, Rawls argues, from behind a "veil of ignorance," a position strikingly similar to that of the child who cuts the cake evenly, unsure of which piece he or she will eventually have. Although all those in Rawls' hypothetical situation seek to protect their own interest, they are prevented from choosing a principle of distribution that will benefit themselves at the expense of others. Thus they are likely to reject a utilitarian principle of justice under which the happiness of a few might be sacrificed to maximize total well-being or a notion of justice in which distribution depends in part upon luck, skill, natural endowments, or social position. Rawls believes that they would select egalitarian principles.

Some critics have challenged Rawls' claim that rational persons acting from behind a veil of ignorance would choose egalitarian principles of justice. Rawls assumes that all people are egoists, and he fails to take account of the gamblers among us. Others ask whether the choice of egalitarian principles by uninformed egoists is really enough to justify them ethically. A possible defense of Rawls' argument involves an appeal to the Kantian ethical principle examined in the introduction to the text. Kant held that one test of the ethical acceptability of a principle is whether it can be made into a universal law without contradiction. By placing us behind a hypothetical veil of ignorance, Rawls asks us to choose principles of justice which apply to ourselves and all others equally. As a universal law, Rawls seems to be saying, only the egalitarian theory of justice is fully consistent.

Because he gives everyone a voice in what the principle of justice is to be, and because equal treatment seems to recognize every person's intrinsic worth, Rawls' theory of justice also seems to satisfy the second Kantian test, the treatment of all people as ends in themselves. It is not clear, however, that the egalitarian way is the only way to treat people as ends in themselves. Robert Nozick's libertarianism, which emphasizes individual rights instead of equal distribution, might also be susceptible to a Kantian defense.

Unlike Rawls, Nozick focuses his attention not on what each person ends up with, but on how each person acquired what he or she has. Justice for Nozick is historical; it resides in the process of acquisition. A theory of justice thus consists of setting forth rules for just acquisition, and something that has been justly acquired justly belongs to its owner even if this means that some people will receive a far greater share of benefits or burdens than others.

Nozick objects to the attempt to bring about justice by imposing a preconceived pattern of distribution, such as the egalitarian one, because he believes that no such pattern can be realized without violating people's rights. As the word *libertarian* suggests, the right most heavily emphasized by Nozick is a barrier right, the right of freedom, or noninterference. Interference, he holds, is permitted only when the rights of others are being violated. Second is the right to property that has been justly acquired. Under a libertarian theory of justice, taxation to redistribute and equalize wealth is a violation of human rights, an appropriation of the fruit of other people's freedom akin to forced labor. One might also look upon it as the treatment of others as means. The only way to treat people as ends in themselves, a libertarian might argue, is to grant them freedom from coercion. The only just pattern of distribution, libertarians claim, is not a pattern at all, but the product of a multitude of free, individual choices.

Critics of the libertarian theory generally attack what they view as its truncated conception of human rights. It may be true, they say, that persons have rights of noninterference. But surely there are other human rights more positive in nature. If persons have a right to life, for example, it could be argued that they also have welfare rights to certain things they need in order to live: food, clothing, shelter, and so on. If this is true, their right to these things might sometimes override someone else's right to noninterference. For example, Nozick himself admits that it is unjust for one person to appropriate the entire supply of something necessary for life, as in the example of the waterhole mentioned above. If it is correct that there are welfare rights that supersede the right to noninterference, libertarianism needs reexamining.

J.J.C. Smart's utilitarian theory of justice differs from both Nozick's and Rawls' in that it neither attempts to make distribution conform to a specific pattern nor focuses on the process by which distribution takes place. As a utilitarian, Smart is concerned with the maximization of happiness or pleasure, and approves of any distribution of goods that accomplishes this goal. Thus, utilitarian justice could be compatible with either an equal or an unequal distribution of goods, depending on which of the two is shown to provide the greater total happiness. Although in general Smart believes that an egalitarian distribution of benefits and burdens is most likely to maximize happiness, he is in no way committed to equality as a principle of distribution. On the contrary, if he were to find that extreme inequalities maximize happiness, he would be committed to these strategies. Utilitarianism, in short, is interested in the maximization of happiness and not in its distribution.

Some thinkers find utilitarianism's stress on the sum total of happiness to be incompatible with the very idea of justice, and Smart admits that justice is only a subordinate interest for utilitarians. Under utilitarianism, people may be denied what they deserve because that denial increases total happiness.

JUSTICE AND ECONOMIC SYSTEMS

Rawls, Nozick, and Smart offer three different theories of economic justice. They have made no claims, however, about how their principles of justice might best be embodied in an economic system. Rawls, for example, might assert that his theory is compatible with both capitalism and socialism. In articles by Irving Kristol and Kai Nielsen we examine the soundness of the concepts of justice underlying two quite different economic systems. Irving Kristol offers a defense of what he views as the capitalist conception of justice; Kai Nielsen's article presents a moral case for socialism.

Perhaps the two most important characteristics of capitalism are (1) the private ownership of the means of production (as opposed to common or government ownership), such that most of us must work for others and earn wages to make a living, and (2) a free market system, in which prices and wages are not controlled by the government or by a small, powerful group, but are allowed to fluctuate. The key word here is freedom. Essential to the system is free competition: workers must be able to move freely from job to job as they choose, and everyone must be free to enter the market to buy and sell. It is on this second characteristic that Kristol focuses in his discussion of capitalism.

Clearly, a free market system will not provide everyone with an equal share of social benefits and burdens. Indeed, the conception of justice that lies at the heart of capitalism, Kristol claims, is fundamentally *anti*egalitarian. Equality of rights and equality of opportunity—which are cornerstones of political equality—are essential to capitalism, but the system makes no guarantee of economic equality. It is interesting to note that Kristol does not believe, as Rawls does, that equality of opportunity requires us to give special compensation to the disadvantaged. For Kristol, equality of opportunity means only that there are no official barriers to opportunity. Luck will thus play an important role in success under a capitalist system.

But the fact that capitalism is consistent with economic inequality, Kristol argues, does not make it unfair. He claims that the only way to achieve economic equality is through the redistribution of wealth by a centralized government authority—a solution that violates individual liberty. Like Nozick, Kristol defends the capitalist conception of justice because he believes that it best respects people's rights and maximizes freedom.

Capitalism does more than protect liberty, Kristol argues. Even though inequalities do exist in a capitalist system, everyone, or nearly everyone, is better off than he or she would be under a different economic system. A capitalist economy maximizes efficiency, for example, and provides a far greater range of goods and services than a planned economy does. If capitalism truly benefits everybody, as Kristol claims, it might win approval not only from Nozick, but from Rawls and Smart as well.

Does everyone really benefit under a capitalist system, however? Some critics argue that the truth of this claim depends on the freedom of the market—a freedom, they hold, that is largely illusory. Because of limitations due to lack of education, poverty, or social position, it is claimed, workers are not free to move from job to job and can thus become trapped in work that is hazardous or low-paying. The influence of powerful, giant corporations skews the market. Individuals are not able to compete on the same terms as large conglomerates, and thus competition is not truly free. Kristol's picture of capitalism, critics might say, fails to take account of the very real constraints felt by people even in a free market system. For this reason, it is not clear that every person is better off in a capitalist economy.

These objections do not challenge the concept of justice presented by Kristol. They suggest only that capitalist systems fail to achieve the justice they claim. But criticisms have also been leveled at the idea of justice that underlies capitalism. Capitalist justice as Kristol describes it ignores claims of need, for example. People are free to give to others in a capitalist economy, but the needy have no real right to demand that their needs be satisfied. Thus, critics have concluded, capitalism sanctions poverty and extreme inequality, and pits human beings against each other in a fierce, competitive struggle. Even if everyone does benefit from a capitalist economy, it might be argued, it is not clear that everyone receives what he or she deserves—the criterion we referred to earlier as the mark of justice.

Capitalism not only fails to reward people equally, Kristol tells us, it also fails to reward them in proportion to merit, hard work, or contribution to society. In a capitalist system, people are rewarded solely for their contribution to the economy as defined by the market. Again, for Kristol this is one of the strengths of an admittedly imperfect system, for to achieve distributions according to criteria such as merit or hard work would require restrictions on freedom and centralized planning on a scope and scale that he could not tolerate.

Taken in its entirety Kristol's discussion defines the moral space, so to speak, in which capitalism operates. Proponents of capitalism, like Kristol, are willing to accept economic inequality in return for economic efficiency, political freedom, and minimal government interference in economic life. However, these values, which in the end are *moral* values, are not the only ones around which an economic system can be organized. In contrast to Kristol, for example, Kai Nielsen argues that a very different economic system—socialism—should be undertaken in the interest of social justice. In large part, it is because capitalism is inconsistent with social justice that socialists like Nielsen reject it.

According to Nielsen, capitalism should be rejected because it is consistent with a high degree of inequality. Placing ownership in private hands, socialists believe, creates a class system in which wealth is concentrated in the hands of a few, and the rich get richer at the expense of the poor. These economic inequalities lead to inequalities in liberty and power as well. According to socialists, a capitalist society can never be truly democratic, even in a democratic political system, because the wealthy few are far more free and powerful than others.

These problems can be solved, socialists claim, by public ownership of the means of production and careful, systematic planning. Public ownership would eliminate the need for private profit, decrease prices, and allow enterprises to better serve the public. Planning would direct the economy for the public interest, rather than allow it to be controlled randomly by the self-interested actions of a few. Socialists do not believe that planning will interfere with individual liberty and democracy, Nielsen explains. Rather, socialists are committed to democratic planning in which the people vote to determine economic goals and directions. In fact, socialism, as Nielsen presents it, sees itself as more democratic than capitalism because it involves the extension of democracy from the political into the economic arena.

Nielsen's argument is specifically a *moral* argument for socialism. He believes that moral principles should take precedence over the demand for profit. The rationale for production in capitalism is profit and capital accumulation. But in socialism, Nielsen argues, the rationale is to meet human needs. Moreover, he claims that democratic socialism will produce greater autonomy, more nearly equal life chances, and a greater equality of opportunity. Thus, in his view, an economy based on democratic socialism would be a more humane and just system than capitalism.

FROM THEORY TO PRACTICE

In Chapter 2 we turn from an examination of the justice of economic systems to an investigation of ethical business decision making within the system at a concrete, specific level. Some of the issues and difficulties businesspersons face when making ethical business decisions are illustrated in the cases at the end of Part One. For example, in "Why Should My Conscience Bother Me?", Kermit Vandivier's discussion of his own part in the B.F. Goodrich aircraft brake scandal highlights the importance of ethics in business decision making. Striking in Goodrich's decision to market a defective brake are the lack of clarity concerning corporate values, the evasion of responsibility, and the refusal or inability of managers to engage in ethical reflection. Although Vandivier and his associates recognized that they were trapped in an ethical dilemma, they lacked the conceptual and analytic tools to state this dilemma clearly and to make their concerns affect corporate policy in an effective way.

These tools are discussed in detail in the articles by Michael Josephson, and Craig Dreilinger and Dan Rice. These articles examine what is required for ethical decisions on a personal level, and describe a decision making process managers can use when confronted with an ethical decision. Josephson defines a series of essential terms which he uses in his discussion of ethical values and principles. He also analyzes some of the more common misconceptions about ethics, and goes over excuses and rationalizations for acting unethically. He concludes that using principled ethical decision making procedures helps accomplish two important things. The first is to distinguish ethical from unethical responses. All too often business people do not consider the ethical dimensions of their choices, or they assume that business or legal principles take precedence over ethics. This leads them to accept unethical choices, or even to fail to acknowledge that ethics is a factor in the decision. The second thing using principled ethical decision making accomplishes is to help rank acceptable ethical alternatives. For a variety of reasons (for instance, crucial facts about the consequences of a certain decision are unknown or ambiguous), some of the alternatives may be better than others.

Craig Dreilinger and Dan Rice discuss a systematic model for analyzing ethical decisions. The components of the model include identifying desired outcomes; defining the problem; examining obstacles; developing alternatives; selecting the best solution; delineating specific steps; and identifying reactions. As a part of their discussion, they describe three conditions under which it is impossible to resolve ethical issues. These are conditions that preclude obtaining the required knowledge, that preclude exercising freedom of choice, and conditions under which a manager lacks the power to influence the outcome. These three conditions in effect describe circumstances that excuse inaction and block moral blame from attaching to managers. Not all moral problems that one knows about are something that one can do something about.

It should be emphasized that the procedure Dreilinger and Rice propose is not intended to be a deterministic algorithm that invariably generates an acceptable solution to ethical issues. It is instead a heuristic that, for its proper application, makes great demands on the judgment, discernment, and sensitivity of the persons who use it. But that is not surprising, given the complexity and difficulty of most ethical problems.

In the next article James Waters and Frederick Bird provide a way of conceptualizing the kinds of ethical decisions managers make. They propose a four part typology of morally questionable managerial acts: non-role against the firm; role failure against the firm; role distortion for the firm; and role assertion for the firm. According to this typology, the acts that Vandivier and his associates engaged in were role distortion for the firm. As Waters and Bird point out, acts that fall in this particular category receive less managerial attention because they occur more often in the corporate life of typical managers.

In the final two articles in Chapter 2, a popular method of evaluating business decisions is discussed in articles by Steven Kelman and Herman Leonard and Richard Zeckhauser. Kelman sees in this widely used technique for business decision making—cost–benefit analysis—a close resemblance to the utilitarian principle examined in the general introduction. He uses theoretical ethics to illuminate cost–benefit analysis and to argue for his claim that it should not be used as the primary tool in making ethical decisions. Commitment to cost–benefit analysis, as Kelman describes it, implies that costs and benefits should be totaled and weighed against each other in making a decision, that an act should not be undertaken unless its benefits exceed its costs, and that benefits and costs must be assigned dollar values so that they can be compared on a common scale.

We have already encountered the primary objections to utilitarianism in the introduction to the text. Kelman reiterates some of these. Utilitarianism identified what is right with what maximizes benefits and minimizes costs, Kelman explains. But he argues that there are instances—those involving the breaking of a promise, for example, or the violation of a human right—in which an act may be wrong even if its benefits outweigh its costs. Kelman cites examples to illustrate his claim that the utilitarian principle permits or even requires some actions which we are inclined to feel are morally repugnant.

Kelman also challenges the possibility of placing dollar values on nonmarket items such as clean air, health and safety, and human life. And even if it were possible to determine prices for these goods that truly reflect their value to society, he holds, it would not be advisable to do so. Certain items like life and health are "priceless," and the very act of placing a price on them may distort their perceived value in society. Kelman fears that placing a price on these things declares that they are for sale; thus a worker's health may be traded because its dollar value is less than that of the equipment required to protect it. Cost–benefit analysis is particularly inappropriate, Kelman argues, when such "specially valued things" are at stake.

Leonard and Zeckhauser attempt to rebut several of the objections Kelman raises against cost–benefit analysis. They argue cost–benefit analysis is an appropriate tool for making decisions affecting the public interest. They concede that not everything of value can be represented within the framework of cost–benefit analysis, but they point out that this does not diminish its usefulness. It may be true that more is at stake than can be measured in terms of costs and benefits, but that does not say that they are unimportant. Finally, they note that cost–benefit analysis is particularly valuable in decisions involving the imposition of risk. They say it is the most practical of the ethically defensible decision-making methods available. It is not without flaws, but it is better than the alternatives.

The reader should keep cost–benefit analysis in mind when reading the other two cases in this part, "Dorrence Corporation" and "AIDS and the Availability of AZT." One of the most famous examples of the use of cost–benefit analysis—the Ford Pinto—is one of the cases in Part Four.

Theories of Economic Justice

Justice as Fairness

John Rawls
Conant University Professor of Philosophy Emeritus, Harvard University

THE MAIN IDEA OF THE THEORY OF JUSTICE

My aim is to present a conception of justice which generalizes and carries to a higher level of abstraction the familiar theory of the social contract as found, say, in Locke, Rousseau, and Kant. In order to do this we are not to think of the original contract as one to enter a particular society or to set up a particular form of government. Rather, the guiding idea is that the principles of justice for the basic structure of society are the object of the original agreement. They are the principles that free and rational persons concerned to further their own interests would accept in an initial position of equality as defining the fundamental terms of their association. These principles are to regulate all further agreements: they specify the kinds of social cooperation that can be entered into and the forms of government that can be established. This way of regarding the principles of justice I shall call justice as fairness.

Thus we are to imagine that those who engage in social cooperation choose together, in one joint act, the principles which are to assign basic rights and duties and to determine the division of social benefits. Men are to decide in advance how they are to regulate their claims against one another and what is to be the foundation charter of their society. Just as each person must decide by rational reflection what constitutes his good, that is, the system of ends which it is rational for him to pursue, so a group of persons must decide once and for all what is to count among them as just and unjust. The choice which rational men would make in this hypothetical situation of equal liberty, assuming for the present that this choice problem has a solution, determines the principles of justice.

In justice as fairness the original position of equality corresponds to the state of nature in the

---

traditional theory of the social contract. This original position is not, of course, thought of as an actual historical state of affairs, much less as a primitive condition of culture. It is understood as a purely hypothetical situation characterized so as to lead to a certain conception of justice. Among the essential features of this situation is that no one knows his place in society, his class position or social status, nor does any one know his fortune in the distribution of natural assets and abilities, his intelligence, strength, and the like. I shall even assume that the parties do not know their conceptions of the good or their special psychological propensities. The principles of justice are chosen behind a veil of ignorance. This ensures that no one is advantaged or disadvantaged in the choice of principles by the outcome of natural chance or the contingency of social circumstances. Since all are similarly situated and no one is able to design principles to favor his particular condition, the principles of justice are the result of a fair agreement or bargain. For given the circumstances of the original position, the symmetry of everyone's relations to each other, this initial situation is fair between individuals as moral persons, that is, as rational beings with their own ends and capable, I shall assume, of a sense of justice. The original position is, one might say, the appropriate initial status quo, and thus the fundamental agreements reached in it are fair. This explains the propriety of the name "justice as fairness": it conveys the idea that the principles of justice are agreed to in an initial situation that is fair. The name does not mean that the concepts of justice and fairness are the same, any more than the phrase "poetry as metaphor" means that the concepts of poetry and metaphor are the same.

Justice as fairness begins, as I have said, with one of the most general of all choices which persons might make together, namely, with the choice of the first principles of a conception of justice which is to regulate all subsequent criticism and reform of institutions. Then, having chosen a conception of justice, we can suppose that they are to choose a constitution and a legislature to enact laws, and so on, all in accordance with the principles of justice initially agreed upon. Our social situation is just if it is such that by this sequence of hypothetical agreements we would have contracted into the general system of rules which defines it.

It may be observed that once the principles of justice are thought of as arising from an original agreement in a situation of equality, it is an open question whether the principle of utility would be acknowledged. Offhand it hardly seems likely that persons who view themselves as equals, entitled to press their claims upon one another, would agree to a principle which may require lesser life prospects for some simply for the sake of a greater sum of advantages enjoyed by others. Since each desires to protect his interests, his capacity to advance his conception of the good, no one has a reason to acquiesce in an enduring loss for himself in order to bring about a greater net balance of satisfaction. In the absence of strong and lasting benevolent impulses, a rational man would not accept a basic structure merely because it maximized the algebraic sum of advantages irrespective of its permanent effects on his own basic rights and interests. Thus it seems that the principle of utility is incompatible with the conception of social cooperation among equals for mutual advantage. It appears to be inconsistent with the idea of reciprocity implicit in the notion of a well-ordered society. Or, at any rate, so I shall argue.

I shall maintain instead that the persons in the initial situation would choose two rather different principles: the first requires equality in the assignment of basic rights and duties, while the second holds that social and economic inequalities, for example inequalities of wealth and authority, are just only if they result in compensating benefits for everyone, and in particular for the least advantaged members of society. These principles rule out justifying institutions on the grounds that the hardships of some are offset by a greater good in the aggregate. It may be expedient but it is not just that some should have less in order that others may prosper. But there is no injustice in the greater benefits earned by a few provided that the situation of persons not so fortunate is thereby improved. The intuitive idea is that since everyone's well-being depends upon a scheme of cooperation without which no one could have a satisfactory life, the division of advantages should be such as to draw forth the willing cooperation of everyone taking part in it, including those less well situated. Yet this can be expected only if reasonable terms are proposed. The two principles mentioned seem to be a fair agreement on the basis of which those better endowed, or more fortunate in their social position, neither of which we can be said to deserve, could expect the willing cooperation of others when some workable scheme is a necessary condition of the welfare of all.[1] Once we decide to look for a conception of justice that nullifies the accidents of natural endowment and the contingencies of social circumstance as counters in quest for political and economic advantage, we are led to these principles. They express the result of leaving aside those aspects of the social world that seem arbitrary from a moral point of view.

The idea of the original position is to set up a fair procedure so that any principles agreed to will be just. Somehow we must nullify the effects of specific contingencies which put men at odds and tempt them to exploit social and natural circumstances to their own advantage. Now in order to do this I assume that the parties are situated behind a veil of ignorance. They do not know how the various alternatives will affect their own particular case and they are obliged to evaluate principles solely on the basis of general considerations.[2] The veil of ignorance enables us to make vivid to ourselves the restrictions that it seems reasonable to impose on arguments for principles of justice, and therefore on these principles themselves. Thus it seems reasonable and generally acceptable that no one should be advantaged or disadvantaged by natural fortune or social circumstances in the choice of principles. It also seems widely agreed that it should be impossible to tailor principles to the circumstances of one's own case. We should insure further that particular inclinations and aspirations, and persons' conceptions of their good do not affect the principles adopted. The aim is to rule out those principles that it would be rational to propose for acceptance, however little the chance of success, only if one knew certain things that are irrelevant from the standpoint of justice. For example, if a man knew that he was wealthy, he might find it rational to advance the principle that various taxes for welfare measures be counted unjust; if he knew that he was poor, he would most likely propose the contrary principle. To represent the desired restrictions one imagines a situation in which everyone is deprived of this sort of information. One excludes the knowledge of those contingencies which sets men at odds and allows them to be guided by their prejudices.

It is assumed, then, that the parties do not know certain kinds of particular facts. First of all, no one knows his place in society, his class position or social status; nor does he know his fortune in the distribution of natural assets and abilities, his intelligence and strength, and the like. Nor, again, does anyone know his conception of the good, the particulars of his rational plan of life, or even the special features of his psychology such as his aversion to risk or liability to optimism or pessimism. More than this, I assume that the parties do not know the particular circumstances of their own society. That is, they do not know its economic or political situation, or the level of civilization and culture it has been able to achieve. The persons in the original position have no information as to which generation they belong. These broader restrictions on knowledge are appropriate in part because questions of social justice arise between generations as well as within them, for example, the question of the appropriate rate of capital saving and of the conservation of natural resources and the environment of nature. There is also, theoretically anyway, the question of a reasonable genetic policy. In these cases too, in order to carry through the idea of the original position, the parties must not know the contingencies that set them in opposition. They must choose principles the consequences of which they are prepared to live with whatever generation they turn out to belong to. As far as possible, then, the only particular facts which the parties know is that their society is subject to the circumstances of justice and whatever this implies.

The restrictions on particular information in the original position are of fundamental importance. The veil of ignorance makes possible a unanimous choice of a particular conception of justice. Without these limitations on knowledge the bargaining problem of the original position would be hopelessly complicated. Even if theoretically a solution were to exist, we would not, at present anyway, be able to determine it.

The Rationality of the Parties

I have assumed throughout that the persons in the original position are rational. In choosing between principles each tries as best he can to advance his interests. But I have also assumed that the parties do not know their conception of the good. This means that while they know that they have some rational plan of life, they do not know the details of this plan, the particular ends and interests which it is calculated to promote. How, then, can they decide which conceptions of justice are most to their advantage? Or must we suppose that they are reduced to mere guessing? To meet this difficulty, I postulate that they would prefer more primary social goods rather than less (i.e., rights and liberties, powers and opportunities, income and wealth and self-respect). Of course, it may turn out, once the veil of ignorance is removed, that some of them for religious or other reasons may not, in fact, want more of these goods. But from the standpoint of the original position, it is rational for the parties to suppose that they do want a larger share, since in any case they are not compelled to accept more if they do not wish to nor does a person suffer from a greater liberty. Thus even though the parties are deprived of information about their particular ends, they have enough knowledge to rank the alternatives. They know that in general they must try to protect their liberties, widen their opportunities, and enlarge their means for promoting their aims whatever these are. Guided by the theory of the good and the general facts of moral psychology, their deliberations are no longer guesswork. They can make a rational decision in the ordinary sense.

The assumption of mutually disinterested rationality, then, comes to this: the persons in the original position try to acknowledge principles which advance their system of ends as far as possible. They do this by attempting to win for themselves the highest index of primary social goods, since this enables them to promote their conception of the good most effectively whatever it turns out to be. The parties do not seek to confer benefits or to impose injuries on one another; they are not moved by affection or rancor. Nor do they try to gain relative to each other; they are not envious or vain. Put in terms of a game, we might say: they strive for as high an absolute score as possible. They do not wish a high or a low score for their opponents, nor do they seek to maximize or minimize the difference between their successes and those of others. The idea of a game does not really apply, since the parties are not concerned to win but to get as many points as possible judged by their own system of ends.

I shall now state in a provisional form the two principles of justice that I believe would be chosen in the original position. The first statement of the two principles reads as follows.

- First: each person is to have an equal right to the most extensive basic liberty compatible with a similar liberty for others.
- Second: social and economic inequalities are to be arranged so that they are both (a) reasonably expected to be to everyone's advantage, and (b) attached to positions and offices open to all.

By way of general comment, these principles primarily apply, as I have said, to the basic structure of society. They are to govern the assignment of rights and duties and to regulate the distribution of social and economic advantages. As their formulation suggests, these principles presuppose that the social structure can be divided into two more or less distinct parts, the first principle applying to the one, the second to the other. They distinguish between those aspects of the social system that define and secure the equal liberties of citizenship and those that specify and establish social and economic inequalities. The basic liberties of citizens are, roughly speaking, political liberty (the right to vote and to be eligible for public office) together with freedom of speech and assembly; liberty of conscience and freedom of thought; freedom of the person along with the right to hold (personal) property; and freedom from arbitrary arrest and seizure as defined by the concept of the rule of law. These liberties are all required to be equal by the first principle, since citizens of a just society are to have the same basic rights.

The second principle applies, in the first approximation, to the distribution of income and wealth and to the design of organizations that make use of differences in authority and responsibility, or chains of command. While the distribution of wealth and income need not be equal, it must be to everyone's advantage, and at the same time, positions of authority and offices of command must be accessible to all. One applies the second principle by holding positions open, and then, subject to this constraint, arranges social and economic inequalities so that everyone benefits.

These principles are to be arranged in a serial order with the first principle prior to the second. This ordering means that a departure from the institutions of equal liberty required by the first principle cannot be justified by, or compensated for, by greater social and economic advantages. The distribution of wealth and income, and the hierarchies of authority, must be consistent with both the liberties of equal citizenship and equality of opportunity.

It is clear that these principles are rather specific in their content, and their acceptance rests on certain assumptions that I must eventually try to explain and justify. For the present, it should be observed that the two principles (and this holds for all formulations) are a special case of a more general conception of justice that can be expressed as follows.

> All social values—liberty and opportunity, income and wealth, and the bases of self-respect—are to be distributed equally unless an unequal distribution of any, or all, of these values is to everyone's advantage.

Injustice, then, is simply inequalities that are not to the benefit of all. Of course, this conception is extremely vague and requires interpretation.

As a first step, suppose that the basic structure of society distributes certain primary goods, that is, things that every rational man is presumed to want. These goods normally have a use whatever a person's rational plan of life. For simplicity, assume that the chief primary goods at the disposition of society are rights and liberties, powers and opportunities, income and wealth. These are the social primary goods. Other primary goods such as health and vigor, intelligence and imagination, are natural goods; although their possession is influenced by the basic structure, they are not so directly under its control. Imagine, then, a hypothetical initial arrangement in which all the social primary goods are equally distributed: everyone has similar rights and duties, and income and wealth are evenly shared. This state of affairs provides a benchmark for judging improvements. If certain inequalities of wealth and organizational powers would make everyone better off than in this hypothetical starting situation, then they accord with the general conception.

Now it is possible, at least theoretically, that by giving up some of their fundamental liberties men are sufficiently compensated by the resulting social and economic gains. The general conception of justice imposes no restrictions on what sort of inequalities are permissible; it only requires that everyone's position be improved.

The second principle insists that each person benefit from permissible inequalities in the basic structure. This means that it must be reasonable for each relevant representative man defined by this structure, when he views it as a going concern, to prefer his prospects with the inequality to his prospects without it. One is not allowed to justify differences in income or organizational powers on the ground that the disadvantages of those in one position are outweighed by the greater advantages of those in another. Much less can infringements of liberty be counterbalanced in this way. Applied to the basic structure, the principle of utility would have us maximize the sum of expectations of representative men (weighted by the number of persons they represent, on the classical view); and this would permit us to compensate for the losses of some by the gains of others. Instead, the two principles require that everyone benefit from economic and social inequalities.

The Tendency to Equality

I wish to conclude this discussion of the two principles by explaining the sense in which they express an egalitarian conception of justice. Also I should like to forestall the objection to the principle of fair opportunity that it leads to a callous meritocratic society. In order to prepare the way for doing this, I note several aspects of the conception of justice that I have set out.

First we may observe that the difference principle gives some weight to the considerations singled out by the principle of redress. This is the principle that undeserved inequalities call for redress; and since inequalities of birth and natural endowment are undeserved, these inequalities are to be somehow compensated for.[3] Thus the principle holds that in order to treat all persons equally, to provide genuine equality of opportunity, society must give more attention to those with fewer native assets and to those born into the less favorable social positions. The idea is to redress the bias of contingencies in the direction of equality. In pursuit of this principle greater resources might be spent on the education of the less rather than the more intelligent, at least over a certain time of life, say the earlier years of school.

Now the principle of redress has not to my knowledge been proposed as the sole criterion of justice, as the single aim of the social order. It is plausible as most such principles are only as a prima facie principle, one that is to be weighed in the balance with others. For example, we are to weigh it against the principle to improve the average standard of life, or to advance the common good. But whatever other principles we hold, the claims of redress are to be taken into account. It is thought to represent one of the elements in our conception of justice. Now the difference principle is not of course the principle of redress. It does not require society to try to even out handicaps as if all were expected to compete on a fair basis in the same race. But the difference principle would allocate resources in education, say, so as to improve the long-term expectation of the least favored. If this end is attained by giving more attention to the better endowed, it is permissible; otherwise not. And in making this decision, the value of education should not be assessed only in terms of economic efficiency and social welfare. Equally if not more important is the role of education in enabling a person to enjoy the culture of his society and to take part in its affairs, and in this way to provide for each individual a secure sense of his own worth.

Thus although the difference principle is not the same as that of redress, it does achieve some of the intent of the latter principle. It transforms the aims of the basic structure so that the total scheme of institutions no longer emphasizes social efficiency and technocratic values. We see then that the difference principle represents, in effect, an agreement to regard the distribution of natural talents as a common asset and to share in the benefits of this distribution whatever it turns out to be. Those who have been favored by nature, whoever they are, may gain from their good fortune only on terms that improve the situation of those who have lost out. The naturally advantaged are not to gain merely because they are more gifted, but only to cover the costs of training and education and for using their endowments in ways that help the less fortunate as well. No one deserves his greater natural capacity nor merits a more favorable starting place in society. But it does not follow that one should eliminate these distinctions. There is another way to deal with them. The basic structure can be arranged so that these contingencies work for the good of the least fortunate. Thus we are led to the difference principle if we wish to set up the social system so that no one gains or loses from his arbitrary place in the distribution of natural assets or his initial position in society without giving or receiving compensating advantages in return.

The natural distribution of talents is neither just nor unjust; nor is it unjust that men are born into society at some particular position. These are simply natural facts. What is just and unjust is the way that institutions deal with these facts. Aristocratic and caste societies are unjust because they make these contingencies the ascriptive basis for belonging to more or less enclosed and privileged social classes. The basic structure of these societies incorporates the arbitrariness found in nature. But there is no necessity for men to resign themselves to these contingencies. The social system is not an unchangeable order beyond human control but a pattern of human action. In justice as fairness men agree to share one another's fate. In designing institutions they undertake to avail themselves of the accidents of nature and social circumstance only when doing so is for the common benefit. The two principles are a fair way of meeting the arbitrariness of fortune; and while no doubt imperfect in other ways, the institutions which satisfy these principles are just.

There is a natural inclination to object that those better situated deserve their greater advantages whether or not they are to the benefit of others. At this point it is necessary to be clear about the notion of desert. It is perfectly true that given a just system of cooperation as a scheme of public rules and the expectations set up by it, those who, with the prospect of improving their condition, have done what the system announces that it will reward are entitled to their advantages. In this sense the more fortunate have a claim to their better situation; their claims are legitimate expectations established by social institutions, and the community is obligated to meet them. But this sense of desert presupposes the existence of the cooperative scheme; it is irrelevant to the question whether in the first place the scheme is to be designed in accordance with the difference principle or some other criterion.

Perhaps some will think that the person with greater natural endowments deserves those assets and the superior character that made their development possible. Because he is more worthy in this sense, he deserves the greater advantages that he could achieve with them. This view, however, is surely incorrect. It seems to be one of the fixed points of our considered judgments that no one deserves his place in the distribution of native endowments, any more than one deserves one's initial starting place in society. The assertion that a man deserves the superior character that enables him to make the effort to cultivate his abilities is equally problematic; for his character depends in large part upon fortunate family and social circumstances for which he can claim no credit. The notion of desert seems not to apply to these cases. Thus the more advantaged representative man cannot say that he deserves and therefore has a right to a scheme of cooperation in which he is permitted to acquire benefits in ways that do not contribute to the welfare of others. There is no basis for his making this claim. From the standpoint of common sense, then, the difference principle appears to be acceptable both to the more advantaged and to the less advantaged individual.

NOTES

1. For the formulation of this intuitive idea I am indebted to Allan Gibbard.
2. The veil of ignorance is so natural a condition that something like it must have occurred to many. The closest express statement of it known to me is found in J. C. Harsanyi, "Cardinal Utility in Welfare Economics and in the Theory of Risk-Taking." *Journal of Political Economy,* vol. 61 (1953). Harsanyi uses it to develop a utilitarian theory.
3. See Herbert Spiegelberg, "A Defense of Human Equality," *Philosophical Review,* vol. 53 (1944), pp. 101, 113–123; and D. D. Raphael, "Justice and Liberty," *Proceedings of the Aristotelian Society,* vol. 51 (1950–1951), pp. 187f.

Distributive Justice

Robert Nozick
Porter Professor of Philosophy, Harvard University

The minimal state is the most extensive state that can be justified. Any state more extensive violates people's rights. Yet many persons have put forth reasons purporting to justify a more extensive state. It is impossible within the compass of this book to examine all the reasons that have been put forth. Therefore, I shall focus upon those generally acknowledged to be most weighty and influential, to see precisely wherein they fail. In this paper we consider the claim that a more extensive state is justified, because necessary (or the best instrument) to achieve distributive justice.

The term "distributive justice" is not a neutral one. Hearing the term "distribution," most people presume that some thing or mechanism uses some principle or criterion to give out a supply of things. Into this process of distributing shares some error may have crept. So it is an open question, at least, whether *re*distribution should take place; whether we should do again what has already been done once, though poorly. However, we are not in the position of children who have been given portions of pie by someone who now makes last minute adjustments to rectify careless cutting. There is no *central* distribution, no person or group entitled to control all the resources, jointly deciding how they are to be doled out. What each person gets, he gets from others who give to him in exchange for something, or as a gift. In a free society, diverse persons control different resources, and new holdings arise out of the voluntary exchanges and actions of persons. There is no more a distributing or distribution of shares than there is a distributing of mates in a society in which persons choose whom they shall marry. The total result is the product of many individual decisions which the different individuals involved are entitled to make.

THE ENTITLEMENT THEORY

The subject of justice in holdings consists of three major topics. The first is the *original acquisition of holdings,* the appropriation of unheld things. This includes the issues of how unheld things may come to be held, the process, or processes, by which unheld things may come to be held, the things that may come to be held by these processes, the extent of what comes to be held by a particular process, and so on. We shall refer to the complicated truth about this topic, which we shall not formulate here, as the principle of justice in acquisition. The second topic concerns the *transfer of holdings* from one person to another. By what processes may a person transfer holdings to another? How may a person acquire a holding from another who holds it? Under this topic come general descriptions of voluntary exchange, and gift and (on the other hand) fraud, as well as reference to particular conventional details fixed upon in a given society. The complicated truth about this subject (with placeholders for conventional details) we shall call the principle of justice in transfer. (And we shall suppose it also includes principles governing how a person may divest himself of a holding, passing it into an unheld state.)

If the world were wholly just, the following inductive definition would exhaustively cover the subject of justice in holdings.

1. A person who acquires a holding in accordance with the principle of justice in acquisition is entitled to that holding.
2. A person who acquires a holding in accordance with the principle of justice in transfer, from someone else entitled to the holding, is entitled to the holding.
3. No one is entitled to a holding except by (repeated) applications of 1 and 2.

The complete principle of distributive justice would say simply that a distribution is just if everyone is entitled to the holdings they possess under the distribution.

A distribution is just if it arises from another just distribution by legitimate means. The legitimate means of moving from one distribution to another are specified by the principle of justice in transfer. The legitimate first "moves" are specified by the principle of justice in acquisition. Whatever arises from a just situation by just steps is itself just. The means of change specified by the principle of justice in transfer preserve justice. As correct rules of inference are truth-preserving, and any conclusion deduced via repeated application of such rules from only true premises is itself true, so the means of transition from one situation to another specified by the principle of justice in transfer are justice-preserving, and any situation actually arising from repeated transitions in accordance with the principle from a just situation is itself just. The parallel between justice-preserving transformations and truth-preserving transformations illuminates where it fails as well as where it holds. That a conclusion could have been deduced by truth-preserving means from premises that are true suffices to show its truth. That from a just situation a situation *could* have arisen via justice-preserving means does *not* suffice to show its justice. The fact that a thief's victims voluntarily *could* have presented him with gifts does not entitle the thief to his ill-gotten gains. Justice in holdings is historical; it depends upon what actually has happened. We shall return to this point later.

Not all actual situations are generated in accordance with the two principles of justice in holdings: the principle of justice in acquisition and the principle of justice in transfer. Some people steal from others, or defraud them, or enslave them, seizing their product and preventing them from living as they choose, or forcibly exclude others from competing in exchanges. None of these are permissible modes of transition from one situation to another. And some persons acquire holdings by means not sanctioned by the principle of justice in acquisition. The existence of past injustice (previous violations of the first two principles of justice in holdings) raises the third major topic under justice in holdings: the rectification of injustice in holdings. If past injustice has shaped present holdings in various ways, some identifiable and some not, what now, if anything, ought to be done to rectify these injustices? What obligations do the performers of injustice have toward those whose position is worse than it would have been had the injustice not been done? Or, than it would have been had compensation been paid promptly? How, if at all, do things change if the beneficiaries and those made worse off are not the direct parties in the act of injustice, but, for example, their descendants? Is an injustice done to someone whose holding was itself based upon an unrectified injustice? How far back must one go in wiping clean the historical slate of injustices? What may victims of injustice permissibly do in order to rectify the injustices being done to them, including the many injustices done by persons acting through their government? I do not know of a thorough or theoretically sophisticated treatment of such issues. Idealizing greatly, let us suppose theoretical investigation will produce a principle of rectification. This principle uses historical information about previous situations and injustices done in them (as defined by the first two principles of justice and rights against interference), and information about the actual course of events that flowed from these injustices, until the present, and it yields a description (or descriptions) of holdings in the society. The principle of rectification presumably will make use of its best estimate of subjunctive information about what would have occurred (or a probability distribution over what might have occurred, using the expected value) if the injustice had not taken place. If the actual description of holdings turns out not to be one of the descriptions yielded by the principle, then one of the descriptions yielded must be realized.

The general outlines of the theory of justice in holdings are that the holdings of a person are just if he is entitled to them by the principles of justice in acquisition and transfer, or by the principle of rectification of injustice (as specified by the first two principles). If each person's holdings are just, then the total set (distribution) of holdings is just. To turn these general outlines into a specific theory we would have to specify the details of each of the three principles of justice in holdings: the principle of acquisition of holdings, the principle of transfer of holdings, and the principle of rectification of violations of the first two principles. I shall not attempt that task here. (Locke's principle of justice in acquisition is discussed below.)

HISTORICAL PRINCIPLES AND END-RESULT PRINCIPLES

The general outlines of the entitlement theory illuminate the nature and defects of other conceptions of distributive justice. The entitlement theory of justice in distribution is *historical;* whether a distribution is just depends upon how it came about. In contrast, *current time-slice principles* of justice hold that the justice of a distribution is determined by how things are distributed (who has what) as judged by some *structural* principle(s) of just distribution. A utilitarian who judges between any two distributions by seeing which has the greater sum of utility and, if the sums tie, applies some fixed equality criterion to choose the more equal distribution, would hold a current time-slice principle of justice. As would someone who had a fixed schedule of trade-offs between the sum of happiness and equality. According to a current time-slice principle, all that needs to be looked at, in judging the justice of a distribution, is who ends up with what; in comparing any two distributions one need look only at the matrix presenting the distributions. No further information need be fed into a principle of justice. It is a consequence of such principles of justice that any two structurally identical distributions are equally just. (Two distributions are structurally identical if they present the same profile, but perhaps have different persons occupying the particular slots. My having ten and your having five, and my having five and your having ten are structurally identical distributions.) Welfare economics is the theory of current time-slice principles of justice. The subject is conceived as operating on matrices representing only current information about distribution. This, as well as some of the usual conditions (for example, the choice of distribution is invariant under relabeling of columns), guarantees that welfare economics will be a current time-slice theory, with all of its inadequacies.

Most persons do not accept current time-slice principles as constituting the whole story about distributive shares. They think it relevant in assessing the justice of a situation to consider not only the distribution it embodies, but also how that distribution came about. If some persons are in prison for murder or war crimes, we do not say that to assess the justice of the distribution in the society we must look only at what this person has, and that person has, and that person has, . . . at the current time. We think it relevant to ask whether someone did something so that he *deserved* to be punished, deserved to have a lower share.

PATTERNING

The entitlement principles of justice in holdings that we have sketched are historical principles of justice. To better understand their precise character, we shall distinguish them from another subclass of the historical principles. Consider, as an example, the principle of distribution according to moral merit. This principle requires that total distributive shares vary directly with moral merit; no person should have a greater share than anyone whose moral merit is greater. Or consider the principle that results by substituting "usefulness to society" for "moral merit" in the previous principle. Or instead of "distribute according to moral merit," or "distribute according to usefulness to society," we might consider "distribute according to the weighted sum of moral merit, usefulness to society, and need," with the weights of the different dimensions equal. Let us call a principle of distribution *patterned* if it specifies that a distribution is to vary along with some natural dimension, weighted sum of natural dimensions, or lexicographic ordering of natural dimensions. And let us say a distribution is patterned if it accords with some patterned principle. The principle of distribution in accordance with moral merit is a patterned historical principle, which specifies a patterned distribution. "Distribute according to I.Q." is a patterned principle that looks to information not contained in distributional matrices. It is not historical, however, in that it does not look to any past actions creating differential entitlements to evaluate a distribution; it requires only distributional matrices whose columns are labeled by I.Q. scores. The distribution in a society, however, may be composed of such simple patterned distributions, without itself being simply patterned. Different sectors may operate different patterns, or some combination of patterns may operate in different proportions across a society. A distribution composed in this manner, from a small number of patterned distributions, we also shall term "patterned." And we extend the use of "pattern" to include the overall designs put forth by combinations of end-state principles.

Almost every suggested principle of distributive justice is patterned: to each according to his moral merit, or needs, or marginal product, or how hard he tries, or the weighted sum of the foregoing, and so on. The principle of entitlement we have sketched is *not* patterned. There is no one natural dimension or weighted sum or combination of a small number of natural dimensions that yields the distributions generated in accordance with the principle of entitlement. The set of holdings that results when some persons receive their marginal products, others win at gambling, others receive a share of their mate's income, others receive gifts from foundations, others receive interest on loans, others receive gifts from admirers, others receive returns on investment, others make for themselves much of what they have, others find things, and so on, will not be patterned.

To think that the task of a theory of distributive justice is to fill in the blank in "to each according to his ___" is to be predisposed to search for a pattern; and the separate treatment of "from each according to his ___" treats production and distribution as two separate and independent issues. On an entitlement view these are *not* two separate questions. Whoever makes something, having bought or contracted for all other held resources used in the process (transferring some of his holdings for these cooperating factors), is entitled to it. The situation is *not* one of something's getting made, and there being an open question of who is to get it. Things come into the world already attached to people having entitlements over them. From the point of view of the historical entitlement conception of justice in holdings, those who start afresh to complete "to each according to his ___" treat objects as if they appeared from nowhere, out of nothing. A complete theory of justice might cover this limited case as well; perhaps here is a use for the usual conceptions of distributive justice.

So entrenched are maxims of the usual form that perhaps we should present the entitlement conception as a competitor. Ignoring acquisition and rectification, we might say:

> From each according to what he chooses to do, to each according to what he makes for himself (perhaps with the contracted aid of others) and what others choose to do for him and choose to give him of what they've been given previously (under this maxim) and haven't yet expended or transferred.

This, the discerning reader will have noticed, has its defects as a slogan. So as a summary and great simplification (and not as a maxim with any independent meaning) we have:

> From each as they choose, to each as they are chosen.

HOW LIBERTY UPSETS PATTERNS

It is not clear how those holding alternative conceptions of distributive justice can reject the entitlement conception of justice in holdings. For suppose a distribution favored by one of these non-entitlement conceptions is realized. Let us suppose it is your favorite one and let us call this distribution D_1; perhaps everyone has an equal share, perhaps shares vary in accordance with some dimension you treasure. Now suppose that Wilt Chamberlain is greatly in demand by basketball teams, being a great gate attraction. (Also suppose contracts run only for a year, with players being free agents.) He signs the following sort of contract with a team: In each home game, twenty-five cents from the price of each ticket of admission goes to him. (We ignore the question of whether he is "gouging" the owners, letting them look out for themselves.) The season starts, and people cheerfully attend his team's games; they buy their tickets, each time dropping a separate twenty-five cents of their admission price into a special box with Chamberlain's name on it. They are excited about seeing him play; it is worth the total admission price to them. Let us suppose that in one season one million persons attend his home games, and Wilt Chamberlain winds up with $250,000, a much larger sum than the average income and larger even than anyone else has. Is he entitled to this income? Is this new distribution D_2 unjust? If so, why? There is *no* question about whether each of the people was entitled to the control over the resources they held in D_1; because that was the distribution (your favorite) that (for the purposes of argument) we assumed was acceptable. Each of these persons *chose* to give twenty-five cents of their money to Chamberlain. They could have spent it on going to the movies, or on candy bars, or on copies of *Dissent* magazine, or of *Monthly Review*. But they all, at least one million of them, converged on giving it to Wilt Chamberlain in exchange for watching him play basketball. If D_1 was a just distribution, and people voluntarily moved from it to D_2, transferring parts of their shares they were given under D_1 (what was it for if not to do something with?), isn't D_2 also just? If the people were entitled to dispose of the resources to which they were entitled (under D_1), didn't this include their being entitled to give it to, or exchange it with, Wilt Chamberlain? Can anyone else complain on grounds of justice? Each other person already has his legitimate share under D_1. Under D_1, there is nothing that anyone has that anyone else has a claim of justice against. After someone transfers something to Wilt Chamberlain, third parties *still* have their legitimate shares; *their* shares are not changed. By what process could such a transfer among two persons give rise to a legitimate claim of distributive justice on a portion of what was transferred, by a third party who had no claim of justice on any holding of the others *before* the transfer? To cut off objections irrelevant here, we might imagine the exchanges occurring in a socialist society, after hours. After playing whatever basketball he does in his daily work, or doing whatever other daily work he does, Wilt Chamberlain decides to put in *overtime* to earn additional money. (First his work quota is set; he works time over that.) Or imagine it is a skilled juggler people like to see, who puts on shows after hours.

The general point illustrated by the Wilt Chamberlain example and the example of the entrepreneur in a socialist society is that no end-state principle or distributional patterned principle of justice can be continuously realized without continuous interference with people's lives. Any favored pattern would be transformed into one unfavored by the principle, by people choosing to act in various ways; for example, by people exchanging goods and services with other people, or giving things to other people, things the transferrers are entitled to under the favored distributional pattern. To maintain a pattern one must either continually interfere to stop people from transferring resources as they wish to, or continually (or periodically) interfere to take from some persons resources that others for some reason chose to transfer to them.

Patterned principles of distributive justice necessitate *re*distributive activities. The likelihood is small that any actual freely-arrived-at set of holdings fit a given pattern; and the likelihood is nil that it will continue to fit the pattern as people exchange and give. From the point of view of an entitlement theory, redistribution is a serious matter indeed, involving, as it does, the violation of people's rights. (An exception is those takings that fall under the principle of the rectification of injustices.) From other points of view, also, it is serious.

Taxation of earnings from labor is on a par with forced labor. Some persons find this claim obviously true: taking the earnings of n hours labor is like taking n hours from the person; it is like forcing the person to work n hours for another's purpose. Others find the claim absurd. But even these, *if* they object to forced labor, would oppose forcing unemployed hippies to work for the benefit of the needy. And they would also object to forcing each person to work five extra hours each week for the benefit of the needy. But a system that takes five hours' wages in taxes does not seem to them like one that forces someone to work five hours, since it offers the person forced a wider range of choice in activities than does taxation in kind with the particular labor specified.

Whether it is done through taxation on wages or on wages over a certain amount, or through seizure of profits, or through there being a big *social pot* so that it's not clear what's coming from where and what's going where, patterned principles of distributive justice involve appropriating the actions of other persons. Seizing the results of someone's labor is equivalent to seizing hours from him and directing him to carry on various activities. If people force you to do certain work, or unrewarded work, for a certain period of time, they decide what you are to do and what purposes your work is to serve apart from your decisions. This process whereby they take this decision from you makes them a *part-owner* of you; it gives them a property right in you. Just as having such partial control and power of decision, by right, over an animal or inanimate object would be to have a property right in it.

LOCKE'S THEORY OF ACQUISITION

We must introduce an additional bit of complexity into the structure of the entitlement theory. This is best approached by considering Locke's attempt to specify a principle of justice in acquisition. Locke views property rights in an unowned object as originating through someone's mixing his labor with it.

This gives rise to many questions. What are the boundaries of what labor is mixed with? If a private astronaut clears a place on Mars, has he mixed his labor with (so that he comes to own) the whole planet, the whole uninhabited universe, or just a particular plot? Which plot does an act bring under ownership?

Locke's proviso that there be "enough and as good left in common for others" is meant to ensure that the situation of others is not worsened. I assume that any adequate theory of justice in acquisition will contain a proviso similar to Locke's. A process normally giving rise to a permanent bequeathable property right in a previously unowned thing will not do so if the position of others no longer at liberty to use the thing is thereby worsened. It is important to specify *this* particular mode of worsening the situation of others, for the proviso does not encompass other modes. It does not include the worsening due to more limited opportunities to appropriate, and it does not include how I "worsen" a seller's position if I appropriate materials to make some of what he is selling, and then enter into competition with him. Someone whose appropriation otherwise would violate the proviso still may appropriate provided he compensates the others so that their situation is not thereby worsened; unless he does compensate these others, his appropriation will violate the proviso of the principle of justice in acquisition and will be an illegitimate one. A theory of appropriation incorporating this Lockean proviso will handle correctly the cases (objections to the theory lacking the proviso) where someone appropriates the total supply of something necessary for life.

A theory which includes this proviso in its principle of justice in acquisition must also contain a more complex principle of justice in transfer. Some reflection of the proviso about appropriation constrains later actions. If my appropriating all of a certain substance violates the Lockean proviso, then so does my appropriating some and purchasing all the rest from others who obtained it without otherwise violating the Lockean proviso. If the proviso excludes someone's appropriating all the drinkable water in the world, it also excludes his purchasing it all. (More weakly, and messily, it may exclude his charging certain prices for some of his supply.) This proviso (almost?) never will come into effect; the more someone acquires of a scarce substance which others want, the higher the price of the rest will go, and the more difficult it will become for him to acquire it all. But still, we can imagine, at least, that something like this occurs: someone makes simultaneous secret bids to the separate owners of a substance, each of whom sells assuming he can easily purchase more from the other owners; or some natural catastrophe destroys all of the supply of something except that in one person's possession. The total supply could not be permissibly appropriated by one person at the beginning. His later acquisition of it all does not show that the original appropriation violated the proviso. Rather, it is the combination of the original appropriation *plus* all the later transfers and actions that violates the Lockean proviso.

Each owner's title to his holding includes the historical shadow of the Lockean proviso on appropriation. This excludes his transferring it into an agglomeration that does violate the Lockean proviso and excludes his using it in a way, in coordination with others or independently of them, so as to violate the proviso by making the situation of others worse than their baseline situation. Once it is known that someone's ownership runs afoul of the Lockean proviso, there are stringent limits on what he may do with (what it is difficult any longer unreservedly to call) "his property." Thus a person may not appropriate the only water hole in a desert and charge what he will. Nor may he charge what he will if he possesses one, and unfortunately it happens that all the water holes in the desert dry up, except for his. This unfortunate circumstance, admittedly no fault of his, brings into operation the Lockean proviso and limits his property rights. Similarly, an owner's property right in the only island in an area does not allow him to order a castaway from a shipwreck off his island as a trespasser, for this would violate the Lockean proviso.

Notice that the theory does not say that owners do not have these rights, but that the rights are overridden to avoid some catastrophe. (Overridden rights do not disappear; they leave a trace of a sort absent in the cases under discussion.) There is no such external (and *ad hoc?*) overriding. Considerations internal to the theory of property itself, to its theory of acquisition and appropriation, provide the means for handling such cases.

I believe that the free operation of a market system will not actually run afoul of the Lockean proviso. If this is correct, the proviso will not provide a significant opportunity for future state action.

Distributive Justice and Utilitarianism

J. J. C. Smart
Center for Information Science Research, The Australian National University

INTRODUCTION

In this paper I shall not be concerned with the defense of utilitarianism against other types of ethical theory. Indeed I hold that questions of ultimate ethical principle are not susceptible of proof, though something can be done to render them more acceptable by presenting them in a clear light and by clearing up certain confusions which (for some people) may get in the way of their acceptance. Ultimately the utilitarian appeals to the sentiment of generalized benevolence, and speaks to others who feel this sentiment too and for whom it is an overriding feeling.[1] (This does not mean that he will always act from this over-riding feeling. There can be backsliding and action may result from more particular feelings, just as an egoist may go against his own interests, and may regret this.) I shall be concerned here merely to investigate certain consequences of utilitarianism, as they relate to questions of distributive justice. The type of utilitarianism with which I am concerned is act utilitarianism.

THE PLACE OF JUSTICE IN UTILITARIAN THEORY

The concept of justice as a fundamental ethical concept is really quite foreign to utilitarianism. A utilitarian would compromise his utilitarianism if he allowed principles of justice which might conflict with the maximization of happiness (or more generally of goodness, should he be an "ideal" utilitarian). He is concerned with the maximization of happiness[2] and not with the distribution of it. Nevertheless he may well deduce from his ethical principle that certain ways of distributing the means to happiness (e.g., money, food, housing) are more conducive to the general good than are others. He will be interested in justice in so far as it is a political or legal or quasi-legal concept. He will consider whether the legal institutions and customary sanctions which operate in particular societies are more or less conducive to the utilitarian end than are other possible institutions and customs. Even if the society consisted entirely of utilitarians (and of course no actual societies have thus consisted) it might still be important to have legal and customary sanctions relating to distribution of goods, because utilitarians might be tempted to backslide and favour non-optimistic distributions, perhaps because of bias in their own favour. They might be helped to act in a more nearly utilitarian way because of the presence of these sanctions.

As a utilitarian, therefore, I do not allow the concept of justice as a fundamental moral concept, but I am nevertheless interested in justice in a subordinate way, as a means to the utilitarian end. Thus even though I hold that it does not matter in what way happiness is distributed among different persons, provided that the total amount of happiness is maximized, I do of course hold that it can be of vital importance that the means to happiness should be distributed in some ways and not in others. Suppose that I have the choice of two alternative actions as follows: I can either give $500 to each of two needy men, Smith and Campbell, or

---

Excerpted from "Distributive Justice and Utilitarianism," published in *Justice and Economic Distribution,* edited by John Arthur and William H. Shaw, Englewood Cliffs, N.J.: Prentice-Hall, 1978. Reprinted by permission of the author.

else give $1000 to Smith and nothing to Campbell. It is of course likely to produce the greatest happiness if I divide the money equally. For this reason utilitarianism can often emerge as a theory with egalitarian consequences. If it does so this is because of the empirical situation, and not because of any moral commitment to egalitarianism as such. Consider, for example, another empirical situation in which the $500 was replaced by a half-dose of a life saving drug, in which case the utilitarian would advocate giving two half-doses to Smith or Campbell and none to the other. Indeed if Smith and Campbell each possessed a half-dose it would be right to take one of the half-doses and give it to the other. (I am assuming that a whole dose would preserve life and that a half-dose would not. I am also assuming a simplified situation: in some possible situations, especially in a society of nonutilitarians, the wide social ramifications of taking a half-dose from Smith and giving it to Campbell might conceivably outweigh the good results of saving Campbell's life.) However, it is probable that in most situations the equal distribution of the means to happiness will be the right utilitarian action, even though the utilitarian has no ultimate moral commitment to egalitarianism. If a utilitarian is given the choice of two actions, one of which will give 2 units of happiness to Smith and 2 to Campbell, and the other of which will give 1 unit of happiness to Smith and 9 to Campbell, he will choose the latter course.[3] It may also be that I have the choice between two alternative actions, one of which gives −1 unit of happiness to Smith and +9 units to Campbell, and the other of which gives +2 to Smith and +2 to Campbell. As a utilitarian I will choose the former course, and here I will be in conflict with John Rawls' theory, whose maximin principle would rule out making Smith worse off.

UTILITARIANISM AND RAWLS' THEORY

Rawls deduces his ethical principles from the contract which would be made by a group of rational egoists in an 'original position' in which they thought behind a 'veil of ignorance,' so that they would not know who they were or even what generation they belonged to.[4] Reasoning behind this veil of ignorance, they would apply the maximin principle. John Harsanyi earlier used the notion of a contract in such a position of ignorance, but used not the maximin principle but the principle of maximizing expected utility.[5] Harsanyi's method leads to a form of rule utilitarianism. I see no great merit in this roundabout approach to ethics *via* a contrary to fact supposition, which involves the tricky notion of a social contract and which thus appears already to presuppose a moral position. The approach seems also too Hobbesian: it is anthropologically incorrect to suppose that we are all originally little egoists. I prefer to base ethics on a principle of generalized benevolence, to which some of those with whom I discuss ethics may immediately respond. Possibly it might show something interesting about our common moral notions if it could be proved that they follow from what would be contracted by rational egoists in an 'original position,' but as a utilitarian I am more concerned to advocate a normative theory which might replace our common moral notions than I am to explain these notions. Though some form of utilitarianism might be deducible (as by Harsanyi) from a contract or original position theory, I do not think that it either ought to be or need be defended in this sort of way.

Be that as it may, it is clear that utilitarian views about distribution of happiness do differ from Rawls' view. I have made a distinction between justice as a moral concept and justice as a legal or quasi-legal concept. The utilitarian has no room for the former, but he can have strong views about the latter, though *what* these views are will depend on empirical considerations. Thus whether he will prefer a political theory which advocates a completely socialist state, or whether he will prefer one which advocates a minimal state (as Robert Nozick's book does[6]), or whether again he will advocate something between the two, is something which depends on the facts of economics, sociology, and so on. As someone not expert in these fields I have no desire to dogmatize on these empirical matters. (My own private non-expert opinion is that probably neither extreme leads to maximization of happiness, though I have a liking for rather more socialism than exists in Australia or U.S.A. at present.) As a utilitarian my approach to political theory has to be tentative and empirical. Not believing in moral rights as such I can not deduce theories about the best political arrangements by making deductions (as Nozick does) from propositions which purport to be about such basic rights.

Rawls deduces two principles of justice.[7] The first of these is that 'each person is to have an equal right to the most extensive basic liberty compatible with a similar liberty for others,' and the second one is that 'social and economic inequalities are to be arranged so that they are both (a) reasonably expected to be to everyone's advantage, and (b) attached to positions and offices open to all.' Though a utilitarian could (on empirical grounds) be very much in sympathy with both of these principles, he could not accept them as universal rules. Suppose that a society which had no danger of nuclear war could be achieved only by reducing the liberty of one per cent of the world's population. Might it not be right to bring about such a state of affairs if it were in one's power? Indeed might it not be right greatly to reduce the liberty of 100% of the world's population if such a desirable outcome could be achieved? Perhaps the present generation would be pretty miserable and would hanker for their lost liberties. However we must also think about the countless future generations which might exist and be happy provided that mankind can avoid exterminating itself, and we must also think of all the pain, misery and genetic damage which would be brought about by nuclear war even if this did not lead to the total extermination of mankind.

Suppose that this loss of freedom prevented a war so devastating that the whole process of evolution on this planet would come to an end. At the cost of the loss of freedom, instead of the war and the end of evolution there might occur an evolutionary process which was not only long lived but also beneficial: in millions of years there might be creatures descended from *homo sapiens* which had vastly increased talents and capacity for happiness. At least such considerations show that Rawls' first principle is far from obvious to the utilitarian, though in certain mundane contexts he might accede to it as a useful approximation. Indeed I do not believe that restriction of liberty, in our present society, could have beneficial results in helping to prevent nuclear war, though a case could be made for certain restrictions on the liberty of all present members of society so as to enable the government to prevent nuclear blackmail by gangs of terrorists.

Perhaps in the past considerable restrictions on the personal liberties of a large proportion of citizens may have been justifiable on utilitarian grounds. In view of the glories of Athens and its contributions to civilization it is possible that the Athenian slave society was justifiable. In one part of his paper, 'Nature and Soundness of the Contract and Coherence Arguments,'[8] David Lyons has judiciously discussed the question of whether in certain circumstances a utilitarian would condone slavery. He says that it would be unlikely that a utilitarian could condone slavery as it has existed in modern times. However he considers the possibility that less objectionable forms of slavery or near slavery have existed. The less objectionable these may have been, the more likely it is that utilitarianism would have condoned them. Lyons remarks that our judgments about the relative advantages of different societies must be very tentative because we do not know enough about human history to say what were the social alternatives at any juncture.[9]

Similar reflections naturally occur in connection with Rawls' second principle. Oligarchic societies, such as that of eighteenth century Britain, may well have been in fact better governed than they would have been if posts of responsibility had been available to all. Certainly to resolve this question we should have to go deeply into empirical investigations of the historical facts. (To prevent misunderstanding, I do think that in our present society utilitarianism would imply adherence to Rawls' second principle as a general rule.)

A utilitarian is concerned with maximizing total happiness (or goodness, if he is an ideal utilitarian). Rawls largely concerns himself with certain 'primary goods,' as he calls them. These include 'rights and liberties, powers and opportunities, income and wealth.'[10] A utilitarian would regard these as mere means to the ultimate good. Nevertheless if he is proposing new laws or changes to social institutions the utilitarian will have to concern himself in practice with the distribution of these 'primary goods' (as Bentham did).[11] But if as an approximation we neglect this distinction, which may be justifiable to the extent that there is a correlation between happiness and the level of these 'primary goods,' we may say that according to Rawls an action is right only if it is to the benefit of the least advantaged person. A utilitarian will hold that a redistribution of the means to happiness is right if it maximizes the general happiness, even though some persons, even the least advantaged ones, are made worse off. A position which is intermediate between the utilitarian position and Rawls' position would be one which held that one ought to maximize some sort of trade-off between total happiness and distribution of happiness. Such a position would imply that sometimes we should redistribute in such a way as to make some persons, even the least advantaged ones, worse off, but this would happen less often than it would according to the classical utilitarian theory.

UTILITARIANISM AND NOZICK'S THEORY

General adherence to Robert Nozick's theory (in his *Anarchy, State and Utopia*)[12] would be compatible with the existence of very great inequality indeed. This is because the whole theory is based quite explicitly on the notion of *rights:* in the very first sentence of the preface of his book we read 'Individuals have rights. . . .' The utilitarian would demur here. A utilitarian legislator might tax the rich in order to give aid to the poor, but a Nozickian legislator would not do so. A utilitarian legislator might impose a heavy tax on inherited wealth, whereas Nozick would allow the relatively fortunate to become even more fortunate, provided that they did not infringe the *rights* of the less fortunate. The utilitarian legislator would hope to increase the total happiness by equalizing things a bit. How far he should go in this direction would depend on empirical considerations. He would not want to equalize things too much if this led to too much weakening of the incentive to work, for example. Of course according to Nozick's system there would be no reason why members of society should not set up a utilitarian utopia, and voluntarily equalize their wealth, and also give wealth to poorer communities outside. However it is questionable whether such isolated utopias could survive in a modern environment, but if they did survive, the conformity of the behaviour of their members to utilitarian theory, rather than the conformity to Nozick's theory, would be what would commend their societies to me.

SUMMARY

In this article I have explained that the notion of justice is not a fundamental notion in utilitarianism, but that utilitarians will characteristically have certain views about such things as the distribution of wealth, savings for the benefit of future generations and for the third world countries and other practical matters. Utilitarianism differs from John Rawls' theory in that it is ready to contemplate some sacrifice to certain individuals (or classes of individuals) for the sake of the greater good of all, and in particular may allow certain limitations of personal freedom which would be ruled out by Rawls' theory. *In practice,* however, the general tendency of utilitarianism may well be towards an egalitarian form of society.

NOTES

1. In hoping that utilitarianism can be rendered acceptable to some people by presenting it in a clear light, I do not deny the possibility of the reverse happening. Thus I confess to a bit of a pull the other way when I consider Nozick's example of an 'experience machine'. See Robert Nozick, *Anarchy, State and Utopia* (Oxford: Blackwell, 1975), pp. 42–45, though I am at least partially reassured by Peter Singer's remarks towards the end of his review of Nozick, *New York Review of Books,* March 6, 1975. Nozick's example of an experience machine is more worrying than the more familiar one of a pleasure inducing machine, because it seems to apply to ideal as well as to hedonistic utilitarianism.
2. In this paper I shall assume a hedonistic utilitarianism, though most of what I have to say will be applicable to ideal utilitarianism too.
3. There are of course difficult problems about the assignment of cardinal utilities to states of mind, but for the purposes of this paper I am assuming that we

can intelligibly talk, as utilitarians do, about units of happiness.
4. John Rawls, *A Theory of Justice* (Cambridge, Mass: Harvard University Press, 1971).
5. John C. Harsanyi, 'Cardinal Utility in Welfare Economics and the Theory of Risk-Taking', *Journal of Political Economy,* **61** (1953), 434–435, and 'Cardinal Welfare, Individualistic Ethics, and Interpersonal Comparisons of Utility', *ibid.,* **63** (1955), 309–321. Harsanyi has discussed Rawls' use of the maximin principle and has defended the principle of maximizing expected utility instead, in a paper 'Can the Maximin Principle Serve as a Basis for Morality? A Critique of John Rawls' Theory', *The American Political Science Review,* **69** (1975), 594–606. These articles have been reprinted in John C. Harsanyi, *Essays on Ethics, Social Behavior, and Scientific Explanation* (Dordrecht, Holland: D. Reidel, 1976).
6. Robert Nozick, *Anarchy, State and Utopia.* (See note 1 above.)
7. Rawls, *A Theory of Justice,* p. 60.
8. In Norman Daniels (ed.), *Reading Rawls* (Oxford: Blackwell, 1975), pp. 141–167. See pp. 148–149.
9. Lyons, *op. cit.,* p. 149, near top.
10. Rawls, *op. cit.,* p. 62.
11. On this point see Brian Barry, *The Liberal Theory of Justice* (London: Oxford University Press, 1973), p. 55.
12. See note 1.

A Capitalist Conception of Justice

Irving Kristol
Senior fellow, American Enterprise Institute, and co-editor of *The Public Interest.*

It is fashionable these days for social commentators to ask, "Is capitalism compatible with social justice?" I submit that the only appropriate answer is "No." Indeed, this is the only possible answer. The term "social justice" was invented in order *not* to be compatible with capitalism.

What is the difference between "social justice" and plain, unqualified "justice?" Why can't we ask, "Is capitalism compatible with justice?" We can, and were we to do so, we would then have to explore the idea of justice that is peculiar to the capitalist system, because capitalism certainly does have an idea of justice.

"Social justice," however, was invented and propagated by people who were not much interested in understanding capitalism. These were nineteenth-century critics of capitalism—liberals, radicals, socialists—who invented the term in order to insinuate into the argument a quite different conception of the good society from the one proposed by liberal capitalism. As it is used today, the term has an irredeemably egalitarian and authoritarian thrust. Since capitalism as a socioeconomic or political system is neither egalitarian nor authoritarian, it is in truth incompatible with "social justice."

Let us first address the issue of egalitarianism. In a liberal or democratic capitalist society there is, indeed, a connection between justice and equality. Equality before the law and equality of political rights are fundamental to a liberal capitalist system and, in historical fact, the ideological Founding Fathers of liberal capitalism all did believe in equality before the law and in some form of equality of political rights. The introduction of the term "social justice" represents an effort to stretch the idea of justice that is compatible with capitalism to cover *economic* equality as well. Proponents of something called "social justice" would persuade us that economic equality is as much a right as are equality before the law and equality of political rights. As a matter of fact, these proponents move in an egalitarian direction so formidably that inevitably *all* differences are seen sooner or later to be unjust. Differences between men and women, differences between parents and children, differences between human beings and animals—all of these, as we have seen in the last ten or fifteen years, become questionable and controversial.

Excerpted from "A Capitalist Conception of Justice" found in *Ethics, Free Enterprise, and Public Policy: Original Essays on Moral Issues in Business,* edited by Richard T. DeGeorge and Joseph A. Pichler.

A person who believes in "social justice" is an egalitarian. I do not say that he or she necessarily believes in perfect equality; I do not think anyone believes in perfect equality. But "social justice" advocates are terribly interested in far more equality than a capitalist system is likely to deliver. Capitalism delivers many good things but, on the whole, economic equality is not one of them. It has never pretended to deliver economic equality. Rather, capitalism has always stood for equality of economic opportunity, reasonably understood to mean the absence of official barriers to economic opportunity.

We are now in an egalitarian age when Harvard professors write books wondering whether there is a problem of "social justice" if some people are born of handsome parents and are therefore more attractive than others. This is seriously discussed in Cambridge and in other learned circles. Capitalism is not interested in that. Capitalism says there ought to be no *official* barriers to economic opportunity. If one is born of handsome or talented parents, if one inherits a musical skill, or mathematical skill, or whatever, that is simply good luck. No one can question the person's right to the fruits of such skills. Capitalism believes that, through equal opportunity, each individual will pursue his happiness as he defines it, and as far as his natural assets (plus luck, good or bad) will permit. In pursuit of that happiness everyone will, to use that familiar phrase of Adam Smith, "better his condition."

Thus, capitalism says that equal opportunity will result in everyone's bettering his or her condition. And it does. The history of the world over the past 200 years shows that capitalism did indeed permit and encourage ordinary men and women in the pursuit of their happiness to improve their condition. Even Marx did not deny this. We are not as poor as our grandparents. We are all better off because individuals in pursuit of happiness, and without barriers being put in their way, are very creative, innovative, and adept at finding ways for societies to be more productive, thereby creating more wealth in which everyone shares.

Now, although individuals do better their condition under capitalism, they do not better their conditions equally. In the pursuit of happiness, some will be more successful than others. Some will end up with more than others. Everyone will end up with *somewhat* more than he had—everyone. But some people will end up with a lot more than they had and some with a little more than they had. Capitalism does not perceive this as a problem. It is assumed that since everyone gets more, everyone ought to be content. If some people get more than others, the reason is to be found in their differential contributions to the economy. In a capitalist system, where the market predominates in economic decision making, people who—in whatever way—make different productive inputs into the economy receive different rewards. If one's input into the economy is great, one receives a large reward; if one's input is small, one receives a modest reward. The determination of these rewards is by public preferences and public tastes as expressed in the market. If the public wants basketball players to make $400,000 a year, then those who are good at basketball can become very, very rich. If the public wants to purchase certain paintings for $1 million or $2 million, then certain artists can become very, very rich. On the other hand, croquet players, even brilliant croquet players, won't better their condition to the same degree. And those who have no particular skill had better be lucky.

This is the way the system works. It rewards people in terms of their contribution to the economy as measured and defined by the marketplace—namely, in terms of the free preferences of individual men and women who have money in their pockets and are free to spend it or not on this, that, or the other as they please. Economic justice under capitalism means the differential reward to individuals is based on their productive input *to the economy.* I emphasize "to the economy" because input is measured by the marketplace.

Is it "just" that Mr. Ray Kroc, chairman of the board of McDonald's, should have made so much money by merely figuring out a new way of selling hamburgers? They are the same old hamburgers, just better made, better marketed. Is it fair? Capitalism says it is fair. He is selling a good product; people want it; it is fair. It is "just" that he has made so much money.

However, capitalism doesn't say only that. It

also understands that it is an exaggeration to say that literally *everyone* betters his condition when rewards are based on productive input. There are some people who are really not capable of taking part in the race at all because of mental illness, physical illness, bad luck, and so on. Such persons are simply not able to take advantage of the opportunity that does exist.

Capitalism as originally conceived by Adam Smith was not nearly so heartless a system as it presented itself during the nineteenth century. Adam Smith didn't say that people who could make no productive input into the economy through no fault of their own should be permitted to starve to death. Though not a believer, he was enough of a Christian to know that such a conclusion was not consistent with the virtue of charity. He understood that such people had to be provided for. There has never been any question of that. Adam Smith wrote two books. The book that first made him famous was not *The Wealth of Nations* but *The Theory of Moral Sentiments,* in which he said that the highest human sentiment is sympathy—the sympathy that men and women have for one another as human beings. Although *The Wealth of Nations* is an analysis of an economic system based on self-interest, Adam Smith never believed for a moment that human beings were strictly economic men or women. It took some later generations of economists to come up with that idea. Adam Smith understood that people live in a society, not just in an economy, and that they feel a sense of social obligation to one another, as well as a sense of engaging in mutually satisfactory economic transactions.

In both these books, but especially in *The Theory of Moral Sentiments,* Adam Smith addressed himself to the question, "What do the rich do with their money once they get it?" His answer was that they reinvest some of it so that society as a whole will become wealthier and everyone will continue to be able to improve his or her condition to some degree. Also, however, the rich will engage in one of the great pleasures that wealth affords: the expression of sympathy for one's fellow human beings. Smith said that the people who have money can only consume so much. What are they going to do with the money aside from what they consume and reinvest? They will use it in such a way as to gain a good reputation among their fellow citizens. He said this will be the natural way for wealthy people to behave under capitalism. Perhaps he was thinking primarily of Scotsmen. Still, his perceptiveness is interesting. Although capitalism has long been accused of being an inhumane system, we forget that capitalism and humanitarianism entered the modern world together. Name a modern, humane movement—criminal reform, decent treatment of women, kindness to animals, etc. Where does it originate? They all came from the rising bourgeoisie at the end of the eighteenth century. They were all middle-class movements. The movements didn't begin with peasants or aristocrats. Peasants were always cruel to animals and aristocrats could not care less about animals, or about wives, for that matter. It was the bourgeoisie, the capitalist middle class, that said animals should be treated with consideration, that criminals should not be tortured, that prisons should be places of punishment, yes, but humane places of punishment. It was the generation that helped establish the capitalist idea and the capitalist way of thinking in the world that brought these movements to life. Incidentally, the anti-slavery movement was also founded by middle-class men and women who had a sense of social responsibility toward their fellow citizens.

So it is simply and wholly untrue that capitalism is a harsh, vindictive, soulless system. A man like Adam Smith would never have dreamed of recommending such a system. No, he recommended the economic relations which constitute the market system, the capitalist system, on the assumption that human beings would continue to recognize their social obligations to one another and act upon this recognition with some degree of consistency. Incidentally, he even seems to have believed in a progressive income tax.

However, something very peculiar happened after Adam Smith. Something very odd and very bad happened to the idea of capitalism and its reputation after the first generation of capitalism's intellectual Founding Fathers. The economics of capitalism became a "dismal science." One cannot read *The Wealth of Nations* and have any sense that economics is a dismal science. It is an inquiry into the causes of the wealth of nations that tells people how to get rich. It says, "If you organize your economic activities this way, everyone will get richer." There is nothing pessimistic about that, nothing dismal about that. It was an exhilarating message to the world.

Unfortunately, what gave capitalism a bad name in the early part of the nineteenth century was not the socialist's criticism of capitalism but, I fear, the work of the later capitalist economists. We do not even have a really good intellectual history of this episode because people who write histories of economic thought tend not to be interested in intellectual history, but in economics. For some reason, Malthus and then Ricardo decided that capitalist economics should not deal with the production of wealth but rather with its distribution. Adam Smith had said everyone could improve his condition. Malthus said the situation was hopeless, at least for the lower classes. If the lower classes improved their condition, he argued, they would start breeding like rabbits and shortly they would be right back where they started. Ricardo came along and said that the expanding population could not all be fed because there is a shortage of fertile land in the world. In his view, the condition of the working class over the long term was unimprovable.

This was the condition of capitalist economics for most of the nineteenth century. It is a most extraordinary and paradoxical episode in modern intellectual history. Throughout the nineteenth century, ordinary men and women, the masses, the working class, were clearly improving their condition. There is just no question that the working classes in England were better off in 1860 than they had been in 1810. In the United States there was never any such question and in France, too, it was quite clear that the system was working as Adam Smith had said it would. Yet all the economists of the School of Malthus and Ricardo kept saying. "It cannot happen. Sorry, people, but you're doomed to live in misery. There is nothing we can do about it. Just have fewer children and exercise continence." To which the people said, "Thank you very much. We do not much like this system you are recommending to us," as well they might not.

When the possibility of helping the average man and woman through economic growth is rejected loudly and dogmatically by the leading economists of the day, many will believe it. When they conclude that their condition cannot be improved by economic growth, they will seek to improve it by redistribution, by taking it away from others who have more. It is nineteenth-century capitalist economic thought, with its incredible emphasis on the impossibility of improving the condition of the working class—even as the improvement was obviously taking place—that gave great popularity and plausibility to the socialist critique of capitalism and to the redistributionist impulse that began to emerge. This impulse, which is still so appealing, makes no sense. A nation can redistribute to its heart's content and it will not affect the average person one bit. There just isn't ever enough to redistribute. Nevertheless, once it became "clear" in the nineteenth century that there was no other way, redistribution became a very popular subject.

Because capitalism after Adam Smith seemed to be associated with a hopeless view of the world, it provoked egalitarian impulses. Is it not a natural human sentiment to argue that, if we're all in a hopeless condition, we should be hopeless equally? Let us go down together. If that indeed is our condition, equality becomes a genuine virtue. Egalitarianism became such a plausible view of the world because capitalist apologists, for reasons which I do not understand, kept insisting that this is the nature of capitalism. Those who talk about "social justice" these days do not say that the income tax should be revised so that the rich people will get more, although there may be an economic case for it. (I am not saying there is, even though there might be.) "Social justice," the term, the idea, is intimately wedded to the notion of egalitarianism as a proper aim of social and economic policy, and capitalism is criticized as lacking in "social justice" because it does not achieve this equality. In fact, it does not, cannot, and never promised to achieve this result.

However, I think the more important thrust of the term "social justice" has to do with its authoritarian meaning rather than its egalitarian meaning. The term "social" prefixed before the word "justice" has a purpose and an effect which is to abolish the distinction between the public and the private sectors, a distinction which is absolutely crucial for a liberal society. It is the very definition of a liberal society that there be a public sector and a large, private sector where people can do what they want without government bothering them. What is a "social problem?" Is a social problem something that government can ignore? Would anyone say we have a social problem but it is not the business of government? Of course not.

The term "social justice" exists in order to identify those issues about which government should get active. A social problem is a problem that gives rise to a governmental policy, which is why people who believe in the expansion of the public sector are always inventing, discovering, or defining more and more social problems in our world. The world has not become any more problematic than it ever was. The proliferation of things called "social problems" arises out of an effort to get government more and more deeply involved in the lives of private citizens in an attempt to "cope with" or "solve" these "problems." Sometimes real problems are posed. Rarely are they followed by real solutions.

The idea of "social justice," however, assumes not only that government will intervene but that government will have, should have, and can have an authoritative knowledge as to what everyone merits or deserves in terms of the distribution of income and wealth. After all, if we do not like the inequality that results from the operation of the market, then who is going to make the decision as to the distribution of services and wealth? Some authority must be found to say so-and-so deserves more than so-and-so. Of course, the only possible such authority in the modern world is not the Church but the State. To the degree that one defines "social justice" as a kind of protest against the capitalist distribution of income, one proposes some other mechanism for the distribution of income. Government is the only other mechanism that can make the decisions as to who gets what, as to what he or she "deserves," for whatever reason.

The assumption that the government is able to make such decisions wisely, and therefore that government should make such decisions, violates the very premises of a liberal community. A liberal community exists on the premise that there is no such authority. If there were an authority which knew what everyone merited and could allocate it fairly, why would we need freedom? There would be no point in freedom. Let the authority do its work. Now, we have seen the experience of non-liberal societies, and not all of it is bad. I would not pretend that a liberal society is the only possible good society. If one likes the values of a particular non-liberal society, it may not be bad at all. There are many non-liberal societies I admire: monasteries are non-liberal societies, and I do not say they are bad societies. They are pretty good societies—but they are not liberal societies. The monk has no need for liberty if he believes there is someone else, his superior, who knows what is good for him and what reward he merits.

Once we assume that there is a superior authority who has authoritative knowledge of the common good and of the merits and demerits of every individual, the ground of a liberal society is swept away, because the very freedoms that subsist and thrive in a liberal society all assume that there is no such authoritative knowledge. Now, this assumption is not *necessarily* true. Maybe there is someone who really does have an authoritative knowledge of what is good for all of us and how much we all merit. We who choose a liberal society are skeptical as to the possibility. In any case, we think it is more likely that there will be ten people all claiming to have different versions of what is good for all of us and what we should all get, and therefore we choose to let the market settle it. It is an amicable way of not getting involved in endless philosophical or religious arguments about the nature of the true, the good, and the beautiful.

The notion of a "just society" existing on earth

is a fantasy, a utopian fantasy. That is not what life on earth is like. The reason is that the world is full of other people who are different from you and me, alas, and we have to live with them. If they were all like us, we would live fine; but they are not all like us, and the point of a liberal society and of a market economy is to accept this difference and say, "Okay, you be you and I'll be I. We'll disagree, but we'll do business together. We'll mutually profit from doing business together, and we'll live not necessarily in friendship but at least in civility with one another."

I am not saying that capitalism is a just society. I am saying that there is a capitalist conception of justice which is a workable conception of justice. Anyone who promises you a just society on this earth is a fraud and a charlatan. I believe that this is not the nature of human destiny. It would mean that we all would be happy. Life is not like that. Life is doomed not to be like that. But if you do not accept this view, and if you really think that life can indeed be radically different from what it is, if you really believe that justice can prevail on earth, then you are likely to start taking phrases like "social justice" very seriously and to think that the function of politics is to rid the world of its evils: to abolish war, to abolish poverty, to abolish discrimination, to abolish envy, to abolish, abolish, abolish. We are not going to abolish any of those things. If we push them out one window, they will come in through another window in some unforeseen form. The reforms of today give rise to the evils of tomorrow. That is the history of the human race.

If one can be somewhat stoical about this circumstance, the basic precondition of social life, capitalism becomes much more tolerable. However, if one is not stoical about it, if one demands more of life than life can give, then capitalism is certainly the wrong system because capitalism does not promise that much and does not give you that much. All it gives is a greater abundance of material goods and a great deal of freedom to cope with the problems of the human condition on your own.

A Moral Case for Socialism

Kai Nielsen
Professor of Philosophy Emeritus, University of Calgary

I.

In North America socialism gets a bad press. It is under criticism for its alleged economic inefficiency and for its moral and human inadequacy. I want here to address the latter issue.[1] Looking at capitalism and socialism, I want to consider, against the grain of our culture, what kind of moral case can be made for socialism.

The first thing to do, given the extensive, and, I would add, inexcusably extensive, confusions about this, is to say what socialism and capitalism are. That done I will then, appealing to a cluster of values which are basic in our culture, concerning which there is a considerable and indeed a reflective consensus, examine how capitalism and socialism fare with respect to these values.[2] Given that people generally, at least in Western societies, would want it to be the case that these values have a stable exemplification in our social lives, it is appropriate to ask the question: which of these social systems is more likely stably to exemplify them? I shall argue, facing the gamut of a careful comparison in the light of these values, that, everything considered, socialism comes out better than capitalism. And this, if right, would give us good reason for believing that socialism is preferable—indeed morally preferable—to capitalism if it also turns out to be a feasible socio-economic system.

What, then, are socialism and capitalism? Put most succinctly, capitalism requires the existence of private *productive* property (private ownership of the means of production) while socialism works toward its abolition. What is essential for socialism is public ownership and control of the means of production and public ownership means just what

From *Critical Review,* Vol. 3, Nos. 3 & 4 (Summer/Fall, 1989,) pp. 542–553. Reprinted by permission of *Critical Review,* 275 W. Park Ave., New Haven, CT 06511.

it says: *ownership by the public.* Under capitalism there is a domain of private property rights in the means of production which are not subject to political determination. That is, even where the political domain is a democratic one, they are not subject to determination by the public; only an individual or a set of individuals who own that property can make the final determination of what is to be done with that property.[3] These individuals make that determination and not citizens at large, as under socialism. In fully developed socialism, by contrast, there is, with respect to productive property, no domain which is not subject to political determination by the public, namely by the citizenry at large. Thus, where this public ownership and control is genuine, and not a mask for control by an elite of state bureaucrats, it will mean genuine popular and democratic control over productive property. What socialism is *not* is *state* ownership in the absence of, at the very least, popular sovereignty, i.e., genuine popular control over the state apparatus including any economic functions it might have.

The property that is owned in common under socialism is the means of existence—the productive property in the society. Socialism does not proscribe the ownership of private personal property, such as houses, cars, television sets and the like. It only proscribes the private ownership of the means of production.

The above characterizations catch the minimal core of socialism and capitalism, what used to be called the essence of those concepts.[4] But beyond these core features, it is well, in helping us to make our comparison, to see some other important features which characteristically go with capitalism and socialism. Minimally, capitalism is private ownership of the means of production but it is also, at least characteristically, a social system in which a class of capitalists owns and controls the means of production and hires workers who, owning little or no means of production, sell their labor-power to some capitalist or other for a wage. This means that a capitalist society will be a class society in which there will be two principal classes: capitalists and workers. Socialism by contrast is a social system in which every able-bodied person is, was or will be a worker. These workers commonly own and control the means of production (this is the characteristic form of public ownership).[5] Thus in socialism we have, in a perfectly literal sense, a classless society for there is no division between human beings along class lines.[6]

There are both pure and impure forms of capitalism and socialism.[7] The pure form of capitalism is competitive capitalism, the capitalism that Milton Friedman would tell us is the real capitalism while, he would add, the impure form is monopoly or corporate capitalism. Similarly the pure form of socialism is democratic socialism, with firm workers' control of the means of production and an industrial as well as a political democracy, while the impure form is state bureaucratic socialism.

Now it is a noteworthy fact that, to understate it, actually existing capitalisms and actually existing socialisms tend to be the impure forms. Many partisans of capitalism lament the fact that the actually existing capitalisms overwhelmingly tend to be forms of corporate capitalism where the state massively intervenes in the running of the economy. It is unclear whether anything like a fully competitive capitalism actually exists—perhaps Hong Kong approximates it—and it is also unclear whether many of the actual players in the major capitalist societies (the existing capitalists and their managers) want or even expect that it is possible to have laissez-faire capitalism again (if indeed we ever had it). Some capitalist societies are further down the corporate road than other societies, but they are all forms of corporate, perhaps in some instances even monopoly, capitalism. Competitive capitalism seems to be more of a libertarian dream than a sociological reality or even something desired by many informed and tough-minded members of the capitalist class. Socialism has had a similar fate. Its historical exemplifications tend to be of the impure forms, namely the bureaucratic state socialisms.[8] Yugoslavia is perhaps to socialism what Hong Kong is to capitalism. It is a candidate for what might count as an exemplification, or at least a near approximation, of the pure form.

This paucity of exemplifications of pure forms of either capitalism or socialism raises the question of whether the pure forms are at best unstable social systems and at worse merely utopian ideals. I shall not try directly to settle that issue here. What I shall do instead is to compare *models* with *models*. In asking about the moral case for socialism, I shall compare forms that a not inconsiderable number of the theoretical protagonists of each take to be pure forms but which are still, they believe, historically feasible. But I will also be concerned to ask whether these models—these pure forms—can reasonably be expected to come to have a home. If they are not historically feasible models, then, even if we can make a good theoretical moral case for them, we will have hardly provided a good moral case for socialism or capitalism. To avoid bad utopianism we must be talking about forms which could be on the historical agenda. (I plainly here do not take "bad utopianism" to be pleonastic.)

II.

Setting aside for the time being the feasibility question, let us compare the pure forms of capitalism and socialism—that is to say, competitive capitalism and democratic socialism—as to how they stand with respect to sustaining and furthering the values of freedom and autonomy, equality, justice, rights and democracy. My argument shall be that socialism comes out better with respect to those values.

Let us first look at freedom and autonomy. An autonomous person is a person who is able to set her ends for herself and in optimal circumstances is able to pursue those ends. But freedom does not only mean being autonomous; it also means the absence of unjustified political and social interference in the pursuit of one's ends. Some might even say that it is just the absence of interference with one's ends. Still it is self-direction—autonomy—not non-interference which is *intrinsically* desirable. Non-interference is only valuable where it is an aid to our being able to do what we want and where we are sufficiently autonomous to have some control over our wants.

How do capitalism and socialism fare in providing the social conditions which will help or impede the flourishing of autonomy? Which model society would make for the greater flourishing of autonomy? My argument is (a) that democratic socialism makes it possible for more people to be more fully autonomous than would be autonomous under capitalism; and (b) that democratic socialism also interferes less in people's exercise of their autonomy than any form of capitalism. All societies limit liberty by interfering with people doing what they want to do in some ways, but the restrictions are more extensive, deeper and more undermining of autonomy in capitalism than in democratic socialism. Where there is private ownership of productive property, which, remember, is private ownership of the means of life, it cannot help but be the case that a few (the owning and controlling capitalist class) will have, along with the managers beholden to them, except in periods of revolutionary turmoil, a firm control, indeed a domination, over the vast majority of people in the society. The capitalist class with the help of their managers determines whether workers (taken now as individuals) can work, how they work, on what they work, the conditions under which they work and what is done with what they produce (where they are producers) and what use is made of their skills and the like.[9] As we move to welfare state capitalism—a compromise still favoring capital which emerged out of long and bitter class struggles—the state places some restrictions on some of these powers of capital. Hours, working conditions and the like are controlled in certain ways. Yet whether workers work and continue to work, how they work and on what, what is done with what they produce, and the rationale for their work are not determined by the workers themselves but by the owners of capital and their managers; this means a very considerable limitation on the autonomy and freedom of workers. Since workers are the great majority, such socio-economic relations place a very considerable limitation on human freedom and indeed on the very most important freedom that people have, namely their being able to live in a self-directed manner, when compared with the industrial democracy of democratic socialism. Under capitalist arrangements it simply cannot fail to be the case that a very large number of people will lose control over a very central set of facets of their lives, namely central aspects of their work and indeed in many instances, over their very chance to be able to work.

Socialism would indeed prohibit capitalist acts between consenting adults; the capitalist class would lose its freedom to buy and sell and to control the labor market. There should be no blinking at the fact that socialist social relations would impose some limitations on freedom, for there is, and indeed can be, no society without norms and some sanctions. In any society you like there will be some things you are at liberty to do and some things that you may not do.[10] However, democratic socialism must bring with it an industrial democracy where workers by various democratic procedures would determine how they are to work, on what they are to work, the hours of their work, under what conditions they are to work (insofar as this is alterable by human effort at all), what they will produce and how much, and what is to be done with what they produce. Since, instead of there being "private ownership of the means of production," there is in a genuinely socialist society "public ownership of the means of production," the means of life are owned by everyone and thus each person has a *right* to work: she has, that is, a right to the means of life. It is no longer the private preserve of an individual owner of capital but it is owned in common by us all. This means that each of us has an equal right to the means of life. Members of the capitalist class would have a few of their liberties restricted, but these are linked with owning and controlling capital and are not the important civil and political liberties that we all rightly cherish. Moreover, the limitation of the capitalist liberties to buy and sell and the like would make for a more extensive liberty for many, many more people.

One cannot respond to the above by saying that workers are free to leave the working class and become capitalists or at least petty bourgeoisie. They may indeed all in theory, taken *individually*, be free to leave the working class, but if many in fact try to leave the exits will very quickly become blocked.[11] Individuals are only free on the condition that the great mass of people, taken collectively, are not. We could not have capitalism without a working class and the working class is not free within the capitalist system to cease being wage laborers. We cannot all be capitalists. A people's capitalism is nonsense. Though a petty commodity production system (the family farm writ large) is a logical possibility, it is hardly a stable empirical possibility and, what is most important for the present discussion, such a system would not be a capitalist system. Under capitalism, most of us, if we are to find any work at all, will just have to sell (or *perhaps* "rent" is the better word) our labor-power as a commodity. Whether you sell or rent your labor power or, where it is provided, you go on welfare, you will not have much control over areas very crucial to your life. If these are the only feasible alternatives facing the working class, working class autonomy is very limited indeed. But these are the only alternatives under capitalism.

Capitalist acts between consenting adults, if they become sufficiently widespread, lead to severe imbalances in power. These imbalances in power tend to undermine autonomy by creating differentials in wealth and control between workers and capitalists. Such imbalances are the name of the game for capitalism. Even if we (perversely I believe) call a system of petty commodity production capitalism, we still must say that such a socioeconomic system is inherently unstable. Certain individuals would win out in this exchanging of commodities and in fairly quick order it would lead to a class system and the imbalances of power—the domination of the many by the few—that I take to be definitive of capitalism. By abolishing capitalist acts between consenting adults, then (but leaving personal property and civil and political liberties untouched), socialism protects more extensive freedoms for more people and in far more important areas of their lives.

III.

So democratic socialism does better regarding the value that epitomizes capitalist pride (*hubris*, would, I think, be a better term), namely autonomy. It also does better, I shall now argue, than capitalism with respect to another of our basic values, namely democracy. Since this is almost a corollary of what I have said about autonomy I can afford to be briefer. In capitalist societies, democracy must simply be *political* democracy. There can in the nature of the case be no genuine or thorough workplace democracy. When we enter the sphere of production, capitalists and not workers own, and therefore at least ultimately control, the means of production. While capitalism, as in some workplaces in West Germany and Sweden, sometimes can be pressured into allowing an ameliorative measure of worker control, once ownership rights are given up, we no longer have private productive property but public productive property (and in that way social ownership): capitalism is given up and we have socialism. However, where worker control is restricted to a few firms, we do not yet have socialism. What makes a system socialist or capitalist depends on what happens across the whole society, not just in isolated firms.[12] Moreover, managers can become very important within capitalist firms, but as long as ownership, including the ability to close the place down and liquidate the business, rests in the hands of capitalists we can have no genuine workplace democracy. Socialism, in its pure form, carries with it, in a way capitalism in any form cannot, workplace democracy. (That some of the existing socialisms are anything but pure does not belie this.)[13]

Similarly, whatever may be said of existing socialisms or at least of some existing socialisms, it is not the case that there is anything in the very idea of socialism that militates against political as well as industrial democracy. Socialists are indeed justly suspicious of some of the tricks played by parliamentary democracy in bourgeois countries, aware of its not infrequent hypocrisy and the limitations of its stress on purely legal and formal political rights and liberties. Socialists are also, without at all wishing to throw the baby out with the bath water, rightly suspicious of any simple reliance on majority rule, unsupplemented by other democratic procedures and safeguards.[14] But there is nothing in socialist theory that would set it against political democracy and the protection of political and civil rights; indeed there is much in socialism that favors them, namely its stress on both autonomy and equality.

The fact that political democracy came into being and achieved stability within capitalist societies may prove something about conditions necessary for its coming into being, but it says nothing about capitalism being necessary for sustaining it. In Chile, South Africa and Nazi Germany, indeed, capitalism has flourished without the protection of civil and political rights or anything like a respect for the democratic tradition. There is nothing structural in socialism that would prevent it from continuing those democratic traditions or cherishing those political and civil rights. That something came about under certain conditions does not establish that these conditions are necessary for its continued existence. That men initially took an interest in chess does not establish that women cannot quite naturally take an interest in it as well. When capitalist societies with long-flourishing democratic traditions move to socialism there is no reason at all to believe that they will not continue to be democratic. (Where societies previously had no democratic tradition or only a very weak one, matters are more problematic.)

IV.

I now want to turn to a third basic value, equality. In societies across the political spectrum, *moral* equality (the belief that everyone's life matters equally) is an accepted value.[15] Or, to be somewhat cynical about the matter, at least lip service is paid to it. But even this lip service is the compliment that vice pays to virtue. That is to say, such a belief is a deeply held considered conviction in modernized societies, though it has not been at all times and is not today a value held in all societies. This is most evident concerning moral equality.

While this value is genuinely held by the vast majority of people in capitalist societies, it can hardly be an effective or functional working norm where there is such a diminishment of autonomy as we have seen obtains unavoidably in such societies. Self-respect is deeply threatened where so many people lack effective control over their own lives, where there are structures of domination, where there is alienated labor, where great power differentials and differences in wealth make for very different (and often very bleak) life chances. For not inconsiderable numbers, in fact, it is difficult to maintain self-respect under such conditions unless they are actively struggling against the system. And, given present conditions, fighting the system, particularly in societies such as the United States, may well be felt to be a hopeless task. Under such conditions any real equality of opportunity is out of the question. And the circumstances are such, in spite of what is often said about these states, that equality of condition is an even more remote possibility. But without at least some of these things moral equality cannot even be approximated. Indeed, even to speak of it sounds like an obscene joke given the social realities of our lives.

Although under welfare-state capitalism some of the worst inequalities of capitalism are ameliorated, workers still lack effective control over their work, with repercussions in political and public life as well. Differentials of wealth cannot but give rise to differentials in power and control in politics, in the media, in education, in the direction of social life and in what options get seriously debated. The life chances of workers and those not even lucky enough to be workers (whose ranks are growing and will continue to grow under capitalism) are impoverished compared to the life chances of members of the capitalist class and its docile professional support stratum.

None of these equality-undermining features would obtain under democratic socialism. Such societies would, for starters, be classless, eliminating the power and control differentials that go with the class system of capitalism. In addition to political democracy, industrial democracy and all the egalitarian and participatory control that goes with that would, in turn, reinforce moral equality. Indeed it would make it possible where before it was impossible. There would be a commitment under democratic socialism to attaining or at least approximating, as far as it is feasible, equality of condition; and this, where approximated, would help make for real equality of opportunity, making equal life chances something less utopian than it must be under capitalism.

In fine, the very things, as we have seen, that make for greater autonomy under socialism than under capitalism, would, in being more equally distributed, make for greater equality of condition, greater equality of opportunity and greater moral equality in a democratic socialist society than in a capitalist one. These values are values commonly shared by both capitalistically inclined people and those who are socialistically inclined. What the former do not see is that in modern industrial societies, democratic socialism can better deliver these goods than even progressive capitalism.

There is, without doubt, legitimate worry about bureaucratic control under socialism.[16] But that is a worry under any historically feasible capitalism as well, and it is anything but clear that state bureaucracies are worse than great corporate bureaucracies. Indeed, if socialist bureaucrats were, as the socialist system requires, really committed to production for needs and to achieving equality of condition, they might, bad as they are, be the lesser of two evils. But in any event democratic socialism is not bureaucratic state socialism, and there is no structural reason to believe that it must—if it arises in a society with skilled workers committed to democracy—give rise to bureaucratic state socialism. There will, inescapably, be some bureaucracy, but in a democratic socialist society it must and indeed will be controlled. This is not merely a matter of optimism about the will of socialists, for there are more mechanisms for democratic control of bureaucracy within a democratic socialism that is both a political and an industrial democracy, than there can be under even the most benign capitalist democracies—democracies which for structural reasons can never be industrial democracies. If, all that notwithstanding, bureaucratic creepage is inescapable in modern societies, then that is just as much a problem for capitalism as for socialism.

The underlying rationale for production under capitalism is profit and capital accumulation. Capitalism is indeed a marvelous engine for building up the productive forces (though clearly at the expense of considerations of equality and autonomy). We might look on it, going back to earlier historical times, as something like a forced march to develop the productive forces. But now that the productive forces in advanced capitalist societies are wondrously developed, we are in a position to direct them to far more humane and more equitable uses under a socio-economic system whose rationale for production is to meet human needs (the needs of everyone as far as this is possible). This egalitarian thrust, together with the socialists' commitment to attaining, as far as that is possible, equality of condition, makes it clear that socialism will produce more equality than capitalism.

V.

In talking about autonomy, democracy and equality, we have, in effect, already been talking about justice. A society or set of institutions that does better in these respects than another society will be a more just society than the other society.[17]

Fairness is a less fancy name for justice. If we compare two societies and the first is more democratic than the second; there is more autonomy in the first society than in the second; there are more nearly equal life chances in the first society than in the second and thus greater equality of opportunity; if, without sacrifice of autonomy, there is more equality of condition in the first society than in the second; and if there is more moral equality in the first society than in the second, then we cannot but conclude that the first society is a society with more fairness than the second and, thus, that it is the more just society. But this is exactly how socialism comes out vis-à-vis even the best form of capitalism.[18]

A society which undermines autonomy, heels in democracy (where democracy is not violating rights), makes equality impossible to achieve and violates rights cannot be a just society. If, as I contend, that is what capitalism does, and cannot help doing, then a capitalist society cannot be a just society. Democratic socialism, by contrast, does not need to do any of those things, and we can predict that it would not, for there are no structural imperatives in democratic socialism to do so and there are deep sentiments in that tradition urging us not to do so. I do not for a moment deny that there are similar sentiments for autonomy and democracy in capitalist societies, but the logic of capitalism, the underlying structures of capitalist societies—even the best of capitalist societies—frustrate the realization of the states of affairs at which those sympathies aim.[19] A radical democrat with a commitment to human rights, to human autonomy and moral equality and fair equality of opportunity ought to be a democratic socialist and a firm opponent of capitalism—even a capitalism with a human face.

NOTES

1. For arguments about efficiency see David Schweickart, *Capitalism or Worker Control?* (New York: Praeger, 1980) and Samuel Bowles, David M. Gordon and Thomas E. Weisskopf, *Beyond the Waste-land: A Democratic Alternative to Economic Decline* (New York: Anchor Doubleday, 1983).
2. Andrew Levine's work is very important here and my own account has been extensively influenced by his. See Andrew Levine, *Arguing for Socialism* (London: Routledge & Kegan Paul, 1984); Andrew Levine, "On Arguing for Socialism—Theoretical Considerations," *Socialism and Democracy* (Spring/Summer 1968): 19–28; and Andrew Levine, *The Withering Away of the State* (London: Verso, 1987).
3. That this is a system which is distinctive of capitalism and to which there are many working alternatives is shown by A.M. Honoré, "Property, Title and Redistribution" in Virginia Held, ed., *Property, Profits and Economic Justice* (Belmont, Calif.: Wadsworth Publishing, 1980), 84–92.
4. This is carefully argued for by Andrew Levine. See the references in my second note.
5. Kai Nielsen, "Capitalism, Socialism and Justice" in Tom Regan and Donald Van De Veere, eds., *And Justice for All* (Totowa, N.J.: Rowman and Littlefield, 1982), 264–96.
6. G.A. Cohen, "The Structure of Proletarian Unfreedom," *Philosophy and Public Affairs* 12, no. 1 (Winter 1983): 2–33 and John Exdell, "Liberty, Equality and Capitalism," *Canadian Journal of Philosophy* II, no. 3 (September 1981): 457–72.
7. Nielsen, "Capitalism, Socialism and Justice," 264–69.
8. Ferenc Fehér, Agnes Heller, György Markus, *Dictatorship over Needs: An Analysis of Soviet Societies* (Oxford: Basil Blackwell, 1983).
9. Cohen, "The Structure of Proletarian Unfreedom."
10. G.A. Cohen, "Freedom, Justice and Capitalism,"

New Left Review no. 26 (March/April 1981) and his "Illusions About Private Property and Freedom," *Issues in Marxist Philosophy,* vol. IV, ed. John Mepham and David-Hillel Ruben (Sussex: Harvester Press, 1981), 223–39.

11. G.A. Cohen, *Karl Marx's Theory of History* (Oxford: Clarendon Press, 1978) 73–7.
12. Levine, *Arguing for Socialism,* 1–11.
13. How far they are from that is shown by Fehér, Heller and Markus, *Dictatorship over Needs.*
14. Claus Offe, *Disorganized Capitalism* (Cambridge, Mass.: MIT Press, 1985), 259–99.
15. Thomas Nagel, *Mortal Questions* (Cambridge: Cambridge University Press, 1979), 106–27.
16. Fehér, Heller and Markus, *Dictatorship over Needs.*
17. John Rawls, *A Theory of Justice* (Cambridge, Mass.: Harvard University Press, 1971); Kai Nielsen, *Equality and Liberty: A Defense of Radical Egalitarianism* (Totowa, N.J.: Rowman and Allanheld, 1985); and Samuel Bowles and Herbert Gintis, *Democracy and Capitalism* (New York: Basic Books, 1986).
18. Levine citations in n 2 above and Nielsen, *Equality and Liberty.*
19. See Richard C. Edwards, Michael Reich and Thomas E. Weisekopf, eds., *The Capitalist System,* 3rd ed. (Englewood Cliffs, N.J.: Prentice-Hall, 1986), and Samuel Bowles and Richard Edwards, *Understanding Capitalism* (New York: Harper and Row, 1985).

QUESTIONS FOR DISCUSSION

1. You have been asked to distribute a sum of money *justly* among the following people. Think of your funds as a pie to be divided into six pieces, and rank the six people listed below from highest (the one to whom you would give the most money) to lowest. You may assign one or more of the candidates an equal rank. Defend your distribution, explaining *why* you think it is just. How would your distribution be assessed by Rawls, Nozick, and Smart?

- **a.** A man who lives off the interest on his inherited wealth
- **b.** An unemployed man from the inner city
- **c.** A single mother of five who works as a rest room attendant during the day and moonlights as a prostitute
- **d.** A blue-collar worker on an automobile plant assembly line
- **e.** A high-level manager of a consumer products company, male, married
- **f.** A married woman who holds an exactly comparable position in a similar consumer products company

2. Rawls argues that just principles are those which would be chosen by rational, self-interested people if they were placed behind a "veil of ignorance." What is the purpose of Rawls' "veil of ignorance"? Do you think that people placed behind such a veil really would choose the principles Rawls claims they would choose?

3. Nozick rejects a system that tries to ensure *equality* among persons, because he believes such a system would inevitably interfere with people's *liberty.* Would people be equally *free* under a Nozickian system of justice? If not, can we call Nozick's theory of justice a truly "libertarian" one?

4. Why does Smart believe that the general tendency of utilitarianism is toward equality? What would be the exceptions to this tendency? What might Rawls and Nozick have to say about Smart's theory of justice?

5. Kristol argues for a "capitalist conception of justice." Yet he also states, "Is capitalism compatible with social justice? I submit that the answer is 'No.' " Is Kristol contradicting himself? What does he mean by "capitalist conception of justice"? By "social justice"?

6. Nielsen claims that socialism is a more just system than capitalism, but he has little to say about which system is more efficient. Is capitalism a more efficient system? Must it be? Assuming it is, and assuming that socialism is more just, which should we accept: economic efficiency at the cost of justice, or justice at the cost of economic efficiency? How might the decision be made?

Ethics and Business Decision Making

Teaching Ethical Decision Making and Principled Reasoning

Michael Josephson
President, Josephson Institute for the Advancement of Ethics

The ethical quality of our society is determined by the separate actions of public officials and their staffs, employers and their employees, parents and their children, teachers and their students, professionals and their clients, individuals and their friends. Each of us is almost always in one or more of these roles and our decisions are important. They are important on an individual level because they establish and define our ethical character. They are important on a social level because they produce significant direct consequences and, indirectly, help to set the moral tone of all social interactions.

Every day we face situations which test our ethical consciousness and commitment. Sometimes, the ethical implications of our decisions are apparent. Our consciences are awake and active, warning us to be good. In such cases, we know we will be held accountable for our conduct and we do not tell big lies, steal or break important promises.

Most of our decisions, however, are more mundane. They deal with our basic personal and occupational relationships and activities and there are no sirens causing us to view the choice as an ethical one. We rely heavily on habits, common sense and our perceptions of custom (i.e., what we think is generally considered acceptable by those engaged in similar activities). The dominant consideration is expediency—accomplishing our tasks, getting what we want, with as little hassle as possible.

Most of us do pretty well in dealing with the big and obvious ethical decisions. We tend to judge ourselves, and would like others to judge us by, these self-conscious choices which usually display our virtue. Unfortunately, we are more likely to be judged, and tripped up, by the way we handle the hundreds of ethical "sleepers" that cumulatively shape our reputations.

In recent years we have witnessed a growing concern about the way people are behaving. In fact,

Excerpted from *Ethics: Easier Said Than Done* (Winter 1988). Reprinted by permission of the Josephson Institute for the Advancement of Ethics.

the proliferation of well-publicized examples of dishonesty, hypocrisy, cheating and greed has created some alarm about the state of personal ethics. If these incidents are indicative of a trend, there is much reason for concern because they reflect a level of selfishness, shortsightedness and insensitivity that could undermine the moral fabric of our society.

ETHICS EDUCATION

In response to this new awareness, there has been a revived interest in ethics education. The pendulum of social conscience seems to be swinging the other way and there is a call for a return to traditional moral values and value-centered education. It has become clear to many that "value clarification," "situational ethics," and "ethical relativism" do not provide the inspiration, motivation or training to generate either the good will or discipline that are essential to moral conduct. Moreover, most academic courses which teach *about* ethics do not seem to engage students on a level that is likely to affect their behavior. The goal of the reformers is to find a way to increase ethical conduct.

We know that ethics are "learned" or "developed," yet many are not sure if ethics can be "taught." We do know that attitudes and character traits are not conveyed in the same way we convey other forms of knowledge (i.e., ethics is not something that can be taught like history or geography). Basic moral education occurs during the process of growing up. We learn from parents, teachers, religious leaders, coaches, employers, friends and others and, as a result, most of us reach adulthood with our character essentially formed and with a basic understanding of, and fundamental respect for, ethical values.

But, the presumptive values adopted in our youth are not immutably etched in our character. We know that values are constantly shuffled and prioritized, for better and for worse, in response to life experiences. Thus, youthful idealism is tested as we are emancipated into a world where important and binding decisions must be made. Only then do we discover what we are really willing to do to get and hold a job and be successful in a competitive society. By the same process, the blind competitiveness and materialism of young adulthood will later be challenged by life-changing experiences (e.g., illness, parenthood, divorce, death of a loved one) or the simple fact of maturation, causing one to reflect on the meaning of life (sometimes inducing a "mid-life crisis").

The point, and it has enormous significance for ethics educators, is that the formation, refinement and modification of a person's operational value system—the attitudes and beliefs that motivate conduct—are an ongoing process which continues throughout one's adult life. It is never too late.

APPROACHES TO ETHICS EDUCATION

One approach to conduct-oriented ethics education deals directly with the development of character and the inculcation and reinforcement of basic moral values such as honesty, caring, fairness and accountability. This approach has potential in the education of children and adolescents, but it is not likely to be effective in dealing with young adults and mature professionals.

The second approach focuses on the development of qualities beyond character—qualities that can be developed or enhanced even in adults. Ethical behavior is the result of ethical decisions, and ethical decision making requires: 1) *ethical commitment*—the personal resolve to act ethically, to do the right thing; 2) *ethical consciousness*—the ability to perceive the ethical implications of a situation; 3) *ethical competency*—the ability to engage in sound moral reasoning and develop practical problem solving strategies.

The purpose of this article is to present a theory of ethics education and to describe a framework for analyzing ethical problems which can be taught in college, postgraduate professional courses, and ethical decision making workshops.

SETTING REASONABLE GOALS

> I am only one, but still I am one. I cannot do everything, but I can do something. And, because I cannot do everything, I will not refuse to do what I can.
> —Edwin Hale

Those who believe they can do something are probably right, and so are those who believe they can't.
—Unknown

It is important to recognize the limitations of ethics education. Many people will simply not respond to appeals to conscience or moral principle. Many people are unwilling, or at a particular point in their lives, unready, to examine the ethical quality of their conduct and change their priorities. Thus, the most appropriate target for ethics programs is not bad and selfish people who knowingly do wrong, but the vast majority of decent people who are already disposed to act with propriety but who, because of lack of insight, rigorous moral reasoning or practical problem solving ability, lose sight of their ethical aspirations and make wrong decisions.

The importance and value of ethics education does not depend on the eradication of all misconduct. If just some of the people act more ethically just some of the time, the effort is worthwhile.

DEFINING TERMS

In order to avoid the semantic quicksand that often engulfs discussions about ethics, it is necessary to define the essential terms and concepts involved.

Ethics refers to a system or code of conduct based on moral duties and obligations which indicate how we should behave; it deals with the ability to distinguish right from wrong and the commitment to do what is right.

Morals refers to what is good and right in character and conduct. The term is essentially interchangeable with ethics, though in common usage, "morality" often implies particular dogmatic views of propriety, especially as to sexual and religious matters. Since the term "ethics" does not carry these same connotations, it is more neutral.

Personal ethics refers to an individual's operational code of ethics based on personal values and beliefs as to what is right or good.

Values are core beliefs which guide or motivate attitudes and actions. Many values have nothing to do with ethics.

Ethical values are beliefs (e.g., honesty and fairness) which are inherently concerned with what is intrinsically good or right and the way one should act.

Nonethical values are ethically neutral values (e.g., wealth, security, comfort, prestige and approval). They are not necessarily inconsistent with ethical values, but often there is a conflict.

Ethical principles are standards or rules describing the kind of behavior an ethical person should and should not engage in. For example, the value of honesty translates into principles demanding truthfulness and candor and forbidding deception and cheating.

ETHICAL NORMS

What is morality in any given time or place? It is what the majority then and there happen to like and immorality is what they dislike
—Alfred North Whitehead

The so-called new morality is too often the old immorality condoned.
—Lord Shawcross

In matters of principle stand like a rock; in matters of taste swim with the current.
—Thomas Jefferson

It is critical to effective ethics education to overcome the cynicism of ethical relativism—the view that ethics is just a matter of opinion and personal belief as in politics or religion. Though debatable beliefs regarding sexual matters and religion often do travel under the passport of morality, there are ethical norms that transcend cultures and time.

While ethics educators must be aware that sermonizing and moralizing about particular ethical principles are not generally effective—after all, "No one likes to be 'should' upon" (a wonderful phrase from *How Can I Help?* by Ram Dass and Paul Gorman, Knopf 1985)—it is not constructive to be so value neutral that everyone is allowed to think that ethics is simply a matter of personal opinion and that one person's answer is necessarily as good as that of another's.

In fact, the study of history, philosophy and religion reveal a strong consensus as to certain universal and timeless values essential to the ethical life:

1) *Honesty,* 2) *Integrity,* 3) *Promise-Keeping,* 4) *Fidelity,* 5) *Fairness,* 6) *Caring for Others,* 7) *Respect for Others,* 8) *Responsible Citizenship,* 9) *Pursuit of Excellence,* and 10) *Accountability.*

These ten core values yield a series of *principles,* do's and don'ts, which delineate right and wrong in general terms and, therefore, provide a guide to behavior. Individuals may want to edit or augment the list, but we have found it to be a valuable tool in examining the ethical implications of a situation and providing solid reference points for ethical problem solving.

Ethical Principles

Honesty Be truthful, sincere, forthright, straightforward, frank, candid; do not cheat, steal, lie, deceive, or act deviously.

Integrity Be principled, honorable, upright, courageous and act on convictions; do not be two-faced, or unscrupulous or adopt an end-justifies-the-means philosophy that ignores principle.

Promise-Keeping Be worthy of trust, keep promises, fulfill commitments, abide by the spirit as well as the letter of an agreement; do not interpret agreements in a technical or legalistic manner in order to rationalize noncompliance or create excuses for breaking commitments.

Fidelity Be faithful and loyal to family, friends, employers, and country; do not use or disclose information learned in confidence; in a professional context, safeguard the ability to make independent professional judgments by scrupulously avoiding undue influences and conflicts of interest.

Fairness Be fair and open-minded, be willing to admit error and, where appropriate, change positions and beliefs, demonstrate a commitment to justice, the equal treatment of individuals, and tolerance for diversity; do not overreach or take undue advantage of another's mistakes or adversities.

Caring for Others Be caring, kind and compassionate; share, be giving, serve others; help those in need and avoid harming others.

Respect for Others Demonstrate respect for human dignity, privacy, and the right to self-determination of all people; be courteous, prompt, and decent; provide others with the information they need to make informed decisions about their own lives; do not patronize, embarrass or demean.

Responsible Citizenship Obey just laws (if a law is unjust, openly protest it); exercise all democratic rights and privileges responsibly by participation (voting and expressing informed views), social consciousness and public service; when in a position of leadership or authority, openly respect and honor democratic processes of decision making, avoid unnecessary secrecy or concealment of information, and assure that others have the information needed to make intelligent choices and exercise their rights.

Pursuit of Excellence Pursue excellence in all matters; in meeting personal and professional responsibilities, be diligent, reliable, industrious, and committed; perform all tasks to the best of your ability, develop and maintain a high degree of competence, be well informed and well prepared; do not be content with mediocrity but do not seek to win "at any cost."

Accountability Be accountable, accept responsibility for decisions and the foreseeable consequences of actions and inactions, and for setting an example for others. Parents, teachers, employers, many professionals and public officials have a special obligation to lead by example, to safeguard and advance the integrity and reputation of their families, companies, professions and the government; avoid even the appearance of impropriety and take whatever actions are necessary to correct or prevent inappropriate conduct of others.

The first question in ethical decision making is: "Which ethical principles are involved in the decision?" Considering the above list is an excellent way to isolate the relevant issues involved.

ETHICAL THEORIES

Though we run the risk of alienating many philosophy-oriented ethicists, in the Institute's programs we have not found it particularly useful to dwell on ethical theories. Our time with audiences is limited and most want to get immediately to the heart of ethical problem solving.

In fact, we present a variation of philosopher W. D. Ross' notion that there are certain *prima facie obligations* which impose ethical duties that can be avoided only in order to perform superior ethical duties—a kind of compromise between Kant's strict duty theory and John Stuart Mill's utilitarianism. Thus, implicit in our analysis of practical decision making situations is the principle that ethical duties are real, important and binding, and that they can be overborne only by other ethical duties.

The Golden Rule On the other hand, we have found it helpful to emphasize the Golden Rule: "Do unto others as you would have them do unto you; and love thy neighbor as thyself." Most of the ethical principles listed above can be derived from these simple statements.

This approach to ethical decision making is surprisingly effective. In many cases, simply by asking, "How would I want to be treated in this situation?" the ethical response becomes clear. We do not want to be lied to or deceived, so we should not lie to or deceive others. We want people to keep their promises and treat us fairly, so we should keep our promises and treat others fairly.

The major problem with the Golden Rule is that in complex cases, where a decision is likely to affect different people in different ways, a more sophisticated method of sorting out ethical responsibilities is necessary.

Stakeholder Analysis To deal with these complex situations, we advocate an analytical tool developed in the corporate responsibility literature. Since a decision is often likely to affect an entire network of people with differing interests, it is necessary to carefully sort out the interests by determining, in a systematic way, which people have a stake in the decision. Thus, a threshold question in analyzing a problem is: "Who are the stakeholders and how is the decision likely to affect them?" This method does not solve the problem, but it helps the decision maker see all the ethical implications of conduct and reduces the likelihood of inadvertent harm.

ETHICAL BEHAVIOR

> Would the boy you were be proud of the man you are?
>
> —Laurence Peter

> The trouble with the rat race is that even if you win, you're still a rat.
>
> —Lily Tomlin

Ethics education works best when it builds upon our positive inclinations. Most people want to be ethical; they want to be worthy of the respect and admiration of others and they want to be proud of themselves and what they do for a living. Self-esteem and self-respect depend on the private assessment of our own character. Very few people can accept the fact that they are less ethical than others. In fact, most people believe that they are more ethical.

Because of the importance of this positive self-image, many people will alter their conduct if they discover it is inconsistent with their espoused values. Thus, it is important to discuss candidly the common misconceptions and normal excuses, rationalization, and temptations which impede ethical conduct. Although some level of confrontation may be necessary to cut through natural defenses, it is critical to avoid an adversary atmosphere which will merely produce resistance. The most successful methods present participants with the opportunity to discuss pertinent and specific problems with peers and help them to clarify their ethical aspirations, engage in moral reflection, and enhance their ethical issue-spotting, reasoning and problem-solving abilities.

Common Misconceptions

Ethics Are Only Concerned with Misconduct Most discussions about ethics focus on misconduct and improprieties—the negative dimension of ethics. But, as is apparent from our list of ethical principles, an equally important dimension of ethics focuses on positive actions, doing the right thing, on producing good, helping and caring, rather than on avoiding wrongdoing. Under this affirmative perspective, ethical principles are not merely burdens and limitations; they are also guidelines for the constructive role a person of virtue can play in society.

If It's Legal, It's Ethical Law abidingness is an aspect of responsible citizenship and an ethical principle especially important in a democracy. We should not, however, confuse ethics with legality. Laws and written codes of ethics are minimalist in nature—they only establish the lines of consensus impropriety.

Ethics requires more of a person than technical compliance with rules. Everything that is lawful is not, *ipso facto,* ethical. Thus, the fact that certain conduct escapes the label of illegality, including the fact that a person has been formally acquitted of a criminal charge, does not, in itself, provide moral exoneration.

People we regard as ethical do not measure their conduct in terms of minimal standards of virtue. They do not walk the line, nor consistently resort to legalistic rationales to circumvent legitimate standards of behavior or the spirit of their agreements. Ethical persons consciously advance ethical principles by choosing to do more than they have to and less than they have a right to do.

The ethical person may, however, occasionally choose to openly violate a law believed to be unjust. The ethical value of lawfulness can be overborne by other conscience driven values. Thus, civil disobedience, the open and deliberate refusal to abide by certain laws, has a long and honorable history. The thing that makes such lawbreaking ethically justifiable is the integrity of the violator and the courage of convictions shown by the willingness to publicly challenge the law and bear the consequences. On the other hand, it is not ethical to break a law one disagrees with in the hope of not being found out. The kind of covert lawlessness that characterized the darker side of the Iran-Contra scandal does not qualify as civil disobedience.

There Is a Single Right Answer An ethical decision maker does not proceed on the assumption that there is a single "right" answer to all ethical dilemmas. In most situations, there are a number of ethical responses. The first task is to distinguish ethical from unethical responses; the second, is to choose the best response from the ethically appropriate ones. Although there may be several ethical responses to a situation, all are not equal. Some are more ethical than others, and some are more consistent with an individual's personal goals and value system than others.

Excuses, Rationalizations and Temptations

It is important to try to understand why people tend to act unethically. An easy answer is that they are just plain bad. This is simply not so. The truth is that a great deal of improper conduct is committed by fundamentally decent people who believe in and are committed to ethical values. There are three major reasons that ethically concerned persons fail to conform to their own moral principles: 1) *unawareness and insensitivity,* 2) *selfishness,* consisting of self-indulgence, self-protection, and self-righteousness, and 3) *defective reasoning.*

Unawareness and Insensitivity

> At the turn of the century, a Russian noblewoman attended an opera and wept out of compassion at the death of a poor peasant. She was still weeping when she left the opera house and found that her footman had frozen to death while waiting for her as he was instructed to do. She became angry, cursing his ignorance and her inconvenience, making no connection between her compassion and her conduct.

Moral blindness, the failure to perceive all the ethical implications of conduct, is a major source of impropriety. In some cases, this blindness results from the operation of subconscious defense mechanisms which protect the psyche from having to cope with the fact that many of the things we do and want to do are not consistent with our ethical beliefs. Elaborate and internally persuasive excuses and rationalizations are used to fool our consciences. Among the most potent are:

- Everyone does it.
- To get along, go along.
- They don't understand.
- I can't do anyone any good if I lose my job.
- I have no time for ethical subtleties.
- Ethics is a luxury I can't afford right now.
- It's not my job/worry/problem.

> You can't learn too soon that the most useful thing about principle is that it can always be sacrificed to expediency.
>
> —Somerset Maugham

> Senators who go down in defeat in defense of a single principle will not be on hand to fight for that or any other principle in the future.
>
> —John F. Kennedy

A common context for this ethical self-deception is occupational behavior. Most occupations develop the "insider syndrome" which rationalizes ethically dubious conduct and immunizes the occupation from the criticism of outsiders on the grounds that the critics simply don't understand the necessities and values that insiders take for granted.

Insider rationales are particularly effective at making expediency a new ethical principle which overrides integrity, honesty and accountability in order to achieve the "greater good" (i.e., the end justifies the means). For example, politicians are viewed as frequently relying on insider rationales to justify various forms of deception, the leaking of confidential information, and cynical manipulation of campaign financing and outside income rules. Journalists are thought to justify the use of stolen documents, invasions of privacy, and arrogant and offensive interviewing behavior—all based upon vague notions of the public's right to know, though the public regularly denounces such press tactics.

Selfishness Implicit in all ethical theories is the notion of caring for and respecting others. In many cases, this requires us to forego personal benefits or bear personal burdens; some level of self-sacrifice is essential to consistent ethical conduct. Thus, selfishness continually assaults the conscience with temptations and rationalizations.

The natural inclination to selfishness has been amplified by certain self-actualizing philosophies coming out of the 1960's and 1970's which either advocated or were misinterpreted to condone selfishness. In the 1980's these philosophies seemed to spawn a generation of greedy people whose dominant values stress materialism.

Although there are many who proudly proclaim their individualistic "everyone for himself/herself" creed, most do not. Most still believe in the primacy of traditional values such as integrity, loyalty, giving, and sharing, but they are influenced by their environment and the ample supply of excuses and justifications developed to defend the new faith. Selfishness comes in three major forms: 1) self-indulgence, 2) self-protection, and 3) self-righteousness.

Self-Indulgence Perhaps the most common and easily identifiable source of unethical conduct is self-indulgence. Although few people are as open as Ivan Boesky was when he publicly asserted that "greed is good," many people lie, break commitments, violate or evade laws, and fail to demonstrate caring, compassion and charity in order to advance narrow personal interests. They often cover-up the selfish motive with noble sounding sentiments, e.g., "I'm doing it for my family"; "I'm creating (or protecting) jobs"; "If the business doesn't survive it will be worse for everyone"; "It's in the interests of all the shareholders (or the public)"; and, "My constituency needs me."

Self-Protection The instinct for self-protection often generates lying, deception and cover-ups, including big and little lies (e.g., "I knew nothing about this"; "The check is in the mail"; "Tell him I'm not in"), concealment, blameshifting, and even document destruction. These actions frequently result from a fear of, or unwillingness to accept, the consequences of prior behavior. The temptation to sacrifice ethical principles is particularly great when it is believed that the consequences will be unfair or disproportionate—an easy thing to believe when you are the one to suffer the consequences.

Self-Righteousness A particularly troublesome type of selfishness results from a form of arrogance arising from self-righteousness. For example, Colonel Oliver North demonstrated a type of integrity when he decided to "go above the law" by shredding documents, lying and deceiving, and withholding vital information to advance his strong personal convictions. The ethical problem arises, however, from the fact that he knew that his beliefs were at variance with honest good faith beliefs of others who had at least an equal right to participate in the decision making process. His conduct denied these people the ability to exercise personal autonomy and deprived them of the ability to carry out their constitutional responsibilities. He did not openly disagree with the Congressional mandates and statutes; instead, he sought to privately nullify them by ignoring them. To accomplish his goals he violated ethical principles of honesty, promise-keeping, respect for others, and responsible democratic citizenship.

Defective Reasoning In addition to sorting out the various values involved and those stakeholders affected, a substantial amount of factual analysis and prediction of consequences is necessary to ethical decision making. This requires sophisticated reasoning skills; defects in reasoning or mistakes in evaluation can result in decisions which are inconsistent with ethical principles. We find two common errors: people consistently overestimate the costs of doing the right thing, and underestimate the cost of failing to do the right thing.

Principled reasoning directs the decision maker to recognize where information is incomplete, uncertain or ambiguous, and to make reasonable efforts to get additional information and clarify the ambiguities! After evaluating the facts, the next step is to predict, with as much certainty as is reasonably possible, the likely consequences of contemplated conduct on all those affected by a decision (i.e., stakeholders).

Another defective reasoning problem, related to the selfishness issues, emanates from the fact that unethical conduct normally yields short-run benefits which, when looked at through the distorted lens of self-interest, seem to outweigh the *possibility* of long-range harms which may flow from unethical conduct. Often, it is easier to lie, deceive, conceal or disregard commitments than to confront a problem head on and accept the costs inherent in honesty and integrity.

The fact is that an ethical person must often sacrifice short-term benefits to achieve long-term advantages. He or she must also be prepared to sacrifice physical or material gains for abstract intangibles such as self-esteem, the respect of others, reputation and a clear conscience. An ethical person must be able to distinguish between short-term and long-term benefits and costs.

ETHICAL DECISION MAKING

Ethical decision making refers to a process of choosing (i.e., principled reasoning) which systematically considers and evaluates alternate courses of conduct in terms of the list of ethical principles. It does not proceed on the assumption that there is a single "right" answer to most problems. To the contrary, it recognizes that though some responses would be unethical, in most situations there are a number of ethical ways of dealing with a situation.

The first task of ethical decision making is to distinguish ethical from unethical responses; the second is to choose the best response from the ethically appropriate ones. Although there may be several ethical responses to a situation, all are not equal.

Making the distinctions necessary is much more difficult and complex than is normally thought because, in so many real world situations, there are a multitude of competing interests and values, and crucial facts are unknown or ambiguous. Since our actions are likely to benefit some at the expense of others, ethical decision makers also attempt to foresee the likely consequences of their actions.

We cannot solve all problems by resorting to some mechanistic formula, but we can be more effective if we have a structure. A process which systematically takes into account the ethical principles involved in a decision tends to prevent inadvertent unethical conduct and allows us to consciously choose which values to advance—to determine whom to aid and whom to harm.

When one is in the trenches, it is difficult, if not impossible, to analyze problems fully and objectively. While most people do not want more rules telling them what to do, they do want assistance in perceiving the ethical implications of their decisions and in developing realistic, morally-centered approaches for resolving ethical dilemmas. . . .

In the "real world" there are many shades of gray, even in routine decision making. Most of these decisions are made in the context of economic, professional, and social pressures which compete with ethical goals and conceal or confuse the moral issues. We must, therefore, be ever vigilant to use principled reasoning in the pursuit of ethical decision making. The essential skills *can* be taught to adults; their subsequent behavior *can* be more ethical. It may not always be simple to do, but, then again, ethics truly are "easier said than done."

Ethical Decision Making in Business

Craig Dreilinger and Dan Rice
Dreilinger—President, The Dreiford Group
Rice—Senior Consultant, The Dreiford Group

In essence, an ethical issue is a problem where some of the components suggest that values or moral judgments may come into conflict. Therefore, it makes eminent sense to approach such an issue by using a systematic problem-solving model to clarify the elements and issues involved in the problem, to generate possible solutions to the problem, and to provide a framework for choosing among those solutions. Because it provides a deliberate and considered approach, we have found that the problem-solving model presented here is of especial benefit in assisting one to resolve ethically related problems.

1. Identify Desired Outcome
2. Define the Problem
3. Examine Difficulties and Obstacles
4. Develop Alternative Solutions
5. Select Best Solution
6. Delineate Specific Steps
7. Identify Reactions/Rewards

The first (of seven) steps in this problem-solving model requires that the decision maker *identify the desired outcome for the entire situation.* What, exactly, are you attempting to accomplish in dealing with the problem? In addition to the problem having been solved, what else should or should not occur when you have achieved the desired result? What is the ideal outcome? What outcome(s) might you be willing to "settle for"—i.e., are there "less-than-ideal" outcomes that are acceptable if the ideal outcome proves impossible or impractical to attain?

Once you feel assured that you thoroughly understand your desired outcome, you should then *define the problem* by asking yourself questions about its antecedents and about the environment in which it is occurring. What, precisely, created or is causing this situation? Is the problem you have recognized the "real" concern, or is it actually symptomatic of a more basic, underlying problem? Who, exactly, is involved in generating or exacerbating this problem? Who, specifically, is it affecting?

When and where does this problem occur? Is this a short-term problem which is likely to be resolved with a reasonable degree of immediacy, or is it a long-term problem requiring a sustained effort to resolve? The more questions you find to ask regarding the problem, the more successful you will be in defining and comprehending the issues with which you are struggling.

After you have defined the problem as thoroughly as possible, you then need to *examine the difficulties involved in solving the problem.* In order to further clarify the solutions that may be available to you, you need to be aware of the specific difficulties that have prevented or may prevent the problem from being solved. Are there reasons that you have avoided or would like to avoid dealing with for solving the problem? Are there reasons that you or others have perpetuated the problem or allowed it to occur or persist? Why has this problem not been solved previously, or by others? What are the costs (not just financially, but also in terms of such factors as harm to others, or

---

Written for this edition of the book. Printed by permission of The Dreiford Group, 6917 Arlington Road, Bethesda, MD 20814.

damage to the organization's image or ability to function, etc.) of not solving the problem? What costs are associated with solving it? Is it more costly to solve the problem or more costly to allow it to continue?

When examining the difficulties involved in solving the problem, you also need to be aware that obstacles or conditions may exist which will make it arduous or impossible to do so.

Obstacles which make it *arduous* to resolve ethical issues are those which *can* be overcome by the decision maker involved. These obstacles suggest areas of responsibility to which you will need to attend in order to ensure that decisions are properly made. The following obstacles make it arduous to resolve ethical issues:

The true facts of the situation are unclear or incomplete Any decision must be made on the basis of the facts available. The ramifications or consequences of decisions involving ethical issues are often unclear or obscured by other considerations. Therefore, it is especially important that you expend every effort to uncover all the data available in regard to ethical considerations when making such decisions.

However, you should not ignore hunches just because you do not yet have all the facts to support them. Often, a sense of discomfort is an important clue in identifying ethical issues; likewise, a feeling that the resolution to a problem lies in a certain direction may be an indication as to where to begin in searching for further information about the situation.

Words used to describe the issue are "loaded" Ethical issues are often described in terms of "fairness," "justice," or "doing right." Such words or phrases mean different things to different people and may make it onerous for them to agree upon the facts concerned. Such words also carry an emotional content which may create an unwarranted bias towards selecting one of a possible number of alternatives. Whenever possible, avoid using "loaded" words in defining or describing ethical issues.

Subjectivity and personal perceptions create barriers to objectivity It is important that decisions involving ethical issues be made rationally and objectively. They must be supported by the facts of the situation. Examine your personal viewpoints on the matter to determine whether or not your feelings may be preventing you from impartially considering the facts or otherwise assessing the issue. Again, however, your instincts (or those of others) may provide you with information about the situation and should be examined rather than ignored.

Emotions get in the way of logic This especially occurs when ethical issues are being discussed with others. Even when you have attempted to rationally and impersonally analyze the facts of the matter, you may find that pertinent discussions become so emotionally charged that logic and clear-sightedness are unable to prevail. When you find yourself in such a situation, attempt to diffuse its intensity before allowing yourself or others to commit to adamant positions. When logic seems to conflict with your values or those of others, that may indicate a need to further explore the situation.

Obstacles which make it *impossible* to resolve ethical issues are those which impede such issues from being fully considered. The best choice for a decision maker under these conditions is to refuse to take action at all, if possible. These are situations to avoid, or if inescapable, they are situations in which no responsibility can be reasonably assigned. Often, the culture of an organization may be responsible for creating the conditions which lead to these impossible obstacles. These fall into three categories (DeGeorge, 1982).[1]

Conditions preclude obtaining the required knowledge These conditions make it impossible for you to acquire the knowledge necessary to make the decision or to anticipate its outcome. The first of these conditions is "excusable ignorance," where you have made every effort to gather the facts about the situation, but could not have been reasonably expected to recognize, understand, or acquire all the relevant facts. The second of these conditions is "invincible ignorance," where it is impossible for you to know about or understand all of the facts involved. If you suspect that important data about a situation lies beyond your grasp, you should either avoid making a decision regarding the ethical issue until such time as you can gather or understand further data, or you should pass the decision on to those better equipped to make it, if at all feasible.

Conditions preclude exercising the required freedom These conditions make it impossible to employ the freedom of choice. They include the absence of alternatives, a lack of the control or power to influence the decision, or overwhelming coercion. Under these circumstances it is best not to take action at all. If that is not an option, you cannot be expected to assume responsibility for the consequences of decisions into which you were forced.

Conditions preclude the possibility of action These conditions apply most often to situations in which harm or, less likely, benefit to others is anticipated if you fail to act. Ethically-related actions may be impossible to perform, or you may not have the ability or opportunity to perform them (e.g., "I know that X may occur and may cause harm to others, but there is nothing *I* can do to prevent X from occurring"). In such instances, your best alternative may be to alert those who might have the ability to take the action or take control of the circumstances.

Awareness of the obstacles to resolving ethical issues can assist you to take steps to overcome them, or may warn you away from involvement or decision making in those instances where overcoming the obstacles is impossible.

Having identified desirable outcomes, defined the problem, and examined the difficulties and obstacles involved in solving it, you should be in a position to *develop alternative solutions to the problem.* By their very nature, problems have alternative solutions. If there is only one possible solution, the difficulty you face is not in solving the problem, but rather in acting upon the solution. In such a case, you need to change your focus from problem-solving to determining why the solution has not been implemented.

Use brainstorming or similar techniques to generate as many alternative solutions to the problem as possible. Avoid rejecting any solution until you have examined it carefully.

Developing alternative solutions often proves easier than selecting the best of those solutions. The following two "frameworks" are designed to be applied at this stage of problem solving. Each provides a systematic approach for screening alternative solutions and selecting the one best suited to resolving the issue you are faced with. There is no "better" framework; you might select one based on its practicality or theoretical appeal, or you may wish to use both of them, choosing the one that seems to best fit the situation at hand.

THE FOUR FACTOR PROCESS

Henderson (1982)[2] noted that there are four factors related to business which can serve as checkpoints when ethical issues arise: goals, methods, motives, and consequences. Examining the components of each of these factors results in a process that facilitates decision making.

The *goals* of an organization can be examined from three perspectives, the first of which is *goal multiplicity.* In any given situation, the organization may be pursuing more than one goal. For example, a corporation may wish to reduce pollution for a number of reasons: to comply with laws, to improve the corporate image, in accordance with a genuine commitment to cleaner air, etc. Additionally, an organization has a number of stakeholders whose goals must be taken into account. You need to clearly identify and set priorities for the various goals that may play a part in making the decision.

Next, you need to determine *stakeholder priorities,* and which stakeholders' priorities take precedence. There may be times when goal priorities and stakeholder priorities come into conflict. This circumstance can direct your attention to further considerations that need to be made in deciding which goals are to be paramount in resolving the issue.

Finally, a check should be made to ensure *goal compatibility,* that is, that the goals decided upon are not mutually exclusive or in conflict. If this proves to be the case, further priorities need to be determined.

Once you have decided upon the goals that need to be achieved in the given situation, you then need to settle on the *methods* for accomplishing them. First, *stakeholder acceptability* needs to be determined. This involves once again examining the stakeholders and ascertaining whether proposed methods will be acceptable to them, or whether these methods will violate the values they hold.

Then, you need to think about whether to select *methods that satisfy or maximize goals.* Should you choose methods that simply accommodate the goals in question or should you pick those which attempt to achieve the maximum potential possible? For example, should you just comply with the minimum acceptable standards for decreasing air pollution, or should you attempt to reduce pollution as much as you possibly can?

Finally, you should determine whether the methods you are contemplating are *essential, incidental, or extraneous.* Are they essential for achieving goals? Are they incidental, in that they might work and so might be worth attempting? Or are they extraneous and based mainly on personal whims or predilections? Weeding out incidental and extraneous methods diminishes the possibility that the methodology selected will miscarry or have unforeseen consequences.

The *motivation* behind the goals or methods embraced can have an effect on outcomes or on others' perceptions of decisions. Are your motives *hidden or evident?* Concealed motives often cause others to become suspicious of or misinterpret decision makers' intentions. At the very least, you should be aware of your own motives and those of others involved, and should know when to reveal them.

Are motives *shared or selfish?* Decision makers need to determine whether their motives are self-centered or are shared by others. Mutually held motives imply that there is a consensus regarding the decision to be made, which enhances its chances for success.

What is the *value orientation* regarding your approach to the situation? Do the motives underlying goals and methods reflect both your own and the organization's values?

As a last step, you should review the goals, methods, and motives you have identified as being relevant to the ethical issue to be resolved. You need to examine the possible *consequences* of the alternatives under consideration on the stakeholders and others, and need to determine whether or not that impact will be affected by time or by possible outside influences. Consider all the imaginable repercussions of the course of action you are contemplating. Once you have done so, you are ready to select the alternative that is most likely to achieve the desired results.

THE THREE APPROACHES METHOD

In an article prepared for the Harvard Business School, Kenneth Goodpaster[3] proposed a process for resolving ethical issues which entails examining three different approaches to ethical problems. This method is helpful for both generating and selecting alternative solutions. Goodpaster suggests that decision makers first determine the answers to two questions:

1. Who are my stakeholders and what, precisely, are the ethical issues that must be resolved in regard to each stakeholder?
2. What are the critical ethical values and assumptions pertaining to or held by each of these stakeholders?

Once the answers to these questions have been satisfactorily determined, Goodpaster recommends that they be re-examined in light of three different approaches:

Approach 1: What are the actions I can take that give each stakeholder the greatest cost/benefit ratio? What facts support these conclusions?

Approach 2: What are the actions I can take that best respect the rights of each stakeholder and ensure that they are treated fairly? What facts support these conclusions?

Approach 3: Given my duties and obligations to each stakeholder, which take priority? Why?

Having approached the situation from these three

viewpoints, you are now in position to answer a final set of questions which should enable you to choose a best solution to the problem:

3. Do the three approaches examined above converge on a particular course of action, or do they suggest divergent actions?
4. If they suggest divergent courses of action, which should take precedence over the others?
5. Are there other ethically relevant considerations which have not been covered by the three approaches? What are they?
6. What is my decision or plan for action?

Having developed alternative solutions, and applied and reviewed appropriate frameworks, you should now be able to make your selection of the best alternative solution.

At this point, you need to carefully *delineate the specific steps that will be required* to put the solution you have selected into action. For each step, you need to define the indicators that will enable you to determine whether that step is succeeding or failing. Decide how and when you should alter your proposed solution-steps if they do not appear to be working. Develop criteria that you can use to decide whether to continue with the effort to carry out your selected solution, or when and whether you should abandon it and attempt a new solution.

Finally, you need to *identify likely reactions to and rewards for your solution.* Remain aware of your own and others' reactions to your solution as it is being carried out. Are there things you or others are doing, either consciously or otherwise, to sabotage the solution in order to "keep the problem"? What recompense do you and others need in order to make the steps towards your solution work? Are these rewards forthcoming? Once the problem has been initially resolved to your satisfaction, you also need to ensure that those involved (including yourself) are sufficiently repaid for your efforts, to guarantee that the endeavor to implement the solution will continue.

Many other problem-solving methodologies than the one we have outlined above exist, and you may find another that you feel will work better for you. Whatever the technique you choose to use, however, we suggest that when you are faced with resolving problems with *ethically related* components, it is highly important that you first have the clearest possible understanding of the problem, that you recognize the need to be aware of obstacles to resolving the problem, and that you employ a means that will serve you as a filter for selecting among alternatives the solution that will best enable you to resolve the ethical issue you have identified.

NOTES

1. DeGeorge, Richard T. *Business Ethics.* New York. Macmillan, 1982.
2. Henderson, Verne E. "The Ethical Side of Enterprise." *Sloan Management Review.* Vol. 23, No. 3, 1982.
3. Goodpaster, Kenneth E. "Some Avenues for Ethical Analysis in General Management." Harvard Business School case 9-383-007.

Attending to Ethics in Management

James A. Waters
Frederick Bird
Waters—Former Graduate Dean, William Carroll Graduate School of Management, Boston College
Bird—Professor of Theology, Concordia University

Consider the following examples of morally questionable managerial acts:

- cheating on an expense report
- conducting a superficial performance appraisal
- bribing a purchasing agent in order to make a sale
- closing a plant in a region of high unemployment

In a very broad sense, these are all examples of ethical issues that may arise in a managerial context and require management attention. At the same time, however, it is obvious that these examples

Found in *Journal of Business Ethics* 8: 493–97, 1989.

differ from one another in important ways. Given these differences among such issues, it may be very difficult to understand what is meant if a CEO or other senior executive states simply that he or she is concerned about ethical issues in an organization. Talking about ethical issues at a global level of abstraction or aggregation can be at best uninformative and at worst misleading because important distinctions among the various types of such issues are obscured. A finer grained language with respect to ethical conduct and ethical questions can help senior managers to clarify and communicate their concerns more effectively. One purpose of this article then is to present a typology of morally questionable managerial acts which managers can use to develop and communicate a more differentiated appreciation of the variety of ethical issues that can arise in their own organizations. The typology was derived from analysis of the results of interviews we conducted with a wide variety of managers about the ethical questions that arise in their work lives (Waters, *et al.,* 1986).

A second purpose of this article is to draw attention to the fact that the different types of morally questionable managerial acts typically receive very different amounts of attention from senior managers. We will suggest that, ironically, the kinds of issues that receive the most attention are those that are the least problematic for most managers; and that the issues which are the most troublesome for most managers are relatively ignored in most organizations. Appreciation of this typically unbalanced attention to ethical issues has implications for how senior managers act on their concerns in this area of organizational life.

TYPES OF MORALLY QUESTIONABLE ACTS

The phrase "ethical issues" is frequently used to refer to questions or dilemmas which involve moral judgement. In that popular usage of the phrase, relatively unambiguous actions like expense account cheating are excluded. To avoid this slipperiness in the usage of the phrase "ethical issues" and to ensure that the entire range of behavior for which ethical judgement is salient receives attention, the discussion builds on the idea of morally questionable acts.

A four part typology of morally questionable managerial acts is proposed for use, distinguishing among the acts on the basis in which the managerial role is used or observed. The typology is summarized in Figure 1.

Non-role acts are those in which the actor is acting outside his or her role as manager, they are managerial primarily in the sense that they take place in organizations and frequently involve peo-

FIGURE 1
Types of morally questionable managerial acts

Type	*Direct Effect*	*Examples*
1. Non-role	against-the-firm	• expense account cheating • embezzlement • stealing supplies
2. Role-failure	against-the-firm	• superficial performance appraisal • not confronting expense account cheating • palming off a poor performer with inflated praise
3. Role-distortion	for-the-firm	• bribery • price fixing • manipulation of suppliers
4. Role-assertion	for-the-firm	• invest in South Africa • utilize nuclear technology for energy generation • do not withdraw product line in face of initial allegations of inadequate safety

ple who may also be managers. Examples might include embezzlement of company funds, stealing supplies, cheating on expense reports, making false claims for sick leave, utilizing suppliers in which one has a financial interest, insider trading, directing the company's maintenance department to paint one's private residence and the like. In all these examples, the costs are borne directly by the organization and the payoffs are gained directly by the individual. These are morally questionable acts committed against the organization; in the short-form notation used in Figure 1, the direct effect of such acts is "against-the firm".

The second category, also with against-the-firm direct effect, concerns what we term *role-failure acts.* In contrast to non-role, these activities essentially involve a failure to perform the managerial role. Thus, managers may fail to conduct candid performance appraisals or fail to confront a subordinate cheating on his/her expense report in order to avoid the personal stress of such confrontations. They may deny promotion or training opportunities to high-performers in order to keep such subordinates in their own department, or they "palm off" a poor performer to another department with inflated words of praise. They may undercut their bosses behind the scenes or slant proposals or withhold information to suit their own emotional commitments. Though the element of financial gain is not part of these examples, there is still the theme of direct personal gain at the expense of the organization (and, in many of these cases, at the expense of some other person's best interests).

In contrast to non-role and role-failure acts, the direct effects of the next two types of morally questionable acts are described as "for-the-firm", i.e., they are committed on behalf of the organization of which the actor is a member. From the vantage point of the long-run welfare of a given firm and the industry and society in which it is embedded, all illegal and unethical acts may be considered as committed against the best interests of the firm. Similarly, in a kind of economic calculus of human behaviour, all actions may be said to be taken to further the self-interest, however conceived, of the individual focal actor. However, in terms of how morally questionable acts are experienced by the focal actor and those affected by the act, the distinction between against-the-firm and for-the-firm direct effect is reasonably clear in the short run. In contrast to the former, acts in the latter category involve direct gain for the organization and only indirectly benefit the individual actor; direct costs are borne largely by parties outside the organization.

Role-distortion acts are those in which the actor is pursuing his or her role mandate (e.g. increase sales, reduce costs, etc.) but is distorting that mandate in the sense that widely accepted moral standards, implicitly part of the role mandate, are not being observed. Examples of role-distortion acts might include bribery, price-fixing, unjustified differential pricing, padding insurance claims, falsifying product safety test results, manipulating suppliers and the like. Though such acts would, if they were widely known, be regarded with disapproval in most organizations, their direct effect is gain for the organization at the expense of outside parties such as customers, suppliers and competitors.

In contrast to role-distortion acts which involve failure to observe generally accepted moral principles, *role-assertion acts* involve situations which have something of a one-of-a-kind quality where little authoritative direction from law, precedent or customary practice exists. In the absence of generally accepted moral principles, the corporate position must be more or less asserted in public debate (Waters, 1980). Role assertion acts typically are morally defensible. They are often controversial because cogent moral arguments can be and are invoked to argue for competing alternative responses to a given question. Examples in this category might include withdrawing investment in South Africa, utilizing nuclear energy for power generation, investing in weapons manufacturing, failure to cooperate openly with regulatory agencies, production of dangerous chemicals, selling non-union picked produce, closing a plant in an area of high unemployment and the like.

Implicit in the examples cited above is the image that role assertion acts involve major questions with potentially great impact on the character of the organization, and that they are highly visible in terms of media attention, senior management involvement and public announcements of decisions. These attributes will often characterize role-assertion acts, but they are not definitive. In our interview research, we identified a small number of examples where mid-level managers unobtrusively asserted moral positions on smaller scope questions. Thus, for example, lower-level managers may "bend the rules" in their treatment of employees caught stealing or suffering from alcoholism, or in making arrangements for severance benefits for discharged employees. What is definitive in identifying role-assertion acts is that moral arguments are involved to justify actions as morally acceptable or at least morally neutral, and these arguments are used to counter the positions of others who would or do judge those actions to be morally unacceptable.

In summary then, we are suggesting that all morally questionable managerial acts can be classified in one of four categories depending on how the managerial role is used (role-assertion), used (role-failure and role-distortion) or ignored (non-role). The value of such a typology rests on the extent to which it directs attention to differences among the categories which are important to management and management research. It is to that question we now turn.

THE TYPICAL FOCUS OF MANAGEMENT ATTENTION

Given the four different types of morally questionable managerial acts, how much management attention does each typically receive in large organizations? It has been observed that conventional accounting and control systems are almost exclusively concerned with against-the-firm acts of the non-role type (Waters and Chant, 1982). There is some evidence also that these non-role type acts are the primary focus of corporate codes of ethics. In a preliminary report on a review of corporate codes of ethics of a large sample of Fortune 500 firms, Mathews (1986) reports that it was rare to find proscriptions dealing with for-the-firm type acts, and that the most prominent theme in these codes was protection of the firm against what we are labelling here as non-role acts. A survey conducted in 1979 for the Ethics Resource Center found that of those firms having formal codes of ethics, 94% prohibited conflict of interest activities, and 97% specifically prohibited the taking of bribes or favors to influence decisions. Also, 62% of the firms reported that their codes specifically prohibited the abuse of expense accounts, special allowances and perquisites (Opinion Research Corporation, 1979; also see Taylor, 1980).

Thus, we can say with some confidence that non-role acts receive a great deal of attention in many large organizations. What then of the other three categories? Role assertion acts frequently receive a great deal of attention because, as noted, these often are high-stakes public issues in which the most senior managers are directly involved. The very nature of such acts, involving questions for which generally accepted societal positions have not crystallized and where competing moral arguments are publicly invoked (witness, for example, debate about nuclear energy or compulsory airbags in automobiles), make them popular targets of interest for managers, media representatives, social critics, and case teachers in business schools. In some organizations, this attention has given rise to the formation of staff groups specifically concerned with so-called social issues in management.

In contrast to the managerial attention directed at non-role acts and role-assertion acts, that directed at role-failure acts and role-distortion acts appears quite minimal. We make that assertion based on our own experiences in different organizations, informal conversations over the years with many managers, and interviews with a variety of managers about the ethical questions they face (Waters *et al.,* 1986). The picture that emerges from all these sources is that role-distortion and role-failure acts seldom receive systematic attention in most organizations and they certainly receive less attention than is given to the other two categories.

The irony of this unbalanced attention to the different kinds of morally questionable acts is that the kinds of acts that are most salient and indeed troublesome for most managers on a day to day basis are the kinds that receive the least attention in terms of proactive management and control. When managers are asked to describe the ethical questions that come up in their own professional lives and in their organizations, their responses are predominantly in the role-failure and role-distortion categories (Waters *et al.,* 1986).[1]

This idea that the "high-attention" categories are least problematic for most managers is readily understandable when one considers their nature. Little ambiguity and few competing standards surround conduct that we have labelled non-role. There is no subtlety to fraud, embezzlement or cheating on expense reports and the overwhelmingly majority of managers do not engage in such activities and view them with repugnance. Managers rarely are placed in a moral dilemma regarding how they ought to respond to this type of conduct.

The other "high-attention" category, role-assertion acts, also tends to be non-problematic for most managers, but for different reasons. Here, a great deal of ambiguity and many competing principles surround the issues and, as noted earlier, reasonable people can disagree on the best course of action. More to the point though, these issues most typically are unique, arise infrequently, and are the province of the most senior managers and directors. While these kinds of issues may attract the most attention from philosophers and journalists, they are simply a less critical aspect of most managers' consciousness with respect to everyday ethical concerns in management.

These observations are not made in order to denigrate the importance of these issues or suggest that they should receive less attention in management circles. Rather, it is to suggest that the two neglected categories, the two which in fact are most salient for most managers, should receive more attention. Widely shared standards exist to guide managers in developing their own responses to situations which can lead to role-failure and role distortion acts (e.g., honesty in communication, fair treatment, fair competition, etc.) (Bird and Waters, 1986). However, these standards are inherently abstract and frequently in conflict and as a result are typically not experienced by managers as being very helpful in providing concrete direction in specific situations. When does legitimate entertainment become bribery? At what point does legitimate concealment of a basic position in negotiating with an employee or supplier become dishonesty? These are the types of difficult questions with which managers must grapple on an everyday basis. Such questions resist easy generalizations; trade-offs and compromises will often be required in response to particular conditions and situations. Given the very overt pressure for performance in most organizations, a failure on the part of senior managers to devote systematic attention to the potential problems of role-failure and role-distortion acts puts a great deal of stress on the members of their organizations. It is only through increased conscious attention on the part of organization leaders to such problems that the moral instincts of all organizational members can be supported and reinforced in the face of competitive pressures.

We have made suggestions elsewhere about how that increased attention might be shaped and acted upon. These include encouragement of dialogue and debate (Waters, 1978), internal control mechanisms to monitor the attention given to such issues (Waters and Chant, 1982) and systematic management of "the moral dimension of organizational culture" (Waters and Bird, 1986). Our intention here has been to highlight the lack of balanced attention to the full range of morally questionable acts in most organizations. Awareness of the different types of morally qustionable acts and of the relative neglect of role-failure and role-distortion acts can help managers to see ethical issues more clearly and to attend more effectively to their own moral concerns.

NOTE

1. More specifically, of 122 examples which directly referenced morally questionable acts, 57 percent concerned role-distortion acts, 23 percent concerned role-failure acts, 17 percent concerned role-assertion acts and 3 percent concerned non-role acts.

REFERENCES

Bird, Frederick and James A. Waters: 1987, 'The nature of managerial moral standards', *Journal of Business Ethics* 6. No. 1, 1–3.

Matthew, M. Cash: August 1986, 'Self-regulation: The effect of codes of ethics on corporate illegalities', paper presented at Academy of Management.

Opinion Research Corporation: June 1979, 'Codes of ethics in corporations and trade associations and the teaching of ethics in graduate business schools', a survey conducted for Ethics Resource Center, ORC Study No. 65302.

Taylor, Mark L: 1980, *A Study of Corporate Ethical Policy Statements* (Dallas: The Foundation of the Southwestern Graduate Schools of Banking).

Waters, James A: Winter 1980, 'Of saints, sinners and socially responsible executives', *Business and Society* 19-2 and 20-1.

Waters, James A: Spring 1978. 'Catch 20.5: Corporate morality as an organizational phenomenon', *Organizational Dynamics.*

Waters, James A. and Frederick Bird: 1987, 'The moral dimension of organizational culture', *Journal of Business Ethics* 6, No. 1, 15–22.

Waters, James A., Frederick Bird and Peter D. Chant: 1986. 'Everyday moral issues experienced by managers', *Journal of Business Ethics* 5, No. 5, 373–384.

Waters, James A. and Peter D. Chant: Spring 1982, 'Internal control of management integrity: Beyond accounting systems', *California Management Review.*

Cost-Benefit Analysis: An Ethical Critique

Steven Kelman

Administrator of the Office of Federal Procurement Policy, Office of Management and Budget; formerly at the Kennedy School of Government, Harvard University

At the broadest and vaguest level, cost-benefit analysis may be regarded simply as systematic thinking about decision-making. Who can oppose, economists sometimes ask, efforts to think in a systematic way about the consequences of different courses of action? The alternative, it would appear, is unexamined decision-making. But defining cost-benefit analysis so simply leaves it with few implications for actual regulatory decision-making. Presumably, therefore, those who urge regulators to make greater use of the technique have a more extensive prescription in mind. I assume here that their prescription includes the following views:

1. There exists a strong presumption that an act should not be undertaken unless its benefits outweigh its costs.
2. In order to determine whether benefits outweigh costs, it is desirable to attempt to express all benefits and costs in a common scale or denominator, so that they can be compared with each other, even when some benefits and costs are not traded on markets and hence have no established dollar values.
3. Getting decision-makers to make more use of cost-benefit techniques is important enough to warrant both the expense required to gather the data for improved cost-benefit estimation and the political efforts needed to give the activity higher priority compared to other activities, also valuable in and of themselves.

My focus is on cost-benefit analysis as applied to environmental, safety, and health regulation. In that context, I examine each of the above propositions from the perspective of formal ethical theory, that is, the study of what actions it is morally right to undertake. My conclusions are:

1. In areas of environmental, safety, and health regulation, there may be many instances where a certain decision might be right even though its benefits do not outweigh its costs.
2. There are good reasons to oppose efforts to put dollar values on non-marketed benefits and costs.
3. Given the relative frequency of occasions in the areas of environmental, safety, and health regulation where one would not wish to use a benefits-outweigh-costs test as a decision rule, and given the reasons to oppose the monetizing of non-marketed benefits or costs that is a prerequisite for cost-benefit analysis, it is not justifiable to devote major resources to the generation of data for cost-benefit calculations or to undertake efforts to "spread the gospel" of cost-benefit analysis further.

Excerpted from "Cost-Benefit Analysis: An Ethical Critique," *Regulation,* January–February 1981. Reprinted by permission of the publisher.

I

How do we decide whether a given action is morally right or wrong and hence, assuming the desire to act morally, why it should be undertaken or refrained from? Like the Molière character who spoke prose without knowing it, economists who advocate use of cost-benefit analysis for public decisions are philosophers without knowing it: the answer given by cost-benefit analysis, that actions should be undertaken so as to maximize net benefits, represents one of the classic answers given by moral philosophers—that given by utilitarians. To determine whether an action is right or wrong, utilitarians tote up all the positive consequences of the action in terms of human satisfaction. The act that maximizes attainment of satisfaction under the circumstances is the right act. That the economists' answer is also the answer of one school of philosophers should not be surprising. Early on, economics was a branch of moral philosophy, and only later did it become an independent discipline.

Before proceeding further, the subtlety of the utilitarian position should be noted. The positive and negative consequences of an act for satisfaction may go beyond the act's immediate consequences. A facile version of utilitarianism would give moral sanction to a lie, for instance, if the satisfaction of an individual attained by telling the lie was greater than the suffering imposed on the lie's victim. Few utilitarians would agree. Most of them would add to the list of negative consequences the effect of the one lie on the tendency of the person who lies to tell other lies, even in instances when the lying produced less satisfaction for him than dissatisfaction for others. They would also add the negative effects of the lie on the general level of social regard for truth-telling, which has many consequences for future utility. A further consequence may be added as well. It is sometimes said that we should include in a utilitarian calculation the feelings of dissatisfaction produced in the liar (and perhaps in others) because, by telling a lie, one has "done the wrong thing." Correspondingly, in this view, among the positive consequences to be weighed into a utilitarian calculation of truth-telling is satisfaction arising from "doing the right thing." This view rests on an error, however, because it *assumes* what it is the purpose of the calculation to *determine*—that telling the truth in the instance in question is indeed the right thing to do. Economists are likely to object to this point, arguing that no feeling ought "arbitrarily" to be excluded from a complete cost-benefit calculation, including a feeling of dissatisfaction at doing the wrong thing. Indeed, the economists' cost-benefit calculations would, at least ideally, include such feelings. Note the difference between the economist's and the philosopher's cost-benefit calculations, however. The economist may choose to include feelings of dissatisfaction in his cost-benefit calculation, but what happens if somebody asks the economist, "Why is it right to evaluate an action on the basis of a cost-benefit test?" If an answer is to be given to that question (which does not normally preoccupy economists but which does concern both philosophers and the rest of us who need to be persuaded that cost-benefit analysis is right), then the circularity problem reemerges. And there is also another difficulty with counting feelings of dissatisfaction at doing the wrong thing in a cost-benefit calculation. It leads to the perverse result that under certain circumstances a lie, for example, might be morally right if the individual contemplating the lie felt no compunction about lying and morally wrong only if the individual felt such a compunction!

This error is revealing, however, because it begins to suggest a critique of utilitarianism. Utilitarianism is an important and powerful moral doctrine. But it is probably a minority position among contemporary moral philosophers. It is amazing that economists can proceed in unanimous endorsement of cost-benefit analysis as if unaware that their conceptual framework is highly controversial in the discipline from which it arose—moral philosophy.

Let us explore the critique of utilitarianism. The logical error discussed before appears to suggest that we have a notion of certain things being right or wrong that *predates* our calculation of costs and benefits. Imagine the case of an old man in Nazi Germany who is hostile to the regime. He is wondering whether he should speak out against Hitler.

If he speaks out; he will lose his pension. And his action will have done nothing to increase the chances that the Nazi regime will be overthrown: he is regarded as somewhat eccentric by those around him, and nobody has ever consulted his views on political questions. Recall that one cannot add to the benefits of speaking out any satisfaction from doing "the right thing," because the purpose of the exercise is to determine whether speaking out *is* the right thing. How would the utilitarian calculation go? The benefits of the old man's speaking out would, as the example is presented, be nil, while the costs would be his loss of his pension. So the costs of the action would outweigh the benefits. By the utilitarians' cost-benefit calculation, it would be *morally wrong* for the man to speak out.

To those who believe that it would not be morally wrong for the old man to speak out in Nazi Germany, utilitarianism is insufficient as a moral view. We believe that some acts whose costs are greater than their benefits may be morally right and, contrariwise, some acts whose benefits are greater than their costs may be morally wrong.

This does not mean that the question whether benefits are greater than costs is morally irrelevant. Few would claim such. Indeed, for a broad range of individual and social decisions, whether an act's benefits outweigh its costs is a sufficient question to ask. But not for all such decisions. These may involve situations where certain duties—duties not to lie, break promises, or kill, for example—make an act wrong, even if it would result in an excess of benefits over costs. Or they may involve instances where people's rights are at stake. We would not permit rape even if it could be demonstrated that the rapist derived enormous happiness from his act, while the victim experienced only minor displeasure. We do not do cost-benefit analyses of freedom of speech or trial by jury. The Bill of Rights was not RARGed.*

As the United Steelworkers noted in a comment on the Occupational Safety and Health Administration's economic analysis of its proposed rule to reduce worker exposure to carcinogenic coke-oven emissions, the Emancipation Proclamation was not subjected to an inflationary impact statement. The notion of human rights involves the idea that people may make certain claims to be allowed to act in certain ways or to be treated in certain ways, even if the sum of benefits achieved thereby does not outweigh the sum of costs. It is this view that underlies the statement that "workers have a right to a safe and healthy work place" and the expectation that OSHA's decisions will reflect that judgment.

In the most convincing versions of nonutilitarian ethics, various duties or rights are not absolute. But each has a *prima facie* moral validity so that, if duties or rights do not conflict, the morally right act is the act that reflects a duty or respects a right. If duties or rights do conflict, a moral judgment, based on conscious deliberation, must be made. Since one of the duties non-utilitarian philosophers enumerate is the duty of beneficence (the duty to maximize happiness), which in effect incorporates all of utilitarianism by reference, a non-utilitarian who is faced with conflicts between the results of cost-benefit analysis and non-utility-based considerations will need to undertake such deliberation. But in that deliberation, additional elements, which cannot be reduced to a question of whether benefits outweigh costs, have been introduced. Indeed, depending on the moral importance we attach to the right or duty involved, cost-benefit questions may, within wide ranges, become irrelevant to the outcome of the moral judgment.

In addition to questions involving duties and rights, there is a final sort of question where, in my view, the issue of whether benefits outweigh costs should not govern moral judgment. I noted earlier that, for the common run of questions facing individuals and societies, it is possible to begin and end our judgment simply by finding out if the benefits of the contemplated act outweigh the costs. This very fact means that one way to show the great importance, or value, attached to an area is to say that decisions involving the area should not be determined by cost-benefit calculations. This applies, I think, to the view many environmentalists have of

---

**Editor's note:* The Regulatory Analysis Review Group (RARG) was created by President Carter to improve the cost-benefit analysis of regulatory policy. It was subsequently disbanded by President Reagan.

decisions involving our natural environment. When officials are deciding what level of pollution will harm certain vulnerable people—such as asthmatics or the elderly—while not harming others, one issue involved may be the right of those people not to be sacrificed on the altar of somewhat higher living standards for the rest of us. But more broadly than this, many environmentalists fear that subjecting decisions about clean air or water to the cost-benefit tests that determine the general run of decisions removes those matters from the realm of specially valued things.

II

In order for cost-benefit calculations to be performed the way they are supposed to be, all costs and benefits must be expressed in a common measure, typically dollars, including things not normally bought and sold on markets, and to which dollar prices are therefore not attached. The most dramatic example of such things is human life itself; but many of the other benefits achieved or preserved by environmental policy—such as peace and quiet, fresh-smelling air, swimmable rivers, spectacular vistas—are not traded on markets either.

Economists who do cost-benefit analysis regard the quest after dollar values for non-market things as a difficult challenge—but one to be met with relish. They have tried to develop methods for imputing a person's "willingness to pay" for such things, their approach generally involving a search for bundled goods that *are* traded on markets and that vary as to whether they include a feature that is, *by itself,* not marketed. Thus, fresh air is not marketed, but houses in different parts of Los Angeles that are similar except for the degree of smog are. Peace and quiet is not marketed, but similar houses inside and outside airport flight paths are. The risk of death is not marketed, but similar jobs that have different levels of risk are. Economists have produced many often ingenious efforts to impute dollar prices to non-marketed things by observing the premiums accorded homes in clean air areas over similar homes in dirty areas or the premiums paid for risky jobs over similar nonrisky jobs.

These ingenious efforts are subject to criticism on a number of technical grounds. It may be difficult to control for all the dimensions of quality other than the presence or absence of the non-marketed thing. More important, in a world where people have different preferences and are subject to different constraints as they make their choices, the dollar value imputed to the nonmarket things that most people would wish to avoid will be lower than otherwise, because people with unusually weak aversion to those things or unusually strong constraints on their choices will be willing to take the bundled good in question at less of a discount than the average person. Thus, to use the property value discount of homes near airports as a measure of people's willingness to pay for quiet means to accept as a proxy for the rest of us the behavior of those least sensitive to noise, of airport employees (who value the convenience of a near-airport location) or of others who are susceptible to an agent's assurances that "it's not so bad." To use the wage premiums accorded hazardous work as a measure of the value of life means to accept as proxies for the rest of us the choices of people who do not have many choices or who are exceptional risk-seekers.

A second problem is that the attempts of economists to measure people's willingness to pay for non-marketed things assume that there is no difference between the price a person would require for *giving up* something to which he has a preexisting right and the price he would pay to *gain* something to which he enjoys no right. Thus, the analysis assumes no difference between how much a homeowner would need to be paid in order to give up an unobstructed mountain view that he already enjoys and how much he would be willing to pay to get an obstruction moved once it is already in place. Available evidence suggests that most people would insist on being paid far more to assent to a worsening of their situation than they would be willing to pay to improve their situation. The difference arises from such factors as being accustomed to and psychologically attached to that which one believes one enjoys by right. But this creates a circularity problem for any attempt to use cost-benefit analysis to determine *whether* to assign to, say, the homeowner the right to an unobstructed mountain view. For willingness to pay will be different depending on whether the right is assigned initially or not. The value judgment about whether to assign the right must thus be made first. (In order to set an upper bound on the value of the benefit, one might hypothetically assign the right to the person and determine how much he would need to be paid to give it up.)

Third, the efforts of economists to impute willingness to pay invariably involve bundled goods exchanged in *private* transactions. Those who use figures garnered from such analysis to provide guidance for *public* decisions assume no difference between how people value certain things in private individual transactions and how they would wish those same things to be valued in public collective decisions. In making such assumptions, economists insidiously slip into their analysis an important and controversial value judgment, growing naturally out of the highly individualistic microeconomic tradition—namely, the view that there should be no difference between private behavior and the behavior we display in public social life. An alternative view—one that enjoys, I would suggest, wide resonance among citizens—would be that public, social decisions provide an opportunity to give certain things a higher valuation than we choose, for one reason or another, to give them in our private activities.

Thus, opponents of stricter regulation of health risks often argue that we show by our daily risk-taking behavior that we do not value life infinitely, and therefore our public decisions should not reflect the high value of life that proponents of strict regulation propose. However, an alternative view is equally plausible. Precisely because we fail, for whatever reasons, to give lifesaving the value in everyday personal decisions that we in some general terms believe we should give it, we may wish our social decisions to provide us the occasion to display the reverence for life that we espouse but do not always show. By this view, people do not have fixed unambiguous "preferences" to which they give expression through private activities and which therefore should be given expression in public decisions. Rather, they may have what they themselves regard as "higher" and "lower" preferences. The latter may come to the fore in private decisions, but people may want the former to come to the fore in public decisions. They may sometimes display racial prejudice, but support antidiscrimination laws. They may buy a certain product after seeing a seductive ad, but be skeptical enough of advertising to want the government to keep a close eye on it. In such cases, the use of private behavior to impute the values that should be entered for public decisions, as is done by using willingness to pay in private transactions, commits grievous offense against a view of the behavior of the citizen that is deeply engrained in our democratic tradition. It is a view that denudes politics of any independent role in society, reducing it to a mechanistic, mimicking recalculation based on private behavior.

Finally, one may oppose the effort to place prices on a non-market thing and hence in effect incorporate it into the market system out of a fear that the very act of doing so will reduce the thing's perceived value. To place a price on the benefit may, in other words, reduce the value of that benefit. Cost-benefit analysis thus may be like the thermometer that, when placed in a liquid to be measured, itself changes the liquid's temperature.

Examples of the perceived cheapening of a thing's value by the very act of buying and selling it abound in everyday life and language. The disgust that accompanies the idea of buying and selling human beings is based on the sense that this would dramatically diminish human worth. Epithets such as "he prostituted himself," applied as linguistic analogies to people who have sold something, reflect the view that certain things should not be sold because doing so diminishes their value. Praise that is bought is worth little, even to the person buying it. A true anecdote is told of an economist who retired to another university community and complained that he was having difficulty making friends. The laconic response of a critical colleague—"If you want a friend why don't you buy yourself one"—illustrates in a pithy way the intuition that, for some things, the very act of placing a price on them reduces their perceived value.

The first reason that pricing something decreases its perceived value is that, in many circumstances, non-market exchange is associated with the production of certain values not associated with market exchange. These may include spontaneity and various other feelings that come from personal relationships. If a good becomes less associated with the production of positively valued feelings because of market exchange, the perceived value of the good declines to the extent that those feelings are valued. This can be seen clearly in instances where a thing may be transferred both by market and by non-market mechanisms. The willingness to pay for sex bought from a prostitute is less than the perceived value of the sex consummating love. (Imagine the reaction if a practitioner of cost-benefit analysis computed the benefits of sex based on the price of prostitute services.)

Furthermore, if one values in a general sense the existence of a non-market sector because of its connection with the production of certain valued feelings, then one ascribes added value to any non-marketed good simply as a repository of values represented by the non-market sector one wishes to preserve. This seems certainly to be the case for things in nature, such as pristine streams or undisturbed forests: for many people who value them, part of their value comes from their position as repositories of values the non-market sector represents.

The second way in which placing a market price on a thing decreases its perceived value is by removing the possibility of proclaiming that the thing is "not for sale," since things on the market by definition are for sale. The very statement that something is not for sale affirms, enhances, and protects a thing's value in a number of ways. To begin with, the statement is a way of showing that a thing is valued for its own sake, whereas selling a thing for money demonstrates that it was valued only instrumentally. Furthermore, to say that something cannot be transferred in that way places it in the exceptional category—which requires the person interested in obtaining that thing to be able to offer something else that is exceptional, rather than allowing him the easier alternative of obtaining the thing for money that could have been obtained in an infinity of ways. This enhances its value. If I am willing to say "You're a really kind person" to whoever pays me to do so, my praise loses the value that attaches to it from being exchangeable only for an act of kindness.

In addition, if we have already decided we value something highly, one way of stamping it with a cachet affirming its high value is to announce that it is "not for sale." Such an announcement does more, however, than just reflect a preexisting high valuation. It signals a thing's distinctive value to others and helps us persuade them to value the thing more highly than they otherwise might. It also expresses our resolution to safeguard that distinctive value. To state that something is not for sale is thus also a source of value for that thing, since if a thing's value is easy to affirm or protect, it will be worth more than an otherwise similar thing without such attributes.

If we proclaim that something is not for sale, we make a once-and-for-all judgment of its special value. When something is priced, the issue of its perceived value is constantly coming up, as a standing invitation to reconsider that original judgment. Were people constantly faced with questions such as "how much money could get you to give up your freedom of speech?" or "how much would you sell your vote for if you could?", the perceived value of the freedom to speak or the right to vote would soon become devastated as, in moments of weakness, people started saying "maybe it's not worth *so much* after all." Better not to be faced with the constant questioning in the first place. Something similar did in fact occur when the slogan "better red than dead" was launched by some pacifists during the Cold War. Critics pointed out that the very posing of this stark choice—in effect, "would you *really* be willing to give up your life in exchange for not living under communism?"—reduced the value people attached to freedom and thus diminished resistance to attacks on freedom.

Finally, of some things valued very highly it is stated that they are "priceless" or that they have "infinite value." Such expressions are reserved for a subset of things not for sale, such as life or health. Economists tend to scoff at talk of pricelessness. For them, saying that something is priceless is to state a willingness to trade off an infinite quantity of all other goods for one unit of the priceless good, a situation that empirically appears highly unlikely. For most people, however, the word priceless is pregnant with meaning. Its value-affirming and value-protecting functions cannot be bestowed on expressions that merely denote a determinate, albeit high, valuation. John Kennedy in his inaugural address proclaimed that the nation was ready to "pay any price [and] bear any burden . . . to assure the survival and the success of liberty." Had he said instead that we were willing to "pay a high price" or "bear a large burden" for liberty, the statement would have rung hollow.

III

An objection that advocates of cost-benefit analysis might well make to the preceding argument should be considered. I noted earlier that, in cases where various non-utility-based duties or rights conflict with the maximization of utility, it is necessary to make a deliberative judgment about what act is finally right. I also argued earlier that the search for commensurability might not always be a desirable one, that the attempt to go beyond expressing benefits in terms of (say) lives saved and costs in terms of dollars is not something devoutly to be wished.

In situations involving things that are not expressed in a common measure, advocates of cost-benefit analysis argue that people making judgments "in effect" perform cost-benefit calculations anyway. If government regulators promulgate a regulation that saves 100 lives at a cost of $1 billion, they are "in effect" valuing a life at (a minimum of) $10 million, whether or not they say that they are willing to place a dollar value on a human life. Since, in this view, cost-benefit analysis "in effect" is inevitable, it might as well be made specific.

This argument misconstrues the real difference in the reasoning processes involved. In cost-benefit analysis, equivalencies are established *in advance* as one of the raw materials for the calculation. One determines costs and benefits, one determines equivalencies (to be able to put various costs and benefits into a common measure), and then one sets to toting things up—waiting, as it were, with bated breath for the results of the calculation to come out. The outcome is determined by the arithmetic; if the outcome is a close call or if one is not good at long division, one does not know how it will turn out until the calculation is finished. In the kind of deliberative judgment that is performed without a common measure, no establishment of equivalencies occurs in advance. Equivalencies are not aids to the decision process. In fact, the decision-maker might not even be aware of what the "in effect" equivalencies were, at least before they are revealed to him afterwards by someone pointing out what he had "in effect" done. The decision-maker would see himself as simply having made a deliberative judgment; the "in effect" equivalency number did not play a causal role in the decision but at most merely reflects it. Given this, the argument against making the process explicit is the one discussed earlier in the discussion of problems with putting specific values on things that are not normally quantified—that the very act of doing so may serve to reduce the value of those things.

My own judgment is that modest efforts to assess levels of benefits and costs are justified, although I do not believe that government agencies ought to sponsor efforts to put dollar prices on non-market things. I also do not believe that the cry for more cost-benefit analysis in regulation is, on the whole, justified. If regulatory officials were so insensitive about regulatory costs that they did not provide acceptable raw material for deliberative judgments (even if not of a strictly cost-benefit nature), my conclusion might be different. But a good deal of research into costs and benefits already occurs—actually, far more in the U.S. regulatory process than in that of any other industrial society. The danger now would seem to come more from the other side.

Cost-Benefit Analysis Defended

Herman B. Leonard and Richard Zeckhauser
Leonard—Academic Dean, Kennedy School of Government, Harvard University
Zeckhauser—Ramsey Professor of Political Economy, Kennedy School of Government, Harvard University

Cost-benefit analysis, particularly as applied to public decisions involving risks to life and health, has not been notably popular. A number of setbacks—Three Mile Island is perhaps the most memorable—have called into question the reliability of analytic approaches to risk issues. We believe that the current low reputation of cost-benefit analysis is unjustified, and that a close examination of the objections most frequently raised against the method will show that it deserves wider public support.

Society does not and indeed could not require the explicit consent of every affected individual in order to implement public decisions that impose costs or risks. The transactions costs of assembling unanimous consent would be prohibitive, leading to paralysis in the status quo. Moreover, any system that required unanimous consent would create incentives for individuals to misrepresent their beliefs so as to secure compensation or to prevent the imposition of relatively small costs on them even if the benefits to others might be great.

If actual individual consent is an impractically strong standard to require of centralized decisions, how should such decisions be made? Our test for a proposed public decision is whether the net benefits of the action are positive. The same criterion is frequently phrased: Will those favored by the decision gain enough that they would have a net benefit even if they fully compensated those hurt by the decision? Applying this criterion to all possible actions, we discover that the chosen alternative should be the one for which benefits most exceed costs. We believe that the benefit-cost criterion is a useful way of defining "hypothetical consent" for centralized decisions affecting individuals with widely divergent interests: hypothetically, if compensation could be paid, all would agree to the decision offering the highest net benefits. We turn now to objections commonly raised against this approach.

From *The Report from The Institute for Philosophy and Public Policy,* Vol. 3, No. 3 (Summer 1983.) Reprinted by permission of The Institute for Philosophy and Public Policy, University of Maryland at College Park, College Park, MD 20742.

COMPENSATION AND HYPOTHETICAL CONSENT

An immediate problem with the pure cost-benefit criterion is that it does not require the actual payment of compensation to those on whom a given decision imposes net costs. Our standard for public decision-making does not require that losers be compensated, but only that they *could* be if a perfect system of transfers existed. But unless those harmed by a decision are *actually* compensated, they will get little solace from the fact that someone is reaping a surplus in which they could have shared.

To this we make two replies. First, it is typically infeasible to design a compensation system that ensures that all individuals will be net winners. The transactions costs involved in such a system would often be so high as to make the project as a whole a net loss. But it may not even be desirable to construct full compensation systems, since losers will generally have an incentive under such systems to overstate their anticipated losses in order to secure greater compensation.

Second, the problem of compensation is probably smaller in practice than in principle. Society tends to compensate large losses where possible or to avoid imposing large losses when adequate compensation is not practical. Moreover, compensation is sometimes overpaid; having made allowances *ex ante* for imposing risks, society still chooses sometimes to pay additional compensation *ex post* to those who actually suffer losses.

Libertarians raise one additional argument about the ethical basis of a system that does not require full compensation to losers. They argue that a public decision process that imposes uncompensated losses constitutes an illegal taking of property by the state and should not be tolerated. This objection, however strongly grounded ethically, would lead to an untenable position for society by unduly constraining public decisions to rest with the status quo.

ATTENTION TO DISTRIBUTION

Two distinct types of distributional issue are relevant in cost-benefit analysis. First, we can be concerned about the losers in a particular decision, whoever they may be. Second, we can be concerned with the transfers between income classes (or other defined groups) engendered by a given project. If costs are imposed differentially on groups that are generally disadvantaged, should the decision criterion include special consideration of their interests? This question is closely intertwined with the issue of compensation, because it is often alleged that the uncompensated costs of projects evaluated by cost-benefit criteria frequently fall on those who are disadvantaged to start with.

These objections have little to do with cost-benefit analysis as a method. We see no reason why any widely agreed upon notion of equity, or weighting of different individuals' interests, cannot in principle be built into the cost-benefit decision framework. It is merely a matter of defining carefully what is meant by a benefit or a cost. If, in society's view, benefits (or costs) to some individuals are more valuable (costly) than those to others, this can be reflected in the construction of the decision criterion.

But although distribution concerns could be systematically included in cost-benefit analyses, it is not always—or even generally—a good idea to do so. Taxes and direct expenditures represent a far more efficient means of effecting redistribution than virtually any other public program; we would strongly prefer to rely on one consistent comprehensive tax and expenditure package for redistribution than on attempts to redistribute within every project.

First, if distributional issues are considered everywhere, they will probably not be adequately, carefully, and correctly treated anywhere. Many critics of cost-benefit analysis believe that project-based distributional analysis would create a net addition to society's total redistributive effort; we suggest that is likely, instead, to be only an inefficient substitution.

Second, treating distributional concerns within each project can only lead to transfers within the group affected by a project, often only a small subset of the community. For example, unisex rating of auto insurance redistributes only among drivers. Cross-subsidization of medical costs affects only those who need medical services. Why should not the larger society share the burden of redistribution?

Third, the view that distributional considerations should be treated project-by-project reflects a presumption that on average they do not balance out—that is, that some groups systematically lose more often than others. If it were found that some groups were severely and systematically disadvantaged by the application of cost-benefit analyses that ignore distributional concerns, we would favor redressing the balance. We do not believe this is generally the case.

SENSITIVE SOCIAL VALUES

Cost-benefit analysis, it is frequently alleged, does a disservice to society because it cannot treat important social values with appropriate sensitivity. We believe that this view does a disservice to society by unduly constraining the use of a reasonable and helpful method for organizing the debate about public decisions. We are not claiming that every important social value can be represented effectively within the confines of cost-benefit analysis. Some values will never fit in a cost-benefit framework and will have to be treated as "additional considerations" in coming to a final decision. Some, such as the inviolability of human life, may simply be binding constraints that cannot be traded off to obtain other gains. Nor can we carry out a cost-benefit analysis to decide which values should be included and which treated separately—this decision will always have to be made in some other manner.

These considerations do not invalidate cost-benefit analysis, but merely illustrate that more is at stake than just dollar measures of costs and benefits. We would, however, make two observations. First, we must be very careful that only genuinely important and relevant social values be permitted to outweigh the findings of an analysis. Second, social values that frequently stand in the way of important efficiency gains have a way of breaking down and being replaced over time, so that in the long run society manages to accommodate itself to some form of cost-benefit criterion. If nuclear power were 1000 times more dangerous for its employees but 10 times less expensive than it is, we might feel that ethical considerations were respected and the national interest well served if we had rotating cadres of nuclear power employees serving short terms in high-risk positions, much as members of the armed services do. In like fashion, we have fire-fighters risk their lives; universal sprinkler systems would be less dangerous, but more costly. Such policies reflect an accommodation to the costs as a recognition of the benefits.

MEASURABILITY

Another objection frequently raised against cost-benefit analysis is that some costs and benefits tend to be ignored because they are much more difficult to measure than others. The long-term environmental impacts of large projects are frequently cited as an example. Cost-benefit analysis is charged with being systematically biased toward consideration of the quantifiable aspects of decisions.

This is unquestionably true: cost-benefit analysis is *designed* as a method of quantification, so it surely is better able to deal with more quantifiable aspects of the issues it confronts. But this limitation is in itself ethically neutral unless it can be shown that the quantifiable considerations systematically push decisions in a particular direction. Its detractors must show that the errors of cost-benefit analysis are systematically unjust or inefficient—for example, that it frequently helps the rich at the expense of the poor, or despoils the environment to the benefit of industry, or vice versa. We have not seen any carefully researched evidence to support such assertions.

We take some comfort in the fact that cost-benefit analysis is sometimes accused of being biased toward development projects and sometimes of being biased against them. Cost-benefit analyses have foiled conservation efforts in national forests—perhaps they systematically weight the future too little. But they have also squelched clearly silly projects designed to bring "economic development" to Alaska—and the developers argued that the analysis gave insufficient weight to the "unquantifiable" value of future industrialization.

In our experience, cost-benefit analysis is often a tool of the "outs"—those not currently in control of the political process. Those who have the political power to back the projects they support often have little need of analyses. By contrast, analysis can be an effective tool for those who are otherwise not strongly empowered politically.

ANALYZING RISKS

Even those who accept the ethical propriety of cost-benefit analysis of decisions involving transfers of money or other tangible economic costs and benefits sometimes feel that the principles do not extend to analyzing decisions involving the imposition of risks. We believe that such applications constitute a *particularly* important area in which cost-benefit analysis can be of value. The very difficulties of reaching appropriate decisions where risks are involved make it all the more vital to employ the soundest methods available, both ethically and practically.

Historically, cost-benefit analysis has been applied widely to the imposition and regulation of risks, in particular to risks of health loss or bodily harm. The cost-benefit approach is particularly valuable here, for several reasons. Few health risks can be exchanged on a voluntary basis. Their magnitude is difficult to measure. Even if they could be accurately measured, individuals have difficulty interpreting probabilities or gauging how they would feel should the harm eventuate. Compounding these problems of valuation are difficulties in contract, since risks are rarely conveyed singly between one individual and another.

The problem of risks conveyed in the absence of contractual approval has been addressed for centuries through the law of torts, which is designed to provide compensation after a harm has been received. If only a low-probability risk is involved, it is often efficient to wait to see whether a harm occurs, for in the overwhelming majority of circumstances transactions costs will be avoided. This approach also limits debate over the magnitude of a potential harm that has not yet eventuated. The creator of the risk has the incentive to gauge accurately, for he is the one who must pay if harm does occur.

While in principle it provides efficient results, the torts approach encounters at least four difficulties when applied to many of the risks that are encountered in a modern technological society. The option of declaring bankruptcy allows the responsible party to avoid paying and so to impose risks that it should not impose. Causality is often difficult to assign for misfortunes that may have alternative or multiple (and synergistically related) causes. Did the individual contract lung cancer from air pollution or from his own smoking, or both? Furthermore, the traditional torts requirement that individuals be made whole cannot be met in many instances (death, loss of a limb). Finally, paying compensation after the fact may also produce inappropriate incentives, and hence be inefficient. Workers who can be more or less careful around dangerous machinery, for example, are likely to be more careful if they will not be compensated for losing an appendage.

Our normal market and legal system tends to break down when substantial health risks are imposed on a relatively large population. These are, therefore, precisely the situations in which the cost-benefit approach is and should be called into play. Cost-benefit analysis is typically used in just those situations where our normal risk decision processes run into difficulty. We should therefore not expect it to lead to outcomes that are as satisfactory as those that evolve when ordinary market and private contractual trade are employed. But we should be able to expect better outcomes than we would achieve by muddling through unsystematically.

We have defended cost-benefit analysis as the most practical of ethically defensible methods and the most ethical of practically usable methods for conducting public decision-making. It cannot substitute for—nor can it adequately encompass, analyze, or consider—the sensitive application of social values. Thus it cannot be made the final arbiter of public decisions. But it does add a useful structure to public debate, and it does enable us to quantify some of the quantifiable aspects of public decisions. Our defense parallels Winston Churchill's argument for democracy: it is not perfect, but it is better than the alternatives.

QUESTIONS FOR DISCUSSION

1. Use the guidelines developed by Michael Josephson, or those developed by Craig Dreilinger and Dan Rice, to discuss the case "AIDS and the Availability of AZT."
2. Waters and Bird argue that certain categories of unethical acts receive less attention from management than they should. What are they? Do you agree with Waters and Bird that management should direct more attention toward these acts? If so, how should management focus more attention to these kinds of acts? If not, why not?
3. In "Dorrence Corporation Tradeoffs" the firm faces a number of difficult decisions that have both economic and ethical consequences. Analyze and discuss those decisions using the techniques developed in the articles in this chapter. Compare and contrast the methods used by Josephson, for example, and cost/benefit analysis.
4. Turn to the cost-benefit analysis performed by the Ford Motor Company in Part Four. How might Kelman respond to this example? How might Leonard and Zeckhauser reply?

Ethics and Business: From Theory to Practice

AIDS and the Availability of AZT

Tom L. Beauchamp
Senior Research Scholar, Kennedy Institute of Ethics, Georgetown University

The realization that AIDS can potentially harm millions of people worldwide has promoted responses from both government and business. In September 1984 the U.S. National Cancer Institute (NCI) conducted a screening program to discover a drug that would kill, or at least deactivate, the human immunodeficiency virus (HIV) that causes AIDS. Five months later, the Burroughs Wellcome Company, a pharmaceutical company in Research Triangle Park, North Carolina, sent samples of zidovudine (formerly azidothymidine, or AZT) to the NCI for virological, immunological, and pharmacological testing. Burroughs Wellcome had experimented with the drug in the early 1980s as a possible antibacterial agent. NCI scientists, led by current NCI Director Dr. Samuel Broder, discovered that AZT slowed the growth of the AIDS virus in the test tube. Following extensive testing and governmental clinical pharmacology studies, Burroughs Wellcome submitted a new drug application (NDA) to the U.S. Food and Drug Administration (FDA) for permission to sell AZT.

On March 19, 1987, the FDA approved the drug for sale, and a year later (on February 9, 1988) Burroughs Wellcome gained an exclusive license to market AZT under the brand name Retrovir. As is the case with all patents, Burroughs Wellcome received exclusive proprietary rights over AZT for 17 years, until February 9, 2005.

Because AIDS is believed to be inevitably fatal and there is no promising alternative treatment, many argue that compassion dictates making the drug available to all HIV-infected persons. The practice of prescribing AZT to patients with HIV infection, with or without symptoms, has spread, due in part to the drug's increasing availability and effectiveness for certain purposes.

Federal regulations require that new drugs be tested extensively before market sale. One standard

From *Case Studies in Business, Society, and Ethics,* Third Edition (Prentice-Hall, 1993). This case was prepared by Tom L. Beauchamp, with assistance by Jeffrey P. Kahn, John Cuddihy, and David L. Parver.

test is to select two similar groups and give one the new drug and the other a harmless placebo. Burroughs Wellcome, in compliance with federal regulations, created a placebo-controlled trial of AZT to determine its efficacy and its toxicity for HIV-infected patients. However, critics argued that a placebo-controlled trial under such extreme circumstances was morally unacceptable, because the trial itself denied 10,000 patients the only promising drug for treating AIDS. Critics argued that the demands for scientific rigor could not be resolved with justice and compassion for HIV patients. However, trial defenders insisted that it was necessary to determine both AZT's efficacy and whether its negative side effects would outweigh its benefits. Dr. Samuel Broder of NCI denied that "compassion and science are in conflict," on grounds that "we have to be concerned with people who have AIDS both now and in the future." He noted that "serious errors—irredeemable errors . . . can be introduced if we don't undertake appropriately controlled studies. It would be a catastrophe if we dismissed a 'good drug' or if we allowed a 'bad drug' to become the standard of therapy."[1]

Use has shown that AZT neither cures AIDS nor eliminates the virus, and its side effects can often be severe, particularly on bone marrow that produces red and white blood cells. Some patients experience other adverse effects, including nausea, muscle pain, insomnia, and moderate to severe headaches. AZT's toxicity forces many recipients over time to cease the treatment, while others select reduced doses.

The FDA eventually began to give quick approval to other new drugs that could combat AIDS or HIV illnesses. In February 1989 the FDA approved aerosol pentamidine for use under a federal program that allows seriously ill patients access to promising new drugs before formal FDA approval. The program allows legal prescription, but it requires that use be monitored before actual licensing can be approved. In June 1989 the FDA also approved Ganciclovir and Erythropoietin without subjecting the drugs to rigorous clinical trials. In October 1991 dideoxyinosine (DDI) received FDA approval "for use in adult and pediatric AIDS patients who are intolerant to or whose health has significantly deteriorated while on zidovudine (AZT)."[2] The FDA approved the drug for market sale six months after Bristol-Myers's Squibb Co. submitted a new drug application for DDI to be marketed under the trade name Videx. HHS Assistant Secretary for Health James O. Mason, M.D., said that "DDI has benefitted through its development from a number of innovative measures FDA has taken to expedite the availability of potentially promising experimental AIDS therapies."[3] These cases constitute a departure from normal FDA drug testing policy.

Though drugs such as DDI and Ganciclovir have received FDA approval for use to combat AIDS and AIDS-related complex (ARC), AZT is currently the only drug that has been awarded *full* marketing approval. (In order to receive treatment with DDI, patients must have first exhausted AZT treatment options without success.) As the sole AZT producer, Burroughs Wellcome is free to set the drug price. Pharmaceutical companies typically recover research and development costs by charging whatever the market will bear before competition and new drugs enter the market, even if the cost exceeds some consumers' budgets. Controversy has long surrounded this practice because of the potential for abuse of profit.

Burroughs Wellcome originally listed a $10,000 retail price (the company then wholesaled the drug for $8,300) for a year's supply of the drug, with a projected use by up to 30,000 patients. Estimated (anticipated) annual revenue at this cost was between $130 and $250 million. By October 1989 the AZT full dosage price had been lowered to approximately $650 per month, or $7,800 per year retail, and by late 1991 the retail price had dropped (partially through lowering dosage) to approximately $3,000. (This retail price derives from Burroughs Wellcome's wholesale price of $1.20 for each 100 mg capsule.)

Industry analysts believe that Burroughs Wellcome's cost for bringing AZT onto the market ranged from $80 to $180 million. Sales quickly exceeded $220 million annually after it was brought to market. In 1990 Retrovir sales earned the Wellcome Foundation, the British-based parent company, approximately $287 million.[4] Early in 1990 scientists confirmed that AZT benefited not only patients ill with HIV-related conditions, but also some asymptomatic HIV-infected persons. With increased use by patients infected with the AIDS virus but showing no symptoms, sales could reach $1 billion annually. Company figures already show large increases in Retrovir's volume sales, which increased 53 percent in 1990 from 1989 levels.

Burroughs Wellcome, with assistance from experts at the Infectious Disease Society of America, originally set strict criteria to ensure the best utilization of AZT and a continuous supply for patients with the greatest need and the most substantial probability of medical benefit. The criteria excluded children, pregnant women, and nursing mothers, due to the lack of information then available about the drug's effects on children, fetuses, and newborns. However, testing eventually showed AZT to be as effective on AIDS-infected children as on adults, prolonging life and dramatically reversing mental deterioration and dementia, symptoms common to AIDS patients. In May 1990 the FDA announced that AZT would be widely distributed to children for the first time. This action ended what some critics have called an unconscionable delay in administering AZT to children after tests showed that it could prolong their lives and reverse mental deterioration.

Critics have long charged that the company's AZT price was unreasonably high and created a potential hardship for patients who lack any real alternative. In January 1988 police arrested 19 people in a civil disobedience protest at Burroughs Wellcome's Burlingame, California, distribution center. Many physicians and consumer advocates still demand that Burroughs Wellcome justify what appears to them to be an exorbitant price.

Burroughs Wellcome has defended the AZT price as fair and necessary because of the costs it incurred, citing the lengthy and expensive process of manufacturing AZT, as well as intensive and financially burdensome labor and technology. However, the company has consistently refused to provide precise figures on costs to Congress, claiming confidentiality. It does state that it committed $80 million to the drug's research and development, including $10 million in free AZT administered to 4,500 clinical trial patients.

Mr. T. E. Haigler, Jr., president and CEO of Burroughs Wellcome, testified that the company's calculation of the AZT product's cost included the following:

> [The] costs of developing, producing and marketing the drug, the high costs of research, and the need to generate revenues to cover these continuing costs . . . [including] the possible advent of new therapies, and profit margins customarily generated by significant new medicines. . . . We also examined factors that might be considered to be unique with respect to Retrovir. These included the very real high cost of producing this drug and the very real needs of the patients for whom this drug was developed.[5]

Burroughs Wellcome also claimed that AZT merits its price because it will reduce the costs of treating each AIDS patient by 25 percent, and the costs of each ARC patient by 60 percent. The prolongation of life and the reduced incidence of infections achieved by the AZT drug will also result in fewer hospitalizations for AIDS patients.[6]

Some individuals with AIDS, many of whom are young, indigent, and uninsured, cannot pay AZT's market price. Therefore, public programs such as Medicaid have borne much of the treatment cost. The financial burden of obtaining AZT has prompted one physician to say, "Either it'll be on the taxpayer's back, or patients will be robbing pharmacies. These are desperate, dying patients."

In September 1988 a $30 million federal allocation for AIDS patients was exhausted. Congress did not renew the funds but did twice extend funding to allow states more time to develop their own programs. However, many state and local governments in the United States have not assumed the costs of combating the disease. In some states, health officials have stopped accepting new applications for AZT under existing programs. Many public officials have expressed fears that new funding bills would open a Pandora's box that could lead to enormous federal and state expenditures.

In response to public pressure and the skyrocketing number of reported AIDS cases, U.S. government agencies have implemented streamlined drug approval programs for potential AIDS treatments. Consequently, drugs such as DDI have gained quicker access to the marketplace and needy AIDS patients. However, many people still face severe financial obstacles to AZT treatment. AIDS activists, pharmaceutical companies, and U.S. government representatives therefore contend that Burroughs Wellcome's monopoly on AZT production should be broken, to allow generic AZT production. According to some economic and pharmaceutical experts, competitive production of AZT would sharply lower the drug's retail price. Dr. Stephen Schondelmeyer, director of Purdue University's Pharmaceutical Economic Research Center, states, "Many generic drugs enter the market for one-half to two-thirds the price of the innovator drug. I think that the same kind of savings could be achieved with zidovudine (AZT)."[7] Consequently, Burroughs Wellcome has had to face legal motions that aim to invalidate the U.S. patent that gives the company exclusive production rights on AZT until February 2005.

On March 18, 1991, Public Citizen, a law firm founded by Ralph Nader, filed suit in Washington, DC, federal court on behalf of the People With AIDS Health Group, hoping to invalidate Burroughs Wellcome's six AIDS-related patents. This group argued that the firm wrongly took credit for developing AZT as an AIDS therapy away from federal scientists and researchers. According to a Public Citizen lawyer, "We cannot allow our government to give away an invention that it paid for and made while at the same time asking people with AIDS and the taxpayers to shoulder the monopoly prices charged by Burroughs Wellcome."[8] Burroughs Wellcome filed a motion to dismiss Public Citizen's lawsuit on May 13, 1991. At this writing, the case remains unresolved.

Some people familiar with the AZT controversy consider the Public Citizen lawsuit "to be part of a larger attempt by scientists at the NCI—where much of the work on the drug was conducted—to be given what they feel is due recognition for their work."[9] The National Institutes of Health (NIH) unsuccessfully negotiated with Burroughs Wellcome through May 1991 to have NCI scientists included on the patent as co-inventors of AZT. NIH Director Bernadine Healy commented during a May 1991 press conference that "The intellectual and scientific contributions made by NCI to the evolution of AZT were essential components of the AZT therapy for AIDS, and deserve recognition."[10]

The patent dispute and collapse of negotiations between NIH and Burroughs Wellcome was related to Burroughs Wellcome's second legal crisis, involving a patent challenge by Barr Laboratories. Barr, a Pomona, NY-based pharmaceuticals firm, filed an abbreviated new drug application (ANDA) with the FDA on March 19, 1991, asking permission to produce a generic equivalent to Retrovir. On April 9 Barr executives informed Burroughs Wellcome they intended to challenge the company's AZT-related patents. In response, Burroughs Wellcome sued Barr for patent infringement on May 14 in a Raleigh, North Carolina, federal court.

Barr contends that a generic version of AZT would sell for 40 percent less than the current prices. Edwin A. Cohen, Barr Laboratories' president and CEO, said, "We would like to see zidovudine become available at the lowest possible price." On July 17, 1991, NIH Director Healy announced that the NIH had granted to Barr a "nonexclusive patent license to market AZT as a treatment for AZT infection."[11] According to Healy, "The availability of AZT from additional commercial sources and the resulting competition should cause a marked decrease in the price of AZT."[12] The NIH also gave Barr the right to litigate the government's alleged inventorship and ownership in the AZT patents, and it has agreed to cooperate with Barr in the lawsuit filed by Burroughs Wellcome. According to one pharmaceuticals publication, "The NIH would also allow Barr a credit on future royalty payments if the [legal] dispute resulted in generic zidovudine being marketed."[13]

According to industry observers, "It is rare for the government to step in and take sides in a patent dispute."[14] Although the Barr-NIH agreement is hollow unless Barr succeeds in invalidating Burroughs Wellcome's exclusive patent, the consequences to the British subsidiary are potentially devastating. According to one pharmaceutical consultant, "Burroughs Wellcome can lose at least half their business in the first year a copy drug reaches the market."[15] However, should Barr win the lawsuit against Burroughs Wellcome and be granted FDA approval to market a generic AZT, the 1984 Waxman/Hatch Act provides Burroughs Wellcome with an exclusive right to market AZT for another five years. This act, which regulates the approval process for copycat products, allows the FDA to award three- and five-year exclusivities in cases where a sponsor (here Burroughs Wellcome) has invested time and money in clinical trials. Should the court uphold Burroughs Wellcome's patents, Barr must wait until 2005 and the end of the 17-year exclusive patent.

Despite the intricacies surrounding the controversy, industry analysts predict that Burroughs Wellcome will eventually prevail in the legal contest. One observer states, "It's a convoluted patent situation, but I put this in the don't-hold-your breath category."[16]

While the challenges to Burroughs Wellcome progress through the American legal system, other companies continue to manufacture potential AIDS vaccines. Glaxo Holdings, a British firm, has begun human testing of 3TC, a chemical cousin to AZT originally manufactured by IAF BioChem International, Inc., a Laval, Quebec-based company. Preliminary results show that 3TC "had very good activity against the AIDS virus," according to one NCI official.[17] Hoffman-LaRoche Inc., a U.S. subsidiary of Roche Holding, Ltd., is also conducting advanced tests of DDC, a nucleoside with potential to combat AIDS.

Although the NIH is helping Barr in its struggle to produce a generic AZT product (which would considerably reduce the government's AZT purchase costs), the federal government has not addressed the issues surrounding the AIDS treatment costs. The federal government does not recognize a social obligation to control the allocation of AIDS-effective drugs by fixing or lowering the market price, or to establish primary need groups among those afflicted. Each state has established priorities in categories (for example, the blind, aged, permanently and totally disabled, and the like) and financial tests (for income and assets) that applicants must meet in order to receive Medicaid assistance for purchasing AZT. As a result, many AIDS patients are still economically ineligible for public assistance and financially unable to purchase the drug.

NOTES

1. The following sources were used to develop the early history of the problems presented in this case study: "AIDS Drug Is Raising Host of Thorny Issues," *New York Times,* September 28, 1986, Sec. 1, p. 38; M. A. Fischl, D. D. Richman, M. H. Grieco, et al., "The Efficacy of Azidothymidine (AZT) in the Treatment of Patients with AIDS and AIDS-Related Complex: A Double-Blind, Placebo-Controlled Trial," *New England Journal of Medicine* 317 (1987), pp. 185–91; D. D. Richman, et al., "The Toxicity of Azidothymidine (AZT) in the Treatment of Patients with AIDS and AIDS-Related Complex: A Double-Blind, Placebo-Controlled Trial," *New England Journal of Medicine* 317 (1987), pp. 192–97; Robin Levin Penslar and Richard D. Lamm, "Who Pays for AZT?," *Hastings Center Report,* September/October 1989, pp. 30–32; Philip J. Hilts, "AZT to Be Widely Given Out to Children with AIDS Virus," *New York Times,* October 26, 1989, pp. A1, A22; Philip J. Hilts, "F.D.A., in Big Shift, Will Permit Use of Experimental AIDS Drug," *New York Times,* September 29, 1989, pp. A1, A16; and Martin Delaney, "The Case for Patient Access to Experimental Therapy," *Journal of Infectious Diseases* 159 (1989), pp. 412–15.
2. *HS News* 4, Department of Health and Human Services press release, October 9, 1991.
3. Ibid.
4. The Wellcome Group, *Annual Report 1990,* p. 17.
5. T. E. Haigler, Jr., president and CEO, Burroughs Wellcome, in testimony before the Subcommittee on Health and the Environment of the House Committee on Energy and Commerce, March 10, 1987, p. 12.
6. Ibid., p. 13.
7. David Kramer and Diana LeBas, "Barr Files Application to Manufacture Generic AZT," Barr Laboratories, Inc., press release, April 18, 1991.
8. Malcolm Gladwell, "Lawsuit on AIDS-Drug Patent Seeks to End Firm's Monopoly," *Washington Post,* March 20, 1991, p. A2.
9. Ibid.
10. Malcolm Gladwell, "NIH May Seek to Void Firm's

Patent on AZT," *Washington Post,* May 29, 1991, p. A1.
11. Public statement of Bernadine Healy, director, National Institutes of Health, July 17, 1991.
12. Ibid.
13. *Scrip,* no. 1637, July 26, 1991, p. 9.
14. Robin Goldwyn Blumenthal, "Barr Labs Granted Conditional License for AZT; Patent Fight Remains a Hurdle," *Wall Street Journal,* July 18, 1991, p. 1.
15. Lourdes Lee Valeriano, "Barr Laboratories Applies to the FDA for Approval to Make an AIDS Drug," *Wall Street Journal,* April 19, 1991, p. 4.
16. Stephen Britten, "Barr Seeks to Make Generic Version of AZT," *Rockland Journal News,* April 19, 1991, p. 2.
17. Michael Waldholz, "Glaxo Holdings Begins Human Testing of AIDS Drug That Is Similar to AZT," *Wall Street Journal,* July 30, 1991, p. B4.

Dorrence Corporation* Trade-offs

Hans A. Wolf
Vice chairman and chief administrative officer (retired), Syntax Co.

Arthur Cunningham, chief executive officer of the Dorrence Corporation, was reflecting on the presentations by the various divisions of the company of their operating plans and financial budgets for the next three years, which he had heard during the past several days. A number of critical decisions would have to be made at tomorrow's meeting of the nine senior executives who formed Dorrence's Corporate Operating Committee. Although the company's tradition was one of consensus management, Cunningham knew that he was expected to exercise leadership and would have the final word on, as well as the ultimate responsibility, for subsequent performance.

Dorrence, a large U.S.-based pharmaceutical company with sales and operations throughout the world, had achieved an outstanding long-term record of growth in sales and profits. It had not incurred a loss in any year since 1957 and profits had increased over the prior year in 28 out of the past 32 years. During the past 10 years, sales had grown at an average compound rate of 12 percent per year and profits had increased at a 15 percent average annual rate. Profits as a percent of sales was considerably higher than that of the average U.S. industrial concern. (See Exhibit 1).

The growth had produced a huge increase in the value of the company's stock. There are approximately 30,000 shareholders, with a small number of owners—pension and mutual funds, university endowments, and insurance companies—holding about 65 percent of the total. Dorrence grants stock options to its executives and permits employees in the U.S. and several other countries to purchase Dorrence stock through the company's savings plan. Executives own about two percent of the company's shares and all other employees about one percent. Thus, directly and indirectly, Dorrence is owned by many people, throughout the country, and perhaps around the world; all are affected to some degree by the policies and operations of the company, particularly as they affect the earnings and market price of Dorrence shares.

Dorrence's fine record of growth had also brought benefits to its customers, employees and the communities in which it had operations. It has steadily expanded its research expenditures at a greater rate than its sales growth and has developed important new products that improved the quality of life—or extended life—for hundreds of thousands of people. Because of its profitability, the company has been able to pay higher than average compensation to its employees, including sizeable incentive awards to middle and upper management and profit-related bonuses to all employees. Dorrence's growth has also provided unusual opportunities for employees' career development. Its managers have prided themselves on the company as a good citizen in the communities in which its laboratories and factories are located. It regularly contributes to local charities and encourages its employees to work constructively in community organizations.

*Name of company and all data related to it have been disguised.

Cunningham found that 1989 earnings were, however, very disappointing. The company fell short of the goals established for the year. Growth in sales and profits was far below the rate of recent years and, what hurt the most, below the levels achieved by several of Dorrence's competitors in the pharmaceutical industry. Management incentive awards and employee bonuses were, therefore, about 5 percent smaller than those distributed for 1988. The value of Dorrence stock had lost about a fifth of its value since its recent high.

Cunningham considered it important that Dorrence commit itself to achieving at least a 13 percent profit growth in 1990, and higher rates in the two following years. He recognized that such an achievement would not be easy. Not only would it demand the best efforts of the entire organization, but it would also require some tough managerial decisions.

The 1990 budgets proposed by the divisions added up to a growth rate of only 8 percent in profit-after-taxes, five percentage points below what Cunningham considered a minimum acceptable level. As a rough rule of thumb each percentage point increase in profit growth rate would require about $8 million additional profit-before-taxes. Thus, each percentage point improvement could be achieved in a number of ways: $13 million additional sales volume accompanied by normal incremental costs, $8 million additional revenue from price increases, $8 million of additional interest income on the company's invested cash, or an $8 million reduction in expenditures. During the course of a three-day division-by-division presentation, he had identified several possibilities for such improvements. In his notes he had summarized them as follows:

1. Size of the research budget: Dorrence's total expenditures for research and development (R&D) had climbed annually, not only in absolute dollars but also as a percent of sales. During the current year they totaled about 17 percent of sales, one of the higher levels in the industry.

The proposed budget included a further increase for R&D, and Cunningham knew that many promising projects required additional funding if the company were to demonstrate the safety and efficacy of important new drugs in a timely manner. He also knew that pharmaceutical R&D are very risky activities. The failure rate was high, with many years elapsing before managers knew if an effort was either a success or a failure. Typically, it took seven to 10 years from the identification of a potential new drug to Food & Drug Administration (FDA) approval for market sales. Approval also had to be sought from similar regulatory agencies in foreign countries, if the company was to sell the product abroad. On average, a pharmaceutical company brought to market only one new drug or product for each $100 million of R&D expenditures.

Clearly, there was a trade-off between investing for future growth and achieving acceptable profits in the short run. On Cunningham's list of possible changes in the proposed 1990 budget was a $10 million reduction in the amount of money requested for R&D.

2. Export sales: The International Division had presented an opportunity for a $4 million sale of Savolene to the Philippine government, not included in the 1990 budget because of lack of product availability. It was a new Dorrence-developed injectable drug for the treatment of serious viral infections, including measles. The drug was difficult and expensive to manufacture and had been in very short supply since its introduction.

A large lot, costing about $1 million, had been rejected for the U.S. market on the basis of a new, very sensitive test for endotoxin recently required by the FDA, in addition to a standard test that had been used for many years. The new test had shown a very low level of endotoxin on this batch of Savolene, even though no endotoxin has been revealed by the older test.

Cunningham had asked whether this ruled out shipping the batch to the Philippines. The company's chief medical safety officer had answered:

> Officially the Philippines and a lot of other countries still rely only on the old test. It always takes them a while to follow U.S. practice, and sometimes they never do. Endotoxin might cause high fever when injected into patients, but I can't tell you that the level in this batch is high enough to cause trouble. But how

can we have a double standard, one for the U.S. and one for the Third World countries?

However, when Cunningham asked Dorrence's export vice president the same question, she said:

> It's not our job to over-protect other countries. The health authorities in the Philippines know what they're doing. Our FDA always takes an extreme position. Measles is a serious illness. Last year in the Philippines half the kids who had measles died. It's not only good business but also good ethics to send them the only batch of Savolene we have available.

3. Capital investments: Among the capital investments that had been included in the proposed budgets was a $200 million plant-automation program for Dorrence's Haitian chemical plant. The purpose of the investment was to permit a dramatic reduction in the cost of Libam, Dorrence's principal product whose U.S. patent would expire in a couple of years. Patent protection had already ended in most other countries and chemical manufacturers in Italy, Hungary and India were selling Libam's active ingredient at very low prices. Once there was no longer patent protection in the U.S., companies based abroad and those in the U.S. could capture a large share of Dorrence's existing sales unless Dorrence were able to match their low prices. Automating the Haitian plant was essential to achieving such a match. Successful implementation of the new technology would enable the plant to achieve the required output with far fewer people than currently employed in the domestic plant. If U.S. plants were closed, the company would have to contend with longtime employees thrown out of work. He did not know whether many of them or if any could be transferred to other plants.

Dorrence was currently earning about 9 percent interest on its cash funds. The proposed automation project would use up $200 million of them and thus reduce interest income. Spending funds on the project would have reduced interest income for 1990 by about $9 million. If the automation program were stretched out over a longer period, almost half of that "loss" of income would be postponed a year, thus adding $4 million to 1990 profits. The down-side was that a slowdown in constructing the automated plant would mean delays in its production, needed to meet the expected competition.

4. Employee health insurance costs: Like all U.S. companies Dorrence was experiencing rapid escalation in the cost of its employee health insurance program. Dorrence paid 100 percent of the premium for its employees and 80 percent of the premiums for their dependents. After meeting certain deductibles, employees were reimbursed 80 percent to 90 percent of their medical and dental costs. The company's cost of maintaining the plan was budgeted to increase 22 percent, or $12 million in 1990. An important issue, therefore, was whether the plan should be changed to shift all or a portion of that cost increase to the employees through reducing the company's share of premiums, increasing deductibles, reducing reimbursements, or some combination of these changes.

5. Closing Dorrence's plant in Argentina: Dorrence had purchased a small pharmaceutical company in Argentina in the early 1950s when prospects for growth in the local market seemed excellent. However, in most years since then Argentina has been plagued by hyperinflation. With rapidly rising wage rates and other costs on the one hand, and strictly controlled drug prices, on the other, Dorrence's Argentine subsidiary had consistently lost money. The 1990 budget projected a loss of $4 million.

For the past year the company had tried to find a buyer for the subsidiary—a buyer who would retain the present sales force of 120 and continue to operate the Buenos Aires plant with its 250 employees. No such buyer had been found, but recently a local company had offered to purchase the rights to Dorrence's product line. It would manufacture them in its own under-utilized plant, distributing them through its own sales force. If Dorrence accepted this offer, the 370 company employees in Argentina would be laid off. Dorrence had already created a financial reserve for the government-mandated severance payments. Thus if he recommended ending the operations in Argentina, corporate profits would improve by $4 million in 1990.

6. Price increase on principal product sold in the U.S.: The budget proposed by Dorrence's U.S. pharmaceutical division already assumed a five percent price increase on all its current products at the end of the first quarter of the year, producing a $40 million increase in sales revenues. A substantially higher price increase on Libam, its largest selling product, could probably be implemented without adversely affecting sales to volume. For example, if the budgeted price increase were 10 percent instead of five percent, an additional $12 million would be generated. Alternately, if two five-percent price increases were implemented six months apart, Dorrence would earn $4 million above the proposed budget. Libam is used by chronically ill patients, many of them elderly.

In most countries pharmaceutical prices are controlled by the government. The United States is one of the few countries in which pharmaceutical companies are free to decide what prices to charge for their drugs. Physicians generally prescribe the drug which they feel will be most beneficial to their patients regardless of price. Unless the patent on a drug has expired and a generic equivalent is available, the demand for a prescription drug is not very sensitive to its price. Consequently, drug prices in the United States are substantially higher than in most other countries.

Cunningham was very conscious, however, of the growing public concern about health care costs. Although drugs constitute only a small fraction of the nation's total health care bill, drug prices are an easily identified target and drug companies were becoming increasingly under attack for their price increases.

7. New Costa Rican manufacturing plant: $10 million in sales of a new life-saving drug developed by Dorrence had been removed from the budget because of an unexpected problem at the new plant, which had been expected to be in operation this year, supplying the drug.

Three years earlier Dorrence had built the plant in a small Costa Rican town after evaluating various possible sites. The town had won the company's choice because it offered inexpensive land, relatively low wages, certain tax concessions, and a promise by the local government to build a new municipal waste treatment facility by the time the plant would be completed. In addition, Dorrence managers felt they would be fulfilling the company's social responsibilities by creating jobs in an area of high unemployment.

A few days before Dorrence's budget meeting the company had learned that completion of the municipal waste treatment plant was delayed at least a year. Although Costa Rica's environmental regulations are less stringent than those of industrialized countries, local law prohibits the discharge of untreated factory waste water into streams. Without a means of disposing of its waste water, the Dorrence plant could not operate.

A message from the Dorrence plant manager received yesterday seemed to solve the problem. The city sanitation commissioner had given Dorrence a special exemption that would allow it to discharge its waste water into a stream behind the plant until the city's waste treatment facility was completed. Cunningham had immediately asked for a fuller report on the situation. The plant manager had sent the following additional details:

> The stream is used to irrigate sugar-cane fields and small vegetable plots on which people in this area depend. There is, therefore, a chance that substances in the waste water would be absorbed by the crops that people are going to eat. I wonder if that is acceptable? On the other hand, I fear that all the good we have accomplished here will go down the drain if we don't begin manufacturing operations. Construction of the plant was completed on schedule three months ago. Building our own waste treatment facility now would add $5 million to the cost of the plant and would take at least 12 months. I've already hired over 100 workers and have given them extensive training. We obviously can't pay the workers for a year to sit around in an idle plant. Losing their jobs would be devastating to them and the whole community. Besides, there is no other Dorrence facility or plant of another company that could accomplish the synthesis required for this product. Lots of people in the United States are anxiously waiting for this new drug.

8. Pricing of an important new product: Finally, there was the issue of what price to charge for another new Dorrence drug, Miracule, which was expected to be introduced later in the year. In most cases patients for whom Miracule was prescribed would require the drug for the rest of their lives, unless an even more effective drug became available. The budget had assumed a price that would result in a daily cost of $1.75 (including wholesaler and drug store markups) for the average patient. A price of $2.50 would yield an additional $8 million profit to Dorrence during 1990 and far greater sums in subsequent years.

Despite the difficulties surrounding each of the issues Cunningham had identified, he felt it was critical that the 1990 budget be improved to aim for 13 percent profit growth over 1989. He believed that a second year in a row of below average profit growth would be viewed very negatively by the investment community, be demoralizing to the company's managers, and could result in a substantial drop in the value of the company's stock as investors switched to pharmaceutical companies with better 1990 results. He also recognized that large institutional investors, such as pension funds, were taking a more active role in demanding better performance from the managements of the companies in which they invested the funds entrusted to them. He worried that another year of disappointing growth might make them supportive of a take-over of the Dorrence Corporation.

EXHIBIT 1

DORRENCE CORPORATION

Financial & Other Data

	1979	1980	1981	1982	1983	1984
SALES—$MILLIONS	826	1,074	1,181	1,259	1,333	1,453
PROFIT*—$MILLIONS	132	164	175	204	224	222
PROFIT* AS % OF SALES	16.0	15.3	14.8	16.2	16.8	15.3
EMPLOYEES	12,500	12,900	13,500	13,600	13,800	14,000
STOCKHOLDERS OF RECORD	26,500	25,000	23,900	23,300	22,300	21,700

	1985	1986	1987	1988	1989
SALES—$MILLIONS	1,466	1,703	2,063	2,493	2,572
PROFIT*—$MILLIONS	241	312	413	524	558
PROFIT* AS % OF SALES	16.4	18.3	20.0	21.8	21.7
EMPLOYEES	13,300	13,100	13,500	13,900	14,700
STOCKHOLDERS OF RECORD	20,300	21,200	24,500	28,900	29,800

*After taxes.

Why Should My Conscience Bother Me?

Kermit Vandivier
Retired writer and Sunday editor, *Troy Daily News*, Troy, OH

The B.F. Goodrich Co. is what business magazines like to speak of as "a major American corporation." It has operations in a dozen states and as many foreign countries, and of these far-flung facilities, the Goodrich plant at Troy, Ohio, is not the most imposing. It is a small, one-story building, once used to manufacture airplanes. Set in the grassy flatlands of west-central Ohio, it employs only about six hundred people. Nevertheless, it is one of the three largest manufacturers of aircraft wheels and brakes, a leader in a most profitable industry. Goodrich wheels and brakes support such well-known planes as the F111, the C5A, the Boeing 727, the XB70 and many others. Its customers include almost every aircraft manufacturer in the world.

Contracts for aircraft wheels and brakes often run into millions of dollars, and ordinarily a contract with a total value of less than $70,000, though welcome, would not create any special stir of joy in the hearts of Goodrich sales personnel. But purchase order P-23718, issued on June 18, 1967, by the LTV Aerospace Corporation, and ordering 202 brake assemblies for a new Air Force plane at a total price of $69,417, was received by Goodrich with considerable glee. And there was good reason. Some ten years previously, Goodrich had built a brake for LTV that was, to say the least, considerably less than a rousing success. The brake had not lived up to Goodrich's promises, and after experiencing considerable difficulty, LTV had written off Goodrich as a source of brakes. Since that time, Goodrich salesmen had been unable to sell so much as a shot of brake fluid to LTV. So in 1967, when LTV requested bids on wheels and brakes for the new A7D light attack aircraft it proposed to build for the Air Force, Goodrich submitted a bid that was absurdly low, so low that LTV could not, in all prudence, turn it down.

Goodrich had, in industry parlance, "bought into the business." Not only did the company not expect to make a profit on the deal; it was prepared, if necessary, to lose money. For aircraft brakes are not something that can be ordered off the shelf. They are designed for a particular aircraft, and once an aircraft manufacturer buys a brake, he is forced to purchase all replacement parts from the brake manufacturer. The $70,000 that Goodrich would get for making the brake would be a drop in the bucket when compared with the cost of the linings and other parts the Air Force would have to buy from Goodrich during the lifetime of the aircraft. Furthermore, the company which manufactures brakes for one particular model of an aircraft quite naturally has the inside track to supply other brakes when the planes are updated and improved.

Thus, that first contract, regardless of the money involved, is very important, and Goodrich, when it learned that it had been awarded the A7D contract, was determined that while it may have slammed the door on its own foot ten years before, this time, the second time around, things would be different. The word was soon circulated throughout the plant: "We can't bungle it this time. We've got to give them a good brake, regardless of the cost."

There was another factor which had undoubtedly influenced LTV. All aircraft brakes made today are of the disk type, and the bid submitted by Goodrich called for a relatively small brake, one containing four disks and weighing only 106 pounds. The weight of any aircraft part is extremely important. The lighter a part is, the heavier the plane's payload can be. The four-rotor, 106-pound brake promised by Goodrich was about as light as could be expected, and this undoubtedly had helped move LTV to award the contract to Goodrich.

The brake was designed by one of Goodrich's most capable engineers, John Warren. A tall, lanky blond and a graduate of Purdue, Warren had come from the Chrysler Corporation seven years before and had become adept at aircraft brake design. The happy-go-lucky manner he usually maintained belied a temper which exploded whenever anyone ventured to offer any criticism of his work, no matter how small. On these occasions, Warren would turn red in the face, often throwing or slamming something and then stalking from the scene. As his coworkers learned the consequences of criticizing him, they did so less and less readily, and when he submitted his preliminary design for the A7D brake, it was accepted without question.

Warren was named project engineer for the A7D, and he, in turn, assigned the task of producing the final production design to a newcomer to the Goodrich engineering stable, Searle Lawson. Just turned twenty-six, Lawson had been out of the Northrup Institute of Technology only one year when he came to Goodrich in January 1967. Like Warren, he had worked for a while in the automotive industry, but his engineering degree was in aeronautical and astronautical sciences, and when the opportunity came to enter his special field, via Goodrich, he took it. At the Troy plant, Lawson had been assigned to various "paper projects" to break him in, and after several months spent reviewing statistics and old brake designs, he was beginning to fret at the lack of challenge. When told he was being assigned to his first "real" project, he was elated and immediately plunged into his work.

The major portion of the design had already been completed by Warren, and major assemblies for the brake had already been ordered from Goodrich suppliers. Naturally, however, before Goodrich could start making the brakes on a production basis, much testing would have to be done. Lawson would have to determine the best materials to use for the linings and discover what minor adjustments in the design would have to be made.

Then, after the preliminary testing and after the brake was judged ready for production, one whole brake assembly would undergo a series of grueling, simulated braking stops and other severe trials called qualification tests. These tests are required by the military, which gives very detailed specifications on how they are to be conducted, the criteria for failure, and so on. They are performed in the Goodrich plant's test laboratory, where huge machines called dynamometers can simulate the weight and speed of almost any aircraft. After the brakes pass the laboratory tests, they are approved for production, but before the brakes are accepted for use in military service, they must undergo further extensive flight tests.

Searle Lawson was well aware that much work had to be done before the A7D brake could go into production, and he knew that LTV had set the last two weeks in June, 1968, as the starting dates for flight tests. So he decided to begin testing immediately. Goodrich's suppliers had not yet delivered the brake housing and other parts, but the brake disks had arrived, and using the housing from a brake similar in size and weight to the A7D brake, Lawson built a prototype. The prototype was installed in a test wheel and placed on one of the big dynamometers in the plant's test laboratory. The dynamometer was adjusted to simulate the weight of the A7D and Lawson began a series of tests, "landing" the wheel and brake at the A7D's landing speed, and braking it to a stop. The main purpose of these preliminary tests was to learn what temperatures would develop within the brake during the simulated stops and to evaluate the lining materials tentatively selected for use.

During a normal aircraft landing the temperatures inside the brake may reach 1000 degrees, and occasionally a bit higher. During Lawson's first simulated landings, the temperature of his prototype brake reached 1500 degrees. The brake glowed a bright cherry-red and threw off incandescent particles of metal and lining material as the temperature reached its peak. After a few such stops, the brake was dismantled and the linings were found to be almost completely disintegrated. Lawson chalked this first failure up to chance and, ordering new lining materials, tried again.

The second attempt was a repeat of the first. The brake became extremely hot, causing the lining materials to crumble into dust.

After the third such failure, Lawson, inexperienced though he was, knew that the fault lay not in defective parts or unsuitable lining material but in the basic design of the brake itself. Ignoring Warren's original computations, Lawson made his own, and it didn't take him long to discover where the trouble lay—the brake was too small. There simply was not enough surface area on the disks to stop the aircraft without generating the excessive heat that caused the linings to fail.

The answer to the problem was obvious but far from simple—the four-disk brake would have to be scrapped, and a new design, using five disks, would have to be developed. The implications were not lost on Lawson. Such a step would require the junking of all the four-disk-brake subassemblies, many of which had now begun to arrive from the various suppliers. It would also mean several weeks of preliminary design and testing and many more weeks of waiting while the suppliers made and delivered the new subassemblies.

Yet, several weeks had already gone by since LTV's order had arrived, and the date for delivery of the first production brakes for flight testing was only a few months away.

Although project engineer John Warren had more or less turned the A7D over to Lawson, he knew of the difficulties Lawson had been experiencing. He had assured the young engineer that the problem revolved around getting the right kind of lining material. Once that was found, he said, the difficulties would end.

Despite the evidence of the abortive tests and Lawson's careful computations, Warren rejected the suggestion that the four-disk brake was too light for the job. Warren knew that his superior had already told LTV, in rather glowing terms, that the preliminary tests on the A7D brake were very successful. Indeed, Warren's superiors weren't aware at this time of the troubles on the brake. It would have been difficult for Warren to admit not only that he had made a serious error in his calculations and original design but that his mistakes had been caught by a green kid, barely out of college.

Warren's reaction to a five-disk brake was not unexpected by Lawson, and, seeing that the four-disk brake was not to be abandoned so easily, he took his calculations and dismal test results one step up the corporate ladder.

At Goodrich, the man who supervises the engineers working on projects slated for production is called, predictably, the projects manager. The job was held by a short, chubby and bald man named Robert Sink. A man truly devoted to his work, Sink was as likely to be found at his desk at ten o'clock on Sunday night as ten o'clock on Monday morning. His outside interests consisted mainly of tinkering on a Model-A Ford and an occasional game of golf. Some fifteen years before, Sink had begun working at Goodrich as a lowly draftsman. Slowly, he worked his way up. Despite his geniality, Sink was neither respected nor liked by the majority of the engineers, and his appointment as their supervisor did not improve their feelings about him. They thought he had only gone to high school. It quite naturally rankled those who had gone through years of college and acquired impressive specialties such as thermodynamics and astronautics to be commanded by a man whom they considered their intellectual inferior. But, though Sink had no college training, he had something even more useful: a fine working knowledge of company politics.

Puffing upon a Meerschaum pipe, Sink listened gravely as young Lawson confided his fears about the four-disk brake. Then he examined Lawson's calculations and the results of the abortive tests. Despite the fact that he was not a qualified engineer, in the strictest sense of the word, it must certainly have been obvious to Sink that Lawson's calculations were correct and that a four-disk brake would never have worked on the A7D.

But other things of equal importance were also obvious. First, to concede that Lawson's calculations were correct would also mean conceding that Warren's calculations were incorrect. As projects manager, he not only was responsible for Warren's activities, but, in admitting that Warren had erred, he would have to admit that he had erred in trusting Warren's judgment. It also meant that, as projects manager, it would be he who would have to explain the whole messy situation to the Goodrich hierarchy, not only at Troy but possibly on the corporate level at Goodrich's Akron offices. And, having taken Warren's judgment of the four-disk brake at face value (he was forced to do this since, not being an engineer, he was unable to exercise any engineering judgment of his own), he had assured LTV, not once but several times, that about all there was left to do on the brake was pack it in a crate and ship it out the back door.

There's really no problem at all, he told Lawson. After all, Warren was an experienced engineer, and if he said the brake would work, it would work. Just keep on testing and probably, maybe even on the very next try, it'll work out just fine.

Lawson was far from convinced, but without the support of his superiors there was little he could do except keep on testing. By now, housings for the four-disk brake had begun to arrive at the plant, and Lawson was able to build up a production model of the brake and begin the formal qualification tests demanded by the military.

The first qualification attempts went exactly as the tests on the prototype had. Terrific heat developed within the brakes and, after a few, short, simulated stops, the linings crumbled. A new type of lining material was ordered and once again an attempt to qualify the brake was made. Again, failure.

On April 11, the day the thirteenth test was completed, I became personally involved in the A7D situation.

I had worked in the Goodrich test laboratory for five years, starting first as an instrumentation engineer, then later becoming a data analyst and technical writer. As part of my duties, I analyzed the reams and reams of instrumentation data that came from the many testing machines in the laboratory, then transcribed it to a more usable form for the engineering department. And when a new-type brake had successfully completed the required qualification tests, I would issue a formal qualification report.

Qualification reports were an accumulation of all the data and test logs compiled by the test technicians during the qualification tests, and were documentary proof that a brake had met all the requirements established by the military specifications and was therefore presumed safe for flight testing. Before actual flight tests were conducted on a brake, qualification reports had to be delivered to the customer and to various government officials.

On April 11, I was looking over the data from the latest A7D test, and I noticed that many irregularities in testing methods had been noted on the test logs.

Technically, of course, there was nothing wrong with conducting tests in any manner desired, so long as the test was for research purposes only. But qualification test methods are clearly delineated by the military, and I knew that this test had been a formal qualification attempt. One particular notation on the test logs caught my eye. For some of the stops, the instrument which recorded the brake pressure had been deliberately miscalibrated so that, while the brake pressure used during the stops was recorded as 1000 psi (the maximum pressure that would be available on the A7D aircraft), the pressure had actually been 1100 psi!

I showed the test logs to the test lab supervisor, Ralph Gretzinger, who said he had learned from the technician who had miscalibrated the instrument that he had been asked to do so by Lawson. Lawson, said Gretzinger, readily admitted asking for the miscalibration, saying he had been told to do so by Sink.

I asked Gretzinger why anyone would want to miscalibrate the data-recording instruments.

"Why? I'll tell you why," he snorted. "That brake is a failure. It's way too small for the job, and they're not ever going to get it to work. They're getting desperate, and instead of scrapping the damned thing and starting over, they figure they can horse around down here in the lab and qualify it that way."

An expert engineer, Gretzinger had been responsible for several innovations in brake design. It was he who had invented the unique brake system used on the famous XB70. A graduate of Georgia Tech, he was a stickler for detail and he had some very firm ideas about honesty and ethics. "If you want to find out what's going on," said Gretzinger, "ask Lawson, he'll tell you."

Curious, I did ask Lawson the next time he came into the lab. He seemed eager to discuss the A7D and gave me the history of his months of frustrating efforts to get Warren and Sink to change the brake design. "I just can't believe this is really happening," said Lawson, shaking his head slowly. "This isn't engineering, at least not what I thought it would be. Back in school, I thought that when you were an engineer, you tried to do your best, no matter what it cost. But this is something else."

He sat across the desk from me, his chin propped in his hand. "Just wait," he warned. "You'll get a chance to see what I'm talking about. You're going to get in the act, too, because I've already had the word that we're going to make one more attempt to qualify the brake, and that's it. Win or lose, we're going to issue a qualification report!"

I reminded him that a qualification report could only be issued after a brake had successfully met all military requirements, and therefore, unless the next qualification attempt was a success, no report would be issued.

"You'll find out," retorted Lawson. "I was already told that regardless of what the brake does on test, it's going to be qualified." He said he had been told in those exact words at a conference with Sink and Russell Van Horn.

This was the first indication that Sink had brought his boss, Van Horn, into the mess. Although Van Horn, as manager of the design engineering section, was responsible for the entire department, he was not necessarily familiar with all phases of every project, and it was not uncommon for those under him to exercise the what-he-doesn't-know-won't-hurt-him philosophy. If he was aware of the full extent of the A7D situation, it meant that matters had truly reached a desperate stage—that Sink had decided not only to call for help but was looking toward that moment when blame must be borne and, if possible, shared.

Also, if Van Horn had said, "regardless what the brake does on test, it's going to be qualified," then it could only mean that, if necessary, a false qualification report would be issued! I discussed this possibility with Gretzinger, and he assured me that under no circumstances would such a report ever be issued.

"If they want a qualification report, we'll write them one, but we'll tell it just like it is," he declared emphatically. "No false data or false reports are going to come out of this lab."

On May 2, 1968, the fourteenth and final attempt to qualify the brake was begun. Although the same improper methods used to nurse the brake through the previous tests were employed, it soon became obvious that this too would end in failure.

When the tests were about half completed, Lawson asked if I would start preparing the various engineering curves and graphic displays which were normally incorporated in a qualification report. "It looks as though you'll be writing a qualification report shortly," he said.

I flatly refused to have anything to do with the matter and immediately told Gretzinger what I had been asked to do. He was furious and repeated his previous declaration that under no circumstances would any false data or other matter be issued from the lab.

"I'm going to get this settled right now, once and for all," he declared. "I'm going to see Line [Russell Line, manager of the Goodrich Technical Services Section, of which the test lab was a part] and find out just how far this thing is going to go!" He stormed out of the room.

In about an hour, he returned and called me to his desk. He sat silently for a few moments, then muttered, half to himself, "I wonder what the hell they'd do if I just quit?" I didn't answer and I didn't ask him what he meant. I knew. He had been beaten down. He had reached the point when the decision had to be made. Defy them now while there was still time—or knuckle under, sell out.

"You know," he went on uncertainly, looking down at his desk, "I've been an engineer for a long time, and I've always believed that ethics and integrity were every bit as important as theorems and formulas, and never once has anything happened to change my beliefs. Now this. . . . Hell, I've got two sons I've got to put through school and I just. . . ." His voice trailed off.

He sat for a few more minutes, then, looking over the top of his glasses, said hoarsely, "Well, it looks like we're licked. The way it stands now, we're to go ahead and prepare the data and other things for the graphic presentation in the report, and when we're finished, someone upstairs will actually write the report.

"After all," he continued, "we're just drawing some curves, and what happens to them after they leave here, well, we're not responsible for that."

He was trying to persuade himself that as long as we were concerned with only one part of the puzzle and didn't see the completed picture, we really weren't doing anything wrong. He didn't believe what he was saying, and he knew I didn't believe it either. It was an embarrassing and shameful moment for both of us.

I wasn't at all satisfied with the situation and decided that I too would discuss the matter with Russell Line, the senior executive in our section.

Tall, powerfully built, his teeth flashing white, his face tanned to a coffee-brown by a daily stint with a sun lamp, Line looked and acted every inch the executive. He was a crossword-puzzle enthusiast and an ardent golfer, and though he had lived in Troy only a short time, he had been accepted into the Troy Country Club and made an official of the golf committee. He commanded great respect and had come to be well liked by those of us who worked under him.

He listened sympathetically while I explained how I felt about the A7D situation, and when I had finished, he asked me what I wanted him to do about it. I said that as employees of the Goodrich Company we had a responsibility to protect the company and its reputation if at all possible. I said I was certain that officers on the corporate level would never knowingly allow such tactics as had been employed on the A7D.

"I agree with you," he remarked, "but I still want to know what you want me to do about it."

I suggested that in all probability the chief engineer at the Troy plant, H. C. "Bud" Sunderman, was unaware of the A7D problem and that he, Line, should tell him what was going on.

Line laughed, good-humoredly. "Sure, I could, but I'm not going to. Bud probably already knows about this thing anyway, and if he doesn't, I'm sure not going to be the one to tell him."

"But why?"

"Because it's none of my business, and it's none of yours. I learned a long time ago not to worry about things over which I had no control. I have no control over this."

I wasn't satisfied with this answer, and I asked him if his conscience wouldn't bother him if, say, during flight tests on the brake, something should happen resulting in death or injury to the test pilot.

"Look," he said, becoming somewhat exasperated, "I just told you I have no control over this thing. Why should my conscience bother me?"

His voice took on a quiet, soothing tone as he continued. "You're just getting all upset over this thing for nothing. I just do as I'm told, and I'd advise you to do the same."

He had made his decision, and now I had to make mine.

I made no attempt to rationalize what I had been asked to do. It made no difference who would falsify which part of the report or whether the actual falsification would be by misleading numbers or misleading words. Whether by acts of commission or omission, all of us who contributed to the fraud would be guilty. The only question left for me to decide was whether or not I would become a party to the fraud.

Before coming to Goodrich in 1963, I had held a variety of jobs, each a little more pleasant, a little more rewarding than the last. At forty-two, with seven children, I had decided that the Goodrich Company would probably be my "home" for the rest of my working life. The job paid well, it was pleasant and challenging, and the future looked reasonably bright. My wife and I had bought a home and we were ready to settle down into a comfortable, middle-age, middle-class rut. If I refused to take part in the A7D fraud, I would have to either resign or be fired. The report would be written by someone anyway, but I would have the satisfaction of knowing I had had no part in the matter. But bills aren't paid with personal satisfaction, nor house payments with ethical principles. I made my decision. The next morning, I telephoned Lawson and told him I was ready to begin on the qualification report.

In a few minutes, he was at my desk, ready to begin. Before we started, I asked him, "Do you realize what we are going to do?"

"Yeah," he replied bitterly, "we're going to screw LTV. And speaking of screwing," he continued, "I know now how a whore feels, because that's exactly what I've become, an engineering whore. I've sold myself. It's all I can do to look at myself in the mirror when I shave. I make me sick."

I was surprised at his vehemence. It was obvious that he too had done his share of soul-searching and didn't like what he had found. Somehow, though, the air seemed clearer after his outburst, and we began working on the report.

I had written dozens of qualification reports, and I knew what a "good" one looked like. Resorting to the actual test data only on occasion, Lawson and I proceeded to prepare page after page of elaborate, detailed engineering curves, charts, and test logs, which purported to show what had happened during the formal qualification tests. Where temperatures were too high, we deliberately chopped them down a few hundred degrees, and where they were too low, we raised them to a value that would appear reasonable to the LTV and military engineers. Brake pressure, torque values, distances, times—everything of consequence was tailored to fit the occasion.

Occasionally, we would find that some test either hadn't been performed at all or had been conducted improperly. On those occasions, we "conducted" the test—successfully, of course—on paper.

For nearly a month we worked on the graphic presentation that would be a part of the report. Meanwhile, the fourteenth and final qualification attempt had been completed, and the brake, not unexpectedly, had failed again.

During that month, Lawson and I talked of little else except the enormity of what we were doing. The more involved we became in our work, the more apparent became our own culpability. We discussed such things as the Nuremberg trials and how they related to our guilt and complicity in the A7D situation. Lawson often expressed his opinion that the brake was downright dangerous and that, once on flight tests, "anything is liable to happen."

I saw his boss, John Warren, at least twice during that month and needled him about what we were doing. He didn't take the jibes too kindly but managed to laugh the situation off as "one of those things." One day I remarked that what we were doing amounted to fraud, and he pulled out an engineering handbook and turned to a section on laws as they related to the engineering profession.

He read the definition of fraud aloud, then said, "Well, technically I don't think what we're doing can be called fraud. I'll admit it's not right, but it's just one of those things. We're just kinda caught in the middle. About all I can tell you is, do like I'm doing. Make copies of everything and put them in your SYA file."

"What's an 'SYA' file?" I asked.

"That's a 'save your ass' file." He laughed.

On June 5, 1968, the report was officially published and copies were delivered in person to the Air Force and LTV. Within a week, flight tests were begun at Edwards Air Force Base in California. Searle Lawson was sent to California as Goodrich's representative. Within approximately two weeks, he returned because some rather unusual incidents during the tests had caused them to be canceled.

His face was grim as he related stories of several near crashes during landings—caused by brake troubles. He told me about one incident in which, upon landing, one brake was literally welded together by the intense heat developed during the test stop. The wheel locked, and the plane skidded for nearly 1500 feet before coming to a halt. The plane was jacked up and the wheel removed. The fused parts within the brake had to be pried apart.

Lawson had returned to Troy from California that same day, and that evening, he and others of the Goodrich engineering department left for Dallas for a high-level conference with LTV.

That evening I left work early and went to see my attorney. After I told him the story, he advised that, while I was probably not actually guilty of fraud, I was certainly part of a conspiracy to defraud. He advised me to go to the Federal Bureau of Investigation and offered to arrange an appointment. The following week he took me to the Dayton office of the FBI, and after I had been warned that I would not be immune from prosecution, I disclosed the A7D matter to one of the agents. The agent told me to say nothing about the episode to anyone and to report any further incident to him. He said he would forward the story to his superiors in Washington.

A few days later, Lawson returned from the conference in Dallas and said that the Air Force, which had previously approved the qualification report, had suddenly rescinded that approval and was demanding to see some of the raw test data taken during the tests. I gathered that the FBI had passed the word.

Finally, early in October 1968, Lawson submitted his resignation, to take effect on October 25. On October 18, I submitted my own resignation, to take effect on November 1. In my resignation, addressed to Russell Line, I cited the A7D report and stated: "As you are aware, this report contained numerous deliberate and willful misrepresentations which, according to legal counsel, constitute fraud and expose both myself and others to criminal charges of conspiracy to defraud. . . . The events of the past seven months have created an atmosphere of deceit and distrust in which it is impossible to work. . . ."

On October 25, I received a sharp summons to the office of Bud Sunderman. As chief engineer at the Troy plant, Sunderman was responsible for the entire engineering division. Tall and graying, impeccably dressed at all times, he was capable of producing a dazzling smile or a hearty chuckle or immobilizing his face into marble hardness, as the occasion required.

I faced the marble hardness when I reached his office. He motioned me to a chair. "I have your resignation here," he snapped, "and I must say you have made some rather shocking, I might even say irresponsible, charges. This is very serious."

Before I could reply, he was demanding an explanation. "I want to know exactly what the fraud is in connection with the A7D and how you can dare accuse this company of such a thing!"

I started to tell some of the things that had happened during the testing, but he shut me off saying, "There's nothing wrong with anything we've done here. You aren't aware of all the things that have been going on behind the scenes. If you had known the true situation, you would never have made these charges." He said that in view of my apparent "disloyalty" he had decided to accept my resignation "right now," and said it would be better for all concerned if I left the plant immediately. As I got up to leave he asked me if I intended to "carry this thing further."

I answered simply, "Yes," to which he replied, "Suit yourself." Within twenty minutes, I had cleaned out my desk and left. Forty-eight hours later, the B. F. Goodrich Company recalled the qualification report and the four-disk brake, announcing that it would replace the brake with a new, improved, five-disk brake at no cost to LTV.

Ten months later, on August 13, 1969, I was the chief government witness at a hearing conducted before Senator William Proxmire's Economy in Government Subcommittee of the Congress's Joint Economic Committee. I related the A7D story to the committee, and my testimony was supported by Searle Lawson, who followed me to the witness stand. Air Force officers also testified, as well as a four-man team from the General Accounting Office, which had conducted an investigation of the A7D brake at the request of Senator Proxmire. Both Air Force and GAO investigators declared that the brake was dangerous and had not been tested properly.

Testifying for Goodrich was R. G. Jeter, vice-president and general counsel of the company, from the Akron headquarters. Representing the Troy plant was Robert Sink. These two denied any wrongdoing on the part of the Goodrich Company, despite expert testimony to the contrary by Air Force and GAO officials. Sink was quick to deny any connection with the writing of the report or of directing any falsifications, claiming to be on the West Coast at the time. John Warren was the man who supervised its writing, said Sink.

As for me, I was dismissed as a high-school graduate with no technical training, while Sink testified that Lawson was a young, inexperienced engineer. "We tried to give him guidance," Sink testified, "but he preferred to have his own convictions."

About changing the data and figures in the report, Sink said: "When you take data from several different sources, you have to rationalize among those data what is the true story. This is part of your engineering know-how." He admitted that changes had been made in the data, "but only to make them more consistent with the overall picture of the data that is available."

Jeter pooh-poohed the suggestion that anything improper occurred, saying: "We have thirty-odd engineers at this plant . . . and I say to you that it is incredible that these men would stand idly by and see reports changed or falsified. . . . I mean you just do not have to do that working for anybody. . . . Just nobody does that."

The four-hour hearing adjourned with no real conclusion reached by the committee. But, the following day the Department of Defense made sweeping changes in its inspection, testing and reporting procedures. A spokesman for the DOD said the changes were a result of the Goodrich episode.

The A7D is now in service, sporting a Goodrich-made five-disk brake, a brake that works very well, I'm told. Business at the Goodrich plant is good. Lawson is now an engineer for LTV and has been assigned to the A7D project. And I am now a newspaper reporter.

At this writing, those remaining at Goodrich are still secure in the same positions, all except Russell Line and Robert Sink. Line has been rewarded with a promotion to production superintendent, a large step upward on the corporate ladder. As for Sink, he moved up into Line's old job.

PART TWO

THE NATURE OF THE CORPORATION

In Part One we examined the ethical dimensions of the economic system in which business operates. Here, we turn attention to the nature and role of the corporation within that system. Reflection on the nature of the corporation is important, in part because our understanding of the corporation shapes our beliefs about the corporation's responsibilities. If we hold that a corporation is a privately owned enterprise designed to make a profit, for example, we are likely to have a narrower view of corporate responsibility than if we hold it to be a quasi-public institution. In Chapter 3 we approach the problem of the nature of the corporation from the perspective of the corporate social responsibility debate.

It is not clear that we can attribute any responsibilities to corporations at all, however, unless we can look upon them as moral agents in some sense. Does it make sense to regard corporations as moral agents, analogous to individuals? Who or what is "Gulf Oil" or "Ford Motor Company"? Chapter 4 explores these and other questions about the identity and agency of corporations.

Finally, we investigate the nature of the corporation from the perspective of its internal structure and governance. In the first three articles in Chapter 5 we focus on the corporate board of directors. Who should sit on the board? What is and what should be the relationship between the board, management, and stockholders? How far should the board's power extend? In the remaining articles in Chapter 5 we investigate some potential consequences of the misuse of corporate power for two stockholder groups: stockholders and employees.

THE CORPORATE SOCIAL RESPONSIBILITY DEBATE

Traditionally it has been held that the major responsibility of business in American society is to produce goods and services and to sell them for a profit. This conception of business's role has been one of the cornerstones of its legitimacy—of society's belief in the right of business to exist. Recently, however, the traditional view has been questioned. Increasingly, business is being asked not only to refrain from harming society, but to contribute actively and directly to public well-being. Business firms are expected not only to obey a multitude of legal requirements, but also to go beyond the demands of the law and exercise moral judgment in making decisions. What are the reasons for this changing conception of corporate social responsibility?

In the context of the traditional view, businesses are understood as private property, instruments of their owners designed primarily to make money. Because the pressure of an "invisible hand" ensures that each entrepreneur's pursuit of his or her own profit will result in the good of the whole, and because businesses are the property of their owners to do with as they please, business has no other responsibility than to perform efficiently its economic function. As economist Milton Friedman, one of the most forceful exponents of the traditional ideology, puts it, "the social responsibility of business is to increase its profits."

Why has the old view begun to erode and a new one begun to take its place? One answer is that today's giant corporations no longer seem to fit the old model. Usually we associate ownership with control, but the modern corporation is owned by stockholders who have little or no psychological or operational involvement in it. Some thinkers have argued that corporations can no longer accurately be viewed as private property. As ownership separates from control, corporations seem less like mere instruments of their owners and more like autonomous entities capable of their own goals and decisions.

The tremendous impact on and power over our society exerted by corporations also casts doubt on their private character. Many thinkers argue that social power inevitably implies social responsibility, and they suggest that those who fail to exercise a responsibility commensurate with their power should lose that power. As the power of business has grown, we have become increasingly aware of the external costs—pollution, hazardous products, job dissatisfaction—corporations have passed on to society at large. These costs in turn call into question a basic assumption of the old view: the identity of individual and social well-being.

The corporation's evolution away from the kind of enterprise described in the traditional view leaves us with at least two alternatives. We can explicitly acknowledge the new idea that corporations have extensive social responsibilities, or we can attempt to make reality fit the old view once again. Some, such as Christopher Stone, Thomas Donaldson, and William Evan and Edward Freeman, take the first option, arguing that corporations are no longer merely economic institutions, but sociological institutions as well. Milton Friedman opts for the second alternative.

Friedman holds fast to the traditional values of a free market system and rejects the idea of corporate social responsibility because he feels it is "fundamentally subversive" of these values. For Friedman, the sole social responsibility of business is to increase its profits while staying within the legal and moral "rules of the game."

It is important to realize that Friedman is not claiming that the corporation has no responsibilities or obligations. Rather, he is arguing that corporations are directly responsible only to one set of people—their stockholders. Regardless of the actual relationship between ownership and control in the modern corporation, Friedman believes they ought not to be separate. Because the stockholders own the corporation and hire managers to run it for them, Friedman argues, managers are "fiduciaries" of the stockholders; they have an obligation to act in stockholders' interest, which means, according to Friedman, that they should maximize profit. To demand that corporate managers exercise responsibility to society at large is to ask them to violate their obligations to stockholders.

Managers who assume "social responsibility," Friedman argues, are actually using stockholders' money to solve social problems without their permission. They are in effect "taxing" stockholders, but because they are private employees rather than publicly elected officials, their actions lack authority and legitimacy. Behind Friedman's argument lies a conviction that each social institution exists to perform a particular function. The legitimacy of corporate activity depends on executives confining themselves to the role of agents serving the interests of those who own stock in the corporation. "Social responsibility" is the job of government, not business.

In "Why Shouldn't Corporations Be Socially Responsible?" Christopher Stone critically examines several arguments that might be used to support Friedman's position. It is often suggested that management has made a promise to maximize the profits of corporate stockholders and ought to stand by its promise; but, Stone argues, this is simply not the case. There is no explicit promise or contract between managers and stockholders. Nor is it true that managers are bound by an implicit contract because they have been hired by the owners of the corporation. In reality, says Stone, stockholders have neither much power nor much interest in selecting the management of the corporation.

Even if such a contract did exist, Stone continues, it would not mean that management has an obligation to maximize profits in every possible way, or that the contract would supersede all other obligations. Business may have an obligation not to sell products that are dangerous to consumers, for example, even if by doing so it will make a profit. A contract that required one to subordinate all moral considerations to considerations of profit would be an immoral contract, one that undermines the basis of contract itself. If such a promise has been made, Stone claims, it would be morally right to break it.

There seems to be no firm basis, Stone concludes, for the claim that management's only obligation is to produce a profit for corporate stockholders. To be sure, managers may have this obligation, but that does not relieve them of all other responsibilities. There are obligations more fundamental than the one Friedman describes; these may include responsibilities to consumers, employees, the surrounding community, and future generations.

Thomas Donaldson further investigates the relation between business and society in "The Social Contract: Norms for a Corporate Conscience." He focuses on the idea of an implied contract between business and society in an attempt to specify what the social obligations of business might be. According to Donaldson, the very right of corporations to exist and operate is granted to them by society. It is society that recognizes productive organizations as single agents with special status under the law and that permits them to use natural resources and hire employees. In return, society should be permitted to demand at least that the benefits of authorizing the existence of corporations outweigh the costs. If Donaldson is correct, the corporation is a social entity—not merely an economic one—from the moment of inception. His social contract theory implies that the legitimacy of corporate activity lies in the successful exercise of social responsibility.

In contrast to Friedman's view that the modern corporation should be managed solely for the benefit of the stockholders, in "A Stakeholder Theory of the Modern Corporation," William Evan and Edward Freeman argue that the corporation should be managed for the benefit of *stakeholders,* which are those individuals or groups that have a stake in or claim on the firm. Basing their theory on the Kantian idea that persons should be treated as ends in themselves and not merely as means to some end, Evan and Freeman argue that stockholder property rights are not absolute, and do not justify or license using persons as means to corporate profit. The ethical challenge for management is thus to meet the claims made by a variety of corporate stakeholders, which includes, of course, those who hold stock in the corporation. Sometimes one of these groups may benefit at the expense of others, but management's job is is to keep the balance between them as best it can, coordinating and maximizing their joint interests.

As Evan and Freeman are careful to point out, their proposal essentially redefines the purpose of the corporation. Some possible difficulties with this redefinition are explored by George Brenkert in the final article in the third chapter, "Private Corporations and Public Welfare." In his article Brenkert considers an objection to the idea that corporations have social responsibility. The objection is that requiring corporations to engage in creating public welfare involves illegitimate interference by private organizations into public interests. He notes that corporations may be inflexible and insensitive to real community needs, that the programs of social responsibility they develop may be ill conceived or even harmful, and that corporations may deal paternalistically with stakeholders who have no real voice in corporate decisions. Given the potential for harm that corporate social programs have, Brenkert considers whether large corporations should be made more fully public, in effect converting them into public instruments of social policy. He points out that this is something opposed by many, and thus that we remain at a crossroads between one view of the corporation as a private competitive enterprise and another view of corporations as quasi-public institutions. He concludes that if one rejects the idea that corporations should become more fully public institutions, then one should also reject the idea that corporations have responsibilities for public welfare.

THE CORPORATION AS A MORAL AGENT

The authors included in Chapter 3 examine the issue of whether the corporation ought to have moral responsibilities and offered suggestions as to what these might be. They do not, however, ask whether the corporation is the kind of entity that is capable of having responsibilities at all. Normally we associate moral responsibility with individual persons. But corporations are not individual persons. They are collections of individuals who work together to establish corporate policy, make corporate decisions, and execute corporate actions.

What does it mean to say that the Ford Motor Company or Gulf Oil is responsible for a particular action? Who is to blame for an immoral corporate action? Does it make sense to look at the corporation as a moral agent, analogous to a person? And if not, does this mean that we cannot judge corporate actions according to ethical standards?

Kenneth Goodpaster and John Matthews argue that there is an analogy between individual and organizational behavior, and that for this reason corporate conduct can be evaluated in moral terms. Some thinkers have claimed that only persons are capable of moral responsibility in the fullest sense, because such responsibility presupposes the ability to reason, to have intentions, and to make autonomous choices. But although the corporation is not a person in a literal sense, Goodpaster and Matthews respond, it is made up of persons. For this reason, we can project many of the attributes of individual human beings to the corporate level. We already speak of corporations having goals, values, interests, strategies. Why, ask Goodpaster and Matthews, shouldn't we also speak of the corporate conscience?

Thinkers who assume that corporations cannot exercise moral responsibility advocate trust in the "invisible hand" of the market system to "moralize" the actions of corporations. Milton Friedman is one of these. Others feel that the "hand of the government" is required to ensure moral corporate behavior. Both of these views, however, fail to locate the source of responsible corporate action in the corporation itself. Both rely upon systems and forces external to the corporation. Goodpaster and Matthews argue for a third alternative: endowing the corporation with a conscience analogous to that of an individual, recognizing the ability of corporations to exercise independent moral judgment, and locating the responsibility for corporate behavior in the hands of corporate managers. This "hand of management" alternative, they admit, is not without its problems—and it requires more thorough analysis on both the conceptual and practical levels. But Goodpaster and Matthews believe that it is the best alternative of the three because it provides a framework for an inventory of corporate responsibilities and accepts corporations as legitimate members of the moral community.

Peter French develops the analogy between individual persons and corporations in detail in his article. One of the most important elements in the notion of responsibility, French points out, is that of intention. In general we do not hold persons morally responsible for unintentional acts. If we wish the idea of corporate responsibility to make sense, we must be able to discover a corporate intention. But how can a collective intend? French suggests that we make use of what he calls the Corporate Internal Decision (CID) Structure to understand the meaning of corporate intention.

The CID Structure has two major components: an organizational flowchart which indicates the "rules of the game"—the levels of responsibility within the corporate hierarchy (French calls this "the grammar of corporate decision making")—and a corporate policy that includes the beliefs, principles, and goals of the organization. Some have argued that it is precisely these characteristics that make corporations nonmoral and fundamentally different from individuals. Here French uses them in the service of corporate responsibility. A decision is a corporate decision—intended by the corporation—if it has been made in accordance with the operational flowchart and if it reflects corporate policy.

It is a crucial aspect of French's theory that a corporate intention or decision is not identical to the intentions or decisions of those within the organization. It is true that corporate action is dependent on the action of individuals in that a corporation cannot act without some human being acting. French holds that the CID Structure literally "incorporates" the actions of individuals. A corporate act is different from the acts of which it is incorporated, just as the activity of an organism is different from the activity of its parts.

If French is correct, corporations must be regarded as genuine, independent moral agents, on an equal footing with human beings. It is precisely this feature of French's position that John Danley attacks. Corporate and individual agency are not the same, argues Danley. The reasons in favor of "anthropological bigotry" become clear when we focus on the "moral moves" which take place after an agent has done something—especially on those of blame and punishment.

French holds that only those actions which are done in accordance with the organizational flowchart and guided by corporate policy can be counted as "corporate acts." Presumably corporate policy includes the provisions of the corporate charter, which grants corporations the right to do business as long as they obey the law. But if the members of the corporation voted to act illegally, then, Danley claims, their decision could not be described as a "corporate action" at all. It is unclear whether corporations can ever act illegally under French's theory.

Even if corporations can perform illegal acts, it is difficult to see how moral sanctions can be applied to them. Only individuals can be punished. Fines can be levied on corporations, but ultimately individuals—stockholders, consumers, employees—pay the cost. If French is correct in saying that a corporate act is not identical to the acts of individuals, however, it does not make sense to go inside the corporation to punish an individual: This is to punish a person for something she did not do. Either corporations cannot be punished at all under French's theory, Danley argues, or individuals are made to suffer in their place, and are thus relegated to the status of second-rate citizens of the moral community. French's view of the corporation, concludes Danley, has some serious drawbacks. He suggests that a machine, the activities of which are dependent on persons, is a more adequate model for understanding corporate morality.

CORPORATE ACCOUNTABILITY AND THE BOARD OF DIRECTORS

Central to the issue of corporate legitimacy, responsibility, and liability taken up in Chapter 4 is the issue of corporate accountability. To whom ought corporations be accountable? How can such accountability be implemented? The authors included in Chapter 5 look not to regulations imposed on the corporation from outside, but on the corporate internal structure itself for answers to these questions. Because historically the board of directors has been conceived of as one important locus of corporate accountability and because suggestions for changes in the role, election, and staffing of boards have been at the heart of several important proposals for reform, it is appropriate that they focus their attention on the nature, role, and composition of corporate boards.

Traditionally, corporate governance has been conceived on a rough analogy with the American political system. As the owners of the corporation, stockholders elect representatives—the board of directors—to establish broad objectives and direct corporate activities. The directors in turn select corporate officers to execute their policies. Management is thus accountable to the board of directors, and the board to stockholders.

But it is increasingly unclear that this picture represents the reality of corporate governance. Such writers as Ralph Nader, Mark Green, and Joel Seligman hold that management really controls the election of board members through its power over the machinery of proxy voting. The board, they claim, does not provide a check on the power of management; it does not really make policies or select executive officers, but routinely rubber-stamps the decisions of management.

Furthermore, as a 1978 press release from the Senate Committee on Governmental Affairs indicates, corporate boards are so tightly interlocked that what power they do have is concentrated in the hands of a small elite. The overwhelming potential for conflicts of interest further impedes boards ability to check management power.

Nader, Green, and Seligman see an urgent need for a truly effective board that will make accountable the unbridled power of management. Their suggestions for achieving this goal include a revamping of the shareholder electoral system; the institutionalizing of a new profession, that of the professional director who devotes full time to supervising the activities of the corporation; and the prohibition of interlocking directorates.

Still other issues of corporate governance are raised by the vast power of the corporation in modern society. The traditional model of corporate governance assumes that the most important constituency of the corporation is its stockholders, and that it is primarily to stockholders that the corporation ought to be accountable. But perhaps this is not so. The view that the crucial form of corporate accountability is accountability to stockholders is based on the assumption that the corporation is a piece of private property; the stockholders are the owners of the corporation and therefore the corporation is answerable only to them. But we have already noted that this assumption has been challenged. Brenkert pointed out that social responsibility seems to require that the corporation not be thought of as private, but as a public institution. If this is true, presumably there ought to be some way to represent all relevant constituencies of the corporation in its internal structure. Milton Friedman has argued that to ask corporations to exercise "social" power is to make them into miniature governments; but Nader, Green, and Seligman claim that corporations do in fact exert such power and that they are governments in a sense for this reason. To ask corporations to be accountable only to stockholders is to permit governments to exist without the consent of the governed, an idea which is fundamentally at odds with the political philosophy of the United States. The election of "public interest directors," each of whom is placed in charge of overseeing such areas as consumer protection, employee welfare, and stockholder rights, may be one way to ensure corporate accountability to those whom it affects. And Nader, Green, and Seligman propose that the board should be made up only of "outside" directors—persons who have no other relationship to the corporation.

The interpretation of the corporation as a public institution is precisely what Irving Shapiro objects to in his essay on corporate governance. Corporations are not analogous to governments, he argues. They are private enterprises formed to execute the essential task of providing goods and services—a task, Shapiro suggests, government could not perform efficiently. The corporation has an important external locus of accountability government does not: the competition engendered by the free market system. For these reasons Shapiro defends the rationale behind the present system of corporate governance. He does not believe that a radical overhaul is required.

Shapiro does not look favorably on proposals that the board contain more "outside" directors representative of various interest groups. Although independence of judgment is crucial in a corporate director, he fears that outside directors may lack the depth of understanding of an industry's problems necessary for informed decision making. Such directors might find themselves dependent on the explanations of the chief executive officer, and thus unable to exert adequate control over management activities. And although the presence of public interest directors on the board could generate a healthy tension, it might also lead to conflicts of interest and paralysis. A clear division of labor between boards of directors and management and a conscientious execution of their respective tasks, Shapiro concludes, are all that is necessary to produce an effective system of corporate governance that ensures accountability.

In "Who Should Control the Corporation?" Henry Mintzberg hopes to clarify the debate about who should control the corporation. He argues that the answer we eventually accept will determine what kind of society we and our children will live in. He identifies a number of different possibilities for controlling the corporation, such as nationalize it, regulate it, trust it, and ignore it. He considers the implications of the various alternatives, and concludes that the one thing we cannot do is hope for the best and ignore the power and influence of corporations. They are much too influential a force in our lives. The challenge, he concludes, is to find ways to direct and channel the power of corporations in ways that ensure that they remain responsive to our interests.

In the next two articles in Chapter 5 we consider some of the consequences of management control of corporations. In "Corporate Governance: Who Is In Control Here?," Dan Dalton argues that despite some pressures to the contrary, management remains firmly in charge of publicly traded corporations. To illustrate management's ability to retain control even in the face of determined attempts to wrench it away, he uses a scenario involving an apartment complex to show how managers can manipulate the outcome of battles for corporate control. He describes how managers and others can use a variety of devices to their advantage and to the detriment of one of the primary stakeholders, those who own shares in the corporation. These devices—golden parachutes, greenmail, poison pills, scorched earth, and so on—can be used by management to prevent the corporation from being sold to the highest bidder, and thus prevent the stockholders from getting the best price for their stock. Dalton argues that although these devices are legal, they are not in the interests of stockholders and thus are not acceptable.

In the final article in this chapter Anthony Buono investigates the consequences of management control for another stakeholder group, the employees. Due to downsizing and restructuring, in recent years many large corporations have drastically reduced the size of their workforce, sometimes eliminating thousands of employees in a single day. Clearly, the power to affect the lives of so many people in such a fundamental way must be used with the utmost care and only in situations where no realistic alternative exists. If there is no such alternative, Buono says, downsizing and restructuring are not inherently unethical business practices. Sometimes, for example, these actions are taken out of economic necessity. But all too often, he argues, management's approach to restructuring ignores the real human costs involved. This leads to a decrease in loyalty and an increase in cynicism among employees, which is detrimental to creating an ethical corporate climate.

Buono points out that many employees of large corporations assumed a kind of psychological contract between themselves and the corporation, a set of expectations based on a sense of reciprocity between employees and employers. People came to believe that a job was more than just a paycheck—that they would be rewarded for their good work with steady employment and growth opportunities. But today, Buono says, termination decisions are all too often not based on performance. They are nothing other than cost containment strategies that give little thought to the impact on employees' lives.

Buono concludes that if there are to be moral corporate cultures—cultures in which employees are treated as ends and not mere means—managers must have empathy for employees and not employ coercive tactics. This means that restructuring corporations must take place in an ethical framework that does not devalue persons or treat them as counters in a utilitarian calculus.

The articles by Dalton and Buono provide a stark illustration of one of Mintzberg's main points. Regardless of how we decide to control the modern corporation, the one thing we cannot afford to do is ignore it. Corporations are one of the most powerful forces in our society, and with power comes the potential for the abuse of power. In the past that potential has often been realized, sometimes leading to devastating economic and social consequences. To assume that nothing can be done to control the abuse of corporate power and prevent such consequences, or to pretend that they cannot or will not occur in the future, is to invite calamity.

CHAPTER 3

Legitimacy and Responsibility

The Social Responsibility of Business Is to Increase Its Profits

Milton Friedman
Senior Research Fellow, Hoover Institution, Stanford University, and Nobel Prize-winning economist

When I hear businessmen speak eloquently about the "social responsibilities of business in a free-enterprise system," I am reminded of the wonderful line about the Frenchman who discovered at the age of 70 that he had been speaking prose all his life. The businessmen believe that they are defending free enterprise when they declaim that business is not concerned "merely" with profit but also with promoting desirable "social" ends; that business has a "social conscience" and takes seriously its responsibilities for providing employment, eliminating discrimination, avoiding pollution and whatever else may be the catchwords of the contemporary crop of reformers. In fact they are—or would be if they or anyone else took them seriously—preaching pure and unadulterated socialism. Businessmen who talk this way are unwitting puppets of the intellectual forces that have been undermining the basis of a free society these past decades.

The discussions of the "social responsibilities of business" are notable for their analytical looseness and lack of rigor. What does it mean to say that "business" has responsibilities? Only people can have responsibilities. A corporation is an artificial person and in this sense may have artificial responsibilities, but "business" as a whole cannot be said to have responsibilities, even in this vague sense. The first step toward clarity in examining the doctrine of the social responsibility of business is to ask precisely what it implies for whom.

Presumably, the individuals who are to be responsible are businessmen, which means individual proprietors or corporate executives. Most of the discussion of social responsibility is directed at corporations, so in what follows I shall mostly neglect the individual proprietors and speak of corporate executives.

In a free-enterprise, private-property system, a corporate executive is an employee of the owners

From *The New York Times Magazine,* September 13, 1970.

of the business. He has direct responsibility to his employers. That responsibility is to conduct the business in accordance with their desires, which generally will be to make as much money as possible while conforming to the basic rules of the society, both those embodied in law and those embodied in ethical custom. Of course, in some cases his employers may have a different objective. A group of persons might establish a corporation for an eleemosynary purpose—for example, a hospital or a school. The manager of such a corporation will not have money profit as his objectives but the rendering of certain services.

In either case, the key point is that, in his capacity as a corporate executive, the manager is the agent of the individuals who own the corporation or establish the eleemosynary institution, and his primary responsibility is to them.

Needless to say, this does not mean that it is easy to judge how well he is performing his task. But at least the criterion of performance is straightforward, and the persons among whom a voluntary contractual arrangement exists are clearly defined.

Of course, the corporate executive is also a person in his own right. As a person, he may have many other responsibilities that he recognizes or assumes voluntarily—to his family, his conscience, his feelings of charity, his church, his clubs, his city, his country. He may feel impelled by these responsibilities to devote part of his income to causes he regards as worthy, to refuse to work for particular corporations, even to leave his job, for example, to join his country's armed forces. If we wish, we may refer to some of these responsibilities as "social responsibilities." But in these respects he is acting as a principal, not as an agent; he is spending his own money or time or energy, not the money of his employers or the time or energy he has contracted to devote to their purposes. If these are "social responsibilities," they are the social responsibilities of individuals, not of business.

What does it mean to say that the corporate executive has a "social responsibility" in his capacity as businessman? If this statement is not pure rhetoric, it must mean that he is to act in some way that is not in the interest of his employers. For example, that he is to refrain from increasing the price of the product in order to contribute to the social objective of preventing inflation, even though a price increase would be in the best interests of the corporation. Or that he is to make expenditures on reducing pollution beyond the amount that is in the best interests of the corporation or that is required by law in order to contribute to the social objective of improving the environment. Or that, at the expense of corporate profits, he is to hire "hard-core" unemployed instead of better qualified available workmen to contribute to the social objective of reducing poverty.

In each of these cases, the corporate executive would be spending someone else's money for a general social interest. Insofar as his actions in accord with his "social responsibility" reduce returns to stockholders, he is spending their money. Insofar as his actions raise the price to customers, he is spending the customers' money. Insofar as his actions lower the wages of some employees, he is spending their money.

The stockholders or the customers or the employees could separately spend their own money on the particular action if they wished to do so. The executive is exercising a distinct "social responsibility," rather than serving as an agent of the stockholders or the customers or the employees, only if he spends the money in a different way than they would have spent it.

But if he does this, he is in effect imposing taxes, on the one hand, and deciding how the tax proceeds shall be spent, on the other.

This process raises political questions on two levels: principle and consequences. On the level of political principle, the imposition of taxes and the expenditure of tax proceeds are governmental functions. We have established elaborate constitutional, parliamentary and judicial provisions to control these functions, to assure that taxes are imposed so far as possible in accordance with the preferences and desires of the public—after all, "taxation without representation" was one of the battle cries of the American Revolution. We have a system of checks and balances to separate the legislative function of imposing taxes and enacting expenditures from the executive function of collecting taxes and administering expenditure programs and from the judicial function of mediating disputes and interpreting the law.

Here the businessman—self-selected or appointed directly or indirectly by stockholders—is to be simultaneously legislator, executive and jurist. He is to decide whom to tax by how much and for what purpose, and he is to spend the proceeds—all this guided only by general exhortations from on high to restrain inflation, improve the environment, fight poverty and so on and on.

The whole justification for permitting the corporate executive to be selected by the stockholders is that the executive is an agent serving the interests of his principal. This justification disappears when the corporate executive imposes taxes and spends the proceeds for "social" purposes. He becomes in effect a public employee, a civil servant, even though he remains in name an employee of a private enterprise. On grounds of political principle, it is intolerable that such civil servants—insofar as their actions in the name of social responsibility are real and not just window-dressing—should be selected as they are now. If they are to be civil servants, then they must be elected through a political process. If they are to impose taxes and make expenditures to foster "social" objectives, then political machinery must be set up to make the assessment of taxes and to determine through a political process the objectives to be served.

This is the basic reason why the doctrine of "social responsibility" involves the acceptance of the socialist view that political mechanisms, not market mechanisms, are the appropriate way to determine the allocation of scarce resources to alternative uses.

On the grounds of consequences, can the corporate executive in fact discharge his alleged "social responsibilities"? On the other hand, suppose he could get away with spending the stockholders' or customers' or employees' money. How is he to know how to spend it? He is told that he must contribute to fighting inflation. How is he to know what action of his will contribute to that end? He is presumably an expert in running his company—in producing a product or selling it or financing it. But nothing about his selection makes him an expert on inflation. Will his holding down the price of his product reduce inflationary pressure? Or, by leaving more spending power in the hands of his customers, simply divert it elsewhere? Or, by forcing him to produce less because of the lower price, will it simply contribute to shortages? Even if he could answer these questions, how much cost is he justified in imposing on his stockholders, customers and employees for this social purpose? What is his appropriate share and what is the appropriate share of others?

And, whether he wants to or not, can he get away with spending his stockholders', customers' or employees' money? Will not the stockholders fire him? (Either the present ones or those who take over when his actions in the name of social responsibility have reduced the corporation's profits and the price of its stock.) His customers and his employees can desert him for other producers and employers less scrupulous in exercising their social responsibilities.

This facet of "social responsibility" doctrine is brought into sharp relief when the doctrine is used to justify wage restraint by trade unions. The conflict of interest is naked and clear when union officials are asked to subordinate the interest of their members to some more general purpose. If the union officials try to enforce wage restraint, the consequence is likely to be wildcat strikes, rank-and-file revolts and the emergence of strong competitors for their jobs. We thus have the ironic phenomenon that union leaders—at least in the U.S.—have objected to Government interference with the market far more consistently and courageously than have business leaders.

The difficulty of exercising "social responsibility" illustrates, of course, the great virtue of private competitive enterprise—it forces people to be responsible for their own actions and makes it difficult for them to "exploit" other people for either selfish or unselfish purposes. They can do good—but only at their own expense.

Many a reader who has followed the argument this far may be tempted to remonstrate that it is all well and good to speak of Government's having the responsibility to impose taxes and determine expenditures for such "social" purposes as controlling pollution or training the hard-core unemployed, but that the problems are too urgent to wait on the slow course of political processes, that the exercise of social responsibility by businessmen is a quicker and surer way to solve pressing current problems.

Aside from the question of fact—I share Adam Smith's skepticism about the benefits that can be expected from "those who affected to trade for the public good"—this argument must be rejected on grounds of principle. What it amounts to is an assertion that those who favor the taxes and expenditures in question have failed to persuade a majority of their fellow citizens to be of like mind and that they are seeking to attain by undemocratic procedures what they cannot attain by democratic procedures. In a free society, it is hard for "evil" people to do "evil," especially since one man's good is another's evil.

I have, for simplicity, concentrated on the special case of the corporate executive, except only for the brief digression on trade unions. But precisely the same argument applies to the newer phenomenon of calling upon stockholders to require corporations to exercise social responsibility (the recent G.M. crusade for example). In most of these cases, what is in effect involved is some stockholders trying to get other stockholders (or customers or employees) to contribute against their will to "social" causes favored by the activists. Insofar as they succeed, they are again imposing taxes and spending the proceeds.

The situation of the individual proprietor is somewhat different. If he acts to reduce the returns of his enterprise in order to exercise his "social responsibility," he is spending his own money, not someone else's. If he wishes to spend his money on such purposes, that is his right, and I cannot see that there is any objection to his doing so. In the process, he, too, may impose costs on employees and customers. However, because he is far less likely than a large corporation or union to have monopolistic power, any such side effects will tend to be minor.

Of course, in practice the doctrine of social responsibility is frequently a cloak for actions that are justified on other grounds rather than a reason for those actions.

To illustrate, it may well be in the long-run interest of a corporation that is a major employer in a small community to devote resources to providing amenities to that community or to improving its government. That may make it easier to attract desirable employees, it may reduce the wage bill or lessen losses from pilferage and sabotage or have other worthwhile effects. Or it may be that, given the laws about the deductibility of corporate charitable contributions, the stockholders can contribute more to charities they favor by having the corporation make the gift than by doing it themselves, since they can in that way contribute an amount that would otherwise have been paid as corporate taxes.

In each of these—and many similar—cases, there is a strong temptation to rationalize these actions as an exercise of "social responsibility." In the present climate of opinion, with its widespread aversion to "capitalism," "profits," the "soulless corporation" and so on, this is one way for a corporation to generate goodwill as a by-product of expenditures that are entirely justified in its own self-interest.

It would be inconsistent of me to call on corporate executives to refrain from this hypocritical window-dressing because it harms the foundations of a free society. That would be to call on them to exercise a "social responsibility"! If our institutions, and the attitudes of the public make it in their self-interest to cloak their actions in this way, I cannot summon much indignation to denounce them. At the same time, I can express admiration for those individual proprietors or owners of closely held corporations or stockholders of more broadly held corporations who disdain such tactics as approaching fraud.

Whether blameworthy or not, the use of the cloak of social responsibility, and the nonsense spoken in its name by influential and prestigious businessmen, does clearly harm the foundations of a free society. I have been impressed time and again by the schizophrenic character of many businessmen. They are capable of being extremely far-sighted and clear-headed in matters that are internal to their businesses. They are incredibly short-sighted and muddle-headed in matters that are outside their businesses but affect the possible survival of business in general. This short-sightedness is strikingly exemplified in the calls from many businessmen for wage and price guidelines or controls or income policies. There is nothing that could do more in a brief period to destroy a market system and replace it by a centrally controlled system than effective governmental control of prices and wages.

The short-sightedness is also exemplified in speeches by businessmen on social responsibility. This may gain them kudos in the short run. But it helps to strengthen the already too prevalent view that the pursuit of profits is wicked and immoral and must be curbed and controlled by external forces. Once this view is adopted, the external forces that curb the market will not be the social consciences, however highly developed, of the pontificating executives; it will be the iron fist of government bureaucrats. Here, as with price and wage controls, businessmen seem to me to reveal a suicidal impulse.

The political principle that underlies the market mechanism is unanimity. In an ideal free market resting on private property, no individual can coerce any other, all cooperation is voluntary, all parties to such cooperation benefit or they need not participate. There are no values, no "social" responsibilities in any sense other than the shared values and responsibilities of individuals. Society is a collection of individuals and of the various groups they voluntarily form.

The political principle that underlies the political mechanism is conformity. The individual must serve a more general social interest—whether that be determined by a church or a dictator or a majority. The individual may have a vote and say in what is to be done, but if he is overruled, he must conform. It is appropriate for some to require others to contribute to a general social purpose whether they wish to or not.

Unfortunately, unanimity is not always feasible. There are some respects in which conformity appears unavoidable, so I do not see how one can avoid the use of the political mechanism altogether.

But the doctrine of "social responsibility" taken seriously would extend the scope of the political mechanism to every human activity. It does not differ in philosophy from the most explicitly collectivist doctrine. It differs only by professing to believe that collectivist ends can be attained without collectivist means. That is why, in my book "Capitalism and Freedom," I have called it a "fundamentally subversive doctrine" in a free society, and have said that in such a society, "there is one and only one social responsibility of business—to use its resources and engage in activities designed to increase its profits so long as it stays within the rules of the game, which is to say, engages in open and free competition without deception or fraud."

Why Shouldn't Corporations Be Socially Responsible?

Christopher D. Stone
Crocker Professor of Law, University of Southern California

The opposition to corporate social responsibility comprises at least four related though separable positions. I would like to challenge the fundamental assumption that underlies all four of them. Each assumes in its own degree that the managers of the corporation are to be steered almost wholly by profit, rather than by what they think proper for society on the whole. Why should this be so? So far as ordinary morals are concerned, we often expect human beings to act in a fashion that is calculated to benefit others, rather than themselves, and commend them for it. Why should the matter be different with corporations?

THE PROMISSORY ARGUMENT

The most widespread but least persuasive arguments advanced by the "antiresponsibility" forces take the form of a moral claim based upon the corporation's supposed obligations to its shareholders. In its baldest and least tenable form, it is presented as though management's obligation rested upon the keeping of a promise—that the management of the corporation "promised" the shareholders that it would maximize the shareholders' profits. But this simply isn't so.

Consider for contrast the case where a widow left a large fortune goes to a broker, asking him to invest and manage her money so as to maximize her return. The broker, let us suppose, accepts the money and the conditions. In such a case, there would be no disagreement that the broker had made a promise to the widow, and if he invested her money in some venture that struck his fancy for any reason other than that it would increase her fortune, we would be inclined to advance a moral (as well, perhaps, as a legal) claim against him. Generally, at least, we believe in the keeping of promises; the broker, we should say, had violated a promissory obligation to the widow.

But that simple model is hardly the one that obtains between the management of major corporations and their shareholders. Few if any American shareholders ever put their money into a corporation upon the express promise of management that the company would be operated so as to maximize their returns. Indeed, few American shareholders ever put their money directly *into* a corporation at all. Most of the shares outstanding today were issued years ago and found their way to their current shareholders only circuitously. In almost all cases, the current shareholder gave his money to some prior shareholder, who, in turn, had gotten it from B, who, in turn, had gotten it from A, and so on back to the purchaser of the original issue, who, many years before, had bought the shares through an underwriting syndicate. In the course of these transactions, one of the basic elements that exists in the broker case is missing: The manager of the corporation, unlike the broker, was never even offered a chance to refuse the shareholder's "terms" (if they were that) to maximize the shareholder's profits.

There are two other observations to be made about the moral argument based on a supposed promise running from the management to the shareholders. First, even if we do infer from all the circumstances a "promise" running from the management to the shareholders, but not one, or not one of comparable weight running elsewhere (to the company's employees, customers, neighbors, etc.), we ought to keep in mind that as a moral matter (which is what we are discussing here) sometimes it is deemed morally justified to break promises (even to break the law) in the furtherance of other social interests of higher concern. Promises can advance moral arguments, by way of creating presumptions, but few of us believe that promises, per se, can end them. My promise to appear in class on time would not ordinarily justify me from refusing to give aid to a drowning man. In other words, even if management *had* made an express promise to its shareholders to "maximize your profits," (a) I am not persuaded that the ordinary person would interpret it to mean "maximize *in every way you can possibly get away with,* even if that means polluting the environment, ignoring or breaking the law"; and (b) I am not persuaded that, even if it were interpreted as so blanket a promise, most people would not suppose it ought—morally—to be broken in some cases.

Finally, even if, in the face of all these considerations, one still believes that there is an overriding, unbreakable, promise of some sort running from management to the shareholders, I do not think that it can be construed to be any stronger than one running to existent shareholders, arising from their expectations as measured by the price they paid. That is to say, there is nothing in the argument from promises that would wed us to a regime in which management was bound to maximize the income of shareholders. The argument might go so far as to support compensation for existent shareholders if the society chose to announce that henceforth management would have other specified obligations, thereby driving the price of shares to a lower adjustment level. All future shareholders would take with "warning" of, and a price that discounted for, the new "risks" of shareholding (i.e., the "risks" that management might put corporate resources to pro bonum ends).

THE AGENCY ARGUMENT

Related to the promissory argument but requiring less stretching of the facts is an argument from agency principles. Rather than trying to infer a promise by management to the shareholders, this argument is based on the idea that the shareholders designated the management their agents. This is the position advanced by Milton Friedman in his *New York Times* article. "The key point," he says, "is that . . . the manager is the agent of the individuals who own the corporation. . . ."[1]

Friedman, unfortunately, is wrong both as to the state of the law (the directors are *not* mere agents of the shareholders)[2] and on his assumption as to the facts of corporate life (surely it is closer to the truth that in major corporations the shareholders are *not,* in any meaningful sense, selecting the directors; management is more often using its control over the proxy machinery to designate who the directors shall be, rather than the other way around).

What Friedman's argument comes down to is that for some reason the directors ought morally to consider themselves more the agents for the shareholders than for the customers, creditors, the state, or the corporation's immediate neighbors. But why? And to what extent? Throwing in terms like "principal" and "agent" begs the fundamental questions.

What is more, the "agency" argument is not only morally inconclusive, it is embarrassingly at odds with the way in which supposed "agents" actually behave. If the managers truly considered themselves the agents of the shareholders, as agents they would be expected to show an interest in determining how their principals wanted them to act—and to act accordingly. In the controversy over Dow's production of napalm, for example, one would expect, on this model, that Dow's management would have been glad to have the napalm question put to the shareholders at a shareholders' meeting. In fact, like most major companies faced with shareholder requests to include "social action" measures on proxy statements, it fought the proposal tooth and claw.[3] It is a peculiar agency where the "agents" will go to such lengths (even spending tens of thousands of dollars of their "principals' " money in legal fees) to resist the determination of what their "principals" want.

THE ROLE ARGUMENT

An argument so closely related to the argument from promises and agency that it does not demand extensive additional remarks is a contention based upon supposed considerations of *role.* Sometimes in moral discourse, as well as in law, we assign obligations to people on the basis of their having assumed some role or status, independent of any specific verbal promise they made. Such obligations are assumed to run from a captain to a seaman (and vice versa), from a doctor to a patient, or from a parent to a child. The antiresponsibility forces are on somewhat stronger grounds resting their position on this basis, because the model more nearly accords with the facts—that is, management never actually promised the shareholders that they would maximize the shareholders' investment, nor did the shareholders designate the directors their agents for this express purpose. The directors and top management are, as lawyers would say, fiduciaries. But what does this leave us? So far as the directors are fiduciaries of the shareholders in a legal sense, of course they are subject to the legal limits on fiduciaries—that is to say, they cannot engage in self-dealing, "waste" of corporate assets, and the like. But I do not understand any proresponsibility advocate to be demanding such corporate largesse as would expose the officers to legal liability; what we are talking about are expenditures on, for example, pollution control, above the amount the company is required to pay by law, but less than an amount so extravagant as to constitute a violation of these legal fiduciary duties. (Surely no court in America would enjoin a corporation from spending more to reduce pollution than the law requires.) What is there about assuming the role of corporate officer that makes it immoral for a manger to involve a corporation in these expenditures? A father, one would think, would have stronger obligations to his children by virtue of his status than a corporate manager to the corporation's shareholders. Yet few would regard it as a compelling moral argument if a father were to distort facts about his child on a scholarship application form on the grounds that he had obligations to advance his child's career; nor would we consider it a strong moral argument if a father were to leave unsightly refuse piled on his lawn, spilling over into the street, on the plea that he had obligations to give every moment of his attention to his children, and was thus too busy to cart his refuse away.

Like the other supposed moral arguments, the one from role suffers from the problem that the strongest moral obligations one can discover have at most only prima facie force, and it is not apparent why those obligations should predominate over some contrary social obligations that could be advanced.

Then too, when one begins comparing and weighing the various moral obligations, those running back to the shareholder seem fairly weak by comparison to the claims of others. For one thing, there is the consideration of alternatives. If the shareholder is dissatisfied with the direction the corporation is taking, he can sell out, and if he does so quickly enough, his losses may be slight. On the other hand, as Ted Jacobs observes, "those most vitally affected by corporate decisions—people who work in the plants, buy the products, and consume the effluents—cannot remove themselves from the structure with a phone call."[4]

THE "POLESTAR" ARGUMENT

It seems to me that the strongest moral argument corporate executives can advance for looking solely to profits is not one that is based on a supposed express, or even implied promise to the shareholder. Rather, it is one that says, if the managers act in such fashion as to maximize profits—if they act *as though* they had promised the shareholders they would do so—then it will be best for all of us. This argument might be called the polestar argument, for its appeal to the interests of the shareholders is not justified on supposed obligations to the shareholders per se, but as a means of charting a straight course toward what is best for the society as a whole.

Underlying the polestar argument are a number of assumptions—some express and some implied. There is, I suspect, an implicit positivism among its supporters—a feeling (whether its proponents own up to it or not) that moral judgments are peculiar, arbitrary, or vague—perhaps even "meaningless" in the philosophic sense of not being amenable to rational discussion. To those who take this position, profits (or sales, or price-earnings ratios) at least provide some solid, tangible standard by which participants in the organization can measure their successes and failures, with some efficiency, in the narrow sense, resulting for the entire group. Sometimes the polestar position is based upon a related view—not that the moral issues that underlie social choices are meaningless, but that resolving them calls for special expertise. "I don't know any investment adviser whom I would care to act in my behalf in any matter except turning a profit. . . . The value of these specialists . . . lies in their limitations; they ought not allow themselves to see so much of the world that they become distracted."[5] A slightly modified point emphasizes not that the executives lack moral or social expertise per se, but that they lack the social authority to make policy choices. Thus, Friedman objects that if a corporate director took "social purposes" into account, he would become "in effect a public employee, a civil servant. . . . On grounds of political principle, it is intolerable that such civil servants . . . should be selected as they are now."[6]

I do not want to get too deeply involved in each of these arguments. That the moral judgments underlying policy choices are vague, I do not doubt—although I am tempted to observe that when you get right down to it, a wide range of actions taken by businessmen every day, supposedly based on solid calculations of "profit," are probably as rooted in hunches and intuition as judgments of ethics. I do not disagree either that, ideally, we prefer those who have control over our lives to be politically accountable; although here, too, if we were to pursue the matter in detail we would want to inspect both the premise of this argument, that corporate managers are not *presently* custodians of discretionary power over us anyway, and also its logical implications: Friedman's point that "if they are to be civil servants, then they must be selected through a political process"[7] is not, as Friedman regards it, a *reductio ad absurdum*—not, at any rate, to Ralph Nader and others who want publicly elected directors.

The reason for not pursuing these counterarguments at length is that, whatever reservations one might have, we can agree that there is a germ of validity to what the "antis" are saying. But their essential failure is in not pursuing the alternatives. Certainly, *to the extent* that the forces of the market and the law can keep the corporation within desirable bounds, it may be better to trust them than to have corporate managers implementing their own vague and various notions of what is best for the rest of us. But are the "antis" blind to the fact that there are circumstances in which the law—and the forces of the market—are simply not competent to keep the corporation under control? The shortcomings of these traditional restraints on corporate conduct are critical to understand, not merely for the defects they point up in the "antis" position. More important, identifying where the traditional forces are inadequate is the first step in the design of new and alternative measures of corporate control.

NOTES

1. *New York Times,* September 12, 1962, sect. 6. p. 33, col. 2.
2. See, for example, *Automatic Self-Cleansing Filter Syndicate Co. Ltd. v. Cunninghame* (1906) 2 Ch. 34.
3. "Dow Shalt Not Kill," in S. Prakash Sethi, *Up Against the Corporate Wall,* Englewood Cliffs, N.J.: Prentice-Hall, 1971), pp. 236–266, and the opinion of Judge Tamm in *Medical Committee for Human Rights v.* S.E.C., 432 F.2d 659 (D.C. Cir. 1970), and the dissent of Mr. Justice Douglas in the same case in the U.S. Supreme Court, 404 U.S. 403, 407–411 (1972).
4. Theodore J. Jacobs, "Pollution, Consumerism, Accountability," *Center Magazine* 5, 1 (January-February 1971): 47.
5. Walter Goodman, "Stocks Without Sin." *Harper's,* August 1971, p. 66.
6. *New York Times,* September 12, 1962, sec. 6, p. 122, col. 3.
7. Ibid., p. 122, cols. 3–4.

A Stakeholder Theory of the Modern Corporation: Kantian Capitalism

William M. Evan and R. Edward Freeman

Evan—Professor of Sociology and Management, The Wharton School, University of Pennsylvania.

Freeman—Olsson Professor of Business Administration, The Darden School, University of Virginia.

INTRODUCTION

> Corporations have ceased to be merely legal devices through which the private business transactions of individuals may be carried on. Though still much used for this purpose, the corporate form has acquired a larger significance. The corporation has, in fact, become both a method of property tenure and a means of organizing economic life. Grown to tremendous proportions, there may be said to have evolved a "corporate system"—which has attracted to itself a combination of attributes and powers, and has attained a degree of prominence entitling it to be dealt with as a major social institution.[1]

Despite these prophetic words of Berle and Means (1932), scholars and managers alike continue to hold sacred the view that managers bear a special

From *Ethical Theory and Business,* Tom L. Beauchamp and Norman E. Bowie, eds., 3rd edition (Englewood Cliffs, NJ: Prentice-Hall, Inc., 1988.) Reprinted by permission of the authors.

relationship to the stockholders in the firm. Since stockholders own shares in the firm, they have certain rights and privileges, which must be granted to them by management, as well as by others. . . . Sanctions, in the form of "the law of corporations," and other protective mechanisms in the form of social custom, accepted management practice, myth, and ritual, are thought to reinforce the assumption of the primacy of the stockholder.

The purpose of this paper is to pose several challenges to this assumption, from within the framework of managerial capitalism, and to suggest the bare bones of an alternative theory, *a stakeholder theory of the modern corporation.* We do not seek the demise of the modern corporation, either intellectually or in fact. Rather, we seek its transformation. In the words of Neurath, we shall attempt to "rebuild the ship, plank by plank, while it remains afloat."[2]

Our thesis is that we can revitalize the concept of managerial capitalism by replacing the notion that managers have a duty to stockholders with the concept that managers bear a fiduciary relationship to stakeholders. Stakeholders are those groups who have a stake in or claim on the firm. Specifically we include suppliers, customers, employees, stockholders, and the local community, as well as management in its role as agent for these groups. We argue that the legal, economic, political, and moral challenges to the currently received theory of the firm, as a nexus of contracts among the owners of the factors of production and customers, require us to revise this concept along essentially Kantian lines. That is, each of these stakeholder groups has a right not to be treated as a means to some end, and therefore must participate in determining the future direction of the firm in which they have a stake.[3] . . .

The crux of our argument is that we must reconceptualize the firm around the following question: For whose benefit and at whose expense should the firm be managed? We shall set forth such a reconceptualization in the form of a *stakeholder theory of the firm.* We shall then critically examine the stakeholder view and its implications for the future of the capitalist system.

THE ATTACK ON MANAGERIAL CAPITALISM

The Legal Argument

The basic idea of managerial capitalism is that in return for controlling the firm, management vigorously pursues the interests of stockholders. Central to the managerial view of the firm is the idea that management can pursue market transactions with suppliers and customers in an unconstrained manner.[4]

The law of corporations gives a less clear-cut answer to the question: In whose interest and for whose benefit should the modern corporation be governed? While it says that the corporations should be run primarily in the interests of the stockholders in the firm, it says further that the corporation exists "in contemplation of the law" and has personality as a "legal person," limited liability for its actions, and immortality, since its existence transcends that of its members.[5] Therefore, directors and other officers of the firm have a fiduciary obligation to stockholders in the sense that the "affairs of the corporation" must be conducted in the interest of the stockholders. And stockholders can theoretically bring suit against those directors and managers for doing otherwise. But since the corporation is a legal person, existing in contemplation of the law, managers of the corporation are constrained by law.

Until recently, this was no constraint at all. In this century, however, . . . the law has evolved to effectively constrain the pursuit of stockholder interests at the expense of other claimants on the firm. It has, in effect, required that the claims of customers, suppliers, local communities, and employees be taken into consideration, though in general they are subordinated to the claims of stockholders. . . .

For instance, the doctrine of "privity of contract," as articulated in *Winterbottom v. Wright* in 1842, has been eroded by recent developments in products liability law. Indeed, *Greenman v. Yuba Power* gives the manufacturer strict liability for damage caused by its products, even though the seller has exercised all possible care in the preparation and sale of the product and the consumer has not bought the product from nor entered into any contractual arrangement with the manufacturer. Caveat emptor has been replaced, in large part, with caveat venditor.[6] The Consumer Product Safety Commission has the power to enact product recalls, and in 1980 one U.S. automobile company recalled more cars than it built. . . . Some industries are required to provide information to customers about a product's ingredients, whether or not the customers want and are willing to pay for this information.[7]

In short, the supplier-firm-customer chain is far from that visualized by managerial capitalism. In their roles as customers and suppliers, firms have benefitted from these constraints, but they have been harmed to the degree to which the constraints have meant loss of profit. . . .

The same argument is applicable to management's dealings with employees. The National Labor Relations Act gave employees the right to unionize and to bargain in good faith. It set up the National Labor Relations Board to enforce these rights with management. The Equal Pay Act of 1963 and Title VII of the Civil Rights Act of 1964 constrain management from discrimination in hiring practices; these have been followed with the Age Discrimination in Employment Act of 1967.[8] The emergence of a body of administrative case law arising from labor-management disputes and the historic settling of discrimination claims with large employers such as AT&T have caused the emergence of a body of practice in the corporation that is consistent with the legal guarantee of the rights of the employees. . . . The law has protected the due process rights of those employees who enter into collective bargaining agreements with management. As of the present, however, only 30 percent of the labor force are participating in such agreements; this has prompted one labor law scholar to propose a statutory law prohibiting dismissals of the 70 percent of the work force not protected.[9] . . .

The law has also protected the interests of local communities. The Clean Air Act and Clean Water Act have constrained management from "spoiling the commons." In an historic case, *Marsh v. Alabama,* the Supreme Court ruled that a company-owned town was subject to the provisions of the U.S. Constitution, thereby guaranteeing the rights of local citizens and negating the "property rights" of the firm. Some states and municipalities have gone further and passed laws preventing firms from moving plants or limiting when and how plants can be closed. In sum, there is much current legal activity in this area to constrain management's pursuit of stockholders' interests at the expense of the local communities in which the firm operates. . . .

We have argued that the result of such changes in the legal system can be viewed as giving some rights to those groups that have a claim on the firm, for example, customers, suppliers, employees, local communities, stockholders, and management. It raises the question, at the core of a theory of the firm: In whose interest and for whose benefit should the firm be managed? The answer proposed by managerial capitalism is clearly "the stockholders," but we have argued that the law has been progressively circumscribing this answer.

The Economic Argument

In its pure ideological form managerial capitalism seeks to maximize the interests of stockholders. In its perennial criticism of government regulation, management espouses the "invisible hand" doctrine. It contends that it creates the greatest good for the greatest number, and therefore government need not intervene. However, we know that externalities, moral hazards, and monopoly power exist in fact, whether or not they exist in theory. Further, some of the legal apparatus mentioned above has evolved to deal with just these issues.

The problem of the "tragedy of the commons" or the free-rider problem pervades the concept of public goods such as water and air. No one has an incentive to incur the cost of clean-up or the cost of nonpollution, since the marginal gain of one firm's action is small. Every firm reasons this way, and the result is pollution of water and air. Since the industrial revolution, firms have sought to internalize the benefits and externalize the costs of their actions. The cost must be borne by all, through taxation and regulation; hence we have the emergence of the environmental regulations of the 1970s.

Similarly, moral hazards arise when the purchaser of a good or service can pass along the cost of that good. There is no incentive to economize, on the part of either the producer or the consumer, and there is excessive use of the resources involved. The institutionalized practice of third-party payment in health care is a prime example.

Finally, we see the avoidance of competitive behavior on the part of firms, each seeking to monopolize a small portion of the market and not compete with one another. In a number of industries, oligopolies have emerged, and while there is questionable evidence that oligopolies are not the most efficient corporate form in some industries, suffice it to say that the potential for abuse of market power has again led to regulation of managerial activity. In the classic case, AT&T, arguably one of the great technological and managerial achievements of the century, was broken up into eight separate companies to prevent its abuse of monopoly power.

Externalities, moral hazards, and monopoly power have led to more external control on managerial capitalism. There are de facto constraints, due to these economic facts of life, on the ability of management to act in the interests of stockholders. . . .

A STAKEHOLDER THEORY OF THE FIRM

Foundations of a Theory

Two themes are present throughout our argument. The first is concerned with the rights and duties of the owners (and their agents) of private property, and the effects of this property on the rights of others. The second theme is concerned with the consequences of managerial capitalism and the effects of the modern corporation on the welfare of others. These themes represent two branches of modern moral theory, Kantianism and consequentialism, and they are pitted together as the main tension in most existing moral theories. Our purpose here is to argue that the stockholder theory of the firm seems to give precedence to one or the other interpretation, but that both are important in grounding a theory of the modern corporation. In other words, we need a theory that balances the rights of the claimants on the corporation with the consequences of the corporate form.

Those who question the legitimacy of the modern corporation altogether because of the evils of excessive corporate power usually believe that the corporation should have no right to decide how things are going to be for its constituents. While we believe that each person has the right to be treated not as a means to some corporate end but as an end in itself, we would not go so far as to say that the corporation has no rights whatsoever. Our more moderate stance is that if the modern corporation requires treating others as means to an end, then these others must agree on, and hence participate (or choose not to participate) in, the decisions to be used as such. Thus, property rights are legitimate but not absolute, particularly when they conflict with important rights of others. And any theory that is to be consistent with our considered judgment about rights must take such a balanced view. The right to property does not yield the right to treat others as means to an end, which is to say that property rights are not a license to ignore Kant's principle of respect for persons.

Those who question the legitimacy of the modern corporation altogether because of the resulting possibility of externalities or harm usually do not see that the corporation can be held accountable for its actions. We maintain that persons (even legal persons) are responsible for the consequences of their actions, regardless of how those actions are mediated, and must be able and willing to accept responsibility for them. Therefore, any theory that seeks to justify the corporate form must be based at least partially on the idea that the corporation and its managers as moral agents can be the cause of and can be held accountable for their actions.

In line with these two themes of rights and effects, . . . we suggest two principles that will serve as working rules, not absolutes, to guide us in addressing some of the foundational issues. We will not settle the thorny issues that these principles raise, but merely argue that any theory, including the stakeholder theory, must be consistent with these principles.

Principle of Corporate Rights (PCR). The corporation and its managers may not violate the legitimate rights of others to determine their own future.

Principle of Corporate Effects (PCE). The corporation and its managers are responsible for the effects of their actions on others.

The Stakeholder Concept

Corporations have stakeholders, that is, groups and individuals who benefit from or are harmed by, and whose rights are violated or respected by, corporate actions. The notion of stakeholder is built around the Principle of Corporate Rights (PCR) and the Principle of Corporate Effect (PCE). . . . The concept of stakeholders is a generalization of the notion of stockholders, who themselves have some special claim on the firm. Just as stockholders have a right to demand certain actions by management, so do other stakeholders have a right to make claims. The exact nature of these claims is a difficult question that we shall address, but the logic is identical to that of the stockholder theory. Stakes require action of a certain sort, and conflicting stakes require methods of resolution. . . .

Freeman and Reed (1983)[10] distinguish two senses of *stakeholder*. The "narrow definition" includes those groups who are vital to the survival and success of the corporation. The "wide-definition" includes any group or individual who can affect or is affected by the corporation. While the wide definition is more in keeping with PCE and PCR, it raises too many difficult issues. We shall begin with a more modest aim: to articulate a stakeholder theory using the narrow definition.

Stakeholders in the Modern Corporation

Figure 1 depicts the stakeholder in a typical large corporation. The stakes of each are reciprocal, since each can affect the other in terms of harms and benefits as well as rights and duties. The stakes of each are not univocal and would vary by particular corporation. We merely set forth some general notions that seem to be common to many large firms.

Owners have financial stake in the corporation in the form of stocks, bonds, and so on, and they expect some kind of financial return from them. Either they have given money directly to the firm, or they have some historical claim made through a series of morally justified exchanges. The firm affects their livelihood or, if a substantial portion of their retirement income is in stocks or bonds, their ability to care for themselves when they can no longer work. Of course, the stakes of owners will differ by type of owner, preferences for money, moral preferences, and so on, as well as by type of firm. The owners of AT&T are quite different from

FIGURE 1
A Stakeholder Model of the Corporation.

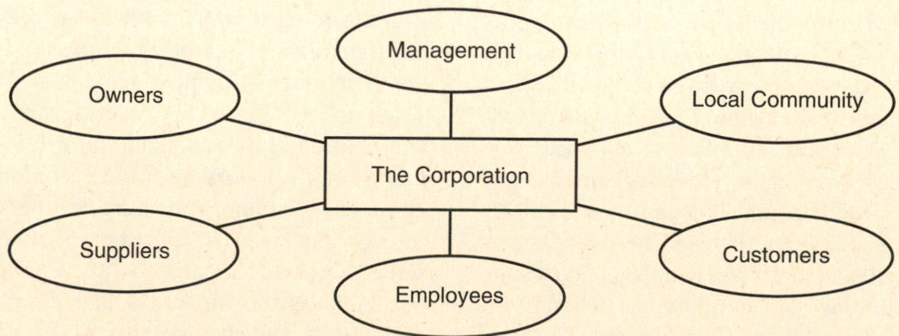

the owners of Ford Motor Company, with stock of the former company being widely dispersed among 3 million stockholders and that of the latter being held by a small family group as well as by a large group of public stockholders.

Employees have their jobs and usually their livelihood at stake; they often have specialized skills for which there is usually no perfectly elastic market. In return for their labor, they expect security, wages, benefits, and meaningful work. In return for their loyalty, the corporation is expected to provide for them and carry them through difficult times. Employees are expected to follow the instructions of management most of the time, to speak favorably about the company, and to be responsible citizens in the local communities in which the company operates. Where they are used as means to an end, they must participate in decisions affecting such use. The evidence that such policies and values as described here lead to productive company-employee relationships is compelling. It is equally compelling to realize that the opportunities for "bad faith" on the part of both management and employees are enormous. "Mock participation" in quality circles, singing the company song, and wearing the company uniform solely to please management all lead to distrust and unproductive work.

Suppliers, interpreted in a stakeholder sense, are vital to the success of the firm, for raw materials will determine the final product's quality and price. In turn the firm is a customer of the supplier and is therefore vital to the success and survival of the supplier. When the firm treats the supplier as a valued member of the stakeholder network, rather than simply as a source of materials, the supplier will respond when the firm is in need. Chrysler traditionally had very close ties to its suppliers, even to the extent that led some to suspect the transfer of illegal payments. And when Chrysler was on the brink of disaster, the suppliers responded with price cuts, accepting late payments, financing, and so on. Supplier and company can rise and fall together. Of course, again, the particular supplier relationships will depend on a number of variables such as the number of suppliers and whether the supplies are finished goods or raw materials.

Customers exchange resources for the products of the firm and in return receive the benefits of the products. Customers provide the lifeblood of the firm in the form of revenue. Given the level of reinvestment of earnings in large corporations, customers indirectly pay for the development of new products and services. Peters and Waterman (1982)[11] have argued that being close to the customer leads to success with other stakeholders and that a distinguishing characteristic of some companies that have performed well is their emphasis on the customer. By paying attention to customers' needs, management automatically addresses the needs of suppliers and owners. Moreover, it seems that the ethic of customer service carries over to the community. Almost without fail the "excellent companies" in Peters and Waterman's study have good reputations in the community. We would argue that Peters and Waterman have found multiple applications of Kant's dictum, "Treat persons as ends unto themselves," and it should come as no surprise that persons respond to such respectful treatment, be they customers, suppliers, owners, employees, or members of the local community. The real surprise is the novelty of the application of Kant's rule in a theory of good management practice.

The local community grants the firm the right to build facilities and, in turn, it benefits from the tax base and economic and social contributions of the firm. In return for the provision of local services, the firm is expected to be a good citizen, as is any person, either "natural or artificial." The firm cannot expose the community to unreasonable hazards in the form of pollution, toxic waste, and so on. If for some reason the firm must leave a community, it is expected to work with local leaders to make the transition as smoothly as possible. Of course, the firm does not have perfect knowledge, but when it discovers some danger or runs afoul of new competition, it is expected to inform the local community and to work with the community to overcome any problem. When the firm mismanages its relationship with the local community, it is in the same position as a citizen who commits a crime. It has violated the implicit social contract with the community and should expect to be distrusted and ostracized. It should not be surprised when punitive measures are invoked.

We have not included "competitors" as stakeholders in the narrow sense, since strictly speaking they are not necessary for the survival and success of the firm; the stakeholder theory works equally well in monopoly contexts. However, competitors and government would be the first to be included in an extension of this basic theory. It is simply not true that the interests of competitors in an industry are always in conflict. There is no reason why trade associations and other multiorganizational groups cannot band together to solve common problems that have little to do with how to restrain trade. Implementation of stakeholder management principles, in the long run, mitigates the need for industrial policy and an increasing role for government intervention and regulation.

The Role of Management

Management plays a special role, for it too has a stake in the modern corporation. On the one hand, management's stake is like that of employees, with some kind of explicit or implicit employment contract. But, on the other hand, management has a duty of safeguarding the welfare of the abstract entity that is the corporation. In short, management, especially top management, must look after the health of the corporation, and this involves balancing the multiple claims of conflicting stakeholders. Owners want higher financial returns, while customers want more money spent on research and development. Employees want higher wages and better benefits, while the local community wants better parks and day-care facilities.

The task of management in today's corporation is akin to that of King Solomon. The stakeholder theory does not give primacy to one stakeholder group over another, though there will surely be times when one group will benefit at the expense of others. In general, however, management must keep the relationships among stakeholders in balance. When these relationships become imbalanced, the survival of the firm is in jeopardy.

When wages are too high and product quality is too low, customers leave, suppliers suffer, and owners sell their stocks and bonds, depressing the stock price and making it difficult to raise new capital at favorable rates. Note, however, that the reason for paying returns to owners is not that they "own" the firm, but that their support is necessary for the survival of the firm, and that they have a legitimate claim on the firm. Similar reasoning applies in turn to each stakeholder group.

A stakeholder theory of the firm must redefine the purpose of the firm. The stockholder theory claims that the purpose of the firm is to maximize the welfare of the stockholders, perhaps subject to some moral or social constraints, either because such maximization leads to the greatest good or because of property rights. The purpose of the firm is quite different in our view. If a stakeholder theory is to be consistent with the principles of corporate effects and rights, then its purpose must take into account Kant's dictum of respect for persons. The very purpose of the firm is, in our view, to serve as a vehicle for coordinating stakeholder interests. It is through the firm that each stakeholder group makes itself better off through voluntary exchanges. The corporation serves at the pleasure of its stakeholders, and none may be used as a means to the ends of another without full rights of participation in that decision. We can crystallize the particular applications of PCR and PCE to the stakeholder theory in two further principles. These stakeholder management principles will serve as a foundation for articulating the theory. They are guiding ideals for the immortal corporation as it endures through generations of particular mortal stakeholders.

Stakeholder Management Principles

P1: The corporation should be managed for the benefit of its stakeholders: its customers, suppliers, owners, employees, and local communities. The rights of these groups must be ensured, and, further, the groups must participate, in some sense, in decisions that substantially affect their welfare.

P2: Management bears a fiduciary relationship to stakeholders and to the corporation as an abstract entity. It must act in the interests of the stakeholders as their agent, and it must act in the interests of the corporation to ensure the survival of the firm, safeguarding the long-term stakes of each group.

P1, which we might call The Principle of Corporate Legitimacy, redefines the purpose of the firm to be in line with the principles of corporate effects and rights. It implies the legitimacy of stakeholder claims on the firm. Any social contract that justifies the existence of the corporate form includes the notion that stakeholders are a party to that contract. Further, stakeholders have some inalienable rights to participate in decisions that substantially affect their welfare or involve their being used as a means to another's ends. We bring to bear our arguments for the incoherence of the stockholder view as justification for P1. If in fact there is no good reason for the stockholder theory, and if in fact there are harms, benefits, and rights of stakeholders involved in running the modern corporation, then we know of no other starting point for a theory of the corporation than P1.

P2, which we might call The Stakeholder Fiduciary Principle, explicitly defines the duty of management to recognize these claims. It will not always be possible to meet all claims of all stakeholders all the time, since some of these claims will conflict. Here P2 recognizes the duty of management to act in the long-term best interests of the corporation, conceived as a forum of stakeholder interaction, when the interests of the group outweigh the interests of the individual parties to the collective contract. The duty described in P2 is a fiduciary duty, yet it does not suffer from the difficulties surrounding the fiduciary duty to stockholders, for the conflicts involved there are precisely those that P2 makes it mandatory for management to resolve. Of course, P2 gives no instructions for a magical resolution of the conflicts that arise from prima facie obligations to multiple parties. An analysis of such rules for decision making is a subject to be addressed on another occasion, but P2 does give these conflicts a legitimacy that they do not enjoy in the stockholder theory. It gives management a clear and distinct directive to pay attention to stakeholder claims.

P1 and P2 recognize the eventual need for changes in the law of corporations and other governance mechanisms if the stakeholder theory is to be put into practice. P1 and P2, if implemented as a major innovation in the structure of the corporation, will make manifest the eventual legal institutionalization of sanctions. . . .

Structural Mechanisms

We propose several structural mechanisms to make a stakeholder management conception practicable. We shall offer a sketch of these here and say little by way of argument for them.

1. *The Stakeholder Board of Directors.* We propose that every corporation of a certain size yet to be determined, but surely all those that are publicly traded or are of the size of those publicly traded, form a Board of Directors comprised of representatives of five stakeholder groups, including employees, customers, suppliers, stockholders, and members of the local community, as well as a representative of the corporation, whom we might call a "metaphysical director" since he or she would be responsible for the metaphysical entity that is "the corporation." Whether or not each representative has an equal voting right is a matter that can be decided by experimentation; issues of governance lend themselves naturally to both laboratory and organizational experiments.

These directors will be vested with the duty of care to manage the affairs of the corporation in concert with the interests of its stakeholders. Such a Board would ensure that the rights of each group would have a forum, and by involving a director for the corporation, would ensure that the corporation itself would not be unduly harmed for the benefit of a particular group. In addition, by vesting each director with the duty of care for all stakeholders, we ensure that positive resolutions of conflicts would occur. . . . The task of the metaphysical director, to be elected unanimously by the stakeholder representatives, is especially important. The fact that the director has no direct constituency would appear to enhance management control. However, nothing could be further from the truth. To represent the abstract entity that is the corporation would be a most demanding job. Our metaphysical director would be responsible for convincing both stakeholders and management that a certain course of action was in the interests of the long-term health of the corporation, especially when that action implies the sacrifice of the interests of all. The metaphysical director would be a key link between the stakeholder representatives and management, and would spearhead the drive to protect the norms of the interests of all stakeholders. . . .

2. *Corporate Law.* The law of corporations needs to be redefined to recognize the legitimate purpose of the corporation as stated in P1. This has in fact developed in some areas of the law, such as products liability, where the claims of customers to safe products has emerged, and labor law, where the claims of employees have been safeguarded. Indeed, in such pioneering cases as *Marsh v. Alabama* the courts have come close to a stakeholder perspective. We envision that a body of case law will emerge to give meaning to "the proper claims of stakeholders," and in effect that the "wisdom of Solomon" necessary to make the stakeholder theory work will emerge naturally through the joint action of the courts, stakeholders, and management.

While much of the above may seem utopian, there are some very practical transitional steps that could occur. Each large corporation could form a stakeholder advisory board, which would prepare a charter detailing how the organization is to treat the claims of each stakeholder. Initially this stakeholder advisory board would serve as an advisor to the current board of directors, and eventually it would replace that board. Simultaneously, a group of legal scholars and practitioners, such as the American Law Institute, could initiate discussion of the legal proposals and methods to change corporate charters, while business groups such as the Business Roundtable could examine the practical consequences of our proposals. Given the emergence of some consensus, we believe that a workable transition can be found. . . .

NOTES

1. Cf. A. Berle and G. Means, *The Modern Corporation and Private Property* (New York: Commerce Clearing House, 1932), 1. For a reassessment of Berle and Means' argument after 50 years, see *Journal of Law and Economics* 26 (June 1983), especially G. Stigler and C. Friedland, "The Literature of Economics: The Case of Berle and Means," 237–68; D. North, "Comment on Stigler and Friedland," 269–72; and G. Means, "Corporate Power in the Marketplace," 467–85.
2. The metaphor of rebuilding the ship while afloat is attributed to Neurath by W. Quine, *Word and Object* (Cambridge: Harvard University Press, 1960), and W. Quine and J. Ullian, *The Web of Belief* (New York: Random House, 1978). The point is that to keep the ship afloat during repairs we must replace a plank with one that will do a better job. Our argument is that Kantian capitalism can so replace the current version of managerial capitalism.
3. Kant's notion of respect for persons (i.e., that each person has a right not to be treated as a means to an end) can be found in (1) Kant, *Critique of Practical Reason* (1838 edition). See J. Rawls, *A Theory of Justice* (Cambridge: Harvard University Press, 1971) for an eloquent modern interpretation.
4. For an introduction to the law of corporations see A. Conard, *Corporations in Perspective* (Mineola, NY: The Foundation Press, 1976), especially section 19; and R. Hamilton, *Corporations* (St. Paul: West Publishing, 1981), Chapter 8.
5. For a modern statement of managerial capitalism, see the literature in managerial economics, for example R. Coase, "The Nature of the Firm," *Economica* 4 (1937): 386–405; M. Jensen and W. Meckling, "Theory of the Firm: Managerial Behavior, Agency Costs and Ownership Structure," *Journal of Financial Economics* 3 (1976): 305–60; and O. Williamson, *The Economics of Discretionary Behavior* (London: Kershaw Publishing, 1965).
6. See R. Charan and E. Freeman, "Planning for the Business Environment of the 1980s," *The Journal of Business Strategy* 1 (1980): 9–19, especially p. 15 for a brief account of the major developments in products liability law.
7. See S. Breyer, *Regulation and Its Reform* (Cambridge: Harvard University Press, 1983), 133, for an analysis of food additives.
8. See I. Millstein and S. Katsh, *The Limits of Corporate Power* (New York: Macmillan, 1981), Chapter 4.
9. Cf. C. Summers, "Protecting All Employees Against

Unjust Dismissal," *Harvard Business Review* 58 (1980): 136, for a careful statement of the argument.

10. See E. Freeman and D. Reed, "Stockholders and Stakeholders: A New Perspective on Corporate Governance," in C. Huizinga, ed., *Corporate Governance: A Definitive Exploration of the Issues* (Los Angeles: UCLA Extension Press, 1983).
11. See T. Peters and R. Waterman, *In Search of Excellence* (New York: Harper and Row, 1982).

The Social Contract: Norms for a Corporate Conscience

Thomas Donaldson
Connelly Professor of Business Ethics, Georgetown University

In a speech to the Harvard Business School in 1969, Henry Ford II stated:

> The terms of the contract between industry and society are changing. . . . Now we are being asked to serve a wider range of human values and to accept an obligation to members of the public with whom we have no commercial transactions.

The "contract" to which Henry Ford referred concerns a corporation's *indirect* obligations. It represents not a set of formally specified obligations, but a set of binding, abstract ones. A social contract for business, if one exists, is not a typewritten contract in the real world, but a metaphysical abstraction not unlike the "social contract" between citizens and government that philosophers have traditionally discussed. Such a contract would have concrete significance, for it would help to interpret the nature of a corporation's indirect obligations, which are notoriously slippery.

The aim of this paper is to discover a corporation's indirect obligations by attempting to clarify the meaning of business's so-called "social contract." The task is challenging. Although people speak frequently of such a contract, few have attempted to specify its meaning. Although businesspeople, legislators, and academics offer examples of supposed infractions of the "contract," few can explain what justifies the contract itself.

Corporations, unlike humans, are artifacts, which is to say *we* create them. We *choose* to create corporations and we might choose either not to create them or to create different entities. Corporations thus are like political states in their need for justification.

The social contract has typically (though not always) been applied to governments. Is there any reason to suppose it is applicable to economic institutions? To productive organizations such as General Motors? One reason for doing so is that companies like General Motors are social giants. They affect the lives of millions of people, influence foreign policy, and employ more people than live in many countries of the world. Equally important is the fact that General Motors exists only through the cooperation and commitment of society. It draws its employees from society, sells its goods to society, and is given its status by society. All of this may suggest the existence of an implied agreement between it and society. If General Motors holds society responsible for providing the condition of its existence, then for what does society hold General Motors responsible? What are the terms of the social contract?

The simplest way of understanding the social contract is in the form: "We (the members of society) agree to do *X*, and you (the productive organizations) agree to do *Y*." Applying this form to General Motors (or any productive organization) means that the task of a social contract argument is to specify *X*, where *X* refers to the obligations of society to productive organizations, and to specify *Y*, where *Y* refers to the obligations of productive organizations to society.

It is relatively easy in this context to specify *X*, because what productive organizations need from society is:

1. Recognition as a single agent, especially in the eyes of the law.

---

2. The authority: (a) to own or use land and natural resources, and (b) to hire employees.

It may appear presumptuous to assume that productive organizations must be warranted by society. Can one not argue that any organization has a *right* to exist and operate? That they have this right *apart* from the wishes of society? When asking such questions, one must distinguish between claims about rights of mere organizations and claims about rights of organizations with special powers, such as productive organizations. A case can be made for the unbridled right of the Elks Club, whose members unite in fraternal activities, to exist and operate (assuming it does not discriminate against minorities or women); but the same cannot be said for Du Pont Corporation, which not only must draw on existing stores of mineral resources, but must find dumping sites to store toxic chemical by-products. Even granted that people have an inalienable right to form and operate organizations, and even granted that this right exists apart from the discretion of society, the productive organization requires special status under the law and the opportunity to use society's resources: two issues in which every member of society may be said to have a vested interest.

Conditions 1 and 2 are obviously linked to each other. In order for a productive organization to use land and hire employees (conditions of 2), it must have the authority to perform those acts as if it were an individual agent (the condition of 1). The philosophical impact of 1 should not be exaggerated. To say that productive organizations must have the authority to act as individual agents is not necessarily to affirm that they are abstract, invisible persons. Rather it is a means of stating the everyday fact that productive organizations must, for a variety of purposes, be treated as individual entities. For example, a corporation must be able to hire new employees, to sign contracts, and to negotiate purchases without getting the O.K. from *all* its employees and stockholders. The corporation *itself,* not its stockholders or managers, must be considered to be the controller of its equipment and land; for its stockholders or managers may leave, sell their shares, or die. If they do, the organization still controls its resources; it still employs its work force, and it still is obliged to honor its previous contracts and commitments.

Defining the *Y* side of the contract is as difficult as defining the *X* side is easy. It is obvious that productive organizations must be allowed to exist and act. But it is not obvious precisely why societies should allow them to exist, that is, what specific benefits society should hope to gain from the bargain. What specific functions should society expect from productive organizations? What obligations should it impose? Only one assumption can be made readily: that the members of society should demand at a minimum that the benefits from authorizing the existence of productive organizations outweigh the detriments of doing so. This is nothing other than the expectation of all voluntary agreements: that no party should be asked to conclude a contract which places him or her in a position worse than before.

Two principal classes of people stand to benefit or be harmed by the introduction of productive organizations: (1) people who consume the organizations' products, i.e., consumers; and (2) people who work in such organizations, i.e., employees. The two classes are broadly defined and not mutually exclusive. "Consumer" refers to anyone who is economically interested; hence virtually anyone qualifies as a consumer. "Employee" refers to anyone who contributes labor to the productive process of a productive organization, including managers, laborers, part-time support personnel, and (in corporations) members of the board of directors.

From the standpoint of our hypothetical consumers, productive organizations promise to *enhance the satisfaction of economic interests.* That is to say, people could hope for the introduction of productive organizations to better satisfy their interests for shelter, food, entertainment, transportation, health care, and clothing. The prima facie benefits for consumers include:

1. Improving efficiency through:
   a. Maximizing advantages of specialization.
   b. Improving decision-making resources.
   c. Increasing the capacity to use or acquire expensive technology and resources.

2. Stabilizing levels of output and channels of distribution.
3. Increasing liability resources.

From the standpoint of consumers, productive organizations should minimize:

1. Pollution and the depletion of natural resources.
2. The destruction of personal accountability.
3. The misuse of political power.

Productive organizations should also be viewed from the standpoint of their effects on people as workers, that is, from the standpoint of their effects upon individual laborers and craftsmen in the state of individual production who opt to work for productive organizations.

It is not difficult to discover certain prima facie benefits, such as the following:

1. Increasing income potential (and the capacity for social contributions).
2. Diffusing personal liability.
3. Adjusting personal income allocation.

From the standpoint of workers, productive organizations should minimize:

1. Worker alienation.
2. Lack of worker control over work conditions.
3. Monotony and dehumanization of the worker.

Thus the social contract will specify that these negative consequences be minimized.

Finally, a caveat must be made concerning justice. Society will grant productive organizations the conditions necessary for their existence only if they agree not to violate certain minimum standards of justice—however these are to be specified. For example, it would refuse to enact the contract if it knew that the existence of productive organizations would systematically reduce a given class of people to an inhuman existence, subsistence poverty, or enslavement.

This point, in turn, provides a clue to one of the specific tenets of the contract. Although the contract might allow productive organizations to undertake actions requiring welfare trade-offs, it would prohibit organizational acts of injustice. It might allow a corporation to lay off, or reduce the salaries of, thousands of workers in order to block skyrocketing production costs; here, worker welfare would be diminished while consumer welfare would be enhanced. But it is another matter when the company commits gross injustices in the process—for example, if it lies to workers, telling them that no layoffs are planned merely to keep them on the job until the last minute. Similarly, it is another matter when the organization follows discriminatory hiring policies, refusing to hire blacks or women, in the name of "consumer advantage." These are clear injustices of the kind that society would want to prohibit as a condition of the social contract. We may infer, then, that a tenet of the social contract will be that productive organizations are to remain within the bounds of the general canons of justice.

Determining what justice requires is a notoriously difficult task. The writings of Plato, Aristotle, and more recently, John Rawls, have shed considerable light on this subject, but unfortunately we must forego a general discussion of justice here. At a minimum, however, the application of the concept of justice to productive organizations appears to imply *that productive organizations avoid deception or fraud, that they show respect for their workers as human beings, and that they avoid any practice that systematically worsens the situations of a given group in society.* Despite the loud controversy over what justice means, most theorists would agree that justice means at least this much for productive organizations.

Our sketch of a hypothetical social contract is now complete. By utilizing the concept of rational people existing in a state of individual production, we have indicated the terms of a contract which they would require for the introduction of productive organizations. The questions asked in the beginning were: Why should corporations exist at all? What is the fundamental justification for their activities? How can we measure their performance, to say when they have performed poorly or well? A social contract helps to answer these questions. Corporations considered as productive organizations exist to enhance the welfare of society through the satisfaction of consumer and worker interests, in a way which relies on exploiting corporations' special advantages and minimizing disadvantages. This is the *moral foundation* of the corporation when considered as a productive organization. The social contract also serves as a tool to measure the performance of productive organizations. That is, when such organizations fulfill the terms of the contract, they have done well. When they do not, then society is morally justified in condemning them.

Productive organizations (whether corporations or not) that produce quality goods at low prices, that reject government favoritism, and that enhance the well-being of workers receive high marks by the standards of the social contract. Those that allow inefficiency, charge high prices, sell low-quality products, and fail to enhance the well-being of workers receive low marks. The latter organizations have violated the terms of the social contract. They must reform themselves, or lose their moral right to exist.

PRIVATE CORPORATIONS AND PUBLIC WELFARE

George G. Brenkert
Professor of Philosophy, University of Tennessee

I

The doctrine of corporate social responsibility comes in many varieties.[1] Its most developed version demands that corporations help alleviate "public welfare deficiencies," by which is understood problems of the inner city, drug problems, poverty, crime, illiteracy, lack of sufficient funding for educational institutions, inadequate health care delivery systems, chronic unemployment, etc.

In short, social responsibility, it is contended, requires that corporations assume part of the responsibility for the basic prerequisites of individual and social life within a community or society. Social responsibility demands this even though, it is claimed, corporations are not causally responsible for these conditions and doing so may not enhance their profits.

In response, corporations today provide job training for the hardcore unemployed, help renovate parks, sponsor clean-up programs, establish manufacturing plants in ghetto areas, offer seminars to high school students on how effectively to seek employment, support minority business adventures, provide educational films as well as additional instructors and tutors to public schools (i.e. "adopt" schools), etc.[2]

Such projects have, seemingly, met with a great deal of approval. Indeed, during a time when the welfare of many is deficient, one wonders how anyone could object to such activities. It might seem that any objections to such corporate behavior would stem not from their participating in these activities, but from their not participating even more.

Nevertheless, a number of objections to corporations engaging in such activities have been raised and are well-known. Many of these criticisms are not very good and will not be reviewed here. There is, however, one objection that is much more interesting, even if it is rarely developed. The essence of this objection is that corporate social responsibility to produce directly the public welfare involves the illegitimate encroachment of private organizations into the public realm. There is much greater merit to it than might appear at first glance.

II

This objection takes various forms. Theodore Levitt, for example, claims that the essence of free enterprise is the production of high-level profits. Private business corporations tend to impose this narrowly materialistic view on whatever they touch. Accordingly, corporate responsibility for welfare threatens to reduce pluralism and to create a monolithic society.[3] George C. Lodge similarly maintains that "the demand that business apply itself to problems which government is finding it increasingly difficult to comprehend or affect . . . is

---

From *Public Affairs Quarterly,* Vol. 6, Issue 2 (April 1992,) pp. 155–68. Reprinted by permission of *Public Affairs Quarterly.*

. . . absurd. Corporations, whatever else they may be, are not purveyors of social assistance."[4] Unelected businessmen, he claims, have "neither the right nor the competence" to define or establish the goals and the criteria by which society should repair or remake itself.[5] Finally, Richard DeGeorge claims that

> there is great danger in expecting corporations to take upon themselves the production of public welfare, because they already have enormous power and are not answerable for its use to the general public. Politicians are elected by the public and are expected to have the common good as their end. We should not expect corporations to do what they are neither competent nor organized to do . . .[6]

These criticisms question the right as well as the competence of corporations to contribute directly to the public welfare. Further, they challenge the influence which corporations in so acting may gain over society. Both increased corporate power and a decrease of social pluralism are feared results.[7]

Unfortunately, these criticisms are, more often than not, simply noted, rather than elaborated upon. In particular, the suggestion implicit within them that the provision of public welfare by private corporations runs afoul of an important distinction between what is public and what is private has not been discussed in recent literature. It is this point which requires greater attention.

The argument offered here is that corporate responsibility for public welfare threatens to reduce, transform, and in some cases eliminate important public dimensions of social life. For this reason we must be wary of it and reluctant to accept it in its present forms. Several characteristics of this argument should be noted at the outset. First, it does not pretend to show that all corporate measures that address public welfare deficiencies are (by themselves or individually) wrong, mischievous, or mistaken. Still, we must not be overly impressed by particular instances and thereby miss the systematic and general implications that are thereby promoted. It is not uncommon for individually rational actions to lead to collectively irrational or morally problematic results.

Second, this argument does not address corporate social responsibilities with regard to damages that corporations may themselves directly cause to the environment, employees, members of society, etc. For all these harms it is reasonable to believe that corporations do have responsibilities. The question this paper addresses concerns the implications of demanding that corporations go beyond correcting the damages they have brought about and assume responsibility for public welfare deficiencies for which they are not causally responsible.

Finally, if we could identify the harms that corporations directly *and* indirectly cause, then the arena of responsibilities that corporations have to society might significantly increase and the deficiencies in public welfare (assuming corporations fulfilled their responsibilities) might correspondingly decrease. This paper presupposes that, even in such a situation, there would remain public welfare deficiencies for which corporations are said to be socially responsible and for which they are neither directly nor indirectly causally responsible.[8]

The present argument has four parts. To begin with, it is important to highlight the different relation that exists between an individual (or group) who is aided by a private corporation, and the relation between such an individual (or group) and public attempts to aid their welfare. The differences in these relations will, in practice, often be insignificant—especially when things go well. However, when problems arise theoretical and practical differences can be important. Surely cases could be identified in which corporations have successfully enhanced the public welfare. However, it is not to be expected that corporations will always act so successfully or so clearly in accord with public needs.

The point here is not that corporations may act in misguided ways so much as what happens in those instances where there are problems. Obviously appeals and complaints can be made to the corporation. However, the fact remains that appeals to the corporation tend to be appeals from external constituencies. Inasmuch as those aided by the corporation are not members of the corporation, they have no standing, as it were, within the corporation other than the one the corporation decides to give them. They have no "constitutional" rights against corporations as they do against public endeavors. They are not "citizens" of the corporation. Thus, they have, in principle, no internal access to the corporation's decision-making processes. They are part of that process only if the corporation allows it. Those who make the decisions to undertake various programs cannot be voted out of office—there is no political, and little legal control, over them. Accordingly, to advocate corporate provision of, and responsibility for, public welfare is to advocate that the basic requisites for human well being are to be provided by institutions whose deliberations, at least at present, do not in principle include representation of those whose interests are affected. Those deficient in welfare lack formal control or power over those agencies from whom they obtain their welfare. Further, since those deficient in welfare tend to be those who are (in general) powerless, the advocacy of corporate responsibility for welfare tends to continue their powerlessness. Corporate social responsibility, in excluding any formal relation between those who are recipients of corporate aid and the corporation, maintains a division between the powerless and the powerful. A democratic society, one would suppose, would seek to moderate, rather than increase, the inequality presupposed in this division.

This situation contrasts with the state or other public bodies which provide, as part of their nature, various forms of administrative, legal and political redress.[9] The state's activities on behalf of its citizenry are hemmed in (at least in principle) by safeguards and guarantees (voting, representation, public hearings, sunshine laws, etc.) which are not imposed on corporations. Indeed, such public forms of access and standing are generally said to be contrary to the corporation's private status. Accordingly, whenever people outside the private corporation are granted such access it is simply due to the benevolence of the corporation.

Now this different relation between individuals and the agencies (private or public) which provide support for them is particularly crucial when that support concerns their basic welfare, i.e. items to which one might reasonably claim a right: e.g., minimal health care, educational opportunities, physical security, shelter, and food. Surely various private institutions such as corporations, churches, etc. may appropriately give aid to those who are deficient in such welfare, when this occurs on an occasional or special basis. Accordingly, private institutions may aid the welfare of their members (those who have access and voice within the organization) as well as non-members (those who do not have such access and voice).

However, those who advocate that this become the normal situation are (implicitly at least) also advocating a condition that places the recipients in a tenuous position vis-à-vis the granting agencies. Though recipients may receive various goods and/or services they need from private corporations, not only are such individuals dependent on those agencies for the aid they receive, but they also lose any formal or "constitutional" voice in the agency which purports to aid them. In effect, any right they have to such welfare is degraded to an act of benevolence on the part of the contributing organization. They can no longer insist or demand that they be treated in various ways, but must play the role of supplicants.

It is in this kind of situation that the view attributed to Andrew Carnegie can arise unchecked by formal mechanisms to control it: "In the exercise of his trust he was responsible only to his own conscience and judgment of what was best for the community."[10] Recipients of such aid lack means of redress which, in matters of basic importance such as welfare, are terribly significant.

Furthermore, when the institutions (i.e. large business corporations) involved in providing welfare are not themselves dedicated to the welfare of others but primarily focused on their own self-interested economic ends, and when these organizations are extremely large and powerful, then we must reflect on the implications of the lack of membership, and hence the lack of redress and voice, within those organizations. Specifically, we need to consider whether these needs ought not to be met by organizations which will grant those receiving such aid the voice and access which has traditionally protected people who are dependent upon others.

In short, when corporations are asked to undertake public welfare on an ongoing basis, the welfare they give is privatized in a manner that eliminates an important relation for those receiving such welfare. To the extent that it formalizes a relation between the powerful and the powerless, it exposes the recipients of such aid to abuses of power. At the same time, the equality that democracy implies is also jeopardized.[11]

Second, a variation on the preceding point concerns the standards by which decisions on the nature and means of implementing corporate welfare measures are made. Again, this might not appear to be a significant problem with regard to the construction or reconstruction of an inner-city park, a neighborhood clean-up campaign, or reading tutors in the schools.[12] Surely corporations will, by and large, consult with the people involved to get their ideas and approval. On other occasions, the people involved will seek out a corporation to aid them. But this does not lay the issue to rest since the standards the corporation seeks to follow may be primarily private in nature, rather than public or general.[13]

Suppose, for instance, that the welfare measures which the corporation seeks to provide (and to which their recipients agree) are of questionable constitutionality. They agree, perhaps, on educational films with a religious or a racist message for the public schools. Or, suppose they agree on an educational program but the corporation liberally sprinkles the presentation with its corporate logo, mascot, jingo, and the like. Suppose that in training of the hard-core unemployed they aim at white, rather than black or Hispanic, populations. The point at issue concerns the legitimacy of these decisions.

The standards according to which the public welfare is fulfilled must be a matter for the public (through its representatives) to determine, not the private corporation.[14] Two reasons lie behind this claim. Such welfare concerns what is common among the citizens, what holds the members of a society together, and what is the nature of their basic prerequisites. It constitutes a statement about how we, as a community or society, believe that we should live. Fulfillment of welfare deficiencies for some that manifests prejudice against other groups, or works to their disadvantage, requires special justification and close public scrutiny, if it is allowed to stand.

In addition, to the extent that corporate contributions to public welfare are tax deductible, the foregone tax revenues constitute a public contribution to itself, through the agency of the corporation. Since public monies are committed through such contributions, the public has a right to assure itself that the standards according to which such monies are expended meet its (minimal) standards.[15]

Accordingly, the legitimacy of the decisions the private corporation makes regarding public welfare cannot be judged simply according to its own private standards. Thus, if the corporation tries to impose its own view and standards, it is crossing an important line between the private and the public. It is naive, then, simply to argue that people's welfare is the responsibility of corporations, without providing for social determination and direction of the activities which corporations undertake.[16]

In those instances in which corporate contributions are of a charitable (or prudential) nature *and* the objects of their actions are wholly private, it would seem that corporations might legitimately give to those individuals or organizations which promote their own values and ideas. In this way, their gifts may reflect their own idiosyncratic standards. Accordingly, some object to business giving to private universities whose faculty advocate ideas opposed to capitalism.[17] However, in contrast, the direction and satisfaction of public welfare according to private standards is not appropriate, since the public welfare is not to be determined simply by this or that individual corporation's ideas and values, but by a political process and, ideally a community dialogue, on what those values should be.[18]

Finally, if corporations are said to be responsible for remedying certain deficient levels of public welfare, but are not given control (both in terms of applicable standards and practical direction) over how such remedies are to be emplaced, then when these measures fail the corporation can hardly be held accountable. Nevertheless, since they will be associated with such efforts, they will often be faulted for their lack of success. Hence, if corporations are required to engage in social responsibility efforts, there will be an understandable tendency for them to seek control over the situations in which they participate. This means, however, supplanting (or reducing) public control and substituting their own judgments and standards for those of the public. Consequently, the demand for corporate social responsibility is a demand that encourages the substitution of private standards, authority and control for those of the public.

III

Third, the demand for corporate social responsibility arises, it has been assumed, due to deficient public welfare, which stems, at least in part, from inadequate public funding. Corporate opposition to higher taxes has played a contributing role to this situation, since taxes are viewed as coercive takings of corporate property.[19] The lower the taxes the greater the return on investment corporations make and the greater the flexibility corporations have to use their resources as they choose. Part of the appeal of corporate social responsibility for public welfare is that the aid that is given is voluntary. Provision of such aid heads off higher taxes, government regulation and hence coercion. In short, behind the demand for corporate social responsibility is a view that holds that the public realm and the state constitute a sphere of coercion, while the private realm and the actions it takes are voluntary.[20]

This is illustrated in Friedman's comment that "the political principle that underlies the political mechanism is conformity. . . . It is appropriate for some to require others to contribute to a general social purpose whether they wish to or not."[21] Corporate social responsibility, then, explicitly seeks to reduce the realm of the public, by reducing the area within which coercion and force might be used.

Now if the public were simply a realm of coercion, such a view would seem unexceptionable. On the contrary, however, such a view arguably distorts the realm of the public. Corporate social responsibility implies that the public is simply an area within which individual prudential interests are worked out and coercion imposed by the state. Both eliminate an important sense of the public.

The public is also the area within which general and common interests are articulated. It is what binds people together, in contrast to the private realm within which people are separated from each other and view each other as limitations upon their freedom.[22] Accordingly, it is the realm of the "we," rather than the "you" or "I." It is what is done in all our names, and not just yours or mine. It is the area, some have even held, within which freedom is only possible.[23] There is (or can be) a different sense of accomplishment when the community builds or creates something rather than simply this or that private organization. Conversely, there is a different sense of loss when a public figure, a President or Prime Minister dies, rather than the head of a private corporation.

Now charity is an extension of the private into this public realm. It is personal, self-given, and can't be demanded in particular cases. It need not be based on political discussion or compromise so much as on one's own willingness to aid others. Those who receive do not have grounds upon which they can demand or negotiate beyond which the charitable organization allows. Charity does not necessarily involve any political or public process by which recipient and contributor are bound together. Thus, Hannah Arendt comments, "The bond of charity between people . . . is incapable of founding a public realm of its own . . ."[24] In short, charity cannot be the basis of a public or political dimension between people.

As such, corporate social responsibility drives out the political and the public. The appeal to corporate responsibility is a confession that the public or political realm has broken (or is breaking) down. It is an unwitting manifestation of liberal individualism extending the realm of the private to encompass the public.

Consequently, Friedman is quite wrong when he complains that the doctrine of social responsibility "taken serious would extend the scope of the political mechanism to every human activity."[25] This is plausible only in that case when the corporation and its executives both engage in social responsibility activities *and,* as a result, become subject to political election procedures since they are viewed as "civil servants."[26] On the other hand, if this does not happen (and there is little present evidence that it will), then the doctrine of social responsibility extends the nature of private activities to many activities in the public or political realm. In short, quite the opposite of what Friedman contends, it extends the scope of the private "to every human activity."

The problem with this approach is that it is implausible to treat society as simply an example of an ideal market situation. This is implied by the above comments on the nature of the public. Not all public (or private) values can be produced or sustained by market exchanges. Friedman slips from discussion of market activities to talk of society without argument. Thus, after he portrays the voluntary nature of the ideal free market, he immediately goes on (without argument) to equate such exchanges with society itself.[27] However, it does not follow (and it is not plausible) to think of society as itself simply an ideal free market. Once again, then, corporate social responsibility involves views and demands which question legitimate distinctions between the private and the public.

IV

Finally, though the relation of the public and the private is a shifting relation, we must guard against collapsing one—either one—term of this relation into the other. The view that the public is simply the arena in which individual actions affect others without their voluntary approval impoverishes the notion of the public.[28] As noted above, the public is more and different than this. The public is what binds a people together and relates them to each other.[29] It is what is done in their common name; it is what makes them a people, rather than simply a random collection of individuals. It embodies the values, norms and ideals we strive towards even if we fail fully to achieve them. It is the responsibility of public agencies (the state or its government) to foster (at least) the minimal conditions under which the public may exist. To be a citizen is to owe allegiance to the government as it works to realize these principles and values.

Now suppose that the government does not fulfill its responsibilities to individuals for basic welfare. The demand that private corporations—rather than the government—dispense public welfare is a step in the privatization of the public realm. The benefits that individuals receive from the government have long been thought to play an important role in their obligations to the state and, hence, their citizenship within the state.[30] If these benefits come from private groups, rather than the state, then one would expect loyalties and obligations to be modified accordingly.

Consequently, if a corporation provides training for the hard-core unemployed, renovates the local park, or provides the house which shelters the sick, it is to the corporation that those aided will be grateful and indebted, not to the community or society of which they are members.[31] It is the corporation to which one's loyalties will be turned, and not to the city or state of which one is a citizen. Indeed, the very notion of citizenship thereby becomes impoverished. The grounds upon which the state has been said to acquire the obligations of its citizenry have been narrowed. In its place develop isolated (groups of) individuals beholden to private institutions of which they are not members (or citizens) and over which they have no formal control.

Surely in these days of popular advertising, the corporation may seem more personal, less abstract, than the community or the state. Through logos, jingoes and mascots corporations seek to get people to identify with them and their products. And through corporate measures to aid their welfare, individuals would have concrete reason to be indebted to them, even if not members or citizens of them. But to accept or promote this situation, and the view of the individual's relations to private and public institutions which it involves, merely reveals the state of poverty to which our notions of the public and citizenship have come. Such corporations encourage us to seek a common identity, rather than to foster our common (public) interests.[32] We are invited to replace the realm of the public which unavoidably involves impersonality with a personal and privatized realm. We transform a realm laden with political meanings into a private and psychologized realm.[33]

However, the danger here does not simply stem from the implications of the altered identifications and loyalties that characterize citizens. The increasing privatization of the public realm that we see in shopping malls, corporate housing developments, the suburban environment, and corporate attempts to establish their own identity and role models within the schools carry other consequences to which we must be keenly sensitive. For example, in private shopping malls people may be prevented from political speech; in corporate housing developments, they may be prohibited from having children and remaining in their home; and cultural exhibits may be skewed to suit corporate purposes.[34] Rights which all citizens share may be, wittingly or unwittingly, foregone through private efforts uninformed by public reflection and participation. In short, the public values and interests of a society can be threatened not simply by an authoritarian government but also by self-interested, though well-meaning, private groups and institutions which lack a sense of the significance of the public realm and the meaning of citizenship.

V

In conclusion, several comments are appropriate. First, it may be allowed that many objections which can be brought against corporate attempts to secure public welfare can also be brought against government or public attempts. Thus, both government and corporations may be inflexible, insensitive, impersonal, non-innovative, as well as hard to move or get through to. They may produce programs which are misconceived, uncoordinated, and/or precipitously stopped, leaving people in the lurch. The production of such programs may increase their power, size and influence; they may also deal paternalistically with those they seek to aid. One would be tempted to abandon all attempts to aid those deficient in welfare were it not for the fact that many people continue to suffer grievously from inadequate welfare. Thus, the question is a complex and messy one. There is no easy and neat answer.

Second, large corporations, however, will continue to be part of our social and political landscape. Their significant economic and political power are obvious. In this situation, the thrust of the public/private argument is two-sided. It can be taken to urge the separation of private corporations and public institutions. This is fraught with all the problems of bureaucratization, distant government, powerful but indifferent corporations, and failed efforts to satisfy public welfare needs. This is not to say that these problems could not be overcome within a fairly strict separation of the private and the public.[35] Still, this would involve a recommitment (and rediscovery!) of the public realm that might be difficult in countries such as the U.S.

On the other hand, the above argument can also be taken to recommend that we require such large corporations be made more fully public, social organizations. Indeed, many argue that large corporations are no longer simply private organizations. George C. Lodge, for example, comments that "it is now obvious that our large public corporations are not private property at all . . . The best we can say," he continues, "is that the corporation is a sort of collective, floating in philosophic limbo, dangerously vulnerable to the charge of illegitimacy and to the charge that it is not amenable to community control."[36] Thus, that corporations increasingly are called to participate in the production of public welfare is not so surprising given their present, quasi-public nature. The further claim that has been made is that this quasi-public nature needs to be institutionalized so as to make it amenable to greater public control and direction. This direction, however, is one that others violently oppose.

Thus, we stand at a crossroads. This juncture is part and parcel of that "tension between self-reliant competitive enterprise and a sense of public solidarity espoused by civic republicans" that some have identified as "the most important unresolved problem in American history."[37] If one rejects the view that corporations must more fully take on the character of public institutions, then demands for corporate social responsibility for public welfare should be seriously curtailed.

The preceding arguments do not show conclusively that corporations ought never to aid public welfare. They are one set of considerations which might, in some circumstances, be overridden. However, they do indicate important reasons why we should be more reluctant to proceed down the path that many have been encouraging us to take. When we are repeatedly told that the sight of corporate social responsibility is so lovely, and that the prospects of corporate responsibility for public welfare are so rosy, one may rightfully come to suspect that we are being led down the garden path.[38]

NOTES

1. "Private corporation" will be used to refer exclusively to private corporations engaged in the production of goods and services for profit.
2. Sandra L. Holmes reports in a study of how executives perceive social responsibility that 78% of the executives surveyed either strongly agreed or agreed more than they disagreed with the statement that "Business possesses the ability and means to be a *major* force in the alleviation of social problems" (pp. 39–40). It is clear from the context that by "social problems" is meant the kinds of problems listed in the text under "public welfare." Cf. Sandra L. Holmes, "Executive Perceptions of Corporate Social Responsibility," *Business Horizons* (June, 1976).
3. Theodore Levitt, "The Dangers of Social Responsibility," *Harvard Business Review,* vol. 36 (September–October, 1958), pp. 44–47.
4. George C. Lodge, *The New American Ideology* (New York: Alfred A. Knopf, 1975), p. 189.
5. *Ibid.,* p. 190. Cf., also p. 218.
6. DeGeorge, *Business Ethics,* 3rd ed. (New York: Macmillan Publishing Co., 1986), p. 171.
7. Cf. Levitt, "The Dangers of Social Responsibility."
8. The importance of indirect causal factors and the resulting responsibility of corporations has been defended by Larry May in his comments, "Corporate Philanthropy and Social Responsibility," given on an earlier version of this paper, before the Society for Business Ethics meeting in Boston, MA, on December 28, 1990. How we might determine for which harms corporations are directly or indirectly causally responsible is not addressed in this paper. Both topics, but especially the latter, raise significant problems.
9. Even if this is not true in any particular case, it is still appropriate to demand such access and forms of redress of present (i.e., democratic or republican) forms of government.
10. Robert H. Bremner, *American Philanthropy* (2nd ed.; Chicago: The University of Chicago Press, 1988), p. 101.
11. This argument allows that other private organizations, such as churches, etc., may legitimately contribute to individuals' welfare needs. The smaller the organization, the more individual the contribution, and the greater the identity of the organization is bound up with promoting the public good, the less there is a problem. On the other hand, some organizations, such as churches, run into problems (e.g., First Amendment issues and attempts to convert others rather than simply aid them) that other private groups do not.
12. Even the park example is not all that simple. There are questions that need to be asked before the park can be built or renovated: what will be the nature and form of the park? Who will maintain it (will anyone?)? Will trash containers be put out and regularly emptied (by whom?)? Is the construction of this park likely to require increased police patrols? Are additional burdens being placed on the city recreational department, trash department, police department? If so, who decides and upon what basis? Admittedly, these questions must be faced whether the city *or* a corporation builds the park. However, the important point is that when corporations aid public welfare many important questions remain to be answered. The city or the public is not suddenly let off the hook.
13. The problem is even more complex since those individuals the corporation addresses in the public forum may themselves primarily hold private values. That is, their vision of themselves and society may have lost any sense of the public. Bellah et al document the degree to which "Americans . . . are genuinely ambivalent about public life" (Bellah et al, *Habits of the Heart* [Berkeley: University of California Press, 1985], p. 250).
14. Similarly for a host of other projects there are questions which demand social or public decision, which only the public through the government can legitimately give. For example, it might be asked whether it is really so bad for corporations to provide tutors for secondary schools to help with basic reading skills. But are these tutors trained in teaching? Do they serve to justify inadequate teaching staffs? Do they undercut the demands of teachers for adequate social commitment for education? What programs are they trained to teach? Do they constitute an influx of business oriented courses rather than human-

ity courses, or science courses? These are serious issues which need to be addressed on the social and public level, not simply on the private corporate level.

Likewise, it might be asked whether it is wrong for corporations (e.g., McDonald's) to start drives for houses for relatives of the seriously ill to stay in while at the hospital. But again, supposing that the rest of the community contributes the preponderant amount, why should the community not get the credit for the house? Why doesn't the name of the house reflect public values or ideals?

We need not assume that public answers to all these questions may be easily arrived at. However, if corporations (or other private groups) simply operate on their own standards, the public discussion which may lead to public standards and agreement will be short-circuited. As a result, the public will be impoverished.

15. This claim applies to similar contributions that come from other private groups, e.g., churches, the Audubon Society, etc. When such contributions come from small and numerous groups, there is less reason for concern, since they may counterbalance each other. It is reasonable for a society to encourage such contributions. Nevertheless, society may legitimately review the nature of their contributions, given that their contributions are tax deductible and they enjoy (where applicable) tax-exempt status.

    This issue is particularly of concern, however, when such contributions come from large corporations which can bring significant power and resources to bear. Similarly, when churches or other private groups become large and their powers significant, the consideration raised in the text applies as well. In short, when the contributions of private groups are supported by the public through tax deductions and when those contributions may in particular cases have a significant effect on the public, the public may legitimately review the standards according to which the contributions are made.
16. For example, Control Data's program, called "City Venture," which sought to write blueprints for economic rebirth of down-and-out city neighborhoods had to be withdrawn: "A bossy, 'we know what's best' attitude offended prickly independent community groups in Minneapolis and Miami, forcing City Venture to be withdrawn" (Neil R. Peirce, "To Corporate Social Involvement," *The Knoxville Journal,* 1982, p. A4).
17. Robert H. Malott, "Corporate Support of Education: Some Strings Attached," *Harvard Business Review,* vol. 56 (1978), pp. 133–38.
18. This is not to say that corporations, or anyone, must (or should) give to causes they believe to be wrongheaded. Rather, if corporations (or other organizations) are given responsibility for public welfare, they may not simply apply their own idiosyncratic standards. This allows, of course, that they could choose, from a range of public welfare needs, to support those compatible with their own views. Since the issue concerns basic deficiencies from which people suffer, this should not be impossible.
19. Similarly Levitt argues: "American capitalism also creates, fosters, and acquiesces in enormous social and economic cancers. Indeed, it fights against the achievement of certain forms of economic and social progress, pouring millions into campaigns against things which people have a right to expect from their government . . ." (Levitt, "The Dangers of Social Responsibility," p. 48).
20. Since corporate social responsibility is, usually, viewed either as charitable or as prudential in nature, corporations can make their own, voluntary choices as to when, what and how much they will do. The alternative is to have the public (the state or the government) take more from them in order to fulfill the public welfare needs. Because this restricts their choices—their freedom (as they would see it)—they argue against state action here. In short, corporate social responsibility is an expression of the liberal view of society. It is also an expression of an individualistic view: "utilitarian individualism" and "expressive individualism" (Bellah et al, Habits of the Heart, p. 27ff). These views contrast with what they call "civic republicanism."
21. Milton Friedman, "The Social Responsibility of Business is to Increase its Profits, in Milton Snoeyenbos, Robert Almeder, James Humber (eds.), *Business Ethics* (Buffalo, New York: Prometheus Books, 1983), p. 78.
22. *Ibid.,* pp. 245, 248.
23. Nancy L. Schwartz, "Distinction Between Public and Private Life," *Political Theory,* vol. 7 (1979), p. 245.
24. Hannah Arendt, *The Human Condition* (Chicago: The University of Chicago Press, 1958), p. 53.
25. Milton Friedman, "The Social Responsibility of Business is to Increase its Profits," in Milton Snoeyenbos, Robert Almeder, James Humber (eds.),

Business Ethics (Buffalo, New York: Prometheus Books, 1983), p. 79.

26. Friedman, "The Social Responsibility of Business is to Increase its Profits, p. 75.
27. *Ibid.*
28. Cf. John Dewey, *The Public and its Problems* (Chicago: Gateway Books, 1946).
29. Cf. Hannah Arendt, "The public realm, as the common world, gathers us together and yet prevents our falling over each other, so to speak"; *The Human Condition* (Chicago: The University of Chicago Press, 1958), p. 52.
30. Cf. A. John Simmons, *Moral Principles and Political Obligations* (Princeton: Princeton University Press, 1979), pp. 157–90.
31. The following comes from a letter to an editor from a mother of a child in a school adopted by IBM. She was responding to objections that others had raised because children in the school were preparing posters and having assemblies to thank IBM for adopting their school. She argues: "to say that this is taking away from the children's learning time is not true. What better learning experience is there than to teach our children what's going on in their schools and to have them have a special program to thank these companies? . . . I believe it is very important that these adopting companies realize, by way of parents and children, that we are honored and grateful that they are willing to help 'our' children with their education" (Letters to the Editor, *The Knoxville News-Sentinel,* November 28, 1986).
32. Cf. Richard Sennett who complains that as part of the end of public culture "the pursuit of common interests is destroyed in the search for a common identity" (p. 261); *The Fall of Public Man* (New York: Vintage Books, 1976).
33. Cf. Sennett, *Ibid.*
34. IBM, for example, "barred the display of computer-art works designed for the equipment of a major business competitor, Macintosh, in the company's heretofore prestigious IBM Gallery of Science and Art in midtown Manhattan"; Susan Davis, "IBM Nixes Macintosh," *Art in America,* vol. 76 (1990), p. 47. The works barred were part of a touring show organized by the Walker Art Center. IBM, which finances its namesake galleries, "bars its competition 'as a matter of policy' " (*Ibid.,* p. 47).
35. It would not, for example, prohibit linking education and business in various ways. Various courses of study in schools might be coordinated with job opportunities in private business, without corporations providing for those courses or other educational needs. Public and government welfare measures would have to be tied much more closely to local needs and allowed much greater flexibility in resolving those needs.
36. Lodge, *The New American Ideology,* p. 18.
37. Bellah et al, *Habits of the Heart,* p. 256.
38. I am indebted to John Hardwig, W. Michael Hoffman, Larry May, Richard Nunan, and an anonymous referee for their perceptive and helpful comments on earlier versions of this paper.

QUESTIONS FOR DISCUSSION

1. How might Friedman respond to Donaldson's social contract view of corporate responsibility? Could he plausibly argue, for example, that the social contract is best fulfilled by firms maximizing profit?
2. What are the main limitations on what Stone calls Friedman's "agency argument"? Does Friedman have an effective response to Stone?
3. Evan and Freeman argue that the interests of stakeholders should be balanced by corporate managers. Can you think of any method for doing this that does not favor one group over another? What happens if the interests of different groups are incompatible?
4. Brenkert argues that we should be very wary of corporations participating in the production of public welfare. What are the main points of his argument? Does it imply a reduced role for the interests of some corporate stakeholders (for example, communities)?

CHAPTER 4

IDENTITY AND AGENCY

Can a Corporation Have a Conscience?

Kenneth E. Goodpaster
John B. Matthews, Jr.
Goodpaster—Professor and Koch Endowed Chair in Business Ethics, The University of St. Thomas.
Matthews—Former Wilson Professor of Business Administration, Emeritus, Harvard University

During the severe racial tensions of the 1960s, Southern Steel Company (actual case, disguised name) faced considerable pressure from government and the press to explain and modify its policies regarding discrimination both within its plants and in the major city where it was located. SSC was the largest employer in the area (it had nearly 15,000 workers, one-third of whom were black) and had made great strides toward removing barriers to equal job opportunity in its several plants. In addition, its top executives (especially its chief executive officer, James Weston) had distinguished themselves as private citizens for years in community programs for black housing, education, and small business as well as in attempts at desegregating all-white police and local government organizations.

SSC drew the line, however, at using its substantial economic influence in the local area to advance the cause of the civil rights movement by pressuring banks, suppliers, and the local government:

> As individuals we can exercise what influence we may have as citizens," James Weston said, "but for a corporation to attempt to exert any kind of economic compulsion to achieve a particular end in a social area seems to me to be quite beyond what a corporation should do and quite beyond what a corporation can do. I believe that while government may seek to compel social reforms, any attempt by a private organization like SSC to impose its views, its beliefs, and its will upon the community would be repugnant to our American constitutional concepts and that appropriate steps to correct this abuse of corporate power would be universally demanded by public opinion.

Reprinted by permission of the *Harvard Business Review*. Excerpts from "Can a Corporation Have a Conscience?" by Kenneth E. Goodpaster and John B. Matthews, Jr. (January–February 1982).

Weston could have been speaking in the early 1980s on any issue that corporations around the United States now face. Instead of social justice, his theme might be environmental protection, product safety, marketing practice, or international bribery. His statement for SSC raises the important issue of corporate responsibility. Can a corporation have a conscience?

Weston apparently felt comfortable saying it need not. The responsibilities of ordinary persons and of "artificial persons" like corporations are, in his view, separate. Persons' responsibilities go beyond those of corporations. Persons, he seems to have believed, ought to care not only about themselves but also about the dignity and well-being of those around them—ought not only to care but also to act. Organizations, he evidently thought, are creatures of, and to a degree prisoners of, the systems of economic incentive and political sanction that give them reality and therefore should not be expected to display the same moral attributes that we expect of persons.

Others inside business as well as outside share Weston's perception. One influential philosopher—John Ladd—carries Weston's view a step further:

"It is improper to expect organizational conduct to conform to the ordinary principles of morality," he says. "We cannot and must not expect formal organizations, or their representatives acting in their official capacities, to be honest, courageous, considerate, sympathetic, or to have any kind of moral integrity. Such concepts are not in the vocabulary, so to speak, of the organizational language game."[1]

In our opinion, this line of thought represents a tremendous barrier to the development of business ethics both as a field of inquiry and as a practical force in managerial decision making. This is a matter about which executives must be philosophical and philosophers must be practical. A corporation can and should have a conscience. The language of ethics does have a place in the vocabulary of an organization. There need not be and there should not be a disjunction of the sort attributed to SSC's James Weston. Organizational agents such as corporations should be no more and no less morally responsible (rational, self-interested, altruistic) than ordinary persons.

We take this position because we think an analogy holds between the individual and the corporation. If we analyze the concept of moral responsibility as it applies to persons, we find that projecting it to corporations as agents in society is possible.

DEFINING THE RESPONSIBILITY OF PERSONS

When we speak of the responsibility of individuals, philosophers say that we mean three things: someone is to blame, something has to be done, or some kind of trustworthiness can be expected.

We apply the first meaning, what we shall call the *causal* sense, primarily to legal and moral contexts where what is at issue is praise or blame for a past action. We say of a person that he or she was responsible for what happened, is to blame for it, should be held accountable. In this sense of the word, *responsibility* has to do with tracing the causes of actions and events, of finding out who is answerable in a given situation. Our aim is to determine someone's intention, free will, degree of participation, and appropriate reward or punishment.

We apply the second meaning of *responsibility* to rule following, to contexts where individuals are subject to externally imposed norms often associated with some social role that people play. We speak of the responsibilities of parents to children, of doctors to patients, of lawyers to clients, of citizens to the law. What is socially expected and what the party involved is to answer for are at issue here.

We use the third meaning of *responsibility* for decision making. With this meaning of the term, we say that individuals are responsible if they are trustworthy and reliable, if they allow appropriate factors to affect their judgment; we refer primarily to a person's independent thought processes and decision making, processes that justify an attitude of trust from those who interact with him or her as a responsible individual.

The distinguishing characteristic of moral responsibility, it seems to us, lies in this third sense of the term. Here the focus is on the intellectual and emotional processes in the individual's moral reasoning. Philosophers call this "taking a moral point of view" and contrast it with such other processes as being financially prudent and attending to legal obligations.

To be sure, characterizing a person as "morally responsible" may seem rather vague. But vagueness is a contextual notion. Everything depends on how we fill in the blank in "vague for ___ purposes."

In some contexts the term "six o'clockish" is vague, while in others it is useful and informative. As a response to a space-shuttle pilot who wants to know when to fire the reentry rockets, it will not do, but it might do in response to a spouse who wants to know when one will arrive home at the end of the workday.

We maintain that the processes underlying moral responsibility can be defined and are not themselves vague, even though gaining consensus on specific moral norms and decisions is not always easy.

What, then, characterizes the processes underlying the judgment of a person we call morally responsible? Philosopher William K. Frankena offers the following answer:

"A morality is a normative system in which judgments are made, more or less consciously, [out of a] consideration of the effects of actions . . . on the lives of persons . . . including the lives of others besides the person acting. . . . David Hume took a similar position when he argued that what speaks in a moral judgment is a kind of sympathy. . . . A little later, . . . Kant put the matter somewhat better by characterizing morality as the business of respecting persons as ends and not as means or as things. . . ."[2]

Frankena is pointing to two traits, both rooted in a long and diverse philosophical tradition:

1. *Rationality.* Taking a moral point of view includes the features we usually attribute to rational decision making, that is, lack of impulsiveness, care in mapping out alternatives and consequences, clarity about goals and purposes, attention to details of implementation.
2. *Respect.* The moral point of view also includes a special awareness of and concern for the effects of one's decisions and policies on others, special in the sense that it goes beyond the kind of awareness and concern that would ordinarily be part of rationality, that is, beyond seeing others merely as instrumental to accomplishing one's own purposes. This is respect for the lives of others and involves taking their needs and interests seriously, not simply as resources in one's own decision making but as limiting conditions which change the very definition of one's habitat from a self-centered to a shared environment. It is what philosopher Immanuel Kant meant by the "categorical imperative" to treat others as valuable in and for themselves.

It is this feature that permits us to trust the morally responsible person. We know that such a person takes our point of view into account not merely as a useful precaution (as in "honesty is the best policy") but as important in its own right.

These components of moral responsibility are not too vague to be useful. Rationality and respect affect the manner in which a person approaches practical decision making: they affect the way in which the individual processes information and makes choices. A rational but not respectful Bill Jones will not lie to his friends *unless* he is reasonably sure he will not be found out. A rational but not respectful Mary Smith will defend an unjustly treated party *unless* she thinks it may be too costly to herself. A rational *and* respectful decision maker, however, notices—and cares—whether the consequences of his or her conduct lead to injuries or indignities to others.

Two individuals who take "the moral point of view" will not of course always agree on ethical matters, but they do at least have a basis for dialogue.

PROJECTING RESPONSIBILITY TO CORPORATIONS

Now that we have removed some of the vagueness from the notion of moral responsibility as it applies to persons, we can search for a frame of reference in which, by analogy with Bill Jones and Mary Smith, we can meaningfully and appropriately say that corporations are morally responsible. This is the issue reflected in the SSC case.

To deal with it, we must ask two questions: Is it meaningful to apply moral concepts to actors who are not persons but who are instead made up of persons? And even if meaningful, is it advisable to do so?

If a group can act like a person in some ways, then we can expect it to behave like a person in other ways. For one thing, we know that people organized into a group can act as a unit. As business people well know, legally a corporation is considered a unit. To approach unity, a group usually has some sort of internal decision structure, a system of rules that spell out authority relationships and specify the conditions under which certain individuals' actions become official actions of the group.[3]

If we can say that persons act responsibly only if they gather information about the impact of their actions on others and use it in making decisions, we can reasonably do the same for organizations. Our proposed frame of reference for thinking about and implementing corporate responsibility aims at spelling out the processes associated with the moral responsibility of individuals and projecting them to the level of organizations. This is similar to, though an inversion of, Plato's famous method in the *Republic*, in which justice in the community is used as a model for justice in the individual.

Hence, corporations that monitor their employment practices and the effects of their production processes and products on the environment and human health show the same kind of rationality and respect that morally responsible individuals do. Thus, attributing actions, strategies, decisions, and moral responsibilities to corporations as entities distinguishable from those who hold offices in them poses no problem.

And when we look about us, we can readily see differences in moral responsibility among corporations in much the same way that we see differences among persons. Some corporations have built features into their management incentive systems, board structures, internal control systems, and research agendas that in a person we would call self-control, integrity, and conscientiousness. Some have institutionalized awareness and concern for consumers, employees, and the rest of the public in ways that others clearly have not.

As a matter of course, some corporations attend to the human impact of their operations and policies and reject operations and policies that are questionable. Whether the issue be the health effects of sugared cereal or cigarettes, the safety of tires or tampons, civil liberties in the corporation or the community, an organization reveals its character as surely as a person does.

Indeed, the parallel may be even more dramatic. For just as the moral responsibility displayed by an individual develops over time from infancy to adulthood,[4] so too we may expect to find stages of development in organizational character that show significant patterns.

EVALUATING THE IDEA OF MORAL PROJECTION

Concepts like moral responsibility not only make sense when applied to organizations but also provide touchstones for designing more effective models than we have for guiding corporate policy.

Now we can understand what it means to invite SSC as a corporation to be morally responsible both in-house and in its community, but *should* we issue the invitation? Here we turn to the question of advisability. Should we require the organizational agents in our society to have the same moral attributes we require of ourselves?

Our proposal to spell out the processes associated with moral responsibility for individuals and then to project them to their organizational counterparts takes on added meaning when we examine alternative frames of reference for corporate responsibility.

Two frames of reference that compete for the allegiance of people who ponder the question of corporate responsibility are emphatically opposed to this principle of moral projection—what we might refer to as the "invisible hand" view and the "hand of government" view.

The Invisible Hand

The most eloquent spokesman of the first view is Milton Friedman (echoing many philosophers and economists since Adam Smith). According to this pattern of thought, the true and only social responsibilities of business organizations are to make profits and obey the laws. The workings of the free and competitive marketplace will "moralize" corporate behavior quite independently of any attempts to expand or transform decision making via moral projection.

A deliberate amorality in the executive suite is encouraged in the name of systemic morality: the common good is best served when each of us and our economic institutions pursue not the common good or moral purpose, advocates say, but competitive advantage. Morality, responsibility, and conscience reside in the invisible hand of the free market system, not in the hands of the organizations within the system, much less the managers within the organizations.

To be sure, people of this opinion admit, there is a sense in which social or ethical issues can and should enter the corporate mind, but the filtering of such issues is thorough: they go through the screens of custom, public opinion, public relations, and the law. And, in any case, self-interest maintains primacy as an objective and a guiding star.

The reaction from this frame of reference to the suggestion that moral judgment be integrated with corporate strategy is clearly negative. Such an integration is seen as inefficient and arrogant, and in the end both an illegitimate use of corporate power and an abuse of the manager's fiduciary role. With respect to our SSC case, advocates of the invisible hand model would vigorously resist efforts, beyond legal requirements, to make SSC right the wrongs of racial injustice. SSC's responsibility would be to make steel of high quality at least cost, to deliver it on time, and to satisfy its customers and stockholders. Justice would not be part of SSC's corporate mandate.

The Hand of Government

Advocates of the second dissenting frame of reference abound, but John Kenneth Galbraith's work has counterpointed Milton Friedman's with insight and style. Under this view of corporate responsibility, corporations are to pursue objectives that are rational and purely economic. The regulatory hands of the law and the political process rather than the invisible hand of the marketplace turns these objectives to the common good.

Again, in this view, it is a system that provides the moral direction for corporate decision making—a system, though, that is guided by political managers, the custodians of the public purpose. In the case of SSC, proponents of this view would look to the state for moral direction and responsible management, both within SSC and in the community. The corporation would have no moral responsibility beyond political and legal obedience.

What is striking is not so much the radical difference between the economic and social philosophies that underlie these two views of the source of corporate responsibility but the conceptual similarities. Both views locate morality, ethics, responsibility, and conscience in the systems of rules and incentives in which the modern corporation finds itself embedded. Both views reject the exercise of independent moral judgment by corporations as actors in society.

Neither view trusts corporate leaders with stewardship over what are often called noneconomic values. Both require corporate responsibility to march to the beat of drums outside. In the jargon of moral philosophy, both views press for a rule-centered or a system-centered ethics instead of an agent-centered ethics. These frames of reference countenance corporate rule-following responsibility for corporations but not corporate decision-making responsibility.

The Hand of Management

To be sure, the two views under discussion differ in that one looks to an invisible moral force in the market while the other looks to a visible moral force in government. But both would advise against a principle of moral projection that permits or encourages corporations to exercise independent, noneconomic judgment over matters that face them in their short- and long-term plans and operations.

Accordingly, both would reject a third view of corporate responsibility that seeks to affect the thought processes of the organization itself—a sort of "hand of management" view—since neither seems willing or able to see the engines of profit regulate themselves to the degree that would be implied by taking the principle of moral projection seriously. Cries of inefficiency and moral imperialism from the right would be matched by cries of insensitivity and illegitimacy from the left, all in the name of preserving us from corporations and managers run morally amok.

Better, critics would say, that moral philosophy

be left to philosophers, philanthropists, and politicians than to business leaders. Better that corporate morality be kept to glossy annual reports, where it is safely insulated from policy and performance.

The two conventional frames of reference locate moral restraint in forces external to the person and the corporation. They deny moral reasoning and intent to the corporation in the name of either market competition or society's system of explicit legal constraints and presume that these have a better moral effect than that of rationality and respect.

Although the principle of moral projection, which underwrites the idea of a corporate conscience and patterns it on the thought and feeling processes of the person, is in our view compelling, we must acknowledge that it is neither part of the received wisdom, nor is its advisability beyond question or objection. Indeed, attributing the role of conscience to the corporation seems to carry with it new and disturbing implications for our usual ways of thinking about ethics and business.

Perhaps the best way to clarify and defend this frame of reference is to address the objections to the principle found in the last pages of this article. There we see a summary of the criticisms and counterarguments we have heard during hours of discussion with business executives and business school students. We believe that the replies to the objections about a corporation having a conscience are convincing.

LEAVING THE DOUBLE STANDARD BEHIND

We have come some distance from our opening reflection on Southern Steel Company and its role in its community. Our proposal—clarified, we hope, through these objections and replies—suggests that it is not sufficient to draw a sharp line between individuals' private ideas and efforts and a corporation's institutional efforts but that the latter can and should be built upon the former.

Does this frame of reference give us an unequivocal prescription for the behavior of SSC in its circumstances? No, it does not. Persuasive arguments might be made now and might have been made then that SSC should not have used its considerable economic clout to threaten the community into desegregation. A careful analysis of the realities of the environment might have disclosed that such a course would have been counterproductive, leading to more injustice than it would have alleviated.

The point is that some of the arguments and some of the analyses are or would have been moral arguments, and thereby the ultimate decision that of an ethically responsible organization. The significance of this point can hardly be overstated, for it represents the adoption of a new perspective on corporate policy and a new way of thinking about business ethics. We agree with one authority, who writes that "the business firm, as an organic entity intricately affected by and affecting its environment, is as appropriately adaptive . . . to demands for responsible behavior as for economic service."[5]

The frame of reference here developed does not offer a decision procedure for corporate managers. That has not been our purpose. It does, however, shed light on the conceptual foundations of business ethics by training attention on the corporation as a moral agent in society. Legal systems of rules and incentives are insufficient, even though they may be necessary, as frameworks for corporate responsibility. Taking conceptual cues from the features of moral responsibility normally expected of the person in our opinion deserves practicing managers' serious consideration.

The lack of congruence that James Weston saw between individual and corporate moral responsibility can be, and we think should be, overcome. In the process, what a number of writers have characterized as a double standard—a discrepancy between our personal lives and our lives in organizational settings—might be dampened. The principle of moral projection not only helps us to conceptualize the kinds of demands that we might make of corporations and other organizations but also offers the prospect of harmonizing those demands with the demands that we make of ourselves.

IS A CORPORATION A MORALLY RESPONSIBLE "PERSON"?

Objection 1 to the Analogy

Corporations are not persons. They are artificial legal constructions, machines for mobilizing economic investments toward the efficient production of goods and services. We cannot hold a corporation responsible. We can only hold individuals responsible.

Reply

Our frame of reference does not imply that corporations are persons in a literal sense. It simply means that in certain respects concepts and functions normally attributed to persons can also be attributed to organizations made up of persons. Goals, economic values, strategies, and other such personal attributes are often usefully projected to the corporate level by managers and researchers. Why should we not project the functions of conscience in the same way? As for holding corporations responsible, recent criminal prosecutions such as the case of Ford Motor Company and its Pinto gas tanks suggest that society finds the idea both intelligible and useful.

Objection 2

A corporation cannot be held responsible at the sacrifice of profit. Profitability and financial health have always been and should continue to be the "categorical imperatives" of a business operation.

Reply

We must of course acknowledge the imperatives of survival, stability, and growth when we discuss corporations, as indeed we must acknowledge them when we discuss the life of an individual. Self-sacrifice has been identified with moral responsibility in only the most extreme cases. The pursuit of profit and self-interest need not be pitted against the demands of moral responsibility. Moral demands are best viewed as containments—not replacements—for self-interest.

This is not to say that profit maximization never conflicts with morality. But profit maximization conflicts with other managerial values as well. The point is to coordinate imperatives, not deny their validity.

Objection 3

Corporate executives are not elected representatives of the people, nor are they anointed or appointed as social guardians. They therefore lack the social mandate that a democratic society rightly demands of those who would pursue ethically or socially motivated policies. By keeping corporate policies confined to economic motivations, we keep the power of corporate executives in its proper place.

Reply

The objection betrays an oversimplified view of the relationship between the public and the private sector. Neither private individuals nor private corporations that guide their conduct by ethical or social values beyond the demands of law should be constrained merely because they are not elected to do so. The demands of moral responsibility are independent of the demands of political legitimacy and are in fact presupposed by them.

To be sure, the state and the political process will and must remain the primary mechanisms for protecting the public interest, but one might be forgiven the hope that the political process will not substitute for the moral judgment of the citizenry or other components of society such as corporations.

Objection 4

Our system of law carefully defines the role of agent or fiduciary and makes corporate managers accountable to shareholders and investors for the use of their assets. Management cannot, in the name of corporate moral responsibility, arrogate to itself the right to manage those assets by partially noneconomic criteria.

Reply

First, it is not so clear that investors insist on purely economic criteria in the management of their assets, especially if some of the shareholders' resolutions and board reforms of the last decade are any indication. For instance, companies doing buisness in South Africa have had stockholders question their activities, other companies have instituted audit committees for their boards before such auditing was mandated, and mutual funds for which "socially responsible behavior" is a major investment criterion now exist.

Second, the categories of "shareholder" and "investor" connote wider time spans than do immediate or short-term returns. As a practical matter, considerations of stability and long-term return on investment enlarge the class of principals to which managers bear a fiduciary relationship.

Third, the trust that managers hold does not and never has extended to "any means available" to advance the interests of the principals. Both legal and moral constraints must be understood to qualify that trust—even, perhaps, in the name of a larger trust and a more basic fiduciary relationship to the members of society at large.

Objection 5

The power, size, and scale of the modern corporation—domestic as well as international—are awesome. To unleash, even partially, such power from the discipline of the marketplace and the narrow or possibly nonexistent moral purpose implicit in that discipline would be socially dangerous. Had SSC acted in the community to further racial justice, its purposes might have been admirable, but those purposes could have led to a kind of moral imperialism or worse. Suppose SSC had thrown its power behind the Ku Klux Klan.

Reply

This is a very real and important objection. What seems not to be appreciated is the fact that power affects when it is used as well as when it is not used. A decision by SSC not to exercise its economic influence according to "noneconomic" criteria is inevitably a moral decision and just as inevitably affects the community. The issue in the end is not whether corporations (and other organizations) should be "unleashed" to exert moral force in our society but rather how critically and self-consciously they should choose to do so.

The degree of influence enjoyed by an agent, whether a person or an organization, is not so much a factor recommending moral disengagement as a factor demanding a high level of moral awareness. Imperialism is more to be feared when moral reasoning is absent than when it is present. Nor do we suggest that the "discipline of the marketplace" be diluted; rather, we call for it to be supplemented with the discipline of moral reflection.

Objection 6

The idea of moral projection is a useful device for structuring corporate responsibility only if our understanding of moral responsibility at the level of the person is in some sense richer than our understanding of moral responsibility on the level of the organization as a whole. If we are not clear about individual responsibility, the projection is fruitless.

Reply

The objection is well taken. The challenge offered by the idea of moral projection lies in our capacity to articulate criteria or frameworks of reasoning for the morally responsible person. And though such a challenge is formidable, it is not clear that it cannot be met, at least with sufficient consensus to be useful.

For centuries, the study and criticism of frameworks have gone on, carried forward by many disciplines, including psychology, the social sciences, and philosophy. And though it would be a mistake to suggest that any single framework (much less a decision mechanism) has emerged as the right one, it is true that recurrent patterns are discernible and well enough defined to structure moral discussion.

In the body of the article, we spoke of rationality and respect as components of individual responsibility. Further analysis of these components would translate them into social costs and benefits, justice in the distribution of goods and services, basic rights and duties, and fidelity to contracts. The view that pluralism in our society has undercut all possibility of moral agreement is anything but self-evident. Sincere moral disagreement is, of course, inevitable and not clearly lamentable. But a process and a vocabulary for articulating such values as we share is no small step forward when compared with the alternatives. Perhaps in our exploration of the moral projection we might make some surprising and even reassuring discoveries about ourselves.

Objection 7

Why is it necessary to project moral responsibility to the level of the organization? Isn't the task of defining corporate responsibility and business ethics sufficiently discharged if we clarify the responsibilities of men and women in business as individuals? Doesn't ethics finally rest on the honesty and integrity of the individual in the business world?

Reply

Yes and no. Yes, in the sense that the control of large organizations does finally rest in the hands of managers, of men and women. No, in the sense that what is being controlled is a cooperative system for a cooperative purpose. The projection of responsibility to the organization is simply an acknowledgment of the fact that the whole is more than the sum of its parts. Many intelligent people do not an intelligent organization make. Intelligence needs to be structured, organized, divided, and recombined in complex processes for complex purposes.

Studies of management have long shown that the attributes, successes, and failures of organizations are phenomena that emerge from the coordination of persons' attributes and that explanations of such phenomena require categories of analysis and description beyond the level of the individual. Moral responsibility is an attribute that can manifest itself in organizations as surely as competence or efficiency.

Objection 8

Is the frame of reference here proposed intended to replace or undercut the relevance of the "invisible hand" and the "government hand" views, which depend on external controls?

Reply

No. Just as regulation and economic competition are not substitutes for corporate responsibility, so corporate responsibility is not a substitute for law and the market. The imperatives of ethics cannot be relied on—nor have they ever been relied on—without a context of external sanctions. And this is true as much for individuals as for organizations.

This frame of reference takes us beneath, but not beyond, the realm of external systems of rules and incentives and into the thought processes that interpret and respond to the corporation's environment. Morality is more than merely part of that environment. It aims at the projection of conscience, not the enthronement of it in either the state or the competitive process.

The rise of the modern large corporation and the concomitant rise of the professional manager demand a conceptual framework in which these phenomena can be accommodated to moral thought. The principal of moral projection furthers such accommodation by recognizing a new level of agency in society and thus a new level of responsibility.

Objection 9

Corporations have always taken the interests of those outside the corporation into account in the sense that customer relations and public relations generally are an integral part of rational economic decision making. Market signals and social signals that filter through the market mechanism inevitably represent the interests of parties affected by the behavior of the company. What, then, is the point of adding respect to rationality?

Reply

Representing the affected parties solely as economic variables in the environment of the company is treating them as means or resources and not as ends in themselves. It implies that the only voice which affected parties should have in organizational decision making is that of potential buyers, sellers, regulators, or boycotters. Besides, many affected parties may not occupy such roles, and those who do may not be able to signal the organization with messages that effectively represent their stakes in its actions.

To be sure, classical economic theory would have us believe that perfect competition in free markets (with modest adjustments from the state) will result in all relevant signals being "heard," but the abstractions from reality implicit in such theory make it insufficient as a frame of reference for moral responsibility. In a world in which strict self-interest was congruent with the common good, moral responsibility might be unnecessary. We do not, alas, live in such a world.

The element of respect in our analysis of responsibility plays an essential role in ensuring the recognition of unrepresented or underrepresented voices in the decision making of organizations as agents. Showing respect for persons as ends and not mere means to organizational purposes is central to the concept of corporate moral responsibility.

NOTES

1. See John Ladd, "Morality and the Ideal of Rationality in Formal Organizations," *The Monist,* October 1970, p. 499.
2. See William K. Frankena, *Thinking About Morality* (Ann Arbor: University of Michigan Press, 1980), p. 26.
3. See Peter French, "The Corporation as a Moral Person," *American Philosophical Quarterly,* July 1979, p. 207.
4. A process that psychological researchers from Jean Piaget to Lawrence Kohlberg have examined carefully; see Jean Piaget, *The Moral Judgement of the Child* (New York: Free Press, 1965) and Lawrence Kohlberg, *The Philosophy of Moral Development* (New York: Harper & Row, 1981).
5. See Kenneth R. Andrews, *The Concept of Corporate Strategy,* revised edition (Homewood, Ill.: Dow Jones–Irwin, 1980), p. 99.

Corporate Moral Agency

Peter A. French
Lennox Distinguished Professor of the Humanities, Trinity University

1. In one of his *New York Times* columns of not too long ago Tom Wicker's ire was aroused by a Gulf Oil Corporation advertisement that "pointed the finger of blame" for the energy crisis at all elements of our society (and supposedly away from the oil company). Wicker attacked Gulf Oil as the major, if not the sole, perpetrator of that crisis and virtually every other social ill, with the possible exception of venereal disease. I do not know if Wicker was serious or sarcastic in making all of his charges; I have a sinking suspicion that he was in deadly earnest, but I have doubts as to whether Wicker understands or if many people understand what sense such ascriptions of moral responsibility make when their subjects are corporations. My interest is to argue for a theory that accepts corporations as members of the moral community, of equal standing with the traditionally acknowledged residents—biological human beings—and hence treats Wicker-type responsibility ascriptions as unexceptionable instances of a perfectly proper sort without having to paraphrase them. In short, I shall argue that corporations should be treated as full-fledged moral persons and hence that they can have whatever privileges, rights, and duties as are, in the normal course of affairs, accorded to moral persons.

2. There are at least two significantly different types of responsibility ascriptions that I want to distinguish in ordinary usage (not counting the laudatory recommendation, "He is a responsible lad.") The first type pins responsibility on someone or something, the who-dun-it or what-dun-it sense. Austin has pointed out that it is usually used when an event or action is thought by the speaker to be untoward. (Perhaps we are more interested in the failures rather than the successes that punctuate our lives.)

The second type of responsibility ascription, parasitic upon the first, involves the notion of accountability.[1] "Having a responsibility" is interwoven with the notion "Having a liability to answer," and having such a liability or obligation seems to imply (as Anscombe has noted[2]) the existence of some sort of authority relationship either between people, or between people and a deity, or in some weaker versions between people and social norms. The kernel of insight that I find intuitively compelling is that

---

From "The Corporation as a Moral Person" by Peter A. French. Paper presented at the Ethics and Economics Conference, University of Delaware, November 11, 1977.
[*Author's note:* I am grateful to Professors Donald Davidson, J. L. Mackie, Howard Wettstein, and T. E. Uehling for their helpful comments on earlier versions of this paper. I wish also to acknowledge the support of the University of Minnesota Graduate School.]

for someone to legitimately hold someone else responsible for some event, there must exist or have existed a responsibility relationship between them such that in regard to the event in question the latter was answerable to the former. In other words, a responsibility ascription of the second type is properly uttered by someone Z if he or she can hold X accountable for what he or she has done. Responsibility relationships are created in a multitude of ways, e.g., through promises, contracts, compacts, hirings, assignments, appointments, by agreeing to enter a Rawlsian original position, etc. The "right" to hold responsible is often delegated to third parties; but importantly, in the case of moral responsibility, no delegation occurs because no person is excluded from the relationship; moral responsibility relationships hold reciprocally and without prior agreements among all moral persons. No special arrangement needs to be established between parties for anyone to hold someone morally responsible for his or her acts or, what amounts to the same thing, every person is a party to a responsibility relationship with all other persons as regards the doing or refraining from doing of certain acts: those that take descriptions that use moral notions.

Because our interest is in the criteria of moral personhood and not the content or morality, we need not pursue this idea further. What I have maintained is that moral responsibility, although it is neither contractual nor optional, is not a class apart but an extension of ordinary, garden-variety responsibility. What is needed in regard to the present subject, then, is an account of the requirements in *any* responsibility relationship.[3]

3. A responsibility ascription of the second type amounts to the assertion that the person held responsible is the cause of an event (usually an untoward one) and that the action in question was intended by the subject or that the event was the direct result of an intentional act of the subject. In addition to what it asserts, it implies that the subject is liable to account to the speaker (who the speaker is or what the speaker is, a member of the "moral community," a surrogate for that aggregate). The primary focus of responsibility ascriptions of the second type is on the subject's intentions rather than, though not to the exclusion of, occasions.[4]

4. For a corporation to be treated as a responsible agent it must be the case that some things that happen, some events, are describable in a way that makes certain sentences true, sentences that say that some of the things a corporation does were intended by the corporation itself. That is not accomplished if attributing intentions to a corporation is only a shorthand way of attributing intentions to the biological persons who comprise, for example, its board of directors. If that were to turn out to be the case, then on metaphysical if not logical grounds there would be no way to distinguish between corporations and mobs. I shall argue, however, that a corporation's CID Structure (the *C*orporate *I*nternal *D*ecision Structure) is the requisite redescription device that licenses the predication of corporate intentionality.

It is obvious that a corporation's doing something involves or includes human beings' doing things and that the human beings who occupy various positions in a corporation usually can be described as having reasons for *their* behavior. In virtue of those descriptions they may be properly held responsible for their behavior, *ceteris paribus*. What needs to be shown is that there is sense in saying that corporations, and not just the people who work in them, have reasons for doing what they do. Typically, we will be told that it is the directors, or the managers, etc. that really have the corporate reasons and desires, etc. and that although corporate actions may not be reducible without remainder, corporate intentions are always reducible to human intentions.

5. Every corporation must have an internal decision structure. The CID Structure has two elements of interest to us here: (1) an organizational or responsibility flow chart that delineates stations and levels within the corporate power structure and (2) corporate decision recognition rule(s) (usually embedded in some-

thing called "corporate policy"). The CID Structure is the personnel organization for the exercise of the corporation's power with respect to its ventures, and as such its primary function is to draw experience from various levels of the corporation into a decision-making and ratification process. When operative and properly activated, the CID Structure accomplishes a subordination and synthesis of the intentions and acts of various biological persons into a corporate decision. When viewed in another way the CID Structure licenses the descriptive transformation of events seen under another aspect as the acts of biological persons (those who occupy various stations on the organizational chart) as corporate acts by exposing the corporate character of those events. A functioning CID Structure *incorporates* acts of biological persons. For illustrative purposes, suppose we imagine that an event E has at least two aspects, that is, can be described in two nonidentical ways. One of those aspects is "Executive X's doing *y*" and one is "Corporation C's doing *z*." The corporate act and the individual act may have different properties: indeed they have different causal ancestors though they are causally inseparable.[5]

Although I doubt he is aware of the metaphysical reading that can be given to this process, J. K. Galbraith rather neatly captures what I have in mind when he writes in his recent popular book on the history of economics:

> From [the] interpersonal exercise of power, the interaction . . . of the participants, comes the *personality* of the corporation.[6]

I take Galbraith here to be quite literally correct, but it is important to spell out how a CID Structure works this "miracle."

In philosophy in recent years we have grown accustomed to the use of games as models for understanding institutional behavior. We all have some understanding of how rules of games make certain descriptions of events possible that would not be so if those rules were nonexistent. The CID Structure of a corporation is a kind of constitutive rule (or rules) analogous to the game rules with which we are familiar. The organization chart of, for example, the Burlington Northern Corporation distinguishes "players" and clarifies their rank and the interwoven lines of responsibility within the corporation. The Burlington chart lists only titles, not unlike King, Queen, Rook, etc. in chess. What it tells us is that anyone holding the title "Executive Vice President for Finance and Administration" stands in a certain relationship to anyone holding the title "Director of Internal Audit" and to anyone holding the title "Treasurer," etc. Also it expresses, or maps, the interdependent and dependent relationships that are involved in determinations of corporate decisions and actions. In effect, it tells us what anyone who occupies any of the positions is vis-à-vis the decision structure of the whole. The organizational chart provides what might be called the grammar of corporate decision-making. What I shall call internal recognition rules provide its logic.[7]

Recognition rules are of two sorts. Partially embedded in the organizational chart are the procedural recognitors: we see that decisions are to be reached collectively at certain levels and that they are to be ratified at higher levels (or at inner circles, if one prefers the Galbraithean model). A corporate decision is recognized internally not only by the procedure of its making, but by the policy it instantiates. Hence every corporation creates an image (not to be confused with its public image) or a general policy, what G. C. Buzby of the Chilton Company has called the "basic belief of the corporation,"[8] that must inform its decisions for them to be properly described as being those of that corporation. "The moment policy is sidestepped or violated, it is no longer the policy of that company."[9]

Peter Drucker has seen the importance of the basic policy recognitors in the CID Structure (though he treats matters rather differently from the way I am recommending). Drucker writes:

> Because the corporation is an institution it must have a basic policy. For it must subordinate individual ambitions and decisions to the *needs* of the corporation's welfare and survival. That means that it must have a set of principles and a rule of conduct which limit and direct individual actions and behavior.[10]

6. Suppose, for illustrative purposes, we activate a CID Structure in a corporation, Wicker's favorite, the Gulf Oil Corporation. Imagine then that three executives X, Y, and Z have the task of deciding whether or not Gulf Oil will join a world uranium cartel (I trust this may catch Mr. Wicker's attention and hopefully also that of Jerry McAfee, current Gulf Oil Corporation president). X, Y, and Z have before them an Everest of papers that have been prepared by lower echelon executives. Some of the reports will be purely factual in nature, some will be contingency plans, some will be in the form of position papers developed by various departments, some will outline financial considerations, some will be legal opinions, and so on. Insofar as these will all have been processed through Gulf's CID Structure system, the personal reasons, if any, individual executives may have had when writing their reports and recommendations in a specific way will have been diluted by the subordination of individual inputs to peer group input even before X, Y, and Z review the matter. X, Y, and Z take a vote. Their taking of a vote is authorized procedure in the Gulf CID Structure, which is to say that under these circumstances the vote of X, Y, and Z can be redescribed as the corporation's making a decision: that is, the event "X Y Z voting" may be redescribed to expose an aspect otherwise unrevealed, that is quite different from its other aspects, e.g., from X's voting in the affirmative.

But the CID Structure, as already suggested, also provides the grounds in its nonprocedural recognitor for such an attribution of corporate intentionality. Simply, when the corporate act is consistent with the implementation of established corporate policy, then it is proper to describe it as having been done for corporate reasons, as having been caused by a corporate desire coupled with a corporate belief and so, in other words, as corporate intentional.

An event may, under one of its aspects, be described as the conjunctive act "X did *a* (or as X intentionally did *a*) and Y did *a* (or as Y intentionally did *a*) and Z did *a* (or as Z intentionally did *a*)" (where *a* = voted in the affirmative on the question of Gulf Oil joining the cartel). Given the Gulf CID Structure—formulated in this instance as the conjunction of rules: when the occupants of positions A, B, and C on the organizational chart unanimously vote to do something and if doing that something is consistent with an implementation of general corporate policy, other things being equal, then the corporation has decided to do it for corporate reasons—the event is redescribable as "the Gulf Oil Corporation did *j* for corporate reasons *f*" (where *j* is "decided to join the cartel" and *f* is any reason [desire + belief] consistent with basic policy of Gulf Oil, e.g., increasing profits) or simply as "Gulf Oil Corporation intentionally did *j*." This is a rather technical way of saying that in these circumstances the executives voting are, given its CID Structure, also the corporation deciding to do something, and that regardless of the personal reasons the executives have for voting as they do, and even if their reasons are inconsistent with established corporate policy or even if one of them has no reason at all for voting as he does, the corporation still has reasons for joining the cartel; that is, joining is consistent with the inviolate corporate general policies as encrusted in the precedent of previous corporate actions and its statements of purpose as recorded in its certificate of incorporation, annual reports, etc. The corporation's only method of achieving its desires or goals is the activation of the personnel who occupy its various positions. However, if X voted affirmatively purely for reasons of personal monetary gain (suppose he had been bribed to do so), that does not alter the fact that the corporate reason for joining the cartel was to minimize competition and hence pay higher dividends to its shareholders. Corporations have reasons because they have interests in doing those things that are likely to result in realization of their established corporate goals regardless of the transient self-interest of directors, managers, etc. If there is a difference between corporate goals and desires and those of human beings, it is probably that the corporate ones are relatively stable and not very wide ranging, but that is only because corporations can do relatively fewer things than human beings, being confined in action pre-

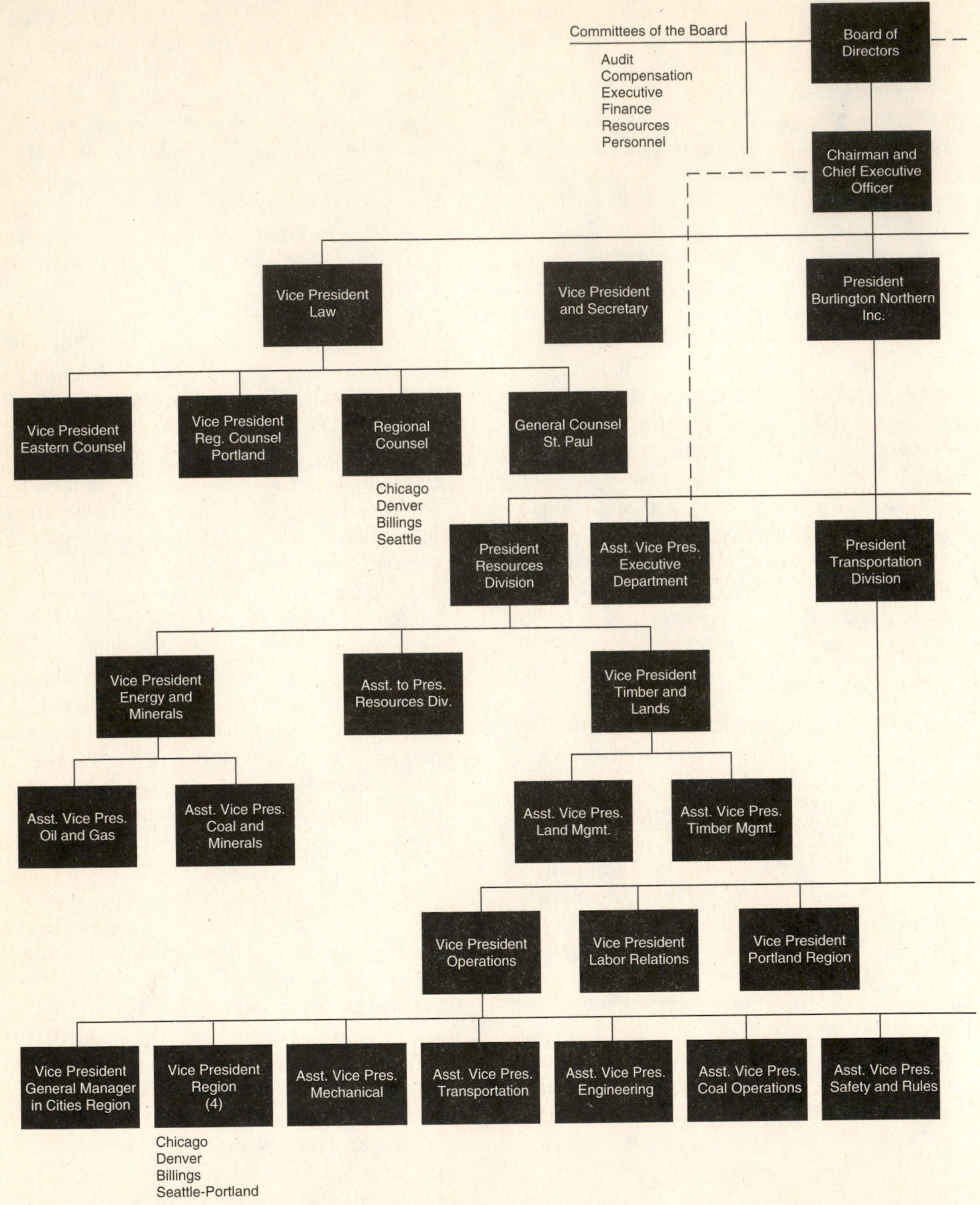

Burlington Northern top management organization chart, January 1, 1977.

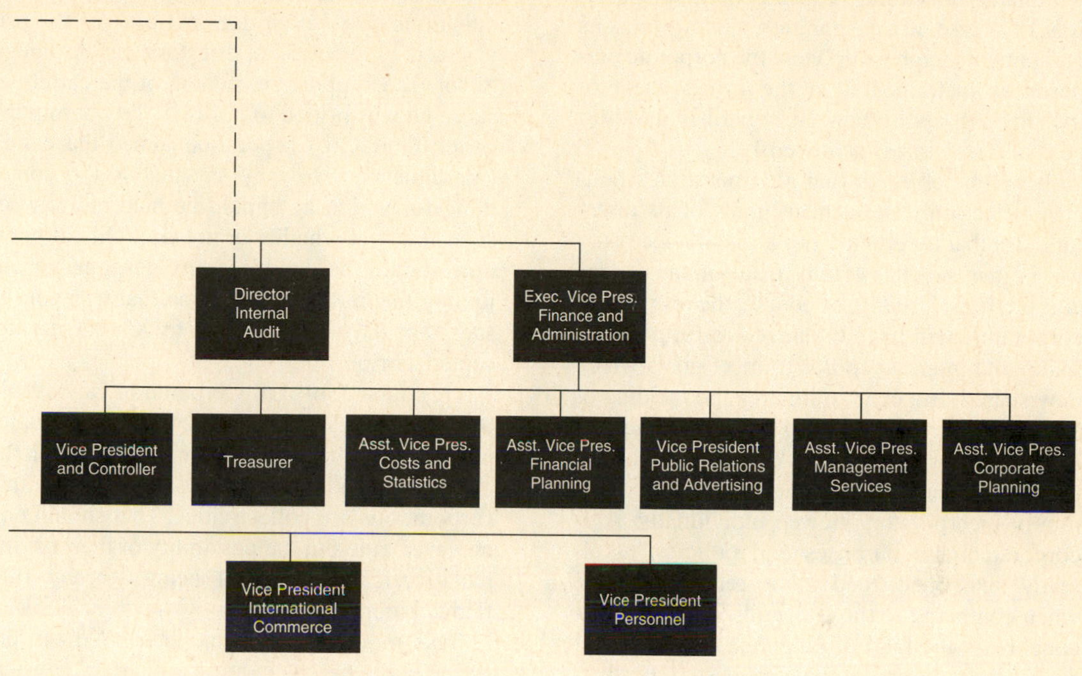
Director
Internal
Audit
Exec. Vice Pres.
Finance and
Administration
Vice President
and Controller
Treasurer
Asst. Vice Pres.
Costs and
Statistics
Asst. Vice Pres.
Financial
Planning
Vice President
Public Relations
and Advertising
Asst. Vice Pres.
Management
Services
Asst. Vice Pres.
Corporate
Planning
Vice President
International
Commerce
Vice President
Personnel

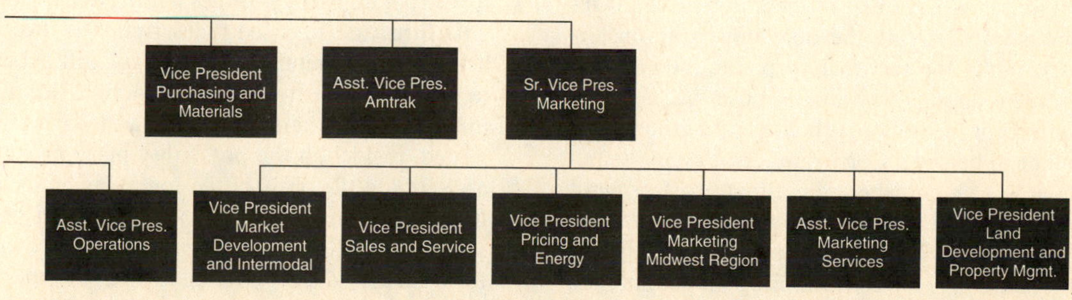
Vice President
Purchasing and
Materials
Asst. Vice Pres.
Amtrak
Sr. Vice Pres.
Marketing
Asst. Vice Pres.
Operations
Vice President
Market
Development
and Intermodal
Vice President
Sales and Service
Vice President
Pricing and
Energy
Vice President
Marketing
Midwest Region
Asst. Vice Pres.
Marketing
Services
Vice President
Land
Development and
Property Mgmt.

dominately to a limited socioeconomic sphere. It is, of course, in a corporation's interest that its component membership view the corporate purposes as instrumental in the achievement of their own goals. (Financial reward is the most common way this is achieved.)

It will be objected that a corporation's policies reflect only the current goals of its directors. But that is certainly not logically necessary nor is it in practice totally true for most large corporations. Usually, of course, the original incorporators will have organized to further their individual interests and/or to meet goals which they shared. But even in infancy the melding of disparate interests and purposes gives rise to a corporate long-range point of view that is distinct from the intents and purposes of the collection of incorporators viewed individually. Also corporate basic purposes and policies, as already mentioned, tend to be relatively stable when compared to those of individuals and not couched in the kind of language that would be appropriate to individual purposes. Furthermore, as histories of corporations will show, when policies are amended or altered it is usually only peripheral issues and matters of style that are involved. Radical policy alteration constitutes a new corporation. This point is captured in the incorporation laws of such states as Delaware. ("Any power which is not enumerated in the charter or which cannot be inferred from it is *ultra vires*[11] of the corporation.") Obviously underlying the objection is an uneasiness about the fact that corporate intent is dependent upon policy and purpose that is but an artifact of the sociopsychology of a group of biological persons. Corporate intent seems somehow to be a tarnished, illegitimate, offspring of human intent. But this objection is a form of the anthropocentric bias that pervades traditional moral theory. By concentrating on possible descriptions of events and by acknowledging only that the possibility of describing something as an agent depends upon whether or not it can be properly described as having done something for a reason, we avoid the temptation of trying to reduce all agents to human referents.

The CID Structure licenses redescriptions of events as corporate and attributions of corporate intentionality while it does not obscure the private acts of executives, directors, etc. Although X voted to support the joining of the cartel because he was bribed to do so, X did not join the cartel: Gulf Oil Corporation joined the cartel. Consequently, we may say that X did something for which he should be held morally responsible, yet whether or not Gulf Oil Corporation should be held morally responsible for joining the cartel is a question that turns on issues that may be unrelated to X's having accepted a bribe.

Of course Gulf Oil Corporation cannot join the cartel unless X or somebody who occupies position A on the organization chart votes in the affirmative. What that shows, however, is that corporations are collectivities. That should not, however, rule out the possibility of their having metaphysical status and being thereby full-fledged moral persons.

This much seems to me clear: We can describe many events in terms of certain physical movements of human beings and we also can sometimes describe those events as done for reasons by those human beings, but further we also can sometimes describe those events as corporate and still further as done for corporate reasons that are qualitatively different from whatever personal reasons, if any, component members may have for doing what they do.

Corporate agency resides in the possibility of CID Structure licensed redescription of events as corporate intentional. That may still appear to be downright mysterious, although I do not think it is, for human agency, as I have suggested, resides in the possibility of description as well. On the basis of the foregoing analysis, however, I think that grounds have been provided for holding corporations *per se* to account for what they do, for treating them as metaphysical persons *qua* moral persons.

A. A. Berle has written:

> The medieval feudal power system set the "lords spiritual" over and against the "lords temporal." These were the men of learning and of the church who in theory were able to say to the greatest power in the

world: "You have committed a sin; therefore either you are excommunicated or you must mend your ways." The lords temporal could reply: "I can kill you." But the lords spiritual could retort: "Yes that you can, but you cannot change the philosophical fact." In a sense this is the great lacuna in the economic power system today.[12]

I have tried to fill that gap by providing reasons for thinking that the moral world is not necessarily composed of homogeneous entities. It is sobering to keep in mind that the Gulf Oil Corporation certainly knows what "You are held responsible for payment in full of the amount recorded on your statement" means. I hope I have provided the beginnings of a basis for an understanding of what "The Gulf Oil Corporation should be held responsible for destroying the ecological balance of the bay" means.

NOTES

1. For which there are good lexical grounds. See *Oxford English Dictionary,* especially entry, Accountability.
2. G. E. M. Anscombe, "Modern Moral Philosophy," *Philosophy* 33, 1958, pp. 1–19.
3. For a more detailed discussion, see my *Foundations of Corporate Responsibility,* forthcoming. In that book I show that the notion of the juristic person does not provide a sufficient account. For example, the deceased in a probate case cannot be *held* responsible in the relevant way by anyone, even though the deceased is a juristic person, a subject of rights.
4. L. Austin, "Three Ways of Spilling Ink," in *Philosophical Papers* (Oxford: Clarendon Press, 1970), p. 273. "In considering responsibility, few things are considered more important than to establish whether a man *intended* to do A, or whether he did A intentionally." Moreover, to be the subject of a responsibility ascription of the second type, to be a party in responsibility relationships, hence to be a moral person, the subject must be, at minimum, what I shall call a Davidsonian agent. If corporations are moral persons, they will be noneliminatable Davidsonian agents. See, for example, Donald Davidson, "Agency," in *Agent, Action, and Reason,* ed. Binkley, Bronaugh and Marros (Toronto: University of Toronto Press, 1971).
5. The causal inseparability of these acts I hope to show is a product of the CID Structure, X's doing y is not the cause of C's doing z nor is C's doing z the cause of X's doing y, although if X's doing y causes Event E then C's doing z causes E and vice versa.
6. John Kenneth Galbraith, *The Age of Uncertainty* (Boston: Houghton Mifflin, 1977), p. 261.
7. By "recognition rule(s)" I mean what Hart, in another context, calls "conclusive affirmative indication" that a decision on act has been made or performed for corporate reasons. H. L. A. Hart, *The Concept of Law* (Oxford: Clarendon Press, 1961), Chap. VI.
8. G. C. Buzby, "Policies—A Guide to What a Company Stands For," *Management Record* (March 1962), p. 5.
9. Ibid.
10. Peter Drucker, *Concept of the Corporation* (New York: John Day Co., 1946/1972), pp. 36–37.
11. Beyond the legal competence.
12. A. A. Berle, "Economic Power and the Free Society," *The Corporate Take-Over,* ed. Andrew Hacker (Garden City, N.Y.: Doubleday, 1964), p. 99.

Corporate Moral Agency: The Case for Anthropological Bigotry

John R. Danley
Professor of Philosophy, Southern Illinois University

In "Corporate Moral Agency,"[1] Peter A. French argues for a position, increasingly popular, which would accept "corporations as members of the moral community, of equal standing with the traditionally acknowledged residents—biological human beings." This is but one implication of accepting the claim that one can legitimately ascribe moral responsibility to corporations. To put the matter somewhat differently, again in French's words, "corporations should be treated as full-fledged moral persons and hence . . . have whatever

---

From *Action and Responsibility: Bowling Green Studies in Applied Philosophy,* Vol. II, 1980. Reprinted by permission of the publisher.

privileges, rights, and duties as are, in the normal course of affairs, accorded to moral persons."

Unwilling to rest content with the usual assaults on prejudices against real persons based on race, creed, sex, religion, or national origin, French is among those[2] seeking to open yet another new front. The struggle is now being extended beyond real persons to eliminate discrimination against a particular class of *personae fictae,* fictitious persons, namely the corporation. Before too hastily endorsing this new "corporate" liberation movement let us pause for reflection. If after serious consideration we do vote to admit these peculiar entities into our rather exclusivist and elitist community of moral beings, we should insist on their having equal standing with the rest of us run-of-the-mill featherless bipeds. After all, what moral neighborhood worthy of the name would allow second-class citizens? After examining the case for admission, however, I find myself driven to the uncomfortable position of defending apartheid, biological apartheid that is, of defending anthropological bigotry. I contend that corporations should not be included in the moral community; they should not be granted full-fledged moral status. Within this emotionally charged atmosphere it is tempting to employ the standard *ad hominems* of bigotry ("Think of the value of your property"; or, "Before you know it your daughter will bring a corporation home to dinner"; "What about the children?"; and so forth), but I will attempt to ward off these temptations. My claim is that the corporatist programs of the kind represented by French would seriously disturb the logic of our moral discourse. Indeed, the corporatist position, while offering no substantial advantages, would entail the reduction of biological persons to the status of second-class citizens. Let us turn now to the dispute.

I

There is little doubt that we often speak of corporations as being responsible for this or that sin or charitable act, whether of microscopic or cosmic proportions. The question is what we mean when we speak in that way. Sometimes all we mean is that the corporation is the cause of such and such. In these instances we are isolating a cause for an event or state of affairs, an exercise not much more (or less) troublesome than saying "The icy pavement caused the accident." The debate revolves around a fuller sense of "responsibility," a sense which includes more than the idea of "causing to happen." In this richer sense, we ascribe responsibility only if the event or state of affairs caused was also intended by the agent.

When the concept of responsibility is unpacked in this fashion, the traditionalists appear to have victory already in hand. Whatever else we may say of them, collective entities are surely not the kinds of things capable of intending. Individuals within the corporation can intend, lust, have malice aforethought, and so forth, but the corporation cannot. Traditionalists, like myself, maintain that only persons, i.e., entities with particular physical and mental properties, can be morally responsible. Corporations lack these. For the traditionalists, to speak of corporations being responsible is simply elliptical for speaking of certain individuals within the corporation being responsible. On this point, and perhaps this one alone, I do not believe Milton Friedman[3] to be in error.

Undaunted by this venerable line of reasoning, the corporatists proceed to press their case. Although it is French's view that I am treating, I am concerned not so much with the details of his argument as with the general outlines of the corporatist position. Using French's theory as representative, however, provides us with one of the most forceful, sophisticated theories developed. French has worked for years in the area of collective responsibility.[4] His strategy is to accept the traditionalists' analysis of "responsibility," and then to attempt to show that some sense can be made of ascribing "intentions" to a corporation.

The key to making some sense of corporate "intentions" is what French calls the Corporate Internal Decision Structure, the CID. The CID is that which allows one, "licenses" one, to redescribe the actions of certain individuals within a corporation as actions of the corporation. Although the notion is complicated, a CID contains two elements which are particularly relevant:

1. an organization or responsibility flow chart delineating stations and levels within the corporate power structure and
2. corporate decision recognition rules.

As French puts it, the organizational chart provides the grammar for corporate decision making; the recognition rules provide the logic. The purpose of the organizational chart is to locate which procedures will count as decisions for the corporation, and who may or must participate in those procedures. The recognition rules, we are informed, are of two sorts. The first sort are procedural recognitors, "partially embedded in the organizational chart." What these amount to, it seems, are directives more explicit than those contained in the chart, expanding upon it. The second sort of recognition rules are expressed primarily in corporate policy.

Employing the cumbersome apparatus of the CID, some acts may now be described in two non-identical ways, or so it is claimed.

> One of these . . . is 'Executive X's doing y' and one is 'Corporation C's doing z.' The corporate act, and the individual act may have different properties; indeed, they have different causal ancestors though they are causally inseparable.

The effect of this, of course, is that when certain individuals as specified by the organizational chart, engage in certain procedures as specified by the organizational chart and some recognition rules, and act in accordance with other recognition rules (corporate policy), then French claims we can redescribe the action as a corporate act, an intentional corporate act. It is critical to the corporatist position that the two descriptions are non-identical. Saying that "Corporation C did z" is not reducible to the statement that "Executives X, Y, and Z, voted to do y," even though y and z are the same. Since they are non-identical the traditionalist is supposedly prevented from ascribing responsibility only to these individuals. The acts of the individuals are necessary for a corporate act but not identical with it.

Like a child with a new toy, one is strongly inclined by the glitter of this technical hardware to dismantle it, to try to find out how it all works, to see whether it really fits together, to see how and whether it can handle hard cases. To be sure, there are some problems which one can detect immediately. Let me mention two. First of all, it is unclear what French means by an organizational chart. Since his examples are those of nice neat black lines and boxes on a page, like the ones found in business textbooks and corporate policy manuals, one is left with the impression that this is what he has in mind. If so, there are severe difficulties. Most everyone is aware of the extent to which corporate reality departs from the ethereal world of black lines and boxes. Will French maintain that any decisions made by the managers of corporations which do not conform to the organizational chart are not decisions of the corporation? Biting the bullet here may be the best course but it is probable that most decisions are not strictly corporate decisions then. Few corporations act at all, if this criterion is used. French needs a more positivistic interpretation[5] of the organizational chart, one which would insure that the flow chart realistically captured the actual procedures and personages holding the powers. The difficulty with this modification, however, is that the CID begins to lose its function as a normative criterion by which to determine which acts are corporate acts and which are not. The positivistic interpretation would mean that a corporate act is whatever some powerful person within the corporation manages to get others in the corporation to perform, or gets others outside to accept as a corporate act. That will not work at all. The CID appears nestled upon the familiar horns of a dilemma. At least more work is necessary here.

There is a second difficulty. A basic component of the CID must be the corporate charter. Recently the general incorporation charters have become little more than blank tablets for the corporation to engage in business for "any lawful purpose," although some aspects of the organizational chart and a few recognition rules are delineated. Even these permissive rules of recognition have pertinence for French. Suppose every aspect of the CID was followed except that the board of directors voted unanimously to engage the corporation in some unlawful activity. According to the charter, a part of the CID, this is not possible. One could not redescribe such an act as a corporate act. The result of this is that corporations can never act illegally.

Unlike the Augustinian doctrine that for fallen man it is not possible not to sin, the French doctrine appears to be that for the corporation it is not possible to sin at all.

These are but two of many queries which might be addressed to French's proposal. However, it is not my concern to dwell on such technical points here, lest we be distracted from the larger issue. Suppose, for the sake of argument, that we accept some mode of redescribing individual acts such that one could identify these acts as constituting a corporate intentional act. Accept French's. Would that establish the corporatist case? I think not. French tips his hand, for instance, when he writes that what "needs to be shown is that there is sense in saying that corporations, and not just the people who work in them, have reasons for doing what they do." But, obviously, French needs to show much more. All that is established by a device which redescribes, is that there is *a sense* in saying that corporations have intentions. The significant question is whether that sense of "intend" is the one used by the traditionalist when explicating "responsibility," and when denying that corporations can have intentions. The traditionalists can easily, and quite plausibly, claim that the corporatist is equivocating on "intend." The sense in which a corporation intends is much different from that in which a biological person intends. The corporatist has further laid the foundation for this charge by finding it necessary to construct the apparatus so that the sense of "intend" involved can be made clear. The more clearly this sense of "intend" is articulated, the more clearly it diverges from what we usually mean by "intend." The arbitrariness of constructing a sense of "intend" should be evident when we consider the possibility of ascribing intentions to numerous other entities, such as plants, animals, or machines. One could go to extraordinary lengths to provide a sense for attributing intentionality to many of these. Yet, few would contend that it was very similar to what we mean in attributing "intention" to humans.

Consider a computer programmed to play chess which learns from previous mistakes. There is a sense in which the computer intends to respond P-K4 to my king pawn opening, but is this the same sense of "intend" as when I intended P-K4? Furthermore, even ascribing an intention to the computer by no means entails that we would be ready to ascribe responsibility to it. The point is that it remains for the corporatist to demonstrate the relationship between the sense of "intend" and the sense involved in ascriptions of responsibility to humans. Hence, a rather difficult task remains for the corporatist before the case is made.

II

Thus far I have established only that the corporatist has failed to establish the position. I must admit that I am not entirely enamored of the preceding line of argument. The dispute smacks of the theological controversies concerning whether "wisdom" or "goodness" when attributed to God have the same sense as when predicated of humans. Nonetheless, the corporatist has moved the debate in that direction by attempting to equate two markedly different senses. There are, fortunately, other factors to be considered in evaluating the corporatist position. These factors appear when one expands the focus of attention beyond the narrow conditions for ascribing "responsibility," and begins to examine the concept as it functions in the broader context of moral discourse.

Much hangs in the balance when ascribing "responsibility." Affixing responsibility is a prelude to expressing approbation or disapprobation—praise or blame. When the agent responsible is praised, that is the final move in the moral game. (Morality never pays very well.) But, when the responsibility is affixed and the agent in question is blame worthy, that is far from the end of the matter. In this case, affixing responsibility and expressing disfavor is itself a prelude to many further permissible or obligatory moves. Minimally, the blameworthy party is expected to express regret or remorse. More importantly, the agent may be required to pay compensation or be subject to punishment. Ascribing responsibility opens the door for these major moral moves. (There are other door openers as well, for example, the notion of cause in strict liability.) Any understanding of the concept of responsibility is incomplete without incorporating the role it plays in relation to these other moral moves. It is this which is lacking from the previous discussion of "intend." Such an analysis cannot be provided here. What can be done, however, is to sketch briefly how ascribing responsibility to corporations effectively blocks these moves, sundering many of the threads which tie "responsibility" so intimately with concepts like remorse, regret, compensation, or punishment. Let me elaborate.

An indication of the consequences of admitting the corporation into the moral community have been foreshadowed by admission into the legal corpus as a person. That legacy is an odious one, marred by an environment within which the corporation has enjoyed nearly all of the benefits associated with personhood while shouldering but few of the burdens or risks. Much the same would result from admission into the moral world. That legacy is not solely to be explained by jaundiced justices or bad judicial judgments, but is a natural consequence of attempting to pretend that the corporation is just another pretty face. While the law early began holding the corporation liable (read: responsible) for certain specified acts, and the scope of things for which it was liable has dramatically increased over the years, there has been a hesitancy to judge that corporations could be subject to most criminal statutes. One of the major stumbling blocks was just the one which is the subject of this paper. It was clear that many of the criminal statutes required criminal intent, or a criminal state of mind, and unable to locate the corporate mind, it was judged that the corporation was not subject to these. The relevance of proposals such as French's is that the justices would now have a method for determining when the corporation acts with intent, with malice aforethought, with premeditation or out of passion. What I am anxious to bring to light, however, is that these proposals offer no advantage over the traditionalist view and in fact create further problems. Consider now the moral moves involved in extracting compensation from, or punishing, a guilty person. How is one to make these moral moves against a corporate person? One cannot. An English jurist put the point well in an often quoted quip to the effect that corporations have no pants to kick, no soul to damn. We may concur with the sentiment of that jurist who concluded that "by God they ought to have both," but they have neither, although French has given them a surrogate soul, the CID.

The corporation cannot be kicked, whipped, imprisoned, or hanged by the neck until dead. Only individuals of the corporation can be punished. What of punishment through the pocketbook, or extracting compensation for a corporate act? Here too, the corporation is not punished, and does not pay the compensation. Usually one punishes the stockholders who in the present corporate climate have virtually no control over corporate actions. Or, if the corporation can pass on the cost of a fiscal punishment or compensation, it is in the end the consumer who pays for the punishment or compensation. If severe enough, hitting the pocketbook may result in the reduction of workforce, again resting the burden on those least deserving, more precisely, on those not responsible at all. Sooner or later, usually sooner, someone hits upon the solution of punishing those individuals of the corporation most directly responsible for the corporate act. There are also moral difficulties associated with this alternative. For example, many top executives are protected through insurance policies, part of the perks of the job. That would be satisfactory if the intent is simply to compensate, but it neutralizes any deterrent or retributive effect. But let us pass over these considerations and examine more closely these recommendations to "go inside" the corporation to punish an individual, whether stockholder, employee, agent, manager, or director of the corporation.

For the traditionalist there is little difficulty. The traditionalist recognizes the corporation as a legal fiction which for better or worse may have equal protection under the law of other persons, but the traditionalist may accept those legal trappings as at best a useful way of treating the corporation for legal purposes. For the traditionalist it makes moral sense for the law to go inside the corporation. After all, morally the corporation is not responsible: only individuals are. As long as those within the corporation pay for the deed, there is no theoretical difficulty.

What of the corporatist's position? The single

advantage is that the adoption of that position would mean that some sense could be made of pointing an accusing finger or raising a fist in moral outrage at a fictitious person, a behavior which might otherwise appear not only futile but ridiculous. In the new corporatist scheme the behavior would no longer be ridiculous, only futile. The disadvantages, on the other hand, are apparent when one attempts to follow the responsibility assignment with the normally attendant moral moves as I have just shown. Either those moves are blocked entirely, since one may find no method by which to punish, or the moves are diverted away from the genuine culprit (the fictitious moral agent) and directed toward someone inside the corporation (non-fictitious moral agent). Either alternative is unacceptable. The former would entail that some citizens of the moral community, namely corporate persons, were not subject to the full obligations of membership. That reduces biological members to the status of second-class citizens, shouldering as they do all the burdens. The latter alternative, "going inside," is equally offensive. This alternative means that biological agents are sacrificed vicariously for the sins of the corporation. This solution not only reduces the biological agents to second-class citizens, but would make scapegoats or worse, sacrificial lambs, of them. Thus would the admission of the corporation into the moral community threaten to disturb the logic associated with the ascription of responsibility.

In addition to these problems, the corporatists face other theoretical obstacles. It is not clear that "going inside" a corporation is often, if ever, intelligible, given the analysis of a corporate act. To counter the traditionalist's claim that only individuals are responsible, French claims that the corporate act is not identical with the acts of individuals in the corporation. Given this, how is it possible now to reverse that claim and hold individuals responsible for something which they did not do? All they did at most was to vote for the corporation to do something, or to pay for something to be done on behalf of the corporation. The claim that individual acts and corporate acts are not identical opens the door to criminalless crime, a possibility admitted openly by French in another earlier paper. French there notes that a collective entity may be responsible yet no individual in that collectivity be responsible. Far from being an extreme case, that outcome may include all corporate acts. As mentioned above, such an alternative is unacceptable. But, again, can one make intelligible going inside to make one or more individuals responsible? In order to do so the corporatist must shift ground and concede that the individual acts and the corporate acts are identical, or perhaps that the individuals, by voting on a course of illegal or immoral action, coerced the hapless corporation to go along with the deed.

III

Although I have offered what I take to be a satisfactory defense of the traditionalist position, I would like to close by suggesting an alternative model for viewing the corporation. An alternative is needed because the corporatist's model has largely succeeded in warping many of our intuitions and is reinforced not only by legal idioms, but by managerial vocabulary. In many a corporatist's eye the corporation is an organism, and perhaps even much like a biological person. It has a brain, nerve receptors, muscle, it moves, reproduces, expands, develops, grows, in some periods the "fat is cut off," processes information, makes decisions, and so on. It adjusts to the environment. Such a metaphor may be useful but we have now begun to be victimized by the metaphorical model. Unfortunately, reformers have found it useful to accept that language and that model. It is useful to personify and then to vilify. The model, I fear, stands behind many attempts to endow the corporation with moral agency and personhood.

A more adequate model, especially for those who are reform minded, I would maintain provides a different perspective from which to view contemporary trends. The corporation is more like a machine than an organism.[6] Like machines they are human inventions, designed by humans, modified by humans, operated by humans. Like many machines they are controlled by the few for the benefit of the few. They are no longer simple, easily understandable, organizations, but as complicated as the latest piece of electronic hardware. It takes years of training to learn how to operate and direct one. Like machines they are created, yet they create and shape humans.

If a complicated machine got out of hand and ravaged a community, there seems something perverse about expressing our moral outrage and indignation to the machine. More appropriately, our fervor should be addressed to the operators and to the designers of the machine. They, not the machines, are morally responsible. To ascribe responsibility to such machines, no matter how complicated, is tantamount to mistaking the created for the creator. This mystification is a contemporary form of animism. Such is the case for anthropological bigotry.

NOTES

1. The basic argument of the article appears in a more detailed version in French's forthcoming book *Foundations of Corporate Responsibility.* I have not had the opportunity to consult that book. See also his article in the *American Philosophical Quarterly,* Vol. 13, No. 3, 1976.
2. Of those who apparently espouse this view to some degree are Norman Bowie and Tom L. Beauchamp in *Ethical Theory and Business* (Englewood Cliffs, N.J., Prentice-Hall, Inc., 1979) e.g. Chapter 1 and comments on page 128 and Christopher Stone in *Where The Law Ends* (Harper Colophon, New York, 1975).
3. See *Capitalism and Freedom,* (Chicago, IL, University of Chicago Press, 1962), pp. 133–136.
4. One of French's earliest works is "Morally Blaming Whole Populations," which appears in *Philosophy, Morality, and International Affairs* (New York, Oxford University Press, 1974) edited by Virginia Held et al., pp. 266–285.
5. The positive interpretation is suggested by, among other things, French's references to Austin and H. L. A. Hart. The distinction between organizational chart and recognition rules also resembles the positivistic distinction between secondary and primary rules.
6. Although I do not follow Ladd's argument, one good example of taking this alternative model seriously is demonstrated in his "Morality and the Ideal of Rationality in Formal Organizations," in *The Monist,* Vol. 54 (October 1970), pp. 488–516.

QUESTIONS FOR DISCUSSION

1. What do Goodpaster and Matthews mean when they say that the "invisible hand" view and the "hand of government" view of the corporation are "conceptually similar"? How does their proposed "hand of management" view differ?
2. Consolidated Industries, Inc., a chemical company, has a company policy containing the clause, "Consolidated Industries, Inc., regards the safety of employees, consumers, and the surrounding community as of paramount importance. All reasonable precautions must be taken to make the operation of our plants as safe as possible." One day, carelessness at Consolidated's Topeka, Alabama, plant results in an explosion and a chemical leak, causing injury and death to hundreds of people. Under French's view, is Consolidated Industries morally responsible for the action? Would Consolidated Industries be morally responsible if its company policy were different? How would Danley respond to these questions?

CHAPTER 5

Governance and Structure

Who Rules the Corporation?

Ralph Nader
Mark Green
Joel Seligman
Nader—Founder of Public Citizen, Inc. and Center for the Study of Responsive Law.
Green—Director, The Corporate Accountability Research Group.
Seligman—Professor, School of Law, University of Michigan.

All modern state corporation statutes describe a common image of corporate governance, an image pyramidal in form. At the base of the pyramid are the shareholders or owners of the corporation. Their ownership gives them the right to elect representatives to direct the corporation and to approve fundamental corporate actions such as mergers or bylaw amendments. The intermediate level is held by the board of directors, who are required by a provision common to nearly every state corporation law "to manage the business and affairs of the corporation." On behalf of the shareholders, the directors are expected to select and dismiss corporate officers; to approve important financial decisions; to distribute profits; and to see that accurate periodic reports are forwarded to the shareholders. Finally, at the apex of the pyramid are the corporate officers. In the eyes of the law, the officers are the employees of the shareholder owners. Their authority is limited to those responsibilities which the directors delegate to them.

In reality, this legal image is virtually a myth. In nearly every large American business corporation, there exists a management autocracy. One man—variously titled the President, or the Chairman of the Board, or the Chief Executive Officer—or a small coterie of men rule the corporation. Far from being chosen by the directors to run the corporation, this chief executive or executive clique chooses the board of directors and, with the acquiescence of the board, controls the corporation.

The common theme of many instances of mismanagement is a failure to restrain the power of these senior executives. A corporate chief executive's decisions to expand, merge, or even violate the law can often be made without accountability to outside scrutiny. There is, for example, the de-

---

Excerpted from Ralph Nader, Mark Green, and Joel Seligman, *Taming the Giant Corporation* (New York; W.W. Norton, 1976).

tailed disclosures of the recent bribery cases. Not only do these reports suggest how widespread corporate foreign and domestic criminality has become; they also provide a unique study in the pathology of American corporate management.

At Gulf Corporation, three successive chief executive officers were able to pay out over $12.6 million in foreign and domestic bribes over a 15-year period without the knowledge of "outside" or non-employee directors on the board. At Northrop, chairman Thomas V. Jones and vice president James Allen were able to create and fund the Economic and Development Corporation, a separate Swiss company, and pay $750,000 to Dr. Hubert Weisbrod, a Swiss attorney, to stimulate West German jet sales without the knowledge of the board or, apparently, other senior executives. At 3M, chairman Bert Cross and finances vice president Irwin Hansen ordered the company insurance department to pay out $509,000 for imaginary insurance and the bookkeeper to fraudulently record the payments as a "necessary and proper" business expense for tax purposes. Ashland Oil Corporation's chief executive officer, Orwin E. Atkins, involved at least eight executives in illegally generating and distributing $801,165 in domestic political contributions, also without question.

The legal basis for such a consolidation of power in the hands of the corporation's chief executive is the proxy election. Annually the shareholders of each publicly held corporation are given the opportunity of either attending a meeting to nominate and elect directors or returning proxy cards to management or its challengers signing over their right to vote. Few shareholders personally attend meetings. Sylvan Silver, a Reuters correspondent who covers over 100 Wilmington annual meetings each year, described representative 1974 meetings in an interview: At Cities Service Company, the 77th largest industrial corporation with some 135,000 shareholders, 25 shareholders actually attended the meeting; El Paso Natural Gas with 125,000 shareholders had 50 shareholders; at Coca Cola, the 69th largest corporation with 70,000 shareholders, 25 shareholders attended the annual meeting; at Bristol Meyers with 60,000 shareholders a like 25 shareholders appeared. Even "Campaign GM," the most publicized shareholder challenge of the past two decades, attracted no more than 3,000 of General Motors' 1,400,000 shareholders, or roughly two-tenths of one percent.

Thus, corporate directors are almost invariably chosen by written proxies. Yet management so totally dominates the proxy machinery that corporate elections have come to resemble the Soviet Union's euphemistic "Communist ballot"—that is, a ballot which lists only one slate of candidates. Although federal and state laws require the annual performance of an elaborate series of rituals pretending there is "corporate democracy," in 1973, 99.7 percent of the directorial elections in our largest corporations were uncontested.

THE BEST DEMOCRACY MONEY CAN BUY

The key to management's hegemony is money. Effectively, only incumbent management can nominate directors—because it has a nearly unlimited power to use corporate funds to win board elections while opponents must prepare separate proxies and campaign literature entirely at their own expense.

There is first management's power to print and post written communications to shareholders. In a typical proxy contest, management will "follow up" its initial proxy solicitation with a bombardment of five to ten subsequent mailings. As attorneys Edward Aranow and Herb Einhorn explain in their treatise, *Proxy Contests for Corporate Control:*

> Perhaps the most important aspect of the followup letter is its role in the all-important efforts of a soliciting group to secure the *latest-dated* proxy from a stockholder. It is characteristic of every proxy contest that a large number of stockholders will sign and return proxies to one faction and then change their minds and want to have their stock used for the opposing faction.

The techniques of the Northern States Power Company in 1973 are illustrative. At that time, Northern States Power Company voluntarily employed cumulative voting, which meant that only 7.2 percent of outstanding shares was necessary to elect one director to Northern's 14-person board. Troubled by Northern's record on environmental and consumer issues, a broadly based coalition of public interest groups called the Citizens' Advocate for Public Utility Responsibility (CAPUR) nominated Ms. Alpha Snaby, a former Minnesota state legislator, to run for director. These groups then successfully solicited the votes of over 14 percent of all shareholders, or more than twice the votes necessary to elect her to the board.

Northern States then bought back the election. By soliciting proxies a second, and then a third time, the Power Company was able to persuade (or confuse) the shareholders of 71 percent of the 2.8 million shares cast for Ms. Snaby to change their votes.

Larger, more experienced corporations are usually less heavyhanded. Typically, they will begin a proxy campaign with a series of "buildup" letters preliminary to the first proxy solicitation. In Campaign GM, General Motors elevated this strategy to a new plateau by encasing the Project on Corporate Responsibility's single 100-word proxy solicitation within a 21-page booklet specifically rebutting each of the Project's charges. The Project, of course, could never afford to respond to GM's campaign. The postage costs of soliciting GM's 1,400,000 shareholders alone would have exceeded $100,000. The cost of printing a document comparable to GM's 21-page booklet, mailing it out, accompanied by a proxy statement, a proxy card, and a stamped return envelope to each shareholder might have run as high as $500,000.

Nor is it likely that the Project or any other outside shareholder could match GM's ability to hire "professional" proxy solicitors such as Georgeson & Company, which can deploy up to 100 solicitors throughout the country to personally contact shareholders, give them a campaign speech, and urge them to return their proxies. By daily tabulation of returned proxies, professional solicitors are able to identify on a day-by-day basis the largest blocks of stock outstanding which have yet to return a favorable vote.

THE STATE OF THE BOARD

But does not the board of directors with its sweeping statutory mandate "to manage the business and affairs of every corporation" provide an internal check on the power of corporate executives? No. Long ago the grandiloquent words of the statutes ceased to have any operative meaning. "Directors," William O. Douglas complained in 1934, "do not direct." "[T]here is one thing all boards have in common, regardless of their legal position." Peter Drucker has written. *"They do not function."* In Robert Townsend's tart analysis. "[M]ost big companies have turned their boards of directors into nonboards. . . . In the years that I've spent on various boards I've never heard a single suggestion from a director (made as a director *at* a board meeting) that produced any result at all."

Recently these views are corroborated by Professor Myles Mace of the Harvard Business School, the nation's leading authority on the performance of boards of directors. In *Directors—Myth and Reality,* Mace summarized the results of hundreds of interviews with corporate officers and directors.

Directors do not establish the basic objectives, corporate strategies or broad policies of large and medium-size corporations, Mace found. Management creates the policies. The board has a right of veto but rarely exercises it. As one executive said, "Nine hundred and ninety-nine times out of a thousand, the board goes along with management. . . ." Or another, "I can't think of a single time when the board has failed to support a proposed policy of management or failed to endorse the recommendation of management."

The board does not select the president or other chief executive officers. "What is perhaps the most common definition of a function of the board of directors—namely, to select the president—was found to be the greatest myth," reported Mace. "The board of directors in most companies, except in a crisis, does not select the president. The president usually chooses the man who succeeds him to that position, and the board complies with the legal amenities in endorsing and voting his election." A corporate president agreed: "The former company president tapped me to be president, and I assure you that I will select my successor when the time comes." Even seeming exceptions such as RCA's 1975 ouster of Robert Sarnoff frequently turn out to be at the instigation of senior operating executives rather than an aroused board.

The board's role as disciplinarian of the corporation is more apparent than real. As the business-supported Conference Board conceded, "One of the most glaring deficiencies attributed to the corporate board . . . is its failure to monitor and evaluate the performance of the chief executive in a concrete way." To cite a specific example, decisions on executive compensation are made by the president—with perfunctory board approval in most situations. In the vast majority of corporations, Professor Mace found, the compensation committee, and the board which approves the recommendations of the compensation committee, "are not decisionmaking bodies."

Exceptions to this pattern become news events. In reporting on General Motors' 1971 annual shareholders' meeting, the *Wall Street Journal* noted that, "The meeting's dramatic highlight was an impassioned and unprecedented speech by the Rev. Leon Sullivan, GM's recently appointed Negro director, supporting the Episcopal Church's efforts to get the company out of South Africa. It was the first time that a GM director had ever spoken against management at an annual meeting." Now Rev. Sullivan is an unusual outside director, being General Motor's first black director and only "public interest" director. But what makes Leon Sullivan most extraordinary is that he was the first director in *any* major American corporation to come out publicly against his own corporation when its operations tended to support apartheid.

REVAMPING THE BOARD

The modern corporation is akin to a political state in which all powers are held by a single clique. The senior executives of a large firm are essentially not accountable to any other officials within the firm. These are precisely the circumstances that, in a democratic political state, require a separation of powers into different branches of authority. As James Madison explained in the *Federalist No. 47:*

> The accumulation of all powers, legislative, executive, and judiciary, in the same hands, whether of one, a few or many, and whether hereditary, self-appointed, or elective, may justly be pronounced the very definition of tyranny. Were the federal constitution, therefore, really chargeable with this accumulation of power, or with a mixture of powers, having a dangerous tendency to such an accumulation, no further arguments would be necessary to inspire a universal reprobation of the system.

A similar concern over the unaccountability of business executives historically led to the elevation of a board of directors to review and check the actions of operating management. As a practical matter, if corporate governance is to be reformed, it must begin by returning the board to this historical role. The board should serve as an internal auditor of the corporations, responsible for constraining executive management from violations of law and breach of trust. Like a rival branch of government, the board's function must be defined as separate from operating management. Rather than pretending directors can "manage" the corporation, the board's role as disciplinarian should be clearly described. Specifically, the board of directors should:

- establish and monitor procedures that assure that operating executives are informed of and obey applicable federal, state, and local laws:
- approve or veto all important executive management business proposals such as corporate bylaws, mergers, or dividend decisions:
- hire and dismiss the chief executive officer and be able to disapprove the hiring and firing of the principal executives of the corporation; and
- report to the public and the shareholders how well the corporation has obeyed the law and protected the shareholders' investment.

It is not enough, however, to specify what the board should do. State corporations statutes have long provided that "the business and affairs of a corporation shall be managed by a board of directors," yet it has been over a century since the boards of the largest corporations have actually performed this role. To reform the corporation, a federal chartering law must also specify the manner in which the board performs its primary duties.

First, to insure that the corporation obeys federal and state laws, the board should designate executives responsible for compliance with these laws and require periodic signed reports describing the effectiveness of compliance procedures. Mechanisms to administer spot checks on compliance with the principal statutes should be created. Similar mechanisms can insure that corporate "whistle blowers" and nonemployee sources may communicate to the board—in private and without fear of retaliation—knowledge of violations of law.

Second, the board should actively review important executive business proposals to determine their full compliance with law, to preclude conflicts of interest, and to assure that executive decisions are rational and informed of all foreseeable risks and costs. But even though the board's responsibility here is limited to approval or veto of executive initiatives, it should proceed in as well-informed a manner as practicable. To demonstrate rational business judgment, the directorate should require management "to prove its case." It should review the studies upon which management relied to make a decision, require management to justify its decision in terms of costs or rebutting dissenting views, and, when necessary, request that outside experts provide an independent business analysis.

Only with respect to two types of business decisions should the board exceed this limited review role. The determination of salary, expense, and benefit schedules inherently possesses such obvious conflicts of interest for executives that only the board should make these decisions. And since the relocation of principal manufacturing facilities tends to have a greater effect on local communities than any other type of business decision, the board should require management to prepare a "community impact statement." This public report would be similar to the environmental impact statements presently required by the National Environmental Policy Act. It would require the corporation to state the purpose of a relocation decision; to compare feasible alternative means; to quantify the costs to the local community; and to consider methods to mitigate these costs. Although it would not prevent a corporation from making a profit-maximizing decision, it would require the corporation to minimize the costs of relocation decisions to local communities.

To accomplish this restructuring of the board requires the institutionalization of a new profession: the full-time "professional" director. Corporate scholars frequently identify William O. Douglas' 1940 proposal for "salaried, professional experts [who] would bring a new responsibility and authority to directorates and a new safety to stockholders" as the origin of the professional director idea. More recently, corporations including Westinghouse and Texas Instruments have established slots on their boards to be filled by full-time directors. Individuals such as Harvard Business School's Myles Mace and former Federal Reserve Board chairman William McChesney Martin consider their own thorough-going approach to boardroom responsibilities to be that of a "professional" director.

To succeed, professional directors must put in the substantial time necessary to get the job done. One cannot monitor the performance of Chrysler's or Gulf's management at a once-a-month meeting; those firms' activities are too sweeping and complicated for such ritual oversight. The obvious minimum here is an adequate salary to attract competent persons to work as full-time directors and to maintain the independence of the board from executive management.

The board must also be sufficiently staffed. A few board members alone cannot oversee the activities of thousands of executives. To be able to appraise operating management, the board needs a trim group of attorneys, economists, and labor and consumer advisors who can analyze complex business proposals, investigate complaints, spot-check accountability, and frame pertinent inquiries.

The board also needs timely access to relevant corporate data. To insure this, the board should be empowered to nominate the corporate financial auditor, select the corporation's counsel, compel the forwarding and preservation of corporate records, require all corporate executives or representatives to answer fully all board questions respecting corporate operations, and dismiss any executive or representative who fails to do so.

This proposed redesign for corporate democracy attempts to make executive management accountable to the law and shareholders without diminishing its operating efficiency. Like a judiciary within the corporation, the board has ultimate powers to judge and sanction. Like a legislature, it oversees executive activity. Yet executive management substantially retains its powers to initiate and administer business operations. The chief executive officer retains control over the organization of the executive hierarchy and the allocation of the corporate budget. The directors are given ultimate control over a narrow jurisdiction: Does the corporation obey the law, avoid exploiting consumers or communities, and protect the shareholders' investment? The executive contingent retains general authority for all corporate operations.

No doubt there will be objections that this structure is too expensive or that it will disturb the "harmony" of executive management. But it is unclear that there would be any increased cost in adopting an effective board. The true cost to the corporation could only be determined by comparing the expense of a fully paid and staffed board with the savings resulting from the elimination of conflicts of interest and corporate waste. In addition, if this should result in a slightly increased corporate expense, the appropriateness must be assessed within a broader social context: should federal and state governments or the corporations themselves bear the primary expense of keeping corporations honest? In our view, this cost should be placed on the corporations as far as reasonably possible.

It is true that an effective board will reduce the "harmony" of executive management in the sense that the power of the chief executive or senior executives will be subject to knowledgeable review. But a board which monitors rather than rubberstamps management is exactly what is necessary to diminish the unfettered authority of the corporate chief executive or ruling clique. The autocratic power these individuals presently possess has proven unacceptably dangerous: it has led to recurring violations of law, conflicts of interest, productive inefficiency, and pervasive harm to consumers, workers, and the community environment. Under normal circumstances there should be a healthy friction between operating executives and the board to assure that the wisest possible use is made of corporate resources. When corporate executives are breaking the law, there should be no "harmony" whatsoever.

ELECTION OF THE BOARD

Restructuring the board is hardly likely to succeed if boards remain as homogeneously white, male, and narrowly oriented as they are today. Dissatisfaction with current selection of directors is so intense that analysts of corporate governance, including Harvard Law School's Abram Chayes, Yale political scientist Robert Dahl, and University of Southern California Law School Professor Christopher Stone, have each separately urged that the starting point of corporate reform should be to change the way in which the board is elected.

Professor Chayes, echoing John Locke's principle that no authority is legitimate except that granted "the consent of the governed," argues that employees and other groups substantially affected by corporate operations should have a say in its governance:

> Shareholder democracy, so-called, is misconceived because the shareholders are not the governed of the corporations whose consent must be sought. . . . Their interests are protected if financial information is made available, fraud and overreaching are prevented, and a market is maintained in which their shares may be sold. A priori, there is no reason for them to have any voice, direct or representational, in [corporate decision making]. They are no more affected than nonshareholding neighbors by these decisions. . . .
>
> A more spacious conception of 'membership,' and one closer to the facts of corporate life, would include all those having a relation of sufficient intimacy with the corporation or subject to its powers in a sufficiently specialized way. Their rightful share in decisions and the exercise of corporate power would be exercised through an institutional arrangement appro-

> priately designed to represent the interests of a constituency of members having a significant common relation to the corporation and its power.

Professor Dahl holds a similar view: "[W]hy should people who own shares be given the privileges of citizenship in the government of the firm when citizenship is denied to other people who also make vital contributions to the firm?" he asks rhetorically. "The people I have in mind are, of course, employees and customers, without whom the firm could not exist, and the general public, without whose support for (or acquiescence in) the myriad protections and services of the state the firm would instantly disappear. . . ." Yet Dahl finds proposals for interest group representation less desirable than those for worker self-management. He also suggests consideration of codetermination statutes such as those enacted by West Germany and ten other European and South American countries under which shareholders and employees separately elect designated portions of the board.

From a different perspective, Professor Stone has recommended that a federal agency appoint "general public directors" to serve on the boards of all the largest industrial and financial firms. In certain extreme cases such as where a corporation repeatedly violates the law, Stone recommends that the federal courts appoint "special public directors" to prevent further delinquency.

There are substantial problems with each of those proposals. It seems impossible to design a general "interest group" formula which will assure that all affected constituencies of large industrial corporations will be represented and that all constituencies will be given appropriate weight. Even if such a formula could be designed, however, there is the danger that consumer or community or minority or franchisee representatives would become only special pleaders for their constituents and otherwise lack the loyalty or interest to direct generally. This defect has emerged in West Germany under codetermination. Labor representatives apparently are indifferent to most problems of corporate management that do not directly affect labor. They seem as deferential to operating executive management as present American directors are. Alternatively, federally appointed public directors might be frozen out of critical decision-making by a majority of "privately" elected directors, or the appointing agency itself might be biased.

Nonetheless, the essence of the Chayes-Dahl-Stone argument is well taken. The boards of directors of most major corporations are, as CBS's Dan Rather criticized the original Nixon cabinet, too much like "twelve grey-haired guys named George." The quiescence of the board has resulted in important public and, for that matter, shareholder concerns being ignored.

An important answer is structural. The homogeneity of the board can only be ended by giving to each director, in addition to a general duty to see that the corporation is profitably administered, a separate oversight responsibility, a separate expertise, and a separate constituency so that each important public concern would be guaranteed at least one informed representative on the board. There might be nine corporate directors, each of whom is elected to a board position with one of the following oversight responsibilities:

1. Employee welfare
2. Consumer protection
3. Environmental protection and community relations
4. Shareholder rights
5. Compliance with law
6. Finances
7. Purchasing and marketing
8. Management efficiency
9. Planning and research

By requiring each director to balance responsibility for representing a particular social concern against responsibility for the overall health of the enterprise, the problem of isolated "public" directors would be avoided. No individual director is likely to be "frozen out" of collegial decision-making because all directors would be of the same character. Each director would spend the greater part of his or her time developing expertise in a different area; each director would have a motivation to insist that a different aspect of a business decision be considered. Yet each would simultaneously be responsible for participating in all board decisions, as directors now are. So the specialized area of each director would supplement but not supplant the director's general duties.

To maintain the independence of the board from the operating management it reviews also requires that each federally chartered corporation shall be directed by a purely "outside" board. No executive, attorney, representative, or agent of a corporation should be allowed to serve simultaneously as a director of that same corporation. Directorial and executive loyalty should be furthered by an absolute prohibition of interlocks. No director, executive, general counsel, or company agent should be allowed to serve more than one corporation subject to the Federal Corporate Chartering Act.

Several objections may be raised. First, how can we be sure that completely outside boards will be competent? Corporate campaign rules should be redesigned to emphasize qualifications. This will allow shareholder voters to make rational decisions based on information clearly presented to them. It is also a fair assumption that shareholders, given an actual choice and role in corporate governance, will want to elect the men and women most likely to safeguard their investments.

A second objection is that once all interlocks are proscribed and a full-time outside board required, there will not be enough qualified directors to staff all major firms. This complaint springs from that corporate mentality which, accustomed to 60-year-old white male bankers and businessmen as directors, makes the norm a virtue. In fact, if we loosen the reins on our imagination, America has a large, rich, and diverse pool of possible directorial talent from academics and public administrators and community leaders to corporate and public interest lawyers.

But directors should be limited to four two-year terms so that boards do not become stale. And no director should be allowed to serve on more than one board at any one time. Although simultaneous service on two or three boards might allow key directors to "pollinize" directorates by comparing their different experiences, this would reduce their loyalty to any one board, jeopardize their ability to fully perform their new directorial responsibilities, and undermine the goal of opening up major boardrooms to as varied a new membership as is reasonable.

The shareholder electoral process should be made more democratic as well. Any shareholder or allied shareholder group which owns .1 percent of the common voting stock in the corporation or comprises 100 or more individuals and does not include a present executive of the corporation, nor act for a present executive, may nominate up to three persons to serve as directors. This will exclude executive management from the nomination process. It also increases the likelihood of a diverse board by preventing any one or two sources from proposing all nominees. To prevent frivolous use of the nominating power, this proposal establishes a minimum shareownership condition.

Six weeks prior to the shareholders' meeting to elect directors, each shareholder should receive a ballot and a written statement on which each candidate for the board sets forth his or her qualifications to hold office and purposes for seeking office. All campaign costs would be borne by the corporation. These strict campaign and funding rules will assure that all nominees will have an equal opportunity to be judged by the shareholders. By preventing directorates from being bought, these provisions will require board elections to be conducted solely on the merit of the candidates.

Finally, additional provisions will require cumulative voting and forbid "staggered" board elections. Thus any shareholder faction capable of jointly voting approximately 10 percent of the total number of shares cast may elect a director.

A NEW ROLE FOR SHAREHOLDERS

The difficulty with this proposal is the one that troubled Juvenal two millennia ago: *Quis custodiet ipsos custodes,* or Who shall watch the watchmen? Without a full-time body to discipline the board, it would be so easy for the board of directors and executive management to become friends. Active vigilance could become routinized into an uncritical partnership. The same board theoretically elected to protect shareholder equity and internalize law might instead become management's lobbyist.

Relying on shareholders to discipline directors may strike many as a dubious approach. Historically, the record of shareholder participation in corporate governance has been an abysmal one. The monumental indifference of most shareholders is worse than that of sheep; sheep at least have some sense of what manner of ram they follow. But taken together, the earlier proposals—an outside, full-time board, nominated by rival shareholder groups and voted on by beneficial owners—will increase involvement by shareholders. And cumulative voting insures that an aroused minority of shareholders—even one as small as 9 or 10 percent of all shareholders—shall have the opportunity to elect at least one member of the board.

But that alone is hardly sufficient. At a corporation the size of General Motors, an aggregation of 10 percent of all voting stock might require the allied action of over 200,000 individuals—which probably could occur no more than once in a generation. To keep directors responsive to law and legitimate public concerns requires surer and more immediate mechanisms. In a word, it requires arming the victims of corporate abuses with the powers to swiftly respond to them. For only those employees, consumers, racial or sex minorities, and local communities harmed by corporate depredations can be depended upon to speedily complain. By allowing any victim to become a shareholder and by permitting any shareholder to have an effective voice, there will be the greatest likelihood of continuing scrutiny of the corporation's directorate.

Shareholders are not the only ones with an incentive to review decisions of corporate management; nor, as Professors Chayes and Dahl argue, are shareholders the only persons who should be accorded corporate voting rights. The increasing use by American corporations of technologies and materials that pose direct and serious threats to the health of communities surrounding their plants requires the creation of a new form of corporate voting right. When a federally chartered corporation engages, for example, in production or distribution of nuclear fuels or the emissions of toxic air, water, or solid waste pollutants, citizens whose health is endangered should not be left, at best, with receiving money damages after a time-consuming trial to compensate them for damaged property, impaired health, or even death.

Instead, upon finding of a public health hazard by three members of the board of directors or 3 percent of the shareholders, a corporate referendum should be held in the political jurisdiction affected by the health hazard. The referendum would be drafted by the unit triggering it—either the three board members or a designate of the shareholders. The affected citizens by majority vote will then decide whether the hazardous practice shall be allowed to continue. This form of direct democracy has obvious parallels to the initiative and referendum procedures familiar to many states—except that the election will be paid for by a business corporation and will not necessarily occur at a regular election.

This type of election procedure is necessary to give enduring meaning to the democratic concept of "consent of the governed." To be sure, this proposal goes beyond the traditional assumption that the only affected or relevant constituents of the corporation are the shareholders. But no longer can we accept the Faustian bargain that the continued toleration of corporate destruction of local health and property is the cost to the public of doing business. In an equitable system of governance, the perpetrators should answer to their victims.

Power and Accountability: The Changing Role of the Corporate Board of Directors

Irving S. Shapiro
Former chairman and CEO, E.I. duPont de Nemours & Company

The proper direction of business corporations in a free society is a topic of intense and often heated discussion. Under the flag of corporate governance there has been a running debate about the performance of business organizations, together with a

Excerpted from a paper presented in the Fairless Lecture Series, Carnegie-Mellon University, Oct. 24, 1979. Reprinted by permission.

flood of proposals for changes in the way corporate organizations are controlled.

It has been variously suggested that corporate charters be dispensed by the Federal Government as distinct from those of the states (to tighten the grip on corporate actions); that only outsiders unconnected to an enterprise be allowed to sit on its board of directors or that, as a minimum, most of the directors should qualify as "independent"; that seats be apportioned to constituent groups (employees, women, consumers and minorities, along with stockholders); that boards be equipped with private staffs, beyond the management's control (to smoke out facts the hired executives might prefer to hide or decorate); and that new disclosure requirements be added to existing ones (to provide additional tools for outside oversight of behavior and performance).

Such proposals have come from the Senate Judiciary Committee's antitrust arm; from regulatory agency spokesmen, most notably the current head of the Securities and Exchange Commission, Harold Williams, and a predecessor there, William Cary; from the professoriat in schools of law and business; from the bench and bar; and from such observers of the American scene as Ralph Nader and Mark Green.[1]

Suggestions for change have sometimes been offered in sympathy and sometimes in anger. They have ranged from general pleas for corporations to behave better, to meticulously detailed reorganization charts. The span in itself suggests part of the problem: "Corporate Governance" (like Social Responsibility before it) is not a subject with a single meaning, but is a shorthand label for an array of social and political as well as economic concerns. One is obliged to look for a way to keep discussion within a reasonable perimeter.

There appears to be one common thread. All of the analyses, premises, and prescriptions seem to derive in one way or another from the question of accountability: Are corporations suitably controlled, and to whom or what are they responsible? This is the central public issue, and the focal point for this paper.

One school of opinion holds that corporations cannot be adequately called to account because there are systemic economic and political failings. In this view, nothing short of a major overhaul will serve. What is envisioned, at least by many in this camp, are new kinds of corporate organizations constructed along the lines of democratic political institutions. The guiding ideology would be communitarian, with the needs and rights of the community emphasized in preference to profit-seeking goals now pursued by corporate leaders (presumably with Darwinian abandon, with natural selection weeding out the weak, and with society left to pick up the external costs).

BOARDS CHANGING FOR BETTER

Other critics take a more temperate view. They regard the present system as sound and its methods of governance as morally defensible. They concede, though, that changes are needed to reflect new conditions. Whether the changes are to be brought about by gentle persuasion, or require the use of a two-by-four to get the mule's attention, is part of the debate.

This paper sides with the gradualists. My position, based on a career in industry and personal observation of corporate boards at work, is that significant improvements have been made in recent years in corporate governance, and that more changes are coming in an orderly way: that with these amendments, corporations are accountable and better monitored than ever before; and that pat formulas or proposals for massive "restructuring" should be suspect. The formula approach often is based on ignorance of what it takes to run a large enterprise, on false premises as to the corporate role in society, or on a philosophy that misreads the American tradition and leaves no room for large enterprises that are both free and efficient.

The draconian proposals would almost certainly yield the worst of all possibilities, a double-negative tradeoff: They would sacrifice the most valuable qualities of the enterprise system to gain the least attractive features of the governmental system. Privately owned enterprises are geared to a primary economic task, that of joining human talents and natural resources in the production and distribution of goods and services. That task is essential, and two centuries of national experience suggest these conclusions: The United States has been uncommonly successful at meeting economic needs through reliance on private initiative; and the competitive marketplace is a better course-correction device than governmental fiat. The enterprise system would have had to have failed miserably before the case could be made for replacing it with governmental dictum.

Why should the public have any interest in the internal affairs of corporations? Who cares who decides? Part of the answer comes from recent news stories noting such special problems as illegal corporate contributions to political campaigns, and tracking the decline and fall of once-stout companies such as Penn Central. Revelations of that kind raise questions about the probity and competence of the people minding the largest stores. There is more to it than this, though. There have always been cases of corporate failures. Small companies have gone under too, at a rate far higher than their larger brethren.[2] Instances of corruption have occurred in institutions of all sizes, whether they be commercial enterprises or some other kind.

Corporate behavior and performance are points of attention, and the issue attaches to size, precisely because people do not see the large private corporation as entirely private. People care about what goes on in the corporate interior because they see themselves as affected parties whether they work in such companies or not.

There is no great mystery as to the source of this challenge to the private character of governance. Three trends account for it. First is the growth of very large corporations. They have come to employ a large portion of the workforce, and have become key factors in the nation's technology, wealth and security. They have generated admiration for their prowess, but also fear of their imputed power.

The second contributing trend is the decline of owner-management. Over time, corporate shares have been dispersed. The owners have hired managers, entrusted them with the power to make decisions, and drifted away from involvement in corporate affairs except to meet statutory requirements (as, for example, to approve a stock split or elect a slate of directors).

That raises obvious practical questions. If the owners are on the sidelines, what is to stop the managers from remaining in power indefinitely, using an inside position to control the selection of their own bosses, the directors? Who is looking over management's shoulder to monitor performance?

The third element here is the rise in social expectations regarding corporations. It is no longer considered enough for a company to make products and provide commercial services. The larger it is, the more it is expected to assume various obligations that once were met by individuals or communities, or were not met at all.

With public expectations ratcheting upward, corporations are under pressure to behave more like governments and embrace a universe of problems. That would mean, of necessity, that private institutions would focus less on problems of their own choice.

If corporations succumbed to that pressure, and in effect declared the public's work to be their own, the next step would be to turn them into institutions accountable to the public in the same way that units of government are accountable.

But the corporation does not parallel the government. The assets in corporate hands are more limited and the constituents have options. There are levels of appeal. While the only accountability in government lies within government itself—the celebrated system of checks and balances among the executive, legislative, and judicial branches—the corporation is in a different situation: It has external and plural accountability, codified in the law and reinforced by social pressure. It must "answer" in one way or another to all levels of government, to competitors in the marketplace who would be happy to have the chance to increase their own market share, to employees who can strike or quit, and to consumers who can keep their wallets in their pockets. The checks are formidable even if one excludes for purposes of argument the corporation's initial point of accountability, its stockholders (many of whom do in fact vote their shares, and do not just use their feet).

The case for major reforms in corporate governance rests heavily on the argument that past governmental regulation of large enterprises has been impotent or ineffectual. This is an altogether remarkable assertion, given the fact that the nation has come through a period in which large corporations have been subjected to an unprecedented flood of new legislation and rule making. Regulation now reaches into every corporate nook and cranny—including what some people suppose (erroneously) to be the sanctuary of the boardroom.

Market competition, so lightly dismissed by some critics as fiction or artifact, is in fact a vigorous force in the affairs of almost all corporations. Size lends no immunity to its relentless pressures. The claim that the largest corporations somehow have set themselves above the play of market forces or, more likely, make those forces play for themselves, is widely believed. Public opinion surveys show that. What is lacking is any evidence that this is so. Here too, the evidence goes the other way. Objective studies of concentrated industries (the auto industry, for instance) show that corporate size does not mean declining competitiveness, nor does it give assurance that the products will sell.

Everyday experience confirms this. Consider the hard times of the Chrysler Corporation today, the disappearance of many once-large companies from the American scene, and the constant rollover in the membership list of the "100 Largest," a churning process that has been going on for years and shows no signs of abating.[3]

If indeed the two most prominent overseers of corporate behavior, government and competition, have failed to provide appropriate checks and balances, and if that is to be cited as evidence that corporations lack accountability, the burden of proof should rest with those who so state.

The basics apply to Sears Roebuck as much as to Sam's appliance shop. Wherever you buy the new toaster, it should work when it is plugged in. Whoever services the washing machine, the repairman should arrive at the appointed time, with tools and parts.

Special expectations are added for the largest firms, however. One is that they apply their resources to tasks that invite economies of scale, providing goods and services that would not otherwise be available, or that could be delivered by smaller units only at considerable loss of efficiency. Another is that, like the elephant, they watch where they put their feet and not stamp on smaller creatures through clumsiness or otherwise.

A second set of requirements can be added, related not to the markets selected by corporations individually, but to the larger economic tasks that must be accomplished in the name of the national interest and security. In concert with others in society, including big government, big corporations are expected to husband scarce resources and develop new ones, and to foster strong and diverse programs of research and development, to the end that practical technological improvements will emerge and the nation will be competitive in the international setting.

Beyond this there are softer but nonetheless important obligations: To operate with respect for the environment and with careful attention to the health and safety of people, to honor and give room to the personal qualities employees bring to their jobs, including their need to make an identifiable mark and to realize as much of their potential as possible; to lend assistance in filling community needs in which corporations have some stake; and to help offset community problems which in some measure corporations have helped to create.

This is not an impossible job, only a difficult one. Admitting that the assignment probably is not going to be carried out perfectly by any organization, the task is unlikely to be done even half well unless some boundary conditions are met. Large corporations cannot fulfill their duties unless they remain both profitable and flexible. They must be able to attract and hold those volunteer owners; which is to say, there must be the promise of present or future gain. Companies must have the wherewithal to reinvest significant amounts to revitalize their own capital plants, year after year in unending fashion. Otherwise, it is inevitable that they will go into decline versus competitors elsewhere, as will the nation.

Flexibility is no less important. The fields of endeavor engaging large business units today are dynamic in nature. Without an in-and-out flow of products and services, without the mobility to adapt to shifts in opportunities and public preferences, corporations would face the fate of the buggywhip makers.

Profitability and flexibility are easy words to say, but in practice they make for hard decisions. A company that would close a plant with no more than a passing thought for those left unemployed would and should be charged with irresponsibility; but a firm that vowed never to close any of its plants would be equally irresponsible, for it might be consigning itself to a pattern of stagnation that could ultimately cost the jobs of the people in all of its plants.

The central requirement is not that large corporations take the pledge and bind themselves to stated actions covering all circumstances, but that they do a thoughtful and informed job of balancing competing (and ever changing) claims on corporate resources, mediating among the conflicting (also changing) desires of various constituencies, and not giving in to any one-dimensional perspective however sincerely felt. It is this that describes responsible corporate governance.

Certainly, corporations do not have the public mandate or the resources to be what Professor George Lodge of the Harvard Business School would have them be, which is nationally chartered community-oriented collectives.[4] Such a mission for corporations would be tolerable to society only if corporations were turned into mini-governments—but that takes us back to the inefficiency problem noted earlier. The one task governments have proven they almost always do badly is to run production and distribution organizations. The only models there are to follow are not attractive. Would anyone seriously argue that the public would be ahead if General Motors were run along the lines of Amtrak, or Du Pont were managed in the manner of the U.S. Postal System?

Once roles are defined, the key to success in running a large corporation is to lay out a suitable division of labor between the board and the management, make that division crystal clear on both sides, and staff the offices with the right people. Perhaps the best way to make that split is to follow the pattern used in the U.S. Constitution, which stipulates the powers of the Federal Government and specifies that everything not covered there is reserved to the states or the people thereof. The board of directors should lay claim to five basic jobs, and leave the rest to the paid managers.

The duties the board should not delegate are these:

1. The determination of the board policies and the general direction the efforts of the enterprise should take.
2. The establishment of performance standards—ethical as well as commercial—against which the management will be judged, and the communication of these standards to the management in unambiguous terms.
3. The selection of company officers, and attention to the question of succession.
4. The review of top management's performance in following the overall strategy and meeting the board's standards as well as legal requirements.
5. The communication of the organization's goals and standards to those who have a significant stake in its activities (insiders and outsiders both) and of the steps being taken to keep the organization responsive to the needs of those people.

The establishment of corporate strategy and performance standards denotes a philosophy of active stewardship, rather than passive trusteeship. It is the mission of directors to see that corporate resources are put to creative use, and in the bargain subjected to calculated risks rather than simply being tucked into the countinghouse for safekeeping.

That in turn implies certain prerequisites for board members of large corporations which go beyond those required of a school board member, a trustee of a charitable organization, or a director of a small, local business firm. In any such assignments one would look for personal integrity, interest and intelligence, but beyond these there is a dividing line that marks capability and training.

The stakes are likely to be high in the large corporation, and the factors confronting the board and management usually are complex. The elements weighing heavily in decisions are not those with which people become familiar in the ordinary course of day-to-day life, as might be the case with a school board.

Ordinarily the management of a corporation attends to such matters as product introductions, capital expansions, and supply problems. This in no way reduces the need for directors with extensive business background, though. With few exceptions, corporate boards involve themselves in strategic decisions and those involving large capital commitments. Directors thus need at least as much breadth and perspective as the management, if not as much detailed knowledge.

If the directors are to help provide informed and principled oversight of corporate affairs, a good number of them must provide windows to the outside world. That is at least part of the rationale for outside directors, and especially for directors who can bring unique perspective to the group. There is an equally strong case, though, for directors with an intimate knowledge of the company's business, and insiders may be the best qualified to deliver that. What is important is not that a ratio be established, but that the group contain a full range of the competences needed to set courses of action that will largely determine the long-range success of the enterprise.

BOARDS NEED WINDOWS

The directors also have to be able and willing to invest considerable time in their work. In this day and age, with major resources on the line and tens of thousands of employees affected by each large corporation, there should be no seat in the boardroom for people willing only to show up once a month to pour holy water over decisions already made. Corporate boards need windows, not window dressing!

There are two other qualities that may be self-evident from what has been said, but are mentioned for emphasis. Directors must be interested in the job and committed to the overall purpose of the organization. However much they may differ on details of accomplishment, they must be willing to work at the task of working with others on the board. They ought to be able to speak freely in a climate that encourages open discussion, but to recognize the difference between attacking an idea and attacking the person who presents it. No less must they see the difference between compromising tactics to reach consensus and compromising principles.

Structures and procedures, which so often are pushed to the fore in discussions of corporate governance, actually belong last. They are not unimportant, but they are subordinate.

Structure follows purpose, or should, and that is a useful principle for testing some of the proposals for future changes in corporate boards. Today, two-thirds to three-quarters of the directors of most large corporations are outsiders, and it is being proposed that this trend be pushed still farther, with the only insider being the chief executive officer, and with a further stipulation that he not be board chairman. This idea has surfaced from Harold Williams, and variations on it have come from other sources.

The idea bumps into immediate difficulties. High-quality candidates for boards are not in large supply as it is. Conflicts of interest would prohibit selection of many individuals close enough to an industry to be familiar with its problems. The disqualification of insiders would reduce the selection pool to a still smaller number, and the net result could well be corporate boards whose members were less competent and effective than those now sitting.

Experience would also suggest that such a board would be the most easily manipulated of all. That should be no trick at all for a skillful CEO, for he would be the only person in the room with a close, personal knowledge of the business.

The objective is unassailable: Corporate boards need directors with independence of judgment; but in today's business world, independence is not enough. In coping with such problems as those confronting the electronics corporations beset by heavy foreign competition, or those encountered by international banks which have loans outstanding in countries with shaky governments, boards made up almost entirely of outsiders would not just have trouble evaluating nuances of the management's performance; they might not even be able to read the radar and tell whether the helmsman was steering straight for the rocks.

If inadequately prepared individuals are placed on corporate boards, no amount of sincerity on their part can offset the shortcoming. It is pure illusion to suppose that complex business issues and organizational problems can be overseen by people with little or no experience in dealing with such problems. However intelligent such people might be, the effect of their governance would be to expose the people most affected by the organization—employees, owners, customers, suppliers—to leadership that would be (using the word precisely) incompetent.

It is sometimes suggested that the members of corporate boards ought to come from the constituencies—an employee-director, a consumer-director, an environmentalist-director, etc. This Noah's Ark proposal, which is probably not to be taken seriously, is an extension of the false parallel between corporations and elected governments. The flaw in the idea is all but self evident: People representing specific interest groups would by definition be committed to the goals of their groups rather than any others; but it is the responsibility of directors (not simply by tradition but as a matter of law as well) to serve the organization as a whole. The two goals are incompatible.

If there were such boards they would move at glacial speed. The internal political maneuvering would be Byzantine, and it is difficult to see how the directors could avoid an obvious challenge of accountability. Stockholder suits would pop up like dandelions in the spring.

One may also question how many people of ability would stand for election under this arrangement. Quotas are an anathema in a free society, and their indulgence here would insult the constituencies themselves—a woman on the board not because she is competent but only because she is female; a black for black's sake; and so on ad nauseam.

A certain amount of constituency pleading is not all bad, as long as it is part of a corporate commitment. There is something to be said for what Harold Williams labels "tension," referring to the divergence in perspective of those concerned primarily with internal matters and those looking more at the broader questions. However, as has been suggested by James Shepley, the president of Time, Inc., "tension" can lead to paralysis, and is likely to do so if boards are packed with groups known to be unsympathetic to the management's problems and business realities.

As Shepley commented, "The chief executive would be out of his mind who would take a risk-laden business proposition to a group of directors who, whatever their other merits, do not really understand the fine points of the business at hand, and whose official purpose is to create 'tension.' "[5]

Students of corporate affairs have an abundance of suggestions for organizing the work of boards, with detailed structures in mind for committees on audit, finance, and other areas; plus prescriptions for membership. The danger here is not that boards will pick the wrong formula—many organization charts could be made to work—but that boards will put too much emphasis on the wrong details.

The idea of utilizing a committee system in which sub-groups have designated duties is far more important than the particulars of their arrangement. When such committees exist, and they are given known and specific oversight duties, it is a signal to the outside world (and to the management) that performance is being monitored in a no-nonsense fashion.

It is this argument that has produced the rule changes covering companies listed on the New York Stock Exchange, calling for audit committees chaired by outside directors, and including no one currently active in management. Most large firms have moved in that direction, and the move makes sense, for an independently minded audit committee is a potent instrument of corporate oversight. Even a rule of that kind, though, has the potential of backfiring.

Suppose some of the directors best qualified to perform the audit function are not outsiders? Are the analytical skills and knowledge of career employees therefore to be bypassed? Are the corporate constituencies well served by such an exclusionary rule, keeping in mind that all directors, insiders or outsiders, are bound by the same legal codes and corporate books are still subject to independent, outside audit? It is scarcely a case of the corporate purse being placed in the hands of the unwatched.

Repeatedly, the question of structure turns on the basics: If corporations have people with competence and commitment on their boards, structure and process fall into line easily; if people with the needed qualities are missing or the performance standards are unclear, corporations are in trouble no matter whose guidebook they follow. Equally, the question drives to alternatives: The present system is surely not perfect, but what is better?

By the analysis presented here the old fundamentals are still sound, no alternative for radical change has been defended with successful argument, and the best course appears to be to stay within the historical and philosophical traditions of American enterprise, working out the remaining problems one by one.

NOTES

1. U.S. Senate, Committee on the Judiciary Subcommittee on Antitrust, Monopoly & Business Rights; Address by Harold M. Williams, *Corporate Accountability,* Fifth Annual Securities Regulation Institute, San Diego, California (January 18, 1978); W. Cary, *A Proposed Federal Corporate Minimum Standards Act,* 29 Bus. Law. 1101 (1974) and W. Cary, *Federalism & Corporate Law: Reflections Upon Delaware,* 83 Yale L.J., 663 (1974); D. E. Schwartz, *A Case for Federal Chartering of Corporations,* 31 Bus. Law. 1125 (1976); M. A. Eisenberg, *Legal Modes of Management Structure in the Modern Corporation; Officers, Directors & Accountants,* 63 Calif. L. Rev. 375 (1975); A. J. Goldberg, *Debate on Outside Directors, New York Times,* October 29, 1972 (§3, p. 1); Ralph Nader & Mark Green, *Constitutionalizing the Corporation: The Case for Federal Chartering of Giant Corporations* (1976).
2. *See* "Sixty Years of Corporate Ups, Downs & Outs," *Forbes,* September 15, 1977, p. 127 et seq.
3. *See* Dr. Betty Bock's Statement before Hearings on S.600, Small and Independent Business Protection Act of 1979, April 25, 1979.
4. G. Lodge, *The New American Ideology* (1975).
5. Shepley, *The CEO Goes to Washington,* Remarks to Fortune Corporation Communications Seminar, March 28, 1979.

Who Should Control the Corporation?

Henry Mintzberg
Professor of Management, McGill University

Who should control the corporation? How? And for the pursuit of what goals? Historically, the corporation was controlled by its owners—through direct control of the managers if not through direct management—for the pursuit of economic goals. But as shareholding became dispersed, owner control weakened; and as the corporation grew to very large size, its economic actions came to have increasing social consequences. The giant, widely held corporation came increasingly under the implicit control of its managers, and the concept of social responsibility—the voluntary consideration of public social goals alongside the private economic ones—arose to provide a basis of legitimacy for their actions.

To some, including those closest to the managers themselves, this was accepted as a satisfactory arrangement for the large corporation. "Trust it" to the goodwill of the managers was their credo; these people will be able to achieve an appropriate balance between social and economic goals.

But others viewed this basis of control as fundamentally illegitimate. The corporation was too large, too influential, its actions too pervasive to be left free of the direct and concerted influence of outsiders. At the extreme were those who believed that legitimacy could be achieved only by subject-

---

ing managerial authority to formal and direct external control. "Nationalize it," said those at one end of the political spectrum, to put ultimate control in the hands of the government so that it will pursue public social goals. No, said those at the other end, "restore it" to direct share holder control, so that it will not waiver from the pursuit of private economic goals.

Other people took less extreme positions. "Democratize it" became the rallying cry for some, to open up the governance of the large, widely held corporation to a variety of affected groups—if not the workers, then the customers, or conservation interests, or minorities. "Regulate it" was also a popular position, with its implicit premise that only by sharing their control with government would the corporation's managers attend to certain social goals. Then there were those who accepted direct management control so long as it was tempered by other, less formal types of influence. "Pressure it," said a generation of social activists, to ensure that social goals are taken into consideration. But others argued that because the corporation is an economic instrument, you must "induce it" by providing economic incentives to encourage the resolution of social problems.

Finally, there were those who argued that this whole debate was unnecessary, that a kind of invisible hand ensures that the economic corporation acts in a socially responsible manner. "Ignore it" was their implicit conclusion.

This article is written to clarify what has become a major debate of our era, *the* major debate revolving around the private sector: Who should control the corporation, specifically the large, widely held corporation, how, and for the pursuit of what goals? The answers that are eventually accepted will determine what kind of society we and our children shall live in. . . .

As implied earlier, the various positions of who should control the corporation, and how, can be laid out along a political spectrum, from nationalization at one end to the restoration of shareholder power at the other. From the managerial perspective, however, those two extremes are not so far apart. Both call for direct control of the corporation's managers by specific outsiders, in one case the government to ensure the pursuit of social goals, in the other case the shareholders to ensure the pursuit of economic ones. It is the moderate positions—notably, trusting the corporation to the social responsibility of its managers—that are farthest from the extremes. Hence, we can fold our spectrum around so that it takes the shape of a horseshoe.

Figure 1 shows our "conceptual horseshoe," with "nationalize it" and "restore it" at the two ends. "Trust it" is at the center, because it postulates a natural balance of social and economic goals. "Democratize it," "regulate it," and "pressure it" are shown on the left side of the horseshoe, because all seek to temper economic goals with social ones. "Induce it" and "ignore it," both of which favor the exclusive pursuit of economic goals, are shown on the right side.

This conceptual horseshoe provides a basic framework to help clarify the issues in this important debate. We begin by discussing each of these positions in turn, circling the horseshoe from left to right. Finding that each (with one exception) has a logical context, we conclude—in keeping with our managerial perspective—that they should be thought of as forming a portfolio from which society can draw to deal with the issue of who should control the corporation and how.

"NATIONALIZE IT"

Nationalization of the corporation is a taboo subject in the United States—in general, but not in particular. Whenever a major corporation runs into serious difficulty (i.e., faces bankruptcy with possible loss of many jobs), massive government intervention, often including direct nationalization, inevitably comes up as an option. This option has been exercised: U.S. travellers now ride on Amtrak; Tennessee residents have for years been getting their power from a government utility; indeed, the Post Office was once a private enterprise. Other nations have, of course, been much more ambitious in this regard.

From a managerial and organizational perspective, the question is not whether nationalization is legitimate, but whether it works—at least in partic-

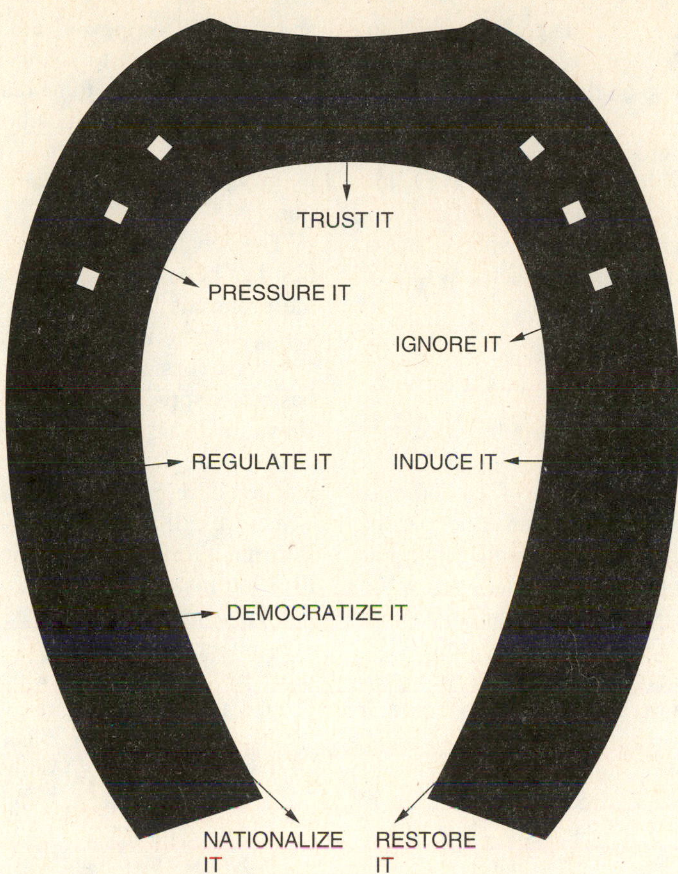

FIGURE 1 **The Conceptual Horseshoe**

ular, limited circumstances. As a response to concerns about the social responsibility of large corporations, the answer seems to be no. The evidence suggests that social difficulties arise more from the size of an organization and its degree of bureaucratization than from its form of ownership.[1] On the other hand, contrary to popular belief in the United States, nationalization does not necessarily harm economic efficiency. Over the years, Renault has been one of the most successful automobile companies outside Japan; it was nationalized by the French government shortly after World War II. . . . When people believe that government ownership leads to interference, politicization, and inefficiency, that may be exactly what happens. However, when they believe that nationalization *has* to work, then state-owned enterprises may be able to attract the very best talent in the country and thereby work well.

But economic efficiency is no reason to favor nationalization any more than is concern about social responsibility. Nationalization does, however, seem to make sense in at least two particular circumstances. The first is when a mission deemed necessary in a society will not be provided adequately by the private sector. That is presumably why America has its Amtrak, and why Canada created its Canadian National. . . . The second is when the activities of an organization must be so intricately tied to government policy that it is best managed as a direct arm of the state. The Canadian government created Petrocan to act as a "window" and a source of expertise on the sensitive oil industry.

Thus, it is not rhetoric but requirement that should determine the role of this position as a solution to who should control the corporation. "Nationalize it" should certainly not be embraced as a panacea, but neither should it be rejected as totally inapplicable.

"DEMOCRATIZE IT"

A less extreme position—at least in the context of the American debate—is one that calls for formal devices to broaden the governance of the corporation. The proponents of this position either accept the legal fiction of shareholder control and argue that the corporation's power base is too narrow, or else they respond to the emergent reality and question the legitimacy of managerial control. Why, they ask, do stockholders or self-selected managers have any greater right to control the profound decisions of these major institutions than do workers or customers or the neighbors downstream.

This stand is not to be confused with what is known as "participative management." The call to "democratize it" is a legal, rather than ethical one and is based on power, not generosity. Management is not asked to share its power voluntarily; rather, that power is to be reallocated constitutionally. That makes this position a fundamental and important one, *especially* in the United States with its strong tradition of pluralist control of its institutions.

The debate over democratization of the corporation has been confusing, in part because many of the proposals have been so vague. We can bring some order to it by considering, in organizational terms, two basic means of democratization and two basic constituencies that can be involved. As shown in Table 1, they suggest four possible forms of corporate democracy. One means is through the election of representatives to the board of directors, which we call *representative democracy*. The other is through formal but direct involvement in internal decision making processes, which we call *participatory democracy*. Either can focus on the *workers*—either all the employees or just those in operating tasks—or else on a host of outside interest groups, the latter giving rise to a *pluralistic* form of democracy. These are basic forms of corporate democracy in theory. With one exception, they have hardly been approached—let alone achieved—in practice. But they suggest where the "democratize it" debate may be headed. . . .

TABLE 1

FOUR BASIC FORMS OF CORPORATE DEMOCRACY

		Groups Involved: Internal Employees	Groups Involved: External Interest Groups
Focus of Attention	Board of Directors	Worker Representative Democracy (European style, e.g., "co-determination" or worker ownership)	Pluralistic Representative Democracy (American style, e.g., "public interest" directors)
	Internal Decision-Making Process	Worker Participatory Democracy (e.g., works councils)	Pluralistic Participatory Democracy (e.g., outsiders on new product committees)

Critics . . . have pointed out the problems of defining constituencies and finding the means to hold elections. "One-person, one-vote" may be easily applied to electing representatives of the workers, but no such simple rule can be found in the case of the consumer or environmental representatives, let alone ones of the "public interest." Yet it is amazing how quickly things become workable in the United States when Americans decide to put their collective mind to it. Indeed, the one case of public directors that I came across is telling in this regard. According to a Conference Board report, the selection by the Chief Justice of the Supreme Court of New Jersey of 6 of the 24 members of the board of Prudential Insurance as public directors has been found by the company to be "quite workable."[2]

Despite its problems, representative democracy is crystal clear compared with participatory democracy. What the French call "auto-gestion" (as opposed to "co-gestion," or co-determination) seems to describe a kind of bottom-up, grassroots democracy in which the workers participate directly in decision making (instead of overseeing management's decisions from the board of directors) and also elect their own managers (who then become more administrators than bosses). Yet such proposals are inevitably vague, and I have heard of no large mass production or mass service firm—not even one owned by workers or a union—that comes close to this.

What has impeded worker participatory democracy? In my opinion, something rather obvious has stood in its way; namely, the structure required by the very organizations in which the attempts have been made to apply it. Worker participatory democracy—and worker representative democracy too, for that matter—has been attempted primarily in organizations containing large numbers of workers who do highly routine, rather unskilled jobs that are typical of most mass production and service—what I have elsewhere called Machine Bureaucracies.[3] The overriding requirement in Machine Bureaucracy is for tight coordination, the kind that can only be achieved by central administrators. For example, the myriad of decisions associated with producing an automobile at Volvo's Kalmar works in Sweden cannot be made by autonomous groups, each doing as it pleases. The whole car must fit together in a particular way at the end of the assembly process. These decisions require a highly sophisticated system of bureaucratic coordination. That is why automobile companies are structured into rigid hierarchies of authority, not because their managers lust for power (though lust for power some of them no doubt do). . . .

Participatory democracy *is* approached in other kinds of organizations. These are not the large, mass output corporations, but rather the autonomous professional institutions such as universities and hospitals, which have very different needs for central coordination. . . . But the proponents of democracy in organizations are not lobbying for changes in hospitals or universities. It is the giant mass producers they are after, and unless the operating work in these corporations becomes largely skilled and professional in nature, nothing approaching participative democracy can be expected.

In principal, the pluralistic form of participatory democracy means that a variety of groups external to the corporation can somehow control its decision-making processes directly. In practice, of course, this concept is even more elusive than the worker form of participatory democracy. To fully open up the internal decision-making processes of the corporation to outsiders would mean chaos. Yet certain very limited forms of outside participation would seem to be not only feasible but perhaps even desirable. . . . Imagine telephone company executives resolving rate conflicts with consumer groups in quiet offices instead of having to face them in noisy public hearings.

To conclude, corporate democracy—whether representative or participatory in form—may be an elusive and difficult concept, but it cannot be dismissed. It is not just another social issue, like conservation or equal opportunity, but one that strikes at the most fundamental of values. Ours has become a society of organizations. Democracy will have decreasing meaning to most citizens if it cannot be extended beyond political and judicial processes to those institutions that impinge upon them in their daily lives—as workers, as consumers, as neighbors. This is why we shall be hearing a great deal more of "democratize it."

"REGULATE IT"

In theory, regulating the corporation is about as simple as democratizing it is complex. In practice, it is, of course, another matter. To the proponents of "regulate it," the corporation can be made responsive to social needs by having its actions subjected to the controls of a higher authority—typically government, in the form of a regulatory agency or legislation backed up by the courts. Under regulation, constraints are imposed externally on the corporation while its internal governance is left to its managers. . . .

To some, regulation is a clumsy instrument that should never be relied upon; to others, it is a panacea for the problems of social responsibility. At best, regulation sets minimum and usually crude standards of acceptable behavior; when it works, it does not make any firm socially responsible so much as stop some from being grossly irresponsible. Because it is inflexible, regulation tends to be applied slowly and conservatively, usually lagging public sentiment. Regulation often does not work because of difficulties in enforcement. The problems of the regulatory agencies are legendary—limited resources and information compared with the industries they are supposed to regulate, the cooptation of the regulators by industries, and so on. When applied indiscriminately, regulation either fails dramatically or else succeeds and creates havoc.

Yet there are obvious places for regulation. A prime one is to control tangible "externalities"—costs incurred by corporations that are passed on to the public at large. When, for example, costly pollution or worker health problems can be attributed directly to a corporation, then there seems to be every reason to force it (and its customers) to incur these costs directly, or else to terminate the actions that generate them. Likewise, regulation may have a place where competition encourages the unscrupulous to pull all firms down to a base level of behavior, forcing even the well-intentioned manager to ignore the social consequences of his actions. Indeed, in such cases, the socially responsible behavior is to encourage sensible regulation. "Help us to help ourselves," businessmen should be telling the government.

Although the public has generally been sympathetic to it, "regulate it," even in highly limited form, has hardly been the position of businessmen. . . . Most discouraging is Theodore Levitt's revelation some years ago that business has fought every piece of proposed regulatory or social legislation throughout this century, from the Child Labor Acts on up. In Levitt's opinion, much of that legislation has been good for business—dissolving the giant trusts, creating a more honest and effective stock market, and so on. Yet, "the computer is programmed to cry wolf."[4] One reason why so much legislation has been excessive and ineffective may be because it has been enacted with the support of the general public but over the obstinate resistance of businessmen.

In summary, regulation is a clumsy instrument but not a useless one. Were the business community to take a more enlightened view of it, regulation could be applied more appropriately, and we would not need these periodic housecleanings to eliminate the excesses.

"PRESSURE IT"

"Pressure it" is designed to do what "regulate it" fails to do: provoke corporations to act beyond some base level of behavior, usually in an area that regulation misses entirely. Here, activists bring ad hoc campaigns of pressure to bear on one or a group of corporations to keep them responsive to the activists' interpretation of social needs. . . .

"Pressure it" is a distinctively American position. While Europeans debate the theories of nationalization and corporate democracy in their cafés, Americans read about the exploits of Ralph Nader et al. in their morning newspapers. Note that "pressure it," unlike "regulate it," implicitly accepts management's right to make the final decisions. Perhaps this is one reason why it is favored in America.

While less radical than the other positions so far discussed, "pressure it" has nevertheless proved far more effective in eliciting behavior sensitive to social needs. . . .

Activist groups have pressured for everything from the dismemberment of diversified corporations to the development of day care centers. Of special note is the class action suit, which has opened up a whole new realm of corporate social issues. But the effective use of the pressure campaign has not been restricted to the traditional activist. President Kennedy used it to roll back U.S. Steel price increases in the early 1960s, and business leaders in Pittsburgh used it in the late 1940s by threatening to take their freight-haulage business elsewhere if the Pennsylvania Railroad did not replace its coal burning locomotives to help clean up their city's air.

"Pressure it" as a means to change corporate behavior is informal, flexible, and focused; hence, it has been highly successful. Yet it is irregular and ad hoc, with different pressure campaigns sometimes making contradictory demands on management. Compared to the positions to its right on the horseshoe, "pressure it," like the other positions to its left, is based on confrontation rather than cooperation.

"TRUST IT"

To a large and vocal contingent, which parades under the banner of "social responsibility," the corporation has no need to act irresponsibly, and therefore there is no reason for it to either be nationalized by the state, democratized by its different constituencies, regulated by the government, or pressured by activists. This contingent believes that the corporation's leaders can be trusted to attend to social goals for their own sake, simply because it is the noble thing to do. (Once this position was known as *noblesse oblige,* literally "nobility obliges.")

We call this position "trust it," or, more exactly, "trust the corporation to the goodwill of its managers," although looking from the outside in, it might just as well be called "socialize it." We place it in the center of our conceptual horseshoe because it alone postulates a natural balance between social and economic goals—a balance which is to be attained in the heads (or perhaps the hearts) of responsible businessmen. And, as a not necessarily incidental consequence, power can be left in the hands of the managers; the corporation can be trusted to those who reconcile social and economic goals.

The attacks on social responsibility, from the right as well as the left, boil down to whether corporate managers should be trusted when they claim to pursue social goals; if so, whether they are capable of pursuing such goals; and finally, whether they have any right to pursue such goals.

The simplest attack is that social responsibility is all rhetoric, no action. E.F. Cheit refers to the "Gospel of Social Responsibility" as "designed to justify the power of managers over an ownerless system. . . .

Others argue that businessmen lack the personal capabilities required to pursue social goals. Levitt claims that the professional manager reaches the top of the hierarchy by dedication to his firm and his industry; as a result, his knowledge of social issues is highly restricted.[5] Others argue that an orientation to efficiency renders business leaders inadept at handling complex social problems (which require flexibility and political finesse, and sometimes involve solutions that are uneconomic). . . .

The most far reaching criticism is that businessmen have no right to pursue social goals. "Who authorized them to do that?", asks Braybrooke, attacking from the left.[6] What business have they—self-selected or at best appointed by shareholders—to impose *their* interpretation of the public good on society. Let the elected politicians, directly responsible to the population, look after the social goals.

But this attack comes from the right, too. Milton Friedman writes that social responsibility amounts to spending other people's money—if not that of shareholders, then of customers or employees. Drawing on all the pejorative terms of right-wing ideology, Friedman concludes that social responsibility is a "fundamentally subversive doctrine," representing "pure and unadulterated socialism," supported by businessmen who are "unwitting puppets of the intellectual forces that have been undermining the basis of a free society these past decades." To Friedman, "there is one and only one social responsibility of business—to use its resources and engage in activities designed to increase its profits so long as it stays within the rules of the game."[7] Let businessmen, in other words, stick to their own business, which is business itself.

The modern corporation has been described as a rational, amoral institution—its professional managers "hired guns" who pursue "efficiently" any goals asked of them. The problem is that efficiency really means measurable efficiency, so that the guns load only with goals that can be quantified. Social goals, unlike economic ones, just don't lend themselves to quantification. As a result, the performance control systems—on which modern corporations so heavily depend—tend to drive out social goals in favor of economic ones. As Robert Ackerman concluded in a study of performance control systems:

> The financial reporting system may actually inhibit social responsiveness. By focusing on economic performance . . . such a system directs energy and resources to achieving results measured in financial terms. It is the only game in town, so to speak, at least the only one with an official scorecard.[8]

In the contemporary large corporation, professional amorality turns into economic morality. When the screws of the performance control systems are turned tight—as they were, for example, in the General Electric price fixing scandal of the early 1960s—economic morality can turn into social immorality. And it happens often: *A Fortune* writer found that "a surprising number of [big companies] have been involved in blatant illegalities" in the 1970s, at least 117 of 1,043 firms studied.[9]

Even when the chief executive is personally committed to social goals, the control systems he must rely upon to manage far flung operations may preclude him from doing anything about them. Thus, while he sings the praises of social responsibility, his employees are forced to march to the tune of economic performance. And then they respond to questionnaires with complaints about having to compromise their ethics.

How, then, is anyone to "trust it"?

The fact is that we have to trust it, for two reasons. First, the strategic decisions of large organizations inevitably involve social as well as economic consequences that are inextricably intertwined. The neat distinction between economic goals in the private sector and social goals in the public sector just doesn't hold up in practice. Every important decision of the large corporation—to introduce a new product line, to close an old plant, whatever—generates all kinds of social consequences. There is no such thing as purely economic decisions in big business. Only a conceptual ostrich, with his head deeply buried in the abstractions of economic theory, could possibly use the distinction between economic and social goals to dismiss social responsibility.

The second reason we have to "trust it" is that there is always some degree of discretion involved in corporate decision making, discretion to thwart social needs or to attend to them. Things could be a lot better in today's corporation, but they could also be an awful lot worse. It is primarily our ethics that keep us where we are. If the performance control systems favored by diversified corporations cut too deeply into our ethical standards, then our choice is clear: to reduce these standards or call into question the whole trend toward diversification.

To dismiss social responsibility is to allow corporate behavior to drop to the lowest level, propped up only by external controls such as regulation and pressure campaigns. Solzhenitsyn, who has experienced the natural conclusion of unrestrained bureaucratization, warns us (in sharp contrast to Friedman) that "a society with no other scale but the legal one is not quite worthy of man . . . A society which is based on the letter of the law and never reaches any higher is scarcely taking advantage of the high level of human possibilities."[10]

This is not to suggest that we must trust it completely. We certainly cannot trust it unconditionally by accepting the claim popular in some quarters that only business can solve the social ills of society. Business has no business using its resources without constraint in the social sphere—whether to support political candidates or to dictate implicitly through donations how non-profit institutions should allocate their efforts. But where business is inherently involved, where its decisions have social consequences, that is where social responsibility has a role to play: where business creates externalities that cannot be measured and attributed to it (in other words, where regulation is ineffective); where regulation would work if only business would cooperate with it; where the corporation can fool its customers, or suppliers, or government through superior knowledge; where useful products can be marketed instead of wasteful or destructive ones. In other words, we have to realize that in many spheres we must trust it, or at least socialize it (and perhaps change it) so that we can trust it. Without responsible and ethical people in important places, our society is not worth very much.

"IGNORE IT"

"Ignore it" differs from the other positions on the horseshoe in that explicitly or implicitly it calls for no change in corporate behavior. It assumes that social needs are met in the course of pursuing economic goals. We include this position in our horseshoe because it is held by many influential people and also because its validity would preempt support for the other positions. We must, therefore, investigate it alongside the others.

It should be noted at the outset that "ignore it" is not the same position as "trust it." In the latter, to be good is the right thing to do; in the present case, "it pays to be good." The distinction is subtle but important, for now it is economics, not ethics, that elicits the desired behavior. One need not strive to be ethical; economic forces will ensure that social needs fall conveniently into place. Here we have moved one notch to the right on our horseshoe, into the realm where the economic goals dominate. . . .

"Ignore it" is sometimes referred to as "enlightened self-interest," although some of its proponents are more enlightened than others. Many a true believer in social responsibility has used the argument that it pays to be good to ward off the attacks from the right that corporations have no business pursuing social goals. Even Milton Friedman must admit that they have every right to do so if it pays them economically. The danger of such arguments, however—and a prime reason "ignore it" differs from "trust it"—is that they tend to support the status quo: corporations need not change their behavior because it already pays to be good.

Sometimes the case for "ignore it" is made in terms of corporations at large, that the whole business community will benefit from socially responsible behavior. Other times the case is made in terms of the individual corporation, that it will benefit directly from its own socially responsible actions. A popular claim in the 1960s, for example, was that satisfied workers lead to greater productivity. "Treat them well, get them involved, and you will make money," we were told by a generation of industrial psychologists. This particular claim has been largely discredited, but many others have taken its place—for example, that companies that are good neighbors by polluting less are more profitable. Others make the case for "ignore it" in "social investment" terms, claiming that socially responsible behavior pays off in a better image for the firm, a more positive relationship with customers, and ultimately a healthier and more stable society in which to do business.

Then, there is what I like to call the "them" argument: "If we're not good, *they* will move in"—"they" being Ralph Nader, the government, whoever. In other words, "Be good or else." The trouble with this argument is that by reducing social responsibility to simply a political tool for sustaining managerial control of the corporation in the face of outside threats, it tends to encourage general pronouncements instead of concrete actions (unless, of course, "they" actually deliver with pressure campaigns). . . .

The "ignore it" position rests on some shaky ground. It seems to encourage average behavior at best; and where the average does not seem to be good enough, it encourages the status quo. In fact, ironically, "ignore it" makes a strong case for "pressure it," since the whole argument collapses in the absence of pressure campaigns. Thus while many influential people take this position, we question whether in the realities of corporate behavior it can really stand alone.

"INDUCE IT"

Continuing around to the right, our next position drops all concern with social responsibility per se and argues, simply, "pay it to be good," or, from the corporation's point of view, "be good only where it pays." Here, the corporation does not actively pursue social goals at all, whether as ends in themselves or as means to economic ends. Rather, it undertakes socially desirable programs only when induced economically to do so—usually through government incentives. If society wishes to clean up urban blight, then let its government provide subsidies for corporations that renovate buildings; if pollution is the problem, then let corporations be rewarded for reducing it.

"Induce it" faces "regulate it" on the opposite side of the horseshoe for good reason. While one penalizes the corporation for what it does do, the other rewards it for doing what it might not otherwise do. Hence these two positions can be direct substitutes: pollution can be alleviated by introducing penalties for the damage done or by offering incentives for the improvements rendered.

Logic would, however, dictate a specific role for each of these positions. Where a corporation is doing society a specific, attributable harm—as in the case of pollution—then paying it to stop hardly seems to make a lot of sense. If society does not wish to outlaw the harmful behavior altogether, then surely it must charge those responsible for it—the corporation and, ultimately, its customers. Offering financial incentives to stop causing harm would be to invite a kind of blackmail—for example, encouraging corporations to pollute so as to get paid to stop. And every citizen would be charged for the harm done by only a few.

On the other hand, where social problems exist which cannot be attributed to specific corporations, yet require the skills of certain corporations for solution, then financial incentives clearly make sense (so long, of course, as solutions can be clearly defined and tied to tangible economic rewards). Here, and not under "trust it," is where the "only business can do it" argument belongs. When it is true that only business can do it (and business has not done it to us in the first place), then business should be encouraged to do it. . . .

"RESTORE IT"

Our last position on the horseshoe tends to be highly ideological, the first since "democratize it" to seek a fundamental change in the governance and the goals of the corporation. Like the proponents of "nationalize it," those of this position believe that managerial control is illegitimate and must be replaced by a more valid form of external control. The corporation should be restored to its former status, that is, returned to its "rightful" owners, the shareholders. The only way to ensure the relentless pursuit of economic goals—and that means the maximization of profit, free of the "subversive doctrine" of social responsibility—is to put control directly into the hands of those to whom profit means the most.

A few years ago this may have seemed to be an obsolete position. But thanks to its patron saint Milton Friedman . . . it has recently come into prominence. . . .

Friedman has written:

> In a free-enterprise, private-property system, a corporate executive is an employee of the owners of the business. He has direct responsibility to his employers. That responsibility is to conduct the business in accordance with their desires, which generally will be to make as much money as possible while conforming to the basic rules of the society, both those embodied in law and those embodied in ethical custom.[11]

Interestingly, what seems to drive Friedman is a belief that the shift over the course of this century from owner to manager control, with its concerns about social responsibility, represents an unstoppable skid around our horseshoe. In the opening chapter of his book *Capitalism and Freedom,* Friedman seems to accept only two possibilities—traditional capitalism and socialism as practiced in Eastern Europe. The absence of the former must inevitably lead to the latter.

> The preservation and expansion of freedom are today threatened from two directions. The one threat is obvious and clear. It is the external threat coming from the evil men in the Kremlin who promise to bury us. The other threat is far more subtle. It is the internal threat coming from men of good intentions and good will who wish to reform us.[12]

The problem of who should control the corporation thus reduces to a war between two ideologies—in Friedman's terms, "subversive" socialism and "free" enterprise. In this world of black and white, there can be no middle ground, no moderate position between the black of "nationalize it" and the white of "restore it," none of the grey of "trust it." Either the owners will control the corporation or else the government will. Hence: " 'restore it' or else." Anchor the corporation on the right side of the horseshoe, Friedman seems to be telling us, the only place where "free" enterprise and "freedom" are safe.

All of this, in my view, rests on a series of assumptions—technical, economic, and political—which contain a number of fallacies. First is the fallacy of the technical assumption of shareholder control. Every trend in ownership during this century seems to refute the assumption that small shareholders are either willing or able to control the large, widely held corporation. The one place where free markets clearly still exist is in stock ownership, and that has served to detach ownership from control. When power is widely dispersed—among stockholders no less than workers or customers—those who share it tend to remain passive. It pays no one of them to invest the effort to exercise their power. Hence, even if serious shareholders did control the boards of widely held corporations (and one survey of all the directors of the *Fortune 500* in 1977 found that only 1.6% of them represented significant shareholder interests),[13] the question remains open as to whether they would actually try to control the management.

The economic assumptions of free markets have been discussed at length in the literature. Whether there exists vibrant competition, unlimited entry, open information, consumer sovereignity, and labor mobility is debatable. Less debatable is the conclusion that the larger the corporation, the greater is its ability to interfere with these processes. The issues we are discussing center on the giant corporation. . . .

Those who laid the foundation for conventional economic theory—such as Adam Smith and Alfred Marshall—never dreamed of the massive amounts now spent for advertising campaigns, most of them designed as much for affect as for effect; of the waves of conglomeration that have combined all kinds of diverse businesses into single corporate entities; of chemical complexes that cost more than a billion dollars; and of the intimate relationships that now exist between giant corporations and government, as customer and partner not to mention subsidizer. The concept of arm's length relationships in such conditions is, at best, nostalgic. What happens to consumer sovereignty when Ford knows more about its gas tanks than do its customers? And what does labor mobility mean in the presence of an inflexible pension plan, or commitment to a special skill, or a one-factory town? It is an ironic twist of conventional economic theory that the worker is the one who typically stays put, thus rendering false the assumption of labor mobility, while the shareholder is the mobile one, thus spoiling the case for owner control.

The political assumptions are more ideological in nature, although usually implicit. These assumptions are that the corporation is essentially amoral, society's instrument for producing goods and services, and, more broadly, that a society is "free" and "democratic" so long as its governmental leaders are elected by universal suffrage and do not interfere with the legal activities of businessmen. But many people—a large majority of the general public, if polls are to be believed—seem to subscribe to one or more assumptions that contradict these "free enterprise" assumptions.

One assumption is that the large corporation is a social and political institution as much as an economic instrument. Economic activities, as noted previously, produce all kinds of social consequences. Jobs get created and rivers get polluted, cities get built and workers get injured. These social consequences cannot be factored out of corporate strategic decisions and assigned to government.

Another assumption is that society cannot achieve the necessary balance between social and economic needs so long as the private sector attends only to economic goals. Given the pervasiveness of business in society, the acceptance of Friedman's prescriptions would drive us toward a one-dimensional society—a society that is too utilitarian and too materialistic. Economic morality, as noted earlier, can amount to a social immorality.

Finally, the question is asked: Why the owners? In a democratic society, what justifies owner control of the corporation any more than worker control, or consumer control, or pluralistic control? Ours is not Adam Smith's society of small proprietors and shopkeepers. His butcher, brewer, and baker have become Iowa Beef Packers, Anheuser-Busch, and ITT Continental Baking. What was once a case for individual democracy now becomes a case for oligarchy. . . .

I see Friedman's form of "restore it" as a rather quaint position in a society of giant corporations, managed economies, and dispersed shareholders—a society in which the collective power of corporations is coming under increasing scrutiny and in which the distribution between economic and social goals is being readdressed.

Of course, there are other ways to "restore it." "Divest it" could return the corporation to the business or central theme it knows best, restoring the role of allocating funds between different businesses to capital markets instead of central headquarters. Also, boards could be restored to positions of influence by holding directors legally responsible for their actions and by making them more independent of managers . . . We might even wish to extend use of "reduce it" where possible, to decrease the size of those corporations that have grown excessively large on the basis of market or political power rather than economies of scale, and perhaps to eliminate certain forms of vertical integration. In many cases it may prove advantageous, economically as well as socially, to have the corporation trade with its suppliers and customers instead of being allowed to ingest them indiscriminately.[14]

I personally doubt that these proposals could be any more easily realized in today's society than those of Friedman, even though I believe them to be more desirable. "Restore it" is the nostalgic position on our horseshoe, a return to our fantasies of a glorious past. In this society of giant organizations, it flies in the face of powerful economic and political forces.

CONCLUSION: IF THE SHOE FITS . . .

I believe that today's corporation cannot ride on any one position any more than a horse can ride on part of a shoe. In other words, we need to treat the conceptual horseshoe as a portfolio of positions from which we can draw, depending on circumstances. Exclusive reliance on one position will lead to a narrow and dogmatic society, with an excess concentration of power. We have learned about the dangers of unrestrained government ownership. No less menacing is the unrestrained pursuit of the economic interests of the shareholders, or of the oligarchy of ostensibly "socially responsible" managers. Lord Acton taught us that absolute power corrupts absolutely. In contrast, the use of a variety of positions can encourage the pluralism I believe most of us feel is necessary to sustain democracy. If the shoe fits, then let the corporation wear it.

I do not mean to imply that the eight positions do not represent fundamentally different values and, in some cases, ideologies as well. Clearly they do. But I also believe that anyone who makes an honest assessment of the realities of power in and around today's large corporations must conclude that a variety of positions have to be relied upon. Anyone can tilt to the left, right, or center of our horseshoe, favoring popular, shareholder, or managerial control, along with social or economic goals or both in balance. But even the most devoted adherent of conventional economic theory cannot, for example, dismiss regulation totally, any more than the most flaming radical can deny the place of economic goals in the corporation.

I tilt to the left of center, as has no doubt been obvious in my comments to this point. Let me summarize my own prescriptions as follows, and in the process provide some basis for evaluating the relevant roles of each of the eight positions.

First "Trust It," or at Least "Socialize It." Despite my suspicions about much of the rhetoric that passes for social responsibility and the discouraging evidence about the behavior of large contemporary organizations (not only corporations), I remain firmly convinced that without honest and responsible people in important places, we are in deep trouble. We need to trust it because, no matter how much we rely on the other positions, managers will always retain a great deal of power. And that power necessarily has social no less than economic consequences. The positions on the right side of our horseshoe ignore these social consequences while some of those on the left fail to recognize the difficulties of influencing these consequences in large, hierarchical organizations. Sitting between these two sets of positions, managers can use their discretion to satisfy or to subvert the wishes of the public. Ultimately, what managers do is determined by their sense of responsibility as individual members of society.

Although we must "trust it," we cannot *only* "trust it." As I have argued, there is an appropriate and limited place for social responsibility—essentially to get the corporation's own house in order and to encourage it to act responsibly in its own sphere of operations. Beyond that, social responsibility needs to be tempered by other positions around our horseshoe.

Then "Pressure It," Ceaselessly. As we have seen, too many forces interfere with social responsibility. The best antidote to these forces is the ad hoc pressure campaign, designed to pinpoint unethical behavior and raise social consciousness about issues. . . .

In fact, "pressure it" underlies the success of most of the other positions. Pressure campaigns have brought about necessary new regulations and have highlighted the case for corporate democracy. As we have seen, the "ignore it" position collapses without "pressure it." Indeed, what if not a pressure campaign is the media blitz of Milton Friedman to "restore it."

After That, Try to "Democratize It." A somewhat distant third in my portfolio is "democratize it," a position I view as radical only in terms of the current U.S. debate, not in terms of fundamental American values. Democracy matters most where it affects us directly—in the water we drink, the jobs we perform, the products we consume. How can we call our society democratic when many of its most powerful institutions are closed to governance from the outside and are run as hierarchies of authority from within?

As noted earlier, I have no illusions about having found the means to achieve corporate democracy. But I do know that Americans can be very resourceful when they decide to resolve a problem—and this is a problem that badly needs resolving. Somehow, ways must be found to open the corporation up to the formal influence of the constituencies most affected by it—employees, customers, neighbors, and so on—without weakening it as an economic institution. At stake is nothing less than the maintenance of basic freedoms in our society.

Then, Only Where Specifically Appropriate, "Regulate It" and "Induce It." Facing each other on the horseshoe are two positions that have useful if limited roles to play. Regulation is neither a panacea nor a menace. It belongs where the corporation can abuse the power it has and can be penalized for that abuse—notably where externalities can be identified with specific corporations. Financial inducements belong, not where a corporation has created a problem, but where it has the capability to solve a problem created by someone else.

Occasionally, Selectively, "Nationalize It" and "Restore It," but Not in Friedman's Way. The extreme positions should be reserved for extreme problems. If "pressure it" is a scalpel and "regulate it" a cleaver, then "nationalize it" and "restore it" are guillotines.

Both these positions are implicitly proposed as alternatives to "democratize it." One offers public control, the other "shareholder democracy." The trouble is that control by everyone often turns out to be control by no one, while control by the owners—even if attainable—would remove the corporation even further from the influence of those most influenced by it.

Yet, as noted earlier, nationalization sometimes makes sense—when private enterprise cannot provide a necessary mission, at least in a sufficient or appropriate way, and when the activities of a corporation must be intricately tied in to government policy.

As for "restore it," I believe Friedman's particular proposals will aggravate the problems of political control and social responsibility, strengthening oligarchical tendencies in society and further tilting what I see as the current imbalance between social and economic goals. In response to Friedman's choice between "subversive" socialism and "free" enterprise, I say "a pox on both your houses." Let us concentrate our efforts on the intermediate positions around the horseshoe. . . . I stand with Friedman in wishing to see competitive markets strengthened; it is just that I believe his proposals lead in exactly the opposite direction.

Finally, Above All, Don't "Ignore It." I leave one position out of my portfolio altogether, because it contradicts the others. The one thing we must not do is ignore the large, widely-held corporation. It is too influential a force in our lives. Our challenge is to find ways to distribute the power in and around our large organizations so that they will remain responsive, vital, and effective.

REFERENCES

1. E. M. Epstein, for example, finds the social record of nationalized firms in the U.K. not much better than the private ones, a conclusion reinforced by C. Jenkins, who advocates nationalization. E. M. Epstein. "The Social Role of Business Enterprise in Britain: An American Perspective; Part II," *The Journal of Management Studies* (1977), pp. 281–316; and C. Jenkins, *Power at the Top* (Westport, CT: Greenwood Press, 1976).
2. From J. Bacon and J. K. Brown. *Corporate Directorship Practices: Role, Selection and Legal Status of the Board* (The Conference Board and the American Society of Corporate Secretaries, Inc., 1975), p. 48.
3. See, Henry Mintzberg, *Structure in Fives: Designing Effective Organizations* (Englewood Cliffs, NJ: Prentice-Hall, 1983).
4. T. Levitt, "Why Business Always Loses," *Harvard Business Review* (March/April 1968), p. 83.
5. Levitt, op. cit.
6. D. Braybrooke, "Skepticism of Wants, and Certain Subversive Effects of Corporations on American Values," in S. Hook, ed., *Human Values and Economic Policy* (New York, NY: New York University Press, 1967), p. 224.
7. Milton Friedman, "A Friedman Doctrine: The Social Responsibility of Business is to Increase its Profits," *The New York Times Magazine,* September 13, 1970, pp. 126, 33, 126.
8. Robert W. Ackerman, *The Social Challenge to Business* (Cambridge, MA: Harvard University Press, 1975), p. 56.
9. I. Ross, "How Lawless are the Big Companies?" *Fortune,* December 1, 1980, p. 57.
10. Aleksander Solzhenitsyn, from "Why The West Has Succumbed to Cowardice," *The Montreal Star: News and Review,* June 10, 1978, p. B1.
11. Friedman, op. cit., p. 33.
12. Milton Friedman, *Capitalism and Freedom* (Chicago, IL: University of Chicago Press, 1962), p. 20.
13. L. Smith, "The Boardroom Is Becoming a Different Scene," *Fortune,* May 8, 1978, pp. 150–154, 158, 162, 166, 168.
14. A number of these proposals would be worthwhile to pursue in the public and parapublic sectors as well, to divide up overgrown hospitals, school systems, social service agencies, and all kinds of government departments.

Corporate Governance: Who Is In Control Here?

Dan R. Dalton
Dow Professor of Management, Indiana University

There is really very little question about who is in control of our nation's businesses. Despite recent posturing regarding increased stockholder activism, greater scrutiny by institutional investors,

---

challenges to boards of directors for better informed, independent judgment, and a host of other pressures, the management of the publicly traded corporation in the United States remains firmly in charge. Some might say that "entrenched" is a better choice of terms.

There are probably any number of developments to which I could turn to provide some justification for this view, but perhaps I should focus on a timely issue regarding corporate governance, "the battle for corporate control." This battle's trendline clearly establishes the firm hand by which management holds the reins. The continuing saga of corporate takeovers, leveraged buyouts, and other transactions may lead some to the conclusion that the magnitude of corporate control by management does not always lead to outcomes in the best interest of the shareholders.

As a vehicle for addressing this issue, I would like to share with you the apocryphal story of Mr. Mitchell, apartment complex manager, and you, who for purposes of this tale will be the owner of a 120-unit apartment complex. Welcome to the trials and tribulations of commercial property ownership.

Please remember, however, that although our story considers the relationship between you, property manager Mitchell, and a certain financial transaction, this journey is a metaphor for similar transactions of the CEO and the shareholders of the typical publicly traded corporation. I hope that the commercial property analogy provides a provocative perspective.

CHAPTER I: THE BATTLE FOR CORPORATE CONTROL ('TIL DEATH DO US PART)

Consider the following (outrageous, it is hoped) scenario. Suppose that Kevin Mitchell works for you. He has served as apartment manager and lead maintenance person for your 120-unit apartment complex. He oversees a relatively small staff of employees who prepare the units between rentals, collect the rents, do routine maintenance, attend to the care of the grounds, and have a variety of other duties. You have owned this apartment complex for some 20 years.

It remains upscale, is in a prestigious area of the community, and enjoys a lengthy waiting list of persons who would like to live on the premises should a vacancy occur. There is an adjoining piece of property on a separate deed that you also own. On this parcel is a beautiful clubhouse, olympic pool, two jacuzzis, several half-court basketball areas, and four well-maintained tennis courts, along with a host of additional recreational facilities. These facilities are for the exclusive use of the tenants. There is no separate charge for this use. Also on this separate deed there are approximately five undeveloped acres. Your best estimate of the value of this complex is $60,000 a unit, a total of some $7,200,000. This evaluation includes the separated deeded parcel as well.

The mortgage on this property has recently been paid in full. Aside from normal obligations (for example, utilities for the common areas, property taxes), the complex is debt-free. You no longer live in the immediate vicinity. In fact, some years ago you moved to the Southwest and are semi-retired. Because Kevin Mitchell has thoroughly distinguished himself as the manager of these apartment units over the years, you have given him a great deal of discretion regarding the day-to-day operations of this business. He, for example, hires additional help as the need arises. He contracts for extraordinary repairs—those in which his full-time staff would not normally be involved (for example, replacing roofs, repaving driveways and common areas).

Moreover, Mr. Mitchell has access to a discretionary account of some $300,000. Basically, this fund includes a certain percentage of the units' income that is set aside for preventive maintenance (for example, external painting) and provision for the more extraordinary repairs. This fund has been used judiciously over the years and accounts in part for the continuing high quality of the units and their high demand.

A Friendly—and Potentially Lucrative—Visit

Unbeknownst to you, a person drops by the rental office late on a Tuesday afternoon and asks to speak to the person in charge. As it happens, your manager, Mr. Mitchell, is in the office at the time, introduces himself, and asks of what service he can be.

"Could you provide me with the name and address of the owner or owners of this apartment complex?" asked the stranger. "I would like to speak with them concerning the purchase of this property. My partners and I are prepared to make what we believe to be a generous offer."

"I am afraid that will not be possible," countered Mr. Mitchell. "The owner is semi-retired and has enchartered me with the full responsibility of managing this property. Frankly, the owner prefers not to be bothered with the normal operations of his properties. If you are comfortable discussing this matter with me, however, I will be pleased to consider your offer, submit it for scrutiny to our accountant and our attorney, and with their approval make the owner aware of your proposal."

"That will be fine," responded the stranger. "I will have my attorney draw up a preliminary offer and have it delivered to your office Monday a.m."

And so he did. On the following Monday a bona fide offer for the apartment complex arrived by courier. The offer was for $10 million, some 40 percent higher than our earlier estimate of $7.2 million. The stranger and his partners were apparently true to their word: It is a generous offer indeed.

Management's Counteroffensive

Mr. Mitchell, the property manager, has a bit of a problem. It occurs to him—and he is correct—that his job is seriously threatened. The group who has made the offer for the property has a rather impressive, in-place management and maintenance team that attends to their other properties. Obviously, this team will have the responsibility for this complex as well if its offer is accepted.

Mr. Mitchell really has done an excellent job over the years, is very well compensated, and would prefer not to be displaced. Although the offer for the property certainly appears to be in the best interests of the owner, it would not seem in the immediate interests of the property manager.

But, to Mr. Mitchell's credit, he realizes that the argument enunciated in the prior paragraph is suspect. He is frankly not entirely sure what a fiduciary responsibility is, but he thinks it has something to do with the notion that he, as property manager, should never put his interests above those of the owner. That being the case, he knows that few people will be sympathetic to his position that he will lose his job. Accordingly, he had better think of an argument that will play a little better.

After some careful thought, he independently arrives at a line of reasoning that—unknown to him—is time tested. Well, he thinks to himself, that the offer of $10 million is well above the "market price" of $7.2 million is puzzling. I do not know what exactly accounts for the difference, but I do know one thing. No rational person would knowingly offer more for a property than it is worth.

Actually, he figures, in a commercial transaction the price should reflect an offer that includes some concept of gain. After all, if the bidding party did not believe that there was some profit to be made on the transaction either in the near or longer term, what would be the point of buying the property? Presumably, commercial transactions are not entered into for the purposes of breaking even.

If that is true—and any sober individual would have to concede that Mr. Mitchell has a point—the $10 million offer is actually something less than the property is worth. The $7.2 million estimate of value is almost certainly understated. If we are patient, the value of the property will be re-evaluated and the actual price *must* be something higher than $10 million.

Yes, Mr. Mitchell is convinced that this logic is flawless on its face. No point, then, in making the owner aware of this offer. The offer is clearly inadequate. Rather than bothering the owner with the burdensome nonsense of realizing an overnight 40 percent of his property, he decides to reject the offer out of hand.

And, that is exactly what Mr. Mitchell does. The owner is not made aware of the offer. The stranger and his associates are surprised by the rejection, but regroup to find alternative properties.

Mr. Mitchell, the near-erstwhile property manager, returns to his day-to-day responsibilities, secure once again in his employment.

An Aside

For purposes of this tale, let's project for a moment. Put yourself in the place of the owner of this property, the value of which you believe to be $7.2

million. Now, it is not as though you arrived at this figure through divination. It may have been based on the purchase prices of similar properties in the region; it may have been based on replacement cost; it may have been based on the professional opinion of appraisers; it may have been based on some combination of all these.

Nevertheless, it comes to your attention that someone—for whatever reason—offered you $10 million for the property and your manager did not choose even to make you aware of the offer. May we assume that you would not react to this information with calm introspection and total equanimity. On the contrary, I suspect that many of us would have to be sedated.

CHAPTER II: BUT . . . IT COULD HAVE BEEN WORSE

At the conclusion of the last chapter, the bidding stranger and his associates retired to consider alternative properties. Suppose, however, that they were less accommodating to Mr. Mitchell. Instead of peacefully withdrawing to other endeavors, they are adamant that their offer be presented to the owner. They insist on an opportunity to have the actual owner, not his management, consider the offer.

Mr. Mitchell, as we have come to expect, is not comfortable with this arrangement. After all, it is possible that the owner might actually elect to sell the property, with it the attendant demise of Mr. Mitchell's employment. It is at this point that Mr. Mitchell decides that he must devise certain strategies to dissuade the stranger and his associates from their relentless crusade to own this property. Owing to what he believes is his inherent creativity—again not realizing that this ground has been thoroughly furrowed before—Mr. Mitchell employs the following tactics in no particular order.

The Apartment Management Golden Parachute

Mr. Mitchell decides that he and his staff cannot be expected to continue to perform at their high level under this purchase-proposal threat. He knows that there is a certain paradox at work here. He explains to his staff that part of the reason that this bid is so high is related to the incredible job they have been doing. In other words, if the property were not so well maintained, were not so well managed, then the bid would have been correspondingly lower.

Obviously, the staff can not reasonably be expected to continue their work at the current, competent level if such behavior will only result in job insecurity: The better they do, the more likely there will be a job-security threatening bid. Accordingly, Mr. Mitchell promises his managerial staff a "golden parachute." This is a promise that if the property is purchased each of these staff members (and himself, of course) will receive five years' pay. Understand that Mr. Mitchell does not suggest that these people will receive their pay over the next five years. This is not an employment contract. Rather, if the property is transferred to the new owners, these golden parachute individuals will receive the five years' pay at once.

Mr. Mitchell realizes that this will accomplish a couple of objectives. Certainly, it does provide security to the employees. Beyond that, it provides a disincentive to future bidders. Obviously, the price of any bid would have to include the amount necessary to pay these managers their five years' pay. Incidentally, Mr. Mitchell has included another nice touch. He or his managers do not actually have to be replaced by the new firm to open this golden parachute. It is sufficient that the property has been acquired. The managers and Mr. Mitchell—if the property is acquired—may leave of their own volition and still collect the golden parachute. Nice touch!

On second thought, Mr. Mitchell decides that it is really unfair only to include the higher-level management employees in this golden parachute arrangement. Why not include all the employees? We probably won't give them five years' severance, he thinks, but we should certainly give them something. Mr. Mitchell coins the term "tin parachute" for this plan.

Apartment Management Greenmail

Mr. Mitchell would really prefer that the stranger and his associates just withdraw their offer. Obviously, that would be the most efficient method to deal with this "problem." So . . . Mr. Mitchell uses the $300,000 maintenance fund to encourage such a retreat.

Mr. Mitchell gives the money to the bidding stranger and partners to cover their "expenses" in this transaction. Incidentally, the bidding stranger—presumably in return for this courtesy—withdraws the offer and promises not to pursue another offer for this property for five, ten years or so. Mr. Mitchell is a little concerned about this strategy. He realizes that this approach might encourage other bidders who are much more interested in the "expense" payment than the property. Oh well, he decides to deal with that when the time comes.

Apartment Management Super Majority Amendment

It is only fair that the tenants should have some input in such a decision. Accordingly, Mr. Mitchell notifies the tenants that the acquisition of this property by others could only be approved by a 80 percent (maybe 95 percent would be better) majority vote of the tenants. The tenants—generally averse to change like the rest of us—may fear that the rents may be increased, the units converted to condos, or whatever. Accordingly, they would not be prone to endorse much of a transaction. Gee, I guess the deal is off. This strategy could be readily put in motion by amending the current leases to give the tenants the right of refusal concerning new ownership.

Apartment Management Super Shares

Mr. Mitchell is fairly confident that the "super majority" provision will work nicely. But one can never be too sure. He thinks of a nice twist to that strategy. Perhaps what he should do is contact the people who have been residents in the apartment complex for the longest time. These may include some elderly tenants for whom increased rents, condo conversion, or ultimately moving would really constitute a burden. Since these individuals are the least likely to "vote" for the new owners, perhaps we should have a program which weights their vote disproportionately.

This is easily done. For their leases, Mr. Mitchell provides language that gives them 10, or 100, or a 1,000 votes instead of one vote. That way a few of the key tenants could outvote the remaining tenants (who only have one vote per unit) even if they were overwhelmingly supportive of the sale among the remaining tenants. This is nice because now Mr. Mitchell will only have to pander to a few key tenants—those with the super weighted votes. If he can keep them content, then the view of the other tenants is largely mute.

Apartment Management Poison Pill

Once again, the object of this exercise is to dissuade this current bidder and, not incidentally, any future bidders with these "hostile" intentions from pursuing this particular property. As regards tenant involvement, Mr. Mitchell has a true master stroke.

Mr. Mitchell goes to all the tenants and promises them a new lease. This lease will be for five years and the monthly rent will be *one-half* of the amount they are currently paying. The tenants sign this lease (obviously) and so does Mr. Mitchell. There is only one stipulation. This new lease is only enforceable if, and only if, the property is transferred to new owners—any new owners.

The effect of this is clear, if not diabolical. If any bidder successfully bids for this property, the new owner will have to assume the rights and conditions of the new leases. Presumably, no persons in their right minds would buy a property under these circumstances. If successful in the transaction, the new owner would receive only half the market rate for all leases over the next five years. At the risk of repeating myself, this truly is a master stroke.

Nice additional touches might include lease provisions for new carpeting at ridiculously short intervals, yearly repainting, company-paid cable television, company-paid utilities. You get the picture.

The Apartment Management People Pill

Another thought. Mr. Mitchell decides that it would be greatly disruptive if—given an acquisition of the property—all the employees quit. Presumably, the bidders would think twice about acquiring the property if the transition period promised to be very difficult. Accordingly, Mr. Mitchell persuasively influences all the management employees to agree to quit if the complex is sold. Mr. Mitchell coins—a bit late—the term "people pill" to refer to this strategy.

The Apartment Management Lockup

You may recall that you own the 120 apartment units on one deed and a rather extensive adjoining recreational area on another. Given the separate deeds, Mr. Mitchell has yet another brainstorm. This strategy is clearly on a par with the poison pill for its demonic impact.

Suppose that the value of the property and improvements on the second deed is $1 million. Mr. Mitchell finds a buyer who is willing to buy this property for $250,000, a presumably trivial exercise. The contract is signed. But wait. There is an important condition to this sale. The contract can be executed only if the ownership of the larger (120-unit) parcel is transferred. Only at that time is the purchase contract enforceable.

So, the first order of business to which the new owner will have to attend is to sell a $1 million dollar property for $250,000. Not only that, but the tenants will no longer have the use of these marvelous facilities. Do you think that would affect the value of the acquisition? Subsequent rents? Will the existence of such a contract dissuade a potential bidder? Mr. Mitchell likes to refer to this brilliant strategy as a lockup. I wonder who ought to be locked up.

Apartment Management Scorched Earth

When conceiving of this ploy, Mr. Mitchell has truly outdone himself—and undone you. This is a gorgeous strategy, if for no other reason than for its simplicity.

One of the reasons why this property is initially appealing is that it is virtually debt-free. There are no mortgages, extraordinary expenses, contracts, liens, judgments, or other items to sully the transaction. That being the case, Mr. Mitchell has any number of options to reduce the attractiveness of this property, all of which might be reasonably grouped together as "scorched earth" strategies.

Suppose, for example, that Mr. Mitchell contracts to have 25 (or 50, or whatever will fit) additional tennis courts built on the five undeveloped acres and mortgages the balance due over a number of years. Never mind that these additional tennis courts are a preposterous overkill as an addition to an apartment complex that already has four prime courts. The point is hardly to provide additional amenities to the tenants; rather, the object of this expansion is to add debt that a new bidder will have to consider and assume when purchasing this property.

Other far more insidious options are available. Mr. Mitchell could contract to have many more apartment units built on the undeveloped area. These could be unusually large and lavishly appointed (read very expensive). They could be far too exclusive for the area, thereby insuring a large vacancy rate. It goes without saying that the new mortgage will still be due although it is unlikely that it can be satisfactorily serviced.

Again, the effect of this strategy is to burden the property with high levels of debt. It seems clear that such a strategy will have the desired effect of reducing the overall attractiveness of the property to those who might otherwise bid. Did I mention that the overall effect on the owner of the property should be noticeable as well?

The Apartment Management Leveraged Buyout

This may be considered the coup de grace of apartment management. The aforementioned strategies—as clever and effective as they may be—only serve to secure Mr. Mitchell's current employment. These strategies, either singly or in concert, do operate to dissuade potential bidders for the property. Mr. Mitchell would strongly prefer that no such bid be successful simply because he believes—and rightly so—that the new owners will rely on different management. Ergo, unemployment.

But it could be better. Mr. Mitchell decides that what he really needs is a tactic that not only secures his employment but improves his financial condition as well. His advantage here will simply be superior knowledge. Presumably, there is nobody who knows more about the day-to-day operations of this apartment complex than does Mr. Mitchell. Mr. Mitchell may know, for example, that the current rents are lagging well behind the market rate. He may know that a large, competing complex has been approved for conversion to condominiums. This will obviously enhance the market for his units and allow the rents to ease even higher.

He may realize that the current maintenance schedules, while most appealing for the tenants, are really too ambitious. There is no necessity for the frequent repainting, carpeting, and so forth at the current intervals. He may know that several of his maintenance contracts (for example, lawn maintenance, pest control) are due for rebid. He also knows that several businesses have contacted him and are prepared to submit aggressive bids for this business at rates below those of current contracts.

He may, in short, know a lot of things. More importantly, there is probably no person on the planet who knows all this. And most certainly the absentee owner does not.

Mr. Mitchell knows something else, something that he did not choose to share with the owner. He has a much higher quality estimate of the value of the property. The owner believes that it is worth about $7.2 million. The manager knows otherwise: he has, after all, seen a bona fide bid for $10 million. Given the wealth of additional information, Mr. Mitchell realizes that even the $10 million may be a bit modest. There just has to be a way to exploit this spread.

Suppose . . .

Mr. Mitchell and others who he has recruited for these purposes decide that he himself will submit a bid for the property. Certainly, they want to be "fair" to the owner so they decide to bid $7.7 million, $500,000 above the "market" value of the property. Surely, the owner will be pleased with this offer, especially the $500,000 windfall.

Mr. Mitchell and his friends decide to call this transaction an apartment leveraged buyout. They do not have a lot of money so they will provide the absolute minimum down payment, borrow the balance, and rely on the cash flow of the property to pay off the mortgage. Accordingly, they will purchase (buy out) the owner's property interest in this deal which will be heavily leveraged.

Mr. Mitchell may really be on to something now. Given his inside information about the operations of the property, not to mention its value, he has come upon the proverbial gold mine. This allows him to own the property a few years, manage it much more efficiently than he did for the owner, "adjust" the income of the property to a level at which it should have operated from the onset, and then play his trump card.

In a couple of years—or instantly for that matter—Mr. Mitchell can sell the property. Suppose that he sells it for $10 million (although it will almost certainly be more). What has happened here? Your apartment manager and fiduciary, Mr. Mitchell, has parlayed a very modest down payment into $2.3 million dollars ($10 million–$7.7 million) in two years. It is a shame that the owner could not have shared in this bonanza. Well, I guess that owning apartment complexes is just a tough business.

Another Aside

Early on in this story, we had a scenario whereby Mr. Mitchell, your manager, did not choose to acquaint you with the $10 million offer on your property. I think we concluded that you, as the owner, would probably have to be sedated to control your anger at this breach of duty. "Control your anger" may be one of the great understatements. More likely, you could be easily induced—or at least be sorely tempted—to contract for the demise of Mr. Mitchell.

But, as you see, this was only a proverbial tip of the iceberg. Can we agree that you would find it inconceivable that Mr. Mitchell might actually engage in these other behaviors—golden parachutes, greenmail, supermajority amendments, poison pills, people pills, lock-ups, scorched earth, and leveraged buyouts?

Surely, I exaggerate. This could not actually happen. At a minimum, wouldn't the apartment manager be civilly, even criminally, liable for such behavior (some sort of conspiracy, fraud)? And, if not that, do these behaviors not constitute the grossest sort of suspension of fiduciary responsibility? Minimally, do we have a textbook case of unethical behavior?

Apparently not.

DENOUEMENT

Suppose I had asked you early on who has control of the typical owner/apartment manager relationship. We would certainly agree that the owner is firmly in control. Having spun this tale, however, we probably both agree that the apartment manager was clearly in control, even to the detriment of the owner. Earlier on, I described this story as "outrageous, it is hoped." And, in the context of commercial property, it goes well beyond outrageous. It is unthinkable. Sadly, however, our metaphor is altogether reasonable, not even overstated. No, in the real world of corporate governance, I immodestly suggest that our analogy is compelling.

The overwhelming majority of shareholders are certainly the equivalent of our apartment complex owner. They are owners in absentia. They rely on their property manager (high-ranking officers of the corporation) to keep them fairly appraised and to operate in a manner not inconsistent with the owner's objectives. They deliberately delegate the day-to-day operations of the corporate enterprise to its managers. Presumably, however, this is not a total abdication.

Every single strategy that I ascribed to Mr. Mitchell has been practiced, and in most cases continues to be practiced, in the battle for corporate control. Golden parachutes, greenmail, supermajority provisions, supershares, poison pills, lock-ups, scorched earth, and leveraged buyouts are real. Not only are they real, they are hardly esoteric. Such strategies are absolutely commonplace. Incidentally, these tactics that we have introduced are not exhaustive, merely representative. They by no means capture the breadth of alternatives available to management to prevent a firm from being purchased by another person or enterprise. In many ways, they are truly creative, even brilliant. Although the exact manner in which many of these strategies operate varies considerably, they all reflect a common theme as regards their impact. They all may very well prevent owners from exercising an option to sell their property to a higher bidder.

Suppose that you own 1,000 shares of Business Horizons, Ltd., a publicly traded U.S. corporation, the common stock of which is currently trading for $72 on the New York Stock Exchange. Suppose further that someone offers the management of this corporation in which you own a property right (1,000 shares) $100 per share to purchase the company in its entirety.

Do you think, under these circumstances, that it is reasonable that you as the stockholder be made aware of this offer?

I could cite you many, many instances in which the management of the company in parallel situations has decided that the offer is "inadequate." Moreover, I could cite you case after case in which the company has made provisions for the high-ranking managers of the company to receive generous severance packages (often millions of dollars) if the company should be purchased (referred to as a "golden parachute"), paid the bidder a premium to forestall their offer and promise not to reinstitute it for the reasonable future (referred to as "greenmail"), required an outrageous percentage of stockholders to agree to the purchase (referred to as "super majority"), and gave 10 votes, or 100, or more to certain stockholders rather than abide by the common one share, one vote principle (referred to as "super shares").

Furthermore, it would be a trivial exercise to demonstrate that management has promised its stockholders that they could buy one share of stock *at half price* for every share they already own, but only if the company is actually taken over (referred to as a "poison pill"). Companies have actually threatened that, if taken over, the entire contingent of upper management will quit at once (referred to as a "people pill"). Moreover, companies have actually contracted to sell certain of its assets at bargain basement prices. The only condition for the execution of the sale is that the company must be taken over (referred to as a "lock-up").

Any number of examples could be detailed in which companies have deliberately utilized strategies (for example, purchasing other companies) for the purpose of drastically increasing their debt. This strategy is presumably relied on to "adjust" the balance sheet to make the company unattractive. Such debt adjustments are often referred to as "scorched earth" policies.

Lastly, the practice of management—with their privileged, high quality information—of being party to groups that attempt themselves to purchase the very company they manage is epidemic. This tactic is generally referred to as a "leveraged buyout."

Given the availability and apparent legality (there are jurisdictions, although certainly not all jurisdictions, in which the lockup and certain varieties of poison pill have been voided) of such tactics, I now ask you once again, "who is in control?"

I would respond, unequivocally, management. Frankly, I would be comfortable with that arrangement if I believed that these actions were in the interests of the shareholders. For the most part, I do not believe that.

Anyone reading the apartment management scenario would come away appalled. The behavior I have described on the part of the apartment manager is unacceptable on its face. I must admit to some surprise that identical behaviors in a corporate forum evidently lead to less urgency.

Moral Corporate Cultures in a Down-Sized, Restructured World

Anthony F. Buono
Professor of Management and Research Fellow, Center for Business Ethics, Bentley College

As we enter the 1990s, increased attention is being placed on the creation of ethical structures and organizational cultures—codes of conduct, ethics hotlines, review committees, ombudsmen, shared value systems, and related self-regulatory phenomena—throughout corporate America. Most of these frameworks and prescriptions, however, largely examine what might be referred to as the "light side" of our efforts to create moral corporate cultures. When I refer to the "light side" of such cultures, I'm not suggesting that we observe them in a humorous vein, but rather that we typically look at them in the daylight, that dimension of organizational life that we want public and visible. The expanding number of corporate training efforts and the growth of ethics resource centers are examples of this public view. These initiatives, which are a very real part of the present business environment, are a reflection that things are indeed beginning to change.

It is important to emphasize, however, that these endeavors are only *part* of what is happening. Running on a very different, some might argue collision, course with these ethical principles, codes and structures is a decidedly disparate set of circumstances and conditions. Thus, instead of praising what has been done to enhance the moral and ethical dimensions of life in Corporate America, this essay delves into the shadows of organizational life,[1] what might be referred to as the "dark side" of corporate culture that is currently reverberating through our business sector and its ramifications for our attempts to create moral corporate cultures.

ORGANIZATIONAL CONSOLIDATION, DOWNSIZING AND RESTRUCTURING

The recent wave of interorganizational consolidation, downsizing and restructuring in Corporate America has significant ramifications for our attempts to create moral corporate cultures. There is a tendency, of course, to look at the past with a certain nostalgia. We do tend to romanticize previous decades as times when people knew how to work and how to be loyal, and American business knew how to get the job done. The tales that characterized our beliefs were that there were opportunities for all to get a good job, to get ahead, to make something of one's self. Yet, as we take a closer look at that same period we often see a different story—tales of hard and often dangerous working

---

Revised version of an article appearing in E.J. Trunfio, B.C. Auday, and M.A. Reid (eds.) *Developing Moral Corporate Cultures* (Wenham, MA: Gordon College Institute for Applied Ethics, 1992, pp. 77–100.) Reprinted by permission of the author.
Acknowledgement: I would like to thank Stephen Zwicker, my graduate research assistant, for his help with bibliographic research.

conditions, mundane, dehumanized and boring jobs, restricted opportunities for women and racial minorities, and clearly unethical business practices by today's standards. The rosy depiction that many of our myths about the past suggest are hardly ever matched by the realities of that world.[2] And yet, by every conceivable measure of attitudes toward and behaviors in the work place, there are ample signs that the levels of disaffection and discontent with our corporate world are currently at all time highs. National surveys reveal that in 1960, 75 percent of the population reported that they trusted politicians; 60 percent trusted big business. By the late 1980s, similar surveys reveal that the situation has changed dramatically, with politicians now being trusted less than big business—but the proportions are startlingly different with favorability ratings of 15 percent for big business and 14 percent for politicians.[3]

Upon examination, there appears to be good reason for such a loss of faith in our business system. Rather than creating a true context for moral corporate cultures, the corporate motto of the 1980s appears to have been "downsize, debt and dismantle," characterized by a wide variety of painful actions taken by corporations to pacify and enrich short-term investors.[4] Over the past decade, counting friendly deals and hostile takeovers, more than one third of the companies in the Fortune 500 industrials were either swallowed up by other concerns or went private.[5] Familiar scenarios, that are still occurring literally on a daily basis, include jobs that are redesigned and structures that are reorganized, new products and programs that are launched and quickly abandoned, long-term organizational members that are riffed or reassigned, and new management techniques that are introduced and rapidly replaced by others. Typical battle cries of the past decade—"Down with Tired Management! Up with Debt to Wipe Out Waste!"—promised rejuvenation, greater efficiency, and a return to competitive eminence. Instead, what might be referred to as "dealmania"—characterized by financial types who did not have any sense of how to run a company, supported by billions of dollars of junk bonds, other people's money—has turned corporate America into something that *Fortune* magazine recently described as more closely resembling a "sick ward in a MASH unit" than a healthy, invigorated, competitive economy.[6] The *Fortune* article went on to pose the question as to whether all this sound and fury were worth it. Its plain and simple conclusion—NO.

A recent survey of Fortune 500 and Service 500 chief executive officers reveals that, in their opinion, (1) the last wave of hostile takeovers hurt rather than helped the economy, and (2) the high levels of debt used to finance many LBOs damaged competitiveness and hurt rather than enhanced efficiency.[7] Ironically, it has gotten to the point where prepackaged bankruptcy filings are being lauded as the latest strategic management tool.[8] These prepackaged plans are essentially quick, uncontested restructurings that are carried out under the auspices of the bankruptcy court, and involve out-of-court arrangements between a company and its creditors, a bankruptcy filing, and the confirmation of a reorganization plan. Although it is often argued that such actions are in the best interest of a firm's customers, suppliers and employees, the legacies associated with such plans include imposed financial settlements on unwilling parties, questionable service arrangements, and large-scale layoffs for organizational members. As one economist recently argued, "Management has discovered with a vengeance that labor is a variable," with employees increasingly viewed as being "as dispensable as Kleenex" instead of valued resources.[9] Perhaps most troublesome in all of this, is that the survey of Fortune and Service 500 CEOs noted above feel that the threat of takeover is likely to increase rather than decrease in the future. Corporate America, in essence, is undergoing a fundamental transformation.

As a result of volatile and often chaotic changes in the external environment, of course, few companies have escaped some form of restructuring over the past 10 to 15 years.[10] It is important to underscore that downsizing and restructuring are not inherently unethical business practices. In fact, part of the dilemma we are faced with is that in an increasing number of instances, organizations are going through these changes, not by choice but by necessity. The reality is that organizations and their members must change in order to compete and survive in a rapidly changing, globally competitive world. Yet, a basic problem associated with these restructuring efforts is that far too many firms take what appear to them to be the most straightforward, direct, cost-controlled approach, namely terminating employees, cutting costs, and selling off underperforming businesses. True restructuring, however, involves much more than simply adding or selling a business, trimming staffs, or reorganizing departmental configurations. Those restructuring efforts with the highest probability of creating long-term value focus on a restructuring of employee attitudes, values, and orientations. Unfortunately, these less tangible dimensions of organizational life are usually the last factors to be addressed in a restructuring program because they are the most difficult for senior managers to control.

Much of my research over the past decade has focused on the ways in which our business organizations treat people during large-scale corporate consolidations. These studies—tracking organizations over the years following mergers and acquisitions—do not provide a rosy picture.[11] Instead of being the well planned, carefully calculated strategic acts they are typically portrayed to be, mergers and acquisitions appear to be more appropriately characterized as literally having a life of their own, with shifting periods of waiting and frenzied activities, cascading minor changes, rising tensions and conflicts, and stressful uncertainties. There is usually (1) an overly narrow and restricted focus on technical concerns at the expense of broader organizational realities, (2) an emphasis on finances and tactics at the expense of production, service, innovation and long-term strategies, (3) an emphasis on short-term shareholder value at the expense of broader stakeholder needs, and, perhaps most troublesome, (4) an emphasis on power and political machinations at the expense of the individuals who are caught up in the process. As our research has found, even initially friendly and collaborative combinations can quickly deteriorate into secrecy and deception, political gamesmanship, open warfare, and a variety of other tactics which, from an ethical vantagepoint, would be considered questionable at best.

Even if a merger or takeover fails to materialize, the latest takeover wave has still had severe human costs and repercussions. In its effort to stave off unwanted advances from Revlon, for example, Gillette Company restructured the firm by laying off thousands of employees, selling off what it considered to be marginal businesses, and more than doubling its long-term debt in a poison pill strategy. After each layoff, the firm promised its employees that the terminations would be the last, only to have wave after wave of termination and reductions in force follow.[12] Ask any Gillette employee to compare life in the firm today with that of only a decade ago.

In today's environment, what might be referred to as a "Theory X" approach to such consolidation and change does not necessarily only occur within the context of a merger or acquisition. Consider recent events at Proctor & Gamble, a company that just a few years ago was lauded as one of the exemplars of U.S. corporate superiority in Peters and Waterman's best seller, *In Search of Excellence.*[13] The *Wall Street Journal* ran a series of articles about restructuring plans at P&G, and cited unidentified sources who said that the head of P&G's food division had resigned under pressure and that some unprofitable divisions might be sold. P&G's top management was outraged that the story had been leaked to the press. After its own internal investigation failed to turn up any guilty parties, the company went to the police. Using a relatively obscure Ohio law that states it is a felony to transmit valuable trade secrets and a misdemeanor to disclose "any confidential matter or information" without a company's consent, P&G sought and successfully received a subpoena ordering Cincinnati Bell to electronically sift through the records of all customers in southwestern Ohio—over 35 million records—and list those who called the home or office of the *Wall Street Journal* reporter who wrote the article from March 1st to June 15th (1991). The police failed to find sufficient evidence to file charges related to the leaks, and no charges are expected. Internally, however, P&G employees have become increasingly disturbed by the company's rather stern handling of the incident and its associated message—"Clam up or ship out." In addition, complaints by the press and civil liberties experts about possible constitutional violations promise to create a bigger public relations problem for the consumer products giant than all the rumors that the firm's trademark is a satanic symbol. The basic question I would pose is whether these actions reflect the ways in which a company will succeed in developing and maintaining commitment to higher level, moral principles in the workplace.

Cynicism and "Free Agent" Managers

The ramifications of these trends for our managerial and professional workforce, and our attempts to ensure moral corporate cultures are ominous. Over the 1980s, it is estimated that over 1 million managers lost their jobs in organizational restructurings, and cutbacks and retrenchment efforts appear to be continuing, literally unabated. It has gotten to the point where a noted management scholar recently suggested that intelligent managers and business professionals should withhold their commitment from the organizations they work for.[14] Instead of being loyal corporate citizens, managers are being told that they should become more like *free agents,* in the sense that, like professional baseball players, as a manager you should look out for yourself and your career, find out how much you are worth, avoid being assigned to any long-term projects, and seek out and consider offers from other firms on a regular basis. The underlying philosophy increasingly appears to be to that "loyalty no longer pays off—self-interest does." Although this scenario might be difficult to initially accept, the reality is that given current trends organizational members are unlikely to stay with any organization over the long term. If you don't "do it" to your company, the company is likely to "do it" to you.

Other studies have found a similar increase in such cynicism—a sense of being deceived, betrayed and used by others—which has grown to the point where a disconcerting number of managers and employees feel that idealism and involvement have few payoffs in organizational life, and that social distance and emotional detachment are superior ways to deal with their day to day responsibilities.[15] The underlying belief in corporate America seems increasingly to be that you cannot trust what others tell you and, given the opportunity, the organization you work for and its management will take advantage of you. Recent surveys of job and organizational satisfaction among middle-level managers, for example, reveal increasing frustration and discontent.[16] The question I would pose, once again, is whether these attitudes and orientations are truly conducive for the creation of a moral corporate culture.

THE DARK SIDE OF EMPLOYEE INVOLVEMENT STRATEGIES

One of the implicit themes in most discussions of corporate ethical conduct concerns the importance of employee participation and involvement in building such cultures. I wholeheartedly agree. Moral corporate cultures do not simply filter down from the top or emerge as part of a grassroots movement. Instead, they must be gradually cultivated, influenced and supported by example, by resource allocation, and by institution-wide involvement and participation. Corporate codes of conduct or related initiatives simply handed down from the top are unlikely to have a significant effect on behavior.

A problematic aspect of such employee involvement strategies, however, is typically glossed over. The dark side of our efforts to create the appropriate level of psychological investment and commitment necessary for true moral cultures is that they also lead to a psychology of entitlement. Once we feel that we are important to an organization, that we are valued members, we also expect to be treated accordingly and to be acknowledged and rewarded for our efforts. One of the paradoxes underlying the hyped-up, high hopes created by executives in their dinner speeches and promises to employees about their importance to the firm and the value of their participation is that at one point I think employees actually bought into the image. Unfortunately, when high hopes and expectations go unfulfilled, it ultimately leads to frustration, discontent and higher levels of cynicism. This is exactly what has happened in the employee involvement arena.

A recurring theme in most management and organizational behavior courses, for example, is the Maslowian notion of self-actualization and its reflection in quality of work life and employee participation programs. A growing number of organizational members, however, have developed a highly jaundiced view of such programs. Consider the case of an assembly line worker, who was part of a labor-management participation program under which he and his coworkers were given the opportunity to plan and carry out the work for themselves, without supervision by a foreman and the typical assembly line mentality of punching into work. His perception: "What this is all about is that the bosses are positioning themselves so that when they close the plant, they can blame us for it. They'll say it was our fault, that they gave us the chance and we blew it."[17] As this feeling reflects, employee involvement strategies are increasingly being viewed by employees themselves as little more than "empty promises."

Within the field of organizational behavior, the bond that holds an individual and an organization together is referred to as a *psychological contract*—an implicit and unwritten set of expectations based on a sense of reciprocity and mutual influence between organizations and their members. The ways in which organizations treat their members, the kinds of authority and power structures which are utilized, and the kinds of norms and values which operate simultaneously affect employee attitudes, expectations and behaviors. The strength and importance of such contracts can best be seen by examining what happens when they are violated. Breakdowns of the psychological contract, since they involve elements of trust, go beyond dissatisfaction and perceptions of inequity. Instead there are usually deep feelings of betrayal and deep psychological distress. As an employee captured the essence of the reciprocal nature of such contracts—"Employee loyalty to the company began to erode when company loyalty to the employee began to erode."[18]

People in the workplace—especially long-term employees—had come to believe that there was more to a job than simply money, that if they supplied their firm with loyalty and good work performance, they would be rewarded with steady employment and job-related challenge and growth-related opportunities. Today, however, employee termination decisions—which are increasingly large-scale in nature—are completely independent of incompetence or poor performance. In all too many instances, terminations are based on cost-containment strategies to reduce debt loads associated with acquisitions, LBOs or other quick profit strategies devised by a firm's top management that ultimately failed.[19] Moreover, instead of developing the necessary trust and credibility among organizational members, CEOs and other top level executives appear more and more concerned about the ramifications that organizational restructuring and consolidation poses for their own perks and golden parachutes than their companies and their stakeholders. The thousands of employees that might lose their jobs and security in a merger, acquisition or corporate retrenchment strategy, of course, are no different—except that the CEOs have the power and position to fight back for themselves.[20] Yet, one of the ironies that I've witnessed is that at the same time these senior executives are providing for themselves, they've become increasingly adept at hiding behind a cloak of utilitarianism to defend their actions—that some individuals and groups must bear some pain so that the majority can prosper. Such rationalizations are little more than body count morality at its very worst. The present generation of CEOs and COOs, who are often cash-flow experts with little savvy in operations, marketing or human resources, appear all too willing to abandon many employee morale and community service programs.[21]

In the wake of the unprecedented level of failure and resultant cutback and consolidation of the Boston banking community, for example, investigation reveals a disconcertingly higher level of loans to insiders—executives and directors of the banks—than is recommended. While high levels of insider loans do not necessarily doom a bank to failure and most of these loans are well within the law, bank regulators consider them an indication of poor management. Moreover, critics contend that they reflect "criss-crossing loyalties" and that they "violate the spirit of laws designed to prevent financial institutions from being used as private piggy banks."[22] The collapse of the real estate market in Massachusetts has not only jeopardized these loans, but as a result, the very stability of the banks. Given such experiences, even the so-called survivors often find it very difficult to buy into the ethos and the emerging moral orientations of the consolidated entity, instead witnessing a growing wall of distrust between them and their employers. In fact, one of the fallouts of the recent wave of corporate merger, acquisition and consolidation is a concomitant rise in dysfunctional employee behaviors—ranging from relatively mild withdrawal behaviors such as tardiness and absenteeism, to outright theft, dishonesty, and sabotage.[23] In my own research, I have even seen the emergence of an organizational counterculture that took on as one of its main goals the mission to work against what the merged firm and its CEO were attempting to accomplish. The question I would pose one more time is whether this is conducive to the creation of moral corporate cultures.

CREATING MORAL CORPORATE CULTURES

The long-term effects of this loss of loyalty and commitment, of course, are quite ominous for both corporate America and our country as a whole—especially if we have gotten to the point where management experts are advising people to care less and less for their companies and more and more for themselves. The ways in which consolidations, restructurings, downsizings and divestitures are currently managed do very little to generate the type of organizational culture and climate necessary for the creation of a true moral corporate culture. Instead, these strategies undermine loyalty and turn once-committed employees into "free agents." A myopic focus on the financial efficiencies that can be derived from a corporate consolidation or restructuring often serves only to disrupt the human fabric of the organization, a firm's true resource in a post-industrial world.

It is increasingly clear that there is a fundamental shift in the ways in which the corporation is structured or, perhaps I should say, restructured. An underlying problem is that the focus of most assessments of ethical conduct in organizations have a relatively stable, unitary view of organizations—independent, autonomous entities creating a series of interlocking norms and codes to ensure adherence to a set of ethical standards agreed to up and down the hierarchy. The business world that I see emerging, and have attempted to capture in this essay, seems far removed from this view.

The challenge is to guide the transition, some might argue transformation, using those roles, processes, and structures that have taken us this far—training programs, codes of conduct, organizational ombudsmen, social audits, and public affairs departments—and reorienting them to the realities of the restructuring and realignment taking place in corporate America. The essence of moral corporate cultures refers to building and sustaining commitment in organizations to socially responsible and ethical decisions and actions. It involves incorporating the idea of ethics and social responsibility into the corporate planning and strategy process. Such institutionalization of social and ethical policies requires the strong support of top management and explicit efforts to: 1) allocate resources and responsibilities; 2) design and use systems to monitor performance; and 3) shape decision processes to reinforce commitment.

The easy way out, which an increasing number of critics appear to have taken, is to suggest that the business schools are somehow the real culprit, focusing especially on their failure to instill a sense of business ethics on the part of our students. There is some truth to this argument, and business ethics need not be considered an oxymoron in our curricula. However, true ethical leadership must start at the top of organizations—by example rather than policy statement, by behavior rather than speeches, and by actions rather than codes—and filter down through the organization. If organizations don't begin changing—here I'm referring to basic value orientations about the importance and role of organizational members and the role of the corporation in the larger society—then organizational members will increasingly make the rules that define commitment, dedication, and ethical behavior, in ways that may not be to the liking of corporate America and the larger society.

A revolutionary thought, though it really shouldn't be, is that in order to create moral corporate cultures, organizations will have to provide their employees with the opportunity to do their jobs differently,[24] without the sort of pressures and organizational expectations that precipitate unethical practices. To recapture employee loyalty and commitment—and I want to stress the need to recapture rather than simply create loyalty and commitment—firms must be willing to share true power with their employees. And this means *sharing the gains as well as the risks* involved: providing important information about the business, ensuring that organizational members have the requisite knowledge and skills, delegating responsibility for performance management, sharing power and decision-making authority, and allocating rewards based on corporate success.[25]

Underlying this effort is the need to combine a sense of direction ("what business are we in?") with commitment to a sense of purpose or values ("what do we stand for?").[26] If moral corporate cultures are indeed to take hold in corporate America, firms must initially create cultures that focus not so much on explicit questions of right or wrong, but rather cultures that respect and enhance the role of the individual. From a managerial perspective, this means having empathy for those you interact with, avoiding the tendency to use others to achieve your own goals and objectives, and attempting to convince and influence others by reason rather than by coercion.[27] Only by creating an atmosphere in which people are given true responsibility and authority will we create organizations that ultimately encourage rather than discourage ethical actions in the workplace.

REFERENCES

1. The metaphor of the "dark" or "shadow side" of organizational life was influenced by A. F. Buono & J. L. Bowditch, "Organizational Countercultures: The Dark Side of Post-Merger Integration," paper presented at the 46th Annual Meeting of the Academy of Management, Chicago, Illinois, August, 1986; and a symposium at the 51st Annual Meeting of the Academy of Management meeting entitled "Perspectives on the Dark Side of Organizational Life," Miami Beach, Florida, August, 1991.
2. See D. Kanter & P. Mirvis, *The Cynical Americans: Living and Working in an Age of Discontent and Disillusion* (San Francisco: Jossey-Bass, 1989).
3. P. Mirvis, "Cynicism at Work," paper presented at the 51st Annual Meeting of the Academy of Management, Miami Beach, Florida, August, 1991.
4. P. Hirsch, *Pack Your Own Parachute: How to Survive Mergers, Takeovers, and Other Corporate Disasters* (Reading: Addison-Wesley, 1987).
5. See E. Faltermayer, "The Deal Decade: Verdict on the '80s," *Fortune,* August 26, 1991, pp. 58–70.
6. Faltermayer, "The Deal Decade."
7. R. S. Teitelbaum, "LBOs Really Didn't Pay, Say the Chiefs," *Fortune,* August 26, 1991, pp. 73–76.
8. R. M. Miller, "Commentary: Prepackaged Bankruptcies," *Across the Board,* 1991, *28* (9), 55–56.
9. Quoted in S. Overman, "The Layoff Legacy," *HR Magazine,* 1991, *36* (8), pp 29, 32.
10. See N. F. Whiteley, Jr., "Commentary: Why Restructurings Fail," *Across the Board,* 1991, *28* (9), 13–14; and H. P. Weinstein & M. S. Leibman, "Corporate Scale Down, What Comes Next," *HR Magazine,* 1991 *36* (8), 33–37.
11. A. F. Buono & J. L. Bowditch, *The Human Side of Mergers and Acquisitions: Managing Collisions Between People, Cultures, and Organizations* (San Francisco: Jossey-Bass, 1989); A. F. Buono and J. L. Bowditch, "Ethical Considerations in Merger and Acquisition Management: A Human Resource Perspective," *SAM Advanced Management Journal,* 1990, *55* (4), 18–23; and A. F. Buono and A. J. Nurick, "Intervening in the Middle: Coping Strategies in Mergers and Acquisitions," *Human Resource Planning,* 1992, *15* (2), 19–33.
12. See A. Beam, "For Gillette, Life Not the Same After Arrival of Perelman," *Boston Globe,* June 19, 1987, pp. 69, 74; and M. L. Marks, "The Disappearing Company Man," *Psychology Today,* 1988 (September), 34–39.
13. The material on Procter & Gamble was drawn from "No Charges Seen In Probe of P&G Leaks," *Boston Globe,* August 15, 1991, p. 48; "Headliners: Lunar

Probe," *New York Times,* August 18, 1991, p. E7; and "Investigator in P&G case an employee, company says," *Boston Globe,* August 20, 1991, p. 53.

14. Hirsch, *Pack Your Own Parachute.*
15. Kanter & Mirvis, *The Cynical Americans.*
16. See A. B. Fisher, "Morale Crisis," *Fortune,* November 18, 1991, pp. 70–80.
17. This quote was adapted from S. Lynd's forward to D. M. Wells, *Empty Promises: Quality of Working Life Programs and the Labor Movement* (New York: Monthly Review Press, 1987), pp. ix–x.
18. W. W. Tornow, "Contract Redesign," *Personnel Administration,* 1988 (October), 97–101.
19. K. P. DeMeuse & W. W. Tornow, "The Tie that Binds—Has Become Very, Very Frayed!" *Human Resource Planning,* 1990, *13* (3), 203–213.
20. See J. Solomon, "Looking for Mr. Right: Bank Mergers, Like Marriages, Hinge on Chemistry and Egos," *Boston Globe,* September 15, 1991, pp. A37, A41.
21. See Marks, "Disappearing Company Man."
22. M. Zucker, "Insider Lending Proves Dangerous," *Boston Globe,* September 4, 1991, pp. 1, 68.
23. See "Merger Fallout: Beware Employee Dishonesty," *Wall Street Journal,* October 19, 1989, p. B1.
24. W. A. Kiechell, III, "Your New Employment Contract," *Fortune,* July 6, 1987, pp. 109–110.
25. DeMeuse & Tornow, "The Tie That Binds"; and D. E. Bowen and E. E. Lawler III, "The Empowerment of Service Workers: What, Why, How, and When," *Sloan Management Review,* 1992, *33* (3), 31–39.
26. R. E. Freeman & D. R. Gilbert, *Corporate Strategy and the Search for Ethics* (Englewood Cliffs: Prentice-Hall, 1988).
27. See Freeman & Gilbert, *Corporate Strategy,* Chapter 8.

QUESTIONS FOR DISCUSSION

1. Nader, Green, and Seligman quote Peter Drucker's comment "There is one thing all boards have in common, regardless of their legal position. *They do not function.*" What are the traditional functions of the corporate board? According to Nader, Green, Seligman, and Mintzburg, how do boards sometimes fail to fulfill that function? How would Nader, Green, and Seligman like to see the function of the board changed?

2. Mintzberg details a number of ways that corporations might be controlled. Which do you think is most likely to succeed? Why? Is it plausible to suppose, as he does, that all of them (except "ignore it") should and can be used, depending on the circumstances?

3. Dalton and Buono show how management can subvert the interests of stakeholder groups in the pursuit of personal or corporate goals. Can you think of any other examples of the misuses, or apparent misuses, of management power? Do any of Mintzberg's ideas about controlling the corporation suggest concrete methods of combating such abuses?

THE NATURE OF THE CORPORATION

Tennessee Coal & Iron (A & B) Condensed

John B. Matthews
Former Wilson Professor of Business Administration, Emeritus, Harvard University

In the early 1960s the Tennessee Coal & Iron Division (TCI) of United States Steel Corporation (USS) was one of that corporation's largest divisions. Originally an independent company, TCI became a subsidiary of USS in 1907. It continued to grow, adding quarries, mines, reservoirs, electric power systems, coke, and wire. Many other kinds of plants and steel facilities were attached over the years. By the beginning of World War II, TCI was by far the largest producer of primary steel and many other products in the 11-state southern region that it served. It moved from subsidiary to divisional status in 1953.

TCI's peak employment was in 1942, when a total of 33,000 employees was attained. A number of factors, including the decline in steel demand and a switch to imported ores, reduced the number of TCI employees to about 24,000 in 1955–1957 and to 16,000 in 1964. Nearly 12,000 of these were production and maintenance employees, and about one-third of the 12,000 were blacks. Nearly all of the production and maintenance employees were covered by a contract between USS and the United Steelworkers of America (USW). Despite the decline in its employment rolls, TCI continued to be by far the largest employer in Birmingham and the Jefferson County area of Alabama. Arthur Wiebel, president of TCI, estimated that the next largest employer was about one-third the size of TCI. Birmingham had a civilian male labor force of 78,000 and Jefferson County, of which Birmingham was the center, had a civilian male labor force of about 155,000. The ratio of whites to blacks was about 2 to 1 in Jefferson County, and about 2 to $1\frac{1}{3}$ in Birmingham itself.

TCI'S EMPLOYMENT RECORD AND RACIAL INTEGRATION

In 1963 the nation's attention was focused on racial disturbances in various parts of the South, with some of the most violent occurrences in Birmingham. Bombings of black churches, incidents of personal violence, and threats of all types occurred as the drive toward racial integration kindled or kept alive old racial hatreds.

The movement toward integration was also taking place inside TCI's many plants in and around Birmingham. USS had had, orally since 1902 and in writing since 1918, a policy that employment would be made available without regard to race, color, creed, or national origin. This policy, however, was affected by labor agreements, and a portion of the USS policy manual had, for several years, read as follows: "Application of this policy as it relates to union-represented employees will be in accordance with applicable provisions of labor agreements."

Thus for many years prior to the 1960s, the combined effects of seniority, contracts at individual plant and local union levels, strike threats, and local racial customs had resulted in a high degree of racial segregation within TCI's plants. It was against this backdrop that senior officials of USS, TCI, and the USW had to work to bring about a lessening of racial discrimination within TCI.

Three major events occurred to help these officials in their efforts. (1) A human relations committee was formed in 1960 by 11 major steel producers and the USW as a mechanism for exploring and solving common problems. (2) In March 1961 President John F. Kennedy issued executive order 10925 which was intended to prevent discrimination within companies bidding for or holding government contracts. The order also established the Committee on Equal Employment Opportunity (CEEO) and Vice President Lyndon B. Johnson was appointed its chairman. (3) Finally, there was a continuing decline in demand for TCI's products, which made it more difficult for senior employees to hold their jobs in spite of the more than 1,000 separate and rigid lines of promotion among the production and maintenance workers.

These factors, plus months of hard and laborious work by company and union officials, bore fruit. Lines of promotion were broadened and all claims of racial discrimination brought before the CEEO were closed out by June 1963. As a result of these actions and a new 1962 contract between the USW and the 11 major steel producers that provided for sweeping changes, Hobart Taylor, Jr., executive vice chairman of the CEEO, wrote a letter to USS which included the following paragraph: "May I thank you, too, for the example which U.S. Steel has given the rest of the managers in this country by its courageous move in Birmingham at a time of great social tension in the area. This was an important milestone toward true equal employment opportunity. You have earned the gratitude of those of us who are also working toward this important national goal."

TCI'S ROLE IN THE COMMUNITY

In spite of the major accomplishments toward integration within TCI's plants and mines, however, TCI's role in the community had been an issue for some time and was to become a major one in summer 1963. The remainder of this case concerns that issue.

By summer's end 1963, officials of the United States Steel Corporation and its Tennessee Coal & Iron Division believed that the problems of job integration among TCI's 12,000 white and black production and maintenance workers had been solved in a satisfactory fashion. In addition, the physical violence that had permeated the Birmingham area in the spring and early summer of 1963 had greatly abated.

The tension that had preceded and accompanied the violence, however, continued to exist in the community at large. In discussing the situation, James Reston made the following (excerpted) comments in the *New York Times* on September 22, 1963:

> The point, then, is not that Birmingham is lacking in young leaders, and not that it is lacking in biracial committees, but that the real power structure of the city—the older men who run the industries, banks

and insurance companies that in turn influence the stores and big law firms—are not leading the peace effort.

There are about a dozen men in this group, some of whom have worked quietly for a compromise, some of whom have tried and then withdrawn. But at no time have they all worked together.

[The Reston story listed 13 prominent Birmingham businessmen and lawyers, among them "Arthur W. Wieble (sic), president of the Tennessee Coal & Iron Division of United States Steel." . . .]

There is general agreement here that these men, working together with the leaders of the local clergy of both races, could do more to produce a compromise in a month than Federal troops, Federal officials and all the national Negro organizations put together could in years.

The question is who, if anybody, can get them together. They damn "The Kennedys" and concede that Senator Goldwater would carry Alabama against the president tomorrow, but even this prospect only creates a new dilemma.[1]

THE USE OF ECONOMIC INFLUENCE

On October 22, 1963, a *New York Times* reporter met with Wiebel, C. Thomas Spivey (TCI director of personnel services), and Clinton Milstead (TCI director of public relations) in Wiebel's conference room. The meeting lasted from 9:00 a.m. until 2:30 p.m. and was largely concerned with the work of TCI and union officials in bringing about job integration within TCI.

During his visit, the reporter also asked Wiebel whether TCI would use its economic power to speed integration in the community itself. According to Wiebel, the reporter suggested that TCI might put pressure on its suppliers, its bank connections, and some of its customers to aid the cause of Birmingham's blacks.

Both the question and the suggestion came as a surprise to Wiebel and his associates. In the preceding months, TCI officials had held extended conversations with union officers, representatives of the president's Committee on Equal Employment Opportunity, General Royall and Colonel Blaik, and black leaders. No question about the use of economic pressure by TCI had arisen in any discussion with these groups, and no suggestions concerning its use had been made officially, although unofficially USS had been criticized in the press.

Wiebel told the reporter that there were two major reasons why TCI would not resort to economic coercion as the area's largest employer to try to solve Birmingham's racial problems. He pointed out that neither TCI nor USS had sufficient economic power in the area to solve the problem, and that neither had the right to tell people what they ought or ought not to do. He also stated that, if TCI were to do what the reporter suggested, charges would be made that TCI and USS were trying to run Birmingham.

One Media's Interpretation of Events

Three days later, under an October 22 dateline, the *New York Times* carried a two-column story about TCI and racial integration in Birmingham. Much of the story concerned activities within TCI. Only the lead paragraphs, which discussed the issue of the division's economic influence in the community are reproduced below from the *New York Times*, October 25, 1963:

> The United States Steel Corporation, the largest employer in Birmingham, appears to be making significant strides in opening up Negro job opportunities in its Alabama plants.
>
> But the nation's biggest steel maker appears to be making little effort to wield its economic influence to help solve the community's racial problems.
>
> These conclusions emerge from talks with officials of U.S. Steel's Tennessee Coal & Iron Division here, as well as with others in both the North and South familiar with the situation.
>
> Critics have contended that Roger M. Blough, U.S. Steel chairman, could contribute greatly toward stemming the racial strife here by simply instructing local officials to exert their power toward that end.
>
> **Progress in Plants**
>
> But the company officials here insist they do not have that much power, and in any event they show no signs of using what power they do have on the community's racial front.[2]

Blough's Response

On October 29, at a press conference called to announce the results of USS operations during the preceding quarter, Roger M. Blough, chairman of the USS board of directors, was asked to comment on USS policies in its TCI operation and, more particularly, on the use of its "economic influence" in the Birmingham area as a means of influencing local opinion. The portion of his response dealing with the latter issue follows below:

> Now, the criticism that U.S. Steel hasn't used what some people refer to as . . . economic influence, which I presume to mean some kind of economic force to bring about some kind of a change, is, I think, an improper matter upon which to criticize either Mr. Wiebel or U.S. Steel. I think I would have to take considerable time to fully explain this point, but very briefly, I'd like to say this—that I do not either believe that it would be a wise thing for U.S. Steel to be other than a good citizen in a community, or to attempt to have its ideas of what is right for the community enforced upon that community by some sort of economic means. This is repugnant to me personally, and I am sure it is repugnant to my fellow officers in U.S. Steel. I doubt very much that this in principle is a good thing for any corporation to follow. When we as individuals are citizens in a community, we can exercise what small influence we may have as citizens, but for a corporation to attempt to exert any kind of economic compulsion to achieve a particular end in the social area seems to me to be quite beyond what a corporation should do, and I will say also, quite beyond what a corporation can do.
>
> . . . we have fulfilled our responsibility in the Birmingham area—whatever responsibility we have as a corporation or as individuals working with a corporation, because, after all, a corporation is nothing but individuals.

Further Public Responses

The October 30 issue of the *New York Times* carried a front-page story devoted primarily to Blough's comments about the Birmingham-TCI situation, and on October 31 the following editorial appeared in the paper:

> **Corporate Race Relations** When it comes to speaking out on business matters Roger Blough, chairman of the United States Steel Corporation does not mince words. Mr. Blough is a firm believer in freedom of action for corporate management, a position he made clear in his battle with the Administration last year. But he also has put some severe limits on the exercise of corporate responsibility, for he rejects the suggestion that U.S. Steel, the biggest employer in Birmingham, Ala., should use its economic influence to erase racial tensions. Mr. Blough feels that U.S. Steel has fulfilled its responsibilities by following a nondiscriminatory hiring policy in Birmingham, and looks upon any other measures as both "repugnant" and "quite beyond what a corporation should do" to improve conditions.
>
> The hands-off strategy surely underestimates the potential influence of a corporation as big as U.S. Steel, particularly at the local level. It could, without affecting its profit margins adversely or getting itself directly involved in politics, actively work with those groups in Birmingham trying to better race relations. Steel is not sold on the retail level, so U.S. Steel has not been faced with the economic pressure used against the branches of national chain stores.
>
> Many corporations have belatedly recognized that it is in their own self-interest to promote an improvement in Negro opportunities. As one of the nation's biggest corporations, U.S. Steel and its shareholders have as great a stake in eliminating the economic imbalances associated with racial discrimination as any company. Corporate responsibility is not easy to define or to measure, but in refusing to take a stand in Birmingham, Mr. Blough appears to have a rather narrow, limited concept of his influence.[3]

Also on October 31, the *Congressional Record* contained remarks made by Representative Ryan of the State of New York:

> Mr. Speaker, yesterday's *New York Times* carried two stories—one of high corporate indifference, the other of high corporate profits. The statement of Roger

Blough, Chairman of the Board of United States Steel Corp., that the corporation should not use its influence to improve racial conditions in strife-torn Birmingham is the epitome of corporate irresponsibility and callousness.

United States Steel willingly accepts all the benefits of our laws and constitution which guarantee the rights of corporations and of private property, but refuses to accept its obligation to support the same laws and constitution which also declare all men equal.

Apparently United States Steel sees its only responsibility as to make profits. Public welfare is not its concern. This callous attitude is a giant step backward by a giant corporation.

It is ironic that, in the same conference, Roger Blough reported a sharp increase in third quarter sales and earnings. Who is responsible for these profits? Roger Blough in his plush New York office did not bring this about by himself. Behind the profits are some 15,000 steelworkers in Birmingham, many of whom are black, who mine the ore, melt the steel, cut it, shape it, and by their hard labor create the product with which the profits are made. These steelworkers and their families live in a town of terror—a town with segregated schools and bigoted police where our citizens are denied their constitutional rights. United States Steel says to these workers, "Give us your labor but do not expect us to be concerned with your lives or the lives of your children."

United States Steel also says to American Society, "We will benefit from the advantages of American Society and its economic system and its laws but do not expect us to share any responsibility for improving human relations in that society."

Even a schoolboy knows that citizenship has obligations as well as privileges. If all citizens, whether private or corporate, insisted on privileges while refusing obligations, our free democratic society would disintegrate.

Mr. Speaker, power without responsibility is tyranny. United States Steel's policy of inaction is in reality a policy of action. Birmingham and other southern cities are permitted to abuse American citizens and deny to them the right to live decently because the so-called respectable and responsible people and organizations remain silent. In the case of United States Steel this unconscionable silence in Birmingham is shocking. As a giant of industry, it has a moral obligation to speak out. In Birmingham, where it is the largest employer, this corporation could use its tremendous influence to bring about substantial and constructive change.

I urge all members and all citizens to raise their voice in protest against this callous irresponsibility and indifference. It is time for United States Steel to put people ahead of profits.

President Kennedy, at a press conference on November 1, was asked to comment on Blough's stand. The question and the president's answer follow below:

Question: The United States Steel Corporation has rejected the idea that it should use economic pressure in an effort to improve race relations in Birmingham, Alabama. Do you have any comment on that position, and do you have any counsel for management and labor in general as to their social responsibility in the areas of tension of this kind?

President Kennedy: Actually, Mr. Blough has been somewhat helpful in one or two cases that I can think of in Birmingham. I don't think he should narrowly interpret his responsibility for the future. That is a very influential company in Birmingham, and he wants to see that city prosper, as do we all. Obviously, the federal government cannot solve this matter. So that business has a responsibility—labor and, of course, every citizen. So I would think that particularly a company which is as influential as United States Steel in Birmingham I would hope would use its influence on the side of comity between the races.

Otherwise, the future of Birmingham, of course, is not as happy as we hope it would be. In other words, it can't be decided—this matter—in Washington. It has to be decided by citizens everywhere. Mr. Blough is an influential citizen. I am sure he will do the best he can.

On November 4, the *Congressional Record* carried the following remarks by Representative George Huddleston, Jr., of Alabama:

Mr. Speaker, in recent days, what I consider unjustifiable criticism has been lodged at Mr. Roger M. Blough, chairman of the board of the United States

Steel Corp., as a result of comments he made in a press conference held in New York on Tuesday, October 29, in which he discussed the role of business in race relations, with particular reference to the Birmingham situation. Some misunderstanding has arisen as a result of this criticism and I feel that, in all fairness to the United States Steel Corp., Mr. Blough, and the people of Birmingham, the record should be clarified. For this purpose, I insert herewith in the *Congressional Record* a verbatim transcript of Mr. Blough's press conference of October 29.

I want to especially call the attention of the Members of Congress to Mr. Blough's comments regarding whether business should attempt to apply economic sanctions to a community in order to further so-called social or moral reforms. Mr. Blough states that such effort by business is repugnant to him and his company, and I think I speak for the overwhelming majority of the citizens of Birmingham in applauding his firm and forthright stand. For any enterprise, government or private, to attempt to exert economic pressures on the people of any community to bring about social changes is truly repugnant to the American way of life.

We in Birmingham are proud of the contributions that United States Steel's TCI division has over the years made to the economy of our city and look forward to continued cooperation for our mutual benefit in the future.

Blough's Reply

The *New York Times* of November 7 contained a letter from Blough:[4]

To the Editor of the New York Times:

From your Oct. 31 editorial "Corporate Race Relations" it would appear that you are under considerable misapprehension as to what I said in my press conference of the previous day concerning the policy and actions of United States Steel in Birmingham. For example, you said:

"Mr. Blough feels that U.S. Steel has fulfilled its responsibilities by following a nondiscriminatory hiring policy in Birmingham, and looks upon any other measures as both 'repugnant' and 'quite beyond what a corporation should' do to improve conditions."

Quite to the contrary, I recounted in some detail the efforts of U.S. Steel management to use its influence in Birmingham to promote better communications and better understanding between the races—not just during the recent crises but over a period of many years.

Unfortunately, the able representatives of the *Times* who attended that press conference made only casual reference to this part of my remarks in their stories. For your information therefore, and for the information of your readers, I should like to summarize the specific statements I made on this point:

The present president of our Tennessee Coal & Iron Division, Arthur Wiebel, has been working since 1946 toward developing understanding and strengthening communications between the races in Birmingham.

In 1949 he became a trustee of the Jefferson County Coordinating Council of Social Forces devoted to civic and social improvement.

In 1951 an interracial committee of this council, with Mr. Wiebel as a member, was formed to improve the lot of the Negroes in many fields: health, sanitation, safety, business, housing and cultural and recreational opportunities. That same year the committee made a formal request that the Birmingham city government employ Negro policemen. That request was denied.

Mr. Wiebel worked, for example, for a Negro upper-middle-class housing project considered as attractive as any in that economic range anywhere in the nation. He helped get Negro insurance companies and investors in Birmingham to make home mortgage money available to Negroes.

From 1953 to 1961 he was a trustee of Tuskegee Institute, an outstanding Negro institution of higher learning.

As a member of the Senior Citizens Committee, last May when serious racial problems occurred in Birmingham he devoted as much time and effort as anyone there in trying to resolve this matter. More recently, he has worked in cooperation with General Royall and Colonel Blaik, and was one of 44 business leaders endorsing a recent public appeal for the employment of qualified Negroes on the Birmingham police force.

Mr. Wiebel has also been active in the United Fund, which supports Negro welfare activities, and in the Red Cross. He is a charter member of the Committee of a Hundred, devoted to bringing new industry to Birmingham, and in more ways than I can recount he has tried to carry out what is our overall U.S. Steel policy of being a good citizen in the community in which we live.

I also said that as individuals we can exercise what influence we may have as citizens, but for a corporation to attempt to exert any kind of economic compulsion to achieve a particular end in the social area seems to me to be quite beyond what a corporation should do and quite beyond what a corporation can do.

To recapitulate, then, let me make our position perfectly clear:

I believe that U.S. Steel in its own plants should provide equal opportunities for all employees, and that it does so in Birmingham, as the *Times* recently reported.

I believe that U.S. Steel management people, as citizens, should use their influence persuasively to help resolve the problems of their communities wherever they may be—and that they are doing so in Birmingham.

I believe that while government—through the proper exercise of its legislative and administrative powers—may seek to compel social reforms, any attempt by a private organization like U.S. Steel to impose its views, its beliefs and its will upon the community by resorting to economic compulsion or coercion would be repugnant to our American constitutional concepts, and that appropriate steps to correct this abuse of corporate power would be universally demanded by public opinion, by Government and by the *New York Times.*

So, even if U.S. Steel possessed such economic power—which it certainly does not—I would be unalterably opposed to its use in this fashion.

We shall, however, continue to use our best efforts in Birmingham to be as helpful as possible.

Roger Blough
Chairman, Board of Directors
United States Steel Corporation
New York, Nov. 2, 1963

National Media Response to the Issues Raised

The matter of the possible use of economic pressure by business firms to speed the process of racial integration drew considerable attention in newspapers throughout the country. News stories, editorials, and letters from readers took various positions on Blough's stand and on President Kennedy's remarks. Several such comments follow below:

Somehow Mr. Blough seems to say that the injunction "we are our brother's keepers" does not apply to corporations, or at least not to U.S. Steel. I am sure that even a most casual examination of this proposition will destroy it. Many large enterprises, including U.S. Steel, have made substantial contributions to the welfare of the community or the nation, beyond the necessities of profit and loss.

What I am afraid Mr. Blough means is that in the current effort to eliminate all the remaining vestiges of a servile history he would prefer to be neutral, at least in deed if not in thought. If we cannot be sure as to what is morally correct in this struggle, when ever will we be able to know right from wrong?

If U.S. Steel strong and great as it is, will not exert its strength for justice, what can be expected from lesser mortals? What strength U.S. Steel has in Birmingham is best known to it, but that it should be used, I have no doubt.

Carl Rachlin
General Counsel, CORE
New York, Nov. 8, 1963

Big Steel and Civil Rights What is the extent of the moral responsibilities of the modern, impersonal, publicly owned corporation? The question has been raised in acute fashion in Birmingham, Ala., where the city's largest single employer is the Tennessee Coal & Iron Division of U.S. Steel Corp.

U.S. Steel, and Tennessee president Arthur Wiebel in particular, have been under pressure from civil rights activists to do more to promote the individual rights of Negroes in that embattled city. In response to criticism, the corporation recently disclosed that it has been moving quietly to erase some traditional barriers that have held hundreds of Negroes to low paying jobs. U.S. Steel has merged into one line previously separate lines of promotion for Negroes and whites in its steel plants. For instance, Negroes in the open hearth shop can now rise along with whites to a job class which pays $3.83 an hour and offers a 40% incentive. Previously they had been limited to a maximum job class offering $2.78 and a 15% incentive. Moreover, in the corporation's Fairfield plant, whites are working under Negroes for the first time. The situation reportedly has caused some discontent among white workers. But U.S. Steel has been strict in the application of its policy. Workers who object are sent home. According to a corporation official, the objectors usually return quickly to the plant. Jobs, after all, are not so easy to get in the steel industry these days.

Beyond taking these forthright steps in its own operations in Birmingham, however, U.S. Steel is inclined to go no further. According to Roger M. Bough, U.S. Steel chairman, the idea that a company should "attempt to have its ideas of what is right for the community enforced upon that community by some sort of economic means" is "clearly repugnant to me personally" and "repugnant to my fellow officers" at U.S. Steel. "We have fulfilled our responsibility in the Birmingham area," Mr. Blough said at the corporation's recent third quarter press conference. For a corporation to attempt to exert any kind of economic compulsion to achieve a particular end in the social area "seems to be quite beyond what a corporation should do, and . . . quite beyond what a corporation can do." But corporate officials who are citizens in a community "can exercise what small influence we may have as citizens," Mr. Blough said. Apparently, U.S. Steel's chairman was referring among other things to Mr. Wiebel's recent support of a move to put Negro policemen on the Birmingham police force.

A careful study of America's industrial past would probably make it difficult for Mr. Blough to support in factual detail the argument that corporations are prevented from achieving particular ends in "the social area." State and local taxes, for instance, clearly play an important social role in the community, and large corporations can wield enormous influence over tax policy. But Birmingham is a unique situation, as puzzling to politicians as it is to businessmen. Even the federal government has been reluctant to apply economic sanctions by withholding federal funds from states which defy Negro rights. Can U.S. Steel be expected to do more?

Indeed Big Steel has left little doubt of its sincerity in advancing civil rights in its own operations. If other businesses . . . and more particularly unions . . . were to follow the corporation's example of on-the-job reforms in the South, the civil rights problems of cities like Birmingham would be a lot closer to solution.

In the realm of morality, one positive example may be worth a dozen damaging sanctions in promoting a worthy end.[5]

The Company in the Community There are still a lot of people around who remember the old "company town"—those communities so dominated by one business enterprise that the politics, the business and very often even the social customs of the people were ordained in the company boardroom.

Some of these company towns were run badly. But many were actually run very well, the company management having a sincere interest in the well-being of the community. In many places the company out of necessity provided housing, streets, schools, hospitals, recreation centers, churches and a host of other things which the people would otherwise not have had. Often the resulting municipal government was a model of good management.

Yet even in the best run such communities the people always chafed. However high-minded the motives, high-handed power was rightly resented and people found intolerable the economic power that could tell the banker to whom he should lend, the shopkeeper whom he should hire, the town councillors what laws they should pass. Thus today companies make their very considerable contributions to the community in other ways—in good jobs, in gifts to local services and in lending their influence to civic progress—and, like other outmoded institutions, the "company town" has passed without mourning.

Or anyway, so it was until lately. Now in the new context of the civil rights struggle, there are voices demanding that our large corporations use exactly this sort of power to force their desired moral standards on the communities in which they live.

Specifically this has been urged by otherwise

thoughtful people in the case of Birmingham. Just the other day Roger Blough of U.S. Steel had to devote the major part of a business press conference to "explaining" why the company did not use its economic power to compel that unhappy city to mend its ways.

The question here was not about U.S. Steel's own practices. Nationwide it follows a practice of nondiscrimination in employment; upwards of 10% of its employees are Negroes, including a number in clerical jobs, supervisory assignments, skilled trades and professional positions. In Birmingham itself, according to Mr. Blough, the U.S. Steel subsidiary has about 30% Negroes among its employees.

Nor, is there any argument here about the duty of a company or its officers to provide moral leadership for what they believe to be right, whether in Birmingham or anywhere else.

In this instance the present president of the U.S. Steel division in Birmingham, Arthur Wiebel, has since 1946 been active in groups working for better race relations; since 1951 he has served on the integration committee formed by local citizens, white and Negro; he is a trustee of Tuskegee Institute, a Negro college; and in the latest difficulties he played an active and prominent role in the quiet citizens' group which has worked hard to improve the situation for Negroes in Birmingham.

Mr. Blough made it quite clear that he approved and encouraged this kind of leadership. But to the voices of impatience this is not enough. It is said by some that companies like U.S. Steel should not merely persuade but coerce the community into adopting the policies they believe to be right.

It is probably true, as these voices say, that a company as large as U.S. Steel could wield powerful weapons against the people of Birmingham. It could, as some clamor that it should, boycott local suppliers who did not act as U.S. Steel thinks they should; it could threaten to take away all or a part of its business if the city authorities didn't do as it wishes; it could even halt its contributions to local civic organizations, from hospitals to recreation facilities, if they did not conduct their affairs in an approved fashion.

Perhaps, although we gravely doubt it, such coercion might win some immediate point for the Negroes of Birmingham. But it would certainly do so at an injury to all the people of Birmingham and most of all at a grievous injury to good government and society everywhere.

Mr. Blough himself put it well: "I do not believe it would be a wise thing for U.S. Steel to be other than a good citizen in a community, or to attempt to have its ideas of what is right for the community enforced upon the community."

As a good citizen, business can use its influence for good, but the old fashioned "company town" is better buried. And no one—least of all those who seek wider democracy—should wish for its resurrection.[6]

NOTES

1. © 1963 by the New York Times Company. Reprinted by permission.
2. Ibid.
3. Ibid.
4. Reprinted by permission of United States Steel Corporation.
5. *American Metal Market,* November 11, 1963. Reprinted with permission.
6. Reprinted by permission of *The Wall Street Journal.* © Dow Jones & Company, Inc. (November 4, 1963). All rights reserved.

Directorships of Major U.S. Corporations Tightly Interlocked

For the first time in over a decade, a Congressional committee has taken a comprehensive look at interlocking directorships among the Nation's largest corporations.

Initiated by the late Sen. Lee Metcalf (D-Mont.) as chairman of the Subcommittee on Reports, Accounting and Management, the study, prepared by the subcommittee's staff, identifies and analyzes 530 direct and 12,193 indirect interlocks among

Senate Committee on Governmental Affairs press release. April 23, 1978

130 of the nation's top industrials, financial institutions, retailing organizations, transportation companies, utilities, and broadcasting companies. The companies in the study represented about 25 percent of the assets of all U.S. corporations.

The study disclosed an extraordinary pattern of directorate concentration:

- 123 of these major firms each connected on an average with half of the other major companies in the study.
- The 13 largest firms not only were linked together, but accounted for 240 direct and 5,547 indirect interlocks, reaching an average of more than 70 percent of the other 117 corporations. The 13 largest corporations ranked by assets were: American Telephone and Telegraph, BankAmerica, Citicorp, Chase Manhattan, Prudential, Metropolitan Life, Exxon, Manufacturers Hanover, J.P. Morgan, General Motors, Mobil, Texaco, and Ford.
- The leading competitors in the fields of automotives, energy, telecommunications, and retailing met extensively on boards of America's largest financial institutions, corporate customers, and suppliers.
- The largest commercial bankers clustered on major insurance company boards and insurance directors joined on the banking company boards.
- A direct interlock occurs when two companies have a common director. An indirect interlock occurs when two companies each have a director on the board of a third company.
- The nation's largest airlines and electric utilities were substantially interlocked with major lending institutions.
- The boardrooms of four of the largest banking companies (Citicorp, Chase Manhattan, Manufacturers Hanover, and J.P. Morgan), two of the largest insurance companies (Prudential and Metropolitan Life) and three of the largest nonfinancial companies (AT&T, Exxon, and General Motors) looked like virtual summits for leaders in American business.

These patterns of director interrelationships imply an overwhelming potential for antitrust abuse and possible conflicts of interest which could affect prices, supply and competition, and impact on the shape and direction of the American economy, said the staff.

Use of the Senate Computer Center enabled the staff to compile master lists of the direct and indirect interlocks among the major companies studied for the year 1976. These lists and accompanying computer analyses are included in the study, along with directorships of officials of the Business Council, Conference Board and Business Roundtable. The study also identifies 256 directors who each sat on the boards of from six to thirteen corporations and the 74 persons who each sat on from three to six of the 130 major corporations.

The subcommittee staff recommended, among other things, that Congress consider:

1. Prohibiting interlocking directorates between corporations with over $1 billion in sales or assets. The proscription would apply to all lines of business, including regulated and nonregulated enterprises. It would be a flat prohibition against multiple management representation involving two or more companies above the $1 billion threshold. Such legislation, said the staff, may be more palatable to both the business and the political sectors since it seeks to reach concentration by restructuring the composition of corporate boards rather than the corporate organizations themselves.
2. Amending the Clayton Act to prohibit all types of horizontal interlocks between actual and potential competitors and vertical interlocks between a company and its customers, suppliers and sources of credit and capital. Such prohibitions, said the staff, may have to be specially tailored to meet the interlock problems within regulatory jurisdictions, but in the nonregulated areas, they should be given sweeping effect.
3. In cooperation with regulatory agencies, legislate a Business in the Sunshine Act requiring open corporate board meetings, subject to closure when trade secrets, privileged and/or special financial information or personnel matters are to be discussed.

Regulatory agencies, the staff proposed, should

1. Adopt rules requiring public representation on the boards of large corporations, and

2. Collect and make public current and complete reports on interlocking directorships of companies under their jurisdiction.

Commenting on the disarray of Federal records regarding corporate ownership and control, the staff said that prosecutors and the average citizen should "no longer have to hunt and pick their way through incomplete and inaccurate Government and private information sources. Computerization is far enough advanced to provide a central and up-to-date source for that information."

The Securities and Exchange Commission should take a lead role in collecting and disseminating such data, the staff suggested, adding that the executive branch could require such action under the Federal Reports Act if cooperation among regulatory agencies was not forthcoming.

Are Executive Pay Scales Off Balance?

RALPH V. WHITWORTH
President, United Shareholders Association

The recent controversy over the excessive compensation of chief executives at many of America's largest companies has exposed one glaring example of a deeply rooted problem: the lack of accountability of top executives to the owners of the companies they manage.

Last spring's reports about CEO pay levels left little doubt that there is virtually no connection between pay and performance for America's top corporate executives. *Business Week*'s survey of management compensation at major American corporations reported that total average annual CEO pay rose by 7 percent in 1990 to more than $1.9 million in a year when corporate profits fell by 7 percent.

Actually, shareholders are less concerned about how much CEOs get paid than how they get paid. Shareholders do not want to dictate CEO pay levels but they are increasingly demanding a rational process for setting executive compensation. These demands include calls for compensation committees made up of nonmanagement directors and the use of compensation consultants who are hired by and report directly to the compensation committee, not management.

These safeguards would represent a substantial improvement over current practice. But the ultimate remedy must include a mechanism allowing shareholders to elect truly independent directors who will advocate the owners', not the management's, interests. Also, the Securities and Exchange Commission should stiffen compensation disclosure requirements and open the proxy voting process to allow more direct input from shareholders on management compensation.

The irrationality of compensation is not only a concern for shareholders, it also has an insidious effect on our national competitiveness. Management is quick to cite the pressures of the financial markets as forcing a short-term orientation on corporate decisions. But management's own compensation is often based on the shortest of short-term factors. The seven-figure salaries and annual cash bonuses for CEOs have more to do with the short-term perspective of corporate America than the functioning of our financial markets. Reforms in the compensation process should focus on creating incentives for management to raise the efficiency, productivity, and competitiveness of the corporation over the long term.

YOU SCRATCH MY BACK, I'LL SCRATCH YOURS

Instead of encouraging long-term thinking, executive pay is typically tied to size-based factors such as revenues or corporate assets. But company size says little about efficiency, profitability, and, most important, how much value is created for the owners of the corporation. This irrational approach reflects a bankrupt corporate governance system.

In theory, shareholders elect a board of directors to represent their interests in corporate affairs including formulating management compensation

From *Business and Society Review,* No. 79 (Fall 1991). Reprinted by permission of the publisher.

packages. The board of directors in turn selects a management team to manage the corporation's day-to-day business.

In reality, however, the theory is turned upside down. For all practical purposes, boards are appointed by management and whether shareholders vote for them, against them, or not at all, they get management's slate. There is no competition for board seats and, worse yet, no mechanism for shareholders to nominate directors. Board members are dependent upon—and thus beholden to—the CEO for their position, pay, and perks. Not surprisingly, there is not much argument when it comes to approving the CEO's pay package. What prevails is a you-scratch-my-back-I'll-scratch-yours system of corporate governance that puts no real check on management avarice.

Simply put, corporate executives are virtually free to devise their own pay schemes. Not surprisingly, they do exactly what we would expect in pursuit of their self-interest; they constantly increase their own pay regardless of year-by-year corporate performance. Like a bear loose in a honey factory, we don't expect an unaccountable CEO to exercise much self-restraint. That restraint is supposed to be imposed by the shareholders through the board of directors. But management has captured the board of directors by controlling the selection and election of board members.

While some 70 percent of corporate board members are now nonemployee "independent" outsiders, 63 percent of all directors are CEOs of other corporations. Compounding the problem, the CEO of one company will often invite a CEO from another company to serve on the board and reciprocate by serving on the board of the second CEO.

The lack of accountability in compensation is recognized by large numbers of middle managers. A recent readership survey by *Industry Week* magazine found that 73.3 percent of respondents believe that directors do not act responsibly in setting top executive compensation, and 27.3 percent said CEO pay should be approved by shareholder vote. The comment of one middle manager quoted by the magazine was typical: "The buddy system is too entrenched in the executive levels of most corporations." Senior-level and middle-management employees comprised some 80 percent of the respondents to the poll.

PHANTOM COMPETITION

One often-heard justification for runaway CEO compensation is that such pay levels are needed to attract and keep the highest quality executives. Supposedly, the price of a CEO—represented by the level of compensation—is being bid up in a constantly churning CEO market with intense competition for open positions. Visions are conjured of free-agent CEO batting champions who can write their own ticket with virtually any team that they choose. But there is no evidence of a competitive and open market for CEOs. In fact, it is a phantom market that exists only in the mind of the CEO's hand-picked compensation committee.

According to a 1987 study by Harvard Business School, 75 percent of CEOs are selected from the ranks of inside management. These CEOs typically have worked for the company for more than 20 years. There is undoubtedly a high level of competition within the senior ranks of the corporation for the mantle of CEO. And certainly, one of the key attractions of the position is the lavish pay. But that is not to say that, considering the plentiful perks and prestige that come with being a captain of industry, an aspiring CEO would turn down the job were it offered for less pay. As University of California at Berkeley Professor Graef Crystal has pointed out, the pay gap between the CEO and other senior-level executives is wide and getting wider, with the average CEO earning 57 percent more than the second highest paid executive of a company. Logic suggests that a CEO candidate would accept the position even if this gap was substantially narrower.

Were the hypothesis correct that stratospheric and constantly rising pay is necessary to attract and retain talented executives, one would also expect to see evidence of competition among companies to hire each other's CEOs. After all, in a truly free market those executives with a proven track record at one or more companies would be in demand, offering their services to the highest bidder, with those who fail to excel falling by the wayside. But, again, there is scant evidence of such movement among CEOs. According to the 1987 Harvard study, nearly 80 percent of all CEOs who held the position between 1960 and 1984 served out "normal" tenures and left their job upon retirement. Only 6 percent resigned to pursue other career interests, and less than 5 percent were removed for poor performance.

In short, there is no "free" market functioning to deliver the services of American CEOs. That term implies a balancing of risk and reward. But the heightened interest in CEO compensation has exposed the fact that the risk-reward profile of the American CEO is so heavily biased toward reward that any element of risk has been virtually eliminated. No other segment of our society is accorded such privilege. The only parallel that seems appropriate to the position of CEO in American culture is that of royalty in some European countries.

INDEPENDENT DIRECTORS ARE KEY

But the tools are available to end the era of monarchy for American CEOs and restore sanity to their compensation packages. The key is providing shareholders with the ability to use the proxy system to nominate and elect independent directors who will be responsive and accountable to the interests of shareholders.

The Securities and Exchange Commission (SEC) is conducting a detailed and comprehensive review of its proxy rules to determine whether changes are required. The SEC review was spurred, in part, by submissions from the California Public Employees' Retirement System and the United Shareholders Association (USA). In March 1990, USA submitted a formal rulemaking petition to the SEC calling for major reform of the proxy rules to allow for a higher level of shareholder participation in the corporate governance process. Key features of USA's proposal would allow qualified shareholders increased access to the proxy to enable them to nominate directors, make proposals, and respond to management proposals; require confidential proxy voting to eliminate the intimidating and potentially coercive environment within which shareholders currently cast their votes; and liberalize the SEC's proxy filing and review requirements that inhibit free and open communication among shareholders.

In addition to these rule changes, the SEC should act immediately to allow submission of shareholder proposals relating to executive compensation. Until recently, SEC interpretation of the shareholder proposal rules precluded proposals concerning compensation. Such proposals were deemed as relating to the "ordinary business" affairs of management and thus were not a proper subject for shareholder proposals.

REFORMS NECESSARY

It appears that the SEC has begun to reinterpret these guidelines. In 1990, the SEC staff ruled that proposals relating to the awarding of "golden parachute" executive severance contracts were a proper subject for shareholder proposals. In the current 1991 proxy season, proposals relating to the appointment of compensation committees and consultants were introduced, although the staff was not asked for a formal interpretation on whether the proposals were acceptable. To clear up any lingering uncertainty, the SEC should further relax its restrictions on compensation-related proposals and allow submission of any proposals relating to the process and criteria by which executive compensation is determined.

The SEC should also act to require "plain English" disclosure of compensation to shareholders while at the same time requiring increased disclosure of compensation policies. For a shareholder, attempting to understand the value of an executive's compensation plan by examining the proxy statement can be like deciphering a secret code. Management should be required to state the total value of all compensation due the executives every year. The SEC should also act immediately to require management to disclose the criteria and process by which executive compensation is determined.

With greater access and information, shareholders will be able to make more educated investment decisions and exercise their rights more responsibly. These reforms would positively alter management's incentives and give shareholders the tools to ensure that their interests are being served by management.

PART THREE

WORK IN THE CORPORATION

In Part Two we examined the notion that business organizations have obligations not only, or even primarily, to their shareholders, but also to other stakeholders in the firm. One of the most important of these groups of stakeholders is the corporation's employees. They provide the productive and decision-making power of the business. In a very real sense, they are the corporation.

What obligations hold between a company and its employees? The traditional view of the relation between employer and employee has been that it is a free agreement or contract between the two parties for their mutual benefit. According to this contract, the primary responsibility of the employer is to pay fair wages. In return, employees owe the company loyalty, obedience, and satisfactory job performance. Either party can terminate the contract at any time, and traditionally, this power to terminate has been thought sufficient to protect the interests of both employers and employees. Like the traditional understanding of the corporation itself, however, this simple model of employer-employee relations has been challenged. Some thinkers argue that the employee's interests are not sufficiently protected by the right to quit. In the past two decades, a strong interest has emerged in securing more extensive rights for employees to protect them from potential abuses of power in the workplace. In Chapter 6, we examine the rights and duties of employees, with a special focus on the employee rights movement and on the issues of privacy and health and safety. The rights of free speech and dissent in the workplace have also received increasing attention, as "whistle-blowing" incidents—cases in which employees go above their supervisors or to the public to reveal corporate wrongdoing—have become more and more common. We devote Chapter 7 to the ethical issues raised by the practice of whistle blowing.

In 1971 a study on work in America commissioned by the Department of Health, Education and Welfare reported that a large majority of Americans are dissatisfied with work. Since then, several other studies have supported this finding. Comparisons with work styles in Japan and West Germany, where productivity is particularly high, have also raised questions about the quality of working life in the United States. In the past decade, issues surrounding work have received a growing amount of attention. The selections included in Chapter 8 address questions of job satisfaction and the quality of working life.

In Chapter 9 we turn to a variety of other workplace issues, including the relation between businesses and family life, sexual harassment, affirmative action, and diversity. These issues have been the subject of much controversy and legislative action, particularly discrimination and sexual harassment. The elimination of harassment and discrimination is essential both to a truly free society and to a truly efficient market. As a major social institution, business has a significant role to play in the perpetuation or termination of harassment and discrimination in U.S. society. But how should business exercise this role? How should corporations regulate interactions between men and women in the workplace? Should they eliminate racial discrimination by adopting a policy of "preferential hiring"? And what policies should business have about family life? How should businesses handle the increasing amount of racial and ethnic diversity in the workplace? All of these issues are examined in our selections.

EMPLOYEE RIGHTS AND DUTIES

Until recently employee rights have been restricted to those specified in the contract between employee and employer. Generally these had to do with wages, job description, hours, pension, and other benefits. If an employee did not like the treatment he or she received at the hands of an employer, did not wish to carry out an order, or disagreed with company policy, he or she could leave the job. Conversely, employers were permitted to fire employees for any reason or for no reason at all. Both parties, then, were free to terminate their contract at any time. But because jobs have usually been harder to find than employees, many felt that employers held the power and that employees were relatively powerless and required protection.

Today corporations are subject to laws governing minimum wages and maximum hours, specifying health and safety standards, and forbidding discrimination in hiring, firing, and promotion. An employer cannot fire an employee for union activity. But within these limits, argues David Ewing in his "An Employee Bill of Rights," corporations retain a great deal of power over their employees. The structure of most business organizations is still an authoritarian one. The relationship of employer to employee remains that of a superior to a subordinate.

According to Ewing, employees in the workplace lack many of the most basic civil liberties guaranteed by the Constitution. A number of corporations give their employees honesty tests, collect extensive information about them, and attempt to dictate their behavior off the job. For the most part, employees are permitted little control over matters that directly affect their work lives. They can be fired for dissenting from company views or for refusing to execute an order, even if they believe that the order is immoral or illegal. Frequently there is no grievance procedure within the organization and no means for ensuring that employees receive just treatment. In effect, Ewing holds, the workplace represents a "black hole" in American rights. Most citizens are virtually without rights from nine to five.

The civil liberties specified in the Bill of Rights were designed to protect citizens against possible abuses of power by government. But, Ewing points out, many corporations today have bigger "populations" than the largest of the original thirteen colonies. The gross annual income of some of the largest conglomerates exceeds the gross national product of such countries as Austria, Norway, and Greece. When corporate power reaches the magnitude of a minigovernment, argues Ewing, it is necessary to protect those subject to that power by an explicit recognition of their rights. His proposed employee bill of rights, which would guarantee employees the rights of free speech, dissent, privacy, and due process, represents one way in which this task might be accomplished.

Not all thinkers believe that steps should be taken to protect employee rights. Donald Martin, for example, argues that an employee bill of rights such as that suggested by Ewing is not necessary. Citizens need a bill of rights to protect them against the government, Martin acknowledges, but this is because the cost of moving to a different country is very high. The cost of changing jobs, however, he claims, is relatively low. The ability of employees to move from job to job thus is enough to protect their interests. If personal liberty is restricted on the job, Martin argues, it is not because employers are tyrannizing employees, but because employee rights are costly and employees have "chosen" fewer rights in exchange for higher earning power. An employee bill of rights would not only be expensive, it would also limit the freedom of employees to trade their rights for higher salaries. Martin would probably favor letting job market forces decide whether polygraph testing and drug testing are acceptable. The case "Johnson Controls" highlights some of the issues raised by Martin. In this case, one of the questions is whether a corporation should protect women from health risks against their will, or whether the women should be allowed to take risks in order to obtain the same high-paying jobs as men.

Another important workplace problem—drug use by employees—has been estimated to cost business millions of dollars in the form of lowered productivity, absenteeism, employee error, and other problems. Drug use also carries the risk of serious physical injury to consumers, the public, or employees themselves. To counter these problems, many companies have instituted programs to test applicants and current employees for drug use. Many Fortune 500 firms, as well as numerous smaller companies, now employ some kind of drug test. Are such programs a threat to employee privacy? Joseph Des Jardins and Ronald Duska claim that they are. Des Jardins and Duska argue that employers have a right to information that is directly related to job performance. But drug use, they claim, is not directly relevant. People use drugs differently, and drugs can have varied effects. Some drug users will be impaired on the job, but others will not. The commonly used drug tests, moreover, do not give much information about impairment. They show only the presence of the drug's metabolite in the urine and not the kind of drug, the amount that is present, or how long ago the drug was taken. An astute supervisor can spot impairment in the form of absenteeism, carelessness, low productivity, or psychological problems. If these problems do arise, the supervisor may discipline the employee for these reasons alone. There is no need to inquire into the employee's use of drugs. However, if no performance problems show up, there is no impairment—the employee is doing the job. Again, drug testing is not necessary. Moreover, as the "Video Game" case shows, there are ways to judge impaired performance that do not require extreme intrusions into employee privacy. Thus, Des Jardins and Duska conclude, if what the employer is truly interested in is performance, drug test results are either superfluous or irrelevant. Testing is only justified, they argue, in jobs in which drug use poses a "clear and present" danger to others. In a *Wall Street Journal* interview conducted by Michael Waldholz, two corporate executives debate the acceptability of drug testing, touching on several of the issues raised by Des Jardins and Duska.

If employees are to protect their rights effectively by exercising their power to change jobs, at the very least they must have adequate information about the ways in which their jobs may threaten their interests. This is particularly difficult in the area of health and safety risks, since employees may not know the risks they face until it is too late to avoid them. The Occupational Safety and Health Administration (OSHA) sets minimum standards for safety in the workplace, but no job can be entirely riskfree. Ruth Faden and Tom Beauchamp argue that employees have a right to know about the health and safety risks they face on the job. Their article explores the extent of employees' right to know and the corresponding duty of an employer to disclose the relevant information. Faden and Beauchamp also point out that the right to know is not effective unless it is accompanied by a real ability to alter working conditions by changing jobs, filing complaints with OSHA, or refusing to perform unusually hazardous assignments.

WHISTLE BLOWING

Occasionally an employee discovers, or is asked to participate in, an activity he or she believes to be unethical or illegal. In such a situation the employee may choose to "blow the whistle" or reveal the activity, either to someone higher up within the corporation (usually called "internal" whistle blowing) or to the public ("external" whistle blowing). Readers will recall Kermit Vandivier's dilemma at B.F. Goodrich in Part One. Another example is the case "GE's Drive to Purge Fraud," which is included as one of the cases in Part Three.

Do employees have the right, or perhaps even the obligation, to blow the whistle on corporate wrongdoing? Should they receive legal protection from such retaliations by their employer as firing, blackballing, or attacks on professional integrity? Some, such as Ralph Nader, recommend not only that whistle blowing receive protection but that it be actively encouraged as a means of improving corporate responsibility. Others are violently opposed to whistle blowing, feeling that it violates the duties of employees to their employer. States James M. Roche, former chairman of General Motors Corporation:

> Some of the enemies of business now encourage an employee to be disloyal to the enterprise. They want to create suspicion and disharmony and pry into the proprietary interests of the business: However this is labeled—industrial espionage, whistle blowing, or professional responsibility—it is another tactic for spreading disunity and creating conflict.

Legally, an employee is regarded as the agent of the corporation for which he or she works. Agency law states that employees have a duty to obey the directions of their employers, to act solely in their employers' interests in all matters related to their employment, and to refrain from disclosing confidential information that, if revealed, might harm their employers. The law does not require employees to carry out commands that are illegal or immoral, but neither does it authorize them to reveal such commands to the public or (for the most part) protect them from reprisals if they do so.

In Chapter 7 Richard De George argues that because it is a form of disloyalty, and because it can cause harm to the firm, whistle blowing needs moral justification. De George believes that whistle blowing is only morally permissible under certain conditions: when serious (physical) harm is threatened and when the employee has already exhausted channels within the corporation in an attempt to correct the problem. De George regards whistle blowing as a supererogatory, self-sacrificing, or heroic act and believes that employees very rarely have an obligation to blow the whistle. For such an obligation to be present, De George believes, an employee must have documented evidence of serious potential harm and good reason to believe that blowing the whistle will actually succeed in averting the harm. The best solution to the problem of whistle blowing in the workplace, claims De George, is to encourage channels of communication and response inside the corporation so that employees are not forced to be "moral heroes."

In response, Gene James believes that De George's criteria are too strict. Harms such as sexual harassment, fraud, or invasion of privacy may also justify blowing the whistle, he believes, even though these do not involve the physical harm that De George finds necessary. James also believes that whistle blowing is more often obligatory than De George admits. Employees who are aware of the potentially harmful consequences of a corporate act and who fail to blow the whistle, James holds, bear part of the responsibility for those consequences. In these cases, the duty to blow the whistle outweighs both the risk of job loss and the duty of loyalty to the corporation.

It is not always clear that a dissenting employee is being disloyal to the corporation. In many cases, corporations could have saved themselves thousands of dollars in lawsuits and a tarnished public image by responding to dissenting employees. In part, whether a dissenting employee is acting in the interest of the corporation depends upon how broadly we interpret the nature, function, and goals of business. If the function of business is to produce a reliable product and refrain from harming its stakeholders as well as making a profit, then it could be argued that top management—not Kermit Vandivier or the GE whistle blower—acted against the interest of their companies.

THE QUALITY OF WORKING LIFE

> I start the automobile, the first welds . . . the welding gun's got a square handle with a button on the top for high voltage and a button on the bottom for low. . . . I stand in one spot, about a two- or three-feet area, all night. The only time a person stops is when the line stops. We do about thirty-two jobs per car, per unit. Forty-eight units an hour, eight hours a day. Thirty-two times forty-eight times eight. Figure it out. That's how many times I push that button. . . . Repetition is such that if you were to think about the job itself, you'd slowly go out of your mind. . . . I don't understand why more guys don't flip. Because you're nothing but a machine when you hit this type of thing. They give better care to that machine than they will to you. They'll have more respect, give more attention to the machine. . . . If that machine breaks down, there's somebody out there to fix it right away. If I break down, I'm just pushed over to the other side until another man takes my place. The only thing they have in their mind is to keep that line running.

The feelings of this spot welder at a Ford assembly plant are not unique. Thousands of Americans hold jobs in which they experience fragmentation, repetition, the feeling of being a mere cog in a machine. This has become even more true in recent years as many major corporations have slashed jobs or moved factories overseas as a way of saving money.

Nor is the dissatisfaction confined to blue-collar workers, although they are the primary focus of the readings included in this chapter. One executive describes his job:

> I don't know of any situation in the corporate world where an executive is completely free and sure of his job from moment to moment. . . . The danger starts as soon as you become a district manager. You have men working for you and you have a boss above—you're caught in a squeeze. . . . There's always the insecurity. You bungle a job. You're fearful of losing a big customer. You're fearful so many things will appear on your record, stand against you. You're always fearful of a big mistake. You've got to be careful when you go to corporation parties. Your

wife, your children have got to behave properly. You've got to fit in the mold. You've got to be on guard. . . . The executive is a lonely animal in the jungle who doesn't have a friend. . . .

I left that world because suddenly the power and the status were empty. I'd been there, and when I got there it was nothing. . . . So when the corporation was sold, my share of the sale was such . . . I didn't have to go back into the jungle. I don't have to fight to the top. I've been to the mountain top. . . . It isn't worth it.

How do we go about decreasing these feelings of dissatisfaction? Proposed solutions include structuring jobs to give workers more challenge, more mobility, more variety, and a greater sense of accomplishment. Often this involves decreasing specialization and replacing assembly lines with teams of three or four workers who assemble an entire unit of machinery. Other important suggestions are increased democracy in the workplace, with more worker participation in running the business, and more cooperation between workers and management. Another suggestion is giving workers a bigger "stake" in the business through stock ownership or profit-sharing plants. Any or all these may be included in what union leader Irving Bluestone calls a "quality of working life program."

In the first article in Chapter 8 Bluestone claims that the workforce has changed dramatically in the past few decades and that the workplace must change to meet it. He sees increased democracy in the workplace as the most important goal of a quality of working life (QWL) program, and calls for union support of QWL. Bluestone regards QWL as an extension of, not a departure from, the traditional goal of unions. QWL programs, he claims, benefit both unions and management. Benefits include lowered absenteeism and turnover, fewer disciplinary actions against employees, a decrease in grievances filed by employees, and improved product quality.

Mike Parker and Dwight Hansen are more skeptical about the benefits of QWL programs for workers and unions in their Chapter 8 article. They fear that the programs upset the traditional adversarial relationship between unions and management, eroding the power of the unions. Because they emphasize cooperation between workers and management, Parker and Hansen believe, QWL programs undercut union solidarity and divide workers against each other, undermining the power to act collectively, which has been the mainstay of workers since unionism began. They believe that the cooperation offered by QWL programs have been used to wring concessions from workers, concessions that have not been outweighed by the benefits of QWL.

In the final article in Chapter 8 Mitchell Fein argues against QWL programs for different reasons. He questions the assumption of thinkers like Bluestone that participation and personal fulfillment are essential characteristics of a satisfying job. Not all workers want more autonomy, more challenge, and more variety in their work, he argues. If they did, there would be more union emphasis on QWL programs at the bargaining table. In fact, he believes, most workers are satisfied with their jobs. Fein fears that workers will suffer because management will impose preconceived ideas on them about what makes work satisfying, and he suggests that QWL programs represent an exploitation of workers' job satisfaction for gains in productivity.

THE MODERN WORKPLACE: TRANSITION TO EQUALITY AND DIVERSITY

For many years in the United States work in the corporation was dominated by one group—white males. Middle- and upper-level management were the exclusive preserve of white males. Lower level jobs were all that women, Afro-Americans, and other minorities could hope for. There was no real possibility of advancement for women and minorities. They were excluded, sometimes subtly, sometimes callously, from full participation in corporate life.

This is gradually changing. As a consequence of legislation and different social realities and attitudes, management is no longer composed solely of white males. This, we hope and anticipate, will continue in the future. However, it brings with it many new problems for corporations and those who run them. Many of these problems are discussed in the articles in Chapter 9.

In the first article, Fran Sussner Rodgers and Charles Rodgers consider the relation between work and family life. They note that the traditional view of work and family—the man at work and the woman at home—no longer applies. Changing demographics and new attitudes toward work are bringing more and more women into the workplace. But with both parents working, and with the increasing number of single parents in the workforce, dependent care becomes a major issue for workers. Companies need to recognize this new reality, they argue, by providing access to child care, alternative work hours, and flexible work schedules for parents. If they do not, then they are likely to be passed over by the best and most productive employees, who will search for a job that grants them the freedom they need to deal with family issues.

Another major issue in the workplace is sexual harassment. For years sexual harassment was dismissed or ignored by corporate management. It was just a fact of work life that women had to deal with as best they could, even though it was clearly a pernicious and ethically repugnant practice. Recently, however, this has begun to change. Legislation has been passed to prohibit sexual harassment, and corporations have at last begun to take action against it. In their article in Chapter 9, Ellen Bravo and Ellen Cassedy offer a commonsense definition of sexual harassment as offering sexual attention to someone who didn't ask for it and doesn't want it. They note that there are two kinds of sexual harassment: quid pro quo harassment in which an employee must submit to keep her job or receive a raise or promotion; and hostile environment harassment in which unwelcome sexual conduct creates an environment in which an employee cannot reasonably be expected to perform her job satisfactorily. By using a number of scenarios and examples, they show how these concepts apply, and they dispel a number of myths about sexual harassment.

Bravo and Cassedy also point out that the "reasonable person" standard so often used by courts to gauge behavior has been replaced by the "reasonable woman" standard as the law has evolved to take account of the perspective of women in the workplace. In their conclusion, however, they argue that despite this, the law and enforcement system still pose formidable obstacles for victims of harassment.

The next two articles in Chapter 9 discuss the perennially controversial topics of affirmative action and reverse discrimination. Louis Pojman approaches the issue of affirmative action by first defining a number of key terms, such as discrimination, prejudice, bias, equal opportunity, and affirmative action. He then outlines seven arguments on each side of the issue. Arguments supporting affirmative action include, for example, the equal results argument, the compensation argument, and the diversity argument. Some arguments against affirmative action are that it requires discrimination against a different group, that it encourages mediocrity, and that it has not been successful. He concludes that there is a real danger that well-intentioned people, in their attempts to redress the inequities of the past, are engaging in new forms of unjust discrimination.

In "What Is Wrong with Reverse Discrimination?" Edwin Hettinger defends from a utilitarian point of view the hiring of slightly less qualified blacks and women rather than slightly more qualified white males. This is justified, he argues, since the ultimate goal is the elimination of racial and sexual inequality. He identifies two objections to reverse discrimination as troubling: that people are judged on the basis of characteristics over which they have no control; and that white males are not compensated for the burden they bear in achieving an egalitarian society. He concludes that these two objections are relatively minor when weighed against the injustices of racial and sexual inequality. The reader may want to test Hettinger's conclusions against the "Kantian Utilitarian" principle proposed in the last section of the introduction to this text.

The final two articles in Chapter 9 address issues of gender and diversity in the workplace. Felice Schwartz argues that it costs more to employ women than men in management, but that what increases their cost is not simply that women are different from men, but the policies and practices of male-led corporations. What needs to be done, she says, is to reduce that expense by becoming more responsive to the needs of women. Only in this way can corporations ensure that they have the best employees. Talented and creative women will gravitate toward firms that recognize their value and make real efforts to provide them with what they need to succeed.

R. Roosevelt Thomas points out that today more than half the U.S. workforce consists of minorities, immigrants, and women. White males are still dominate but are a statistical minority and will continue to make up less and less of the workforce. In the future, he says, affirmative action will no longer be as important, simply because of demographic changes. What minorities and women need is not entry into work, but a chance to achieve their potential without artificial barriers imposed on them by shortsighted corporate practices. Thomas sees affirmative action as a necessary and useful step toward true diversity in the workplace, but it does not ensure that those recruited via affirmative action programs get an opportunity to fulfill their potential. He proposes ten guidelines to enable a company to move beyond affirmative action to managing diversity. This, he argues, is how companies can maintain competitive advantage in the global economy. It is also, we suggest, an ethical imperative demanded by the Kantian principle that people should be treated as ends in themselves and not merely as means.

CHAPTER 6

EMPLOYEE RIGHTS AND DUTIES

An Employee Bill of Rights

David Ewing
Writer and former editor of the *Harvard Business Review*

For nearly two centuries Americans have enjoyed freedom of press, speech, and assembly, due process of law, privacy, freedom of conscience, and other important rights—in their homes, churches, political forums, and social and cultural life. But Americans have not enjoyed these civil liberties in most companies, government agencies, and other organizations where they work. Once a U.S. citizen steps through the plant or office door at 9 *a.m.,* he or she is nearly rightless until 5 *p.m.,* Monday through Friday. The employee continues to have political freedoms, of course, but these are not the significant ones now. While at work, the important relationships are with bosses, associates, and subordinates. Inequalities in dealing with these people are what really count for an employee.

To this generalization there are important exceptions. In some organizations, generous managements have seen fit to assure free speech, privacy, due process, and other concerns as privileges. But there is no guarantee the privileges will survive the next change of chief executive. As former Attorney General Ramsey Clark once said in a speech, "A right is not what someone gives you; it's what no one can take from you." Defined in this manner, rights are rare in business and public organizations.

In effect, U.S. society is a paradox. The Constitution and Bill of Rights light up the sky over political campaigners, legislators, civic leaders, families, church people, and artists. But not so over employees. The employee sector of our civil liberties universe is more like a black hole, with rights so compacted, so imploded by the gravitational forces of legal tradition, that, like the giant black stars in the physical universe, light can scarcely escape.

Perhaps the most ironic thing is that only in recent years have Americans made many noises about this paradox. It is as if we took it for granted and assumed there was no alternative. "Organizations have always been this way and always have to be," we seem to say. One is reminded of an observation attributed to Marshall McLuhan: "Anybody's total surround, or environment, creates a condition of nonperception."

To put the situation in focus, let us make a brief review of rights in the workplace.

SPEECH

In many private and public organizations there is a well-oiled machinery for providing relief to an employee who is discharged because of his or her race, religion, or sex. But we have no mechanisms for granting similar relief to an employee who is discharged for exercising the right of free speech. The law states that all employers "may dismiss their employees at will . . . for good cause, for no cause, or even for cause morally wrong, without being thereby guilty of legal wrong."[1]

Of course, discharge is only the extreme weapon; many steps short of discharge may work well enough—loss of a raise in pay, demotion, assignment to the boondocks, or perhaps simply a cutback of normal and expected benefits.

Consider the case of a thirty-five-year-old business executive whom I shall call "Mike Z." He was a respected research manager in a large company. He believed that his company was making only superficial efforts to comply with newly enacted pollution laws. In a management meeting and later in social groups he spoke critically of top management's attitude. Soon strange things began to happen to him, different only in degree from what happens to a political dissenter in the Soviet Union. First, his place in the company parking lot was canceled. Then his name was "accidentally" removed from the office building directory inside the main entrance. Soon routine requests he made to attend professional meetings began to get snarled up in red tape or were "lost." Next he found himself harassed by directives to rewrite routine reports. Then his budget for clerical service was cut, followed by a drastic slash in his research budget. When he tried to protest this treatment, he met a wall of top management silence. Rather than see his staff suffer further for his dissidence, he quit his job and moved his family to another city.

Mike Z. could be almost anyone in thousands of companies, government agencies, and other organizations. It should not be surprising, therefore, that when it comes to speaking out on issues of company policy or management practice, employees make about as much noise as fish swimming.

So well-established is the idea that any criticism of the company is "ratting" or "finking" that some companies hang out written prohibitions for all to see. For instance, a private bus company on the West Coast puts employees on notice with this rule:

> The company requires its employees to be loyal. It will not tolerate words or acts of hostility to the company, its officers, agents, or employees, its services, equipment or its condition, or . . . criticisms of the company to others than . . . superior officers.

CONSCIENTIOUS OBJECTION

There is very little protection in industry for employees who object to carrying out immoral, unethical, or illegal orders from their superiors. If the employee doesn't like what he or she is asked to do, the remedy is to pack up and leave. This remedy seems to presuppose an ideal economy, where there is another company down the street with openings for jobs just like the one the employee left. But what about the real world? Here resignation may mean having to uproot one's family and move to a strange city in another state. Or it may mean, for an employee in the semifinals of a career, or for an employee with a specialized competence, not being able to find another suitable job anywhere.

In 1970 Shirley Zinman served as a secretary in a Philadelphia employment agency called LIB Services. One day she was instructed by her bosses to record all telephone conversations she might have with prospective clients. This was to be done for "training purposes," she was told, although the callers were not to be told that their words were being taped. The office manager would monitor the conversations on an extension in her office. Ms. Zinman refused to play along with this game, not only because it was unethical, in her view, but illegal as well—the telephone company's regulations forbade such unannounced telephone recordings.

So Ms. Zinman had to resign. She sought unemployment compensation. The state unemployment pay board refused her application. It reasoned that her resignation was not "compelling and necessitous." With the help of attorneys from the American Civil Liberties Union, she appealed her case to the Pennsylvania Commonwealth Court. In a ruling hailed by civil rights leaders, the court in 1973 reversed the pay board and held that Ms. Zinman was entitled to unemployment compensation because her objection to the unethical directive was indeed a "compelling" reason to quit her job.[2]

What this interesting case leaves unsaid is as important as what it does say: Resignation continues to be the accepted response for the objecting employee. The Pennsylvania court took a bold step in favor of employee rights, for prior to this decision there was little reason to think that the Shirley Zinmans of industry could expect any help at all from the outside world. But within the organization itself, an employee is expected to sit at the feet of the boss's conscience.

SECURITY AND PRIVACY

When employees are in their homes, before and after working hours, they enjoy well-established rights to privacy and to protection from arbitrary search and seizure of their papers and possessions. But no such rights protect them in the average company, government agency, or other organization; their superiors need only the flimsiest pretext to search their lockers, desks, and files. The boss can rummage through an employee's letters, memoranda, and tapes looking for evidence that (let us say) he or she is about to "rat" on the company. "Ratting" might include reporting a violation of safety standards to the Occupational Safety and Health Administration (which is provided for by law), or telling Ralph Nader about a product defect, or giving the mayor's office requested information about a violation of energy-use regulations.

CHOICE OF OUTSIDE ACTIVITIES AND ASSOCIATIONS

In practice, most business employees enjoy no right to work after hours for the political, social, and community organizations of their choice. To be sure, in many companies an enlightened management will encourage as much diversity of choice in outside activities as employees can make. As noted earlier, however, this is an indulgence which can disappear any time, for most states do not mandate such rights, and even in those that do, the rights are poorly protected. An employee who gets fired for his or her choice of outside activities can expect no damages for his loss even if he or she wins a suit against the employer. The employee may only "secure the slight satisfaction of seeing his employer suffer the statutory penalties."[3]

Ironically, however, a company cannot discriminate against people whose politics it dislikes when it *hires* them.[4] It has to wait a few days before it can exercise its prerogatives.

DUE PROCESS

"Accidents will occur in the best-regulated families," said Mr. Micawber in *David Copperfield.* Similarly, accidents of administration occur even in the best-managed companies, with neurotic, inept, or distracted supervisors inflicting needless harm on subordinates. Many a subordinate who goes to such a boss to protest would be well-advised to keep one foot in the stirrups, for he is likely to be shown to the open country for his efforts.

This generalization does not hold for civil service employees in the federal government, who can resort to a grievance process. Nor does it hold for unionized companies, which also have grievance procedures. But it holds for *most* other organizations. A few organizations voluntarily have established a mechanism to ensure due process.

The absence of a right to due process is especially painful because it is the second element of constitutionalism in organizations. As we shall think of it in this book, employee constitutionalism consists of a set of clearly defined rights, and a means of protecting employees from discharge, demotion, or other penalties imposed when they assert their rights.

Why bother about rightlessness in corporations, government agencies, and other organizations? They are much smaller than state and federal governments, are they not? Must an organization that "rules" an employee only for forty or so hours per week be treated as a government?

For one answer, let us turn to the Founding Fathers. Of course, they did not know or conceive of the modern corporation and public agency, so we cannot read what their thoughts about all this might have been. Perhaps we can make a reasonable guess, however, by comparing some numbers.

If the original thirteen colonies were large and powerful enough to concern the Founding Fathers, it seems likely that those men, if here today, would want to extend their philosophy to other assemblages of equivalent size and magnitude. In the writings of James Madison, Thomas Jefferson, George Mason, Jonas Phillips, Richard Henry Lee, Elbridge Gerry, Luther Martin, and others, there is no inference that human rights were seen as a good thing only some of the time or for some places. Instead, the Fathers saw rights as a universal need.[5]

In 1776, and in 1789, when the Bill of Rights (first ten amendments to the Constitution) was passed by Congress and sent to the states for ratification, trading companies and government agencies were tiny organizations incapable of harboring bureaucracy. Indeed, to use Mr. Micawber's phrase, there was hardly room in them to swing a cat, much less create layer on layer of hierarchy and wall after wall of departmental structure.

Today all that has changed. Some of our corporate and public organizations have larger "populations" than did the thirteen colonies. And a truly vast number of organizations have large enough "populations" to rank as real powers in people's everyday lives. For instance:

- AT&T has more than 939,000 employees, nearly twice the size of the largest colony, Virginia, which had about 493,000 inhabitants in 1776.
- General Motors, with 681,000 employees, is nearly two and one-half times the size of the second largest colony, Pennsylvania, which had a population of about 284,000 people in 1776.
- Westinghouse, the thirteenth largest corporate employer today with 166,000 employees, is four times the size of the thirteenth largest colony, Delaware, which had a population of 41,400. Westinghouse's "population" is also larger than that in 1776 of South Carolina, New Jersey, New Hampshire, Rhode Island, and Georgia.

In fact, 125 corporations have larger "populations" than did Delaware, the smallest colony, in 1776. But can employee workforces legitimately be compared with state populations? Of course, there are important differences—the twenty-four-hours-per-day jurisdiction of the state as opposed to only eight hours per day for an employer, the fact that the state has courts and military forces while the employer does not, and others. Yet it is not an apples-and-oranges comparison. Decades ago, and long before corporations and public agencies achieved anything like their current size, political scientists were noting many important similarities between the governments of organizations and political governments. In 1908, for example, Arthur Bentley wrote:

> A corporation is government through and through . . . Certain technical methods which political government uses, as, for instance, hanging, are not used by corporations, generally speaking, but that is a detail.[6]

In numerous ways, sizable corporations, public agencies, and university administrations qualify as "minigovernments." They pay salaries and costs. They have medical plans. They provide for retirement income. They offer recreational facilities. They maintain cafeterias. They may assist an employee with housing, educational loans, personal training, and vacation plans. They schedule numerous social functions. They have "laws," conduct codes, and other rules. Many have mechanisms for resolving disputes. A few even keep chaplains on the payroll or maintain facilities for religious worship.

Accordingly, it seems foolish to dismiss minigovernments as possible subjects of rights, or to exclude employees from discussions of civil liberties. We have assumed that rights are not as important for employees as for political citizens. Our assumption is in error.

The bill of rights that follows is one person's proposal, a "working paper" for discussion, not a platform worked out in committee.

1. *No organization or manager shall discharge, demote, or in other ways discriminate against any employee who criticizes, in speech or press, the ethics, legality, or social responsibility of management actions.*
   Comment: What this right does not say is as important as what it does say. Protection does not extend to employees who make nuisances of themselves or who balk, argue, or contest managerial decisions on normal operating and planning matters, such as the choice of inventory accounting method, whether to diversify the product line or concentrate it, whether to rotate workers on a certain job or specialize them, and so forth. "Committing the truth," as Ernest Fitzgerald called it, is protected only for speaking out on issues where we consider an average citizen's judgment to be as valid as an expert's—truth in advertising, public safety standards, questions of fair disclosure, ethical practices, and so forth.
2. *No employee shall be penalized for engaging in outside activities of his or her choice after working hours, whether political, economic, civic, or cultural, nor for buying products and services of his or her choice for personal use, nor for expressing or encouraging views contrary to top management's on political, economic, and social issues.*
   Comment: Many companies encourage employees to participate in outside activities, and some states have committed this right to legislation. Freedom of choice of products and services for personal use is also authorized in various state statutes as well as in arbitrators' decisions. The third part of the statement extends the protection of the First Amendment to the employee whose ideas about government, economic policy, religion, and society do not conform with the boss's.

   Note that this provision does not authorize an employee to come to work "beat" in the morning because he or she has been moonlighting. Participation in outside activities should enrich employees' lives, not debilitate them; if on-the-job performance suffers, the usual penalties may have to be paid.
3. *No organization or manager shall penalize an employee for refusing to carry out a directive that violates common norms of morality.*
   Comment: The purpose of this right is to afford job security to subordinates who cannot perform an action because they consider it unethical or illegal. It is important that the conscientious objector in such a case hold to a view that has some public acceptance. Fad moralities—messages from flying saucers, mores of occult religious sects, and so on—do not justify refusal to carry out an order. Nor in any case is the employee entitled to interfere with the boss's finding another person to do the job requested.
4. *No organization shall allow audio or visual recordings of an employee's conversations or actions to be made without his or her prior knowledge and consent. Nor may an organization require an employee or applicant to take personality tests, polygraph examinations, or other tests that constitute, in his opinion, an invasion of privacy.*
   Comment: This right is based on policies that some leading organizations have already put into practice. If an employee doesn't want his working life monitored, that is his privilege so long as he demonstrates (or, if an applicant, is willing to demonstrate) competence to do a job well.
5. *No employee's desk, files, or locker may be examined in his or her absence by anyone but a senior manager who has sound reason to believe that the files contain information needed for a management decision that must be made in the employee's absence.*
   Comment: The intent of this right is to grant people a privacy right as employees similar to that which they enjoy as political and social citizens under the "searches and seizures"

guarantee of the Bill of Rights (Fourth Amendment to the Constitution). Many leading organizations in business and government have respected the principle of this rule for some time.

6. *No employer organization may collect and keep on file information about an employee that is not relevant and necessary for efficient management. Every employee shall have the right to inspect his or her personnel file and challenge the accuracy, relevance, or necessity of data in it, except for personal evaluations and comments by other employees which could not reasonably be obtained if confidentiality were not promised. Access to an employee's file by outside individuals and organizations shall be limited to inquiries about the essential facts of employment.*
   Comment: This right is important if employees are to be masters of their employment track records instead of possible victims of them. It will help to eliminate surprises, secrets, and skeletons in the clerical closet.
7. *No manager may communicate to prospective employers of an employee who is about to be or has been discharged gratuitous opinions that might hamper the individual in obtaining a new position.*
   Comment: The intent of this right is to stop blacklisting. The courts have already given some support for it.
8. *An employee who is discharged, demoted, or transferred to a less desirable job is entitled to a written statement from management of its reasons for the penalty.*
   Comment: The aim of this provision is to encourage a manager to give the same reasons in a hearing, arbitration, or court trial that he or she gives the employee when the cutdown happens. The written statement need not be given unless requested; often it is so clear to all parties why an action is being taken that no document is necessary.
9. *Every employee who feels that he or she has been penalized for asserting any right described in this bill shall be entitled to a fair hearing before an impartial official, board, or arbitrator. The findings and conclusions of the hearing shall be delivered in writing to the employee and management.*
   Comment: This very important right is the organizational equivalent of due process of law as we know it in political and community life. Without due process in a company or agency, the rights in this bill would all have to be enforced by outside courts and tribunals, which is expensive for society as well as time-consuming for the employees who are required to appear as complainants and witnesses. The nature of a "fair hearing" is purposely left undefined here so that different approaches can be tried, expanded, and adapted to changing needs and conditions.

Note that the findings of the investigating official or group are not binding on top management. This would put an unfair burden on an ombudsperson or "expedited arbitrator," if one of them is the investigator. Yet the employee is protected. If management rejects a finding of unfair treatment and then the employee goes to court, the investigator's statement will weigh against management in the trial. As a practical matter, therefore, employers will not want to buck the investigator-referee unless they fervently disagree with the findings.

Every sizable organization, whether in business, government, health, or another field, should have a bill of rights for employees. Only small organizations need not have such a statement—personal contact and oral communications meet the need for them. However, companies and agencies need not have identical bills of rights. Industry custom, culture, past history with employee unions and associations, and other considerations can be taken into account in the wording and emphasis given to different provisions.

NOTES

1. See Lawrence E. Blades, "Employment at Will vs. Individual Freedom: On Limiting the Abusive Exercise of Employer Power," *Columbia Law Review* 67 (1967):1405.
2. 8 Pa. Comm. Ct. Reports 649,304 A. 2nd 380 (1973). Also see *New York Times,* August 26, 1973.

3. Blades, 1412.
4. See 299 F. Supp. 1100, cited in *Employee Relations in Action,* August 1971 (New York, N.Y., Man & Manager), pp. 1–2.
5. See, for example, Bernard Schwartz, *The Bill of Rights: A Documentary History.* Vol. 1 (Toronto and New York: Chelsea House Publishers in association with McGraw-Hill Book Company, 1971), pp. 435 ff.
6. Arthur Bentley, *The Process of Government,* cited in Arthur Selwyn Miller, *The Modern Corporate State* (Westport, Conn.: Greenwood Press, 1976), p. 188.

Is an Employee Bill of Rights Needed?

Donald L. Martin
Formerly of the Law and Economics Center, University of Miami School of Law

The perception of the corporation as an industrial form of government in which management plays the role of the governor and labor the role of the governed has been particularly popular since the end of World War II. "Industrial democracy" has been the slogan of the labor movement in the industrial relations community. This analogy has recently given rise to demands for an "Employee Bill of Rights."[1] Such a bill would guarantee the worker the same *due process* that the Constitution guarantees the citizen. It would protect the worker from the arbitrary and inequitable exercise of managerial discretion.

WHERE THE INDUSTRIAL DEMOCRACY ANALOGY FALTERS

But, the industrial democracy analogy surely must be false. Two important considerations obviate it. First, a crucial distinction between government at any level and private economic organization, corporate or otherwise, is the right entrusted to government to exercise legitimate and reasonable force in its relations with its citizens. Second, the cost to a citizen of switching affiliation between governments is far greater than the cost to an employee of switching affiliations between firms. Since governments will surely violate public trust through their police powers, and since the costs to citizens of changing leaders or residences are relatively high, citizens will seek institutions to insulate themselves from the arbitrary and exploitative use of such powers by their elected and appointed representatives. These institutions include the first ten amendments to the United States Constitution (the Bill of Rights) and the Fourteenth Amendment (guaranteeing due process).

THE PROBLEM OF THE MONOPSONISTIC LABOR MARKET

Something close to an analogous use of exploitative power in the private sector occurs in the world of monopsonistic labor markets. In those labor markets, would-be employees have few, if any, alternative job opportunities, either because of an absence of immediate competitive employers or because of the presence of relatively high costs of moving to available job alternatives in other markets. With few or no job alternatives, workers are more likely to be the unwilling subjects of employer prejudice, oppression, and personal discretion than if labor market competition prevails.

No one would claim that the American economy is completely free of monopsony power. There is not a shred of evidence, on the other hand, that such power exists in the large American corporation of today. Indeed, there is impressive evidence to suggest that monopsony is not likely to be found in large, private corporations. Robert Bunting's examination of labor market concentration throughout the United States among large firms, for example, finds that employment concentration (measured by the fraction of total employees in a geographic area who are employed by the largest reporting firm in that area) is related inversely to labor market size, while firm size is correlated positively with labor market size.[2]

It is well known that monopsonistic powers reside in the collusive owners of professional sports teams, precisely because these powers are exempt from antitrust laws in the United States.[3] Professional sports firms, however, do not number among the large corporations at which "Employee Bill of Rights" proposals are directed.

Interestingly, monopsonistic power in the labor market may be a significant factor at the local government level. Evidence of monopsony exists in such fields as public education, fire and police protection, and nursing.[4]

THE NATURE OF EMPLOYER-EMPLOYEE AGREEMENTS

The Constitution of the United States does not extend the Bill of Rights and the due process clause of the Fourteenth Amendment to the private sector unless agents of the latter are performing public functions [*Marsh v. State of Alabama,* 66 S. Ct. 276 (1946)]. Instead of interpreting this limitation as an oversight of the founding fathers, the preceding discussion suggests that the distinctive treatment accorded governments reflects the conscious belief that market processes, more than political processes, yield a degree of protection to their participants that is closer to levels that those participants actually desire. It also suggests that this inherent difference justifies the institutionalization of civil liberties in one form of activity (political) and not in the other form (market).

This interpretation is consistent with the repeated refusal of the United States Supreme Court to interfere with the rights of employers and employees (corporate or otherwise) to make mutually agreeable arrangements concerning the exercise of civil liberties (otherwise protected under the Constitution) on the job or in connection with job-related activities. (The obvious legislative exceptions to this generalization are the Wagner Act of 1935 and the Taft-Hartley Act of 1947. These acts proscribe the free speech rights of employers with regard to their possible influence over union elections on their own property, while allowing labor to use that same property for similar purposes.)

In the absence of monopsonistic power, the substantive content of an employer-employee relationship is the result of explicit and implicit bargaining that leaves both parties better off than they would be if they had not entered into the relationship. That both are better off follows because each is free to end the employment relationship at will—unless, of course, contractual relationships specify otherwise. Americans have demonstrated at an impressive rate a willingness to leave current employment for better pecuniary and nonpecuniary alternatives. During non-recessionary periods, employee resignations contribute significantly to turnover statistics. In an uncertain world, the workers who resign generate valuable information about all terms and conditions under which firms and would-be employees can reach agreement.

THE COSTS OF WORKPLACE CIVIL LIBERTIES

If information about each party to employment and information about potential and actual performance are costly, both firms *and* employees seek ways to economize. Indeed, the functions of a firm, from the viewpoint of employees, are to screen job applicants and to monitor on-the-job activities. A firm's final output is often a result of the joint efforts of workers rather than a result of the sum of the workers' separate efforts. This jointness of production makes individual effort difficult to measure, and on-the-job shirking becomes relatively inexpensive for any given employee. The reason is precisely that all employees must share the cost of one employee's "goldbricking." As a consequence, shirking, if done excessively, threatens the earning opportunities of other workers. Other white collar crimes, such as pilfering finished products or raw materials, have similar consequences.

To protect themselves from these threats, workers use the firm as a monitoring agent, implicitly authorizing it to direct work, manage tools, observe work practices and other on-the-job employee activities, and discipline transgressors. If employers function efficiently, the earnings of workers will be higher than if the monitoring function were not provided.[5]

Efficient *employer* activities, however, may appear to others, including some employees, to be flagrant violations of personal privacy from the perspective of the First, Fourth, Fifth, and Ninth Amendments to the Constitution. These employer activities, on the contrary, are the result of implied agreements between employers and employees, consummated by demand and supply forces in the labor market. The reduction in personal liberty that workers sustain in a firm has a smaller value for them, at the margin, than the increase in earning power that results. Thus, limitations on personal liberty in a firm, unlike such limitations in governments, are not manifestations of tyranny; they are, instead, the product of a mutually preferred arrangement.

It should not be surprising that higher-paying firms and firms entrusting more valuable decision-making responsibility to some employees would invest relatively more resources than would other firms in gathering potentially revealing information about the qualifications of prospective employees and about the actions of existing employees. Since the larger a firm is, by asset size or by employee number, the more likely it is to be a corporation, it should also not be surprising that corporations are among the firms that devote relatively large amounts of resources to gathering information of a personal nature about employees.

Prohibiting the gathering of such information by superimposing an "Employee Bill of Rights" on the employment relationship has the effect of penalizing a specific group of employees. This group is composed of those persons who cannot otherwise compete successfully for positions of responsibility, trust, or loyalty because the high cost of information makes it unprofitable for them to distinguish themselves from other workers without desirable job characteristics. Thus, federal protection of the civil liberties of employees in the marketplace may actually harm those who wish to waive such rights as a less expensive way of competing.

Under an "Employee Bill of Rights," the process of searching for new employees and the process of managing existing employees are relatively more costly for an employer. This greater cost will be reflected not only in personnel policy but also in the cost of producing final outputs and in the prices consumers pay for them. An effect of an "Employee Bill of Rights" would be limited dimensions on which employees may compete with each other. Although there are precedents for such limitations (for example, federal minimum wage laws), it is important to recognize that this kind of protection may have unintended effects on the welfare of large numbers of employees. The anticompetitive effects of institutionalizing due process and civil liberties have long been recognized by trade unions. These effects constitute an important reason for the interest unions have in formalizing the procedures employers use in hiring, firing, promoting, demoting, rewarding, and penalizing union employees. It is false to argue, nevertheless, that an absence of formal procedures and rules in nonunionized firms is evidence that workers are at the mercy of unfettered employers, or that workers are more likely to be exploited if they are located in corporations rather than in noncorporate forms of organization.

Even the most powerful corporations must go to an effectively competitive labor market for their personnel. Prospective employees see arbitrary and oppressive personnel policies as relatively unattractive working conditions requiring compensation of pecuniary and nonpecuniary differentials over and above what they would receive from alternative employments. Those workers who want more certainty in the exercise of civil liberties pay for that certainty by forgoing these compensating differentials. This reasoning suggests that the degree of desired democracy in the labor market is amenable to the same forces that determine wages and working conditions. There is neither evidence nor persuasive arguments that suggest that workers in large corporations somehow have been excluded from the process that determines the degree of democracy they want.

NOTES

1. Ralph Nader, Mark Green and Joel Seligman, *Taming the Giant Corporation.* (New York: Norton, 1976), pp. 180–197.
2. Robert L. Bunting, *Employer Concentration in Local Labor Markets.* (Chapel Hill: The University of North Carolina Press, 1962). And "A Note on Large Firms and Labor Market Concentration," *Journal of Political Economy* 74 (August 1966), pp. 403–406.

3. James S. Mofsky, *Blue Sky Restrictions on New Business Promotions.* (New York: Matthew Bender, 1971).
4. Eugene J. Devine, *An Analysis of Manpower Shortages in Local Government.* (New York: Praeger, 1970).
5. Armen A. Alchian and Harold Demsetz, "Production, Information Costs, and Economic Organization," *American Economic Review* 62 (December 1972), pp. 777–795.

Drug Testing in Employment

Joseph R. Des Jardins
Ronald Duska
Des Jardins—Department of Philosophy, College of St. Benedict.
Duska—Department of Philosophy, Rosemont College; and Executive Director, Society for Business Ethics

According to one survey, nearly one-half of all *Fortune* 500 companies were planning to administer drug tests to employees and prospective employees by the end of 1987.[1] Counter to what seems to be the current trend in favor of drug testing, we will argue that it is rarely legitimate to override an employee's or applicant's right to privacy by using such tests or procedures.[2]

OPENING STIPULATIONS

We take privacy to be an "employee right" by which we mean a presumptive moral entitlement to receive certain goods or be protected from certain harms in the workplace.[3] Such a right creates a *prima facie* obligation on the part of the employer to provide the relevant goods or, as in this case, refrain from the relevant harmful treatment. These rights prevent employees from being placed in the fundamentally coercive position where they must choose between their job and other basic human goods.

Further, we view the employer-employee relationship as essentially contractual. The employer-employee relationship is an economic one and, unlike relationships such as those between a government and its citizens or a parent and a child, exists primarily as a means for satisfying the economic interests of the contracting parties. The obligations that each party incurs are only those that it voluntarily takes on. Given such a contractual relationship, certain areas of the employee's life remain their own private concern and no employer has a right to invade them. On these presumptions we maintain that certain information about an employee is rightfully private, i.e. the employee has a right to privacy.

THE RIGHT TO PRIVACY

According to George Brenkert, a right to privacy involves a three-place relation between a person A, some information X, and another person B. The right to privacy is violated only when B deliberately comes to possess information X about A, and no relationship between A and B exists which would justify B's coming to know X about A.[4] Thus, for example, the relationship one has with a mortgage company would justify that company's coming to know about one's salary, but the relationship one has with a neighbor does not justify the neighbor's coming to know that information.

Hence, an employee's right to privacy is violated whenever personal information is requested, collected and/or used by an employer in a way or for any purpose that is *irrelevant to* or *in violation of* the contractual relationship that exists between employer and employee.

Since drug testing is a means for obtaining information, the information sought must be relevant to the contract in order for the drug testing not to violate privacy. Hence, we must first decide if knowledge of drug use obtained by drug testing is job relevant. In cases where the knowledge of drug

---

Excerpted from "Drug Testing in Employment" by J.R. Des Jardins and R. Duska, *Business and Professional Ethics Journal,* volume 6, number 3, Fall 1987, pp. 3–21. Copyright by J.R. Des Jardins and R. Duska. Printed by permission of the authors. [*Authors' note:* Versions of this paper were read to the Department of Philosophy at Southern Connecticut State College and to the Society of Business Ethics. The authors would like to thank those people, as well as Robert Baum and Norman Bowie, the editors of *Business and Professional Ethics Journal,* for their many helpful comments.]

use is *not* relevant, there appears to be no justification for subjecting employees to drug tests. In cases where information of drug use is job relevant, we need to consider if, when, and under what conditions using a means such as drug testing to obtain that knowledge is justified.

IS KNOWLEDGE OF DRUG USE JOB RELEVANT INFORMATION?

There seem to be two arguments used to establish that knowledge of drug use is job relevant information. The first argument claims that drug use adversely affects job performance thereby leading to lower productivity, higher costs, and consequently lower profits. Drug testing is seen as a way of avoiding these adverse effects. According to some estimates twenty-five billion ($25,000,000,000) dollars are lost each year in the United States because of drug use.[5] This occurs because of loss in productivity, increase in costs due to theft, increased rates in health and liability insurance, and such. Since employers are contracting with an employee for the performance of specific tasks, employers seem to have a legitimate claim upon whatever personal information is relevant to an employee's ability to do the job.

The second argument claims that drug use has been and can be responsible for considerable harm to the employee him/herself, fellow employees, the employer, and/or third parties, including consumers. In this case drug testing is defended because it is seen as a way of preventing possible harm. Further, since employers can be held liable for harms done both to third parties, e.g. customers, and to the employee or his/her fellow employees, knowledge of employee drug use will allow employers to gain information that can protect themselves from risks such as liability. But how good are these arguments? We turn to examine the arguments more closely.

THE FIRST ARGUMENT: JOB PERFORMANCE AND KNOWLEDGE OF DRUG USE

The first argument holds that drug use leads to lower productivity and consequently implies that a knowledge of drug use obtained through drug testing will allow an employer to increase productivity. It is generally assumed that people using certain drugs have their performances affected by such use. Since enhancing productivity is something any employer desires, any use of drugs that reduces productivity affects the employer in an undesirable way, and that use is, then, job relevant. If such production losses can be eliminated by knowledge of the drug use, then knowledge of that drug use is job relevant information.

On the surface this argument seems reasonable. Obviously some drug use in lowering the level of performance can decrease productivity. Since the employer is entitled to a certain level of performance and drug use adversely affects performance, knowledge of that use seems job relevant.

But this formulation of the argument leaves an important question unanswered. To what level of performance are employers entitled? Optimal performance, or some lower level? If some lower level, what? Employers have a valid claim upon some *certain level* of performance, such that a failure to perform up to this level would give the employer a justification for disciplining, firing or at least finding fault with the employee. But that does not necessarily mean that the employer has a right to a maximum or optimal level of performance, a level above and beyond a certain level of acceptability. It might be nice if the employee gives an employer a maximum effort or optimal performance, but that is above and beyond the call of the employee's duty and the employer can hardly claim a right at all times to the highest level of performance of which an employee is capable.

That there are limits on required levels of performance and productivity becomes clear if we recognize that job performance is person-related. It is person-related because one person's best efforts at a particular task might produce results well below the norm, while another person's minimal efforts might produce results abnormally high when compared to the norm. For example a professional baseball player's performance on a ball field will be much higher than the average person's since the average person is unskilled at baseball. We have all encountered people who work hard with little or no results as well as people who work little with phenomenal results. Drug use by very talented people might diminish their performance or productivity, but that performance would still be better than the performance of the average person or someone totally lacking in the skills required. That being said, the important question now is whether the employer is entitled to an employee's maximum effort and best results, or merely to an effort sufficient to perform the task expected.

If the relevant consideration is whether the employee is producing as expected (according to the normal demands of the position and contract) not whether he/she is producing as much as possible, then knowledge of drug use is irrelevant or unnecessary. Let's see why.

If the person is producing what is expected, knowledge of drug use on the grounds of production is irrelevant since, *ex hypothesi* the production is satisfactory. If, on the other hand, the performance suffers, then, to the extent that it slips below the level justifiably expected, the employer has *prima facie* grounds for warning, disciplining or releasing the employee. But the justification for this is the person's unsatisfactory performance, not the person's use of drugs. Accordingly, drug use information is either unnecessary or irrelevant and consequently there are not sufficient grounds to override the right of privacy. Thus, unless we can argue that an employer is entitled to optimal performance, the argument fails.

This counter-argument should make it clear that the information which is job relevant, and consequently which is not rightfully private, is information about an employee's level of performance and not information about the underlying causes of that level. The fallacy of the argument which promotes drug testing in the name of increased productivity is the assumption that each employee is obliged to perform at an optimal, or at least, quite high level. But this is required under few, if any, contracts. What is required contractually is meeting the normally expected levels of production or performing the tasks in the job-description adequately (not optimally). If one can do that under the influence of drugs, then on the grounds of job performance at least, drug use is rightfully private. If one cannot perform the task adequately, then the employee is not fulfilling the contract, and knowledge of the cause of the failure to perform is irrelevant on the contractual model.

Of course, if the employer suspects drug use or abuse as the cause of the unsatisfactory performance, then she might choose to help the person with counseling or rehabilitation. However, this does not seem to be something morally required of the employer. Rather, in the case of unsatisfactory performance, the employer has a *prima facie* justification for dismissing or disciplining the employee.

THE SECOND ARGUMENT: HARM AND THE KNOWLEDGE OF DRUG USE TO PREVENT HARM

Even though the performance argument is inadequate, there is an argument that seems somewhat stronger. This is an argument that takes into account the fact that drug use often leads to harm. Using a type of Millian argument that allows interference with a person's rights in order to prevent harm, we could argue that drug testing might be justified if such testing led to knowledge that would enable an employer to prevent harm.

Drug use certainly can lead to harming others. Consequently, if knowledge of such drug use can prevent harm, then, knowing whether or not one's employee uses drugs might be a legitimate concern of an employer in certain circumstances. This second argument claims that knowledge of the employee's drug use is job relevant because employees who are under the influence of drugs can pose a threat to the health and safety of themselves and others, and an employer who knows of that drug use and the harm it can cause has a responsibility to prevent it. Employers have both a general duty to prevent harm and the specific responsibility for harms done by their employees. Such responsibilities are sufficient reason for an employer to claim that information about an employee's drug use is relevant if that knowledge can prevent harm by giving the employer grounds for dismissing the employee or not allowing him/her to perform potentially harmful tasks. Employers might even claim a right to reduce unreasonable risks, in this case the risks involving legal and economic liability for harms caused by employees under the influence of drugs, as further justification for knowing about employee drug use.

But let us examine this more closely. Upon examination, certain problems arise, so that even if there is a possibility of justifying drug testing to prevent harm, some caveats have to be observed and some limits set out.

Jobs with Potential to Cause Harm

In the first place, it is not clear that every job is one with a potential to cause harm, or at least with potential to cause harm sufficient to override a *prima facie* right to privacy. To say that employers can use drug testing where that can prevent harm is not to say that every employer has the right to know about the drug use of every employee. Not every job poses a serious enough threat to justify an employer coming to know this information.

In deciding which jobs pose serious enough threats certain guidelines should be followed. First the potential for harm should be *clear* and *present.* Perhaps all jobs in some extended way pose potential threats to human well-being. We suppose an accountant's error could pose a threat of harm to someone somewhere. But some jobs like those of airline pilots, school bus drivers, public transit drivers and surgeons, are jobs in which unsatisfactory performance poses a clear and present danger to others. It would be much harder to make an argument that job performances by auditors, secretaries, executive vice-presidents for public relations, college teachers, professional athletes, and the like, could cause harm if those performances were carried on under the influence of drugs. They would cause harm only in exceptional cases.[6]

Not Every Person Is to Be Tested

But, even if we can make a case that a particular job involves a clear and present danger for causing harm if performed under the influence of drugs, it is not appropriate to treat everyone holding such a job the same. Not every job-holder is equally threatening. There is less reason to investigate an airline pilot for drug use if that pilot has a twenty-year record of exceptional service than there is to investigate a pilot whose behavior has become erratic and unreliable recently, or than one who reports to work smelling of alcohol and slurring his words. Presuming that every airline pilot is equally threatening is to deny individuals the respect that they deserve as autonomous, rational agents. It is to ignore previous history and significant differences. It is also probably inefficient and leads to the lowering of morale. It is the likelihood of causing harm, and not the fact of being an airline pilot *per se,* that is relevant in deciding which employees in critical jobs to test.

So, even if knowledge of drug use is justifiable to prevent harm, we must be careful to limit this justification to a range of jobs and people where the potential for harm is clear and present. The jobs must be jobs that clearly can cause harm, and the specific employee should not be someone who is reliable with a history of such reliability. Finally, the drugs being tested should be those drugs, the use of which in those jobs is really potentially harmful.

LIMITATIONS ON DRUG TESTING POLICIES

Even when we identify those jobs and individuals where knowledge of drug use would be job relevant information, we still need to examine whether some procedural limitations should not be placed upon the employer's testing for drugs. We have said that in cases where a real threat of harm exists and where evidence exists suggesting that a particular employee poses such a threat, an employer could be justified in knowing about drug use in order to prevent the potential harm. But we need to recognize that as long as the employer has the discretion for deciding when the potential for harm is clear and present, and for deciding which employees pose the threat of harm, the possibility of abuse is great. Thus, some policy limiting the employer's power is called for.

Just as criminal law places numerous restrictions protecting individual dignity and liberty on the state's pursuit of its goals, so we should expect that some restrictions be placed on an employer in order to protect innocent employees from harm (including loss of job and damage to one's personal and professional reputation). Thus, some system of checks upon an employer's discretion in these matters seems advisable. Workers covered by collective bargaining agreements or individual contracts might be protected by clauses in those agreements that specify which jobs pose a real threat of harm (e.g. pilots but not cabin attendants) and what constitutes a just cause for investigating drug use. Local, state, and federal legislatures might do the same for workers not covered by employment contracts. What needs to be set up is a just employment relationship—one in which an employee's expectations and responsibilities are specified in advance and in which an employer's discretionary authority to discipline or dismiss an employee is limited.

Beyond that, any policy should accord with the nature of the employment relationship. Since that relationship is a contractual one, it should meet the condition of a morally valid contract, which is informed consent. Thus, in general, we would argue that only methods that have received the informed consent of employees can be used in acquiring information about drug use.[7]

A drug-testing policy that requires all employees to submit to a drug test or to jeopardize their job would seem coercive and therefore unacceptable. Being placed in such a fundamentally coercive position of having to choose between one's job and one's privacy does not provide the conditions for a truly free consent. Policies that are unilaterally established by employers would likewise be unacceptable. Working with employees to develop company policy seems the only way to insure that the policy will be fair to both parties. Prior notice of testing would also be required in order to give employees the option of freely refraining from drug use. It is morally preferable to prevent drug use than to punish users after the fact, since this approach treats employees as capable of making rational and informed decisions.

Further procedural limitations seem advisable as well. Employees should be notified of the results of the test, they should be entitled to appeal the results (perhaps through further tests by an independent laboratory) and the information obtained through tests ought to be kept confidential. In summary, limitations upon employer discretion for administering drug tests can be derived from the nature of the employment contract and from the recognition that drug testing is justified by the desire to prevent harm, not the desire to punish wrong doing.

EFFECTIVENESS OF DRUG TESTING

Having declared that the employer might have a right to test for drug use in order to prevent harm, we still need to examine the second argument a little more closely.

It is important to keep in mind that: (1) if the knowledge doesn't help prevent the harm, the testing is not justified on prevention grounds; (2) if the testing doesn't provide the relevant knowledge it is not justified either; and finally, (3) even if it was justified, it would be undesirable if a more effective means of preventing harm were discovered.

Upon examination, the links between drug testing, knowledge of drug use, and prevention of harm are not as clear as they are presumed to be. As we investigate, it begins to seem that the knowledge of the drug use even though relevant in some instances is not the most effective means to prevent harm.

Let us turn to this last consideration first. Is drug testing the most effective means for preventing harm caused by drug use?

Consider. If someone exhibits obviously drugged or drunken behavior, then this behavior itself is grounds for preventing the person from continuing in the job. Administering urine or blood tests, sending the specimens out for testing and waiting for a response, will not prevent harm in this instance. Such drug testing because of the time lapse involved, is equally superfluous in those cases where an employee is in fact under the influence of drugs, but exhibits no or only subtly impaired behaviour.

Thus, even if one grants that drug testing somehow prevents harm an argument can be made that there might be much more effective methods of preventing potential harm such as administering dexterity tests of the type employed by police in possible drunk-driving cases, or requiring suspect pilots to pass flight simulator tests.[8] Eye-hand coordination, balance, reflexes, and reasoning ability can all be tested with less intrusive, more easily administered, reliable technologies which give instant results. Certainly if an employer has just cause for believing that a specific employee presently poses a real threat of causing harm, such methods are just more effective in all ways than are urinalysis and blood testing.

Even were it possible to refine drug tests so that accurate results were immediately available, that knowledge would only be job relevant if the drug use was clearly the cause of impaired job performance that could harm people. Hence, testing behavior still seems more direct and effective in preventing harm than testing for the presence of drugs *per se*.

In some cases, drug use might be connected with potential harms not by being causally connected to motor-function impairment, but by causing personality disorders (e.g. paranoia, delusions, etc.) that affect judgmental ability. Even though in such cases a *prima facie* justification for urinalysis or blood testing might exist, the same problems of effectiveness persist. How is the knowledge of the drug use attained by urinalysis and/or blood testing supposed to prevent the harm? Only if there is a causal link between the use and the potentially harmful behavior would such knowledge be relevant. Even if we get the results of the test immediately, there is the necessity to have an established causal link between specific drug use and anticipated harmful personality disorders in specific people.

But even when this link is established, it would seem that less intrusive means could be used to detect the potential problems, rather than relying upon the assumption of a causal link. Psychological tests of judgment, perception and memory, for example, would be a less intrusive and more direct means for acquiring the relevant information, which is, after all, the likelihood of causing harm and not the presence of drugs *per se*. In short, drug testing even in these cases doesn't seem to be very effective in preventing harm on the spot.

Still, this does not mean it is not effective at all. Where it is most effective in preventing harm is in its getting people to stop using drugs or in identifying serious drug addiction. Or to put it another way, urinalysis and blood tests for drug use are most effective in preventing potential harm when they serve as a deterrent to drug use *before* it occurs, since it is very difficult to prevent harm by diagnosing drug use *after* it has occurred but before the potentially harmful behavior takes place.

Drug testing can be an effective deterrent when there is regular or random testing of all employees. This will prevent harm by inhibiting (because of the fear of detection) drug use by those who are occasional users and those who do not wish to be detected.

It will probably not inhibit or stop the use by the chronic addicted user, but it will allow an employer to discover the chronic user or addict, assuming that the tests are accurately administered and reliably evaluated. If the chronic user's addiction would probably lead to harmful behavior to others, the harm is prevented by taking that user off the job. Thus regular or random testing will prevent harms done by deterring the occasional user and by detecting the chronic user.

But we have said that testing without probable cause is unacceptable. Any type of regular testing of all employees is unacceptable. We have argued that testing employees without first establishing probable cause is an unjustifiable violation of employee privacy. Given this, and given the expense of general and regular testing of all employees (especially if this is done by responsible laboratories), it is more likely that random testing will be employed as the means of deterrence. But surely testing of randomly selected innocent employees is as intrusive to those tested as is regular testing. The argument that there will be fewer tests is correct on quantitative grounds, but qualitatively the intrusion and unacceptability are the same. The claim that employers should be allowed to sacrifice the well-being of (some few) innocent employees to deter (some equally few) potentially harmful employees seems, on the face of it, unfair. Just as we do not allow the state randomly to tap the telephones of just any citizen in order to prevent crime, so we ought not to allow employers to drug test all employees randomly to prevent harm. To do so is again to treat innocent employees solely as a means to the end of preventing potential harm.

This leaves only the use of regular or random drug testing as a deterrent in those cases where probable cause exists for believing that a particular employee poses a threat of harm. It would seem that in this case, the drug testing is acceptable. In such cases only the question of effectiveness remains: Are the standard techniques of urinalysis and blood testing more effective means for preventing harms than alternatives such as dexterity tests? It seems they are effective in different ways. The dexterity tests show immediately if someone is incapable of performing a task, or will perform one in such a way as to cause harm to others. The urinalysis and blood-testing will prevent harm indirectly by getting the occasional user to curtail their use, and by detecting the habitual or addictive user, which will allow the employer to either give treatment to the addictive personality or remove them from the job. Thus we can conclude that drug testing is effective in a limited way, but aside from inhibiting occasional users because of fear of detection, and discovering habitual users, it seems problematic that it does much to prevent harm that couldn't be achieved by other means.

In summary, then, we have seen that drug use is not always job relevant, and if drug use is not job relevant, information about it is certainly not job relevant. In the case of performance it may be a cause of some decreased performance, but it is the performance itself that is relevant to an employee's position, not what prohibits or enables him to do the job. In the case of potential harm being done by an employee under the influence of drugs, the drug use seems job relevant, and in this case drug testing to prevent harm might be legitimate. But how this is practical is another question. It would seem that standard motor dexterity or mental dexterity tests, immediately prior to job performance, are more efficacious ways of preventing harm, unless one concludes that drug use invariably and necessarily leads to harm. One must trust the individuals in any system in order for that system to work. One cannot police everything. It might work to randomly test people, to find drug users, and to weed out the few to forestall possible future harm, but are the harms prevented sufficient to over-ride the rights of privacy of the people who are innocent and to overcome the possible abuses we have mentioned? It seems not.

Clearly, a better method is to develop safety checks immediately prior to the performance of a job. Have a surgeon or a pilot or a bus driver pass a few reasoning and motor-skill tests before work. The cause of the lack of a skill, which lack might lead to harm, is really a secondary issue.

NOTES

1. *The New Republic,* March 31, 1986.
2. This trend primarily involves screening employees for such drugs as marijuana, cocaine, amphetamines, barbiturates, and opiates (e.g., heroin, methadone and morphine). While alcohol is also a drug that can be abused in the workplace, it seldom is among the drugs mentioned in conjunction with employee testing. We believe that testing which proves justified for controlled substances will, *a fortiori,* be justified for alcohol as well.
3. "A Defense of Employee Rights," Joseph Des Jardins and John McCall, *Journal of Business Ethics* 4, (1985). We should emphasize that our concern is with the *moral* rights of privacy for employees and not with any specific or prospective *legal* rights. Readers interested in pursuing the legal aspects of employee drug testing should consult: "Workplace Privacy Issues and Employer Screening Policies" by Richard Lehr and David Middlebrooks in *Employee Relations Law Journal* (Vol. 11, no. 3) pp. 407–21; and "Screening Workers for Drugs: A Legal and Ethical Framework" by Mark Rothstein, in *Employee Relations Law Journal* (Vol. 11, no. 3) pp. 422–36.
4. "Privacy, Polygraphs, and Work," George Brenkert, *Journal of Business and Professional Ethics* vol. 1, no. 1 (Fall 1981). For a more general discussion of privacy in the workplace see "Privacy in Employment" by Joseph Des Jardins, in *Moral Rights in the Workplace* edited by Gertrude Ezorsky, (SUNY Press, 1987). A good resource for philosophical work on privacy can be found in "Recent Work on the Concept of Privacy" by W.A. Parent, in *American Philosophical Quarterly* (Vol. 20, Oct. 1983) pp. 341–56.
5. *U.S. News & World Report* Aug. 1983; *Newsweek* May 1983.
6. Obviously we are speaking here of harms that go beyond the simple economic harm which results from unsatisfactory job performance. These economic harms were discussed in the first argument above. Further, we ignore such "harms" as providing bad role-models for adolescents, harms often used to justify drug tests for professional athletes. We think it

unreasonable to hold an individual responsible for the image he/she provides to others.

7. The philosophical literature on informed consent is often concerned with "informed consent" in a medical context. For an interesting discussion of informed consent in the workplace, see Mary Gibson, *Worker's Rights* (Rowman and Allanheld, 1983) especially pp. 13–14 and 74–75.
8. For a reiteration of this point and a concise argument against drug testing see Lewis L. Maltby, "Why Drug Testing Is a Bad Idea," *Inc.* June, 1987, pp. 152–153. "But the fundamental flaw with drug testing is that it tests for the wrong thing. A realistic program to detect workers whose condition puts the company or other people at risk would test for the condition that actually creates the danger. The reason drunk or stoned airline pilots and truck drivers are dangerous is their reflexes, coordination, and timing are deficient. This impairment could come from many situations—drugs, alcohol, emotional problems—the list is almost endless. A serious program would recognize that the real problem is workers' impairment, and test for that. Pilots can be tested in flight simulators. People in other jobs can be tested by a trained technician in about 20 minutes—at the job site." p. 152.

Drug Testing in the Workplace: Whose Rights Take Precedence?

Michael Waldholz
Staff reporter, *The Wall Street Journal*

Amid growing national concern over substance abuse, drug testing in the workplace has become an explosive issue.

To those who support it, testing, which is commonly done through urinalysis, is often a question of protecting business interests. "For us, it is the financial security of billions of dollars entrusted to us by clients," says Edwin A. Weihenmayer, vice president and director of the human-resources group at Kidder, Peabody & Co. The New York-based investment bank began drug testing this summer as part of a comprehensive drug-prevention program.

Critics, for their part, tend to view such measures as unnecessarily or even unconstitutionally invasive. "For us, it just doesn't make good business sense to police our employees' private lives," says Lewis L. Maltby, vice president of Drexelbrook Engineering Co. The small instrumentation company in Horsham, Pa., has decided against drug tests.

What follows is a debate organized by *The Wall Street Journal* between the two executives.

Mr. Maltby: We've considered testing and totally rejected it. One reason is the accuracy problem. In an often-cited study, the U.S. Centers for Disease Control got false positive results of up to 66% from 13 randomly chosen private labs. The CDC said none of the labs were reliable. That isn't a very strong base to build a program on.

Mr. Weihenmayer: You've hit on the one controversial aspect of drug-prevention programs. Our program consists of policy statements and a lot of communication: manager-awareness training, employee-assistance programs. And, yes, testing—of new hires, and just recently we began unannounced testing of current employees too.

We want to create a workplace mentality where people say, "If I work at Kidder, I don't do drugs." I see our workers accepting that objective, and I believe it's due to an umbrella of programs. It wouldn't be happening just with testing, but testing gives our program teeth.

Testing can be inaccurate if you use lousy labs, fail to monitor movement of the urine specimens, don't do reconfirmation tests. But we've addressed those problems. When an employee provides a sample, it is sealed and signed. Prescription-drug use is noted. Everywhere the sample moves, it's signed. If a test is positive for drugs, we feel we have an obligation to reconfirm. And if that's positive, we go back and give the employee a chance to explain any extenuating circumstance before we act.

Mr. Maltby: Ed is right: If the only test you use is the inexpensive test, which costs $15 or so but which is highly unreliable, you'll have serious problems. But the state-of-the-art test for reconfirmation costs from $75 to $100, which will multiply your costs an order of magnitude or so. Spending that much money isn't cost-justified for most companies. But unless you do, you're going to be firing people who shouldn't be fired.

Mr. Weihenmayer: If it's an important business issue, you'll spend the money. We'll spend over $100,000 this year on our drug program. And that's just direct costs. A lot more cost is involved in dialoguing with our 7,000 employees, explaining why we test, answering all their questions. But I don't think you can put a price tag on the comfort that our clients have with the way we're processing and managing their money.

Mr. Maltby: I think we disagree on the relevance of the information you get from testing. Kidder tests, at least in part, to assure its customers. Our only concern is job performance. But drug testing isn't a job-performance test. For instance, traces of drugs can remain in the system for days. I can't tell, if an employee takes a drug test on Monday, whether he is impaired now, whether he is sober as a judge or whether he had a couple of puffs on a joint Saturday night.

Mr. Weihenmayer: We're concerned about performance. We're concerned about the effects of alcohol, but I can tell from someone's behavior if they come to work drunk. Not so with drugs. About 80% of performance problems from drugs are invisible. I equate our concern with that of the airline industry. When you walk on a plane, you don't want pilots to just appear drug free. You want to be absolutely sure they are.

We're also concerned about the potential pressures that result from drug use, whether it's done at work or not. Drug use can be expensive, and can exert financial demands—temptations—we don't want on employees who are dealing with transactions worth millions of dollars.

Mr. Maltby: I challenge the idea that you can't detect drug-related deterioration in job performance. In my experience, a really good supervisor who's paying attention is the best way to detect a problem. A supervisor should be watching if employees come in late, if they are sick often on Mondays, whether their error rate is up or their attention span is down. A well-tuned-in supervisor is a much better indicator of whether an employee has a problem than some testing program.

I really don't think, as Ed is saying, that for the sake of client perception you can fire someone for what they did on Saturday night if it's not affecting their job performance.

Mr. Weihenmayer: I can tell you there are situations where supervisors were paying attention, where performance seemed fine, but that until an account problem surfaced through computer controls we didn't know we had a drug-related problem. We just aren't prepared to tolerate a problem until it arises, just as the airline industry can't tolerate drug use until a collision makes it visible.

Our program isn't designed to get rid of people. We invest a lot of money to find people and train them. And what we want to do is influence them toward working in our way, which is drug free. We want people to say, "I used marijuana casually, but this job is so important I quit." We can't afford to risk whatever results from that casual use, whether it affects the job or a person's financial integrity. Security in an industry dealing with billions of dollars demands that.

Mr. Maltby: We just don't think you need to test to keep the workplace drug free. After all, drugs are just a symptom of something else. What you really want is a committed, dedicated work force, people who like their jobs and care enough not to come to work stoned. What we do is select and nurture employees that are going to do a good job. We think if we do that, the drug problem takes care of itself.

We're incredibly careful about the people we hire. We do multiple reference checks, even for floor sweepers. And then we take a lot of time and trouble to really know our people. Our supervisors know their people's families; they work to build trust and rapport. If they have problems financial or otherwise, (the supervisors) want to know about it, and we have programs to provide them help. We've found that with that kind of trust people will confide in you when a problem arises, before they feel they must use drugs in a dangerous way. I think the proof is that we believe drug problems affect only about 1% of our work force.

Mr. Weihenmayer: The relationship and concern expressed here is commendable, and everyone should strive for that. But the point is you think your drug incidence is 1%, but you don't know. Even if you do a thorough check, someone's going to get exposed to drugs after they join you.

Mr. Maltby: The implication is that we have employees running around with problems and we don't know it. We produce precision instrumentation for chemical plants and refineries. If we had drug problems at work, it would affect our product and cause life-threatening problems, and we'd be up to our eyeballs in lawsuits.

Mr. Weihenmayer: Our belief, put simply, is that certain industries require this type of assured security—pilots, air-traffic controllers, for instance. I think protecting a person's savings is crucial too. We want people to feel Kidder is doing everything possible to protect their savings. At the same time, we are trying to be very sensitive to the needs of our employees.

Mr. Maltby: You're saying you can have a testing program *and* the kind of employee relations I'm talking about. I say you can't. The two are inimical. Ours is based on a relationship that doesn't just come from a paycheck. When you say to an employee, "You're doing a great job; just the same, I want you to pee in this jar and I'm sending someone to watch you," you've undermined that trust.

Mr. Weihenmayer: I'll grant you it makes it more difficult. It bothers us if they're bothered. That's why we spend so much time explaining our objectives. Also, when we test a department, everyone from top to bottom is tested. For most employees who test positive, we reexplain our policy, ask them to commit themselves to be drug free and to undergo periodic testing. The company makes available, at its expense, help if they feel they need it. But if they test positive again, they are subject to immediate termination.

We've had employees who say in good conscience they can't take the test. We treat that person with respect, but we explain that on this matter we have to call the shots. You may anguish a bit over the damage which is done, but it's extremely important for the program's integrity that everyone take the test.

We don't have watchers. It would make the program more accurate, but we have drawn the line because it would be too embarrassing.

Mr. Maltby: But that's the kind of swamp you get into with testing. Right now, the threat to the program is small. But as people learn how to beat the system, the only way you're going to keep people from monkeying around is to watch them.

Mr. Weihenmayer: I don't think it will be a problem. Who is going to carry a urine sample around 365 days of the year?

The Right to Risk Information and the Right to Refuse Health Hazards in the Workplace

Ruth R. Faden
Tom L. Beauchamp
Faden—Senior Research Scholar, Kennedy Institute of Ethics, Georgetown University
Beauchamp—Senior Research Scholar, Kennedy Institute of Ethics, Georgetown University

In recent years, the right of employees to know about health hazards in the workplace has emerged as a major issue in occupational health policy.[1] This paper focuses on several philosophical and policy-oriented problems about the right to know

From *Ethical Theory and Business,* Tom L. Beauchamp and Norman E. Bowie, eds., 3rd edition (Englewood Cliffs, NJ: Prentice-Hall, Inc., 1988,) pp. 226–33.

[*Author's note:* We are indebted to Ilise Feitshans for helpful comments and criticisms on the 1987 revision. Parts of the earlier article had appeared in the *Canadian Journal of Philosophy,* Supplementary Volume, 1982.]

and correlative duties to disclose. Also addressed are related rights, such as the right to refuse hazardous work and the right of workers to contribute to the development of safety standards in the workplace.

I

A general consensus has gradually evolved in government and industry that there is a right to know, and correlatively that there is both a moral and legal obligation to disclose relevant information to workers. The National Institute for Occupational Safety and Health (NIOSH) and other U.S. federal agencies informed the U.S. Senate as early as July 1977 that "workers have the right to know whether or not they are exposed to hazardous chemical and physical agents regulated by the Federal Government."[2] The Occupational Safety and Health Administration (OSHA) promulgated regulations guaranteeing workers access to medical and exposure records in 1980,[3] and then developed regulations in 1983 and 1986 pertaining to the right to know about hazardous chemicals and requiring right-to-know training programs in many industries.[4] Legislation has also passed in numerous states and municipalities that are often more stringent than federal requirements.[5] For example, one of the earliest state bills, in New York, declared that employees and their representatives have a right to "*all* information relating to toxic substances"—a right that cannot be "waived as a condition of employment."[6] Many corporations—including Monsanto, DuPont, and Hercules—have also initiated right-to-know programs.

Although the general view that workers have some form of right to information about health hazards is now well established under law, there is no consensus about the nature and extent of an employer's moral or legal obligation to disclose such information. Considerable ambiguity also attends the nature and scope of the right—that is, which protections and actions the right entails, and to whom these rights apply.[7] For example, there is often a failure to distinguish between disclosing already available information, seeking information through literature searches or new research, and communicating about hazards through educational or other training programs. It is also often unclear whether there exists an affirmative duty to disclose information about health hazards to workers or merely a duty to honor worker-initiated or physician-initiated requests for access to records. What corporations owe their workers over and above the demands of federal and state requirements is likewise little discussed in the literature.

II

The belief that citizens and communities in general (and sometimes workers in particular) have a right to know about significant risks is reflected in a diverse set of recent laws and federal regulations in the United States. These include The Freedom of Information Act; The Federal Insecticide, Fungicide, and Rodenticide Amendments and Regulations; The Motor Vehicle and School Bus Safety Amendments; The Truth-in-Lending Act; The Pension Reform Act; The Real Estate Settlement Procedures Act; The Federal Food, Drug, and Cosmetic Act; The Consumer Product Safety Act; and The Toxic Substances Control Act. These acts commonly require manufacturers and other businesses to make available guidebooks, explanations of products, and warranties. Taken together, the implicit message of this corpus of legislation is that manufacturers and other businesses have a moral (and in some cases a legal) obligation to disclose information without which individuals could not adequately decide about matters of participation, usage, employment, or enrollment.[8]

Recent legal developments in the employee's right-to-know controversy have been consistent with this general trend toward disclosure and have included a more sweeping notion of corporate responsibility to provide adequate information to workers than had previously prevailed. These developments could have a pervasive and revolutionary effect on major American corporations. Until the 1983 final OSHA Hazard Communication Standard went into effect in 1986,[9] workers did not routinely receive extensive information from many employers. Now some corporations are beginning to establish model programs. For example, the

Monsanto Company has a right-to-know program in which it distributes information on hazardous chemicals at its 53 plants, screens its employees, and both notifies and monitors past and current employees exposed to carcinogenic chemicals. Hercules Inc. has training sessions using videotapes with frank discussions of workers' anxieties. The tapes include depictions of dangers and of on-the-job accidents. Those employees who have seen the Hercules film are then instructed how to read safety data and how to protect themselves.[10]

That such programs are needed in many corporations is evident from the sobering statistics on worker exposure and injury and on dangerous chemicals in the workplace. The annual Registry of Toxic Effects of Chemical Substances lists over 25,000 hazardous chemicals, at least 8,000 of which are present in the workplace. As OSHA pointed out in the preamble to its final Hazard Communication Standard, an estimated 25 million largely uninformed workers in North America (1 in 4 workers) are exposed to toxic substances regulated by the federal government. About 6,000 American workers die from workplace injuries each year, and perhaps as many as 100,000 deaths annually are caused in some measure by workplace exposure and consequent disease. One percent of the labor force is exposed to known carcinogens, and over 44,000 U.S. workers are exposed *fulltime* to OSHA-regulated carcinogens.[11]

III

The most developed models of general disclosure obligations and the right to know are presently found in the extensive literature on informed consent, which also deals with informed refusal. This literature developed largely in the context of fiduciary relationships between physicians and patients, where there are broadly recognized moral and legal obligations to disclose known risks (and benefits) associated with a proposed treatment or research maneuver.

No parallel obligation has traditionally been recognized in nonfiduciary relationships, such as that between management and workers. Risks in this environment have traditionally been handled largely by workmen's compensation laws that were originally designed for problems of accident in instances of immediately assessable damage. Duties to warn or to disclose are irrelevant under the "no-fault" conception operative in workmen's compensation, and thus these duties went undeveloped.

However, needs for information in clinical medicine and in the workplace have become more similar in light of recent knowledge about occupational disease—in particular, knowledge about the serious long-term risks of injury, disease, and death from exposure to toxic substances. In comparison to traditional accident and safety issues, these recently discovered risks to health in the workplace carry with them *increased* need for information on the basis of which a person may wish to take various actions, including choosing to forego employment completely, to refuse certain work environments within a place of employment, to request improved protective devices, or to request lowered levels of exposure.

Employee-employer relationships—unlike physician-patient relationships—are often confrontational, with few goals shared in common, and therefore with undisclosed risk to workers a constant danger. This danger of harm to employees and their relative powerlessness in the employer-employee relationship may not be sufficient to justify employer disclosure obligations in *all* industries, but few would deny that placing relevant information in the hands of workers seems morally appropriate in at least some cases. By what criteria, then, shall such disclosure obligations be determined?

One plausible argument is the following: Because large employers, unions, and government agencies must deal with multiple employees and complicated causal conditions, no standard should be *more* demanding than the so-called objective reasonable person standard. This is the standard of what a fair and informed member of the relevant community believes is needed. Under this standard, no employer, union, or other party should be held responsible for disclosing information beyond that needed to make an informed choice about the adequacy of safety precautions, industrial hygiene, long-term hazards, and the like, as determined by what the reasonable person in the community would judge to be the worker's need for information material to a decision about employment or working conditions.

It does not follow, however, that this general standard of disclosure is adequate for all individual disclosures. At least in the case of serious hazards—such as those involved in short-term, but concentrated doses of radiation—a *subjective* standard may be more appropriate.[12] In cases where disclosures to *individual* workers may be expected to have significant subjective impact that varies with each individual, the reasonable person standard should perhaps be supplemented by a standard that takes account of each worker's personal informational needs. A viable alternative might be to include the following as a component of all general disclosures under the reasonable person standard: "If you are concerned about the possible effect of hazards on your individual health, and you seek clarification or personal information, a company physician may be consulted by making an appointment." Perhaps the most satisfactory solution to the problem of a general standard is a compromise between a reasonable-person and a subjective standard: Whatever a reasonable person would judge material to the decision-making process should be disclosed, and in addition any remaining information that is material to an individual worker should be provided through a process of asking whether he or she has any additional or special concerns.[13]

This standard is indifferent as to which groups of workers will be included. Former workers, for example, often have as much or even more need for the information than do presently employed workers. The federal government has the names of approximately 250,000 former workers whose risk of cancer, heart disease, and lung disease has been increased by exposure to asbestos, polyvinyl chloride, benzene, arsenic, betanaphthyalamine, and dozens of other chemicals. Employers have the names of several million such workers. Legislation has been in and out of the U.S. Congress to notify workers at greatest risk so that checkups and diagnosis of disease can be made before an advanced stage.[14] At this writing, neither industry nor the government has developed a systematic program, claiming that the expense of notification would be enormous, that many workers would be unduly alarmed, and that existing screening and surveillance programs should prove adequate to the task of monitoring and treating disease. Critics charge, however, that existing programs are far from adequate and that, in any event, there are duties to inform workers so that they can pursue potential problems at their own initiative.[15]

IV

Despite the apparent consensus on the appropriateness of having some form of right to know in the workplace, there are reasons why it will prove difficult to implement this right. There are, for example, complicated questions about the kinds of information to be disclosed, by whom, to whom, and under what conditions. Trade secrets have also been a long-standing thorn in the side of progress, because companies resist disclosing information about an ingredient or process that they claim is a trade-secret.[16]

There is also the problem of what to do if workers are inhibited from taking actions they otherwise would take because of economic or other constraints. For example, in industries where ten people stand in line for every available position, bargaining for increased protection is an unlikely event. However, we must set most of these problems aside here in order to consider perhaps the most perplexing difficulty about the right to know in the workplace: the right to refuse hazardous work assignments and to have effective mechanisms for workers to reduce the risks they face.

In a limited range of cases, it is possible for informed workers to reject employment because they regard health and safety conditions as unacceptable. This decision is most likely to be reached in a job market where workers have alternative employment opportunities or where a worker is being offered a new assignment with the option of remaining in his or her current job. More commonly, however, workers are not in a position to respond to information about health hazards by seeking employment elsewhere. For the information to be useful, it must be possible for workers to effect changes on the job.

The United States Occupational Safety and

Health Act of 1970 (OSH Act)[17] confers a series of rights on employees that appear to give increased significance to the duty to disclose hazards in the workplace. Specifically, the OSH Act grants workers the right to request an OSHA inspection if they believe an OSHA standard has been violated or an imminent hazard exists. Under the Act, employees also have the right to "walk-around," that is, to participate in OSHA inspections of the worksite and to consult freely with the inspection officer. Most importantly, the OSH Act expressly protects employees who request an inspection or otherwise exercise their rights under the OSH Act from discharge or any discriminatory treatment in retaliation for legitimate safety and health complaints.[18]

While these worker rights under the OSH Act are important, they are not strong enough to assure that all workers have effective mechanisms for initiating inspections of suspected health hazards. Small businesses (those with fewer than ten workers) and federal, state, and municipal employees are not covered by the OSH Act. There are also questions about the ability of the Occupational Safety and Health Administration (OSHA) to enforce these provisions of the OSH Act. If workers are to make effective use of disclosed information about health hazards, they must have access to an effective and efficient regulatory system.

It is also essential that workers have an adequately protected right to refuse unsafe work. It is difficult to determine the extent to which this right is legally protected at the present time. Although the OSH Act does not grant a general right to refuse unsafe work,[19] provisions to this effect exist in some state occupational safety laws. In addition, the Secretary of Labor has issued a regulation that interprets the OSH Act as including a limited right to refuse unsafe work, a right that was upheld by the United States Supreme Court in 1980.[20] A limited right of refusal is also protected in the Labor-Management Relations Act (LMRA) and implicitly in the National Labor Relations Act (NLRA).[21]

Unfortunately, these statutory protections vary significantly in the conditions under which they grant a right to refuse and in the consequences they permit to follow from such refusals. For example, the OSHA regulation allows workers to walk off the job where there is a "real danger of death or serious injury," while the LMRA permits refusals only under "abnormally dangerous conditions."[22] Thus, under the LMRA, the nature of the occupation determines the extent of danger justifying refusal, while under OSHA the character of the threat, or so-called "imminent danger," is determinative. By contrast, under the NLRA a walk-out by two or more workers may be justified for even minimal safety problems, so long as the action can be construed as a "concerted activity" for mutual aid and protection and there does not exist a no-strike clause in any collective bargaining agreements.[23] While the NLRA would appear to provide the broadest protection to workers, employees refusing to work under the NLRA may lose the right to be reinstated in their positions if permanent replacements can be found.[24]

The relative merits of the different statutes are further confused by questions of overlapping authority, called "preemption." It is not always clear (1) whether a worker is eligible to claim protection under a given law, (2) which law affords a worker maximum protections or remedies in a particular circumstance, and (3) whether or under what conditions a worker can seek relief under another law or through the courts, once a claim under a given law has not prevailed.

The current legal situation concerning the right to refuse hazardous work leaves many other questions unresolved as well. Consider, for example, whether a meaningful right to refuse hazardous work entails an obligation to continue to pay nonworking employees, or to award the employees back pay if the issue is resolved in their favor. On the one hand, workers without union strike benefits or other income protections would be unable to exercise their right to refuse unsafe work because of economic pressures. On the other hand, to permit such workers to draw a paycheck is to legitimate strike with pay, a practice generally considered unacceptable by management and by Congress. Also unresolved is whether the right to refuse unsafe work should be restricted to cases of obvious, imminent, and serious risks to health or life (the current OSHA and LMRA position) or should be expanded to include lesser risks and uncertain risks—for example, exposure to suspected toxic or carcinogenic substances that although not immediate threats, may prove more dangerous over time. If "the right to know" is to lead to meaningful worker action, workers must be able to remove themselves from exposure to suspected hazards, as well as obvious or known hazards.

Related to this issue is the question of the proper standard for determining whether a safety walkout is justified. At least three different standards have been applied in the past: a good-faith subjective standard, which requires only a determination that the worker honestly believes that the health hazard exists; a reasonable person standard, which requires that the belief be reasonable under the circumstances as well as sincerely held; and an objective standard, which requires evidence—generally established by expert witnesses—that the threat actually exists. Although the possibility of worker abuse of the right to refuse has been a major factor in a current trend to reject the good faith standard, recent commentary has argued that this trend raises serious equity issues in the proper balancing of this concern with the needs of workers confronted with basic self-preservation issues.[25]

No less important is whether the right to refuse hazardous work should be protected only until a formal review of the situation is initiated (at which time the worker must return to the job) or whether the walkout should be permitted until the alleged hazard is at least temporarily removed. So long as the hazards covered under a right to refuse are restricted to risks that are obvious in the environment and that are easily established as health hazards, this issue is relatively easy to resolve. However, if the nature of the risk is less apparent, a major function of any meaningful right to refuse will be to call attention to an alleged hazard and to compel regulatory action. If this chain of events is set in motion, then requirements that workers continue to be exposed while OSHA or the NLRB conduct investigations may be unacceptable to workers and certainly will be unacceptable if the magnitude of potential harm is perceived to be significant. However, compelling employers to remove suspected hazards during the evaluation period may also result in intolerable economic burdens. We therefore need a delineation of the conditions under which workers may be compelled to return to work while an alleged hazard is being evaluated, and the conditions under which employers must be compelled to remove immediately alleged hazards.

V

Legal rights will be of no practical consequence if workers remain ignorant of their options. It is doubtful that many workers, particularly nonunion workers, are aware that they have a legally protected right to refuse hazardous work, let alone that there are at least three statutory provisions protecting that right.[26] Even if workers were aware of such a right, it is unlikely that they could weave their way through the maze of legal options unaided. If there is to be a meaningful right to know in the workplace, there will also have to be an adequate program to educate workers about their rights and how to exercise them, as well as adequate legal protection of this and related worker rights.

It is to be hoped that many corporations will follow the model guidelines and programs established by Monsanto and Hercules on the right to know and will make these rights as meaningful as possible by confirming a right to (at least temporarily) refuse work under unduly hazardous conditions. Potentially effective programs of information and training in hazards are as important for managers as for the workers they manage. In several recent court cases executives of corporations have been tried—and in some cases convicted—for murder because of negligence in causing the deaths of workers by failing to warn them of hazards. The Los Angeles District Attorney has announced that he will investigate all occupational deaths as possible homicides, and similar cases of criminal action have been prosecuted in Chicago.[27] A better system of corporate responsibility in disclosing risks thus stands to benefit management no less than employees.

NOTES

1. For developments in this area, see *Protecting Workplace Secrets, A Manager's Guide to Workplace Confidentiality* (New York: Joseph P. O'Reilly Executive Enterprises, 1985); Elihu D. Richter, "The Worker's Right to Know: Obstacles, Ambiguities,

and Loopholes," *Journal of Health Politics, Policy and Law* 6 (1981): 340; George Miller, "The Asbestos Coverup," *Congressional Record,* May 17, 1979, pp. E2362–E2364, and "Asbestos Health Hazards and Company Morality," *Congressional Record,* May 24, 1979, pp. E2523–E2524; *The "Right to Know" Law: Special Report to the Governor and Legislature,* NY State Bureau of Toxic Substances, Department of Labor, March 1983.

2. NIOSH et al., "The Right to Know: Practical Problems and Policy Issues Arising from Exposures to Hazardous Chemical and Physical Agents in the Workplace," a report prepared at the request of the Subcommittee on Labor and Committee on Human Resources, U.S. Senate (Washington, D.C.: July 1977), 1, 5; Ilise L. Feitshans, "Hazardous Substances in the Workplace: How Much Does the Employee Have the Right to Know?" *Detroit Law Review III* (1985).
3. Occupational Safety and Health Administration, "Access to Employee Exposure and Medical Records—Final Rules," *Federal Register,* May 23, 1980, pp. 35212–35277. (Hereafter referred to as OSHA *Access* regulations.)
4. OSHA, *Access* regulations 29 CFR 1910.1200 et seq; printed in 48 FR 53278 (1983) and (1986). See also *United Steelworkers v. Auchter,* No. 83-3554 et al.; 763 F.2d 728 (3rd Cir. 1985).
5. See Barry Meier, "Use of Right-to-Know Rules Increasing," *Wall Street Journal,* May 23, 1986. p. 10; Vilma R. Hunt, "Perspective on Ethical Issues in Occupational Health," in *Biomedical Ethics Reviews 1984,* ed. J. Humber and R. Almeder (Clifton, N.J.: Humana Press, 1984), p. 194; and "Bhopal Has Americans Demanding the Right to Know," *Business Week,* February 18, 1985.
6. State of New York, 1979–1980 Regular Sessions, 7103-D, Article 28, para. 880.
7. 762 F.2d 728.
8. On this point, cf. Harold J. Magnuson, "The Right to Know," *Archives of Environmental Health 32* (1977): 40–44.
9. 29 CFRs 1910. 1200; 48 FR 53,280 (1983). See also Mary Melville, "Risks on the Job: The Worker's Right to Know," *Environment* 23 (1981): 12–20, 42–45.
10. Laurie Hays, "New Rules on Workplace Hazards Prompt Intensified On the Job Training Programs," *Wall Street Journal,* July 8, 1986, p. 31; Cathy Trost, "Plans to Alert Workers to Health Risks Stir Fears of Lawsuits and High Costs," *Wall Street Journal,* March 28, 1986, p. 15.
11. See 48 CFR 53, 282 (1983); Office of Technology Assessment, *Preventing Illness and Injury in the Workplace* (Washington, D.C.: Government Printing Office, 1985); "Suit Challenges OSHA Limits on Worker's Right to Know Standards," *The Nation's Health* (July 1984): 1; U.S. Department of Labor, *"An Interim Report to Congress on Occupational Disease"* (Washington, D.C.: Government Printing Office, 1980), pp. 1–2; NIOSH et al., "The Right to Know," pp. 3–9.
12. For an account that in effect demands a subjective standard for carcinogens, see Andrea Hricko, "The Right to Know," in *Public Information in the Prevention of Occupational Cancer: Proceedings of a Symposium,* 2–3 December, 1976, ed. Thomas P. Vogl (Washington, D.C.: National Academy of Science, 1977), esp. p. 72.
13. As more and more data are gathered regarding the effects of workplace hazards on particular predisposing conditions, the need for disclosure of such information can be identified through preemployment physical examinations without the worker's needing to ask questions.
14. High Risk Occupational Disease Notification and Prevention Act, HR 1309.
15. See Trost, "Plans to Alert Workers," p. 15; Peter Perl, "Workers Unwarned," *Washington Post,* January 14, 1985, pp. A1, A6.
16. OSHA initially asserted that by regulating the "worst" areas of illness, it had "preempted" (or replaced) state "Right-to-Know" laws when it promulgated OSHA's Hazard Communication Standard. OSHA also claimed that its broad definition of trade secret exemptions for employers superceded state trade secret laws. Connecticut, New York, and New Jersey joined with several other states and challenged both of these assertions in *United Steelworkers v. Auchter* (763 F.2d 728 (3rd Cir. 1985). The Steelworkers court held that OSH Act enabled the Secretary to promulgate *minimum* standards to protect workers, but that in the absence of coverage, states remain free to "fill the void" (between the need for regulation and actual hazards) with valid state laws. Consequently, insofar as OSHA's standard does not cover workers, there can be no "preemption" of state laws.
17. 29 U.S.C. S 651–658 (1970).
18. OSH Act 29 USC S 661 (c). Note, if the health or

safety complaint is not determined to be legitimate, there are no worker protections.

19. Susan Preston, "A Right Under OSHA to Refuse Unsafe Work or A Hobson's Choice of Safety or Job?," *University of Baltimore Law Review* 8 (Spring 1979): 519–550.
20. The Secretary's interpretation of the OSH Act was upheld by the Supreme Court on February 26, 1980. *Whirlpool* v. *Marshall* 445 US 1 (1980).
21. Preston, "A Right Under OSHA to Refuse Unsafe Work," pp. 519–550.
22. 20 U.S.C. S143 (1976), and 29 CFR S 1977.12 (1978).
23. Nicholas Ashford and Judith P. Katz, "Unsafe Working Conditions: Employee Rights Under the Labor Management Relations Act and the Occupational Safety and Health Act," *Notre Dame Lawyer* 52 (June 1977): 802–837.
24. Preston, "A Right Under OSHA to Refuse Unsafe Work," p. 543.
25. Nancy K. Frank, "A Question of Equity: Workers' Right to Refuse Under OSHA Compared to the Criminal Necessity Defense," *Labor Law Journal* 31 (October 1980): 617–626.
26. In most states, these rights are not extended to public employees or domestic workers.
27. See *Illinois* v. *Chicago Magnet Wire Corporation,* No. 86–114, *Amicus Curiae* for The American Federation of Labor and Congress of Industrial Organizations; Jonathan Tasini, "The Clamor to Make Punishment Fit the Corporate Crime," *Business Week,* February 10, 1986, p. 73; Aric Press et al., "Murder in the Front Office," *Newsweek,* July 8, 1985; Bill Richards, "Ex-Officials Get 25-Year Sentences in Worker's Death," *Wall Street Journal,* July 2, 1985, p. 14; and *Illinois* v. *Chicago Magnet Wire Corporation,* No. 86-114, *Amicus Curiae* for The American Federation of Labor and Congress of Industrial Organizations.

QUESTIONS FOR DISCUSSION

1. Ewing argues for an "Employee Bill of Rights" similar to the Bill of Rights guaranteed to U.S. citizens. How does the relationship between citizens and their government differ from the relationship between employees and their employer? How, if at all, does this affect Ewing's argument?
2. Some argue that employers are entitled to "job relevant" information about their employees but that acquiring information that is not job relevant violates employees' privacy. What could be meant by "job relevant" information? Why do Des Jardins and Duska argue that the information revealed by drug tests isn't really job relevant?
3. You are director of personnel for a large company that produces insecticides. The president of the company asks for your advice on instituting a drug-testing program. Should one be instituted, he wants to know? If not, why not? If so, what is the fairest possible way to do so? Having read all the readings in this chapter, draft a memo to the president with your answer.
4. Des Jardins and Duska argue that an employer is entitled to satisfactory job performance from employees but not to "peak" performance. Do you agree? What would be some of the implications of accepting the idea that employers are entitled to "peak" performance?
5. In the past decade, job security (protection against job loss) has become a central concern for employees, even more important than the traditional concerns of salary and benefits. How, if at all, does this affect Martin's thesis that working conditions are a result of mutually beneficial agreement and that employee rights are adequately protected?

CHAPTER 7

WHISTLE BLOWING

Whistle Blowing

Richard T. De George
Distinguished Professor of Philosophy, University of Kansas

We shall restrict our discussion to a specific sort of whistle blowing, namely, *nongovernmental, impersonal, external whistle blowing*. We shall be concerned with (1) employees of profit-making firms, who, for moral reasons, in the hope and expectation that a product will be made safe, or a practice changed, (2) make public information about a product or practice of the firm that due to faulty design, the use of inferior materials, or the failure to follow safety or other regular procedures or state of the art standards (3) threatens to produce serious harm to the public in general or to individual users of a product. We shall restrict our analysis to this type of whistle blowing because, in the first place, the conditions that justify whistle blowing vary according to the type of case at issue. Second, financial harm can be considerably different from bodily harm. An immoral practice that increases the cost of a product by a slight margin may do serious harm to no individual, even if the total amount when summed adds up to a large amount, or profit. (Such cases can be handled differently from cases that threaten bodily harm.) Third, both internal and personal whistle blowing cause problems for a firm, which are for the most part restricted to those within the firm. External, impersonal whistle blowing is of concern to the general public, because it is the general public rather than the firm that is threatened with harm.

As a paradigm, we shall take a set of fairly clear-cut cases, namely, those in which serious bodily harm—including possible death—threatens either the users of a product or innocent bystanders because of a firm's practice, the design of its product, or the action of some person or persons within the firm. (Many of the famous whistle-blowing cases are instances of such situations.) We shall assume clear cases where serious, preventable harm will result unless a company makes changes in its product or practice.

Cases that are less clear are probably more numerous, and pose problems that are difficult to solve, for example, how serious is *serious,* and how does one tell whether a given situation is serious? We choose not to resolve such issues, but rather to construct a model embodying a number of distinctions that will enable us to clarify the moral status of whistle blowing, which may, in turn, provide a basis for working out guidelines for more complex cases.

Finally, the only motivation for whistle blowing we shall consider here is moral motivation. Those who blow the whistle for revenge, and so on, are not our concern in this discussion.

Corporations are complex entities. Sometimes those at the top do not want to know in detail the difficulties encountered by those below them. They wish lower-management to handle these difficulties as best they can. On the other hand, those in lower-management frequently present only good news to those above them, even if those at the top do want to be told about difficulties. Sometimes, lower-management hopes that things will be straightened out without letting their superiors know that anything has gone wrong. For instance, sometimes a production schedule is drawn up, which many employees along the line know cannot be achieved. Each level has cut off a few days of the production time actually needed, to make his projection look good to those above. Because this happens at each level, the final projection is weeks, if not months, off the mark. When difficulties develop in actual production, each level is further squeezed and is tempted to cut corners in order not to fall too far behind the overall schedule. The cuts may be that of not correcting defects in a design, or of allowing a defective part to go through, even though a department head and the workers in that department know that this will cause trouble for the consumer. Sometimes a defective part will be annoying; sometimes it will be dangerous. If dangerous, external whistle blowing may be morally mandatory.

The whistle blower usually fares very poorly at the hands of his company. Most are fired. In some instances, they have been blackballed in the whole industry. If they are not fired, they are frequently shunted aside at promotion time, and treated as pariahs. Those who consider making a firm's wrongdoings public must therefore be aware that they may be fired, ostracized, and condemned by others. They may ruin their chances of future promotion and security; and they also may make themselves a target for revenge. Only rarely have companies praised and promoted such people. This is not surprising, because the whistle blower forces the company to do what it did not want to do, even if, morally, it was the right action. This is scandalous. And it is ironic that those guilty of endangering the lives of others—even of indirectly killing them—frequently get promoted by their companies for increasing profits.

Because the consequences for the whistle blower are often so disastrous, such action is not to be undertaken lightly. Moreover, whistle blowing may, in some cases, be morally justifiable without being morally mandatory. The position we shall develop is a moderate one, and falls between two extreme positions: that defended by those who claim that whistle blowing is always morally justifiable, and that defended by those who say it is never morally justifiable.

WHISTLE BLOWING AS MORALLY PERMITTED

The kind of whistle blowing we are considering involves an employee somehow going public, revealing information or concerns about his or her firm in the hope that the firm will change its product, action, or policy, or whatever it is that the whistle blower feels will harm, or has harmed others, and needs to be rectified. We can assume that when one blows the whistle, it is not with the consent of the firm, but against its wishes. It is thus a form of disloyalty and of disobedience to the corporation. Whistle blowing of this type, we can further assume, does injury to a firm. It results in either adverse publicity or in an investigation of some sort, or both. If we adopt the principle that one ought not to do harm without sufficient reason, then, if the act of whistle blowing is to be morally permissible, some good must be achieved that outweighs the harm that will be done.

There are five conditions, which, if satisfied,

change the moral status of whistle blowing. If the first three are satisfied, the act of whistle blowing will be morally justifiable and permissible. If the additional two are satisfied, the act of whistle blowing will be morally obligatory.

Whistle blowing is morally permissible if—

> 1. The firm, through its product or policy, will do serious and considerable harm to the public, whether in the person of the user of its product, an innocent bystander, or the general public.

Because whistle blowing causes harm to the firm, this harm must be offset by at least an equal amount of good, if the act is to be permissible. We have specified that the potential or actual harm to others must be serious and considerable. That requirement may be considered by some to be both too strong and too vague. Why specify "serious and considerable" instead of saying, "involve more harm than the harm that the whistle blowing will produce for the firm?" Moreover, how serious is "serious?" And how considerable is "considerable?"

There are several reasons for stating that the potential harm must be serious and considerable. First, if the harm is not serious and considerable, if it will do only slight harm to the public, or to the user of a product, the justification for whistle blowing will be at least problematic. We will not have a clear case. To assess the harm done to the firm is difficult; but though the harm may be rather vague, it is also rather sure. If the harm threatened by a product is slight or not certain, it might not be greater than the harm done to the firm. After all, a great many products involve some risk. Even with a well-constructed hammer, one can smash one's finger. There is some risk in operating any automobile, because no automobile is completely safe. There is always a trade-off between safety and cost. It is not immoral not to make the safest automobile possible, for instance, and a great many factors enter into deciding just how safe a car should be. An employee might see that a car can be made slightly safer by modifying a part, and might suggest that modification: but not making the modification is not usually grounds for blowing the whistle. If serious harm is not threatened, then the slight harm that is done, say by the use of a product, can be corrected after the product is marketed (e.g., as a result of customer complaint). Our society has a great many ways of handling minor defects, and these are at least arguably better than resorting to whistle blowing.

To this consideration should be added a second. Whistle blowing is frequently, and appropriately, considered an unusual occurrence, a heroic act. If the practice of blowing the whistle for relatively minor harm were to become a common occurrence, its effectiveness would be diminished. When serious harm is threatened, whistle blowers are listened to by the news media, for instance, because it is news. But relatively minor harm to the public is not news. If many minor charges or concerns were voiced to the media, the public would soon not react as it is now expected to react to such disclosures. This would also be the case if complaints about all sorts of perceived or anticipated minor harm were reported to government agencies, although most people would expect that government agencies would act first on the serious cases, and only later on claims of relatively minor harm.

There is a third consideration. Every time an employee has a concern about possible harm to the public from a product or practice we cannot assume that he or she makes a correct assessment. Nor can we assume that every claim of harm is morally motivated. To sift out the claims and concerns of the disaffected worker from the genuine claims and concerns of the morally motivated employee is a practical problem. It may be claimed that this problem has nothing to do with the moral permissibility of the act of whistle blowing; but whistle blowing is a practical matter. If viewed as a technique for changing policy or actions, it will be justified only if effective. It can be trivialized. If it is, then one might plausibly claim that little harm is done to the firm, and hence the act is permitted. But if trivialized, it loses its point. If whistle blowing is to be considered a serious act with serious consequences, it should be reserved for disclosing potentially serious harm, and will be morally justifiable in those cases.

Serious is admittedly a vague term. Is an increase in probable automobile deaths, from 2 in

100,000 to 15 in 100,000 over a one-year period, serious? Although there may be legitimate debate on this issue, it is clear that matters that threaten death are prima facie serious. If the threatened harm is that a product may cost a few pennies more than otherwise, or if the threatened harm is that a part or product may cause minor inconvenience, the harm—even if multiplied by thousands or millions of instances—does not match the seriousness of death to the user or the innocent bystander.

The harm threatened by unsafe tires, which are sold as premium quality but that blow out at 60 or 70 mph, is serious, for such tires can easily lead to death. The dumping of metal drums of toxic waste into a river, where the drums will rust, leak, and cause cancer or other serious ills to those who drink the river water or otherwise use it, threatens serious harm. The use of substandard concrete in a building, such that it is likely to collapse and kill people, poses a serious threat to people. Failure to x-ray pipe fittings, as required in building a nuclear plant, is a failure that might lead to nuclear leaks; this involves potential serious harm, for it endangers the health and lives of many.

The notion of *serious* harm might be expanded to include serious financial harm, and kinds of harm other than death and serious threats to health and body. But as we noted earlier, we shall restrict ourselves here to products and practices that produce or threaten serious harm or danger to life and health. The difference between producing harm and threatening serious danger is not significant for the kinds of cases we are considering.

> 2. Once an employee identifies a serious threat to the user of a product or to the general public, he or she should report it to his or her immediate superior and make his or her moral concern known. Unless he or she does so, the act of whistle blowing is not clearly justifiable.

Why not? Why is not the weighing of harm sufficient? The answer has already been given in part. Whistle blowing is a practice that, to be effective, cannot be routinely used. There are other reasons as well. First, reporting one's concerns is the most direct, and usually the quickest, way of producing the change the whistle blower desires. The normal assumption is that most firms do not want to cause death or injury, and do not willingly and knowingly set out to harm the users of their products in this way. If there are life-threatening defects, the normal assumption is, and should be, that the firm will be interested in correcting them—if not for moral reasons, at least for prudential reasons, viz., to avoid suits, bad publicity, and adverse consumer reaction. The argument from loyalty also supports the requirement that the firm be given the chance to rectify its action or procedure or policy before it is charged in public. Additionally, because whistle blowing does harm to the firm, harm in general is minimized if the firm is informed of the problem and allowed to correct it. Less harm is done to the firm in this way, and if the harm to the public or the users is also averted, this procedure produces the least harm, on the whole.

The condition that one report one's concern to one's immediate superior presupposes a hierarchical structure. Although firms are usually so structured, they need not be. In a company of equals, one would report one's concerns internally, as appropriate.

Several objections may be raised to this condition. Suppose one knows that one's immediate superior already knows the defect and the danger. In this case reporting it to him or her would be redundant, and condition two would be satisfied. But one should not presume without good reason that one's superior does know. What may be clear to one individual may not be clear to another. Moreover, the assessment of risk is often a complicated matter. To a person on one level what appears as unacceptable risk may be defensible as legitimate to a person on a higher level, who may see a larger picture, and knows of offsetting compensations, and the like.

However, would not reporting one's concern effectively preclude the possibility of anonymous whistle blowing, and so put one in jeopardy? This might of course be the case; and this is one of the considerations one should weigh before blowing the whistle. We will discuss this matter later on. If the reporting is done tactfully, moreover, the voicing of one's concerns might, if the problem is apparent to others, indicate a desire to operate within the firm, and so make one less likely to be the one assumed to have blown the whistle anonymously.

By reporting one's concern to one's immediate superior or other appropriate person, one preserves and observes the regular practices of firms, which on the whole promote their order and efficiency; this fulfills one's obligation of minimizing harm, and it precludes precipitous whistle blowing.

> 3. If one's immediate superior does nothing effective about the concern or complaint, the employee should exhaust the internal procedures and possibilities within the firm. This usually will involve taking the matter up the managerial ladder, and, if necessary—and possible—to the board of directors.

To exhaust the internal procedures and possibilities is the key requirement here. In a hierarchically structured firm, this means going up the chain of command. But one may do so either with or without the permission of those at each level of the hierarchy. What constitutes exhausting the internal procedures? This is often a matter of judgment. But because going public with one's concern is more serious for both oneself and for the firm, going up the chain of command is the preferable route to take in most circumstances. This third condition is satisfied of course if, for some reason, it is truly impossible to go beyond any particular level.

Several objections may once again be raised. There may not be time enough to follow the bureaucratic procedures of a given firm; the threatened harm may have been done before the procedures are exhausted. If, moreover, one goes up the chain to the top and nothing is done by anyone, then a great deal of time will have been wasted. Once again, prudence and judgment should be used. The internal possibilities may sometimes be exhausted quickly, by a few phone calls or visits. But one should not simply assume that no one at any level within the firm will do anything. If there are truly no possibilities of internal remedy, then the third condition is satisfied.

As we mentioned, the point of the three conditions is essentially that whistle blowing is morally permissible if the harm threatened is serious, and if internal remedies have been attempted in good faith but without a satisfactory result. In these circumstances, one is morally justified in attempting to avert what one sees as serious harm, by means that may be effective, including blowing the whistle.

We can pass over as not immediately germane the questions of whether in nonserious matters one has an obligation to report one's moral concerns to one's superiors, and whether one fulfills one's obligation once one has reported them to the appropriate party.

WHISTLE BLOWING AS MORALLY REQUIRED

To say that whistle blowing is morally permitted does not impose any obligation on an employee. Unless two other conditions are met, the employee does not have a moral obligation to blow the whistle. To blow the whistle when one is not morally required to do so, and if done from moral motives (i.e., concern for one's fellow man) and at risk to oneself, is to commit a supererogatory act. It is an act that deserves moral praise. But failure to so act deserves no moral blame. In such a case, the whistle blower might be considered a moral hero. Sometimes he or she is so considered, sometimes not. If one's claim or concern turns out to be ill-founded, one's subjective moral state may be as praiseworthy as if the claim were well-founded, but one will rarely receive much praise for one's action.

For there to be an obligation to blow the whistle, two conditions must be met, in addition to the foregoing three.

> 4. The whistle blower must have, or have accessible, documented evidence that would convince a reasonable, impartial observer that one's view of the situation is correct, and that the company's product or practice poses a serious and likely danger to the public or to the user of the product.

One does not have an obligation to put oneself at serious risk without some compensating advantage to be gained. Unless one has documented evidence that would convince a reasonable, impartial observer, one's charges or claims, if made public, would be based essentially on one's word. Such grounds may be sufficient for a subjective feeling of certitude about one's charges, but they are not usually sufficient for others to act on one's claims. For instance, a newspaper is unlikely to print a story based simply on someone's undocumented assertion.

Several difficulties emerge. Should it not be the responsibility of the media or the appropriate regulatory agency or government bureau to carry out an investigation based on someone's complaint? It is reasonable for them to do so, providing they have some evidence in support of the complaint or claim. The damage has not yet been done, and the harm will not, in all likelihood, be done to the complaining party. If the action is criminal, then an investigation by a law-enforcing agency is appropriate. But the charges made by whistle blowers are often not criminal charges. And we do not expect newspapers or government agencies to carry out investigations whenever anyone claims that possible harm will be done by a product or practice. Unless harm is imminent, and very serious (e.g., a bomb threat), it is appropriate to act on evidence that substantiates a claim. The usual procedure, once an investigation is started or a complaint followed up, is to contact the party charged.

One does not have a moral obligation to blow the whistle simply because of one's hunch, guess, or personal assessment of possible danger, if supporting evidence and documentation are not available. One may, of course, have the obligation to attempt to get evidence if the harm is serious. But if it is unavailable—or unavailable without using illegal or immoral means—then one does not have the obligation to blow the whistle.

> 5. The employee must have good reason to believe that by going public the necessary changes will be brought about. The chance of being successful must be worth the risk one takes and the danger to which one is exposed.

Even with some documentation and evidence, a potential whistle blower may not be taken seriously, or may not be able to get the media or government agency to take any action. How far should one go, and how much must one try? The more serious the situation, the greater the effort required. But unless one has a reasonable expectation of success, one is not obliged to put oneself at great risk. Before going public, the potential whistle blower should know who (e.g., government agency, newspaper, columnist, TV reporter) will make use of his or her evidence, and how it will be handled. He or she should have good reason to expect that the action taken will result in the kind of change or result that he or she believes is morally appropriate.

The foregoing fourth and fifth conditions may seem too permissive to some and too stringent to others. They are too permissive for those who wish everyone to be ready and willing to blow the whistle whenever there is a chance that the public will be harmed. After all, harm to the public is more serious than harm to the whistle blower, and, in the long run, if everyone saw whistle blowing as obligatory, without satisfying the last two conditions, we would all be better off. If the fourth and fifth conditions must be satisfied, then people will only rarely have the moral obligation to blow the whistle.

If, however, whistle blowing were mandatory whenever the first three conditions were satisfied, and if one had the moral obligation to blow the whistle whenever one had a moral doubt or fear about safety, or whenever one disagreed with one's superiors or colleagues, one would be obliged to go public whenever one did not get one's way on such issues within a firm. But these conditions are much too weak, for the reasons already given. Other, stronger conditions, but weaker than those proposed, might be suggested. But any condition that makes whistle blowing mandatory in large numbers of cases, may possibly reduce the effectiveness of whistle blowing. If this were the result, and the practice were to become widespread, then it is doubtful that we would all be better off.

Finally, the claim that many people very often have the obligation to blow the whistle goes against the common view of the whistle blower as a moral hero, and against the commonly held feeling that whistle blowing is only rarely morally mandatory. This feeling may be misplaced. But a very strong argument is necessary to show that although the general public is morally mistaken in its view, the moral theoretician is correct in his or her assertion.

A consequence of accepting the fourth and fifth conditions stated is that the stringency of the moral obligation of whistle blowing corresponds with the common feeling of most people on this issue. Those in higher positions and those in professional positions in a firm are more likely to have the obligation to change a firm's policy or product—even by whistle blowing, if necessary—than are lower-placed employees. Engineers, for instance, are more likely to have access to data and designs than are assembly-line workers. Managers generally have a broader picture, and more access to evidence, than do nonmanagerial employees. Management has the moral responsibility both to see that the expressed moral concerns of those below them have been adequately considered and that the firm does not knowingly inflict harm on others.

The fourth and fifth conditions will appear too stringent to those who believe that whistle blowing is always a supererogatory act, that it is always moral heroism, and that it is never morally obligatory. They might argue that, although we are not permitted to do what is immoral, we have no general moral obligation to prevent all others from acting immorally. This is what the whistle blower attempts to do. The counter to that, however, is to point out that whistle blowing is an act in which one attempts to prevent harm to a third party. It is not implausible to claim both that we are morally obliged to prevent harm to others at relatively little expense to ourselves, and that we are morally obliged to prevent great harm to a great many others, even at considerable expense to ourselves.

The five conditions outlined can be used by an individual to help decide whether he or she is morally permitted or required to blow the whistle. Third parties can also use these conditions when attempting to evaluate acts of whistle blowing by others, even though third parties may have difficulty determining whether the whistle blowing is morally motivated. It might be possible successfully to blow the whistle anonymously. But anonymous tips or stories seldom get much attention. One can confide in a government agent, or in a reporter, on condition that one's name not be disclosed. But this approach, too, is frequently ineffective in achieving the results required. To be effective, one must usually be willing to be identified, to testify publicly, to produce verifiable evidence, and to put oneself at risk. As with civil disobedience, what captures the conscience of others is the willingness of the whistle blower to suffer harm for the benefit of others, and for what he or she thinks is right.

PRECLUDING THE NEED FOR WHISTLE BLOWING

The need for moral heroes shows a defective society and defective corporations. It is more important to change the legal and corporate structures that make whistle blowing necessary than to convince people to be moral heroes.

Because it is easier to change the law than to change the practices of all corporations, it should be illegal for any employer to fire an employee, or to take any punitive measures, at the time or later, against an employee who satisfies the first three aforementioned conditions and blows the whistle on the company. Because satisfying those conditions makes the action morally justifiable, the law should protect the employee in acting in accordance with what his or her conscience demands. If the whistle is falsely blown, the company will have suffered no great harm. If it is appropriately blown, the company should suffer the consequences of its actions being made public. But to protect a whistle blower by passing such a law is no easy matter. Employers can make life difficult for whistle blowers without firing them. There are many ways of passing over an employee. One can be relegated to the back room of the firm, or be given unpleasant jobs. Employers can find reasons not to promote one or to give one raises. Not all of this can be prevented by law, but some of the more blatant practices can be prohibited.

Second, the law can mandate that the individuals responsible for the decision to proceed with a faulty product or to engage in a harmful practice be penalized. The law has been reluctant to interfere with the operations of companies. As a result, those in the firm who have been guilty of immoral and illegal practices have gone untouched even though the corporation was fined for its activity.

A third possibility is that every company of a certain size be required, by law, to have an inspector general or an internal operational auditor, whose job it is to uncover immoral and illegal practices. This person's job would be to listen to the moral concerns of employees, at every level, about the firm's practices. He or she should be independent of management, and report to the audit committee of the board, which, ideally, should be a committee made up entirely of outside board members. The inspector or auditor should be charged with making public those complaints that should be made public if not changed from within. Failure on the inspector's part to take proper action with respect to a worker's complaint, such that the worker is forced to go public, should be prima facie evidence of an attempt to cover up a dangerous practice or product, and the inspector should be subject to criminal charges.

In addition, a company that wishes to be moral, that does not wish to engage in harmful practices or to produce harmful products, can take other steps to preclude the necessity of whistle blowing. The company can establish channels whereby those employees who have moral concerns can get a fair hearing without danger to their position or standing in the company. Expressing such concerns, moreover, should be considered a demonstration of company loyalty and should be rewarded appropriately. The company might establish the position of ombudsman, to hear such complaints or moral concerns. Or an independent committee of the board might be established to hear such complaints and concerns. Someone might even be paid by the company to present the position of the would-be whistle blower, who would argue for what the company should do, from a moral point of view, rather than what those interested in meeting a schedule or making a profit would like to do. Such a person's success within the company could depend on his success in precluding whistle blowing, as well as the conditions that lead to it.

Whistle Blowing: Its Moral Justification

Gene G. James
Professor of Philosophy, Memphis State University

Whistle blowing may be defined as the attempt of an employee or former employee of an organization to disclose what he or she believes to be wrongdoing in or by the organization. Like blowing a whistle to call attention to a thief, whistle blowing is an effort to make others aware of practices one considers illegal or immoral. If the wrongdoing is reported to someone higher in the organization, the whistle blowing may be said to be *internal.* If the wrongdoing is reported to outside individuals or groups, such as reporters, public interest groups, or regulatory agencies, the whistle blowing is *external.* If the harm being reported is primarily harm to the whistle blower alone, such as sexual harassment, the whistle blowing may be said to be *personal.* If it is primarily harm to other people that is being reported, the whistle blowing is *impersonal.* Most whistle blowing is done by people currently employed by the organization on which they are blowing the whistle. However, people who have left an organization may also blow the whistle. The former may be referred to as *current* whistle blowing, the latter as *alumni* whistle blowing. If the whistle blower discloses his or her identity, the whistle blowing may be said to be *open;* if the whistle blower's identity is not disclosed, the whistle blowing is *anonymous.*

Whistle blowers almost always experience retaliation. If they work for private firms and are not protected by unions or professional organizations, they are likely to be fired. They are also likely to receive damaging letters of recommendation and may even be blacklisted so that they cannot find

---

 This article is a revision of the earlier article "In Defense of Whistle Blowing" which appeared in the first edition of this book. Because the argument has been considerably revised and expanded, it seemed preferable to give it a new title to avoid confusion.

work in their profession. If they are not fired, they are still likely to be transferred, given less interesting work, denied salary increases and promotions, or demoted. Their professional competence is usually attacked. They are said to be unqualified to judge, misinformed, etc. Since their actions may threaten both the organization and their fellow employees, attacks on their personal lives are also frequent. They are called traitors, rat finks, disgruntled, known trouble makers, people who make an issue out of nothing, self-serving, and publicity seekers. Their life-styles, sex lives, and mental stability may be questioned. Physical assaults, abuse of their families, and even murder are not unknown as retaliation for whistle blowing.

WHISTLE BLOWING AND THE LAW[1]

The law does not at present offer whistle blowers very much protection. Agency law, the area of common law which governs relations between employees and employers, imposes a duty on employees to keep confidential any information learned through their employment that might be detrimental to their employers. However, this duty does not hold if the employee has knowledge that the employer either has committed or is about to commit a felony. In this case the employee has a positive obligation to report the offense. Failure to do so is known as misprision and makes one subject to criminal penalties.

One problem with agency law is that it is based on the assumption that unless there are statutes or agreements to the contrary, contracts between employees and employers can be terminated at will by either party. It therefore grants employers the right to discharge employees at any time for any reason or even for no reason at all. The result is that most employees who blow the whistle, even those who report felonies, are fired or suffer other retaliation. One employee of thirty years was even fired the day before his pension became effective for testifying under oath against his employer, without the courts doing anything to aid him.

This situation has begun to change somewhat in recent years. In *Pickering v. Board of Education* in 1968 the Supreme Court ruled that government employees have the right to speak out on policy issues affecting their agencies provided doing so does not seriously disrupt the agency. A number of similar decisions have followed, and the right of government employees to speak out on policy issues now seems firmly established. But employees in private industry cannot criticize company policies without risking being fired. In one case involving both a union and a company doing a substantial portion of its business with the federal government, federal courts did award back pay to an employee fired for criticizing the union and the company but did not reinstate or award him punitive damages.

A few state courts have begun to modify the right of employers to dismiss employees at will. Courts in Oregon and Pennsylvania have awarded damages to employees fired for serving on juries. A New Hampshire court granted damages to a woman fired for refusing to date her foreman. A West Virginia court reinstated a bank employee who reported illegal interest rates. The Illinois Supreme Court upheld the right of an employee to sue when fired for reporting and testifying about criminal activities of a fellow employee. However, a majority of states still uphold the right of employers to fire employees at will unless there are statutes or agreements to the contrary. To my knowledge only one state, Michigan, has passed a law prohibiting employers from retaliating against employees who report violations of local, state, or federal laws.

A number of federal statutes contain provisions intended to protect whistle blowers. The National Labor Relations Act, Fair Labor Standards Act, Title VII of the 1964 Civil Rights Act, Age Discrimination Act, and the Occupational Safety and Health Act all have sections prohibiting employers from taking retaliatory actions against employees who report or testify about violations of the acts. Although these laws seem to encourage and protect whistle blowers, to be effective they must be enforced. A 1976 study[2] of the Occupational Safety and Health Act showed that only about 20 percent of the 2300 complaints filed in fiscal years 1975 and 1976 were judged valid by OSHA investigators. About half of these were settled out of court. Of the sixty cases taken to court at the time of the study in November 1976, one had been won, eight lost, and the others were still pending. A more recent study[3] showed that of the 3100 violations reported in 1979, only 270 were settled out of court and only sixteen litigated.

Since the National Labor Relations Act guarantees the right of workers to organize and bargain collectively, and most collective bargaining agreements contain a clause requiring employers to have just cause for discharging employees, these agreements would seem to offer some protection for whistle blowers. In fact, however, arbitrators have tended to agree with employers that whistle blowing is an act of disloyalty which disrupts business and injures the employer's reputation. Their attitude seems to be summed up in a 1972 case in which the arbitrator stated that one should not "bite the hand that feeds you and insist on staying for future banquets."[4] One reason for this attitude, pointed out by David Ewing, is that unions are frequently as corrupt as the organizations on which the whistle is being blown. Such unions he says, "are not likely to feed a hawk that comes to prey in their own barnyard."[5] The record of professional societies is not any better. They have generally failed to come to the aid or defense of members who have attempted to live up to their codes of professional ethics by blowing the whistle on corrupt practices.

THE MORAL JUSTIFICATION OF WHISTLE BLOWING

Under what conditions, if any, is whistle blowing morally justified? Some people have argued that whistle blowing is never justified because employees have absolute obligations of confidentiality and loyalty to the organization for which they work. People who argue this way see no difference between employees who reveal trade secrets by selling information to competitors and whistle blowers who disclose activities harmful to others.[6] This position is similar to another held by some business people and economists that the sole obligation of corporate executives is to make a profit for stockholders. If this were true, corporate executives would have no obligations to the public. However, no matter what one's special obligations, one is never exempt from the general obligations we have to our fellow human beings. One of the most fundamental of these obligations is to not cause avoidable harm to others. Corporate executives are no more exempt from this obligation than other people.

Just as the special obligations of corporate executives to stockholders cannot override their more fundamental obligations to others, the special obligations of employees to employers cannot override their more fundamental obligations. In particular, obligations of confidentiality and loyalty cannot take precedence over the fundamental duty to act in ways that prevent unnecessary harm to others. Agreements to keep something secret have no moral standing unless that which is to be kept secret is itself morally justifiable. For example, no one can have an obligation to keep secret a conspiracy to murder someone, because murder is an immoral act. It is for this reason also that employees have a legal obligation to report an employer who has committed or is about to commit a felony. Nor can one justify participation in an illegal or immoral activity by arguing that one was merely following orders. Democratic governments repudiated this type of defense at Nuremberg.

It has also been argued that whistle blowing is always justified because it is an exercise of the right to free speech. However, the right to free speech is not absolute. An example often used to illustrate this is that one does not have the right to shout "Fire" in a crowded theater because that is likely to cause a panic in which people may be injured. Analogously, one may have a right to speak out on a particular subject, in the sense that there are no contractual agreements which prohibit one from doing so, but it nevertheless be the case that it would be morally wrong for one to do so because it would harm innocent people, such as one's fellow workers and stockholders who are not responsible for the wrongdoing being disclosed. The mere fact that one has the right to speak out does not mean that one ought to do so in every case. But this kind of consideration cannot create an absolute prohibition against whistle blowing, because one must weigh the harm to fellow workers and stockholders caused by the disclosure against the harm to others caused by allowing the organizational wrong to continue. Furthermore, the moral principle that one must consider all people's interests equally prohibits giving priority to one's own group. There is, in fact, justification for not giving as much weight to the interests of the stockholders as to those of the public, because stockholders investing in corporate firms do so with the knowledge that they undergo financial risk if management acts in imprudent, illegal, or immoral ways. Similarly, if the employees of a company know that it is engaged in illegal or immoral activities and do not take action, including whistle blowing, to terminate the activities, then they too must bear some of the guilt for the actions. To the extent that these conditions hold, they nullify the principle that one ought to refrain from whistle blowing because speaking out would cause harm to the organization. Unless it can be shown that the harm to fellow workers and stockholders would be *significantly greater* than the harm caused by the organizational wrongdoing, the obligation to avoid unnecessary harm to the public must take precedence. Moreover, as argued above, this is true even when there are specific agreements which prohibit one from speaking out, because such agreements are morally void if the organization is engaged in illegal or immoral activities. In that case one's obligation to the public overrides one's obligation to maintain secrecy.

CRITERIA FOR JUSTIFIABLE WHISTLE BLOWING

The argument in the foregoing section is an attempt to show that unless special circumstances hold, one has a obligation to blow the whistle on illegal or immoral actions—an obligation that is grounded on the fundamental human duty to avoid preventable harm to others. In this section I shall attempt to spell out in greater detail the conditions under which blowing the whistle is morally obligatory. Since Richard De George has previously attempted to do this, I shall proceed by examining the criteria he has suggested.[7]

De George believes there are three conditions that must hold for whistle blowing to be morally permissible and two additional conditions that must hold for it to be morally obligatory. The three conditions that must hold for it to be morally permissible are:

1. The firm, through its product or policy, will do serious and considerable harm to the public, whether in the person of the user of its product, an innocent bystander, or the general public.
2. Once an employee identifies a serious threat to the user of a product or to the general public, he or she should report it to his or her immediate superior and make his or her moral concern known. Unless he or she does so, the act of whistle blowing is not clearly justifiable.
3. If one's immediate superior does nothing effective about the concern or complaint, the employee should exhaust the internal procedures and possibilities within the firm. This usually will involve taking the matter up the managerial ladder, and, if necessary—and possible—to the board of directors.

The two additional conditions which De George thinks must hold for whistle blowing to be morally obligatory are:

4. The whistle blower must have, or have accessible, documented evidence that would convince a reasonable, impartial observer that one's view of the situation is correct and that the company's product or practice poses a serious and likely danger to the public or to the user of the product.
5. The employee must have good reason to believe that by going public the necessary changes will be brought about. The chance of being successful must be worth the risk one takes and the danger to which one is exposed.[8]

De George intends for the proposed criteria to apply to situations in which a firm's policies or products cause physical harm to people. Indeed, the first criterion he proposes is intended to restrict the idea of harm even more narrowly to threats of serious bodily harm or death.

De George apparently believes that situations which involve threats of serious bodily harm or death are so different from those involving other types of harm, that the kind of considerations which justify whistle blowing in the former situations could not possibly justify it in the latter. Thus, he says, referring to the former type of whistle blowing: "As a paradigm, we shall take a set of fairly clear-cut cases, namely, those in which serious bodily harm—including possible death—threatens either the users of a product or innocent bystanders."[9]

One problem in restricting discussion to clear-cut cases of this type, regarding which one can get almost universal agreement that whistle blowing is justifiable, is that it leaves us with no guidance when we are confronted with more usual situations involving other types of harm. Although De George states that his "analysis provides a model for dealing with other kinds of whistle blowing as well,"[10] his criteria in fact provide no help in deciding whether one should blow the whistle in situations involving such wrongs as sexual harassment, violations of privacy, industrial espionage, insider trading, and a variety of other harmful actions.

No doubt, one of the reasons De George restricts his treatment the way he does is to avoid having to define harm. This is indeed a problem. For if we fail to put any limitations on the idea of harm, it seems to shade into the merely offensive or distasteful and thus offer little help in resolving moral problems. But, on the other hand, if we restrict harm to physical injury, as De George does, it then applies to such a limited range of cases that it is of minimal help in most of the moral situations which confront us. One way of dealing with this problem is by correlating harm with violations of fundamental human rights such as the rights to due process, privacy, and property, in addition to the right to freedom from physical harm. Thus, not only situations which involve threats of physical harm, but also those involving actions such as sexual harassment which violate the right to privacy and causes psychological harm, compiling unnecessary records on people, and financial harm due to fraudulent actions, are situations which may justify whistle blowing.

A still greater problem with De George's analysis is that even in cases where there is a threat of serious physical harm or death, he believes that this only makes whistle blowing morally permissible, rather than creating a strong *prima facie* obligation in favor of whistle blowing. His primary reasons for believing this seem to be those stated in criterion 5. Unless one has reason to believe that the whistle blowing will eliminate the harm, and the cost to oneself is not too great, he does not believe whistle blowing is morally obligatory. He maintains that this is true even when the person involved is a professional whose code of ethics requires her or him to put the public good ahead of private good. He argued in an earlier article, for example, that:

> The myth that ethics has no place in engineering has . . . at least in some corners of the engineering profession . . . been put to rest. Another myth, however, is emerging to take its place—the myth of the engineer as moral hero. . . . The zeal . . . however, has gone too far, piling moral responsibility upon moral responsibility on the shoulders of the engineer. This emphasis . . . is misplaced. Though engineers are members of a profession that holds public safety paramount, we cannot reasonably expect engineers to be willing to sacrifice their jobs each day for principle and to have a whistle ever at their sides.[11]

He contends that engineers have only the obligation "to do their jobs the best they can."[12] This includes reporting their concerns about the safety of products to management, but does *not* include "the obligation to insist that their perceptions or . . . standards be accepted. They are not paid to do that, they are not expected to do that, and they have no moral or ethical obligation to do that."[13]

To take a specific case, De George maintains that even though some Ford engineers had grave misgivings about the safety of Pinto gas tanks, and several people had been killed when tanks exploded after rear-end crashes, the engineers did not have an obligation to make their misgivings public. De George's remarks are puzzling because the Pinto case would seem to be exactly the kind of clear-cut situation which he says provides the paradigm for justified whistle blowing. Indeed, if the Ford engineers did not have an obligation to blow the whistle, it is difficult to see what cases could satisfy his criteria. They knew that if Pintos were struck from the rear by vehicles traveling thirty miles per hour or more, their gas tanks were likely to explode, seriously injuring or killing people. They also knew that if they did not speak out, Ford would continue to market the Pinto. Finally, they were members of a profession whose code of ethics requires them to put public safety above all other obligations.

De George's remarks suggest that the only obligation the Ford engineers had was to do what management expected of them by complying with their job descriptions and that so long as they did that no one should find fault with them or hold them accountable for what the company did. It is true that when people act within the framework of an organization, it is often difficult to assess individual responsibility. But the fact that one is acting as a member of an organization does not relieve one of moral obligations. The exact opposite is true. Because most of the actions we undertake in organizational settings have more far-reaching consequences than those we undertake in our personal lives, our moral obligation to make sure that we do not harm others is *increased* when we act as a member of an organization. The amount of moral responsibility one has for any particular organizational action depends on the extent to which: (1) the consequences of the action are foreseeable, and (2) one's own action or failure to act is a cause of those consequences. It is important to include failure to act here, because frequently it is easier to determine what will happen if we do not act than if we do, and because we are morally responsible for not preventing harm as well as for causing it.

De George thinks that the Ford engineers would have had an obligation to blow the whistle only if they believed doing so would have been likely to prevent the harm involved. But we have an obligation to warn others of danger even if we believe they will ignore our warnings. This is especially true if the danger will come about partly because we did not speak out. De George admits that the public has a right to know about dangerous products. If that is true, then those who have knowledge about such products have an obligation to inform the public. This is not usurping the public's right to decide acceptable risk: it is simply supplying people with the information necessary to exercise that right.

De George's comments also seem to imply that in general it is not justifiable to ask people to blow the whistle if it would threaten their jobs. It is true that we would not necessarily be justified in demanding this if it would place them or their families' lives in danger. But this is *not* true if only their jobs are at stake. It is especially not true if the people involved are executives and professionals, who are accorded respect and high salaries, not only because of their specialized knowledge and skills, but also because of the special responsibilities we entrust to them. Frequently, as in the case of engineers, they also subscribe to codes of ethics which require them to put the public good ahead of their own or the organization's good. Given all this, it is difficult to understand why De George does not think the Ford engineers had an obligation to blow the whistle in the Pinto case.

The belief that whistle blowing is an act of disloyalty and disobedience seems to underlie De George's second and third criteria for justifiable whistle blowing: The whistle blower must have first reported the wrongdoing to his or her immediate superior and, if nothing was done, have taken the complaint as far up the managerial ladder as possible. Some of the problems with adopting these suggestions as general criteria for justified whistle blowing are: (1) It may be one's immediate supervisor who is responsible for the wrongdoing. (2) Organizations differ considerably in both their procedures for reporting, and how they respond to, wrongdoing. (3) Not all wrongdoing is of the same type. If the wrongdoing is of a type that threatens people's health or safety, exhausting channels of protest within the organization may result in unjustified delay in correcting the problem. (4) Exhausting internal channels of protest may give people time to destroy evidence needed to substantiate one's allegations. (5) Finally, it may expose the employee to possible retaliation, against which she or he might have some protection if the wrongdoing were reported to an external agency.

His fourth criterion, that the whistle blower have documented evidence which would convince an impartial observer, is intended to reduce incidences of whistle blowing by curbing those who would blow the whistle on a mere suspicion of wrongdoing. It is true that one should not make claims against an organization based on mere guesses or hunches, because if they turn out to be false one will have illegitimately harmed the organization and innocent people affiliated with it. But, De George also wishes to curb whistle blowing, because he thinks that if it were widespread, that would reduce its effectiveness. De George's fourth and fifth criteria are, therefore, deliberately formulated in such a way that if they are satisfied, "people will only rarely have the moral obligation to blow the whistle."[14]

De George's fear, that unless strict criteria of justification are applied to whistle blowing it might become widespread, is unjustified. If it is true, as he himself claims, that there is a strong tradition in America against "ratting," that most workers consider themselves to have an obligation of loyalty to their organization, and that whistle blowers are commonly looked upon as traitors, then it is unlikely that whistle blowing will ever be a widespread practice. De George believes that if one is unable to document wrongdoing without recourse to illegal or immoral means, this relieves one of the obligation to blow the whistle. He argues:

> One does not have an obligation to blow the whistle simply because of one's hunch, guess, or personal assessment of possible danger, if supporting evidence and documentation are not available. One may, of course, have the obligation to attempt to get evidence if the harm is serious. But if it is unavailable—or unavailable without using illegal or immoral means—then one does not have the obligation to blow the whistle.[15]

I have already indicated above that I do not think one has an obligation to blow the whistle on possible wrongdoing on the basis of a mere guess or hunch because this might harm innocent people. But if one has good reason to believe that wrongdoing is occurring even though one cannot document it without oneself engaging in illegal or immoral actions, this does not relieve one of the obligation to blow the whistle. Indeed, if this were true one would almost never have an obligation to blow the whistle, because employees are rarely in a position to satisfy De George's fourth criterion that the whistle blower "must have, or have accessible, documented evidence that would convince a reasonable, impartial observer that one's view of the situation is correct." Indeed, it is precisely because employees are rarely ever in a position to supply this type of documentation without themselves resorting to illegal or immoral actions, that they have an obligation to inform others who have the authority to investigate the possible wrongdoing. The attempt to secure such evidence on one's own may even thwart the gathering of evidence by the proper authorities. Thus, instead of De George's criterion being a necessary condition for justifiable whistle blowing, the attempt to satisfy it would prevent its occurrence. One has an obligation to gather as much evidence as one can so that authorities will have probable cause for investigation. But, if one is convinced that wrongdoing is occurring, one has an obligation to report it even if one is unable to adequately document it. One will have then done one's duty even if the authorities ignore the report.

The claim that it is usually necessary for the whistle blower to speak out openly for whistle blowing to be morally justified implies that anonymous whistle blowing is rarely, if ever, justified. Is this true? It has been argued that anonymous whistle blowing is never justified because it violates the right of people to face their accusers. But, as Frederick Elliston has pointed out, although people should be protected from false accusations, it is not necessary for the identity of whistle blowers to be known to accomplish this. "It is only necessary that accusations be properly investigated, proven true or false, and the results widely disseminated."[16]

Some people believe that because the whistle blower's motive is not known in anonymous whistle blowing, this suggests that the motive is not praiseworthy and in turn raises questions about the moral justification of anonymous whistle blowing. De George apparently believes this, because in addition to stating that only public whistle blowing by previously loyal employees who display their sincerity by their willingness to suffer is likely to be effective and morally justified, he mentions at several places that he is restricting his attention to whistle blowing for moral reasons. He says, e.g., that "the only motivation for whistle blowing we shall consider . . . is moral motivation."[17] However, in my opinion, concern with the whistle blower's motive is irrelevant to the moral justification of whistle blowing. It is a red herring which takes attention away from the genuine moral issue involved: whether the whistle blower's claim that the organization is doing something harmful to others is true. If the claim is true, then the whistle blowing is justified regardless of the motive. If the whistle blower's motives are not moral, that makes the act less praiseworthy, but this is a totally different issue. As De George states, whistle blowing is a "practical matter." But precisely because this is true, the justification of whistle blowing turns on the truth or falsity of the disclosure, not on the motives of the whistle blower. Anonymous whistle blowing is justified because it can both protect the whistle blower from unjust attacks and prevent those who are accused of wrongdoing from shifting the issue away from their wrongdoing by engaging in an irrelevant *ad hominem* attack on the whistle blower. Preoccupation with the whistle blower's motives facilitates this type of irrelevant diversion. It is only if the accusations prove false or inaccurate that the motives of the whistle blower have any moral relevance. For it is only then, and not before, that the whistle blower rather than the organization should be put on trial.

The view that whistle blowing is *prima facie* wrong because it goes against the tradition that "ratting" is wrong is indefensible because it falsely assumes both that we have a general obligation to not inform others about wrongdoing and that this outweighs our fundamental obligation to prevent harm to others. The belief that whistle blowers should suffer in order to show their moral sincerity, on the other hand, is not only false and irrelevant to the issue of the moral justification of whistle blowing, but is perverse. There are *no* morally justifiable reasons a person who discloses wrongdoing should be put at risk or made to suffer. The contradictory view stated by De George that "one does not have an obligation to put oneself at serious risk without some compensating advantage to be gained,"[18] is also false. Sometimes doing one's duty requires one to undertake certain risks. However, both individuals and society in general should attempt to reduce these risks to the minimum. In the next section I consider some of the actions whistle blowers can take to both make whistle blowing effective and avoid unnecessary risk. In the last section I briefly consider some of the ways society can reduce the need for whistle blowing.

FACTORS TO CONSIDER IN WHISTLE BLOWING

Since whistle blowing usually involves conflicting moral obligations and a wide range of variables and has far-reaching consequences for everyone concerned, the following is not intended as a recipe or how-to-do list. Like all complicated moral actions, whistle blowing cannot be reduced to such a list. Nevertheless, some factors can be stated which whistle blowers should consider in disclosing wrongdoing if they are to also act prudently and effectively.

Make Sure the Situation Is One That Warrants Whistle Blowing

Make sure the situation is one that involves illegal or immoral actions which harm others, rather than one in which you would be disclosing personal matters, trade secrets, customer lists, or similar material. If the disclosure would involve the latter as well, make sure that the harm to be avoided is great enough to offset the harm from the latter.

Examine Your Motives

Although it is not necessary for the whistle blower's motives to be praiseworthy for whistle blowing to be morally justified, examining your motives can help in deciding whether the situation is one that warrants whistle blowing.

Verify and Document Your Information

Try to obtain information that will stand up in regulatory hearings or court. If this is not possible, gather as much information as you can and indicate where and how additional information might be obtained. If the *only* way you could obtain either of these types of information would be through illegal procedures, make sure the situation is one in which the wrongdoing is so great that it warrants this risk. Although morality requires that in general we obey the law, it sometimes requires that we break it. Daniel Ellsberg's release of the Pentagon papers was a situation of this type in my opinion. If you do have to use illegal methods to obtain information, try to find alternative sources for any evidence you uncover so that it will not be challenged in legal hearings. Keep in mind also that if you use illegal methods to obtain information you are opening yourself to *ad hominem* attacks and possible prosecution. In general illegal methods should be avoided unless substantial harm to others is involved.

Determine the Type of Wrongdoing Involved and to Whom It Should Be Reported

Determining the exact nature of the wrongdoing can help you both decide what kind of evidence to obtain and to whom it should be reported. For example, if the wrongdoing consists of illegal actions such as the submission of false test reports to government agencies, bribery of public officials, racial or sexual discrimination, violation of safety, health, or pollution laws, then determining the nature of the law being violated will help indicate which agencies have authority to enforce the law. If, on the other hand, the wrongdoing is not illegal, but is nevertheless harmful to the public, determining this will help you decide whether you have an obligation to publicize the actions and if so how to go about it. The best place to report this type of wrongdoing is usually to a public interest group. Such an organization is more likely than the press to: (1) be concerned about and advise the whistle blower how to avoid retaliation. (2) maintain confidentiality if that is desirable, (3) investigate the allegations to try to substantiate them, rather than sensationalizing them by turning the issue into a "personality dispute." If releasing information to the press is the best way to remedy the wrongdoing, the public interest group can help with or do this.

State Your Allegations in an Appropriate Way

Be as specific as possible without being unintelligible. If you are reporting a violation of law to a government agency, and if possible to do so, include technical data necessary for experts to verify the wrongdoing. If you are disclosing wrongdoing that does not require technical data to substantiate it, still be as specific as possible in stating the type of illegal or harmful activity involved, who is being harmed and how.

Stick to the Facts

Avoid name calling, slander, and being drawn into a mud-slinging contest. As Peter Raven-Hansen wisely points out: "One of the most important points . . . is to focus on the disclosure. . . . This rule applies even when the whistle blower believes that certain individuals are responsible. . . . The disclosure itself usually leaves a trail for others to follow the miscreants."[19] Sticking to the facts also helps the whistle blower minimize retaliation.

Decide Whether the Whistle Blowing Should Be Internal or External

Familiarize yourself with all available internal channels for reporting wrongdoing and obtain as much data as you can both on how people who have used these channels were treated by the organization and what was done about the problems they reported. If people who have reported wrongdoing in the past have been treated fairly and the problems corrected, use internal channels. If not, find out which external agencies would be the most appropriate to contact. Try to find out also how these agencies have treated whistle blowers, how much aid and protection they have given them, etc.

Decide Whether the Whistle Blowing Should Be Open or Anonymous

If you intend to blow the whistle anonymously, decide whether partial or total anonymity is required. Also document the wrongdoing as thoroughly as possible. Finally, since anonymity may be difficult to preserve, anticipate what you will do if your identity becomes known.

Decide Whether Current or Alumni Whistle Blowing Is Required

Sometimes it is advisable to resign one's position and obtain another before blowing the whistle. This is because alumni whistle blowing helps protect one from being fired, receiving damaging letters of recommendation, or even being blacklisted in one's profession. However, changing jobs should not be thought of as an alternative to whistle blowing. If one is aware of harmful practices, one has a moral obligation to try to do something about them, which cannot be escaped by changing one's job or location. Many times people who think the wrongdoing involved is personal, harming only them, respond to a situation by simply trying to remove themselves from it. They believe that "personal whistle blowing is, in general, morally permitted but not morally required."[20] For example, a female student subjected to sexual harassment, and fearful that she will receive low grades and poor letters of recommendation if she complains, may simply change departments or schools. However, tendencies toward wrongdoing are rarely limited to specific victims. By not blowing the whistle the student allows a situation to exist in which other students are likely to be harassed also.

Make Sure You Follow Proper Guidelines in Reporting the Wrongdoing

If you are not careful to follow any guidelines that have been established by organizations or external agencies for a particular type of whistle blowing, including using the proper forms, meeting deadlines, etc., wrongdoers may escape detection or punishment because of "technicalities."

Consult a Lawyer

Lawyers are advisable at almost every stage of whistle blowing. They can help determine if the wrongdoing violates the law, aid in documenting it, inform you of any laws you might break in documenting it, assist in deciding to whom to report it, make sure reports are filed correctly and promptly, and help protect you from retaliation. If you cannot afford a lawyer, talk with an appropriate public interest group that may be able to help. However, lawyers frequently view problems within a narrow legal framework, and decisions to blow the whistle are moral decisions, so in the final analysis you will have to rely on your own judgment.

Anticipate and Document Retaliation

Although not as certain as Newton's law of motion that for every action there is an equal reaction, whistle blowers whose identities are known can expect retaliation. Furthermore, it may be difficult to keep one's identity secret. Thus whether the whistle blowing is open or anonymous, personal or impersonal, internal or external, current or alumni, one should anticipate retaliation. One should, therefore, protect oneself by documenting every step of the whistle blowing with letters, tape recordings of meetings, etc. Without this documentation, the whistle blower may find that regulatory agencies and the courts are of little help in preventing or redressing retaliation.

BEYOND WHISTLE BLOWING

What can be done to eliminate the wrongdoing which gives rise to whistle blowing? One solution would be to give whistle blowers greater legal protection. Another would be to change the nature of organizations so as to diminish the need for whistle blowing. These solutions are of course not mutually exclusive.

Many people are opposed to legislation to protect whistle blowers because they think that it is unwarranted interference with the right to freedom of contract. However, if the right to freedom of contract is to be consistent with the public interest, it cannot serve as a shield for wrongdoing. It does this when threat of dismissal prevents people from blowing the whistle. The right of employers to dismiss at will has been previously restricted by labor laws which prevent employers from dismissing employees for union activities. It is ironic that we have restricted the right of employers to fire employees who are pursuing their economic self-interest but allowed them to fire employees acting in the public interest. The right of employers to dismiss employees in the interest of efficiency should be balanced against the right of the public to know about illegal, dangerous, and unjust practices of organizations. The most effective way to achieve this goal would be to pass a federal law protecting whistle blowers.

Laws protecting whistle blowers have also been opposed on the grounds that: (1) employees would use them to mask poor performance, (2) they would create an "informer ethos," and (3) they would take away the autonomy of business, strangling it in red tape.

The first objection is illegitimate because only those employees who could show that an act of whistle blowing preceded their being penalized or dismissed, and that their employment records were adequate up to the time of the whistle blowing, could seek relief under the law.

The second objection is more formidable but nevertheless invalid. A society that encourages snooping, suspicion, and mistrust does not conform to most people's idea of the good society. Laws which encourage whistle blowing for self-interested reasons, such as the federal tax law which pays informers part of any money that is collected, could help bring about such a society.[21] However, laws protecting whistle blowers from being penalized or dismissed are quite different. They do not reward the whistle blower; they merely protect him or her from unjust retaliation. It is unlikely that state or federal laws of this type would promote an informer society.

The third objection is also unfounded. Laws protecting whistle blowers would not require any positive duties on the part of organizations—only the negative duty of not retaliating against employees who speak out in the public interest.

However not every act of apparent whistle blowing should be protected. If (1) the whistle blower's accusations turn out to be false and, (2) it can be shown that she or he had no probable reasons for assuming wrongdoing, then the individual should not be shielded from being penalized or dismissed. Both of these conditions should be satisfied before this is allowed to occur. People who can show that they had probable reasons for believing that wrongdoing existed should be protected even if their accusations turn out to be false. If the accusation has not been disproved, the burden of proof should be on the organization to prove that it is false. If it has been investigated and proven false, then the burden of proof should be on the individual to show that she or he had probable reasons for believing wrongdoing existed. If it is shown that the individual did not have probable reasons for believing wrongdoing existed, and the damage to the organization from the false charge is great, it should be allowed to sue or seek other restitution. Since these provisions would impose some risks on potential whistle blowers, they would reduce the possibility of frivolous action. If, on the other hand, it is found that the whistle blower had probable cause for the whistle blowing and the organization has penalized or fired him or her, then that person should be reinstated, awarded damages, or both. If there is further retaliation, additional sizeable damages should be awarded.

What changes could be made in organizations to prevent the need for whistle blowing? Some of the suggestions which have been made are that organizations develop effective internal channels for reporting wrongdoing, reward people with salary increases and promotions for using these channels, and appoint senior executives, board members, ombudspersons, etc., whose primary obligations would be to investigate and eliminate organizational wrongdoing. These changes could be undertaken by organizations on their own or mandated by law. Other changes which might be mandated are requiring that certain kinds of records be kept, assessing larger fines for illegal actions, and making executives and other professionals personally liable for filing false reports, knowingly marketing dangerous products, failing to monitor how policies are being implemented, and so forth. Although these reforms could do much to reduce the need for whistle blowing, given human nature it is highly unlikely that this need can ever be totally eliminated. Therefore, it is important to have laws which protect whistle blowers and for us to state as clearly as we can both the practical problems and moral issues pertaining to whistle blowing.

NOTES

1. For discussion of the legal aspects of whistle blowing see Lawrence E. Blades, "Employment at Will

vs. Individual Freedom: On Limiting the Abusive Exercise of Employer Power," *Columbia Law Review,* vol. 67 (1967); Philip Blumberg, "Corporate Responsibility and the Employee's Duty of Loyalty and Obedience: A Preliminary Inquiry," *Oklahoma Law Review,* vol. 24 (1967); Clyde W. Summers, "Individual Protection Against Unjust Dismissal: Time for a Statue," *Virginia Law Review,* vol. 62 (1976); Arthur S. Miller, "Whistle Blowing and the Law," in Ralph Nader, Peter J. Petkas, and Kate Blackwell, *Whistle Blowing,* New York: Grossman Publishers, 1972; Alan F. Westin, *Whistle Blowing!,* New York: McGraw-Hill, 1981. See also vol. 16, no. 2, Winter 1983, *University of Michigan Journal of Law Reform,* special issue, "Individual Rights in the Workplace: The Employment-At-Will Issue."

2. For a discussion of this study which was conducted by Morton Corn see Frank von Hipple, "Professional Freedom and Responsibility: The Role of the Professional Society," *Newsletter on Science, Technology and Human Values,* vol. 22, January 1978.
3. See Westin, *Whistle Blowing!*
4. See Martin H. Marlin, "Protecting the Whistleblower from Retaliatory Discharge," in the special issue of the *University of Michigan Journal of Law Reform.*
5. David W. Ewing, *Freedom inside the Organization,* New York: E. P. Dutton, 1977, pp. 165–166.
6. For a more detailed discussion of this argument see Gene G. James, "Whistle Blowing: Its Nature and Justification," *Philosophy in Context,* vol. 10 (1980).
7. See Richard T. De George, 2d ed., *Business Ethics,* New York: Macmillan, 1986. Earlier versions of De George's criteria can be found in the first edition (1982), and in "Ethical Responsibilities of Engineers in Large Organizations," *Business and Professional Ethics Journal,* vol. 1, no. 1. Fall 1981.
8. De George, *Business Ethics,* pp. 230–234.
9. *Ibid.,* p. 223.
10. *Ibid.,* p. 237.
11. De George, "Ethical Responsibilities of Engineers," p. 1.
12. *Ibid.,* p. 5.
13. *Ibid.*
14. De George, *Business Ethics,* p. 235.
15. *Ibid.,* p. 234.
16. Frederick A. Ellison, "Anonymous Whistleblowing," *Business and Professional Ethics Journal,* vol. 1, no. 2, Winter 1982.
17. De George, *Business Ethics,* p. 223.
18. *Ibid.,* p. 234.
19. Peter Raven-Hansen, "Dos and Don'ts for Whistleblowers: Planning for Trouble," *Technology Review,* May 1980, p. 30. My discussion in this section is heavily indebted to this article.
20. De George, *Business Ethics,* p. 222.
21. People who blow the whistle on tax evaders in fact rarely receive any money because the law leaves payment to the discretion of the Internal Revenue Service.

QUESTIONS FOR DISCUSSION

1. "Employees owe their employers loyalty and obedience, therefore they should never blow the whistle." Make a case for or against this statement, keeping in mind the arguments of De George and James.

2. De George believes that employees are obligated to blow the whistle only if they have documented evidence of a serious harm, and if they have reason to believe that whistle blowing will be effective in preventing the harm. Why does James think these criteria are too strict? Do you agree with De George or James, and why?

CHAPTER 8

MEANINGFUL WORK

Labor's Stake in Improving the Quality of Working Life

Irving Bluestone
University Professor of Labor Studies, Wayne State University, and former vice-president of the United Auto Workers

In the play *Fiddler on the Roof,* Tevye, bound by tradition, must face the challenge of changing times and circumstances. He finds himself compelled to grapple with new societal concepts of life as the generation he has helped spawn no longer pays obeisance to his traditions. In a sense, the industrial scene in these "modern times" in the United States is facing a similar challenge as changes in society demand a reassessment of the authoritarian practices of the past and present and influence certain basic shifts in managerial attitudes toward the workers and the structure of the work place.

In the ten-year period from 1970 to 1980 in the United States, for instance, the composition of the work force underwent significant change, and current forecasts presage a continuing transformation.

- Workers completing at least one year of college: blue collar—16 percent up from 7 percent in 1970; service—18 percent up from 8 percent in 1970; white collar—57 percent up from 45 percent in 1970. (Overall, workers today have about four more years of education than was true a generation ago.)
- The nature of the education process has changed, as students are more prone to question the authority of the teacher—even at the grade school level.
- Women as a proportion of the U.S. civilian labor force have increased from 38.1 percent in 1970 to 42.2 percent in 1979. (It is estimated that, in 1980, 53 percent of all women were in the work force and this proportion will rise to 60 percent in the next several years.)
- A recent Conference Board study projects that 86 percent of U.S. families will have two incomes

From *The Quality of Working Life and the 1980's,* Harvey Kolodny and Hans van Beinum, eds. (Praeger Publishers, a division of Greenwood Press, New York 1983,) pp. 33–41.

by 1990. There is a constant upward shift in the number of multiple income families.

- Persons age 45 and over as a percent of the civilian labor force have declined from 38.1 percent in 1970 to 30.8 percent in 1979 (to 30.3 percent in 1980).

Daniel Yankelovich, in his widely noted study, *The New Morality,* summed up his findings in part as follows:

> Today's generation of young people is less fearful of economic insecurity than generations in the past. They want interesting and challenging work, but they assume that their employers cannot—or will not—provide it. By their own say-so, they are inclined to take "less crap" than older workers. They are not as automatically loyal to the organization as their fathers, and they are far more cognizant of their own needs and rights. Nor are they as awed by organizational and hierarchical authority. Being less fearful of discipline and the threat of losing their jobs, they feel free to express their discontent in myriad ways, from fooling around on the job to sabotage. They are better educated than their parents, even without a college degree. They want more freedom and opportunity and will struggle hard to achieve it. [1974, p. 37]

It is commonplace to hear business managers anchored in the customary management hierarchical structure—in which the boss makes the decisions and gives the orders, and the employees take the orders and do as they are told—complain that workers today:

- are less attentive to the quality of the product or service in the performance of their job;
- exhibit a surly, cynical attitude toward management;
- run the gamut from apathy to rebelliousness;
- are more prone to unwarranted absenteeism and lateness;
- have no "loyalty" to the employer.

It is evident that these are the imputations of those managers who fail to comprehend the comparatively rapid changes occurring in society and the world of work and who have not yet realized the need to alter their own behavior in relation to their employees. Fortunately, however, an increasing number of business executives have perceived that the old authoritarian mode is not only morally and philosophically incompatible with a society rooted in democratic values, but is moreover antagonistic to their own self-interests.

Furthermore, world competition, not only from Japan and Europe but increasingly from developing nations as well, is compelling a reevaluation of the current system of business administration. Long term planning, the best uses of capital and investment, a review of research and development processes and programs, and the upgrading of managerial skills are some of the aspects of business administration coming under sharp scrutiny. No less so is the vitally important subject of the effective utilization of human resources. Every company proclaims that its employees are its most valuable resource. Most often, however, the proclamation is rhetoric without substance.

A primary function of unions is to make of this proclamation a reality. Toward this end a union represents workers in order to improve their living standards, enhance their job and income security, and establish enforceable negotiated work place rights for them. Essential to the purposes and goals of a union as well is to create a work place climate in which the workers will enjoy job satisfaction derived from recognition of their desire for dignity and self-realization—a knowledge that what they are as adult human beings counts more than being an extension of the tool, and that what they do is intrinsically meaningful.

The process of creating a work life of "quality" embraces those concepts that afford the opportunity for the employees at all levels—middle management, white collar, and blue collar—to be adult citizens in the work place as they are in society. To achieve this objective requires a departure from the all encompassing authoritarian managerial control of the decision-making process; it requires a system in which the employees participate significantly in the process of decision making.

For management this may be a disconcerting development since it represents a challenge to certain long established management prerogatives—

especially those relating to decisions over the methods, means, and processes of production or, as the case may be, providing services. Yet the forces of change are impelling business executives to "think anew." For unions these recent developments should be viewed as a further step along the road of unionism's persistent historical goal—to bring a greater measure of democracy to the work place.

For both management and unions, the break with tradition does not come easy. For all that, it is, however, equally apparent that not all traditions are worthy of rigid preservation. From the point of view of the union, embracing the concept of improving the quality of work life raises anxieties, both expressed and latent, that should be thoroughly aired and dispelled.

First of all there is the problem of definition. What, after all, is the quality of working life (QWL)? Definitions abound, and the following are several of them for consideration:

> The essence of QWL is the opportunity for employees at all levels in an organization to have substantial influence over their work environment by participating in decisions related to their work, thereby enhancing their self-esteem and satisfaction from their work. [Greenberg and Glaser 1980, p. 19]
>
> Quality of work life is neither a single event nor a packaged program. It is a general label attached to systematic programs that involve employees designing and carrying out improvements in their work conditions. The details vary widely. Sometimes QWL involves representative worker-management problem solving committees or task forces. Sometimes, it involves the creation of worker teams that might take on responsibility for quality control, for distribution of work assignments, and sometimes even for daily supervision.
>
> QWL practices aim at extending growth, challenge, participation, responsibility and control to all employees. [Bell Telephone Magazine 1970, p. 15] Improving the quality of work life is a people-oriented process dedicated to altering attitudes in the union-management relationship, developing mutual respect between management and labor and a cooperative effort toward achievement and mutually desirable and beneficial goals. Essential to its success is the meaningful involvement of workers in the decision-making process. Its primary thrust is to increase job satisfaction, self-worth, self-fulfillment at work and to enhance the dignity of the individual worker.
>
> Improving the quality of work life is not a substitute for collective bargaining, but it can be complementary to collective bargaining subjects of mutual concern. It may cover a wide variety of non-controversial aspects of labor-management relations. It is not, and must not be, a management gimmick manipulated simply to increase production and profit.
>
> It is essential to establish a relationship of co-equality between union and management in planning, designing and implementing the QWL program.
>
> Fundamentally, improving the quality of work life is rooted in the democratic way of life. To the fullest extent possible, it means that the citizen as worker should be able to enjoy democratic values at the work place in the same sense that he enjoys democratic values as a citizen in a free society. [Bluestone, 1981]

Since QWL is a process derived largely from the unique circumstances existing in each individual situation, the definition will vary with the envisioned objectives. A fairly consistent thread runs through the various definitions, however, namely: the right of the employees to participate significantly in the decision-making process. This is as basic to the concept as it is foreign to the more familiar structure of work organization, and it therefore requires sincere, steadfast commitment on the part of both management and labor.

COMMITMENT TO THE QWL CONCEPT

A prerequisite to change in managerial behavior toward the employees is the commitment to the essential concept of QWL. It is not enough for management at all levels to be persuaded of the need and the justification for embarking on the QWL process. The union at its various levels of authority must likewise be convinced. While the cultural and societal changes described earlier provide motivation for managerial attitudinal change, principles of sound patterns of human behavior should impel it. In fact, however, it is the success of the QWL process where it currently exists that in the final analysis may be the more influential persuader.

Concrete examples of vastly increased employee satisfaction through the QWL process and the resultant benefits to management, the workers, the union (and the community and consumers as well) serve to dispel doubts about the value of the QWL concept. In any event, firm commitment to the QWL process at the various levels of the management and the union hierarchies is a primary ingredient for the required initiative, its development, and its success.

COEQUAL STATUS

The constancy of the commitment is best assured within a climate in which both management and the union share coequal status responsibility in planning, designing, and implementing the QWL process. Without the cooperation of management, the union, no matter how deeply dedicated, will find it impossible to initiate, much less fully implement, the program. While management, on the other hand, might succeed in initially installing a QWL program without union cooperation, before long union opposition to such unilateral action will doom the program to ultimate failure. Moreover, a program that is designed and controlled solely by management, even with union acquiescence (but not union support) soon will lay itself open to abuse and exploitation by management itself, since there will be no countervailing force (the union) to protect the workers' interests and preserve the primary purpose of the QWL process: to enhance the dignity of the worker and provide the vehicle for worker self-fulfillment and self-satisfaction at work by assuring that the process remains primarily relevant to the needs of the workers.

SEPARATION OF QWL AND THE LABOR CONTRACT

One of the guidelines that the contracting parties accept as a matter of course when initiating the QWL process is that the negotiated labor contract provisions remain inviolate. Management should not contemplate that the mere agreement to undertake the QWL process through joint, cooperative endeavor means automatic change in the labor contract requirements. Maintaining a clear-cut separation between QWL and the negotiated labor contract is vitally important to both parties and to the workers. This is not to say the parties may not reach the conclusion that "bending" or even modifying certain negotiated contract provisions is desirable under given circumstances. It is up to the parties to the labor contract to reach such a decision, in which case, of course, they have the authority to act on their decision, subject to the usual ratification procedures.

BENEFITS OF QWL

By its very definition, the QWL process is designed for and on behalf of the worker. Its philosophic base, rooted in the principles of democracy and participation, is people-oriented. From labor's point of view, therefore, the QWL process, properly effected, represents an extension of unionism's historic goals.

The benefits that workers and the union derive from the QWL process have also been manifested in other concrete ways—and are benefits of value to management as well.

Improved Product Quality

Workers know a great deal more about how to manage their jobs, and have greater concern for the quality of the product or service, than most managements are willing to give them credit for. If, like automatons, they are simply to be programmed and obey orders, they are deprived of the initiative to respond as problem solvers. As the Japanese system has proven to the chagrin of most industrialized nations, the floodgates of innovation and ingenuity, once opened to the workers, create near miracles of quality service—given the time, the opportunity, and the motivation. They recognize that good quality is tied inevitably to improved job security through assured sales.

It is well established that improved quality is a direct benefit derived from the QWL process—a benefit commonly desired by the workers, the union, the management, and, naturally, the consumer.

Reduced Absenteeism and Labor Turnover

The problem of unwarranted absenteeism is more often than not considered an issue solely of concern to management. Obviously, high unwarranted absentee rates are costly, jeopardize continuous high standards of quality excellence, and are disruptive of operations. For the workers who are present, absenteeism often means being moved from jobs that they find desirable to fill in on jobs with which they are not thoroughly familiar. They resent the reassignment and are critical of the union. Habitually absent workers are subject to disciplinary action, even discharge, creating grievance problems for the union representatives. An overall reduction in unwarranted absenteeism rates is desirable from the point of view of the workers and the union as well as management.

Successful QWL programs have demonstrated that increased job satisfaction results in a decline in such absenteeism rates—a mutually desirable objective.

Similarly, labor turnover, costly to management but also troublesome to the union, declines as the work place becomes more conducive to the fulfillment of employees' needs. Reduction in labor turnover makes for greater stability in the work force, which, in turn, makes for a more stable and effective union.

Reduction in Discharges, Disciplinary Layoffs, and Grievance Load

It is a truism that over time the QWL process results in a sharp reduction in the number of disciplinary actions assessed against employees and a notable decline in the number of written grievances. The change in managerial behavior and attitude appears to lengthen the managerial temper fuse; it causes management to seek out the causes of "employee discontent" rather than view only its results. The reasons for the reduction in the number of discharges and disciplinary layoffs may be inexplicable without in-depth research; nevertheless, it is a welcome fact.

The decline in the number of written grievances is attributable essentially to the fact that complaints at the work place are resolved more readily as they arise, through consultation and discussion between the union representative and floor supervision with the grievant. The process of change wrought by the parties' commitment to QWL influences the collective bargaining relationship. Issues that previously appeared hard core and controversial in nature become the targets of mutual problem solvers rather than problem creators—an altogether salutary development for all concerned.

Election of Union Officials

While it is not universally demonstrable, it is nevertheless a fact that, with few exceptions, union officials who are proponents of the QWL process and are actively involved in planning and implementing the program, are reelected to office. The acknowledged betterment in the quality of working life is the direct result of union effort as a coequal with management. The workers are quick to recognize and appreciate the union's role in bringing a better life into the work place. It is only natural, therefore, that at election time, they will vote for the incumbents who were prime movers in bringing it all to pass. The function of a union representative is to provide service to the constituents and advance their welfare. It is only natural that the constituents in turn support those union representatives who best fulfill that role in their behalf.

Reward System

Job satisfaction, enhanced dignity and self-realization, a feeling that one counts in the scheme of things, is for some reward enough. Financial reward or other types of reward systems may be the handmaiden to a successful QWL process. Profit sharing, gain sharing, paid time off, pay for knowledge, and so on, comprise some of the reward system approaches compatible with the QWL process—usually the subject of the customary collective bargaining procedures. Whatever may be negotiated between the parties will represent a mutually desirable and mutually agreeable pact, which both negotiating parties and the workers consider beneficial.

GUIDELINES

Among the guidelines that the parties might well consider adopting as they enter upon the cooperative process of QWL—over and above the separation of QWL from labor contract provisions and the coequal status position of the parties as noted earlier—are:

- The work pace should not be increased by reason of the QWL program. (Naturally, increased production due to technological change is another matter.)
- The program should be voluntary for all employees.
- The employee should experience genuinely that he is not simply the adjunct to the tool, but that his bent toward being creative, innovative, and inventive, plays a significant role in the production or service process.
- The employee should be assured that his participation in decision making will not erode his job security or that of his fellow workers.
- Job functions should be engineered to fit the employee; the current system is designed to make the employee fit the job on the theory that this is a more efficient production or service system and that, in any event, economic gain is the employee's only reason for working. This theory is, I believe, wrong on both counts.
- The employee should be assured the widest possible latitude of self-management, responsibility, and the opportunity for use of his "brain power." Gimmickry or manipulation of the employees must not be used.
- The changes in job content and function, the added responsibility and involvement in decision making should be accompanied by an appropriate reward system.
- The employees should be able to foresee opportunities for growth in their work and for promotion.
- The employees' role in the business should enable them to relate to the product being produced, or the services being rendered, and to its meaning in society; in a broader sense it should enable them as well to relate constructively to their role in society.

Achieving human dignity by bringing a meaningful measure of democratic values into the work place lies at the heart of the QWL process. And that, after all, is what unionism is all about. The marriage between unionism and its goals on the one hand and the QWL process on the other is a natural culmination of the historic march of labor toward a better life. Labor's stake in the success of the QWL process commands, therefore, that unions be in the forefront of advocacy; that, as has been so often true in the past, they become the initiators, the movers and doers in accelerating the process toward workers' participation in decision making and enjoying the better life.

NOTES

Bell Telephone Magazine 1970. "Quality of Work Life on the Bell System Drawing Board," edition 4. Bluestone, Irving 1981. Unpublished paper distributed for classroom discussion to students in the Master of Arts in Industrial Relations program. Mich.: Wayne State University.

Greenberg, Paul D. and Edward Glaser 1980. *Some Issues in Joint Union-Management Quality of Worklife Improvement Efforts.* Kalamazoo, Mich.: W. E. Upjohn Institute for Employment Research. Yankelovich, Daniel 1974. *The New Morality.* New York: McGraw-Hill.

The Circle Game

Mike Parker
Dwight Hansen
Parker—Consultant to unions and educational institutions, and former industrial electrician.
Hansen—Former tool and die maker and member of the United Auto Workers

Every Wednesday, at a stamping plant in Dearborn, Michigan, twelve of the 120 workers and one of the five foremen interrupt what they are doing and walk away from the assembly line where front sections for the Ford Escort are welded. For an hour, they brainstorm in a clean office lined with graphs and slogan-packed posters. "Circle 81," as this group calls itself, grapples with a single problem for several meetings. This time, it's how to keep the flanges on the front-end aprons from getting bent during production.

Each participant comes up with an idea to add to a list of possible solutions, and no suggestion is criticized or even discussed until the brainstorm has subsided. When the list has made the rounds, circle members rank the proposals according to handbook instructions the company has given the group's "facilitator." By consensus, members decide to have a chute realigned, so the aprons can slide smoothly off the line.

Circle 81 is pleased when, in this instance, the solution works out. One member is concerned about the worker who has had the job of hammering bent flanges back into shape, but the foreman offers reassurance: No jobs will be lost because of quality improvements. The Employee Involvement Circle, as it's known officially, puts another problem on its agenda and moves on.

In Flint, about fifty miles north, thirty-six female fashion models parade around in the latest styles while workers continue to turn out fifty-five cars an hour. A plant spokeswoman says Fashion Day would not have been possible at the Buick factory before General Motors brought in "quality-of-worklife" programs. But now, she says, "these people have become so trustworthy and so adept they can handle a show on the sideline. It doesn't take away from their work at all."

"It used to be like a concentration camp here when I first came six years ago," plant manager Lee Furse told the *Detroit Free Press*. "Now it's a fun place to work. For years we just hired the workers' hands. Now we treat them like people."

GM's quality-of-worklife (QWL) efforts and Ford's Employee Involvement Circles have counterparts at other companies, where they are variously known as Labor-Management Participation Teams or Quality Circles. Whatever they are called, the programs are part of a growing QWL movement—the centerpiece of the New Industrial Relations, the "non-adversarial relationship" heralded in some labor and business publications. QWL encompasses a vast range of schemes, from renamed employee suggestion systems to redrawn plant chain-of-command maps. Some programs concentrate on "hard" issues, such as product quality or productivity, while others focus on attitudes and factory relations. All bring workers and managers together to improve efficiency at the point of production.

Ten years ago, there was little interest in QWL except among a few academics, maverick business leaders, and unionists who drew their models from social democratic Scandinavia. In the last three years, however, QWL has swept through the nation's private and public sectors, thanks, in part, to support from most of organized labor. The United Auto Workers, the United Steelworkers, the Communication Workers of America, and several other AFL-CIO unions actively promote some form of QWL. Many labor leaders see QWL as a counterweight to contract concessions or as a demonstration of labor "statesmanship." Not surprisingly, then, it is the concession-wracked UAW that is blazing the QWL trail. GM and Ford have set up hundreds of circles and teams. GM has spent $1.6 million on QWL just at its plant in Tarrytown, New York.

Corporations have not been prompted to invest in QWL by some new-found concern for workers' needs, however. Big business has discovered that QWL is a convenient way to tighten control over the workforce. Nonetheless, union leaders are buying into the concept for their own reasons.

For many unionists, QWL is a job-security strategy. Workers at the Ford Rouge Glass Plant south of Detroit point to a recently completed construction project they helped salvage through QWL. Management was about to scrap a planned improvement because outside bids were too high, but members of the employee involvement program said the job could be done with in-house labor. The work was finished on time and at about half the original projected cost, turning John Gutzman, president of the Maintenance and Construction unit of UAW Local 600, from a skeptic of QWL into a booster.

The construction project, Gutzman says, "is a good example of the positive benefits that can result when UAW members are given a voice in decision-making and when we all work together. The talent and potential of our membership is unlimited, and when this talent is tapped, we all benefit—as in the glass plant. The maintenance and construction unit members got a large amount of additional work which everyone enjoyed and really worked hard on. Management saved almost one-half of a million dollars and got a better quality job [and] the glass plant unit gained increased job security."

QWL can also be an inspiring personal experience for some workers. Carla, a custodial worker at a Detroit-area GM plant, describes an encounter with QWL-enlightened management as "the best thing that ever happened to me": "Imagine, I was sitting with the superintendent, and I'm just a janitor. He was asking *me* questions. We talked and we were equals. I really like it."

In fact, the promise of a new, personal relationship to one's work—of equality, respect, and dignity on the job—are QWL's strongest appeals to workers. But even when there is neither heightened personal fulfillment nor a big job-saving success story, QWL at least means a chance to get off the line for an hour to chat over coffee. And if only a fraction of the promises of QWL were to work out, it would be a giant step forward. Who could oppose the idea?

Not many have. One measure of QWL's popularity is that union leaders commonly invoke it at election time. According to *Fortune* magazine, "Leaders in quality-of-worklife plants find themselves politically more popular than ever. To date [1981] according to UAW leaders, virtually every slate of the union's officers who campaigned by supporting an established quality-of-worklife effort has won." Even union dissidents are embracing QWL in surprising numbers, despite its emphasis on productivity and cooperation with management. Many QWL showcases involve locals with militant histories. Unionists with militant reputations are often selected to head QWL programs. Bob Evans coordinates QWL for Oldsmobile Local 652 in Lansing, Michigan, and Bob Roth, who had been fired five times for leading wildcat strikes, directs QWL for Buick Local 599 in Flint.

Its champions believe, for the most part, that QWL will significantly improve the lives of working people. Yet QWL eats away at the power of unions: The main point of QWL is to convince workers that their security and future are tied to the success of the company (or plant, or department) instead of to their union—or class. It pushes the message, *We* have to make *our* company profitable if we are to save our jobs.

Thus, UAW International Representative Al Hendricks told unionists in Ford Local 600 that *we* must make the company competitive with the Japanese in order to undercut GM and Chrysler—hardly the way to build trade union solidarity throughout the auto industry. Moreover, since the industry is set up so that divisions and individual plants bid on jobs from the parent company, QWL encourages UAW members at, say, the Ford Dearborn stamping plant to find a way to produce at lower cost than fellow unionists at the Ford Woodhaven stamping plant down the road. And jobs depend on such competition: The president of GM Buick Local 599, Al Christner, proudly explains how QWL enabled his division to underbid a GM Pontiac division, and GM Oldsmobile workers, long-time UAW activists, boast that their QWL program helped them win work from GM Buick.

The divisiveness does not stop there. Once workers are persuaded that job security depends on increasing *our* company's productivity, their attitudes change toward other workers in the plant. The older workers are now "slow," and employees who didn't mind "carrying" them in the past now see them as a drag on productivity. Production workers begin to bad-mouth "do-nothing" skilled workers. A Ford local president who supports QWL admits he has a problem with circle members who blame production snags on alcoholics and others with personal problems. Carla, the janitor and QWL enthusiast, acknowledges that custodial workers in her plant are capable of finishing their daily assignments in less than eight hours. "I don't want to give anything away and have sixty janitors mad," she says. "But I don't want to lie to these [management] people, if you are going to have trust and make changes." Carla says she feels "caught."

It may be that all of organized labor is caught in a QWL bind. While unions have historically defended workplaces from what bosses called "rationalization," when the word meant nothing more than speed-ups or job reductions, they now push that same old process in a new form. QWL paints productivity and competition as the paths to job security, and so anything that gets in the way is suspect, including union-negotiated work rules, "excessive" concern for the environment or workplace safety, and absenteeism.

Because it creates a competitive climate, QWL has turned out to be a favorite tool of union busters. The California Hospital Personnel Management Association conducts seminars on the use of QWL in the fight against unions. The Council on Union-Free Environment publishes a how-to pamphlet on starting "circle" programs and staving off unionization. And the National Association of Manufacturers estimates there are "roughly 32,000 quality circles in [South] Korea and 1,200 registered in Taiwan." To which the United Electrical Workers' *News* responded: "No better recommendation can be had for the enemies of trade union organization."

QWL is a sort of union version of Reaganomics: Help the company make more profits so that some of the wealth will trickle down in the form of more jobs. Indeed, UAW Vice President Donald Ephlin takes pleasure in noting the correlation between active QWL programs and local votes in favor of the Ford concessions contract—a pattern that also showed up in the GM contract vote. The case for concessions advanced by both the UAW leadership and the automakers echoes their endorsement of QWL; concessions, like QWL-induced efficiency, will save jobs in the face of the Japanese onslaught and stiffer domestic competition.

But QWL "victories" have not offset contract concessions. At the Ford Rouge plant, site of the successful Employee Involvement construction project, hourly employment is down more than 50 per cent in three years while Ford looks overseas for more parts. What's more, the concessions Ford is demanding are actually quality-of-worklife takebacks. The company is pressing to place more restrictions on workers' rights to change jobs; trying to change line rules in the name of efficiency; combining job classifications, and reducing the number of skilled jobs in the process. A union activist who supports QWL says Ford has become hard-nosed over grievances and is "refusing to move, particularly on terminations, because they have all the replacements they want on the layoff list." Management's "cooperative spirit" at the Rouge plant surfaces only when it serves to increase productivity, cut costs, or clamp down on absenteeism.

QWL is, in a sense, providing the ideological grease for concessions by sowing competitiveness. Ford is homing in on individual plants—even though contracts have long been signed—and threatening to ship work to other Ford factories if workers do not approve give-backs. (GM is pursuing the same strategy.) Among the reasons Local 1250 of the Cleveland engine plant refused to be taken for a ride was that Ford would not guarantee a new engine job in return for concessions. The company then assigned the work to its plant in Lima, Ohio, which had agreed to concessions. The UAW International stood by and watched.

The UAW response to the companies' divide-and-conquer strategy has, in fact, been to campaign for QWL programs. In throwing in its lot with QWL, the union tells workers to identify with the problems of plant management. And, far from breaking new ground, union backing for the concept reinforces a narrow, purely contractual vision of trade unionism engendered during the prosperity of the 1950s and 1960s. Consider how AFL-CIO Secretary-Treasurer Thomas Donahue reconciles QWL to trade unionism:

"The adversarial role, appropriate to the conflict of collective bargaining, ought to be limited to the period of negotiation. And during the lifetime of a contract so arrived at, it ought to be replaced by a period of cooperation, aimed at maximizing the potential success of the joint enterprise, i.e., the company's business or production."

Donahue's perspective raises an obvious question: Why don't unions just step aside between contracts and let managers manage? From the viewpoint of corporations, unions do serve a useful purpose from contract to contract—as conduits for workforce discipline and as efficient consolidators of such workplace discontent as is risked in a time of near-record unemployment. And if unionism is being turned into a management tool, QWL may be the tool's handle.

Can organized labor redeem QWL? Robert Cole, a sociologist at the University of Michigan, has spelled out a common union approach. Cole warns union leaders to make sure that "circles do not take up matters which fall under collective bargaining agreements." But he continues, "Now, you can tell this to the circle members and management and even get it in writing. But in some companies the local union found it had to insist on a union committee man being present at every meeting to be sure that this principle was maintained at least for the first several months before the ground rules were clear."

The message conveyed to the rank and file by having a union official assume the watchdog role is that the union itself is threatened, and scrambling to protect its position. Yet almost anything that affects working conditions at the plant level can be won in collective bargaining, either directly at contract time or in the continuing struggle to interpret the contract and set useful precedents. Union collaboration in setting up the circles therefore makes concrete the notion that a union defends the worker only at contract time. The ideology of QWL places management inside the workers' concept of "we" and simultaneously positions the union as "them." QWL success stories hint at union impotence: Why should it take a circle meeting to get splash shields installed so machine operators don't get sprayed with coolant?

What makes QWL different from yesterday's management fads is that QWL gives bosses a way around the union to the shop floor. This allows them to draw off those workers who are dissatisfied with their jobs but who have leadership skills and self-confidence—that is, potential union leaders. Quality circles become a Junior Achievement-style management training ground where people learn to think and act like managers. The more advanced QWL programs are explicitly organized so that, in the words of the former GM director of organizational development, "each team is like a small business."

The teams play in what one local union leader described as "a company ball game, with company umpires, on company turf."

The gloss of QWL appears to wear thin after a year or two. Some of the QWL success stories of a few years ago, such as Rushton Mine and Harmon Industries, have ended in bitterness on all sides. In Japan, some managers worry that quality circle activities are becoming ritualized and counterproductive. An expanding economy can paper over a lot of problems, but in bad times discussions cannot sustain enthusiasm. Sooner or later, QWL programs have to come up against the reality of capitalist industrial relations: Managers run the company, and their bottom line is profits; labor is a major production cost, and management's job is to cut it.

Some QWL consultants recognize that the attraction fades, and therefore have plans to expand and improve the process. (One cynical observer calls this "a bigger-participation fix.") Next steps include "gains sharing"—financial incentives for the suggestions generated by circles—and plant redesign. GM is experimenting with "pay-for-knowledge" systems and "self-managing" departments.

But increased participation is not the same thing as power. It is not even a step toward power when the participation undermines the only real power workers still have—the power to act collectively. Managers assume QWL programs will lead workers to cooperate in their own undoing because they are allowed to help in choosing the means. Business leaders are also betting that QWL will not raise expectations about the right to respect and dignity on the job, or if it does, that workers will not turn their anger and disappointment into anything more than cynicism.

Whether worker discontent is channeled into building a stronger union depends, in large measure, on whether the union has discredited itself during the QWL experience. An appropriate union response to QWL has to be determined by the specific situation; where a union has a solid reputation as an active fighter it can simply refuse to take part. The in-plant leaders of UAW Local 595 in Linden, New Jersey, turned their back on QWL and explained the decision with an educational campaign. Some locals of the International Association of Machinists (IAM) and the United Electrical Workers (UE) have entered into negotiations over QWL; their demands for the release of information on hazardous chemicals, investment, and production plans exposed the companies' hidden QWL agendas. One UE local ended a QWL program by publicizing the antiunion record of the company's QWL consultant. The national leaders of both the IAM and the UE are against QWL. Says the IAM newspaper, "The simple reason is that we don't like cooperating on the shop floor while we're being mugged by management at the plant gate."

But these are exceptions. The argument that QWL will weaken unions has not seemed compelling to workers who are already alienated from their union; to them, QWL promises some relief. Union militants often face QWL programs imposed from above by their international leadership or already entered upon by past union officers. In these situations, direct opposition to QWL could easily be misunderstood and thus ineffective. On the other hand, the grudging support some unions have given QWL has reinforced the image of a union bureaucracy threatened by new approaches to shop-floor life.

One of the lessons of labor history is that skillful organizers find ways to bend to union purposes all manner of employer-initiated programs. Indeed, even pure company unions have been transformed into real ones in some industries. If a similar approach is to be tried on QWL, it will take aggressive organizing.

First, unions must try to convince workers in QWL circles to think of themselves as union representatives. Where election of representatives to circles is possible, it helps employees feel accountable to their fellow workers.

In one case, circle members were elected because there were more volunteers than management wanted. "People took it seriously," said Susan Greene, a circle participant at a Bell Telephone garage in Chicago. "We won some things at first, including a fan in the club room and a bike rack. . . . But as time went on, people who were not on the circle began to get upset with our lack of progress and put pressure on us." When Bell tried to reduce overtime pay, the circle convened a meeting of all garage workers; they decided that the best protest would be a mass resignation. The experience demonstrated that a circle can be bent toward building worker solidarity.

Where elections are not possible because QWL programs are already in place, unions can still make workers "circle reps," and perhaps assign them union duties such as handling the first stages of grievance procedures. A model for this once existed in the auto industry, when "working stewards" (often called "blue button" or "line" stewards) tied the union to its grass-roots members.

Second, unions must develop plans to cope with technological advances and train circle representatives to protect workers from job cutbacks. QWL participants should be taught to see increased productivity in terms of its effect on the quantity and quality of work. The union can counter the tendency, inherent in QWL, for workers to identify with corporate management; cross-departmental and even cross-company meetings of unionized circle members can strengthen workers' identification with the union—and with each other.

Finally, unions should work to change the accepted jurisdiction of QWL circles, insisting, as the IAM does, that "every aspect of the employer-employee relationship is subject to negotiation through collective bargaining." A union that decides to buy into QWL would do well to make circles the vehicle for greater rank-and-file participation in the collective bargaining process.

Of course, none of these steps can be taken unless the unions are rebuilt to wage ideological war. Unions must not only be able to challenge this or that company's strategy; they must instill a collective union consciousness in the ranks. In short, unions must project a political program that offers workers a way out of their dead-end dependency on corporate profits as the source of job security.

The Myth of Job Enrichment

Mitchell Fein
Formerly in the Department of Industrial Engineering, New York University; President, Mitchell Fein, Inc.

Practically all writing that deals with worker boredom and frustration starts with the idea that the nature of work in industry and offices degrades the human spirit, is antithetical to workers' needs and damages their mental health, and that the redesign of work is socially desirable and beneficial to workers. Curiously, however, this view is not supported by workers or their unions. If workers faced the dire consequences of deprivation projected by the behaviorists, they should be conscious of the need to redesign and enrich their jobs. (The term "behaviorist" is used in this article to include psychologists, social scientists, and others who favor the redesign of work and job enrichment as a way to enhance the quality of working life. Many behaviorists, in fact, may not hold these views. Still, there is a sharp difference of opinion between what workers say they want and what behaviorists say workers want.)

WHO SPEAKS FOR WORKERS?

Workers' feelings about their work and what goes on at the workplace are expressed quite freely by workers themselves and their spokesmen in the unions. Since no union has yet raised the issue of work boredom and the redesign of jobs, is it not reasonable to assume that the question is not important to workers? Workers are not bashful in their demands, and worker representatives are quite vocal in championing workers' needs. One might argue that workers do not comprehend the harm that is done to them by their work and that they must be shown that many of their problems and troubles really stem from the nature of their jobs. But that assumes that workers are naive or stupid, which is not the case.

This article first appeared in *The Humanist* issue of September/October 1973 and is reprinted by permission.

The judgments of those advocating job changes derive from people whom Abraham Maslow would characterize as "superior people (called self-actualizers) who are also superior perceivers, not only of facts but of values, . . . their ultimate values [are then used] as possibly the ultimate values for the whole species."[1] These advocates of change maintain that healthy progress for people is toward self-fulfillment through work, and they see most jobs as dull, repetitive, seemingly meaningless tasks, offering little challenge or autonomy. They view the nature of work as the main deterrent to more fulfilling lives for the workers and the redesign of jobs as the keystone of their plans for accomplishing the desired changes.

Paul Kurtz has stated: "Humanists today attack all those social forces which seek to destroy man: they deplore the dehumanization and alienation of man within the industrial and technological society. . . . and the failure of modern man to achieve the full measure of his potential excellence. The problem for the humanist is to create the conditions that would emancipate man from oppressive and corruptive social organization, and from the denigration and perversion of his human talents . . ."[2] Humanists' goals and behaviorists' objectives appear similar. Both accept Maslow's self-actualization concepts as the preferred route to fulfillment. But by what divine right does one group assume that its values are superior to others and should be accepted as normal? Both the selection of goals and attitudes toward work are uniquely personal. The judges of human values have no moral right to press their normative concepts on others as preferable.

SATISFACTION AND ACHIEVEMENT

The fundamental question is whether or not the nature of work prevents people from achieving the full measure of their potential. When behaviorists view people at work, they see two main groups: those who are satisfied and those who are not. They examine the satisfied and like what they see. These are eager, energetic people, who are generally enthusiastic about their jobs and life in general. The behaviorists hold them up as ideal and prepare to convert the dissatisfied.

In contrasting the satisfied workers with the dissatisfied ones, behaviorists see the nature of the work performed as the main difference. So they propose to change the work of the dissatisfied to more closely resemble that performed by the satisfied. But there is a large "if" in this approach: What if the nature of the work is not the reason for the satisfaction?

It could very well be that the satisfied have more drive, which creates greater material wants and higher goals, which in turn motivates them to make more effective efforts in the workplace and to bid for more highly skilled jobs, and so on. Restructuring the work and creating new opportunities may make some people enthusiastic, but to what extent is the nature of the work the determinant of a person's drive?

There are no data that definitively show that restructuring and enriching jobs will increase the will to work or give workers greater satisfaction. Similarly, I have not seen any research data that show that a person with drive is deterred from reaching his potential by the nature of the work.

I believe that ethical considerations alone should keep behaviorists from setting up their values as the ideals for society. In addition, I will attempt to demonstrate that the behaviorists' views on redesigning jobs are misguided; they do not understand the work process in plants, and they misjudge workers' attitudes toward their jobs.

WORKERS' ATTITUDES TOWARD THEIR WORK

A 1972 Gallup Poll found that 80 to 90 percent of American workers are satisfied with their jobs. A 1973 poll by Thomas C. Sorenson found that from 82 to 91 percent of blue- and white-collar workers like their work. He asked, "If there were one thing you could change about your job, what would it be?" He found that "Astonishingly, very few mentioned making their jobs 'less boring' or 'more interesting.' "[3]

Behaviorists and humanists find it difficult to understand how workers can possibly say they like their work when it appears so barren to intellectuals. This view was recently expressed by the behavioral scientist David Sirota, after making a study in a garment plant. He was surprised to find that most sewing-machine operators found their work interesting. Since the work appeared highly repetitive to him, he had expected that they would say that they were bored and that their talents were not fully utilized. These workers' views are supported in a study by Emanuel Weintraub of 2,535 female sewing-machine operators in seventeen plants from Massachusetts to Texas. He found that "most of the operators like the nature of their work."[4] What the behaviorists find so difficult to comprehend is really quite simply explained: Workers have similar attitudes toward their work because *they are not a cross-section of the population, but rather a select group.*

There is greater choice in the selection of jobs by workers than is supposed. The selection process in factories and offices goes on without conscious direction by either workers or management. The data for white- and blue-collar jobs show that there is tremendous turnover in the initial employment period but that the turnover drops sharply with time on the job. What occurs is that a worker comes onto a new job, tries it out for several days or weeks, and decides whether or not the work suits his needs and desires. Impressions about a job are a composite of many factors: pay, proximity to home, nature of work, working conditions, attitude of supervision, congeniality of fellow workers, past employment history of the company, job security, physical demands, possibilities for advancement, and many others. Working conditions may be bad, but if the pay and job security are high, the job may be tolerable. To a married woman, the pay may be low, but if the job is close to home and working conditions are good, it may be desirable. There are numerous combinations of factors that influence a worker's disposition to stay on the job or not.

There is a dual screening process that sifts out many of those who will be dissatisfied with the work. The process operates as follows: The worker in the first instance decides whether or not to stay on the job; management then has the opportunity to determine whether or not to keep him beyond the trial period. The combination of the worker's choice to remain and management's decision regarding the worker's acceptability screens out many workers who might find the job unsatisfying.

Some workers find highly repetitive work in factories intolerable, so they become truck drivers, where they can be out on the road with no supervisor on their back all day. Others prefer to work in gas stations, warehouses, retail stores, and other such places. Increasingly workers are taking white-collar jobs that in many ways are similar to repetitive factory jobs but which have cleaner physical surroundings and better working conditions. In times of high unemployment, workers stay in safe jobs for continuity of income; but, as the job market improves, the rate of turnover increases and selection of jobs resumes.

There would undoubtedly be much greater dissatisfaction among workers if they were not free to make changes and selections in the work they do. Some prefer to remain in highly repetitive, low-skilled work even when they have an opportunity to advance to more highly skilled jobs through job bidding. A minority of workers strive to move into the more skilled jobs, such as machinists, maintenance mechanics, setup men, group leaders, and utility men, where work is discretionary and the workers have considerable autonomy in the tasks they perform.

The continued evaluation of workers by management and the mobility available to workers in the job market refine the selection process. A year or two after entering a plant, most workers are on jobs or job progressions that suit them or which they find tolerable.

However, the work force in the plant is not homogeneous. There are two main groups, the achievers and the nonachievers. Their attitudes toward work and their goals are vastly different. A minority of the work force, which I find to be 15 percent, have a drive for achievement and identify with their work. These workers' attitudes match the ideal projected by behaviorists. They dislike repetitive work and escape from it by moving into more skilled jobs, which have the autonomy and interest they look for in their work. Only a minority of jobs in industry and offices are in the skilled category, and fortunately only a minority of workers aspire to these jobs. About 85 percent of workers do not identify with their work, do not prefer more complicated and restructured jobs, and simply work in order to eat. Yet they, too, like their work and find it interesting.[5]

For different reasons, both groups of workers find their work interesting and satisfying. The work of the 85 percent who are nonachievers is interesting to them though boring to the other 15 percent. And the 15 percent who are achievers find their work interesting, though it is not sufficiently appealing for the majority to covet it. The selection process does amazingly well in matching workers and jobs.

What blinds behaviorists to this process is their belief that the achievement drive is an intrinsic part of human nature, that fulfillment at work is essential to sound mental health, and that, given the opportunity, workers would choose to become more involved in their work and take on larger and more complicated tasks. Once behaviorists take this view, they cannot understand what really happens on the plant floor or why workers do one thing rather than another.

WHY DO BEHAVIORISTS CLAIM TO SPEAK FOR WORKERS?

Behaviorists' insistence that they know more about what workers want than workers themselves is largely based on a number of job-enrichment case histories and studies of workers over the past decade. It is claimed that these studies show that workers really want job enrichment and benefit from it. But when these studies are examined closely, four things are found. (1) What actually occurred was quite different from what was reported by the behaviorists. (2) Most of the studies were conducted with hand-picked employees, usually working in areas or plants isolated from the main operation, and they do not reflect a cross-section of the working population. Practically all are in nonunion plants. (3) Only a handful of job-enrichment cases have been reported in the past ten years, despite the behaviorists' claims of gains for employees and management obtained through job changes. (4) In all instances, the experiments were initiated by management, never by workers or unions.

The *Survey of Working Conditions,* conducted for the United States Department of Labor by the Survey Research Center of the University of Michigan, contained serious errors.[6] The General Foods-Topeka case reported by Richard E. Walton[7] omits important information that shows that the sixty-three workers for this plant were handpicked from seven hundred applicants. Texas Instruments, which conducted the longest and broadest experiments, only attracted 10 percent of its employees to the program.[8] The Texas Instruments cleaning-employees case, as well as others, was grossly misreported in HEW's *Work in America.*

There are no job-enrichment successes that bear out the predictions of the behaviorists, because the vast majority of workers reject the concept. A small proportion of workers who desire job changes are prevented from participating by the social climate in the plant. They find involvement by moving into skilled jobs. Perhaps behaviorists do not recognize the moral issues raised by their proposals to redesign work—for example: intrusion upon a person's right to personal decisions; exploitation of workers' job satisfaction for company gains; distortion of the truth.

The boundless wisdom of this country's founders in separating religion from government and public practices has been revealed in countless ways. But along comes a new faith that proclaims that people should derive satisfaction from their work. When up to 90 percent of workers are reported to be satisfied with their work, the behaviorists say that workers do not really know what satisfaction is and that they will lead them to a superior kind. This sounds oddly like the proselytizing of a missionary. If behaviorists called for making enriched work available for those who want it, I would support them because I believe a minority of workers do want it. But I oppose foisting these practices on workers who do not call for it. In any case, I believe the minority has all the enrichment they want.

Exploiting workers' job satisfaction for management's gain can backfire dangerously. Workers expect management to develop new approaches and production processes to increase productivity; they are prepared for continuous pressure for more output. But when these changes are designed primarily to create a more receptive worker attitude toward greater productivity, they may see that they have been "had." If management's gains are real, while workers' benefits are only in their minds, who has really benefited? The behaviorists now say that workers should also share in productivity gains. But these statements have come late and are couched in such vague terms as to be meaningless.

When a supposedly good thing must be put into fancy wrappings to enhance it, something is amiss. Why must the job-enrichment cases be distorted to make the final results appealing? Why must behaviorists use phrases such as "work humanization" to describe their proposals, as though work were now inhuman? Workers understand the meaning of money, job security, health benefits, and retirement without fancy explanations. If the enrichment and redesign of work is such a good thing, why is it rejected by those who would benefit from it? The so-called new industrial democracy is not really democracy but a new autocracy of "we know better than you what's good for you."

NOTES

1. Abraham Maslow, *The Farther Reaches of Human Nature* (New York: Viking, 1971), p. 10.
2. Paul Kurtz, "What Is Humanism?" in *Moral Problems in Contemporary Society: Essays in Humanistic Ethics,* ed. P. Kurtz (Buffalo: Prometheus Books, 1973), p. 11.
3. Thomas C. Sorenson, "Do Americans Like Their Jobs?" *Parade,* June 3, 1973.
4. Emanuel Weintraub, "Has Job Enrichment Been Oversold?" an address to the 25th annual convention of the American Institute of Industrial Engineers, May 1973, *Technical Papers,* p. 349.
5. A more complete discussion and supporting data for the 15/85 worker composition is contained in M. Fein's "Motivation for Work," in *Handbook of Work Organization and Society,* ed. Robert Dubin (Skokie, Ill.: Rand-McNally, 1973).
6. *Survey of Working Conditions* (Washington, D.C.:

U.S. Dept. of Labor, 1971). These errors were disclosed in my analysis in "The Real Needs and Goals of Blue Collar Workers," *The Conference Board Record,* Feb. 1973.

7. Richard E. Walton, "How To Counter Alienation in the Plant," *Harvard Business Review,* Nov.–Dec. 1972, pp. 70–81.
8. Fein, "Motivation for Work."

QUESTIONS FOR DISCUSSION

1. How might an adversarial relationship between workers and employers protect workers? How might cooperation with management work against the interests of labor?
2. In what ways are the interests of workers and management interdependent? How might cooperation between workers and management benefit both?

CHAPTER 9

The Modern Workplace: Transition to Equality and Diversity

Business and the Facts of Family Life

Fran Sussner Rodgers and Charles Rodgers
Fran S. Rodgers—CEO, Charles Rodgers—Principal, Work/Family Directions, Inc., and President, Rodgers and Associates.

Business is a good thing.

Family is also a good thing.

These are simple, self-evident propositions.

Yet the awkward fact is that when we try to combine these two assertions in the new labor force, they stop being safe, compatible, and obvious and become difficult, even antagonistic. Sometimes the most complex and controversial challenges we face have commonsense truths at their roots.

Consider these variations on the same theme:

Our economy needs the most skilled and productive work force it can possibly find in order to remain competitive.

That same work force must reproduce itself and give adequate care to the children who are the work force of the future.

People with children—women especially—often find themselves at a serious disadvantage in the workplace.

Among Western democracies, the United States ranks number three in dependence on women in the work force, behind only Scandinavia and Canada.

In short, we value both business and family, and they are increasingly at loggerheads.

THE FAMILY AS A BUSINESS ISSUE

At one time, women provided the support system that enabled male breadwinners to be productive outside the home for at least 40 hours every week. That home-based support system began to recede a generation ago and is now more the exception than the rule. The labor force now includes more than 70% of all women with children between the ages of 6 and 17 and more than half the women with children less than 1 year old. This new reality has had a marked effect on what the family requires of

Reprinted by permission of *Harvard Business Review*. "Business and the Facts of Family Life," by Fran Sussner Rodgers and Charles Rodgers, (November–December 1989).

each family member—and on what employers can expect from employees. It is not only a question of who is responsible for very young children. There is no longer anyone home to care for adolescents and the elderly. There is no one around to take in the car for repair or to let the plumber in. Working families are faced with daily dilemmas: Who will take care of a sick child? Who will go to the big soccer game? Who will attend the teacher conference?

Yet employees from families where all adults work are still coping with rules and conditions of work designed, as one observer put it, to the specifications of Ozzie and Harriet. These conditions include rigid adherence to a 40-hour workweek, a concept of career path inconsistent with the life cycle of a person with serious family responsibilities, notions of equity formed in a different era, and performance-evaluation systems that confuse effort with results by equating hours of work with productivity.

Despite the growing mismatch between the rules of the game and the needs of the players, few companies have made much effort to accommodate changing lifestyles. For that matter, how serious can the problem really be? After all, employees still get to work and do their jobs. Somehow the plumber manages to find the key. We know that children and the elderly are somewhere. Why start worrying now? Women's entry into the labor force has been increasing for 20 years, and the system still appears to function.

Nevertheless, we are seeing a rapidly growing corporate interest in work-and-family issues. There are four principal *business* reasons:

First, work force demographics are changing. Most of the increase in the number of working women has coincided with the baby boom. Any associated business fallout—high turnover, lost productivity, absenteeism—occurred in the context of a large labor surplus. Most people were easily replaced, and there was plenty of talent willing to make the traditional sacrifices for success—like travel, overtime, relocation. With the baby boom over and a baby bust upon us, there are now higher costs associated with discouraging entry into the labor force and frustrating talented people who are trying to act responsibly at home as well as at work. In some parts of the country, labor is already so scarce that companies are using progressive family policies as a means of competing for workers.

Second, employee perceptions are changing. Unless we rethink our traditional career paths, the raised aspirations of many women are now clearly on a collision course with their desire to be parents. Before the emergence of the women's movement in the 1960s, many suburban housewives thought their frustrations were uniquely their own. Similarly, for 20 years corporate women who failed to meet their own high expectations considered it a personal failing. But now the invisible barriers to female advancement are being named, and the media take employers to task for their inflexibility.

This shift in women's perceptions greatly changes the climate for employers. Women and men in two-career and single-parent families are much better able to identify policies that will let them act responsibly toward their families and still satisfy their professional ambitions. Companies that don't act as partners in this process may lose talent to companies that do rise to the challenge. No one knows how many women have left large companies because of cultural rigidity. It is even harder to guess at the numbers of talented women who have never even applied for jobs because they assume big companies will require family sacrifices they are unwilling to make.

And it's not just women. In two studies at Du Pont, we found that men's reports of certain family-related problems nearly doubled from 1985 to 1988. (Interestingly, on a few of these items, women's reported problems decreased proportionally, which suggests that one reason women experience such great difficulty with work-and-family issues is that men experience so little.)

In fact, men's desire for a more active role in parenting may be unacceptable to their peers. Numerous reports show that few men take advantage of the formal parental leave available to them in many companies. Yet a recent study shows that many men do indeed take time off from work after the birth of a child, but that they do so by piecing together other forms of leave—vacation, personal leave, sick leave—that they see as more acceptable.[1]

A third reason why more companies are addressing work-and-family issues is increasing evidence that inflexibility has an adverse effect on productivity. In a study at Merck in 1984, employees who perceived their supervisors as unsupportive on family issues reported higher levels of stress, greater absenteeism, and lower job satisfaction.[2] Other studies show that supportive companies attract new employees more easily, get them back on the job more quickly after maternity leave, and benefit generally from higher work-force morale.[3]

Fourth, concern about America's children is growing fast. Childhood poverty is up, single-parent families are on the increase, SAT scores are falling, and childhood literacy, obesity, and suicide rates are all moving in the wrong direction.

So far, the business community has expressed its concern primarily through direct efforts to improve schools. Yet in our studies, one-third to one-half of parents say they do not have the workplace flexibility to attend teacher conferences and important school events. It is certainly possible that adapting work rules to allow this parent-school connection—and trying to influence schools to schedule events with working parents in mind—might have as great a positive effect on education as some direct interventions.

For companies that want to use and fully develop the talents of working parents and others looking for flexibility, the agenda is well defined. There are three broad areas that require attention:

1. Dependent care, including infants, children, adolescents, and the elderly.
2. Greater flexibility in the organization, hours, and location of work, and creation of career paths that allow for family responsibility as well as professional ambition.
3. Validation of family issues as an organizational concern by means of company statements and manager training.

Few companies are active in all three areas. Many are active in none. The costs and difficulties are, after all, considerable, and the burden of change does not fall on only employers. There is plenty for government to do. Individual employees too will have to take on new responsibilities. Corporate dependent-care programs often mean purchasing benefits or programs from outside providers and may entail substantial community involvement. Workplace flexibility demands reexamination of work assumptions by employees as well as employers and often meets with line resistance. A corporate commitment to family takes time to work its way down to the front-line supervisory levels where most of the work force will feel its effects.

DEPENDENT CARE

Dependent care is a business issue for the obvious reason that employees cannot come to work unless their dependents are cared for. Study after study shows that most working parents have trouble arranging child care, and that those with the most difficulty also experience the most frequent work disruptions and the greatest absenteeism. Moreover, the lack of child care is still a major barrier to the entry of women into the labor force.

Child-care needs vary greatly in any employee population, and most companies have a limited capacity to address them. But, depending on the company's location, financial resources, the age of its work force, and the competitiveness of its labor market, a corporate child-care program might include some or all of the following:

- Help in finding existing child care and efforts to increase the supply of care in the community, including care for sick children.
- Financial assistance for child care, especially for entry level and lower level employees.
- Involvement with schools, Ys, and other community organizations to promote programs for school-age children whose parents work.
- Support for child-care centers in locations convenient to company employees.
- Efforts to move government policies—local and federal—toward greater investment in children.

Existing child care is often hard to find because so much of the country's care is provided by the woman down the street, who does not advertise and is not usually listed in the yellow pages or anywhere else. Even where lists do exist—as the result, say, of state licensing requirements—they are often out-of-date. (Turnover in family day-care, as this form of child care is called, is estimated at 50% per year.) And lists don't give vacancy information, so parents can spend days making unsuccessful phone calls. Sometimes existing care is invisible because it operates in violation of zoning rules or outside of onerous or inefficient regulatory systems.

In other places—suburban neighborhoods where many women work outside the home or where family income is so high that few need the extra money—there is virtually no child care. Often, too, land prices make centers unaffordable. Infant care is especially scarce because it requires such a high ratio of adults to children. Care for children before and after school and during the many weeks when school is out is in short supply just about everywhere, as is care for "off hour" workers such as shift workers, police officers, and hospital employees.

In addition to the difficulty of finding child care, quality and affordability are always big questions. Cost depends greatly on local standards. In Massachusetts, for example, infant care in centers runs from $150 to more than $200 per week per child due to a combination of high labor costs and strict state licensing standards. Even the highest standards, however, still mean that an infant-care staff member has more to do all day—and more responsibility—than a new parent caring for triplets. In states with lower standards, one staff member may care for as many as eight infants at a time. Up to now, child care in many places has been made affordable by paying very low wages—the national average for child-care staff is $5.35 an hour—and by reducing the standards of quality and safety below what common sense would dictate.[4]

Given all these problems, is it any wonder the companies that want to help feel stymied? While few companies provide significant child-care support today, a very large number are exploring the possibility. We think that number will increase geometrically as the competition for labor grows and more members of the labor force need such support.

One increasingly popular way for companies to address these issues is through resource and referral services. Typically, such services do three things: they help employees find child care suited to their circumstances; they make an effort to promote more care of all types in the communities where employees live; and they try to remove regulatory and zoning barriers to care facilities. Resource and referral services (R & Rs) meet standards of equity by assisting parents regardless of their incomes and their children's ages. And R & Rs work as well for a few workers as for thousands. When the service is delivered through a network of community-based R & Rs, moreover corporate involvement can also strengthen the community at large.

Although R & R programs can be very helpful, they have limitations. By themselves, they have little effect on affordability, for example, and only an indirect effect on quality, primarily through consumer education and provider training. Also, R & Rs cannot dig up a supply of care where market conditions are highly unfavorable.

A small but growing number of companies provide, subsidize, or contract with outside providers to operate on-site or near-site centers that are available to employees at fees covering at least most of the cost. A North Carolina software company, SAS Institute Inc., provides child care at an on-site center at no cost to employees. The company reports that its turnover rates are less than half the industry average and feels the center's extra expense is justified because it decreases the extremely high cost of training new workers.[5]

Companies that get involved with child-care centers, however, find themselves making difficult trade-offs as a result of the high cost of good care. Many companies won't associate themselves even indirectly with any child care that doesn't meet the highest standards, which means that without a subsidy, only higher income employees can afford the service. But if a company does subsidize child care, it must justify giving this considerable benefit to one group of parents while other parents, who buy child care in some other place or way, get none. One way of avoiding this dilemma is to give child-care subsidies to all lower income employees as an extension of the R & R service, the approach recently announced by NCNB, the banking corporation.

Companies sometimes capitalize centers by donating space or land along with renovation costs or by providing an initial subsidy until the centers are self-supporting. In this way, Du Pont helped a number of community not-for-profit organizations establish and expand existing child-care centers in Delaware. Of course, costs can vary hugely. If a building is already available, renovation and startup costs could be as low as $100,000. In most cases, the bill will run from several hundred thousand to several million dollars.

Businesses are also working more closely with schools to encourage before-school, after-school, and vacation care programs. Such a partnership has been established between the American Bankers Insurance Group and the Dade County, Florida school system. The school system actually operates a kindergarten and a first- and second-grade school in a building built by the insurance company. In Charlotte, North Carolina, the 19 largest employers have joined forces with the public sector to expand and improve the quality of care.

In any case, employee interest in child care is great, and employees often fix on the issue of on-site care as a solution to the work-and-family conflicts they experience. But helping employees with child care, given the enormity of the problem in the society at large, is a complicated question. More and more companies are taking the kinds of steps described here, but as the pressure grows, business as a whole is likely to focus more attention on public policy.

Of course, dependent care is not just a question of care for children. Studies at Travelers Insurance Company and at IBM show that 20% to 30% of employees have some responsibility for the care of an adult dependent. Traditionally, the wife stayed home and cared for the elderly parents of both spouses, but as women entered the work force, this support system began to disappear. Since the most recent growth in the female work force involves comparatively younger women whose parents are not yet old enough to require daily assistance, the workplace has probably not yet felt the full effects of elder-care problems.

As in the case of child care, studies show that productivity suffers when people try to balance work and the care of parents. Some people quit their jobs entirely. The most immediate need is for information about the needs and problems of the aging and about available resources. Most young people know nothing at all about government programs like Medicare and Medicaid. More often than not, children know very little about their own parents' financial situations and need help simply to open communication.

Unlike child care, elder care is often complicated by distance. In our experience with some 12,000 employees with elderly dependents, more than half lived more than 100 miles from the person they were concerned about. Crises are common. The elderly suffer unexpected hospitalizations, for example, and then come out of the hospital too weak to care for themselves. A service that can help with referrals and arrangements in another city can spare employees time, expense, and anguish. Also, people often need to compare resources in several states where different siblings live in order to make decisions about such things as where parents should live when their health begins to deteriorate.

CONDITIONS OF WORK

A study at two high-tech companies in New England showed that the average working mother logs in a total workweek of 84 hours between her home and her job, compared with 72 hours for male parents and about 50 hours for married men and women with no children. In other words, employed parents—women in particular—work the equivalent of two full-time jobs.[6] No wonder they've started looking for flexible schedules, part-time employment, and career-path alternatives that allow more than one model of success. For that matter, is it even reasonable to expect people who work two jobs to behave and progress along exactly the same lines as those with no primary outside responsibilities?

Until now, most companies have looked at job flexibility on a case-by-case basis and have offered it sparingly to valued employees as a favor. But increasing competition for the best employees will make such flexibility commonplace. A smaller labor supply means that workers will no longer have to take jobs in the forms that have always been offered. Companies will have to market their own employment practices and adapt their jobs to the demands of the work force.

We all know that the way we did things in the past no longer works for many employees. Our research shows that up to 35% of working men and women with young children have told their bosses they will not take jobs involving shift work, relocation, extensive travel, intense pressure, or lots of overtime. Some parents are turning down promotions that they believe might put a strain on family life. Women report more trade-offs than men, but even the male numbers are significant and appear to be increasing. In our study, nearly 25% of men with young children had told their bosses they would not relocate.

Interestingly enough, few employees seem angry about such trade-offs. They value the rewards of family life, and, by and large, they don't seem to expect parity with those willing to sacrifice their family lives for their careers. Nevertheless, they *are* bothered by what they see as unnecessary barriers to success. Most believe they could make greater contributions and go farther in their own careers—despite family obligations—if it weren't for rigid scheduling, open-ended expectations, and outmoded career definitions. They long for alternative scenarios that would allow them more freedom to determine the conditions of their work and the criteria for judging their contributions.

The question is whether a willingness to sacrifice family life is an appropriate screen for picking candidates for promotions. It would be wrong to suppose that these employees are any less talented or less ambitious than those who don't make the family trade-off. A study we conducted at NCNB showed no evidence of any long-term difference in ambition between people with and without child-care responsibilities. Since fewer and fewer people in our diverse labor force are willing to pay the price for traditional success, to insist on it is only to narrow the funnel of opportunity and, eventually, to lower the quality of the talent pool from which we draw our leaders.

Flexible Schedules. In addition to time away from work to care for newborn or newly adopted children, employees with dependent-care responsibilities have two different needs for flexibility. One is the need for working hours that accommodate their children's normal schedules and their predictable special requirements such as doctor's appointments, school conferences, and soccer championships. The other is the need to deal with the emergencies and unanticipated events that are part and parcel of family life—sudden illness, an early school closing due to snow, a breakdown in child-care arrangements.

The most common response to both needs has been flextime. Flextime can be narrowly designed to permit permanent alterations of a basically rigid work schedule by, say, half an hour or an hour, or it can be more broadly defined to allow freewheeling variations from one workday to the next.

Pioneered in this country by Hewlett-Packard, flextime is now used by about 12% of all U.S. workers, while half the country's large employers offer some kind of flextime arrangement. Its effects on lateness, absenteeism, and employee morale have been highly positive.[7] The effects on the family are not as easily measured, but most employees say they find it helpful, and the more scheduling latitude it offers, the more helpful they seem to find it.

A number of companies are considering ways of further expanding the notion of flextime. One alternative, called "weekly balancing," lets employees set their own hours day-to-day as long as the weekly total stays constant. In Europe, some companies offer monthly and yearly balancing. Clearly, this is most difficult to do in situations where production processes require a predictable level of staffing.

In November 1988, Eastman Kodak announced a new work-schedule program that permits four kinds of alternative work arrangements:

1. Permanent changes in regular, scheduled hours.
2. Supervisory flexibility in adjusting daily schedules to accommodate family needs.
3. Temporary and permanent part-time schedules at all levels.
4. Job sharing.

Aetna Life and Casualty too has recently launched an internal marketing effort and training program to help its supervisors adapt to, plan for, and implement unconventional work schedules.

Employees also must assume new roles. In the job-sharing program at Rolscreen Company, for example, employees are responsible for locating compatible partners for a shared job and for ensuring that the arrangement works and that business needs are met.[8] Also, employees are often expected to make themselves available when business emergencies arise. In the best flexible arrangements, employers and employees work as partners.

Part-Time Employment. Studies show that a third to half of women with young children want to work less than full time for at least a while, despite the loss of pay and other benefits. Yet we have found in our work with dozens of companies that managers at all levels show firm resistance to part-time work. They seem to regard the 40-hour week as sacred and cannot imagine that anyone working fewer hours could be doing anything useful. Even in companies that accept the need for part-time work, we see managers who refuse to believe it will work in their own departments. Indeed, even the term "part-time" seems to have a negative connotation.

Research on part-time productivity is sometimes hard to interpret, but the studies we've seen indicate that the productivity of part-time workers is, in certain cases, better than their full-time counterparts and, in all cases, no worse. One study comparing part-time and full-time social workers found that, hour for hour, the part-time employees carried greater caseloads and serviced them with more attention.[9]

Part-time is not necessarily the same as half-time, as many managers assume. Many parents want 4-day or 30-hour workweeks. Many other assumptions about less than full-time employment are also unwarranted. For example, managers often insist that customers will not work with part-time employees, but few have asked their customers if this is true.

Another axiom is that supervisory and managerial personnel must always be full-time, since it is a manager's role "to be there" for subordinates. This article of faith ignores the fact that managers travel, attend meetings, close their doors, and are otherwise unavailable for a good part of every week.

Career-Path Alternatives. It takes a lot of ingenuity and cultural adaptability to devise meaningful part-time work opportunities and to give employees individual control of their working hours. But an even greater challenge is to find ways of fitting these flexible arrangements into long-term career paths. If the price of family responsibility is a label that reads "Not Serious About Career," frustrations will grow. But if adaptability and labor-market competitiveness are the goals, then the usual definition of fast-track career progression needs modification.

The first step, perhaps, is to find ways of acquiring broad business experience that are less disruptive to the family. For example, Mobil Oil has gradually concentrated a wide range of facilities at hub locations, partly in order to allow its employees a greater variety of work experience without relocation.

Another essential step is to reduce the tendency to judge productivity by time spent at work. Nothing is more frustrating to parents than working intensely all day in order to pick up a child on time, only to be judged inferior to a coworker who has to stay late to produce as much. For many hardworking people, hours certainly do translate into increased productivity. Not for all. And dismissing those who spend fewer hours at the workplace as lacking dedication ignores the fact that virtually all employees go through periods when their working hours and efficiency rise or fall, whether the cause is family, health, or fluctuating motivation.

CORPORATE MISSION

Fertility in the United States is below replacement levels. Moreover, the higher a woman's education level, the more likely she is to be employed and the less likely to have children. The choice to have a family is complex, yet one study shows that two-thirds of women under 40 who have reached the upper echelons in our largest companies and institutions are childless, while virtually all men in leadership positions are fathers.[10] If we fail to alter the messages and opportunities we offer young men and women, and if they learn to see a demanding work life as incompatible with a satisfying family life, we could create an economy in which more and more leaders have traded family for career success.

There are four things a company needs to do in order to create an environment where people with dependents can do their best work without sacrificing their families' welfare. It needs to develop a corporate policy that it communicates to all its employees; it needs to train and encourage supervisors to be adaptable and responsible; it needs to give supervisors tools and programs to work with; and it needs to hold all managers accountable for the flexibility and responsiveness of their departments.

The key people in all this are first-line managers and supervisors. All the policies and programs in the world don't mean much to an employee who has to deal with an unsupportive boss, and the boss is often unsupportive because of mixed signals from above.

We have seen companies where the CEO went on record in support of family flexibility but where supervisors were never evaluated in any way for their sensitivity to family issues. In one company, managers were encouraged to provide part-time work opportunities, yet head-count restrictions reckoned all employees as full-time. In another, maternity leave was counted against individual managers when measuring absenteeism, a key element in their performance appraisals. As a general rule, strict absenteeism systems designed to discourage malingerers often inadvertently punish the parents of young children. Yet such systems coexist with corporate admonitions to be flexible. Where messages are mixed and performance measurement has not changed since the days of the "give an inch, they'll take a mile" personnel policy, it is hardly surprising that supervisors and managers greet lofty family-oriented policy statements with some cynicism.

Training is critical. IBM, Johnson & Johnson, Merck, and Warner-Lambert have all established training programs to teach managers to be more sensitive to work-and-family issues. The training lays out the business case for flexibility, reviews corporate programs and policies, and presents case studies that underline the fact that there are often no right answers or rule books to use as guides in the complicated circumstances of real life.

Perhaps the thorniest issue facing businesses and managers is that of equity. Most managers have been trained to treat employees identically and not to adjudicate the comparative merits of different requests for flexibility. But what equity often means in practice is treating everyone as though they had wives at home. On the other hand, it is difficult to set up guidelines for personalized responses, since equity is a touchstone of labor relations and human resource management. Judging requests individually, on the basis of business and personal need, is not likely to lead to identical outcomes.

Seniority systems also need rethinking. Working second or third shift is often the only entry to a well-paying job for nonprofessional employees, but for a parent with a school-age child, this can mean not seeing the child at all from weekend to weekend. Rotating shifts wreak havoc with child-care arrangements and children's schedules. Practices that worked fine when the labor force consisted mostly of men with wives at home now have unintended consequences.

Finally, the message top management sends to all employees is terribly important. In focus groups at various large companies, we hear over and over again a sense that companies pay lip service to the value of family and community but that day-to-day practice is another story altogether. We hear what we can only describe as a yearning for some tangible acknowledgment from top management that family issues are real, complex, and important.

Johnson & Johnson, which sees its 40-year-old corporate credo as central to its culture, recently added the statement, "We must be mindful of ways to help our employees fulfill their family obligations." Du Pont has developed a mission statement that commits it, in part, to "making changes in the workplace and fostering changes in the community that are sensitive to the changing family unit and the increasingly diverse work force."

Throughout Europe, governments have required companies to treat the parenting of babies as a special circumstance of employment and have invested heavily in programs to support the children of working parents. In this country, recent surveys indicate almost universal popular support for parental leave. But our instincts oppose government intervention into internal business practices. We leave decisions about flexibility and the organization of work to individual companies, which means that the decisions of first-line managers in large part create our national family policy.

In this, the United States is unique. But then we are also unique in other ways, including the depth of our commitment to business, to fairness, to equal opportunity, to common sense. Many of our young women now strive to become CEOs. No one intended that the price for business success should be indifference to family or that the price of having a family should be to abandon professional ambition.

REFERENCES

1. Joseph Pleck, "Family-Supportive Employer Policies and Men's Participation," unpublished paper, Wheaton College, 1989.
2. From research conducted by Ellen Galinsky at Merck and Company, Rahway, New Jersey, 1983, 1984, and 1986.
3. Terry Bond, *Employer Supports for Child Care*, report for the National Council of Jewish Women, Center for the Child, New York, August 1988.
4. Marcy Whitebook, Carollee Howes, and Deborah Phillips, "Who Cares: Child Care Teachers and the Quality of Care in America," National Child Care Staffing Study, Child Care Employee Project, Oakland, California, 1989.
5. "On-site Child Care Results in Low Turnover at Computer Firm." *National Report on Work and Family,* vol. 2, no. 13 (Washington, D.C.: Buraff Publications, June 9, 1989, p. 3.
6. Dianne Burden and Bradley Googins, *Boston University Balancing Job and Homelife Study* (Boston University School of Social Work, 1986).
7. Kathleen Christensen, *A Look at Flexible Staffing and Scheduling in U.S. Corporations* (New York: Conference Board, 1989); and Jon L. Pierce et al., *Alternative Work Schedules* (Newton, Mass.: Allyn and Bacon, 1988).
8. *Work and Family: A Changing Dynamic* (Washington, D.C.: Bureau of National Affairs Special Report, 1986), pp. 78–80.
9. *Part-Time Social Workers in Public Welfare* (New York: Catalyst, 1971), cited in *Alternative Work Schedules,* p. 81.
10. *The Corporate Woman Officer* (Chicago, Ill.: Heidrick and Struggles, Inc., 1986); *Korn/Ferry International's Executive Profile: Corporate Leaders in the Eighties* (New York: Korn/Ferry International, 1986).

Sexual Harassment in the Workplace

Ellen Bravo and Ellen Cassedy
Bravo—Executive Director, 9 to 5, National Association of Working Women
Cassedy—A founder of 9 to 5, National Association of Working Women

SECTION 1: WHAT SEXUAL HARASSMENT IS—AND IS NOT

Louette Colombano was one of the first female police officers in her San Francisco district. While listening to the watch commander, she and the other officers stood

---

at attention with their hands behind their backs. The officer behind her unzipped his fly and rubbed his penis against her hands.

Diane, a buyer, was preparing to meet an out-of-town client for dinner when she received a message: her boss had informed the client that she would spend the night with him. Diane sent word that she couldn't make it to dinner. The next day she was fired.

Few people would disagree that these are clear-cut examples of sexual harassment. Touching someone in a deliberately sexual way, demanding that an employee engage in sex or lose her job—such behavior is clearly out of bounds. But in less obvious cases, many people are confused about where to draw the line.

Is all sexual conversation inappropriate at work? Is every kind of touching off limits? Consider the following examples. In your opinion, which, if any, constitute sexual harassment?

- A male manager asks a female subordinate to lunch to discuss a new project.
- A man puts his arm around a woman at work.
- A woman tells an off-color joke.
- These comments are made at the workplace:
  "Your hair looks terrific."
  "That outfit's a knockout."
  "Did you get any last night?"

The answer in each of these cases is, "It depends." Each one *could* be an example of sexual harassment—or it could be acceptable behavior.

Take the case of the manager asking a female subordinate to lunch to discuss a new project. Suppose this manager often has such lunchtime meetings with his employees, male and female. Everyone is aware that he likes to get out of the office environment in order to get to know the associates a little better and to learn how they function—for example, whether they prefer frequent meetings or written reports, detailed instructions or more delegation of responsibility. The female subordinate in this case may feel she's being treated just like other colleagues and be glad to receive the individual attention.

On the other hand, suppose this subordinate has been trying for some time, unsuccessfully, to be assigned to an interesting project. The only woman who does get plum assignments spends a lot of time out of the office with the boss; the two of them are rumored to be sleeping together. The lunch may represent an opportunity to move ahead, but it could mean that the manager expects a physical relationship in return. In this case, an invitation to lunch with the boss is laden with unwelcome sexual overtones.

An arm around the shoulder, an off-color joke, comments about someone's appearance, or even sexual remarks may or may not be offensive. What matters is the relationship between the two parties and how each of them feels.

"Your hair looks terrific," for instance, could be an innocuous compliment if it were tossed off by one coworker to another as they passed in the hall. But imagine this same phrase coming from a male boss bending down next to his secretary's ear and speaking in a suggestive whisper. Suddenly, these innocent-sounding words take on a different meaning. The body language and tone of voice signify something sexual. While the comment itself may not amount to much, the secretary is left to wonder *what else the boss has in mind.*

On the other hand, even words that may seem grossly inappropriate—"Did you get any last night?"—can be harmless in certain work situations. One group of male and female assemblyline workers talked like this all the time. What made it okay? They were friends and equals—no one in the group had power over any of the others. They were all comfortable with the banter. They hadn't drawn up a list specifying which words were acceptable to the group and which were not. But they had worked together for some time and knew one another well. Their remarks were made with affection and accepted as good-natured. No one intended to offend—and no one was offended. The assembly-line area was relatively isolated, so the workers weren't in danger of bothering anyone outside their group. Had a new person joined the group who wasn't comfortable with this kind of talk, the others would have stopped it. They might have thought the new person uptight, they might not have liked the new atmosphere, but they would have respected and honored any request to eliminate the remarks.

This is the essence of combating sexual harassment—creating a workplace that is built on mutual respect.

Try assessing whether each of the following scenarios constitutes sexual harassment. Then consider the analysis that follows.

Scenario 1

Justine works in a predominantly male department. She has tried to fit in, even laughing on occasion at the frequent sexual jokes. The truth is, though, that she gets more irritated by the jokes each day. It is well known in the department that Justine has an out-of-town boyfriend whom she sees most weekends. Nonetheless, Franklin, one of Justine's coworkers, has said he has the "hots" for her and that—boyfriend or not—he's willing to do almost anything to get a date with her. One day, Sarah, another of Justine's coworkers, overheard their boss talking to Franklin in the hallway. "If you can get her to go to bed with you," the boss said, "I'll take you out to dinner. Good luck." They chuckled and went their separate ways. *(From the consulting firm of Jane C. Edmonds & Associates, Inc.,* Boston Globe, *10/24/91.)*

The boss is out of line. True, he probably didn't intend anyone to overhear him. But why was he having this conversation in the hallway? What was he doing having the conversation at all? The boss is responsible for keeping the workplace free of harassment. Instead, he's giving Franklin an incentive to make sexual advances to a coworker and then to brag about it.

The conversation may constitute harassment not only of Justine but also of Sarah, who overheard the conversation. A reasonable woman might easily wonder, "Who's he going to encourage to go after *me?"* Ideally, Sarah should tell the two men she was offended by their remarks. But given that one of them is her boss, it would be understandable if she were reluctant to criticize his behavior.

Franklin isn't just romantically interested in Justine; he "has the hots" for her and is willing to "do almost anything" to get a date with her. Justine could well be interested in a "fling" with Franklin. But she's irritated by the sexual remarks and innuendoes in the workplace. It's unlikely that she would be flattered by attention from one of the men responsible for this atmosphere.

Justine can just say no to Franklin. But she may well object to having to say no over and over. And most women are not pleased to be the brunt of jokes and boasts. Some may argue that whether Franklin and Justine get together is a personal matter between the two of them. The moment it becomes the subject of public boasting, however, Franklin's interest in Justine ceases to be just a private interaction.

The law doesn't say Justine should be tough enough to speak up on her own—it says the company is responsible for providing an environment free of offensive or hostile behavior. As the person in charge, the boss ought to know what kind of remarks are being made in the workplace and whether employees are offended by them. Instead of making Franklin think the way to win favor with him is to pressure a coworker into bed, the manager might want to arrange for some training on sexual harassment.

Scenario 2

Freda has been working for Bruce for three years. He believes they have a good working relationship. Freda has never complained to Bruce about anything and appears to be happy in her job. Bruce regularly compliments Freda on her clothing; in his opinion, she has excellent taste and a good figure. Typically, he'll make a remark like "You sure look good today." Last week, Freda was having a bad day and told Bruce that she was "sick and tired of being treated like a sex object." Bruce was stunned. *(From the consulting firm of Jane C. Edmonds & Associates, Inc.,* Boston Globe, *10/24/91.)*

There's really not enough information to come to any conclusions in this case. The scenario explains how Bruce feels, but not Freda. In the past, when he said, "Hey, you look good today," did Freda usually answer, "So do you"? Or did he murmur, "Mmm, you look go-o-o-o-d," and stare at her chest while she crossed her arms and said, "Thank you, sir"? In addition to complimenting Freda's appearance, did Bruce ever praise her work? Did he compliment other women? men?

It is plausible that Freda might have been upset earlier. She probably wouldn't say she was tired of being treated like a sex object unless she'd felt that way before. Why didn't she speak up sooner? It's not uncommon for someone in Freda's situation to be reluctant to say anything for fear of looking foolish or appearing to be a "bad sport." Remember, Bruce is her boss.

Bruce states that he was stunned when Freda blew up at him. He needs to consider whether Freda might have given him any signals he ignored. He should ask himself how his compliments fit in with the way he treats other employees. Has he really given Freda an opening to object to his remarks?

The most comfortable solution might be for Bruce and Freda to sit down and talk. Perhaps Freda doesn't really mind the compliments themselves but wants more attention paid to her work. If Freda has been upset about the compliments all along, Bruce is probably guilty only of not paying close attention to her feelings. He should let her know that he values her work *and* her feelings, listen carefully to what she has to say, and encourage her to speak up promptly about issues that may arise in the future.

Scenario 3

Barbara is a receptionist for a printing company. Surrounding her desk are five versions of ads printed by the company for a beer distributor. The posters feature women provocatively posed with a can of beer and the slogan, "What'll you have?" On numerous occasions, male customers have walked in, looked at the posters, and commented, "I'll have you, baby." When Barbara tells her boss she wants the posters removed, he responds by saying they represent the company's work and he's proud to display them. He claims no one but Barbara is bothered by the posters.

The legal standard in this case is not how the boss feels, but whether a "reasonable woman" might object to being surrounded by such posters. The company has other products it could display. Barbara has not insisted that the company refuse this account or exclude these posters from the company portfolio. She has merely said she doesn't want the posters displayed around *her* desk. Barbara's view is substantiated by how she's been treated; the posters seem to give customers license to make suggestive remarks to her.

Scenario 4

Therese tells Andrew, her subordinate, that she needs him to escort her to a party. She says she's selecting him because he's the most handsome guy on her staff. Andrew says he's busy. Therese responds that she expects people on her staff to be team players.

Therese may have wanted Andrew merely to accompany her to the party, not to have a sexual relationship with her. And Andrew might have been willing to go along if he hadn't been busy. Nevertheless, a reasonable employee may worry about what the boss means by such a request, particularly when it's coupled with remarks about personal appearance.

Andrew might not mind that Therese finds him handsome. But most people would object to having their job tied to their willingness to make a social appearance with the boss outside of work. The implicit threat also makes Therese's request unacceptable. The company should prohibit managers from requiring subordinates to escort them to social engagements.

Scenario 5

Darlene invites her coworker Dan for a date. They begin a relationship that lasts several months. Then Darlene decides she is no longer interested and breaks up with Dan. He wants the relationship to continue. During the workday, he frequently calls her on the interoffice phone and stops by her desk to talk. Darlene tries to brush him off, but with no success. She asks her manager to intervene. The manager says he doesn't get involved in personal matters.

Most managers are rightly reluctant to involve themselves in employees' personal relationships. Had Darlene asked for help dealing with Dan outside of work, the manager would have been justified in staying out of it. He could have referred her to the employee assistance program, if the company had one.

Once Dan starts interfering with Darlene's work, however, it's a different story. The company has an obligation to make sure the work environment is free from harassment. If Darlene finds herself less able to do her job or uncomfortable at work because of Dan and if her own efforts have failed, the manager has both the right and the responsibility to step in and tell Dan to back off.

Scenario 6

Susan likes to tell bawdy jokes. Bob objects. Although he doesn't mind when men use such language in the office, he doesn't think it's appropriate for women to do so.

An employee who objects to off-color jokes shouldn't have to listen to them at work, and management should back him up. Bob's problem, however, is restricted to jokes told by women. If he doesn't have the same problem when men tell such jokes, it's his problem—not the company's. Management can't enforce Bob's double standard.

Scenario 7

Janet is wearing a low-cut blouse and short shorts. John, her coworker, says, "Now that I can see it, you gotta let me have some." Janet tells him to buzz off. All day, despite Janet's objections, John continues to make similar remarks. When Janet calls her supervisor over to complain, John says, "Hey, can you blame me?"

The company has a right to expect clothing appropriate to the job. If Janet's clothes are inappropriate, management should tell her so. But Janet's outfit doesn't give John license to say or do whatever he likes. Once she tells him she doesn't like his comments, he should stop—or be made to do so.

Scenario 8

Someone posts a *Hustler* magazine centerfold in the employee men's room. No women use this room.

Some would say that if the women aren't aware of the pinups in the men's room, they can't be offensive. But when men walk out of the restroom with such images in their mind's eye, how do they view their female coworkers? And when the women find out about the pinups—as they will—how will they feel? As the judge ruled in a 1991 Florida case involving nude posters at a shipyard, the presence of such pictures, even if they aren't intended to offend women, "sexualizes the work environment to the detriment of all female employees."

A COMMON-SENSE DEFINITION

Sexual harassment is not complicated to define. To harass someone is to bother him or her. Sexual harassment is bothering someone in a sexual way. The harasser offers sexual attention to someone who didn't ask for it and doesn't welcome it. The unwelcome behavior might or might not involve touching. It could just as well be spoken words, graphics, gestures or even looks (not any look—but the kind of leer or stare that says, "I want to undress you").

Who decides what behavior is offensive at the workplace? The recipient does. As long as the recipient is "reasonable" and not unduly sensitive, sexual conduct that offends him or her should be changed.

That doesn't mean there's a blueprint for defining *sexual harassment.* "Reasonable" people don't always agree. Society celebrates pluralism. Not everyone is expected to have the same standards of morality or the same sense of humor. Still, reasonable people will agree *much of the time* about what constitutes offensive behavior or will recognize that certain behavior or language can be expected to offend some others. Most people make distinctions between how they talk to their best friends, to their children, and to their elderly relatives. Out of respect, they avoid certain behavior in the presence of certain people. The same distinctions must be applied at work.

Sexual harassment is different from the innocent mistake—that is, when someone tells an off-color joke, not realizing the listener will be offended, or gives what is meant as a friendly squeeze of the arm to a coworker who doesn't like to be touched. Such behavior may represent insensitivity, and that may be a serious problem, but it's usually not sexual harassment. In many cases, the person who tells the joke that misfires or who pats an unreceptive arm *knows right away* that he or she has made a mistake. Once aware or made aware, this individual will usually apologize and try not to do it again.

DO THEY MEAN IT?

Some offensive behavior stems from what University of Illinois psychologist Louise Fitzgerald calls "cultural lag." "Many men entered the workplace at a time when sexual teasing and innuendo were commonplace," Fitzgerald told the *New York Times*. "They have no idea there's anything wrong with it." Education will help such men change their behavior.

True harassers, on the other hand, *mean* to offend. Even when they know their talk or action is offensive, they continue. Sexual harassment is defined as behavior that is not only unwelcome but *repeated.* (Some kinds of behavior are *always* inappropriate, however, even if they occur only once. Grabbing someone's breast or crotch, for example, or threatening to fire a subordinate who won't engage in sexual activity does not need repetition to be deemed illegal.)

The true harasser acts not out of insensitivity but precisely because of the knowledge that the behavior will make the recipient uncomfortable. The harasser derives pleasure from the momentary or continuing powerlessness of the other individual. In some cases, the harasser presses the victim to have sex, but sexual pleasure itself is not the goal. Instead, the harasser's point is to dominate, to gain power over another. As University of Washington psychologist John Gottman puts it, "Harassment is a way for a man to make a woman vulnerable."

Some harassers target the people they consider the most likely to be embarrassed and least likely to file a charge. Male harassers are sometimes attempting to put "uppity women" in their place. In certain previously all-male workplaces, a woman who's simply attempting to do her job may be considered uppity. In this instance, the harassment is designed to make the woman feel out of place, if not to pressure her out of the job. Such harassment often takes place in front of an audience or is recounted to others afterwards ("pinch and tell"). . . .

PART OF THE JOB

Some harassers who don't consciously set out to offend are nevertheless unwilling to curb their behavior even after they're told it's offensive. If a woman doesn't like it, they figure that's her problem. And some harassers consider sexual favors from subordinates to be a "perk," as much a part of the job as a big mahogany desk and a private executive bathroom.

Men can be harassed by women, or both harasser and victim can be of the same sex. Overwhelmingly, however, sexual harassment is an injury inflicted on women by men. While the number of hardcore harassers is small, their presence is widely felt. Sexual harassment is ugly. And it's damaging—to the victims, to business, and to society as a whole.

SECTION 2: COUNTERING THE MYTHS ABOUT SEXUAL HARASSMENT

From the Senate chambers to the company mailroom, from the executive suite to the employee lounge, from the locker room to the bedroom, a debate is raging over sexual harassment. No matter what the forum, the same arguments arise. Here are some of the most common myths about harassment rebutted by the facts.

Myth: Sexual harassment doesn't deserve all the attention it's getting. It's a rare disorder unique to a few sick people.

Fact: No exact figures exist, but a large body of research conducted at workplaces and universities suggests that at least 50 percent of women—as well as a smaller percentage of men—have been sexually harassed, either on the job or on campus. Very few people are considered to be "chronic harassers," but most of these are not psychopaths. Many men in the workplace, whether intentionally or not, end up encouraging or condoning harassment.

Myth: Sexual harassment is a fact of life that people might as well get used to. It's so widespread that it's pointless to try to stamp it out.

Fact: To expect men to engage in abusive behavior is insulting. The notion that women should take responsibility for preventing harassers from behaving offensively at the workplace is also a myth. Like other forms of sexual abuse, harassment is usually a means of exerting power, not of expressing a biological urge. Yes, sexual harassment is widespread, but the answer is to stop it, not to accept it.

Myth: Most men accused of harassment don't really intend to offend women.

Fact: A small percentage of men are dead serious about engaging in abusive behavior on the job. They know their behavior makes women uncomfortable; that's why they do it.

Other men are surprised to find that what they intend as innocent teasing isn't received that way. They need to make some simple changes in behavior. After all, beginning in early childhood, most people are taught that different settings require different codes of behavior. Children learn not to use swear words at Grandma's dinner table and not to insult the teacher. At the workplace, it's safest to assume that a coworker *won't* like sexual comments or gestures. If you find out you've offended someone, simply apologize.

Myth: If women want to be treated equally on the job, they can't expect special treatment—whether at the construction site or in the executive boardroom.

Fact: Women don't want special treatment. They want *decent* treatment—the same decent treatment most men want for themselves.

Myth: Many charges of sexual harassment are false—the women are either fantasizing or lying in order to get men in trouble.

Fact: According to a survey of Fortune 500 managers conducted by *Working Woman* magazine (December 1988), false reports are rare. "Every story I hear is very specific and very detailed," said one survey respondent, "too much so to be made up." Said another respondent, "More than 95 percent of our complaints have merit."

There's little incentive for women to come forward with false harassment charges. The real problem is not that reports are fraudulent but that women who *are* suffering severe harassment remain silent for fear of being humiliated and derailing their careers.

Myth: A man's career can be destroyed by an accusation of sexual harassment, while the woman who accuses him suffers no consequences.

Fact: A woman's *life* can be destroyed by sexual harassment, at least for a time. Offensive behavior *should* bring consequences for the perpetrator. But most cases don't result in heavy penalties.

A good corporate policy, however, protects both the accuser and the accused by ensuring confidentiality and a fair hearing. A range of disciplinary action is needed—from warnings and reprimands to suspensions and terminations—depending on the severity of the offense.

As things stand now, it's usually the victim who suffers a career setback. Many harassers receive only a slap on the wrist or no reprisals at all, even for serious offenses.

Myth: You can't blame a guy for looking. Women bring harassment on themselves by the way they dress.

Fact: Truly provocative clothing doesn't belong at the workplace, and management shouldn't allow it. Yet under no circumstances does a woman's appearance give men license to break the law.

Many employers require women to dress in a way that calls attention to their physical appearance. Waitresses, for example, may be required to wear uniforms with short skirts or low necklines. In 1991, Continental Airlines reservation clerk Teresa Fischette was summarily fired when she refused to wear makeup on the job. Only after the *New York Times* publicized her case and she appeared on a television talk show did she win back her position.

Without questioning the importance of being well groomed, many women resent having to conform to a highly specific "look" for the benefit of clients or coworkers. Not only is it expensive and time-consuming, it can lead others to treat them like sex objects at the workplace.

Myth: Women send mixed signals. Half the time when they say no, they really mean yes.

Fact: Men can't assume they're the ones who know best what women "really want." Especially at the workplace, some women can't put up strong resistance to sexual pressure without fear of endangering their jobs. Dr. Michelle Paludi, a psychologist at Hunter College in New York City, finds that "90 percent of women who have been sexually harassed want to leave, but can't because they need their job." Take a no as a no.

Myth: Women who make clear that they don't welcome sexual attention don't get harassed. If a woman doesn't like what's happening, she can say so.

Fact: Most hard-core harassers know their conduct is unwelcome; that's why they continue. Some women do say no again and again and find that their resistance is simply ignored. Others hesitate to speak up because they fear being ridiculed or ostracized.

While women do have a responsibility to communicate when sexual attention is unwelcome, the employer has a prior legal responsibility: to create an environment where no woman is punished for refusing to accept offensive behavior.

Myth: All this attention to harassment will give women ideas, causing them to imagine problems where there are none.

Fact: In the short run, defining *sexual harassment* and providing women with ways to speak up probably *will* lead to an increase in the number of reports filed, most of them concerning legitimate, not imagined, offenses. In the long run, however, public discussion of the issue will cut down on unwelcome sexual attention on the job. The result will be fewer harassment complaints and a more harmonious and productive work world for all.

Myth: Cracking down on sexual harassment will lead to a boring and humorless workplace.

Fact: Antiharassment policies are aimed at repeated, unwelcome sexual attention, not at friendly relations among coworkers. Social interaction that's mutually enjoyable is fine, so long as it doesn't interfere with work or offend others.

The aim of a sexual-harassment policy is to eliminate *offensive* interactions, not *all* interactions. Most encounters defined as sexual harassment have nothing to do with a romantic agenda. They involve an assertion of power, not of affection.

But sex between managers and their subordinates—or between faculty and students—is a different story. Many employers and college administrators recognize that romantic relationships are fraught with danger when one party to the affair has economic or academic power over the other. Even when it seems that both parties have entered freely into the relationship, management is right to worry about the potential for exploitation and adverse effects on the workplace or academic setting.

SECTION 3: WHAT THE LAW SAYS

What words would you use to describe sexual harassment? Participants in workplace training sessions are always full of answers. "Humiliating," they call out. "Unwelcome." "Repeated." "Power abuse." The list goes on. Yet in session after session, at one workplace after another, no one but the instructor states a word that's just as important as all the rest: *illegal.* Sexual harassment is against the law.

It's not surprising that most people are uninformed about the law on sexual harassment. Not until 1977 did a federal court uphold a harassment charge. The Supreme Court did not do so until 1986. Until a short time ago, sexual harassment was a problem without a name or a remedy.

Employees and employers alike can be thankful

that sexual harassment is unlawful. Those who use the laws to file charges aren't the only ones who benefit. For *all* employees, simply knowing they have a right to a harassment-free workplace makes it easier to insist on fair treatment. For many potential harassers, the laws are an effective deterrent. And for employers seeking to enforce appropriate workplace behavior, the laws are invaluable. . . .

FEDERAL LAW DEFINES HARASSMENT

Title VII of the Civil Rights Act of 1964 makes it illegal to discriminate against employees on the basis of race, color, religion, sex, or national origin. As enforced by the Equal Employment Opportunity Commission (EEOC), the law gives every employee the right to work in an environment free of intimidation, insult, or ridicule based on race, religion, or sex.

Here's how the EEOC, a Washington-based agency with regional offices, defines *sexual harassment:*

> Unwelcome sexual advances, requests for sexual favors, and other verbal or physical conduct of a sexual nature constitute sexual harassment when
>
> 1. submission to such conduct is made either explicitly or implicitly a term or condition of an individual's employment or academic advancement,
> 2. submission to or rejection of such conduct by an individual is used as the *basis for employment decisions* or academic decisions affecting such individual, or
> 3. such conduct has the purpose or effect of unreasonably *interfering with an individual's work* or academic performance or creating an intimidating, *hostile,* or offensive working or academic *environment.*

Illegal sexual harassment falls into four categories: *quid pro quo,* hostile environment, sexual favoritism, and harassment by nonemployees.

QUID PRO QUO

Quid pro quo means something given in return for something else. In this type of sexual harassment, a supervisor makes unwelcome sexual advances and either states or implies that the victim *must* submit if she wants to keep her job or receive a raise, promotion, or job assignment.

These cases are the most clear-cut. The courts generally hold the employer liable for any such harassment, whether he knew about it or not. That's because anyone who holds a supervisory position, with power over terms of employment, is considered to be an "agent" of the employer, that is, "acting for" the employer.

> *Deborah, an office manager at a small firm, couldn't stop Bill, the sales and marketing manager, from coming by her desk to complain about his unsatisfying sex life with his wife. She insisted again and again that she wasn't interested in hearing about his personal affairs, but nothing she said would deter him. Finally, Deborah went to their boss for help. "Put your faith in God," was all he had to say. Deborah did her best to avoid Bill, but then a corporate restructuring took place and he became president of the firm. "I'm on the other side of the desk now," he told Deborah in their first meeting. "Either we engage in a sexual relationship, or I no longer need an office manager." Deborah filed a charge and won.*

Hostile Environment

An employee doesn't have to be fired, demoted, or denied a raise or promotion to be "harmed"—and to file a charge. Even if no threat is involved, unwelcome sexual conduct can have the effect of "poisoning" the victim's work environment. Sexually explicit jokes, pinups, graffiti, vulgar statements, abusive language, innuendoes; and overt sexual conduct can create a hostile environment.

In these cases, the employer is considered liable if he knew or should have known of the harassment and did nothing to stop it. If the harassment is out in the open, if everyone except the employer knows all about it, then he *ought* to have known—whether or not anyone brings the matter to his attention.

Where no *quid pro quo* is involved, the courts generally don't rule in favor of the victim unless the incidents of harassment are repeated, pervasive, and harmful to the victim's emotional well-being. A single incident isn't enough to prove the existence of a hostile environment, unless the incident is extreme. An employer can let a vulgar remark or two go by without being found in violation of the law. But if someone intentionally *touches* an employee in a sexual way on the job even once and the employer ignores the behavior, then the EEOC will generally find that harassment has occurred.

Hostile environment cases may leave more room for argument than *quid pro quo* cases.

The victim will strengthen his or her case by complaining or protesting at the time of the harassment, preferably in writing. This kind of documentation will prove that the victim finds the sexual attention unwelcome—and will also help prove that the offensive behavior occurred in the first place, if the employer is inclined to deny it.

But a verbal or written protest is not absolutely necessary to winning a case—the EEOC recognizes that it's not always possible to speak up. Even if the employer claims, as a defense, that there was a grievance procedure and the victim never used it, the EEOC will examine what may have deterred the victim from doing so. How often has the grievance procedure been used? Do all employees know it exists? Have other harassment victims felt comfortable using it?

> *Carol Zabkowicz, a warehouse worker, was tormented by a group of male coworkers who enjoyed upsetting her by calling out her name and then exposing their genitals or buttocks when she looked up. Carol complained to management, to no avail. "If we didn't see it, it didn't happen" was the company's position. Even when she brought witnesses with her and submitted evidence in the form of obscene cartoons that had been left at her workstation, management did nothing. When the case went to court, the company was found guilty of "malicious, blatant discrimination."*

The employer's best defense will be to take the strong preventive and remedial action recommended in the EEOC's guidelines:

> The employer should affirmatively raise the subject with all supervisory and nonsupervisory employees, express strong disapproval, and explain the sanctions for harassment. The employer should also have a procedure for resolving sexual harassment complaints. The procedure should be designed to encourage victims of harassment to come forward and should not require a victim to complain first to the offending supervisor. It should ensure confidentiality as much as possible and provide effective remedies and protection of victims and witnesses against retaliation.

If the employer takes strong action immediately upon finding out about a "hostile environment" problem, the EEOC may find that the situation has been resolved satisfactorily and close the case . . .

Sexual Favoritism

In this type of harassment, a supervisor rewards only those employees who submit to sexual demands. The *other* employees, those who are *denied* raises or promotions, can claim that they're penalized by the sexual attention directed at the favored coworkers.

> *Catherine A. Broderick, an attorney with the federal Securities and Exchange Commission, filed a suit charging that the agency was run "like a brothel." Senior attorneys were having affairs with secretaries and junior attorneys and rewarding them with cash bonuses and promotions. When Broderick complained, she received poor reviews and was threatened with firing. She won her case, receiving $128,000 in back pay and a promotion.*

Harassment by Nonemployees

An employer can be held responsible for harassment by people outside the company—such as customers, vendors, or contractors—if the employer has control or could have control over their actions.

> *The owner of an office building required a female elevator operator to wear a sexy uniform. People riding the elevator made lewd remarks and propositioned her. The operator complained to the owner and said she refused to wear the uniform. For this she was fired. She brought suit against the employer and won.*

THE LEGAL HISTORY OF SEXUAL HARASSMENT

The legal history of sexual harassment is surprisingly short. Not until 1964 was sex discrimination itself declared illegal—and only by a fluke. During the debate over the proposed Civil Rights Act at that time, a Southern member of Congress proposed what he considered an absurd amendment, making sex discrimination illegal along with race discrimination. His intent was only to make sure the bill wouldn't pass; to his chagrin, however, the plan backfired. The bill became law with his amendment intact, and discrimination on the basis of sex as well as race was outlawed.

Eight years later, in 1972, Congress passed the Equal Employment Opportunity Act giving enforcement powers to the EEOC. That same year, President Nixon signed the Education Amendments, forbidding discrimination by any education program receiving federal funds. . . .

In the precedent-setting *Barnes v. Costle* case, sexual harassment victims gained a foothold in the courts. The U.S. Court of Appeals for the District of Columbia ruled in 1977 in favor of a woman whose government job was abolished because she wouldn't submit to her boss's demand for sexual favors. "But for her womanhood," the court said, "the woman wouldn't have lost her job." If she'd been a man, in other words, she wouldn't have been treated this way. Therefore, the harassment was not just an isolated instance of supervisory misbehavior; it was illegal sex discrimination. . . .

Hostile Environment: An Uphill Battle

While the concept of *quid pro quo* harassment was accepted by courts in the 1970s, victims of hostile environment harassment fought an uphill battle in the 1980s. . . .

At last, in June 1986, the Supreme Court upheld the concept of *hostile environment harassment.* In *Meritor Savings Bank v. Vinson,* the court affirmed that harassment is illegal even if the victim hasn't lost any job benefits—even if it's not a *quid pro quo* situation. Employees have "the right to work in an environment free from discriminatory intimidation, ridicule, and insult," the Court said.

Mechelle Vinson, a bank teller who worked her way up to a position as an assistant branch manager, claimed that her supervisor repeatedly pressured her to have sex with him. At first she resisted; finally, afraid of losing her job, she gave in to his advances. Over the next several years, he fondled her in front of other employees, followed her into the restroom, and exposed himself at work. He had sex with her 40 or 50 times and raped her on more than one occasion. Finally, she went on leave and was fired. Her employer's defense was that she'd made up the whole story, dressed provocatively, and never used the grievance procedure.

Voluntary?

The lower court found that if there was a sexual relationship between Vinson and her supervisor, it was a voluntary one, and that the employer wasn't liable because Vinson hadn't complained. But the court of appeals disagreed. Even though Vinson had indeed agreed to have sex with the supervisor, said the court, her participation couldn't fairly be called "voluntary" because she was afraid she'd lose her job if she refused. Further, regardless of whether she had lodged a complaint, the bank was liable because a supervisor is an agent of the employer.

The bank appealed to the Supreme Court, which affirmed the court of appeals. The Court said that the question was not whether Vinson had made a voluntary decision to have sex with her supervisor, but whether the sexual relationship was welcome or unwelcome to her.

The Court also asserted that merely having a sexual harassment policy and a grievance procedure didn't automatically excuse the employer from liability. But the Court didn't go so far as to say that employers were always liable for the actions of supervisors. Where no *quid pro quo* threats are made, the Court said, the employer's liability must be determined on a case-by-case basis.

The Case of the Reasonable Woman

It's common practice in the courtroom to examine behavior through the eyes of the hypothetical "reasonable person," the so-called "man in the street." But in 1991, in *Ellison v. Brady,* the U.S. Court of Appeals for the Ninth Circuit created a new standard: the "reasonable woman."

Kerry Ellison, an agent for the Internal Revenue Service in San Mateo, California, charged that a coworker persisted in pressuring her for dates even though she kept refusing him. He sent her bizarre "love letters" that she found frightening. "I know that you are worth knowing with or without sex," said one letter. "I have enjoyed you so much over the past few months. Watching you. Experiencing you from so far away." When Ellison complained to a supervisor, the coworker was transferred. He filed a grievance, however, and won a return to Ellison's office. At this point, Ellison filed a harassment charge.

A district court dismissed the case, calling the coworker's conduct "isolated and genuinely trivial." But the Ninth Circuit of the U.S. Court of Appeals disagreed. The "severe and pervasive" harassment directed at Ellison, the court wrote, had created "an abusive working environment." And while IRS managers told the coworker to stop his illegal harrassment, they didn't subject him to any disciplinary action—no reprimand, no probation, no threat of termination. They even decided to transfer him back to Ellison's office without consulting her.

In the court's view, the reasonable-person standard could end up simply reinforcing discrimination. After all, if harassment is common and widespread, doesn't it follow that an average, "reasonable" person can engage in harassment? Fairness demands that the law take note of women's unique perspective. The court wrote:

> Conduct that many men consider unobjectionable may offend many women. Because women are disproportionately victims of rape and sexual assault, women have a stronger incentive to be concerned with sexual behavior. Women who are victims of mild forms of sexual harassment may understandably worry whether a harasser's conduct is merely a prelude to a violent sexual assault. Men, who are rarely victims of sexual assault, may view sexual conduct in a vacuum without a full appreciation of the social setting or the underlying threat of violence that a woman may perceive.

Robinson v. Jacksonville Shipyards: Workplace Pornography Banned

Another breakthrough came in 1991. For the first time, a court ruled that pornography at the workplace constituted sex discrimination.

Lois Robinson, a welder, was one of only six women among over 800 skilled craftworkers at a Florida shipyard. When female employees reported demeaning jokes and comments to managers, their complaints were not taken seriously. In addition, pictures of nude women were displayed—sometimes by managers—throughout the workplace. One pinup showed a meat spatula pressed against a woman's pubic area. Another picture featured a nude woman holding a whip. A drawing on the wall featured a nude woman's body with "USDA Choice" stamped across it as if it were a piece of meat. . . .

The district court upheld Robinson's harassment charge, finding that pornography may be far more threatening to women in the workplace than it is outside. "Pornography on an employer's wall or desk communicates a message about the way he views women, a view strikingly at odds with the way women wish to be viewed in the workplace," the court decision declared. Further, "a preexisting atmosphere that deters women from entering or continuing in a profession or job" is as bad as "a sign declaring 'Men Only.' "

The shipyard was ordered to remove the offensive pictures and to implement an antiharassment policy drafted by the National Organization for Women Legal Defense and Education Fund. Two employees were held personally liable for harassment, and the company was ordered to pay Robinson's legal fees, as well as $1 in damages.

An Abridgment of Free Speech?

The employer, with the approval of the American Civil Liberties Union, protested that being forced to remove the posters and graffiti would mean abridging employees' freedom of speech. But many women's groups strongly backed the court's ruling. The messages contained in the pornographic posters would be called sexual harassment—and declared illegal—if they were stated out loud at the workplace. Why should pictures be allowed to convey what workers aren't allowed to say on the job? The "right" of supervisors and male workers to express themselves offensively before a captive audience of female workers must be balanced against other goals, like avoiding discrimination and getting the work done. . . .

Victims Win Right to Collect Damages Under Federal Law

Until the end of 1991, federal law didn't allow harassment victims—or victims of any other form of sex discrimination—to collect much money. All they could win under Title VII were remedies that would make them "whole"—reinstatement if they'd been fired, a promotion if they'd been denied one, back pay, and attorney's fees. There were no remedies for out-of-pocket expenses like medical bills or for emotional pain and suffering. Nor was there any way to assess punitive damages against the employer.

Under the circumstances, many harassment victims saw little reason to sue under Title VII, especially if they didn't want their job back or hadn't been fired in the first place. They couldn't collect a penny, nor would their employer suffer any significant consequences. Victims also found it difficult to interest attorneys in their cases, since there was no chance of collecting damages, even if they won.

In 1991, however, in the wake of Anita Hill's testimony on sexual harassment before the Senate Judiciary Committee, Congress passed legislation strengthening several aspects of civil rights law. The Civil Rights Act of 1991 gives victims of sex, race, and religious discrimination the right to sue for both *compensatory* and *punitive* damages. Victims can sue to collect compensation for the abuse they've suffered, as well as to collect penalties designed to punish the employer. This makes it easier for victims to interest attorneys in taking their cases on a contingent-fee basis. (The lawyer receives little or no payment up front but takes a percentage of the total award, if any, once the case is resolved.) Out-of-pocket medical expenses can now be recovered as well. Further, the law gives the right to trial by jury, and juries are generally acknowledged to be more sympathetic to the victim than judges.

In February 1992, the Supreme Court affirmed that Title IX of the Education Amendments of 1972 gives students the right to recover damages from schools and school officials for sexual harassment and other forms of sex discrimination. . . .

THE LAW EVOLVES

Despite the few big-money settlements that have grabbed headlines and the steady progress in court decisions, both the law and the enforcement system still pose formidable obstacles for the victim of harassment. The burden is on the victim to prove both that harassment took place and that the offender's conduct was unwelcome. Too often, the courtroom inquiry tends to focus not on what the offender did but on how the victim responded—how strongly she resisted, how quickly she protested, how sincere her objections were. Frequently, judges and juries fail to recognize how hard it is to speak up against harassment if the offender is your boss.

As new statutes are passed and new cases decided, sexual harassment law continues to evolve. In coming years, strides may be made toward more effectively preventing harassment, protecting the victim, and imposing appropriate penalties on harasser and employer.

SECTION 4: WHAT EVERY GOOD EMPLOYER SHOULD DO

After the Clarence Thomas hearings in October 1991 and the passage of the federal Civil Rights Act shortly thereafter, many managers examined their policies on sexual harassment. What they saw ranged from an effective preventive program to no policy at all.

"A THRIVING WORKPLACE DEPENDS ON A HARASSMENT-FREE ENVIRONMENT"

Managers who promote this view are most successful in combating sexual harassment. Smart managers do want to avoid legal liability. But above all, they should root out anything that seriously interferes with employee morale, well-being, and productivity. They should recognize that sexual harassment can happen anywhere and that no matter how careful the hiring and promotion practices, no workplace has a guarantee against insensitivity or misconduct. They should work to prevent harassment from occurring, while dealing with it promptly if it does take place.

Managers in this category will understand that no employee is indispensable. Even if an employee brings in money or prestige, his misconduct should not be tolerated.

Many companies with well-developed policies,

such as AT&T and Du Pont, have had them in place for more than a decade. Texas Industries began to develop its policy as soon as it started placing women in traditionally male jobs, such as driving and production engineering. While some companies began devising or reworking policies after the Supreme Court first ruled against harassment in 1986, firms like Merck & Co. said the ruling merely affirmed the policies they had already instituted. . . .

DEVELOPING OR REVISING AN IN-HOUSE POLICY ON SEXUAL HARASSMENT

There's no one model for a good sexual harassment policy. Employers need to develop procedures based on their particular circumstances. But all policies should be designed to send a clear message: "We will not tolerate sexual harassment. We will do everything in our power to prevent it from happening. If you have a complaint, we will listen to it. We will follow the most effective course of action to stop the offensive behavior as speedily and thoroughly as possible."

A good sexual harassment policy should incorporate the following elements:

Employee Involvement

Employees who have been or could be the targets of harassment should have a voice. Men who might otherwise feel defensive should also help to develop the policy. Rather than selecting one or two employee "representatives" at the outset, solicit comments and suggestions companywide. Through a union or professional association, some employees may know of a strong policy elsewhere; encourage them to pass on any information that may be helpful. . . .

Written Policy

A written policy tailored to the company should be included in any employee handbook and orientation materials. The policy should define what harassment is and is not, describe how harassment will be handled within the company, explain how to file a charge with a government agency, and spell out what the law says. But set *higher standards* than the law requires; for example, federal law does not prohibit harassment against homosexuals, but in-house policy should make clear that such harassment will not be tolerated. . . .

Publicity

Publicize the policy by every means used to communicate business goals. "Employers ought constantly to reinforce their commitment to a work force free from sexual harassment, using whatever the usual trusted mechanisms of the company are," says consultant Freada Klein. That could be anything from a newsletter to posters to global voice mail. "Some companies send a statement stapled to employee paychecks," says Klein. "Others send periodic memos about the number of complaints they've had and what the resolution has been."

Support from the Top

It's important to have visible support from top management. After the Thomas hearings, Richard Teerlink, the CEO of Harley-Davidson, gave a ten-minute talk about harassment to the top 150 managers. "He talked very candidly and told us, 'This is serious stuff that goes along with our values of respecting the individual,' " said Margaret Crawford, director of the company's human resources department. " 'It's not just an issue of what's legal or illegal, but what's right and wrong and how do you treat people in the workplace. Managers will be held accountable for the environment your workers have to live in.' That ten-minute off-the-cuff presentation did more than anything else could have done. Word was out in the hallways. People came forward with questions, some situations they were uncomfortable about. They saw this as a very strong message that the company will not take harassment lightly."

Prevention

A successful policy depends on *education of all employees*. Training should be *ongoing*, not a one-time session, and presented *on paid time*. The program should aim to help all employees to understand the issues and the seriousness of the problem, ensure that those experiencing harassment know their rights, and inform any hardcore offenders that they won't get away with harassment. . . .

Clearly Defined Procedures that Protect the Complainant—and the Accused

The policy must clearly spell out the complaint procedures, including where to report problems, what steps will follow, timetables, methods of investigation, and follow-up. To maximize options for the complainant, the policy must allow for *several different channels.* The procedure should not require the complainant to report the problem to her supervisor, since that person may be the harasser. At least one option should be to complain to an employee through an affirmative action committee, women's committee, or other employee committee. If feasible, designate an ombudsperson to counsel victims. Du Pont Company has a sexual harassment hotline with a toll-free number listed in the company's telephone directory. Four staff specially trained in sexual harassment and rape prevention are assigned to the hotline; each carries a beeper.

The policy must state unequivocally that no one will be punished for coming forward and that *every* complaint will be taken seriously. No retaliatory action should be permitted against a complainant. But make clear, too, that false accusations will not be condoned and that *due process* will be followed. . . .

The Moral Status of Affirmative Action

Louis P. Pojman
Professor of Philosophy, University of Mississippi

> "A ruler who appoints any man to an office, when there is in his dominion another man better qualified for it, sins against God and against the State."
>
> (The *Koran*).

> "[Affirmative Action] is the meagerest recompense for centuries of unrelieved oppression."
>
> (quoted by Shelby Steele as the justification for Affirmative Action).

Hardly a week goes by but that the subject of Affirmative Action does not come up. Whether in the guise of reverse discrimination, preferential hiring, non-traditional casting, quotas, goals and time tables, minority scholarships, or race-norming, the issue confronts us as a terribly perplexing problem. Last summer's Actor's Equity debacle over the casting of the British actor, Jonathan Pryce, as a Eurasian in Miss Saigon; Assistant Secretary of Education Michael Williams' judgement that Minority Scholarships are unconstitutional; the "Civil Rights Bill of 1991," reversing recent decisions of the Supreme Court which constrain preferential hiring practices; the demand that Harvard Law School hire a black female professor; grade stipends for black students at Pennsylvania State University and other schools; the revelations of race norming in state employment agencies; as well as debates over quotas, underutilization guidelines, and diversity in employment; all testify to the importance of this subject for contemporary society.

There is something salutary as well as terribly tragic inherent in this problem. The salutary aspect is the fact that our society has shown itself committed to eliminating unjust discrimination. Even in the heart of Dixie there is a recognition of the injustice of racial discrimination. Both sides of the affirmative action debate have good will and appeal to moral principles. Both sides are attempting to bring about a better society, one which is color blind, but they differ profoundly on the morally proper means to accomplish that goal.

And this is just the tragedy of the situation: good people on both sides of the issue are ready to tear each other to pieces over a problem that has no easy or obvious solution. And so the voices become shrill and the rhetoric hyperbolic. The same spirit which divides the pro-choice movement from the right to life movement on abortion divides liberal pro-Affirmative Action advocates from liberal anti-Affirmative Action advocates. This problem,

From *Public Affairs Quarterly,* Vol. 6, Issue 2 (April 1992), pp 181–206. Reprinted by permission of *Public Affairs Quarterly.*

more than any other, threatens to destroy the traditional liberal consensus in our society. I have seen family members and close friends who until recently fought on the same side of the barricades against racial injustice divide in enmity over this issue. The anti-affirmative liberals ("liberals who've been mugged") have tended towards a form of neo-conservativism and the pro-affirmative liberals have tended to side with the radical left to form the "politically correct ideology" movement.

In this paper I will confine myself primarily to Affirmative Action policies with regard to race, but much of what I say can be applied to the areas of gender and ethnic minorities.

I. DEFINITIONS

First let me define my terms:

Discrimination is simply judging one thing to differ from another on the basis of some criterion. "Discrimination" is essentially a good quality, having reference to our ability to make distinctions. As rational and moral agents we need to make proper distinctions. To be rational is to discriminate between good and bad arguments, and to think morally is to discriminate between reasons based on valid principles and those based on invalid ones. What needs to be distinguished is the difference between rational and moral discrimination, on the one hand, and irrational and immoral discrimination, on the other hand.

Prejudice is a discrimination based on irrelevant grounds. It may simply be an attitude which never surfaces in action, or it may cause prejudicial actions. A prejudicial discrimination in action is immoral if it denies someone a fair deal. So discrimination on the basis of race or sex where these are not relevant for job performance is unfair. Likewise, one may act prejudicially in applying a relevant criterion on insufficient grounds, as in the case where I apply the criterion of being a hard worker but then assume, on insufficient evidence, that the black man who applies for the job is not a hard worker.

There is a difference between *prejudice* and *bias*. Bias signifies a tendency towards one thing rather than another where the evidence is incomplete or based on non-moral factors. For example, you may have a bias towards blondes and I towards red-heads. But prejudice is an attitude (or action) where unfairness is present—where one *should* know or do better, as in the case where I give people jobs simply because they are red-heads. Bias implies ignorance or incomplete knowledge, whereas prejudice is deeper, involving a moral failure—usually a failure to pay attention to the evidence. But note that calling people racist or sexist without good evidence is also an act of prejudice. I call this form of prejudice "defamism," for it unfairly defames the victim. It is a contemporary version of McCarthyism.

Equal Opportunity is offering everyone a fair chance at the best positions that society has at its disposal. Only native aptitude and effort should be decisive in the outcome, not factors of race, sex or special favors.

Affirmative Action is the effort to rectify the injustice of the past by special policies. Put this way, it is Janus-faced or ambiguous, having both a backward-looking and a forward-looking feature. The backward-looking feature is its attempt to correct and compensate for past injustice. This aspect of Affirmative Action is strictly deontological. The forward-looking feature is its implicit ideal of a society free from prejudice; this is both deontological and utilitarian.

When we look at a social problem from a backward-looking perspective we need to determine who has committed or benefited from a wrongful or prejudicial act and to determine who deserves compensation for that act.

When we look at a social problem from a forward-looking perspective we need to determine what a just society (one free from prejudice) would look like and how to obtain that kind of society. The forward-looking aspect of Affirmative Action is paradoxically race-conscious, since it uses race to bring about a society which is not race-conscious, which is colorblind (in the morally relevant sense of this term).

It is also useful to distinguish two versions of Affirmative Action. *Weak Affirmative Action* involves such measures as the elimination of segregation (namely the idea of "separate but equal"), widespread advertisement to groups not previously represented in certain privileged positions, special scholarships for the disadvantaged classes (e.g., all the poor), using underrepresentation or a history of past discrimination as a tie breaker when candidates are relatively equal, and the like.

Strong Affirmative Action involves more positive steps to eliminate past injustice, such as reverse discrimination, hiring candidates on the basis of race and gender in order to reach equal or near equal results, proportionate representation in each area of society.

II. ARGUMENTS FOR AFFIRMATIVE ACTION

Let us now survey the main arguments typically cited in the debate over Affirmative Action. I will briefly discuss seven arguments on each side of the issue.

1. *Need For Role Models*

This argument is straightforward. We all have need of role models, and it helps to know that others like us can be successful. We learn and are encouraged to strive for excellence by emulating our heroes and role models.

However, it is doubtful whether role models of one's own racial or sexual type are necessary for success. One of my heroes was Gandhi, an Indian Hindu, another was my grade school science teacher, one Miss DeVoe, and another was Martin Luther King. More important than having role models of one's own type is having genuinely good people, of whatever race or gender, to emulate. Furthermore, even if it is of some help to people with low self-esteem to gain encouragement from seeing others of their particular kind in leadership roles, it is doubtful whether this need is a sufficient condition to justify preferential hiring or reverse discrimination. What good is a role model who is inferior to other professors or business personnel? Excellence will rise to the top in a system of fair opportunity. Natural development of role models will come more slowly and more surely. Proponents of preferential policies simply lack the patience to let history take its own course.

2. *The Need of Breaking the Stereotypes*

Society may simply need to know that there are talented blacks and women, so that it does not automatically assign them lesser respect or status. We need to have unjustified stereotype beliefs replaced with more accurate ones about the talents of blacks and women. So we need to engage in preferential hiring of qualified minorities even when they are not the most qualified.

Again, the response is that hiring the less qualified is neither fair to those better qualified who are passed over nor an effective way of removing inaccurate stereotypes. If competence is accepted as the criterion for hiring, then it is unjust to override it for purposes of social engineering. Furthermore, if blacks or women are known to hold high positions simply because of reverse discrimination, then they will still lack the respect due to those of their rank. In New York City there is a saying among doctors, "Never go to a black physician under 40," referring to the fact that AA has affected the medical system during the past fifteen years. The police use "Quota Cops" and "Welfare Sergeants" to refer to those hired without passing the standardized tests. (In 1985 180 black and hispanic policemen, who had failed a promotion test, were promoted anyway to the rank of sergeant.) The destruction of false stereotypes will come naturally as qualified blacks rise naturally in fair competition (or if it does not—then the stereotypes may be justified). Reverse discrimination sends the message home that the stereotypes are deserved—otherwise, why do these minorities need so much extra help?

3. *Equal Results Argument*

Some philosophers and social scientists hold that human nature is roughly identical, so that on a fair playing field the same proportion from every race and gender and ethnic group would attain to the highest positions in every area of endeavor. It would follow that any inequality of results itself is evidence for inequality of opportunity. John

Arthur, in discussing an intelligence test, Test 21, puts the case this way.

> History is important when considering governmental rules like Test 21 because low scores by blacks can be traced in large measure to the legacy of slavery and racism: segregation, poor schooling, exclusion from trade unions, malnutrition, and poverty have all played their roles. Unless one assumes that blacks are naturally less able to pass the test, the conclusion must be that the results are themselves socially and legally constructed, not a mere given for which law and society can claim no responsibility.
>
> The conclusion seems to be that genuine equality eventually requires equal results. Obviously blacks have been treated unequally throughout US history, and just as obviously the economic and psychological effects of that inequality linger to this day, showing up in lower income and poorer performance in school and on tests than whites achieve. Since we have no reason to believe that differences in performance can be explained by factors other than history, equal results are a good benchmark by which to measure progress made toward genuine equality.[1]

The result of a just society should be equal numbers in proportion to each group in the work force.

However, Arthur fails even to consider studies that suggest that there are innate differences between races, sexes, and groups. If there are genetic differences in intelligence and temperament within families, why should we not expect such differences between racial groups and the two genders? Why should the evidence for this be completely discounted?

Perhaps some race or one gender is more intelligent in one way than another. At present we have only limited knowledge about genetic differences, but what we do have suggests some difference besides the obvious physiological traits.[2] The proper use of this evidence is not to promote discriminatory policies but to be *open* to the possibility that innate differences may have led to an over-representation of certain groups in certain areas of endeavor. It seems that on average blacks have genetic endowments favoring them in the development of skills necessary for excellence in basketball.

Furthermore, on Arthur's logic, we should take aggressive AA against Asians and Jews since they are over-represented in science, technology, and medicine. So that each group receives its fair share, we should ensure that 12% of the philosophers in the United States are Black, reduce the percentage of Jews from an estimated 15% to 2%—firing about 1,300 Jewish philosophers. The fact that Asians are producing 50% of Ph.D's in science and math and blacks less than 1% clearly shows, on this reasoning, that we are providing special secret advantages to Asians.

But why does society have to enter into this results game in the first place? Why do we have to decide whether all difference is environmental or genetic? Perhaps we should simply admit that we lack sufficient evidence to pronounce on these issues with any certainty—but if so, should we not be more modest in insisting on equal results? Here is a thought experiment. Take two families of different racial groups, Green and Blue. The Greens decide to have only two children, to spend all their resources on them, to give them the best education. The two Green kids respond well and end up with achievement test scores in the 99th percentile. The Blues fail to practice family planning. They have 15 children. They can only afford 2 children, but lack of ability or whatever prevents them from keeping their family down. Now they need help for their large family. Why does society have to step in and help them? Society did not force them to have 15 children. Suppose that the achievement test scores of the 15 children fall below the 25th percentile. They cannot compete with the Greens. But now enters AA. It says that it is society's fault that the Blue children are not as able as the Greens and that the Greens must pay extra taxes to enable the Blues to compete. No restraints are put on the Blues regarding family size. This seems unfair to the Greens. Should the Green children be made to bear responsibility for the consequences of the Blues' voluntary behavior?

My point is simply that Arthur needs to cast his net wider and recognize that demographics and childbearing and -rearing practices are crucial factors in achievement. People have to take some responsibility for their actions. The equal results argument (or axiom) misses a greater part of the picture.

4. *The Compensation Argument*

The argument goes like this: blacks have been wronged and severely harmed by whites. Therefore white society should compensate blacks for the injury caused them. Reverse discrimination in terms of preferential hiring, contracts, and scholarships is a fitting way to compensate for the past wrongs.

This argument actually involves a distorted notion of compensation. Normally, we think of compensation as owed by a specific person *A* to another person *B* whom *A* has wronged in a specific way *C*. For example, if I have stolen your car and used it for a period of time to make business profits that would have gone to you, it is not enough that I return your car. I must pay you an amount reflecting your loss and my ability to pay. If I have only made $5,000 and only have $10,000 in assets, it would not be possible for you to collect $20,000 in damages—even though that is the amount of loss you have incurred.

Sometimes compensation is extended to groups of people who have been unjustly harmed by the greater society. For example, the United States government has compensated the Japanese-Americans who were interred during the Second World War, and the West German government has paid reparations to the survivors of Nazi concentration camps. But here a specific people have been identified who were wronged in an identifiable way by the government of the nation in question.

On the face of it the demand by blacks for compensation does not fit the usual pattern. Perhaps Southern States with Jim Crow laws could be accused of unjustly harming blacks, but it is hard to see that the United States government was involved in doing so. Furthermore, it is not clear that all blacks were harmed in the same way or whether some were *unjustly* harmed or harmed more than poor whites and others (e.g. short people). Finally, even if identifiable blacks were harmed by identifiable social practices, it is not clear that most forms of Affirmative Action are appropriate to restore the situation. The usual practice of a financial payment seems more appropriate than giving a high level job to someone unqualified or only minimally qualified, who, speculatively, might have been better qualified had he not been subject to racial discrimination. If John is the star tailback of our college team with a promising professional future, and I accidentally (but culpably) drive my pick-up truck over his legs, and so cripple him, John may be due compensation, but he is not due the tailback spot on the football team.

Still, there may be something intuitively compelling about compensating members of an oppressed group who are minimally qualified. Suppose that the Hatfields and the McCoys are enemy clans and some youths from the Hatfields go over and steal diamonds and gold from the McCoys, distributing it within the Hatfield economy. Even though we do not know which Hatfield youths did the stealing, we would want to restore the wealth, as far as possible, to the McCoys. One way might be to tax the Hatfields, but another might be to give preferential treatment in terms of scholarships and training programs and hiring to the McCoys.[3]

This is perhaps the strongest argument for Affirmative Action, and it may well justify some weak versions of AA, but it is doubtful whether it is sufficient to justify strong versions with quotas and goals and time tables in skilled positions. There are at least two reasons for this. First, we have no way of knowing how many people of group *G* would have been at competence level *L* had the world been different. Secondly, the normal criterion of competence is a strong prima facie consideration when the most important positions are at stake. There are two reasons for this: (1) society has given people expectations that if they attain certain levels of excellence they will be awarded appropriately and (2) filling the most important positions with the best qualified is the best way to insure efficiency in job-related areas and in society in general. These reasons are not absolutes. They can be overridden. But there is a strong presumption in their favor so that a burden of proof rests with those who would override them.

At this point we get into the problem of whether

innocent non-blacks should have to pay a penalty in terms of preferential hiring of blacks. We turn to that argument.

5. *Compensation from Those who Innocently Benefited from Past Injustice*

White males as innocent beneficiaries of unjust discrimination of blacks and women have no grounds for complaint when society seeks to rectify the tilted field. White males may be innocent of oppressing blacks and minorities (and women), but they have unjustly benefited from that oppression or discrimination. So it is perfectly proper that less qualified women and blacks be hired before them.

The operative principle is: He who knowingly and willingly benefits from a wrong must help pay for the wrong. Judith Jarvis Thomson puts it this way. "Many [white males] have been direct beneficiaries of policies which have down-graded blacks and women . . . and even those who did not directly benefit . . . had, at any rate, the advantage in the competition which comes of the confidence in one's full membership [in the community], and of one's right being recognized as a matter of course."[4] That is, white males obtain advantages in self respect and self-confidence deriving from a racist system which denies these to blacks and women.

Objection. As I noted in the previous section, compensation is normally individual and specific. If *A* harms *B* regarding *x*, *B* has a right to compensation from *A* in regards to *x*. If *A* steals *B*'s car and wrecks it, *A* has an obligation to compensate *B* for the stolen car, but *A*'s son has no obligation to compensate *B*. Furthermore, if *A* dies or disappears, *B* has no moral right to claim that society compensate him for the stolen car—though if he has insurance, he can make such a claim to the insurance company. Sometimes a wrong cannot be compensated, and we just have to make the best of an imperfect world.

Suppose my parents, divining that I would grow up to have an unsurpassable desire to be a basketball player, bought an expensive growth hormone for me. Unfortunately, a neighbor stole it and gave it to little Lew Alcindor, who gained the extra 18 inches—my 18 inches—and shot up to an enviable 7 feet 2 inches. Alias Kareem Abdul Jabbar, he excelled in basketball, as I would have done had I had my proper dose.

Do I have a right to the millions of dollars that Jabbar made as a professional basketball player—the unjustly innocent beneficiary of my growth hormone? I have a right to something from the neighbor who stole the hormone, and it might be kind of Jabbar to give me free tickets to the Laker basketball games, and perhaps I should be remembered in his will. As far as I can see, however, he does not *owe* me anything, either legally or morally.

Suppose further that Lew Alcindor and I are in high school together and we are both qualified to play basketball, only he is far better than I. Do I deserve to start in his position because I would have been as good as he is had someone not cheated me as a child? Again, I think not. But if being the lucky beneficiary of wrong-doing does not entail that Alcindor (or the coach) owes me anything in regards to basketball, why should it be a reason to engage in preferential hiring in academic positions or highly coveted jobs? If minimal qualifications are not adequate to override excellence in basketball, even when the minimality is a consequence of wrong-doing, why should they be adequate in other areas?

6. *The Diversity Argument*

It is important that we learn to live in a pluralistic world, learning to get along with those of other races and cultures, so we should have fully integrated schools and employment situations. Diversity is an important symbol and educative device. Thus preferential treatment is warranted to perform this role in society.

But, again, while we can admit the value of diversity, it hardly seems adequate to override considerations of merit and efficiency. Diversity for diversity's sake is moral promiscuity, since it obfuscates rational distinctions, and unless those hired are highly qualified the diversity factor threatens to become a fetish. At least at the higher levels of business and the professions, competence far outweighs considerations of diversity. I do not care whether the group of surgeons operating on me reflect racial or gender balance, but I do care that they are highly qualified. And likewise with airplane pilots, military leaders, business executives, and, may I say it, teachers and professors. Moreover, there are other ways of learning about other cultures besides engaging in reverse discrimination.

7. *Anti-Meritocratic (Desert) Argument to Justify Reverse Discrimination: "No One Deserves His Talents"*

According to this argument, the competent do not deserve their intelligence, their superior character, their industriousness, or their discipline; therefore they have no right to the best positions in society; therefore society is not unjust in giving these positions to less (but still minimally) qualified blacks and women. In one form this argument holds that since no one deserves anything, society may use any criteria it pleases to distribute goods. The criterion most often designated is social utility. Versions of this argument are found in the writings of John Arthur, John Rawls, Bernard Boxill, Michael Kinsley, Ronald Dworkin, and Richard Wasserstrom. Rawls writes, "No one deserves his place in the distribution of native endowments, any more than one deserves one's initial starting place in society. The assertion that a man deserves the superior character that enables him to make the effort to cultivate his abilities is equally problematic; for his character depends in large part upon fortunate family and social circumstances for which he can claim no credit. The notion of desert seems not to apply to these cases."[5] Michael Kinsley is even more adamant:

> Opponents of affirmative action are hung up on a distinction that seems more profoundly irrelevant: treating individuals versus treating groups. What is the moral difference between dispensing favors to people on their "merits" as individuals and passing out society's benefits on the basis of group identification?
>
> Group identifications like race and sex are, of course, immutable. They have nothing to do with a person's moral worth. But the same is true of most of what comes under the label "merit." The tools you need for getting ahead in a meritocratic society—not all of them but most: talent, education, instilled cultural values such as ambition—are distributed just as arbitrarily as skin color. They are fate. The notion that people somehow "deserve" the advantages of these characteristics in a way they don't "deserve" the advantage of their race is powerful, but illogical.[6]

It will help to put the argument in outline form.

1. Society may award jobs and positions as it sees fit as long as individuals have no claim to these positions.
2. To have a claim to something means that one has earned it or deserves it.
3. But no one has earned or deserves his intelligence, talent, education or cultural values which produce superior qualifications.
4. If a person does not deserve what produces something, he does not deserve its products.
5. Therefore better qualified people do not deserve their qualifications.
6. Therefore, society may override their qualifications in awarding jobs and positions as it sees fit (for social utility or to compensate for previous wrongs).

So it is permissible if a minimally qualified black or woman is admitted to law or medical school ahead of a white male with excellent credentials or if a less qualified person from an "underutilized" group gets a professorship ahead of a far better qualified white male. Sufficiency and underutilization together outweigh excellence.

Objection Premise 4 is false. To see this, reflect that just because I do not deserve the money that I have been given as a gift (for instance) does not mean that I am not entitled to what I get with that money. If you and I both get a gift of $100 and I bury mine in the sand for 5 years while you invest yours wisely and double its value at the end of five years, I cannot complain that you should split the increase 50/50 since neither of us deserved the original gift. If we accept the notion of responsibility at all, we must hold that persons deserve the fruits of their labor and conscious choices. Of course, we might want to distinguish moral from legal desert and argue that, morally speaking, effort is more important than outcome, whereas, legally speaking, outcome may be more important. Nevertheless, there are good reasons in terms of efficiency, motivation, and rough justice for holding a strong prima facie principle of giving scarce high positions to those most competent.

The attack on moral desert is perhaps the most radical move that egalitarians like Rawls and company have made against meritocracy, but the ramifications of their attack are far reaching. The following are some of its implications. Since I do not deserve my two good eyes or two good kidneys, the social engineers may take one of each from me to give to those needing an eye or a kidney—even if they have damaged their organs by their own voluntary actions. Since no one deserves anything, we do not deserve pay for our labors or praise for a job well done or first prize in the race we win. The notion of moral responsibility vanishes in a system of levelling.

But there is no good reason to accept the argument against desert. We do act freely and, as such, we are responsible for our actions. We deserve the fruits of our labor, reward for our noble feats and punishment for our misbehavior.

We have considered seven arguments for Affirmative Action and have found no compelling case for Strong AA and only one plausible argument (a version of the compensation argument) for Weak AA. We must now turn to the arguments against Affirmative Action to see whether they fare any better.[7]

III. ARGUMENTS AGAINST AFFIRMATIVE ACTION

1. *Affirmative Action Requires Discrimination Against a Different Group*

Weak Affirmative Action weakly discriminates against new minorities, mostly innocent young white males, and Strong Affirmative Action strongly discriminates against these new minorities. As I argued in II.5, this discrimination is unwarranted, since, even if some compensation to blacks were indicated, it would be unfair to make innocent white males bear the whole brunt of the payments. In fact, it is poor white youth who become the new pariahs on the job market. The children of the wealthy have no trouble getting into the best private grammar schools and, on the basis of superior early education, into the best universities, graduate schools, managerial and professional positions. Affirmative Action simply shifts injustice, setting blacks and women against young white males, especially ethnic and poor white males. It does little to rectify the goal of providing equal opportunity to all. If the goal is a society where everyone has a fair chance, then it would be better to concentrate on support for families and early education and decide the matter of university admissions and job hiring on the basis of traditional standards of competence.

2. *Affirmative Action Perpetuates the Victimization Syndrome*

Shelby Steele admits that Affirmative Action may seem "the meagerest recompense for centuries of unrelieved oppression" and that it helps promote diversity. At the same time, though, notes Steele, Affirmative Action reinforces the spirit of victimization by telling blacks that they can gain more by emphasizing their suffering, degradation and helplessness than by discipline and work. This message holds the danger of blacks becoming permanently handicapped by a need for special treatment. It also sends to society at large the message that blacks cannot make it on their own.

Leon Wieseltier sums up the problem this way.

> The memory of oppression is a pillar and a strut of the identity of every people oppressed. It is no ordinary marker of difference. It is unusually stiffening. It instructs the individual and the group about what to expect of the world, imparts an isolating sense of aptness. . . . Don't be fooled, it teaches, there is only repetition. For that reason, the collective memory of an oppressed people is not only a treasure but a trap.
>
> In the memory of oppression, oppression outlives itself. The scar does the work of the wound. That is the real tragedy: that injustice retains the power to distort long after it has ceased to be real. It is a posthumous victory for the oppressors, when pain be-

> comes a tradition. And yet the atrocities of the past must never be forgotten. This is the unfairly difficult dilemma of the newly emancipated and the newly enfranchised: an honorable life is not possible if they remember too little and a normal life is not possible if they remember too much.[8]

With the eye of recollection, which does not "remember too much," Steele recommends a policy which offers "educational and economic development of disadvantaged people regardless of race and the eradication from our society—through close monitoring and severe sanctions—of racial and gender discrimination."[9]

3. *Affirmative Action Encourages Mediocrity and Incompetence*

Last Spring Jesse Jackson joined protesters at Harvard Law School in demanding that the Law School faculty hire black women. Jackson dismissed Dean of the Law School, Robert C. Clark's standard of choosing the best qualified person for the job as "Cultural anemia." "We cannot just define who is qualified in the most narrow vertical academic terms," he said. "Most people in the world are yellow, brown, black, poor, non-Christian and don't speak English, and they can't wait for some White males with archaic rules to appraise them."[10] It might be noted that if Jackson is correct about the depth of cultural decadence at Harvard, blacks might be well advised to form and support their own more vital law schools and leave places like Harvard to their archaism.

At several universities, the administration has forced departments to hire members of minorities even when far superior candidates were available. Shortly after obtaining my Ph.D. in the late 70's I was mistakenly identified as a black philosopher (I had a civil rights record and was once a black studies major) and was flown to a major university, only to be rejected for a more qualified candidate when it discovered that I was white.

Stories of the bad effects of Affirmative Action abound. The philosopher Sidney Hook writes that "At one Ivy League university, representatives of the Regional HEW demanded an explanation of why there were no women or minority students in the Graduate Department of Religious Studies. They were told that a reading of knowledge of Hebrew and Greek was presupposed. Whereupon the representatives of HEW advised orally: 'Then end those old fashioned programs that require irrelevant languages. And start up programs on relevant things which minority group students can study without learning languages.' "[11]

Nicholas Capaldi notes that the staff of HEW itself was one-half women, three-fifths members of minorities, and one-half black—a clear case of racial over-representation.

In 1972 officials at Stanford University discovered a proposal for the government to monitor curriculum in higher education: the "Summary Statement . . . Sex Discrimination Proposed HEW Regulation to Effectuate Title IX of the Education Amendment of 1972" to "establish and use internal procedure for reviewing curricula, designed both to ensure that they do not reflect discrimination on the basis of sex and to resolve complaints concerning allegations of such discrimination, pursuant to procedural standards to be prescribed by the Director of the office of Civil Rights." Fortunately, Secretary of HEW Caspar Weinberger when alerted to the intrusion, assured Stanford University that he would never approve of it.[12]

Government programs of enforced preferential treatment tend to appeal to the lowest possible common denominator. Witness the 1974 HEW Revised Order No. 14 on Affirmative Action expectations for preferential hiring: "Neither minorities nor female employees should be required to possess higher qualifications than those of the lowest qualified incumbents."

Furthermore, no tests may be given to candidates unless it is *proved* to be relevant to the job.

> No standard or criteria which have, by intent or effect, worked to exclude women or minorities as a class can be utilized, unless the institution can demonstrate the necessity of such standard to the performance of the job in question.
>
> Whenever a validity study is called for . . . the user should include . . . an investigation of suitable alter-

native selection procedures and suitable alternative methods of using the selection procedure which have as little adverse impact as possible. . . . Whenever the user is shown an alternative selection procedure with evidence of less adverse impact and substantial evidence of validity for the same job in similar circumstances, the user should investigate it to determine the appropriateness of using or validating it in accord with these guidelines.[13]

At the same time Americans are wondering why standards in our country are falling and the Japanese are getting ahead. Affirmative Action with its twin idols, Sufficiency and Diversity, is the enemy of excellence. I will develop this thought below (III.6).

4. *Affirmative Action Policies Unjustly Shift the Burden of Proof*

Affirmative Action legislation tends to place the burden of proof on the employer who does not have an "adequate" representation of "underutilized" groups in his work force. He is guilty until proven innocent. I have already recounted how in the mid-eighties the Supreme Court shifted the burden of proof back onto the plaintiff, while Congress is now attempting to shift the burden back to the employer. Those in favor of deeming disproportional representation "guilty until proven innocent" argue that it is easy for employers to discriminate against minorities by various subterfuges, and I agree that steps should be taken to monitor against prejudicial treatment. But being prejudiced against employers is not the way to attain a just solution to discrimination. The principle: innocent until proven guilty, applies to employers as well as criminals. Indeed, it is clearly special pleading to reject this basic principle of Anglo-American law in this case of discrimination while adhering to it everywhere else.

5. *An Argument from Merit*

Traditionally, we have believed that the highest positions in society should be awarded to those who are best qualified—as the Koran states in the quotation at the beginning of this paper. Rewarding excellence both seems just to the individuals in the competition and makes for efficiency. Note that one of the most successful acts of integration, the recruitment of Jackie Robinson in the late 40's, was done in just this way, according to merit. If Robinson had been brought into the major league as a mediocre player or had batted .200 he would have been scorned and sent back to the minors where he belonged.

Merit is not an absolute value. There are times when it may be overridden for social goals, but there is a strong prima facie reason for awarding positions on its basis, and it should enjoy a weighty presumption in our social practices.

In a celebrated article Ronald Dworkin says that "Bakke had no case" because society did not owe Bakke anything. That may be, but then why does it owe anyone anything? Dworkin puts the matter in Utility terms, but if that is the case, society may owe Bakke a place at the University of California/Davis, for it seems a reasonable rule-utilitarian principle that achievement should be rewarded in society. We generally want the best to have the best positions, the best qualified candidate to win the political office, the most brilliant and competent scientist to be chosen for the most challenging research project, the best qualified pilots to become commercial pilots, only the best soldiers to become generals. Only when little is at stake do we weaken the standards and content ourselves with sufficiency (rather than excellence)—there are plenty of jobs where "sufficiency" rather than excellence is required. Perhaps we now feel that medicine or law or university professorships are so routine that they can be performed by minimally qualified people—in which case AA has a place.

But note, no one is calling for quotas or proportional representation of *underutilized* groups in the National Basketball Association where blacks make up 80% of the players. But if merit and merit alone reigns in sports, should it not be valued at least as much in education and industry?

6. *The Slippery Slope*

Even if Strong AA or Reverse Discrimination could meet the other objections, it would face a tough question: once you embark on this project, how do you limit it? Who should be excluded from reverse discrimination? Asians and Jews are over-represented, so if we give blacks positive quotas, should we place negative quotas to these other groups? Since white males, "WMs," are a minority which is suffering from reverse discrimination, will we need a New Affirmative Action policy in the 21st century to compensate for the discrimination against WMs in the late 20th century?

Furthermore, Affirmative Action has stigmatized the *young* white male. Assuming that we accept reverse discrimination, the fair way to make sacrifices would be to retire *older* white males who are more likely to have benefited from a favored status. Probably the least guilty of any harm to minority groups is the young white male—usually a liberal who has been required to bear the brunt of ages of past injustice. Justice Brennan's announcement that the Civil Rights Act did not apply to discrimination against white shows how the clearest language can be bent to serve the ideology of the moment.[14]

7. The Mounting Evidence Against the Success of Affirmative Action

Thomas Sowell of the Hoover Institute has shown in his book *Preferential Policies: An International Perspective* that preferential hiring almost never solves social problems. It generally builds in mediocrity or incompetence and causes deep resentment. It is a short term solution which lacks serious grounding in social realities.

For instance, Sowell cites some disturbing statistics on education. Although twice as many blacks as Asian students took the nationwide Scholastic Aptitude Test in 1983, approximately fifteen times as many Asian students scored above 700 (out of a possible 800) on the mathematics half of the SAT. The percentage of Asians who scored above 700 in math was also more than six times higher than the percentage of American Indians and more than ten times higher than that of Mexican Americans—as well as more than double the percentage of whites. As Sowell points out, in all countries studied, "intergroup performance disparities are huge" (108).

> There are dozens of American colleges and universities where the median combined verbal SAT score and mathematics SAT score total 1200 or above. As of 1983 there were less than 600 black students in the entire US with combined SAT scores of 1200. This meant that, despite widespread attempts to get a black student "representation" comparable to the black percentage of the population (about 11%), there were not enough black students in the entire country for the Ivy League alone to have such a "representation" without going beyond this pool—even if the entire pool went to the eight Ivy League colleges.[15]

Often it is claimed that a cultural bias is the cause of the poor performance of blacks on SAT (or IQ tests), but Sowell shows that these test scores are actually a better predictor of college performance for blacks than for Asians and whites. He also shows the harmfulness of the effect on blacks of preferential acceptance. At the University of California, Berkeley, where the freshman class closely reflects the actual ethnic distribution of California high school students, more than 70% of blacks fail to graduate. All 312 black students entering Berkeley in 1987 were admitted under "Affirmative Action" criteria rather than by meeting standard academic criteria. So were 480 out of 507 Hispanic students. In 1986 the median SAT score for blacks at Berkeley was 952, for Mexican Americans 1014, for American Indians 1082 and for Asian Americans 1254. (The average SAT for all students was 1181.)

The result of this mismatching is that blacks who might do well if they went to a second tier or third tier school where their test scores would indicate they belong, actually are harmed by preferential treatment. They cannot compete in the institutions where high abilities are necessary.

Sowell also points out that Affirmative Action policies have mainly assisted the middle class black, those who have suffered least from discrimination. "Black couples in which both husband and wife are college-educated overtook white couples of the same description back in the early 1970's and continued to at least hold their own in the 1980's" (115).

Sowell's conclusion is that similar patterns of

results obtained from India to the USA wherever preferential policies exist. "In education, preferential admissions policies have led to high attrition rates and substandard performances for those preferred students . . . who survived to graduate." In all countries the preferred tended to concentrate in less difficult subjects which lead to less remunerative careers. "In the employment market, both blacks and untouchables at the higher levels have advanced substantially while those at the lower levels show no such advancement and even some signs of retrogression. These patterns are also broadly consistent with patterns found in countries in which majorities have created preferences for themselves . . ." (116).

The tendency has been to focus at the high level end of education and employment rather than on the lower level of family structure and early education. But if we really want to help the worst off improve, we need to concentrate on the family and early education. It is foolish to expect equal results when we begin with grossly unequal starting points—and discriminating against young white males is no more just than discriminating against women, blacks or anyone else.

CONCLUSION

Let me sum up. The goal of the Civil Rights movement and of moral people everywhere has been equal opportunity. The question is: how best to get there. Civil Rights legislation removed the legal barriers to equal opportunity, but did not tackle the deeper causes that produced differential results. Weak Affirmative Action aims at encouraging minorities in striving for the highest positions without unduly jeopardizing the rights of majorities, but the problem of Weak Affirmative Action is that it easily slides into Strong Affirmative Action where quotas, "goals," and equal results are forced into groups, thus promoting mediocrity, inefficiency, and resentment. Furthermore, Affirmative Action aims at the higher levels of society—universities and skilled jobs—yet if we want to improve our society, the best way to do it is to concentrate on families, children, early education, and the like. Affirmative Action is, on the one hand, too much, too soon and on the other hand, too little, too late.

Martin Luther said that humanity is like a man mounting a horse who always tends to fall off on the other side of the horse. This seems to be the case with Affirmative Action. Attempting to redress the discriminatory iniquities of our history, our well-intentioned social engineers engage in new forms of discriminatory iniquity and thereby think that they have successfully mounted the horse of racial harmony. They have only fallen off on the other side of the issue.[16]

NOTES

1. John Arthur, *The Unfinished Constitution* (Belmont, CA, 1990), p. 238.
2. See Phillip E. Vernon's excellent summary of the literature in *Intelligence: Heredity and Environment* (New York, 1979) and Yves Christen "Sex Differences in the Human Brain" in Nicholas Davidson (ed.) *Gender Sanity* (Lanham, 1989) and T. Bouchard, *et al.,* "Sources of Human Psychological Differences: The Minnesota Studies of Twins Reared Apart," *Science,* vol. 250 (1990).
3. See Michael Levin, "Is Racial Discrimination Special?" *Policy Review,* Fall issue (1982).
4. Judith Jarvis Thomson, "Preferential Hiring" in Marshall Cohen, Thomas Nagel and Thomas Scanlon (eds.), *Equality and Preferential Treatment* (Princeton, 1977).
5. John Rawls, *A Theory of Justice* (Cambridge, 1971), p. 104; See Richard Wasserstrom "A Defense of Programs of Preferential Treatment," *National Forum* (Phi Kappa Phi Journal), vol. 58 (1978). See also Bernard Boxill, "The Morality of Preferential Hiring," *Philosophy and Public Affairs,* vol. 7 (1978).
6. Michael Kinsley, "Equal Lack of Opportunity," *Harper's,* June issue (1983).
7. There is one other argument which I have omitted. It is one from precedence and has been stated by Judith Jarvis Thomson in the article cited earlier:

"Suppose two candidates for a civil service job have equally good test scores, but there is only one job available. We could decide between them by coin-tossing. But in fact we do allow for declaring for *A* straightaway, where *A* is a veteran, and *B* is not. It may be that *B* is a non-veteran through no fault of his own . . . Yet the fact is that *B* is not a veteran and *A* is. On the assumption that the veteran has served his country, the country owes him something. And it is plain that giving him preference is not an unjust way in which part of that debt of gratitude can be paid" (p. 379f).

The two forms of preferential hiring are analogous. Veteran's preference is justified as a way of paying a debt of gratitude; preferential hiring is a way of paying a debt of compensation. In both cases innocent parties bear the burden of the community's debt, but it is justified.

My response to this argument is that veterans should not be hired in place of better qualified candidates, but that benefits like the GI scholarships are part of the contract with veterans who serve their country in the armed services. The notion of compensation only applies to individuals who have been injured by identifiable entities. So the analogy between veterans and minority groups seems weak.

8. Quoted in Jim Sleeper, *The Closest of Strangers* (New York, 1990), p. 209.
9. Shelby Steele, "A Negative Vote on Affirmative Action," *New York Times,* May 13, 1990 issue.
10. *New York Times,* May 10, 1990 issue.
11. Nicholas Capaldi, *op. cit.,* p. 85.
12. Cited in Capaldi, *op. cit.,* p. 95.
13. *Ibid.*
14. The extreme form of this New Speak is incarnate in the Politically Correct Movement ("PC" ideology) where a new orthodoxy has emerged, condemning white, European culture and seeing African culture as the new savior of us all. Perhaps the clearest example of this is Paula Rothenberg's book *Racism and Sexism* (New York, 1987) which asserts that there is no such thing as black racism; only whites are capable of racism (p. 6). Ms. Rothenberg's book has been scheduled as required reading for all freshmen at the University of Texas. See Joseph Salemi, "Lone Star Academic Politics," no. 87 (1990).
15. Thomas Sowell, *op. cit.,* p. 108.
16. I am indebted to Jim Landesman, Michael Levin, and Abigail Rosenthal for comments on a previous draft of this paper. I am also indebted to Nicholas Capaldi's *Out of Order* for first making me aware of the extent of the problem of Affirmative Action.

What Is Wrong with Reverse Discrimination?

Edwin C. Hettinger
Department of Philosophy, College of Charleston

Many people think it obvious that reverse discrimination is unjust. Calling affirmative action reverse discrimination itself suggests this. This discussion evaluates numerous reasons given for this alleged injustice. Most of these accounts of what is wrong with reverse discrimination are found to be deficient. The explanations for why reverse discrimination is morally troubling show only that it is unjust in a relatively weak sense. This result has an important consequence for the wider issue of the moral justifiability of affirmative action. If social policies which involve minor injustice are permissible (and perhaps required) when they are required in order to overcome much greater injustice, then the mild injustice of reverse discrimination is easily overridden by its contribution to the important social goal of dismantling our sexual and racial caste system.

By 'reverse discrimination' or 'affirmative action' I shall mean hiring or admitting a slightly less well qualified woman or black, rather than a slightly more qualified white male, for the purpose of helping to eradicate sexual and/or racial inequality, or for the purpose of compensating women and blacks for the burdens and injustices they have suffered due to past and ongoing sexism and racism. There are weaker forms of affirmative action, such as giving preference to minority candidates only when qualifications are equal, or providing special educational opportunities for youths in disadvan-

From *Business & Professional Ethics Journal* (Fall 1987), pp 39–51. Reprinted by permission of the author.

taged groups. This paper seeks to defend the more controversial sort of reverse discrimination defined above. I begin by considering several spurious objections to reverse discrimination. In the second part, I identify the ways in which this policy is morally troubling and then assess the significance of these negative features.

SPURIOUS OBJECTIONS

1. Reverse Discrimination as Equivalent to Racism and Sexism

In a discussion on national television, George Will, the conservative news analyst and political philosopher, articulated the most common objection to reverse discrimination. It is unjust, he said, because it is discrimination on the basis of race or sex. Reverse discrimination against white males is the same evil as traditional discrimination against women and blacks. The only difference is that in this case it is the white male who is being discriminated against. Thus if traditional racism and sexism are wrong and unjust, so is reverse discrimination, and for the very same reasons.

But reverse discrimination is not at all like traditional sexism and racism. The motives and intentions behind it are completely different, as are its consequences. Consider some of the motives underlying traditional racial discrimination. Blacks were not hired or allowed into schools because it was felt that contact with them was degrading, and sullied whites. These policies were based on contempt and loathing for blacks, on a feeling that blacks were suitable only for subservient positions and that they should never have positions of authority over whites. Slightly better qualified white males are not being turned down under affirmative action for any of these reasons. No defenders or practitioners of affirmative action (and no significant segment of the general public) think that contact with white males is degrading or sullying, that white males are contemptible and loathsome, or that white males—by their nature—should be subservient to blacks or women.

The consequences of these two policies differ radically as well. Affirmative action does not stigmatize white males; it does not perpetuate unfortunate stereotypes about white males; it is not part of a pattern of discrimination that makes being a white male incredibly burdensome. Nor does it add to a particular group's "already overabundant supply" of power, authority, wealth, and opportunity, as does traditional racial and sexual discrimination. On the contrary, it results in a more egalitarian distribution of these social and economic benefits. If the motives and consequences of reverse discrimination and of traditional racism and sexism are completely different, in what sense could they be morally equivalent acts? If acts are to be individuated (for moral purposes) by including the motives, intentions, and consequences in their description, then clearly these two acts are not identical.

It might be argued that although the motives and consequences are different, the act itself is the same: reverse discrimination is discrimination on the basis of race and sex, and this is wrong in itself independently of its motives or consequences. But discriminating (i.e., making distinctions in how one treats people) on the basis of race or sex is not always wrong, nor is it necessarily unjust. It is not wrong, for example, to discriminate against one's own sex when choosing a spouse. Nor is racial or sexual discrimination in hiring necessarily wrong. This is shown by Peter Singer's example in which a director of a play about ghetto conditions in New York City refuses to consider any white applicants for the actors because she wants the play to be authentic.[1] If I am looking for a representative of the black community, or doing a study about blacks and disease, it is perfectly legitimate to discriminate against all whites. Their whiteness makes them unsuitable for my (legitimate) purposes. Similarly, if I am hiring a wet-nurse, or a person to patrol the women's change rooms in my department store, discriminating against males is perfectly legitimate.

These examples show that racial and sexual discrimination are not wrong in themselves. This is not to say that they are never wrong; most often they clearly are. Whether or not they are wrong, however, depends on the purposes, consequences, and context of such discrimination.

2. Race and Sex as Morally Arbitrary and Irrelevant Characteristics

A typical reason given for the alleged injustice of all racial and sexual discrimination (including affirmative action) is that it is morally arbitrary to consider race or sex when hiring, since these characteristics are not relevant to the decision. But the above examples show that not all uses of race or sex as a criterion in hiring decisions are morally arbitrary or irrelevant. Similarly, when an affirmative action officer takes into account race and sex, use of these characteristics is not morally irrelevant or arbitrary. Since affirmative action aims to help end racial and sexual inequality by providing black and female role models for minorities (and non-minorities), the race and sex of the job candidates are clearly relevant to the decision. There is nothing arbitrary about the affirmative action officer focusing on race and sex. Hence, if reverse discrimination is wrong, it is not wrong for the reason that it uses morally irrelevant and arbitrary characteristics to distinguish between applicants.

3. Reverse Discrimination as Unjustified Stereotyping

It might be argued that reverse discrimination involves judging people by alleged average characteristics of a class to which they belong, instead of judging them on the basis of their individual characteristics, and that such judging on the basis of stereotypes is unjust. But the defense of affirmative action suggested in this paper does not rely on stereotyping. When an employer hires a slightly less well qualified woman or black over a slightly more qualified white male for the purpose of helping to overcome sexual and racial inequality, she judges the applicants on the basis of their individual characteristics. She uses this person's sex or skin color as a mechanism to help achieve the goals of affirmative action. Individual characteristics of the white male (his skin color and sex) prevent him from serving one of the legitimate goals of employment policies, and he is turned down on this basis.

Notice that the objection does have some force against those who defend reverse discrimination on the grounds of compensatory justice. An affirmative action policy whose purpose is to compensate women and blacks for past and current injustices judges that women and blacks on the average are owed greater compensation than are white males. Although this is true, opponents of affirmative action argue that some white males have been more severely and unfairly disadvantaged than some women and blacks. A poor white male from Appalachia may have suffered greater undeserved disadvantages than the upper-middle class woman or black with whom he competes. Although there is a high correlation between being female (or being black) and being especially owed compensation for unfair disadvantages suffered, the correlation is not universal.

Thus defending affirmative action on the grounds of compensatory justice may lead to unjust treatment of white males in individual cases. Despite the fact that certain white males are owed greater compensation than are some women or blacks, it is the latter that receive compensation. This is the result of judging candidates for jobs on the basis of the average characteristics of their class, rather than on the basis of their individual characteristics. Thus compensatory justice defenses of reverse discrimination may involve potentially problematic stereotyping. But this is not the defense of affirmative action considered here.

4. Failing to Hire the Most Qualified Person Is Unjust

One of the major reasons people think reverse discrimination is unjust is because they think that the most qualified person should get the job. But why should the most qualified person be hired?

A. Efficiency One obvious answer to this question is that one should hire the most qualified person because doing so promotes efficiency. If job qualifications are positively correlated with job performance, then the more qualified person will tend to do a better job. Although it is not always true that there is such a correlation, in general there is, and hence this point is well taken. There are short term efficiency costs of reverse discrimination as defined here.

Note that a weaker version of affirmative action has no such efficiency costs. If one hires a black or woman over a white male only in cases where qualifications are roughly equal, job performance will not be affected. Furthermore, efficiency costs will be a function of the qualifications gap between the black or woman hired, and the white male rejected: the larger the gap, the greater the efficiency costs. The existence of efficiency costs is also a function of the type of work performed. Many of the jobs in our society are ones which any normal person can do (e.g., assembly line worker, janitor, truck driver, etc.). Affirmative action hiring for these positions is unlikely to have significant efficiency costs (assuming whoever is hired is willing to work hard). In general, professional positions are the ones in which people's performance levels will vary significantly, and hence these are the jobs in which reverse discrimination could have significant efficiency costs.

While concern for efficiency gives us a reason for hiring the most qualified person, it in no way explains the alleged injustice suffered by the white male who is passed over due to reverse discrimination. If the affirmative action employer is treating the white male unjustly, it is not because the hiring policy is inefficient. Failing to maximize efficiency does not generally involve acting unjustly. For instance, a person who carries one bag of groceries at a time, rather than two, is acting inefficiently, though not unjustly.

It is arguable that the manager of a business who fails to hire the most qualified person (and thereby sacrifices some efficiency) treats the owners of the company unjustly, for their profits may suffer, and this violates one conception of the manager's fiduciary responsibility to the shareholders. Perhaps the administrator of a hospital who hires a slightly less well qualified black doctor (for the purposes of affirmative action) treats the future patients at that hospital unjustly, for doing so may reduce the level of health care they receive (and it is arguable that they have a legitimate expectation to receive the best health care possible for the money they spend). But neither of these examples of inefficiency leading to injustice concern the white male "victim" of affirmative action, and it is precisely this person who the opponents of reverse discrimination claim is being unfairly treated.

To many people, that a policy is inefficient is a sufficient reason for condemning it. This is especially true in the competitive and profit oriented world of business. However, profit maximization is not the only legitimate goal of business hiring policies (or other business decisions). Businesses have responsibilities to help heal society's ill's, especially those (like racism and sexism) which they in large part helped to create and perpetuate. Unless one takes the implausible position that business' only legitimate goal is profit maximization, the efficiency costs of affirmative action are not an automatic reason for rejecting it. And as we have noted, affirmative action's efficiency costs are of no help in substantiating and explaining its alleged injustice to white males.

B. The Most Qualified Person Has a Right to the Job One could argue that the most qualified person for the job has a right to be hired in virtue of superior qualifications. On this view, reverse discrimination violates the better qualified white male's right to be hired for the job. But the most qualified applicant holds no such right. If you are the best painter in town, and a person hires her brother to paint her house, instead of you, your rights have not been violated. People do not have rights to be hired for particular jobs (though I think a plausible case can be made for the claim that there is a fundamental human right to employment). If anyone has a right in this matter, it is the employer. This is not to say, of course, that the employer cannot do wrong in her hiring decision; she obviously can. If she hires a white because she loathes blacks, she does wrong. The point is that her wrong does not consist in violating the right some candidate has to her job (though this would violate other rights of the candidate).

C. The Most Qualified Person Deserves the Job It could be argued that the most qualified person should get the job because she deserves it in virtue of her superior qualifications. But the assumption that the person most qualified for a job is the one who most deserves it is problematic. Very often people do not deserve their qualifications, and hence they do not deserve anything on the basis of those qualifications. A person's qualifications are a function of at least the following factors: (a) innate abilities, (b) home environment, (c) socio-economic class of parents, (d) quality of the schools attended, (e) luck, and (f) effort or perseverance. A person is only responsible for the last factor on this list, and hence one only deserves one's qualifications to the extent that they are a function of effort.

It is undoubtedly often the case that a person who is less well qualified for a job is more deserving of the job (because she worked harder to achieve those lower qualifications) than is someone with superior qualifications. This is frequently true of women and blacks in the job market: they worked harder to overcome disadvantages most (or all) white males never faced. Hence, affirmative action policies which permit the hiring of slightly less well qualified candidates may often be more in line with considerations of desert than are the standard meritocratic procedures.

The point is not that affirmative action is defensible because it helps insure that more deserving candidates get jobs. Nor is it that desert should be the only or even the most important consideration in hiring decisions. The claim is simply that hiring the most qualified person for a job need not (and quite often does not) involve hiring the most deserving candidate. Hence the intuition that morality requires one to hire the most qualified people cannot be justified on the grounds that these people deserve to be hired.

D. The Most Qualified Person Is Entitled to the Job One might think that although the most qualified person neither deserves the job nor has a right to the job, still this person is entitled to the job. By 'entitlement' in this context, I mean a natural and legitimate expectation based on a type of social promise. Society has implicitly encouraged the belief that the most qualified candidate will get the job. Society has set up a competition and the prize is a job which is awarded to those applying with the best qualifications. Society thus reneges on an implicit promise it has made to its members when it allows reverse discrimination to occur. It is dashing legitimate expectations it has encouraged. It is violating the very rules of a game it created.

Furthermore, the argument goes, by allowing reverse discrimination, society is breaking an explicit promise (contained in the Civil Rights Act of 1964) that it will not allow race or sex to be used against one of its citizens. Title VII of that Act prohibits discrimination in employment on the basis of race or sex (as well as color, religion, or national origin).

In response to this argument, it should first be noted that the above interpretation of the Civil Rights Act is misleading. In fact, the Supreme Court has interpreted the Act as allowing race and sex to be considered in hiring or admission decisions.[2] More importantly, since affirmative action has been an explicit national policy for the last twenty years (and has been supported in numerous court cases), it is implausible to argue that society has promised its members that it will not allow race or sex to outweigh superior qualifications in hiring decisions. In addition, the objection takes a naive and utopian view of actual hiring decisions. It presents a picture of our society as a pure meritocracy in which hiring decisions are based solely on qualifications. The only exception it sees to these meritocratic procedures is the unfortunate policy of affirmative action. But this picture is dramatically distorted. Elected government officials, political appointees, business managers, and many others clearly do not have their positions solely or even mostly because of their qualifications. Given the widespread acceptance in our society of procedures which are far from meritocratic, claiming that the most qualified person has a socially endorsed entitlement to the job is not believable.

5. Undermining Equal Opportunity for White Males

It has been claimed that the right of white males to an equal chance of employment is violated by affirmative action. Reverse discrimination, it is said, undermines equality of opportunity for white males.

If equality of opportunity requires a social environment in which everyone at birth has roughly the same chance of succeeding through the use of his or her natural talents, then it could well be argued that given the social, cultural, and educational disadvantages placed on women and blacks, preferential treatment of these groups brings us closer to equality of opportunity. White males are full members of the community in a way in which women and blacks are not, and this advantage is diminished by affirmative action. Affirmative action takes away the greater than equal opportunity white males generally have, and thus it brings us closer to a situation in which all members of society have an equal chance of succeeding through the use of their talents.

It should be noted that the goal of affirmative action is to bring about a society in which there is equality of opportunity for women and blacks without preferential treatment of these groups. It is not the purpose of the sort of affirmative action defended here to disadvantage white males in order to take away the advantage a sexist and racist society gives to them. But noticing that this occurs is sufficient to dispel the illusion that affirmative action undermines the equality of opportunity for white males.

LEGITIMATE OBJECTIONS

The following two considerations explain what is morally troubling about reverse discrimination.

1. Judging on the Basis of Involuntary Characteristics

In cases of reverse discrimination, white males are passed over on the basis of membership in a group they were born into. When an affirmative action employer hires a slightly less well qualified black (or woman), rather than a more highly qualified white male, skin color (or sex) is being used as one criterion for determining who gets a very important benefit. Making distinctions in how one treats people on the basis of characteristics they cannot help having (such as skin color or sex) is morally problematic because it reduces individual autonomy. Discriminating between people on the basis of features they can do something about is preferable, since it gives them some control over how others act towards them. They can develop the characteristics others use to give them favorable treatment and avoid those characteristics others use as grounds for unfavorable treatment.

For example, if employers refuse to hire you because you are a member of the American Nazi Party, and if you do not like the fact that you are having a hard time finding a job, you can choose to leave the party. However, if a white male is having trouble finding employment because slightly less well qualified women and blacks are being given jobs to meet affirmative action requirements, there is nothing he can do about this disadvantage, and his autonomy is curtailed.

Discriminating between people on the basis of their involuntary characteristics is morally undesirable, and thus reverse discrimination is also morally undesirable. Of course, that something is morally undesirable does not show that it is unjust, nor that it is morally unjustifiable.

How morally troubling is it to judge people on the basis of involuntary characteristics? Notice that our society frequently uses these sorts of features to distinguish between people. Height and good looks are characteristics one cannot do much about, and yet basketball players and models are ordinarily chosen and rejected on the basis of precisely these features. To a large extent our intelligence is also a feature beyond our control, and yet intelligence is clearly one of the major characteristics our society uses to determine what happens to people.

Of course there are good reasons why we distinguish between people on the basis of these sorts of involuntary characteristics. Given the goals of basketball teams, model agencies, and employers in general, hiring the taller, better looking, or more intelligent person (respectively) makes good sense. It promotes efficiency, since all these people are likely to do a better job. Hiring policies based on these involuntary characteristics serve the legitimate purposes of these businesses (e.g., profit and serving the public), and hence they may be morally justified despite their tendency to reduce the control people have over their own lives.

This argument applies to reverse discrimination as well. The purpose of affirmative action is to help eradicate racial and sexual injustice. If affirmative action policies help bring about this goal, then they can be morally justified despite their tendency to reduce the control white males have over their lives.

In one respect this sort of consequentialist argument is more forceful in the case of affirmative action. Rather than merely promoting the goal of efficiency (which is the justification for businesses hiring naturally brighter, taller, or more attractive individuals), affirmative action promotes the nonutilitarian goal of an egalitarian society. In general, promoting a consideration of justice (such as equality) is more important than is promoting efficiency or utility. Thus in terms of the importance of the objective, this consequentialist argument is stronger in the case of affirmative action. If one can justify reducing individual autonomy on the grounds that it promotes efficiency, one can certainly do so on the grounds that it reduces the injustice of racial and sexual inequality.

2. Burdening White Males without Compensation

Perhaps the strongest moral intuition concerning the wrongness of reverse discrimination is that it is unfair to job seeking white males. It is unfair because they have been given an undeserved disadvantage in the competition for employment; they have been handicapped because of something that is not their fault. Why should white males be made to pay for the sins of others?

It would be a mistake to argue for reverse discrimination on the grounds that white males deserve to be burdened and that therefore we should hire women and blacks even when white males are better qualified. Young white males who are now entering the job market are not more responsible for the evils of racial and sexual inequality than are other members of society. Thus, reverse discrimination is not properly viewed as punishment administered to white males.

The justification for affirmative action supported here claims that bringing about sexual and racial equality necessitates sacrifice on the part of white males who seek employment. An important step in bringing about the desired egalitarian society involves speeding up the process by which women and blacks get into positions of power and authority. This requires that white males find it harder to achieve these same positions. But this is not punishment for deeds done.

Thomas Nagel's helpful analogy is state condemnation of property under the right of eminent domain for the purpose of building a highway. Forcing some in the community to move in order that the community as a whole may benefit is unfair. Why should these individuals suffer rather than others? The answer is: Because they happen to live in a place where it is important to build a road. A similar response should be given to the white male who objects to reverse discrimination with the same "Why me?" question. The answer is: Because job seeking white males happen to be in the way of an important road leading to the desired egalitarian society. Job-seeking white males are being made to bear the brunt of the burden of affirmative action because of accidental considerations, just as are homeowners whose property is condemned in order to build a highway.[3]

This analogy is extremely illuminating and helpful in explaining the nature of reverse discrimination. There is, however, an important dissimilarity that Nagel does not mention. In cases of property condemnation, compensation is paid to the owner. Affirmative action policies, however, do not compensate white males for shouldering this burden of moving toward the desired egalitarian society. So affirmative action is unfair to job seeking white males because they are forced to bear an unduly large share of the burden of achieving racial and sexual equality without being compensated for this sacrifice. Since we have singled out job seeking white males from the larger pool of white males who should also help achieve this goal, it seems that some compensation from the latter to the former is appropriate.

This is a serious objection to affirmative action policies only if the uncompensated burden is substantial. Usually it is not. Most white male "victims" of affirmative action easily find employment. It is highly unlikely that the same white male will repeatedly fail to get hired because of affirmative action. The burdens of affirmative action should be spread as evenly as possible among all the job seeking white males. Furthermore, the burden job seeking white males face—of finding it somewhat more difficult to get employment—is inconsequential when compared to the burdens ongoing discrimination places on women and blacks. Forcing job seeking white males to bear an extra burden is acceptable because this is a necessary step toward achieving a much greater reduction in the unfair burdens our society places on women and blacks. If affirmative action is a necessary mechanism for a timely dismantlement of our racial and sexual caste system, the extra burdens it places on job seeking white males are justified.

Still the question remains: Why isn't compensation paid? When members of society who do not deserve extra burdens are singled out to sacrifice for an important community goal, society owes them compensation. This objection loses some of its force when one realizes that society continually places undeserved burdens on its members without compensating them. For instance, the burden of seeking efficiency is placed on the shoulders of the least naturally talented and intelligent. That one is born less intelligent (or otherwise less talented) does not mean that one deserves to have reduced employment opportunities, and yet our society's meritocratic hiring procedures make it much harder for less naturally talented members to find meaningful employment. These people are not compensated for their sacrifices either.

Of course, pointing out that there are other examples of an allegedly problematic social policy does not justify that policy. Nonetheless, if this analogy is sound, failing to compensate job-seeking white males for the sacrifices placed on them by reverse discrimination is not without precedent. Furthermore, it is no more morally troublesome than is failing to compensate less talented members of society for their undeserved sacrifice of employment opportunities for the sake of efficiency.

CONCLUSION

This article has shown the difficulties in pinpointing what is morally troubling about reverse discrimination. The most commonly heard objections to reverse discrimination fail to make their case. Reverse discrimination is not morally equivalent to traditional racism and sexism since its goals and consequences are entirely different, and the act of treating people differently on the basis of race or sex is not necessarily morally wrong. The race and sex of the candidates are not morally irrelevant in all hiring decisions, and affirmative action hiring is an example where discriminating on the basis of race or sex is not morally arbitrary. Furthermore, affirmative action can be defended on grounds that do not involve stereotyping. Though affirmative action hiring of less well qualified applicants can lead to short run inefficiency, failing to hire the most qualified applicant does not violate this person's rights, entitlements, or deserts. Additionally, affirmative action hiring does not generally undermine equal opportunity for white males.

Reverse discrimination is morally troublesome in that it judges people on the basis of involuntary characteristics and thus reduces the control they have over their lives. It also places a larger than fair share of the burden of achieving an egalitarian society on the shoulders of job seeking white males without compensating them for this sacrifice. But these problems are relatively minor when compared to the grave injustice of racial and sexual inequality, and they are easily outweighed if affirmative action helps alleviate this far greater injustice.

NOTES

I thank Cheshire Calhoun, Beverly Diamond, John Dickerson, Jasper Hunt, Glenn Lesses, Richard Nunan, and Martin Perlmutter for helpful comments.

1. Peter Singer, "Is Racial Discrimination Arbitrary?" *Philosophia*, vol. 8 (November 1978), pp. 185–203.
2. See Justice William Brennan's majority opinion in

United Steel Workers and Kaiser Aluminum v. Weber, United States Supreme Court, *443 U.S. 193* (1979). See also Justice Lewis Powell's majority opinion in the University of California v. Bakke, United States Supreme Court, *438 U.S. 265* (1978).

3. Thomas Nagel, "A Defense of Affirmative Action" in *Ethical Theory and Business,* 2nd edition, ed. Tom Beauchamp and Norman Bowie (Englewood Cliffs, NJ: Prentice-Hall, 1983), p. 484.

Women Cost a Company More—But Are Worth It

Felice N. Schwartz
President Emerita, Catalyst Company, New York, NY

The cost of employing women in management is greater than the cost of employing men. This is a jarring statement, partly because it is true, but mostly because it is something people are reluctant to talk about. A new study by one multinational corporation shows that the rate of turnover in management positions is 2 1/2 times higher among top-performing women than it is among men. A large producer of consumer goods reports that one-half of the women who take maternity leave return to their jobs late or not at all. And we know that women also have a greater tendency to plateau or to interrupt their careers in ways that limit their growth and development. But we have become so sensitive to charges of sexism and so afraid of confrontation, even litigation, that we rarely say what we know to be true. Unfortunately, our bottled-up awareness leaks out in misleading metaphors ("glass ceiling" is one notable example), veiled hostility, lowered expectations, distrust and reluctant adherence to Equal Employment Opportunity requirements.

Career interruptions, plateauing and turnover are expensive. The money corporations invest in recruitment, training and development is less likely to produce top executives among women than among men, and the invaluable company experience that developing executives acquire at every level as they move up through management ranks is more often lost.

The studies just mentioned are only the first of many, I'm quite sure. Demographic realities are going to force corporations all across the country to analyze the cost of employing women in managerial positions, and what they will discover is that women cost more.

But here is another startling truth: The greater cost of employing women is not a function of inescapable gender differences. Women are different from men, but what increases their cost to the corporations is principally the clash of their perceptions, attitudes and behavior with those of men, which is to say, with the policies and practices of male-led corporations.

It is terribly important that employers draw the right conclusions from the studies now being done. The studies will be useless—or worse, harmful—if all they teach us is that women are expensive to employ. What we need to learn is how to reduce that expense, how to stop throwing away the investments we make in talented women, how to become more responsive to the needs of the women that corporations must employ if they are to have the best and the brightest of all those now entering the work force.

The gender differences relevant to business fall into two categories: those related to maternity and those related to the differing traditions and expectations of the sexes. Maternity is biological rather than cultural. We can't alter it, but we can dramatically reduce its impact on the workplace and in many cases eliminate its negative effect on employee development. We can accomplish this by addressing the second set of differences, those between male and female socialization. Today, these differences exaggerate the real costs of maternity

Reprinted by permission of *Harvard Business Review.* An excerpt from "Management Women and the New Facts of Life" by Felice N. Schwartz (January–February 1989).

and can turn a relatively slight disruption in work schedule into a serious business problem and a career derailment for individual women. If we are to overcome the cost differential between male and female employees, we need to address the issues that arise when female socialization meets the male corporate culture and masculine rules of career development—issues of behavior and style, of expectation, of stereotypes and preconceptions, of sexual tension and harassment, of female mentoring, lateral mobility, relocation, compensation and early identification of top performers.

There is no question that the management ranks of business will include increasing numbers of women. There remains, however, the question of how these women will succeed—how long they will stay, how high they will climb, how completely they will fulfill their promise and potential, and what kind of return the corporation will realize on its investment in their training and development.

There is ample business reason for finding ways to make sure that as many of these women as possible will succeed. The first step in this process is to recognize that women are not all alike. Like men, they are individuals with differing talents, priorities and motivations. For the sake of simplicity, let me focus on . . . what I call the career-primary woman and the career-and-family woman.

Like many men, some women put their careers first. They are ready to make the same trade-offs traditionally made by the men who seek leadership positions. They make a career decision to put in extra hours, to make sacrifices in their personal lives, to make the most of every opportunity for professional development. For women, of course, this decision also requires that they remain single or at least childless or, if they do have children, that they be satisfied to have others raise them. Some 90 percent of executive men but only 35 percent of executive women have children by the age of 40. The automatic association of all women with babies is clearly unjustified.

The secret to dealing with such women is to recognize them early, accept them and clear artificial barriers from their path to the top. After all, the best of these women are among the best managerial talent you will ever see. And career-primary women have another important value to the company that men and other women lack. They can act as role models and mentors to younger women who put their careers first. Since upwardly mobile career-primary women still have few role models to motivate and inspire them, a company with women in its top echelon has a significant advantage in the competition for executive talent.

Men at the top of the organization—most of them over 55, with wives who tend to be traditional—often find career women "masculine" and difficult to accept as colleagues. Such men miss the point, which is not that these women are just like men but that they are just like the best men in the organization. And there is such a shortage of the best people that gender cannot be allowed to matter. It is clearly counterproductive to disparage in a woman with executive talent the very qualities that are most critical to the business and that might carry a man to the CEO's office.

Clearing a path to the top for career-primary women has four requirements:

1. Identify them early.

2. Give them the same opportunity you give to talented men to grow and develop and contribute to company profitability. Give them client and customer responsibility. Expect them to travel and relocate, to make the same commitment to the company as men aspiring to leadership positions.

3. Accept them as valued members of your management team. Include them in every kind of communication. Listen to them.

4. Recognize that the business environment is more difficult and stressful for them than for their male peers. They are always a minority, often the only woman. The male perception of talented, ambitious women is at best ambivalent, a mixture of admiration, resentment, confusion, competitiveness, attraction, skepticism, anxiety, pride and animosity. Women can never feel secure about how they should dress and act, whether they should speak out or grin and bear it when they encounter discrimination, stereotyping, sexual harassment and paternalism. Social interaction and travel with

male colleagues and with male clients can be charged. As they move up, the normal increase in pressure and responsibility is compounded for women because they are women.

Stereotypical language and sexist day-to-day behavior do take their toll on women's career development. Few male executives realize how common it is to call women by their first names while men in the same group are greeted with surnames, how frequently female executives are assumed by men to be secretaries, how often women are excluded from all-male social events where business is being transacted. With notable exceptions, men are still generally more comfortable with other men, and as a result women miss many of the career and business opportunities that arise over lunch, on the golf course or in the locker room.

The majority of women, however, are what I call career-and-family women, women who want to pursue serious careers while participating actively in the rearing of children. These women are a precious resource that has yet to be mined. Many of them are talented and creative. Most of them are willing to trade some career growth and compensation for freedom from the constant pressure to work long hours and weekends.

Most companies today are ambivalent at best about the career-and-family women in their management ranks. They would prefer that all employees were willing to give their all to the company. They believe it is in their best interest for all managers to compete for the top positions so the company will have the largest possible pool from which to draw its leaders.

"If you have both talent and motivation," many employers seem to say, "we want to move you up. If you haven't got that motivation, if you want less pressure and greater flexibility, then you can leave and make room for a new generation." These companies lose on two counts. First, they fail to amortize the investment they made in the early training and experience of management women who find themselves committed to family as well as career. Second, they fail to recognize what these women could do for their middle management.

The ranks of middle managers are filled with people on their way up and people who have stalled. Many of them have simply reached their limits, achieved career growth commensurate with or exceeding their capabilities, and they cause problems because their performance is mediocre, but they still want to move ahead. The career-and-family woman is willing to trade off the pressures and demands that go with promotion for the freedom to spend more time with her children. She's very smart, she's talented, she's committed to her career, and she's satisfied to stay at the middle level, at least during the early child-rearing years. Compare her with some of the people you have there now.

Consider a typical example, a woman who decides in college on a business career and enters management at age 22. For nine years, the company invests in her career as she gains experience and skills and steadily improves her performance. But at 31, just as the investment begins to pay off in earnest, she decides to have a baby. Can the company afford to let her go home, take another job, or go into business for herself? The common perception now is yes, the corporation can afford to lose her, unless, after six or eight weeks or even three months of disability and maternity leave, she returns to work on a full-time schedule with the same vigor, commitment and ambition that she showed before.

But what if she doesn't? What if she wants or needs to go on leave for six months or a year or, heaven forbid, five years? In this worst-case scenario, she works full time from age 22 to 31 and from 36 to 65—a total of 38 years as opposed to the typical male's 43 years. That's not a huge difference. Moreover, my typical example is willing to work part time while her children are young, if only her employer will give her the opportunity. There are two rewards for companies responsive to this need: higher retention of their best people and greatly improved performance and satisfaction in their middle management.

The high-performing career-and-family woman can be a major player in your company. She can give you a significant business advantage as the competition for able people escalates. Sometimes, too, if you can hold on to her, she will switch gears in mid-life and reenter the competition for the top. The price you must pay to retain these women is threefold: You must plan for and manage maternity; you must provide the flexibility that will allow them to be maximally productive: and you must take an active role in helping to make family supports and high-quality, affordable child care available to all women.

We have come a tremendous distance since the days when the prevailing male wisdom saw women as lacking the kind of intelligence that would allow them to succeed in business. For decades, even women themselves have harbored an unspoken belief that they couldn't make it because they couldn't be just like men, and nothing else would do. But now that women have shown themselves the equal of men in every area of organizational activity, now that they have demonstrated that they can be stars in every field of endeavor, now we can all venture to examine the fact that women and men are different.

On balance, employing women is more costly than employing men. Women can acknowledge this fact today because they know that their value to employers exceeds the additional cost and because they know that changing attitudes can reduce the additional cost dramatically. Women in management are no longer an idiosyncrasy of the arts and education. They have always matched men in natural ability. Within a very few years, they will equal men in numbers as well in every area of economic activity.

The demographic motivation to recruit and develop women is compelling. But an older question remains: Is society better for the change? Women's exit from the home and entry into the work force has certainly created problems—an urgent need for good, affordable child care: troubling questions about the kind of parenting children need; the costs and difficulties of diversity in the workplace: the stress and fatigue of combining work and family responsibilities. Wouldn't we all be happier if we could turn back the clock to an age when men were in the workplace and women in the home, when male and female roles were clearly differentiated and complementary?

Nostalgia, anxiety, and discouragement will urge many to say yes, but my answer is emphatically no. Two fundamental benefits that were unattainable in the past are now within our reach. For the individual, freedom of choice—in this case the freedom to choose career, family, or a combination of the two. For the corporation, access to the most gifted individuals in the country. These benefits are neither self-indulgent nor insubstantial. Freedom of choice and self-realization are too deeply American to be cast aside for some wistful vision of the past. And access to our most talented human resources is not a luxury in this age of explosive international competition but rather the barest minimum that prudence and national self-preservation require.

From Affirmative Action to Affirming Diversity

R. Roosevelt Thomas, Jr.
President, The American Institute for Managing Diversity, Inc., Atlanta, GA; and Secretary of the College, Morehouse College

Sooner or later, affirmative action will die a natural death. Its achievements have been stupendous, but if we look at the premises that underlie it, we find assumptions and priorities that look increasingly shopworn. Thirty years ago, affirmative action was invented on the basis of these five appropriate premises:

1. Adult, white males make up something called the U.S. business mainstream.
2. The U.S. economic edifice is a solid, unchanging institution with more than enough space for everyone.

3. Women, blacks, immigrants, and other minorities should be allowed in as a matter of public policy and common decency.
4. Widespread racial, ethnic, and sexual prejudice keeps them out.
5. Legal and social coercion are necessary to bring about the change.

Today all five of these premises need revising. Over the past six years, I have tried to help some 15 companies learn how to achieve and manage diversity, and I have seen that the realities facing us are no longer the realities affirmative action was designed to fix.

To begin with, more than half the U.S. work force now consists of minorities, immigrants, and women, so white, native-born males, though undoubtedly still dominant, are themselves a statistical minority. In addition, white males will make up only 15% of the increase in the work force over the next ten years. The so-called mainstream is now almost as diverse as the society at large.

Second, while the edifice is still big enough for all, it no longer seems stable, massive, and invulnerable. In fact, American corporations are scrambling, doing their best to become more adaptable, to compete more successfully for markets and labor, foreign and domestic, and to attract all the talent they can find.

Third, women and minorities no longer need a boarding pass, they need an upgrade. The problem is not getting them in at the entry level; the problem is making better use of their potential at every level, especially in middle-management and leadership positions. This is no longer simply a question of common decency, it is a question of business survival.

Fourth, although prejudice is hardly dead, it has suffered some wounds that may eventually prove fatal. In the meantime, American businesses are now filled with progressive people—many of them minorities and women themselves—whose prejudices, where they still exist, are much too deeply suppressed to interfere with recruitment. The reason many companies are still wary of minorities and women has much more to do with education and perceived qualifications than with color or gender. Companies are worried about productivity and well aware that minorities and women represent a disproportionate share of the undertrained and undereducated.

Fifth, coercion is rarely needed at the recruitment stage. There are very few places in the United States today where you could dip a recruitment net and come up with nothing but white males. Getting hired is not the problem—women and blacks who are seen as having the necessary skills and energy can get *into* the work force relatively easily. It's later on that many of them plateau and lose their drive and quit or get fired. It's later on that their managers' inability to manage diversity hobbles them and the companies they work for.

In creating these changes, affirmative action had an essential role to play and played it very well. In many companies and communities it still plays that role. But affirmative action is an artificial, transitional intervention intended to give managers a chance to correct an imbalance, an injustice, a mistake. Once the numbers mistake has been corrected, I don't think affirmative action alone can cope with the remaining long-term task of creating a work setting geared to the upward mobility of *all* kinds of people, including white males. It is difficult for affirmative action to influence upward mobility even in the short run, primarily because it is perceived to conflict with the meritocracy we favor. For this reason, affirmative action is a red flag to every individual who feels unfairly passed over and a stigma for those who appear to be its beneficiaries.

Moreover, I doubt very much that individuals who reach top positions through affirmative action are effective models for younger members of their race or sex. What, after all, do they model? A black vice president who got her job through affirmative action is not necessarily a model of how to rise through the corporate meritocracy. She may be a model of how affirmative action can work for the people who find or put themselves in the right place at the right time.

If affirmative action in upward mobility meant that no person's competence and character would ever be overlooked or undervalued on account of race, sex, ethnicity, origins, or physical disability, then affirmative action would be the very thing we need to let every corporate talent find its niche. But what affirmative action means in practice is an unnatural focus on one group, and what it means too often to too many employees is that someone is playing fast and loose with standards in order to favor that group. Unless we are to compromise our standards, a thing no competitive company can even contemplate, upward mobility for minorities and women should always be a question of pure competence and character unmuddled by accidents of birth.

And that is precisely why we have to learn to manage diversity—to move beyond affirmative action, not to repudiate it. Some of what I have to say may strike some readers—mostly those with an ax to grind—as directed at the majority white males who hold most of the decision-making posts in our economy. But I am speaking to all managers, not just white males, and I certainly don't mean to suggest that white males somehow stand outside diversity. White males are as odd and as normal as anyone else.

THE AFFIRMATIVE ACTION CYCLE

If you are managing diverse employees, you should ask yourself this question: Am I fully tapping the potential capacities of everyone in my department? If the answer is no, you should ask yourself this follow-up: Is this failure hampering my ability to meet performance standards? The answer to this question will undoubtedly be yes.

Think of corporate management for a moment as an engine burning pure gasoline. What's now going into the tank is no longer just gas, it has an increasing percentage of, let's say, methanol. In the beginning, the engine will still work pretty well, but by and by it will start to sputter, and eventually it will stall. Unless we rebuild the engine, it will no longer burn the fuel we're feeding it. As the work force grows more and more diverse at the intake level, the talent pool we have to draw on for supervision and management will also grow increasingly diverse. So the question is: Can we burn this fuel? Can we get maximum corporate power from the diverse work force we're now drawing into the system?

Affirmative action gets blamed for failing to do things it never could do. Affirmative action gets the new fuel into the tank, the new people through the front door. Something else will have to get them into the driver's seat. That something else consists of enabling people, in this case minorities and women, to perform to their potential. This is what we now call managing diversity. Not appreciating or leveraging diversity, not even necessarily understanding it. Just managing diversity in such a way as to get from a heterogeneous work force the same productivity, commitment, quality, and profit that we got from the old homogeneous work force.

The correct question today is not "How are we doing on race relations?" or "Are we promoting enough minority people and women?" but rather "Given the diverse work force I've got, am I getting the productivity, does it work as smoothly, is morale as high, as if every person in the company was the same sex and race and nationality?" Most answers will be, "Well, no, of course not!" But why shouldn't the answer be, "You bet!"?

When we ask how we're doing on race relations, we inadvertently put our finger on what's wrong with the question and with the attitude that underlies affirmative action. So long as racial and gender equality is something we grant to minorities and women, there will be no racial and gender equality. What we must do is create an environment where no one is advantaged or disadvantaged, an environment where "we" is everyone. What the traditional approach to diversity did was to create a cycle of crisis, action, relaxation, and disappointment that companies repeated over and over again without ever achieving more than the barest particle of what they were after.

Affirmative action pictures the work force as a pipeline and reasons as follows: "If we can fill the pipeline with *qualified* minorities and women, we can solve our upward mobility problem. Once recruited, they will perform in accordance with our promotional criteria and move naturally up our regular developmental ladder. In the past, where minorities and women have failed to progress, they were simply unable to meet our performance standards. Recruiting qualified people will enable us to avoid special programs and reverse discrimination."

This pipeline perspective generates a self-perpetuating, self-defeating, recruitment-oriented cycle with six stages:

1. *Problem Recognition.* The first time through the cycle, the problem takes this form—We need more minorities and women in the pipeline. In later iterations, the problem is more likely to be defined as a need to retain and promote minorities and women.

2. *Intervention.* Management puts the company into what we may call an Affirmative Action Recruitment Mode. During the first cycle, the goal is to recruit minorities and women. Later, when the cycle is repeated a second or third time and the challenge has shifted to retention, development, and promotion, the goal is to recruit *qualified* minorities and women. Sometimes, managers indifferent or blind to possible accusations of reverse discrimination will institute special training, tracking, incentive, mentoring, or sponsoring programs for minorities and women.

3. *Great Expectations.* Large numbers of minorities and women have been recruited, and a select group has been promoted or recruited at a higher level to serve as highly visible role models for the newly recruited masses. The stage seems set for the natural progression of minorities and women up through the pipeline. Management leans back to enjoy the fruits of its labor.

4. *Frustration.* The anticipated natural progression fails to occur. Minorities and women see themselves plateauing prematurely. Management is upset (and embarrassed) by the failure of its affirmative action initiative and begins to resent the impatience of the new recruits and their unwillingness to give the company credit for trying to do the right thing. Depending on how high in the hierarchy they have plateaued, alienated minorities and women either leave the company or stagnate.

5. *Dormancy.* All remaining participants conspire tacitly to present a silent front to the outside world. Executives say nothing because they have no solutions. As for those women and minorities who stayed on, calling attention to affirmative action's failures might raise doubts about their qualifications. Do they deserve their jobs, or did they just happen to be in the right place at the time of an affirmative action push? So no one complains, and if the company has a good public relations department, it may even wind up with a reputation as a good place for women and minorities to work.

If questioned publicly, management will say things like "Frankly, affirmative action is not currently an issue," or "Our numbers are okay," or "With respect to minority representation at the upper levels, management is aware of this remaining challenge."

In private and off the record, however, people say things like "Premature plateauing is a problem, and we don't know what to do," and "Our top people don't seem to be interested in finding a solution," and "There's plenty of racism and sexism around this place—whatever you may hear."

6. *Crisis.* Dormancy can continue indefinitely, but it is usually broken by a crisis of competitive pressure, governmental intervention, external pressure from a special interest group, or internal unrest. One company found that its pursuit of a Total Quality program was hampered by the alienation of minorities and women. Senior management at another corporation saw the growing importance of minorities in their customer base and decided they needed minority participation in their managerial ranks. In another case, growing expressions of discontent forced a break in the conspiracy of silence even after the company had received national recognition as a good place for minorities and women to work.

Whatever its cause, the crisis fosters a return to the Problem Recognition phase, and the cycle begins again. This time, management seeks to explain the shortcomings of the previous affirmative action push and usually concludes that the problem is recruitment. This assessment by a top executive is typical: "The managers I know are decent people. While they give priority to performance, I do not believe any of them deliberately block minorities or women who are qualified for promotion. On the contrary, I suspect they bend over backward to promote women and minorities who give some indication of being qualified.

"However, they believe we simply do not have the necessary talent within those groups, but because of the constant complaints they have heard about their deficiencies in affirmative action, they feel they face a no-win situation. If they do not promote, they are obstructionists. But if they promote people who are unqualified, they hurt performance and deny promotion to other employees unfairly. They can't win. The answer, in my mind, must be an ambitious new recruitment effort to bring in quality people."

And so the cycle repeats. Once again blacks, Hispanics, women, and immigrants are dropped into a previously homogeneous, all-white, all-Anglo, all-male, all native-born environment, and the burden of cultural change is placed on the newcomers. There will be new expectations and a new round of frustration, dormancy, crisis, and recruitment.

TEN GUIDELINES FOR LEARNING TO MANAGE DIVERSITY

The traditional American image of diversity has been assimilation: the melting pot, where ethnic and racial differences were standardized into a kind of American puree. Of course, the melting pot is only a metaphor. In real life, many ethnic and most racial groups retain their individuality and express it energetically. What we have is perhaps some kind of American mulligan stew; it is certainly no puree.

At the workplace, however, the melting pot has been more than a metaphor. Corporate success has demanded a good deal of conformity, and employees have voluntarily abandoned most of their ethnic distinctions at the company door.

Now those days are over. Today the melting pot is the wrong metaphor even in business, for three good reasons. First, if it ever was possible to melt down Scotsmen and Dutchmen and Frenchmen into an indistinguishable broth, you can't do the same with blacks, Asians, and women. Their differences don't melt so easily. Second, most people are no longer willing to be melted down, not even for eight hours a day—and it's a seller's market for skills. Third, the thrust of today's nonhierarchical, flexible, collaborative management requires a ten- or twentyfold increase in our tolerance for individuality.

So companies are faced with the problem of surviving in a fiercely competitive world with a work force that consists and will continue to consist of *unassimilated diversity.* And the engine will take a great deal of tinkering to burn that fuel.

What managers fear from diversity is a lowering of standards, a sense that "anything goes." Of course, standards must not suffer. In fact, competence counts more than ever. The goal is to manage diversity in such a way as to get from a diverse work force the same productivity we once got from a homogeneous work force, and to do it without artificial programs, standards—or barriers.

Managing diversity does not mean controlling or containing diversity, it means enabling every member of your work force to perform to his or her potential. It means getting from employees, first, everything we have a right to expect, and, second—if we do it well—everything they have to give. If the old homogeneous work force performed dependably at 80% of its capacity, then the first result means getting 80% from the new heterogeneous work force too. But the second result, the icing on the cake, the unexpected upside that diversity can perhaps give as a bonus, means 85% to 90% from everyone in the organization.

For the moment, however, let's concentrate on the basics of how to get satisfactory performance from the new diverse work force. There are few adequate models. So far, no large company I know of has succeeded in managing diversity to its own satisfaction. But any number have begun to try.

On the basis of their experience, here are my ten guidelines:

1. *Clarify Your Motivation.* A lot of executives are not sure why they should want to learn to manage diversity. Legal compliance seems like a good reason. So does community relations. Many executives believe they have a social and moral responsibility to employ minorities and women. Others want to placate an internal group or pacify an out-

side organization. None of these are bad reasons, but none of them are business reasons, and given the nature and scope of today's competitive challenges, I believe only business reasons will supply the necessary long-term motivation. In any case, it is the business reasons I want to focus on here.

In business terms, a diverse work force is not something your company ought to have; it's something your company does have, or soon will have. Learning to manage that diversity will make you more competitive.

2. *Clarify Your Vision.* When managers think about a diverse work force, what do they picture? Not publicly, but in the privacy of their minds?

One popular image is of minorities and women clustering on a relatively low plateau, with a few of them trickling up as they become assimilated into the prevailing culture. Of course, they enjoy good salaries and benefits, and most of them accept their status, appreciate the fact that they are doing better than they could do somewhere else, and are proud of the achievements of their race or sex. This is reactionary thinking, but it's a lot more common than you might suppose.

Another image is what we might call "heightened sensitivity." Members of the majority culture are sensitive to the demands of minorities and women for upward mobility and recognize the advantages of fully utilizing them. Minorities and women work at all levels of the corporation, but they are the recipients of generosity and know it. A few years of this second-class status drives most of them away and compromises the effectiveness of those that remain. Turnover is high.

Then there is the coexistence-compromise image. In the interests of corporate viability, white males agree to recognize minorities and women as equals. They bargain and negotiate their differences. But the win-lose aspect of the relationship preserves tensions, and the compromises reached are not always to the company's competitive advantage.

"Diversity and equal opportunity" is a big step up. It presupposes that the white male culture has given way to one that respects difference and individuality. The problem is that minorities and women will accept it readily as their operating image, but many white males, consciously or unconsciously, are likely to cling to a vision that leaves them in the driver's seat. A vision gap of this kind can be a difficulty.

In my view, the vision to hold in your own imagination and to try to communicate to all your managers and employees is an image of fully tapping the human resource potential of every member of the work force. This vision sidesteps the question of equality, ignores the tensions of coexistence, plays down the uncomfortable realities of difference, and focuses instead on individual enablement. It doesn't say, "Let *us* give *them* a chance." It assumes a diverse work force that includes us and them. It says, "Let's create an environment where everyone will do their best work."

Several years ago, an industrial plant in Atlanta with a highly diverse work force was threatened with closing unless productivity improved. To save their jobs, everyone put their shoulders to the wheel and achieved the results they needed to stay open. The senior operating manager was amazed.

For years he had seen minorities and women plateauing disproportionately at the lower levels of the organization, and he explained that fact away with two rationalizations. "They haven't been here that long," he told himself. And "This is the price we pay for being in compliance with the law."

When the threat of closure energized this whole group of people into a level of performance he had not imagined possible, he got one fleeting glimpse of people working up to their capacity. Once the crisis was over, everyone went back to the earlier status quo—white males driving and everyone else sitting back, looking on—but now there was a difference. Now, as he put it himself, he had been to the mountaintop. He knew that what he was getting from minorities and women was nowhere near what they were capable of giving. And he wanted it, crisis or no crisis, all the time.

3. *Expand Your Focus.* Managers usually see affirmative action and equal employment opportunity as centering on minorities and women, with very little to offer white males. The diversity I'm talking about includes not only race, gender, creed, and ethnicity but also age, background, education, function, and personality differences. The objec-

tive is not to assimilate minorities and women into a dominant white male culture but to create a dominant heterogeneous culture.

The culture that dominates the United States socially and politically is heterogeneous, and it works by giving its citizens the liberty to achieve their potential. Channeling that potential, once achieved, is an individual right but still a national concern. Something similar applies in the workplace, where the keys to success are individual ability and a corporate destination. Managing disparate talents to achieve common goals is what companies learned to do when they set their sights on, say, Total Quality. The secrets of managing diversity are much the same.

4. *Audit Your Corporate Culture.* If the goal is not to assimilate diversity into the dominant culture but rather to build a culture that can digest unassimilated diversity, then you had better start by figuring out what your present culture looks like. Since what we're talking about here is the body of unspoken and unexamined assumptions, values, and mythologies that make your world go round, this kind of cultural audit is impossible to conduct without outside help. It's a research activity, done mostly with in-depth interviews and a lot of listening at the water cooler.

The operative corporate assumptions you have to identify and deal with are often inherited from the company's founder. "If we treat everyone as a member of the family, we will be successful" is not uncommon. Nor is its corollary "Father Knows Best."

Another widespread assumption, probably absorbed from American culture in general, is that "cream will rise to the top." In most companies, what passes for cream rising to the top is actually cream being pulled or pushed to the top by an informal system of mentoring and sponsorship.

Corporate culture is a kind of tree. Its roots are assumptions about the company and about the world. Its branches, leaves, and seeds are behavior. You can't change the leaves without changing the roots, and you can't grow peaches on an oak. Or rather, with the proper grafting, you *can* grow peaches on an oak, but they come out an awful lot like acorns—small and hard and not much fun to eat. So if you want to grow peaches, you have to make sure the tree's roots are peach friendly.

5. *Modify Your Assumptions.* The real problem with this corporate culture tree is that every time you go to make changes in the roots, you run into terrible opposition. Every culture, including corporate culture, has root guards that turn out in force every time you threaten a basic assumption.

Take the family assumption as an example. Viewing the corporation as a family suggests not only that father knows best; it also suggests that sons will inherit the business, that daughters should stick to doing the company dishes, and that if Uncle Deadwood doesn't perform, we'll put him in the chimney corner and feed him for another 30 years regardless. Each assumption has its constituency and its defenders. If we say to Uncle Deadwood, "Yes, you did good work for 10 years, but years 11 and 12 look pretty bleak; we think it's time we helped you find another chimney," shock waves will travel through the company as every family-oriented employee draws a sword to defend the sacred concept of guaranteed jobs.

But you have to try. A corporation that wants to create an environment with no advantages or disadvantages for any group cannot allow the family assumption to remain in place. It must be labeled dishonest mythology.

Sometimes the dishonesties are more blatant. When I asked a white male middle manager how promotions were handled in his company, he said, "You need leadership capability, bottom-line results, the ability to work with people, and compassion." Then he paused and smiled. "That's what they say. But down the hall there's a guy we call Captain Kickass. He's ruthless, mean-spirited, and he steps on people. That's the behavior they really value. Forget what they say."

In addition to the obvious issue of hypocrisy, this example also raises a question of equal opportunity. When I asked this young middle manager if he thought minorities and women could meet the Captain Kickass standard, he said he thought they probably could. But the opposite argument can certainly be made. Whether we're talking about blacks in an environment that is predominantly white, whites in one predominantly black, or women in one predominantly male, the majority culture will not readily condone such tactics from a member of a minority. So the corporation with the unspoken kickass performance standard has at least one criterion that will hamper the upward mobility of minorities and women.

Another destructive assumption is the melting pot I referred to earlier. The organization I'm arguing for respects differences rather than seeking to smooth them out. It is multicultural rather than culture blind, which has an important consequence: When we no longer force people to "belong" to a common ethnicity or culture, then the organization's leaders must work all the harder to define belonging in terms of a set of values and a sense of purpose that transcend the interests, desires, and preferences of any one group.

6. *Modify Your Systems.* The first purpose of examining and modifying assumptions is to modify systems. Promotion, mentoring, and sponsorship comprise one such system, and the unexamined cream-to-the-top assumption I mentioned earlier can tend to keep minorities and women from climbing the corporate ladder. After all, in many companies it is difficult to secure a promotion above a certain level without a personal advocate or sponsor. In the context of managing diversity, the question is not whether this system is maximally efficient but whether it works for all employees. Executives who only sponsor people like themselves are not making much of a contribution to the cause of getting the best from every employee.

Performance appraisal is another system where unexamined practices and patterns can have pernicious effects. For example, there are companies where official performance appraisals differ substantially from what is said informally, with the result that employees get their most accurate performance feedback through the grapevine. So if the grapevine is closed to minorities and women, they are left at a severe disadvantage. As one white manager observed, "If the blacks around here knew how they were really perceived, there would be a revolt." Maybe so. More important to your business, however, is the fact that without an accurate appraisal of performance, minority and women employees will find it difficult to correct or defend their alleged shortcomings.

7. *Modify Your Models.* The second purpose of modifying assumptions is to modify models of managerial and employee behavior. My own personal hobgoblin is one I call the Doer Model, often an outgrowth of the family assumption and of unchallenged paternalism. I have found the Doer Model alive and thriving in a dozen companies. It works like this:

Since father knows best, managers seek subordinates who will follow their lead and do as they do. If they can't find people exactly like themselves, they try to find people who aspire to be exactly like themselves. The goal is predictability and immediate responsiveness because the doer manager is not there to manage people but to do the business. In accounting departments, for example, doer managers do accounting, and subordinates are simply extensions of their hands and minds, sensitive to every signal and suggestion of managerial intent.

Doer managers take pride in this identity of purpose. "I wouldn't ask my people to do anything I wouldn't do myself," they say. "I roll up my sleeves and get in the trenches." Doer managers love to be in the trenches. It keeps them out of the line of fire.

But managers aren't supposed to be in the trenches, and accounting managers aren't supposed to do accounting. What they are supposed to do is create systems and a climate that allow accountants to do accounting, a climate that enables people to do what they've been charged to do. The right goal is doer subordinates, supported and empowered by managers who manage.

8. *Help Your People Pioneer.* Learning to manage diversity is a change process, and the managers involved are change agents. There is no single tried and tested "solution" to diversity and no fixed right way to manage it. Assuming the existence of a single or even a dominant barrier undervalues the importance of all the other barriers that face any company, including, potentially, prejudice, personality, community dynamics, culture, and the ups and downs of business itself.

While top executives articulate the new company policy and their commitment to it, middle managers—most or all of them still white males, remember—are placed in the tough position of having to cope with a forest of problems and simultaneously develop the minorities and women who represent their own competition for an increasingly limited number of promotions. What's more, every time they stumble they will themselves be labeled the major barriers to progress. These managers need help, they need a certain amount of sympathy, and, most of all, perhaps, they need to be told that they are pioneers and judged accordingly.

In one case, an ambitious young black woman was assigned to a white male manager, at his request, on the basis of her excellent company record. They looked forward to working together, and for the first three months, everything went well. But then their relationship began to deteriorate, and the harder they worked at patching it up, the worse it got. Both of them, along with their superiors, were surprised by the conflict and seemed puzzled as to its causes. Eventually, the black woman requested and obtained reassignment. But even though they escaped each other, both suffered a sense of failure severe enough to threaten their careers.

What could have been done to assist them? Well, empathy would not have hurt. But perspective would have been better yet. In their particular company and situation, these two people had placed themselves at the cutting edge of race and gender relations. They needed to know that mistakes at the cutting edge are different—and potentially more valuable—than mistakes elsewhere. Maybe they needed some kind of pioneer training. But at the very least they needed to be told that they were pioneers, that conflicts and failures came with the territory, and that they would be judged accordingly.

9. *Apply the Special Consideration Test.* I said earlier that affirmative action was an artificial, transitional, but necessary stage on the road to a truly diverse work force. Because of its artificial nature, affirmative action requires constant attention and drive to make it work. The point of learning once and for all how to manage diversity is that all that energy can be focused somewhere else.

There is a simple test to help you spot the diversity programs that are going to eat up enormous quantities of time and effort. Surprisingly, perhaps, it is the same test you might use to identify the programs and policies that created your problem in the first place. The test consists of one question: Does this program, policy, or principle give special consideration to one group? Will it contribute to everyone's success, or will it only produce an advantage for blacks or whites or women or men? Is it designed for *them* as opposed to *us?* Whenever the answer is yes, you're not yet on the road to managing diversity.

This does not rule out the possibility of addressing issues that relate to a single group. It only underlines the importance of determining that the issue you're addressing does not relate to other groups as well. For example, management in one company noticed that blacks were not moving up in the organization. Before instituting a special program to bring them along, managers conducted interviews to see if they could find the reason for the impasse. What blacks themselves reported was a problem with the quality of supervision. Further interviews showed that other employees too—including white males—were concerned about the quality of supervision and felt that little was being done to foster professional development. Correcting the situation eliminated a problem that affected everyone. In this case, a solution that focused only on blacks would have been out of place.

Had the problem consisted of prejudice, on the other hand, or some other barrier to blacks or minorities alone, a solution based on affirmative action would have been perfectly appropriate.

10. *Continue Affirmative Action.* Let me come full circle. The ability to manage diversity is the ability to manage your company without unnatural advantage or disadvantage for any member of your diverse work force. The fact remains that you must first have a work force that is diverse at every level, and if you don't, you're going to need affirmative action to get from here to there.

The reason you then want to move beyond affirmative action to managing diversity is because affirmative action fails to deal with the root causes of prejudice and inequality and does little to develop the full potential of every man and woman in the company. In a country seeking competitive advantage in a global economy, the goal of managing diversity is to develop our capacity to accept, incorporate, and empower the diverse human talents of the most diverse nation on earth. It's our reality. We need to make it our strength.

QUESTIONS FOR DISCUSSION

1. Rodgers and Rodgers say that the thorniest issue facing business and managers is that of equity. What do they mean by "equity"? Do some of the problems they discuss imply that equity should be abandoned as a corporate goal? What are the ethical implications of this? Might there be any unintended consequences of the policies they advocate?
2. Using the guidelines developed by Bravo and Cassedy, decide what you would do in the "Case of the Mismanaged Ms."
3. Discuss "The Case of the Unequal Opportunity" in light of the arguments given by Pojman and Hettinger. What do you think Thomas would have to say about the case?
4. How do the theories of Rawls, Nozick, and Smart (from Chapter One) apply to the debate about affirmative action?
5. Thomas says that we should "move beyond affirmative action." What does he mean by this? Why does he think that affirmative action is inadequate by itself? Why does he believe we need to rethink the seniority system? Do you agree or disagree with his views?

WORK IN THE CORPORATION

LANSCAPE

Ernest Kallman and John Grillo
Kallman—Professor of Computer Information Systems, and Research Fellow, Center for Business Ethics, Bentley College
Grillo—Professor of Computer Information Systems, and Research Fellow, Center for Business Ethics, Bentley College

Clare Valerian is a systems analyst at Califon, Inc., a large distributor of electronic equipment. Her primary responsibility is to make certain that the 127 end users in Califon's U.S. headquarters can access data, post to accounts, send and receive e-mail, and perform all other daily activities through their use of the corporate Local Area Network. She describes herself as a facilitator and trouble shooter. She must respond quickly to the users' complaints and needs, even so far as to provide training for novice users. It's a demanding and time-consuming job, and until the appearance two weeks ago of the LANSCAPE utility, Clare was spending up to 12 hours a day one-on-one with her users. Much of that time was travel time. She seemed to spend more time on the escalators and elevators, in the stairwells, and riding the interoffice shuttle carts than with her users. The telephone couldn't help, because Clare had to see for herself exactly what the users saw on their terminals. LANSCAPE has changed her workday completely. She now uses the utility program and the telephone at her desk without ever having to go directly to the users' workstations and terminals. The program allows Clare to view and actually take over the activities of network users. Typically, her first task upon arriving at her desk is to check her e-mail messages for trouble spots, print them out, fire up LANSCAPE, and call each user with a problem one at a time.

"John, this is Clare in Systems. You left me a message about a problem with the inventory re-order module. I've got your screen up on my terminal now. Can you get out of the word processor and transfer to the inventory system? . . . Good, I see the main menu . . . now, the re-order module . . . go ahead and repeat the steps that got you into trouble yesterday. OK, . . . fine . . . oops, I see what you did. The system asks for 'ENTER' and you hit

Found in Ernest A. Kallman and John P. Grillo, *Ethical Decision Making and Information Technology: An Introduction with Cases,* pp. 36–38.

'RETURN.' What kind of keyboard do you have? . . . That's what I thought. For now, remember to hit 'ENTER.' I'll get the maintenance programmer to change the module to accept 'RETURN' too. Sorry about that. . . . Thanks, 'bye."

"Bill, this is Clare in Systems. Your word processor bombed? Why don't you call it up and repeat the . . . Oh, I see the problem. You're working with the buggy Version 2.3. I'll delete it from the system. You'll have to remember to use V2.4 from now on . . . No problem, 'bye."

Clare is delighted with the LANSCAPE utility. She roves electronically from one troubled user to another, seeing on her screen exactly what they see. The amount of time it takes to solve the problems is about the same, but because she can solve them from her desk, she has eliminated the frustrating delays of travel time. She is at her desk when the users call, and they are pleased at the fast response time.

Clare even has time to scan users' activities without their making a request. Her troubleshooting has become more proactive than reactive. She can scan a number of users without their knowledge and when she finds one in trouble she can interrupt and help.

"Harry, this is Clare in Systems. I'm looking at your screen now . . . I know you didn't call, but I thought I'd beat you to the punch . . . You can speed up that multiple posting to a single customer by using the tab key instead of updating the record for each entry . . . Yes, like that . . . Glad to be of service. 'Bye."

Last week, Clare and her boss, the Director of User Support, met with the Vice President of Information Systems Art Betony, to discuss LANSCAPE and the way it has helped to solve several tough technical problems.

Clare said, "Without this program, I'd have to control the activities of every user in every system test, and move from one building to the other to guide their activities. With LANSCAPE, I can watch over their shoulders without being there. LANSCAPE is inexpensive and easy to use. I fully endorse its continued use and recommend we obtain additional copies and make it available to all support personnel."

Both managers are pleased with the results. They have solved the problem of slow and costly user support with the best of all solutions, one that is both more efficient and cost effective. They not only get an increase in user satisfaction but also an increase in productivity.

Yesterday Art was having his usual Tuesday lunch with his boss, the Executive Vice President, Alberta Wilson. They use these meetings to discuss any information systems issues that may be pending. This time, though, Art couldn't stop praising the successful implementation and use of LANSCAPE.

"With your background in human resources and production planning, I know you can appreciate the importance of the productivity gains we've made. And they're truly important. But from the information systems point of view, I am even more pleased that we are able to use the power of the computer itself to help us make it a more effective business tool."

Ms. Wilson seemed especially interested. She asked, "You mean you can tell me any time what people are doing?"

"Not quite," Art answered, "We can only see the screens of the users who are logged in. But of course that's exactly what my people need for their purposes."

"But the people you observe this way . . . they know they're being observed, right?"

"No, not unless I tell them. The LANSCAPE program doesn't change anything on their screens. Of course, that's a necessary feature of the system, because my people have to see exactly what the users see."

"Could you install LANSCAPE on my terminal, in my office?", she asked.

Art replied, "Of course, we could, but what value would that be?"

Alberta leaned forward and whispered, "I shouldn't reveal this outside the Human Resources Department, but I think I will in order to enlist your support. We may have one or more persons at Headquarters dealing in drugs. We have suspects but no proof. Somehow these people are taking orders and making deliveries right on the premises during company time. I suspect that they are using the phone and maybe even the computer to make their deals. We have tried various surveillance methods to no avail. What I want to do is use LANSCAPE to randomly check on what the known suspects are doing. Then if we catch them 'red-handed,' we'll have our evidence and we can prosecute."

Art frowned and said "Gee, I don't know if I should give you that software, Alberta. Let me think about it and get back to you."

A Video Game That Tells if Employees Are Fit for Work

Joan O. C. Hamilton
Correspondent, *Business Week Magazine*

For fun, Robert Anguay likes to take his two stepsons out to play video games. He often drops a few quarters himself. But every day before he begins work at Silicon Valley's Ion Implant Services Inc., Anguay lines up with his fellow delivery drivers, stands in front of a console, and "plays" a short video game. There's no fooling around here: Unless the machine spits out a receipt confirming that the drivers have passed the video test, they can't climb behind the wheel.

Using random drug testing to promote workplace safety is an issue that has been bedeviling employers and civil libertarians. Now, a tiny Alameda (Calif.) company, Performance Factors Inc. (PFI), is pushing a simple, computer-based test that could go a lot further toward determining an employee's fitness for work than drug tests ever have. Instead of detecting chemicals in the blood, PFI's Factor 1000 software system tests a worker's hand-eye coordination to measure fitness for duty.

Such big companies as the diversified food processor Cargill Inc. and defense contractor Hercules Inc. have joined a handful of smaller concerns as customers of PFI. The company now is testing workers who perform a range of tasks, from machine tooling to driving tour buses to handling poisonous gases and high-voltage equipment. The privately held, two-year-old company has also raised roughly $2 million from some blue-ribbon financial backers, including San Francisco billionaire Gordon Getty, Chicago's Pritzker family, and Itel Corp. Chairman Samuel Zell. How come? Simple. The idea seems to be working. Results from companies who've been using the Factor 1000 system are impressive—and sometimes surprising.

Companies annually pay PFI about $200 per employee to install software and a small console hooked up to a personal computer. When employees report to work, they go to the computer then type in an ID code. Next, they use a knob to center a diamond-shaped image swaying between two posts on the screen. Experience shows Factor 1000 demands considerable concentration and practice: This reporter (cold sober) failed miserably in four attempts.

When Factor 1000 is in actual use, companies have employees perform the test many times to establish a base average. Then, they're measured against their average, which is stored in the computer. What to do with an employee who keeps failing? Administer a drug test? Fire the person? That is the toughest issue, employers acknowledge. What Factor 1000 provides them, however, is a precise, performance-related basis for action.

If a worker fails, some companies refer the individual to a superior, others to an employee-assistance program. Repeated test failures could lead to disciplinary action or outright dismissal, though PFI says it doesn't know of any such cases yet. In any event, an impaired worker can be kept away from dangerous tasks.

Intriguingly, most failures so far don't appear to involve drug or alcohol use, says Marc Silverman, PFI's president and co-founder. He adds: "Severe fatigue or illness can be more dangerous than a disgusting drunk [person] because it's not visible." Companies report that it's common for some employees who fail to admit that they are so distracted with personal problems they're not fit to perform a sensitive job on a given day.

That's consistent with other evidence that suggests mandatory drug testing isn't helping to deter accidents: A recent Federal Railroad Administration report, for example, found only 3.2% of work-

---

ers involved in railroad accidents tested positively for drugs. Cliff Palefsky, an employment attorney who urged Silverman to form PFI, argues that the PFI approach could help prevent those accidents. Results of urine tests, he observes, "only arrive in time for the funerals." H. Lewis Page, general manager of Paumier Co., a tool-and-die company based in Canton, Ohio, that's using Factor 1000, says: "If people are performing their job properly, I don't care what they're doing at home."

Curiously, the software itself is nothing new. PFI licenses it from a Hawthorne (Calif.) research outfit called Systems Technology Inc. that developed computer programs for the Air Force in the late 1950s to help pick pilots capable of flying unstable aircraft. The so-called "critical tracking task" was later modified for research on drunk driving, but until recently it wasn't sold for industrial uses.

Silverman claims he has been swamped by inquiries from businesses, ranging from insurance companies looking to urge Factor 1000 on clients with safety problems to a major appliance company considering putting consoles in trucks rigged so they won't start unless the driver can pass the test. It seems inevitable that competitors sooner or later will give PFI a run for its money. But for now, the little outfit is scrambling to market an idea that seems so obvious it's hard to figure why nobody thought of it before.

Woman vs. Womb: Johnson Controls, Inc.

Ellen Goodman
Columnist, *The Boston Globe* and *The Washington Post*

When "The Handmaid's Tale" was published in 1986, the stark parable was written and read against the real-life background of the rising religious right. The country of Gilead was created as a joyless and perverse paradise of fundamentalism that reduced a woman to the sum of her reproductive parts.

But when Margaret Atwood's novel reappeared in film this month, something had changed in the atmosphere. This time, this eye was more conscious of Gilead as a toxic wasteland plagued by infertility. This time it was a land in which children were rare and longed-for. And a land in which motherhood was not empowered or enshrined but enforced.

The tale looked less like a warning about politics and more like a parable about the pitfalls of protection, female protection, fetal protection. In 1990, the very words "fetal protection" have taken on a meaning in real life that is nearly as chilling as "The Handmaid's Tale" is on the screen. They are used now to pit fetus against the woman. Indeed, when we talk about protecting the fetus, the woman is now designated as its enemy.

No case makes this more evident than the true story that will be retold before the Supreme Court. On March 26, the Court decided to hear a case brought by eight women who were forced to choose between their fertility and their jobs.

The Leadworker's Tale began back in 1982, when a Milwaukee battery manufacturer banned "women with childbearing capacity" from work in jobs that involved high lead exposure. Eventually a group of workers, one a 50-year-old single woman, another a 25-year-old who submitted to sterilization, charged Johnson Controls, Inc., with sex discrimination.

The company countered that they were not discriminating against women but protecting the fetus from the effects of lead exposure. So this case entered the public consciousness as another example of "the rights of women versus the fetus." Once again, woman against her womb. But it is not as simple, not as stark as that.

By any measure, Johnson Controls, Inc., is less interested in fetal protection from lead than in self-protection from *liability suits.* If they win this case, any woman "with childbearing capacity" could be banned from jobs as diverse as those of flight attendant and silicon-chip maker. Some 20 million industrial jobs could be closed to women whether or not they planned to get pregnant.

So in many ways, The Leadworker's Tale goes to the very heart of the old question: Is a woman's life from 12 to 50 to be governed by the possibility of pregnancy?

The appeals court that upheld the Johnson policy said yes and based their reasoning on a profound mistrust. They said, in effect, that a woman "might somehow rationally discount this clear risk" to her fetus. They defended a policy to guard any potential fetus against all fertile women.

In contrast, another judge—the Reagan appointed conservative Frank Easterbrook—wrote in a stinging dissent, "No legal or ethical principle, compels or allows Johnson to assume that women are less able than men to make intelligent decisions about the welfare of the next generation . . ."

But even if we assume the overriding importance of protecting the fetus, we still have to ask whether policies like Johnson's make sense. Banning women from the workplace is, after all, no health-insurance policy. Another dissenting judge compared the relative prospects of a "pregnant woman, unemployed or working for minimum wage . . . ill-housed, fed and doctored" to that of her pregnant sister at Johnson and asked: "Whose fetus is at greater risk?"

And what of the *father?* A baby's health, like the baby itself, is the product of both parents. Male exposure to lead, research suggests, also affects their offspring. The passion to "protect" fertile women doesn't extend to men, but they are hardly invulnerable to reproductive damage. Ask the Vietnam vets exposed to agent orange or the British workers in a nuclear power station whose children have leukemia.

The parallels of this leadworker's tale are rich enough to provide the stuff of a sequel. In the fantasyland of Gilead, after all, men were not tested for infertility, fertile women were not free and the countryside was a wasteland.

In America, "fetal protection policies" protect women out of their jobs and leave men at risk to their health. But worst of all, the comforting myth leaves companies free to do their dirty business.

Under a Civil Rights Cloud, Fetal Protection Looks Dismal: Johnson Controls, Inc.

Eric Felten
Editorial writer, *Washington Times,* and author of *The Ruling Class*

Those who lose at the Supreme Court do not have many options open to them. If the case is decided on a constitutional principle, they can press for a constitutional amendment, but few do—the odds of success are infinitesimally small. If the court is interpreting a statute, the losers can ask Congress to override the decision by changing the law, and this is done far more frequently. The civil rights measure (known to its opponents as the quotas bill) currently before Congress is one such example: an effort to reverse a series of Supreme Court decisions limiting lawsuit victories under the Civil Rights Act of 1964.

But usually those whose arguments have been rejected just take their lumps, and that is just what manufacturers with fetal protection plans are going to do, now that a unanimous court has declared that such policies illegally discriminate against women.

Denise Zutz, a spokesman for Johnson Controls Inc., the company whose plan was struck down, says the Milwaukee-based firm has not figured out in what way it will abide by the decision, but that it will certainly obey the law. The company's policy was to keep fertile women out of jobs that could injure their fetuses if they became pregnant. John Maciarz, a spokesman for General Motors Corp., which has had a similar fetal protection policy since 1953, says that GM too will obey the law in whatever way the company's lawyers recommend.

The companies still think they were right to have the policies, saying they protected fetuses from birth defects and the companies from being sued years later by children so injured. But there are no plans to cart these arguments up to the Capi-

---

tol, where they are seen to be less welcome than they were across the street in the Supreme Court. "It's such an emotional issue that it would be an uphill battle all the way," says Quentin Riegel, deputy general counsel for the National Association of Manufacturers. "With the current debate on the civil rights act, I can see how this proposal would be received well."

So the manufacturers are left with only a few alternatives. Mona Zeiberg, senior labor counsel for the U.S. Chamber of Commerce, says companies either will just pay the cost of lawsuits by injured children or they will use robotics or move the operation out of the country.

Those are the options being considered by Johnson Controls. "The two longer-term solutions," says Zutz, "are, one, to take the people out through automation and, second, to consider moving offshore—not for the purpose of reducing the amount of protection given workers, but where you wouldn't be held accountable for the liability."

In Johnson Controls' case, that liability comes from workers' exposure to lead. The company's Globe Battery division has lead battery plants in 10 states that employ about 5,000 workers. Many of them come in contact with levels of lead that could cause birth defects in their children should they become pregnant.

In 1977, the company adopted a policy of recommending that women who planned to have children not take jobs exposing them to lead. By 1982, however, eight women had become pregnant while in such jobs, and the company made the policy mandatory. Women who could not prove they were sterile were not allowed in the lead-exposed jobs, which because of the higher risk were higher paying.

A class action lawsuit was brought in 1984 by eight current and former employees of the company, together with the United Auto Workers union, arguing that the policy was discriminating and illegal under Title VII of the Civil Rights Act. Johnson Controls responded that the differential treatment of fertile women was a business necessity and that the sterility requirement was a so-called bona fide occupational qualification. A U.S. District Court ruled in the company's favor with a summary judgment, and the Chicago-based U.S. Court of Appeals for the 7th Circuit affirmed that decision.

But the Supreme Court reversed the appellate court, saying the policy was on its face discriminatory and that the company had not shown that women were more likely to suffer reproductive damage from lead than were men. The court also said the potential for lawsuits against the company was not an issue because acting in compliance with civil rights requirements would provide manufacturers with a defense.

Business lawyers were astonished, and not at all comforted, by the high court's belief that injured children would not be able to bring lawsuits. "If they allow women into the workplace under conditions that pose a substantial risk to the fetus, then there will likely be litigation down the road despite the Supreme Court's hope that there won't be," says Riegel.

"A mother can waive her own right to sue, but she can't waive the right of a child to bring a suit," says Zeiberg. "So five or 10 years down the line you might see children born with cognitive disabilities, and they could independently sue businesses." Various states have upheld a child's right to sue for injuries suffered during gestation.

The UAW does not dispute that claim. Indeed, spokesman Reg McGhee says the threat of lawsuits will give the union leverage to push for greater workplace safety. "We've always thought it is better to make the workplace safer than to construct artificial situations for avoiding lawsuits."

"What are companies going to do?" asks Riegel. "Well, obviously they can't have a fetal protection policy. They've either got to include women in the workplace and pay the consequences or exclude fertile men from the workplace."

Riegel thinks that the wording of the court's majority opinion, which pointed out that there was some evidence of a risk to children whose fathers had high blood-lead levels, may allow for fetal protection policies as long as men capable of fathering children are kept out of the jobs as well. The opinion, written by Justice Harry A. Blackmun, said part of the problem was that "fertile men, but not fertile women, are given a choice as to whether they wish to risk their reproductive health for a particular job."

Zeiberg doubts though that the court would look favorably on a unisex sterility policy, which in the justices' view, she says, would still violate the pregnancy clauses of the civil rights law.

The decision affects not only heavy manufacturers, such as Johnson Controls and GM battery plants, but also chemical companies and some hospitals that have also set fetal protection policies. The hospital policies have applied to radiologists and X-ray technicians, whose exposure to radiation could cause fetal abnormalities. And chemical companies have had policies to protect against a variety of reproductive toxicants.

According to a Du Pont Co. spokesman, that company has tried to limit exposure to fetal toxins, such as one of its products, tetraethyl lead, "first by engineering controls, second by personnel protection and last by alternative company employment." But Du Pont was careful not to force those excluded from contact with the toxins—some 500 of the company's 440,000 employees—into lower-paying jobs. "Unlike some other companies, no employee has suffered a loss of pay or position as a result of the alternative employment," says the spokesman. Even so, Du Pont plans to alter its policy in light of the court's decision.

Johnson Controls is not giving up on its fetal protection plan altogether. The company will likely return to the voluntary scheme it recommended before 1982. Zutz says that aside from the issue of legal liability, Johnson Controls has to take an interest in the health of children. "We felt we needed to protect fetuses, children," she says. "To me, part of what's outrageous here is that basically the court said it's none of our business, which strikes us as fairly odd."

Whistle Blowing: GE's Drive to Purge Fraud

Amal Kumar Naj
Staff Reporter, *The Wall Street Journal*

General Electric Co., subject of several high-profile corporate scandals over the past decade, now has one of the most elaborate programs in corporate America to head off further embarrassments. Its centerpiece is a program to motivate employees who suspect anything fishy to report it immediately to GE officials.

The effort GE makes is remarkable. Besides seminars and videos for employees, the company goes so far as to spring pop quizzes on workers in hallways, asking, for instance, "What are the three ways to report wrongdoing?" Correct answers win a coffee mug.

Yet today, GE is expected to plead guilty and pay $70 million to settle charges arising from a case in which an employee didn't use the internal compliance system, but instead kept his suspicions to himself for years while gathering evidence, and eventually filed suit against the company and alerted government authorities.

The employee is Chester Walsh, and the wrongdoing he spotted was a scheme by a high GE official and an Israeli general to divert U.S. aid for Israel into their personal accounts. With phony bills for projects that were never started by GE, the scheme defrauded the U.S. of about $42 million.

COLLECTING A BOUNTY?

Why would an employee such as Mr. Walsh decline to use a compliance system GE had developed with such care? The question entails issues of concern not only to GE but to other corporations that must devise programs to prevent wrongdoing by employees. And it bears on the merits of a statute that is a kind of whistle-blower protection act, the False Claims Act.

That law permits employees whose tips result in federal fines or assessments against U.S. contractors to receive as much as 25% of the sums. And to GE, this law goes a long way to explain why Mr. Walsh kept his suspicions to himself. GE contends that he allowed the fraud to spread for four years after he discovered it in order to collect a larger bounty. Under the act, Mr. Walsh could receive as much as $17.5 million of GE's $70 million settlement, and at the very least he is likely to receive millions.

But Mr. Walsh has a different explanation. He says that despite GE's vociferous protestations, GE workers who blow the whistle on suspected wrongdoers aren't always protected. "I did a lot of research to see what happened to people who went up the chain of command and reported wrongdoings," says the 60-year-old Mr. Walsh. "All I found was they lost their jobs, their security, they lost everything."

INVESTIGATIONS APLENTY

Without question, fraud remains a concern at General Electric. Only two years ago, the Defense Department formed a special unit solely to investigate allegations of wrongdoing at GE.

And few of those allegations are emanating from GE's self-policing program. Of the 60 cases the unit has referred to various criminal investigative agencies, only 11 were voluntarily disclosed by GE; government auditors and whistle blowers like Mr. Walsh accounted for the rest, according to a spokesman at the Defense Logistics Agency, the Pentagon's procurement arm.

GE says that the large number of cases the special unit is investigating doesn't mean criminal charges are imminent. It notes that of 27 cases investigated and closed since 1985 by a different agency, the Defense Criminal Investigative Service, only one resulted in criminal charges, while many others ended with GE paying restitution for improper pricing and other problems. Many of these cases were voluntarily disclosed by GE.

PERFORMANCE PRESSURE

Mr. Walsh and other GE employees who have gone outside to blow the whistle say GE's self-policing system is hampered by a culture that puts extreme emphasis on profit. They say that culture is fostered at the top, where Chairman John F. Welch Jr. demands ever-rising earnings—even though Mr. Welch has personally pushed the campaign to root out wrongdoing internally.

"If you have ever worked at GE you know that every quarter you make a phenomenal effort to generate income," says Mr. Walsh, echoing many other former and current GE employees.

Says GE: "We feel that competitiveness and integrity are utterly compatible. . . . You bet we compete. You bet we demand performance. Otherwise we wouldn't be the world leader in businesses."

Worker fear about turning in corporate wrongdoers is hardly limited to GE. Emil Stache, a quality control manager at Teledyne Inc., says he complained in 1990 to Teledyne's "ethics person," then to its vice president of quality, that some co-workers were falsifying test results of electronic components used in missile-guidance systems. But all that happened was that he got laid off, says Mr. Stache. In September 1990, he and a co-worker filed a whistle-blower suit that the Justice Department has joined as a plaintiff. Teledyne declines to comment.

Throughout the defense industry, "if you're an employee and you complain [of wrongdoing] you take your career in your hand," says Jay Gourley, editor of DOJ Alert, a journal covering the Department of Justice.

In this climate, prosecutors say the False Claims Act is invaluable in fighting fraud. Since Congress increased the payout to whistle blowers in 1986, nearly 500 suits have been filed under the act, and about a quarter turned out to have merit, says the Justice Department. This month, in the largest payout yet, a court awarded $7.5 million to an ex-employee of a Binghamton, N.Y., military contractor for exposing fraud.

But GE contends that the law undermines corporate compliance programs. It would like the statute changed so that whistle blowers couldn't bring suit unless they had tried to report their suspicions to a company compliance program and gotten no response.

At GE, its officials say, much has changed since the day in 1983 when a worker named John Gravitt complained to his division head about time-card cheating among supervisors and co-workers. Dismissed that very day, Mr. Gravitt sued GE in 1984, and GE settled after acknowledging time-card alterations.

That and other cases prompted Mr. Welch in 1985 to declare war on fraud. GE began training employees to keep an eye out for wrongdoing and to report it quickly. GE established toll-free numbers, special forms, even avenues for sending anonymous notes to Mr. Welch. It also began requiring nonunion workers to sign documents every year affirming that they knew of no wrongdoing. An instruction manual said: "If confronted with apparent conflicts between the demands of their jobs and the highest standards of conduct, employees should be guided by their sense of honor until the inconsistency has been reconciled."

ADDING BEEF

But despite those measures, some GE workers continued going outside the company to blow the whistle. So GE beefed up the system even more, and it cites its Philadelphia aerospace division as an example of the self-policing it is doing throughout the company.

That operation boasts 160 interactive video terminals that offer mandatory compliance courses for the division's 30,000 employees. The courses, implemented 18 months ago, feature hypothetical situations dramatized by actors, with cameo appearances by top managers.

Training programs assure employees they needn't wait for "a preponderance of evidence" to report wrongdoing, says William Lytton, general counsel of GE Aerospace. GE officials strongly deny that whistle blowers are punished, adding that most whistle-blowing is anonymous anyway. Mr. Lytton says the company is evaluating approaches to take the fear out of reporting wrongdoing.

There is a need for that, say several former and current GE whistle blowers. They say they would have been encouraged to use the internal reporting system if GE had rewarded others for doing so.

"That hasn't happened at all," says Edward Russell, a former vice president of GE's Superabrasives division who has sued GE charging wrongful dismissal. Mr. Russell claims he was dismissed because he alleged that a meeting between certain GE officials and a South African cartel was for the purpose of fixing industrial diamond prices, a charge the Justice Department is investigating. GE denies that charge and says Mr. Russell was fired for poor performance.

GE also says employees shouldn't have to be rewarded for being ethical. "It's part of every employee's code of honor," says Mr. Lytton.

BIG REGRETS

But some employees say they're honorably unemployed because they followed compliance procedures. Patricia Della Croce, a government property administrator in GE's Lynn, Mass., engine plant, says that in 1990 she told supervisors that some coworkers in her unit were unfairly billing the government for parts in an engine development program. "I was told I wasn't a team player and was ostracized," she says. Mrs. Della Croce, 59 years old and a 25-year GE employee, says that early this year she was abruptly told her job had been eliminated. "Actually, it was me whom they eliminated," she says.

When she appealed her dismissal to an ombudsman at the plant, a GE attorney, compliance representative and accountant also showed up. "It was like a jury trial. They pounded their fists on the table. I was in tears," she says. GE says it investigated Mrs. Della Croce's case and found no wrongdoing; it says her job was among many eliminated in deep staff cuts prompted by a shrinking defense budget.

Salvatore Cimorelli, who worked in the parts department of GE's Lynn, Mass., engine facility, tells a similar story. He says he was dismissed in 1989 after complaining to his boss and to GE's legal department about employees altering time vouchers and overcharging the government on a test engine being developed at the plant. GE won't comment, citing a whistle-blower suit that Mr. Cimorelli filed in federal court in Boston. Mr. Cimorelli, who had worked at GE for 29 years, says: "What it tells me is that Chester Walsh did the right thing keeping his mouth shut."

HIGH-LEVEL TREACHERY

The Israeli scandal illustrates how GE's compliance program can fail when a high-level executive is involved. The scheme was plotted by a powerful Israeli Air Force general, Rami Dotan, and Herbert Steindler, who was in charge of GE's military marketing in Israel and was considered the "Israeli desk" within GE for his deep contacts in that country.

Over a period of years, Mr. Steindler and Gen. Dotan diverted about $42 million of U.S. aid to Israel into personal accounts, say government officials. To account for the funds, Mr. Steindler, with the help of other GE employees, submitted false documents for nonexistent military projects whose completion Gen. Dotan attested to. Investigators say some of the money represented a bribe to Gen. Dotan to induce him to place actual orders for GE F-110 jet engines.

When Mr. Walsh learned of the scheme, he could have told his immediate boss, Robert Garvin. But he says Mr. Garvin was a close friend of Mr. Steindler's. GE says that Mr. Garvin is retired and isn't available for comment.

Another person Mr. Walsh could have reported the matter to was Brian Brimelow, then general manager for the F-110 engine program in Cincinnati. But according to Mr. Walsh, and to other GE employees who were in a position to detect the scheme, documents authorizing projects and payments that passed between Cincinnati and Tel Aviv bore Mr. Brimelow's signature. Mr. Brimelow was also on the compliance board of the GE aircraft engine unit that's supposed to investigate frauds. "Who the hell do you report it to?" asks Mr. Walsh. (Mr. Brimelow eventually was demoted from the head of the government products division to chief systems engineer, says GE, but it won't say whether he was accused of involvement in the scheme. He declines to comment.)

How about the 800 number? Mr. Walsh says that since he was the only GE man stationed in Israel and privy to the paper trail, "the call would have been easily traced back to me."

REMAINING MUM

With people as senior as Mr. Steindler possibly involved in the scheme, Mr. Walsh decided against disclosing what he knew to superiors. Instead he read up on the False Claims Act, and hired an attorney. Then he began collecting documents and recording conversations with GE employees in Cincinnati.

After Mr. Walsh filed suit under the False Claims Act, GE fired Mr. Steindler, who faces criminal charges brought by the Department of Justice. He declines to comment. Gen. Dotan, convicted in Israel of bribery and other crimes, drew a 13-year sentence. GE fired or disciplined more than 20 other workers it said knew or should have known about the scheme and reported it.

Yet at least one GE employee, David McDonald, manager of the international engine support operation in Cincinnati, did report his suspicions to his bosses, nearly 20 months before Mr. Walsh filed suit. In a March 10, 1989, letter to Mr. Steindler—with copies to Mr. Brimelow and Ken Bowman, Mr. McDonald's boss—Mr. McDonald noted that GE had received "advance payment in full" for two projects that hadn't even been started. Because recording payment for incomplete projects violates compliance policies, the letter should have raised an immediate alarm at the top of that division, say former GE employees familiar with the letter.

Instead, it went unheeded. And in the wake of the government investigation of the GE-Israeli scandal, GE earlier this year fired Mr. McDonald, a 29-year veteran, for what it called "shortfall in compliance culture." Mr. McDonald declines to comment, citing a termination agreement he signed with GE.

A number of the GE employees fired for acts of

"omission" in the scandal say that in the frenzy of meeting sales goals there was little time to scrutinize the phony transactions. Several say that when they did try to verify the existence of "test cells" and "support systems," they were rebuffed by Gen. Dotan and Mr. Steindler, who told them the projects were situated in "highly secured areas." The GE employees say they were afraid of alienating Israel, GE's second largest defense customer after the U.S. "GE taught me how to go through the brick wall [to] support the customer, and that's what we were doing," says one dismissed worker.

Mr. Lytton, the GE attorney, who is also an aerospace-division vice president, contends fraud isn't a widespread problem at the company. He says that "occasional instances of unauthorized illegal behavior" by GE's 275,000-member work force is "minuscule" compared with crime rates in cities of that size.

At the same time, he says, there is increasing pressure within the company "to make sure that every time we give a performance message—make your number—we also give a compliance message."

The Case of the Mismanaged Ms.

Sally Seymour
Former Lecturer in Communication, Management Communication, Harvard Business School

It started out as one of those rare quiet mornings when I could count on having the office to myself. The Mets had won the World Series the night before, and most of the people in the office had celebrated late into the night at a bar across the street. I'm a fan too, but they all like to go to one of those bars where the waitresses dress like slave girls and the few women customers have to run a mine field of leers when they go to a ladies' room labeled "Heifers." Instead, I watched the game at home with my husband and escaped a hangover.

So I was feeling pretty good, if a little smug, when Ruth Linsky, a sales manager here at Triton, stormed past my secretary and burst into my office. Before I could say good morning, she demanded to know what business it was of the company who she slept with and why. I didn't know what she was talking about, but I could tell it was serious. In fact, she was practically on the verge of tears, but I knew she wasn't the type to fly off the handle.

Ruth had been with the company for three years, and we all respected her as a sensible and intelligent woman. She had been top in her class at business school and we recruited her hand when she graduated, but she didn't join us for a couple of years. She's since proved to be one of our best people in sales, and I didn't want to lose her. She fumed around the room for a while, not making much sense, until I talked her into sitting down.

"I've had it with this place and the way it treats women!" she shouted.

I allowed her to let off some more steam for a minute or two, and then I tried to calm her down. "Look, Ruth," I said, "I can see you're upset, but I need to know exactly what's going on before I can help you."

"I'm not just upset, Barbara," she said, "I'm damned mad. I came over to Triton because I thought I'd get more chances to advance here, and I just found out that I was passed over for director of the marketing division and Dick Simon got it instead. You know that I've had three outstanding years at the company, and my performance reviews have been excellent. Besides, I was led to believe that I had a pretty good shot at the job."

"What do you mean, 'led to believe'?"

"Steve heard through the grapevine that they were looking for a new marketing director, and he suggested I put in my name," she said. "He knows my work from when we worked together over at Forge Techtronics, and he said he'd write a letter in support. I wouldn't have even known they were

---

Reprinted by permission of *Harvard Business Review*. An excerpt from "The Case of the Mismanaged MS." by Sally Seymour (November–December 1987).

looking for someone if Steve hadn't tipped me off."

Steve Baines is vice president of manufacturing. He's certainly a respected senior person in the company and he pulls some weight, but he doesn't have sole control of the marketing position. The hierarchy doesn't work that way, and I tried to get Ruth to see that. "Okay, so Steve wrote a letter for you, but he's only one of five or six VPs who have input in executive hiring decisions. Of course it helps to have his support, but lots of other factors need to be considered as well."

"Come off it, Barbara," Ruth snapped. "You know as well as I do there's only one thing that really matters around here and that's whether you're one of the boys. I've got a meeting this afternoon with my lawyer, and I'm going to file a sexual discrimination suit, a sexual harassment suit, and whatever other kind of suit she can come up with. I've had it with this old-boy crap. The only reason I'm here is that, as human resources director, you should know what's going on around here."

So the stakes were even higher than I had thought; not only did it look like we might lose Ruth, but we also might have a lawsuit on our hands. And to top it off, with the discrimination issue Ruth might be trying to get back at us for promoting Dick. I felt strongly about the importance of this legal remedy, but I also knew that using it frivolously would only undermine women's credibility in legitimate cases.

"Ruth," I said, "I don't doubt your perceptions, but you're going to need some awfully strong evidence to back them up."

"You want evidence? Here's your evidence. Number one: 20% of the employees in this company are women. Not one is on the board of directors, and not one holds an executive-level position. You and I are the only two in mid-level positions. Number two: there's no way for women to move into the mid-level positions because they never know when they're available. When a vacancy comes up, the VPs—all men, of course—decide among themselves who should fill it. And then, over and over again I hear that some guy who hasn't worked half as hard as most of the women at his level has been given the plum. Number three: there are plenty of subtle and sometimes not-so-subtle messages around here that women are less than equal."

"Ruth, those are still pretty vague accusations," I interrupted. "You're going to have to come up with something more specific than feelings and suppositions."

"Don't worry, Barbara. Just keep listening and maybe you'll learn something about how this company you think so highly of operates. From the day Ed Coulter took over as vice president of marketing and became my boss, he's treated me differently from the male sales managers. Instead of saying good morning, he always has some comment about my looks—my dress is nice, or my hair looks pretty, or the color of my blouse brings out my eyes. I don't want to hear that stuff. Besides, he never comments on a guy's eyes. And then there's that calendar the sales reps have in their back office. Every time I go in there for a sales meeting, I feel like I've walked into a locker room."

So far, this all seemed pretty harmless to me, but I didn't want Ruth to feel I wasn't sympathetic. "To tell you the truth, Ruth, I'm not so sure all women here find compliments like that insulting, but maybe you can give me other examples of discriminatory treatment."

"You bet I can. It's not just in the office that these things happen. It's even worse in the field. Last month Ed and I and Bill, Tom, and Jack went out to Dryden Industries for a big project meeting. I'll admit I was a little nervous because there were some heavy hitters in the room, so I kept my mouth shut most of the morning. But I was a team member and I wanted to contribute.

"So when Ed stumbled at one point, I spoke up. Well, it was like I had committed a sacrilege in church. The Dryden guys just stared at me in surprise, and then they seemed actually angry. They ignored me completely. Later that afternoon, when I asked Ed why I had gotten that reaction, he chuckled a little and explained that since we hadn't been introduced by our specific titles, the Dryden guys had assumed I was a research assistant or a secretary. They thought I was being presumptuous. But when Ed explained who I was, they admitted that I had made an important point.

"But that wasn't all," she went on. "The next day, when we explained to them that I would be interviewing some of the factory foremen for a needs assessment, one of the executives requested that someone else do it because apparently there's a superstition about women on the factory floor bringing bad luck. Have you ever heard of anything so stupid? But that's not the worst of it. Ed actually went along with it. After I'd pulled his bacon out of the fire the day before. And when I nailed him for it, he had the gall to say 'Honey, whatever the client wants, the client gets.'

"Well, we got the contract, and that night we all went out to dinner and everything was hurray for our team. But then, when I figured we'd all go back to the hotel for a nightcap, Ed and the guys just kind of drifted off."

"Drifted off?" I asked.

"Yeah. To a bar. They wanted to watch some basketball game."

"And you weren't invited?"

"I wasn't invited and I wasn't disinvited," she said. "They acted like they didn't know what to say."

By this point Ruth had cooled down quite a bit, and although she still seemed angry, she was forthright in presenting her case. But now her manner changed. She became so agitated that she got up from her chair to stare out the window. After a few minutes, she sort of nodded her head, as if she had come to some private, difficult decision, and then crossed the room to sit down again. Looking at her lap and twisting a paper clip around in her hands, she spoke so softly that I had to lean forward to hear her.

"Barbara," she began, "what I'm going to tell you is, I hope, in confidence. It's not easy for me to talk about this because it's very personal and private, but I trust you and I want you to understand my position. So here goes. When Steve Baines and I were both at Forge, we had a brief affair. I was discreet about it; it never interfered with business, and we ended it shortly after we both came to work here. But we're still very close friends, and occasionally we have dinner or a drink together. But it's always as friends. I think Ed found out about it somehow. The day after I notified the head office that I wanted to be considered for the director position, Ed called me into his office and gave me a rambling lecture about how we have to behave like ladies and gentlemen these days because of lawsuits on sexual harassment.

"At the time, I assumed he was referring somehow to one of our junior sales reps who had gotten drunk at the Christmas party and made a fool of himself with a couple of secretaries; but later I began to think that the cryptic comment was meant for me. What's more, I think Ed used that rumor about my relationship with Steve to block my promotion. And that, Barbara, is pure, sexist, double-standard hypocrisy because I can name you at least five guys at various levels in this company who have had affairs with colleagues and clients, and Ed is at the top of the list."

I couldn't deny the truth of Ruth's last statement, but that wasn't the point, or not yet. First I had to find out which, if any, of her accusations were true. I told her I needed some time and asked if she could give me a week before calling in a lawyer. She said no way. Having taken the first step, she was anxious to take the next, especially since she didn't believe things would change at Triton anyway. We dickered back and forth, but all I could get from her was a promise to hold off for 24 hours. Not much of a concession, but it was better than nothing.

Needless to say, I had a lot to think about and not very much time to do it in. It was curious that this complaint should come shortly after our organization had taken steps to comply with affirmative action policies by issuing a companywide memo stating that we would continue to recruit, employ, train, and promote individuals without regard to race, color, religion, sex, age, national origin, physical or mental handicap, or status as a disabled veteran or veteran of the Vietnam era. And we did this to prevent any problems in the future, not because we'd had trouble in the past. In fact, in my five years as HRM director, I'd never had a sexual discrimination or harassment complaint.

But now I was beginning to wonder whether there had never been grounds for complaint or whether the women here felt it was useless or even dangerous to complain. If it was the latter, how had

I contributed to allowing that feeling to exist? And this thought led me to an even more uncomfortable one: Had I been co-opted into ignoring injustices in a system that, after all, did pretty well by me? Was I afraid to slap the hand that buttered my bread?

Questioning one's own motives may be enlightening, but it's also time consuming, and I had more pressing matters to deal with before I could indulge in what would likely be a painful self-analysis. I asked my secretary to find George Drake, CEO of Triton, and get him on the phone. In the meantime, I wrote down as much as I could remember of what Ruth had just told me. When George finally called, I told him I knew his schedule was full but we had an emergency of sorts on our hands and I needed an hour of his time this morning. I also asked that Ed Coulter be called into the meeting. George told me I had the hour.

When I got to George's office, Ed and George were already waiting. They were undoubtedly curious about why I had called this meeting, but as I've seen people do in similar situations, they covered their anxiety with chitchat about ball games and hangovers. I was too impatient for these rituals, so I cut the conversation short and told them that we were going to have a serious lawsuit on our hands in a matter of days if we didn't act very quickly. That got their attention, so I proceeded to tell Ruth's story. When I began, George and Ed seemed more surprised than anything else, but as I built up Ruth's case their surprise turned to concern. When I finished, we all sat in silence for I don't know how long and then George asked Ed for comments.

"Well, George," Ed said, "I don't know what to say. Ruth certainly was a strong contender for the position, and her qualifications nearly equaled Dick's, but it finally came down to the fact that Dick had the seniority and a little more experience in the industrial sector. When you've got two almost equally qualified candidates, you've got to distinguish them somehow. The decision came down to the wire, which in this case was six months seniority and a few more visits to factory sites."

"Were those the only criteria that made a difference in the decision?" George wanted to know.

"Well, not exactly. You know as well as I do that we base hiring decisions on a lot of things. On one hand, we look at what's on paper: years at the company, education, experience, recommendations. But we also rely on intuition, our feel for the situation. Sometimes, you don't know exactly why, but you just feel better about some people than others, and I've learned that those gut reactions are pretty reliable. The other VPs and I all felt good about Dick. There's something about him—he's got the feel of a winner. You know? He's confident—not arrogant—but solid and really sharp. Bruce had him out to the club a couple of times, and I played squash with him all last winter. We got to know him and we liked what we saw; he's a family man, kids in school here, could use the extra money, and is looking to stick around for a while. None of these things mean a lot by themselves, of course, but together they add up.

"Don't get me wrong. I like Ruth too. She's very ambitious and one of our best. On the other hand, I can't say that I or any of the VPs know her as well as we know Dick. Of course, that's not exactly Ruth's fault, but there it is."

I had to be careful with the question I wanted Ed to respond to next because Ruth had asked for my confidence about the affair. I worded it this way: "Ed, did any part of your decision take into account Ruth's relationship with anyone else at the company?"

The question visibly disturbed Ed. He walked across the room and bummed a cigarette from me—he had quit last week—before answering: "Okay, I didn't want to go into this, but since you brought it up. . . . There's a rumor—well it's stronger than a rumor—that Ruth is more than professionally involved with Steve Baines—I mean she's having an, ah, sexual affair with him. Now before you tell me that's none of my business, let me tell you about some homework I did on this stuff. Of course it's real tricky. It turns out there are at least two court cases that found sexual discrimination where an employer involved in a sexual relationship with an employee promoted that person over more qualified candidates.

"So here's what that leaves us with: we've got Steve pushing his girlfriend for the job. You saw the letter he wrote. And we've got Dick with seniority. So if we go with Ruth, what's to keep Dick from charging Steve and the company on two counts of sexual discrimination: sexual favoritism because Ruth is Steve's honey and reverse discrimination because we pass over a better qualified man just to get a woman into an executive position. So we're damned if we do and damned if we don't. We've got lawsuits if we don't advance Dick, and, so you tell me, lawsuits if we don't advance Ruth!"

We let that sink in for a few seconds. Then George spoke up: "What evidence do you have, Ed, that Steve and Ruth are having an affair?" he asked.

"Look, I didn't hire some guy to follow them around with a camera, if that's what you mean," Ed said. "But come on, I wasn't born yesterday; you can't keep that kind of hanky-panky a secret forever. Look at the way she dresses; she obviously enjoys men looking at her, especially Steve. In fact, I saw them having drinks together at Dino's the other night and believe me, they didn't look like they were talking business. All that on top of the rumors, you put two and two together."

Well, that did it for me. I'd been trying to play the objective observer and let Ed and George do all the talking, but Ed's last comment, along with some budding guilt about my own blindness to certain things at Triton that Ruth had pointed out, drove me out in the open. "Come off it, Ed," I said. "That's not evidence, that's gossip."

Now Ed turned on me: "Look," he shouted, "I didn't want to talk about this, but now that you've brought it up, I'll tell you something else. Even if we didn't have to worry about this sexual discrimination business, I still wouldn't back Ruth for the director's job." He calmed down a bit. "No offense, Barbara, but I just don't think women work out as well as men in certain positions. Human resources is one thing. It's real soft, person-to-person stuff. But factories are still a man's world. And I'm not talking about what I want it to be like. I'm talking facts of life.

"You see what happens when we send a woman out on some jobs, especially in the factories. To be any good in marketing you have to know how to relate to your client; that means getting to know him, going out drinking with him, talking sports, hunting, whatever he's interested in. A lot of our clients feel uncomfortable around a woman in business. They know how to relate to their wives, mothers, and girlfriends, but when a woman comes to the office and wants to talk a deal on industrial drills—well, they don't know what to do.

"And then there's the plain fact that you can't depend on a woman the way you can on a guy. She'll get married and her husband will get transferred, or she'll have a baby and want time off and not be able to go on the road as much. I know, Barbara, you probably think I'm a pig, or whatever women's libbers call guys like me these days. But from where I'm sitting, it just made good business sense to choose Dick over Ruth."

"Ed, I don't believe it," I said. "The next thing you'll tell me is that women ought to stay at home, barefoot and pregnant." There was a long silence after that—my guess was that I had hit on exactly what Ed thought. At least he didn't deny it. Ed stared at the rug, and George frowned at his coffee cup. I tried to steer the conversation back to the subject at hand, but it dwindled into another silence. George took a few notes and then told Ed he could go back to work. I assumed I was excused too, but as I started to leave, George called me back.

"Barbara, I'm going to need your help thinking through this mess," he said. "Of course we've got to figure out how we can avoid a lawsuit before the day is out, but I also want to talk about what we can do to avoid more lawsuits in the future. While Ed was talking I took some notes, and I've got maybe four or five points I think we ought to hash out. I'm not saying we're going to come up with all the answers today, but it'll be a start. You ready?"

"Shoot."

"Okay, let's do the big one first," he began. "What should I have done or not done to avoid this situation? I mean, I was just patting myself on the back for being so proactive when I sent out that memo letting everyone know the company policy on discrimination. I wrote it not thinking we had any problem at Triton. But just in case we did, I figured that memo would take care of it."

"Well, it looks like it's not enough just to have a

corporate policy if the people in the ranks aren't on board. Obviously it didn't have much of an effect on Ed."

"So what am I supposed to do? Fire Ed?"

Being asked for my honest opinion by my CEO was a new experience for me and I appreciated it, but I wasn't going to touch that last question with a ten-foot pole. Instead I went on to another aspect: "And even if you get your managers behind you, your policy won't work if the people it's supposed to help don't buy it. Ruth was the first woman to complain around here. Are the others afraid to speak up? Or do they feel like Ed about a woman's place, or have husbands who do? Maybe they lack confidence even to try for better jobs, that is, if they knew about them."

"Okay," he said, "I'll admit that our system of having the VPs make recommendations, our 'old-boy network,' as Ruth called it, does seem to end up excluding women, even though the exclusion isn't intentional. And it's not obvious discrimination, like Ed's claim that Ruth is unqualified for a position because she is a woman. But wouldn't open job posting take away our right to manage as we see fit? Maybe we should concentrate instead on getting more women into the social network, make it an old boys' and old girls' club?"

"To tell you the truth, George, I don't much want to play squash with you," I replied, "but maybe we're getting off the subject. The immediate question seems to be how we're going to get more women into executive positions here, or, more specifically, do we give Ruth the director of marketing position that we just gave Dick?"

"On that score, at least, it seems to me that Ed has a strong argument," George said. "Dick is more qualified. You can't get around that."

I had wanted to challenge Ed on this point when he brought it up earlier, but I wasn't quite sure of myself then. Now that George was asking me for advice and seemed to be taking what I had to say seriously, I began to think that I might have something valuable to offer. So I charged right in. "George, maybe we're cutting too fine a line with this qualifications business. I know a lot of people think affirmative action means promoting the unqualified over the qualified to achieve balance. I think that argument is hogwash at best and a wily diversion tactic at worst. To my mind, Ruth and Dick are equally qualified, or equal enough. And wouldn't it make good business sense to get a diverse set of perspectives—women's, men's, blacks', whites'—in our executive group?"

"But isn't that reverse discrimination—not promoting Dick because he's a man? How would a judge respond to that? That's a question for a lawyer."

George leaned forward. "Let's talk about my last point, the one I think we've both been avoiding. What about this affair between Ruth and Steve? Boy, this is one reason why women in the work force are such trouble—no, just joking, Barbara, sorry about that. Look, I don't like lawsuits any more than anyone else, but I'd do anything to avoid this one. We'd be a laughing stock if it got out that Triton promoted unqualified people because they slept with the boss. I don't know how I'd explain that one to my wife."

"Look, George," I said, "in the first place, Dick's superior qualifications are debatable; in the second place, we have no proof that Ruth and Steve are involved in that way; and in the third place, what if they were once involved but no longer are? Does a past relationship condemn them for life? Isn't there a statute of limitations on that kind of thing, or are we going to make her put a scarlet letter on her briefcase? I thought these discrimination laws were supposed to protect women, but now it looks like a woman can be denied a promotion because someone thinks she's a floozy."

"Wait a second, Barbara. Don't make me look like such a prig," George said. "I realize that when men and women work together sexual issues are bound to crop up. I just don't know what I'm supposed to do about it, if anything. In some cases a woman may welcome a guy coming on to her, but what if it's her boss? And then there's that subtle stuff Ruth brought up—the calendar, dirty jokes, the male employees excluding women by going to bars to watch TV—and other women. And Ruth's treatment at that factory—how can we control our clients? I'm not sure these are things you can set policy on, but I am sure that I can't ignore them any longer."

And there we were. All the issues were on the table, and we had about 21 hours to make our decisions and act on them.

The Case of the Unequal Opportunity

Mary C. Gentile
Lecturer, Harvard Business School

Laura Wollen, group marketing director for ARPCO, Inc., a manufacturer of small electrical tools and appliances, telephoned London from her Columbus, Ohio office. She was getting ready to recommend her best product manager, Charles Lewis, for a position in the London office, a job that would give Lewis the international exposure he would need to progress toward senior management. She and David Abbott, her counterpart in the United Kingdom, had had several conversations about Lewis's candidacy, and Abbott had seemed impressed. Wollen simply wanted to touch base with him before making her recommendation formal.

Only two candidates were serious contenders for the U.K. product manager job: Frank Billings and Charles Lewis. Billings had joined ARPCO the previous year as a product manager for the housewares division. Before that, he had been a sales representative for one of ARPCO's main competitors. Wollen knew Billings fairly well because he had reported to her for several months on a special project. She found him to be intelligent and hardworking.

Yet she believed that Lewis, who had reported to her for three years, had the same innate talents but was better prepared for the job and possessed a creative spark that Billings did not. With a bachelor's degree in business administration and two years of experience selling financial services, Lewis had joined ARPCO as a sales rep in the Midwest. He immediately proved himself a winner. Marketing often recruited high fliers from the sales force, so Lewis was soon offered a job as product manager for power saws.

Within a year, Lewis had such command of his product management job that Wollen asked him to head the introduction of a charging system for ARPCO's new line of cordless power tools. The assignment required more than the usual amount of interdependence and collaboration, but Lewis worked carefully and cautiously to develop the relationships that he needed. The product introduction was a smashing success.

Now the company wanted to launch the charging system along with several cordless power tools in the United Kingdom. It was ARPCO's first entry into the British home workshop market. Its success was important because the company saw the do-it-yourself home maintenance market as a way to compensate for stagnant sales in the housewares division. The company also wanted to maintain visibility in the U.K. while waiting for the economy to recover and for the opportunities that 1992 would bring.

Jobs outside the United States were highly sought after at ARPCO, and only the high performers made the cut. When an opening occurred, marketing directors reviewed their product managers and selected the appropriate candidates. They then discussed the candidates informally with the director who was doing the hiring, and each could recommend one candidate to his or her divisional vice president. The vice presidents typically reviewed the recommendations and passed them on unchanged to the director in the host country. ARPCO encouraged managers to recommend their best people; it rewarded managers for the number of people they put on the fast track and for the performance of those fast trackers in their first six months on the job.

To Wollen's mind, Lewis was a natural for the job. Although she hated to lose him, she was glad he would have the opportunity to demonstrate his ability in such a visible position, and she was eager

---

to play a role in his professional development. But her friendly conversation with Abbott suddenly took an unexpected turn as she learned that Abbott no longer shared her enthusiasm for Lewis.

"You're the group marketing director, Laura, so I can't tell you who to recommend for the position, but I'll go on record as preferring Billings to Lewis." Abbott's British enunciation had an insistent edge.

"That really surprises me," she responded. "I know Billings is bright and motivated and all of that, but his experience is in housewares, just as yours is. Lewis, on the other hand, has three years in the home workshop division. His experience can get the launch off to a good start, and I know how important that is to you."

"You're right, I do have a lot riding on this launch, and it will require a lot of coordination. That's why I'm trying to pull together a team of professionals who can work together in the British environment. I need people who are comfortable with our sales force, our research and support staff, and our buyers. When Billings was here on temporary assignment last fall, he demonstrated that ability. I'm sure he can learn the product line."

"But let's face it," Wollen said. "That assignment was a three-month fill-in in housewares and didn't include any client contact. Besides, Billings has been on line as a product manager for only eleven months. Compared with Lewis, he's less mature, less creative—"

"If you insist on recommending Lewis, fine, I won't refuse the hire," Abbott said crossly. "But I need someone who can work comfortably and constructively with the team I've put together, not some individual contributor whose main concern is the next rung on the career ladder."

Wollen hesitated, then trusting her instincts, said, "We're not really talking about the same thing here, are we David? This isn't about market knowledge or ego. It's about race. You're concerned because Lewis is black, aren't you?"

"You didn't even mention it in our earlier conversations! If one of my managers hadn't mentioned it, I wouldn't have known until he walked in the door for the interview two weeks from now."

"Does it matter? Is it relevant here?" Wollen asked.

"The only thing that matters is that my new product manager is able to work well with the other managers and that he—or she—is able to adjust to the culture. Other managers like Lewis have been uncomfortable here, and we can't afford to botch this introduction. It's the key to our presence in the whole market."

"Look, David," Wollen reasoned, "in the three years Lewis has worked for me, he's had to work with all kinds of coworkers and customers, and they all had their own concerns and assumptions about him. But he managed to build productive relationships despite all those things. If you think he's too sensitive or inflexible, I can point to—"

"Don't misunderstand me, Laura. Lewis looks very good on paper. I'm certain he's very talented and will go far with ARPCO. I just don't believe that he is the most appropriate candidate for this position at this time. And when a manager doesn't last, everyone suffers from the loss of continuity. It will set the product line back months. Our group can recover from that kind of setback, but what about you? A failed recommendation will become part of your record. And just think what it will do to Lewis's career."

Wollen winced. "What would have happened to my career if Ralph Jordan hadn't been willing to take a chance by putting a woman product manager in the home workshop division for the first time? That's all I'm asking of you, that you give Lewis the chance to show what he can do."

"Perhaps this one is a bit too close to home, Laura. Are you sure this isn't just a personal issue?"

Wollen regretted giving Abbott that opening and closed the conversation coolly: "I'll think about what you've said and submit my recommendation by the end of the day."

Wollen hung up the phone and dashed from her office up to the eighth floor conference room for a meeting with the rest of the home workshop marketing directors and Ralph Jordan, their divisional vice president. Much as she tried to shift gears and focus on their planning agenda, she kept thinking about Abbott's question, "Are you sure this isn't a personal issue?"

Wollen had been with ARPCO for nine years, and although she knew the company had its problems, she was proud of it. It was known for making high-quality tools and appliances and for being a responsible employer. The company was full of bright, dedicated people, many of whom had been with ARPCO for more than 20 years. But sitting across the table from Jordan, she found herself thinking about the time five years earlier when she nearly left in disillusionment and defeat. It was Jordan who convinced her to stay.

Having joined ARPCO fresh from her MBA program, Wollen came ready to make her mark on the organization. She was particularly interested in the relatively new home workshop division. Her father was a carpenter, and she had spent many evenings and weekends watching and helping him. She loved that time working quietly beside her father and was proud of the skills he had taught her. She saw the home workshop division as the perfect place for her to combine her talents and interests.

In interviews with the ARPCO recruiters, she had stated her interest in the home workshop division, but they urged her to take a position with housewares. They assured her that if she did well, she could circulate into another area. That began a four-year stint with food processors, vacuum cleaners, and electric knives. Wollen improved the performance of every product she managed, and every time she learned of an opening in the home workshop division, she notified her supervisor of her interest. She was consistently passed over. Finally, after being overlooked yet again, she was ready to leave. Before she did, she made a last-ditch effort by going over her director's head to Ralph Jordan, who was then the divisional vice president of housewares.

Jordan knew Wollen's record, and after listening to her story, he looked into the situation. Six days later, he told her she had an interview for product manager of ARPCO's power drills if she wanted it. She still remembered much of what he had said to her that afternoon: "Laura, you have an outstanding record in housewares, and you deserve to be circulated among other divisions and regions. You have great potential to do well here, both for yourself and for the company. And I'm committed to developing talent whenever I find it.

"But I want you to listen to what I say to you now. Home workshop has never had a woman product manager before, partly because of a lack of interest on the part of our women product managers and also because of a lack of imagination on the part of our marketing directors. At any rate, you'll be working with managers and customer reps who will find you an anomaly. You're taking a risk by leaving housewares. But if you succeed, you will be opening a whole new set of doors for yourself.

"I can't guarantee that you'll succeed. I can't even guarantee you a level playing field. But I can promise you that I will do everything in my power to provide you with the backing you deserve. I will give you the support and authority you merit, just as I would for any talented manager. I believe that the truest test of a manager is his or her ability to develop good people. That's where I prove my stuff. If you make it, I'll feel I've done my job well."

Wollen interviewed for the position, and when it was offered to her, she promptly accepted.

In a way, Wollen did have a personal stake in Lewis's situation. She had embraced Jordan's philosophy of developing talent. When Lewis first went to work for her, Wollen had reflected on the fact that he was the only black manager in her group and one of very few in the division. She was aware that he was not as well knit into the social fabric of the group as other managers hired around the same time. Although Lewis got along with his colleagues professionally, he didn't socialize with them and their families, except for formal ARPCO events.

When the opening arose for a product manager to introduce the charging system for ARPCO's new line of cordless power tools, Wollen had some concern that Lewis's outsider status would cause problems for the project if it meant that he couldn't work himself into the information loop with the other product managers. On the other hand, the social distance could give him a balanced perspective, free of personal loyalties that might complicate the task. Finally, she thought the charging system assignment might be just what Lewis needed to work his way into the product managers' informal network.

The posting provided the opportunity for Lewis and Wollen to begin to develop a close mentoring relationship. Wollen was frank with Lewis, and she made a point of checking in frequently with him during the first few months of his new assignment. This support was an important signal to Lewis and to the other product managers as well. They were made aware of how important the collaborative project was to the entire group. And in fact, this cordless segment of the power tools market had been growing at a rate five times that of the rest of the group over the past two years.

At about the same time Wollen had begun to look around for an international assignment for Lewis, she learned of ARPCO's plan to enter the British home workshop market with the cordless line. The timing and fit seemed perfect.

Back in her office after a difficult lunch discussing cuts in the research budget, Wollen tried to prepare for a 1:30 meeting with Charles Lewis. Lewis had requested the meeting hastily, which meant one thing: he wanted to get to Wollen before she submitted her recommendation. The two of them had discussed the position at great length when it first opened, and initially Lewis was excited but concerned—excited about the implications of such an assignment, concerned about the impact on his family. After many long conversations with his wife, who had just rejoined her law practice after a year-long maternity leave, Lewis had told Wollen that he was willing to make the one-and-a-half to two-year commitment. The concern had vanished, and then it was pure excitement.

As Lewis entered the office, Wollen could see that the concern was back.

"Thanks for seeing me on such short notice," Lewis started. "It's about the U.K. position, of course. I know you haven't promised me anything . . ."

"But I told you you're high on the list. Go on."

"It's just that I've heard rumors from some of the guys over in housewares, and I don't know how much credence to give them."

"What exactly did you hear?" Wollen asked.

"Vague comments, really. When they found out I was being considered for the London slot, they shook their heads and said things like 'I hear it's real conservative over there' and 'Don't expect a lot of warmth.' I thought they were jealous. But then they got more explicit. They told me about a product manager who was assigned there—a black manager. He found the environment very difficult."

"You know we can't promise that all your client contact will be smooth sailing," Wollen said. "You deal with that all the time, and you've always been able to establish your credibility firmly and quietly."

"But that's just it," Lewis replied. "With this other manager, the customers weren't the problem, or not the only one. It was the other managers and even the supervisor, David Abbott. I know I can deal with difficult clients, but I've always counted on my boss's—on your—support. I've got to know there's some authority behind me. I'll need David Abbott's support."

Wollen hoped Lewis couldn't read her face. She knew Lewis was right about needing Abbott's support, and she was undecided about how to handle Abbott's message from the morning's call. She was also concerned about putting ARPCO in legal jeopardy. International assignments were still an evolving area in antidiscrimination law.

Wollen didn't know how much candor she could afford, so she proceeded cautiously. "You know, Charles, when U.S. companies send expatriate managers overseas, there are bound to be obstacles. Sometimes people are outright hostile, if only because they think you're taking opportunities away from them. When you—"

"That's not what I'm talking about," Lewis interrupted. He sat silent for a long, uncomfortable moment, then said, "I've given this opportunity a great deal of thought. My wife and I have considered the pros and cons for both of our careers, for our marriage, and for our daughter. We don't expect it to be easy, but we're ready to face the challenge.

"I'm not asking for any guarantees of success," Lewis continued. "But I am asking you to consider whether or not you think I truly have a shot in this slot. If you don't, then don't recommend me. I'll trust your judgment. Maybe I don't have the right to ask that of you, but you know more about the situation than I do, and I don't see that I have a choice."

Lewis and Wollen ended the meeting with a solemn handshake. Wollen's forced smile faded when Lewis closed the door behind him.

Earlier in the day, Wollen thought nothing could dissuade her from recommending Lewis. Now she sat at her desk poring through the personnel files looking for a reason to change her mind.

The company policies were clear: "promote the most qualified person, regardless of race, gender, or ethnic background" and "capitalize on the considerable investment ARPCO makes in its people by applying their skills in ways that will maximize benefit to the company and the individual." In Wollen's opinion, Lewis was the most qualified, and making him product manager in Britain would leverage his training and experience in the United States. She also wondered how long he would remain at ARPCO if he didn't get this opportunity. Lewis knew international circulation was critical to his career there.

The criteria used to evaluate her performance were also clear. Her vice president would consider the number of product managers she placed on the circulation track and how those managers performed in the first six months of their new assignments. Lewis was her best—virtually her only—shot.

But policies and her own career aside, there were other considerations, such as the realities of the London office and Lewis himself. Abbott was convinced that Lewis wouldn't work out, and Wollen knew that expectations beget reality. Abbott wouldn't have to thwart Lewis. If he believed that efforts to help Lewis would only postpone the inevitable, his passivity alone could do the trick.

Wollen wondered if she should go ahead and recommend Lewis and let him decide for himself whether to accept the position. Of course, if he refused such a competitive appointment, he would be knocked out of the running for some time.

Then she pondered how much support she could provide from a distance. Maybe she could talk to Jordan and enlist his help. But pronouncements from the top wouldn't necessarily improve the situation for Lewis. Real change usually came slowly.

If the lack of support got in the way of Lewis's performance, he was likely to leave the company. His departure would be a permanent loss of talent for ARPCO. And then there was the impact on Lewis himself. Wollen hated the thought of seeing a man with so much promise fail in a job he was basically well prepared to do. And while it would be painful for Wollen if Lewis didn't succeed, it would of course be all the more painful for Lewis and his family.

She had to assess Lewis's real chances for success and decide which candidate to recommend.

PART FOUR

THE CORPORATION IN SOCIETY

In Part Three we examined some aspects of the relationship of business to one of its most important internal constituencies, its employees. Here we turn attention to the relationship between business and its external constituencies—that is, between business and its environment. In Chapter 10, we examine the relationship between business and consumers by looking at some of the ethical aspects of marketing and sales; Chapter 11 explores some ethical dimensions of the relation of business to the natural environment; Chapter 12 takes up ethical problems raised by multinational business operations.

BUSINESS AND CONSUMERS

Business organizations exist by selling goods and services to consumers. Consumers, therefore, are one of business' most important constituencies, literally essential for its survival. Traditionally, the relationship between business and consumers in U.S. society has been defined by the free market, which links business and consumers in what is intended to be a mutually beneficial relationship. Business is free to make as large a profit as possible on its transactions with consumers; but—the theory goes—business succeeds only by giving consumers what they want. Both consumer and business interests are protected by the "invisible hand" of the market. Presumably an unsatisfactory or undesirable product, or one offered at an unreasonable price, will not sell. In such a system, it is often said that "the consumer is king," and sellers must serve the consumer or go out of business.

This system can work in practice, however, only if two conditions are met: (1) there is no deception, and the consumer receives adequate and accurate information about products on the market to make rational market decisions; and (2) the consumer is free to choose what to buy. Does the real world really meet these conditions, however? This question is the takeoff point for some of the most important debates about business and consumer relations in business ethics.

One business activity that has led thinkers to question the accuracy of the traditional picture of business and consumer relations is advertising or marketing. Advertising of some kind is necessary to convey information to consumers and to make them aware of what products are available. But how much information is really conveyed in such slogans as "Coke is the real thing" or "This Bud's for you"? It is not surprising that many observers of advertising conclude that its main purpose is not to inform but to persuade.

Advertisers have been accused not only of failing to inform the public but of creating needs and desires which the consumer otherwise would not have had. This is the charge made by John Kenneth Galbraith in his article "The Dependence Effect." Galbraith argues that in the United States the manufacture of consumer demands is as important as, if not more important than, the manufacture of products which satisfy those demands. The same companies that satisfy wants, he claims, also create those wants by advertising, establishing a self-perpetuating cycle of desire and satisfaction. If consumers truly wanted all the products on the market, Galbraith claims, such creation of desire would not be necessary. Genuine desires originate with the consumer and do not need to be created from outside. Galbraith might regard the extensive advertising campaign for cigarettes as an example of this want creation.

If Galbraith is correct, consumers are being manipulated into buying things they do not really want or need. The consumer is not the "king" in this picture, but a pawn. Recalling our discussion of Kant in the general introduction, we might say that if Galbraith is correct, then consumers are being treated by producers as means to an end rather than as ends in themselves. For rather than responding to consumer needs, producers are creating needs and looking on the consumer as nothing more than an instrument for making profits. Creation of consumer needs is also bad, according to Galbraith, because it encourages the excessive consumption of private goods which are not really essential, and diverts spending away from public goods like clean air, livable cities, parks, and public transportation. People would get a great deal of satisfaction from such public goods, Galbraith believes, but since there is comparatively little advertising to persuade us to spend our money on public goods, private goods tend to dominate. Galbraith feels that although our society is rich in private goods, it is poor in public goods.

But does advertising really manipulate us in the way that Galbraith claims? F.A. von Hayek does not think so. von Hayek agrees that many of our wants are created by production. Living in a society in which many material goods are available generates wants we would not have if we were raised in a different sort of society. But, he claims, this does not mean these wants are not urgent or important. Most of what we regard as our "highest" desires—for art, literature, education—are instilled in us by our culture. If only internally generated wants or needs were legitimate, we would have to conclude that the only important desires are for food, sex, and shelter. Advertising is only one cultural element that shapes our desires, von Hayek concludes. It cannot, by itself, determine our wants.

In the article "Marketing Ethics: Some Dimensions of the Challenge," Paul Camenisch addresses the ethic internal to marketing—that is, the specific purpose that society intends to accomplish by permitting such an activity. He argues that to speak of the goal of marketing from this perspective we need to go beyond the simple idea of selling products, and view marketing as an attempt to increase the likelihood of free, informed, and morally defensible transactions in the marketplace. He says that most marketing does not meet this ideal, but is intended to "hook" the customer by using a number of psychological devices. Thus, given the variety and complexity of products now on the market, and the consumers reliance on advertising to gain product information, marketing often serves to impede rather than enhance free and informed choice by consumers. To the extent that it does, it is a morally questionable practice. He concludes that these problems are better addressed through self-regulation guided by a vision of advertising and business as institutions intended to serve society, and through the marketer's own sense of integrity, than through externally imposed regulation, which brings to the fore difficult questions about censorship in a free society.

As noted by Galbraith and Camenisch, advertisers and salespeople are often accused of deceiving and manipulating the public through techniques such as "puffery" or exaggeration, failure to tell the whole truth about a product, misleading pricing and packaging, and appeals to emotion rather than to rational judgement. In his article, David Holley reviews and analyzes a number of such practices. Such sales techniques are unethical, Holley argues, if they undermine the possibility of a fair and free exchange between buyer and seller. If a consumer is led by a deceptive sales practice to buy a product, for example, he or she purchases that product on a false basis. Deception makes it impossible for the free market to satisfy the consumer's needs. Because the product is not what the consumer intended to buy when he or she made the purchase, the consumer's freedom has been violated.

Another important issue raised by the relationship between business and consumers is that of product safety. If a manufacturer has a responsibility to consumers not to market unsafe products, how far does this responsibility extend? Who should assume the liability if a consumer is injured by a defective product? Here, as in the case of advertising, it is unclear whether the market system by itself really protects the interests of the consumers. If they had adequate information, consumers could freely choose the risks they wish to run, and products considered too risky would be driven off the market. But in most cases, manufacturers need not make explicit the potential hazards of what they sell. Most consumers lack the expertise to assess the safety of today's technologically sophisticated products and must rely at least to some extent on the impression they are given by sellers. Many purchases are "one-shot" deals, which means that the consumer has no opportunity to benefit from his or her experience in the future. And although we are likely to hear about seriously dangerous products, often their danger does not attract attention until some consumers are injured.

Our growing lack of confidence in the market system to protect consumer safety is demonstrated by the increase in consumer protection legislation, and by the establishment of two major consumer protection agencies in the last decade—the Consumer Product Safety Commission and the National Highway Traffic Safety Administration. Some observers of this trend claim that we have moved from a stance of "Let the buyer beware" to one of "Let the manufacturer/seller beware." Moreover, many feel that the responsibility of manufacturers to consumers goes beyond obedience to federal safety regulations. Ford, for example, was asked to pay substantial amounts in settlements for accidents due to the placement of the Pinto's gas tank, even though there were no federal standards for fuel-system integrity at the time the Pinto was produced. One might argue that the manufacturer has an obligation to the consumer to make a product that can be used safely for the purposes for which the consumer has been led to believe it can be used, regardless of federal standards.

No product can be absolutely risk-free, however; some theorists hold that the most that can be demanded of manufacturers is that they exercise "due care" to make all products "reasonably" safe. The National Commission on Product Safety (NCPS) has suggested that risks are reasonable when consumers are aware of them, able to assess their probability and severity, know how to cope with them if they do arise, and voluntarily accept them to receive benefits they could not get otherwise. Risks which could easily be prevented, or which consumers would be willing to pay to prevent if given the choice, the NCPS concluded, are not reasonable. In part, it was the failure of Ford to exercise due care in making a safe product which is at issue in the Pinto case included in this book. But the case is an unusual one because in it Ford is accused of criminal homicide—of knowingly choosing not to exercise due care and trading human lives for profit.

It may seem fair that manufacturers should assume liability for consumer injuries caused by failure to exercise due care. But in recent years, the courts have extended the liability of manufacturers to include all cases in which injuries result from defects in the manufacturing process, even if the manufacturer could not have foreseen or prevented the injury. This doctrine is called "strict products liability." Proponents of the doctrine argue that manufacturers are best able to bear the costs of injuries because they can distribute them to others, and that forcing manufacturers to assume liability is likely to reduce the frequency of accident in the future. These are essentially utilitarian arguments. But do they constitute a justification for strict products liability? George Brenkert is one thinker who does not find them convincing, although he supports the doctrine of strict products liability.

Brenkert questions whether holding manufacturers strictly liable really will reduce the number of accidents and, if it will, whether it is the only way or the best way to do so. And even if a policy of strict products liability would reduce accidents, Brenkert argues, it does not follow that the doctrine is just. Similarly, that manufacturers are best able to bear the costs of injuries does not mean that it is just that they pay those costs.

Nevertheless, Brenkert believes that in the context of a free enterprise system, the doctrine of strict products liability is a just one. Essential to the functioning of a free enterprise system, he argues, is equal opportunity. However unintentionally, a manufacturer whose defective product has injured a consumer has interfered with that consumer's equal opportunity to participate in the system. Just as a team may be penalized for hurting an opposing player's ability to compete, even if the injury was an accident, a manufacturer may be required to compensate a consumer injured by a defective product, whether the defect was foreseen or not. Brenkert concludes that for this reason, it is just to place the burden of liability on the manufacturer.

BUSINESS AND THE ENVIRONMENT

Some of the most urgent questions faced by society today are those raised by the increasing contamination and depletion of our natural resources. The air pollution present in all major United States cities increases the incidence of respiratory disease, heart disease, and lung cancer. Toxic wastes like those dumped in Love Canal by Hooker Chemical find their way into drinking water and pose serious threats to human life and health. The earth's protective ozone layer is deteriorating, leaving us vulnerable to harmful effects from beyond the atmosphere. Researchers predict that if the exponentially rising rate of use of fossil fuels continues, estimated reserves will be depleted rapidly, and global warming is much more likely.

In Chapter 11 we look at some environmental problems raised by the activities of commercial and industrial enterprises. Business is by no means the sole polluter, nor is it the sole consumer of natural resources. But there are several important reasons for focusing on business-related environmental issues.

One reason is that the structure of the free enterprise system itself has been accused of encouraging pollution. At one time air and water were thought of as unlimited and "free" goods, available for anyone's use without charge. The effects—in terms of pollution—of any particular business's use of air or water were negligible, and we were confident of the ability of the environment to absorb them. Today, we realize that the environment can't absorb them. Air and water pollution are costs of production that business has "externalized," or passed on to society as a whole. Market forces encourage this conversion of private to public costs. However, as increasing pollution and the depletion of natural resources force us to adopt what has been called a "spaceship earth" mentality, it seems clear that pollution must be made less desirable by forcing polluters to internalize environmental costs. It is not surprising that business is resisting such attempts, and that some business people view environmental protection measures as contrary to their interests.

A second reason for examining business's role in the environmental crisis is the pervasiveness of the value placed on consumption, which is an integral part of our business society. Although Americans comprise only a small percent of the world's population, we consume more than a third of the world's annual energy resources. We also have the highest gross domestic product of any country in the world. The link between standard of living, economic growth as measured by the GNP, and high levels of pollution and consumption of natural resources cannot be denied. Business has developed into a powerful force in our society because of its ability to satisfy the appetite for consumption. Whether business is responsible for the pervasiveness of consumption as a social value, as Galbraith would suggest, is not clear. But it is clear that the environmental protection movement presents a challenge to private consumption, and therefore to a very important aspect of business activity.

Some thinkers argue that the environmental challenge to business is limited. For example, Norman Bowie, in his article "Money, Morality, and Motor Cars," argues that business's role should be limited to strict adherence to environmental laws and regulations. Business does not have, he argues, an obligation to protect environment over and above what is required by law. To expect business to do otherwise, to expect that business go beyond the law in its efforts to protect the environment, makes impossible demands on business and ignores the impact such activities have on profit.

Using automobile production as an analogy, Bowie claims that the moral requirement to prevent harm is satisfied by auto makers if they adhere to law and regulation. They could, it is true, make a safer car, but society has chosen to make a tradeoff in this area—cars that are less safe are also less expensive. Similarly, society has chosen to endure more pollution and pay less for products than to have less pollution and pay more. Society may decide differently in the future, but until that day comes, business has no special role to play in environmental protection.

Bowie continues, however, by pointing out that business has often acted improperly with regard to the environment in the political arena. Businesses have lobbied strongly against environmental laws and regulation. This is ethically unacceptable, Bowie claims, because it is unwarranted interference with the public's expression of its preferences. Thus, in a sense, business does have an obligation to the environment. But the obligation is not to interfere in the political arena rather than to exceed the requirements of environmental law and regulation.

W. Michael Hoffman expresses a very different view. He argues that business has obligations to protect the environment that go beyond the law. As he sees it, business should show moral leadership in this area, and not wait for government action. He also explores "ecological homocentrism," which claims that society, including business, ought to protect the environment solely because doing so prevents harm to human beings and human interests. He argues that a broader and deeper moral perspective is required, one that goes beyond self-interest and grants moral standing to the environment itself. Not to do so risks the loss of the very insight that grounds ethical concern for the environment in the first place.

In "Environmental Pollution and the Law," Leonard Boonin outlines two ways the law has tried to deal with environmental problems. The "common law" response makes use of traditional liability rules. Individuals who believe they have been harmed can sue for personal and property damage. But this approach, Boonin says, has serious limitations because it provides only a piecemeal response to environmental problems. A newer legislative approach focuses on prevention of harm, with compensation for injury playing only a subsidiary role. An advantage of this method is that it sets performance standards in cases in which actions by individual polluters only marginally increase risk of harm, with no clear threshold point at which demonstrable harm begins to take place. This makes it relatively easy for polluters to deny that their activities created harm and escape penalty under common law. But precise standards offer clearer guidelines as to acceptable conduct. Boonin notes that we also pay a serious price for the administrative-regulatory approach to pollution. Common law leaves individuals free to act as they choose as long as they are willing to accept the consequences, but the new regulatory approach restricts freedom of action, and makes individuals and companies accountable to regulators.

Larry Ruff's "The Economic Common Sense of Pollution" suggests that we should strive, not for no pollution, but for an "optimum" level of pollution at which the cost of further pollution abatement exceeds the benefits. The best way to regulate pollution control, Ruff argues, is to place a price on the right to pollute. The price would be set by a public body, and would allow anyone to pollute as long as he or she is willing to pay the price. Ruff argues that this would lead people to regulate their pollution in the most efficient possible way.

In "At the Shrine of Our Lady of Fatima" Mark Sagoff challenges the idea that environmental issues should be dealt with on purely economic grounds. The economic cost of pollution is only one of the factors to be considered, he says. The American people are not only consumers, they are also citizens, and their interests as citizens may be quite different than their interests as consumers. As consumers, we think about how to get the best deal for ourselves; as citizens our interests are wider. We think about the community as a whole and not just ourselves. For example, Sagoff points out that, as citizens, we may vote for a bottle bill because it helps the community, even though as consumers we hate the process of collecting and returning bottles. It is because we frequently have different interests as consumers and citizens that our society has a political as well as an economic agenda. And it is for this reason, Sagoff argues, that we should resist reducing all political issues to economic ones. Because our interests go beyond the economic, we cannot expect the market or cost-benefit analysis to answer all our political questions. This does not mean that Sagoff rejects cost-benefit analysis altogether. It is an excellent tool for deciding how to reach our goals, but it should not be used to set our goals. We want to achieve our political goals as efficiently as possible, but economic efficiency is a means rather than an end in itself.

In "The Pollution of Environmental Theory" Michael Silverstein argues that it is a mistake to think that economic growth is incompatible with a clean environment. This may have been true in the past, but, he says, in the future economic growth will presuppose sound environmental policies. Thus, traditional antimaterialistic and antigrowth environmentalism is an outdated ideology. The old ways of looking at the relation between the environment and economic growth need to be changed, and replaced with a new understanding of the nature of economic efficiency and its relation to environmental degradation. If this is right, then Sagoff's distinction between consumer and citizen may need to be redrawn. Perhaps the two are not as different as he suggests.

In the final paper in Chapter 11, Karen Blumenfeld uses a case analysis to discuss ethical issues surrounding internal investigations of situations that go beyond strict compliance with environmental regulations. She argues that in the case an auditor has a conflict between legitimate moral obligations. On the one hand, he has a duty to protect the public from possible environmental harm. On the other, he has a fiduciary duty to his employer not to disclose confidential information. She then proposes six tests to determine the circumstances under which the auditor's obligation to the public outweighs his obligations to his employer. These include: the potential environmental harm is significant; the auditor has exhausted all reasonable internal reporting channels; and the hazard is not on a reasonable timetable for remediation.

Determining whether a situation meets all six tests is not simple because environmental risks are open to alternative evaluations. Hence, there is no guarantee that reasonable people using the six tests would all arrive at the same conclusion. Nevertheless, Blumenfeld claims, the six tests offer the best way to judge highly complex ethical situations typical of the kind faced by those in the environmental field.

INTERNATIONAL BUSINESS

Multinational corporations are business organizations that maintain extensive operations in more than one country. Multinational business faces many of the same ethical issues as domestic business, but the fact that multinationals conduct business across national and cultural lines raises special problems. Legal and cultural standards may differ from culture to culture. Practices that are benign in the United States may be inappropriate or even unethical in other contexts. Because they are so large and widely dispersed, multinational corporations do not come under the complete control of any one government, and some fear that their interests diverge from those of both their home and host countries.

Extensive investment by multinational corporations can help the economies of developing nations, but such investment can have harmful effects as well. Multinational investment can lead to extensive dependence on foreign capital and technology, leaving the developing nation powerless and vulnerable. Many multinationals establish foreign operations to get cheap labor or to engage in hazardous production processes without the expense of conforming to U.S. health and safety and environmental regulations. The natural desire of multinational corporations to do business in a secure investment climate sometimes leads them to support authoritarian and repressive regimes. Multinational industry can stifle local enterprise and submerge the characteristic culture of the nations in which the industry operates. Finally, successful private enterprise does not always lead to the satisfaction of the needs of developing countries.

Richard De George suggests that some of the dilemmas that appear to face multinational corporations doing business in the Third World in fact arise from assuming that U.S. standards are universal moral standards. There are important differences in culture and values between First and Third World countries, De George believes, and these should be respected. In spite of these differences, however, De George believes that there are universal moral norms that can be applied across cultures, and he offers seven principles that might serve as guidelines for evaluating the actions of multinational corporations.

Several of the issues mentioned in the De George article are further developed by Thomas Donaldson in his "Moral Minimums for Multinationals." Donaldson concentrates his discussion on human rights. He proposes a series of ten fundamental international rights that include: the right to freedom of physical movement; the right to ownership of property; the right to nondiscriminatory treatment; the right to political participation; and the right to subsistence. He says that multinational corporations have a moral duty to avoid depriving persons of all ten of these rights. However, they should help protect from deprivation only six of the rights, for example, political participation and subsistence, and for none of the ten rights do they have a duty to aid those deprived of them by other institutions.

Donaldson says that although the list of rights he proposes provide a moral minimum for multinational corporations, something else is needed for managers to use in developing the implications of their own moral views. He suggests a moral algorithm for evaluating conflicts between ethical norms of a multinational's home and host country. The algorithm is a two part test of moral practices. In the first part the moral reasons underlying the practice are related to the host country's relative level of economic development; in the second part, the moral reasons underlying the practice are not related to the host country's level of economic development. Donaldson shows how the algorithm applies to a number of different examples. He does not claim that it eliminates the need for a general moral theory; rather its strength lies in its ability to uncover and clarify the implications of moral beliefs held by multinational managers.

In response to Donaldson, Manuel Velasquez questions whether multinational corporations have any moral obligations to contribute to the international common good. He argues that in a restricted but not insignificant portion of international transactions, corporations have no such obligations because, for instance, doing so will put them at a serious competitive disadvantage. He concludes that this shows the need for an international agency capable of forcing all multinationals to contribute to the common good.

In his second article in the chapter, Richard De George brings together some of the issues discussed by Donaldson and Velasquez in his analysis of business ethics in Russia and Eastern Europe. De George first presents an overview of the business and ethical climate in these countries, and then investigates several issues of business ethics from the point of view of their citizens. Finally, he asks what ethical obligations foreign firms have that wish to operate in these countries. He draws three main conclusions from his discussion. The first is that international business ethics cannot be an imposition of American business ethics. The second is that a company that wishes to act with integrity must have a set of values to which it adheres in all countries in which it operates, even in countries, like some of those in Eastern Europe, in which there is social and economic chaos. The third is that there is a need to adopt worldwide agreements and rules that make mutually advantageous trade possible and keep competition within ethically acceptable bounds.

Both De George and Velasquez call for international agreements to provide guidelines for ethical conduct for multinationals. Several of these agreements are already in place, as

William Frederick demonstrates in his article, "The Moral Authority of Transnational Moral Codes." Frederick examines the ethical guidelines for multinational corporations included in a number of international agreements and treaties. The guidelines, which often are not legally enforceable, attempt to influence the practices of multinationals in a number of different areas, such as consumer protection and environmental pollution. He notes that although many difficulties surround the acceptance and enforcement of these international agreements, it is possible to argue that they indicate the emergence of a transcultural corporate ethic.

BRIBERY

The next three articles in Chapter 12 examine a major ethical challenge faced by managers of multinationals abroad: the widespread occurrence of bribery and extortion. In the United States, bribery is illegal and almost universally regarded as unethical. But in some countries, claim U.S. managers, bribery is a way of life, necessary to conducting business. Is it morally permissible to bribe if bribery is a common practice in the culture in which you are doing business? What, really, is wrong with bribery?

Scott Turow explains that the essence of bribery is the attempt to corrupt a public official's impartial judgment, giving the briber an unfair advantage over others. Managers of multinationals who bribe to secure a contract are trying to "buy" the loyalty of foreign officials, loyalty that the officials actually owe to their public. It is easy to see that the practice of bribery is hostile to a free market system. In a free market system, companies compete to offer consumers the best product at the best price. Bribery shifts the terms of competition from quality and price to the size of the sum of money paid to a government official. Widespread bribery would make fair competition impossible. Bribery also injures the consumer, because the selection of an item on any basis other than quality and price often leads to the purchase of an inferior product.

In 1977 Congress passed the Foreign Corrupt Practices Act, which makes payments to foreign political officials to secure or retain business illegal. Its passage has been quite controversial. Although it is generally conceded that bribery is unethical, some argue that the act is an inappropriate response. Mark Pastin and Michael Hooker go so far as to claim that the act itself is immoral.

Pastin and Hooker argue on "end point" or utilitarian grounds that the act is wrong because it does not benefit the majority of the people it affects. In fact, they claim, the Foreign Corrupt Practices Act has serious and far-reaching negative consequences for American business, including loss of sales, loss of jobs, and a weakened ability to compete in foreign markets. Often, they suggest, the only way to secure a superior product for a client is to offer a larger bribe than a competing company which makes an inferior product. And a law forbidding American companies to offer bribes does not stop foreign officials from accepting bribes from non-American businesses.

Pastin and Hooker also offer a "rule assessment" or deontological argument against the act, suggesting that it places U.S. business in a conflict of obligations. By cutting into corporate profits, the act forces organizations to break their promise (1) to shareholders to maximize return on investment and (2) to employees to provide job security.

Robert Frederick believes that Hooker and Pastin's position is not persuasive and that the act has a firm ethical foundation. Accurate end-point, or utilitarian, assessment of the act, he points out, requires objective empirical evidence that Hooker and Pastin do not provide. Does the act really have a serious negative impact on U.S. firms' foreign operations? Frederick cites studies that claim it does not. He also points out that loss of business by U.S. firms is balanced by the gains for the country whose firm does get the business. This means there is no decrease in total utility when a U.S. firm fails to gain a contract, as Hooker and Pastin imply. From the perspective of rule assessment, Frederick argues, Hooker and Pastin's argument is also faulty. The obligation of U.S. corporations to provide jobs and make a profit for shareholders does not include furthering the interest of these groups by illegal or immoral means.

CHAPTER 10

THE CONSUMER

The Dependence Effect

John Kenneth Galbraith
Warburg Professor Emeritus of Economics, Harvard University

The theory of consumer demand, as it is now widely accepted, is based on two broad propositions, neither of them quite explicit but both extremely important for the present value system of economists. The first is that the urgency of wants does not diminish appreciably as more of them are satisfied or, to put the matter more precisely, to the extent that this happens it is not demonstrable and not a matter of any interest to economists or for economic policy. When man has satisfied his physical needs, then psychologically grounded desires take over. These can never be satisfied or, in any case, no progress can be proved. The concept of satiation has very little standing in economics. It is neither useful nor scientific to speculate on the comparative cravings of the stomach and the mind.

The second proposition is that wants originate in the personality of the consumer or, in any case, that they are given data for the economist. The latter's task is merely to seek their satisfaction. He has no need to inquire how these wants are formed. His function is sufficiently fulfilled by maximizing the goods that supply the wants.

The notion that wants do not become less urgent the more amply the individual is supplied is broadly repugnant to common sense. It is something to be believed only by those who wish to believe. Yet the conventional wisdom must be tackled on its own terrain. Intertemporal comparisons of an individual's state of mind do rest on doubtful grounds. Who can say for sure that the deprivation which afflicts him with hunger is more painful than the deprivation which afflicts him with envy of his neighbour's new car? In the time that has passed since he was poor his soul may have become subject to a new and deeper searing. And where a society is concerned, comparisons between marginal satisfactions when it is poor and those when it is affluent will involve not only the same individual at different times but different individuals at different

---

times. The scholar who wishes to believe that with increasing affluence there is no reduction in the urgency of desires and goods is not without points for debate. However plausible the case against him, it cannot be proved. In the defence of the conventional wisdom this amounts almost to invulnerability.

However, there is a flaw in the case. If the individual's wants are to be urgent they must be original with himself. They cannot be urgent if they must be contrived for him. And above all they must not be contrived by the process of production by which they are satisfied. For this means that the whole case for the urgency of production, based on the urgency of wants, falls to the ground. One cannot defend production as satisfying wants if that production creates the wants.

Were it so that man on arising each morning was assailed by demons which instilled in him a passion sometimes for silk shirts, sometimes for kitchenware, sometimes for chamber-pots, and sometimes for orange squash, there would be every reason to applaud the effort to find the goods, however odd, that quenched this flame. But should it be that his passion was the result of his first having cultivated the demons, and should it also be that his effort to allay it stirred the demons to ever greater and greater effort, there would be question as to how rational was his solution. Unless restrained by conventional attitudes, he might wonder if the solution lay with more goods or fewer demons.

So it is that if production creates the wants it seeks to satisfy, or if the wants emerge *pari passu* with the production, then the urgency of the wants can no longer be used to defend the urgency of the production. Production only fills a void that it has itself created.

The even more direct link between production and wants is provided by the institutions of modern advertising and salesmanship. These cannot be reconciled with the notion of independently determined desires, for their central function is to create desires—to bring into being wants that previously did not exist.[1] This is accomplished by the producer of the goods or at his behest. A broad empirical relationship exists between what is spent on production of consumers' goods and what is spent in synthesizing the desires for that production. A new consumer product must be introduced with a suitable advertising campaign to arouse an interest in it. The path for an expansion of output must be paved by a suitable expansion in the advertising budget. Outlays for the manufacturing of a product are not more important in the strategy of modern business enterprise than outlays for the manufacturing of demand for the product. None of this is novel. All would be regarded as elementary by the most retarded student in the nation's most primitive school of business administration. The cost of this want formation is formidable. In 1956 total advertising expenditure—though, as noted, not all of it may be assigned to the synthesis of wants—amounted to about ten thousand million dollars. For some years it had been increasing at a rate in excess of a thousand million dollars a year. Obviously, such outlays must be integrated with the theory of consumer demand. They are too big to be ignored.

But such integration means recognizing that wants are dependent on production. It accords to the producer the function both of making the goods and of making the desires for them. It recognizes that production, not only passively through emulation, but actively through advertising and related activities, creates the wants it seeks to satisfy.

The businessman and the lay reader will be puzzled over the emphasis which I give to a seemingly obvious point. The point is indeed obvious. But it is one which, to a singular degree, economists have resisted. They have sensed, as the layman does not, the damage to established ideas which lurks in these relationships. As a result, incredibly, they have closed their eyes (and ears) to the most obtrusive of all economic phenomena, namely modern want creation.

This is not to say that the evidence affirming the dependence of wants on advertising has been entirely ignored. It is one reason why advertising has so long been regarded with such uneasiness by economists. Here is something which cannot be accommodated easily to existing theory. More previous scholars have speculated on the urgency of desires which are so obviously the fruit of such expensively contrived campaigns for popular attention. Is a new breakfast cereal or detergent so much wanted if so much must be spent to compel in the consumer the sense of want? But there has been little tendency to go on to examine the implications of this for the theory of consumer demand and even less for the importance of production and productive efficiency. These have remained sacrosanct. More often the uneasiness has been manifested in a general disapproval of advertising and advertising men, leading to the occasional suggestion that they shouldn't exist. Such suggestions have usually been ill received.

And so the notion of independently determined wants still survives. In the face of all the forces of modern salesmanship it still rules, almost undefiled, in the textbooks. And it still remains the economist's mission—and on few matters is the pedagogy so firm—to seek unquestioningly the means for filling these wants. This being so, production remains of prime urgency. We have here, perhaps, the ultimate triumph of the conventional wisdom in its resistance to the evidence of the eyes. To equal it one must imagine a humanitarian who was long ago persuaded of the grievous shortage of hospital facilities in the town. He continues to importune the passers-by for money for more beds and refuses to notice that the town doctor is deftly knocking over pedestrians with his car to keep up the occupancy.

And in unravelling the complex we should always be careful not to overlook the obvious. The fact that wants can be synthesized by advertising, catalysed by salesmanship, and shaped by the discreet manipulations of the persuaders shows that they are not very urgent. A man who is hungry need never be told of his need for food. If he is inspired by his appetite, he is immune to the influence of Messrs. Batten, Barton, Durstine and Osborn. The latter are effective only with those who are so far removed from physical want that they do not already know what they want. In this state alone men are open to persuasion.

The general conclusion of these pages is of such importance for this essay that it had perhaps best be put with some formality. As a society becomes increasingly affluent, wants are increasingly created by the process by which they are satisfied. This may operate passively. Increases in consumption, the counterpart of increases in production, act by suggestion or emulation to create wants. Or producers may proceed actively to create wants through advertising and salesmanship. Wants thus come to depend on output. In technical terms it can no longer be assumed that welfare is greater at an all-round higher level of production than at a lower one. It may be the same. The higher level of production has, merely, a higher level of want creation necessitating a higher level of want satisfaction. There will be frequent occasion to refer to the way wants depend on the process by which they are satisfied. It will be convenient to call it the Dependence Effect.

The final problem of the productive society is what it produces. This manifests itself in an implacable tendency to provide an opulent supply of some things and a niggardly yield of others. This disparity carries to the point where it is a cause of social discomfort and social unhealth. The line which divides our area of wealth from our area of poverty is roughly that which divides privately produced and marketed goods and services from publicly rendered services. Our wealth in the first is not only in startling contrast with the meagerness of the latter, but our wealth in privately produced goods is, to a marked degree, the cause of crisis in the supply of public services. For we have failed to see the importance, indeed the urgent need, of maintaining a balance between the two.

This disparity between our flow of private and public goods and services is no matter of subjective judgment. On the contrary, it is the source of the most extensive comment which only stops short of the direct contrast being made here. In the years following World War II, the papers of any major city—those of New York were an excellent example—told daily of the shortages and shortcomings in the elementary municipal and metropolitan services. The schools were old and overcrowded. The police force was under strength and underpaid. The parks and playgrounds were insufficient. Streets and empty lots were filthy, and the sanitation staff was under-equipped and in need of men. Access to the city by those who work there was uncertain and painful and becoming more so. Internal transportation was overcrowded, unhealthful, and dirty. So was the air. Parking on the streets had to be prohibited, and there was no space elsewhere. These deficiencies were not in new and novel services but in old and established ones. Cities have long swept their streets, helped their people move around, educated them, kept order, and provided horse rails for vehicles which sought to pause. That their residents should have a non-toxic supply of air suggests no revolutionary dalliance with socialism.

The contrast was and remains evident not alone to those who read. The family which takes its mauve and cerise, air-conditioned, power-steered, and power-braked car out for a tour passes through cities that are badly paved, made hideous by litter, blighted buildings, billboards, and posts for wires that should long since have been put underground. They pass on into a countryside that has been rendered largely invisible by commercial art. (The goods which the latter advertise have an absolute priority in our value system. Such aesthetic considerations as a view of the countryside accordingly come second. On such matters we are consistent.) They picnic on exquisitely packaged food from a portable icebox by a polluted stream and go on to spend the night at a park which is a menace to public health and morals. Just before dozing off on an air-mattress, beneath a nylon tent, amid the stench of decaying refuse, they may reflect vaguely on the curious unevenness of their blessings. Is this, indeed, the American genius?

The case for social balance has, so far, been put negatively. Failure to keep public services in minimal relation to private production and use of goods is a cause of social disorder or impairs economic performance. The matter may now be put affirmatively. By failing to exploit the opportunity to expand public production we are missing opportunities for enjoyment which otherwise we might have had. Presumably a community can be as well rewarded by buying better schools or better parks as by buying bigger cars. By concentrating on the latter rather than the former it is failing to maximize its satisfactions. As with schools in the community, so with public services over the country at large. It is scarcely sensible that we should satisfy our wants in private goods with reckless abundance, while in the case of public goods, on the evidence of the eye, we practice extreme self-denial. So, far from systematically exploiting the opportunities to derive use and pleasure from these services, we do not supply what would keep us out of trouble.

The conventional wisdom holds that the community, large or small, makes a decision as to how much it will devote to its public services. This decision is arrived at by democratic process. Subject to the imperfections and uncertainties of democracy, people decide how much of their private income and goods they will surrender in order to have public services of which they are in greater need. Thus there is a balance, however rough, in the enjoyments to be had from private goods and services and those rendered by public authority.

It will be obvious, however, that this view depends on the notion of independently determined consumer wants. In such a world one could with some reason defend the doctrine that the consumer, as a voter, makes an independent choice between public and private goods. But given the dependence effect—given that consumer wants are created by the process by which they are satisfied—the consumer makes no such choice. He is subject to the forces of advertising and emulation by which production creates its own demand. Advertising operates exclusively, and emulation mainly, on behalf of privately produced goods and services.[2] Since management and emulative effects operate on behalf of private production, public services will have an inherent tendency to lag behind. Car demand which is expensively synthesized will inevitably have a much larger claim on income than parks or public health or even roads where no such influence operates. The engines of mass communication, in their highest state of development, assail the eyes and ears of the community on behalf of more beer but not of more schools. Even in the conventional wisdom it will scarcely be contended that this leads to an equal choice between the two.

The competition is especially unequal for new products and services. Every corner of the public psyche is canvassed by some of the nation's most talented citizens to see if the desire for some merchantable product can be cultivated. No similar process operates on behalf of the nonmerchantable services of the state. Indeed, while we take the cultivation of new private wants for granted we would be measurably shocked to see it applied to public services. The scientist or engineer or advertising man who devotes himself to developing a new carburetor, cleanser, or depilatory for which the public recognizes no need and will feel none until an advertising campaign arouses it, is one of the valued members of our society. A politician or a public servant who dreams up a new public service is a wastrel. Few public offenses are more reprehensible.

So much for the influences which operate on the decision between public and private production. The calm decision between public and private consumption pictured by the conventional wisdom is, in fact, a remarkable example of the error which arises from viewing social behavior out of context. The inherent tendency will always be for public services to fall behind private production. We have here the first of the causes of social imbalance.

NOTES

1. Advertising is not a simple phenomenon. It is also important in competitive strategy and want creation is, ordinarily, a complementary result of efforts to shift the demand curve of the individual firm at the expense of others or (less importantly, I think) to change its shape by increasing the degree of product differentiation. Some of the failure of economists to identify advertising with want creation may be attributed to the undue attention that its use in purely competitive strategy has attracted. It should be noted, however, that the competitive manipulation of consumer desire is only possible, at least on any appreciable scale, when such need is not strongly felt.
2. Emulation does operate between communities. A new school or a new highway in one community does exert pressure on others to remain abreast. However, as compared with the pervasive effects of emulation in extending the demand for privately produced consumers' goods there will be agreement, I think, that this intercommunity effect is probably small.

The *Non Sequitur* of the "Dependence Effect"

F. A. von Hayek
Former Professor Emeritus of Economics, University of Chicago and University of Freiburg

For well over a hundred years the critics of the free enterprise system have resorted to the argument that if production were only organized rationally, there would be no economic problem. Rather than face the problem which scarcity creates, socialist reformers have tended to deny that scarcity existed. Ever since the Saint-Simonians their contention has been that the problem of production has been solved and only the problem of distribution remains. However absurd this contention must appear to us with respect to the time when it was first advanced, it still has some persuasive power when repeated with reference to the present.

The latest form of this old contention is expounded in *The Affluent Society* by Professor J. K. Galbraith. He attempts to demonstrate that in our affluent society the important private needs are already satisfied and the urgent need is therefore no longer a further expansion of the output of commodities but an increase of those services which are supplied (and presumably can be supplied only) by government. Though this book has been extensively discussed since its publication in 1958, its central thesis still requires some further examination.

I believe the author would agree that his argument turns upon the "Dependence Effect" [p. 407 of this book]. The argument of this chapter starts from the assertion that a great part of the wants which are still unsatisfied in modern society are not wants which would be experienced spontaneously by the individual if left to himself, but are wants which are created by the process by which they are

Excerpted from "The *Non Sequitur* of the 'Dependence Effect' " by F.A. von Hayek, *Southern Economic Journal* (April 1961).

satisfied. It is then represented as self-evident that for this reason such wants cannot be urgent or important. This crucial conclusion appears to be a complete *non sequitur* and it would seem that with it the whole argument of the book collapses.

The first part of the argument is of course perfectly true: we would not desire any of the amenities of civilization—or even of the most primitive culture—if we did not live in a society in which others provide them. The innate wants are probably confined to food, shelter, and sex. All the rest we learn to desire because we see others enjoying various things. To say that a desire is not important because it is not innate is to say that the whole cultural achievement of man is not important.

This cultural origin of practically all the needs of civilized life must of course not be confused with the fact that there are some desires which aim, not as a satisfaction derived directly from the use of an object, but only from the status which its consumption is expected to confer. In a passage which Professor Galbraith quotes, Lord Keynes seems to treat the latter sort of Veblenesque conspicuous consumption as the only alternative "to those needs which are absolute in the sense that we feel them whatever the situation of our fellow human beings may be." If the latter phrase is interpreted to exclude all the needs for goods which are felt only because these goods are known to be produced, these two Keynesian classes describe of course only extreme types of wants, but disregard the overwhelming majority of goods on which civilized life rests. Very few needs indeed are "absolute" in the sense that they are independent of social environment or of the example of others, and that their satisfaction is an indispensable condition for the preservation of the individual or of the species. Most needs which make us act are needs for things which only civilization teaches us to exist at all, and these things are wanted by us because they produce feelings or emotions which we would not know if it were not for our cultural inheritance. Are not in this sense probably all our esthetic feelings "acquired tastes"?

How complete a *non sequitur* Professor Galbraith's conclusion represents is seen most clearly if we apply the argument to any product of the arts, be it music, painting, or literature. If the fact that people would not feel the need for something if it were not produced did prove that such products are of small value, all those highest products of human endeavor would be of small value. Professor Galbraith's argument could be easily employed without any change of the essential terms, to demonstrate the worthlessness of literature or any other form of art. Surely an individual's want for literature is not original with himself in the sense that he would experience it if literature were not produced. Does this then mean that the production of literature cannot be defended as satisfying a want because it is only the production which provokes the demand? In this, as in the case of all cultural needs, it is unquestionably, in Professor Galbraith's words, "the process of satisfying the wants that creates the wants." There have never been "independently determined desires for" literature before literature has been produced and books certainly do not serve the "simple mode of enjoyment which requires no previous conditioning of the consumer." Clearly my taste for the novels of Jane Austen or Anthony Trollope or C. P. Snow is not "original with myself." But is it not rather absurd to conclude from this that it is less important than, say, the need for education? Public education indeed seems to regard it as one of its tasks to instill a taste for literature in the young and even employs producers of literature for that purpose. Is this want creation by the producer reprehensible? Or does the fact that some of the pupils may possess a taste for poetry only because of the efforts of their teachers prove that since "it does not arise in spontaneous consumer need and the demand would not exist were it not contrived, its utility or urgency, ex contrivance, is zero?"

The appearance that the conclusions follow from the admitted facts is made possible by an obscurity of the wording of the argument with respect to which it is difficult to know whether the author is himself the victim of a confusion or whether he skillfully uses ambiguous terms to make the conclusion appear plausible. The obscurity concerns the implied assertion that the wants of the consumers are determined by the producers. Professor Galbraith avoids in this connection any terms as crude and definite as "determine." The expressions he employs, such as that wants are "dependent on" or the "fruits of" production, or that "production creates the wants" do, of course, suggest determination but avoid saying so in plain terms. After what has already been said it is of course obvious that the knowledge of what is being produced is one of the many factors on which it depends what people will want. It would scarcely be an exaggeration to say that contemporary man, in all fields where he has not yet formed firm habits, tends to find out what he wants by looking at what his neighbours do and at various displays of goods (physical or in catalogues or advertisements) and then choosing what he likes best.

In this sense the tastes of man, as is also true of his opinions and beliefs and indeed much of his personality, are shaped in a great measure by his cultural environment. But though in some contexts it would perhaps be legitimate to express this by a phrase like "production creates the wants," the circumstances mentioned would clearly not justify the contention that particular producers can deliberately determine the wants of particular consumers. The efforts of all producers will certainly be directed towards that end: but how far any individual producer will succeed will depend not only on what he does but also on what the others do and on a great many other influences operating upon the consumer. The joint but uncoordinated efforts of the producers merely create one element of the environment by which the wants of the consumers are shaped. It is because each individual producer thinks that the consumers can be persuaded to like his products that he endeavours to influence them. But though this effort is part of the influences which shape consumers' tastes, no producer can in any real sense "determine" them. This, however, is clearly implied in such statements as that wants are "both passively and deliberately the fruits of the process by which they are satisfied." If the producer could in fact deliberately determine what the consumers will want, Professor Galbraith's conclusions would have some validity. But though this is skillfully suggested, it is nowhere made credible, and could hardly be made credible because it is not true. Though the range of choice open to the consumers is the joint result of, among other things, the efforts of all producers who vie with each other in making their respective products appear more attractive than those of their competitors, every particular consumer still has the choice between all those different offers.

A fuller examination of this process would, of course, have to consider how, after the efforts of some producers have actually swayed some consumers, it becomes the example of the various consumers thus persuaded which will influence the remaining consumers. This can be mentioned here only to emphasize that even if each consumer were exposed to pressure of only one producer, the harmful effects which are apprehended from this would soon be offset by the much more powerful example of his fellows. It is of course fashionable to treat this influence of the example of others (or, what comes to the same thing, the learning from the experience made by others) as if it amounted all to an attempt of keeping up with the Joneses and for that reason was to be regarded as detrimental. It seems to me that not only the importance of this factor is usually greatly exaggerated but also that it is not really relevant to Professor Galbraith's main thesis. But it might be worthwhile briefly to ask what, assuming that some expenditure were actually determined solely by a desire of keeping up with the Joneses, that would really prove? At least in Europe we used to be familiar with a type of persons who often denied themselves even enough food in order to maintain an appearance of respectability or gentility in dress and style of life. We may regard this as a misguided effort, but surely it would not prove that the income of such persons was larger than they knew how to use wisely. That the appearance of success, or wealth, may to some people seem more important than many other needs, does in no way prove that the needs they sacrifice to the former are unimportant. In the same way, even though people are often persuaded to spend unwisely, this surely is no evidence that they do not still have important unsatisfied needs.

Professor Galbraith's attempt to give an apparent scientific proof for the contention that the need for the production of more commodities has greatly decreased seems to me to have broken down completely. With it goes the claim to have produced a valid argument which justifies the use of coercion to make people employ their income for those purposes of which he approves. It is not to be denied that there is some originality in this latest version of the old socialist argument. For over a hundred years we have been exhorted to embrace socialism because it would give us more goods. Since it has so lamentably failed to achieve this where it has been tried, we are now urged to adopt it because more goods after all are not important. The aim is still progressively to increase the share of the resources whose use is determined by political authority and the coercion of any dissenting minority. It is not surprising, therefore, that Professor Galbraith's thesis has been most enthusiastically received by the intellectuals of the British Labour Party where his influence bids fair to displace that of the late Lord Keynes. It is more curious that in this country it is not recognized as an outright socialist argument and often seems to appeal to people on the opposite end of the political spectrum. But this is probably only another instance of the familiar fact that on these matters the extremes frequently meet.

Marketing Ethics: Some Dimensions of the Challenge

Paul F. Camenisch
Professor of Religious Studies, DePaul University

The tension between the imperatives of economic survival in the competitive marketplace and ethics is a very real one for many individuals and corporations. Any such tensions can be magnified and complicated in marketing since the marketing firm must not only survive in its own market, but must, as one factor in that survival, deal with the question of what it must do, or what its clients *think* it must do to ensure the clients' survival in their marketplaces. Practitioners must vividly portray these complex and difficult situations for academic ethicists from time to time, lest the ethical analysis and recommendations offered by the latter lose all touch with the harsh realities business people actually face.

At the same time, the integrity of the ethicists' own profession requires that they keep pressing practitioners not to relax the tension they feel by abandoning ethics and capitulating to the demands of the marketplace. Confronting practitioners with hard questions about such matters is not, or certainly need not be, the attack of hostile outsiders determined to expose the soft underbelly of business to a critical public. It can also be the challenge of the loyalist who believes that businesspersons are often sufficiently sensitive to such issues and that business can be sufficiently creative to find ways to be simultaneously successful and ethical.

One way to press such a concern about ethics in business, and specifically in marketing is by holding up the issue of the social responsibility of business, which I understand to refer to the doing of societal good unrelated or minimally related to the business activity in view. It is in some ways a kind of "add-on" ethic for business. Following Milton Friedman many business persons dismiss such social responsibility as an inappropriate add-on for business people and organizations operating in the competitive marketplace. They often maintain not that business does no social good, but that business that does its business well is already performing a number of positive services to society and its members through the creation of jobs, the paying of taxes, and the generating of beneficial and/or desired products and services. Additional social responsibility is simply seen as excessive and inappropriate. While I think the issue of corporate social responsibility cannot be dismissed this easily, I will here focus on another dimension of the business-society relationship by raising the question of the ethics of business activity itself, the question of the ethics which is in some sense internal to that activity. In our current case, that means

Found in *Journal of Business Ethics* 10; 245–248, 1991.

the ethic that is internal to marketing. Here we deal not with some add-on to business but with an element integral to business activity.

One can begin thinking about an ethic internal to a given kind of activity by asking what the goal or purpose of that activity is. By this I mean not the goals or purposes of the various parties engaged in that activity; those are almost unlimited in their variety. I mean rather the purpose or goal of the activity itself, specifically its *societal* purpose, the reason that society permits, encourages, even facilitates such activity.

The goals of marketing have been variously stated and I will not here conclusively answer the question of which is its definitive goal. The goal perhaps most often assumed and supported by common sense observation of the business enterprise is that marketing's goal is to increase the company's profits by increasing the sales of its product. Some students of business and marketing, either because they fear that a focus on profit will give too much of a toehold to the critic, or because they know a company's profits depend on many factors other than marketing, prefer to see the goal of marketing as creating a market, or creating a customer. But to this amateur observer such ideas do not really change the thrust of the first answer. They only buffer it by putting another layer between the activity and its ultimate goal. Why does a company want to create a market except to increase its sales? And why create a customer except to buy its products or services?

However put, such answers may be more or less adequate when marketing is viewed from the side of the marketer. But marketing is a societal enterprise. It occurs in society, with society's permission and support, and purportedly, in part for society's benefit. Presumably it is therefore to some extent subject to the moral regulations and expectations society and potential customers attach to it.

But what is marketing's purpose when seen from other perspectives, specifically those of the larger society and of the customer? These two perspectives are not identical. But given that all of us are customers in much of our lives, this perspective represents the larger society better than does the perspective of businesspersons who represent only a portion of the population.

To speak of the goal of marketing from this perspective we must go beyond the simple idea of moving the product or increasing sales, since these as such serve the larger society only indirectly at best. One might attempt to bring together the goals of marketing as seen by business and as seen by the customer or the larger society by suggesting that the goal of responsible marketing is to inform the customer about the product so that sales will increase. This goal of informing the potential customer can be brought one step closer to specifically moral considerations by drawing on philosopher Richard DeGeorge and others who have suggested that transactions are more likely to be morally defensible if both parties enter it freely and fully informed. Assuming that marketing and marketers want to be part of morally defensible transactions, one might then say that viewed societally, the goal of marketing should be to increase the likelihood and frequency of free and informed transactions in the marketplace. Or, to put it negatively, marketing ought not to decrease the likelihood of such free and informed market transactions.

The information requirement is easy enough to state, even if determining what constitutes being fully informed is not. Unfortunately we are also familiar with the various ways it can be compromised. Blatant untruths would seem to be relatively rare in current advertising. But partial truths, the misleading embellishing of the facts (the fixed focus camera becomes "focus free," the unsized bathrobe becomes "one-size-fits-all"), propositions intentionally implied to be true but not actually stated, still abound. Here we meet a variety of unresolved and perhaps unresolvable matters: How much hard information do customers want and deserve? How much of the relevant information are marketers obligated to provide and how much should potential customers be left to seek out on their own? In planning advertising so as not to mislead the public, are marketers to envision the average citizen, however that elusive will 'o the wisp is defined, or the especially vulnerable or gullible citizen—the child, the aged, the simple-minded? How much of the policing of advertising should be taken on by the government and how much left up to the industry.

But in spite of these and related questions, the most complex part of the problem of morally defensible transactions probably has to do with the question of freedom. Clear, honest information relevant to the goods or services being marketed is almost certain to enhance the potential customer's freedom in the transaction, or at least it will not diminish that freedom. But except for the highly technical information aimed at limited markets such as stereophiles, and price advertising of grocery specials and automobile deals, very little of marketing has to do with hard information about the product. Any student of marketing knows that much of contemporary marketing consists of techniques which can be used to "hook" the potential customer on the product in a way that potentially diminishes clear, rational decision-making about the product or service being offered. These of course include enhancing the symbolic value of products by associating them with celebrities, including them in sexually provocative advertising campaigns, linking them with deeply held values and commitments, or presenting them as solutions to widely shared insecurities and fears. This is not to say that all puffery is inappropriate. But it is to say that the lines between legitimate puffery, distortion, deception and the psychological "hooking" of the potential customer are not easy to draw, and that the more the interaction is cluttered by irrelevant "information," the more likely the seller is trying to prevent a fully informed and free decision by the customer.

Of course some will dismiss this goal of marketing as the recommendation of a well-meaning but idealistic academician. But before doing that, one should consult that almost perennial final appeal of the defender of the marketplace, Adam Smith. The market he was willing to defend is one in which there is no fraud or coercion and in which all participants are adequately informed about the transaction. Of course we will not always agree on what constitutes adequate information. But here we are more interested in the principle of adequate information for the participant than we are in the details of definition or the mechanics of enforcement.

But perhaps most decisive for the argument being made here is the point made by many marketers that the marketplace is not turned into a moral reality only by moral considerations brought to it from the outside—the moral convictions of the various participants, or the societal guidelines established for its conduct. Rather, the marketplace is itself already a moral as well as an economic mechanism even prior to any externally imposed moral requirements. There are moral constraints built into the very dynamics through which marketing works. For example, contemporary marketing practitioners often argue that dishonest marketing will be unsuccessful marketing, that the market will weed out those who violate the common morality. I am not entirely convinced that that is true, at least in the short run. Products that conspicuously and almost immediately fail to perform have been rejected by the public in spite of aggressive and clever marketing campaigns. But that is a very limited category of test cases. Increasingly we deal more in very complex products and services whose performance, especially long-run performance, and potential negative impacts are not easily assessed by the layperson. Just what sort of performance level, length of service, and maintenance and repair costs are reasonable for such products as modern automobiles, or the electronic products which now flood our lives? What are the truly significant potential harms of the countless chemical products from pharmaceuticals to fertilizers we now scatter freely through our lives and our environment? These are much more complex judgements than whether the miracle knife advertised on television can slice both tin cans and ripe tomatoes in that order with equal aplomb, or whether the new copier really does produce X copies per minute with greater clarity than the old machine. The variety and complexity of products most of us now purchase in the consumer society mean that virtually no unassisted layperson can make truly informed rational decisions about such purchases. The question then is whether marketing will be an ally or an obstacle in our making such decisions. Where it is the latter it is clearly morally indefensible on the criteria suggested here. But even if marketing is merely neutral in terms of its impact on the freedom and informed character of the transaction, it is not clear how one would justify the increase it generates in the ultimate cost of the product.

There is another set of concerns which are an element in the issues raised above, but which also have a life of their own in the discussion of advertising ethics. These concerns arise in relation to advertising that critics see as appealing to our baser, darker, less admirable side—our penchant towards violence, exploitative sex, and the desire to control and manipulate other persons. The usual defense of such advertising is that marketers here are simply offering us what we want, whether in the product or service offered, or in the marketing which sells it. Such a defense is backed by the claim that they have discovered what we want both by experience and by marketing research through surveys and focus groups. But given the more than 100 billion dollars poured annually into advertising and the shaping of the consumer's view of the world, it should hardly surprise us that advertisers find in the minds and psyches of many consumers what they have been helping put there for decades. It is no trick to pull a rabbit from a hat as long as one chooses the hat into which one has previously put the rabbit. Nor are advertisers cleared of responsibility for such advertising even if this baser side is rooted in something other than prior marketing efforts, which it no doubt is. The question still remains whether marketing and its clients should not only exploit that side of us for the sake of sales, but legitimate it and give it respectable, public standing by making it seem to be not only a natural and universal, but even the dominant dimension of the human self.

Of course if these questions are to be answered and the answers then enforced by agencies outside the marketing enterprise, we encounter the very complex and troubling issues of censorship in a free society. It is much to be preferred for everyone's sake that marketers and their clients raise these questions in a serious manner that can, where indicated, lead to self-regulation. This is most likely to happen if they look at these issues not just from the perspective of business, but as responsible citizens of a society in which they, their children, families and friends must also join with the rest of us in building and sustaining liveable, humane communities.

This raises the issue, met by many occupational and professional groups, of how we relate our work or our professional roles to our other roles in the society—our roles as responsible citizens, as members of communities responsible for the raising and moral formation of children, as members of religious communities and other voluntary associations. Do these other dimensions of our selves figure into our reflections on appropriate marketplace activity? If so, then economic survival, whether individual or corporate, cannot be the only, or even the last and decisive consideration. Or do we recommend a compartmentalization, a walling off of these various roles from each other that denies the marketer a consistency, an integrity among the various things she is and does? Little need be said here about the individual and societal pathologies that result from such an approach. The only viable alternative seems to be a proper vision of the world which subordinates marketing to business, and business to the goals and purposes of the larger society, so that the tensions among these and the other spheres of one's life are reduced to a minimum and one can fulfill one's various roles with a sense of personal integrity.

My focus has been on the possible moral problems posed by contemporary marketing. That is not because there is no positive case to be made for marketing. It rather reflects my assigned task and the fact that the interesting ethical discussions occur there rather than around the positive side of advertising, such as its alerting us to the availability of new products, the helpful information it does sometimes convey, and the possible reduction in price resulting from the larger volume of sales generated.

It would be an impossible and a pointless task to attempt a cost/benefit analysis on the basis of the above considerations to decide if advertising as a whole is morally defensible. It should be neither impossible nor pointless to do such a calculus about some specific forms of advertising for those who are prepared to acknowledge that marketing must be seen in the context of the larger society, of the sorts of human communities we are trying to build and of the sorts of persons we are trying to become.

The Ethics of Marketing: Nestle's Infant Formula

James E. Post
Professor of Management & Public Policy, Boston University

INTRODUCTION

Among the many different types of dilemmas faced by multinational enterprises are those related to its marketing of consumer products. It has now become apparent that the marketing of First World foods in Third World nations poses a special type of concern to the populations and governments of host nations, and to the would-be marketers themselves. While there are a number of products that one can cite as illustrative of the generic issue, none has so sharply and clearly defined it as the controversy surrounding the marketing and promotion of infant formula in the developing world.

My perspective on the infant formula controversy, industry, and on Nestle in particular, is derived from more than a decade of research. In addition to field research on infant formula marketing in Latin America, Africa, and Southern Asia, I have served as a consultant to the World Health Organization (WHO) in the development of the international marketing code, and testified at congressional and United States Senate hearings on these issues. Most recently, it has included about 18 months of service on the Nestle Infant Formula Audit Commission, which was created to monitor the company's compliance with marketing policies that were drafted for the purpose of implementing the WHO Code.

Rest assured, this is no apologia for Nestle. I know that some of their managers disagree with my interpretation of the evidence. That troubles me little, for I cannot think of an ethical dilemma that does not breed some disagreement among caring participants. Were it otherwise, I doubt it could be called a dilemma. Among the various types of ethical dilemmas confronting the managers of multinational enterprises (MNEs) are those tied to the introduction of products developed and used in one social environment into a significantly different environment. I prefer to term this the introduction of First World Products in Third World Markets.

The infant formula situation involves a product which is not defective in itself. This distinguishes it from such cases as the dumping of products which are unsafe or deemed unacceptable for sale in the United States, but are accepted for sale in another nation (e.g., Tris-treated sleepwear).

Infant formula is also not harmful to the consumer (user) when used properly under appropriate conditions. This distinguishes it from products such as tobacco, which are, in the view of most health professionals, per se dangerous to all users.

Infant formula is the *definitive* example, however, of a First World product which is safe when used properly, but which is *demanding*. That is, when risk conditions are present, it can be—and is—potentially harmful to users.

The fundamental ethical dilemma for MNE managers, then, is whether such a product can be marketed when it cannot be guaranteed, or reasonably expected, that it will be used by people who meet the minimum conditions necessary for safe use.

EVOLUTION OF A PUBLIC ISSUE

The criticism of the infant formula manufacturers for their aggressive marketing behavior in developing nations became a serious issue in 1970. Prior to that time, individual physicians and health workers had criticized promotional practices, but there was nothing to suggest an organized campaign of criticism. In 1970, however, the Protein-Calorie Advi-

---

Excerpted from "Ethical Dilemmas of Multinational Enterprise: An Analysis of Nestle's Traumatic Experience with the Infant Formula Controversy" by James E. Post, in *Ethics and the Multinational Enterprise* edited by W. Michael Hoffmann, Ann E. Lange, and David A. Fedo (Lanham, MD: University Press of America, 1986).

sory Group (PAG) of the United Nations held a meeting in Bogota to discuss the problem of infant malnutrition and disease in developing nations. Participants pointed a finger of blame at the industry, charging that it pushed its products to mothers, many of whom lived in circumstances that made the use of such products a highly risky adventure. First, infant formula must be sold in powdered form in tropical environments, requiring that the mother mix the powder with locally available water. When water supplies are of poor quality, as so often is the case in the developing nations, infants are exposed to disease. Second, since the product must be mixed, preparation instructions are important, and mothers must be able to read. Unfortunately, the rate of illiteracy is very high in many developing nations. Thirdly, since infant formulas are relatively expensive to purchase, there is a temptation to overdilute the powder with water. This effort to "stretch" its uses enables the mother to go a few extra days without buying a new supply. Unfortunately, overdiluted formula preparations provide very poor nutrition to the baby. Thus mothers who came to the health clinics with malnourished babies often reported that a five day supply of formula had been stretched to ten days or more. Having decided to bottlefeed their babies in order to improve their chances for a healthy life, many mothers discovered to their horror that they had actually been starving their little ones. Because corporate advertising by the infant formula companies had promoted the idea that bottlefeeding was better than breastfeeding, a view with which doctors disagreed, there was a sharp condemnation of the industry and its behavior at the Bogota meeting.

Management scholars now understand that public issues often proceed through a predictable series of phases in their evolution. Some refer to this as the "public issue life cycle," modelled after the product life cycle described in marketing research. The public issue life cycle can be thought of as a measure of continuing public concern about an underlying problem.

Phase I of the issue life cycle involved rising awareness and sensitivity to the facts of the issue. In the infant formula controversy, this phase began with the PAG Meeting in 1970 and continued for several years. An important element in the process of rising awareness was the activity of journalist Peter Muller who, with support from the British charity group, War on Want, travelled to Africa in the early 1970s to study allegations of marketing abuses. Muller wrote several articles and a pamphlet which War on Want published in 1974 under the title, *The Baby Killer.* These publications began to draw the attention of a broader public to the problem of sick and dying children, and the connection between commercial practices and this tragedy.

Because Nestle was, and still is, the industry's largest producer and seller of infant formula products, Muller encountered many examples of Nestle advertising and promotional practices in Africa. Indeed, Nestle employees were willing to speak with Muller, while those of other companies were often much less willing. Not surprisingly, then, *The Baby Killer* pamphlet included Nestle actions as examples of unethical industry behavior. This became very important, because a Swiss public action group, Third World Action Group, reprinted the Muller pamphlet in Switzerland under the new title, *Nestle Kills Babies!*

Nestle immediately sued the group for defamation, and in 1975 the case came to trial in Switzerland. Because the trial involved several hearings, with experts from developing nations brought in to testify, the media began to show increasing interest in the story. It became quite clear that although the trial involved only Nestle and the defendants, the entire infant formula industry was being examined and criticized for their actions in the developing nations. Thus, the trial was a turning point in two important ways. First, public interest in the issue expanded greatly as the newspaper stories began to carry the details of what one doctor called "commerciogenic malnutrition"—malnutrition brought about because of corporate commercial practices. Second, the infant formula industry began to respond as an industry, having formed an international association, known as the International Council of Infant Foods Industries (ICIFI). The council, whose existence was announced in Switzerland at the time of the trial, made an immediate effort to develop an international code of marketing which addressed some of the most criticized marketing practices. In this Phase II of the life cycle, both the critics, the media, and the industry recognized that the issue had become an important political matter, as well as a public health concern.

Between 1975 and 1978, the infant formula controversy became increasingly politicized. The media in Europe and the United States paid increasing attention to the conflict. Each newspaper or magazine story brought about more awareness in the general public. The critics highlighted the terrible tragedy of dying and sick children, while the companies, including Nestle, tried to respond to the criticism individually and through ICIFI. The political pressure mounted against the industry. In 1977, an official consumer boycott of Nestle and its products was begun in the United States. Interest in the boycott spread quickly, in part because many member churches of the National Council of Churches had been concerned about the problems of world hunger. The Nestle boycott gave church leaders an opportunity to educate their congregations about the problem of world hunger and suggest a practical course of action that would pressure companies to act responsibly in dealing with the poor and needy of the Third World. The National Council of Churches had been concerned about many corporate responsibility issues, and had a special research and action unit known as the Interfaith Center on Corporate Responsibility (ICCR). ICCR became actively involved in the boycott campaign, and helped spread the message of consumer action to hundreds of thousands of people in the United States.

The high point of Phase II of the infant formula controversy occurred when boycott sponsors were able to convince the staff of United States Senator Edward Kennedy to hold hearings into the infant formula marketing controversy. These hearings were held in May, 1978 in Washington, DC, and occurred at a time when Senator Kennedy was widely rumored to be considering a campaign for the presidency against incumbent President Jimmy Carter. The media followed Kennedy's every action. On the day of the public hearing, every American television network had cameras in the hearing room, and many famous reporters sat at special tables to hear the testimony of witnesses. The witnesses were heard in three groups. First, people who had worked in developing nations told a tale of human tragedy and marketing abuses by the companies. The second panel consisted of experts in public health (Pan American Health Organization, World Health Organization), medicine, and the author of this paper, who was an expert on the industry. The third panel consisted of the company representatives. Nestle was represented by the head of its Brazilian operation, and the three American companies were represented by senior executives from their corporate headquarters.

The Kennedy hearings were a landmark in the history of this controversy. They represented the highest level of media attention and political attention that had been achieved in nearly eight years of conflict. Critics had to be pleased with their success. Moreover, Nestle behaved in a way that actually strengthened the claims of the boycott supporters and organizers. The company's representative charged that the consumer boycott was a conspiracy of church organizations and an indirect attack on the free enterprise system. Senator Kennedy exploded in anger at the charge that the churchmen and health workers were part of a conspiracy to undermine the free enterprise system. The Nestle statement was a political disaster. Every television program featured the testimony and the reaction from the political leaders in attendance. Nestle was denounced for its statement and its foolishness.

Phase III of an evolving public issue occurs when some governmental or other formal action begins to develop. In a single nation, this may take the form of a regulatory standard, a piece of legislation, or a government program. In the infant formula controversy, formal action took the form of an international code of marketing conduct which industry and national governments would support. Following the Kennedy hearings, the Director-General of the World Health Organization agreed to convene a meeting of interested parties to lay the groundwork for international action. An important meeting took place in 1979, with delegates calling upon WHO to draft an international marketing code. The code development process took several years, required extensive negotiation, and eventually produced a document that was adopted by the World Health Assembly (the governing body of WHO) in 1981. Throughout this process, Nestle and other industry members actively participated in the discussions and lobbied for particular terms and provisions. In advance of the World Health Assembly vote, Nestle was the only company to publicly state that it would follow the code if it was adopted.

Phase IV of a public issue involves the process of implementing the new policy throughout the organizations involved. This is called "institutionalizing" the policy action. Nestle considered how to implement the WHO Code's provisions following the World Health Assembly's adoption. But there existed a number of very serious obstacles. Many of the Code's terms were imprecise, leaving unanswered questions about the proper interpretations. WHO was reluctant to provide continuing interpretation and reinterpretation of the Code's terms, as this would require a staff of lawyers and a continuing commitment. In addition, the Nestle boycott continued in both the United States and Europe. Critics continued to pressure the company, and offered alternative interpretations of various code provisions. WHO had no desire to get further drawn into the dispute between the company and its adversaries. Thus, Nestle was left to negotiate proper interpretations with members of what was now called the International Nestle Boycott Committee (INBC).

Since 1981, Nestle has continued to pursue a process of institutionalizing the provisions of the WHO Code by transforming those requirements into policy instructions for its own sales and marketing personnel. A number of innovations have been created to assist this process. These will be discussed below. In early 1984, the international boycott group suspended the Nestle boycott, following extensive negotiations about such critical issues as product labelling, marketing in health facilities, gifts to medical personnel, and provisions of free supplies to health institutions. By October 1984, the INBC leaders had concluded that Nestle's commitment to implement the policies had proceeded well enough to permit them to terminate the boycott. Its conclusion was announced at a joint press conference attended by boycott leaders and senior Nestle managers. Nearly fifteen years after the first formal complaints began, Nestle had managed to close the controversy over its marketing activities.

ETHICAL ISSUES AND LESSONS

Throughout this long conflict, Nestle has faced a variety of difficult ethical issues. Some of the broad issues and lessons are summarized below.

All businesses which sell their products in developing nations must consider two basic questions: (1) Is the product an appropriate one for the people in that country? and (2) Are the proposed tactics for marketing the product proper for selling the products but not misleading consumers for whom the product is not appropriate? As Nestle discovered, both questions are easily overlooked by managers when they are concerned with sales and profits.

Managers should recognize the following points about the appropriateness of products in developing nation markets.

1. Products which are appropriate and acceptable in one social environment may be inappropriate in the social environment of another nation.

Infant formula products are demanding products. There must be pure water with which to prepare them, refrigeration to safely store unused prepared formula, and customers must be able to read instructions and have the income to purchase adequate quantities of the products. The greater the existence of these *risk factors,* the less appropriate the product becomes for marketing. This phenomenon applies to many other consumer products as well.

2. Good products, made without defects, may still be inappropriate because of the inherent riskiness of the environment in which those products are to be used.

Nestle and its competitors often stated that the market they sought to reach consisted only of those who could safely use the product, and who had adequate income. However, the evidence from many developing nations continuously showed that vast numbers of the population did not meet the necessary requirements for safe use of the product. By selling formula products to such people, managers could know with virtual certainty that there would be overdilution, improper mixing, or contamination with impure water. As Nestle discovered, many people would denounce and criticize any company that sought to sell its infant formula products under such conditions. When a large part of the population cannot safely use a product, *and* the company cannot effectively segment the market to ensure that only qualified consumers purchase and use it, there may be no choice for the business but to halt sales in that community.

3. Companies may not close their eyes once a product is sold. There is a continuing responsibility to monitor product use, resale, and consumption to determine who is actually using the product, and how. Post-marketing reviews are a necessary step in this process.

Repeatedly, Nestle and its industry colleagues claimed that they had no desire or intention to see unqualified consumers use their formula products. In 1978 at the United States Senate hearings, representatives from Nestle, Abbott Laboratories, American Home Products, and Bristol-Myers were asked whether they conducted any post-marketing research studies to determine who actually used their products. Each company representative answered that his company did no such research and did not know who actually used its products. Naturally, critics attacked the companies for such a careless attitude toward learning the true facts surrounding their products.

4. Products which have been sold to consumers who cannot safely use them must be demarketed. Demarketing may involve withdrawal or recall of products, limitations of the selling of the product, or even a halting of future sales.

The infant formula controversy raised the issue of whether, and when, companies should demarket products which have been commercially successful, but also harmful to innocent consumers. Nestle and its competitors gradually changed their marketing practices, and recognized that infant formula was not the same "mass market" product that it had once been. The World Health Organization Code specifically indicated that marketing had to be done in ways that guaranteed that the users of formula products had proper information to use the product safely, and to make an intelligent choice about whether or not infant formula was even an appropriate product for them to use. Much of this is to be done by insisting that companies not market directly to mothers, but channel product supplies and advice through health institutions which can ensure that unbiased health information is received by the mother.

5. Marketing strategies must be appropriate to the circumstances of consumers, the social and economic environment in which they live, and to political realities.

Consumer advertising to people for whom product use is highly risky is unacceptable and unethical marketing behavior. Critics of the infant formula industry continued to find evidence of highly aggressive and misleading advertising by companies for many years after the issue became well known. Mass marketing became an unacceptable and inappropriate marketing strategy for infant formula products. The companies, however, had difficulty segmenting their markets and drawing back from the mass market approach. It was only through an industry-wide effort, and then the WHO Code, that managers began to accept that it was more appropriate to focus marketing promotions through the health care system than to consumers directly.

6. Marketing techniques are inappropriate when they exploit a condition of consumer vulnerability.

Many firms in the industry used "milk nurses" during the 1960s and 1970s. These were sales personnel who dressed in nurses uniforms and visited new mothers in hospitals. They would try to encourage the mother to allow their babies to be fed formula, rather than breastfeed, in order to encourage formula adoptions. Since a mother loses the ability to breastfeed after several days of not doing so, such a decision would then require that the baby continue to be fed from a bottle for the next six months. This would be good for formula sales, if the mother could afford to buy it, but might be bad for the baby if the mother had to find a cheaper substitute product to put in the bottle. In South America, for example, members of my own research team saw mothers feeding a mixture of corn starch and water to babies because they had no money to buy formula. Mothers who have given birth are quite vulnerable, and the use of the milk nurses took advantage of that vulnerability in ways that were unethical and unfair. Actions which exploit consumer vulnerability and result in harm are inappropriate marketing tactics.

7. Marketing strategies should be formulated in such a way as to permit flexibility and adjustment to new circumstances.

In the early 1970s, Nestle management knew that critics had a legitimate concern for the sales practices of the industry, but were unable to change their marketing activities in response. The company seemed to be "locked in" to a strategy of resistance, denial, and anger at such charges. In retrospect, it seems that Nestle needed time to change its marketing strategy from a mass-market, consumer-advertising approach, to one which emphasized promotion through the medical and health care system. It took Nestle much longer to change its marketing strategy than it took many of its competitors. This may have been because of pressures from field managers or from the product marketing staff, which denied the truth of the critics' charges. Whatever the case, the company was injured by its slow response to criticism, and its seeming inability to find an alternative way to continue marketing its products. A company which can only market its products in one way is very vulnerable to public issues and political pressures.

CONCLUSION

Nestle's traumatic experience with the infant formula controversy has finally come to an end, but the impact is likely to last for many years. The company suffered a major blow to its reputation and to the morale of its people. It is traumatic and difficult for people to be told they are working for a company which "kills babies." Today, Nestle's senior management is again working to restore the company's economic and cultural fabric. Its future success will depend upon much more than sales and profits. Nestle has been a successful institution as well as a successful business. Institutions represent a structure of values, and it is this structure which was most sharply affected by the long controversy over infant formula.

If a historian writes the history of Nestle one hundred years from now, will he or she include a reference to the infant formula controversy? Very likely yes. The conflict continued for more than ten years, cost the company many millions of dollars of revenue, expenses, and profits, and damaged or destroyed the careers of a number of its promising managers. It is impossible to say how long it will take for the company to regain its good name and for the public to once again think of Nestle as a good corporate citizen.

Multinational corporations must learn to anticipate conflicts of the sort faced by Nestle, and be prepared to respond in ways that not only justify what the company is doing but also deal with the legitimate concerns of the critics. Union Carbide cannot forget its experience in Bhopal, India; Unilever cannot ignore its experience with Persil in England; Johnson & Johnson cannot forget its experience with Tylenol in the United States; and Nestle cannot forget its experience with infant formula. Each of these experiences involved a company with a good reputation, successful business strategies, and a major public credibility problem. The resolution of each dilemma required a careful integration of public affairs strategies with the business strategy for the company. And each situation demanded and required that the company's managers recognize the *common interest* that existed between the corporation and the public. In the long run, there is no other way to harmonize the legitimate interests of companies with the legitimate interests of the public.

A Moral Evaluation of Sales Practices

David M. Holley
Department of Philosophy and Religion, University of Southern Mississippi

In this paper I will attempt to develop a framework for evaluating the morality of various sales practices. Although I recognize that much of the salesforce in companies is occupied exclusively or primarily with sales to other businesses, my discussion will focus on sales to the individual consumer. Most of what I say should apply to any type of sales activity, but the moral issues arise most clearly in cases in which a consumer may or may not be very sophisticated in evaluating and responding to a sales presentation.

My approach will be to consider first the context of sales activities, a market system of production and distribution. Since such a system is generally justified on teleological grounds, I describe several conditions for its successful achievement of key goals. Immoral sales practices are analyzed as attempts to undermine these conditions.

I

The primary justification for a market system is that it provides an efficient procedure for meeting people's needs and desires for goods and services.[1] This appeal to economic benefits can be elaborated in great detail, but at root it involves the claim that people will efficiently serve each other's needs if they are allowed to engage in voluntary exchanges.

A crucial feature of this argument is the condition that the exchange be voluntary. Assuming that individuals know best how to benefit themselves and that they will act to achieve such benefits, voluntary exchange can be expected to serve both parties. On the other hand, if the exchanges are not made voluntarily, we have no basis for expecting mutually beneficial results. To the extent that mutual benefit does not occur, the system will lack efficiency as a means for the satisfaction of needs and desires. Hence, this justification presupposes that conditions necessary for the occurrence of voluntary exchange are ordinarily met.

What are these conditions? For simplicity's sake, let us deal only with the kind of exchange involving a payment of money for some product or service. We can call the person providing the product the *seller* and the person making the monetary payment the *buyer.* I suggest that voluntary exchange occurs only if the following conditions are met:

1. Both buyer and seller understand what they are giving up and what they are receiving in return.
2. Neither buyer nor seller is compelled to enter into the exchange as a result of coercion, severely restricted alternatives, or other constraints on the ability to choose.
3. Both buyer and seller are able at the time of the exchange to make rational judgments about its costs and benefits.

I will refer to these three conditions as the knowledge, noncompulsion, and rationality conditions, respectively.[2] If the parties are uninformed, it is possible that an exchange might accidentally turn out to benefit them. But given the lack of information, they would not be in a position to make a rational judgment about their benefit, and we cannot reasonably expect beneficial results as a matter of course in such circumstances. Similarly, if the exchange is made under compulsion, then the judgment of personal benefit is not the basis of the exchange. It is possible for someone to be forced or manipulated into an arrangement that is in fact beneficial. But there is little reason to think that typical or likely.[3]

It should be clear that all three conditions are subject to degrees of fulfillment. For example, the parties may understand certain things about the exchange but not others. Let us posit a theoretical situation in which both parties are fully informed, fully rational, and enter into the exchange entirely of their own volition. I will call this an *ideal ex-*

Excerpted from "A Moral Evaluation of Sales Practices" by David M. Holley, *Business and Professional Ethics Journal,* Vol. 5, No. 1, circa 1987, pp. 3–21.

change. In actual practice there is virtually always some divergence from the ideal. Knowledge can be more or less adequate. Individuals can be subject to various irrational influences. There can be borderline cases of external constraints. Nevertheless, we can often judge when a particular exchange was adequately informed, rational, and free from compulsion. Even when conditions are not ideal, we may still have an *acceptable exchange*.

With these concepts in mind, let us consider the obligations of sales personnel. I suggest that the primary duty of salespeople to customers is to avoid undermining the conditions of acceptable exchange. It is possible by act or omission to create a situation in which the customer is not sufficiently knowledgeable about what the exchange involves. It is also possible to influence the customer in ways that short-circuit the rational decision-making process. To behave in such ways is to undermine the conditions that are presupposed in teleological justifications of the market system. Of course, an isolated act is not sufficient to destroy the benefits of the system. But the moral acceptability of the system may become questionable if the conditions of acceptable exchange are widely abused. The individual who attempts to gain personally by undermining these conditions does that which, if commonly practiced, would produce a very different system from the one that supposedly provides moral legitimacy to that individual's activities.

II

If a mutually beneficial exchange is to be expected, the parties involved must be adequately informed about what they are giving up and what they are receiving. In most cases this should create no great problem for the seller[4], but what about the buyer? How is she to obtain the information needed? One answer is that the buyer is responsible for doing whatever investigation is necessary to acquire the information. The medieval principle of *caveat emptor* encouraged buyers to take responsibility for examining a purchase thoroughly to determine whether it had any hidden flaws. If the buyer failed to find defects, that meant that due caution had not been exercised.

If it were always relatively easy to discover defects by examination, then this principle might be an efficient method of guaranteeing mutual satisfaction. Sometimes, however, even lengthy investigation would not disclose what the buyer wants to know. With products of great complexity, the expertise needed for an adequate examination may be beyond what could reasonably be expected of most consumers. Even relatively simple products can have hidden flaws that most people would not discover until after the purchase, and to have the responsibility for closely examining every purchase would involve a considerable amount of a highly treasured modern commodity, the buyer's time. Furthermore, many exchange situations in our context involve products that cannot be examined in this way—goods that will be delivered at a later time or sent through the mail, for example. Finally, even if we assume that most buyers, by exercising enough caution, can protect their interests, the system of *caveat emptor* would take advantage of those least able to watch out for themselves. It would in effect justify mistreatment of a few for a rather questionable benefit.

In practice the buyer almost always relies on the seller for some information, and if mutually beneficial exchanges are to be expected, the information needs to meet certain standards of both quality and quantity. With regard to quality, the information provided should not be deceptive. This would include not only direct lies but also truths that are intended to mislead the buyer. Consider the following examples:

1. An aluminum siding salesperson tells customers that they will receive "bargain factory prices" for letting their homes be used as models in a new advertising campaign. Prospective customers will be brought to view the houses, and a commission of $100 will be paid for each sale that results. In fact, the price paid is well above market rates, the workmanship and materials are substandard, and no one is ever brought by to see the houses.[5]
2. A used car salesperson turns back the odometer reading on automobiles by an average of 25,000 to 30,000 miles per car. If customers ask

whether the reading is correct, the salesperson replies that it is illegal to alter odometer readings.

3. A salesperson at a piano store tells an interested customer that the "special sale" will be good only through that evening. She neglects to mention that another "special sale" will begin the next day.
4. A telephone salesperson tells people who answer the phone that they have been selected to receive a free gift, a brand new freezer. All they have to do is buy a year's subscription to a food plan.
5. A salesperson for a diet system proclaims that under this revolutionary new plan the pounds will melt right off. The system is described as a scientific advance that makes dieting easy. In fact, the system is a low-calorie diet composed of foods and liquids that are packaged under the company name but are no different from standard grocery store items.

The possibilities are endless, and whether or not a lie is involved, each case illustrates a salesperson's attempt to get a customer to believe something that is false in order to make the sale. It might be pointed out that these kinds of practices would not deceive a sophisticated consumer. Perhaps so, but whether they are always successful deceptions is not the issue. They are attempts to mislead the customer, and given that the consumer must often rely on information furnished by the salesperson, they are attempts to subvert the conditions under which mutually beneficial exchange can be expected. The salesperson attempts to use misinformation as a basis for customer judgment rather than allowing that judgment to be based on accurate beliefs. Furthermore, if these kinds of practices were not successful fairly often, they would probably not be used.

In the aluminum siding case, the customer is led to believe that there will be a discount in exchange for a kind of service, allowing the house to be viewed by prospective customers. This leaves the impression both that the job done will be of high quality and that the price paid will be offset by commissions. The car salesperson alters the product in order to suggest false information about the extent of its use. With such information, the customer is not able to judge accurately the value of the car. The misleading reply to inquiries is not substantially different from a direct lie. The piano salesperson deceives the customer about how long the product will be obtainable at a discount price. In this case the deception occurs through an omission. The telephone solicitor tries to give the impression that there has been a contest of some sort and that the freezer is a prize. In this way, the nature of the exchange is obscured.

The diet-system case raises questions about how to distinguish legitimate "puffery" from deception. Obviously, the matter will depend to some extent on how gullible we conceive the customer to be. As described, the case surely involves an attempt to get the customer to believe that dieting will be easier under this system and that what is being promoted is the result of some new scientific discovery. If there were no prospect that a customer would be likely to believe this, we would probably not think the technique deceptive. But in fact a number of individuals are deceived by claims of this type.

Some writers have defended the use of deceptive practices in business contexts on the grounds that there are specific rules applying to these contexts that differ from the standards appropriate in other contexts. It is argued, for example, that deception is standard practice, understood by all participants as something to be expected and, therefore, harmless, or that it is a means of self-defense justified by pressures of the competitive context.[6] To the extent that claims about widespread practice are true, people who know what is going on may be able to minimize personal losses, but that is hardly a justification of the practice. If I know that many people have installed devices in their cars that can come out and puncture the tires of the car next to them, that may help keep me from falling victim, but it does not make the practice harmless. Even if no one is victimized, it becomes necessary to take extra precautions, introducing a significant disutility into driving conditions. Analogously, widespread deception in business debases the currency of language, making business communication less efficient and more cumbersome.

More importantly, however, people are victimized by deceptive practices, and the fact that some may be shrewd enough to see through clouds of misinformation does not alter the deceptive intent. Whatever may be said with regard to appropriate behavior among people who "know the rules," it is clear that many buyers are not aware of having entered into some special domain where deception is allowed. Even if this is naive, it does not provide a moral justification for subverting those individuals' capacity for making a reasoned choice.

Only a few people would defend the moral justifiability of deceptive sales practices. However, there may be room for much more disagreement with regard to how much information a salesperson is obligated to provide. In rejecting the principle of *caveat emptor,* I have suggested that there are pragmatic reasons for expecting the seller to communicate some information about the product. But how much? When is it morally culpable to withhold information? Consider the following cases:

1. An automobile dealer has bought a number of cars from another state. Although they appear to be new or slightly used, these cars have been involved in a major flood and were sold by the previous dealer at a discount rate. The salesperson knows the history of the cars and does not mention it to customers.
2. A salesperson for an encyclopedia company never mentions the total price of a set unless he has to. Instead he emphasizes the low monthly payment involved.
3. A real estate agent knows that one reason the couple selling a house with her company want to move is that the neighbors often have loud parties and neighborhood children have committed minor acts of vandalism. The agent makes no mention of this to prospective customers.
4. An admissions officer for a private college speaks enthusiastically about the advantages of the school. He does not mention the fact that the school is not accredited.
5. A prospective retirement home resident is under the impression that a particular retirement home is affiliated with a certain church. He makes it known that this is one of the features he finds attractive about the home. Though the belief is false, the recruiters for the home make no attempt to correct the misunderstanding.

In all these cases the prospective buyer lacks some piece of knowledge that might be relevant to the decision to buy. The conditions for ideal exchange are not met. Perhaps, however, there can be an acceptable exchange. Whether or not this is the case depends on whether the buyer has adequate information to decide if the purchase would be beneficial. In the case of the flood-damaged autos, there is information relevant to evaluating the worth of the car that the customer could not be expected to know unless informed by the seller. If this information is not revealed, the buyer will not have adequate knowledge to make a reasonable judgment. Determining exactly how much information needs to be provided is not always clear-cut. We must in general rely on our assessments of what a reasonable person would want to know. As a practical guide, a salesperson might consider, "What would I want to know if I were considering buying this product?"

Surely a reasonable person would want to know the total price of a product. Hence the encyclopedia salesperson who omits this total is not providing adequate information. The salesperson may object that this information could be inferred from other information about the monthly payment, length of term, and interest rate. But if the intention is not to have the customer act without knowing the full price, then why shouldn't it be provided directly? The admissions officer's failure to mention that the school is unaccredited also seems unacceptable when we consider what a reasonable person would want to know. There are some people who would consider this a plus, since they are suspicious about accrediting agencies imposing some alien standards (e.g., standards that conflict with religious views). But regardless of how one evaluates the fact, most people would judge it to be important for making a decision.

The real estate case is more puzzling. Most real

estate agents would not reveal the kind of information described, and would not feel they had violated any moral duties in failing to do so. Clearly, many prospective customers would want to be informed about such problems. However, in most cases failing to know these facts would not be of crucial importance. We have a case of borderline information. It would be known by all parties to an ideal exchange, but we can have an acceptable exchange even if the buyer is unaware of it. Failure to inform the customer of these facts is not like failing to inform the customer that the house is on the site of a hazardous waste dump or that a major freeway will soon be adjacent to the property.

It is possible to alter the case in such a way that the information should be revealed or at least the buyer should be directed another way. Suppose the buyer makes it clear that his primary goal is to live in a quiet neighborhood where he will be undisturbed. The "borderline" information now becomes more central to the customer's decision. Notice that thinking in these terms moves us away from the general standard of what a reasonable person would want to know to the more specific standard of what is relevant given the criteria of this individual. In most cases, however, I think that a salesperson would be justified in operating under general "reasonable person" standards until particular deviations become apparent.[7]

The case of the prospective retirement home resident is a good example of how the particular criteria of the customer might assume great importance. If the recruiters, knowing what they know about this man's religious preferences, allow him to make his decision on the basis of a false assumption, they will have failed to support the conditions of acceptable exchange. It doesn't really matter that the misunderstanding was not caused by the salespeople. Their allowing it to be part of the basis for a decision borders on deception. If the misunderstanding was not on a matter of central importance to the individual's evaluation, they might have had no obligation to correct it. But the case described is not of that sort.

Besides providing nondeceptive and relatively complete information, salespeople may be obligated to make sure that their communications are understandable. Sales presentations containing technical information that is likely to be misunderstood are morally questionable. However, it would be unrealistic to expect all presentations to be immune to misunderstanding. The salesperson is probably justified in developing presentations that would be intelligible to the average consumer of the product he or she is selling and making adjustments in cases where it is clear that misunderstanding has occurred.

III

The condition of uncompelled exchange distinguishes business dealings from other kinds of exchanges. In the standard business arrangement, neither party is forced to enter the negotiations. A threat of harm would transform the situation to something other than a purely business arrangement. Coercion is not the only kind of compulsion, however. Suppose I have access to only one producer of food. I arrange to buy food from this producer, but given my great need for food and the absence of alternatives, the seller is able to dictate the terms. In one sense I choose to make the deal, but the voluntariness of my choice is limited by the absence of alternatives.

Ordinarily, the individual salesperson will not have the power to take away the buyer's alternatives. However, a clever salesperson can sometimes make it seem as if options are very limited and can use the customer's ignorance to produce the same effect. For example, imagine an individual who begins to look for a particular item at a local store. The salesperson extolls the line carried by his store, warns of the deficiencies of alternative brands, and warns about the dishonesty of competitors, in contrast to his store's reliability. With a convincing presentation, a customer might easily perceive the options to be very limited. Whether or not the technique is questionable may depend on the accuracy of the perception. If the salesperson is attempting to take away a legitimate alternative, that is an attempt to undermine the customer's voluntary choice.

Another way the condition of uncompelled choice might be subverted is by involving a customer in a purchase without allowing her to notice what is happening. This would include opening techniques that disguise the purpose of the encounter so there can be no immediate refusal. The customer is led to believe that the interview is about a contest or a survey or an opportunity to make money. Not until the end does it become apparent that this is an attempt to sell something, and occasionally if the presentation is smooth enough, some buyers can be virtually unaware that they have bought anything. Obviously, there can be degrees of revelation, and not every approach that involves initial disguise of certain elements that might provoke an immediate rejection is morally questionable. But there are enough clear cases in which the intention is to get around, as much as possible, the voluntary choice of the customer. Consider the following examples:

1. A seller of children's books gains entrance to houses by claiming to be conducting an educational survey. He does indeed ask several "survey" questions, but he uses these to qualify potential customers for his product.
2. A salesperson alludes to recent accidents involving explosions of furnaces and, leaving the impression of having some official government status, offers to do a free safety inspection. She almost always discovers a "major problem" and offers to sell a replacement furnace.
3. A man receives a number of unsolicited books and magazines through the mail. Then he is sent a bill and later letters warning of damage to his credit rating if he does not pay.

These are examples of the many variations on attempts to involve customers in exchanges without letting them know what is happening. The first two cases involve deceptions about the purpose of the encounter. Though they resemble cases discussed earlier that involved deception about the nature or price of a product, here the salesperson uses misinformation as a means of limiting the customer's range of choice. The customer does not consciously choose to listen to a sales presentation but finds that this is what is happening. Some psychological research suggests that when people do something that appears to commit them to a course of action, even without consciously choosing to do so, they will tend to act as if such a choice had been made in order to minimize cognitive dissonance. Hence, if a salesperson successfully involves the customer in considering a purchase, the customer may feel committed to give serious thought to the matter. The third case is an attempt to get the customer to believe that an obligation has been incurred. In variations on this technique, merchandise is mailed to a deceased person to make relatives believe that some payment is owed. In each case, an effort is made to force the consumer to choose from an excessively limited range of options.

IV

How can a salesperson subvert the rationality condition? Perhaps the most common way is to appeal to emotional reactions that cloud an individual's perception of relevant considerations. Consider the following cases:

1. A man's wife has recently died in a tragic accident. The funeral director plays upon the husband's love for his wife and to some extent his guilt about her death to get him to purchase a very expensive funeral.
2. A socially insecure young woman has bought a series of dance lessons from a local studio. During the lessons, an attractive male instructor constantly compliments her on her poise and natural ability and tries to persuade her to sign up for more lessons.[8]
3. A life insurance salesperson emphasizes to a prospect the importance of providing for his family in the event of his death. The salesperson tells several stories about people who put off this kind of preparation.
4. A dress salesperson typically tells customers how fashionable they look in a certain dress. Her stock comments also include pointing out that a dress is slimming or sexy or "looks great on you."
5. A furniture salesperson regularly tells customers that a piece of furniture is the last one in stock and that another customer recently

showed great interest in it. He sometimes adds that it may not be possible to get any more like it from the factory.

These cases remind us that emotions can be important motivators. It is not surprising that salespeople appeal to them in attempting to get the customer to make a purchase. In certain cases the appeal seems perfectly legitimate. When the life insurance salesperson tries to arouse the customer's fear and urges preparation, it may be a legitimate way to get the customer to consider something that is worth considering. Of course, the fact that the fear is aroused by one who sells life insurance may obscure to the customer the range of alternative possibilities in preparing financially for the future. But the fact that an emotion is aroused need not make the appeal morally objectionable.

If the appeal of the dress salesperson seems more questionable, this is probably because we are not as convinced of the objective importance of appearing fashionable, or perhaps because repeated observations of this kind are often insincere. But if we assume that the salesperson is giving an honest opinion about how the dress looks on a customer, it may provide some input for the individual who has a desire to achieve a particular effect. The fact that such remarks appeal to one's vanity or ambition does not in itself make the appeal unacceptable.

The furniture salesperson's warnings are clearly calculated to create some anxiety about the prospect of losing the chance to buy a particular item unless immediate action is taken. If the warnings are factually based, they would not be irrelevant to the decision to buy. Clearly, one might act impulsively or hastily when under the spell of such thoughts, but the salesperson cannot be faulted for pointing out relevant considerations.

The case of the funeral director is somewhat different. Here there is a real question of what benefit is to be gained by choosing a more expensive funeral package. For most people, minimizing what is spent on the funeral would be a rational choice, but at a time of emotional vulnerability it can be made to look as if this means depriving the loved one or the family of some great benefit. Even if the funeral director makes nothing but true statements, they can be put into a form designed to arouse emotions that will lessen the possibility of a rational decision being reached.

The dance studio case is similar in that a weakness is being played upon. The woman's insecurity makes her vulnerable to flattery and attention, and this creates the kind of situation in which others can take advantage of her. Perhaps the dance lessons fulfill some need, but the appeal to her vanity easily becomes a tool to manipulate her into doing what the instructor wants.

The key to distinguishing between legitimate and illegitimate emotional appeals lies in whether the appeal clouds one's ability to make a decision based on genuine satisfaction of needs and desires. Our judgment about whether this happens in a particular case will depend in part on whether we think the purchase likely to benefit the customer. The more questionable the benefits, the more an emotional appeal looks like manipulation rather than persuasion. When questionable benefits are combined with some special vulnerability on the part of the consumer, the use of the emotional appeal appears even more suspect.

V

I have attempted to provide a framework for evaluating the morality of a number of different types of sales practices. The framework is based on conditions for mutually beneficial exchange and ultimately for an efficient satisfaction of economic needs and desires. An inevitable question is whether this kind of evaluation is of any practical importance.

If we set before ourselves the ideal of a knowledgeable, unforced, and rational decision on the part of a customer, it is not difficult to see how some types of practices would interfere with this process. We must, of course, be careful not to set the standards too high. A customer may be partially but adequately informed to judge a purchase's potential benefits. A decision may be affected by nonrational and even irrational factors and yet still be rational enough in terms of being plausibly related to the individual's desires and needs. There may be borderline cases in which it is not clear whether acting in a particular way would be morally required or simply overscrupulous, but that is not an objection to this approach, only a recognition of a feature of morality itself.[9]

NOTES

1. The classic statement of the argument from economic benefits is found in Adam Smith, *The Wealth of Nations* (1776) (London: Methusen and Co. Ltd., 1930). Modern proponents of this argument include Ludwig von Mises, Friedrich von Hayek, and Milton Friedman.
2. One very clear analysis of voluntariness making use of these conditions may be found in John Hospers' *Human Conduct: Problems of Ethics*, 2nd ed. (New York: Harcourt Brace Jovanovich, 1982), pp. 385–388.
3. I will refer to the three conditions indifferently as conditions for voluntary exchange or conditions for mutually beneficial exchange. By the latter designation I do not mean to suggest that they are either necessary or sufficient conditions for the occurrence of mutual benefit, but that they are conditions for the reasonable expectation of mutual benefit.
4. There are cases, however, in which the buyer knows more about a product than the seller. For example, suppose Cornell has found out that land Fredonia owns contains minerals that make it twice as valuable as Fredonia thinks. The symmetry of my conditions would lead me to conclude that Cornell should give Fredonia the relevant information unless perhaps Fredonia's failure to know was the result of some culpable negligence.
5. This case is described in Warren Magnuson and Jean Carper, *The Dark Side of the Market-Place* (Englewood Cliffs, N.J.: Prentice Hall, 1968). pp. 3–4.
6. Albert Carr, "Is Business Bluffing Ethical?" *Harvard Business Review* 46 (January–February 1968): 143–153. See also Thomas L. Carson, Richard E. Wokutch, and Kent F. Murrmann, "Bluffing in Labor Negotiations: Legal and Ethical Issues," *Journal of Business Ethics* 1 (1982): 13–22.
7. My reference to a reasonable person standard should not be confused with the issue facing the FTC of whether to evaluate advertising by the reasonable consumer or ignorant consumer standard as described in Ivan Preston, "Reasonable Consumer or Ignorant Consumer: How the FTC Decides," *Journal of Consumer Affairs* 8 (Winter 1974): 131–143. There the primary issue is with regard to whom the government should protect from claims that might be misunderstood. My concern here is with determining what amount of information is necessary for informed judgment. In general I suggest that a salesperson should begin with the assumption that information a reasonable consumer would regard as important needs to be revealed and that when special interests and concerns of the consumer come to light they may make further revelations necessary. This approach parallels the one taken by Tom Beauchamp and James Childress regarding the information that a physician needs to provide to obtain informed consent. See their *Principles of Biomedical Ethics*, 2nd ed. (New York: Oxford University Press, 1983), pp. 74–79.
8. This is adapted from a court case quoted in Braybrooke, pp. 68–70.
9. This paper was written during a sabbatical leave from Friends University at the Center for the Study of Values, University of Delaware. I wish to thank Friends University for the leave and Dr. Norman Bowie for his hospitality during my stay at the Center.

Strict Products Liability and Compensatory Justice

George G. Brenkert
Professor of Philosophy, University of Tennessee

I

Strict products liability is the doctrine that the seller of a product has legal responsibilities to compensate the user of that product for injuries suffered because of a defective aspect of the product, even when the seller has not been negligent in permitting that defect to occur.[1] Thus, even though a manufacturer, for example, has reasonably applied the existing techniques of manufacture and has anticipated and cared for nonintended uses of the product, he may still be held liable for injuries a product user suffers if it can be shown that the product was defective when it left the manufacturer's hands.[2]

To say that there is a crisis today concerning this doctrine would be to utter a commonplace which few in the business community would deny. The development of the doctrine of strict products liability, according to most business people, threatens many businesses financially.[3] Furthermore, strict products liability is said to be a morally questionable doctrine, since the manufacturer or seller has not been negligent in permitting the injury-causing defect to occur. On the other hand, victims of defective products complain that they deserve full compensation for injuries sustained in using a defective product whether or not the seller is at fault. Medical expenses and time lost from one's job are costs no individual should have to bear by himself. It is only fair that the seller share such burdens.

In general, discussions of this crisis focus on the limits to which a business ought to be held responsible. Much less frequently, discussions of strict products liability consider the underlying question of whether the doctrine of strict products liability is rationally justifiable. But unless this question is answered it would seem premature to seek to determine the limits to which business ought to be held liable in such cases. In the following paper I discuss this underlying philosophical question and argue that there is a rational justification for strict products liability which links it to the very nature of the free enterprise system.

II

It should be noted at the outset that strict products liability is not absolute liability. To hold a manufacturer legally (and morally) responsible for any and all injuries which product users might sustain would be morally perverse. First, it would deny the product user's own responsibility to take care in his actions and to suffer the consequences when he does not. It would therefore constitute an extreme form of moral and legal paternalism.

Second, if the product is not defective, there is no significant moral connection between anything the manufacturer has done or not done and the user's injuries other than the production and sale of the product. This provides no basis for holding the manufacturer responsible for the user's injuries. If, because of my own carelessness, I cut myself with my new pocket knife, the fact that I just bought my knife from Blade Manufacturing Company provides no moral reason to hold Blade Manufacturing responsible for my injury.

Finally, though the manufacturer's product might be said to have harmed the person,[4] it is wholly implausible, when the product is not defective and the manufacturer not negligent, to say that the manufacturer has harmed the user. Thus, there would seem to be no moral basis upon which to maintain that the manufacturer has any liability to the product user. Strict products liability, on the other hand, holds that the manufacturer can be held liable when the product can be shown to be defective, even though the manufacturer himself has not been negligent.[5]

Two justifications of strict products liability are predominant in the literature. Both, I believe, are untenable. They are:

1. To hold producers strictly liable for defective products will cut down on the number of accidents and injuries which occur by forcing manufacturers to make their products safer.[6]
2. The manufacturer is best able to distribute to others the costs of injuries which users of his defective products suffer.[7]

There are several reasons why the first justification is unacceptable. First, it has been argued plausibly that almost everything that can be attained through the use of strict liability to force manufacturers to make their products safer can also be attained in other ways through the law.[8] Hence, to hold manufacturers strictly liable will not necessarily help reduce the number of accidents. The incentive to produce safer products already exists, without invoking the doctrine of strict products liability.

Second, at least some of the accidents which have been brought under strict liability have been caused by features of the products which the manufacturers could not have foreseen or controlled. At the time the product was designed and manufactured, the technological knowledge required to discover the hazard and take steps to minimize its effects was not available. It is doubtful that in such cases the imposition of strict liability upon the manufacturer could reduce accidents.[9] Thus, again, this justification for strict products liability fails.[10]

Third, the fact that the imposition of legal restraints and/or penalties would have a certain positive effect—for example, reduce accidents—does not show that the imposition of those penalties would be just. It has been pointed out before that the rate of crime might be cut significantly if the law would imprison the wives and children of men who break the law. Regardless of how correct that claim may be, to use these means in order to achieve a significant reduction in the crime rate would be unjust. Thus, the fact—if fact it be—that strict liability would cut down on the amount of dangerous and/or defective products placed on the market, and thus reduce the number of accidents and injuries, does not justify the imposition of strict liability on manufacturers.

Finally, the above justification is essentially a utilitarian appeal which emphasizes the welfare of the product users. It is not obvious, however, that those who use this justification have ever undertaken the utilitarian analysis which would show that greater protection of the product user's safety would further the welfare of product users. If emphasis on product user safety would cut down on the number and variety of products produced, the imposition of strict liability might not enhance product user welfare: rather, it might lower it. Furthermore, if the safety of product users is the predominant concern, massive public and private education safety campaigns might do as much or more to lower the level of accidents and injuries as strict products liability.

The second justification given for strict products liability is also utilitarian in nature. Among the factors cited in favor of this justification are the following:

1. "An individual harmed by his or her use of a defective product is often unable to bear the loss individually."
2. "Distribution of losses among all users of a product would minimize both individual and aggregate loss."
3. "The situation of producers and marketers in the marketplace enables them conveniently to distribute losses among all users of a product by raising prices sufficiently to compensate those harmed (which is what in fact occurs where strict liability is in force)."[11]

This justification is also defective.

First, the word "best" in the phrase "best able to distribute to others the cost" is usually understood in a nonmoral sense; it is used to signify that the manufacturer can most efficiently pass on the costs of injuries to others. Once this use of "best" is recognized, surely we may ask why these costs ought to be passed on to other consumers and/or users of the same product or line of products. Even if the imposition of strict liability did maximize utility, it might still be unjust to use the producer as the distributor of losses.[12] Indeed, some have objected that to pass along the costs of such accidents to other consumers of a manufacturer's products is unjust to them.[13] The above justification is silent with regard to these legitimate objections.

Second, manufacturers may not always be in the best (that is, most efficient and economical) position to pass costs on to customers. Even in monopoly areas, there are limitations. Furthermore, some products are subject to an elastic demand, preventing the manufacturer from passing along the costs.[14] Finally, the present justification could justify far more than is plausible. If the reason for holding the manufacturer liable is that the manufacturer is the "best" administrator of costs, one might plausibly argue that the manufacturer should pay for injuries suffered not only when he is not negligent but also when the product is not defective. Theoretically, at least, this argument could be extended from cases of strict liability to that of absolute liability.

Whether this argument holds up depends upon contingent facts concerning the nature and frequency of injuries people suffer using products, the financial strength of businesses, and the kinds and levels of products liability insurance available to them. It does not depend on any morally significant elements in the relationship between the producer and the product user. Such an implication, I believe, undercuts the purported moral nature of this justification and reveals it for what it is: an economic, not a moral, justification.

Accordingly, neither of the major current justifications for the imposition of strict liability appears to be acceptable. If this is the case, is strict products liability a groundless doctrine, willfully and unjustly imposed on manufacturers?

III

This question can be asked in two different ways. On the one hand, it can be asked within the assumptions of the free enterprise system. On the other hand, it could be raised with the premise that the fundamental assumptions of that socioeconomic system are also open to revision and change. In the following, I will discuss the question *within* the general assumptions of the free enterprise system. Since these assumptions are broadly made in legal and business circles it is interesting to determine what answer might be given within these constraints. Indeed, I suggest that only within these general assumptions can strict products liability be justified.

To begin with, it is crucial to remember that what we have to consider is the relationship between an entity doing business and an individual.[15] The strict liability attributed to business would not be attributed to an individual who happened to sell some product he had made to his neighbor or a stranger. If Peter sold an article he had made to Paul and Paul hurt himself because the article had a defect which occurred through no negligence of Peter's, we would not normally hold Peter morally responsible to pay for Paul's injuries.

Peter did not claim, we may assume, that the product was absolutely risk-free. Had he kept it, he himself might have been injured by it. Paul, on the other hand, bought it. He was not pressured, forced, or coerced to do so. Peter mounted no advertising campaign. Though Paul might not have been injured if the product had been made differently, he supposedly bought it with open eyes. Peter did not seek to deceive Paul about its qualities. The product, both its good and bad qualities, became his when he bought it.

In short, we assume that both Peter and Paul are morally autonomous individuals capable of knowing their own interests, that such individuals can legitimately exchange their ownership of various products, that the world is not free of risks, and that not all injuries one suffers in such a world can be blamed on others. To demand that Peter protect Paul from such dangers and/or compensate him for injuries resulting from such dangers is to demand that Peter significantly reduce the risks of the product he offers to Paul and to protect Paul from encountering those risks. However, this demand smacks of paternalism and undercuts our basic moral assumptions about such relations. Hence, in such a case, Peter is not morally responsible for Paul's injuries or, because of this transaction, obligated to aid him. Perhaps Peter owes Paul aid because Paul is an injured neighbor or person. Perhaps for charitable reasons Peter ought to help Paul. But Peter has no moral obligation stemming from the sale itself to provide aid.

It is different for businesses. They have been held to be legally and morally obliged to pay the victim for his injuries. Why? What is the difference? The difference is that when Paul is hurt by a defective product from corporation X, he is hurt by something produced in a socioeconomic system purportedly embodying free enterprise. In other words, among other things:

1. Each business and/or corporation produces articles or services it sells for profit.
2. Each member of this system competes with other members of the system in trying to do as well as it can for itself not simply in each exchange, but through each exchange for its other values and desires.
3. Competition is to be "open and free, without deception or fraud."
4. Exchanges are voluntary and undertaken when each party believes it can benefit thereby. One party provides the means for another party's

ends if the other party will provide the first party the means to its ends.[16]

5. The acquisition and disposition of ownership rights—that is, of private property—is permitted in such exchanges.
6. No market or series of markets constitutes the whole of a society.
7. Law, morality, and government play a role in setting acceptable limits to the nature and kinds of exchange in which people may engage.[17]

What is it about such a system which would justify claims of strict products liability against businesses? Calabresi has suggested that the free enterprise system is essentially a system of strict liability.[18] Thus the very nature of the free enterprise system justifies such liability claims. His argument has two parts. First, he claims that "bearing risks is both the function of, and justification for, private enterprise in a free enterprise society."[19] "Free enterprise is prized, in classical economics, precisely because it fosters the creation of entrepreneurs who will take such uninsurable risks, who will, in other words, gamble on uncertainty and demonstrate their utility by surviving—by winning more than others."[20]

Accordingly, the nature of private enterprise requires individual businesses to assume the burden of risk in the production and distribution of its products. However, even if we grant that this characterization of who must bear the risks "in deciding what goods are worthy of producing and what new entrants into an industry are worth having" is correct, it would not follow that individual businesses ought to bear the burden of risk in cases of accidents.

Calabresi himself recognizes this. Thus in the second part of his argument he maintains that there is a close analogy which lets us move from the regular risk-bearing businesses must accept in the marketplace to the bearing of risks in accidents: "although . . . [the above characterization] has concerned *regular* entrepreneurial-product risks, not accident risks, the analogy is extremely close."[21] He proceeds to draw the analogy, however, in the following brief sentence: "As with product-accident risks, our society starts out by allocating ordinary product-production risks in ways which try to maximize the chances that incentives will be placed on those most suited to 'manage' these risks."[22] In short, he asserts that the imposition of strict products liability on business will be the most effective means of reducing such risks.

But such a view does not really require, as we have seen in the previous section, any assumptions about the nature of the free enterprise system. It could be held independently of such assumptions. Further, this view is simply a form of the first justificatory argument we discussed and rejected in the previous section. We can hardly accept it here just by attaching it to the nature of free enterprise.

Nevertheless, Calabresi's initial intuitions about a connection between the assumptions of the free enterprise system and the justification of strict products liability are correct. However, they must be developed in the following, rather different, manner. In the free enterprise system, each person and/or business is obligated to follow the rules and understandings which define this socioeconomic system. Following the rules is expected to channel competition among individuals and businesses to socially positive results. In providing the means to fulfill the ends of others, one's own ends also get fulfilled.

Though this does not happen in every case, it is supposed to happen most of the time. Those who fail in their competition with others may be the object of charity, but not of other duties. Those who succeed, qua members of this socioeconomic system, do not have moral duties to aid those who fail. Analogously, the team which loses the game may receive our sympathy but the winning team is not obligated to help it to win the next game or even to play it better. Those who violate the rules, however, may be punished or penalized, whether or not the violation was intentional and whether or not it redounded to the benefit of the violator. Thus, a team may be assessed a penalty for something that a team member did unintentionally to a member of the other team but which injured the other team's chances of competition in the game by violating the rules.

This point may be emphasized by another instance involving a game that brings us closer to strict products liability. Imagine that you are playing table tennis with another person in his newly constructed table tennis room. You are both avid table tennis players and the game means a lot to both of you. Suppose that after play has begun, you are suddenly and quite obviously blinded by the light over the table—the light shade has a hole in it which, when it turned in your direction, sent a shaft of light unexpectedly into your eyes. You lose a crucial point as a result. Surely it would be unfair of your opponent to seek to maintain his point because he was faultless—after all, he had not intended to blind you when he installed that light shade. You would correctly object that he had gained the point unfairly, that you should not have to give up the point lost, and that the light shade should be modified so that the game can continue on a fair basis. It is only fair that the point be played over.

Businesses and their customers in a free enterprise system are also engaged in competition with each other.[23] The competition here, however, is multifaceted as each tries to gain the best agreement he can from the other with regard to the buying and selling of raw materials, products, services, and labor. Such agreements must be voluntary. The competition which leads to them cannot involve coercion. In addition, such competition must be fair and ultimately result in the benefit of the entire society through the operation of the proverbial invisible hand.

Crucial to the notion of fairness of competition are not simply the demands that the competition be open, free, and honest, but also that each person in a society be given an equal opportunity to participate in the system in order to fulfill his or her own particular ends. Friedman formulates this notion in the following manner:

> . . . the priority given to equality of opportunity in the hierarchy of values . . . is manifested particularly in economic policy. The catchwords were free enterprise, competition, laissez-faire. Everyone was to be free to go into any business, follow any occupation, buy any property, subject only to the agreement of the other parties to the transaction. Each was to have the opportunity to reap the benefits if he succeeded, to suffer the costs if he failed. There were to be no arbitrary obstacles. Performance, not birth, religion, or nationality, was the touchstone.[24]

What is obvious in Friedman's comments is that he is thinking primarily of a person as a producer. Equality of opportunity requires that one not be prevented by arbitrary obstacles from participating (by engaging in a productive role of some kind or other) in the system of free enterprise, competition, and so on in order to fulfill one's own ends ("reap the benefits"). Accordingly, monopolies are restricted, discriminatory hiring policies have been condemned, and price collusion is forbidden.

However, each person participates in the system of free enterprise *both* as a worker/producer *and* as a consumer. The two roles interact; if the person could not consume he would not be able to work, and if there were no consumers there would be no work to be done. Even if a particular individual is only (what is ordinarily considered) a consumer, he or she plays a theoretically significant role in the competitive free enterprise system. The fairness of the system depends upon what access he or she has to information about goods and services on the market, the lack of coercion imposed on that person to buy goods, and the lack of arbitrary restrictions imposed by the market and/or government on his or her behavior.

In short, equality of opportunity is a doctrine with two sides which applies both to producers and to consumers. If, then, a person as a consumer or a producer is injured by a defective product—which is one way his activities might arbitrarily be restricted by the action of (one of the members of) the market system—surely his free and voluntary participation in the system of free enterprise will be seriously affected. Specifically, his equal opportunity to participate in the system in order to fulfill his own ends will be diminished.

Here is where strict products liability enters the picture. In cases of strict liability the manufacturer does not intend for a certain aspect of his product to injure someone. Nevertheless, the person is injured. As a result, he is at a disadvantage both as a consumer and as a producer. He cannot continue to play either role as he might wish. Therefore, he is denied that equality of opportunity which is basic to the economic system in question just as surely as he would be if he were excluded from employment by various unintended consequences of the economic system which nevertheless had racially or sexually prejudicial implications. Accordingly, it is fair for the manufacturer to compensate the person for his losses before proceeding with business as usual. That is, the user of a manufacturer's product may justifiably demand compensation from the manufacturer when its product can be shown to be defective and has injured him and harmed his chances of participation in the system of free enterprise.

Hence, strict liability finds a basis in the notion of equality of opportunity which plays a central role in the notion of a free enterprise system. That is why a business which does *not* have to pay for the injuries an individual suffers in the use of a defective article made by that business is felt to be unfair to its customers. Its situation is analogous to that of a player's unintentional violation of a game rule which is intended to foster equality of competitive opportunity.

A soccer player, for example, may unintentionally trip an opposing player. He did not mean to do it: perhaps he himself had stumbled. Still, he has to be penalized. If the referee looked the other way, the tripped player would rightfully object that he had been treated unfairly. Similarly, the manufacturer of a product may be held strictly liable for a product of his which injures a person who uses that product. Even if he is faultless, a consequence of his activities is to render the user of his product less capable of equal participation in the socioeconomic system. The manufacturer should be penalized by way of compensating the victim. Thus, the basis upon which manufacturers are held strictly liable is compensatory justice.

In a society which refuses to resort to paternalism or to central direction of the economy and which turns, instead, to competition in order to allocate scarce positions and resources, compensatory justice requires that the competition be fair and losers be protected.[25] Specifically, no one who loses should be left so destitute that he cannot reenter the competition. Furthermore, those who suffer injuries traceable to defective merchandise or services which restrict their participation in the competitive system should also be compensated.

Compensatory justice does not presuppose negligence or evil intentions on the part of those to whom the injuries might ultimately be traced. It is not perplexed or incapacitated by the relative innocence of all parties involved. Rather, it is concerned with correcting the disadvantaged situation an individual experiences due to accidents or failures which occur in the normal working of that competitive system. It is on this basis that other compensatory programs which alleviate the disabilities of various minority groups are founded. Strict products liability is also founded on compensatory justice.

An implication of the preceding argument is that business is not morally obliged to pay, as such, for the physical injury a person suffers. Rather, it must pay for the loss of equal competitive opportunity—even though it usually is the case that it is because of a (physical) injury that there is a loss of equal opportunity. Actual legal cases in which the injury which prevents a person from going about his or her daily activities is emotional or mental, as well as physical, support this thesis. If a person were neither mentally nor physically harmed, but still rendered less capable of participating competitively because of a defective aspect of a product, there would still be grounds for holding the company liable.

For example, suppose I purchased and used a cosmetic product guaranteed to last a month. When used by most people it is odorless. On me, however, it has a terrible smell. I can stand the smell, but my co-workers and most other people find it intolerable. My employer sends me home from work until it wears off. The product has not harmed me physically or mentally. Still, on the above argument, I would have reason to hold the manufacturer liable. Any cosmetic product with this result is defective. As a consequence my opportunity to participate in the socioeconomic system is curbed. I should be compensated.

IV

There is another way of arriving at the same conclusion about the basis of strict products liability. To speak of business or the free enterprise system, it was noted above, is to speak of the voluntary exchanges between producer and customer which take place when each party believes he has an opportunity to benefit. Surely customers and producers may miscalculate their benefits; something they voluntarily agreed to buy or sell may turn out not to be to their benefit. The successful person does not have any moral responsibilities to the unsuccessful person—at least as a member of this economic system. If, however, fraud is the reason one person does not benefit, the system is, in principle, undermined. If such fraud were universalized, the system would collapse. Accordingly, the person committing the fraud does have a responsibility to make reparations to the one mistreated.

Consider once again the instance of a person who is harmed by a product he bought or used, a product that can reasonably be said to be defective. Has the nature of the free enterprise system also been undermined or corrupted in this instance? Producer and consumer have exchanged the product but it has not been to their mutual benefit; the manufacturer may have benefited, but the customer has suffered because of the defect. Furthermore, if such exchanges were universalized, the system would also be undone.

Suppose that whenever people bought products from manufacturers the products turned out to be defective and the customers were always injured, even though the manufacturers could not be held negligent. Though one party to such exchanges might benefit, the other party always suffered. If the rationale for this economic system—the reason it was adopted and is defended—were that in the end both parties share the equal opportunity to gain, surely it would collapse with the above consequences. Consequently, as with fraud, an economic system of free enterprise requires that injuries which result from defective products be compensated. The question is: Who is to pay for the compensation?

There are three possibilities. The injured party could pay for his own injuries. However, this is implausible since what is called for is compensation and not merely payment for injuries. If the injured party had simply injured himself, if he had been negligent or careless, then it is plausible that he should pay for his own injuries. No compensation is at stake here. But in the present case the injury stems from the actions of a particular manufacturer who, albeit unwittingly, placed the defective product on the market and stands to gain through its sale.

The rationale of the free enterprise system would be undermined, we have seen, if such actions were universalized, for then the product user's equal opportunity to benefit from the system would be denied. Accordingly, since the rationale and motivation for an individual to be part of this socioeconomic system is his opportunity to gain from participation in it, justice requires that the injured product user receive compensation for his injuries. Since the individual can hardly compensate himself, he must receive compensation from some other source.

Second, some third party—such as government—could compensate the injured person. This is not wholly implausible if one is prepared to modify the structure of the free enterprise system. And, indeed, in the long run this may be the most plausible course of action. However, if one accepts the structure of the free enterprise system, this alternative must be rejected because it permits the interference of government into individual affairs.[26]

Third, we are left with the manufacturer. Suppose a manufacturer's product, even though the manufacturer wasn't negligent, always turned out to be defective and injured those using his products. We might sympathize with his plight, but he would either have to stop manufacturing altogether (no one would buy such products) or else compensate the victims for their losses. (Some people might buy and use his products under these conditions.) If he forced people to buy and use his products he would corrupt the free enterprise system. If he did not compensate the injured users, they would not buy and he would not be able to sell his products. Hence, he could partake of the free enterprise system—that is, sell his products—only if he compensated his user/victims. Accordingly, the sale of this hypothetical line of defective products would be voluntarily accepted as just or fair only if compensation were paid the user/victims of such products by the manufacturer.

The same conclusion follows even if we consider a single defective product. The manufacturer put the defective product on the market. Because of his actions others who seek the opportunity to participate on an equal basis in this system in order to benefit therefrom are unable to do so. Thus, a result of his actions, even though unintended, is to undermine the system's character and integrity. Accordingly, when a person is injured in his attempt to participate in this system, he is owed compensation by the manufacturer. The seller of the defective article must not jeopardize the equal opportunity of the product user to benefit from the system. The seller need not guarantee that the buyer/user will benefit from the purchase of the product; after all, the buyer may miscalculate or be careless in the use of a nondefective product. But if he is not careless or has not miscalculated, his opportunity to benefit from the system is illegitimately harmed if he is injured in its use because of the product's defectiveness. He deserves compensation.

It follows from the arguments in this and the preceding section that strict products liability is not only compatible with the system of free enterprise but that if it were not attributed to the manufacturer the system itself would be morally defective. And the justification for requiring manufacturers to pay compensation when people are injured by defective products is that the demands of compensatory justice are met.[27]

NOTES

1. This characterization of strict products liability is adapted from Alvin S. Weinstein et al., *Products Liability and the Reasonably Safe Product* (New York: John Wiley & Sons, 1978), ch. 1. I understand the seller to include the manufacturer, the retailer, distributors, and wholesalers. For the sake of convenience, I will generally refer simply to the manufacturer.
2. Cf. John W. Wade, "On Product 'Design Defects' and Their Actionability," 33 *Vanderbilt Law Review* 553 (1980); Weinstein et al., *Products Liability and the Reasonably Safe Product,* pp. 8, 28–32; Reed Dickerson, "Products Liability: How Good Does a Product Have to Be?" 42 *Indiana Law Journal* 308–316 (1967). Section 402A of the Restatement (Second) of Torts characterizes the seller's situation in this fashion: "the seller has exercised all possible care in the preparation and sale of his product."
3. Cf. John C. Perham, "The Dilemma in Product Liability," *Dun's Review,* 109 (1977), pp. 48–50. 76. W. Page Keeton, "Products Liability—Design Hazards and the Meaning of Defect," 10 *Cumberland Law Review* 293–316 (1979); Weinstein et al., *Products Liability and the Reasonably Safe Product,* ch. 1.
4. More properly, of course, the person's use of the manufacturer's product harmed the product user.
5. Clearly one of the central questions confronting the notion of strict liability is what is to count as "defective." With few exceptions, it is held that a product is defective if and only if it is unreasonably dangerous. There have been several different standards proposed as measures of the defectiveness or unreasonably dangerous nature of a product. However, in terms of logical priorities, it really does not matter what the particular standard for defectiveness is unless we know whether we may justifiably hold manufacturers strictly liable for defective products. That is why I concentrate in this paper on the justifiability of strict products liability.
6. Michel A. Coccia, John W. Dondanville, and Thomas R. Nelson, *Product Liability: Trends and Implications* (New York: American Management Association, 1970), p. 13; W. Page Keeton, "The Meaning of Defect in Products Liability Law—A Review of Basic Principles," 45 *Missouri Law Review* 580 (1980); William L. Prosser, "The Assault Upon the Citadel (Strict Liability to the Consumer)," 69 *The Yale Law Journal* 119 (1960).
7. Coccia, Dondanville, and Nelson, *Product Liability: Trends and Implications,* p. 13; Keeton, "The Meaning of Defect in Products Liability Law—A Review of Basic Principles," pp. 580–581; David G. Owen, "Rethinking the Policies of Strict Products Liability," 33 *Vanderbilt Law Review* 686 (1980); Prosser, "The Assault Upon the Citadel (Strict Liability to the Consumer)," p. 1120.
8. Marcus L. Plant, "Strict Liability of Manufacturers for Injuries Caused by Defects in Products—An Op-

posing View," 24 *Tennessee Law Review* 945 (1957); Prosser, "The Assault Upon the Citadel (Strict Liability to the Consumer)," pp. 1114, 1115, 1119.

9. Keeton, "The Meaning of Defect in Products Liability Law—A Review of Basic Principles," pp. 594–595; Weinstein et al., *Products Liability and the Reasonably Safe Product,* p. 55.
10. An objection might be raised that such accidents ought not to fall under strict products liability and hence do not constitute a counterexample to the above justification. This objection is answered in Sections III and IV.
11. These three considerations are formulated by Michael D. Smith, "The Morality of Strict Liability in Tort," *Business and Professional Ethics Newsletter,* 3(1979), p. 4. Smith himself, however, was drawing upon Guido Calabresi, "Some Thoughts on Risk Distribution and the Law of Torts," 70 *Yale Law Journal* 499–553 (1961).
12. Smith, "The Morality of Strict Liability in Tort," p. 4. Cf. George P. Fletcher, "Fairness and Utility in Tort Theory," 85 *Harvard Law Review* 537–573 (1972).
13. Rev. Francis E. Lucey, S. J., "Liability Without Fault and the Natural Law," 24 *Tennessee Law Review* 952–962 (1957); Perham, "The Dilemma in Product Liability," pp. 48–49.
14. Plant, "Strict Liability of Manufacturers for Injuries Caused by Defects in Products—An Opposing View," pp. 946–947. By "elastic demand" is meant "a slight increase in price will cause a sharp reduction in demand or will turn consumers to a substitute product" (pp. 946–947).
15. Cf. Prosser, "The Assault Upon the Citadel (Strict Liability to the Consumer)," pp. 1140–1141; Wade, "On Product 'Design Defects' and Their Actionability," p. 569; Coccia, Dondanville, and Nelson, *Product Liability: Trends and Implications,* p. 19.
16. F. A. Hayek emphasizes this point in "The Moral Element in Free Enterprise," in *Studies in Philosophy, Politics, and Economics* (New York: Simon and Schuster, 1967), p. 229.
17. Several of these characteristics have been drawn from Milton Friedman and Rose Friedman, *Free to Choose* (New York: Avon Books, 1980).
18. Calabresi, "Product Liability: Curse or Bulwark of Free Enterprise," 27 *Cleveland State Law Review* 325 (1978).
19. *Ibid.,* p. 321.
20. *Ibid.*
21. *Ibid.,* p. 324.
22. *Ibid.*
23. Cf. H. B. Acton, *The Morals of Markets* (London: Longman Group Limited, 1971), pp. 1–7, 33–37; Milton Friedman and Rose Friedman, *Free to Choose.*
24. Milton Friedman and Rose Friedman, *Free to Choose,* pp. 123–124.
25. I have drawn heavily, in this paragraph, on the fine article by Bernard Boxhill, "The Morality of Reparation," reprinted in *Reverse Discrimination,* ed. Barry R. Gross (Buffalo, New York: Prometheus Books, 1977). pp. 270–278.
26. Cf. Calabresi, "Product Liability: Curse or Bulwark of Free Enterprise," pp. 315–319.
27. I would like to thank the following for providing helpful comments on earlier versions of this paper: Betsy Postow, Jerry Phillips, Bruce Fisher, John Hardwig, and Sheldon Cohen.

QUESTIONS FOR DISCUSSION

1. The CEO of Consumer Products Unlimited opened the annual meeting with a speech about CPU's commitment to "serving the needs of the consumer." At the same meeting, she announced the introduction of a new bath soap into the company's product line, which already contained eleven soaps. She explained that it had the same formula as three of CPU's other soaps, but it would have a French name, would cost more, and would appeal to a more sophisticated consumer. The marketing division, she said, was already beginning an aggressive ad campaign. Do consumers *need* CPU's new soap? Do they want it? If so, in what sense? If not, why not? Would CPU's ads be deceptive if they claimed that the soap contained "unique European skin-care ingredients"?

2. Galbraith claims that U.S. society is rich in private goods, such as those produced by CPU, but poor in public goods such as clean air, parks, and public transportation. According to Galbraith, does this mean that people want public goods less than they want private goods? Explain. Would it make sense to conduct advertising campaigns for public goods? Why or why not?

3. Explain when a manufacturer is liable under the doctrine of strict products liability, and when he is not. What is the point of Brenkert's table-tennis analogy? Are there any other appropriate sports analogies that illuminate strict products liability?
4. Evaluate Nestle's sale of infant formula in developing countries in light of Holley's discussion of the morality of sales practices.

CHAPTER 11

THE ENVIRONMENT

Morality, Money, and Motor Cars

Norman Bowie
Andersen Chair in Corporate Responsibility, University of Minnesota

Environmentalists frequently argue that business has special obligations to protect the environment. Although I agree with the environmentalists on this point, I do not agree with them as to where the obligations lie. Business does not have an obligation to protect the environment over and above what is required by law; however, it does have a moral obligation to avoid intervening in the political arena in order to defeat or weaken environmental legislation. In developing this thesis, several points are in order. First, many businesses have violated important moral obligations, and the violation has had a severe negative impact on the environment. For example, toxic waste haulers have illegally dumped hazardous material, and the environment has been harmed as a result. One might argue that those toxic waste haulers who have illegally dumped have violated a special obligation to the environment. Isn't it more accurate to say that these toxic waste haulers have violated their obligation to obey the law and that in this case the law that has been broken is one pertaining to the environment? Businesses have an obligation to obey the law—environmental laws and all others. Since there are many well-publicized cases of business having broken environmental laws, it is easy to think that business has violated some special obligations to the environment. In fact, what business has done is to disobey the law. Environmentalists do not need a special obligation to the environment to protect the environment against illegal business activity; they need only insist that business obey the laws.

Business has broken other obligations beside the obligation to obey the law and has harmed the environment as a result. Consider the grounding of the Exxon oil tanker *Valdez* in Alaska. That grounding was allegedly caused by the fact that an inadequately trained crewman was piloting the

From *Business, Ethics, and the Environment: The Public Policy Debate*, edited by W. Michael Hoffman, Robert Frederick, and Edward S. Petry, Jr. (Westport, CT: Quorum Books, 1990).

tanker while the captain was below deck and had been drinking. What needs to be determined is whether Exxon's policies and procedures were sufficiently lax so that it could be said Exxon was morally at fault. It might be that Exxon is legally responsible for the accident under the doctrine of respondent superior, but Exxon is not thereby morally responsible. Suppose, however, that Exxon's policies were so lax that the company could be characterized as morally negligent. In such a case, the company would violate its moral obligation to use due care and avoid negligence. Although its negligence was disastrous to the environment, Exxon would have violated no special obligation to the environment. It would have been morally negligent.

A similar analysis could be given to the environmentalists' charges that Exxon's cleanup procedures were inadequate. If the charge is true, either Exxon was morally at fault or not. If the procedures had not been implemented properly by Exxon employees, then Exxon is legally culpable, but not morally culpable. On the other hand, if Exxon lied to government officials by saying that its policies were in accord with regulations and/or were ready for emergencies of this type, then Exxon violated its moral obligation to tell the truth. Exxon's immoral conduct would have harmed the environment, but it violated no special obligation to the environment. More important, none is needed. Environmentalists, like government officials, employees, and stockholders, expect that business firms and officials have moral obligations to obey the law, avoid negligent behavior, and tell the truth. In sum, although many business decisions have harmed the environment, these decisions violated no environmental moral obligations. If a corporation is negligent in providing for worker safety, we do not say the corporation violated a special obligation to employees; we say that it violated its obligation to avoid negligent behavior.

The crucial issues concerning business obligations to the environment focus on the excess use of natural resources (the dwindling supply of oil and gas, for instance) and the externalities of production (pollution, for instance). The critics of business want to claim that business has some special obligation to mitigate or solve these problems. I believe this claim is largely mistaken. If business does have a special obligation to help solve the environmental crisis, that obligation results from the special knowledge that business firms have. If they have greater expertise than other constituent groups in society, then it can be argued that, other things being equal, business's responsibilities to mitigate the environmental crisis are somewhat greater. Absent this condition, business's responsibility is no greater than and may be less than that of other social groups. What leads me to think that the critics of business are mistaken?

William Frankena distinguished obligations in an ascending order of the difficulty in carrying them out: avoiding harm, preventing harm, and doing good.[1] The most stringent requirement, to avoid harm, insists no one has a right to render harm on another unless there is a compelling, overriding moral reason to do so. Some writers have referred to this obligation as the moral minimum. A corporation's behavior is consistent with the moral minimum if it causes no avoidable harm to others.

Preventing harm is a less stringent obligation, but sometimes the obligation to prevent harm may be nearly as strict as the obligation to avoid harm. Suppose you are the only person passing a 2-foot-deep working pool where a young child is drowning. There is no one else in the vicinity. Don't you have a strong moral obligation to prevent the child's death? Our obligation to prevent harm is not unlimited, however. Under what conditions must we be good samaritans? Some have argued that four conditions must exist before one is obligated to prevent harm: capability, need, proximity, and last resort.[2] These conditions are all met with the case of the drowning child. There is obviously a need that you can meet since you are both in the vicinity and have the resources to prevent the drowning with little effort; you are also the last resort.

The least strict moral obligation is to do good—to make contributions to society or to help solve problems (inadequate primary schooling in the inner cities, for example). Although corporations may have some minimum obligation in this regard based on an argument from corporate citizenship, the obligations of the corporation to do good cannot be expanded without limit. An injunction to assist in solving societal problems makes impossible demands on a corporation because at the practical level, it ignores the impact that such activities have on profit.

It might seem that even if this descending order of strictness of obligations were accepted, obligations toward the environment would fall into the moral minimum category. After all, the depletion of natural resources and pollution surely harm the environment. If so, wouldn't the obligations business has to the environment be among the strictest obligations a business can have?

Suppose, however, that a businessperson argues that the phrase "avoid harm" usually applies to human beings. Polluting a lake is not like injuring a human with a faulty product. Those who coined the phrase *moral minimum* for use in the business context defined harm as "particularly including activities which violate or frustrate the enforcement of rules of domestic or institutional law intended to protect individuals against prevention of health, safety or basic freedom."[3] Even if we do not insist that the violations be violations of a rule of law, polluting a lake would not count as a harm under this definition. The environmentalists would respond that it would. Polluting the lake may be injuring people who might swim in or eat fish from it. Certainly it would be depriving people of the freedom to enjoy the lake. Although the environmentalist is correct, especially if we grant the legitimacy of a human right to a clean environment, the success of this reply is not enough to establish the general argument.

Consider the harm that results from the production of automobiles. We know statistically that about 50,000 persons per year will die and that nearly 250,000 others will be seriously injured in automobile accidents in the United States alone. Such death and injury, which is harmful, is avoidable. If that is the case, doesn't the avoid-harm criterion require that the production of automobiles for profit cease? Not really. What such arguments point out is that some refinement of the moral minimum standard needs to take place. Take the automobile example. The automobile is itself a good-producing instrument. Because of the advantages of automobiles, society accepts the possible risks that go in using them. Society also accepts many other types of avoidable harm. We take certain risks—ride in planes, build bridges, and mine coal—to pursue advantageous goals. It seems that the high benefits of some activities justify the resulting harms. As long as the risks are known, it is not wrong that some avoidable harm be permitted so that other social and individual goals can be achieved. The avoidable-harm criterion needs some sharpening.

Using the automobile as a paradigm, let us consider the necessary refinements for the avoid-harm criterion. It is a fundamental principle of ethics that "ought" implies "can." That expression means that you can be held morally responsible only for events within your power. In the ought-implies-can principle, the overwhelming majority of highway deaths and injuries is not the responsibility of the automaker. Only those deaths and injuries attributable to unsafe automobile design can be attributed to the automaker. The ought-implies-can principle can also be used to absolve the auto companies of responsibility for death and injury from safety defects that the automakers could not reasonably know existed. The company could not be expected to do anything about them.

Does this mean that a company has an obligation to build a car as safe as it knows how? No. The standards for safety must leave the product's cost within the price range of the consumer ("ought implies can" again). Comments about engineering and equipment capability are obvious enough. But for a business, capability is also a function of profitability. A company that builds a maximally safe car at a cost that puts it at a competitive disadvantage and hence threatens its survival is building a safe car that lies beyond the capability of the company.

Critics of the automobile industry will express horror at these remarks, for by making capability a function of profitability, society will continue to have avoidable deaths and injuries; however, the situation is not as dire as the critics imagine. Certainly capability should not be sacrificed completely so that profits can be maximized. The decision to build products that are cheaper in cost but are not maximally safe is a social decision that has widespread support. The arguments occur over the line between safety and cost. What we have is a classical trade-off situation. What is desired is some appropriate mix between engineering safety and consumer demand. To say there must be some mix between engineering safety and consumer demand is not to justify all the decisions made by the automobile companies. Ford Motor Company made a morally incorrect choice in placing Pinto gas tanks where it did. Consumers were uninformed, the record of the Pinto in rear-end collisions was worse than that of competitors, and Ford fought government regulations.

Let us apply the analysis of the automobile industry to the issue before us. That analysis shows that an automobile company does not violate its obligation to avoid harm and hence is not in violation of the moral minimum if the trade-off between potential harm and the utility of the products rests on social consensus and competitive realities.

As long as business obeys the environmental laws and honors other standard moral obligations, most harm done to the environment by business has been accepted by society. Through their decisions in the marketplace, we can see that most consumers are unwilling to pay extra for products that are more environmentally friendly than less friendly competitive products. Nor is there much evidence that consumers are willing to conserve resources, recycle, or tax themselves for environmental causes.

Consider the following instances reported in the *Wall Street Journal.*[4] The restaurant chain Wendy's tried to replace foam plates and cups with paper, but customers in the test markets balked. Procter and Gamble offered Downey fabric softener in concentrated form that requires less packaging than ready-to-use products; however the concentrate version is less convenient because it has to be mixed with water. Sales have been poor. Procter and Gamble manufactures Vizir and Lenor brands of detergents in concentrate form, which the customer mixes at home in reusable bottles. Europeans will take the trouble; Americans will not. Kodak tried to eliminate its yellow film boxes but met customer resistance. McDonald's has been testing mini-incinerators that convert trash into energy but often meets opposition from community groups that fear the incinerators will pollute the air. A McDonald's spokesperson points out that the emissions are mostly carbon dioxide and water vapor and are "less offensive than a barbecue." Exxon spent approximately $9,200,000 to "save" 230 otters ($40,000 for each otter). Otters in captivity cost $800. Fishermen in Alaska are permitted to shoot otters as pests.[5] Given these facts, doesn't business have every right to assume that public tolerance for environmental damage is quite high, and hence current legal activities by corporations that harm the environment do not violate the avoid-harm criterion?

Recently environmentalists have pointed out the environmental damage caused by the widespread use of disposable diapers. Are Americans ready to give them up and go back to cloth diapers and the diaper pail? Most observers think not. Procter and Gamble is not violating the avoid-harm criterion by manufacturing Pampers. Moreover, if the public wants cloth diapers, business certainly will produce them. If environmentalists want business to produce products that are friendlier to the environment, they must convince Americans to purchase them. Business will respond to the market. It is the consuming public that has the obligation to make the trade-off between cost and environmental integrity.

Data and arguments of the sort described should give environmental critics of business pause. Nonetheless, these critics are not without counter-responses. For example, they might respond that public attitudes are changing. Indeed, they point out, during the Reagan deregulation era, the one area where the public supported government regulations was in the area of environmental law. In addition, *Fortune* predicts environmental integrity as the primary demand of society on business in the 1990s.[6]

More important, they might argue that environmentally friendly products are at a disadvantage in the marketplace because they have public good characteristics. After all, the best situation for the individual is one where most other people use environmentally friendly products but he or she does not, hence reaping the benefit of lower cost and convenience. Since everyone reasons this way, the real demand for environmentally friendly products cannot be registered in the market. Everyone is understating the value of his or her preference for environmentally friendly products. Hence, companies cannot conclude from market behavior that the environmentally unfriendly products are preferred.

Suppose the environmental critics are right that the public goods characteristic of environmentally friendly products creates a market failure. Does that mean the companies are obligated to stop producing these environmentally unfriendly products? I think not, and I propose that we use the four conditions attached to the prevent-harm obligation to show why not. There is a need, and certainly corporations that cause environmental problems are in proximity. However, environmentally clean firms, if there are any, are not in proximity at all, and most business firms are not in proximity with respect to most environmental problems. In other words, the environmental critic must limit his or her argument to the environmental damage a business actually causes. The environmentalist might argue that Procter and Gamble ought to do something about Pampers; I do not see how an environmentalist can use the avoid-harm criterion to argue that Procter and Gamble should do something about acid rain. But even narrowing the obligation to damage actually caused will not be sufficient to establish an obligation to pull a product from the market because it damages the environment or even to go beyond what is legally required to protect the environment. Even for damage actually done, both the high cost of protecting the environment and the competitive pressures of business make further action to protect the environment beyond the capability of business. This conclusion would be more serious if business were the last resort, but it is not.

Traditionally it is the function of the government to correct for market failure. If the market cannot register the true desires of consumers, let them register their preferences in the political arena. Even fairly conservative economic thinkers allow government a legitimate role in correcting market failure. Perhaps the responsibility for energy conservation and pollution control belongs with the government.

Although I think consumers bear a far greater responsibility for preserving and protecting the environment than they have actually exercised, let us assume that the basic responsibility rests with the government. Does that let business off the hook? No. Most of business's unethical conduct regarding the environment occurs in the political arena.

Far too many corporations try to have their cake and eat it too. They argue that it is the job of government to correct for market failure and then use their influence and money to defeat or water down regulations designed to conserve and protect the environment.[7] They argue that consumers should decide how much conservation and protection the environment should have, and then they try to interfere with the exercise of that choice in the political arena. Such behavior is inconsistent and ethically inappropriate. Business has an obligation to avoid intervention in the political process for the purpose of defeating and weakening environmental regulations. Moreover, this is a special obligation to the environment since business does not have a general obligation to avoid pursuing its own parochial interests in the political arena. Business need do nothing wrong when it seeks to influence tariffs, labor policy, or monetary policy. Business does do something wrong when it interferes with the passage of environmental legislation. Why?

First, such a noninterventionist policy is dictated by the logic of the business's argument to avoid a special obligation to protect the environment. Put more formally:

1. Business argues that it escapes special obligations to the environment because it is willing to respond to consumer preferences in this matter.
2. Because of externalities and public goods considerations, consumers cannot express their preferences in the market.
3. The only other viable forum for consumers to express their preferences is in the political arena.
4. Business intervention interferes with the expression of these preferences.

5. Since point 4 is inconsistent with point 1, business should not intervene in the political process.

The importance of this obligation in business is even more important when we see that environmental legislation has special disadvantages in the political arena. Public choice reminds us that the primary interest of politicians is being reelected. Government policy will be skewed in favor of policies that provide benefits to an influential minority as long as the greater costs are widely dispersed. Politicians will also favor projects where benefits are immediate and where costs can be postponed to the future. Such strategies increase the likelihood that a politician will be reelected.

What is frightening about the environmental crisis is that both the conservation of scarce resources and pollution abatement require policies that go contrary to a politician's self-interest. The costs of cleaning up the environment are immediate and huge, yet the benefits are relatively long range (many of them exceedingly long range). Moreover, a situation where the benefits are widely dispersed and the costs are large presents a twofold problem. The costs are large enough so that all voters will likely notice them and in certain cases are catastrophic for individuals (e.g., for those who lose their jobs in a plant shutdown).

Given these facts and the political realities they entail, business opposition to environmental legislation makes a very bad situation much worse. Even if consumers could be persuaded to take environmental issues more seriously, the externalities, opportunities to free ride, and public goods characteristics of the environment make it difficult for even enlightened consumers to express their true preference for the environment in the market. The fact that most environmental legislation trades immediate costs for future benefits makes it difficult for politicians concerned about reelection to support it. Hence it is also difficult for enlightened consumers to have their preferences for a better environment honored in the political arena. Since lack of business intervention seems necessary, and might even be sufficient, for adequate environmental legislation, it seems business has an obligation not to intervene. Nonintervention would prevent the harm of not having the true preferences of consumers for a clean environment revealed. Given business's commitment to satisfying preferences, opposition to having these preferences expressed seems inconsistent as well.

The extent of this obligation to avoid intervening in the political process needs considerable discussion by ethicists and other interested parties. Businesspeople will surely object that if they are not permitted to play a role, Congress and state legislators will make decisions that will put them at a severe competitive disadvantage. For example, if the United States develops stricter environmental controls than other countries do, foreign imports will have a competitive advantage over domestic products. Shouldn't business be permitted to point that out? Moreover, any legislation that places costs on one industry rather than another confers advantages on other industries. The cost to the electric utilities from regulations designed to reduce the pollution that causes acid rain will give advantages to natural gas and perhaps even solar energy. Shouldn't the electric utility industry be permitted to point that out?

These questions pose difficult questions, and my answer to them should be considered highly tentative. I believe the answer to the first question is "yes" and the answer to the second is "no." Business does have a right to insist that the regulations apply to all those in the industry. Anything else would seem to violate norms of fairness. Such issues of fairness do not arise in the second case. Since natural gas and solar do not contribute to acid rain and since the costs of acid rain cannot be fully captured in the market, government intervention through regulation is simply correcting a market failure. With respect to acid rain, the electric utilities do have an advantage they do not deserve. Hence they have no right to try to protect it.

Legislative bodies and regulatory agencies need to expand their staffs to include technical experts, economists, and engineers so that the political process can be both neutral and highly informed about environmental matters. To gain the respect of business and the public, its performance needs to improve. Much more needs to be said to make any contention that business ought to stay out of the political debate theoretically and practically possible. Perhaps these suggestions point the way for future discussion.

Ironically business might best improve its situation in the political arena by taking on an additional obligation to the environment. Businesspersons often have more knowledge about environmental harms and the costs of cleaning them up. They may often have special knowledge about how to prevent environmental harm in the first place. Perhaps business has a special duty to educate the public and to promote environmentally responsible behavior.

Business has no reticence about leading consumer preferences in other areas. Advertising is a billion-dollar industry. Rather than blaming consumers for not purchasing environmentally friendly products, perhaps some businesses might make a commitment to capture the environmental niche. I have not seen much imagination on the part of business in this area. Far too many advertisements with an environmental message are reactive and public relations driven. Recall those by oil companies showing fish swimming about the legs of oil rigs. An educational campaign that encourages consumers to make environmentally friendly decisions in the marketplace would limit the necessity for business activity in the political arena. Voluntary behavior that is environmentally friendly is morally preferable to coerced behavior. If business took greater responsibility for educating the public, the government's responsibility would be lessened. An educational campaign aimed at consumers would likely enable many businesses to do good while simultaneously doing very well.

Hence business does have obligations to the environment, although these obligations are not found where the critics of business place them. Business has no special obligation to conserve natural resources or to stop polluting over and above its legal obligations. It does have an obligation to avoid intervening in the political arena to oppose environmental regulations, and it has a positive obligation to educate consumers. The benefits of honoring these obligations should not be underestimated.

NOTES

The title for this chapter was suggested by Susan Bernick, a graduate student in the University of Minnesota philosophy department.

1. William Frankena, *Ethics,* 2d ed. (Englewood Cliffs, N.J.: Prentice-Hall, 1973), p. 47. Actually Frankena has four principles of prima facie duty under the principle of beneficence: one ought not to inflict evil or harm; one ought to prevent evil or harm; one ought to remove evil; and one ought to do or promote good.
2. John G. Simon, Charles W. Powers, and Jon P. Gunneman, *The Ethical Investor: Universities and Corporate Responsibility* (New Haven, Conn.: Yale University Press, 1972), pp. 22–25.
3. Ibid., p. 21.
4. Alicia Swasy, "For Consumers, Ecology Comes Second," *Wall Street Journal,* August 23, 1988, p. B1.
5. Jerry Alder, "Alaska after Exxon," *Newsweek,* September 18, 1989, p. 53.
6. Andrew Kupfer, "Managing Now for the 1990s," *Fortune,* September 26, 1988, pp. 46–47.
7. I owe this point to Gordon Rands, a Ph.D. student in the Carlson School of Management. Indeed the tone of the chapter has shifted considerably as a result of his helpful comments.

Business and Environmental Ethics

W. Michael Hoffman
Executive Director, Center for Business Ethics, Bentley College

The business ethics movement, from my perspective, is still on the march. And the environmental movement, after being somewhat silent for the past twenty years, has once again captured our attention—promising to be a major social force in the 1990s. Much will be written in the next few years trying to tie together these two movements. This is one such effort.

Concern over the environment is not new.

From *Business Ethics Quarterly,* Vol. 1, Issue 2, 1991, pp. 169–184. Reprinted by permission of the author.

Warnings came out of the 1960s in the form of burning rivers, dying lakes, and oil-fouled oceans. Radioactivity was found in our food, DDT in mother's milk, lead and mercury in our water. Every breath of air in the North American hemisphere was reported as contaminated. Some said these were truly warnings from Planet Earth of eco-catastrophe, unless we could find limits to our growth and changes in our lifestyle.

Over the past few years Planet Earth began to speak to us even more loudly than before, and we began to listen more than before. The message was ominous, somewhat akin to God warning Noah. It spoke through droughts, heat waves, and forest fires, raising fears of global warming due to the buildup of carbon dioxide and other gases in the atmosphere. It warned us by raw sewage and medical wastes washing up on our beaches, and by devastating oil spills—one despoiling Prince William Sound and its wildlife to such an extent that it made us weep. It spoke to us through increased skin cancers and discoveries of holes in the ozone layer caused by our use of chlorofluorocarbons. It drove its message home through the rapid and dangerous cutting and burning of our primitive forests at the rate of one football field a second, leaving us even more vulnerable to greenhouse gases like carbon dioxide and eliminating scores of irreplaceable species daily. It rained down on us in the form of acid, defoliating our forests and poisoning our lakes and streams. Its warnings were found on barges roaming the seas for places to dump tons of toxic incinerator ash. And its message exploded in our faces at Chernobyl and Bhopal, reminding us of past warnings at Three Mile Island and Love Canal.

Senator Albert Gore said in 1988: "The fact that we face an ecological crisis without any precedent in historic times is no longer a matter of any dispute worthy of recognition."[1] The question, he continued, is not whether there is a problem, but how we will address it. This will be the focal point for a public policy debate which requires the full participation of two of its major players—business and government. The debate must clarify such fundamental questions as: (1) What obligation does business have to help with our environmental crisis? (2) What is the proper relationship between business and government, especially when faced with a social problem of the magnitude of the environment crisis? And (3) what rationale should be used for making and justifying decisions to protect the environment? Corporations, and society in general for that matter, have yet to answer these questions satisfactorily. In the first section of this paper I will briefly address the first two questions. In the final two sections I will say a few things about the third question.

I.

In a 1989 keynote address before the "Business, Ethics and the Environment" conference at the Center for Business Ethics, Norman Bowie offered some answers to the first two questions.

> Business does not have an obligation to protect the environment over and above what is required by law; however, it does have a moral obligation to avoid intervening in the political arena in order to defeat or weaken environmental legislation.[2]

I disagree with Bowie on both counts.

Bowie's first point is very Friedmanesque.[3] The social responsibility of business is to produce goods and services and to make profit for its shareholders, while playing within the rules of the market game. These rules, including those to protect the environment, are set by the government and the courts. To do more than is required by these rules is, according to this position, unfair to business. In order to perform its proper function, every business must respond to the market and operate in the same arena as its competitors. As Bowie puts this:

> An injunction to assist in solving societal problems [including depletion of natural resources and pollution] makes impossible demands on a corporation because, at the practical level, it ignores the impact that such activities have on profit.[4]

If, as Bowie claims, consumers are not willing to respond to the cost and use of environmentally friendly products and actions, then it is not the responsibility of business to respond or correct such market failure.

Bowie's second point is a radical departure from this classical position in contending that business should not lobby against the government's process to set environmental regulations. To quote Bowie:

> Far too many corporations try to have their cake and eat it too. They argue that it is the job of government to correct for market failure and then they use their influence and money to defeat or water down regulations designed to conserve and protect the environment.[5]

Bowie only recommends this abstinence of corporate lobbying in the case of environmental regulations. He is particularly concerned that politicians, ever mindful of their reelection status, are already reluctant to pass environmental legislation which has huge immediate costs and in most cases very long-term benefits. This makes the obligations of business to refrain from opposing such legislation a justified special case.

I can understand why Bowie argues these points. He seems to be responding to two extreme approaches, both of which are inappropriate. Let me illustrate these extremes by the following two stories.

At the Center's First National Conference on Business Ethics, Harvard Business School Professor George Cabot Lodge told of a friend who owned a paper company on the banks of a New England stream. On the first Earth Day in 1970, his friend was converted to the cause of environmental protection. He became determined to stop his company's pollution of the stream, and marched off to put his new-found religion into action. Later, Lodge learned his friend went broke, so he went to investigate. Radiating a kind of ethical purity, the friend told Lodge that he spent millions to stop the pollution and thus could no longer compete with other firms that did not follow his example. So the company went under, 500 people lost their jobs, and the stream remained polluted.

When Lodge asked why his friend hadn't sought help from the state or federal government for stricter standards for everyone, the man replied that was not the American way, that government should not interfere with business activity, and that private enterprise could do the job alone. In fact, he felt it was the social responsibility of business to solve environmental problems, so he was proud that he had set an example for others to follow.

The second story portrays another extreme. A few years ago "Sixty Minutes" interviewed a manager of a chemical company that was discharging effluent into a river in upstate New York. At the time, the dumping was legal, though a bill to prevent it was pending in Congress. The manager remarked that he hoped the bill would pass, and that he certainly would support it as a responsible citizen. However, he also said he approved of his company's efforts to defeat the bill and of the firm's policy of dumping wastes in the meantime. After all, isn't the proper role of business to make as much profit as possible within the bounds of law? Making the laws—setting the rules of the game—is the role of government, not business. While wearing his business hat the manager had a job to do, even if it meant doing something that he strongly opposed as a private citizen.

Both stories reveal incorrect answers to the questions posed earlier, the proof of which is found in the fact that neither the New England stream nor the New York river was made any cleaner. Bowie's points are intended to block these two extremes. But to avoid these extremes, as Bowie does, misses the real managerial and ethical failure of the stories. Although the paper company owner and the chemical company manager had radically different views of the ethical responsibilities of business, both saw business and government performing separate roles, and neither felt that business ought to cooperate with government to solve environmental problems.[6]

If the business ethics movement has led us anywhere in the past fifteen years, it is to the position that business has an ethical responsibility to become a more active partner in dealing with social concerns. Business must creatively find ways to become a part of solutions, rather than being a part of problems. Corporations can and must develop a conscience, as Ken Goodpaster and others have argued—and this includes an environmental conscience.[7] Corporations should not isolate themselves from participation in solving our environmental problems, leaving it up to others to find the answers and to tell them what not to do.

Corporations have special knowledge, expertise, and resources which are invaluable in dealing with the environmental crisis. Society needs the ethical vision and cooperation of all its players to solve its most urgent problems, especially one that involves the very survival of the planet itself. Business must work with government to find appropriate solutions. It should lobby for good environmental legislation and lobby against bad legislation, rather than isolating itself from the legislative process as Bowie suggests. It should not be ethically quixotic and try to go it alone, as our paper company owner tried to do, nor should it be ethically inauthentic and fight against what it believes to be environmentally sound policy, as our chemical company manager tried to do. Instead business must develop and demonstrate moral leadership.

There are examples of corporations demonstrating such leadership, even when this has been a risk to their self-interest. In the area of environmental moral leadership one might cite DuPont's discontinuing its Freon products, a $750-million-a-year-business, because of their possible negative effects on the ozone layer, and Proctor and Gamble's manufacture of concentrated fabric softener and detergents which require less packaging. But some might argue, as Bowie does, that the real burden for environmental change lies with consumers, not with corporations. If we as consumers are willing to accept the harm done to the environment by favoring environmentally unfriendly products, corporations have no moral obligation to change so long as they obey environmental law. This is even more the case, so the argument goes, if corporations must take risks or sacrifice profits to do so.

This argument fails to recognize that we quite often act differently when we think of ourselves as *consumers* than when we think of ourselves as *citizens.* Mark Sagoff, concerned about our over-reliance on economic solutions, clearly characterizes this dual nature of our decision making.[8] As consumers, we act more often than not for ourselves; as citizens, we take on a broader vision and do what is in the best interests of the community. I often shop for things I don't vote for. I might support recycling referendums, but buy products in nonreturnable bottles. I am not proud of this, but I suspect this is more true of most of us than not. To stake our environmental future on our consumer willingness to pay is surely shortsighted, perhaps even disastrous.

I am not saying that we should not work to be ethically committed citizen consumers, and investors for that matter. I agree with Bowie that "consumers bear a far greater responsibility for preserving and protecting the environment than they have actually exercised,"[9] but activities which affect the environment should not be left up to what we, acting as consumers, are willing to tolerate or accept. To do this would be to use a market-based method of reasoning to decide on an issue which should be determined instead on the basis of our ethical responsibilities as a member of a social community.

Furthermore, consumers don't make the products, provide the services, or enact the legislation which can be either environmentally friendly or unfriendly. Grass roots boycotts and lobbying efforts are important, but we also need leadership and mutual cooperation from business and government in setting forth ethical environmental policy. Even Bowie admits that perhaps business has a responsibility to educate the public and promote environmentally responsible behavior. But I am suggesting that corporate moral leadership goes far beyond public educational campaigns. It requires moral vision, commitment, and courage, and involves risk and sacrifice. I think business is capable of such a challenge. Some are even engaging in such a challenge. Certainly the business ethics movement should do nothing short of encouraging such leadership. I feel morality demands such leadership.

II.

If business has an ethical responsibility to the environment which goes beyond obeying environmental law, what criterion should be used to guide and justify such action? Many corporations are making environmentally friendly decisions where they see there are profits to be made by doing so. They are wrapping themselves in green where they see a green bottom line as a consequence. This rationale is also being used as a strategy by environmentalists to encourage more businesses to become environmentally conscientious. In December 1989 the highly respected Worldwatch Institute published an article by one of its senior researchers entitled "Doing Well by Doing Good" which gives numerous examples of corporations improving their pocketbooks by improving the environment. It concludes by saying that "fortunately, businesses that work to preserve the environment can also make a buck."[10]

In a recent Public Broadcast Corporation documentary entitled "Profit the Earth," several efforts are depicted of what is called the "new environmentalism" which induces corporations to do things for the environment by appealing to their self-interest. The Environmental Defense Fund is shown encouraging agribusiness in Southern California to irrigate more efficiently and profit by selling the water saved to the city of Los Angeles. This in turn will help save Mono Lake. EDF is also shown lobbying for emissions trading that would allow utility companies which are under their emission allotments to sell their "pollution rights" to those companies which are over their allotments. This is for the purpose of reducing acid rain. Thus the frequent strategy of the new environmentalists is to get business to help solve environmental problems by finding profitable or virtually costless ways for them to participate. They feel that compromise, not confrontation, is the only way to save the earth. By using the tools of the free enterprise system, they are in search of win-win solutions, believing that such solutions are necessary to take us beyond what we have so far been able to achieve.

I am not opposed to these efforts; in most cases I think they should be encouraged. There is certainly nothing wrong with making money while protecting the environment, just as there is nothing wrong with feeling good about doing one's duty. But if business is adopting or being encouraged to adopt the view that good environmentalism is good business, then I think this poses a danger for the environmental ethics movement—a danger which has an analogy in the business ethics movement.

As we all know, the position that good ethics is good business is being used more and more by corporate executives to justify the building of ethics into their companies and by business ethics consultants to gain new clients. For example, the Business Roundtable's *Corporate Ethics* report states:

> The corporate community should continue to refine and renew efforts to improve performance and manage change effectively through programs in corporate ethics . . . corporate ethics is a strategic key to survival and profitability in this era of fierce competitiveness in a global economy.[11]

And, for instance, the book *The Power of Ethical Management* by Kenneth Blanchard and Norman Vincent Peale states in big red letters on the cover jacket that "Integrity Pays! You Don't Have to Cheat to Win." The blurb on the inside cover promises that the book "gives hard-hitting, practical, *ethical* strategies that build profits, productivity, and long-term success."[12] Who would have guessed that business ethics could deliver all that! In such ways business ethics gets marketed as the newest cure for what ails corporate America.

Is the rationale that good ethics is good business a proper one for business ethics? I think not. One thing that the study of ethics has taught us over the past 2500 years is that being ethical may on occasion require that we place the interests of others ahead of or at least on par with our own interests. And this implies that the ethical thing to do, the morally right thing to do, may not be in our own self-interest. What happens when the right thing is not the best thing for the business?

Although in most cases good ethics may be good business, it should not be advanced as the only or even the main reason for doing business ethically. When the crunch comes, when ethics conflicts with the firm's interests, any ethics program that has not already faced up to this possibility is doomed to fail because it will undercut the rationale of the program itself. We should promote business ethics, not because good ethics is good business, but because we are morally required to adopt the moral point of view in all our dealings—and business is no exception. In business, as in all other human endeavors, we must be prepared to pay the costs of ethical behavior.

There is a similar danger in the environmental movement with corporations choosing or being wooed to be environmentally friendly on the grounds that it will be in their self-interest. There is the risk of participating in the movement for the wrong reasons. But what does it matter if business cooperates for reasons other than the right reasons, as long as it cooperates? It matters if business believes or is led to believe that it only has a duty to be environmentally conscientious in those cases where such actions either require no sacrifice or actually make a profit. And I am afraid this is exactly what is happening. I suppose it wouldn't matter if the environmental cooperation of business was only needed in those cases where it was also in business' self-interest. But this is surely not the case, unless one begins to really reach and talk about that amorphous concept "long-term" self-interest. Moreover, long-term interests, I suspect, are not what corporations or the new environmentalists have in mind in using self-interest as a reason for environmental action.

I am not saying we should abandon attempts to entice corporations into being ethical, both environmentally and in other ways, by pointing out and providing opportunities where good ethics is good business. And there are many places where such attempts fit well in both the business and environmental ethics movements. But we must be careful not to cast this as the proper guideline for business' ethical responsibility. Because when it is discovered that many ethical actions are not necessarily good for business, at least in the short-run, then the rationale based on self-interest will come up morally short, and both ethical movements will be seen as deceptive and shallow.

III.

What is the proper rationale for responsible business action toward the environment? A minimalist principle is to refrain from causing or prevent the causing of unwarranted harm, because failure to do so would violate certain moral rights not to be harmed. There is, of course, much debate over what harms are indeed unwarranted due to conflict of rights and questions about whether some harms are offset by certain benefits. Norm Bowie, for example, uses the harm principle, but contends that business does not violate it as long as it obeys environmental law. Robert Frederick, on the other hand, convincingly argues that the harm principle morally requires business to find ways to prevent certain harm it causes even if such harm violates no environmental law.[13]

However, Frederick's analysis of the harm principle is largely cast in terms of harm caused to human beings and the violation of rights of human beings. Even when he hints at the possible moral obligation to protect the environment when no one is caused unwarranted harm, he does so by suggesting that we look to what we, as human beings, value.[14] This is very much in keeping with a humanistic position of environmental ethics which claims that only human beings have rights or moral standing because only human beings have intrinsic value. We may have duties with regard to nonhuman things (penguins, trees, islands, etc.) but only if such duties are derived from duties we have toward human beings. Nonhuman things are valuable only if valued by human beings.

Such a position is in contrast to a naturalistic view of environmental ethics which holds that natural things other than human beings are intrinsically valuable and have, therefore, moral standing. Some naturalistic environmentalists only include other sentient animals in the framework of being deserving of moral consideration; others include all things which are alive or which are an integral part of an ecosystem. This latter view is sometimes called a biocentric environmental ethic as opposed to the homocentric view which sees all moral claims in terms of human beings and their interests. Some characterize these two views as deep *versus* shallow ecology.

The literature on these two positions is vast and the debate is ongoing. The conflict between them goes to the heart of environmental ethics and is crucial to our making of environmental policy and to our perception of moral duties to the environment, including business'. I strongly favor the biocentric view. And although this is not the place to try to adequately argue for it, let me unfurl its banner for just a moment.

A version of R. Routley's "last man" example[15] might go something like this: Suppose you were the last surviving human being and were soon to die from nuclear poisoning, as all other human and sentient animals have died before you. Suppose also that it is within your power to destroy all remaining life, or to make it simpler, the last tree which could continue to flourish and propagate if left alone. Furthermore you will not suffer if you do not destroy it. Would you do anything wrong by cutting it down? The deeper ecological view would say yes because you would be destroying something that has value in and of itself, thus making the world a poorer place.

It might be argued that the only reason we may find the tree valuable is because human beings generally find trees of value either practically or aesthetically, rather than the atoms or molecules they might turn into if changed from their present form. The issue is whether the tree has value only in its relation to human beings or whether it has a value deserving of moral consideration inherent in itself in its present form. The biocentric position holds that when we find something wrong with destroying the tree, as we should, we do so because we are responding to an intrinsic value in the natural object, not to a value we give to it. This is a view which argues against a humanistic environmental ethic and which urges us to channel our moral obligations accordingly.

Why should one believe that nonhuman living things or natural objects forming integral parts of ecosystems have intrinsic value? One can respond to this question by pointing out the serious weaknesses and problems of human chauvinism.[16] More complete responses lay out a framework of concepts and beliefs which provides a coherent picture of the biocentric view with human beings as a part of a more holistic value system. But the final answer to the question hinges on what criterion one decides to use for determining moral worth—rationality, sentience, or a deeper biocentric one. Why should we adopt the principle of attributing intrinsic value to all living beings, or even to all natural objects, rather than just to human beings? I suspect Arne Naess gives as good an answer as can be given.

> Faced with the ever returning question of 'Why?,' we have to stop somewhere. Here is a place where we well might stop. We shall admit that the value in itself is something shown in intuition. We attribute intrinsic value to ourselves and our nearest, and the validity of further identification can be contested, and *is* contested by many. The negation may, however, also be attacked through a series of 'whys?' Ultimately, we are in the same human predicament of having to start somewhere, at least for the moment. We must stop somewhere and treat where we then stand as a foundation.[17]

In the final analysis, environmental biocentrism is adopted or not depending on whether it is seen to provide a deeper, richer, and more ethically compelling view of the nature of things.

If this deeper ecological position is correct, then it ought to be reflected in the environmental movement. Unfortunately, for the most part, I do not think this is being done, and there is a price to be paid for not doing so. Moreover, I fear that even those who are of the biocentric persuasion are using homocentric language and strategies to bring business and other major players into the movement because they do not think they will be successful otherwise. They are afraid, and undoubtedly for good reason, that the large part of society, including business, will not be moved by arguments regarding the intrinsic value and rights of natural things. It is difficult enough to get business to recognize and act on their responsibilities to human beings and things of human interest. Hence many environmentalists follow the counsel of Spinoza:

> . . . it is necessary that while we are endeavoring to attain our purpose . . . we are compelled . . . to speak in a manner intelligible to the multitude . . . For we can gain from the multitude no small advantages. . . .[18]

I understand the temptation of environmentalists employing a homocentric strategy, just as I understand business ethicists using the rationale that good ethics is good business. Both want their important work to succeed. But just as with the good ethics is good business tack, there are dangers in being a closet ecocentrist. The ethicists in both cases fail to reveal the deeper moral base of their positions because it's a harder sell. Business ethics gets marketed in terms of self-interest, environmental ethics in terms of human interest.

A major concern in using the homocentric view to formulate policy and law is that nonhuman nature will not receive the moral consideration it deserves. It might be argued, however, that by appealing to the interests and rights of human beings, in most cases nature as a whole will be protected. That is, if we are concerned about a wilderness area, we can argue that its survival is important to future generations who will otherwise be deprived of contact with its unique wildlife. We can also argue that it is important to the aesthetic pleasure of certain individuals or that, if it is destroyed, other recreational areas will become overcrowded. In this way we stand a chance to save the wilderness area without having to refer to our moral obligations to respect the intrinsic value of the spotted owl or of the old-growth forest. This is simply being strategically savvy. To trot out our deeper ecological moral convictions runs the risk of our efforts being ignored, even ridiculed, by business leaders and policy makers. It also runs head-on against a barrage of counter arguments that human interests take precedence over nonhuman interests. In any event it will not be in the best interest of the wilderness area we are trying to protect. Furthermore, all of the above homocentric arguments happen to be true—people will suffer if the wilderness area is destroyed.

In most cases, what is in the best interests of human beings may also be in the best interests of the rest of nature. After all, we are in our present environmental crisis in large part because we have not been ecologically intelligent about what is in our own interest—just as business has encountered much trouble because it has failed to see its interest in being ethically sensitive. But if the environmental movement relies only on arguments based on human interests, then it perpetuates the danger of making environmental policy and law on the basis of our strong inclination to fulfill our immediate self-interests, on the basis of our consumer viewpoints, on the basis of our willingness to pay. There will always be a tendency to allow our short-term interests to eclipse our long-term interests and the long-term interest of humanity itself. Without some grounding in a deeper environmental ethic with obligations to nonhuman natural things, then the temptation to view our own interests in disastrously short-term ways is that much more encouraged. The biocentric view helps to block this temptation.

Furthermore, there are many cases where what is in human interest is not in the interest of other natural things. Examples range from killing leopards for stylish coats to destroying a forest to build a golf course. I am not convinced that homocentric arguments, even those based on long-term human interests, have much force in protecting the interests of such natural things. Attempts to make these interests coincide might be made, but the point is that from a homocentric point of view the leopard and the forest have no morally relevant interests to consider. It is simply fortuitous if nonhuman natural interests coincide with human interests, and are thereby valued and protected. Let us take an example from the work of Christopher Stone. Suppose a stream has been polluted by a business. From a homocentric point of view, which serves as the basis for our legal system, we can only correct the problem through finding some harm done to human beings who use the stream. Reparation for such harm might involve cessation of the pollution and restoration of the stream, but it is also possible that the business might settle with the people by paying them for their damages and continue to pollute the stream. Homocentrism provides no way for the stream to be made whole again unless it is in the interests of human beings to do so. In short it is possible for human beings to sell out the stream.[19]

I am not saying that human interests cannot take precedence over nonhuman interests when there are conflicts. For this we need to come up with criteria for deciding on interspecific conflicts of interests, just as we do for intraspecific conflicts of interest among human beings.[20] But this is a different problem from holding that nonhuman natural things have no interests or value deserving of moral consideration. There are times when causing harm to natural things is morally unjustifiable when there are no significant human interests involved and even when there are human interests involved. But only a deeper ecological ethic than homocentrism will allow us to defend this.

Finally, perhaps the greatest danger that biocentric environmentalists run in using homocentric strategies to further the movement is the loss of the very insight that grounded their ethical concern in the first place. This is nicely put by Lawrence Tribe:

> What the environmentalist may not perceive is that, by couching his claim in terms of human self-interest—by articulating environmental goals wholly in terms of human needs and preferences—he may be helping to legitimate a system of discourse which so structures human thought and feeling as to erode, over the long run, the very sense of obligation which provided the initial impetus for his own protective efforts.[21]

Business ethicists run a similar risk in couching their claims in terms of business self-interest.

The environmental movement must find ways to incorporate and protect the intrinsic value of animal and plant life and even other natural objects that are integral parts of ecosystems. This must be done without constantly reducing such values to human interests. This will, of course, be difficult, because our conceptual ideology and ethical persuasion is so dominantly homocentric; however, if we are committed to a deeper biocentric ethic, then it is vital that we try to find appropriate ways to promote it. Environmental impact statements should make explicit reference to nonhuman natural values. Legal rights for nonhuman natural things, along the lines of Christopher Stone's proposal, should be sought.[22] And naturalistic ethical guidelines, such as those suggested by Holmes Rolston, should be set forth for business to follow when its activities impact upon ecosystems.[23]

At the heart of the business ethics movement is its reaction to the mistaken belief that business only has responsibilities to a narrow set of its stakeholders, namely its stockholders. Crucial to the environmental ethics movement is its reaction to the mistaken belief that only human beings and human interests are deserving of our moral consideration. I suspect that the beginnings of both movements can be traced to these respective moral insights. Certainly the significance of both movements lies in their search for a broader and deeper moral perspective. If business and environmental ethicists begin to rely solely on promotional strategies of self-interest, such as good ethics is good business, and of human interest, such as homocentrism, then they face the danger of cutting off the very roots of their ethical efforts.

NOTES

This paper was originally presented as the Presidential Address to the *Society for Business Ethics,* August 10, 1990, San Francisco, CA.

1. Albert Gore, "What is Wrong With Us?" *Time* (January 2, 1989), 66.
2. Norman Bowie, "Morality, Money, and Motor Cars," *Business, Ethics, and the Environment: The Public Policy Debate,* edited by W. Michael Hoffman, Robert Frederick, and Edward S. Petry, Jr. (New York: Quorum Books, 1990), p. 89.
3. See Milton Friedman, "The Social Responsibility of Business Is to Increase Its Profits," *The New York Times Magazine* (September 13, 1970).
4. Bowie, p. 91.
5. Bowie, p. 94.
6. Robert Frederick, Assistant Director of the Center for Business Ethics, and I have developed and written these points together. Frederick has also provided me with invaluable assistance on other points in this paper.
7. Kenneth E. Goodpaster, "Can a Corporation have an Environmental Conscience," *The Corporation, Ethics, and the Environment,* edited by W. Michael Hoffman, Robert Frederick, and Edward S. Petry, Jr. (New York: Quorum Books, 1990).
8. Mark Sagoff, "At the Shrine of Our Lady of Fatima, or Why Political Questions Are Not All Economic," found in *Business Ethics: Readings and Cases in Corporate Morality,* 2nd edition, edited by W. Michael Hoffman and Jennifer Mills Moore (New York: McGraw-Hill, 1990), pp. 494–503.
9. Bowie, p. 94.
10. Cynthia Pollock Shea, "Doing Well By Doing Good," *World-Watch* (November/December, 1989), p. 30.

11. *Corporate Ethics: A Prime Business Asset,* a report by The Business Roundtable, February, 1988, p. 4.
12. Kenneth Blanchard, and Norman Vincent Peale, *The Power of Ethical Management* (New York: William Morrow and Company, Inc., 1988).
13. Robert Frederick, "Individual Rights and Environmental Protection," presented at the Annual Society for Business Ethics Conference in San Francisco, August 10 and 11, 1990.
14. Frederick.
15. Richard Routley, and Val Routley, "Human Chauvinism and Environmental Ethics," *Environmental Philosophy,* Monograph Series, No. 2, edited by Don Mannison, Michael McRobbie, and Richard Routley (Australian National University, 1980), pp. 121ff.
16. See Paul W. Taylor, "The Ethics of Respect for Nature," found in *People, Penguins, and Plastic Trees,* edited by Donald VanDeVeer and Christine Pierce (Belmont, California: Wadsworth, 1986), pp. 178–83. Also see R. and V. Routley, "Against the Inevitability of Human Chauvinism," found in *Ethics and the Problems of the 21st Century,* edited by K. E. Goodpaster and K. M. Sayre (Notre Dame: University of Notre Dame Press, 1979), pp. 36–59.
17. Arne Naess, "Identification as a Source of Deep Ecological Attitudes," *Deep Ecology,* edited by Michael Tobias (San Marcos, California: Avant Books, 1988), p. 266.
18. Benedict de Spinoza, "On the Improvement of the Understanding," found in *Philosophy of Benedict de Spinoza,* translated by R. H. M. Elwes (New York: Tudor Publishing Co., 1936), p. 5.
19. Christopher D. Stone, "Should Trees Have Standing?—Toward Legal Rights for Natural Objects," found in *People, Penguins, and Plastic Trees,* pp. 86–87.
20. See Donald VanDe Veer, "Interspecific Justice," *People, Penguins, and Plastic Trees,* pp. 51–66.
21. Lawrence H. Tribe, "Ways Not to Think about Plastic Trees: New Foundations for Environmental Law," found in *People, Penguins, and Plastic Trees,* p. 257.
22. Stone, pp. 83–96.
23. Holmes Rolston, III, *Environmental Ethics* (Philadelphia: Temple University Press, 1988), pp. 301–13.

Environmental Pollution and the Law

Leonard G. Boonin
Professor of Philosophy, University of Colorado-Boulder

Our society is faced with a host of complex problems relating to the quality of our environment. People are concerned over such matters as air and water pollution, the use of pesticides and other toxic substances, and the disposal of solid and hazardous waste materials.

We are vitally dependent on the use of a great variety of chemical compounds. It has been estimated that some 70,000 different compounds are currently in commercial production—some produced in quantities greater than one billion pounds a year. Most of these are harmless, but a significant number *are* toxic and can pose serious health hazards. Only about 7,000 of these substances have been even partially tested for carcinogenicity. Between 600 and 800 of these are believed to constitute health risks. Through tragic experience we have discovered previously unsuspected compounds to be highly toxic. PCB's, asbestos, benzene, kepone, and dioxin have been added to a list that already included lead, mercury, and radium.

Many of the known toxic substances have valuable social uses, and their complete elimination is hardly possible. Even when such substances are used in comparatively safe ways with adequate protection of those who come in contact with them, serious problems arise over their disposal. Of the approximately 32,000 hazardous waste disposal sites in this country, from 1,200 to 2,000 are estimated to pose significant dangers to human health. About 600 of these sites have been abandoned by their owners.

How has the law sought to deal with problems

From *The Newsletter of the Center for Values and Social Policy,* Vol. XI, No. 2 (Fall 1992). Reprinted by permission of The Center for Values and Social Policy, University of Colorado, Boulder, CO.

of environmental pollution? The "common law" response to such problems makes use of traditional liability rules based on property, tort, and contract law and does not typically involve direct regulation and control. Individuals who believe they have been substantially harmed by specific and identifiable sources of pollution can sue for the personal and property damage they have suffered. The usual remedy in such cases is for monetary damages. Such judgments bring about pollution control only indirectly by providing an incentive to alter conduct. A more direct form of control can be obtained, under fairly restrictive conditions, in the form of injunctive relief prohibiting certain kinds of activity. This remedy applies primarily in suits to abate a nuisance.

The common law approach clearly has serious limitations and fails to provide a systematic and comprehensive response to pollution problems. The plaintiff in such cases has the burden of proving by a preponderance of evidence not only that he or she was harmed but that an identifiable substance was the cause and that the defendant was its source. While this can undoubtedly be established in some cases, in many situations we either lack reliable knowledge about whether a certain substance is harmful or cannot prove that a given harm was caused by that substance or originated with the defendant.

By contrast, the new legislative approach focuses on the prevention of harm, with issues of compensation and fault playing only a subsidiary role. The legislation dealing with such matters as air and water pollution and toxic waste disposal is essentially administrative and regulatory in character. As it is often not completely clear which substances are harmful and at what levels they pose "unreasonable risks" to health and welfare, administrative agencies such as the Environmental Protection Agency have been given authority to conduct research and establish standards. In most traditional tort and criminal law matters one has a fairly clear idea of what constitutes wrongful behavior and can directly see the resulting harm. Many pollution cases do not involve discrete acts which are wrong per se, but rather some socially approved activity which only incrementally increases the likelihood of harm. What conduct is reasonable and unreasonable is often highly judgmental. The common law approach leaves those decisions to the judge or jury in each particular case. The new legislation converts the determination of "unreasonable and unacceptable risks to health and welfare" into technical decisions to be made by administrators. While scientific evidence is clearly relevant in establishing such standards, important kinds of value judgments are also involved.

What is the justification for the new approach? Because usually each polluter only marginally increases the risk of harm with no clear threshold point at which demonstrable harm begins to result, it is easy for each to view his or her conduct as not creating an unreasonable risk. Precise standards settle that question and offer clearer guidance as to acceptable conduct. In addition, they ease administration.

In addition to establishing performance standards, administrative regulations can also introduce design standards specifying how certain activities are to be carried out. Thus power plants may be required to use scrubbers or automobiles catalytic converters as pollution control equipment. This type of standard does not regulate the total amount of pollutants emitted as such but rather the manner or conditions of the emission.

This shift in focus from a primarily retrospective emphasis on fault and causality to a prospective emphasis on prevention is understandable. It is important to note, however, that we pay a serious price in adopting the administrative-regulatory approach. Whereas the law of torts and crimes basically leaves individuals free to act as they choose with the understanding that they must accept the consequences of their actions, the regulatory approach often intervenes in one's activities through detailed design regulations as well as ongoing monitoring. Many who are subject to such regulations object to this interference with their freedom. They also argue that legislators and administrators lack the knowledge to formulate such regulations.

While the use of tort and criminal liability as

well as administrative control through design and performance standards represent the main legal responses to pollution problems, there are other, less direct methods of exercising control that should be considered. Instead of directly mandating specific conduct one can provide incentives for voluntary pollution control. One such method offers subsidies or tax credits to encourage such activities, e.g., tax credits for installing pollution control equipment. Another technique imposes fees or charges on pollution activities. Many economists strongly support these approaches on the grounds that they make effective use of the incentives provided by a market system. They can help set what has been called an "optimum level" of pollution. Such methods also take advantage of the detailed knowledge possessed by those subject to regulation.

Uniform mandatory standards are criticized for failing to take into account the differential costs that may be involved in achieving them. Thus it is much more expensive for eastern industrialized states with coal of high sulfuric content to meet national standards than for western states. Design standards often lock one into existing technology instead of encouraging the discovery of new ways of pollution control. This is not to say that the system of pollution licenses does not have its own difficulties, among which is determining how to set the fee schedule so that "satisfactory levels" of pollution control are realized.

A related technique for arriving at an "optimum level" of pollution is the "bubble" concept. Under that concept a company is permitted to exceed the maximum allowable levels of emissions from one of its point sources, e.g., a particular smokestack, provided it is able to reduce emission by an equal amount at its other pollution sources. The goal is to achieve a certain overall level of pollution control aggregatively rather than distributively at each pollution source. A company may decide the most cost-effective way of arriving at that overall level. This approach can be extended to create a market in pollution rights. If a company pollutes less than its allowable maximum, it can sell its right to pollute to another company which needs to exceed its allowable maximum. The theory underlying these economic techniques is that we can thereby arrive at an optimum level of pollution where the marginal cost of increasing pollution control is equal to the marginal benefit obtained from such control.

We have seen that we can respond to our pollution problems in a variety of ways. The challenge is to develop a "mixed strategy" in which each specific type of problem is dealt with appropriately. Criminal punishment is especially appropriate for willful or repeated violations of environmental standards that create a serious danger to human health or welfare. In cases involving only slight marginal increases in risk, a combination of regulations and market incentives may be appropriate: regulations to ensure that certain basic levels of pollution control are achieved and market incentives to achieve further reductions in a cost-effective way.

All of these different responses are predicated on the importance of providing a legal structure which makes it more likely that essentially self-interested polluters will act in a socially responsible way. To some the solution to our pollution problems lies less in developing sophisticated ways of appealing to individual self-interest than in developing an environment in which individuals act as caring members of a community with genuine concern for the welfare of others as well as for future generations. One can only speculate how many environmental disasters could be avoided or mitigated if decision-makers took a broader view of their role and function. The importance of this culturally imbued sense of social responsibility cannot be overestimated. Even with a well-designed set of laws to address our environmental problems, individuals who are so inclined can prevent these from achieving their intended effect. Of course if legislators and administrators themselves act largely as self-interested individuals we face even greater problems in arriving at responses to our environmental problems which are both appropriate and effective.

The Economic Common Sense of Pollution

Larry E. Ruff
Managing Director, Putnam, Hayes, and Bartlett, Inc., Washington, DC

We are going to make very little real progress in solving the problem of pollution until we recognize it for what, primarily, it is: an economic problem, which must be understood in economic terms. Of course, there are *noneconomic* aspects of pollution, as there are with all economic problems, but all too often, such secondary matters dominate discussion. Engineers, for example, are certain that pollution will vanish once they find the magic gadget or power source. Politicians keep trying to find the right kind of bureaucracy; and bureaucrats maintain an unending search for the correct set of rules and regulations. Those who are above such vulgar pursuits pin their hopes on a moral regeneration or social revolution, apparently in the belief that saints and socialists have no garbage to dispose of. But as important as technology, politics, law, and ethics are to the pollution question, all such approaches are bound to have disappointing results, for they ignore the primary fact that pollution is an economic problem.

MARGINALISM

One of the most fundamental economic ideas is that of *marginalism,* which entered economic theory when economists became aware of the differential calculus in the 19th century and used it to formulate economic problems as problems of "maximization." The standard economic problem came to be viewed as that of finding a level of operation of some activity which would maximize the net gain from that activity, where the net gain is the difference between the benefits and the costs of the activity. As the level of activity increases, both benefits and costs will increase; but because of diminishing returns, costs will increase faster than benefits. When a certain level of the activity is reached, any further expansion increases costs more than benefits. At this "optimal" level, "marginal cost"—or the cost of expanding the activity—equals "marginal benefit," or the benefit from expanding the activity. Further expansion would cost more than it is worth, and reduction in the activity would reduce benefits more than it would save costs. The net gain from the activity is said to be maximized at this point.

This principle is so simple that it is almost embarrassing to admit it is the cornerstone of economics. Yet intelligent men often ignore it in discussion of public issues. Educators, for example, often suggest that, if it is better to be literate than illiterate, there is no logical stopping point in supporting education. Or scientists have pointed out that the benefits derived from "science" obviously exceed the costs and then have proceeded to infer that their particular project should be supported. The correct comparison, of course, is between *additional* benefits created by the proposed activity and the *additional* costs incurred.

The application of marginalism to questions of pollution is simple enough conceptually. The difficult part lies in estimating the cost and benefits functions, a question to which I shall return. But several important qualitative points can be made immediately. The first is that the choice facing a rational society is *not* between clean air and dirty air, or between clear water and polluted water, but rather between various *levels* of dirt and pollution. The aim must be to find that level of pollution abatement where the costs of further abatement begin to exceed the benefits.

The second point is that the optimal combination of pollution control methods is going to be a very complex affair. Such steps as demanding a 10 per cent reduction in pollution from all sources, without considering the relative difficulties and costs of the reduction, will certainly be an inefficient approach. Where it is less costly to reduce

---

Excerpted from "The Economic Sense of Pollution" by Larry E. Ruff, *The Public Interest,* No. 19 (Spring 1970), pp 69–85.

pollution, we want a greater reduction, to a point where an additional dollar spent on control anywhere yields the same reduction in pollution levels.

MARKETS, EFFICIENCY, AND EQUITY

A second basic economic concept is the idea—or the ideal—of the self-regulating economic system. Adam Smith illustrated this ideal with the example of bread in London: the uncoordinated, selfish actions of many people—farmer, miller, shipper, baker, grocer—provide bread for the city dweller, without any central control and at the lowest possible cost. Pure self-interest, guided only by the famous "invisible hand" of competition, organizes the economy efficiently.

The logical basis of this rather startling result is that, under certain conditions, competitive prices convey all the information necessary for making the optimal decision. A builder trying to decide whether to use brick or concrete will weigh his requirements and tastes against the prices of the materials. Other users will do the same, with the result that those whose needs and preferences for brick are relatively the strongest will get brick. Further, profit-maximizing producers will weigh relative production costs, reflecting society's productive capabilities, against relative prices, reflecting society's tastes and desires, when deciding how much of each good to produce. The end result is that users get brick and cement in quantities and proportions that reflect their individual tastes and society's production opportunities. No other solution would be better from the standpoint of all the individuals concerned.

This suggests what it is that makes pollution different. The efficiency of competitive markets depends on the identity of *private* costs and *social* costs. As long as the brick-cement producer must compensate somebody for every cost imposed by his production, his profit-maximizing decisions about how much to produce, and how, will also be socially efficient decisions. Thus, if a producer dumps wastes into the air, river, or ocean; if he pays nothing for such dumping; and if the disposed wastes have no noticeable effect on anyone else, living or still unborn; then the private and social costs of disposal are identical and nil, and the producer's private decisions are socially efficient. *But if these wastes do affect others, then the social costs of waste disposal are not zero. Private and social costs diverge, and private profit-maximizing decisions are not socially efficient.* Suppose, for example, that cement production dumps large quantities of dust into the air, which damages neighbors, and that the brick-cement producer pays these neighbors nothing. In the social sense, cement will be over-produced relative to brick and other products because users of the products will make decisions based on market prices which do not reflect true social costs. They will use cement when they should use brick, or when they should not build at all.

This divergence between private and social costs is the fundamental cause of pollution of all types, and it arises in any society where decisions are at all decentralized—which is to say, in any economy of any size which hopes to function at all. Even the socialist manager of the brick-cement plant, told to maximize output given the resources at his disposal, will use the People's Air to dispose of the People's Wastes; to do otherwise would be to violate his instructions. And if instructed to avoid pollution "when possible," he does not know what to do: how can he decide whether more brick or cleaner air is more important for building socialism? The capitalist manager is in exactly the same situation. Without prices to convey the needed information, he does not know what action is in the public interest, and certainly would have no incentive to act correctly even if he did know.

ESTIMATING THE COSTS OF POLLUTION

Both in theory and practice, the most difficult part of an economic approach to pollution is the measurement of the cost and benefits of its abatement. Only a small fraction of the costs of pollution can be estimated straightforwardly. If, for example, smog reduces the life of automobile tires by 10 per cent, one component of the cost of smog is 10 per cent of tire expenditures. It has been estimated that, in a moderately polluted area of New York City, filthy air imposes extra costs for painting, washing, laundry, etc., of $200 per person per year. Such costs must be included in any calculation of the benefits of pollution abatement, and yet they are only a part of the relevant costs—and often a small part. Accordingly it rarely is possible to justify a measure like river pollution control solely on the basis of costs to individuals or firms of treating water because it usually is cheaper to process only the water that is actually used for industrial or municipal purposes, and to ignore the river itself.

The costs of pollution that cannot be measured so easily are often called "intangible" or "noneconomic," although neither term is particularly appropriate. Many of these costs are as tangible as burning eyes or a dead fish, and all such costs are relevant to a valid economic analysis. Let us therefore call these costs "nonpecuniary."

The only real difference between nonpecuniary costs and the other kind lies in the difficulty of estimating them. If pollution in Los Angeles harbor is reducing marine life, this imposes costs on society. The cost of reducing commercial fishing could be estimated directly: it would be the fixed cost of converting men and equipment from fishing to an alternative occupation, plus the difference between what they earned in fishing and what they earn in the new occupation, plus the loss to consumers who must eat chicken instead of fish. But there are other, less straightforward costs: the loss of recreation opportunities for children and sportsfishermen and of research facilities for marine biologists, etc. Such costs are obviously difficult to measure and may be very large indeed; but just as surely as they are not zero, so too are they not infinite. Those who call for immediate action and damn the cost, merely because the spiney starfish and furry crab populations are shrinking, are putting an infinite marginal value on these creatures. This strikes a disinterested observer as an overestimate.

The above comments may seem crass and insensitive to those who, like one angry letterwriter to the Los Angeles *Times,* want to ask: "If conservation is not for its own sake, then what in the world *is* it for?" Well, what *is* the purpose of pollution control? Is it for its own sake? Of course not. If we answer that it is to make the air and water clean and quiet, then the question arises: what is the purpose of clean air and water? If the answer is, to please the nature gods, then it must be conceded that all pollution must cease immediately because the cost of angering the gods is presumably infinite. But if the answer is that the purpose of clean air and water is to further human enjoyment of life on this planet, then we are faced with the economists' basic question: given the limited alternatives that a niggardly nature allows, how can we best further human enjoyment of life? And the answer is, by making intelligent marginal decisions on the basis of costs and benefits. Pollution control is for lots of things: breathing comfortably, enjoying mountains, swimming in water, for health, beauty, and the general delectation. But so are many other things, like good food and wine, comfortable housing and fast transportation. The question is not which of these desirable things we should have, but rather what combination is most desirable. To determine such a combination, we must know the rate at which individuals are willing to substitute more of one desirable thing for less of another desirable thing. Prices are one way of determining those rates.

But if we cannot directly observe market prices for many of the costs of pollution, we must find another way to proceed. One possibility is to infer the costs from other prices, just as we infer the value of an ocean view from real estate prices. In principle, one could estimate the value people put on clean air and beaches by observing how much more they are willing to pay for property in nonpolluted areas. Such information could be obtained; but there is little of it available at present.

Another possible way of estimating the costs of pollution is to ask people how much they would be willing to pay to have pollution reduced. A resident of Pasadena might be willing to pay $100 a year to have smog reduced 10 or 20 per cent. In Barstow, where the marginal cost of smog is much less, a resident might not pay $10 a year to have smog reduced 10 per cent. If we knew how much it was worth to everybody, we could add up these amounts and obtain an estimate of the cost of a marginal amount of pollution. The difficulty, of course, is that there is no way of guaranteeing truthful responses. Your response to the question, how much is pollution costing *you,* obviously will depend on what you think will be done with this information. If you think you will be compensated for these costs, you will make a generous estimate; if you think that you will be charged for the control in proportion to these costs, you will make a small estimate.

Let us assume that, somehow, we have made an estimate of the social cost function for pollution, including the marginal cost associated with various pollution levels. We now need an estimate of the benefits of pollution—or, if you prefer, of the costs of pollution abatement. So we set the Pollution Control Board (PCB) to work on this task.

The PCB has a staff of engineers and technicians, and they begin working on the obvious question: for each pollution source, how much would it cost to reduce pollution by 10 per cent, 20 per cent, and so on. If the PCB has some economists, they will know that the cost of reducing total pollution by 10 per cent is *not* the total cost of reducing each pollution source by 10 per cent. Rather, they will use the equimarginal principle and find the pattern of control such that an additional dollar spent on control of any pollution source yields the same reduction. This will minimize the cost of achieving any given level of abatement. In this way the PCB can generate a "cost of abatement" function, and the corresponding marginal cost function.

Once cost and benefit functions are known, the PCB should choose a level of abatement that maximizes net gain. This occurs where the marginal cost of further abatement just equals the marginal benefit. If, for example, we could reduce pollution damages by $2 million at a cost of $1 million, we should obviously impose that $1 million cost. But if the damage reduction is only $1/2 million, we should not and in fact should reduce control efforts.

This principle is obvious enough but is often overlooked. One author, for example, has written that the national cost of air pollution is $11 billion a year but that we are spending less than $50 million a year on control; he infers from this that "we could justify a tremendous strengthening of control efforts on purely economic grounds." That *sounds* reasonable, if all you care about are sounds. But what is the logical content of the statement? Does it imply we should spend $11 billion on control just to make things even? Suppose we were spending $11 billion on control and thereby succeeded in reducing pollution costs to $50 million. Would this imply we were spending too *much* on control? Of course not. We must compare the *marginal* decrease in pollution costs to the *marginal* increase in abatement costs.

PUTTING A PRICE ON POLLUTION

Once the optimal pollution level is determined, all that is necessary is for the PCB to enforce the pattern of controls which it has determined to be optimal. But now a new problem arises: how should the controls be enforced?

There is a very simple way to accomplish this. *Put a price on pollution.* A price-based control mechanism would differ from an ordinary market transaction system only in that the PCB would set the prices, instead of their being set by demand-supply forces, and that the state would force payment. Under such a system, anyone could emit any amount of pollution so long as he pays the price which the PCB sets to approximate the marginal social cost of pollution. Under this circumstance, private decisions based on self-interest are efficient. If pollution consists of many components, each with its own social cost, there should be different prices for each component. Thus, extremely dangerous materials must have an extremely high price, perhaps stated in terms of "years in jail" rather than "dollars," although a sufficiently high dollar price is essentially the same thing. In principle, the prices should vary with geographical location, season of the year, direction of the wind, and even day of the week, although the cost of too many variations may preclude such fine distinctions.

Once the prices are set, polluters can adjust to them any way they choose. Because they act on self-interest they will reduce their pollution by every means possible up to the point where further reduction would cost more than the price. Because all face the same price for the same type of pollution, the marginal cost of abatement is the same everywhere. If there are economies of scale in pollution control, as in some types of liquid waste treatment, plants can cooperate in establishing joint treatment facilities. In fact, some enterprising individual could buy these wastes from various plants (at negative prices—i.e., they would get paid for carting them off), treat them, and then sell them at a higher price, making a profit in the process. (After all, this is what rubbish removal firms do now.) If economies of scale are so substantial that the provider of such a service becomes a monopolist, then the PCB can operate the facilities itself.

Obviously, such a scheme does not eliminate the need for the PCB. The board must measure the output of pollution from all sources, collect the fees, and so on. But it does not need to know anything about any plant except its total emission of pollution. It does not control, negotiate, threaten, or grant favors. It does not destroy incentive because development of new control methods will reduce pollution payments.

As a test of this price system of control, let us consider how well it would work when applied to automobile pollution, a problem for which direct control is usually considered the only feasible approach. If the price system can work here, it can work anywhere.

Suppose, then, that a price is put on the emissions of automobiles. Obviously, continuous metering of such emissions is impossible. But it should be easy to determine the average output of pollution for cars of different makes, models, and years, having different types of control devices and using different types of fuel. Through graduated registration fees and fuel taxes, each car owner would be assessed roughly the social cost of his car's pollution, adjusted for whatever control devices he has chosen to install and for his driving habits. If the cost of installing a device, driving a different car, or finding alternative means of transportation is less than the price he must pay to continue his pollution, he will presumably take all the necessary steps. But each individual remains free to find the best adjustment to his particular situation. It would be remarkable if everyone decided to install the same devices which some states currently require; and yet that is the effective assumption of such requirements.

Even in the difficult case of auto pollution, the price system has a number of advantages. Why should a person living in the Mojave desert, where pollution has little social cost, take the same pains to reduce air pollution as a person living in Pasadena? Present California law, for example, makes no distinction between such areas; the price system would. And what incentive is there for auto manufacturers to design a less polluting engine? The law says only that they must install a certain device in every car. If GM develops a more efficient engine, the law will eventually be changed to require this engine on all cars, raising costs and reducing sales. But will such development take place? No collusion is needed for manufacturers to decide unanimously that it would be foolish to devote funds to such development. But with a pollution fee paid by the consumer, there is a real advantage for any firm to be first with a better engine, and even a collusive agreement wouldn't last long in the face of such an incentive. The same is true of fuel manufacturers, who now have no real incentive to look for better fuels. Perhaps most important of all, the present situation provides no real way of determining whether it is cheaper to reduce pollution by muzzling cars or industrial plants. The experts say that most smog comes from cars; but *even if true, this does not imply that it is more efficient to control autos rather than other pollution sources.* How can we decide which is more efficient without mountains of information? The answer is, by making drivers and plants pay the same price for the same pollution, and letting self-interest do the job.

In situations where pollution outputs can be measured more or less directly (unlike the automobile pollution case), the price system is clearly superior to direct control. A study of possible control methods in the Delaware estuary, for example, estimated that, compared to a direct control scheme requiring each polluter to reduce his pollution by a fixed percentage, an effluent charge which would achieve the same level of pollution abatement would be only half as costly—a saving of about \$150 million. Such a price system would also provide incentive for further improvements, a simple method of handling new plants, and revenue for the control authority.

In general, the price system allocates costs in a manner which is at least superficially fair: those who produce and consume goods which cause pollution, pay the costs. But the superior efficiency in control and apparent fairness are not the only advantages of the price mechanism. Equally important is the ease with which it can be put into operation. It is not necessary to have detailed information about all the techniques of pollution reduction, or estimates of all costs and benefits. Nor is it necessary to determine whom to blame or who should pay. All that is needed is a mechanism for estimating, if only roughly at first, the pollution output of all polluters, together with a means of collecting fees. Then we can simply pick a price—any price—for each category of pollution, and we are in business. The initial price should be chosen on the basis of some estimate of its effects but need not be the optimal one. If the resulting reduction in pollution is not "enough," the price can be raised until there is sufficient reduction. A change in technology, number of plants, or whatever, can be accommodated by a change in the price, even without detailed knowledge of all the technological and economic data. Further, once the idea is explained, the price system is much more likely to be politically acceptable than some method of direct control. Paying for a service, such as garbage disposal, is a well-established tradition, and is much less objectionable than having a bureaucrat nosing around and giving arbitrary orders. When businessmen, consumers, and politicians understand the alternatives, the price system will seem very attractive indeed.

An important part of this method of control obviously is the mechanism that sets and changes the pollution price. Ideally, the PCB could choose this price on the basis of an estimate of the benefits and costs involved, in effect imitating the impersonal workings of ordinary market forces. But because many of the costs and benefits cannot be measured, a less "objective," more political procedure is needed. This political procedure could take the form of a referendum, in which the PCB would present to the voters alternative schedules of pollution prices, together with the estimated effects of each. The strongest argument for the price system is not found in idle speculation but in the real world, and in particular, in Germany. The Rhine River in Germany is a dirty stream, recently made notorious when an insecticide spilled into the river and killed millions of fish. One tributary of the Rhine, a river called the Ruhr, is the sewer for one of the world's most concentrated industrial areas. The Ruhr River valley contains 40 per cent of German industry, including 80 per cent of coal, iron, steel and heavy chemical capacity. The Ruhr is a small river, with a low flow of less than half the flow on the Potomac near Washington. The volume of wastes is extremely large—actually exceeding the flow of the river itself in the dry season! *Yet people and fish swim in the Ruhr River.*

This amazing situation is the result of over forty years of control of the Ruhr and its tributaries by a hierarchy of regional authorities. These authorities have as their goal the maintenance of the quality of the water in the area at minimum cost, and they have explicitly applied the equimarginal principle to accomplish this. Water quality is formally defined in a technological rather than an economic way; the objective is to "not kill the fish." Laboratory tests are conducted to determine what levels of various types of pollution are lethal to fish, and from these figures an index is constructed which measures the "amount of pollution" from each source in terms of its fish-killing capacity. This index is different for each source, because of differences in amount and composition of the waste, and geographical locale. Although this physical index is not really a very precise measure of the real economic *cost* of the waste, it has the advantage of being easily measured and widely understood. Attempts are made on an *ad hoc* basis to correct the index if necessary—if, for example, a nonlethal pollutant gives fish an unpleasant taste.

Once the index of pollution is constructed, a price is put on the pollution, and each source is free to adjust its operation any way it chooses. Geographical variation in prices, together with some direct advice from the authorities, encourage new plants to locate where pollution is less damaging. For example, one tributary of the Ruhr has been converted to an open sewer; it has been lined with concrete and landscaped, but otherwise no attempt is made to reduce pollution in the river itself. A treatment plant at the mouth of the river processes all these wastes at low cost. Therefore, the price of pollution on this river is set low. This arrangement, by the way, is a rational, if perhaps unconscious, recognition of marginal principles. The loss caused by destruction of *one* tributary is rather small, if the nearby rivers are maintained, while the benefit from having this inexpensive means of waste disposal is very large. However, if *another* river were lost, the cost would be higher and the benefits lower; one open sewer may be the optimal number.

The revenues from the pollution charges are used by the authorities to measure pollution, conduct tests and research, operate dams to regulate stream flow, and operate waste treatment facilities where economies of scale make this desirable. These facilities are located at the mouths of some tributaries, and at several dams in the Ruhr. If the authorities find pollution levels are getting too high, they simply raise the price, which causes polluters to try to reduce their wastes, and provides increased revenues to use on further treatment. Local governments influence the authorities, which helps to maintain recreation values, at least in certain stretches of the river.

This classic example of water management is obviously not exactly the price system method discussed earlier. There is considerable direct control, and the pollution authorities take a very active role. Price regulation is not used as much as it could be; for example, no attempt is made to vary the price over the season, even though high flow on the Ruhr is more than ten times larger than low flow. If the price of pollution were reduced during high flow periods, plants would have an incentive to regulate their production and/or store their wastes for release during periods when the river can more easily handle them. The difficulty of continuously monitoring wastes means this is not done; as automatic, continuous measurement techniques improve and are made less expensive, the use of variable prices will increase. Though this system is not entirely regulated by the price mechanism, prices are used more here than anywhere else, and the system is much more successful than any other. So, both in theory and in practice, the price system is attractive, and ultimately must be the solution to pollution problems.

At the Shrine of Our Lady of Fátima, or Why Political Questions Are Not All Economic

Mark Sagoff
Director and Senior Research Scholar, Institute for Philosophy and Public Policy, University of Maryland

Lewiston, New York, a well-to-do community near Buffalo, is the site of the Lake Ontario Ordinance Works, where the federal government, years ago, disposed of the residues of the Manhattan Project. These radioactive wastes are buried but are not forgotten by the residents, who say that when the wind is southerly radon gas blows through the town. Several parents at a recent conference I attended there described their terror on learning that cases of leukemia had been found among area children. They feared for their own lives as well. At the other sides of the table, officials from New York State and from local corporations replied that these fears were ungrounded. People who smoke, they said, take greater risks than people who live close to waste disposal sites. One speaker talked in terms of "rational methodologies of decision making." This aggravated the parents' rage and frustration.

The speaker suggested that the townspeople, were to make their own decision in a free market, would choose to live near the hazardous waste facility, if they knew the scientific facts. He told me later they were irrational—he said, "neurotic"—because they refused to recognize or to act upon their own interests. The residents of Lewiston were unimpressed with his analysis of their "willingness to pay" to avoid this risk or that. They did not see

Excerpted from "At the Shrine of Our Lady of Fatima or Why Political Questions are Not all Economic" by Mark Sagoff, 23 *Arizona Law Review*, No 1283 (1981).

what risk-benefit analysis had to do with the issues they raised.

If you take the Military Highway (as I did) from Buffalo to Lewiston, you will pass through a formidable wasteland. Landfills stretch in all directions, where enormous trucks—tiny in that landscape—incessantly deposit sludge which great bulldozers, like yellow ants, then push into the ground. These machines are the only signs of life, for in the miasma that hangs in the air, no birds, not even scavengers, are seen. Along colossal power lines which criss-cross this dismal land, the dynamos at Niagara send electric power south, where factories have fled, leaving their remains to decay. To drive along this road is to feel, oddly, the mystery and awe one experiences in the presence of so much power and decadence.

Henry Adams had a similar response to the dynamos on display at the Paris Exposition of 1900. To him "the dynamo became a symbol of infinity."[1] To Adams, the dynamo functioned as the modern equivalent of the Virgin, that is, as the center and focus of power. "Before the end, one began to pray to it; inherited instinct taught the natural expression of man before silent and infinite force."[2]

Adams asks in his essay "The Dynamo and the Virgin" how the products of modern industrial civilization will compare with those of the religious culture of the Middle Ages. If he could see the landfills and hazardous waste facilities bordering the power stations and honeymoon hotels of Niagara Falls he would know the answer. He would understand what happens when efficiency replaces infinity as the central conception of value. The dynamos at Niagara will not produce another Mont-Saint-Michel. "All the steam in the world," Adams wrote, "could not, like the Virgin, build Chartres."[3]

At the Shrine of Our Lady of Fátima, on a plateau north of the Military Highway, a larger than life sculpture of Mary looks into the chemical air. The original of this shrine stands in central Portugal, where in May, 1917, three children said they saw a Lady, brighter than the sun, raised on a cloud in an evergreen tree.[4] Five months later, on a wet and chilly October day, the Lady again appeared, this time before a large crowd. Some who were skeptical did not see the miracle. Others in the crowd reported, however, that "the sun appeared and seemed to tremble, rotate violently and fall, dancing over the heads of the throng. . . ."[5]

The Shrine was empty when I visited it. The cult of Our Lady of Fátima, I imagine, has only a few devotees. The cult of Pareto optimality, however, has many. Where some people see only environmental devastation, its devotees perceive efficiency, utility, and the maximization of wealth. They see the satisfaction of wants. They envision the good life. As I looked over the smudged and ruined terrain I tried to share that vision. I hoped that Our Lady of Fátima, worker of miracles, might serve, at least for the moment, as the Patroness of cost-benefit analysis. I thought of all the wants and needs that are satisfied in a landscape of honeymoon cottages, commercial strips, and dumps for hazardous waste. I saw the miracle of efficiency. The prospect, however, looked only darker in that light.

I

This essay concerns the economic decisions we make about the environment. It also concerns our political decisions about the environment. Some people have suggested that ideally these should be the same, that all environmental problems are problems in distribution. According to this view there is an environmental problem only when some resource is not allocated in equitable and efficient ways.[6]

This approach to environmental policy is pitched entirely at the level of the consumer. It is his or her values that count, and the measure of these values is the individual's willingness to pay. The problem of justice or fairness in society becomes, then, the problem of distributing goods and services so that more people get more of what they want to buy. A condo on the beach. A snowmobile for the mountains. A tank full of gas. A day of labor. The only values we have, on this view, are those which a market can price.

How much do you value open space, a stand of trees, an "unspoiled" landscape? Fifty dollars? A hundred? A thousand? This is one way to measure value. You could compare the amount consumers would pay for a townhouse or coal or a landfill and the amount they would pay to preserve an area in its "natural" state. If users would pay more for the land with the house, the coal mine, or the landfill, than without—less construction and other costs of development—then the efficient thing to do is to improve the land and thus increase its value. That is why we have so many tract developments. And pizza stands. And gas stations. And strip mines. And landfills. How much did you spend last year to preserve open space? How much for pizza and gas? "In principle, the ultimate measure of environmental quality," as one basic text assures us, "is the value people place on these . . . services or their *willingness to pay.*"[7]

Willingness to pay. What is wrong with that? The rub is this: not all of us think of ourselves simply as *consumers.* Many of us regard ourselves *as citizens* as well. We act as consumers to get what we want *for ourselves.* We act as citizens to achieve what we think is right or best *for the community.* The question arises, then, whether what we want for ourselves individually as consumers is consistent with the goals we would set for ourselves collectively as citizens. Would I vote for the sort of things I shop for? Are my preferences as a consumer consistent with my judgments as a citizen?

They are not. I am schizophrenic. Last year, I fixed a couple of tickets and was happy to do so since I saved fifty dollars. Yet, at election time, I helped to vote the corrupt judge out of office. I speed on the highway; yet I want the police to enforce laws against speeding. I used to buy mixers in returnable bottles—but who can bother to return them? I buy only disposables now, but, to soothe my conscience, I urge my state senator to outlaw one-way containers. I love my car; I hate the bus. Yet I vote for candidates who promise to tax gasoline to pay for public transportation. I send my dues to the Sierra Club to protect areas in Alaska I shall never visit. And I support the work of the American League to Abolish Capital Punishment although, personally, I have nothing to gain one way or the other. (When I hang, I will hang myself.) And of course I applaud the Endangered Species Act, although I have no earthly use for the Colorado squawfish or the Indiana bat. I support almost any political cause that I think will defeat my consumer interests. This is because I have contempt for—although I act upon—those interests. I have an "Ecology Now" sticker on a car that leaks oil everywhere it's parked.

The distinction between consumer and citizen preferences has long vexed the theory of public finance. Should the public economy serve the same goals as the household economy? May it serve, instead, goals emerging from our association as citizens? The question asks if we may collectively strive for and achieve only those items we individually compete for and consume. Should we aspire, instead, to public goals we may legislate as a nation?

The problem, insofar as it concerns public finance, is stated as follows by R. A. Musgrave, who reports a conversation he had with Gerhard Colm.

> He [Colm] holds that the individual voter dealing with political issues has a frame of reference quite distinct from that which underlies his allocation of income as a consumer. In the latter situation the voter acts as a private individual determined by self-interest and deals with his personal wants; in the former, he acts as a political being guided by his image of a good society. The two, Colm holds, are different things.[8]

Are these two different things? Stephen Marglin suggests that they are. He writes:

> The preferences that govern one's unilateral market actions no longer govern his actions when the form of reference is shifted from the market to the political arena. The Economic Man and the Citizen are for all intents and purposes two different individuals. It is not a question, therefore, of rejecting individual . . . preference maps; it is, rather, that market and political preference maps are inconsistent.[9]

Marglin observes that if this is true, social choices optimal under one set of preferences will not be optimal under another. What, then, is the meaning of "optimality"? He notices that if we take a person's true preferences to be those expressed in the market, we may, then, neglect or reject the preferences that person reveals in advocating a political cause or position.

II

On February 19, 1981, President Reagan published Executive Order 12,291 requiring all administrative agencies and departments to support every new major regulation with a cost-benefit analysis establishing that the benefits of the regulation to society outweigh its costs.[10] The Order directs the Office of Management and Budget (OMB) to review every such regulation on the basis of the adequacy of the cost-benefit analysis supporting it. This is a departure from tradition. Traditionally, regulations have been reviewed not by OMB but by the courts on the basis of their relation not to cost-benefit analysis but to authorizing legislation.

A month earlier, in January 1981, the Supreme Court heard lawyers for the American Textile Manufacturers Institute argue against a proposed Occupational Safety and Health Administration (OSHA) regulation which would have severely restricted the acceptable levels of cotton dust in textile plants.[11] The lawyers for industry argued that the benefits of the regulation would not equal the costs. The lawyers for the government contended that the law required the tough standard. OSHA, acting consistently with Executive Order 12,291, asked the Court not to decide the cotton dust case, in order to give the agency time to complete the cost-benefit analysis required by the textile industry. The Court declined to accept OSHA's request and handed down its opinion on June 17, 1981.[12]

The Supreme Court, in a 5–3 decision, found that the actions of regulatory agencies which conform to the OSHA law need not be supported by cost-benefit analysis. In addition, the Court asserted that Congress in writing a statute, rather than the agencies in applying it, has the primary responsibility for balancing benefits and costs. The Court said:

> When Congress passed the Occupational Health and Safety Act in 1970, it chose to place preeminent value on assuring employees a safe and healthful working environment, limited only by the feasibility of achieving such an environment. We must measure the validity of the Secretary's actions against the requirements of that Act.[13]

The opinion upheld the finding of the Appeals Court that "Congress itself struck the balance between costs and benefits in the mandate to the agency."[14]

The Appeals Court opinion in *American Textile Manufacturers* vs. *Donovan* supports the principle that legislatures are not necessarily bound to a particular conception of regulatory policy. Agencies that apply the law, therefore, may not need to justify on cost-benefit grounds the standards they set. These standards may conflict with the goal of efficiency and still express our political will as a nation. That is, they may reflect not the personal choices of self-interested individuals, but the collective judgments we make on historical, cultural, aesthetic, moral, and ideological grounds.

The appeal of the Reagan Administration to cost-benefit analysis, however, may arise more from political than economic considerations. The intention, seen in the most favorable light, may not be to replace political or ideological goals with economic ones but to make economic goals more apparent in regulation. This is not to say that Congress should function to reveal a collective willingness-to-pay just as markets reveal an individual willingness-to-pay. It is to suggest that Congress should do more to balance economic with ideological, aesthetic, and moral goals. To think that environmental or worker safety policy can be based exclusively on aspiration for a "natural" and "safe" world is as foolish as to hold that environmental law can be reduced to cost-benefit accounting. The more we move to one extreme, as I found in Lewiston, the more likely we are to hear from the other.

III

There are some who believe, on principle, that worker safety and environmental quality ought to be protected only insofar as the benefits of protection balance the costs. On the other hand, people argue, also on principle, that neither worker safety nor environmental quality should be treated merely as a commodity, to be traded at the margin for other commodities, but should be valued for its own sake. The conflict between these two principles is logical or moral, to be resolved by argument or debate. The question whether cost-benefit analysis should play a decisive role in policymaking is not to be decided by cost-benefit analysis. A contradiction between principles—between contending visions of the good society—cannot be settled by asking how much partisans are willing to pay for their beliefs.

The role of the *legislator,* the political role, may be more important to the individual than the role of *consumer.* The person, in other words, is not to be treated as merely a bundle of preferences to be juggled in cost-benefit analyses. The individual is to be respected as an advocate of ideas which are to be judged in relation to the reasons for them. If health and environmental statutes reflect a vision of society as something other than a market by requiring protections beyond what are efficient, then this may express not legislative ineptitude but legislative responsiveness to public values. To deny this vision because it is economically inefficient is simply to replace it with another vision. It is to insist that the ideas of the citizen be sacrificed to the psychology of the consumer.

We hear on all sides that government is routinized, mechanical, entrenched, and bureaucratized; the jargon alone is enough to dissuade the most mettlesome meddler. Who can make a difference? It is plain that for many of us the idea of a national political community has an abstract and suppositious quality. We have only our private conceptions of the good, if no way exists to arrive at a public one. This is only to note the continuation, in our time, of the trend Benjamin Constant described in the essay, *De La Liberte des Anciens Comparee a Celle des Modernes.*[15] Constant observes that the modern world, as opposed to the ancient, emphasizes civil over political liberties, the rights of privacy and property over those of community and participation.

Nowhere are the rights of the moderns, particularly the rights of privacy and property, less helpful than in the area of the natural environment. Here the values we wish to protect—cultural, historical, aesthetic, and moral—are public values; they depend not so much upon what each person wants individually as upon what he or she believes we stand for collectively. We refuse to regard worker health and safety as commodities; we regulate hazards as a matter of right. Likewise, we refuse to treat environmental resources simply as public goods in the economist's sense. Instead, we prevent significant deterioration of air quality not only as a matter of individual self-interest but also as a matter of collective self-respect. How shall we balance efficiency against moral, cultural, and aesthetic values in policy for the workplace and the environment? No better way has been devised to do this than by legislative debate ending in a vote. This is not the same thing as a cost-benefit analysis terminating in a bottom line.

IV

It is the characteristic of cost-benefit analysis that it treats all value judgments other than those made on its behalf as nothing but statements of preference, attitude, or emotion, insofar as they are value judgments. The cost-benefit analyst regards as true the judgment that we should maximize efficiency. The analyst believes that this view can be backed by reasons; the analyst does not regard it as a preference or want for which he or she must be willing to pay. The cost-benefit analyst, however, tends to treat all other normative views and recommendations as if they were nothing but subjective reports of mental states. The analyst supposes in all such cases that "this is right" and "this is what we ought to do" are equivalent to "I want this" and "this is what I prefer." Value judgments are beyond criticism if, indeed, they are nothing but expressions of personal preference; they are incorrigible since every person is in the best position to know what he or she wants. All valuation, according to this approach, happens *in foro interno;* debate *in foro publico* has no point. On this approach, the reasons that people give for their views, unless these people are welfare economists, do not count; what counts is how much they are willing to pay to satisfy their wants. Those who are willing to pay the most, for all intents and purposes, have the right view; theirs is the more informed opinion, the better aesthetic judgment, and the deeper moral insight.

The assumption that valuation is subjective, that judgments of good and evil are nothing but expressions of desire and aversion, is not unique to economic theory.[16] There are psychotherapists—Carl Rogers is an example—who likewise deny the objectivity or cognitivity of valuation.[17] For Rogers, there is only one criterion of worth: it lies in "the subjective world of the individual. Only he knows it fully."[18] The therapist shows his or her client that a "value system is not necessarily something imposed from without, but is something experienced."[19] Therapy succeeds when the client "perceives himself in such a way that no self-experience can be discriminated as more or less worthy of positive self-regard than any other. . . ."[20] The client then "tends to place the basis of standards within himself, recognizing that the 'goodness' or 'badness' of any experience or perceptual object is not something inherent in that object, but is a value placed in it by himself."[21]

Rogers points out that "some clients make strenuous efforts to have the therapist exercise the valuing function, so as to provide them with guides for action."[22] The therapist, however, "consistently keeps the locus of evaluation with the client."[23] As long as the therapist refuses to "exercise the valuing function" and as long as he or she practices an "unconditional positive regard"[24] for all the affective states of the client, then the therapist remains neutral among the client's values or "sensory and visceral experiences."[25] The role of the therapist is legitimate, Rogers suggests, because of this value neutrality. The therapist accepts all felt preferences as valid and imposes none on the client.

Economists likewise argue that their role as policymakers is legitimate because they are neutral among competing values in the client society. The political economist, according to James Buchanan, "is or should be ethically neutral: the indicated results are influenced by his own value scale only insofar as this reflects his membership in a larger group."[26] The economist might be most confident of the impartiality of his or her policy recommendations if he or she could derive them formally or mathematically from individual preferences. If theoretical difficulties make such a social welfare function impossible,[27] however, the next best thing, to preserve neutrality, is to let markets function to transform individual preference orderings into a collective ordering of social states. The analyst is able then to base policy on preferences that exist in society and are not necessarily his own.

Economists have used this impartial approach to offer solutions to many outstanding social problems, for example, the controversy over abortion. An economist argues that "there is an optimal number of abortions, just as there is an optimal level of pollution, or purity. . . . Those who oppose abortion could eliminate it entirely, if their intensity of feeling were so strong as to lead to payments that were greater at the margin than the price anyone would pay to have an abortion."[28] Likewise economists, in order to determine whether the war in Vietnam was justified, have estimated the willingness to pay of those who demonstrated against it.[29] Likewise it should be possible, following the same line of reasoning, to decide whether Creationism should be taught in the public schools, whether black and white people should be segregated, whether the death penalty should be enforced, and whether the square root of six is three. All of these questions depend upon how much people are willing to pay for their subjective preferences or wants—or none of them do. This is the beauty of cost-benefit analysis: no matter how relevant or irrelevant, wise or stupid, informed or uninformed, responsible or silly, defensible or indefensible wants may be, the analyst is able to derive a policy from them—a policy which is legitimate because, in theory, it treats all of these preferences as equally valid and good.

V

Consider, by way of contrast, a Kantian conception of value.[30] The individual, for Kant, is a judge of values, not a mere haver of wants, and the individual judges not for himself or herself merely, but as a member of a relevant community or group. The central idea in a Kantian approach to ethics is that some values are more reasonable than others and therefore have a better claim upon the assent of members of the community as such.[31] The world of obligation, like the world of mathematics or the world of empirical fact, is intersubjective, it is public not private, so that objective standards of argument and criticism apply. Kant recognizes that values, like beliefs, are subjective states of mind, but he points out that like beliefs they have an objective content as well; therefore they are either correct or mistaken. Thus Kant discusses valuation in the context not of psychology but of cognition. He believes that a person who makes a value judgment—or a policy recommendation—claims to know what is right and not just what is *preferred.* A value judgment is like an empirical or theoretical judgment in that it claims to be *true,* not merely to be *felt.*

We have, then, two approaches to public policy before us. The first, the approach associated with normative versions of welfare economics, asserts that the only policy recommendation that can or need be defended on objective grounds is efficiency or wealth-maximization. Every policy decision after that depends only on the preponderance of feeling or preference, as expressed in willingness to pay. The Kantian approach, on the other hand, assumes that many policy recommendations other than that one may be justified or refuted on objective grounds. It would concede that the approach of welfare economics applies adequately to some questions, e.g., those which ordinary consumer markets typically settle. How many yo-yos should be produced as compared to how many frisbees? Shall pens have black ink or blue? Matters such as these are so trivial it is plain that markets should handle them. It does not follow, however, that we should adopt a market or quasi-market approach to every public question.

A market or quasi-market approach to arithmetic, for example, is plainly inadequate. No matter how much people are willing to pay, three will never be the square root of six. Similarly, segregation is a national curse and the fact that we are willing to pay for it does not make it better but only makes us worse. Similarly, the case for abortion must stand on the merits; it cannot be priced at the margin. Similarly, the war in Vietnam was a moral debacle and this can be determined without shadow-pricing the willingness to pay of those who demonstrated against it. Similarly, we do not decide to execute murderers by asking how much bleeding hearts are willing to pay to see a person pardoned and how much hard hearts are willing to pay to see him hanged. Our failures to make the right decisions in these matters are failures in arithmetic, failures in wisdom, failures in taste, failures in morality—but not market failures. There are no relevant markets to have failed. What separates these questions from those for which markets are appropriate is this. They involve matters of knowledge, wisdom, morality, and taste that admit of better or worse, right or wrong, true or false—and these concepts differ from that of economic optimality. Surely environmental questions—the protection of wilderness, habitats, water, land, and air as well as policy toward environmental safety and health—involve moral and aesthetic principles and not just economic ones. This is consistent, of course, with cost-effectiveness and with a sensible recognition of economic constraints.

The neutrality of the economist, like the neutrality of Rogers' therapist, is legitimate if private preferences or subjective wants are the only values in question. A person should be left free to choose the color of his or her necktie or necklace—but we cannot justify a theory of public policy or private therapy on that basis. If the patient seeks moral advice or tries to find reasons to justify a choice, the therapist, according to Rogers' model, would remind him or her to trust his visceral and sensory experiences. The result of this is to deny the individual status as a cognitive being capable of responding intelligently to reasons; it reduces him or her to a bundle of affective states. What Rogers' therapist does to the patient the cost-benefit analyst does to society as a whole. The analyst is neutral among our "values"—having first imposed a theory of what value is. This is a theory that is impartial among values and for that reason fails to treat the persons who have them with respect or concern. It does not treat them even as persons but only as locations at which wants may be found. And thus we may conclude that the neutrality of economics is not a basis for its legitimacy. We recognize it as an indifference toward value—an indifference so deep, so studied, and so assured that at first one hesitates to call it by its right name.

VI

The residents of Lewiston at the conference I attended demanded to know the truth about the dangers that confronted them and the reasons for these dangers. They wanted to be convinced that the sacrifice asked of them was legitimate even if it served interests other than their own. One official from a large chemical company dumping wastes in the area told them, in reply, that corporations were people and that people could talk to people about their feelings, interests, and needs. This sent a shiver through the audience. Like Joseph K. in *The Trial,*[32] the residents of Lewiston asked for an explanation, justice, and truth, and they were told that their wants would be taken care of. They demanded to know the reasons for what was continually happening to them. They were given a personalized response instead.

"At the rate of progress since 1900," Henry Adams speculates in his *Education,* "every American who lived into the year 2000 would know how to control unlimited power."[33] Adams thought that the Dynamo would organize and release as much energy as the Virgin. Yet in the 1980s, the citizens of Lewiston, surrounded by dynamos, high tension lines, and nuclear wastes, are powerless. They do not know how to criticize power, resist power, or justify power—for to do so depends on making distinctions between good and evil, right and wrong, innocence and guilt, justice and injustice, truth and lies. These distinctions cannot be made out and have no significance within an emotive or psychological theory of value. To adopt this theory is to imagine society as a market in which individuals trade voluntarily and without coercion. No individual, no belief, no faith has authority over them. To have power to act as a nation, however, we must be able to act, at least at times, on a public philosophy, conviction, or faith. We cannot replace with economic analysis the moral function of public law.

NOTES

1. H. Adams, *The Education of Henry Adams* 380 (1970, 1961).
2. *Id.*
3. *Id.* at 388.
4. For an account, see J. Pelletier, *The Sun Danced At Fatima* (1951).
5. *New Catholic Encyclopedia* 856 (1967).
6. See, e.g., W. Baxter, *People or Penguins: The Case For Optimal Pollution* chap. 1 (1974). See generally A. Freeman III, R. Haveman, A. Kneese, *The Economics of Environmental Policy* (1973).
7. Freeman et al., note 6 *supra* at 23.
8. R. Musgrave, *The Theory of Public Finance* 87–88 (1959).
9. Marglin, "The Social Rate of Discount and the Optimal Rate of Investment," 77 *Q. J. of Econ.* 98 (1963).
10. See 46 *Fed. Reg.* 13193 (February 19, 1981). The Order specifies that the cost-benefit requirement shall apply "to the extent permitted by law."
11. *American Textile Mfgrs. Inst.* v. *Bingham,* 617 F.2d 636 (D.C. Cir. 1979) *cert.* granted *sub nom.* [1980]; *American Textile Mfgrs.* v. *Marshall,* 49 U.S.L.W. 3208.
12. *Textile Mfgrs.* v. *Donovan,* 101 S. Ct. 2478 (1981).
13. *Id.* U.S.L.W. (1981), 4733–34.
14. *Ibid.,* 4726–29.
15. *De la Liberte des Anciens Comparee a Celle des Modernes* (1819).
16. This is the emotive theory of value. For the classic statement, see C. Stevenson, *Ethics and Language* chaps. 1, 2 (1944). For criticism, see Blanshard, "The New Subjectivism in Ethics" 9 *Philosophy and Phenomenological Research* 504 (1949).
17. My account is based on C. Rogers, *On Becoming a Person* (1961); C. Rogers, *Client Centered Therapy* (1965); and Rogers, "A Theory of Therapy, Personality, and Interpersonal Relationships, as Developed in the Client Centered Framework" 3 *Psychology: A Study of a Science* 184 (S. Koch ed., 1959).
18. Rogers, note 17 *supra* at 210.
19. C. Rogers, *Client Centered Therapy* 150 (1965).
20. Rogers, note 17 *supra* at 208.
21. Rogers, note 19 *supra* at 139.
22. *Id.* at 150.
23. *Id.*
24. Rogers, note 17 *supra* at 208.
25. *Id.* at 523–24.
26. Buchanan, "Positive Economics, Welfare Economics, and Political Economy" 2 *J. L. and Econ.* 124, 127 (1959).
27. K. Arrow, *Social Choice and Individual Values* i–v (2d ed., 1963).
28. H. Macaulay and B. Yandle, *Environmental Use and the Market* 120–21 (1978).
29. Cicchetti, Freeman, Haveman, and Knetsch, "On the Economics of Mass Demonstrations: A Case Study

of the November 1969 March on Washington, 61 *Am. Econ. Rev.* 719 (1971).

30. I. *Kant, Foundations of the Metaphysics of Morals* (R. Wolff, ed., L. Beck trans., 1969). I follow the interpretation of Kantian ethics of W. Sellars, *Science and Metaphysics* chap. VII (1968) and Sellars, "On Reasoning about Values" 17 *Am. Phil. Q.* 81 (1980).
31. See A. Macintyre, *After Virtue* 22 (1981).
32. F. Kafka, *The Trial* (rev. ed. trans. 1957).
33. H. Adams, note 1 *supra* at 476.

The Pollution of Environmental Theory

Michael Silverstein
President, Environmental Economics, Philadelphia, PA

The economics of environmentalism has evolved into a kind of anti-economics. Environmentalists, historically, have tended to see industrial growth and the prosperity it generated as unmitigated evils—whatever created material wealth was likely to be regarded as a threat to nature. Indeed, for more than 100 years—from Luddite hostility toward any new technology to the cerebral pastoralism of Thoreau to the work-at-home, sun-powered autarkic fantasy of the 1970s—environmentalism has been at odds with primary economic trends.

The idea that material prosperity goes hand in hand with environmental degradation inevitably leads to the proposition that a choice must be made between the environment and the economy. This zero-sum rhetoric is used by environmentalists and polluters alike. Polluters lament the environmental damage they cause but claim it is necessary to protect jobs and profits. Old line environmentalists, in turn, seeing an either/or proposition, select trees and birds over soft goods and toaster ovens.

Given the opposition they faced, environmentalists have wrought near miracles. Since the latter part of the nineteenth century, the environmental movement has done so much to save vast portions of the American landscape from development. And for decades now, environmentalists have been involved in virtually every legislative battle.

The problem with the traditional, anti-materialistic, anti-economic growth environmentalism is not its past record of achievement but its growing inability to meet the extraordinary environmental challenges of the 1990s and beyond. Often, in human affairs, what originally motivates a far-seeing elite must yield to more popular ideologies in order for that elite's vision to be achieved. Ideas and approaches that once had highly beneficial consequences ossify and become obstructions to further progress.

FADING IDEOLOGIES

Such was the case with ideological socialism, for example. Socialism lost its appeal to many people in the world's developed countries largely because of the political upheaval in Eastern Europe in the past two years. While it may be viewed as a philosophy that played an important part in forcing governments to provide better pay and other benefits to working people, socialism is no longer seen as relevant in meeting current challenges in a highly competitive global marketplace.

Socialism is a fading ideology today because its practitioners were wed to the notion of a "vanguard party" leading the way to a better world for working people—a notion increasingly viewed as politically incompatible with the democratic spirit, and economically incompatible with entrepreneurial innovation.

Socialist thought, in short, is anachronistic. So, too, is traditional environmental thought that regards economic growth as evil. Indeed, this view grows more dated with each passing day and has become a genuinely destructive element in the battle to protect and preserve the environment.

It would be hard to exaggerate the harm to national and world ecosystems that the single, simple choice—jobs versus the environment—has caused in recent years. Countless people from all walks of

---

From *Business and Society Review,* No. 78 (Summer 1991). Reprinted by permission of the publisher.

life—people who would otherwise have become strong supporters of environmental legislation—have turned away because they fear the economic consequences of choosing the environment over economic growth.

This unfortunate situation was greatly magnified as this country slipped into recession. Members of poor minority groups have always looked on the environment as a Yuppie quality-of-life issue that had little relation to their own real world needs. As the recession deepened, a similar view took hold among many Americans who were previously supportive of environmental initiatives. Faced with an apparent choice between the natural environment and a job, they nodded sadly and opted for the latter.

This is the reason California's "Big Green" referendum was defeated on election day 1990. It is why other environmental referenda in all parts of the country went down to similar defeats.

When it is opposed to economic growth, environmentalism thrives only where and when people feel prosperous enough to trade a few consumer perks for the more rarefied satisfactions usually associated with good eco-citizenship. Antimaterialistic environmentalism never had a constituency among the Third World's impoverished. It seems like pure fluff to the poor in America's inner cities. And, as this country begins to pay the economic costs of its past profligacies, it will seem ever less critical to middle-class Americans as well. And when times get tougher, the consequences to the environment will be that much worse. In this way, traditional environmentalist ideology now undermines its own ends.

This situation is tragic because it is so unnecessary. We are a long way from the time when Dickens and Marx wrote, when pollution was synonymous with economic growth and material prosperity. Then, there were no economic penalties for polluting and many economic incentives to do so. Indeed, prosperity and pollution were linked: the dirtier the air above a city, the filthier the water in its river or harbor, the richer the city's fathers and the greater the job opportunities for the city's workers.

Today, an opposite set of circumstances prevails. Poor, local environmental conditions are invariably linked with poor, underdeveloped, or declining local economies.

A large part of this sea change, of course, came about through artificial intrusions into the marketplace—new laws, regulations, and judicial decisions that were designed to protect the environment. Since 1970—the year of the first Earth Day, the year the first federal Clean Air Act was passed, and the year the Environmental Protection Agency was established—new laws, stricter enforcement, and broader interpretations from the courts have, at every level of government, made formerly profitable polluting practices increasingly unprofitable.

These legislative and bureaucratic intrusions are, however, theoretically reversible; they could change should new political priorities and personalities come to the fore, as occurred during the early years of the Reagan administration. But the initiatives of Congress, legislatures, courts, and agencies are only part of the new environmental economics. There are other more basic, underlying—and, hence, less reversible—economic forces at work that fuel the growing synergism between sound environmental behavior by corporations and economic well-being.

The most important of these forces is the emergence of a true world marketplace. The United States—long able to grow by supplying and servicing its own internal markets—grew to depend on manufactured exports to the tune of $316 billion in 1990, up from $287 billion the year before. Meeting competition of foreign companies in the domestic market has become an even more urgent imperative for American corporations.

Thus, the bottom line of American companies, the dividends of their shareholders, and the jobs and benefits of their employees depend increasingly on how efficiently they compete in the world marketplace. And efficient economic activity is synonymous with low-polluting economic behavior.

A perfectly efficient factory, after all, would emit no pollution. It would turn all raw materials into finished goods. There would be no leftovers to go up the smokestack as toxic smoke, nothing nasty would leach into rivers or groundwater, and nothing really dangerous would have to be hauled away in fifty-five gallon drums.

WEALTH AND POVERTY

The reason the world's richest countries—the United States, Japan, and the western part of Germany, for example—also have the most fully articulated policies to protect the environment is because that which today creates wealth also tends to be less destructive to the environment. Conversely, the poorest industrial countries—Poland, for example—are environmental and economic basket cases because stagnant, inefficient economies, which reduce the capacity to generate wealth, are most destructive to the environment.

Good environmental policies are good national industrial policies. And good environmental policies are a precondition for—not an alternative to—economic growth. The choice nations face today is not between the environment and the economy, but between good environments and prosperity or ecological decline and national penury.

One of the dominant characteristics of human societies is inertia. That machines exist to tabulate and transmit information nearly instantaneously does not mean, however, that the people who use these machines change their views any quicker than they used to.

The old ways of looking at the environment-economic nexus—the rhetoric, the confrontational tactics, the demonizing of corporate America—are alive and well. Those views, however, are vestigial remnants of another era.

There are, however, some specific kinds of talk and behavior that can advance the environmental agenda that traditional environmentalism is no longer able to promote.

• When the White House issues statements saying that any proposed new piece of environmental legislation will cost jobs—during the debate over the 1990 Clean Air Act, a Bush Administration official said that the measure would "cost America 600,000 jobs"—do not accept this loss as the price of environmental progress. Rather, look for the job-creating potential of laws that protect the environment.

There are, by government estimates, approximately 65,000 to 70,000 companies in the United States now active in environmental clean-up work. The thirty-seven largest environmental services/pollution control firms alone employed more than 112,000 people at the end of 1989. When financial services, automaking, retailing, and other industries are laying off workers in droves, this is one field where employment gains continue to be very strong. In short, tougher environmental laws and stricter enforcement mean more jobs.

GREAT GREEN GOODS

• Some argue that environmental policies cost the United States business to foreign competitors that operate under less stringent laws. This view neglects the trade-boosting aspects of American policies. In a report released in March 1991, the U.S. Council on Competitiveness, a group of business, labor, and academic leaders, listed emissions reduction, recycling, and waste processing as among the relatively few leading edge technologies at which this country excels and is expected to continue to excel during the next five years.

A 1991 report from the International Trade Administration of the U.S. Department of Commerce sets the 1990 dollar value of environmental spending around the globe—excluding the United States—at $139 billion to $248 billion. Of this sum, an estimated $30 billion to $50 billion in "green" goods, services, and technology takes the form of imports. The United States, because it enacted environmental laws and regulations earlier than most countries, garnered between $3 billion to $6 billion of this market, or more than 10 percent. Thus, tougher environmental laws and better enforcement will be a boost to American exports.

• Another familiar argument is that new or tougher environmental policies hurt corporate profits. Environmental legislation at its very worst, however, simply involves a transfer of wealth: the losses of polluters are the gains of those paid to clean up the pollution. (This also creates a strong incentive for corporations to avoid producing pollution and waste in the first place.)

In America, the environmental clean-up industry now generates between $100 billion to $125 billion in annual revenues. Revenues of the fifty largest companies in the field increased more than 36 percent in 1990 over the previous year; profits grew by a solid 11.2 percent. So, if you want to boost the profits of one of this nation's economic dynamos, pass tougher environmental laws and enforce them better.

• The environmental costs that corporations bear are also sometimes said to reduce their ability to make needed capital investments. It should be noted that capital investment is usually the best way to check present and future pollution. Almost all newer, state-of-the-art manufacturing generates less pollution than older, less efficient methods. Environmental demands are encouraging innovation of new materials, processes, and packaging. In other words, the way to spur corporations into capital spending while lubricating the wheels of inventiveness is to pass tougher environmental laws and enforce them better.

The goals of environmentalism can be best achieved by reaching out to the unconverted in a way that can reasonably be expected to change their polluting ways. The new environmental economics will likely prove to have greater appeal in achieving that end.

Dilemmas of Disclosure: Ethical Issues in Environmental Auditing

Karen Blumenfeld
Former Director, Alliance Technologies Corporation

Environmental auditors occasionally face conflicts between competing moral demands. Situations may arise where an environmental auditor's duty to his or her employer appears to conflict with the duty to protect innocent third parties from harm. This chapter explores a fundamental question of environmental auditing ethics: what is an environmental auditor's ethical responsibility when he or she has identified a potentially serious environmental risk and, after reporting the risk through appropriate company channels, feels that the company is failing to take responsible action? Does the auditor have a moral duty to disclose the potential problem to outside representatives (e.g., the government, the plant's neighbors, or the press), or is any public duty superseded by an obligation to protect the employer's confidentiality?

I will argue that an environmental auditor does not have a special professional duty to protect third parties from harm, but the auditor does have an ordinary moral duty to do so. In the situation described, this ordinary moral duty conflicts with the auditor's fiduciary duty to protect the employer's confidentiality.[1] Both duties represent legitimate moral expectations. A principle for their reconciliation must be defined. In the absence of environmental auditing professional standards or codes of ethics, I propose a series of tests for evaluating auditors' ethical obligations when their duty to the public conflicts with their duty to their employer.

The scope of this chapter is limited in two ways. First, it is limited to ethical issues involved in the disclosure dilemma; legal issues are outside its scope. Second, it focuses exclusively on internal environmental auditors. Because special issues of professional responsibility and liability may arise with outside auditing consultants, I chose to limit the paper's scope to internal environmental auditors.

THE SCENARIO

Ed Anderson is a seasoned environmental auditor. He is a chemical engineer by training and has been with the Western Manufacturing Company for nineteen years. Prior to 1985, Anderson held increasingly responsible positions in three different plants. In 1985, while Anderson was manufacturing engineering director at the Alameda plant, he was offered the opportunity to head the new corporate environmental auditing program. Anderson accepted the offer and now heads a group of four drawn from various company operations. As director of the Environmental Audit Department, Ed

---

From *The Corporation, Ethics, and the Environment,* edited by W. Michael Hoffman, Robert Frederick, and Edward S. Petry, Jr. (Westport, CT: Quorum Books, 1990).

Anderson reports to the company's vice-president for health, safety, and the environment. He is responsible for planning, managing, participating in, and ensuring the proper reporting of periodic environmental audits of company operations.

Western Manufacturing Company established its corporate environmental auditing program in response to a series of small but embarrassing penalties by the Environmental Protection Agency (EPA) for violations of hazardous waste regulations at two plants. In spite of the company's substantially increased investment in environmental controls, the chief executive officer (CEO) did not feel comfortable that he or his senior management team understood the firm's potential environmental exposures. On hearing about the practice of environmental auditing among nearly all his competitors by 1984 and spurred by the Bhopal tragedy, the CEO decided to establish a corporate environmental auditing program. The program would provide top management with independent assurance that company operations are in compliance with applicable environmental laws and regulations. In initiating the program, the CEO made clear to all corporate staff and line managers the company's commitment to protecting the environment and complying with the law. He clearly articulated his intent that compliance problems identified during environmental audits would be remedied. After all, he observed, the company would be foolhardy to identify and document environmental problems if it did not have a serious commitment to fixing them.

Ed Anderson and the vice-president for health, safety, and the environment designed the audit program based on discussions with other environmental professionals and a detailed review of the environmental auditing literature. Figure 1 illustrates the principles of environmental auditing that Anderson and his boss established for the company. Western's environmental auditing program is now running smoothly. The program has virtually full cooperation from plant personnel who generally understand that the program is not designed to punish the plants but rather to protect the company and the plants from unreasonable environmental risks and associated liabilities.

THE AUDITOR'S DISCLOSURE DILEMMA

In January 1989 Ed Anderson and two fellow auditors are on a routine audit at the Columbia plant. At the audit close-out meeting with the plant manager and environmental coordinator, Ed Anderson presents the audit team's findings. He notes that the plant appears to be largely in compliance with applicable laws, regulations, and permit conditions; however, the most serious finding, in his judgment, is a situation that goes beyond compliance. The audit team has observed that the plant has limited preventive maintenance programs and aging physical facilities. Failure of any of several hazardous chemical storage loading and transfer systems could result in contamination of a water supply serving 750,000 people. Ed Anderson is convinced that a major spillage is imminent. He agrees not to document this issue in his audit report since no compliance problem is involved; however, he asks the plant manager to study the problem further to determine the degree of risk posed to the community.

The following week, Ed Anderson prepares the draft audit report and sends it to the Columbia plant manager with copies to the specialty chemicals division manager, the vice-president for health, safety, and the environment, and the office of general counsel. Four weeks later, the Columbia plant manager's response arrives. Follow-up actions have been specified for each of the audit findings with reasonable timetables for their implementation, but no mention is made of the potential spillage risk. While legally the company is not obliged to take action, Anderson feels that from a risk management standpoint, at least a study of the problem should be undertaken. He telephones the plant manager, who disagrees.

Anderson is unable to find support for his position in the company. The cost of corrective action and the company's plan to close the plant in three years have resulted in a management decision to accept the risk that the plant poses, a risk that management believes to be small. "Drop it," Ed Anderson is told. This is the first serious conflict Anderson has faced since joining the corporate staff. He feels strongly that the problem, if not fully ad-

FIGURE 1

WESTERN MANUFACTURING COMPANY ENVIRONMENTAL AUDITING PRINCIPLES

1. *Environmental Audit Definition:* Environmental auditing is a methodical and documented examination of our facilities' operations and practices to evaluate the extent to which they meet environmental laws and regulations.
2. *Environmental Audit Program Objective:* The primary objective of Western Manufacturing Company's environmental audit program is to provide assurance to top management that facility operations are in compliance with environmental laws and regulations, and that reasonable steps are being taken to correct identified environmental problems.
3. *Environmental Audit Program Direction:* Western Manufacturing Company's environmental audit program is sanctioned by the Chief Executive Officer and the Board of Directors. Top management support is demonstrated through our corporate environmental policy statement, which articulates management's desire for Western Manufacturing Company to be in full compliance with environmental requirements and management's commitment to follow-up on audit findings that require corrections.
4. *Environmental Audit Organization:* The environmental audit function is independent of ad line operations being audited. To assure operational independence, the Environmental Audit Department reports to the Vice President for Health, Safety, and the Environment who reports to the CEO through the Executive Vice President for Corporate Affairs.
5. *Environmental Audit Program Staffing:* The Environmental Audit Department is staffed by experienced individuals drawn from company operations. These individuals are drawn both from plant operations and from plant environmental staff positions. All environmental auditors receive initial training in audit skills, knowledge and techniques, as well as continuing education and training during their tenure as auditors. It is expected that some number of auditors will return full-time to plant operations after 3–5 years in the Environmental Audit Department. In addition to providing an important corporate assurance function, the environmental auditing program is also considered to provide a useful training ground for rising professionals in the corporation.
6. *Environmental Audit Program Design:* Typically, an audit begins with pre-audit planning which involves notifying the plant being audited, arranging trip logistics, and reviewing background information. The on-site audit activities normally are conducted in four steps: (1) understand and evaluate internal environmental management systems; (2) collect relevant information; (3) evaluate information collected; and (4) report audit findings. Following the on-site visit, the audit concludes with formal reporting and ensuring that identified deficiencies are corrected. These steps are codified in a series of written audit protocols. The scope of each audit is determined in advance and may include air pollution control and/or water pollution control and/or hazardous and solid waste management. A system has been established for determining audit frequency, but in no case will any plant be audited less than once every 4 years.
7. *Quality Assurance:* Program quality assurance will be ensured by periodic independent reviews of Western Manufacturing Company's program by an outside consultant.

dressed, could cause a major spillage, which would almost certainly contaminate the local water supply; however, it is not his job responsibility to fix environmental problems, only to identify and report them truthfully to company management. Plant management is responsible for fixing the problems. Worse, Ed Anderson is not entirely sure of the probability that a spill may occur. A cursory analysis was equivocal; it would take a considerable amount of effort to evaluate the risk fully.

Anderson feels he is in a moral bind. He believes that as an environmental professional he has a public duty to protect human health and the environment. He views the environmental auditor role as, at least in part, an environmental stewardship responsibility. He suspects he should notify the community about the potential danger even at the risk of losing his job. On the other hand, as a nineteen-year loyal employee of the Western Manufacturing Company, Anderson feels he has a general professional obligation to maintain the confidentiality of information that he obtained during an audit, under the good faith assumption that his findings would be kept confidential. He also wants to be careful not to undermine the audit program, to which the company is firmly committed, and which has important social value.

THE DILEMMA IN ETHICAL TERMS

Underlying Anderson's disclosure dilemma are two legitimate but opposing assumptions. First, he assumes that environmental professionals have a general duty to protect human health and the environment. Second, he assumes that professionals of all kinds have an obligation to protect the confidentiality of their employers. He feels the second obligation keenly in a situation such as his, where, without the assumption of confidentiality, a socially responsible voluntary corporate activity—environmental auditing—would not exist.

Although Ed Anderson is an engineer, not a philosopher, his assumptions each contain two driving principles: one relates to the fundamental duty underlying his actions and the other to the consequences of his actions. The fundamental duty principle assumes that the ethical value of an action is strictly a function of the inherent moral duty from which the action derives. The consequentialist principle assumes that the ethical value of an action is strictly a function of its consequences. Figure 2 illustrates the fundamental duty and consequentialist principles underlying Ed Anderson's dilemma. In practice, these two principles complement and inform each other; however, for the sake of discussion, the two principles are treated separately.

DISCUSSION

This discussion centers on two questions: (1) Is Ed Anderson morally obliged to protect human health and the environment, and if so, on what basis? (2) Is he morally obliged to protect his employer's confidentiality, and on what basis? The discussion is organized around the fundamental duty and consequentialist principles underlying each question.

Is the Environmental Auditor Morally Obliged to Protect Human Health and the Environment?

The first question has to do with Ed Anderson's obligation to protect human health and the environment. His concern is that failure to disclose a hazard that could potentially cause serious harm to human health or the environment is unethical.

The Duty

Ed Anderson believes he has a basic moral duty, derived from his position as an environmental au-

FIGURE 2

THE DILEMMA IN ETHICAL TERMS

Assumption	Underlying Principles	
	Fundamental Duty	Consequences
1. Failure to disclose a hazard which could potentially cause serious harm to human health or the environment is unethical.	There exists a fundamental moral duty to protect innocent third parties from harm.	Disclosure of the hazard might prevent significant human health or environmental damage.
2. Failure of an internal auditor to protect the confidentiality of his or her employer is unethical.	The auditor has a fundamental moral obligation not to disclose company information collected on the assumption that it would	Disclosure of confidential information jeopardizes the trust which underlies all current and future audits.

ditor, to protect human health and the environment. I will argue that he does have such a duty, but it is the same ordinary moral duty held by any individual, not a special duty derived from his position as environmental auditor.

The environmental auditing field is still emerging and is not yet fully professionalized. As a result, environmental auditors do not, in my judgment, currently have a special professional duty to protect the public—analogous, say, to the duties of public accountants.

The ethics literature is rich with descriptions as to what constitutes a profession. Three examples provide a sense of range of definitions:

> Succinctly put, all professions seem to possess: (1) systematic theory, (2) authority, (3) community sanction, (4) ethical codes, and (5) a culture. (Ernest Greenwood in Baumrin and Freedman, 1983, p. 21).

> [A profession has] three necessary features. . . . First, a rather extensive training is required to practice a profession. . . . Second, the training involves a significant intellectual component. . . . Third, the trained ability provides an important service in society. . . . Other features are common to most professions although they are not necessary for professional status. Usually a process of certification or licensing exists. . . . Another feature common to professions is an organization of members. . . . A third common feature of the professional is autonomy in his or her work. (Michael Bayles in Callahan, 1988, p. 28).

> In general, we can agree that a profession has the following:
>
> 1. a clearly defined field of expertise, which distinguishes members of the profession from all other careers;
> 2. a period of prescribed education or training which precedes entry into membership;
> 3. a selective process of entry into the profession, restricting its membership to those qualified;
> 4. a procedure for testing and licensing, generally approved by a state agency under guidance from the profession itself;
> 5. a dedication of the profession to social service, meeting obligations to the society and performing services other groups are not capable of offering;
> 6. correlatively, substitution of service for income and wealth as the primary motivation of members, plus high-quality service regardless of fees received;
> 7. provision of adequate services for the indigent or those in extremis generally with charge;
> 8. the application of differential fees for the same service to different clients, according to circumstances or ability to pay; and
> 9. a set of self-governing rules, inculcating a high code of ethics in relationships among members and in behavior toward society, and requiring provision of service at high levels of competence. (Behrman, 1988, p. 97)

By almost any definition, environmental auditing is not yet formally an established profession. It has no professional standards or self-governing rules, no ethical codes, limited community understanding or sanction, no prescribed training or education, no commonly agreed intellectual component, and no certification of licensure (except in California). Unlike public accountants, who have a rigorous and disciplined set of professional principles and practices, environmental auditors lack a commonly understood mission. As a result, the environmental auditor lacks the financial auditor's recognized position of public trust.

In the absence of explicit professional principles and practices, and an explicit, broadly understood covenant with the public, environmental auditors have no more moral obligation to protect the public than does any other individual.[2] But what is the ordinary obligation to protect the public? Let us look at an example.

Suppose an unemployed bricklayer sitting on the subway overhears a conversation in which a man tells a companion he plans to kill his employer because the employer has discriminated against him. Suppose further that the listener has every reason to believe that the speaker genuinely intends to carry out his threat. The listener has an ordinary moral duty to inform someone, say the police, who may be able to protect the man's employer. His obligation is not derived from any professional duty (indeed the listener is unemployed) but rather from an ordinary moral duty to protect innocent third parties.

One way to derive this ordinary moral duty is to apply a basic test, developed by the philosopher John Rawls, called the "veil of ignorance" test. By situating a person behind a hypothetical veil of ignorance, this test ensures that an individual evaluates various alternatives without regard to how he or she personally would be affected.

The veil of ignorance test is as follows. If one did not know one's position in a matter (e.g., in Ed Anderson's situation, whether one owns Western Manufacturing Company, is one of the 750,000 residents who rely on the local drinking water supply, etc.), what moral rule would one accept? Without knowing one's position in the unemployed bricklayer's case, one would certainly choose a moral rule that required disclosure since, when the veil of ignorance was lifted, one could turn out to be the potential murderer's boss with a gun to her head. Without knowing one's position in Ed Anderson's situation, one would similarly choose a rule that required disclosure since most people would not voluntarily increase their cancer risk by drinking from a contaminated water supply. Because a veil of ignorance test prevents the auditor from knowing whether he will be the auditor, who leaves on the next outbound flight from Columbia, or a local resident who will unknowingly continue to drink from a contaminated water supply, he must choose disclosure.

Suppose the auditor is not certain that a spill is imminent or is not sure that a spill would actually contaminate the local water supply. Is he still obliged to disclose? At this point, the fundamental duty principle and the consequentialist principle overlap, since one can rightfully question whether an auditor has a fundamental moral duty to protect innocent third parties from harm if the harm is insignificant (e.g., the contamination is minuscule and not likely to increase the community's cancer risk). Here we must turn to the consequentialist principle, which complements the fundamental duty principle by adding a significance test.

The Consequences

Ed Anderson believes that if he does not disclose the potential hazard to the public, significant contamination of a water supply could occur, causing harm to the community. From a moral standpoint, the consequentialist principle is persuasive; if his failure to act could cause dire consequences, then not acting is unethical. From a practical standpoint, however, there must be a high threshold for this principle to be adduced.

In a consequentialist analysis, the auditor must consider—in addition to the potential harm that could be prevented by disclosure—the potential harm that disclosure could cause. For example, the costs to the community and company of raising a potential false alarm could be significant. Psychological distress, depressed property values, lost production, and other negative consequences of disclosure need to be balanced against the potential harm that could result if the hazard is not disclosed. Because the costs of disclosure could be quite high, the costs of remaining silent must be even higher in order to justify disclosure.

Viewed another way, the consequentialist argument can be supported by Rawlsian reasoning. Using the veil of ignorance test, one can evaluate the auditor's fundamental duty to disclose in relation to the consequences of the hazard. The reasoning is as follows: An environmental auditor typically is able to make a general judgment as to the type of consequences that might occur if a problem is uncorrected and the general likelihood of its occurrence. He or she is unlikely to know with precision, however, the probability of such an event's occurring or the exact nature of the consequences.

Assuming for the sake of argument that an auditor were able to know, without doubt, the probability and consequences of an environmental event, there are four possible scenarios for the event's occurrence (Figure 3). In my judgment, only the first of the four risks—the high probability–high harm scenario—scenarios clearly justifies the auditor's duty to disclose. In this scenario, the auditor knows with a high degree of certainty that the environmental hazard will cause significant harm to human health and/or the environment. The veil of ignorance test suggests that most people, not knowing whether they were the auditor or a local resident, would prefer to be informed about imminent and severe contamination of their drinking water supply.

FIGURE 3

FOUR ENVIRONMENTAL RISK SCENARIOS

		Severity of Harm to Health or the Environment: High	Severity of Harm to Health or the Environment: Low
Probability of Occurrence	High	1 High Probability High Harm	3 High Probability Low Harm
	Low	2 Low Probability High Harm	4 Low Probability Low Harm

In the second risk scenario (low probability-high harm), people might well choose not to be informed of the potential risk, since we face so many of these risk situations in life (e.g., flying in an airplane) that we often feel better off not being confronted with information about every possible risk. Applying the veil of ignorance test to the third and fourth risk scenarios, both of which involve nonsignificant harm to human health and the environment, I would argue that people do not necessarily want to be informed of these low consequence risks. Clearly risks that are defined by scenarios 2–4 must be characterized and appropriately managed by a corporation. However, public disclosure of such risks is not necessarily dictated by moral obligation.

Summary

The analysis suggests that Ed Anderson's assumption—that failure to disclose a hazard that could potentially cause serious harm to human health or the environment is unethical—is justified by the fundamental duty principle and possibly by the consequentialist principle. More information is needed about the consequences of disclosure and nondisclosure to determine whether the latter principle can be adduced.

The fundamental duty principle states that an auditor has an ordinary moral duty to protect innocent third parties from harm. This duty does not arise from the auditor's occupation. However, since environmental auditors are likely to be exposed to more opportunities than most other people to exercise this duty and since auditors are better trained to evaluate environmental risks than the general public, it can be argued that auditors at least have greater opportunities than other people to protect human health and the environment from harm. The consequentialist principle adds a significance test to the disclosure decision by stating that the consequences of the identified hazard must be significant to justify the auditor's obligation for public disclosure.

Is the Environmental Auditor Morally Obliged to Protect His or Her Employer's Confidentiality?

The next question has to do with Ed Anderson's obligation to protect Western Manufacturing Company's confidentiality. His concern is that failure to protect the confidentiality of his employer is unethical.

The Duty

Ed Anderson believes he has a basic moral duty to protect Western Manufacturing Company's confidentiality. I will argue that he does have such a duty and that it is fundamental to the internal auditor-employer relationship.

Because environmental auditing is only an

emerging profession, we cannot look to environmental auditing standards or codes of ethics to define the auditor's obligations with respect to protecting an employer's confidentiality. On the other hand, when a company empowers an environmental auditor to conduct audits, the company does so on the basis of trust and confidence that the auditor will protect its interests. Indeed, the environmental auditor-employer relationship is fundamentally a fiduciary relationship: "A fiduciary relation[ship is] the relation existing when one person justifiably reposes confidence, faith, and reliance in another whose aid, advice, or protection is sought in some manner" (*Webster's Third New International Dictionary, Unabridged,* 1981).

When a company voluntarily creates an environmental audit function, it does so with a view toward the social good as well as with its financial interests in mind. To preserve the integrity of the audit program, management expects that environmental auditors will protect the confidentiality of information obtained during the course of conducting audits. If management thought otherwise (in the extreme, that auditors would freely disclose confidential information to the outside), audit programs would not voluntarily be undertaken. The purpose of an environmental audit program is to identify and solve problems before they become public threats, and the success of the environmental audit function is predicated on the auditor's ability to elicit sufficient cooperation from plant personnel to be able to identify environmental problems.

How does the presence of a fiduciary relationship govern the environmental auditor's moral behavior? The dictionary offers further guidance: "[In a fiduciary relationship] good conscience requires one to act at all times for the sole benefit and interests of another with loyalty to those interests" (*Webster's Third New International Dictionary, Unabridged,* 1981). Plainly the fiduciary (the environmental auditor) is expected to act at all times in the interests of the beneficiary (the employer). The notion that an auditor should not publicly disclose information obtained during audits is supported by a fundamental moral principle of keeping promises. The company can undertake a self-auditing program only if it trusts its employees to maintain the confidentiality of audit findings. The foundation of a voluntary audit program rests on the principle of keeping promises, with the implicit assumption of reliance and expectation.

With respect to the auditor's fiduciary relationship, the fundamental duty to protect the employer's confidentiality is closely tied to the consequences of breaching that confidentiality. Indeed the fundamental duty and consequentialist principles are almost inseparable.

The Consequences

Ed Anderson believes that if he discloses the hazard to the public, he jeopardizes the trust that underlies all current and future audits. I will argue that he is correct.

A voluntary environmental audit program rests on the trust between auditor and employer. It is difficult to imagine a company that would deliberately ask its employees to identify and document problems and then report those problems to government authorities or the media without the company's permission. It is equally hard to imagine a plant manager or plant environmental staff cooperating with an auditor (by providing the auditor with access to documents, in-plant interviews, and other sources of information) if it was believed that the auditor would publicly reveal potentially embarrassing information collected during the course of the audit.

Since environmental audit programs serve a public good (because they are designed to identify and correct environmental problems before they cause harm to human health or the environment), protection of the trust on which they are based also serves a public good. A breach of this trust would be discreditable to the company and the auditor and could undermine the basic foundation of the audit program, causing management to reconsider whether to continue with the audit program and causing other companies to question their audit programs. This result would serve neither the company's best interest nor the public's.

The obligation to protect the company's confidentiality is based not only on a fundamental moral duty to keep promises but also on a broader notion of protecting the general public interest. Ironically, the principle of protecting the general public interest (by maintaining the integrity of audit programs) may be in direct conflict with the principle of protecting specific members of the public (e.g., the local community served by the Columbia public water supply). In this respect, the auditor faces an almost insoluble dilemma between protecting the greater public good and protecting a specific public good. Clearly some kind of balancing test is needed.

Before concluding the consequentialist evaluation, the auditor must consider the potential negative consequences of not protecting the company's confidentiality. Here the auditor must balance the harm done by violating the company's confidence (e.g., undermining future audits) against the harm done by remaining silent. One could argue, for example, that protecting the company's confidentiality is not necessarily in the company's best interest when such protection could ultimately result in lawsuits, fines and penalties, or public embarrassment to the company. Depending on the circumstances, either choice (to disclose or not to disclose) could be interpreted as fulfilling the auditor's moral obligation to protect the company's relevant interests.

Summary

The analysis suggests that Ed Anderson's second assumption—that failure to protect the confidentiality of his employer is unethical—is justified by the fundamental duty principle and by the consequentialist principle. The fundamental duty principle states that the auditor, because of his fiduciary relationship to the company, is obliged to protect confidential information obtained during the course of an audit. This obligation is inherent in the nature of the fiduciary relationship. The consequentialist principle adds that public disclosure of the hazard would jeopardize the trust on which all present and future audits are built.

CONCLUSIONS

Ed Anderson plainly has a conflict between legitimate moral obligations. If he exercises his ordinary moral duty to protect human health and the environment, he abrogates his fiduciary responsibility to his employer. If he strictly interprets his fiduciary responsibility to his employer and fails to disclose the potential hazard to the public, he abrogates his duty to protect a segment of the public. It is impossible for him to honor both duties at the same time. A method is needed to resolve conflicts between an environmental auditor's obligations to his or her employer and to others. The approach I suggest offers six proposed tests to evaluate when an auditor's duty to the public outweighs his or her duty to the employer.

I begin by assuming that the auditor's primary obligation is to the employer. I make this assumption for two reasons. First, the auditor has a fiduciary responsibility to the employer. This responsibility grows out of a basic trust that is essential to the integrity of voluntary corporate environmental audit programs. In addition, the fiduciary responsibility serves more than just the employer since audit programs ultimately serve the general public good. Second, because the environmental audit occupation does not hold an explicit position of public trust and because there are no environmental auditing standards or codes of ethics specifying an auditor's obligation to the public, the auditor has no special obligation to protect the public.

The question then arises, Under what circumstances does the auditor's ordinary moral obligation to the public outweigh the fiduciary obligation to his or her employer? Six tests can be used to balance these obligations:[3]

1. The potential human health or environmental harm that could result from the hazard is significant.
2. Peer environmental professionals agree that the hazard is potentially significant and is not being adequately addressed by the company.
3. The potential negative consequences of remaining silent outweigh the potential negative consequences of disclosure.
4. The auditor has exhausted all reasonable internal reporting channels.
5. The hazard is not on a reasonable timetable for remediation.

6. The auditor is not primarily motivated by personal gain.

These tests are especially tailored to the environmental auditor. If all six tests are met, the auditor may be justified in making public his or her concerns.

The first test is that the potential human health or environmental harm that could result from the hazard is significant. Granted, reasonable people could disagree about how to define significant (for example, is one death significant, or must multiple deaths occur in order for the consequences to be considered significant?). But the goal here is to determine the potential severity of the problem so the auditor can properly weigh its overall importance.

In Ed Anderson's case, several basic questions must be answered in order to determine the significance of the risk—for example:

- Is Ed Anderson correct in his assessment of imminent (i.e., high probability) spillage?
- Is he right in believing that such spillage would contaminate the local drinking water supply?
- Would the community's excess lifetime cancer risk substantially be increased as a result of the contamination?

In all likelihood, Ed Anderson will not be able to answer these questions alone, nor is it desirable that he do so, since even reasonable people may disagree about probabilities and consequences. This gives rise to the second test: a peer environmental professional must agree that the hazard is potentially significant. Ed Anderson needs to obtain corroboration for his beliefs, as well as supporting data. Ideally he should obtain corroboration from an environmental professional within the company. But if necessary, he should talk to a trusted peer outside the company. This test is to ensure that the auditor is squarely in the midst of a genuine dilemma. No doubt reasonable people could disagree about the seriousness of an environmental hazard or the appropriateness of public disclosure; however, some level of peer corroboration is important for validating the auditor's judgment.

The third test is a balancing test: the potential negative consequences of remaining silent must outweigh the potential negative consequences of disclosure. The auditor has to weigh the negative consequences of disclosure carefully. These may be societal—for example, the costs to the community and the company of a false alarm—or personal—for example, the financial or emotional cost of disagreeing with one's management, jeopardizing a job because of a breach of fiduciary duty to the company, or being harassed or humiliated by people in the company who disagree with the judgment. This test is to ensure that the auditor considers all the consequences of disclosure, not just the potential harm that can be prevented by disclosure.

The fourth test is that the auditor has exhausted all reasonable internal reporting channels. This is critical; the auditor must attempt to give the company every possible opportunity to understand and address the problem. This could mean reporting as high in the company management structure as the company president or even the board of directors. In extreme cases, where an auditor believes that he or she is not being heard by immediate management, the auditor must make every effort to work through the company's internal management before turning to outside authorities. The purpose of this test is to ensure that the auditor has attempted to the fullest extent possible to honor the company's confidentiality while at the same time attempting to ensure correction of the identified hazard.

The fifth test is that the hazard is not adequately being remediated, nor is it on a reasonable timetable for remediation. This is to ensure that the auditor is fully aware of the steps the company is taking (if any) to address the problem.

Finally, the last test is that the auditor not be motivated primarily by personal gain. This test is to ensure that the auditor properly respects his fiduciary obligations and is not acting primarily in a manner to aggrandize himself or herself at the employer's expense.

Determining whether a situation meets the six proposed tests is not simple. In Ed Anderson's case, the most problematic tests are the first two. He does not know with certainty the probability or outcome of a major spill and has not discussed the problem with peer environmental professionals. Ed Anderson would probably elect to disclose the problem publicly if he determined that tests 3–6 were met and that the probability of a major spillage was high, the spill would result in major contamination of the water supply, increasing the community's excess lifetime cancer risk from, say, 10^{-6} to 10^{-5}, and a trusted audit colleague agreed with Ed Anderson's assessment.

In reality, however, environmental risk situations normally are more gray than black and white. Auditors generally do not have the luxury of knowing precisely the probability or outcome of an event. Moreover, there is no guarantee that reasonable people using these tests would draw the same conclusions. The audit practitioner operates in a world of enormous uncertainty. Nevertheless, the six tests offer a way of evaluating a highly complex ethical situation that is quite typical of the kinds of situations faced by environmental auditors.

To elevate the resolution of these dilemmas from the individual to the societal level requires that environmental auditing become more professionalized. Extensive progress already has been made toward environmental audit professionalization. Three environmental audit professional groups exist, and two of them have actively studied the issue of professional standards.[4]

Over the long run, ethical issues will best be addressed through formal professional standards and codes of ethics devoted to environmental auditors. The codes of ethics that exist for engineers, who comprise a large portion of the environmental audit work force, are not quite tailored to environmental auditors' needs because they do not address in depth certain issues unique to the auditor or employer situation, such as the importance of confidentiality to the effectiveness of the audit function. The Institute of Internal Auditors' and Certified Public Accountants' codes of ethics come closer to addressing the special environmental auditor-employer relationship but do not address the substantive issues unique to the environmental audit function, such as the fact that environmental auditors deal with information relevant to human health and welfare. Until professional standards are developed for environmental auditors, tough dilemmas of disclosure will have to be addressed by individual auditors without recourse to written guidance.

NOTES

I am grateful to the following individuals for their thoughtful input to this chapter. Al Alm, Greg Dees, John Palmisano, Steve Poltorzycki, Ralph Rhodes, Ann Smith, and Bill Yodis. They challenged my thinking and generously offered suggestions for improvement. Any errors, omissions, or misconceptions that remain are solely my responsibility.

1. The environmental auditor's duty to protect the confidentiality of audit findings may be overridden by certain legal circumstances, such as a subpoena requiring the disclosure of such information. However, this chapter assumes no legal obligations to disclose audit findings.
2. Environmental auditors usually have training in a specific field (e.g., chemical engineering, environmental sciences). Because of their training and background, many have professional affiliations with groups that have well-established ethical standards, for example, professional engineers. Membership in such a professional association confers special ethical obligations on an auditor. However, this chapter centers on the auditor's obligations qua auditor. Thus, the auditor's ethical obligations that arise from other affiliations are not dealt with here.
3. In the course of evaluating how an auditor might properly weigh his or her ethical obligations, I arrived at the six tests described. A literature search confirmed that several of these are the types of tests ethicists are likely to apply at a more general level to ethical dilemmas. See, for example, Sissela Bok or Gene G. James in Callahan (1988).
4. Three environmental audit professional groups exist as of this writing: the Environmental Audit Roundtable, the Institute for Environmental Auditing, and the Environmental Audit Forum.

The first two groups have addressed the issue of professional standards.

REFERENCES

American Institute of Certified Public Accountants, Inc. 1978. *Ethics in the Accounting Profession.* New York: John Wiley & Sons.

Barry, Vincent E., 1986. *Moral Issues in Business.* Belmont, Calif.: Wadsworth Publishing Company.

Baumrin, Bernard, and Benjamin Freedman, eds. 1983. *Moral Responsibility and the Professions.* New York: Haven Publications.

Bayles, Michael D. 1981. *Professional Ethics.* Belmont, Calif: Wadsworth Publishing Company.

Beauchamp, Tom L., and Norman E. Bowie, eds. 1988. *Ethical Theory and Business.* Englewood Cliffs, N.J.: Prentice-Hall.

Behrman, Jack N., 1988. *Essays on Ethics in Business and the Professions.* Englewood Cliffs, N.J.: Prentice-Hall.

Bureau of National Affairs., 1986. *Codes of Professional Responsibility.* Washington, D.C.: BNA.

Callahan, Joan C., ed. 1988. *Ethical Issues in Professional Life.* New York: Oxford University Press.

Hoffman, W. Michael, and Jennifer Mills Moore, eds. 1984. *Business Ethics.* New York: McGraw-Hill.

QUESTIONS FOR DISCUSSION

1. Do people have a "right to a livable environment"? If so, is this a barrier right (from the section on rights in the introduction) or a welfare right? Depending on your answer, what would this imply about business' responsibility to the environment?
2. What do you believe to be the main point of disagreement between Bowie and Hoffman? Do you think that most businesspeople would agree with Hoffman's proposal about business' responsibility to the environment? Why or why not?
3. What does Ruff mean by an "optimum" level of pollution? How would he go about determining this level? Would Sagoff agree? Why or why not? Is there any way of reconciling the ideas of Ruff and Sagoff?
4. What does Sagoff mean when he says that we are "citizens" as well as "consumers"? What does this imply about the use of economic decision making in the political arena? How do you think Leonard and Zeckhauser (from Chapter 2) would respond to Sagoff?
5. Silverstein argues that good environmental policies are a precondition for economic growth, and that poor economic policies will eventually lead to economic decline. If you were the leader of a less developed nation with few resources at your command, how do you think you would respond to Silverstein?

CHAPTER 12

INTERNATIONAL BUSINESS

Ethical Dilemmas for Multinational Enterprise: A Philosophical Overview

Richard T. De George
Distinguished Professor of Philosophy, University of Kansas

First World multinational corporations (MNCs) are both the hope of the Third World and the scourge of the Third World. The working out of this paradox poses moral dilemmas for many MNCs. I shall focus on some of the moral dilemmas that many American MNCs face.

Third World countries frequently seek to attract American multinationals for the jobs they provide and for the technological transfers they promise. Yet when American MNCs locate in Third World countries, many Americans condemn them for exploiting the resources and workers of the Third World. While MNCs are a means for improving the standard of living of the underdeveloped countries, MNCs are blamed for the poverty and starvation such countries suffer. Although MNCs provide jobs in the Third World, many criticize them for transferring these jobs from the United States. American MNCs usually pay at least as high wages as local industries, yet critics blame them for paying the workers in underdeveloped countries less than they pay American workers for comparable work. When American MNCs pay higher than local wages, local companies criticize them for skimming off all the best workers and for creating an internal brain-drain. Multinationals are presently the most effective vehicle available for the development of the Third World. At the same time, critics complain that the MNCs are destroying the local cultures and substituting for them the tinsel of American life and the worst aspects of its culture. American MNCs seek to protect the interests of their shareholders by locating in an environment in which their enterprise will be safe from destruction by revolutions and confiscation by socialist regimes. When they do so, critics complain that the MNCs thrive in countries with strong, often right-wing, governments.[1]

From *Ethics and the Multinational Enterprise,* edited by W. Michael Hoffman, Ann E. Lange and David A. Fedo (Lanhum, MD: University Press of America, 1986).

The dilemmas the American MNCs face arise from conflicting demands made from opposing, often ideologically based, points of view. Not all of the demands that lead to these dilemmas are equally justifiable, nor are they all morally mandatory. We can separate the MNCs that behave immorally and reprehensibly from those that do not by clarifying the true moral responsibility of MNCs in the Third World. To help do so, I shall state and briefly defend five theses.

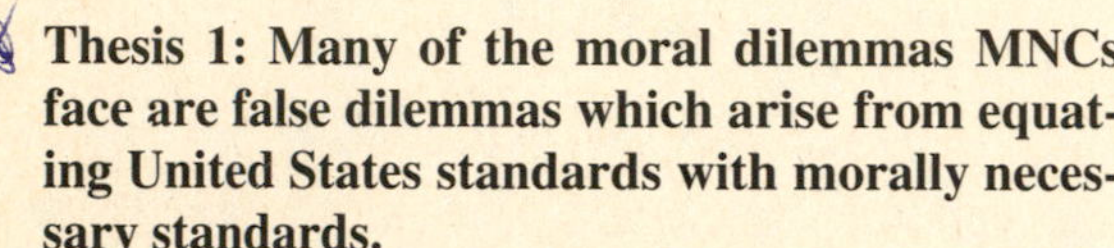

Thesis 1: Many of the moral dilemmas MNCs face are false dilemmas which arise from equating United States standards with morally necessary standards.

Many American critics argue that American multinationals should live up to and implement the same standards abroad that they do in the United States and that United States mandated norms should be followed.[2] This broad claim confuses morally necessary ways of conducting a firm with United States government regulations. The FDA sets high standards that may be admirable. But they are not necessarily morally required. OSHA specifies a large number of rules which in general have as their aim the protection of the worker. However, these should not be equated with morally mandatory rules. United States wages are the highest in the world. These also should not be thought to be the morally necessary norms for the whole world or for United States firms abroad. Morally mandatory standards that no corporation—United States or other—should violate, and moral minima below which no firm can morally go, should not be confused either with standards appropriate to the United States or with standards set by the United States government. Some of the dilemmas of United States multinationals come from critics making such false equations.

This is true with respect to drugs and FDA standards, with respect to hazardous occupations and OSHA standards, with respect to pay, with respect to internalizing the costs of externalities, and with respect to foreign corrupt practices. By using United States standards as moral standards, critics pose false dilemmas for American MNCs. These false dilemmas in turn obfuscate the real moral responsibilities of MNCs.

Thesis 2: Despite differences among nations in culture and values, which should be respected, there are moral norms that can be applied to multinationals.

I shall suggest seven moral guidelines that apply in general to any multinational operating in Third World countries and that can be used in morally evaluating the actions of MNCs. MNCs that respect these moral norms would escape the legitimate criticisms contained in the dilemmas they are said to face.

1. *MNCs should do no intentional direct harm.*
   This injunction is clearly not peculiar to multinational corporations. Yet it is a basic norm that can be usefully applied in evaluating the conduct of MNCs. Any company that does produce intentional direct harm clearly violates a basic moral norm.
2. *MNCs should produce more good than bad for the host country.*
   This is an implementation of a general utilitarian principle. But this norm restricts the extent of that principle by the corollary that, in general, more good will be done by helping those in most need, rather than by helping those in less need at the expense of those in greater need. Thus the utilitarian analysis in this case does not consider that more harm than good might justifiably be done to the host country if the harm is offset by greater benefits to others in developed countries. MNCs will do more good only if they help the host country more than they harm it.
3. *MNCs should contribute by their activities to the host country's development.*
   If the presence of an MNC does not help the host country's development, the MNC can be correctly charged with exploitation, or using the host country for its own purposes at the expense of the host country.
4. *MNCs should respect the human rights of its employees.*
   MNCs should do so whether or not local companies respect those rights. This injunction will preclude gross exploitation of workers, set minimum standards for pay, and prescribe minimum standards for health and safety measures.
5. *MNCs should pay their fair share of taxes.*

Transfer pricing has as its aim taking advantage of different tax laws in different countries. To the extent that it involves deception, it is itself immoral. To the extent that it is engaged in to avoid legitimate taxes, it exploits the host country, and the MNC does not bear its fair share of the burden of operating in that country.

6. *To the extent that local culture does not violate moral norms, MNCs should respect the local culture and work with it, not against it.*
MNCs cannot help but produce some changes in the cultures in which they operate. Yet, rather than simply transferring American ways into other lands, they can consider changes in operating procedures, plant planning, and the like, which take into account local needs and customs.

7. *MNCs should cooperate with the local government in the development and enforcement of just background institutions.*
Instead of fighting a tax system that aims at appropriate redistribution of incomes, instead of preventing the organization of labor, and instead of resisting attempts at improving the health and safety standards of the host country, MNCs should be supportive of such measures.

Thesis 3: Wholesale attacks on multinationals are most often overgeneralizations. Valid moral evaluations can be best made by using the above moral criteria for context-and-corporation-specific studies and analysis.
Broadside claims, such that all multinationals exploit underdeveloped countries or destroy their culture, are too vague to determine their accuracy. United States multinationals have in the past engaged—and some continue to engage—in immoral practices. A case by case study is the fairest way to make moral assessments. Yet we can distinguish five types of business operations that raise very different sorts of moral issues: 1) banks and financial institutions; 2) agricultural enterprises; 3) drug companies and hazardous industries; 4) extractive industries; and 5) other manufacturing and service industries.

If we were to apply our seven general criteria in each type of case, we would see some of the differences among them. Financial institutions do not generally employ many people. Their function is to provide loans for various types of development. In the case of South Africa they do not do much—if anything—to undermine apartheid, and by lending to the government they usually strengthen the government's policy of apartheid. In this case, an argument can be made that they do more harm than good—an argument that several banks have seen to be valid, causing them to discontinue their South African operations even before it became financially dangerous to continue lending money to that government. Financial institutions can help and have helped development tremendously. Yet the servicing of debts that many Third World countries face condemns them to impoverishment for the foreseeable future. The role of financial institutions in this situation is crucial and raises special and difficult moral problems, if not dilemmas.

Agricultural enterprises face other demands. If agricultural multinationals buy the best lands and use them for export crops while insufficient arable land is left for the local population to grow enough to feed itself, then MNCs do more harm than good to the host country—a violation of one of the norms I suggested above.

Drug companies and dangerous industries pose different and special problems. I have suggested that FDA standards are not morally mandatory standards. This should not be taken to mean that drug companies are bound only by local laws, for the local laws may require less than morality requires in the way of supplying adequate information and of not producing intentional, direct harm.[3] The same type of observation applies to hazardous industries. While an asbestos company will probably not be morally required to take all the measures mandated by OSHA regulations, it cannot morally leave its workers completely unprotected.[4]

Extractive industries, such as mining, which remove minerals from a country, are correctly open to the charge of exploitation unless they can show that they do more good than harm to the host country and that they do not benefit only either themselves or a repressive elite in the host country.

Other manufacturing industries vary greatly, but as a group they have come in for sustained charges of exploitation of workers and the undermining of the host country's culture. The above guidelines can serve as a means of sifting the valid from the invalid charges.

Thesis 4: On the international level and on the national level in many Third World countries the lack of adequate just background institutions makes the use of clear moral norms all the more necessary.

American multinational corporations operating in Germany and Japan, and German and Japanese multinational corporations operating in the United States, pose no special moral problems. Nor do the operations of Brazilian multinational corporations in the United States or Germany. Yet First World multinationals operating in Third World countries have come in for serious and sustained moral criticism. Why?

A major reason is that in the Third World the First World's MNCs operate without the types of constraints and in societies that do not have the same kinds of redistributive mechanisms as in the developed countries. There is no special difficulty in United States multinationals operating in other First World countries because in general these countries *do* have appropriate background institutions.[5]

More and more Third World countries are developing controls on multinationals that insure the companies do more good for the country than harm.[6] Authoritarian regimes that care more for their own wealth than for the good of their people pose difficult moral conditions under which to operate. In such instances, the guidelines above may prove helpful.

Just as in the nations of the developed, industrial world the labor movement serves as a counter to the dominance of big business, consumerism serves as a watchdog on practices harmful to the consumer, and big government serves as a restraint on each of the vested interest groups, so international structures are necessary to provide the proper background constraints on international corporations.

The existence of MNCs is a step forward in the unification of mankind and in the formation of a global community. They provide the economic base and substructure on which true international cooperation can be built. Because of their special position and the special opportunities they enjoy, they have a special responsibility to promote the cooperation that only they are able to accomplish in the present world.

Just background institutions would preclude any company's gaining a competitive advantage by engaging in immoral practices. This suggests that MNCs have more to gain than to lose by helping formulate voluntary, UN (such as the code governing infant formulae),[7] and similar codes governing the conduct of all multinationals. A case can also be made that they have the moral obligation to do so.

Thesis 5: The moral burden of MNCs do not exonerate local governments from responsibility for what happens in and to their country. Since responsibility is linked to ownership, governments that insist on part or majority ownership incur part or majority responsibility.

The attempts by many underdeveloped countries to limit multinationals have shown that at least some governments have come to see that they can use multinationals to their own advantage. This may be done by restricting entry to those companies that produce only for local consumption, or that bring desired technology transfers with them. Some countries demand majority control and restrict the export of money from the country. Nonetheless, many MNCs have found it profitable to engage in production under the terms specified by the host country.

What host countries cannot expect is that they can demand control without accepting correlative responsibility. In general, majority control implies majority responsibility. An American MNC, such as Union Carbide, which had majority ownership of its Indian Bhopal plant, should have had primary control of the plant. Union Carbide, Inc. can be held liable for the damage the Bhopal plant caused because Union Carbide, Inc. did have majority ownership.[8] If Union Carbide did not have effective control, it is not relieved of its responsibility. If it could not exercise the control that its responsibility demanded, it should have withdrawn or sold off part of its holdings in that plant. If India had had majority ownership, then it would have had primary responsibility for the safe operation of the plant.

This is compatible with maintaining that if a company builds a hazardous plant, it has an obligation to make sure that the plant is safe and that those who run it are properly trained to run it safely. MNCs cannot simply transfer dangerous technologies without consideration of the people who will run them, the local culture, and similar factors. Unless MNCs can be reasonably sure that the plants they build will be run safely, they cannot morally build them. To do so would be to will intentional, direct harm.

The theses and guidelines that I have proposed are not a panacea. But they suggest how moral norms can be brought to bear on the dilemmas American multinationals face and they suggest ways out of apparent or false dilemmas. If MNCs observed those norms, they could properly avoid the moral sting of their critics' charges, even if their critics continued to level charges against them.

NOTES

1. The literature attacking American MNCs is extensive. Many of the charges mentioned in this paper are found in Richard J. Barnet and Ronald E. Muller, *Global Reach: The Power of the Multinational Corporations,* New York: Simon & Schuster, 1974, and in Pierre Jalee, *The Pillage of the Third World,* translated from the French by Mary Klopper, New York and London: Modern Reader Paperbacks, 1968.
2. The position I advocate does not entail moral relativism, as my third thesis shows. The point is that although moral norms apply uniformly across cultures, U.S. standards are not the same as moral standards, should themselves be morally evaluated, and are relative to American conditions, standard of living, interests, and history.
3. For a fuller discussion of multinational drug companies see Richard T. De George, *Business Ethics,* 2nd ed., New York: Macmillan, 1986, pp. 363–367.
4. For a more detailed analysis of the morality of exporting hazardous industries, see my *Business Ethics,* 367–372.
5. This position is consistent with that developed by John Rawls in his *A Theory of Justice,* Cambridge, Mass.: Harvard University Press, 1971, even though Rawls does not extend his analysis to the international realm. The thesis does not deny that United States, German, or Japanese policies on trade restrictions, tariff levels, and the like can be morally evaluated.
6. See, for example, Theodore H. Moran, "Multinational Corporations: A Survey of Ten Years' Evidence," Georgetown School of Foreign Service, 1984.
7. For a general discussion of UN codes, see Wolfgang Fikentscher, "United Nations Codes of Conduct: New Paths in International Law," *The American Journal of Comparative Law,* 30 (1980), pp. 577–604.
8. The official Indian Government report on the Bhopal tragedy has not yet appeared. The Union Carbide report was partially reprinted in the *New York Times,* March 21, 1985, p. 48. The major *New York Times* reports appeared on December 9, 1984, January 28, 30, and 31, and February 3, 1985.

Moral Minimums for Multinationals

Thomas Donaldson
Connelly Professor of Business Ethics, Georgetown University

When exploring issues of international ethics, researchers frequently neglect multinational corporations. They are prone to forget that these commercial leviathans often rival nation-states in power and organizational skill, and that their remarkable powers imply nonlegal responsibilities. Critics and defenders agree on the enormity of corporate multinational power. Richard Barnet and Ronald Muller, well-known critics of multinationals, remark that the global corporation is the "most powerful human organization yet devised for colonizing the future."[1] The business analyst, P. P.

Excerpted from *The Ethics of International Business* (Oxford: Oxford University Press, 1989), and which appeared in *Ethics and International Affairs,* Vol. 3, 1989, pp. 163–182. Reprinted by permission.

Gabriel, writing in the *Harvard Business Review,* characterizes the multinational as the "dominant institution" in a new era of world trade.[2] Indeed, with the exception of a handful of nation-states, multinationals are alone in possessing the size, technology, and economic reach necessary to influence human affairs on a global basis.

Ethical issues stemming from multinational corporate activities often derive from a clash between the cultural attitudes in home and host countries. When standards for pollution, discrimination, and salary schedules appear lower in a multinational's host country than in the home country, should multinational managers always insist on home-country standards? Or does using home standards imply a failure to respect cultural diversity and national integrity? Is a factory worker in Mexico justified in complaining about being paid three dollars an hour for the same work a U.S. factory worker, employed by the same company, is paid ten dollars?[3] Is an asbestos worker in India justified in criticizing the lower standards for regulating in-plant asbestos pollution maintained by a British multinational relative to standards in Britain, when the standards in question fall within Indian government guidelines and, indeed, are stricter than the standards maintained by other Indian asbestos manufacturers? Furthermore, what obligations, if any, do multinationals have to the people they affect indirectly? If a company buys land from wealthy landowners and turns it to the production of a cash crop, should it ensure that displaced farmers will avoid malnutrition?

I

It is well to remember that multinational power is not a wholly new phenomenon. Hundreds of years ago, the East India Company deployed over 40 warships, possessed the largest standing army in the world, was lord and master of an entire subcontinent, had dominion over 250 million people, and even hired its own church bishops.[4] The modern multinational is a product of the post-World War II era, and its dramatic success has stemmed from, among other factors, spiraling labor costs in developed countries, increasing importance of economies of scale in manufacturing, better communication systems, improved transportation, and increasing worldwide consumer demand for new products.[5] Never far from the evolution of the multinational has been a host of ethical issues, including bribery and corrupt payments, employment and personnel issues, marketing practices, impact on the economy and development of host countries, effects on the natural environment, cultural impacts of multinational operations, relations with host governments, and relations with the home countries.[6]

The formal responsibilities of multinationals as defined in domestic and international law, as well as in codes of conduct, are expanding dramatically. While many codes are nonbinding in the sense that noncompliance will fail to trigger sanctions, these principles, taken as a group, are coming to exert significant influence on multinational conduct. A number of specific reasons lie behind the present surge in international codes and regulations. To begin with, some of the same forces propelling domestic attempts to bring difficult-to-control activities under stricter supervision are influencing multinationals.[7] Consider, for example, hazardous technology, a threat which by its nature recognizes no national boundaries yet must be regulated in both domestic and foreign contexts. The pesticide industry, which relies on such hazardous technology (of which Union Carbide's Bhopal plant is one instance), in 1987 grossed over $13 billion a year and has been experiencing mushrooming growth, especially in the developing countries.[8] It is little surprise that the rapid spread of hazardous technology has prompted the emergence of international codes on hazardous technology, such as the various U.N. resolutions on the transfer of technology and the use of pesticides.

Furthermore, just as a multiplicity of state regulations and laws generates confusion and inefficiency, and stimulates federal attempts to manage conduct, a multiplicity of national regulations stimulates international attempts at control. Precisely this push for uniformity lies behind, for example, many of the international codes of ethics, such as the WHO Code of Marketing Breast Milk Substitutes. Another well-known instance illustrating the need for uniformity involved the collision of French and U.S. law in the sale of equipment by Dresser Industries to the Soviets for the planned European pipeline. U.S. law forbade the sale of such technology to the Soviets for reasons of national security while French law (which affected a Dresser subsidiary) encouraged it in order to stimulate commercial growth. It was neither to the advantage of Dresser Industries nor to the advantage of the French and U.S. governments to be forced to operate in an arena of conflict and inconsistency. For months the two governments engaged in a public standoff while Dresser, and Dresser's public image, were caught in the middle.

National laws, heretofore unchallenged in authority, are now being eclipsed by regulatory efforts falling into four categories: namely, inter-firm, inter-government, cooperative, and world-organizational efforts.[9] The first category of "inter-firm" standards is one which reflects initiatives from industries, firms, and consumer groups, and it includes the numerous inter-industry codes of conduct that are operative for international business, such as the World Health Organization's Code on Pharmaceuticals and Tobacco, and the World Intellectual Property Organization's Revision of the Paris Convention for the Protection of Industrial Patents and Trademarks. The second category of "inter-government" efforts includes specific-purpose arrangements between and among nation-states, such as the General Agreement on Tariffs and Trade (GATT), the International Monetary Fund (IMF), and the World Bank.[10] "Cooperative" efforts, which comprise the third category, involve governments and industries coordinating skills in mutual arrangements that regulate international commerce. The European Community (EC) and the Andean Common Market (ANCOM) are two notable examples of such cooperative efforts.[11]

Finally, the fourth or "world-organizational" category includes efforts from broad-based global institutions such as the World Court, the International Labor Organization (ILO), the Organization for Economic Cooperation and Development (OECD), and the various sub-entities of the United Nations.

II

The growing tradition of international business codes and policies suggests that the investigation of ethical issues in international business is pressing and proper. But what issues deserve attention?

One key set of issues relates to business practices that clearly conflict with the moral attitudes of most multinational's home countries. Consider, for example, the practice of child labor, which continues to plague developing countries. While not the worst example, Central America offers a sobering lesson. In dozens of interviews with workers throughout Central America conducted in the fall of 1987, most respondents said they started working between the ages of 12 and 14.[12] The work week lasts six days, and the median salary (for all workers including adults) is scarcely over a dollar a day. The area is largely non-unionized, and strikes are almost always declared illegal. There is strong similarity between the pressures compelling child labor in Central America and those in early nineteenth-century England during the Industrial Revolution. With unemployment ranging from a low of 24 percent in Costa Rica to a high of 50 percent in Guatemala, and with families malnourished and older breadwinners unable to work, children are often forced to make growth-stunting sacrifices.[13]

Then, too, there are issues about which our moral institutions seem confused, issues which pose difficult questions for researchers. Consider an unusual case involving the sale of banned goods abroad—one in which a developing country argued that being able to buy a banned product was important to meeting its needs. Banned pharmaceuticals, in contrast to other banned goods, have been subject to export restrictions for over 40 years. Yet, in defense of a recent Reagan initiative, drug manufacturers in the United States argued by appealing to differing cultural variables. For example, a spokesman for the American division of Ciba-Geigy Pharmaceuticals justified relaxing restrictions on the sale of its Entero-Vioform, a drug he agrees has been associated with blindness and paralysis, on the basis of culture-specific, cost-benefit analysis. "The government of India," he pointed out, "has requested Ciba-Geigy to continue producing the drug because it treats a dysentery problem that can be life threatening."[14]

III

The task for the international ethicist is to develop or discover concepts capable of specifying the obligations of multinational corporations in cases such as these. One such important concept is that of a human right.

Rights establish minimum levels of morally acceptable behavior. One well-known definition of a right construes it as a "trump" over a collective good, which is to say that the assertion of one's right to something, such as free speech, takes precedence over all but the most compelling collective goals, and overrides, for example, the state's interest in civil harmony or moral consensus.[15] Rights are at the rock bottom of modern moral deliberation. Maurice Cranston writes that the litmus test for whether something is a right or not is whether it protects something of "paramount importance."[16] Hence, it may help to define what minimal responsibilities should be assigned to multinational corporations by asking, "What specific rights ought multinationals to respect?"

The flip side of a right typically is a duty.[17] This, in part, is what gives aptness to Joel Feinberg's well-known definition of a right as a "justified entitlement *to* something *from* someone."[18] It is the "from someone" part of the definition which reflects the assumption of a duty, for without a correlative obligation that attaches to some moral agent or group of agents, a right is weakened—if not beyond the status of a right entirely, then significantly. If we cannot say that a multinational corporation has a duty to keep the levels of arsenic low in the work place, then the worker's right not to be poisoned means little.

Often, duties associated with rights fall upon more than one class of moral agent. Consider, for example, the furor over the dumping of toxic waste in West Africa by multinational corporations. During 1988, virtually every country from Morocco to the Congo on Africa's west coast received offers from companies seeking cheap sites for dumping waste.[19] In the years prior, dumping in the U.S. and Europe had become enormously expensive, in large part because of the costly safety measures mandated by U.S. and European governments. In February of 1988, officials in Guinea-Bissau, one of the world's poorest nations, agreed to bury 15 million tons of toxic wastes from European tanneries and pharmaceutical companies. The companies agreed to pay about $120 million, which is only slightly less than the country's entire gross national product. In Nigeria in 1987, five European ships unloaded toxic waste in Nigeria containing dangerous poisons such as polychlorinated biphenyls, or PCBs. Workers wearing thongs and shorts unloaded the barrels for $2.50 a day, and placed them in a dirt lot in a residential area in the town of Kiko.[20] They were not told about the contents of the barrels.[21]

Who bears responsibility for protecting the workers' and inhabitants' rights to safety in such instances? It would be wrong to place it entirely upon a single agent such as the government of a West African nation. As it happens, the toxic waste dumped in Nigeria entered under an import permit for "non-explosive, nonradioactive and non-self-combusting chemicals." But the permit turned out to be a loophole; Nigeria had not meant to accept the waste and demanded its removal once word about its presence filtered into official channels. The example reveals the difficulty many developing countries have in creating the sophisticated language and regulatory procedures necessary to control high-technology hazards. It seems reasonable in such instances, then, to place the responsibility not upon a single class of agents, but upon a broad collection of them, including governments, corporate executives, host-country companies and officials, and international organizations.

One list receiving significant international attention is the Universal Declaration of Human Rights.[22] However, it and the subsequent International Covenant on Social, Economic and Cultural Rights have spawned controversy, despite the fact that the Declaration was endorsed by virtually all of the important post-World War II nations in 1948 as part of the affirmation of the U.N. Charter. What distinguishes these lists from their predecessors, and what serves also as the focus of controversy, is their inclusion of rights that have come to be called, alternatively, "social," "economic," "positive," or "welfare" rights.

Many have balked at such rights, arguing that no one can have a right to a specific supply of an economic good. Can anyone be said to have a "right," for example, to 128 hours of sleep and leisure each week? And, in the same spirit, some international documents have simply refused to adopt the welfare-affirming blueprint established in the Universal Declaration. For example, the European Convention of Human Rights omits mention of welfare rights, preferring instead to create an auxiliary document (The European Social Charter of 1961) which references many of what earlier had been treated as "rights," as "goals." Similar objections underlie the bifurcated covenants drawn up in an attempt to implement the Universal Declaration: one such covenant, entitled the Covenant on Civil and Political Rights, was drawn up for all signers, including those who objected to welfare rights, while a companion covenant, entitled the Covenant on Social, Economic, and Cultural Rights, was drawn up for welfare rights defenders. Of course, many countries signed both; but some signed only the former.[23]

Many who criticize welfare rights utilize a traditional philosophical distinction between so-called negative and positive rights. A positive right is said to be one that requires persons to act positively to *do* something, while a negative one requires only that people not directly deprive others. Hence, the right to liberty is said to be a negative right, whereas the right to enough food is said to be a positive one. With this distinction in hand, the point is commonly made that no one can be bound to improve the welfare of another (unless, say, that person has entered into an agreement to do so); rather, they can be bound at most to *refrain* from damaging the welfare of another.

Nonetheless, Henry Shue has argued persuasively against the very distinction between negative and positive rights. Consider the most celebrated and best accepted example of a negative right: namely, the right to freedom. The meaningful preservation of the right to freedom requires a variety of positive actions: for example, on the part of the government it requires the establishment and maintenance of a police force, courts, and the military, and on the part of the citizenry it requires ongoing cooperation and diligent (not merely passive) forbearance. The protection of another so-called negative right, the right to physical security, necessitates "police forces; criminal rights; penitentiaries; schools for training police, lawyers, and guards; and taxes to support an enormous system for the prevention, detention, and punishment of violations of personal security."[24]

This is compelling. The maintenance and preservation of many non-welfare rights (where, again, such maintenance and preservation is the key to a right's status as basic) require the support of certain basic welfare rights. Certain liberties depend upon the enjoyment of subsistence, just as subsistence sometimes depends upon the enjoyment of some liberties. One's freedom to speak freely is meaningless if one is weakened by hunger to the point of silence.

What list of rights, then, ought to be endorsed on the international level? Elsewhere I have argued that the rights appearing on such a list should pass the following three conditions:[25] 1) the right must protect something of very great importance; 2) the right must be subject to substantial and recurrent threats; and 3) the obligations or burdens imposed by the right must satisfy a fairness-affordability test.[26]

In turn, I have argued that the list of fundamental international rights generated from these conditions include: 1) the right to freedom of physical movement; 2) the right to ownership of property; 3) the right to freedom from torture; 4) the right to a fair trial; 5) the right to nondiscriminatory treatment (e.g., freedom from discrimination on the basis of such characteristics as race or sex); 6) the right to physical security; 7) the right to freedom of speech and association; 8) the right to minimal education; 9) the right to political participation; and 10) the right to subsistence.

This seems a minimal list. Some will wish to add entries such as the right to employment, to social security, or to a certain standard of living (say, as might be prescribed by Rawls's well-known "difference" principle). The list as presented aims to suggest, albeit incompletely, a description of a *minimal* set of rights and to serve as a point of beginning and consensus for evaluating international conduct. If I am correct, many would wish to add entries, but few would wish to subtract them.

As we look over the list, it is noteworthy that, except for a few isolated instances, multinational corporations have probably succeeded in fulfilling their duty not to actively deprive persons of their enjoyment of the rights at issue. But correlative duties involve more than failing to actively deprive people of the enjoyment of their rights. Shue, for example, notes that three types of correlative duties (i.e., duties corresponding to a particular right) are possible: 1) to avoid depriving; 2) to help protect from deprivation; and 3) to aid the deprived.[27]

While it is obvious that the honoring of rights clearly imposes duties of the first kind, i.e., to avoid depriving directly, it is less obvious, but frequently true, that honoring them involves acts or omissions that help prevent the deprivation of rights. If I receive a note from Murder, Incorporated, and it looks like business, my right to security is clearly threatened. Let's say that a third party (X) has relevant information which, if revealed to the police, would help protect my right to security. In this case, there is no excuse for X to remain silent, claiming that it is Murder, Incorporated, and not X, who wishes to murder me.

Similarly, the duties associated with rights often include ones from the third category, i.e., that of aiding the deprived, as when a government is bound to honor the right of its citizens to adequate nutrition by distributing food in the wake of famine or natural disaster, or when the same government, in the defense of political liberty, is required to demand that an employer reinstate or compensate an employee fired for voting for a particular candidate in a government election.

Which of these duties apply to corporations, and which apply only to governments? It would be unfair, not to mention unreasonable, to hold corporations to the same standards for enhancing and protecting social welfare to which we hold civil governments—since frequently governments are formally dedicated to enhancing the welfare of, and actively preserving the liberties of, their citizens. The profit-making corporation, in contrast, is designed to achieve an economic mission and as a moral actor possesses an exceedingly narrow personality. It is an undemocratic institution, furthermore, which is ill-suited to the broader task of distributing society's goods in accordance with a conception of general welfare. The corporation is an economic animal; although its responsibilities extend beyond maximizing return on investment for shareholders, they are informed directly by its economic mission. Hence, while it would be strikingly generous for multinationals to sacrifice some of their profits to buy milk, grain, and shelter for persons in poor countries, it seems difficult to consider this one of their minimal moral requirements. If anyone has such minimal obligations, it is the peoples' respective governments or, perhaps, better-off individuals.

The same, however, is not true of the second class of duties, i.e., to protect from deprivation. While these duties, like those in the third class, are also usually the province of government, it sometimes happens that the rights to which they correlate are ones whose protection is a direct outcome of ordinary corporate activities. For example, the duties associated with protecting a worker from the physical threats of other workers may fall not only upon the local police but also upon the employer. These duties, in turn, are properly viewed as correlative duties of the right—in this instance, the worker's right—to personal security. This will become clearer in a moment when we discuss the correlative duties of specific rights.

The following list of correlative duties reflects a second-stage application of the fairness-affordability condition to the earlier list of fundamental international rights, and indicates which rights do, and which do not, impose correlative duties upon multinational corporations of the three various kinds.[28]

Let us illustrate the duty to protect from deprivation with specific examples. The right to physical security entails duties of protection. If a Japanese multinational corporation operating in Nigeria hires shop workers to run metal lathes in an assembly factory, but fails to provide them with protective goggles, then the corporation has failed to

MINIMAL CORRELATIVE DUTIES OF MULTINATIONAL CORPORATIONS

Fundamental Rights	To Avoid Depriving	To Help Protect From Deprivation	To Aid the Deprived
Freedom of physical movement	X		
Ownership of property	X		
Freedom from torture	X		
Fair trial	X		
Nondiscriminatory treatment	X	X	
Physical security	X	X	
Freedom of speech and association	X	X	
Minimal education	X	X	
Political participation	X	X	
Subsistence	X	X	

honor the workers' moral right to physical security (no matter what the local law might decree). Injuries from such a failure would be the moral responsibility of the Japanese multinational despite the fact that the company could not be said to have inflicted the injuries directly.

Another correlative duty, to protect the right of education, may be illustrated through the example mentioned earlier: namely, the prevalence of child labor in developing countries. A multinational in Central America is not entitled to hire an eight-year-old for full-time, ongoing work because, among other reasons, doing so blocks the child's ability to receive a minimally sufficient education. While what counts as a "minimally sufficient" education may be debated, and while it seems likely, moreover, that the specification of the right to a certain level of education will depend at least in part upon the level of economic resources available in a given country, it is reasonable to assume that any action by a corporation which has the effect of blocking the development of a child's ability to read or write will be proscribed on the basis of rights.

In some instances, corporations have failed to honor the correlative duty of protecting the right to political participation from deprivation. The most blatant examples of direct deprivation are fortunately becoming so rare as to be nonexistent, namely, cases in which companies directly aid in overthrowing democratic regimes, as when United Fruit, Inc., allegedly contributed to overthrowing a democratically elected regime in Guatemala during the 1950s. But a few corporations have continued indirectly to threaten this right by failing to protect it from deprivation. A few have persisted, for example, in supporting military dictatorships in countries with growing democratic sentiment, and others have blatantly bribed publicly elected officials with large sums of money. Perhaps the most celebrated example of the latter occurred when the prime minister of Japan was bribed with $7 million by the Lockheed Corporation to secure a lucrative Tri-Star Jet contract. The complaint from the perspective of this right is not against bribes or "sensitive payments" in general, but against bribes in contexts where they serve to undermine a democratic system in which publicly elected officials are in a position of public trust.

Even the buying and owning of major segments of a foreign country's land and industry have been criticized in this regard. As Brian Barry has remarked, "The paranoia created in Britain and the United States by land purchases by foreigners (especially the Arabs and the Japanese, it seems) should serve to make it understandable that the citizenry of a country might be unhappy with a state of affairs in which the most important natural resources are in foreign ownership."[29] At what point would Americans regard their democratic control threatened by foreign ownership of U.S. industry and resources? At 20 percent ownership? At 40 percent? At 60 percent? At 80 percent? The answer is debatable, yet there seems to be some point beyond which the right to national self-determination, and in turn national democratic control, is violated by foreign ownership of property.[30]

Corporations also have duties to protect the right to subsistence from deprivation. Consider the following scenario. A number of square miles of land in an underdeveloped country has been used for years to grow black beans. The bulk of the land is owned, as it has been for centuries, by two wealthy landowners. Poorer members of the community work the land and receive a portion of the crop, a portion barely sufficient to satisfy nutritional needs. Next, imagine that a multinational corporation offers the two wealthy owners a handsome sum for the land, and does so because it plans to grow coffee for export. Now if—and this, admittedly, is a crucial "if"—the corporation has reason to *know* that a significant number of people in the community will suffer malnutrition as a result—that is, if it has convincing reasons to believe either those persons will fail to be hired by the company and paid sufficiently or, if forced to migrate to the city, will receive wages insufficient to provide adequate food and shelter—then the multinational may be said to have failed in its correlative duty to protect persons from the deprivation of the right to subsistence. This despite the fact that the corporation would never have stooped to take food from workers' mouths, and despite the fact that the malnourished will, in Coleridge's words, "die so slowly that none call it murder."

In addition to articulating a list of rights and the correlative duties imposed upon multinational corporations, there is also a need to articulate a practical stratagem for use in applying the home-country norms of the multinational manager to the vexing problems arising in developing countries. In particular, how should highly-placed multinational managers, typically schooled in home-country moral traditions, reconcile conflicts between those traditions and ones of the host country? When host-country standards for pollution, discrimination, and salary schedules appear sub-standard from the perspective of the home-country, should the manager take the high road and implement home-country standards? Or does the high road imply a failure to respect cultural diversity and national integrity?

What distinguishes these issues from standard ones about corporate practices is that they involve reference to a conflict of norms, either moral or legal, between home and host country. Consider two actual instances of the problem at issue.

Case #1: A new American bank in Italy was advised by its Italian attorneys to file a tax return that misstated income and expenses and consequently grossly underestimated actual taxes due. The bank learned, however, that most other Italian companies regarded the practice as standard operating procedure and merely the first move in a complex negotiating process with the Italian internal revenue service. The bank initially refused to file a fallacious return on moral grounds and submitted an "American-style" return instead. But because the resulting tax bill was many times higher than what comparable Italian companies were asked to pay, the bank changed policy in later years to agree with the "Italian style."[31]

Case #2: In 1966 Charles Pettis, employee of an American multinational, became resident engineer for one of the company's projects in Peru: a 146-mile, $46 million project to build a highway across the Andes. Pettis soon discovered that Peruvian safety standards were far below those in the United States. The highway design called for cutting through mountains in areas where rock formations were unstable. Unless special precautions were taken, slides could occur. Pettis blew the whistle, complaining first to Peruvian government officials and later to U.S. officials. No special precautions were taken, with the result that 31 men were killed by landslides during the construction of the road. Pettis was fired and had difficulty finding a job with another company.[32]

One may well decide that enforcing home-country standards was necessary in one of the above cases, but not in the other. One may decide that host-country precautions in Peru were unacceptable, while at the same time acknowledging that, however inequitable and inefficient Italian tax mores may be, a decision to file "Italian style" is permissible.

Thus, despite claims to the contrary, one must reject the simple dictum that whenever the practice violates a moral standard of the home country, it is impermissible for the multinational company. Arnold Berleant has argued that the principle of equal treatment endorsed by most U.S. citizens requires that U.S. corporations pay workers in less developed countries exactly the same wages paid to U.S. workers in comparable jobs (after appropriate adjustments are made for cost of living levels in the relevant areas).[33] But most observers, including those from the less developed countries, believe this stretches the doctrine of equality too far in a way that is detrimental to host countries. By arbitrarily establishing U.S. wage levels as the benchmark for fairness, one eliminates the role of the international market in establishing salary levels, and this in turn eliminates the incentive U.S. corporations have to hire foreign workers. Perhaps U.S. firms should exceed market rate for foreign labor as a matter of moral principle, but to pay strictly equal rates would freeze less developed countries out of the international labor market.[34] Lacking a simple formula such as "the practice is wrong when it violates the home country's norms," one seems driven to undertake a more complex analysis of the types and degrees of responsibilities multinationals possess.

What is needed is a more comprehensive test than a simple appeal to rights. Of course the earlier rights-based approach clarifies a moral bottom line regarding, say, extreme threats to workers' safety. But it leaves obscure not only the issue of less extreme threats, but of harms other than physical injury. Granted, the celebrated dangers of asbestos call for recognizing the right to workers' safety no matter how broadly the language of rights is framed. But what are we to say of a less toxic pollutant? Is the level of sulphur-dioxide air pollution we should tolerate in a struggling nation, one with only a few fertilizer plants working overtime to help feed its malnourished population, the same we should demand in Portland, Oregon?

In the end, nothing less than a general moral theory working in tandem with an analysis of the foundations of corporate existence is needed. But at the practical level a need exists for an interpretive mechanism or algorithm that multinational managers could use in determining the implications of their own moral views.

The first step in generating such an ethical algorithm is to isolate the distinct sense in which the norms of the home and host country conflict. If the practice is morally and/or legally permitted in the host country, but not in the home country, then either: 1) the moral reasons underlying the host country's view that the practice is permissible refer to the host country's relative level of economic development; or 2) the moral reasons underlying the host country's view that the practice is permissible are independent of the host country's relative level of economic development.

Let us call the conflict of norms described in (1) a type 1 conflict. In such a conflict, an African country that permits slightly higher levels of thermal pollution from electric power generating plants, or a lower minimum wage than that prescribed in European countries, would do so not because higher standards would be undesirable per se, but because its level of economic development requires an ordering of priorities. In the future, when it succeeds in matching European economic achievements, it may well implement the higher standards.

Let us call the conflict of norms described in (2) a type 2 conflict. In such cases, levels of economic development play no role. For example, low-level institutional nepotism, common in many developing countries, is justified not on economic grounds, but on the basis of clan and family loyalty. Presumably the same loyalties will be operative even after the country has risen to economic success—as the nepotism prevalent in Saudi Arabia would indicate. The Italian tax case also reflects an Italian cultural style with a penchant for personal negotiation and an unwillingness to formalize transactions, more than a strategy based on level of economical development.

The difference in norms between the home and host country, i.e., whether the conflict is of type 1 or 2, does not determine the correctness, or truth value, of the host country's claim that the practice is permissible. The practice may or may not be permissible, whether the conflict is of type 1 or 2. This is not to say that the truth value of the host country's claim is independent of the nature of the conflict. A different test will be required to determine whether the practice is permissible when the conflict is of type 1 as opposed to type 2. In a type 1 dispute, the following formula is appropriate:

> The practice is permissible if and only if the members of the home country would, under conditions of economic development similar to those of the host country, regard the practice as permissible.

Under this test, excessive levels of asbestos pollution would almost certainly not be tolerated by the members of the home country under similar economic conditions, whereas higher levels of thermal pollution would be tolerated. The test, happily, explains and confirms our initial moral intuitions.

Since in type 2 conflicts the dispute between the home and host country depends upon a fundamental difference of perspective, a different test is needed. In type 2 conflicts, the opposing evils of ethnocentricism and ethical relativism must be avoided. A multinational must forego the temptation to remake all societies in the image of its home society, while at the same time rejecting a relativism that conveniently forgets ethics when the payoff is sufficient. Thus, the ethical task is to tolerate cultural diversity while drawing the line at moral recklessness.

Since in type 2 cases the practice is in conflict with an embedded norm of the home country, one should first ask whether the practice is necessary to do business in the host country, for if it is not, the solution clearly is to adopt some other practice that is permissible from the standpoint of the home country. If petty bribery of public officials is unnecessary for the business of the Cummins Engine Company in India, then the company is obliged to abandon such bribery. If, on the other hand, the practice proves necessary for business, one must next ask whether the practice constitutes a direct violation of a basic human right. Here the notion of a fundamental international right outlined earlier, specifying a minimum below which corporate conduct should not fall, has special application. If Toyota, a Japanese company, confronts South African laws that mandate systematic discrimination against non-whites, then Toyota must refuse to comply with the laws. In type 2 cases, the evaluator must ask the following questions: 1) Is it possible to conduct business successfully in the host country without undertaking the practice? and 2) Is the practice a clear violation of a fundamental international right? The practice would be permissible if and only if the answer to both questions is "no."

What sorts of practice might satisfy both criteria? Consider the practice of low-level bribery of public officials in some developing nations. In some South American countries, for example, it is impossible for any company, foreign or national, to move goods through customs without paying low-level officials a few dollars. Indeed, the salaries of such officials are sufficiently low that one suspects they are set with the prevalence of the practice in mind. The payments are relatively small, uniformly assessed, and accepted as standard practice by the surrounding culture. Here, the practice of petty bribery would pass the type 2 test and, barring other moral factors, would be permissible.

The algorithm does not obviate the need for multinational managers to appeal to moral concepts both more general and specific than the algorithm itself. It is not intended as a substitute for a general theory of morality or even an interpretation of the basic responsibilities of multinationals. Its power lies in its ability to tease out implications of the moral presuppositions of a manager's acceptance of "home" morality, and in this sense to serve as a clarifying device for multinational decision-making. The algorithm makes no appeal to a universal concept of morality (as the appeal to fundamental rights does in type 2 cases), save for the purported universality of the ethics endorsed by the home-country culture. When the home country's morality is wrong or confused, the algorithm can reflect this ethnocentricity, leading either to a mild paternalism or to the imposition of parochial standards. For example, the home country's oversensitivity to aesthetic features of the environment may lead it to reject a certain level of thermal pollution, even under strained economic circumstances. This results in a paternalistic refusal to allow such levels in the host country, despite the host country's acceptance of the higher levels and its belief that tolerating such levels is necessary for stimulating economic development. It would be a mistake, however, to exaggerate this weakness of the algorithm; coming up with actual cases in which the force of the algorithm would be relativized is extremely difficult. Indeed, I have been unable to discover a single, non-hypothetical set of facts fitting this description.

IV

How might multinational corporations improve their moral performance and come to embody the normative concepts advanced in this article? Two classes of remedies suggest themselves: external remedies, i.e., those that rely on international associations or agreements on the one hand; and internal remedies, i.e., those that rely on internal, corporate initiative on the other.

Earlier we discussed the dramatic expansion of external remedies in the form of international laws, agreements, and codes of conduct. Again, while many of these are nonbinding in the sense that noncompliance will fail to trigger sanctions, they are as a group coming to exert significant influence on multinational conduct. One of the principal advantages of such global and industry-wide initiatives is that they distribute costs more fairly than initiatives undertaken by individual corporations. When, in line with the WHO Code of Marketing Breast Milk Substitutes, Nestle curtails questionable marketing practices for the sale of infant formula, it does so with the confidence that the other signers of the WHO Code will not be taking unfair advantage by undertaking the same questionable practices, for they must adhere to its provisions. Still another advantage of external remedies stems from the fact that many nation-states, especially developing ones, are unable to gather sufficient information about, much less control, the multinational corporations that operate within their borders. Thus, the use of supra-national entities, whether of an international or inter-industry form, will sometimes augment, or supplement, the power and information-gathering abilities of developing nations. It seems difficult to deny that the growth and maturation of such entities can enhance the ethical conduct of multinational corporations.

The most important change of an internal nature likely to enhance the ethical behavior of multinationals is for multinationals themselves to introduce ethical deliberation, i.e., to introduce factors of ethics into their decision-making mechanisms. That they should do so is a clear implication of the preceding discussion, yet it is a conclusion some will resist. Those who place great confidence in the efficacy of the market may, for example, believe that a corporate policy of moral disinterest and profit maximization will—*pace* Adam Smith's invisible hand—maximize overall global welfare.

This kind of ideological confidence in the international market may have been understandable decades ago. But persisting in the belief that market mechanisms will automatically ensure adequate moral conduct today seems recklessly idealistic. Forces such as Islamic fundamentalism, the global debt bomb, and massive unemployment in developing countries have drastically distorted the operation of the free market in international commerce, and even though a further selective freeing of market forces may enhance global productivity, it cannot solve automatically questions of fair treatment, hazardous technology, or discrimination.

Even adopting the minimal guidelines for corporate conduct advanced here would involve dramatic changes in the decision-making mechanisms of multinational corporations. Such firms would need to alter established patterns of information flow and collection in order to accommodate new forms of morally relevant information. The already complex parameters of corporate decision-making would become more so. Even scholarly research about international business would need to change. At present, research choices tend to be dictated by the goals of increased profits, long-term access to basic commodities needed for manufactured items, and increased global market share; but clearly these goals sometimes conflict with broader moral ends, such as refraining from violating human rights. Revised goals call for a revised program of research. And although we have rejected the view that multinational corporations must shoulder the world's problems of poverty, discrimination, and political injustice because, as economic entities, they have limited social missions, their goals nonetheless must include the aim of not impeding solutions to such problems.

Are such changes in the decision-making of multinational corporations likely or even possible? Resistance will be intense; clearly, there should be no delusions on this score. Yet, without minimizing the difficulties, I do not think the task impossible. At a minimum, corporations are capable of choosing the more ethical alternative in instances where alternative courses of action yield equal profits—and I believe they are capable of even more. Corporations are run by human beings, not beasts. As multinationals continue to mature in the context of an ever-expanding, more sophisticated global economy, we have reason to hope that they are capable of looking beyond their national borders and recognizing the same minimal claims, made in the name of our shared humanity, that they accept at home.

NOTES

1. Richard Barnet and Ronald Muller, *Global Reach: the Power of Multinational Corporations* (New York: Simon and Schuster, 1974) p. 363.
2. P. P. Gabriel, "MNCs in the Third World: Is Conflict Unavoidable?" *Harvard Business Review,* Vol. 56 (March–April 1978) pp. 83–93.
3. An example of disparity in wages between Mexican and U.S. workers is documented in the case study by John H. Haddox, "Twin-Plants and Corporate Responsibilities," in *Profits and Responsibility,* eds. Patricia Werhane and Kendall D'Andrade (New York: Random House, 1985).
4. Barnet and Muller, *Global Reach,* p. 72.
5. J. R. Simpson, "Ethics and Multinational Corporations vis-à-vis Developing Nations," *Journal of Business Ethics,* Vol. 1 (1982) pp. 227–37.
6. I have borrowed this eight-fold scheme of categories from researchers Farr and Stening in Lisa Farr and Bruce W. Stening, "Ethics and the Multinational Corporation" (an unpublished paper) p. 4.
7. An analysis of such reasons, one which also contains many observations on the evolution of international public policy, is Lee E. Preston's "The Evolution of Multinational Public Policy Toward Business: Codes of Conduct," a paper read at the annual meeting of the American Academy of Management, New Orleans, August 1987.
8. Jon R. Luoma, "A Disaster That Didn't Wait," *The New York Times Book Review,* November 29, 1987, p. 16.
9. While I personally have coined the terms, "inter-industry," "inter-government," etc., the basic four-fold division of international initiatives is drawn from Preston, *op. cit.*
10. See, for example, Raymond J. Waldman, *Regulating International Business through Codes of Conduct* (Washington, D.C.: American Enterprise Institute, 1980).
11. See, for example, P. S. Tharp, Jr., "Transnational Enterprises and International Regulation: A Survey of Various Approaches to International Organizations," *International Organization,* Vol. 30 (Winter 1976) pp. 47–73.
12. James LeMoyne, "In Central America, the Workers Suffer Most," *The New York Times,* October 26, 1987, pp. 1 and 4.
13. *Ibid.*
14. Quoted in "Products Unsafe at Home are Still Unloaded Abroad," *The New York Times,* August 22, 1982, p. 22.
15. Ronald Dworkin, *Taking Rights Seriously* (Cambridge: Harvard University Press, 1977). For other standard definitions of rights, see: James W. Nickel, *Making Sense of Human Rights: Philosophical Reflections on the Universal Declaration of Human Rights* (Berkeley: University of California Press, 1987) especially chapter 2; Joel Feinberg, "Duties, Rights and Claims," *American Philosophical Quarterly,* Vol. 3 (1966) pp. 137–44. See also Feinberg, "The Nature and Value of Rights," *Journal of Value Inquiry,* Vol. 4 (1970) pp. 243–57; Wesley N. Hohfeld, *Fundamental Legal Conceptions* (New Haven: Yale University Press, 1964); and H. J. McCloskey, "Rights—Some Conceptual Issues," *Australasian Journal of Philosophy,* Vol. 54 (1976) pp. 99–115.
16. Maurice Cranston, *What Are Human Rights?* (New York: Taplinger, 1973) p. 67.

17. H. J. McCloskey, for example, understands a right as a positive entitlement that need not specify who bears the responsibility for satisfying that entitlement. H. J. McCloskey, "Rights—Some Conceptual Issues," p. 99.
18. Joel Feinberg, "Duties, Rights and Claims," *American Philosophical Quarterly,* Vol. 3 (1966) pp. 137–44. See also Feinberg, "The Nature and Value of Rights," pp. 243–57.
19. James Brooke, "Waste Dumpers Turning to West Africa," *The New York Times,* July 17, 1988, pp. 1 and 7.
20. *Ibid.*
21. *Ibid.,* p. 7. Nigeria and other countries have struck back, often by imposing strict rules against the acceptance of toxic waste. For example, in Nigeria officials now warn that anyone caught importing toxic waste will face the firing squad.
22. See Ian Brownlie, *Basic Documents on Human Rights* (Oxford: Oxford University Press, 1975).
23. James W. Nickel, "The Feasibility of Welfare Rights in Less Developed Countries," in *Economic Justice: Private Rights and Public Responsibilities,* eds. Kenneth Kipnis and Diana T. Meyers (Totowa, N.J.: Rowman and Allenheld, 1985) pp. 217–26.
24. Henry Shue, *Basic Rights: Subsistence, Affluence, and U.S. Foreign Policy* (Princeton: Princeton University Press, 1980) pp. 37–38.
25. Donaldson, *The Ethics of International Business,* see especially chapter 5. My formulation of these three conditions is an adaptation from four conditions presented and defended by James Nickel in James W. Nickel, *Making Sense of Human Rights: Philosophical Reflections on the Universal Declaration of Human Rights* (Berkeley: University of California Press, 1987).
26. The fairness-affordability test implies that in order for a proposed right to qualify as a genuine right, all moral agents (including nation-states, individuals, and corporations) must be able under ordinary circumstances, both economically and otherwise, to assume the various burdens and duties that fall fairly upon them in honoring the right. "Affordable" here means literally capable of paying for; it does not mean "affordable" in the vernacular sense that something is not affordable because it would constitute an inefficient luxury, or would necessitate trading off other more valuable economic goods. This definition implies that—at least under unusual circumstances—honoring a right may be mandatory for a given multinational corporation, even when the result is bankrupting the firm. For example, it would be "affordable" under ordinary circumstances for multinational corporations to employ older workers and refuse to hire eight-year-old children for full-time, ongoing labor, and hence doing so would be mandatory even in the unusual situation where a particular firm's paying the higher salaries necessary to hire older laborers would probably bankrupt the firm. By the same logic, it would probably not be "affordable" for either multinational corporations or nation-states around the world to guarantee kidney dialysis for all citizens who need it. The definition also implies that any act of forbearance (of a kind involved in not violating a right directly) is "affordable" for all moral agents.
27. Shue, *Basic Rights,* p. 57.
28. It is possible to understand even the first four rights as imposing correlative duties to protect from deprivation under highly unusual or hypothetical circumstances.
29. Brian Barry, "The Case for a New International Economic Order," in *Ethics, Economics, and the Law: Nomos XXIV,* eds. J. Roland Pennock and John W. Chapman (New York: New York University Press, 1982).
30. Companies are also charged with undermining local governments, and hence infringing on basic rights, by sophisticated tax evasion schemes. Especially when companies buy from their own subsidiaries, they can establish prices that have little connection to existing market values. This, in turn, means that profits can be shifted from high-tax to low-tax countries, with the result that poor nations can be deprived of their rightful share.
31. Arthur Kelly, "Italian Bank Mores," in *Case Studies in Business Ethics,* ed. by T. Donaldson (Englewood Cliffs, N.J.: Prentice-Hall, 1984) pp. 37–39.
32. Charles Peters and Taylor Branch, *Blowing the Whistle: Dissent in the Public Interest* (New York: Praeger, 1974) pp. 182–85.
33. Arnold Berleant, "Multinationals and the Problem of Ethical Consistency," *Journal of Business Ethics,* Vol. 3 (August 1982) pp. 182–95.
34. Some have argued that insulating the economies of the less developed countries would be advantageous

to the less developed countries in the long run. But whether correct or not, such an argument is independent of the present issue, for it is independent of the claim that if a practice violates the norms of the home country, then it is impermissible.

International Business, Morality, and the Common Good

Manuel Velasquez
Dirksen Professor of Business Ethics, Santa Clara University

During the last few years an increasing number of voices have urged that we pay more attention to ethics in international business, on the grounds that not only are all large corporations now internationally structured and thus engaging in international transactions, but that even the smallest domestic firm is increasingly buffeted by the pressures of international competition.[1] This call for increased attention to international business ethics has been answered by a slowly growing collection of ethicists who have begun to address issues in this field. The most comprehensive work on this subject to date is the recent book *The Ethics of International Business* by Thomas Donaldson.[2]

I want in this article to discuss certain realist objections to bringing ethics to bear on international transactions, an issue that, I believe, has not yet been either sufficiently acknowledged nor adequately addressed but that must be resolved if the topic of international business ethics is to proceed on solid foundations. Even so careful a writer as Thomas Donaldson fails to address this issue in its proper complexity. Oddly enough, in the first chapter where one would expect him to argue that, in spite of realist objections, *businesses* have international moral obligations, Donaldson argues only for the less pertinent claim that, in spite of realist objections, *states* have international moral obligations.[3] But international business organizations, I will argue, have special features that render realist objections quite compelling. The question I want to address, here, then, is a particular aspect of the question Donaldson and others have ignored: Can we say that businesses operating in a competitive international environment have any moral obligations to contribute to the international common good, particularly in light of realist objections? Unfortunately, my answer to this question will be in the negative.

My subject, then, is international business and the common good. What I will do is the following. I will begin by explaining what I mean by the common good, and what I mean by international business. Then I will turn directly to the question whether the views of the realist allow us to claim that international businesses have a moral obligation to contribute to the common good. I will first lay out the traditional realist treatment of this question and then revise the traditional realist view so that it can deal with certain shortcomings embedded in the traditional version of realism. I will then bring these revisions to bear on the question of whether international businesses have any obligations toward the common good, a question that I will answer in the negative. My hope is that I have identified some extremely problematic issues that are both critical and disturbing and that, I believe, need to be more widely discussed than they have been because they challenge our easy attribution of moral obligation to international business organizations.

I should note that what follows is quite tentative. I am attempting to work out the implications of certain arguments that have reappeared recently in the literature on morality in international affairs. I am not entirely convinced of the correctness of my conclusions, and offer them here as a way of trying to get clearer about their status. I should also note that although I have elsewhere argued that it is improper to attribute *moral responsibility* to corporate entities, I here set these arguments aside in order to show that even if we ignore the issue of moral responsibility, it is still questionable whether international businesses have obligations toward the common good.

From *Business Ethics Quarterly*, Vol. 2, Issue 1 (July 1992), pp. 27–40. Reprinted by permission of the author.

I. THE COMMON GOOD

Let me begin by distinguishing a weak from a strong conception of the common good, so that I might clarify what I have in mind when I refer to the common good.

What I have in mind by a weak conception of the common good is essentially the utilitarian notion of the common good. It is a notion that is quite clearly stated by Jeremy Bentham:

> The interest of the community then is—what? The sum of the interests of the several members who compose it. . . . It is vain to talk of the interest of the community, without understanding what is the interest of the individual. A thing is said to promote the interest or to be for the interest of an individual, when it tends to add to the sum total of his pleasure; or what comes to the same thing, to diminish the sum total of his pains.[4]

On the utilitarian notion of the common good, the common good is nothing more than the sum of the utilities of each individual. The reason why I call this the "weak" conception of the common good will become clear, I believe, once it is contrasted with another, quite different notion of the common good.

Let me describe, therefore, what I will call a strong conception of the common good, the conception on which I want to focus in this essay. It is a conception that has been elaborated in the Catholic tradition, and so I will refer to it as the Catholic conception of the common good. Here is how one writer, William A. Wallace, O.P., characterizes the conception:

> A common good is clearly distinct from a *private* good, the latter being the good of one person only, to the exclusion of its being possessed by any other. A common good is distinct also from a *collective* good, which, though possessed by all of a group, is not really participated in by the members of the group; divided up, a collective good becomes respectively the private goods of the members. A true *common* good is universal, not singular or collective, and is distributive in character, being communicable to many without becoming anyone's private good. Moreover, each person participates in the whole common good, not merely in a part of it, nor can any one person possess it wholly.[5]

In the terms used by Wallace, the utilitarian conception of the common good is actually a "collective" good. That is, it is an aggregate of the private goods (the utilities) of the members of a society. The common good in the utilitarian conception is divisible in the sense that the aggregate consists of distinct parts and each part is enjoyable by only one individual. Moreover, the common good in the utilitarian conception is not universal in the sense that not all members of society can enjoy all of the aggregate; instead, each member enjoys only a portion of the aggregate.

By contrast, in the Catholic conception that Wallace is attempting to characterize, the common good consists of those goods that (1) benefit all the members of a society in the sense that all the members of the society have access to each of these goods, and (2) are not divisible in the sense that none of these goods can be divided up and allocated among individuals in such a way that others can be excluded from enjoying what another individual enjoys. The example that Wallace gives of one common good is the "good of peace and order."[6] Other examples are national security, a clean natural environment, public health and safety, a productive economic system to whose benefits all have access, a just legal and political system, and a system of natural and artificial associations in which persons can achieve their personal fulfillment.

It is this strong notion of the common good that the Catholic tradition has had in mind when it has defined the common good as "the sum total of those conditions of social living whereby men are enabled more fully and more readily to achieve their own perfection."[7] It is also the conception that John Rawls has in mind when he writes that "Government is assumed to aim at the common good, that is, at maintaining conditions and achieving objectives that are similarly to everyone's advantage," and "the common good I think of as certain general conditions that are in an appropriate sense equally to everyone's advantage."[8]

The Catholic conception of the common good is

the conception that I have in mind in what follows. It is clear from the characterization of the common good laid out above that we can think of the common good on two different levels. We can think of the common good on a national and on an international level. On a national level, the common good is that set of conditions within a certain nation that are necessary for the citizens of that nation to achieve their individual fulfillment and so in which all of the citizens have an interest.

On an international level, we can speak of the global common good as that set of conditions that are necessary for the citizens of all or of most nations to achieve their individual fulfillment, and so those goods in which all the peoples of the world have an interest. In what follows, I will be speaking primarily about the global common good.

Now it is obvious that identifying the global common good is extremely difficult because cultures differ on their views of what conditions are necessary for humans to flourish. These differences are particularly acute between the cultures of the lesser developed third world nations who have demanded a "new economic order," and the cultures of the wealthier first world nations who have resisted this demand. Nevertheless, we can identify at least some elements of the global common good. Maintaining a congenial global climate, for example is certainly part of the global common good. Maintaining safe transportation routes for the international flow of goods is also part of the global common good. Maintaining clean oceans is another aspect of the global common good, as is the avoidance of a global nuclear war. In spite of the difficulties involved in trying to compile a list of the goods that qualify as part of the global common good, then, it is nevertheless possible to identify at least some of the items that belong on the list.

II. INTERNATIONAL BUSINESS

Now let me turn to the other term in my title: international business. When speaking of international business, I have in mind a particular kind of organization: the multinational corporation. Multinational corporations have a number of well known features, but let me briefly summarize a few of them. First, multinational corporations are businesses and as such they are organized primarily to increase their profits within a competitive environment. Virtually all of the activities of a multinational corporation can be explained as more or less rational attempts to achieve this dominant end. Secondly, multinational corporations are bureaucratic organizations. The implication of this is that the identity, the fundamental structure, and the dominant objectives of the corporation endure while the many individual human beings who fill the various offices and positions within the corporation come and go. As a consequence, the particular values and aspirations of individual members of the corporation have a relatively minimal and transitory impact on the organization as a whole. Thirdly, and most characteristically, multinational corporations operate in several nations. This has several implications. First, because the multinational is not confined to a single nation, it can easily escape the reach of the laws of any particular nation by simply moving its resources or operations out of one nation and transferring them to another nation. Second, because the multinational is not confined to a single nation, its interests are not aligned with the interests of any single nation. The ability of the multinational to achieve its profit objectives does not depend upon the ability of any particular nation to achieve its own domestic objectives.

In saying that I want to discuss international business and the common good, I am saying that I want to discuss the relationship between the global common good and multinational corporations, that is, organizations that have the features I have just identified.

The general question I want to discuss is straightforward: I want to ask whether it is possible for us to say that multinational corporations with the features I have just described have an obligation to contribute toward the global common good. But I want to discuss only one particular aspect of this general question. I want to discuss this question in light of the realist objection.

III. THE TRADITIONAL REALIST OBJECTION IN HOBBES

The realist objection, of course, is the standard objection to the view that agents—whether corporations, governments, or individuals—have moral obligations on the international level. Generally, the realist holds that it is a mistake to apply moral concepts to international activities: morality has no place in international affairs. The classical statement of this view, which I am calling the "traditional" version of realism, is generally attributed to Thomas Hobbes. I will assume that this customary attribution is correct; my aim is to identify some of the implications of this traditional version of realism even if it is not quite historically accurate to attribute it to Hobbes.

In its Hobbsian form, as traditionally interpreted, the realist objection holds that moral concepts have no meaning in the absence of an agency powerful enough to guarantee that other agents generally adhere to the tenets of morality. Hobbes held, first, that in the absence of a sovereign power capable of forcing men to behave civilly with each other, men are in "the state of nature," a state he characterizes as a "war . . . of every man, against every man."[9] Secondly, Hobbes claimed, in such a state of war, moral concepts have no meaning:

> To this war of every man against every man, this also is consequent; that nothing can be unjust. The notions of right and wrong, justice and injustice have there no place. Where there is no common power, there is no law: where no law, no injustice.[10]

Moral concepts are meaningless, then, when applied to state of nature situations. And, Hobbes held, the international arena is a state of nature, since there is no international sovereign that can force agents to adhere to the tenets of morality.[11]

The Hobbsian objection to talking about morality in international affairs, then, is based on two premises: (1) an ethical premise about the applicability of moral terms and (2) an apparently empirical premise about how agents behave under certain conditions. The ethical premise, at least in its Hobbsian form, holds that there is a connection between the meaningfulness of moral terms and the extent to which agents adhere to the tenets of morality: If in a given situation agents do not adhere to the tenets of morality, then in that situation moral terms have no meaning. The apparently empirical premise holds that in the absence of a sovereign, agents will not adhere to the tenets of morality: they will be in a state of war. This appears to be an empirical generalization about the extent to which agents adhere to the tenets of morality in the absence of a third-party enforcer. Taken together, the two premises imply that in situations that lack a sovereign authority, such as one finds in many international exchanges, moral terms have no meaning and so moral obligations are nonexistent.

However, there are a number of reasons for thinking that the two Hobbsian premises are deficient as they stand. I want next, therefore, to examine each of these premises more closely and to determine the extent to which they need revision.

IV. REVISING THE REALIST OBJECTION: THE FIRST PREMISE

The ethical premise concerning the meaning of moral terms, is, in its original Hobbsian form, extremely difficult to defend. If one is in a situation in which others do not adhere to any moral restraints, it simply does not logically follow that in that situation one's actions are no longer subject to moral evaluation. At most what follows is that since such an extreme situation is different from the more normal situations in which we usually act, the moral requirements placed on us in such extreme situations are different from the moral requirements that obtain in more normal circumstances. For example, morality requires that in normal circumstances I am not to attack or kill my fellow citizens. But when one of those citizens is attacking me in a dark alley, morality allows me to defend myself by counterattacking or even killing that citizen. It is a truism that what moral principles require in one set of circumstances is different from what they require in other circumstances. And in extreme circumstances, the requirements of morality may become correspondingly extreme. But there is no reason to think that they vanish altogether.

Nevertheless, the realist can relinquish the Hobbsian premise about the meaning of moral terms, replace it with a weaker and more plausible premise, and still retain much of Hobbes' conclusion. The realist or neo-Hobbsian can claim that although moral concepts can be meaningfully applied to situations in which agents do not adhere to the tenets of morality, nevertheless it is not morally wrong for agents in such situations to also fail to adhere to those tenets of morality, particularly when doing so puts one at a significant competitive disadvantage.

The neo-Hobbsian or realist, then, might want to propose this premise: When one is in a situation in which others do not adhere to certain tenets of morality, and when adhering to those tenets of morality will put one at a significant competitive disadvantage, then it is not immoral for one to likewise fail to adhere to them. The realist might want to argue for this claim, first, by pointing out that in a world in which all are competing to secure significant benefits and avoid significant costs, and in which others do not adhere to the ordinary tenets of morality, one risks significant harm to ones' interests if one continues to adhere to those tenets of morality. But no one can be morally required to take on major risks of harm to oneself. Consequently, in a competitive world in which others disregard moral constraints and take any means to advance their self-interests, no one can be morally required to take on major risks of injury by adopting the restraints of ordinary morality.

A second argument the realist might want to advance would go as follows. When one is in a situation in which others do not adhere to the ordinary tenets of morality, one is under heavy competitive pressures to do the same. And, when one is under such pressures, one cannot be blamed—i.e., one is excused—for also failing to adhere to the ordinary tenets of morality. One is excused because heavy pressures take away one's ability to control oneself, and thereby diminish one's moral culpability.

Yet a third argument advanced by the realist might go as follows. When one is in a situation in which others do not adhere to the ordinary tenets of morality it is not fair to require one to continue to adhere to those tenets, especially if doing so puts one at a significant competitive disadvantage. It is not fair because then one is laying a burden on one party that the other parties refuse to carry.

Thus, there are a number of arguments that can be given in defense of the revised Hobbsian ethical premise that when others do not adhere to the tenets of morality, it is not immoral for one to do likewise. The ethical premise of the Hobbsian or realist argument, then, can be restated as follows:

> In situations in which other agents do not adhere to certain tenets of morality, it is not immoral for one to do likewise when one would otherwise be putting oneself at a significant competitive disadvantage.

In what follows, I will refer to this restatement as the ethical premise of the argument. I am not altogether convinced that this premise is correct. But it appears to me to have a great deal of plausibility, and it is, I believe, a premise that underlies the feelings of many that in a competitive international environment where others do not embrace the restraints of morality, one is under no obligation to be moral.

V. REVISING THE REALIST OBJECTION: THE SECOND PREMISE

Let us turn, then, to the other premise in the Hobbsian argument, the assertion that in the absence of a sovereign, agents will be in a state of war. As I mentioned, this is an apparently empirical claim about the extent to which agents will adhere to the tenets of morality in the absence of a third-party enforcer.

Hobbes gives a little bit of empirical evidence for this claim. He cites several examples of situations in which there is no third party to enforce civility and where, as a result, individuals are in a "state of war."[12] Generalizing from these few examples, he reaches the conclusion that in the absence of a third-party enforcer, agents will always be in a "condition of war." But the meager evidence Hobbes provides is surely too thin to support his rather large empirical generalization. Numerous empirical counterexamples can be cited of people living in peace in the absence of a third-party enforcer, so it is difficult to accept Hobbes' claim as an empirical generalization.

Recently, the Hobbsian claim, however, has been defended on the basis of some of the theoretical claims of game theory, particularly of the prisoner's dilemma. Hobbes' state of nature, the defense goes, is an instance of a prisoner's dilemma, and *rational* agents in a Prisoner's Dilemma necessarily would choose not to adhere to a set of moral norms. Rationality is here construed in the sense that is standard in social theory: having a coherent set of preferences among the objects of choice, and selecting the one(s) that has the greatest probability of satisfying more of one's preferences rather than fewer.[13] Or, more simply, always choosing so as to maximize one's interests.

A Prisoner's Dilemma is a situation involving at least two individuals. Each individual is faced with two choices: he can cooperate with the other individual or he can choose not to cooperate. If he cooperates and the other individual also cooperates, then he gets a certain payoff. If, however, he chooses not to cooperate, while the other individual trustingly cooperates, the noncooperator gets a larger payoff while the cooperator suffers a loss. And if both choose not to cooperate, then both get nothing.

It is a commonplace now that in a Prisoner's Dilemma situation, the most rational strategy for a participant is to choose not to cooperate. For the other party will either cooperate or not cooperate. If the other party cooperates, then it is better for one not to cooperate and thereby get the larger payoff. On the other hand, if the other party does not cooperate, then it is also better for one not to cooperate and thereby avoid a loss. In either case, it is better for one to not cooperate.

Now Hobbes' state of nature, the neo-Hobbsian realist can argue, is in fact a prisoner's dilemma situation. In Hobbes' state of nature each individual must choose either to cooperate with others by adhering to the rules of morality (like the rule against theft), or to not cooperate by disregarding the rules of morality and attempting to take advantage of those who are adhering to the rules (e.g., by stealing from them). In such a situation it is more rational (in the sense defined above) to choose not to cooperate. For the other party will either cooperate or not cooperate. If the other party does not cooperate, then one puts oneself at a competitive disadvantage if one adheres to morality while the other party does not. On the other hand, if the other party chooses to cooperate, then one can take advantage of the other party by breaking the rules of morality at his expense. In either case, it is more rational to not cooperate.

Thus, the realist can argue that in a state of nature, where there is no one to enforce compliance with the rules of morality, it is more rational from the individual's point of view to choose not to comply with morality than to choose to comply. Assuming—and this is obviously a critical assumption—that agents behave rationally, then we can conclude that agents in a state of nature will choose not to comply with the tenets of ordinary morality. The second premise of the realist argument, then, can, tentatively, be put as follows:

> In the absence of an international sovereign, all rational agents will choose not to comply with the tenets of ordinary morality, when doing so will put one at a serious competitive disadvantage.

This is a striking, and ultimately revealing, defense of the Hobbsian claim that in the absence of a third-party enforcer, individuals will choose not to adhere to the tenets of morality in their relations with each other. It is striking because it correctly identifies, I think, the underlying reason for the Hobbsian claim. The Hobbsian claim is not an empirical claim about how most humans actually behave when they are put at a competitive disadvantage. It is a claim about whether agents that are *rational* (in the sense defined earlier) will adopt certain behaviors when doing otherwise would put them at a serious competitive disadvantage. For our purposes, this is significant since, as I claimed above, all, most, or at least a significant number of multinationals are rational agents in the required sense: all or most of their activities are rational means for achieving the dominant end of increasing profits. Multinationals, therefore, are precisely the kind of rational agents envisaged by the realist.

But this reading of the realist claim is also significant, I think, because it reveals certain limits inherent in the Hobbsian claim, and requires revising the claim so as to take these limits into account.

As more than one person has pointed out, moral interactions among agents are often quite unlike Prisoner's Dilemmas situations.[14] The most important difference is that a Prisoner's Dilemma is a single meeting between agents who do not meet again, whereas human persons in the real world tend to have repeated dealings with each other. If two people meet each other in a Prisoner's Dilemma situation, and never have anything to do with each other again, then it is rational (in the sense under discussion) from each individual's point of view to choose not to cooperate. However, if individuals meet each other in repeated Prisoner's Dilemma situations, then they are able to punish each other for failures to cooperate, and the cumulative costs of noncooperation can make cooperation the more rational strategy.[15] One can therefore expect that when rational agents know they will have repeated interactions with each other for an indefinite future, they will start to cooperate with each other even in the absence of a third party enforcer. The two cooperating parties in effect are the mutual enforcers of their own cooperative agreements.

The implication is that the realist is wrong in believing that in the absence of a third-party enforcer, rational individuals will always fail to adhere to the tenets of morality, presumably even when doing so would result in serious competitive disadvantage. On the contrary, we can expect that if agents know that they will interact with each other repeatedly in the indefinite future, it is rational for them to behave morally toward each other. In the international arena, then, we can expect that when persons know that they will have repeated interactions with each other, they will tend to adhere to ordinary tenets of morality with each other, assuming that they tend to behave rationally, even when doing so threatens to put them at a competitive disadvantage.

There is a second important way in which the Prisoner's Dilemma is defective as a characterization of real world interactions. Not only do agents repeatedly interact with each other, but, as Robert Frank has recently pointed out, human agents signal to each other the extent to which they can be relied on to behave morally in future interactions.[16] We humans can determine more often than not whether another person can be relied on to be moral by observing the natural visual cues of facial expression and the auditory cues of tone of voice that tend to give us away; by relying on our experience of past dealings with the person; and by relying on the reports of others who have had past dealings with the person. Moreover, based on these appraisals of each other's reliability, we then choose to interact with those who are reliable and choose not to interact with those who are not reliable. That is, we choose to enter prisoner's dilemmas situations with those who are reliable, and choose to avoid entering such situations with those who are not reliable. As Robert Frank has shown, given such conditions it is, under quite ordinary circumstances, rational to habitually be reliable since reliable persons tend to have mutually beneficial interactions with other reliable persons, while unreliable persons will tend to have mutually destructive interactions with other unreliable persons.

The implication again is that since signaling makes it rational to habitually cooperate in the rules of morality, even in the absence of a third-party enforcer, we can expect that rational humans, who can send and receive fairly reliable signals between each other, will tend to behave morally even, presumably, when doing so raises the prospect of competitive disadvantage.

These considerations should lead the realist to revise the tentative statement of the second premise of his argument that we laid out above. In its revised form, the second premise would have to read as follows:

> In the absence of an international sovereign, all rational agents will choose not to comply with the tenets of ordinary morality, when doing so will put one at a serious competitive disadvantage, provided that interactions are not repeated and that agents are not able to signal their reliability to each other.

This, I believe, is a persuasive and defensible version of the second premise in the Hobbsian argument. It is the one I will exploit in what follows.

VI. REVISED REALISM, MULTINATIONALS, AND THE COMMON GOOD

Now how does this apply to multinationals and the common good? Can we claim that it is clear that multinationals have a moral obligation to pursue the global common good in spite of the objections of the realist?

I do not believe that this claim can be made. We can conclude from the discussion of the realist objection that the Hobbsian claim about the pervasiveness of amorality in the international sphere is false when (1) interactions among international agents are repetitive in such a way that agents can retaliate against those who fail to cooperate, and (2) agents can determine the trustworthiness of other international agents.

But unfortunately, multinational activities often take place in a highly competitive arena in which these two conditions do not obtain. Moreover, these conditions are noticeably absent in the arena of activities that concern the global common good.

First, as I have noted, the common good consists of goods that are indivisible and accessible to all. This means that such goods are susceptible to the free rider problem. Everyone has access to such goods whether or not they do their part in maintaining such goods, so everyone is tempted to free ride on the generosity of others. Now governments can force domestic companies to do their part to maintain the national common good. Indeed, it is one of the functions of government to solve the free rider problem by forcing all to contribute to the domestic common good to which all have access. Moreover, all companies have to interact repeatedly with their host governments, and this leads them to adopt a cooperative stance toward their host government's objective of achieving the domestic common good.

But it is not clear that governments can or will do anything effective to force multinationals to do their part to maintain the global common good. For the governments of individual nations can themselves be free riders, and can join forces with willing multinationals seeking competitive advantages over others. Let me suggest an example. It is clear that a livable global environment is part of the global common good, and it is clear that the manufacture and use of chloroflurocarbons is destroying that good. Some nations have responded by requiring their domestic companies to cease manufacturing or using chloroflurocarbons. But other nations have refused to do the same, since they will share in any benefits that accrue from the restraint others practice, and they can also reap the benefits of continuing to manufacture and use chloroflurocarbons. Less developed nations, in particular, have advanced the position that since their development depends heavily on exploiting the industrial benefits of chloroflurocarbons, they cannot afford to curtail their use of these substances. Given this situation, it is open to multinationals to shift their operations to those countries that continue to allow the manufacture and use of chloroflurocarbons. For multinationals, too, will reason that they will share in any benefits that accrue from the restraint others practice, and that they can meanwhile reap the profits of continuing to manufacture and use chloroflurocarbons in a world where other companies are forced to use more expensive technologies. Moreover, those nations that practice restraint cannot force all such multinationals to discontinue the manufacture or use of chloroflurocarbons because many multinationals can escape the reach of their laws. An exactly parallel, but perhaps even more compelling, set of considerations can be advanced to show that at least some multinationals will join forces with some developing countries to circumvent any global efforts made to control the global warming trends (the so-called "greenhouse effect") caused by the heavy use of fossil fuels.

The realist will conclude, of course, that in such situations, at least some multinationals will seek to gain competitive advantages by failing to contribute to the global common good (such as the good of a hospitable global environment). For multinationals are rational agents, i.e., agents bureaucratically structured to take rational means toward achieving their dominant end of increasing their profits. And in a competitive environment, contributing to the common good while others do not, will fail to achieve this dominant end. Joining this conclusion to the ethical premise that when others do not adhere to the requirements of morality it is not immoral for one to do likewise, the realist can conclude that multinationals are not morally obligated to contribute to such global common goods (such as environmental goods).

Moreover, global common goods often create interactions that are not iterated. This is particularly the case where the global environment is concerned. As I have already noted, preservation of a favorable global climate is clearly part of the global common good. Now the failure of the global climate will be a one-time affair. The breakdown of the ozone layer, for example, will happen once, with catastrophic consequences for us all; and the heating up of the global climate as a result of the infusion of carbon dioxide will happen once, with catastrophic consequences for us all. Because these environmental disasters are a one-time affair, they represent a non-iterated prisoner's dilemma for multinationals. It is irrational from an individual point of view for a multinational to choose to refrain from polluting the environment in such cases. Either others will refrain, and then one can enjoy the benefits of their refraining; or others will not refrain, and then it will be better to have also not refrained since refraining would have made little difference and would have entailed heavy losses.

Finally, we must also note that although natural persons may signal their reliability to other natural persons, it is not at all obvious that multinationals can do the same. As noted above, multinationals are bureaucratic organizations whose members are continually changing and shifting. The natural persons who make up an organization can signal their reliability to others, but such persons are soon replaced by others, and they in turn are replaced by others. What endures is each organization's single-minded pursuit of increasing its profits in a competitive environment. And an enduring commitment to the pursuit of profit in a competitive environment is not a signal of an enduring commitment to morality.

VII. CONCLUSIONS

The upshot of these considerations is that it is not obvious that we can say that multinationals have an obligation to contribute to the global common good in a competitive environment in the absence of an international authority that can force all agents to contribute to the global common good. Where other rational agents can be expected to shirk the burden of contributing to the common good and where carrying such a burden will put one at a serious competitive disadvantage, the realist argument that it is not immoral for one to also fail to contribute is a powerful argument.

I have not argued, of course, nor do I find it persuasive to claim that competitive pressures automatically relieve agents of their moral obligations, although my arguments here may be wrongly misinterpreted as making that claim. All that I have tried to do is to lay out a justification for the very narrow claim that *certain very special kinds of agents, under certain very limited and very special conditions, seem to have no obligations with respect to certain very special kinds of goods.*

This is not an argument, however, for complete despair. What the argument points to is the need to establish an effective international authority capable of forcing all agents to contribute their part toward the global common good. Perhaps several of the more powerful autonomous governments of the world, for example, will be prompted to establish such an international agency by relinquishing their autonomy and joining together into a coherently unified group that can exert consistent economic, political, or military pressures on any companies or smaller countries that do not contribute to the global common good. Such an international police group, of course, would transform the present world order, and would be much different from present world organizations such as the United Nations. Once such an international force exists, of course, then both Hobbes and the neo-realist would say that moral obligations can legitimately be attributed to all affected international organizations.

Of course, it is remotely possible but highly unlikely that multinationals themselves will be the source of such promptings for a transformed world order. For whereas governments are concerned with the well being of their citizens, multinationals are bureaucratically structured for the rational pursuit of profit in a competitive environment, not the pursuit of citizen well-being. Here and there we occasionally may see one or even several multinationals whose current cadre of leadership is enlightened enough to regularly steer the organization toward the global common good. But given time, that cadre will be replaced and profit objectives will reassert themselves as the enduring end built into the on-going structure of the multinational corporation.

NOTES

1. See, for example, the articles collected in W. Michael Hoffman, Ann E. Lange, and David A. Fedo, eds., *Ethics and the Multinational Enterprise* (New York: University Press of America, 1986).
2. Thomas Donaldson, *The Ethics of International Business* (New York: Oxford University Press, 1989).
3. Donaldson discusses the question whether *states* have moral obligations to each other in *op. cit.*, pp. 10–29. The critical question, however, is whether *multinationals,* i.e., profit-driven types of international organizations, have moral obligations. Although Donaldson is able to point out without a great deal of trouble that the realist arguments against morality among nations are mistaken (see pp. 20–23, where Donaldson points out that if the realist were correct, then there would be no cooperation among nations; but since there is cooperation, the realist must be wrong), his points leave untouched the arguments I discuss below which acknowledge that while much cooperation among nations is possible, nevertheless certain crucial forms of cooperation will not obtain among multinationals with respect to the global common good.
4. J. Bentham, *Principles of Morals and Legislation,* 1.4–5.
5. William A. Wallace, O.P., *The Elements of Philosophy, A Compendium for Philosophers and Theologians* (New York: Alba House, 1977), p. 166–67.
6. *Ibid.,* p. 167.
7. "Common Good," *The New Catholic Encyclopedia.*
8. John Rawls, *A Theory of Justice* (Cambridge, MA: Harvard University Press, 1971), p. 233 and 246.
9. Thomas Hobbes, *Leviathan, Parts I and II,* [1651] (New York: The Bobbs-Merrill Company, Inc., 1958), p. 108.
10. *Ibid.* As noted earlier, I am simply assuming what I take to be the popular interpretation of Hobbes' view on the state of nature. As Professor Philip Kain has pointed out to me, there is some controversy among Hobbes scholars about whether or not Hobbes actually held that moral obligation exists in the state of nature. Among those who hold that moral obligation does not exist in Hobbes' state of nature is M. Oakeshott in "The Moral Life in the Writings of Thomas Hobbes" in his *Hobbes on Civil Association* (Berkeley-Los Angeles: University of California Press, 1975), pp. 95–113; among those who hold that moral obligation does exist in Hobbes' state of nature is A. E. Taylor in "The Ethical Doctrine of Hobbes" in *Hobbes Studies,* ed. K. C. Brown (Cambridge: Harvard, 1965), pp. 41ff. Kain suggests that Hobbes simply contradicts himself—holding in some passages that moral obligation does exist in the state of nature and holding in others that it does not—because of his need to use the concept of the state of nature to achieve purposes that required incompatible conceptions of the state of nature; see his "Hobbes, Revolution and the Philosophy of History," in *"Hobbes's 'Science of Natural Justice,'"* ed. C. Walton and P.J. Johnson (Boston: Martinus Nijhoff Publishers, 1987), pp. 203–18. In the present essay I am simply assuming without argument the traditional view that Hobbes made the claim that moral obligation does not exist in the state of nature; my aim is to pursue certain implications of this claim even if I am wrong in assuming that is Hobbes'.
11. See *ibid.,* where Hobbes writes that "yet in all times kings and persons of sovereign authority, because of their independency" are in this state of war.
12. *Ibid.,* pp. 107–8.
13. See Amartya K. Sen, *Collective Choice and Social Welfare* (San Francisco: Holden-Day, Inc., 1970), pp. 2–5.
14. See, for example, Gregory Kavka, "Hobbes' War of All Against All," *Ethics,* 93 (January, 1983), pp. 291–310; a somewhat different approach is that of David Gauthier, *Morals By Agreement* (Oxford: Clarendon Press, 1986) and Russell Hardin, *Morality Within the Limits of Reason* (Chicago: University of Chicago Press, 1988).
15. See Robert Axelrod, *The Evolution of Cooperation* (New York: Basic Books, Inc., 1984), pp. 27–69.
16. Robert Frank, *Passions Within Reason* (New York: W. W. Norton & Company, 1988).

International Business Ethics: Russia and Eastern Europe

Richard T. De George
Distinguished Professor of Philosophy, University of Kansas

An American firm hires Russian scientists for $40 a month, which is above the average wage of the Russian worker but well below what their work is worth to the company. Although the American firm is willing to pay more, the Russian scientists do not want to earn too much more than their colleagues and are content to be able to continue their research. Both the American firm and the Russian scientists benefit. The American firm is accused by Americans of exploitation.

A truck full of toxic waste crosses the border from Germany into Poland and in a Polish border town dumps its hot load into a large, unprotected landfill. The German company has solved its problem of disposing of toxic waste. A group of Polish entrepreneurs has found a way of getting hard currency. What each side does is not against the law. The town's inhabitants, and probably others downstream, will eventually bear the cost.

A small Russian entrepreneur tries to set up a small plumbing business. He finds that all pipe and other supplies are allocated to big industries and that the only way he can get any at all is through bribes. He defends his paying these as being necessary and de facto the way business is done.

A former East German professor, who has lived in his apartment for forty years, is evicted when the building is privatized by the manager and sold to a West-German buyer who raises the rent beyond the professor's means.

These are just a few samples of the ethical issues that form part of daily life in Russia and Eastern Europe as they go through the torturous and unprecedented journey from socialist ownership and a centralized command economy to private ownership and a market economy. Marx claimed that the initial accumulation of capital was a result of plunder and theft of a variety of kinds and that capitalism was based on exploitation of the workers. Many in the former socialist countries seem to believe that this is in fact the situation they now face and that the system they are attempting to adopt is the system of capitalism as described by Marx.

In discussing business ethics in Russia and Eastern Europe I shall do three things. First, I shall present an overview of both the business and the ethical climate in these countries. Second, I shall investigate issues of business ethics for and from the point of view of the citizens of these countries. Third, I shall ask, given these two foundations, what are the obligations of foreign firms—especially American firms—that wish to operate in these countries.

I. THE BUSINESS AND ETHICAL CLIMATE OF PRIVATIZATION

Following the October Revolution in 1917, Lenin and his followers started a new society governed by Marxist principles. The newly established Soviet Union entered unchartered waters as it moved from an early capitalist country to socialism. No country had done what this fledgling country did: seize the private instruments of production—all land, all buildings, all firms and business enterprises, large and small—and convert them to state property. There was no compensation given, no ethical qualms entertained. The exploiters and expropriators held their wealth and position unjustly and had no ethical or legal claim to them under the new rules. In theory, the move from capitalism to socialism was easy. The state simply had to nationalize what previously had been private without thought of weighing owner's rights, competing claims, or other similar considerations. Nonetheless, the years of War Communism following the revolution were an economic disaster. This led Lenin to introduce the New Economic Policy, which permitted some small free enterprise and which allowed the peasants to sell some of their produce on the open market. Stalin put an end to that policy and forcibly collectivized the farms,

From *Social Responsibility: Business, Journalism, Law, Medicine,* Vol. 19, 1993. Reprinted by permission of Society & the Professions, Washington & Lee University.

killing millions of kulaks in the process. The period from 1917 to 1933 can be considered the fifteen years it took to change over from a capitalist economy to a socialist one, and the change involved enormous hardships for the people and cost many lives.

The change from a socialist to a free market economy in the former Soviet Union and in Eastern Europe is unprecedented as well. It is even more difficult and complicated than the change in the other direction. And it cannot be understood or appreciated without our being aware of the socialist background out of which these countries are moving.

I shall touch on only three aspects: the ethical and social background, the development of free enterprises, and the privatization of industry.

A) Government control in the USSR and in the socialist countries of Eastern Europe was ubiquitous. The state or government was the owner of all the means of production, including all the land. Housing was state owned, just as was industry. The government was the sole employer, and it in turn provided highly subsidized housing, free education, free medical care, old age pensions. The standard of living was not very high and productivity was correlatively low. There were laws, but there was no real rule of law. Nonetheless, the state provided security. Government control was total, and hence other sources of control were minimal. In 1961 the Communist Party issued a Moral Code of the Builders of Communism, which listed the norms that were to guide Soviet citizens.[1] The norms were collective. Conscience was not something private to be respected but something social to be molded. Any notion of internal norms was undermined by a view of ethics that was external and in the service of the state.

One result was that the vast majority of the population ignored the official morality. They learned how to get around official rules whenever possible. There was little in the way of a work ethic. The standard joke was, "We pretend to work, and the State pretends to pay us." And there was also little in the way of a shared public ethic. People still valued their families and friends, but the values of the state were never successfully inculcated into the people. Except for those who privately nurtured religious values, the moral fabric of the country was seriously weakened. The old morality had been undermined and the new morality was ineffective. Falsehood was expected from the government and from the Communist Party, and people became immune to Party propaganda. For over seventy years the Soviet Union had preached Marxism-Leninism, and most of those alive today in the former Soviet republics have never known any other approach to history, society, or economics. They think in Marxist terms, and they learned about the West and capitalism from their Marxist texts, which tended to vilify both.

The overthrow of the Communist regime was a protest against the domination by the Party and its control. It was not a fight for capitalism or free enterprise. And how much of socialism the people want to give up is still an open question. The problems are many. Having overthrown communism and repudiated the former system, they are left with little in the way of a system under which to operate. Socialist laws have not yet been effectively replaced by other laws, and the question of which laws to adopt is a continuing topic of debate. With the legal system under revision, the police and the courts are less and less effective—and not free of corruption. As the traditional background institutions that lend stability to a society disintegrate, there is more and more need for morality to function as a source of social order; but there is little public morality left to play that essential role.

The ordinary worker—who has little, who earns an average of 5,000 rubles a month (less than $10 at the May 1993 rate of exchange), and whose savings have disappeared with rampant inflation—considers anyone able to succeed under these circumstances as being crooked: they must be a former communist official or a bureaucrat who is taking advantage of his or her past position; or a member of the "mafia," criminally amassing wealth; or an entrepreneur exploiting others.

This is the social background for the development of free enterprise and for privatization.

B) The development of small entrepreneurs has been officially both encouraged and hampered. It has been encouraged because it is clear that one of the failures of the old system, which relied exclusively on centralized control, was simply not effective. Hence, some of those presently in charge realize, at least in theory, the need for entrepreneurs to develop small businesses and for decentralization to replace the former command economy.

The difficulty is that the former state structures of distribution are for the most part still in place. Large factories and enterprises are still the dominant economic reality, and sources of supplies are still geared toward those enterprises. The result is that small businesses have a very difficult time receiving the wherewithal to conduct their business. If goods are earmarked for the large factories and are not available to the small entrepreneur, the latter effectively cannot operate. The only way they can operate, given the skewed—and, they claim, unfair—allocation system, is by getting what they can where, when, and how they can. In practice, this most often means paying bribes to those who have access to the needed materials—whether they are managers in factories willing to sell what has been allocated to them, or shippers and middle men who divert shipments to the small business for a fee, or black market and other people who steal what they can sell.

The climate for the entrepreneur is very volatile. The laws are constantly changing. The tax rates and rules are similarly in a state of flux. The status of ownership of whatever property they have is uncertain. In addition, there is a growing crime rate, with extortion not uncommon, and there are reports of a Russian mafia becoming more and more powerful.[2] Dmitri Rozanov, a Russian entrepreneur, says, "Without paying off the local powers-that-be, it's almost impossible to stay in business,"[3]—a view that is echoed by most Russian business persons.

C) The status of privatization is equally unsettled. Privatization has been described as the state's selling enterprises worth nothing to people who have nothing. A major difficulty in the present situation is the amassing of industrial capital. The people have savings that amount to only about 4% of the estimated value of state enterprises. Clearly they cannot buy them. But under socialism they were said to be the owners of the means of production: hence they should not have to buy them because they already own them. One problem is that simply owning the factories, shops, stores does no good if they are not productive, and most of them need an influx of money to retool and modernize. A second problem is great confusion about who owns former state property and who has the right to privatize it.

What is the ethically right, the just, the fair way to privatize state property? When Britain privatized its state-owned industries it did so according to established rules. It was clear who owned the industries, who had a right to sell them, and who would get the proceeds. In the former Soviet Union and Eastern Europe none of this is the case. It is not clear who owns what (since in theory everyone owned everything), who has the right to sell anything, and who should get the proceeds. Issues of fairness and justice arise as competing, conflicting, incompatible claims, with no mechanism for dispute resolution in place and a sense of urgency to make the transition quickly, before reactionary forces can turn the clock back to state ownership. Yelena Kotova, former director of Moscow's privatization, says, "Moral notions are essentially inappropriate, because it's a cruel process."[4]

Privatization is proceeding in a number of different ways—none of which is wholly fair to all. In Czechoslovakia and Russia the government has issued vouchers that may be used to purchase shares in firms of the individual's choosing. In October 1992, the Russian government issued vouchers of 10,000 rubles each and expected to make available all small and medium enterprises and about 5,000 large enterprises in 1993.[5] The vouchers may be sold or the stock one buys may be traded, although capital markets are just now being organized and are still rudimentary. The vouchers were originally worth $40 at the current rate of exchange; by February 1993 they were worth $17 and were selling for half that on the commodities exchange.[6] On February 9, 1993, 15.5% of the famous Moscow department store GUM was offered for sale, and buyers were issued 7 shares for each voucher (making each share worth $2.40).[7] The voucher system sounds like a good solution, since everyone in theory owned everything. But one can hardly expect the ordinary Russian citizen to believe that his or her share of the nation's wealth was, at best, $40.

A second form of privatization, followed to a large extent in Poland, consists of turning a factory or enterprise over to the workers. But some of the enterprises were favored under the state system and are productive while others were not. Is it fair to treat them all the same? Is it fair for a worker who has been at a plant for two years to get the same share as one who has been there for twenty years? And is it fair to turn over a non-productive factory to workers who have no prospects of making it productive? What of those who were in the service sector, like teachers? In some cases, managers have taken the initiative and sold the enterprise, sometimes to themselves at ridiculously low prices, sometimes to foreign investors and others who had available cash—again often at ridiculously low prices.

Some firms are being privatized by government auction. Poland has used this method, among others. This provides immediate revenue, but it works only for productive enterprises and has been criticized for turning factories over to foreigners. In an attempt to overcome the former problem, Poland is restructuring and intends to sell whole industries rather than just the strongest companies.[8]

A fourth form of privatization is the selling off of the assets of a company piecemeal to whomever will buy the pieces. This has even been done by military units, which are selling off their arms and even in some instances their tanks to whoever is willing to buy them.[9] A group of generals and administrators went too far in attempting to sell military assets on "a huge scale."[10] Similarly, a group of eight members of a state research institute set up a private firm. They then bought 100 of the institute's computers for the state-subsidized price and resold them at the market price, which was 100 times higher, funneling the profits into their firm.[11] Enterprises belong to the workers—but it is not up to the managers or generals to sell off the parts for their personal gain.

Other forms of privatization include: the state's organizing holding companies (which in fact tend to resemble state-owned enterprises) to help the transition; or, as in Hungary, the selling of individual firms through the State Property Agency to investors who ask to buy them; or allowing companies to go private on their own. Each method has advantages and disadvantages, and from an ethical point of view each raises problems. In Russia, if enterprises were simply turned over to the workers, 70% of the population would be left out.[12]

The situation in East Germany and Poland is further complicated because the new regimes are recognizing the legal claims of former owners on property that the state confiscated from them or their families immediately after the World War II.

The result is a condition of great confusion and uncertainty. The state is ineffective in its new role. Market forces are not yet in place. The transition period has led to high unemployment and the closing of many factories that simply cannot compete. They were able to sell shoddy goods in the former command economy but not in an economy where goods are available from the West. The social services formerly provided by the state are no longer readily available. The status of apartments and housing is often in dispute, and ownership is not clear. Do the apartments belong to the occupants, to the city, to the state? Who is responsible for their upkeep and repair?

It is within this system that I now turn to the question of business ethics, to consider it first from the point of view of the local entrepreneur and then from the point of view of the foreigner.

II. BUSINESS ETHICS AND RUSSIAN ENTREPRENEURS

What can we say of business ethics from the Russian point of view? The first answer is that it is a perceived problem, at least by some. In June 1993 the Academy of National Economy of the Russian Federation Graduate School of International Business sponsored an international conference on "Business Ethics in New Russia." What a conference can do is certainly minimal, and bears on the insignificant. But it is an indication of the realization on the part of at least some that a move to free enterprise is possible only if it is accompanied by a set of background institutions—laws, enforceable contracts, social understandings, accepted business practices, and acceptability by the general population, which is where ethics enters. Ethics provides the legitimation for the system of business, and it provides both the glue that keeps it together and the oil that allows it to function. Without basic trust, no contracts will be signed, no goods delivered. Markets rely on information, and hence truth becomes a value. Property is central, and hence respect for property is essential.

But what can one do in the currently existing situation? I noted earlier that Marx claimed that the initial accumulation of capital by western nations took place through theft and unjust appropriation—the plunder of the Incas and other Indians as well as of other nations, by war and by exploitation of the workers. How are Russia and the countries of Eastern Europe to develop their capital? Some of the countries are better off in this respect than others. The former East Germany has access to the technology and capital of the former West Germany. Czechoslovakia and even Poland were better off to begin with than is Russia. Hungary has been the most attractive to foreign investors. Yet all of them suffer from the breakdown of a public ethic, an inherited distrust of government despite a heavy reliance on it, and lack of managerial skills. The former managers under the Communist regimes tend to be those who were and remain appropriately placed and sufficiently skilled to take over the new enterprises, much to the displeasure of many of the workers.

The issue of ethics in a corrupt system is a difficult one. The claim that in order to operate as a small entrepreneur one must pay bribes and buy supplies where and when one finds them, without questioning their source, is probably correct. Let us suppose that it is. Is one ethically allowed to operate one's business this way? The obvious answer is No, if there is any alternative. But if the allocation system is itself unfair and corrupt, if government bureaucrats get their share of payments and ignore or condone the diverting of goods based on bribes, can the small entrepreneur be held to a standard of ethical behavior proper in a less corrupt environment? To hold one to that standard is, in effect, to preclude one's being a private entrepreneur and to leave all enterprise to the criminal element.

The tax laws keep changing, and no standard method of bookkeeping is in place. In some cases no bookkeeping is required.

Under the circumstances, basic fundamental ethical norms still apply. Extortion, physical harm and threats, robbery, lying, producing defective goods, dumping toxic wastes, all remain unethical—whether or not they are effectively policed. The outright stealing of goods by some of the managers, who receive materials and immediately ship and sell them abroad for below their market value, is unethical by any standard.

But in the given circumstances I believe that some practices that would be clearly wrong, for instance, in the United States, may be ethically justified for people in those circumstances. When, for example, might the paying of bribes to receive legitimate supplies necessary for one's business be allowed? One justifiable answer is that they are justifiable when they are not bribes but part of the cost of doing business. Bribes are payments made to receive special advantage at the expense of others under some orderly system of entitlements. Absent an orderly system of entitlements, and absent the special advantage and the harm done to others, we are no longer describing what is generally thought of as bribery. We have a disorderly system in which goods are not rationally allocated, either by the market or by the government, and in which there is no fair market price. The price of goods is determined by supply and demand in a rough sense. But if all private entrepreneurs are in the same system, and if goods are available to all only through the payment of fees beyond those listed on an invoice (if there is one), then that is the way, and the cost, of doing business. The payments do not undermine a free market but in this case are part of a developing one.

A kind of utilitarian argument might also be mounted according to which both society as a whole and consumers benefit from private entrepreneurs taking the risks of private business and providing goods and services under the present inefficient and chaotic system. Both the entrepreneurs and society will benefit more than if such businesses were not carried on, leaving people without goods and services, and all enterprise to criminal initiatives.

This justification is clearly conditional and temporary. As the system becomes organized and regularized, the status of such payments changes and becomes disruptive rather than productive, unethical rather than justifiable. Moreover, at best this line of reasoning justifies those who are forced to pay what we shall continue to call bribes. It does not justify the actions of government officials who demand bribes, or of police who require bribes to not enforce what law there is. These actions are part of the problem and can in no way be considered a waystation toward the solution.

Similarly, it is difficult for the small entrepreneur to know what his taxes are when the government, for all intents and purposes, does not know and is unable to provide adequate information or to police any rules it does establish. In such a situation, is failure to pay one's taxes unethical? While it is unethical to avoid paying one's fair taxes in an ordinary system, one can hardly call the present Russian situation a system in any functional sense. Hence the small entrepreneur can plausibly follow whatever rules there are that are most favorable to him—possibly even delaying paying where it is not clearly illegal to delay.

The appropriate generalization in these conditions is that more cannot be asked of those in business than the situation warrants. General ethical demands must be placed in context, and in the Russian context the conclusions one comes to, from an ethical point of view, diverge from the conclusions one would come to in a normal situation. That is true primarily because of the lack of any stable or just background institutions.

At the present time it is difficult to know what "just" or "fair" mean in a great many instances having to do with property—because property is a bundle of rights relative to a system of rights. What constitutes property in the United States is a function of our laws that grant property rights and provide a system under which property can be legitimately transferred. Under the Soviet system, private property was not allowed and the system of rights that developed was significantly different from the system of property in the United States. What was fair or just, as well as what was possible under the two systems, differed. But under which system are Russia and the countries of Eastern Europe now, and which notions of property and justice apply? The problem is that no clear system has yet emerged in any of these countries.

This fact makes the problems of privatization and of developing private enterprises very difficult to judge from the point of view of fairness or justice. If what constitutes property, and what is fair with respect to its transfer or control, are a function of a system, then absent a clear system there is no clear answer to the question. The practical difficulty is that privatization is taking place before any coherent system has been put in place. In some ways, then, business ethics requires a background system within which to operate.

This does not mean that there are no norms common to all systems. As we have already seen, both the ordinary citizen and outside observers appropriately condemn violence, outright robbery, the misuse of political or police power for private gain, and the like.

This leads to my third consideration: how should foreign—for instance, American—firms, act in this environment?

III. MULTINATIONALS IN RUSSIA AND EASTERN EUROPE

I have already claimed that the basic norms of respecting life, honoring agreements and contracts, and telling the truth are basic to any society and economic system. The norms are not universally adhered to; but that is consistent with the necessity for basic norms to exist. If basic norms are breached in any significant numbers, the very possibility of social life and hence of doing business is undermined.

Nor does the fact that some moral issues are dependent on the background institutions of a society mean that when in Rome one should do as the Romans do.[13] In the first place, what the Romans do may be unethical and unjustifiable in itself. If some society practices slavery and protects it by law, that does not mean that American companies are ethically allowed to similarly practice slavery in that country. In South Africa under the apartheid laws, American companies could not morally abide by those laws and enforce apartheid within their operations. This led to the Sullivan principles, which precluded firms from following the apartheid laws and yet allowed them to operate in the country in the hope that they could weaken apartheid from within. After ten years, Leon Sullivan, who had proposed the principles in the first place, declared the experiment a failure and maintained that following his principles no longer could provide justification for continued operation in South Africa.

Although American companies are not required to do business in Eastern Europe and Russia exactly as they do in the United States, they are also not allowed to ignore moral norms, even if these are neither enacted into law nor effectively enforced in the host country. The situation of the multinational that can choose whether to operate in these countries, and the conditions under which it will operate, is different from the situation of native entrepreneurs. The latter's choices are much more restricted if they choose to set up a business.

The example of MacDonald's is a case in point. When MacDonald's first started operating in Moscow, it made provision to receive almost all of its supplies from foreign sources because of the unreliability of Soviet sources. Slowly, as it found reliable local suppliers, it switched from foreign to local sources. This option would not be open to local entrepreneurs. But even though the policy was possible for MacDonalds, it is clear that American firms cannot justify bribery and illegality by arguing that because this is the way business is done in Russia, it is the only way our firm can do business there.

Does this not imply a double standard, since I gave a limited defense of local entrepreneurs working within the system? The answer is No. The reason is that the situation of the local entrepreneur and of the American multinational is very different. One can plausibly argue that the local entrepreneur has no choice but to operate within a corrupt system or not to operate at all. The American multinational, on the other hand, has a very real option of not operating there at all, while continuing to operate everywhere else that it already does. Second, the multinational does not need to engage in bribery. It has available hard currency, which is in such great demand that, if anything, it needs to give some attention to the fact that it can skew the allocation of resources to the serious disadvantage of local firms. If bribes are demanded, an American company can and should point to the American Foreign Corrupt Practices Act as an added reason precluding its paying bribes to public officials. If bribes are actually necessary to conduct business, the American company can protest through official governmental and intergovernmental channels; it can use the media to expose the demands; and it can band together with other American companies similarly situated to jointly refuse to pay such demands. In short, an American company has a wide variety of options available that are not available to the local entrepreneur. Therefore, the multinationals have no justification for engaging in such practices.

The multinational in the given context, because of the strength of its position, has a positive obligation to set an example of ethics in business and to encourage the development of background institutions conducive to stability and to business practices that benefit the society as a whole. As an outside interest entering the country for the company's benefit, it should not be exploitive or seek its own good to the disadvantage of the local population. To do otherwise is the carpetbagger syndrome, exploitive and unethical, even if legal.

Of the stories with which we began, clearly the Western firm that transported its toxic waste to Poland and knew it would be dumped in unprotected landfills acted unethically, even though not yet illegally. It took advantage of the need of the people for hard currency and collaborated with a group of private entrepreneurs willing, for their own profit, to endanger a considerable number of people. Even if the town as a whole had consented to the deal and shared in the proceeds, the Western company would have been taking advantage of them. There are some deals, such as selling oneself into slavery, that are not allowable, even if done with the apparent consent of the disadvantaged party. Using one's backyard for toxic wastes indicates either desperation or lack of appreciation of the consequences of one's act; in any case, it shows flagrant disregard for those who will be adversely affected without their consent.

What of the American firm that hired Russian

scientists for $40 a month—as both AT&T and Corning have done? AT&T Bell Laboratories signed a one year agreement with the General Physics Institute of the Russian Academy of Sciences in Moscow, hiring about 100 of the Institute's 1200 scientists and researchers. Corning hired 115 scientists and technicians at Vavilov State Optical Institute in St. Petersburg, which has several thousand scientists.[14] Are the American firms guilty of exploiting the scientists by paying them $4,800 a year, while a comparable top scientist in the U. S. working, say, in fiber optics could command an annual salary of about $70,000? Despite appearances, the answer is No. In these cases the wages were set by the Russian scientists, who know they could get more but who did not want to be paid too much more than their Russian counterparts. Since $40 a month is well above the average Russian worker's wage, it is sufficient to live at a standard common to large numbers of people in that society. The labor is not forced, and the wage is set by the workers, who have the Russian right to patents on whatever they develop. Hence there is no exploitation in this case. There is rather a mutually satisfactory and ethically justifiable arrangement.

The issue of wages is a difficult one for American companies in many countries abroad. If they pay the going wage—which by American standards seems pitifully low—they are accused by Americans of exploiting the local workers. If they pay well above the going wage, they are accused by local companies of stealing away their best workers and of attempting to drive wages up so as to put them out of business. No matter what the going wage, an American multinational can and should pay at least wages that are sufficient for the worker to live at a standard of living considered acceptable in that country, providing that it is at least sufficient for the worker to live in accordance with general norms of human dignity. These guidelines are admittedly vague, and they are necessarily so because there is no one just wage. Above a certain minimum necessary for decent living conditions, the amount of which varies from country to country, the market can ethically be allowed to operate. What is ethically demanded everywhere is respect for the human rights of workers, which means not only adequate wages but fair treatment and relatively safe and sanitary working conditions.

What of the West German who buys the Berlin apartment building? I have already indicated that in Russia and in some other East European countries it is not clear to whom such property belongs. Nor is it clear how to decide what is a fair way to privatize. No one can legitimately sell what does not belong to him. The difficulty facing an outside buyer is to determine that what he is buying legitimately belongs to the seller, that the title the buyer receives will be legally recognized, and that the attached rights will be upheld and enforced.

In the German case, the buyer knows that German law applies. The fact that long-time residents of the apartment building could not pay the new rent and were forced to leave is an unfortunate consequence of privatization. The buyer, the seller, or the government might try to alleviate the residents' plight by helping them relocate. But that is an ethical ideal and not an ethical requirement. In itself the transaction is not unethical. It differs from the toxic dumping case because of the difference in the harm done and foreseen in the two cases. Had the building existed prior to World War II, and had it been nationalized by the East Germans, the former owner might have some claim on it. What that claim amounts to and how such claims are to be adjudicated is presently being decided by German courts. Had the apartments been given to the tenants, as the state has done in many cases in Russia, the situation would obviously be different. The fact that persons who had important positions under the Communist regime and had correspondingly favorable housing are now being forced to relocate to more modest housing does not seem unjust, on the face of it. The German laws are adequate to handle difficult cases of homelessness and eviction rights. This case—as opposed to somewhat similar cases in other East European countries that were not able to adopt wholesale a preexisting system of laws—shows the pain many in Eastern Europe are suffering in the period of transition.

The final issue I shall briefly address is Marx's claim that the primitive accumulation of capital necessarily involved theft and exploitation. Whatever one says about the historical accumulation of capital by the nations of Western Europe, what may we say about Russia and countries of Eastern Europe? Are theft and exploitation necessary and hence by some logic morally justifiable? The response of some western commentators is that the ethics of the method of jumpstarting the economy is irrelevant as long as it starts. Contrary to that view, the more unethical the means used in the conversion from a socialist to a market economy, the more difficulties the countries will have in the long run. There are ways to preclude such ills. Some involve the developed countries of the world helping through loans, grants, technical assistance, remission of debt, and assistance in forging just background institutions. Those countries that have lived through unbridled capitalism have learned to tame it. There is no need to recapitulate that history. But being willing to help the former socialist countries demands some foresight and an understanding that such aid is not only in the interest of the receiving countries but also of the donor countries.

Standing in the wings behind President Yeltsin is a group anxious to use the abuses of the present conditions as an excuse for taking power and returning to socialism. This places additional importance on the positive role that foreign companies can play in helping the positive development of a controlled and ethically justifiable version of capitalism in Russia and the countries of Eastern Europe. It is not clear that without such help both from other countries and from multinationals, it will be possible to avoid the growth of crime, abuse, and exploitation together with the free market in those countries.

What general conclusions can we draw?

The first is that international business ethics is not and cannot be the imposition of American business ethics—whatever one means by that—on all nations. Ethics is one of the restraints on business, and in each country it operates in conjunction with a host of other restraints, demands, and expectations. As we have noted in passing, the system of law, the view of property, the standard of living, and the customs and traditions of the people are all important considerations. This does not imply ethical relativism, or the view that whatever any society says is ethical is in fact ethical—as the cases of slavery and apartheid show. But it does imply that norms appropriately vary in their application, and that one should be cautious of overgeneralization based exclusively on American experience.

A second conclusion has to do with American multinationals. A company that wishes to act with integrity must have its own values to which it adheres. If a company changes its values from country to country, and if the norms it follows are determined exclusively by the enforced local laws, it is questionably a company of integrity. I have suggested that, given the conditions of Eastern Europe and Russia, American companies, and companies from other industrially developed countries, have a special obligation not to abuse the special advantages they have vis-à-vis these countries. They are ethically precluded from exploitation, from cooperating with criminal elements (whether as suppliers or as go-betweens), from paying bribes, and from violating the human rights of workers or consumers—whether or not any of this is precluded by enforced laws.

A third conclusion has to do with international business ethics in general. Business ethics is itself a fairly recent subject of study. It developed in the United States in the 1970s and has grown since then.[15] It has spread to various countries in Europe and more recently to centers in Japan, Brazil, Australia, and elsewhere. But although business is clearly global, there is still a great deal of confusion among both academicians and business people about international or global business ethics: what it means and how it can be implemented. The most significant difference between business ethics in the United States and on a global level is the absence on the global level of what can be called background institutions: laws, agreements, understandings, traditions, and the like. The need worldwide is to adopt agreements, understandings, and rules that make mutually advantageous trade possible and that keep the playing field of competition level.

I suggest that these background institutions should not be established by the imposition of American standards on the world, but that they should be the result of negotiation between all affected parties. Only if all those seriously affected agree to the justice of those institutions will they be stable and perform the function that comparable background institutions play in most developed countries.

Russia and some East European countries are now in a state of economic and social chaos. In such a situation ethics is needed, but even more important are ethically justifiable structures—laws and procedures. The development of such structures is a precondition for any full-fledged consideration of business ethics in Russia and Eastern Europe in the foreseeable future.

NOTES

1. For the Moral Code of the Builders of Communism, see *The Road to Communism: Documents of the 22nd Congress of the Communist Party of the Soviet Union* (Moscow: Foreign Languages Publishing House, 1961, 566–67.)
2. See Stephen Handelman, "Inside Russia's Gangster Economy," *The New York Times Magazine,* January 24, 1993, 12 ff.
3. Cynthia Scharf, "The Wild, Wild East: Everyone's a Capitalist in Russia Today and Nobody Knows the Rules," *Business Ethics,* vol. 6, No. 6, (Nov./Dec. 1992), 21.
4. "Russians Privatize by Looting State Goods," *The Washington Post,* May 17, 1992, A1.
5. "Citizens of Russia To Be Given Share of State's Wealth," *The New York Times,* October 1, 1992, A1, A10. 60–70% of Russian companies will reorganize themselves as joint stock companies. Under one option, employees can get up to 40% of the shares free, with the rest going public; under the second option, managers and employees may buy up to 51% of the enterprise, providing they pay 1.7 times the book value of the shares. No one knows what enterprises are really worth.
6. *Christian Science Monitor,* February 10, 1993, 3.
7. "Russia Sells Off Shares of GUM, Several Plants," *The New York Times,* February 9, 1993, A10.
8. "In East Europe, There's More Than One Capitalist Road," *Chicago Tribune,* October 25, 1992, Sec. 7, 1.
9. "Selling Off Big Red," *Newsweek,* March 1, 1993, 50–51; "Russians Privatize by Looting State Goods," *The Washington Post,* May 17, 1992, A1.
10. "Russia to Fight Private Sell-Offs by Ex-Officials," *The New York Times,* February 29, 1993, A5.
11. "Russians Privatize," *The Washington Post,* A1.
12. "Russia's Big Enterprises Privatize, With Communists at the Ready," *Christian Science Monitor,* February 10, 1993, 3.
13. For a fuller discussion of these issues, see my *Competing With Integrity in International Business* (New York: Oxford University Press, 1993).
14. "Russian Scientists for A. T. & T. and Corning," *The New York Times,* May 27, 1992, D1.
15. Of course, ethics in business is as old as ethics and business themselves.

The Moral Authority of Transnational Corporate Codes

William C. Frederick
Professor of Business Administration, University of Pittsburgh

Moral guidelines for corporations may be found embedded in several multilateral compacts adopted by governments since the end of the Second World War. Taken as a whole, these normative guides comprise a framework for identifying the essential moral behaviors expected of multinational corporations. Corporate actions that transgress these principles are understood to be *de facto,* and in some cases *de jure,* unethical and immoral. This set of normative prescriptions and proscriptions embodies a moral authority that transcends national boundaries and societal differences, thereby invoking or manifesting a universal or transcultural standard of corporate ethical behavior. Although this remarkable development has not run its full course and therefore is not yet all-embracing, it is well enough along for its main outlines to be evident and its central normative significance to be clear.

Found in *Journal of Business Ethics* 10: 165–177, 1991.

LANDMARK MULTILATERAL COMPACTS

The four decades between 1948 and 1988 have been remarkable for the proliferation of intergovernmental agreements, compacts, accords, and declarations that have been intended to put on the public record various sets of principles regulating the activities of governments, groups, and individuals. The core concerns of these compacts have ranged from military security to economic and social development, from the protection of national sovereignty to specifying acceptable actions by multinational enterprises, from condemnations of genocide and slavery to the regulation of capital flows and the transfer of technology, from the political rights of women to the movements of refugees and stateless persons, and many others too numerous to list here. They reflect the many kinds of problems and issues that have confronted governments in the last half of the 20th century (United Nations, 1983).

This paper focuses on six of these intergovernmental compacts, which by their nature, purpose, and comprehensiveness might well be considered to be the most generic or archetypal of such agreements. Collectively they proclaim the basic outlines of a transcultural corporate ethic. This ethic effectively lays down specific guidelines for the formulation of multinational corporate policies and practices. These six compacts and their respective dates of promulgation are:

- The United Nations Universal Declaration of Human Rights (1948) [Abbreviated as UDHR]
- The European Convention on Human Rights (1950) [ECHR]
- The Helsinki Final Act (1975) [Helsinki]
- The OECD Guidelines for Multinational Enterprises (1976) [OECD]
- The International Labor Office Tripartite Declaration of Principles Concerning Multinational Enterprises and Social Policy (1977) [ILO]
- The United Nations Code of Conduct on Transnational Corporations (Not yet completed nor promulgated but originating in 1972.) [TNC Code][1]

The first two compacts are clearly normative in focus and intention, emphasizing human rights, but they are not addressed specifically to multinational enterprises. The principal emphasis of the Helsinki Final Act is the national and political security of the signatory governments, although this accord and its successor protocols carry strong messages concerning human rights and environmental protections, which do concern business operations. The last three compacts are aimed primarily and explicitly at the practices of multinational enterprises across a wide range of issues and problems. While three of the six accords issue primarily from European-North American governments, the other three represent the views of a much wider, even global, range of governments.

NORMATIVE CORPORATE GUIDELINES

By careful reading of these six intergovernmental compacts, one can derive a set of explicitly normative guides for the policies, decisions, and operations of multinational corporations. These guidelines refer to normal business operations, as well as more fundamental responsibilities regarding basic human rights.

Employment Practices and Policies

- MNCs should not contravene the manpower policies of host nations. [ILO]
- MNCs should respect the right of employees to join trade unions and to bargain collectively. [ILO; OECD; UDHR]
- MNCs should develop nondiscriminatory employment policies and promote equal job opportunities. [ILO; OECD; UDHR]
- MNCs should provide equal pay for equal work. [ILO; UDHR]
- MNCs should give advance notice of changes in operations, especially plant closings, and mitigate the adverse effects of these changes. [ILO; OECD]
- MNCs should provide favorable work conditions, limited working hours, holidays with pay, and protection against unemployment. [UDHR]

- MNCs should promote job stability and job security, avoiding arbitrary dismissals and providing severance pay for those unemployed. [ILO; UDHR]
- MNCs should respect local host-country job standards and upgrade the local labor force through training. [ILO; OECD]
- MNCs should adopt adequate health and safety standards for employees and grant them the right to know about job-related health hazards. [ILO]
- MNCs should, minimally, pay basic living wages to employees. [ILO; UDHR]
- MNCs' operations should benefit lower-income groups of the host nation. [ILO]
- MNCs should balance job opportunities, work conditions, job training, and living conditions among migrant workers and host-country nationals. [Helsinki]

Consumer Protection

- MNCs should respect host-country laws and policies regarding the protection of consumers. [OECD; TNC Code]
- MNCs should safeguard the health and safety of consumers by various disclosures, safe packaging, proper labelling, and accurate advertising. [TNC Code]

Environmental Protection

- MNCs should respect host-country laws, goals, and priorities concerning protection of the environment. [OECD; TNC Code; Helsinki]
- MNCs should preserve ecological balance, protect the environment, adopt preventive measures to avoid environmental harm, and rehabilitate environments damaged by operations. [OECD; TNC Code; Helsinki]
- MNCs should disclose likely environmental harms and minimize risks of accidents that could cause environmental damage. [OECD; TNC Code]
- MNCs should promote the development of international environmental standards. [TNC Code; Helsinki]
- MNCs should control specific operations that contribute to pollution of air, water, and soils. [Helsinki]
- MNCs should develop and use technology that can monitor, protect, and enhance the environment. [OECD; Helsinki]

Political Payments and Involvement

- MNCs should not pay bribes nor make improper payments to public officials. [OECD; TNC Code]
- MNCs should avoid improper or illegal involvement or interference in the internal politics of host countries. [OECD; TNC Code]
- MNCs should not interfere in intergovernmental relations. [TNC Code]

Basic Human Rights and Fundamental Freedoms

- MNCs should respect the rights of all persons to life, liberty, security of person, and privacy. [UDHR; ECHR; Helsinki; ILO; TNC Code][2]
- MNCs should respect the rights of all persons to equal protection of the law, work, choice of job, just and favorable work conditions, and protection against unemployment and discrimination. [UDHR; Helsinki; ILO; TNC Code]
- MNCs should respect all persons' freedom of thought, conscience, religion, opinion and expression, communication, peaceful assembly and association, and movement and residence within each state. [UDHR; ECHR; Helsinki; ILO; TNC Code]
- MNCs should promote a standard of living to support the health and well-being of workers and their families. [UDHR; Helsinki; ILO; TNC Code]
- MNCs should promote special care and assistance to motherhood and childhood. [UDHR; Helsinki; ILO; TNC Code]

These guidelines should be viewed as a *collective* phenomenon since all of them do not appear in each of the six compacts. Table I reveals that the OECD compact and the proposed TNC CODE provide the most comprehensive coverage of the guideline categories. The relative lack of guidelines in the ECHR compact may be attributable to the considerable membership overlap with the Organization for Economic Cooperation and Development whose members subscribe to the OECD standards for multinationals. Human rights and employment conditions are clearly the leading guideline categories, while consumer protection and corporate political activity appear infrequently. Table 1 suggests that the respective compacts have "specialized" in different types of normative issues involving corporate practices, the most obvious example being the ILO's emphasis on employment issues. The argument of this paper is that the collective weight of the guidelines is more important than the absence of some of them from specific international agreements. Clearly their inclusion across the board would strengthen the case for a global normative system intended to guide corporate practices.

These normative guidelines have direct implications for a wide range of *specific* corporate programs and policies. They include policies regarding child-care, minimum wages, hours of work, employee training and education, adequate housing and health care, pollution control efforts, advertising and marketing activities, severance pay, privacy of employees and consumers, information concerning on-the-job hazards, and, especially for those companies with operations in South Africa, such additional matters as the place of residence and free movement of employees. Quite clearly, the guidelines are not intended to be, nor do they act as, mere rhetoric. Nor do they deal with peripheral matters. They have *direct* applicability to many of the *central* operations and policies of multinational enterprises.

THE NORMATIVE SOURCES OF THE GUIDELINES

These guides for the practices and policies of multinational companies seem to rest upon and be justified by four normative orientations. Given sets of the guidelines can be tied directly to one or more of these moral sources.

National Sovereignty is one such source. All six compacts invoke the inviolability of national sovereignty. In acting on the compacts' principles, each nation is to take care not to infringe on the sovereignty of its neighbors. Hence, preservation of a nation's integrity and self-interest appears to be one of the moral foundations on which such multilateral accords rest. Multinational enterprises are urged to respect the aims, goals, and directions of a host-country's economic and social development and its cultural and historical traditions. Companies' plans and goals should not contravene these components of a nation's being and sovereignty. Nor should they interfere in the internal po-

TABLE I

NUMBER OF MNC NORMATIVE GUIDELINES BY CATEGORY FOR SIX MULTILATERAL COMPACTS

	UDHR	ECHR	HELSINKI	OECD	ILO	TNC CODE	TOTAL
Employment Practices	6	—	—	4	10	—*	20
Consumer Protection	—	—	—	1	—	2	3
Environmental Protection	—	—	5	4	—	4	13
Political Activity	—	—	—	2	—	3	5
Human Rights (re: work)	5	2	5	—	5	5	22
TOTAL	11	2	10	11	15	14	63

*It is expected, but is not a foregone certainty, that the Transnational Corporate Code of Conduct will incorporate into its provisions regarding employment practices the bulk and central meaning of those set forth in the ILO Tripartite Declaration. Hence, their omission in this Table should not be construed to mean that they have been ignored or overlooked by the drafters of the TNC Code.

litical affairs of host countries through improper political activities, political bribes, or questionable payments of any kind made to political candidates or public officials.

Social Equity is another normative basis underlying some of the specific corporate guidelines. Pay scales are to be established in ways that will insure equity between men and women, racial and ethnic groups, professional and occupational groups, host-country nationals and parent-country expatriates, indigenous employees and migrant workers, and those well-off and those least-advantaged. The same equity principle is advocated for job opportunities, job training, treatment of the unemployed, and the provision of other work-related benefits and services.

Market Integrity is yet another source of moral authority and justification for some of the guidelines identified above, as well as for a large number of other guidelines specified in other agreements that are not treated here which have to do with restrictive business practices, the transnational flow of capital investments, the repatriation of profits, the rights of ownership, and similar matters. Among the normative corporate guidelines listed earlier, those tinged with the notion of market integrity include restrictions on political payments and bribes that might inject non-market considerations into business transactions, a recognition of private collective bargaining (rather than government mandates) as a preferred technique for establishing pay scales, working conditions, and benefits for employees, and some (but not all) of the consumer protections sought in the accords.

By far the most fundamental, comprehensive, widely acknowledged, and pervasive source of moral authority for the corporate guidelines is *human rights and fundamental freedoms.* This concept is given eloquent expression in the UN Universal Declaration of Human Rights. It is then picked up and adopted by the framers of four of the other five accords analyzed in this paper. Only the OECD Guidelines for Multinational Enterprises fail to invoke the specific language or the basic meaning of human rights and fundamental freedoms as the normative principle on which these accords are erected, although the OECD Guidelines incorporate some of these rights and freedoms as specific duties and obligations of multinationals. As previously noted, a number of OECD members are signatories to the European Convention on Human Rights, thereby subscribing to the basic principles of the Universal Declaration of Human Rights.

Essentially, the Declaration of Human Rights proclaims the existence of a whole host of human rights and freedoms, saying that they are inherent in the human condition. "All human beings are born free and equal in dignity and rights." "Equal and inalienable rights" are possessed by "all members of the human family" who also manifest an "inherent dignity." Other language speaks of "fundamental human rights," "the dignity and worth of the human person," "the equal rights of men and women," and "fundamental freedoms." These rights and freedoms exist "without distinction of any kind." They are understood as a common possession of humankind, not dependent on membership in any particular group, organization, nation, or society.

This invocation of human rights, as a philosophical principle, owes much to Immanuel Kant. In effect, the Declaration of Human Rights posits the Kantian person as the fundament of moral authority. The human person is said to possess an inherent worth and dignity, as well as inalienable and equal rights and freedoms. This being true of all human beings, correlative duties and obligations are thereby imposed on everyone to respect and not to interfere with the rights of others. No one person is warranted in using another as a means to promote one's own ends and purposes, absent a freely-given informed consent. Hence, a deceptively simple algorithm based on rights and duties sets the stage for the specification of normative rules of conduct for governments, groups, individuals, and—for present purposes—multinational enterprises.[3]

As powerful and compelling as the human rights principle is, it does compete with the other three normative sources—national sovereignty, social equity, and market integrity. This means that human rights are conditioned by political, social, and economic values. Rights do not stand alone or outside the normal range of human institutions, diverse as those institutions are around the globe and from society to society. The nation remains a sacred repository of group allegiance and fierce loyalty, an institution whose leaders at times are fully capable of depriving their own citizens and others of fundamental rights. Witness South Africa's apartheid system, China's brutal suppression of the student-led democracy movement, and the totalitarian excesses of Romania's communist leaders. In all three cases, the state and nation were invoked as ultimate criteria justifying the denial of human rights.

Moreover, societies everywhere erect systems of social status and class, instilling notions of "just claims" and insisting that most people should "know their place." For example, women around the globe find their rights and their life opportunities restricted by male-dominated economic and political systems. The same can be said of the widest variety of ethnic, religious, and racial groups throughout the world, whose fundamental rights and freedoms are often sacrificed on the altar of "social equity" as defined by dominant and competing groups.

Few economic institutions in modern times have appealed more powerfully than markets, whether directed by decentralized economic actors or by centralized states. Those who safeguard the integrity of markets, including officials responsible for high-level governmental or corporate policies, frequently accept the "market necessity" of closing a plant, shifting operations to lower-wage areas, or "busting" a trade union—all in the alleged interest of "allowing the market to work" or "enhancing national and corporate productivity." Doing so may deprive employees of jobs, living wages, retirement security, and other workplace rights.

Hence, in these several ways, rights everywhere are hedged in by such political, social, and economic features of human society. The behavioral guidelines for multinational corporations seem to have been woven, not from a single philosophic principle but by a blending of normative threads. At the pattern's center stand human rights and fundamental freedoms, for in the international compacts reference is found most frequently to this normative marker. But the strands of national sovereignty, social equity, and market integrity are woven into the overall pattern, coloring and giving form to the expression of human rights. Thus are human rights conditioned by societal factors.

One important trait is responsible for the normative dominance of the human rights principle. The human rights spoken of in the Universal Declaration of Human Rights are transcultural. As a principle, human rights span and disregard cultural and national boundaries, class systems, ethnic groupings, economic levels, and other human arrangements which for a variety of reasons differentiate between individuals and groups. Human rights are just that—human. They inhere in *all* humans, regardless of imposed societal classifications and exclusions. They can be defined, disregarded, or violated but they cannot be eradicated.

A transcultural character cannot be claimed for the other three normative sources. National sovereignty is by definition bound to and expressive of the nation. If "nation" is understood to embrace, not only the nation-state but also identification with and allegiance to an ethnic grouping, then it might be more accurate to speak of "socio-ethnicity" as the kind of sovereignty whose protection is sought. In any event, neither "nation-state" nor "socio-ethnic group" is or can be transcultural.

Similarly, social equity meanings rarely if ever span cultural boundaries, in spite of Marxist class theory to the contrary or even the mightiest efforts of Third World nations to see and organize themselves as the world's exploited underclass. That they *are* a global underclass, mistreated, and denied many opportunities by their more prosperous neighbors has not yet bound them together into a solid bloc that could be called transcultural.

Market integrity remains tied firmly to nation-states, even as regional interstate markets such as the European Common Market and the Andean Common Market emerge. Economic systems based on the market principle bear the marks of their national parent's political and ideological institutions. The relatively freer markets that have emerged during the 1980s in the Soviet Union, Eastern Europe, and China are heavily conditioned by the prevailing governmental philosophies of the respective countries, and their operation is not permitted to contravene the perceived needs of the state. The same may be said of markets in the United States, as one observes the ideological swings that accompany successive presidential administrations, legislative elections, and judicial decisions. United States government-imposed commercial sanctions against South Africa, the Soviet Union, Poland, Cuba, Nicaragua, Libya, and other nations reveal the nation-bound character of market operations.

Except for the human rights principle, all other normative sources that undergird the multinational corporate guidelines are thus culture bound, unable to break out of their respective societal contexts. By contrast, human rights are seen to be transcultural. They are the glue or the linchpin that holds the entire normative system together in a coherent international whole. While conditioned by desires for national (or socio-ethnic) sovereignty, social equity, and market integrity—thus finding their operational meaning within a societal context—human rights express attitudes, yearnings, and beliefs common to all humankind. In that sense, they form the core of a global system whose normative aim is to regulate the practices of multinational corporations.

This rights-based normative system finds justification in two ways. One is through deontological obligations implicit in human rights. Here, the philosopher speaks to us. The other justification is more directly operational, taking the form of lessons learned from human experience about the formation and sustenance of human values. These lessons are taught by social scientists. Each of these rationales calls for further elaboration.

RATIONALE I: DEONTOLOGICAL NORMS

The normative corporate guidelines may be seen as extensions and manifestations of broad deontological, i.e., duty-based, principles of human conduct. These principles provide a philosophic basis for defining the duties and obligations of multinational enterprises.

The concurring governments, in the several compacts mentioned here, are saying to multinational enterprises:

- Because your employees have rights to work, to security, to freedom of association, to healthful and safe work conditions, to a pay scale that sustains them and their families at a dignified level of subsistence, to privacy, and to be free from discrimination at work, the managers of multinational corporations incur duties and obligations to respect such rights, to promote them where and when possible, and to avoid taking actions that would deny these rights to the corporation's employees and other stakeholders.
- Because humans and their communities have rights to security, to health, and to the opportunity to develop themselves to their fullest potentials, corporations have an obligation to avoid harming the ecological balance on which human community life and health depend and a positive duty to promote environmental conditions conducive to the pursuit and protection of human rights.
- Because consumers have rights to safe and effective products and to know the quality and traits of the products and services they need to sustain life, companies are obligated, i.e., they have a duty, to offer such products for sale under conditions that permit a free, uncoerced choice for the consumer.
- Because human beings can lay claim to a set of human rights and fundamental freedoms enumerated in the Universal Declaration of Human Rights, multinational corporations are duty-bound to promote, protect, and preserve those rights and freedoms and to avoid trampling on them through corporate operations. The corporations' Kantian duty is implied in the Kantian rights held by all.

A moral imperative is thus imposed on corporations. The source of this deontological imperative is the rights and freedoms that inhere in all human persons. The corporation is bound, by this moral logic, to respect all persons within the purview of its decisions, policies, and actions. In some such fashion as this, the Universal Declaration of Human Rights serves as the deontological fount, the moral fundament, that defines a corporation's basic duties and obligations toward others. The Declaration's moral principles have been extended to many if not most of the multilateral compacts of the past 40 years, many of whose specific provisions take the form of normative guides for corporate actions across a large range of issues. So goes the moral logic of the accords and compacts.

This philosophic position is compelling and convincing. However, the case for a transcultural corporate ethic need not rest on philosophical arguments alone, or, more positively, the deontological position can be considerably enriched and strengthened by considering the role of human experience as a creator of human values.

RATIONALE II: EXPERIENCE-BASED VALUES

Respect for persons, respect for community integrity, respect for ecological balance, and respect for tested human experience in many spheres of life can be understood both deontologically and as adaptive human value orientations. As value phenomena, they are compatible with the needs and experiences of the world's peoples in a technological era. The need to proclaim many of the rights that appear in the Universal Declaration of Human Rights grew directly out of the gross violations of human rights during the pre-war and war periods of the 1930s and 1940s. Those experiences inspired most of the world's governments to take collective action, in the form of a proclamation, to define an acceptable number of such rights and to urge all to nourish and safeguard them.

Since that time, societies around the globe have felt the bite and seen the promise of technology spawned and applied by multinational corporations and governments. They have experienced the benefits, and have often borne the costs, of business operations undertaken without much regard for environmental, human, and community interests. These experiences have been as compelling, if not as traumatic, as those of the pre-war and war years when human rights were trampled. They have generated widespread agreement and belief in a network of experienced-based values that sustain the lives of individuals, their communities, and their societies. It is these values that have found their way into the several multilateral compacts and accords discussed here. Corporations are urged, not just to tend to their deontological duties but also to support, and not to override, the values that have been found through experience to undergird human flourishing.

Speaking of the role played by experience in formulating value standards, sociologist Robin Williams (1979: 22, 45) reminds us that

> . . . values are learned. This means that they are developed through some kind of experience. . . . Similar repeated and pervasive experiences are often characteristic of large numbers of persons similarly situated in society; such experiences are described, discussed, and appraised by the persons involved. The communication of common appraisals eventually builds value standards, which often become widely accepted across many social and cultural boundaries. . . .
>
> . . . value orientations, repeatedly experienced and reformulated by large numbers of persons over extended periods, will eventually become intellectualized as components of a comprehensive world view.

The gathering together of such experience-derived values concerning the human condition has produced "a comprehensive world view" of what is thought to be morally acceptable behavior by multinational enterprises. The specific "components" of that world view are the normative corporate guidelines described earlier. Humankind is speaking here, making known the basic, minimum, socially acceptable conditions for the conduct of economic enterprise. It is a voice that speaks the language of philosophically inspired rights and duties, as well as the language of a social-scientific conception of experienced-based, adaptive human values. The outcome in both cases is movement toward a transcultural corporate ethic, which is manifested in the six multilateral compacts or codes of conduct discussed here.

Another observer (Dilloway, 1986a: 427) reveals the transcultural moral potential of such international accords:

> The final justification, therefore, for a code of rights is, first, that it defines the conditions in which human potential can develop peacefully in an interdependent

> milieu; and, second, that such a code, whether for the individual or for interstate relations, offers the *only* frame of common ideas that can span the diversity of cultures, religions, living standards, and political and economic systems to create a common nexus of humane practice for an emergent world community.

This view is echoed by Richard Falk (1980: 67, 108):

> To think of human rights in the world as a whole . . . is itself a reflection of the emergence, however weakly, of a planetary perspective based on the notion that persons . . . warrant our normative attention.

Nor is there is any reason to restrict this "frame of common ideas"—this morality of the commons—to multinational enterprises alone. It would apply with equal force to domestic and multinational companies. Where nations have been able to identify and agree upon common ethical principles and common values that reflect the experience of even the most diverse cultures, a moral minimum has been established. It remains within the power of some governments and their citizens and businesses to exceed this minimum, while other governments' powers may be insufficiently dedicated to meet even the minimum moral standards. But this minimum—the international common morality, the "common nexus of humane practice," the planetary perspective—stands as a benchmark to be striven for. While it exists, no corporation, domestic or multinational, can legitimately claim the right to operate without referring its policies and practices to this basic moral standard, this morality of the commons that has been writ large upon the global scene.

RESERVATIONS AND QUALIFICATIONS

Four objections might be raised to the derivation of these normative corporate guidelines.

First, it can rightly be said that the six compacts are agreements among *governments* (except the ILO whose members also include enterprises and employee associations). Multinational enterprises themselves are not parties to these accords and thereby are not *directly* bound by their terms and principles. Only three of the compacts, namely, the OECD Guidelines, the ILO Tripartite Declaration, and the UN TNC Code, are directed explicitly to the activities of multinational enterprises. Therefore, an attempt to expand the intention and purposes of the other three accords—the Declaration of Human Rights, the European Convention on Human Rights, and the Helsinki Final Act—to cover the affairs of multinationals might seem to be unwarranted. In other words, the multinationals were not the authors of these guidelines, did not themselves agree to them, and did not pledge to honor them in practice.

This objection, while fair and logical enough as far as it goes, can be offset by noting that all persons, groups, and organizations falling into the sovereign jurisdiction of the concurring governments are bound also by the agreements made by their governments. Such governments are within their justifiable powers and responsibilities to enter into and conclude agreements that bind their citizens, both natural persons and legal entities (such as corporations), to given courses of action. For that reason, when a government pledges itself to promote any given set of behavioral guidelines for its citizens and business firms, it has *pari passu* defined a desirable course of action for them to follow, and it may subsequently enact specific laws that mandate compliance. In this sense, it does not matter that the signatory parties are governments and not enterprises. The enterprises are subject to the laws and agreements of the respective governments in whose territories they conduct business. Beyond these legal considerations, it also should be noted that the UN Universal Declaration of Human Rights asserts that "every individual and *every organ of society,*" should promote and secure the human rights proclaimed by the Declaration. The phrase, "every organ of society," is obviously broad enough to encompass business corporations.

A second difficulty that might be raised by some is that all six accords rely on voluntary compliance by the signatories, since there is no all-embracing international legal authority to enforce the principles enunciated. Their provisions and principles are recommendatory and expectational, not obligational, in character. It is true that the European Convention on Human Rights established a commission to receive complaints and a court to judge actions thought to be inconsistent with the principles proclaimed, and these organs have functioned as a type of legally sanctioned enforcement machinery (Robertson, 1977). It is true also that the concurring governments of all six compacts, having agreed to abide by the spirit of the proclamations, hold the authority within their own jurisdictions to enact legislation aimed at compliance on their own soil. So it cannot be said without some qualification that the accords, though couched in terms of voluntary, nonenforced agreements, are left entirely to police themselves.

More important than these formal pressures to conform to the agreed principles is the manner in which normative, ethical, and moral forces exert their influence on human perceptions and actions. Human compliance with moral standards is a subtle and complex matter that may include, but need not be limited to, reliance on police power.

Awareness of others' values and others' attitudes toward ethical issues helps shape one's own values and attitudes. Compliance with moral standards occurs most frequently when there is self-awareness of what others believe to be morally correct. Research has shown that most people register an apparent desire to hold values, and to be seen as holding values, that are consistent with others' values and with one's own behavior (Rokeach, 1973, 1979). Studies of moral development by Lawrence Kohlberg and his associates also support the idea that value commitments and various types of moral reasoning are strongly influenced by social interactions and social learning experiences (Kohlberg, 1981).

Without this psychological and socially induced strain toward moral consistency, it is unlikely that governmental coercion by itself would be able to secure compliance with socially acceptable moral standards. This is what is usually meant by those who say that "Morals cannot be legislated." Moral compliance in this sense must rely largely on voluntary acceptance of the core ideas expressed by such standards. Compliance is more a matter of social learning and an understanding of the worthwhileness and serviceability of given moral standards than of an acceptance forced by an authoritarian source. Frequently, people accept moral channeling because it makes sense to them and because it reflects their own experience in coping with knotty moral issues. Hence, the widespread declaration of moral principles founded on voluntary acceptance may symbolize a type of moral commitment that is conceivably stronger and more effective than the use of government police power to secure compliance with moral directives. A somewhat related view has been expressed by Ronald Dworkin (1977).

A third difficulty arises when arguing that normative corporate guidelines form the core of a transcultural corporate ethic. The guidelines are not subscribed to by all governments, and even some of the signatory governments may override or ignore them in some circumstances. Thus, it may be charged that the guidelines fall considerably short of representing a universal world view of what multinational corporations should do. Three of the accords are clearly a product of North American-European concerns and issues, while at least one other, the ILO Tripartite Declaration, tends to express the views of employee representatives from industrial nations. Only the UN Universal Declaration of Human Rights and the UN Code of Conduct for Transnational Corporations speak with a more or less global voice, and the last of these two accords has not yet actually come into existence.

This sceptical view is compelling and must be accepted as true. The world is not yet at a point where it can claim to have formulated or projected a set of normative corporate guidelines that are universally or globally accepted and observed. Very real difficulties and genuine controversies have accompanied efforts to forge multilateral compacts that are acceptable to all parties. As noted earlier, the general absence of effective legal enforcement mechanisms weakens these intergovernmental efforts. Sharp differences between multinationals and trade unions have been prominent (Rowan and Campbell, 1983). The sometimes muted struggle between Third World nations and their richer industrial neighbors is always there as a background factor conditioning negotiations. Social ethnicity and diverse religious affiliations become stumbling blocks to consensus. Geopolitical rivalry and *real politik* frequently frustrate the best efforts to reach multilateral accord. Such obstacles are seen by many to be the essence of the international scene, putting the creation of a universal code of conduct beyond reach (Feld, 1980; Waldman, 1980; Wallace, 1982; Windsor and Preston, 1988).

However, a modicum of hope may exist in the very *process* of trying to achieve consensus, prickly as it often is. If nations can agree on procedural rules for determining a fair distribution of the benefits and costs of joining with others in multilateral compacts, more international collaboration might be forthcoming (Windsor and Preston, 1988). The outcome might then be a gradual lessening of substantive differences and a drawing together of the negotiating parties. Robin Williams (1979; 30) explains how this process works:

> . . . opposition of interests and struggles among individuals and collectivities within a continuing policy and societal system actually can contribute to the establishment and elaboration of generalized values and symbols. . . . If successive contests and conflicts are then successfully resolved without repudiation of the values which legitimate the conflict-resolving process or mechanisms, the more highly generalized values will come more and more to be regarded as axiomatic or unchallengable. Although the specific social implications of the general value principle will be changed through successive occasions, nevertheless, all parties come to have a stake in maintaining the complex value referent as a resource for the future.

This process-based outcome is also thought to be a factor by the UN Centre on Transnational Corporations (United Nations, 1988: 361):

> . . . certain substantive principles are known and relatively undisputed in practice . . . there exists today a large body of authoritative material—agreements, declarations, statements, etc.—on the issues at hand. They are not all identical, of course, . . . but there is also considerable coincidence of views.
>
> . . . Even where binding legal obligations are not created, legitimate expectations may be established as to the application of corresponding standards within reasonable bounds.

It is worth remembering that corporations remain remarkably attuned to public perceptions of their images and reputations, displaying an often surprising sensitivity to public criticism of their policies and actions. The reasons are frequently self protective, rather than stemming from altruistic or socially responsible motives. Even so, the hovering presence and repeated expression of moral principles seemingly accepted by large public blocs and their governments may influence corporate behavior toward voluntary compliance with these normative standards.

A fourth difficulty is that the normative guidelines are obviously an incomplete set of moral instructions to enterprises. They do not cover many important matters and issues related to multinational corporate operations. None of the five categories shown in Table I contains an exhaustive list of all possible issues and needed guidelines. One can easily identify other categories and types of issues relevant to multinational business that apparently have not found their way into this particular group of compacts.

In spite of the relatively limited moral compass of these six accords, an impressively diverse range of issues has been evident in several other multilateral conventions, codes, and treaties enacted and promulgated during the 1970s and 1980s, which are not discussed here. These accords attempt to establish guidelines concerning product liability, safety of consumer products, protection of privacy and personal data, transnational movement of hazardous waste materials, distribution and use of pesticides, business operations in South Africa, elimination of various forms of discrimination, protection of employees from workplace hazards, and reduction and elimination of chlorofluorocarbons. Were these to be added to the normative guidelines already identified earlier, the entire set of normative instructions to multinationals would be much larger and more complete.

The argument of this paper does not require that all possible issues be included nor that all parties accept all of the provisions of the compacts. It is not claimed that we are witnessing more than the bare beginnings of a globally oriented system of normative principles governing corporate behavior. The only claim being made is that the general outlines of such a system are now discernible and partially operational.

LESSONS FOR POLICY MAKERS

Those who set policies, whether for public or private institutions, can find some important lessons in these multinational codes of conduct.

The most compelling lesson is that highly diverse governments and societies have been able to reach a workable consensus about some core normative directives for multinational enterprises. That should send a strong message to corporate leaders everywhere that the world's peoples, speaking through their governments, are capable of setting standards intended to guide corporate practices and policies into morally desirable channels. As noted, there continues to be much disagreement among governments about many of these issues, but failure to agree on everything should not be allowed to cloak an achieved consensus on many other issues.

Wise corporate leaders will be able to interpret this consensus as a framework of public expectations on which the policies of their own companies can be based. Global stakeholders have set out their positions on a large range of problems and issues that matter to them. In effect, corporations are being offered an opportunity to match their own operations to these public expectations. The best ones will do so. The others may wish they had if, in failing to heed the normative messages, they encounter rising hostility and increased governmental intervention in their affairs.

For public policy makers, these agreements betoken a growing consensus among the world's peoples about what is thought to be morally desirable action by governments. It would be as perilous for political leaders to ignore this rising tide of global agreement as for corporate policy makers to turn their backs upon it. The authority and legitimacy of these central economic and political institutions are frequently at risk, as illustrated so dramatically in Eastern Europe in 1989 and 1990. Therefore, it will be vitally important for those charged with making institutional policies to guide their respective societies in ways acceptable to their citizens.

Acting to promote this normative consensus can be encouraged if policy makers understand both the philosophic roots and the experience-based values from which these international agreements draw their meaning and strength. The philosophic concept of the human person that one finds in these multilateral compacts, and the human and humane values that grow out of shared global experiences, are no mere passing fancy of a planetary people. Building policy on these twin foundations will bring government and business into alignment with the deep structure of human aspirations.

BEYOND MULTINATIONALS: THE CULTURE OF ETHICS

The transcultural corporate ethic described here is only one part of a much more comprehensive, universal moral order whose shadowy outlines are only partially apparent. This broader "culture of ethics" includes all of those fundamental values and moral orientations that have been proven through long experience to contribute to the sustenance and flourishing of human persons within their communities (Frederick, 1986). It will be important, and increasingly apparent, that all economic enterprises, public and private, domestic and multinational, are bound to acknowledge the moral force of this culture of ethics and to shape their policies and practices accordingly. This "moral dimension" of economic analysis and corporate decision making can no longer be set aside or treated as a peripheral matter (Etzioni, 1988). As human societies are drawn ever closer together by electronic and other technologies, and as they face the multiple threats posed by the unwise and heedless use of these devices, it will become ever more necessary to reach agreement on the core values and ethical principles that permit a humane life to be lived by all. Such planetary agreement is now visible, though yet feeble in its rudiments. This broadscale culture of ethics draws upon many societal, religious, and philosophical sources. It is a great chorus of human voices, human aspirations, and human experiences, arising out of societal and cultural and individual diversity, that expresses the collective normative needs of a global people.

NOTES

1. The successor protocols subsequently attached to some of these compacts are not treated here, although doing so would strengthen the paper's argument. Of particular importance are the International Covenant on Economic, Social, and Cultural Rights; the International Covenant on Civil and Political Rights; and the Optional Protocol to the International Covenant on Civil and Political Rights. These three instruments, which were adopted by the United Nations General Assembly in 1966, transformed the general principles of the Universal Declaration of Human Rights into legal obligations of the ratifying states. By 1985, about half of the governments had ratified these covenants (Dilloway b: 458–459). Three additional documents, two of them intergovernmental and one privately proclaimed, all with obviously normative messages for multinational corporations, have not been included. They are the World Health Organization's International Code on the Marketing of Breast-milk Substitutes (1981), the European Economic Community's Code of Conduct for Companies with Interests in South Africa (1977), and The Sullivan Principles concerning U.S. corporate operations in South Africa (1977). The normative principles on which these three documents are based are entirely consistent with those found in the six compacts that are the focus of this paper. Hence, the case being made here for the emergence of a normative system of global dimensions is predictably stronger than the evidence adduced.
2. The Helsinki Final Act, the ILO Tripartite Declaration, and the UN Code for Transnational Corporations incorporate a general statement accepting the UN Universal Declaration of Human Rights; hence, each of these accords is shown as expressing those guidelines that are derived from the UN Declaration.

   Of the numerous human rights and freedoms identified in the UN Declaration, only those are included here whose observance or violation would be most closely tied to corporate operations. Many rights and freedoms with a "political" content are thereby not treated here, although it could be further argued that corporate influence on the public policies and political processes of host nations exerts both direct and indirect effect on such rights and freedoms.

   It also should be noted that the UN Universal Declaration of Human Rights takes the form of a resolution of the General Assembly and is not a convention, treaty, or accord to which government representatives affix their signatures. Therefore, it is not technically correct to refer to the "signatories" of the Universal Declaration. Where that usage is employed here, it should be understood as meaning only that the then-voting members of the General Assembly agreed to the Declaration's central message.
3. The algorithm is "deceptively simple" by seeming to overlook the enormous volume of argumentation, qualifications, and exceptions to Kant's views that has been produced by succeeding generations of philosophers. Extended discussion of theories of human rights may be found in Shue (1980) and Nickel (1987). Thomas Donaldson (1989) has developed a far more sophisticated view of ethical algorithms than the one offered here, and I am indebted to him for both the concept and the phrase itself.

REFERENCES

Dilloway, A. J.: 1986a, 'Human Rights and Peace', in Ervin Laszlo and Jong Youl Yoo (eds.), *World Encyclopedia of Peace,* vol. 1 (Pergamon Press, Oxford), p. 427.

Dilloway, A. J.: 1986b, 'International Bill of Rights,' in Ervin Laszlo and Jong Youl Yoo (eds.), *World Encyclopedia of Peace,* vol. 1 (Pergamon Press, Oxford), pp. 458–9.

Donaldson, Thomas: 1989, *The Ethics of International Business* (Oxford University Press, New York).

Dworkin, Ronald: 1977, *Taking Rights Seriously* (Harvard University Press, Cambridge).

Etzioni, Amitai: 1988, *The Moral Dimension: Toward a New Economics* (Free Press, New York).

Falk, Richard: 1980, "Theoretical Foundations of Human Rights', in Paula Newberg (ed.): *The Politics of Human Rights* (New York University Press, New York).

Feld, Werner J.: 1980, *Multinational Corporations and U.N. Politics: The Quest for Codes of Conduct* (Pergamon Press, New York).

Frederick, William C.: 1986, 'Toward CSR3: Why Ethical Analysis is Indispensable and Unavoidable in Corporate Affairs', *California Management Review* 28(3), 126–41.

Kohlberg, Lawrence: 1981, *The Philosophy of Moral Development* (Harper & Row, San Francisco).

Nickel, James W.: 1987, *Making Sense of Human Rights: Philosophical Reflections on the Universal Declaration of Human Rights* (University of California Press, Berkeley).

Robertson, A. H.: 1977, *Human Rights in Europe*, 2nd edition (Manchester University Press, Manchester).

Rokeach, Milton: 1973, *The Nature of Human Values* (Free Press, New York).

Rokeach, Milton: 1979, *Understanding Human Values: Individual and Societal* (Free Press, New York).

Rowan, Richard L. and Duncan C. Campbell: 1983, 'The Attempt to Regulate Industrial Relations through International Codes of Conduct', *Columbia Journal of World Business* 18(2), 64–72.

Shue, Henry, 1980, *Basic Rights: Subsistence, Affluence, and U.S. Foreign Policy* (Princeton University Press, Princeton, N.J.).

United Nations: 1983, *Human Rights: A Compilation of International Instruments* (United Nations, New York).

United Nations: 1988, *Transnational Corporations in World Development: Trends and Prospects* (United Nations, New York).

Waldman, Raymond J.: 1980, *Regulating International Business through Codes of Conduct* (American Enterprise Institute, Washington, D.C.).

Wallace, Cynthia Day: 1982, *Legal Control of the Multinational Enterprise: National Regulatory Techniques and the Prospects for International Controls* (Martinus Nijhoff, The Hague).

Windsor, Duane and Lee E. Preston: 1988. 'Corporate Governance, Social Policy and Social Performance in the Multinational Corporation', in Lee E. Preston (ed.), *Research in Corporate Social Performance and Policy*, vol. 10 (JAI Press, Greenwich, Conn.).

Williams, Robin: 1979, 'Change and Stability in Values and Value Systems', in Milton Rokeach, *Understanding Human Values* (Free Press, New York).

What's Wrong with Bribery

Scott Turow
Partner in the law firm of Sonnenschein Nath & Rosenthal, Chicago, and author of *One L, Presumed Innocent, Burden of Proof*, and *Pleading Guilty*

The question on the floor is what is wrong with bribery? I am not a philosopher and thus my answer to that question may be less systematic than others, but it is certainly no less deeply felt. As a federal prosecutor I have worked for a number of years now in the area of public corruption. Over that course of time, perhaps out of instincts of self-justification, or, so it seems, sharpened moral insights, I have come to develop an abiding belief that bribery is deeply immoral.

We all know that bribery is unlawful and I believe that the legal concepts in this area are in fact grounded in widely accepted moral intuitions. Bribery as defined by the state of Illinois and construed by the United States Court of Appeals for the Seventh Circuit in the case of *United States* v. *Isaacs,* in which the former Governor of Illinois, Otto Kerner, was convicted for bribery, may be said to take place in these instances: Bribery occurs when property or personal advantage is offered, without the authority of law, to a public official with the intent that the public official act favorably to the offeror at any time or fashion in execution of the public official's duties.

Under this definition of bribery, the crime consists solely of an unlawful offer, made or accepted with a prohibited state of mind. No particular act need be specified; and the result is immaterial.

This is merely a matter of definition. Oddly the moral underpinnings of bribery are clearer in the context of another statute—the criminal law against mail fraud. Federal law has no bribery statute of general application; it is unlawful of course to bribe federal officials, to engage in a pat-

Found in *Journal of Business Ethics,* Vol. 4, No. 4 (1985), pp. 249–251.

tern of bribery, or to engage in bribery in certain other specified contexts, e.g., to influence the outcome of a sporting contest. But unlike the states, the Congress, for jurisdictional reasons, has never passed a general bribery statute, criminalizing *all* instances of bribery. Thus, over time the federal mail fraud statute has come to be utilized as the vehicle for some bribery prosecutions. The theory, adopted by the courts, goes to illustrate what lawyers have thought is wrong with bribery.

Mail fraud/bribery is predicated on the theory that someone—the bribee's governmental or private employer—is deprived, by a bribe, of the recipient's undivided loyalties. The bribee comes to serve two masters and as such is an 'unfaithful servant.' This breach of fiduciary duty, when combined with active efforts at concealment becomes actionable under the mail fraud law, assuming certain other jurisdictional requisites are met. Concealment, as noted, is another essential element of the crime. An employee who makes no secret of his dual service cannot be called to task; presumably his employer is thought to have authorized and accepted the divided loyalties. For this reason, the examples of maitre d's accepting payments from customers cannot be regarded as fully analogous to instances of bribery which depend on persons operating under false pretenses, a claimed loyalty that has in truth been undermined.

Some of the stricter outlines of what constitutes bribery, in the legal view, can be demonstrated by example. Among the bribery prosecutions with which I have spent the most time is a series of mail fraud/bribery cases arising out of corruption at the Cook County Board of Appeals. The Board of Appeals is a local administrative agency, vested with the authority to review and revise local real estate property tax assessments. After a lengthy grand jury investigation, it became clear that the Board of Appeals was a virtual cesspool, where it was commonplace for lawyers practicing before the Board to make regular cash payments to some decision-makers. The persons accused of bribery at the Board generally relied on two defenses. Lawyers and tax consultants who made the payments often contended that the payments were, in a fashion, a necessity; the Board was so busy, so overcome by paperwork, and so many other people were paying, that the only way to be sure cases would be examined was to have an 'in' with an official whom payments had made friendly. The first argument also suggests the second: that the payments, whatever their nature, had accomplished nothing untoward, and that any tax reduction petition granted by the bribed official actually deserved the reduction it received.

Neither contention is legally sufficient to remove the payments from the category of bribery. Under the definition above, any effort to cause favorable action constitutes bribery, regardless of the supposedly provocative circumstances. And in practice juries had great difficulty accepting the idea that the lawyers involved had been 'coerced' into making the boxcar incomes—sometimes $300,000 to $400,000 a year—that many of the bribers earned. Nor is the merits of the cases involved a defense, under the above definitions. Again, in practical terms, juries seemed reluctant to believe that lawyers would be passing the Board's deputy commissioners cash under the table if they were really convinced of their cases' merits. But whatever the accuracy of that observation, it is clear that the law prohibits a payment, even to achieve a deserved result.

The moral rationale for these rules of law seems clear to me. Fundamentally, I believe that any payment to a governmental official for corrupt purposes is immoral. The obligation of government to deal with like cases alike is a principal of procedural fairness which is well recognized. But this principal is more than a matter of procedure; it has a deep moral base. We recognize that the equality of humans, their fundamental dignity as beings, demands that each stand as an equal before the government they have joined to create, that each, as Ronald Dworkin has put, has a claim to government's equal concern and respect. Bribery asks that that principal be violated, that some persons be allowed to stand ahead of others, that like cases not be treated alike, and that some persons be preferred. This I find morally repugnant.

Moreover, for this reason, I cannot accept the

idea that bribery, which is wrong here, is somehow more tolerable abroad. Asking foreign officials to act in violation of moral principles must, as an abstract matter, be no less improper than asking that of members of our own government; it even smacks of imperialist attitudes. Furthermore, even dealing with the question on this level assumes that there are societies which unequivocally declare that governmental officials may properly deal with the citizenry in a random and unequal fashion. I doubt, in fact, whether any such sophisticated society exists; more than likely, bribery offends the norms and mores of the foreign country as well.

Not only does bribery violate fundamental notions of equality, but it also endangers the vitality of the institution affected. Most bribery centers on persons in discretionary or decision-making positions. Much as we want to believe that bribery invites gross deviations in duty, a prosecutor's experience is that in many cases there are no objectively correct decisions for the bribed official to make. We discovered that this was the case in the Board of Appeals prosecutions where a variety of competing theories of real estate valuation guaranteed that there was almost always some justification, albeit often thin, for what had been done. But it misses the point to look solely at the ultimate actions of the bribed official. Once the promise of payment is accepted, the public official is no longer the impartial decision-maker he is supposed to be. Whatever claims he might make, it is difficult to conceive of a public official who could convince anyone that he entirely disregarded a secret 'gift' from a person affected by his judgments.

Indeed, part of the evil of bribery inheres in the often indetectable nature of some of its results. Once revealed, the presence of bribery thus robs persons affected of a belief in the integrity of *all* prior decisions. In the absolute case, bribery goes to dissolve the social dependencies that require discretionary decision-making at certain junctions in our social scheme. Bribery, then, is a crime against trust; and to the extent that trust, a belief in the good faith of discretionary decision-makers, is essential to certain bureaucratic and governmental structures, bribery is deeply corrosive.

Because of its costs, the law usually deems bribery to be without acceptable justification. Again, I think this is in line with moral intuitions. Interestingly, the law does not regard extortion and bribery as mutually exclusive; extortion requires an apprehension of harm, bribery desire to influence. Often, in fact, the two are coincident. Morally—and legally, perhaps—it would seem that bribery can be justified only if the bribe-giver is truly without alternatives, including the alternative of refusing payment and going to the authorities. Moreover, the briber should be able to show not merely that it was convenient or profitable to pay the bribe, but that the situation presented a choice of evils in which the bribe somehow avoided a greater peril. The popular example in our discussions has been bribing a Nazi camp guard in order to spare concentration camp internees.

Ethics and the Foreign Corrupt Practices Act

Mark Pastin
Michael Hooker
Pastin—Director, Lincoln Center for Ethics, Arizona State University, and Chair & President, Council of Ethical Organizations, Alexandria, VA.
Hooker—President, University of Massachusetts-Amherst

Not long ago it was feared that as a fallout of Watergate, government officials would be hamstrung by artificially inflated moral standards. Recent events, however, suggest that the scapegoat of post-Watergate morality may have become American business rather than government officials.

One aspect of the recent attention paid to corporate morality is the controversy surrounding payments made by American corporations to foreign officials for the purpose of securing business abroad. Like any law or system of laws, the Foreign Corrupt Practices Act (FCPA), designed to control or eliminate such payments, should be grounded in morality, and should therefore be judged from an ethical perspective. Unfortunately, neither the law nor the question of its repeal has been adequately addressed from that perspective.

HISTORY OF THE FCPA

On December 20, 1977 President Carter signed into law S.305, the Foreign Corrupt Practices Act (FCPA), which makes it a crime for American corporations to offer or provide payments to officials of foreign governments for the purpose of obtaining or retaining business. The FCPA also establishes record keeping requirements for publicly held corporations to make it difficult to conceal political payments proscribed by the Act. Violators of the FCPA, both corporations and managers, face severe penalties. A company may be fined up to $1 million, while its officers who directly participated in violations of the Act or had reason to know of such violations, face up to five years in prison and/or $10,000 in fines. The Act also prohibits corporations from indemnifying fines imposed on their directors, officers, employees, or agents. The Act does not prohibit "grease" payments to foreign government employees whose duties are primarily ministerial or clerical, since such payments are sometimes required to persuade the recipients to perform their normal duties.

At the time of this writing, the precise consequences of the FCPA for American business are unclear, mainly because of confusion surrounding the government's enforcement intentions. Vigorous objections have been raised against the Act by corporate attorneys and recently by a few government officials. Among the latter is Frank A. Weil, former Assistant Secretary of Commerce, who has stated, "The questionable payments problem may turn out to be one of the most serious impediments to doing business in the rest of the world."[1]

The potentially severe economic impact of the FCPA was highlighted by the fall 1978 report of the Export Disincentives Task Force, which was created by the White House to recommend ways of improving our balance of trade. The Task Force identified the FCPA as contributing significantly to economic and political losses in the United States. Economic losses come from constricting the ability of American corporations to do business abroad, and political losses come from the creation of a holier-than-thou image.

The Task Force made three recommendations in regard to the FCPA:

- The Justice Department should issue guidelines on its enforcement policies and establish procedures by which corporations could get advance government reaction to anticipated payments to foreign officials.
- The FCPA should be amended to remove enforcement from the SEC, which now shares enforcement responsibility with the Department of Justice.
- The administration should periodically report to Congress and the public on export losses caused by the FCPA.

In response to the Task Force's report, the Justice Department, over SEC objections, drew up guidelines to enable corporations to check any proposed action possibly in violation of the FCPA. In response to such an inquiry, the Justice Department would inform the corporation of its enforcement intentions. The purpose of such an arrangement is in part to circumvent the intent of the law. As of this writing, the SEC appears to have been successful in blocking publication of the guidelines, although Justice recently reaffirmed its intention to publish guidelines. Being more responsive to political winds, Justice may be less inclined than the SEC to rigidly enforce the Act.

Particular concern has been expressed about the way in which bookkeeping requirements of the Act will be enforced by the SEC. The Act requires that company records will "accurately and fairly reflect the transactions and dispositions of the assets of the issuer." What is at question is the interpretation the SEC will give to the requirement and the degree of accuracy and detail it will demand. The SEC's post-Watergate behavior suggests that it will be rigid in requiring the disclosure of all information that bears on financial relationships between the company and any foreign or domestic public official. This level of accountability in record keeping, to which auditors and corporate attorneys have strongly objected, goes far beyond previous SEC requirements that records display only facts material to the financial position of the company.

Since the potential consequences of the FCPA for American businesses and business managers are very serious, it is important that the Act have a rationale capable of bearing close scrutiny. In looking at the foundation of the FCPA, it should be noted that its passage followed in the wake of intense newspaper coverage of the financial dealings of corporations. Such media attention was engendered by the dramatic disclosure of corporate slush funds during the Watergate hearings and by a voluntary disclosure program established shortly thereafter by the SEC. As a result of the SEC program, more than 400 corporations, including 117 of the Fortune 500, admitted to making more than $300 million in foreign political payments in less than ten years.

Throughout the period of media coverage leading up to passage of the FCPA, and especially during the hearings on the Act, there was in all public discussions of the issue a tone of righteous moral indignation at the idea of American companies making foreign political payments. Such payments were ubiquitously termed "bribes," although many of these could more accurately be called extortions, while others were more akin to brokers' fees or sales commissions.

American business can be faulted for its reluctance during this period to bring to public attention the fact that in a very large number of countries, payments to foreign officials are virtually required for doing business. Part of that reluctance, no doubt, comes from the awkwardly difficult position of attempting to excuse bribery or something closely resembling it. There is a popular abhorrence in this country of bribery directed at domestic government officials, and that abhorrence transfers itself to payments directed toward foreign officials as well.

Since its passage, the FCPA has been subjected to considerable critical analysis, and many practical arguments have been advanced in favor of its repeal.[2] However, there is always lurking in back of such analyses the uneasy feeling that no matter how strongly considerations of practicality and economics may count against this law, the fact remains that the law protects morality in forbidding bribery. For example, Gerald McLaughlin, professor of law at Fordham, has shown persuasively that where the legal system of a foreign country affords inadequate protection against the arbitrary exercise of power to the disadvantage of American corporations, payments to foreign officials may be required to provide a compensating mechanism against the use of such arbitrary power. McLaughlin observes, however, that "this does not mean that taking advantage of the compensating mechanism would necessarily make the payment moral."[3]

The FCPA, and questions regarding its enforcement or repeal, will not be addressed adequately until an effort has been made to come to terms with the Act's foundation in morality. While it may be very difficult, or even impossible, to legislate morality (that is, to change the moral character and sentiments of people by passing laws that regulate their behavior), the existing laws undoubtedly still reflect the moral beliefs we hold. Passage of the FCPA in Congress was eased by the simple connection most Congressmen made between bribery, seen as morally repugnant, and the Act, which is designed to prevent bribery.

Given the importance of the FCPA to American business and labor, it is imperative that attention be given to the question of whether there is adequate moral justification for the law.

ETHICAL ANALYSIS OF THE FCPA

The question we will address is not whether each payment prohibited by the FCPA is moral or immoral, but rather whether the FCPA, given all its consequences and ramifications, is itself moral. It is well known that morally sound laws and institutions may tolerate some immoral acts. The First Amendment's guarantee of freedom of speech allows individuals to utter racial slurs. And immoral laws and institutions may have some beneficial consequences, for example, segregationist legislation bringing deep-seated racism into the national limelight. But our concern is with the overall morality of the FCPA.

The ethical tradition has two distinct ways of assessing social institutions, including laws: *End-Point Assessment* and *Rule Assessment.* Since there is no consensus as to which approach is correct, we will apply both types of assessment of the FCPA.

The End-Point approach assesses a law in terms of its contribution to general social well-being. The ethical theory underlying End-Point Assessment is utilitarianism. According to utilitarianism, a law is morally sound if and only if the law promotes the well-being of those affected by the law to the greatest extent practically achievable. To satisfy the utilitarian principle, a law must promote the well-being of those affected by it at least as well as any alternative law that we might propose, and better than no law at all. A conclusive End-Point Assessment of a law requires specification of what constitutes the welfare of those affected by the law, which the liberal tradition generally sidesteps by identifying an individual's welfare with what he takes to be in his interests.

Considerations raised earlier in the paper suggest that the FCPA does not pass the End-Point test. The argument is not the too facile one that we could propose a better law. (Amendments to the FCPA are now being considered.[4]) The argument is that it may be better to have *no* such law than to have the FCPA. The main domestic consequences of the FCPA seem to include an adverse effect on the balance of payments, a loss of business and jobs, and another opportunity for the SEC and the Justice Department to compete. These negative effects must be weighed against possible gains in the conduct of American business within the United States. From the perspective of foreign countries in which American firms do business, the main consequence of the FCPA seems to be that certain officials now accept bribes and influence from non-American businesses. It is hard to see that who pays the bribes makes much difference to these nations.

Rule Assessment of the morality of laws is often favored by those who find that End-Point Assessment is too lax in supporting their moral codes. According to the Rule Assessment approach: A law is morally sound if and only if the law accords with a code embodying correct ethical rules. This approach has no content until the rules are stated, and different rules will lead to different ethical assessments. Fortunately, what we have to say about Rule Assessment of the FCPA does not depend on the details of a particular ethical code.

Those who regard the FCPA as a worthwhile expression of morality, despite the adverse effects on American business and labor, clearly subscribe to a rule stating that it is unethical to bribe. Even if it is conceded that the payments proscribed by the FCPA warrant classifications as bribes, citing a rule prohibiting bribery does not suffice to justify the FCPA.

Most of the rules in an ethical code are not *categorical* rules; they are *prima facie* rules. A categorical rule does not allow exceptions, whereas a prima facie rule does. The ethical rule that a person ought to keep promises is an example of a prima facie rule. If I promise to loan you a book on nuclear energy and later find out that you are a terrorist building a private atomic bomb, I am ethically obligated not to keep my promise. The rule that one ought to keep promises is "overridden" by the rule that one ought to prevent harm to others.

A rule prohibiting bribery is a prima facie rule. There are cases in which morality requires that a bribe be paid. If the only way to get essential medical care for a dying child is to bribe a doctor, morality requires one to bribe the doctor. So adopting an ethical code which includes a rule prohibiting the payment of bribes does not guarantee that a Rule Assessment of the FCPA will be favorable to it.

The fact that the FCPA imposes a cost on American business and labor weighs against the prima facie obligation not to bribe. If we suppose that American corporations have obligations, tantamount to promises, to promote the job security of their employees and the investments of shareholders, these obligations will also weigh against the obligation not to bribe. Again, if government legislative and enforcement bodies have an obligation to secure the welfare of American business and workers, the FCPA may force them to violate their public obligations.

The FCPA's moral status appears even more dubious if we note that many of the payments prohibited by the Act are neither bribes nor share features that make bribes morally reprehensible. Bribes are generally held to be malefic if they persuade one to act against his good judgement, and consequently purchase an inferior product. But the payments at issue in the FCPA are usually extorted *from the seller.* Further it is arguable that not paying the bribe is more likely to lead to purchase of an inferior product than paying the bribe. Finally, bribes paid to foreign officials may not involve deception when they accord with recognized local practices.

In conclusion, neither End-Point nor Rule Assessment uncovers a sound moral basis for the FCPA. It is shocking to find that a law prohibiting bribery has no clear moral basis, and may even be an immoral law. However, this is precisely what examination of the FCPA from a moral perspective reveals. This is symptomatic of the fact that moral conceptions which were appropriate to a simpler world are not adequate to the complex world in which contemporary business functions. Failure to appreciate this point often leads to righteous condemnation of business, when it should lead to careful reflection on one's own moral preconceptions.

NOTES

1. *National Journal,* June 3, 1978: 880.
2. David C. Gustman, "The Foreign Corrupt Practices Act of 1977," *The Journal of International Law and Economics,* Vol. 13, 1979; 367–401, and Walter S. Surrey, "The Foreign Corrupt Practices Act: Let the Punishment Fit the Crime," *Harvard International Law Journal,* Spring 1979: 203–303.
3. Gerald T. McLaughlin, "The Criminalization of Questionable Foreign Payments by Corporations," *Fordham Law Review,* Vol. 46: 1095.
4. "Foreign Bribery Law Amendments Drafted," *American Bar Association Journal,* February 1980: 135.

Bribery and Ethics: A Reply to Pastin and Hooker

Robert E. Frederick
Research Scholar, Center for Business Ethics, Bentley College.

In their article on the Foreign Corrupt Practices Act, Mark Pastin and Michael Hooker used both "end-point assessment" and "rule assessment" to evaluate the FCPA from a moral point of view.[1] They argue that neither method of assessment supports the FCPA and hence that it "has no clear moral basis, and may even be an immoral law."[2] It seems to me, however, that Pastin and Hooker's arguments are not compelling and that there is a sense in which the FCPA does have a sound moral basis. Thus in the remainder of this paper I will give reasons why I think Pastin and Hooker are mistaken. I will begin with their end-point assessment of the FCPA and then turn to the rule assessment. In the final section I will have some brief comments about extortion and the FCPA.

I

End-point assessment is based on the moral theory of utilitarianism. If we use end-point assessment to evaluate a law, then according to Pastin and Hooker it is a morally sound law "if and only if the law promotes the well-being of those affected by the law to the greatest extent practically achievable."[3] They argue that the FCPA has not promoted the well-being of those affected by the law to the greatest extent practically achievable, since it has led to a loss of business and jobs, it has unfavorably affected the balance of payments, and it is a source of discord between government agencies.[4] Hence, they suggest that the FCPA does not pass the end-point test of moral soundness.

It is difficult to judge the strength of this argument against the FCPA, since it is very difficult to find and evaluate objective empirical evidence that either confirms or disconfirms the economic harm allegedly caused by the FCPA. There is anecdotal evidence that the FCPA has caused some firms a loss of business.[5] In a 1983 study of the data, however, John L. Graham finds that "the FCPA has not had a negative effect on U.S. trade," and in a 1987 analysis of U.S. trade in the Mideast, Kate Gillespie concludes that "The FCPA potential to hurt U.S. exports remains unproved."[6] These studies do not show that the FCPA has promoted the well-being of those affected by it to the greatest extent practically achievable, so they do not show that the FCPA passes the end-point assessment test of moral soundness. Perhaps the best we can say about the studies is that they seem to show, not that we are economically any better off for having the FCPA on the books, but rather that we are not any worse off.

Let us suppose, however, that there is good evidence that the FCPA has caused a loss of U.S. exports and a loss of jobs in U.S. export-related industries. Would this show that the FCPA does not pass the end-point assessment? It seems to me it would not. One of the central tenets of utilitarianism is that the well-being of any one person or group of persons is not to count more or be of more moral weight than the well-being of some other person or group of persons. Thus the well-being of people in the United States does not count more than the well-being of people in France or Uganda or China. Now, if the FCPA causes a U.S. firm to lose an export contract, then some foreign competitor must have gotten that contract. Thus it could be that a loss of exports and jobs in the United States would be offset by an increase in exports and jobs in some foreign country. Assuming the people receiving the goods are as well off with either vendor, and since the well-being of people in the United States does not count more than the well-being of people in the country that got the contract, the net effect of the FCPA on economic well-being, once we consider *everyone* affected by it, might be entirely neutral.

If this argument is correct, it shows that from a utilitarian point of view the FCPA is morally neutral. It neither harms nor enhances total economic well-being. Thus, as long as we consider only economic well-being, end-point assessment does not provide moral grounds for either favoring or opposing the law. Of course, it is possible that the FCPA affects well-being in noneconomic ways. For example, one might argue that insofar as the FCPA discourages the corrupt practice of bribery, people both in the United States and abroad are better off. But it seems to me that considerations of well-being, although important, do not address the central moral issues raised by the FCPA. For that we have to turn to rule assessment.

II

Pastin and Hooker claim that a law passes the rule assessment test of moral soundness "if and only if the law accords with a code embodying correct moral rules."[7] They then try to show that the FCPA does not pass the rule assessment test regardless of the actual content of the moral code. This may seem a little extreme, since it may be that the correct moral code contains a rule such as "under no circumstances is bribery morally permissible." But Pastin and Hooker circumvent this problem by claiming that the rule against bribery is always a prima facie rule, i.e., it can be overridden by other moral considerations in appropriate circumstances. They then seem to claim that in the arena of international competition other moral considerations frequently override the rule. And since the FCPA makes no allowance for such instances—it prohibits bribes even in cases where it is morally permissible to offer a bribe—it does not accord with the moral code and does not pass the end-point assessment.

But is the rule against bribery a prima facie rule? And even if it is, are there moral considerations that frequently override it? I will try to show that for certain types of bribery the moral rule against bribery is not a prima facie rule and that in other cases the considerations Pastin and Hooker mention are not overriding. I will begin with a brief description of what I take to be a central case of bribery, and then, using that case as a focal point for discussion, I will say something about why I think bribery is morally wrong.

Suppose you find yourself in the following situation: You are taking a difficult course required for your major. You work hard, go to class, do all the homework, and are well satisfied with the B you receive for a final grade. You happen to find out, however, that an acquaintance of yours made an A in the course even though he missed most of the classes, didn't do the homework, and didn't even show up for the final exam. You know this person is no genius, so you wonder how he did it. You are so curious, in fact, that you decide to ask him. "Well," he replies, "let's just say I know how to spread some money around where it will do the most good."

You are outraged, since the clear implication is that your acquaintance bribed the professor to give him an A. But exactly why are you outraged? Exactly what is wrong with bribery?

The best way to begin to answer that question is to get as clear as we can about the main characteristics of a central case of bribery, such as the one just described. The first thing to note is that the above situation is a kind of social practice which is governed in all essential respects by an agreement or understanding between the participants. This understanding, parts of which may be explicit and parts implicit, is voluntary, at least in the sense that no one is threatened with unjustifiable harm if he or she does not take the class, and the understanding does not require that any of the participants engage in morally impermissible behavior. In addition, the agreement defines the role, position, or function of each participant in the practice and delineates the kinds of behaviors that are acceptable or unacceptable for each role or position in certain circumstances. For example, even though it may never be explicitly stated, it is a part of the understanding, and undoubtedly a part of your expectations for the course, that all students will be graded solely on the amount and quality of work that they do.

The understanding can be broken in a number of ways, some of which are innocuous and do not involve immoral behavior. But the case of bribery in question is not innocuous. It is an attempt by one student to gain an unfair advantage over the other students by offering the professor something of value in return for the professor violating the understanding by giving the student special treatment. It is, in effect, an attempt by one of the participants to subvert the original understanding by entering into a new one with terms that are incompatible with the terms of the original.

If we put all these things together we can give a complete, although somewhat complex, characterization of central cases of bribery:

> In central cases bribery is a violation of an understanding or agreement which defines a social practice. It is an attempt by one person(s) *X* to secure an unfair advantage over another person(s) *Y* by giving a third person(s) *Z* something of value in exchange for *Z* giving favorable treatment to *X* by violating some prima facie duty *Z* has in virtue of *Z*'s position, role, or function in a morally permissible understanding in which *X, Y,* and *Z* are all voluntary participants.

Thus, if my analysis is correct, central cases of bribery always involve social practices in which there are voluntary and morally permissible agreements or understandings, always involve a three-term relationship, and are always attempts to gain an unfair advantage. Noncentral cases of bribery deviate from central cases in that they apparently either do not involve morally permissible agreements, or voluntary agreements, or there is no three-term relationship, or they are not attempts to gain an unfair advantage.

We are finally in a position to say something about what is wrong with central cases of bribery. To give someone an unfair advantage is to give them special treatment that others do not receive, treatment that cannot be justified under the terms of the original understanding, and treatment that the other parties of the understanding would not acquiesce to if they were to know about it. And to give someone such an advantage is, it seems reasonable to say, morally wrong. To paraphrase Aristotle, it is not to treat equals equally. Hence to *accept* a bribe is morally wrong. This does not explain why *offering* a bribe is morally wrong. But I suggest, as a general moral principle, that if one person attempts to get another person to do something morally wrong, then the attempt is also morally wrong. Hence, if I attempt to bribe you to do something that is morally wrong, my attempt to bribe you is morally wrong regardless of whether you accept the bribe or not.

If the rule against bribery is a prima facie rule,

then, even for central cases of bribery, there must be some possible circumstances in which it can be overridden. But what circumstances might those be? Under what conditions is it morally permissible to give someone an unfair advantage over others? It seems to me there are no such conditions. It is never morally permissible to give someone an unfair advantage, nor is it morally permissible to induce someone to provide an unfair advantage. Hence, for central cases, the rule against bribery is not a prima facie rule. Thus, the FCPA does have a clear moral basis since it prohibits a type of bribery that is always morally wrong.

III

There are two ways that Pastin and Hooker might respond. We concede, they might say, that central cases of bribery are always wrong. Given your characterization of central cases it could hardly be otherwise. Yet in foreign competition such cases hardly ever occur. Noncentral cases are much more common, and in these cases the rule against bribery is prima facie. Their second response would probably be to point out, as they do in their article, that many of the payments prohibited by the FCPA are not bribes at all, but extortions. And, they might continue, since the FCPA as it is presently formulated prohibits noncentral cases of bribery, and since it prohibits most types of extortion, it lacks a completely sound moral basis. The reason is that in many instances it is morally permissible to pay bribes in noncentral cases, or to make extortion payments. Thus, the FCPA does not pass the rule assessment test after all, since the FCPA is not in *complete* accord with the correct moral code.

To some extent I am sympathetic with these responses. They do show, I believe, that there are considerations in favor of *revising* the law.[8] This is not too surprising, since there are many laws that could be improved. But it is important to see that, as long as the FCPA is on the books in its present form, the responses I have attributed to Pastin and Hooker give no justification whatever for violating the law by offering a bribe. Let me explain.

Suppose for a moment that we have not made the distinction between central and noncentral cases of bribery, and suppose Pastin and Hooker are correct about the rule against bribery always being a prima facie rule. If it is, then if one has other moral obligations that override the obligation not to bribe, it is morally permissible to offer a bribe. So, in order to determine whether it is permissible, we need to know something about what kinds of obligations might override the rule against bribery.

It is beyond the scope of this article to examine all the different obligations that might override the rule against bribery, but Pastin and Hooker do mention one that deserves discussion. It is the obligation businesspeople have to protect the financial interests of corporate investors. Pastin and Hooker seem to say that in order to protect these interests businesspeople must sometimes offer bribes. I believe, however, that this mistakes the obligations businesspeople actually have. Except in very unusual circumstances they are only obligated to protect the interests of investors *within* the limits established by law. They simply have no obligation to protect those interests by breaking the law. Thus, investors can have no *moral* complaint against a businessperson if they suffer a financial loss because the businessperson refused to break a law.

There are occasions on which it is morally permissible or obligatory to break the law. If the law is flagrantly unjust, or if following the law is likely to cause severe and irremediable harm, then our moral obligations may outweigh our legal ones. But it has not been established that the FCPA is flagrantly unjust or that following it is likely to cause severe and irremediable harm. Hence, there is no justification for concluding that businesspeople are morally required to violate the FCPA by offering bribes, even assuming the rule against bribery is always prima facie.[9]

IV

One aspect of the FCPA that I have only touched on is the prohibition of most types of extortion payments. Typically extortion is an attempt by one person(s) *X* to gain from another person(s) *Y* something of value to which *X* has no rightful claim by an actual or implied threat to harm unjustifiably *Y*'s legitimate interests unless *Y* yields the thing of value to *X*. For example, if your professor makes it known to you that she will not grade your work fairly unless you give her $100, then she is attempting extortion.

Although there are clear differences between extortion and central cases of bribery, extortion and noncentral cases of bribery are often confused. For example, an illustration Pastin and Hooker use—"bribing" a doctor to get essential medical treatment for a child—seems to me a form of extortion instead of bribery.[10]

It is important to distinguish carefully between extortion and bribery, since the moral relationships in extortion are quite different from the moral relationships in bribery. For example, in extortion, but not in bribery, there is a threat to vital interests. And since, I believe, it is always morally wrong to threaten unjustifiably vital interests, demanding extortion is always morally wrong. But it is sometimes morally permissible to make an extortion payment provided that no other reasonable alternative is available to protect threatened vital interests. Paying the doctor to treat the child is a good example. Thus, there is a sense, absent in cases of bribery, in which someone making an extortion payment is a victim of morally improper behavior.

Pastin and Hooker appear to argue that since it is at least sometimes morally permissible to make extortion payments, and since the FCPA prohibits most types of extortion payments, the FCPA is defective from a moral point of view. But I suggest that we look at the FCPA in a different light. Businesspeople who are forced to make extortion payments to protect threatened interests are victims of a corrupt and immoral practice. We do have moral obligations to protect people from such victimization. How should we do it? It is unlikely that businesspeople acting individually would be able to prevent extortion. What is needed is concerted action, and one effective way to achieve concerted action is through regulation and law.[11] If the FCPA prohibition of extortion payments is strictly enforced, then U.S. firms will not do business in countries where extortion is common. And if we can encourage other countries strictly to enforce laws against extortion, or to pass such laws if they do not have them, then businesspeople in those countries will respond similarly. This will eventually bring pressure on the remaining countries where extortion is common, since it will close them off from products and services that are needed for their economies. And this, in turn, should make them much more likely to enforce laws against demanding extortion. Thus, instead of the FCPA being morally defective, if it is strictly enforced, and if other countries enforce similar laws, the FCPA can advance a worthwhile moral purpose by helping stop the victimization imposed by extortion.

It would be naive to think that extortion can be completely eliminated via the sort of concerted action I have proposed, but I believe it is morally unacceptable to take no action against it at all. Enforcing the FCPA and similar laws is one way to help the international business community avoid falling victim to extortionists' demands. Hence, in my view the FCPA should not be revised to permit extortion payments. If anything, the prohibition of such payments should be strengthened.

There is one misunderstanding I would like to forestall. It might be suggested that prohibiting extortion payments is *imposing* morality. As long as we are concerned with a rule assessment of the FCPA, this is a completely mistaken view. The correct moral code, on which rule assessment is based, is a moral code that applies to everyone at all times. It exempts no one. Thus if a practice is a violation of the code, as I have claimed demanding extortion always is, to refuse to pay extortion is not in any sense imposing morality. It is refusing to participate in and make possible behavior prohibited by the moral code, behavior that is immoral for anyone in any country.

In conclusion I would like to emphasize that my analysis and discussion of bribery and extortion is by no means complete. I have not tried to address many issues that could be raised, and with many others I have undoubtedly raised more questions than I have answered. But I do think I have shown that Pastin and Hooker are incorrect in claiming that the FCPA does not pass either end-point or rule assessment tests of moral soundness. The FCPA may not be a perfect law, but it is not entirely without moral justification.[12]

NOTES

1. Mark Pastin and Michael Hooker, "Ethics and the Foreign Corrupt Practices Act," in *Business Ethics: Readings and Cases in Corporate Morality,* ed. W. Michael Hoffman and Jennifer Mills Moore, 2d ed. (New York: McGraw-Hill Book Company, 1989), pp. 551.
2. Ibid., p. 555.
3. Ibid., p. 553.
4. It is beyond my expertise to say whether, in this case, discord between agencies is a good thing or a bad one, so I will not comment on it.
5. Suk H. Kim, "On Repealing the Foreign Corrupt Practices Act: Survey and Assessment," *Columbia Journal of World Business,* Fall 1981, pp. 16–20. Also see Justin G. Longenecker, Joseph A. McKinney, and Carlos W. Moore, "The Ethical Issue of International Bribery: A Survey of Attitudes among U.S. Business Professionals," *Journal of Business Ethics,* vol. 7, no. 5, May 1988, pp. 341–346.
6. John L. Graham, "Foreign Corrupt Practices: A Manager's Guide," *Columbia Journal of World Business,* Fall 1983, p. 89. Kate Gillespie, "Middle East Response to the Foreign Corrupt Practices Act," *California Management Review,* vol. 29, no. 4, Summer 1987, p. 28.
7. Pastin and Hooker, p. 554.
8. I will argue later that the FCPA prohibition of extortion payments should not be revised.
9. The same sort of argument applies against making extortion payments. However, extortion is more complex, since in some cases severe harm may be caused by refusing to make an extortion payment. The FCPA makes provision for some of these cases. In the final section I will suggest one way such harm might be avoided.
10. There are a number of more difficult cases. For example, it is often said that in some countries bribery is a common practice. But are payments made in such countries bribes or extortion payments? Can bribery be a common practice, or after a certain point does it become institutionalized extortion?
11. Longenecker, McKinney, and Moore, p. 346.
12. My thanks to W. Michael Hoffman and Jennifer Mills Moore for their comments on an earlier draft of this paper.

QUESTIONS FOR DISCUSSION

1. In your opinion, what are some of the most important ethical problems facing multinational corporations operating in developing countries? Do you think the principles offered by De George and Donaldson might help resolve some of these dilemmas? Explain your answer.

2. Can you think of any rights that should be added to Donaldson's list? Are there any that should be deleted? How would you use his "ethical algorithm" to deal with cases like "Tropical Plywood Imports" or "The Project at Moza Island"?

3. Would De George and Donaldson differ in their ideas about multinational business practices in Eastern Europe and Russia? Are De George's recommendations about business in that region of the world consistent with his discussion in "Ethical Dilemmas for Multinational Enterprise"? Be sure to explain why or why not.

4. In your view, exactly what is wrong with bribery? If bribery is a common practice in some countries, why shouldn't U.S. companies be allowed to practice bribery in those countries?

THE CORPORATION IN SOCIETY

Do Ads Lure Youngsters to Drink, Smoke?

Dolores Kong
Medical reporter, *The Boston Globe*

When Dr. Paul Fischer's son was 2 1/2, he picked up a soda straw, pretended to smoke, and said, "When I grow up, I want to be a man. I want to drive fast cars and I want to smoke cigarettes."

That incident in a restaurant nearly four years ago shocked Fischer, an associate professor at the Medical College of Georgia, and launched him on an inquiry into the effects of cigarette advertising on very young children.

The results of Fischer's study of the Old Joe cartoon that pitches Camel cigarettes, issued to widespread publicity in December, have become part of a small but growing body of research—from such diverse fields as child development, marketing and communications—that suggests that tobacco and alcohol ads, intentionally or not, may be having a wide influence on youngsters because of the images the ads use.

Fischer's study provided some of the most startling evidence to date of tobacco advertising's effects. Children as young as three were able to link the Old Joe cartoon with cigarettes; by the age of six, they were able to identify the camel as readily as they could Mickey Mouse.

With alcohol advertising, the most compelling finding came in a 1990 survey by Berkeley researchers for the AAA Foundation for Traffic Safety, a non-profit organization that receives most of its funding from the American Automobile Association. Of nearly 500 11- and 12-year-olds, 88 percent correctly linked "Spuds Mackenzie"—dubbed the "original party animal" in some ads—with Bud Light beer.

With growing evidence of youngsters' early recognition of and possible influence by ads for tobacco and alcohol, the battle lines have been drawn.

On one side, public health officials and advocates charge that advertising, as pervasive and persuasive as it is, is a major factor in causing children to start to smoke or drink as young as 10 or 11, as

Found in *The Boston Globe,* (April 27, 1992). Reprinted courtesy of *The Boston Globe.*

well as a reason that smoking rates among adolescents are not declining as rapidly as they are among adults.

On the other, industry officials say that their ads are not aimed at children and do not cause them to smoke or drink, and that advertising is protected under the First Amendment's guarantee of free speech.

"If you want to know what appeals to children, look at ads that are aimed deliberately at children," says Jean Kilbourne, a Boston-area based advertising critic who lectures internationally. "What do they use? They use cartoon characters. They use animals."

"Those are the same exact things that they use in beer and alcohol ads that they say are not aimed at children," says Kilbourne.

Joe Tye, founder and president of Stop Teenage Addiction to Tobacco, or STAT, a Springfield-based group that has launched a nationwide boycott of Oreo cookies to force RJR Nabisco to stop using the cartoon camel, agreed: "What they're selling these kids is not a product, it's an image."

Another Cartoon Coming

James Bergman, executive director of STAT, says another cartoon character may be selling cigarettes again soon. Kool has begun test marketing an updated cartoon penguin, complete with sunglasses, high-top sneakers and an attitude, a revamp of a 1930s cartoon penguin, according to Bergman. "This time he's going to be real cool, real cool. He's going to have shades. It's clearly going to build on the Joe Camel experience. . . . Everyone knows it worked. It was a dynamite ad campaign."

Last month, Surgeon General Antonia Novello and the American Medical Association criticized RJR Nabisco, maker of Camels, for encouraging youth smoking with the cartoon. In January, even Advertising Age, an industry journal that staunchly opposes restrictions on advertising, called upon RJR to drop the campaign.

Maura Payne, director of public relations for RJ Reynolds Tobacco Company, a division of RJR Nabisco, said in a telephone interview last week that the firm has no plans to stop using the cartoon. "There is just no evidence that more young people are taking up smoking because the Camel campaign exists."

Novello also demanded that the alcohol industry stop using ads that lead youngsters to think that "they can ski, swim, scuba dive or race cars better if they drink."

Others have called for such tough restrictions as a ban on billboard advertising, sports sponsorship and product giveaways by tobacco and alcohol companies, steps which some other countries have taken. In Massachusetts, a bill has been filed to ban cigarette ads on billboards in such places as Fenway Park. In another move to deter smoking, a proposal for a 25-cents-a-pack cigarette tax hike will be on the November ballot.

Bans Could Stand

Legal precedent suggests that governmental restrictions on advertising of such potentially harmful products as tobacco and alcohol would not violate the First Amendment, says Richard Daynard, law professor at Northeastern University and chairman of a tobacco products liability project.

"It's very, very clear that a ban would be upheld," Daynard said. "The real problem is not that. The real problem is political will."

Tobacco and alcohol makers defend their campaigns. They argue that peer pressure and adult influence lead youngsters to pick up the habits, not their advertisements. The campaigns are aimed at making adult smokers switch brands or to establish brand loyalty, they say.

"Are the ads the reason why kids begin smoking? The answer is overwhelmingly 'No,' " says Payne at RJ Reynolds. "They want to be cool, they want to fit in, they want to emulate their older brother or sister."

She cited a December Gallup poll that found that only 3 percent of smokers said advertising played any role in their decision to begin smoking, and a 16-country study by the International Advertising Association, commissioned by the tobacco industry, that found the influence of friends and family members much more important than advertising in youngsters' decisions to start.

In the face of the criticism, however, the tobacco and alcohol industries have started campaigns to discourage youth smoking and irresponsible drinking, with such slogans as "Smoking should not be a part of growing up," or "Know when to say when." They have commissioned counter-studies and critiques of reports suggesting a link between advertising and youth smoking.

Evidence, Not Proof

There is no proof that advertising causes children to smoke or drink, health officials acknowledge.

"But the definitive and conclusive proof of the level that would be required by science has never been required by the policy community when it comes to policy about life and death. They go with the best evidence available," says Kenneth Warner, a University of Michigan public health researcher who edited the 1989 US Surgeon General's report on smoking and health.

And, Warner adds, the best evidence indicates that advertising influences youngsters' attitudes toward smoking and drinking and their health behavior.

The strongest evidence on smoking comes from a study done at the University of Strathclyde in Scotland. In a study of 600 children, aged 11 to 14, those who were more aware of cigarette advertising were more likely a year later to have positive attitudes about smoking.

In addition, the more cigarette ads they recognized, the more likely they were to say a year later that they intended to pick up smoking. Potentially confounding factors, such as whether the children already smoked or whether peers or siblings smoked, were taken into account.

Even so, "We can't say categorically this is a cause-and-effect relationship," concedes Gerard Hastings, director of advertising research at the university and one of the authors of the report, published last year in the British Journal of Addiction. However, he adds, "I can't think of any sensible explanation for this data other than advertising is having this effect."

Image's Power

The power of social image in the minds of young smokers was demonstrated by a study of 550 fifth through seventh graders in Fitchburg, by researchers at the University of Massachusetts Medical School.

Youngsters who smoked were three times as likely to believe the habit would make them popu-

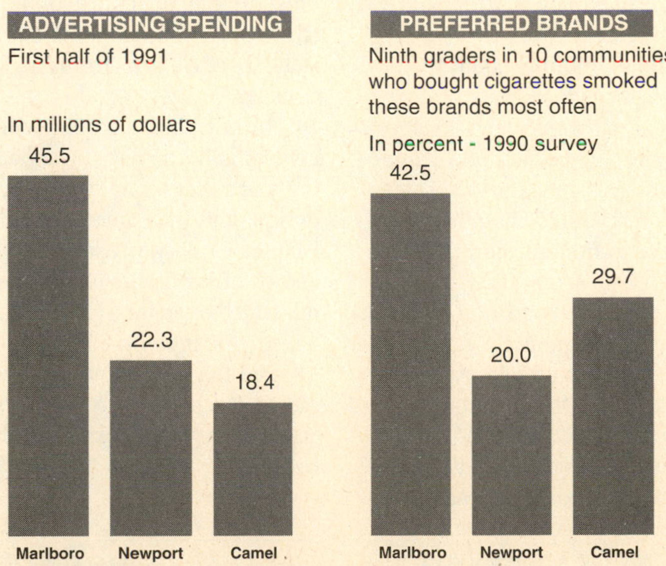

SOURCE: Advertising Age; Centers for Disease Control

lar or attractive, even though they knew the health hazards of smoking as well as their non-smoking peers. The smokers were also significantly less likely to believe ads are deceptive.

Dr. Joseph R. DiFranza, a UMass associate professor of family medicine and one of the researchers involved in the unpublished study, says, "Kids are just like adults. When they make a decision to do something, they think the benefits outweigh the risks." And, he adds, "The benefits of smoking are what you see in the advertisements."

Adolescents are particularly vulnerable to cigarette advertising because psychologically, they need to become independent from their parents, to be accepted by their peers and to develop a positive self-image, DiFranza says.

"For girls, to address independence, you've got, 'You've come a long way, baby," DiFranza says, citing the Virginia Slims campaign.

"For boys, the Marlboro man is the ultimate American image of independence. You get on your horse and ride in every direction. There's nobody to tell you what you can do."

In a separate study also published in December, DiFranza found that the Old Joe "smooth character" is better recognized and more appealing to high school students than to adults. The study concluded that the campaign, launched in 1988, has helped boost Camel's share of cigarettes sold to minors from 0.5 to 32.8 percent.

There have been similar findings about the appeal of alcohol advertising to adolescents.

Child psychologists and communications researchers say cigarette and alcohol ads that feature cartoons or cute animals may appeal especially to young children, who are not yet old enough to want to rebel against parents or to imitate adult behavior by smoking or drinking.

As early as age 3, children zero in on cartoon characters as representing something for them, whether they are in Saturday morning cartoons or ads for adult products, he says. "It's just the sort of thing that would attract a child's attention."

"There is increasing commercialization of youth," says Ellen Wartella, a communications researcher and specialist in the effects of television advertising on children at the University of Illinois, Urbana. "Nobody knows how to talk about it. It's amoeba-like. Nobody can get a handle on it."

The Ford Pinto

W. Michael Hoffman
Executive Director, Center for Business Ethics, Bentley College

I

On August 10, 1978, a tragic automobile accident occurred on U.S. Highway 33 near Goshen, Indiana. Sisters Judy and Lynn Ulrich (ages 18 and 16, respectively) and their cousin Donna Ulrich (age 18) were struck from the rear in their 1973 Ford Pinto by a van. The gas tank of the Pinto ruptured, the car burst into flames, and the three teenagers were burned to death.

Subsequently an Elkhart County grand jury returned a criminal homicide charge against Ford, the first ever against an American corporation. During the following twenty-week trial, Judge Harold R. Staffeldt advised the jury that Ford should be convicted of reckless homicide if it were shown that the company had engaged in "plain, conscious and unjustifiable disregard of harm that might result (from its actions) and the disregard involves a substantial deviation from acceptable standards of conduct."[1]

The key phrase around which the trial hinged, of course, is "acceptable standards." Did Ford knowingly and recklessly choose profit over safety in the design and placement of the Pinto's gas tank? Elkhart County prosecutor Michael A. Cosentino and chief Ford attorney James F. Neal battled dramatically over this issue in a rural Indiana courthouse. Meanwhile, American business anxiously awaited the verdict which could send warning ripples through boardrooms across the nation concerning corporate responsibility and product liability.

II

As a background to this trial some discussion of the Pinto controversy is necessary. In 1977 the magazine *Mother Jones* broke a story by Mark Dowie, general manager of *Mother Jones* business operations, accusing Ford of knowingly putting on the road an unsafe car—the Pinto—in which hundreds of people have needlessly suffered burn deaths and even more have been scarred and disfigured from burns. In his article "Pinto Madness" Dowie charges that:

- Fighting strong competition from Volkswagen for the lucrative small-car market, the Ford Motor Company rushed the Pinto into production in much less than the usual time.
- Ford engineers discovered in preproduction crash tests that rear-end collisions would rupture the Pinto's fuel system extremely easily.
- Because assembly-line machinery was already tooled when engineers found this defect, top Ford officials decided to manufacture the car anyway—exploding gas tank and all—even though Ford owned the patent on a much safer gas tank.
- For more than eight years afterward, Ford successfully lobbied, with extraordinary vigor and some blatant lies, against a key government safety standard that would have forced the company to change the Pinto's fire-prone gas tank.

> By conservative estimates Pinto crashes have caused 500 burn deaths to people who would not have been seriously injured if the car had not burst into flames. The figure could be as high as 900. Burning Pintos have become such an embarrassment to Ford that its advertising agency, J. Walter Thompson, dropped a line from the ending of a radio spot that read "Pinto leaves you with that warm feeling."
>
> Ford knows that the Pinto is a firetrap, yet it has paid out millions to settle damage suits out of court, and it is prepared to spend millions more lobbying against safety standards. With a half million cars rolling off the assembly lines each year, Pinto is the biggest-selling subcompact in America, and the company's operating profit on the car is fantastic. Finally, in 1977, new Pinto models have incorporated a few minor alterations necessary to meet that federal standard Ford managed to hold off for eight years. Why did the company delay so long in making these minimal, inexpensive improvements?

- Ford waited eight years because its internal "cost-benefit analysis," which places a dollar value on human life, said it wasn't profitable to make the changes sooner.[2]

Several weeks after Dowie's press conference on the article, which had the support of Ralph Nader and auto safety expert Byron Bloch, Ford issued a news release attributed to Herbert T. Misch, vice president of Environmental and Safety Engineering, countering points made in the *Mother Jones* article. Their statistical studies conflict significantly with each other. For example, Dowie states that more than 3,000 people were burning to death yearly in auto fires; he claims that, according to a National Highway Traffic Safety Administration (NHTSA) consultant, although Ford makes 24 percent of the cars on American roads, these cars account for 42 percent of the collision-ruptured fuel tanks.[3] Ford, on the other hand, uses statistics from the Fatality Analysis Reporting System (FARS) maintained by the government's NHTSA to defend itself, claiming that in 1975 there were 848 deaths related to fire-associated passenger-car accidents and only 13 of these involved Pintos; in 1976, Pintos accounted for only 22 out of 943. These statistics imply that Pintos were involved in only 1.9 percent of such accidents, and Pintos constitute about 1.9 percent of the total registered passenger cars. Furthermore, fewer than half of those Pintos cited in the FARS study were struck in the rear.[4] Ford concludes from this and other studies that the Pinto was never an unsafe car and has not been involved in some 70 burn deaths annually, as *Mother Jones* claims.

Ford admits that early-model Pintos did not meet rear-impact tests at 20 mph but denies that this implies that they were unsafe compared with other cars of that type and era. In fact, according to Ford, some of its tests were conducted with experimental rubber "bladders" to protect the gas tank, in order to determine how best to have its future cars meet a 20-mph rear-collision standard which Ford itself set as an internal performance goal. The government at that time had no such standard. Ford also points out that in every model year the Pinto met or surpassed the government's own standards, and

> it simply is unreasonable and unfair to contend that a car is somehow unsafe if it does not meet standards proposed for future years or embody the technological improvements that are introduced in later model years.[5]

Mother Jones, on the other hand, presents a different view of the situation. If Ford was so concerned about rear-impact safety, why did it delay the federal government's attempts to impose standards? Dowie gives the following answer:

> The particular regulation involved here was Federal Motor Vehicle Safety Standard 301. Ford picked portions of Standard 301 for strong opposition way back in 1968 when the Pinto was still in the blueprint stage. The intent of 301, and the 300 series that followed it, was to protect drivers and passengers after a crash occurs. Without question the worst post-crash hazard is fire. So Standard 301 originally proposed that all cars should be able to withstand a fixed barrier impact of 20 mph (that is, running into a wall at that speed) without losing fuel.
>
> When the standard was proposed, Ford engineers pulled their crash-test results out of their files. The front ends of most cars were no problem—with minor alterations they could stand the impact without losing fuel. "We were already working on the front end," Ford engineer Dick Kimble admitted. "We knew we could meet the test on the front end." But with the Pinto particularly, a 20 mph rear-end standard meant redesigning the entire rear end of the car. With the Pinto scheduled for production in August of 1970, and with $200 million worth of tools in place, adoption of this standard would have created a minor financial disaster. So Standard 301 was targeted for delay, and with some assistance from its industry associates, Ford succeeded beyond its wildest expectations: the standard was not adopted until the 1977 model year.[6]

Ford's tactics were successful, according to Dowie, not only due to their extremely clever lobbying, which became the envy of lobbyists all over Washington, but also because of the proindustry stance of NHTSA itself.

Furthermore, it is not at all clear that the Pinto was as safe as comparable cars with regard to the positioning of its gas tank. Unlike the gas tank in the Capri, which rode over the rear axle, a "saddle-type" fuel tank on which Ford owned the patent, the Pinto tank was placed just behind the rear bumper. According to Dowie,

> Dr. Leslie Ball, the retired safety chief for the NASA manned space program and a founder of the International Society of Reliability Engineers, recently made a careful study of the Pinto. "The release to production of the Pinto was the most reprehensible decision in the history of American engineering," he said. Ball can name more than 40 European and Japanese models in the Pinto price and weight range with safer gas-tank positioning.
>
> Los Angeles auto safety expert Byron Bloch has made an in-depth study of the Pinto fuel system. "It's a catastrophic blunder," he says. "Ford made an extremely irresponsible decision when they placed such a weak tank in such a ridiculous location in such a soft rear end. It's almost designed to blow up—premeditated."[7]

Although other points could be brought out in the debate between *Mother Jones* and Ford, perhaps the most intriguing and controversial is the cost-benefit analysis study that Ford did entitled "Fatalities Associated with Crash-Induced Fuel Leakage and Fires" released by J. C. Echold, director of automotive safety for Ford. This study apparently convinced Ford and was intended to convince the federal government that a technological improvement costing $11 per car which would have prevented gas tanks from rupturing so easily was not cost effective for society. The costs and benefits are broken down in the following way:

Benefits	
Savings:	180 burn deaths, 180 serious burn injuries, 2,100 burned vehicles
Unit Cost:	$200,000 per death, $67,000 per injury, $700 per vehicle
Total Benefit:	180 × $200,000 + 180 × $67,000 + 2,100 × $700 = *$49.5 million*

Costs	
Sales:	11 million cars, 1.5 million light trucks
Unit Cost:	$11 per car, $11 per truck
Total Cost:	11,000,000 × $11 + 1,500,000 × $11 = *$137 million*

And where did Ford come up with the $200,000 figure as the cost per death? This came from a NHTSA study which broke down the estimated social costs of a death as follows:

Component	**1971 Costs**
Future productivity losses	
Direct	$132,000
Indirect	41,300
Medical costs	
Hospital	700
Other	425
Property damage	1,500
Insurance administration	4,700
Legal and court	3,000
Employer losses	1,000
Victim's pain and suffering	10,000
Funeral	900
Assets (lost consumption)	5,000
Miscellaneous	200
Total per fatality	$200,725

(Although this analysis was on all Ford vehicles, a breakout of just the Pinto could be done.) *Mother Jones* reports it could not find anybody who could explain how the $10,000 figure for "pain and suffering" had been arrived at.[8]

Although Ford does not mention this point in its news release defense, one might have replied that it was the federal government, not Ford, that set the figure for a burn death. Ford simply carried out a cost-benefit analysis based on that figure. *Mother Jones,* however, in addition to insinuating that there was industry-agency (NHTSA) collusion, argues that the $200,000 figure was arrived at under intense pressure from the auto industry to use cost-benefit analysis in determining regulations. *Mother Jones* also questions Ford's estimate of burn injuries: "All independent experts estimate that for each person who dies by an auto fire, many more are left with charred hands, faces and limbs." Referring to the Northern California Burn Center, which estimates the ratio of burn injuries to deaths at ten to one instead of one to one, Dowie states that "the true ratio obviously throws the company's calculations way off."[9] Finally, *Mother Jones* claims to have obtained "confidential" Ford documents which Ford did not send to Washington, showing that crash fires could largely be prevented by installing a rubber bladder inside the gas tank for only $5.08 per car, considerably less than the $11 per car Ford originally claimed was required to improve crashworthiness.[10]

Instead of making the $11 improvement, installing the $5.08 bladder, or even giving the consumer the right to choose the additional cost for added safety, Ford continued, according to *Mother Jones,* to delay the federal government for eight years in establishing mandatory rear-impact standards. In the meantime, Dowie argues, thousands of people were burning to death and tens of thousands more were being badly burned and disfigured for life, while many of these tragedies could have been prevented for only a slight cost per vehicle. Furthermore, the delay also meant that millions of new unsafe vehicles went on the road, "vehicles that will be crashing, leaking fuel and incinerating people well into the 1980s."[11]

In concluding his article Dowie broadens his attack beyond just Ford and the Pinto.

> Unfortunately, the Pinto is not an isolated case of corporate malpractice in the auto industry. Neither is Ford a lone sinner. There probably isn't a car on the road without a safety hazard known to its manufacturer. . . .
>
> Furthermore, cost-valuing human life is not used by Ford alone. Ford was just the only company careless enough to let such an embarrassing calculation slip into public records. The process of willfully trading lives for profits is built into corporate capitalism. Commodore Vanderbilt publicly scorned George Westinghouse and his "foolish" air brakes while people died by the hundreds in accidents on Vanderbilt's railroads.[12]

Ford has paid millions of dollars in Pinto jury trials and out-of-court settlements, especially the latter. *Mother Jones* quotes Al Slechter in Ford's Washington office as saying: "We'll never go to a jury again. Not in a fire case. Juries are just too sentimental. They see those charred remains and forget the evidence. No sir, we'll settle."[13] But apparently Ford thought such settlements would be less costly than the safety improvements. Dowie wonders if Ford would continue to make the same decisions "were Henry Ford II and Lee Iacocca serving twenty-year terms in Leavenworth for consumer homicide."[14]

III

On March 13, 1980, the Elkhart County jury found Ford not guilty of criminal homicide in the Ulrich case. Ford attorney Neal summarized several points in his closing argument before the jury. Ford could have stayed out of the small-car market, which would have been the "easiest way," since Ford would have made more profit by sticking to bigger cars. Instead, Ford built the Pinto "to take on the imports, to save jobs for Americans and to make a profit for its stockholders."[15] The Pinto met every fuel-system standard of any federal, state, or local government, and was comparable to other 1973 subcompacts. The engineers who designed the car thought it was a good, safe car and bought it for themselves and their families. Ford did everything possible to recall the Pinto quickly after NHTSA ordered it to do so. Finally, and more specifically to the case at hand, Highway 33 was a badly designed highway, and the girls were fully stopped when a 4,000-pound van rammed into the rear of their Pinto at least 50 miles an hour. Given the same circumstances, Neal stated, any car would have suffered the same consequences as the Ulrich's Pinto.[16] As reported in the *New York Times* and *Time*, the verdict brought a "loud cheer" from Ford's board of directors and undoubtedly at least a sigh of relief from other corporations around the nation.

Many thought this case was that of a David against a Goliath because of the small amount of money and volunteer legal help Prosecutor Cosentino had in contrast to the huge resources Ford poured into the trial. In addition, it should be pointed out that Cosentino's case suffered from a ruling by Judge Staffeldt that Ford's own test results on pre-1973 Pintos were inadmissible. These documents confirmed that Ford knew as early as 1971 that the gas tank of the Pinto ruptured at impacts of 20 mph and that the company was aware, because of tests with the Capri, that the over-the-axle position of the gas tank was much safer than mounting it behind the axle. Ford decided to mount it behind the axle in the Pinto to provide more trunk space and to save money. The restrictions of Cosentino's evidence to testimony relating specifically to the 1973 Pinto severely undercut the strength of the prosecutor's case.[17]

Whether this evidence would have changed the minds of the jury will never be known. Some, however, such as business ethicist Richard De George, feel that this evidence shows grounds for charges of recklessness against Ford. Although it is true that there were no federal safety standards in 1973 to which Ford legally had to conform and although Neal seems to have proved that all subcompacts were unsafe when hit at 50 mph by a 4,000-pound van, the fact that the NHTSA ordered a recall of the Pinto and not other subcompacts is, according to De George, "*prima facie* evidence that Ford's Pinto gas tank mounting was substandard."[18] De George argues that these grounds for recklessness are made even stronger by the fact that Ford did not give the consumer a choice to make the Pinto gas tank safer by installing a rubber bladder for a rather modest fee.[19] Giving the consumer such a choice, of course, would have made the Pinto gas tank problem known and therefore probably would have been bad for sales.

Richard A. Epstein, professor of law at the University of Chicago Law School, questions whether Ford should have been brought up on criminal charges of reckless homicide at all. He also points out an interesting historical fact. Before 1966 an injured party in Indiana could not even bring civil charges against an automobile manufacturer solely because of the alleged "uncrashworthiness" of a car; one would have to seek legal relief from the other party involved in the accident, not from the manufacturer. But after *Larson v. General Motors Corp.* in 1968, a new era of crashworthiness suits against automobile manufacturers began. "Reasonable" precautions must now be taken by manufacturers to minimize personal harm in crashes.[20] How to apply criteria of reasonableness in such cases marks the whole nebulous ethical and legal arena of product liability.

If such a civil suit had been brought against Ford, Epstein believes, the corporation might have argued, as it did to a large extent in the criminal suit, that the Pinto conformed to all current applicable safety standards and with common industry practice. (Epstein cites that well over 90 percent of United States standard production cars had their gas tanks in the same position as the Pinto.) But in a civil trial the adequacy of industry standards are ultimately up to the jury, and had civil charges been brought against Ford in this case the plaintiffs might have had a better chance of winning.[21] Epstein feels that a criminal suit, on the other hand, had no chance from the very outset, because the prosecutor would have had to establish criminal intent on the part of Ford. To use an analogy, if a hunter shoots at a deer and wounds an unseen person, he may be held civilly responsible but not criminally responsible because he did not intend to harm. And even though it may be more difficult to determine the mental state of a corporation (or its principal agents), it seems clear to Epstein that the facts of this case do not prove any such criminal intent even though Ford may have known that some burn deaths and injuries could have been avoided by a different placement of its Pinto gas tank and that Ford consciously decided not to spend more money to save lives.[22] Everyone recognizes that there are trade-offs between safety and costs. Ford could have built a "tank" instead of a Pinto, thereby considerably reducing risks, but it would have been relatively unaffordable for most and probably unattractive to all potential consumers.

To have established Ford's reckless homicide it would have been necessary to establish the same of Ford's agents, since a corporation can only act through its agents. Undoubtedly, continues Epstein, the reason why the prosecutor did not try to subject Ford's officers and engineers to fines and imprisonment for their design choices is "the good faith character of their judgment, which was necessarily decisive in Ford's behalf as well."[23] For example, Harold C. MacDonald, Ford's chief engineer on the Pinto, testified that he felt it was important to keep the gas tank as far from the passenger compartment as possible, as it was in the Pinto. And other Ford engineers testified that they used the car for their own families. This is relevant information in a criminal case which must be concerned about the intent of the agents.

Furthermore, even if civil charges had been made in this case, it seems unfair and irrelevant to Epstein to accuse Ford of trading cost for safety. Ford's use of cost-benefit formulas, which must assign monetary values to human life and suffering, is precisely what the law demands in assessing civil liability suits. The court may disagree with the decision, but to blame industry for using such a method would violate the very rules of civil liability. Federal automobile officials (NHTSA) had to make the same calculations in order to discharge their statutory duties. In allowing the Pinto design, are not they too (and in turn their employer, the United States) just as guilty as Ford's agents?[24]

IV

The case of the Ford Pinto raises many questions of ethical importance. Some people conclude that Ford was definitely wrong in designing and marketing the Pinto. The specific accident involving the Ulrich girls, because of the circumstances, was simply not the right one to have attacked Ford on. Other people believe that Ford was neither criminally nor civilly guilty of anything and acted completely responsibly in producing the Pinto. Many others, I suspect, find the case morally perplexing, too complex to make sweeping claims of guilt or innocence.

Was Ford irresponsible in rushing the production of the Pinto? Even though Ford violated no federal safety standards or laws, should it have made the Pinto safer in terms of rear-end collisions, especially regarding the placement of the gas tank? Should Ford have used cost-benefit analysis to make decisions relating to safety, specifically placing dollar values on human life and suffering? Knowing that the Pinto's gas tank could have been made safer by installing a protective bladder for a relatively small cost per consumer, perhaps Ford should have made that option available to the public. If Ford did use heavy lobbying efforts to delay and/or influence federal safety standards, was this ethically proper for a corporation to do? One might ask, if Ford was guilty, whether the engineers, the managers, or both are to blame. If Ford had been found guilty of criminal homicide, was the proposed penalty stiff enough ($10,000 maximum fine for each of the three counts equals $30,000 maximum), or should agents of the corporations such as MacDonald, Iacocca, and Henry Ford II be fined and possibly jailed?

A number of questions concerning safety standards are also relevant to the ethical issues at stake in the Ford trial. Is it just to blame a corporation for not abiding by "acceptable standards" when such standards are not yet determined by society? Should corporations like Ford play a role in setting such standards? Should individual juries be determining such standards state by state, incident by incident? If Ford should be setting safety standards, how does it decide how safe to make its product and still make it affordable and desirable to the public without using cost-benefit analysis? For that matter, how does anyone decide? Perhaps it is putting Ford, or any corporation, in a catch-22 position to ask it both to set safety standards and to make a competitive profit for its stockholders.

Regardless of how we answer these and other questions it is clear that the Pinto case raises fundamental issues concerning the responsibilities of corporations, how corporations should structure themselves in order to make ethical decisions, and how industry, government, and society in general ought to interrelate to form a framework within which such decisions can properly be made in the future.

NOTES

1. *The Indianapolis Star,* Sunday, Mar. 9, 1980, Section 3, p. 2.
2. Mark Dowie, "Pinto Madness," *Mother Jones,* September–October, 1977, pp. 18, 20. Subsequently Mike Wallace for "Sixty Minutes" and Sylvia Chase for "20-20" came out with similar exposés.
3. *Ibid.,* p. 30.
4. Ford news release (Sept. 9, 1977), pp. 1–3.
5. *Ibid.,* p. 5.
6. Dowie, p. 29.
7. *Ibid.,* pp. 22–23.
8. *Ibid.,* pp. 24, 28.
9. *Ibid.,* p. 28.
10. *Ibid.,* pp. 28–29.
11. *Ibid.,* p. 30.
12. *Ibid.,* p. 32. Dowie might have cited another example which emerged in the private correspondence which transpired almost a half-century ago between Lammot du Pont and Alfred P. Sloan, Jr., then president of GM. Du Pont was trying to convince Sloan to equip GM's lowest-priced cars, Chevrolets, with safety glass. Sloan replied by saying: "It is not my responsibility to sell safety glass. . . . You can say, perhaps, that I am selfish, but business is selfish. We are not a charitable institution—we are trying to make a profit for our stockholders." [Quoted in Morton Mintz and Jerry S. Cohen, *Power, Inc.* (New York: The Viking Press, 1976), p. 110.]
13. *Ibid.,* p. 31.
14. *Ibid.,* p. 32.
15. Transcript of report of proceedings in *State of Indiana v. Ford Motor Company,* Case No. 11-431, Monday, Mar. 10, 1980, pp. 6202–6203. How Neal reconciled his "easiest way" point with his "making more profit for stockholders" point is not clear to this writer.
16. *Ibid.,* pp. 6207–6209.
17. *Chicago Tribune,* Oct. 13, 1979, p. 1, and Section 2, p. 12; *New York Times,* Oct. 14, 1979, p. 26; *The Atlanta Constitution,* Feb. 7, 1980.
18. Richard De George, "Ethical Responsibilities of Engineers in Large Organizations: The Pinto Case," *Business and Professional Ethics Journal,* vol. 1., No. 1 (Fall 1981), p. 4. *The New York Times,* Oct. 26, 1978, p. 103, also points out that during 1976 and 1977 there were thirteen fiery fatal rear-end collisions involving Pintos, more than double that of other United States comparable cars, with VW Rabbits and Toyota Corollas having none.
19. *Ibid.,* p. 5.
20. Richard A. Epstein, "Is Pinto a Criminal?", *Regulation,* March–April, 1980, pp. 16–17.
21. A California jury awarded damages of $127.8 mil-

lion (reduced later to $6.3 million on appeal) in a Pinto crash in which a youth was burned over 95 percent of his body. See *New York Times,* Feb. 8, 1978, p. 8.

22. Epstein, p. 19.
23. *Ibid.,* pp. 20–21.
24. *Ibid.,* pp. 19–21.

Tropical Plywood Imports, Inc.

LaRue Tone Hosmer
Professor of Corporate Strategy and Managerial Ethics,
University of Michigan

The tropical forests of the world are being destroyed at a rate that is far greater than the annual losses earlier reported by government agencies. Recent surveys taken by satellite reveal that each year 40 million acres[1] of rain forest simply disappear, with the marketable trees cut for timber while the remaining species are so severely damaged by the logging operations they cannot recover. The whole forest may be destroyed shortly afterwards by the "slash and burn" agricultural practices of the inhabitants of the area, who follow the logging roads and trails into cut-over areas. The World Resources Institute, in cooperation with the United Nations, prepared a recent report, based upon satellite surveys. It showed that in the nine largest tropical countries, accounting for 73 percent of the total measured destruction, the actual annual losses of tropical forest acreage were four times greater than the 1985 estimates of government officials in those countries. (See Table 1.)

The satellite surveys revealed that in some countries tropical forest officially classified as state or national preserves and parks were in fact treeless. In a particularly telling comment, the report explained that the figures on actual losses might have been undercounted because smoke from burning brush and logging debris obscured some of the satellite photos; only areas that could be clearly seen to be deforested were included in the official reports. Officials at the World Resource Institute, members of the U. S. Congress, and international economists were dismayed at the newly reported

TABLE 1

ESTIMATED VERSUS ACTUAL LOSSES IN TROPICAL FOREST ACREAGE.

	Annual Acreage Losses Estimated During 1981–85	Annual Acreage Losses Revealed by 1988 satellite survey
Brazil	3,657,000	19,768,000
Cameroon	198,000	247,000
Costa Rica	160,000	306,000
India	363,000	3,707,000
Indonesia	1,482,000	2,224,000
Myanmar (Burma)	254,000	1,673,000
Philippines	227,000	353,000
Thailand	437,000	981,000
Vietnam	161,000	427,000
Total	6,939,000	29,686,000

Source: World Resource Institute, reported in *The New York Times,* June 8, 1990, p. A10.

totals. James Speth, chair of the World Resource Institute said, "Tropical deforestation is an unparalleled tragedy. If we don't reverse the trend now, it will soon be too late."[2] Senator Patrick Leahy, chair of the Agriculture Committee, U. S. Senate, declared, "This is the first reliable data we've had on tropical deforestation in 10 years. A situation we knew was bleak is now shown to be truly horrendous."[3]

Scientists were even more appalled, if that were possible. Sara Oldfield, writing in *The New Scientist* warned that

> The destruction of tropical forests is one of the worst ecological disasters of the 20th century. It is the key to the most serious environmental problems: mass extinctions, global warming, shortages of natural resources, and the displacement and suffering of the tribal people who live in the forest.[4]

There are three reasons the destruction of the tropical forests can be described with such strong adjectives. The first is the possibility of global warming and the greenhouse effect. Green plants absorb carbon dioxide, and through photosynthesis (the action of sunlight upon chlorophyll) convert carbon dioxide and water into carbohydrates that are basic to the growth of all living organisms, both plants and animals. Trees are the largest green plants, and consequently are among the earth's most important plant sinks for carbon dioxide; and among trees, those in tropical forests are exceedingly effective absorbers, since they receive maximum sunlight, heavy rainful and grow the year around.

Carbon dioxide is formed as the result of burning fossil fuels, such as lignite, coal and oil or natural fuels, such as wood or straw, as well as by the weathering of carbonate rocks and volcanic eruptions. The amount of carbon dioxide in the atmosphere has, of course, increased significantly since the beginning of the industrial revolution[5] and the great burning of fossil fuels. Atmospheric carbon dioxide reflects infrared radiation from the earth's surface, much as greenhouse glass does, increasing surface temperatures and changing weather patterns.

Scientists are not sure of the exact relationship of atmospheric carbon dioxide and the greenhouse effect. Separating long-term trends of global temperature from daily, seasonally and yearly variations is not at all easy or simple. Surface temperatures are affected by topography, wind streams, cloud patterns, rainfall, and solar radiation, all interacting in complex, poorly understood ways. Increases in surface temperatures can be definitely established for some regions, but they seem to be at least partially offset by decreases in other regions. Further, global temperatures have varied in the past, as evidenced by the successive ice ages, and those changes are not likely to have been caused by human activity.

The greenhouse effect has not been proven. The concern of many atmospheric scientists and meteorologists is that when it can be proven, which may not be for another two decades when adequate data will have been accumulated, it will be far too late to take remedial action. The amount of carbon dioxide in the atmosphere might be irreversible if the tropical forests no longer exist. If current rates of cutting and burning continue, only scattered remnants in the higher and more inaccessible region may be left.

The possibility of irreversible global warming is only one of the adverse effects of the destruction of the rain forests. The second is the extinction of plant and animal species. Tropical rain forests originally accounted for less than seven percent of the earth's surface, yet they may have held more than half of all of the earth's living species. Many of those still surviving have not been identified and few of these have ever been studied. Many biologists believe that some of the many species, particularly among the plants, may possess materials and substances of great value to human health and well-being.

The third adverse impact of the destruction of the rain forests is the increased poverty of the tropical nations that will come with the final depletion of this resource. The nine nations listed in Table 1, with the exception of Brazil, are Third World countries: poor, under-developed and over-populated. The export value of tropical hardwood timber was reported to be \$7 billion per year in the early 1980s;[6] it was expected to decline to \$2 billion by the year 2000 and become negative in 2010. "Become negative" means that the tropical economies will have to import timber for building and other local uses by that year.

The last, and perhaps the most serious, *proven* and pernicious effects of destroyed rain forests are the ruined cultural life and, often, living conditions inflicted upon indigenous peoples, who have long lived in the forests. The forests have not been unpopulated. They provided a rich environment for people as well as for plants and animals. Tribes, living in small groups or communal villages thrived on fish, game, wild fruit and small cleared plantations of root crops such as sweet potatoes, in the Amazon basin, or manioc, in southeast Asia. Such a life is not possible after deforestation.

Native residents have usually been either forcefully removed from the land prior to cutting, or are economically forced to move after the logging operations end. A particularly poignant aspect of the forced movement was the attitude of the indigenous peoples. Commonly they assume that the forests are, and should be, communal property, owned by all for the benefit of all. The communal belief was reflected in the national law of most tropical countries. Forests were legally owned by the government for the benefit of its citizens. Typically, land could not be sold to timber companies. Instead, "concessions" or rights to cut the timber for a limited number of years were sold. Consequently, "concessionaires," the formal title for timber companies operating in Southeast Asia, had no long-term interest in preserving the forests as a national resource. Their most profitable action was to cut all the marketable trees, drag the logs by tractor to the nearest road, and leave.

When they left, the land rapidly deteriorated even if it were not burned for agricultural use. Tropical forests are not similar to those in the more temperate Northern Hemisphere. The nutrients that support the vegetation of the forests are not found in the soil; instead they are contained in the "biomass" or the decaying debris of plants, vines and trees that lays upon the forest floor. This debris decays rapidly, helped by the heat, the water, the insects and fungi common in the tropics. After trees are cut down, the remaining forest debris is easily washed away by heavy rainfalls, leaving a raw clay that will support little except coarse grass.

Many environmentalists favor "selective logging," taking only a few of the mature trees per acre, and leaving the rest to regenerate. Selective logging is also known as "sustained yield" forestry. If a timber concessionaire were to take out only selected trees during the first cutting, it would then be able to re-cut the land on a 25-year or 40-year cycle harvesting the cumulative growth each time. Harvesting costs, of course, are higher than those of clear cutting, where all the trees in an area are cut at once.

Selective cutting and sustained yield forestry are widely practiced in northern Europe and southeastern United States, but the practices are not easily transferred to the tropics. First, the timber of the temperate forests is predominantly softwood—pine, spruce and fir—growing to a merchantable size in 30 to 50 years. The valuable timber in the tropical rain forests is exclusively hardwood—mahogany, rosewood and teak—and grows much more slowly.

Second, the timberlands in northern Europe easily reproduce themselves through seeding. Timberlands in the tropics contain a much wider variety of species. It is estimated that Indonesia is the home of 700 different trees that grow large enough to be harvested, yet only 20 of those trees produce lumber with the grain, color and "workability" needed for export. A few of the remaining trees have some value for local construction, but many are commercially useless except for pulp, and few pulp and paper mills have been built in the developing countries. When the desired trees are selectively logged, there often are not enough specimens left for natural seeding in the complex, highly competitive ecological environment of tropical forests.

Third, in a tropical forest, the desired, mature trees tend to be huge. They are often encumbered by vines and creepers, connecting and tying them to their various neighbors. When felled, they generally flatten a considerable section of surrounding trees. The logs, of course, are also large and heavy. In mountainous regions—and much of the southeastern Asian tropical landmass is mountainous—large, powerful tractors have to be used to drag them to the nearest road for trucking. Sledding big, massive logs down steep slopes destroys much vegetation. Photographs of tropical forests that allegedly have been selectively logged show a wasted landscape, with broken tree stubs, crushed undergrowth, and churned-up soil that may not be a hospitable seedbed for regenerating another forest.

There is one further reason, seldom discussed at international conferences though well known, why selective logging and sustained growth forestry have not been successful in the tropical rain forests: economic exploitation and political corruption. Profits in logging the concessions offered by the national governments can be immense. The *Far Eastern Economic Review*[7] estimated that a concessionaire in the Philippines, after meeting all reasonable costs and paying all expected taxes, would make a net profit of P100,000 (US $4,673) per hectare[8]. The *Review* also reported that one concessionaire on the island of Palawan, Philippines, had been awarded cutting rights on 168,000 hectares (c. 263 square miles). Simple mathematics converts this award to a potential profit, over the five years of the grant, of $785,000,000. Profits of such a magnitude have been known to fund political influence in industrialized countries, as well as in Third World countries. A writer for the *Review* complained that

> Palawan is being plundered. Its destruction, spurred by a lack of the political will to stop it and administrative neglect, has set the stage for a last-ditch struggle by conservationists. The fight over Palawan's resources contains in miniature the structure and workings of Philippine politics: the interlocking interests of politicians, government officials, military officers and the businessmen who control the province's economy.[9]

Local residents were unable to stop the private destruction of the public forests. The *Review* reported that the concessionaire on Palawan "maintains a considerable number of private security guards and has an intemperate reputation."[10]

The combination of profits, politics, government, and the military was said in 1989 to have defeated an attempt to convert to sustained yield forestry in Thailand. Many villages in the southern portion of that country had been carried away by flash floods in November 1988, or had been buried in mud and logs washed down from hillsides denuded by recent logging, with a resulting loss of 3,500 people. A government report on the causes blamed a "complete failure in the entire system of forestry protection."[11]

> . . . there were 301 logging concessions throughout the country, most of which were granted in 1972. All carried a 30-year lease. Adverse environmental impact would have been minimal if the logging procedures had been strictly observed. Each of the concessions was divided into 30 plots; the concessionaires were to fell systematically only the large trees on one-year-per-plot basis whereby at the end of the lease, smaller trees in the initially logged plots would have grown enough for re-logging. But because of rampant corruption among forestry and other local officials, the scientific logging procedures were ignored.[12]

Selective logging and sustainable forestry have not been successful in the past; unfortunately, there is little hope that these scientific practices for the sound utilization of the forest resources can be successful in the future:

> Corruption, commercial pressures, the high rate of return expected on capital, the ravages of heavy machinery all make sustainable logging a pipedream. . . . The tragedy of the rain forests is that they are being managed neither in the traditional manner, by hunters and shifting cultivators making their livings from the forests without destroying them, nor by strong state forest agencies or large commercial companies willing and able to adopt strategies for the long-term management of a sustainable resource.[13]

In a last ditch effort to save the tropical forests, it has been suggested by environmental groups that the industrialized nations should simply refuse to import tropical hardwoods from areas that have been improperly logged. The suggestion has been strongly rejected by both exporting and importing companies.

Spokespersons for exporting countries argue that such a refusal would be an attack upon national sovereignty, upon nations' right to manage their own resources in their own way for their own interests. Delegates from exporting countries are occasionally willing to acknowledge political corruption as an element in wasteful forest exploitation, but they maintain that the overall results have been beneficial to them, if not to the world. Critics should recognize, they say, that harvesting the tropical rain forests creates rural jobs, increases export earnings and tax revenues, and provides the additional, cleared agricultural land needed for a growing population.

> I worry about the greenhouse effect too", says one of the Brazilian delegates to the ITTO (International Timber Trade Organization) meeting. But why is it the tropical forest countries that have to pay the price to try to do something about it. . . . Environmentalists are always talking about our moral duty, but our people can't live on moral duty.[14]

A Filipino professor, visiting a U.S. university told the case writer:

> Environmentalists from Western Europe, the United States, and Japan have already cut down their forests for economic development and to provide the land needed for agricultural use. Now they want to keep us from doing exactly the same thing.

Managers of importing companies maintain that they are not the cause of the problem. They are merely buying commodity products at market prices, thereby generating domestic employment and foreign exchange for the host countries, while providing needed products for retail and industrial consumers in their home countries.

Tropical Plywood Imports, Inc.[15] is an American importing company. It was recently formed in Seattle, Washington to import meranti plywood from Indonesia. Meranti is a tropical hardwood very similar to mahogany; it is a strong, dense wood without growth rings that can be cut into very thin veneer and then laminated into plywood sheets that are 1/4 inch thick. American softwoods such as Douglas fir and southern pine cannot be cut into such thin veneers because of growth rings. The veneer tears at the soft inner portion of the ring wood. Consequently all plywoods produced in the United States are a minimum of 3/8 inch thick. It would be possible to produce 1/4 inch plywood from the strong and dense American hardwoods, such as birch, maple, cherry or walnut, but those woods are very expensive, and are reserved for fine furniture.

The meranti plywood is ideal for concrete forms. It is much less costly than American plywood used for this purpose, in part because it is thinner and uses less wood and in part because it can more easily be sawn, drilled, and nailed without danger of splitting. Meranti plywood is also used in manufacturing kitchen cabinets and paneling for travel trailers and mobile homes.

Tropical Plywood Imports, Inc. sells approximately $375 million worth of meranti plywood annually to lumber yards and industrial firms throughout the U.S. In an interview with the local newspaper, the founder of the company was quoted as saying that

> Cutting the meranti trees helps provide jobs and income for the Indonesian people, as well as a useable product for the American market. The meranti trees have to be at least 20 inches in diameter, and the timber is harvested in a selective logging method in which smaller trees are left to be cut 35 years from now. Environmentalists disagree with us, of course; they say that you should let the large trees stay there and rot.

The founder admitted, however, that he had never visited the logging sites in Indonesia where the meranti was harvested; he relied upon assurances from the concessionaire and government officials.

NOTES

1. Or 62,500 square miles, equal to a block 250 miles on each side.
2. James Speth, Chairman of World Resource Institute, *The New York Times,* June 8, 1990, p A10.
3. Patrick Leahy, Chairman of the Agriculture Committee of the U.S. Senate, *The New York Times,* June 8, 1990, p A10.
4. Sara Oldfield, "The Tropical Chainsaw Massacre", *New Scientist,* September 23, 1989, p. 55.
5. The atmospheric concentration of CO_2 has risen about 30 percent since the 1850s. See "CO_2 Rise May Favor Trees Over Grassland," *The New York Times,* January 15, 1991.

6. *Futures,* October 1985, p. 451.
7. *Far Eastern Economic Review,* (November 24, 199, p. 50.
8. A metric surface measure equal to 2.471 acres.
9. Ibid, p. 49.
10. Ibid, p. 50.
11. *Far Eastern Economic Review,* January 12, 1989, p. 40.
12. The article continues to describe the actions by which the land, in essence, was denuded of all vegetation. Ibid, p.40.
13. *New Scientist,* Sept. 16, 1989, p. 43.
14. *Far Eastern Economic Review,* January 12, 1989, p. 41.
15. The company's name is disguised.

U.S. and Mexico Confront a Toxic Legacy

Colum Lynch
Writer and regular contributor to *The Boston Globe.*

Here at the Otay Mesa industrial park on the outskirts of Tijuana, subsidiaries of dozens of US corporations sit like a great industrial fortress overlooking Ejido Chilpancingo, a small working-class barrio situated in a valley near the Tijuana River.

Since the industrial park opened over a decade ago, residents of Ejido Chilpancingo say, they have been living in the shadow of a chemical nightmare. Their livestock feed on toxic waste, their air is often blackened by pollutants and their water supply has been fouled by a network of open drainage pipes that poke out over the town from a bluff beneath the industrial park. Its tenants include subsidiaries to such corporate giants as Mobil Oil and Pepsi and to American Optical Corp., a Southbridge, Mass.-based firm that manufactures lenses.

When rain falls upon Ejido Chilpancingo, plant workers release into drainage pipes stockpiled industrial detergents, solvents, heavy metals and petroleum products. The outflow empties into dozens of meandering creeks, rivulets and gulleys before emptying into a river where the town residents bathe.

Ultimately the contaminated waters reach the Rio Tijuana and then flow north back into the United States.

In February, when President George Bush visited Los Angeles and San Antonio to mobilize support for a North American Free Trade Agreement among the United States, Mexico and Canada, he argued that the agreement was the antidote to the environmental problems that afflict communities like Ejido Chilpancingo. By providing benefits to US corporations, he reasoned, the agreement would raise living standards for Mexicans and Americans alike, and "higher standards of living . . . will help people keep the air and water cleaner on both sides of the border."

The agreement has to be ratified by the US Congress, which is unlikely to deal with it until after the November elections.

To deal with the immediate problems, which will cost billions to clean up, Bush has proposed what he called an Integrated Border Plan and asked the US Congress to appropriate $250 million to fund a series of clean-up operations along the US side of the border. (The proposal is now before the House Appropriations Committee.) At the same time, President Carlos Salinas de Gortari promised to commit $460 million over the next three years for environmental clean-up and to improve Mexico's capacity to monitor rampant illegal chemical dumping by foreign corporations along his side of the border.

At Ejido Chilpancingo, where an experiment in free trade has already been going on for over a decade, residents say they can't wait for any benefits from a free trade agreement to trickle down into their community.

US, Japanese and Mexican corporations have already transformed their town into an environmental junk yard. From the Otay Mesa industrial park, poisonous plumes of black smoke rise from the industrial waste being illegally burned, emit-

The Boston Globe, June 15, 1992. Reprinted by permission.

ting an acrid odor of rubber and sulphur. The open-air grounds of a nearby factory are covered with a snowy layer of lead sulphate dust, a compound found in corroded batteries that attacks the central nervous system. Puddles of yellow water collect on the dirt roads of the town square.

Down the road from the square, Jose Juan de Vora, 11, sits wearily on the edge of the single bed in his small one-bedroom home. The boy fell sick months ago. Clumps of his hair have fallen out, a skin infection covered much of his body, and he no longer plays. A rash extends from the top of his ear to his cheekbone.

The boy's mother, Dona Rosa de Vora, 42, says her three grandaughters and many other children of Ejido Chilpancingo have been racked by similar ailments. She says a doctor believes the town's communal water, which often stings the skin upon touch, is responsible for the problems.

The foreign companies that have set up shop at Ejido Chilpancingo over the last 10 years are part of Mexico's *maquiladora* program. The program allows foreign companies to set up *maquiladoras,* or assembly plants, along a 65-mile corridor on the US-Mexico border, and to reap the benefits of low tariffs and cheap Mexican labor. It has drawn hundreds of US firms that manufacture everything from Barbie Dolls to parts for Patriot Missiles. It has also lured hundreds of thousands of Mexican laborers from the interior to take advantage of nearly 100 percent employment, and wages that exceed Mexico's $3 a day minimum.

Under Bush's Free Trade Agreement, towns like Ejido Chilpancingo would sprout up throughout Mexico.

No one is certain what impact the dumping and the fouled waters of Ejido Chilpancingo will ultimately have on the health of residents, but reports of a rare and fatal brain disease among newborns in Brownsville, Tex., which specialists suspect may be linked to pollution, has sent a chill the length of the 2,000-mile US-Mexico border.

A recent study of water samples taken by the Autonomous University of Baja California from one creek in Ejido Chilpancingo found dangerous levels of lead (more than 100 times acceptable levels), zinc, cadmium and chromium (commonly linked to some skin problems) in one stream that runs into the village.

A 1990 government study by Mexico's State Workers Institute of Social Security found that 16.4 percent of the community suffer from skin diseases, and 8.5 percent from respiratory ailments.

"They wouldn't do this in San Diego," thunders Maurilio Pachuca, a crafts merchant who has been organizing residents to stop the toxic dumping in his town. "Well, we're human beings, too!"

But the environmental damage created by industry in Otay Mesa doesn't stop at Ejido Chilpancingo.

On the US side of the border, Jesse Gomez, manager of the Effie May Organic Farm, grows cabbage, beets, carrots, lettuce and broccoli for American consumers on a 130-acre farm along the Rio Tijuana. When heavy rains flood the river, the contaminated water spreads over the land. Business is booming, though he worries that one day his crops will not meet environmental standards if the contamination isn't brought under control.

Gomez says his hopes lie in the construction of a monumental $200 million sewage treatment plant that will process 12 million gallons of raw sewage and toxic soup that run into the United States through the Rio Tijuana. The plant, which would be completed in 1995, is one of the cornerstones of the Bush administration's proposed solution to border pollution.

Some environmentalists say the sewage treatment plant won't solve Gomez's problems. "It's amazing how people in the US could ever feel safe when massive environmental contamination is happening on the other side of an imaginary political line," says Marco Kaltofen, an author of a study for the Boston-based National Toxic Campaign Fund on the impact of the *maquiladora* industry on water pollution along the border.

Kaltofen says sewage treatment plants cannot control the flow of industrial residues like petroleum, heavy metals and pesticides that pollute the Rio Tijuana. "The issue of toxic waste management has to be dealt with in the plants where the chemical waste originates," he says. Otherwise, "It's out the drain one day, on your dinner table in New York a week later," citing the movement of toxic chemicals from the factories into the food chain through farms along the Rio Tijuana.

The Integrated Environmental Plan, as the scheme is officially called, is designed to erect a line of defense against a number of polluted waterways like the Rio Tijuana that flow into the United States. The plan also includes $75 million to improve drinking water and sewage systems in the hundreds of shanty towns that have sprung up along the US side in the last decade. Another $50 million would finance limited air-pollution management, training for Mexican inspectors, and a system for tracking the movement of raw chemicals imported into Mexico for manufacturing purposes.

Under Mexican law, US manufacturers in Mexico are required to return imported raw chemical waste and solvents used in the manufacturing process in the nation of origin. Only a tiny percentage of the chemical waste, however, finds its way back to the United States. As in the Otay Mesa industrial park, much of it is simply poured down drains, dropped in clandestine garbage dumps or buried in canyons. The estimated cost of cleaning up the border area run as high as $9 billion.

J. Michael McCloskey, chairman of the Sierra Club, calls the plan "short-sighted," because it confronts only the existing problem and fails to provide a long-term strategy for increasing funding as free trade extends throughout Mexico.

He also said the plan lacks an "action-forcing mechanism" to require industry to comply with Mexican or US environmental laws. Mexico has a notoriously poor track record on environmental enforcement. And so far, the US Environmental Protection Agency has only asked manufacturers to take voluntary steps to contain illegal dumping and to reduce the use of toxic materials.

According to Kaltofen, who led the water pollution study, the EPA has refused to sanction US corporate dumpers or even to acknowledge the extent of the US corporations' role in creating a toxic waste disaster zone along the border. The EPA, he says, treats pollution as a "made in Mexico" problem.

EPA spokesman Luke Hester acknowledges that border pollution is a "horrendous problem," and he says Mexico is improving its standards daily. Mexico, he says, has doubled the number of border environmental inspectors to 200, and earlier this month the government shut down eight facilities for environmental violations. "We're not going to turn Mexico around overnight," he says, "but there is movement. There's progress."

Environmentalists, meanwhile remain skeptical. Once a free trade agreement is signed, they fear President Bush will lose sight of his vision of a sound environment.

"What assurances," McCloskey asks, "do we have that all of these promises won't be quickly forgotten?"

The Project at Moza Island

John A. Seeger
Balachandran Manyadath
Seeger—Professor of Management, Bentley College
Manyadath—Deputy General Manager, Voltas International LTD, Abu Dhabi

Sameer had just finished a marathon four-hour meeting with Gulf Sargam's General Manager, Joe Fernandes. The meeting had proved, as expected, inconclusive. In his own matter-of-fact and dry manner, Joe had pointed out the magnitude of the loss on the project. A loss this size would wipe out the limited capital of the firm. It would also adversely affect future relations with Bank of Arabia. Worst of all, it would threaten the very existence of the firm. There was no choice but to negotiate for the release of the impounded funds.

Sameer Mustafa did not blame Joe for thinking the way he did. Nor did he blame his partner,

---

Events portrayed in this case have been reproduced faithfully, without change. All names and locations have been disguised, with the knowledge and cooperation of the major companies involved.

Nawab, the Director and Chief Executive (D&CE) of Sargam International. (Figure 1 shows the relationships of the firms.) Nawab had called three times during the last 24 hours, urging Sameer to consider the issue carefully in view of the serious long term effects on the joint venture. Sameer Mustafa shared all the apprehensions. Yet he knew that his role demanded that he look at the issue more broadly. And he strongly believed that inherent values were as important to a company as the necessity to conduct business profitably and increase the wealth of the owners.

COMPANY BACKGROUND

Sameer Mustafa was a Palestinian national with a Jordanian passport and a business degree from the University of Texas. He had extensive connections with the government officials and businessmen in the East Arabian Sultanate, and his Gulf Trading Company had formed joint ventures with several leading multinational firms.

In 1948 Sohsee Brothers, Switzerland, and Sorabhjee Group, India, had joined together to form Sargam International Ltd., one of the ten largest multinational corporations in India. The company specialized in building large turn-key construction projects and had successfully completed many contracts in India, Africa, Southeast Asia and the Middle East. It employed 12,000 people, had 115 offices (108 of them in India), and in 1984 had sales revenues of $700 million (US). Sohese Brothers and Sorabhjee Group still owned 40 percent of the shares of the company, the balance being held by the Indian public.

THE JOINT VENTURE

The salient features of the joint-ventures agreement between Gulf Trading Company and Sargam International were simple:

> 51 percent of Gulf Sargam's capital would be contributed by Gulf Trading Company and 49 percent by Sargam International. Total initial capital was Riyal (R)1,200,000.
>
> Gulf Trading Company would use its good offices to secure contracts from the Government and private firms in East Arabia. It would also arrange for bank facilities for the execution of large projects. Guarantees against such facilities would be provided by Sameer Mustafa in his capacity as the Owner of Gulf Trading Company (Exhibit 1 defines the nature of the guarantees).
>
> Sargam International would operate the joint venture and it would send one of its managers from India for this purpose. All other technical, administrative and support staff would also be provided by Sargam International.
>
> Gulf Trading Company and Sargam International would share profits in the ratio of 55 percent for Gulf, to 45 percent for Sargam International. Losses, if any, would be equally shared.

ORGANIZATION

Joe Fernandes was the first General Manager of Gulf Sargam. A native of Goa, India (an area once claimed by Portugal), he was an engineer by profession. Joe had joined Sargam International in 1974 and had quickly climbed into middle management ranks. His outstanding performance on several complex construction projects made him the unanimous choice to head the new Middle Eastern joint venture.

At Gulf Sargam, Joe's technical and management staff—all from Sargam International—consisted of five field engineers, one financial analyst, and an administrative officer. All other hiring was done locally. Joe had extensive authority and powers for day-to-day operations of the firm, but he had to get the consent of Sameer Mustafa for "non-routine" decisions.

Four divisions reported to Joe Fernandes in 1986. The largest was Construction, which installed mechanical equipment for heating, ventilating and air conditioning (HVAC) as required by contract specifications. Sargam International held the exclusive area licenses for several world-wide brands of this heavy equipment. A separate Service division provided ongoing maintenance of HVAC equipment and serviced elevators and fire alarm systems. An Electrical division constructed and maintained electrical switchgear, transformers, transmission lines and equipment. A small Finance and Administration division completed the organization. Although total employment fluctuated with contracts, Gulf Sargam typically employed 300 to 400 people.

THE ECONOMIC ENVIRONMENT

The economies of the Middle East countries witnessed unprecedented growth during the oil boom period of the 1970's. But beginning in 1980 most of these countries experienced a glut of oil as demand for petroleum leveled off or declined. Their people realized the good times were far behind them. East Arabia was no exception. With the sharp drop in oil prices and the quota imposed by the Organization of Petroleum Exporting Countries (OPEC), the Government's revenues fell sharply, and its development construction activity dropped to 15 percent of the level sustained in the 1970's. For the few new construction projects that were brought to market for bids, competition was intense. A study undertaken by the Sultanate government during this period indicated that competition and the scarcity of business forced firms to accept contracts with margins as low as five to seven percent. Joe Fernandes reported to Sargam International:

> We have no choice in this matter. With a staff of over 250 people, we need projects to keep our people busy, to cover our overhead expenses, and to at least make a nominal profit for our partners. If we refuse to participate in such projects because of low margins, we would be without work and the cash reserves that we currently possess may carry us through only four months. You may say that this is not a healthy situation but we know that better times are ahead and we have to survive to make substantial profits in the future.

Between 1980 and 1983 Sargam won and completed several projects. Most of them were at very low margins, but through effective control and the dedication of its engineers, it was able to make nominal profits for the two partners. In the summer, 1984, however, the picture changed dramatically.

THE DEVELOPMENT PROJECT AT MOZA ISLAND

In June 1983, the Government decided to modernize the living facilities on Moza, an island 150 miles to the southeast of Abu Sidar, where the country's major liquified petroleum gas (LPG) plants were located. Moza was critically important to the Sultanate's income, but the harsh living conditions there and the primitive state of employee living quarters made it nearly impossible to attract good workers. Modernization was essential.

Moza was a contractor's nightmare. The island could only be accessed by air, flying time from Abu Sidar was one hour. In summer, temperatures averaged around 130°F and relative humidity rarely dropped below 95 percent. The air was severely polluted through minor but constant gas leaks, and reeked of hydrogen sulfide (the smell of rotten eggs). Government regulations therefore specified that the maximum "ON" period on the island for any worker should not exceed 12 weeks. Sandstorms were common during the nine summer months and the combination of temperature, humidity, and gas made the island one of the most difficult places in the world for heavy construction.

The East Arabian Sultanate invited bids from international construction firms in early 1983, and in September the contract for the Moza Island Project was awarded, at a price of R100,000,000, to Al Hasker Contracting Company, a Lebanese organization based in Athens. Hasker, primarily a civil engineering contractor, in turn, awarded various subcontracts to local firms in good standing. In April 1984, Gulf Sargam was awarded the mechanical subcontract at a price of R11,000,000—almost ten times the company's original capital. Joe Fernandes recalled:

> Both Sameer Mustafa and Nawab were unhappy over the low margin—only R1,000,000 estimated profit on the project. Nawab in particular felt that the margin was dangerously low for a project spanning 18 months at a remote location. He saw that a large portion of the contract value involved equipment from European sources, and that exchange rate variations would constitute a potent risk. But I convinced them that it was easier for the Company to execute one

large project and earn R1,000,000 than to derive the same benefit from several smaller projects, each of a different type.

To supervise the construction job, the Government employed a prominent consulting firm with offices throughout the Middle East, called Yusuf al Yusuf. This firm in turn appointed Habib Sharif as Engineer-in-Charge and in May 1984, Sharif moved to Moza with his six field engineers. (Yusuf al Yusuf was affiliated with a London consulting firm; several of the supervising engineers were British.)

The contract documents stated that the Engineer-in-Charge was the final authority on every aspect of the project including, but not limited to, approvals of equipment, approval of finished work, approval of variation claims, issue of change orders, interpretation of delays, and grants of extension period. Because the client was the Government of the East Arabian Sultanate, disagreements between contractors and the Engineer-in-Charge could be resolved only by a complex civil arbitration system administered by the government in Abu Sidar.

Joe Fernandes selected Raghu Menon to serve as Moza Island Project Manager for Gulf Sargam. The two men had been associated on several previous projects and Joe knew Raghu as a dedicated, competent, and friendly individual, who got along well with supervising authorities. A good relationship with the Engineer-in-Charge was a necessity on such large projects.

EXECUTION OF THE MOZA ISLAND CONTRACT

From the beginning, Raghu noticed that Habib Sharif often went out of his way to strictly enforce the contract specifications on Gulf Sargam, but not on Al Hasker Construction Company. All construction contracts, by their nature, contain clauses with ambiguous meanings, open to various interpretations; the Moza Island contract was no exception. In normal practice, a contractor would win a favorable interpretation in some of these cases, and would lose in others.

At Moza Island, however, Habib consistently interpreted these clauses to the advantage of the East Arabian Sultanate government, insisting on absolute compliance with the smallest details. Construction drawings, for example, were routinely delayed and then returned for correction of flaws so minute they would not be noticed in normal practice (an example might be a misspelled word like "refrigeration"). In defense, Raghu filed claims for reimbursement of the additional costs Gulf Sargam was forced to pay.

Raghu's weekly report to his head office during this first three months of the Moza Island project regularly reported Habib's attitude of extreme tolerance with Al Hasker Contracting Company and extreme intolerance with Gulf Sargam. His report on the episode of the X-ray welder provided an example:

> On August 4, 1984, our X-ray welder failed the welding test, even though photographs taken on a sample of 60 welds indicated 100 percent finishes. I was furious but helpless. The contract specifies that the British "Code of Welding Practice" sets our standards, and the Code defines the characteristics of both a perfect weld and a perfect workman. An acceptable workman must have basic communication skills in order to handle emergency situations. Habib argued that our worker lacked communication skills, and shut down the job.
>
> Our man had superb technical skills and was fluent in two languages—Hindi and Malayalam (the native tongue of Kerala province in India)—and he could converse in English too. But not well enough to suit Habib in August. We had to fly in a substitute welder. A month later we put the original man through the test again and he passed.

There was no comment about the welder from Habib Sharif, but in Raghu's eyes, a familiar picture was unfolding. Most construction consultants in the region expected to gain personally from their work, but none would ask an outright bribe. The consultant normally initiated the move with subtle "feelers" and awaited responses from the contractor. If a favorable response did not materialize, stronger signals were sent—each signal causing more disruption to the contractor's work than the earlier one. Raghu had faced this situation in several earlier projects and had, through a combination of diplomacy and skill, survived each situation. Sameer Mustafa had strong feelings on the subject:

> The fact that gratuities are often paid in the Middle East does not make it right to pay them. The practice exists because people—very often foreign corporations—pay when they are asked. There is no law saying you must pay. Taking part in a corrupt system is immoral and it perpetuates the corruption. Giving in now would set a precedent for all my other operations.
>
> Habib Shamir is playing a game with us. As always, we must make it clear we don't play by those rules. If we hold fast, the man will see we mean it. He will come around.

The game was a nightmare for Raghu. By June 1985, Gulf Sargam had incurred costs on an additional 9,000 man-hours due to delays in approval of drawings and rejection of site work by Yusuf al Yusuf. Gulf Sargam had filed variation claims totalling R1,000,000 but not a single one had been approved.

By early 1986, the game was still in progress. The delays imposed on Gulf Sargam had slowed the entire Moza Island project, but Habib had not wavered. Joe recalled Raghu's 80th progress report from the site, as the project neared conclusion:

> We are 6 months behind schedule and the situation is worsening every day. Habib rarely approves our work the first time. Al Hasker Contracting Company's approvals are granted from the office without Habib even visiting the job site. Last evening the space frame (a structure covering an indoor swimming pool, made of lightweight aluminum tubing) erected by Hasker between grids E-H and 21–26 came crashing down. Fortunately, no one was hurt. Habib attributed this mishap to metal fatigue not to Hasker's workmanship.
>
> Last night I met Habib at the club and decided to take him on directly as we must resolve this matter before the end of the project. Habib mentioned to me that Al Hasker Contracting Company has taken "good care" of him and he was accordingly reciprocating their gesture. He expressed surprise that Gulf Sargam had not followed the same policy for the last 12 months, a policy that was common in the Middle East and essential for the smooth execution of a project. But, he said, it was still not too late. He had authority to approve variation claims up to a total of R3,000,000 and Gulf Sargam could still make a profit. The cost of this consideration would be R300,000—10 percent of the claims approved for payment.

Habib Sharif argued that, as Engineer-in-Charge on the job, he had every right to enforce the spirit of the contract agreement on Gulf Sargam. He was only, logically, executing his responsibilities in the fullest sense. The firm had bid on the project on the basis of the specifications. They were given an opportunity to review every single part of the contract prior to acceptance and award of the bid. Gulf Sargam's price to his client was based on full knowledge of the job's terms and conditions, and should have allowed for all nuances; after all, the practice of providing gratuities to consultants was hardly new. If the company now wanted "softer" terms, to increase its profits, it was only reasonable to expect that they part with a small portion of the added reward. The government had budgeted a 20 percent increase in contract value, and to allow for change orders and variation claims from contractors, so the funds were available for disbursement, provided Habib, too, shared in the benefits.

Raghu Menon reported on his response to this argument:

> I repeated our company's policy on such financial arrangements, but said I would relay Habib's information to higher authorities. Then I asked how we could be sure he really had the power to deliver. This morning, Habib approved one of my claims—the most dubious one of them all—for R77,000. He has the power.
>
> . . . I am tired and would like to return to India. You cannot match knowledge and expertise with corruption and greed. I suggest that Sameer and you should think over this matter carefully.

CONCLUDING THE MOZA ISLAND PROJECT

On the last day of Ramadam, June 1986, Sameer-Mustafa read Joe's internal memo several times.

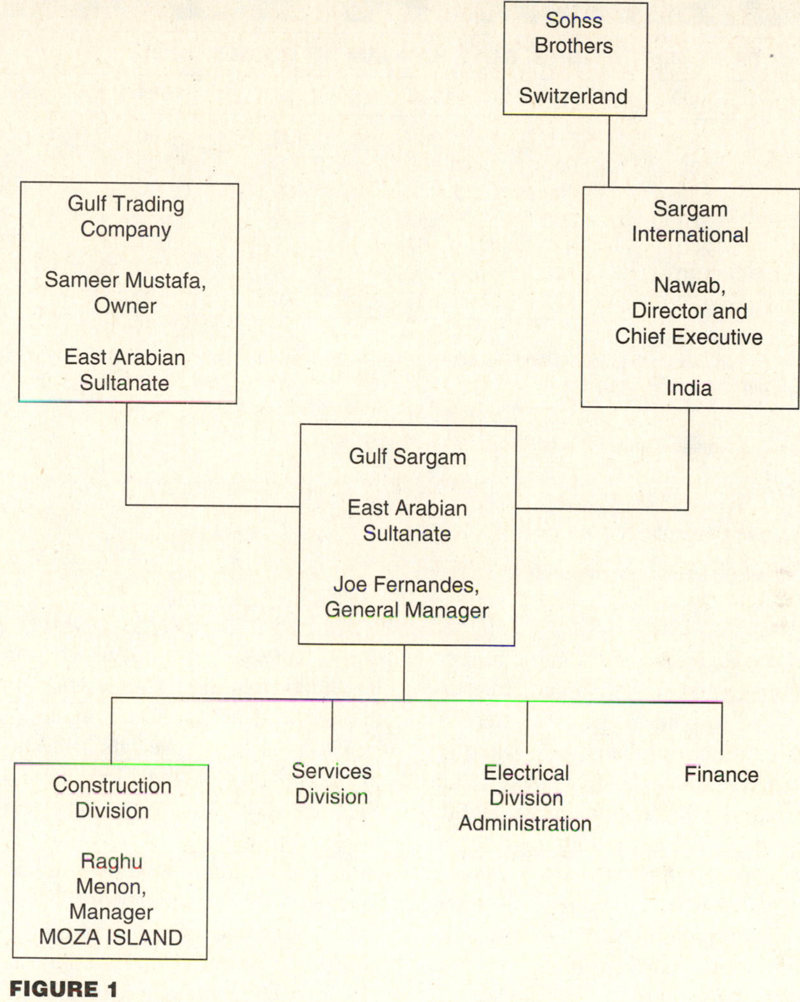

FIGURE 1
Organization of Gulf System

The final scenario was frightening. The Moza Island contract had been completed six months behind schedule, and the firm was exposed to the possibility that Habib could impose the contract's penalty clause. At ten percent of the contract's total value, that would add another R1,100,000 to Gulf Sargam's losses. Even without the penalty, the net loss was R2,138,000 as against an estimated profit of R1,000,000. Variation claims on the client totalled R2,860,000 and only a single one had been approved. Raghu had suffered from exhaustion and had returned to India a month earlier. His last progress report had been appended to Joe's memo, with a copy marked for Nawab:

> You have to decide on the variation claims before Habib finalizes the contract on June 30. I feel that we are in a hopeless position and we must accede to his request in order to recover our losses. Bear in mind that after this date we can pursue our claims only in the Abu Sidar arbitration committee, and I hope you will appreciate that we would be against the Government. Secondly Habib has, at this stage, every right to impose the penalty clause.

EXHIBIT 1

FINANCIAL RESULTS OF OPERATIONS, GULF SARGAM (IN RIYALS[a] 000)

	1980	1981	1982	1983	1984	1985	1986
Sales (Projects)	20	500	1,000	1,400	1,900	12,000[b]	6,000
Sales (Services)	500	600	1,800	2,000	1,800	2000	2,500
Sales (Total)	520	1,100	2,800	3,400	3,700	14,000	8,500
Cost of Sales[c]	320	503	1,643	1,830	2,070	11,470	6,300
Gross Margin	200	597	1,157	1,570	1,630	2,570	2,300
O & A	100	366	800	1,050	1,100	2,000	2,200
Net Profit	100	231	357	520	530	570	100

[a]Exchange rate 3.7 Riyals per U.S. dollar.
[b]Includes Rys 11,000,000 revenue from the Moza Island Project—Booked in 1985 with the concurrence of the auditors for Gulf Trading Co. and Gulf Sargam (a "Big Eight" CPA firm).
[c]Includes cost of goods sold for both projects and services.

Note: Personal Financial Guarantees Given by Sameer Mustafa (in Riyals)

1. Bank overdraft facilities (open line of credit)	3,000,000
2. Letter of credit (guarantees payment for goods received)	2,000,000
3. Tender guarantees (bid bond, forfeited if job not completed)	3,000,000

Joe fully endorsed Raghu's views on the matter. He added that as an employee of Sargam International he was obliged to take all possible steps to avoid losses to his parent company and, since all other avenues were exhausted, he believed that Sameer should endorse the payment to Habib. Sameer's partner, the D&CE of Sargam International, also had a point of view. Nawab's telephone calls had pointed out the Indian government's interest in the performance of joint ventures; financial results were monitored regularly, and a loss of this size would be difficult to explain. While Sameer was a single owner, answering to no one, Nawab had important shareholders who would insist on knowing the details of Gulf Sargam's performance.

Sameer paused and shook his head. The decision was made. He picked up the telephone to summon Joe back to his office.

THE PROJECT AT MOZA ISLAND (B)

Sameer Mustafa held firm. The principle was clear, he said. If he succumbed to the pressure of a blackmailer at Moza Island, which was a relatively small part of his holdings in Gulf Trading Company, then the precedent would be set for all his divisions, and for all his managers. He might say it was "just this once," but every employee who ever faced a similar situation in the future would know he had given in once, and so might do it again.

Gulf Sargam closed its 1987 books with a loss of R2,233,000 on the Moza Island project. Habib Shamir invoked the penalty clause, but Gulf Sargam fought it successfully through the Abu Sidar arbitration procedure. Gulf Sargam also filed claims against the client for R2,300,000, for excess costs on work carried out under duress, beyond the contract's terms. The East Arabian arbitrator allowed R220,000 as reasonable, after a long and costly legal battle. The rest of the claims were dismissed as unsupported.

Gulf Sargam never fully recovered, but continued in business through 1990, earning enough to pay the interest on funds it borrowed to replenish its working capital after the loss. Relations between Sameer Mustafa and his partner Nawab were strained, however, and in mid-1988 Sameer sold Gulf Trading Company to a prominent East Arabian citizen and emigrated to Jordan. Raghu resigned to start a small consulting firm with some close associates. In July 1989, Joe Fernandes tendered his resignation from Gulf Sargam, feeling his future with the firm was limited. Nawab, however, refused to accept the resignation.

PART FIVE

THE FUTURE CORPORATE ETHOS

In earlier parts of the text we explored some of the most important dilemmas faced by American business today. In the final part we reflect on some of the issues raised, and look toward the future of the American corporation. In particular, we wish to ask how the business organization of the future will meet the ethical challenges posed to it by society. Its ability to meet these challenges could prove crucial for business' very survival.

Observers of business sometimes speak as if business had no normative role to play in society, but this view is misleading. The legitimacy of business—the public's acceptance of its right to exist and its belief in the "rightness" of business as an institution—has always rested on business' connection with our highest social values and on its perceived contribution to what we view as the good life or the good society. While business has been essentially a profit-making institution, society has encouraged business to strive for profits in the belief that its doing so would promote the general welfare. Maximizing profits, then, has been the way in which business has discharged its social responsibilities. The "invisible hand" of the market system, it has been assumed, would function automatically to harmonize self-interest and bring about the good of society as a whole. And indeed business has made enormous contributions to American society. It has supported fundamental social values such as freedom of opportunity, productivity, growth, efficiency, and material well-being. It has encouraged enterprise and creativity. No society has a higher standard of living or such an abundance of goods and services.

The legitimacy of business still rests on public confidence in its contribution to a good society. In the past two decades, however, this confidence has eroded, and our conception of a good society has undergone some transformation. Observers of the American scene have concluded that business could be facing a genuine crisis in legitimacy.

Increasingly, people are challenging the belief that economic well-being is identical with social well-being, or that the former leads automatically to the latter. On the contrary, many now feel that some of the same values which contributed to our economic success—

growth, productivity, consumption, the profit motive—have led to unacceptably high social costs, such as environmental damage. Many Americans have lost confidence in the ability of the market system automatically to bring about the general welfare. Rather than encouraging business in the single-minded pursuit of profit and waiting for social well-being to follow, the public is demanding that business broaden the scope of its concerns and assume a more active role in solving social problems and in working for a good society. The social responsibility of business today, the American public seems to be saying, no longer ends with its economic responsibility.

The view that business should assume social as well as economic responsibilities and take an active role in working toward social goals represents a challenge to the traditional understanding of the nature and functions of business. As we have worked through this text, we have seen the impact of this challenge in nearly every aspect of business activity. Traditionally, business organizations have been understood to be the private property of their shareholders. Managers were viewed as agents of the shareholders, bound by an agreement to serve their interests as the shareholders themselves would serve them—which, presumably, was to make a profit. As we have seen, however, the increasing separation or ownership and control and the decreasing confidence in the market system to contribute to public welfare have undermined the idea that management's sole responsibility is to shareholders.

Business is now expected to exercise responsibility toward a range of "stakeholders," including consumers, employees, and the public at large. For example, society now expects corporations not only to supply goods to consumers, but also to exercise care and foresight to make sure that the product is safe for consumer use. Manufacturers' liability for defective products has been extended to include even situations in which manufacturers could not have foreseen and prevented accidents. Society now demands that business avoid undue pollution and depletion of natural resources, and that it operate as much as possible in harmony with the natural environment. Business has been asked not simply to invest where it is most profitable, but to be sensitive to the social consequences of investment and to use its economic power to alleviate social injustice. It is expected not merely to provide jobs for members of the community, but also to offer a safe, healthy, and fulfilling work environment. Many thinkers have called for restrictions on the corporation's freedom to hire and fire, and on the obedience and loyalty it demands from its employees. Increasingly, business organizations are being asked to adopt hiring policies which help solve problems of racism and sexism. As the duties of business organizations are broadened to include social responsibilities, employees who resist or reveal illegal or unethical acts on the part of their employers may in fact be acting in the best interests to the corporation.

Many of the responsibilities corporations are being asked to assume are duties which, until now, have been associated with government. Traditionally, it has been government's job to promote social welfare. The job of business was to make money. Ironically, the government has also been expected to keep its interference with business at a minimum, passing only those regulations necessary to preserve freedom of competition. As public dissatisfaction with business performance has increased, however, the relationship between business and government has shifted. Business is now subject to a multiplicity of "social regulations," many of which it feels are unfair and unnecessary. The restrictions placed on business by these regulations constitute a powerful argument for complying voluntarily with society's new demands.

How is business to respond effectively to public expectations, however, when institutional attitudes and forces encourage corporate managers to place profits first? Often today's manager is rewarded with success and esteem not for cutting down on the pollution of a local river or for improving employee satisfaction, but for maximizing profits. Indeed, as we have seen in many of the cases included in the text, pressures to sacrifice ethical concerns to profits are often severe. The corporation can create a closed context in which behavior that might be condemned elsewhere is found acceptable.

However, this need not be the case. Corporations can take steps to encourage ethical behavior by individuals and enhance an ethical corporate culture. In the first article in this section, "A Blueprint for Corporate Ethical Development," W. Michael Hoffman discusses some of these steps. He argues that corporations should address issues of institutional integrity as well as individual integrity. He points out that individuals do not operate in a vacuum; they gain purpose, meaning and direction from the organizations to which they belong. The social and ethical culture of a corporation can have a profound influence on persons who work for the corporation. Consequently, Hoffman argues, ethical people can be corrupted by bad organizations, just as people with questionable integrity can be uplifted by good ones.

One reason corporations should build ethical cultures is that it is in their self-interest to do so. As Hoffman points out, the costs of unethical business activity are often very high. However, "good ethics is good business" is not the only or the most important reason for building corporate cultures. The most important reason is that we are ethically required to adopt the ethical point of view in all our dealings with other people. Business is no exception to this rule. Sometimes ethical behavior may be expensive. There is no assurance that it will always be cost free. But this is the price, Hoffman says, of maintaining integrity.

A vital component of an ethical corporate culture, Hoffman says, is a code of ethics. Yet it is not enough to merely have a code; it must be integrated into the corporate culture and become a part of the way the company does business. Otherwise it is just another piece of paper to file away and forget. One way to make the code a living document, he continues, is to establish the position of ethics officer, or appoint an ethics committee, to oversee and enforce the code, and to begin ethics training programs for all employees, including those at the top of the corporation. Finally, ethics audits are a valuable tool for identifying and rewarding ethically responsible performance, and for discovering those areas of the corporation where more attention is needed. It is all of these things working together that make up an ethical corporate culture.

Some of the details of putting together a good corporate code are discussed by Lisa Newton in her article, "The Many Faces of the Corporate Code." She points out that interest in corporate codes seems to be increasing. Although, she says, nothing can force people to be moral if they are determined to act otherwise, corporate codes can serve a valuable function for corporations. If properly designed and implemented, written codes reinforce the intention to be ethical, and serve as a reminder and guide for corporate executives who face complex decisions involving the interests of many constituencies.

Successful codes, Newton argues, have three characteristics. The first is that as many employees as possible are included in drafting the code. Codes that are the product of a few people in offices remote from day-to-day work life are not likely to be relevant to the situations most employees face, and thus will not be useful. The second characteristic is that the code must not be the idiosyncratic statement of top management. It must be consistent with generally accepted principle of good ethics, and its provisions must be defended by good arguments. Finally, all levels of management, especially top management, must be committed to following the code. Without the support and compliance of upper management the code is doomed to be put in a bottom drawer and never looked at again. If all of this is done, and if the corporation is committed to taking its status as a moral agent seriously, then a code of ethics can provide an invaluable ethical context for corporate employees by outlining a "moral minimum" that all employees are expected to follow.

If a corporation follows the advice given by Newton and Hoffman, then it will invest a great deal of time and energy in building an ethical corporate culture. Is it possible for a company to spend too much time and effort on ethics? Can the effort to be ethical have bad consequences? This is one of the questions Andrew Singer investigates in his article "Can a Company be too Ethical?" Singer notes that there is a narrower and broader sense of "ethics" as it applies to corporations. The narrower sense covers issues such as bribe taking, theft, and sexual harassment—all of which are clearly prohibited by most people's idea of ethics. In the broader sense, ethics includes issues such as affirmative action, empowering workers, and hiring the hardcore unemployed. It is this sense of "ethics," Singer says, that some corporate executives find problematic. The reason, these executives argue, is that such practices are more harmful to business than helpful. Often they have direct or indirect costs that detract from profits. The best place to be, some claim, is in the middle somewhere—neither too unethical nor too ethical.

An example of a company that may have been too ethical, according to Singer, is Control Data Corporation. Some analysts feel that Control Data devoted too many resources to socially responsible projects, and that this was a major factor in the declining fortunes of the company. There is, according to some of the people quoted in Singer's article, an ethical side of business and a profit side, and the two have to be balanced. If this is correct, however, it seems that becoming ethical is a business decision like any other—one is ethical as long as it is to one's benefit. When being ethical ceases to be beneficial, then ethics are discarded. Neither Newton nor Hoffman would find this view congenial.

Nor would the author of the final article, Norman Bowie. The orthodox view, Bowie says, is that corporations should pursue profit while respecting a moral minimum below which it is unacceptable to operate. This is the view expressed by a number of people quoted in Singer's article. Bowie concedes that he was once an advocate of this position, but that now he thinks it is mistaken. Part of what it means to be a corporation, he now believes, is to cooperate with other corporations and government agencies to help solve social problems.

Bowie's basic argument is that profit should not be the goal of the firm; rather, profit is a byproduct of other goals, such as providing meaningful work for employees. By acting altruistically, he believes, corporations can create a "moral community" in which the moral commitments between the corporation and its various stakeholders are reciprocal—just as the corporation is committed to treat all stakeholders fairly, so stakeholders are committed to the welfare of the corporation.

If we accept Bowie's argument that profit should be a byproduct of other corporate goals, and that ethical relations between the corporation and its stakeholders impose duties on each of them, then we must abandon the traditional idea of the corporation as a purely economic institution. Corporations, on this view, are as much instruments of social policy and change as they are centers for producing and distributing economic goods. If this is the future of the corporation, or if it ought to be, then ethics and the implications of ethics for corporate actions will play as central a role in business in the years to come as profit has played in the past.

CHAPTER 13

REFLECTIONS ON THE MORAL CORPORATION

A Blueprint For Corporate Ethical Development

W. Michael Hoffman
Executive Director, Center for Business Ethics, Bentley College

My father was an architectural engineer. When I was a boy I remember climbing up along side him at his drafting table and asking about the intricate white lines and figures drawn on intriguing blue papers. He told me they were blueprints he designed to give him a detailed plan for building something. When I went with him to the job and saw the concrete being poured and the frame of the building being erected, I watched my father constantly checking his blueprints. As a boy it seemed like magic that the building which I could walk around in and play in had somehow sprung out of those blueprints. But I knew it had and that they were important. Lessons of a father should not be lost on his son. Therefore, this address is based on the belief that in building a moral corporate culture an appropriate blueprint is no less important.

INDIVIDUAL AND INSTITUTIONAL INTEGRITY

With the exception of a few exemplary corporations I think it is safe to say that businesses have paid very little attention to developing ethical environments—at least until quite recently. Part of the reason for this I suspect is the belief that ethics is just an individual matter of personal integrity. Therefore, if corporations hire good people this will result in a good company. Furthermore, corporate wrongdoing happens because certain individuals commit wrongful acts; hence we should focus our attention on developing individual integrity which will then lead to corporate integrity.

There is truth to this claim—corporations act on the basis of decisions made by individuals and cannot be ethical unless the people who comprise them are ethical. However, this position overlooks the essential dynamics and reciprocity between individuals and organizations. Individuals do not oper-

Revised version of an article appearing in E.J. Trunflo, B.C. Auday, and M.A. Reid (eds.), *Developing Moral Corporate Cultures* (Wenham, MA: Gordon College Institute for Applied Ethics, 1992, pp. 37–59. Reprinted by permission of the author.

ate in a vacuum. Just as organizations are made up of individuals, individuals are dependent on organizations. Individuals gain meaning, direction, and purpose by belonging to and acting out of organizations, out of social cultures that are formed around common goals, shared beliefs, and collective duties. As the philosopher John Dewey has put it, "Apart from ties which bind (the individual) to others, (the individual) is nothing." Corporations, like other social organizations, can and do influence individual decisions and actions.

Corporations are social cultures with character—character that can exercise good or bad influences, depending on goals, policies, structures, strategies, and other characteristics that formalize relations among the individuals who make up corporations. Therefore, when a majority of managers of major corporations feel pressure to sacrifice their own personal ethical integrity for corporate goals, as several polls have shown, it is necessary and appropriate that business ethics direct its attention to issues of institutional integrity as well as individual integrity.

I am convinced that a major reason why we have witnessed outbreaks of corporate wrongdoing, recently as well as in the past, is not that business people are less ethical than others, but rather that business has given so little thought to developing a moral corporate culture within which individuals can act ethically. Causes of unethical actions are quite often systemic and not simply the result of rotten apples in the corporate barrel. Ethical people can be brought down by serving in a bad organization, just as people with questionable ethical integrity can be uplifted or at least held in check by serving in a good one. Corporations should examine themselves to see if their structures and relations, which systematically bind and move their employees, are compatible with ethical behavior. And if they are not, then certain steps ought to be taken to change or supplement them.

ETHICS INITIATIVES

Over the past decade many, if not most, corporations have begun to take ethics seriously. In a 1985 survey the Center for Business Ethics asked the *Fortune* 500 industrial and 500 service companies if they were taking any steps to incorporate ethical values into their organizations. Approximately 80 percent of the responding companies indicated that they were, with the goal of being a socially responsible corporation being listed more often than any other as the primary reason for building ethics into the organization. In a 1990 follow-up survey by the Center, 93 percent of the responding *Fortune* companies said they were taking such ethical steps. Furthermore, in the 1990 survey 50 percent responded that they were planning to expand their efforts compared to only 25 percent saying so in 1985. Cautiously generalizing on the surveys and based on my experience at the Center, I believe a truly significant number of attempts are underway to develop ethical corporations and that such attempts will continue to expand and mature.

However, the surveys also indicate that most of these corporate attempts need to go much further before they will be successful. For example, although 75 percent of the 1985 responding companies said they had written codes of ethics, only 14 percent had an ethics committee and only 5 percent had ethics officers. It is difficult to understand how codes can be overseen and enforced adequately without a committee or officer assigned to that task. Also, the communication of the codes seemed suspect. Largely this occurs through printed materials, and less than half the time through advice from a superior or in an entrance interview, and less than 20 percent of the time through a workshop or seminar designed for that purpose. The Center's 1990 survey does reveal some progress in these areas. Approximately 90 percent of the responding companies report having a written code of ethics and 32 percent say they have an ethics committee—more than doubling the report on ethics committees in 1985. Furthermore, 43 percent now report having workshops or seminars to communicate their ethics policies.

But, it seems clear that in most cases a proper blueprint for developing an ethical culture still is not part of corporate ethics initiatives. Writing a code of ethics, which seems to be the extent of most corporate ethics efforts, is an important first step toward building an ethical corporation, but it is just that—a first step. To be effective, it must be backed up by other kinds of support structures throughout the organization to insure its adequate communication, oversight, enforcement, adjudication, and review. And for this you need a blueprint, a plan for building, in this case the building of an ethical corporate culture, starting with the purpose or rationale of the project itself.

RATIONALE

What should be the proper rationale for a corporation's developing an ethical culture? First, let me answer this by saying that unethical business activity is certainly accompanied by enormous risks and costs. White-collar crime, such as embezzlement, bribery, stock manipulations, and antitrust violations, has been conservatively estimated to cost business and society between $50 to $100 billion annually. And fines and penalties run into the millions, as do liability suits filed against corporations. Dramatic examples include Drexel Burnham's fine of $650 million for insider trading and securities fraud, and Manville Corporation's liability suits by asbestos victims which could cost the company over half of its stock. These and other such unethical activities have led to the bankruptcy and downfall of such companies.

But this is only the beginning of the cost. Increased government regulation almost inevitably follows revealed corporate illegality and immorality. In 1980, the Business Roundtable reported that it cost business $100 billion yearly to comply with government regulations. This cost undoubtedly has risen over the past decade. Much of this, of course, is passed along to the consumers in the form of higher prices, but this still affects the outlook of business in its competitive position in the world market and in its ability to attract investors.

Another cost on which it is even more difficult to get clear estimates relates to the damage of a firm's public image resulting from an ethics scandal. This is a cost that is surely real, and perhaps even more economically damaging than any mentioned above. Consumers are becoming more and more sensitive and selective as to which companies they choose to deliver their goods and services. A poor public image also turns off many of today's investors. Moreover, if a company is burdened by public negativism and cynicism, this will surely lead to a hesitancy on the part of the best and the brightest in wanting to make that company their career choice. I suspect this is also true of business in general.

It seems to me then that one reason for corporations to build ethical cultures is that it is in their own self-interest to do so. Although it is impossible to totally prevent unscrupulous people from committing wrongful acts in any organization, nevertheless, by working toward the development of an ethical corporate climate I think we can lessen such acts and support and strengthen individual integrity. I see it along the lines of preventive medicine—a kind of ethical health maintenance organization. I am convinced most people want to do the right thing, just as they want to stay healthy. But in both cases proper awareness programs and guidelines must be developed to strengthen proper habits that are in one's own self-interest. Regular check-ups and follow-ups are also essential. In this way corporations have their best chance to maintain their ethical health and avoid the aforementioned costs.

Am I saying that good ethics is good business? Generally speaking, I do think this is the case, especially over the long run, and not just in terms of avoiding costs. It is true in terms of building an organization for which employees are proud to work, communities are happy to have as neighbors, and with which consumers and investors are confident to do business. An ethical company carries with it a sense of trust, and trust is what drives a successful business.

However, there is a real misconception and danger in basing a corporate ethics initiative on this good-ethics-is-good-business rationale. I am not saying that good ethics is not good business. In most cases I think it is. I am saying that it should not be advanced as the only or even the main reason for doing business ethically or for studying business ethics. The ethical thing to do may not always be in the best interests of the firm. And when the crunch comes, when ethics conflicts with the firm's interest, any ethics program that has not already faced up to this possibility is doomed to fail because it will undercut the rationale of the program itself. We should promote business ethics, not because good ethics is good business, but because we are ethically required to adopt the moral point of view in all our dealings with other people—and business is no exception. In business, as in all other human endeavors, we must be prepared to pay the costs of ethical behavior. The costs may sometimes seem high, but that is the risk we take in valuing and preserving our integrity.

ETHICS CODES

A blueprint for building a corporate moral culture must include a written ethics code. Some corporate codes of ethics are better than others. Of those with which I am familiar, some consist of just a set of specific rules, a list of dos and don'ts usually corresponding to clearly illegal or unethical actions such as bribery, price-fixing, conflicts of interest, improper use of company funds, improper accounting practices, and the acceptance of gifts. Other codes consist largely of general statements putting forth corporate goals and responsibilities, a kind of credo expressing the company's philosophy and values. The better codes consist of both. Rules of conduct without a general credo lack a framework of meaning and purpose; credos without rules of conduct lack specific content.

Codes of ethics also should not be written to imply that whatever is not strictly prohibited is thereby allowed. There is no way that all ethical or unethical conduct can be exhaustively listed and mandated through a code, nor ought to be. Business ethics, like all areas of ethics, has its grey areas that require individual discretion. A good corporate code of ethics should include certain managerial and employee guidelines for ethical decision making. Such guidelines might include the principles and factors that one ought to think about before arriving at a decision. They might include sources both inside and outside the corporation through which advice and counsel could be offered. They could even include cases based on history that might clarify a future ethical dilemma. Whatever these guidelines include, they should make one aware that there may very well be some difficult ethical judgements to make, for which one is accountable, that will have to be made from the spirit of the code, rather than from its letter. This will also place a greater sense of personal ethical responsibility on corporate employees and send a clear message that corporate integrity is in this way dependent on individual integrity.

But recognition of the importance of individual integrity and its accompanying responsibilities must be backed up by strong corporate support. The employee must believe that the corporation will stand behind individual decisions made in keeping with or out of respect for the ethics code. The code, therefore, should have clear support from the very top of the corporation, preferably from the board of directors. In fact, a corporate ethics committee should probably be chaired by a member of the board, or at least report directly to a member of the board. Equally important is that everyone in the corporation should be brought into efforts to develop the ethical corporation—including the ethics code. Unfortunately in most cases this does not happen. Ethics initiatives are strongly orientated toward upper management without much input or representation from lower level employees. A corporate code of ethics lacks overall effectiveness if it is simply handed down and run from on high, so to speak. Corporations must find ways for all their members to feel they have played and continue to play some role in the on-going design and maintenance of the code. The code, of course, will also lack effectiveness and meaning if no appropriately representative committee or board actually addresses employee concerns about the code or potential code violations.

A few blueprint guidelines for writing or redesigning an ethics code are as follows:

- Be clear about the objectives the code is intended to accomplish.
- Try to get support and ideas for the code from all levels of the organization.
- Be aware of the latest developments in the laws and regulations affecting your industry.
- Write as simply and clearly as possible. Be sure the code is legally defensible, but avoid legal jargon.

- Try to give reasons for the various provisions of the code.
- Devise a concrete program for communicating the code and for educating employees about the code and all programs designed to support it.
- Devise a concrete and responsible program for enforcing the code.
- Select competent persons to administer the code and give them the time and resources to get the job done.
- Make sure to provide for changing the code to meet new situations and challenges. Make it a living document by regularly scheduling reviews and reevaluations of all segments of the code and its supporting programs.

ETHICS OFFICERS AND COMMITTEES

Another essential part of the corporate moral culture blueprint consists of an ethics officer and an ethics committee. The ethics officer (EO) oversees the corporate ethics program and helps to steer the company around ethical pitfalls. Many corporations now have an EO, and the Center for Business Ethics is the facilitating institution for a newly formed organization of practicing EOs called the Ethics Officer Association (EOA). The EOA as of this date has 50 Sponsoring Partner companies. In a 1992 Center survey of *Fortune* 500 companies, one-third of the responding companies reported having an EO.

The EO position is so new that it will take some time before these EOs clearly define their role—the topic they spend most of their time in EOA forums discussing. Right now most are expected to be confessor, corporate conscience, investigator, enforcer, and teacher, all rolled into one. To successfully play out all of these various roles, while avoiding conflicts of interest and fitting into the established political structure of the organization, is a difficult task indeed and explains why all the EOs feel the need to begin networking with each other as they try to carve out their proper place in their companies.

All EOs seem to agree that there must be unequivocal and visible support from the top of the corporation for their efforts to be effective. They also must maintain a central position in the organization, having access to everyone in the company from top to bottom. As one EO noted, there is a real danger in becoming identified with upper management. When this happens they are less likely to be brought problems by the rank and file, thereby losing effectiveness. The EO must make sure all possible channels of communication are open in order to find out what is really going on in the company.

The EOs emphasize in their discussions that they must have direct and regular access to the highest levels of the organization, especially when policy and planning decisions are made. Corporate ethical decisions are rarely formed by a simple interpretation of the corporate code. Instead it usually requires a painstaking effort to analyze the general values and principles stated in the code and apply them to specific situations. An EO's responsibility is to help recognize a potential ethical problem that might be obscured by operational or financial considerations and lend expertise in dealing with it. The EOs agree that the toughest problems occur when the ethical conduct of upper management is in question. Therefore, it seems advisable for the EO to also have direct access to the board of directors.

There are many other issues relating to the EO position which need further discussion and refinement. For example, should the EO take only anonymous or nonanonymous calls, or both, in the hotline or reporting procedure? One company only takes anonymous calls and another only takes nonanonymous ones, but most take both. Should the EO get personally involved in investigating allegations of ethical misconduct and administering rewards and sanctions? Or should the EO allow others to conduct investigations and serve only to coordinate and oversee the process? Some do the former; others do the latter. How does the EO insure due process for the rights of the accused? It appears that most EOs do not have a solid handle on this. How does the EO interrelate with other corporate officers, such as legal, human resources, ombudspeople, when ethical issues inevitably spread into their turf? How does the EO avoid a "big brother is watching you" atmosphere, which is too sanction oriented, and create instead an ethical corporate culture which is positive and in which everyone takes pride? Although these questions have yet to be fully resolved with most EOs, the very fact that EOs are discussing them indicates to me that a healthy maturation of the EO position is taking place and that ethics is alive and growing in these companies.

I have often heard the argument that having an EO is a mistake because it gives the impression that ethics is compartmentalized in a certain office, thereby discouraging ethics from truly infiltrating throughout the organization. If ethics is seen to be the responsibility of one person or office, then other areas of the organization and employees generally will think that they don't have to build it into their own decision making. Those decisions will be made by the EO. Although I understand the concern at the base of this argument, it arises due to a misunderstanding of the role of the EO. One of the primary functions of the EO is to proactively encourage responsible ethical decision making throughout every facet of the organization and to promote programs to heighten the ethical awareness and the importance of ethics for all employees. Rather than a corporate guru spewing forth ethical edicts, the EO is a catalyst for corporate ethical thinking. It is the absence of such a catalyst that has impeded the development of corporate moral cultures.

Some companies might have an EO but no ethics committee (EC); others might have an EC but no EO. Our blueprint should include both, and each needs the other. An EO needs an EC from which to gain ideas, to aid in communication of the ethics program throughout the company, and to help assist in decision making and ethics policy review. An EC needs an EO to handle the day to day operations of the ethics program, serve as its spokesperson, and have access to the highest levels of management.

The Center's 1990 survey revealed that of the 32 percent that report having ECs, 70 to 80 percent review, update, and develop policy on ethics, and over half handle infractions of the code. I believe an EC ought to be representative of all levels of the organization in order to give an appropriate voice to all employees. These different voices are important for designing a truly relevant ethics program for the entire company and for making everyone feel he or she is truly a part in building and maintaining the ethical culture. Unfortunately the profile of ECs based on the Center's surveys shows that almost no ECs have members below the board or top management level. If this representative pattern of ECs is to continue to be the case, then EOs and ECs must find effective ways for all levels of the organization to have and perceive that they have a meaningful participatory role in establishing corporate ethics policy. But the Center's surveys show that less than half report that non-management employees have had any impact in the development of ethics policy. I perceive this to be a serious weakness in and challenge for the functions of the EOs and ECs—perhaps the two most fundamental building blocks for a corporate ethical culture blueprint.

ETHICS TRAINING

Another important element in our blueprint design is ethics training for corporate employees. Close to 50 percent of the responding companies in the Center's 1990 survey said they have such training, a 10 to 15 percent increase from the 1985 survey. And 43 percent have ethics workshops or seminars, more than doubling the 1985 response.

Having consulted with many major corporations, I am convinced that ethics seminars are important for a successful corporate ethics training program. Such seminars allow employees to dialogue with each other about the importance of business ethics and about ethics issues that specifically relate to their daily operations in the company. As with ethics codes, some ethics seminars are better than others. Many are not long enough to accomplish anything significant; many do not adequately prepare the participants in advance of the session; and many are not placed in a larger context of an overall corporate ethics development effort. As with any educational program, corporate ethics training seminars require sufficient time for presentation of issues and cases, discussion and debate, and follow-up sessions.

A few blueprint objectives for a corporate ethics seminar are as follows:

- To clarify the ethical values and enhance the ethical awareness of the corporation's employees.
- To uncover and investigate the ethical issues and concerns that directly relate to the corporation.
- To discuss criteria for ethical decision making within the corporation.
- To examine and enrich the structures, strategies, resources, policies, and goals which shape the ethical environments and guide the ethical activities of the corporation.

A corporate ethics seminar should help the participants to see or recognize ethical issues, especially those which may be overlooked if one is not looking for them. That is, such seminars should fit the participants with "moral glasses" through which they will see their world from a moral point of view. But *ethical awareness* is not enough.

Such seminars should also provide participants with some tools for rational ethical analysis and decision making. And further, there should be assistance in how to transfer such *ethical reasoning* into *ethical action* within the corporate context. Finally, such seminars should stress the importance of *ethical leadership* and role modeling. There are leaders at all levels of the organization, and it is difficult to know who might be looking to you to help set their moral compass. The characteristics of a community are shaped out of the dynamics of such role modeling. And a community's ethical character is no exception.

A successful ethics training program should include all levels of the corporation, not just upper and middle management. Much of the ethics training, however, focuses on management. In 1985 only 35 percent of those companies engaged in ethics training involved hourly workers. It is encouraging, at least to see this percentage increasing to 57 percent in 1990. Also, I believe ethics workshops should from time to time mix different levels of the corporation, from hourly workers to executive officers, to even members of the board, in order to promote better understanding and communication among all members of the organization with regard to the ethical problems and commitments of the firm. This, in turn, would build a stronger and more unified ethical corporate culture.

ETHICS AUDITS

Our blueprint should also include an ethics audit, a process for analyzing and measuring the firm's activities in a number of ethically sensitive areas. It makes little sense to implement answers to a company's ethical problems before making sure what the problems are. All the ethics officers I have talked to agree that some procedures need to be devised to determine areas of ethical strain and to provide indicators of how successful their efforts have been to build ethics into the organization.

Both the 1985 and 1990 Center surveys indicate that about 30 percent of the responding companies report having ethical audits in such ethically sensitive areas as equal opportunity employment, compliance, safety, quality of products, protection of the environment, and conduct in multinational operations. However, very little is known about these audits, partly because almost all of the companies reporting that they conduct them only disclose their results to senior executives or the board. Furthermore, the ethics officers don't seem to know much about them. Consequently, I doubt very much that these reported ethics audits are any real integrated part of the ethics programs overseen by corporate EOs. But they certainly should be, and I would argue that their results should be disseminated throughout the company and to the general public. The public not only has a right to know the ethical indicators of corporations who provide their goods and services, but assuming corporations are performing responsibly, it would seem they would improve their ethical image by widely disclosing such ethics audit information.

OTHER DESIGNS FOR AN ETHICAL BLUEPRINT

I have mentioned only some of the more important designs for a blueprint from which to build an ethical corporate culture. Other internal structural features should include the appropriate ethical role and make-up of the governance system—especially that of the board of directors, which is ultimately responsible for the ethical integrity of the firm. Many argue that boards have not understood or carried out their responsibilities to oversee and insure the ethical activities of their companies. Other questions arise concerning the number of inside directors to outside directors and their proper relationship to each other, and concerning the appropriateness of having the same directors serving on the boards of other companies, thereby creating potential conflicts of interest. At the very least our ethical blueprint should certainly include a direct reporting line from the EO and EC to the board, perhaps through a member of the board who is an outside director with specific responsibilities to oversee the ethical activities and climate of the corporation.

Changes also need to be made in the traditional reliance on hierarchical top-down chains of responsibility and decision making. Flatter organizations and bottom-up structures allow for increased responsibility and participatory decision making at lower levels in the organization. At all levels, or perhaps better said in all areas of the organization, ethical responsibilities and guidelines for ethical action should be clearly stated, communicated, and overseen with participation from all affected parties. And such responsibilities should be complemented by equally important statements of rights for all employees. Very few companies have moved toward worker participation in decision making and even fewer have developed bills of rights for employees. A specific threat to employee rights seems to be occurring when investigations of possible violations of corporate ethical policy are conducted without due process being granted to those being investigated. For example, the accused may not be told he or she is the target of such an investigation, may not be "mirandized" before questioning, and may not be allowed to know the source of the allegation. Ethics programs must be designed to insure that all steps taken in the name of ethics can themselves be ethically justified.

I learned from my father that you can't build a good building without a well-designed blueprint. But I also learned from my father that blueprints many times have to be changed depending on the specific problems that arise in the on-site construction. Learning how to adapt the blueprint to the needs that arise in the actual building process is a talent that must be acquired by a good architectural engineer through experience. It is also a talent that must be acquired by those building an ethical corporate culture.

Ideas for a corporate ethical blueprint can be suggested by others, as I have done. Outside construction advice can also be offered. Ultimately, however, this is a project that can only be done by the corporation itself, for it is a process of self-construction involving redevelopment and remodeling. But before the blueprint is designed and the job begins, the corporation must first decide that it needs and is willing to make the investment in the ethical building.

REFERENCES

For more detailed information on the Center for Business Ethics surveys see "Are Corporations Institutionalizing Ethics?" *Journal of Business Ethics,* Vol. 5, #2, April 1986, and "Instilling Ethical Values in Large Corporations." *Journal of Business Ethics,* Vol. 11, #11, November 1992.

For more information on the Center for Business Ethics ethics officer survey see "The Emerging Role of the Ethics Officer" by Judith Kamm, Associate Director of the Center for Business Ethics, *Ethikos,* January/February 1993.

Hoffman, W. Michael, Jennifer Mills Moore, and David A. Fedo, editors. *Corporate Governance and Institutionalizing Ethics: Proceedings of the Fifth National Conference on Business Ethics.* Lexington, Massachusetts: D.C. Heath and Company, 1984.

Hoffman, W. Michael. "Ethics are Good Business." *Business and Society Review,* Fall 1985.

Hoffman, W. Michael. "What is Necessary for Corporate Moral Excellence?" *Journal of Business Ethics,* Vol. 5, #3, June 1986.

Hoffman, W. Michael. "Developing the Ethical Corporation." *Bell Atlantic Quarterly,* Vol. III, #1, Spring 1986. ("A Blueprint for Corporate Ethical Development" is an update of this 1986 paper.)

The Many Faces of the Corporate Code

Lisa H. Newton
Director, Program in Applied Ethics, Fairfield University

INTRODUCTION

We seem to be in another of our code-writing phases. Interest in the development of corporate codes of ethics—by which term we encompass corporate Aspirations, Beliefs, Creeds, Guidelines and so on through the alphabet—has continued to rise since the 1970's, in tandem with the interest in the teaching and taking of ethics, in colleges and workplaces alike. In what follows, I take on some of the dominant themes in the codes of ethics literature, in an attempt to give a partial overview of the state of the art in the formulation of the corporate code.

The attempt turns out to be a study in multiple function. The much-recommended "corporate code of ethics" serves a diversity of functions, and must avoid a similar diversity of pitfalls. Some of these we will survey; to anticipate the end, we will discover that for maximum effectiveness and ethical validity, each code ought to meet three specifications:

1. In its *development and promulgation,* the code must enjoy the maximum participation of the officers and employees of the corporation (the principle of *participation*);
2. In its *content,* the code must be coherent with general ethical principles and the dictates of conscience (the principle of *validity*);
3. In its *implementation,* the code must be, and must be seen to be, coherent with the lived commitments of the company's officers (the principle of *authenticity*).

Found in *Institutionalizing Corporate Ethics Programs,* proceedings of the conference "Corporate Visions and Values," Fairfield University, November 1991, sponsored by the Connecticut Humanities Council and Wright Investors' Service of Bridgeport, CT. Reprinted by permission of the author.

CLEAR AND PRESENT NEED

Businesses ought to have codes of ethics, if for no other reason than to allay real doubts that businessmen are capable of morality at all. Leonard Brooks has recently taken note of the ". . . crisis of confidence about corporate activity. Many corporate representations or claims have low credibility, including those made regarding financial dealings and disclosure, environmental protection, health and safety disclosures related to both employees and customers, and questionable payments." That is quite a list of things to be distrusted about. If we were looking for a blanket indictment of business, that one ought to cover the ballpark.[1] Or as Michael Hoffman and Jennifer Moore put it somewhat more concisely, it is the opinion of many of our wiser heads that ". . . business faces a true crisis of legitimacy."[2]

We cannot, *pace* Milton Friedman, leave the governance of the corporation to the forces of the market. While the market may bring about economic efficiency, Gerald Cavanagh points out, it cannot guarantee that corporate performance will be ethically and socially sensitive. Here the responsibility lies with the Board of Directors and top management, and it is "essential that board and management step up to the task," ascertain the ethical climate already prevailing and guide policy and decision in ethical directions. He adds as a final qualification that "while codes, structures and monitoring can encourage ethical decisions, it is even more important to have ethical people in the firm who want to make ethical judgments, know how to, and are not afraid to do so."[3] This is surely true: there is no structure or device in the universe, let alone within the capability of the American business community, that will keep people moral if they are determined to be immoral. But most people, at least most businesspeople, it seems are really neither one nor the other; they are prepared to be either, depending on the prevailing culture, and that is where the code can help.

There is nothing new in the aspiration to ethical codes. As early as 1961, Fr. Raymond Baumhart's survey of 2000 business managers showed two-thirds of them interested in developing codes of ethics, which they thought would improve the ethical level of business practice.[4] By the seventies, public attention reinforced that view. George Benson traces the current effort on codes to the revelations on foreign and domestic bribery in government investigations 1973–1976, leading to the Foreign Corrupt Practices Act of 1977.[5] In the mid-seventies, W. Michael Blumenthal, then CEO of Bendix, went so far as to propose that the business executives of America organize a professional association to develop a comprehensive code of ethics for business with a review panel to enforce it. The idea died at the time, but might be worth following up at some point.[6] To this day, the most highly placed businessmen support the development of codes of ethics. In a survey conducted by Touche Ross in October, 1987, 1,082 respondents concluded that the most effective way to encourage ethical business behavior was the adoption of a code of ethics—outscoring the adoption of further legislation by 19%.[7] Nor is this support surprising. Ethics pays, not just in public relations but in company work. As the Business Roundtable, an association of Chief Executive Officers of major U. S. companies, concluded in 1988,

> "It may come as a surprise to some that . . . corporate ethics programs are not mounted primarily to improve the reputation of business. Instead, many executives believe that a culture in which ethical concern permeates the whole organization is necessary to the self-interest of the company. . . . In the view of the top executives represented in this study, there is no conflict between ethical practices and acceptable profits. Indeed, the first is a necessary precondition for the second."[8]

To be sure, we can, at least in theory, behave like saints without a code to describe how we are behaving. But a written document reinforces an intention to be ethical—as a reminder, as a guide, and as a focus for the solidarity of the corporate officers in their attempts to run the company along the lines it lays down. And beyond this, there is the first concern mentioned: that the public is, probably justifiably, concerned over the proclivities of the business community and interested in seeing tangible proof of its intention to behave.

So a public commitment to ethics serves at least two functions: it addresses the concerns of the public and it reinforces (and clarifies) a bottom-line-justified interest in ethical behavior on the part of the officers. A third reason to take ethics seriously, address the subject explicitly, and articulate provisions to enforce it, is simple realism. As Freeman and Gilbert point out, as long as organizations are composed of human beings, no organizational task can proceed, nor can any cogent corporate strategy be formulated, without recognizing that these human beings have values. Their "First Axiom of Corporate Strategy"—"Corporate strategy must reflect an understanding of the values of organizational members and stakeholders"—is derived directly from the discovery that the human players in the corporate enterprise very often act in accordance with personal and cultural ethical imperatives. The corporation relegates itself to irrelevance if it fails to recognize this fact. Their second Axiom—"Corporate strategy must reflect an understanding of the ethical nature of strategic choice"—acknowledges the interaction between corporate direction and private value. It is essential that the choices made by management in strategic planning meet the ethical standards implicit in the stakeholders' values.[9] The authors note the current fashion for describing strategy formulation as if persons did not exist, and point out at some length the errors of such attempts.[10]

WHY CODES FAIL

We sometimes take note of "widespread skepticism" as to the effectiveness of codes and the motivation behind their development. That skepticism bears some examination. Oddly, the doubts do not seem to have their roots in the business community, whose opinions are captured above. It seems to originate in the academic community of the business schools, possibly due to misunderstandings on the nature of valid corporate codes. Larue Tone Hosmer states well the prevailing error:

"Ethical codes are statements of the norms and beliefs of an organization. These norms and beliefs are generally proposed, discussed, and defined by the senior executives in the firm and then published and distributed to all of the members. Norms, of course, are standards of behavior; they are the ways the senior people in the organization want the others to act when confronted with a given situation."[11]

Again,

"The beliefs in an ethical code are standards of thought; they are the ways that the senior people in the organization want others to think."[12]

With that understanding, no wonder that he must immediately insist that "[t]his is not censorship"! Although that insistence is hardly reinforced with his following, "the intent is to encourage ways of thinking and patterns of attitudes that will lead towards the wanted behavior."

And with both of those understandings in place, again it is not surprising that his evaluation of codes is negative: "Do ethical codes work? Are they helpful in conveying to all employees the moral standards selected by the board of directors and president? Not really."[13] The problem with the code he describes is not only that it is not effective—taking no essential account of the nature of the business, let alone the pre-existing commitments of the people to whom it is supposed to apply (how could it be?)—but that it is not ethical. The basis for its norms is, it appears, completely subjective, founded on the whim of whomever happens to be in the executive offices the day that it occurs to a CEO to write a code of ethics; its application is coercive, being conceived by a more powerful group to apply to a less powerful group (but not to themselves); and there is no built-in check to see that it will actually help the company and its employees achieve the ends of the business. In short, it fails by any standards of reasonableness, and why on earth any firm would be interested in such a code is puzzling beyond the norm for such writings. (As Richard DeGeorge points out, we are occasionally willing to allow short lists of rules to be simply imposed on us, as long as the author is reliably known to be God. Senior officers, even CEO's, are not God.)[14]

While we have Hosmer's example before us, we may take the opportunity to extract some more general ethical principles from the critique. The code he describes was brought into existence by a few people in a few remote offices, enlisting the energies of none of the lower-ranking employees of the company. For this reason it fails on any measure of democracy, that understanding of governance that holds participation in policy formulation to be a part of justice; and it fails on any estimate of likely relevance to the situation of those excluded employees. The temptations that beset the stockman and secretary are best known to them, and it is inherently unwise to draw up rules without drawing on their experience. To avoid both sets of failures, it is essential to include as many employees as possible in the development process. This imperative we may call the *principle of participation.*

Second, the content of the code is completely unspecified save by reference to its authors—its provisions are those that strike the CEO and his golfing buddies as good, at the time they write it. Given their understandings of justice (see above and below), we are not inspired to confidence in their intuitions, but that is quite beside the point. Subjective presentations of this type can never qualify as imperatives with the authority of ethics. The provisions of a code must be reasoned, logically consistent, defended by reasoned argument, and coherent with the usual understandings of ethics: they must demonstrate respect for the individual, a commitment to justice, and sensitivity to the rights and interests of all parties affected by corporate action. We may call this requirement the *principle of validity.*

Third, it is assumed that the code is written by the senior officers, but that they themselves are not bound by it, and are therefore by implication perfectly free to ignore it or defy it if that is what they want to do. No liberty could be more destructive. People will do not as they are told, but as it is modeled to them; the company's values are trumpeted in the acts of the highest ranking employees, and need appear nowhere else. Again there is a violation of justice, in the development of a set of rules from which a privileged few shall be exempt, and again there is gross inattention to effectiveness. Whatever we may not know about codes, we know for sure that the real culture of a corporation will be embodied in the behavior of the senior officers, especially the CEO, and that it is imperative to secure the allegiance and the compliance of those persons for a code to be taken seriously; we may call this imperative the *principle of authenticity*. Hosmer's understanding of a corporate code violates all three principles, and condemns itself to ineffectiveness through its violations.

In the limiting case, then, a purported "code" can be no more than some authority's attempt to impose whimsical rules, which are bound to fail. A second type of code that is doomed to failure is the oracular code, confined to bare rules or ideals, no matter how derived or promulgated, with no commentary or explanation grounding the rule in experience.

> "The difficulty with many codes is not that they prescribe what is immoral, but that they fail to be truly effective in helping members of the profession or company to act morally. To be moral means not only doing what someone says is right, but also knowing *why* what one does is right, and assuming moral responsibility for the action. How were the provisions of the code arrived at? On what moral bases do the injunctions stand?"[15]

The standard instruction at the end of such codes, to discuss any dilemmas with the legal office, won't do it; they don't know morality. Implicit in this objection is a strong suggestion that the code must serve an educational function. This is correct; we will come back to this point.

A third and common way for codes to fail is through failure of the highest executives to take the provisions seriously, not only as they apply to themselves (the principle of authenticity, above), but as they apply to the company's management policies (especially "management by objectives") and other standard procedures. If the CEO honestly believes in the provisions, and takes the lead in modeling and enforcing them, if top management follows suit, and if the company's reward and punishment structure reinforces those provisions consistently, the code may well achieve its purpose even if it fails as a model of logical coherence. If they do not do so, there is very little chance that anyone else will either, especially when no one is watching. "Management needs to understand the real dynamics of its own organization. For example, how do people get ahead in the company? What conduct is actually rewarded, what values are really being instilled in employees?"[16] And the modeling and enforcement must be spread throughout the company. As Andy Sigler, CEO of Champion International and initiator of one of the best corporate codes in existence, put it, "Making speeches and sending letters just doesn't do it. You need a culture and peer pressure that spells out what is acceptable and isn't and why. It involves training, education, and follow-up."[17] For example, the institutionalization of any code must include protection from retaliation by supervisors against whistleblowers.[18] Kenneth Arrow would go further, arguing that any effective code must not only be fused into the corporate culture, but "accepted by the significant operating institutions and transmitted from one generation of executives to the next through standard operating procedures [and] through education in business schools."[19]

HOW CODES SUCCEED

The first condition for success is a commitment to the promotion of ethical behavior in a company—not to better public relations, nor to more certain deterrence of Federal inspectors, nor to the terror of an occasional bad apple, but to make the whole company a better and finer employer, producer, resident and citizen. For starters, the business community must take a leaf from the book of the professions, who have seen themselves as moral communities from the outset.[20] Like the professions, the corporation must take its status as a moral agent seriously. (There is almost a note of surprise in Leonard Brooks' observation that nowadays, there is a public expectation that if managers are caught *in flagrante delicto,* as they sometimes are, they will be punished. "This is a significant change because it is signalling that our society no longer regards the interests of the corporation or its shareholders to be paramount in importance. Neither corporate executives nor professionals can operate with impunity any longer, because society now expects them to be accountable.")[21] It certainly does.

From that basic commitment should follow a commitment to a process aimed at gathering that ethos from, and infusing it throughout, the entire company. Our first and third specifications, the principle of participation and the principle of authenticity, are two phases of that process commitment. The whole company (starting from the top) must commit itself to the development of the corporate code; the whole company (including the most junior members) must contribute to the process of deliberation; and the whole company (again, especially the top) must be, and feel, bound to obey and to exemplify it.

The imperative of validity is no more than a remote test of the coherence of the content. In accordance with the examples set by the professions, it is not essential for a code to be a model of academic ethics. The requirement that the code be in conformity with theory does not mean that the code must explicitly signal the kind of reasoning that validates it. Earlier in this enterprise academicians were perhaps too insistent, and codecrafters too self-conscious, on this point; earlier discussions of the issue of corporate and professional codes were known to break down on the issue of "consequentialist vs. deontological moral reasoning." Both are necessarily included in the development of a corporate ethic. As Robin and Reidenbach point out, maintaining a certain kind of "ethical profile" (e.g. strong customer orientation for a sales-driven industry) is absolutely essential for the bottom line—there is no more utilitarian requirement. Yet the "core values" extracted from that profile (e.g. "Treat customers with respect and honesty, . . . the way you would want your family treated") can be derived from any system of primary duties, and are deontological in form and function. Any good formulation of a company's creed should be subject to verification by both kinds of moral reasoning.[22]

As Robin and Reidenbach emphasize, the code must be drawn to reflect the aims of the particular set of business practices with which the company is concerned. The ruling ideal of the code might equally be integrity of the practitioners, the excellence of craftsmanship, or the dedication to serve the client/customer, depending on the type of business it is. One of the first principles of "excellence" in the running of any company—the imperative to "stick to the knitting"—entails that a code for one industry, or one kind of company, need not apply with equal force to any others.

Along that line, be it noted that there are many reasons why a code cannot be all things to all people. Critics with certain key areas of interest, for instance, will often discover limits in codes that might not occur to the rest of us. Pat Werhane, for instance, complains that codes "usually tell the employee what he or she is not permitted to do, but they seldom spell out worker rights."[23] She goes on to argue that they tend to turn employees into legalists, obedient to the letter of the regulation but ignorant of its moral spirit.

The solution to both problems may lie in the shift of focus from dead rule to living dialogue. I am inclined to argue that the real value of the code does not lie in the finished product, rules with explanations that all must obey, but in the process by which it came to be. The first call for participation is an invitation to the employee to look into his conscience, discover his own moral commitments, and attempt to prioritize and formulate them. This may be the first time he has ever been asked to take on that job, and the educational value is enormous. The second phase of the participatory process includes the discovery of community consensus, a dialogue in which the employee must test his perceptions against those of others, re-examine and perhaps replace those that do not meet the test, and discover the defenses of those that do. However the code emerges, we will have much more articulate employees at the end of the process than we had at the beginning. And in this articulation is implicit genuine self-awareness: the employee now has his moral beliefs where he can see and get at them, and can be educated to apply them in new and creative ways should the situation around him change.

And it will change. Change was always a fact in the American business community, and very rapid, almost chaotic, change an occasional reality. Now, as Tom Peters points out, partly at his instigation, it has become a conscious policy. The continuation of that dialogue is needed especially as firms radically reorganize themselves, destroying the traditional departmental divisions and job descriptions. In the absence of traditional guides, all members of the corporation will need new and extraordinary norms to govern practice, and there is no substitute for a dialogical process in place as the change happens.[24]

ENDNOTES

1. Leonard J. Brooks, "Corporate Codes of Ethics," *Journal of Business Ethics* 8(1989):117–129. p. 119.
2. W. Michael Hoffman and Jennifer Mills Moore, *Business Ethics,* Second Edition. New York: McGraw-Hill, 1990. page 2.
3. Gerald F. Cavanagh, *American Business Values,* second edition. Englewood Cliffs, New Jersey: Prentice-Hall, 1984. p. 159
4. Raymond C. Baumhart, S.J., "How Ethical Are Businessmen?" *Harvard Business Review* 39(July–August 1961):166–71
5. George C. S. Benson, "Codes of Ethics," *Journal of Business Ethics* 8(1989):305–319.p.306.
6. W. Michael Blumenthal, "New Business Watchdog Needed," *The New York Times,* May 25, 1975, F1; and "R for Reducing the Occasion of Corporate Sin," *Advanced Management Journal* 42 (Winter 1977):4–13.
7. Touche Ross, *Ethics in American Business: An opinion survey of key business leaders on ethical standards and behavior,* New York: Touche Ross, 1988. page 14. The sample included only chief executive officers of companies with $500 million or more in annual sales, deans of business schools and members of Congress.
8. *Corporate Ethics: A Prime Business Asset* New York: The Business Roundtable, 1988. page 9.
9. R. Edward Freeman and Daniel R. Gilbert, Jr. *Corporate Strategy and the Search for Ethics.* Englewood Cliffs, New Jersey: Prentice-Hall, 1988. pp. 6–7.
10. *Loc. cit.* See also p. 138, and p. 197, n. 3.
11. Larue Tone Hosmer, *The Ethics of Management,* Homewood, Illinois: Irwin, 1987, p. 153
12. *Ibid.* p. 154.
13. *Loc.cit.* p. 154.
14. Richard T. DeGeorge, *Business Ethics* Third Edition. New York, Macmillan, 1990. p. 390.
15. DeGeorge, *op. cit* p. 391.
16. William H. Shaw, *Business Ethics,* Belmont, California: Wadsworth Publishing Company, 1991. p. 175
17. Andrew Sigler, CEO of Champion International, cited in "Businesses are Signing Up for Ethics 101," *Business Week,* February 15, 1988. p. 56.
18. Leonard J. Brooks, "Corporate Codes of Ethics," *Journal of Business Ethics* 8(1989):117–129. p. 124.
19. Kenneth J. Arrow, "Social Responsibility and Economic Efficiency," *Public Policy* 21(Summer 1973):42
20. Mark S. Frankel, "Professional Codes: Why, How, and with What Impact?" *Journal of Business Ethics* 8(1989):109–115. p. 110.
21. Brooks, *op. cit.* p. 119
22. Donald P. Robin and R. Eric Reidenbach, *Business Ethics: Where Profits Meet Value Systems.* Englewood Cliffs, New Jersey: Prentice-Hall, 1989.p. 94–95
23. Patricia H. Werhane, *Persons, Rights and Corporations,* Englewood Cliffs, New Jersey: Prentice-Hall, Inc. 1985. p. 159.
24. See Tom Peters, "Get Innovative or Get Dead (part one)," *California Management Review* 33(Fall 1990):9–26.

Can a Company Be Too Ethical?

Andrew W. Singer
Editor and Publisher, *Ethikos*

"A couple of years ago, we were competing on a government contract," recalls Norman Augustine, chairman and CEO of Martin Marietta Corp. "The low bid would win. Two days before we were to submit the bid, we got a brown paper bag with our competitor's bid in it."

Martin Marietta didn't "spend 10 minutes" de-

Found in *Across the Board* (April 1993). Reprinted by permission of *Across the Board* and the author.

bating what to do with this information. Augustine remembers. The company turned the price sheet over to the U.S. government. Martin Marietta also told its competitor what it had received.

"And we did not change our bid."

What happened? "We lost the contract," recalls Augustine. "As a result, some of our employees lost jobs. And our shareholders lost money."

Is this a case of a company being too ethical?

No, answers Augustine. The outcome was only unfavorable in the short term. "We helped establish a reputation that, in the long run, will draw us business." This he accepts as a matter of faith.

"To me, the subject of ethics deals with principles," explains Augustine, "what you believe to be right or wrong." And insofar as ethics deals with principles, it is not possible to be too ethical. "You can't have too much principle."

But not all agree.

"You can spend too much time, too much effort, on almost anything," says Edward Bowman, Reginald Jones Professor of Corporate Management at The Wharton School at the University of Pennsylvania. "It doesn't mean you shouldn't be ethical." But it does suggest that there are limits.

What happens to a company in a highly competitive industry where "sharp" practices are the norm? If it behaves too nobly, might not other corporations succeed in cutting it off at the knees? Or what about companies that pour heaps of money into safety or environmental compliance—above and beyond what is mandated by law? Won't that hurt the bottom line?

A company, too, can pay so much attention to "doing good" that its traditional business suffers. This was a criticism made against Control Data Corp. (now Ceridian Corp.) under William C. Norris in the 1980s. The company ignored its core business at the expense of so-called humanitarian projects, said critics (more on this shortly).

The question—Can a company be too ethical?—admits of no quick or simple answers. In fact, it is difficult even to arrive at a common definition of what one means by ethical. Strictly speaking, ethics is a discipline for dealing with questions of good or bad, right and wrong—but there is also a broader definition, at least in the minds of many executives and ethicists, that embraces issues of so-called social responsibility. (Supererogatory duties, philosophers might call these.) Issues of bribe-taking, the stealing of competitive information, and sexual harassment clearly accord with most people's notion of ethics, but others, such as affirmative action, investing in South Africa, empowering workers, and hiring the hard-core unemployed can be addressed only if one accepts an expanded concept.

Nonetheless, asking the question sheds some light on how business leaders view ethics and the business enterprise. (For the purposes of this inquiry, we examine business ethics in both the strict and expanded senses of the word.)

Thomas Donaldson, John F. Connelly Professor of Business Ethics at Georgetown University, observes that what is understood as business ethics among executives has undergone a sea change in recent decades. In the '60s, for instance, "business executives tended to identify corporate ethics with philanthropy and social-oriented programs, like hiring the hard-core unemployed.

"Now it has to do more with *how one approaches business objectives.*" Is one being attentive to all one's constituencies, or "stakeholders," including employees, customers, suppliers, and the community in which one operates?

Some people say a company can be too ethical if "it pays its employees like kings," notes Donaldson. They reason that it costs money to pay employees so handsomely, and a company's profit margin may deteriorate, which ultimately hurts shareholders and overall business health. In that case, a serious question arises if the company is behaving toward its shareholders, and others, in a less-than-ethical manner.

THE PRICE OF ETHICS

Most will agree that ethics sometimes exacts a price in the short run. "You know that old definition of a pioneer: He's the one with the arrows in his butt," says Tom Stephens, chairman, president, and CEO of the Manville Corp. (formerly Johns-Manville, of asbestos notoriety).

Manville emerged from bankruptcy in 1988.

Today, Stephens feels an obligation for his company to be more ethical than average—given its past and the fact that it was offered a second chance by the courts. (The company, once one of the world's largest manufacturers of asbestos, was subject to 150,000 lawsuits on behalf of individuals whose health was allegedly ruined from asbestos exposure.) Yet this stance has its perils from a short-term profit standpoint.

Take the issue of product labeling. In the late '80s and early '90s, Manville went beyond what the law required in terms of warning labels on its fiberglass products. After the International Agency for Research on Cancer suggested in 1987 that fiberglass was a "possible carcinogen," the company promptly affixed prominent cancer-warning labels to all its fiberglass products. (The company disputes the claim that fiberglass may be a carcinogen, however.)

This in itself is not so unusual: U.S. companies are expected to respond this way in accordance with the Occupational Safety and Health Administration's (OSHA) Hazard Communication Standard. But Manville went further: It put the warning labels on fiberglass products that it shipped to Japan, and translated those warnings into Japanese. Not only was this not required by law, but the Japanese government advised against it.

Government officials there warned "against using the 'C' word," recalls Stephens. (The Japanese have a particular dread of cancer—a legacy of Hiroshima.) They were afraid of frightening the public. Manville's business customers, in turn, were fearful of scaring their workers. Architects worried about alarming lawyers by specifying a possibly carcinogenic building material.

The Japanese said, "We'll tell them what the risks are," according to Stephens. No need to alarm people by affixing such a label.

"But a human being in Japan is no different from a human being in the U.S.," Stephens says. "We told them we had a policy. We had to have a label."

The Japanese response? "The Japanese trade minister said, 'You are very brave.' "

And it *did* have an impact on the company's Japanese sales. (Twenty-five percent of Manville's revenues are derived from outside the United States.) The company lost 40 percent of sales to Japan in one year.

Stephens, Augustine, and others who recount such stories usually add that their business losses are only in the short term. Manville, for instance, was later able to rebuild all of its Japanese business. But do some managers believe that a business can be too ethical—period—and not just in the short term?

Few are likely to say so publicly. "If you ask people directly, they're likely to give you the most socially responsible answer," observes John Delaney, professor of management at the University of Iowa. But Delaney, who has collected dozens of ethical dilemmas submitted by business executives (including those from a study he conducted of Columbia University business-school graduates), suspects that some executives privately believe a company can, in fact, be too ethical.

He offers this case, which was reported by a corporate auditor at a large, well-known pharmaceutical company:

"The FDA was reviewing our application to place a new drug on the market," the auditor told Delaney. The persistent questioning of the FDA reviewer regarding the application, however, made the auditor uneasy, so he asked to review his company's research-and-development records.

Photocopies of the data provided evidence of "double books." "One set of raw data, completely fabricated, had been provided to me to present to the FDA, while another set of raw data, showing failing results, were the true data," the auditor recalled to Delaney.

The auditor reported his findings, in accordance with corporate procedure, to the international legal department. Eventually, he was asked to testify before the company's board of directors.

"The corporation, as a consequence of the hearing, made me a 'deal.' They would give me all the resources possible to get the drug approval by the FDA. But they promised they would never market the drug. They did not want the embarrassment of the fraud uncovered. . . . I cooperated in the deal, and the company cooperated in its part. Ten years later, the drug is still not on the market."

Subsequent to this "deal," however, the company rewrote the auditor's job description. Its aim seemed to be to make it more unlikely that improprieties of this sort would be uncovered in the future. The new corporate policy prohibited "surprise" audits, for instance. And corporate audit policy was placed directly in the hands of the CEO.

According to Delaney, this suggests that the pharmaceutical concern saw real "costs" in being too ethical. It didn't want to be blatantly unethical—foisting a flawed drug on the public (nor did it fire or demote the whistle-blowing auditor)—but by the same token, it wasn't too keen about uncovering any more episodes of this sort. Hence, it curtailed the audit function. The company seemed to be saying, "Whoa, we don't want to be too ethical. That could lead to real trouble!"

Nor is this stance entirely without financial justification. Back in 1975, the Wharton School's Bowman co-authored "A Strategic Posture Toward Corporate Social Responsibility," a study of 100 companies in the food-processing industry that sought to establish if there was a connection between corporate social responsibility and profits. (Bowman acknowledges that social responsibility is not the same thing as ethics but suggests that the two are related.)

Did the link exist? "If you plot the relationship, the association is curvilinear," says Bowman. That is, as one moves from companies that exhibit little or no social responsibility to those that demonstrate a modest degree, profitability rises. It peaks somewhere in the middle.

(What constituted a socially responsible company? Such factors as concern for the environment and eagerness to hire minorities. An unusually responsible corporation might be one that granted employees paid leaves of absence to work in the local community, for instance.)

"But over on the far right [i.e., among the *most* socially responsible firms], profitability drops off." It is a matter of diminishing marginal returns.

"You can spend too much money on advertising, on computers, on research and development," says Bowman. "Can a company concerned with its overall health spend too much on social responsibility? The answer is yes."

Nonetheless, as a matter of record, "The number of firms that have gotten in trouble for being too ethical is very small," observes David Vogel, professor of business and public policy at the Haas School of Business at the University of California at Berkeley.

While acknowledging that ethics and profits are not always compatible, and a company facing constraints could in theory be too ethical for its own good—such as failing to lay off workers when its sales plummet—in point of fact, "few firms, when faced with that tension, don't give in to the economic constraints," says Vogel.

THE LEGACY OF CONTROL DATA

One of the few examples in which a company might have been harmed by being too good, Vogel acknowledges, is Control Data, which may have sapped its resources with humanitarian programs in the early and mid-'80s.

Indeed, the name of Control Data comes up again and again when one asks if a company can be too ethical. (Rightly or wrongly, people seem to accept a broader definition of ethics here: one that goes beyond questions of right and wrong, and encompasses social responsibility.) The computer company has become a paradigm in the minds of some of a company that faltered for being too good.

Under Norris, its visionary founder, Control Data built factories in riot-torn inner cities in the late 1960s and 1970s. It saw this as doing its part to ameliorate the social situation. "You can't do business in a society that is burning," Norris said at the time. The company had an exemplary record of hiring minority men and women with little formal education and few qualifications, and allowing them to rise through the ranks and become foremen and plant managers.

The company also spent $900 million between 1963 and 1980 trying to develop computer-based education programs for schools. The basic idea was that through computer-based instruction, students could learn at their own rate—unlike a classroom, where everyone must adapt to the teacher's pace. Control Data developed programs for everything from third-grade arithmetic to Farsi and Japanese.

While the company remained profitable, it garnered accolades. In 1983, a poll of Wall Street analysts and corporate directors rated Control Data one of the most admired corporations in the United States.

But then the company's core business began to flounder under the onslaught of intense Japanese competition, particularly in the computer-peripherals business. The corporation lost $568 million in 1985. That year, a new Wall Street poll showed Control Data to be among the country's *least* admired companies.

Norris, who resigned as chairman in 1986, has long disputed the view that he was too attached to socially responsible programs. Control Data was not engaged in sundry humanitarian projects, he insists, but rather in "addressing unmet social needs as business opportunities." Although the computer-based education program proved economically untenable, for example, there is no denying that the market for education and training was—and is—potentially enormous.

"I never felt that criticism was appropriate," Norris tells *Across the Board.* The company devoted no more than 5 percent of its resources to these nontraditional projects, he says. But they were in high-profile areas and were dependent on the cooperation of the public sector, such as local and state governments.

Might he have dedicated too much of his own time and energy, if not the company's resources, to such projects, to the detriment of the company's core business?

"The problem that plagued Control Data was a problem that plagued a lot of companies, but it hit us first," says Norris. "We were moving to a world economy. We didn't recognize it as fast as I would have hoped."

Max DePree, chairman of Herman Miller Inc., the furniture manufacturer, knew Norris "a little bit, and admired him greatly." DePree confirms in an interview that he, too, gained an impression that Norris may have devoted too many resources to socially responsible projects. But that isn't the same thing as saying the company was too ethical, even if that is the idea that has taken hold in the public mind.

"If Control Data had problems [in the mid-1980s], it was probably for the same reasons we all did: We underestimated the competition and we didn't stay focused on what we do," DePree says.

Control Data's socially responsible projects may have diminished Norris' focus, DePree acknowledges—but then the answer would have been to appoint a CEO to handle the core business, something that Norris may have resisted doing.

In any event, "I can't accept that Control Data failed because it was too ethical," DePree says.

Interestingly, Norris himself believes that "there are instances where a company can be too ethical." (And here we are back to a strict definition of ethics.) "But it's often a matter of failing to use common sense.

"One example when I was at Control Data occurred in Mexico. Bribes were commonplace at that time. In fact, government officials were expected to make part of their income through bribes. We had a situation where we shipped an expensive computer there. It was sitting on the dock, and the local official said we had to pay $500 if we wanted to move it out.

"Well, common sense says that you better pay that $500" even if the company has a policy against such payments. "The computer could get stolen; it could rain." Control Data made the payment.

THE MORALITY OF MANAGEMENT

Many view the way a corporation treats its employees as an ethical issue. Does the company treat its workers with dignity, as "ends" in themselves? Or are employees simply a "means" toward greater corporate profits? Companies that have sought to "empower" their workers by giving them a greater say in design and production matters, for instance, often view these actions as having an ethical—as well as a business—component. One is reaffirming employees as "ends" in themselves. But can a company take this notion too far?

Consultant Verne E. Henderson, while supporting worker empowerment generally, believes such a danger exists. In his book *What's Ethical in Business?* (McGraw-Hill, 1992), Henderson looks at People Express Airlines, the discount-fare carrier of the early 1980s.

Philosophy Meets Fiscal Reality

The notion that a company or individual cannot be too ethical reflects a view of ethics and the world that ultimately can be traced back to Aristotle.

Aristotle, it may be recalled, defined virtue as the mean between two blameworthy extremes. Courage, a virtue, represents the mean between cowardice and recklessness. Friendliness, a virtue, is the mean between the extremes of obsequiousness (the desire to please too much) and irascibility (the desire to please too little).

In business, an Aristotelian might see ethics as a sort of balancing act. One has to take into account the demands and needs of various constituencies, or "stakeholders": shareholders, employees, customers, suppliers, and the larger community. No single group can dominate at the expense of any other.

"If one deals with one stakeholder group in an imbalanced way, you do that at the expense of other stakeholders," Guiseppe Bassani, NCR Corp.'s vice president of stakeholder relations, told *ethikos* in September 1991. "In the short term, you can do that. But in the long term, it will kill the company.

"Many times, expectations are not reasonable," he said. A customer may want the company's products for little or nothing. The customer has to be told, "We can't do this. If we do, we'll go out business.

"For me, business ethics is telling people what we can do and what we can't do," Bassani added.

The ethical challenge for Aristotelians is finding that balance, that virtuous mean. A company that refuses to close a failing plant or lay off redundant workers—and subsequently goes bankrupt—is not too ethical, according to this view, but insufficiently ethical. It has slighted one of its key constituencies (shareholders) and probably a second (the remaining workers) at the expense of a third constituency (redundant workers). By failing to achieve that proper balance, management is found lacking in ethical skill.

"Aristotle tells us that ethics is more like building a house than it is like physics," says Georgetown University's Thomas Donaldson. "You learn to build a house by building houses. You learn to be an ethical manager by managing," not by reading textbooks on philosophy.

Professional philosophers sometimes view the practice of business ethics as a theoretical pursuit, continues Donaldson. "It's not. It is an art. It can't be reduced to a science."

For an Aristotelian, it's impossible for a company to be too ethical.

"It is like the question, 'Can a person be too rich, or too thin?' " says Donaldson. In the broadest sense, "a company cannot be too ethical."

But Aristotle's isn't the only perspective on the question. There is another position, one that might be referred to as the Kantian view.

Immanuel Kant, perhaps the most influential moral philosopher of the modern era, viewed moral conduct as something of a struggle. One performs one's moral duty often *in spite* of one's inclinations, or even one's interest. And things don't always work out so well in the end. (Kant's famous example of the individual who refuses to lie, even to save another person's life, is perhaps an extreme illustration of this.)

Many of us would clearly recognize situations in which a person acts ethically and suffers, and not just in the short term. A small-businessman refuses to pay "protection" money, and the mob puts him out of business. Can we really say he was insufficiently ethical for not taking into account stakeholders' interests? Or is it more the case that he was really too ethical—too high-minded—for an imperfect world?

Or consider the struggling entrepreneur who insists on paying his creditors 100 cents on the dollar—even though he could probably force them to accept less—because "a debt is an implied promise, and promises are meant to be kept." He depletes precious working capital and the business fails. Might he not have been more successful if he had fewer scruples?

Can a company be too ethical? "I think if you just take the question at face value, the answer is yes, you can be too ethical," says The Wharton School's Edward Bowman. "But you have to be awfully careful by what you mean by ethical."—**A.S.**

The company's founder, Donald Burr, "was considered a motivational genius," writes Henderson. "His management style was unique. Employees were called managers, no matter how insignificant their assignment. Productivity, job satisfaction, and initial customer enthusiasm reached new highs for an airline company. Every employee became a shareholder with stock value that grew in most cases to equal one's annual salary in less than four years. His achievement was remarkable, considering the kind of change he introduced. Employees didn't own the company, but they owned the work."

People Express faltered, however, and it was eventually taken over by Frank Lorenzo's Texas Air. The company may have been a victim, at least in some part, of its own good intentions, suggests Henderson in an interview. "The company tried so hard to impart dignity to individual workers and managers that it led to attitudes that were not viable over the long term."

People Express told its employees to do what's right—"even when no one is there to help you. They invited people to be entrepreneurs in an industry where it didn't really work. If the captain has a problem with the airplane, he doesn't call a meeting of the passengers to discuss it." Something of the sort occurred at the company, he suggests.

But a case such as People Express may be the exception, not the rule. "If you listed all the companies that failed, you won't find too many like People Express that failed for doing the right thing," DePree tells *Across the Board.* There are many popular misconceptions about what is meant by a "participative environment," adds DePree, who as chairman of Herman Miller has been credited with forging strong bonds between employees and managers.

"We never talk about everyone voting," he continues. Rather, the company seeks decision-making at its most competent level, "and you can't limit that to the talents of the people at the top." In other words, empowerment doesn't mean that everyone votes on every issue. But it does require more input from a wider range of people than is found at most traditional, command-and-control-type companies.

Asking whether a company can be too ethical "is a bit of a conundrum," says DePree. "I can't imagine where we could be too ethical."

According to Martin Marietta CEO Augustine, it is naive to equate good ethics with profits, at least in the short run.

Martin Marietta is a large NASA contractor. It launches spacecraft for the government, and it earns a substantial incentive bonus when those vehicles are launched successfully.

As an illustration of how a company can lose money in the short term by hewing to its principles, Augustine offers this example:

"One day, our insurance department heard about an insurance policy that would insure our launch bonus, for a low premium. For one nickel on the dollar, we could guarantee the dollar."

On the face of it, such an insurance policy looked like a win-win situation. If the company launched the spacecraft successfully, it would get the bonus from the government. If the launch failed, the insurance company would pay the bonus.

But the deal raised some troubling questions. Why was the customer—the U.S. government, in this instance—providing the company with the incentive? Obviously, it was to make sure that the company did everything in its power, to ensure a successful launch. Wouldn't an insurance policy of the sort described undermine the government's *intent* in offering the launch bonus?

"Our engineers said: 'It would not make a difference,' " recalls Augustine. They would put forth the same 100 percent effort in any case. "And I believed them," he adds. The company's lawyers raised questions of fiduciary responsibility: Didn't the corporation have an obligation to its shareholders to take the insurance policy? There was, notes Augustine, "big money" at stake.

What to do? Augustine's answer was to call the customer—in this case, a general in the U.S. Air Force.

After explaining the insurance matter, "I said: 'Would you care?' " Augustine explained that it was still *his* decision to make, and not the general's, but he would weigh seriously what the general said in making that decision.

"He said he hadn't heard of such a thing, and wondered if others might already be doing it," recalls Augustine. "But he also said he wanted a couple of days to think it over."

Several days later, he called back. The general, upon reflection, reported that "they 'cared' a lot."

"We finally decided not to buy the insurance. And we subsequently had a loss."

In the final analysis, Augustine believes, matters of principle are not for compromise. One behaves as one does because it is right, he suggests (even if determining what is right sometimes takes some doing, such as consulting with the Air Force general). The so-called bad outcomes are only in the short term. "It always pays off in the long term."

But that is unlikely to convince realpolitikers like Henderson. "If a company is too ethical, it can go out of business," he observes. "There's an ethical side and a profit side of the enterprise, and they have to be balanced."

New Directions in Corporate Social Responsibility

Norman Bowie
Andersen Chair in Corporate Responsibility, University of Minnesota

Among philosophers writing in business ethics, something of a consensus has emerged in the past ten years regarding the social responsibility of business. Although these philosophers were critical of the classical view of Milton Friedman (the purpose of the corporation is to make profits for stockholders), the consensus view had much in common with Friedman, so much so that I referred to my own statement of this position as the neoclassical view of corporate responsibility (Bowie 1982). The heart of the neoclassical view was that the corporation was to make a profit while avoiding inflicting harm. In other formulations the corporation was to make a profit while (1) honoring the moral minimum or (2) respecting individual rights and justice. Tom Donaldson arrived at a similar neoclassical description of the purpose of the corporation by arguing that such a view is derived from the social contract that business has with society (1989).

The stakeholder theory made popular by Ed Freeman does seem to represent a major advance over the classical view (Freeman 1984; Evan and Freeman 1988). It might seem inappropriate to refer to the stakeholder position as neoclassical. Rather than argue that the job of the manager was to maximize profits for stockholders, Freeman argued that the manager's task was to protect and promote the rights of the various corporate stakeholders. Stakeholders were defined by Freeman as members of groups whose existence was necessary for the survival of the firm—stockholders, employees, customers, suppliers, the local community, and managers themselves.

Despite the vast increase in scope of managerial obligations, a Friedmanite might try to bring stakeholder theory under his or her umbrella. Of course, the managers must worry about the rights and interests of the other corporate stakeholders. If you don't look after them, these other stakeholders will not be as productive and profits will fall. A good manager is concerned with all stakeholders while increasing profits for stockholders. In the Friedmanite view, the stakeholder theorist does not give us an alternative theory of social responsibility; rather, he or she reminds us how an enlightened Friedmanite, as opposed to an unenlightened one, is supposed to manage. The unenlightened Friedmanite exploits stakeholders to increase profits. Although that strategy might succeed in the short run, the morale and hence the productivity of the other stakeholders plummets, and as a result long-run profits fall. To protect long-run profits, the enlightened manager is concerned with the health, safety, and family needs (day care) of employees, a no-question-asked return policy, stable long-term relations with suppliers, and civic activities in the local community. In this way, long-run

---

profitability is protected or even enhanced. In the classical view, the debate between Milton Friedman and Ed Freeman is not a debate about corporate ends, but rather about corporate means to that end.

Moreover, some classicists argue, the neoclassical concern with avoiding harm or honoring the moral minimum does not add anything to Friedman's theory. In *Capitalism and Freedom* (1962) he argues that the manager must obey the law and moral custom. The quotation goes like this:

> In such an economy, there is one and only one social responsibility of business—to use its resources and engage in activities designed to increase its profits so long as it stays within the rules of the game, which is to say, engages in open and free competition, without deception or fraud.

If there really is a social contract that requires business to honor a moral minimum, then a business manager on the Friedmanite model is duty-bound to obey it. To the extent that the moral minimum involves duties to not cause avoidable harm, or to honor individual stakeholder rights, or to adhere to the ordinary canons of justice, then the Friedmanite manager has these duties as well. Even if Friedman didn't emphasize the manager's duties to law and common morality, the existence of the duties are consistent with Friedman's position.

Unfortunately, the compatibility of the classical Friedmanite position with obedience to law and morality is undercut by some of Friedman's most well-known followers. The late Albert Carr (1968) substituted the morality of poker for ordinary morality. Indeed he argued that ordinary morality was inappropriate in business:

> Poker's own brand of ethics is different from the ethical ideals of civilized human relationships. The game calls for distrust of the other fellow. It ignores the claim of friendship. Cunning deception and concealment of one's strength and intentions, not kindness and openheartedness, are vital in poker. No one thinks any the worse of poker on that account. And no one should think the worse of the game of business because its standards of right and wrong differ from the prevailing traditions of morality in our society. . . .

Even more pervasive has been the influence of former *Harvard Business Review* editor Theodore Levitt. He defends various deceptive practices in advertising, which seem to be in violation of ordinary morality, as something consumers really like after all (1970):

> Rather than deny that distortion and exaggeration exist in advertising, in this article I shall argue that embellishment and distortion are among advertising's legitimate and socially desirable purpose: and that illegitimacy in advertising consists only of falsification with larcenous intent. . . . But the consumer suffers from an old dilemma. He wants "truth," but he also wants and needs the alleviating imagery and tantalizing promise of the advertiser and designer.

The writings of these authors give Friedman's theory that "anything for profit" ring that its critics hear. But Friedman need not be interpreted in that way. Many profit-oriented business people do not espouse that interpretation; neither do some academic Friedmanites. What needs to be done is for the Friedmanite school to declare Carr and Levitt heretics and excommunicate them from the faith. The Friedmanites also need to include as part of their canon some statement of the moral minimum idea so the phrase "rules of the game" in *Capitalism and Freedom* has some flesh and bone.

On one important point the neoclassical theorists and the Friedmanites are already in explicit agreement. Both positions argue that it is *not* the purpose of business to do good. The neoclassicists agree with Levitt that providing for the general welfare is the responsibility of government. A business is not a charitable organization.

> Business will have a much better chance of surviving if there is no nonsense about its goals—that is, if long-run profit maximization is one dominant objective in practice as well as in theory. Business should recognize what government's functions are and let it go at that, stopping only to fight government where government directly intrudes itself into business. It should let government take care of the general welfare so that business can take care of the more material aspects of welfare. (Levitt 1958)

Both the classicists and the neoclassicists have

elaborate arguments to support their views. The classicist arguments focus on legitimacy. Corporate boards and managers are not popularly elected. Politicians are. Hence, government officials have a legitimacy in spending tax dollars for public welfare that corporate managers don't. Moreover, the corporate board and managers are agents of the stockholders. Unless the stockholders authorize charitable contributions, the corporate officers have no right to give the stockholders' money away and violate their fiduciary responsibility in doing so.

Levitt (1958) gives the legitimacy argument a final twist. It is the job of the government to provide for the general welfare; but if business starts doing the government's job, the government will take over business. As a result, business and government will coalesce into one powerful group at the expense of our democratic institutions.

Levitt seems to hold the traditional American view, adopted from Montesquieu, that the existence of a democracy requires a balance of competing powers among the main institutions of society. Levitt and Friedman both see the competing institutions as business, government, and labor, each with its distinct and competing interests. If business starts to take on the task of government, the balance of power is upset.

The neoclassical arguments are much more pragmatic. Corporations don't have the resources to solve social problems. Moreover, since the obligation to do good is an open-ended one, society cannot expect corporations to undertake it. A corporation that tries to solve social problems is an institutional Mother Teresa. What it does is good, but its actions, in the language of ethics, are supererogatory.

Some of the neoclassicists add a little sophistication to the argument by showing that competitive pressure will prevent corporations from doing good, even if the competitors all want to. If company X spends more of its money solving social problems than company Y, company Y gains a competitive advantage. Even if company Y wants to contribute to solving social problems, it will try to get company X to contribute even more. Company X has thought this all through; as a result it can't contribute (or contribute as much as it would like). The conclusion is that all competitive companies believe they can't focus on solving social problems even if they want to.

As a result of the arguments, a fairly orthodox position has developed both in theory and in practice. American corporations do not have an obligation to solve social problems. Whatever the notion of corporate responsibility means, it does not mean that. However, the orthodox position does have its critics, and these critics have arguments of their own.

Perhaps the three strongest arguments are based on the duties of gratitude and citizenship and the responsibilities of power. With respect to gratitude, defenders of a duty to help solve social problems argue that society provides tremendous resources to corporations. The local community provides public education that trains workers, a legal system complete with police and courts to enforce corporate contracts, and a huge infrastructure of highways, sewage and garbage disposal, and public health facilities. Corporate taxes are not sufficient payment for the corporations' share of these resources, therefore corporations have a duty out of gratitude to help solve social problems. Moreover, even if corporate taxes did cover their fair share, corporations are citizens morally similar to individual citizens: as a result, they have a similar obligation to help solve social problems. Thus, corporations have a duty based on citizenship to help solve social problems. Finally, the moral use of power requires that power be used responsibly. The term "stewardship" is often used to describe the responsibilities of those who have great power and resources. Individual corporate leaders make reference to the duties of stewardship when they establish private foundations. Carnegie and Rockefeller are two prominent examples.

In addition to the intellectual arguments on behalf of a duty to help solve social problems, there are many actual cases where corporations have acted on that duty. It is part of the corporate culture in the Twin Cities (Minneapolis and St. Paul). Indeed, it seems to be part of the Minnesota corporate culture. Three chambers of commerce annually compile a list of the corporations who give 2 to 5 percent of their pre-tax profits to charitable organizations. The list contains a number of *Fortune* 500 companies, including General Mills, Honeywell, Pillsbury, and the H.B. Fuller Co. The Minneapolis offices of the accounting firms of Arthur Andersen, Price Waterhouse, Peat Marwick and Mitchell, and Touche Ross and Company are also on the list.

The number of academics who support the view that corporate responsibility involves an obligation to help solve social problems is even smaller than the number of corporations who support the view. Moreover, the corporate culture of the Minnesota business community is considered unique. The orthodox view is that a socially responsible corporation pursues profit while respecting the moral minimum. I have been an adherent of that position, but I now think the position is mistaken. Part of what it means for a corporation to be socially responsible is cooperation with other corporations and with nonprofit social and government agencies to help solve social problems.

SOCIAL RESPONSIBILITY AND THE DUTY TO SOLVE SOCIAL PROBLEMS

I began this section with an argument for a duty to solve social problems. This argument resembles one a Friedmanite could use to defend an obligation on the part of corporate managers to honor the needs and rights of corporate stakeholders. As you recall, a Friedmanite could argue that a concern with the needs and rights of corporate stakeholders is required for long-term profits. Treating one's customers, employees, and suppliers well is a means to profit.

That theme provides a rationale for an instrumental duty of business to solve social problems. The argument I shall make rests on a number of complicated and controversial empirical claims, and I have neither the expertise—nor the space to argue for these empirical claims here. However, these empirical claims constitute something of a conventional wisdom on this subject.

Among the social problems the U.S. faces, most of the more important ones have a severe impact on the quality of the work force. The problem of drug use and other forms of substance abuse, the abysmal quality of public education, the decline in work ethic values, the instability of the family, and the short-term orientation of all corporate stakeholders all affect the firm negatively. The impact is especially acute on employees and suppliers. If the work force is poorly educated, affected with substance abuse, poorly motivated, and short-term oriented, productivity suffers both in quantity and quality.

In future international competition, the quality of the work force is the most important asset a company can have. If capital markets are open, the cost of capital will even out, so any advantage a country might gain through lower costs of capital is short-term. If a country gains an advantage through a technological discovery, highly developed technological competitors will reverse engineer the discovery so the advantage is short-term as well. The one advantage that is relatively long lasting is the quality of one's work force.

In that respect America is at a disadvantage. All the problems pointed out earlier have affected the quality of our work force more severely than in other countries. In addition, racial, religious, and ethnic tensions in our pluralistic work force affect productivity, putting us at a disadvantage against industrial societies with a more homogeneous work force. Thus, if America is to remain competitive, social problems that affect work-force productivity must be addressed.

However, the traditional institutional source for resolving social problems—government—seems to have neither the will nor the power to do so. After all, the costs are high and Americans—as events in the past decade have demonstrated—don't like taxes. In addition to being high, the costs are also immediate. However, the benefits, though higher, are very distant. Politicians have difficulty with a time frame beyond the next election. Therefore, there is little incentive for a politician to pay the costs now. A well worked-out statement of this view can be found in Alan Blinder's *Hard Heads Soft Hearts* (1987).

To make matters worse, our high national debt, the recent war with Iraq, the S&L debacle, and our aging infrastructure will only drain resources from social problems. If international competition requires that such problems be solved, but government is unwilling and perhaps unable to do so, it would seem that business has no choice but to become involved. The long-term competitiveness and hence long-term profitability of business is at stake. If the scenario I have painted is at all accurate, then even a Friedmanite could argue that business should help solve social problems. Business initiative in that area is justified on the grounds that such action is necessary to increase profits.

There certainly is nothing inconsistent with a Friedmanite arguing that business should help solve social problems to increase profit, so long as the dangers from not doing so outweigh the dangers discussed earlier. But I doubt that people like Levitt would ever agree that the increase in profitability would be worth the cost of lost independence now enjoyed by the business community. Even though Friedmanites in theory could support a view of corporate responsibility that included a corporate duty to help solve social problems, in all probability they would not.

On the chance some Friedmanite might support such an expanded concept of social responsibility, let me argue why a Friedmanite approach to an obligation to help solve social problems would probably fail. My argument here is tied up with issues of motivation and intentionality.

Consider what philosophers call "the hedonic paradox": the more people consciously seek happiness the less likely they are to achieve it. The reader is invited to test this assertion by getting up tomorrow and framing his or her activities with a conscious goal of happiness. In other words, do everything to be happy. If you do, almost certainly you will fail to achieve happiness.

To understand the paradox, we must distinguish between the intended end of an action and the feelings we get when we succeed (achieve the goal). If you are thirsty, you seek a glass of water to extinguish the thirst. When you quench your thirst you feel pleasure or contentment. But you didn't get the glass of water to get the contentment that goes with quenching your thirst. And you generally don't act to be happy. You are happy when you succeed in obtaining the goals that constitute the basis of your actions. Happiness is not one of those goals; it is a state one achieves when one successfully gains one's other goals.

What does this have to do with profit? Should profit be a conscious goal of the firm, or the result of achieving other corporate goals? For simplicity's sake let us say there is some relation between providing meaningful work for employees, quality products for customers, and corporate profits. What is the nature of that relationship? Do you achieve meaningful work for employees and quality products for customers by aiming at profits (by making profits your goal), or do you aim at providing meaningful work for employees and quality products for customers (make them your goal) and achieve profits as a result? A Friedmanite is committed to making profits the goal. As we saw in the discussion of stakeholder theory, a Friedmanite will respect the needs and rights of the other stakeholders to increase profits for the stockholders. But for a genuine stakeholder theorist, the needs and rights of the various stakeholders take priority. Management acts in response to those needs: profits are often the happy result.

Both Friedmanites and non-Friedmanites can posit a relationship between profits and meeting stakeholder needs. What divides them is the strength of the causal arrow, a difference over which one should be the conscious objective of management. A Friedmanite argues for profit. A stakeholder theorist argues for the needs and rights of stakeholders. A Friedmanite argues that you treat employees and customers well to make a profit: good treatment is a means to an end. A stakeholder theorist argues that a manager should treat employees and customers well because it is the right thing to do; the needs and rights of the corporate stakeholders are the ends the manager should aim at. Profits are the happy results that usually accompany these ends.

American corporations have thought like Friedmanites even when they speak the language of stakeholder theorists. They introduce quality circles or ESOPS to increase profits. Some of our international competitors have thought like stakeholder theorists even though they have achieved Friedman-like results.

With respect to the duty to help solve social

problems, should that duty be taken on because by doing so profits may be increased, or because it is a moral responsibility to do so? To answer that question, I suggest we visit the work of Cornell economist Robert Frank (1988) and consider the spotty success of the introduction of quality circles and other forms of "enlightened" labor management in the U.S.

Frank's point, buttressed by a large amount of empirical evidence from psychology, sociology, and biology, is that an altruistic person (a person who will not behave opportunistically even when he or she can get away with it) is the most desirable person to make a deal with. After all, if you have a contractual relationship with someone, the best person you can deal with is someone you know will honor the terms of the contract even if he or she could get away with not honoring them. An employer wants employees who won't steal or cheat even if they could. A marriage partner wants a spouse who won't cheat even if he or she could. Altruists rather than profit maximizers make the best business partners.

Frank then goes on to make the point Immanuel Kant would make. You can't adopt altruism as a strategy like "honesty is the best policy" and gain the advantages of altruism. After all, if I knew you were being an altruist because it paid, I would conclude that in any case where altruism didn't pay, you would revert to opportunism. My ideal business partner is someone who doesn't merely adopt altruism because it pays but adopts it because he or she is committed to it. She or he is not an opportunist because opportunism is wrong. As Frank says:

> For the model to work, satisfaction from doing the right thing must not be premised on the fact that material gains may later follow; rather it must be *intrinsic* to the act itself. Otherwise a person will lack the necessary motivation to make self-sacrificing choices, and once others sense that, material gains will not, in fact, follow. Under the commitment model, moral sentiments do not lead to material advantage unless they are heartfelt.

Frank's theoretical account of the advantages of committed altruism over reciprocal altruism as the best payoff strategy helps explain the spotty record of "enlightened" employee management techniques. Techniques like quality circles that work very well in Japan and Sweden don't work as well in the U.S. Why? Cultural difference is not a sufficiently specific answer. What cultural differences make the transfer difficult? I hypothesize that since labor/management relations in the U.S. are opportunistically based, labor assumes—probably correctly—that such reforms are motivated not by employer concern for employees but by profit. If that is the motivation, labor reasons, why should labor embrace the reforms? The elements of trust created by genuine concern for employees are missing in the American context. Indeed, both labor and management assume the other will behave opportunistically. Academics assume that too, and agency theory provides a model for the opportunistic framework. Given that cultural and intellectual context, it is no surprise that labor would distrust an employer whose concern with an improved working environment was not genuinely altruistic.

This discussion affects the duty to help solve social problems. If the resolution of these problems would improve America's human capital, that result would be most likely to occur if the investment in human capital were altruistically motivated. The one good thing about corporate efforts to solve social problems is that it is easy to show that with respect to the individual firm, such efforts must be altruistic. After all, an improved labor force is a classic case of a public good. There is no guarantee that the money spent by an individual firm will benefit that firm. If a firm adopts an inner city elementary school and pours resources into it, there is no reason to think that firm will get its investment back. The reason need not be that many of the students of that elementary school won't work for the supporting firm. After all, it might gain employees from other schools supported by other firms. Rather, the reason is that some firms will ride free off the expenditures of the moral firms. Thus, employees who understand these considerations can be sure that the employers who give money to solve social problems are altruistic.

If this analysis is correct the following conclusions can be drawn:

1. It is in the interest of business to adopt an extended view of corporate social responsibility that includes a duty to help solve social problems.
2. If business adopts that duty because it thinks it will benefit, its actions will be viewed cynically.
3. Moreover, because an improved labor force is a public good for business, the only real reason for an individual firm to help solve social problems is altruistic.
4. Thus, employees and other corporate stakeholders have a good reason to believe that corporate attempts to solve social problems are altruistic.

OBLIGATIONS OF VARIOUS STAKEHOLDERS IN A SOCIALLY RESPONSIBLE CORPORATION

In the previous section I gave an argument to show that everyone has good reason to believe that corporate attempts to solve social problems are genuinely altruistic. What are the implications of this for the various corporate stakeholders, especially customers?

Our ordinary way of speaking is to say the corporation ought to respect stakeholder needs and rights. Thus, we say that the corporation should produce quality products for customers, or that the corporation should not subject its employees to lie detector tests. We speak of the obligation of the firm (firm's management) to employees, customers, and local community. However, this way of speaking tends to give a one-sided emphasis to the moral obligations of the corporation.

My concern is that within the firm conceived of as a moral community, we speak as if all the obligations fall on the firm, or its managers and stockholders. In a previous article, "The Firm as a Moral Community" (Bowie 1991), I argued that Kant's third formulation of the categorical imperative best captures the moral relations that exist among corporate stakeholders. Kant would view a corporation as a moral community in which all of the stakeholders would both create the rules that govern them and be bound to one another by these same rules.

Moral relations are reciprocal. In addition to the obligations of managers, what of the obligations of the employees, customers, or local community to the firm (firm's management)? For example, business ethicists are critical of the so-called employment-at-will doctrine under which employees can be let go for "any reason, no reason, or reason immoral." Such a doctrine is unresponsive to the needs and rights of employees; it permits a manager to ignore both the quality of an employee's work performance and the number of years he or she has been with the firm.

Similarly, business ethicists are critical of the noneconomic layoffs that often accompany a hostile takeover. An example of noneconomic layoffs is when people are fired just because they worked for the old company. The new managers simply want their people in those positions—an understandable view, but one that does not take into account the interests of the employees let go. Those people might have served the target company for 20 years with great loyalty and distinction. Now they find themselves out of work through no fault of their own.

However, these business ethicists seldom criticize employees who leave a corporation on short notice simply to get a better job. Business firms argue that they invest huge amounts of money in training new employees, and losses from turnover are very high. Sometimes the employee might have been given educational benefits or even paid leave to resolve personal problems such as alcohol and drug abuse. Others may have received company financial support for further education—perhaps even an M.B.A. Yet these employees think nothing of leaving the proven loyal employer for a better job elsewhere. As managers often remind us, loyalty is not a one-way street.

What needs to be decided is the nature of the employment relationship. Because it is among people, it cannot be merely an economic relationship. Although some currently refer to it as such, they are mistaken. All employment relationships have some contractual elements attached to them. A contract represents a kind of promise; even the standard employment relationship is in part moral. Some argue that legally the employment contract is nothing more than an agreement that the employer can let the employee go whenever he or she wants, and the employee can leave whenever he or she wants. There is true reciprocity here, even if the relationship is rather limited morally.

However, in the world of actual business practice one side or the other often behaves in ways that go far beyond the limited legal contractual relationship, thus adding moral capital to the relationship. Loyal employees who may have passed up other jobs are let go; employees leave loyal employers who have invested heavily in their welfare for a slightly better-paying job. Both actions are morally wrong because the duties of reciprocity and gratitude have been breached. Social responsibility under a stakeholder model requires that each stakeholder has reciprocal duties with others. Thus, if an employee has a duty of loyalty to an employer, an employer has a duty of loyalty to an employee.

Let us apply this analysis to a triadic stakeholder relationship—the firm's management, its customers, and the local community. One of the moral problems facing any community is environmental pollution. As with the employment-at-will doctrine, most business ethicists focus on the obligations of the firm. But what of the obligations of the consumers who buy and use the firm's products?

Consider the following instances reported by Alicia Swasy in a recent *Wall Street Journal* article (1988). Wendy's tried to replace foam plates and cups with paper, but customers in the test markets balked.

Procter and Gamble offered Downy fabric softener in a concentrated form that requires less packaging than ready-to-use products. However, the concentrate version is less convenient because it has to be mixed with water. Sales have been poor. Procter and Gamble also manufactures Vizir and Lenor brands of detergents in concentrate form. Europeans will take the trouble; Americans will not.

Kodak tried to eliminate its yellow film boxes but met customer resistance. McDonald's has been testing mini-incinerators that convert trash into energy but often meets opposition from community groups that fear the incinerators will pollute the air. A McDonald's spokesperson points out that the emissions are mostly carbon dioxide and water vapor and are "less offensive than a barbecue."

And Jerry Alder reports in *Newsweek* (1989) that Exxon spent approximately $40,000 each to "save" 230 otters. Otters in captivity cost $800. Fishermen in Alaska are permitted to shoot otters as pests.

Recently environmentalists have pointed out the environmental damage caused by the wide-spread use of disposable diapers. However, are Americans ready to give up Pampers and go back to cloth diapers and the diaper pail? Most observers think not.

If environmentalists want business to produce products that are more friendly to the environment, they must convince Americans to purchase them. Business will respond to the market. It is the consuming public that has the obligation to make the trade-off between cost and environmental integrity.

Yet another example involves corporate giving. Earlier I cited the Twin Cities, Minnesota business community as providing an example of a local community where many of the firms gave either 2 percent or 5 percent of their pretax profits back to the community. I have never heard anyone argue that on the principle of reciprocity, citizens of the Twin Cities have obligations to these firms. Yet I would argue that these citizens have an obligation to support socially responsible firms over firms that are either socially irresponsible or indifferent to social responsibility. The relation of a local citizen to the companies that do business locally is again not simply economic. Citizens who consider only price in choosing between two department stores are behaving in a socially irresponsible way. If one department store contributes to the local community and the other doesn't, that factor should be taken into account when citizens in that community decide on where to shop. It's more than a matter of price.

The Target department store chain is a branch of the Dayton Hudson Company. It has a special program for hiring the disabled, and even assists these people with up to one-third of their rent. At Christmas it closes its stores to the general public and opens them to the elderly and disabled. These people receive an additional 10 percent discount and free gift wrapping. In many stores 75 percent of the trash generated is recycled. Target is a member of the 5 percent club. The list of its activities that support the community goes on and on. Target's competitors, WalMart and K mart, have nothing comparable. I maintain that Target's superior social performance creates an obligation for members of the community to shop at Target.

All these examples lead to a general point. For too long corporate responsibility has been analyzed simply in terms of the responsibilities of the firm (firm's management) to all other corporate stakeholders except stockholders. I exclude stockholders because the cost of honoring stakeholder obligations comes almost exclusively from their profits. If we are to have a truly comprehensive theory of corporate social responsibility, we must develop a theory for determining the appropriate *reciprocal* duties that exist among corporate stakeholders. If the managers and stockholders have a duty to customers, suppliers, employees, and the local community, then the local community, employees, suppliers, and customers have a duty to managers and stockholders. What these duties are has barely been discussed.

THE COMPLICATIONS OF MORAL PLURALISM

A great complication that exists for any attempt to determine reciprocal stakeholder duties occurs when the existence of moral pluralism is taken into account. For purposes of this paper, moral pluralism is a descriptive term that applies to the widespread disagreement about moral matters that exists among the American people. People disagree as to what is right and wrong. Some consider drug testing to be right. Others think it's wrong. People also disagree about the priorities given to various rights and responsibilities. For example, does the firm's obligation to protect its customers override its obligation to protect the privacy of its employees? And suppose it is decided that the safety of the customers does take priority? Is testing all employees or random testing more fair? The general point is this: If people cannot agree as to what is right and wrong and how to set priorities when our duties conflict, what advice can be given to managers and other corporate stakeholders regarding what their duties are?

The unhappy situation that befell Dayton Hudson in late 1990 illustrates the point exactly. Dayton Hudson has long been a member of the Twin Cities 5 percent club. The funds are distributed through the Dayton Hudson Foundation. For many years Planned Parenthood has been the recipient of relatively small grants of a few thousand dollars. Abortion opponents have charged Planned Parenthood with various degrees of complicity in abortion activities.

In 1990 Dayton Hudson announced that to avoid becoming embroiled in the abortion debate, it would no longer support Planned Parenthood. No decision could have gotten it more embroiled in the debate. Pro-choice forces announced an immediate boycott of Dayton Hudson and its Target stores; hundreds of people cut up their Dayton Hudson credit cards and mailed them back to the company. In a few days Dayton Hudson relented and agreed to provide a grant to Planned Parenthood as it had done in the past. Now the anti-abortion forces were enraged. They organized boycotts and demonstrations that continued into the holiday season.

Dayton Hudson officials were both embarrassed and angry, but they indicated they would not retreat from their position to give 5 percent of their pretax income to charity. Although little was said publicly, the Dayton Hudson public relations disaster gave many executives pause. Perhaps the Friedmanites were right. They were giving away stockholder money for causes deemed inappropriate. Obviously some stockholders would not approve of the company's choices, just as some of Dayton's customers and citizens of the local community didn't.

In addition some executives were rumored to have taken the following position:

1. The money is ours;
2. If people don't like how we spend our money, then we won't spend it on charity at all.

These corporate officials saw Dayton Hudson's protesting customers and citizens in the Twin Cities as ungrateful and unappreciative of the largesse Dayton Hudson had given over the years. These ingrates did not deserve corporate support. Whether corporate support for charities in the Twin Cities will fall off over the next few years remains to be seen.

Should the Dayton Hudson problem become more widespread, a serious impediment toward any corporation's decision to help solve social problems will have arisen. How should such difficulties be resolved? To answer that question we need to return to our model of the firm as a nexus of moral relationships among stakeholders. From that perspective I might suggest some principles that can be used to help resolve the problems created by moral pluralism.

First, if a corporation really has a duty to help solve social problems, we can ask whether the corporation, through its managers, should have sole say as to how the money is to be spent. I think the answer to that question must be "no." A firm as constituted by its stakeholders is not narrowly defined. To let the managers have the sole say is to allow one stakeholder to make the decisions on behalf of all. How can that be justified?

Some argue that legal ownership justifies the decision. On this view the decision should be made by the stockholders, because they are the legal owners. To my knowledge, no corporation decides either the amount of charity or determines those organizations that receive charity by taking a vote of the stockholders. Of course, the matter could be settled in this way, but I have argued elsewhere (Bowie 1990) that the limited short-term view of most stockholders undercuts any moral claim that ownership might have to make the sole decision here.

These arguments, if valid, also count against any view that would justify the manager making this decision as the agent of the stockholder. If the stockholders have no right to make the sole determination in these matters, neither do the stockholders' agents. If no one stakeholder should settle these issues, it seems reasonable to think that all stakeholders should have a voice. How this voice is exercised can be decided in a number of ways.

Some corporations might focus on providing funds to groups that have broad public support, such as the United Way. Agencies like the United Way reflect community decisions concerning which charities are considered worthwhile. Undoubtedly some people in the community will object to the list, and agencies like the United Way have been criticized for leaving out controversial nonprofits that really fight social problems while keeping "middle class" charities such as the Boy Scouts. Despite these objections, deferring to local agencies recognizes the voice of the local community in decisions that are made. Alternatively, a corporation might put community people on its foundation board or community affairs council. I would recommend the first approach. The latter approach runs the risk of filling a board or council with individuals who speak only to narrow interests. Moreover, in line with my argument that moral duties fall on all corporate stakeholders, I would argue that it is the moral responsibility of the community to structure the United Way and other social agencies to meet genuine social needs. It is up to the local community to find a place for unpopular but socially concerned and effective nonprofits. It is up to the local community to solve the problems of representation.

Many corporations have given voice to their employees by matching employee contributions to charity. If an employee gives $100 to his or her college alma mater, the company will kick in $100 as well. Corporations also support charitable organizations in cities and towns where they have plants. They might extend this to cities and towns where their suppliers are located as well. These strategies should be adopted as policy by other corporations unless other defensible ways of giving voice to employees and suppliers can be found.

As for customers, they are part of the local community; unless there are some special circumstances that should be taken into account. I think our analysis will suffice. Customers are given voice the same way the local community is—by supporting local agencies through the United Way or some other similar organization.

Finally, I turn to stockholders. Although I have argued that the amount and type of corporate support given to help solve social problems should not be decided by the stockholders alone, they certainly should have some say in the decisions. Management might poll stockholders to determine their interests or get them to specifically approve the company's program in this area when they cast their annual proxy vote for the election of the board and other matters.

As the tenor of these remarks suggest, we are further along than might have been suspected with regard to giving all stakeholders a voice in corporate decisions. However, we have a way to go, and I have made some suggestions as to the directions we might take.

Let me close by making a point that will seem obvious to philosophers but less obvious to others. In essence I have approached the issues raised by ethical pluralism by process rather than substance. I have not tried to argue that one position on these matters is morally correct and the others morally flawed. Rather, I have tried to elucidate a just process so the various stakeholder voices in these matters can be heard and have some influence on the decision. To put my perspective in Rawls's language (1971), I think the issues presented by ethical pluralism can only be handled by just procedures rather than aiming at just results. In Rawls's language, I am suggesting a system of imperfect procedural justice to address this issue.

REFERENCES

Jerry Alder. "Alaska After Exxon," *Newsweek,* September 18, 1989, pp. 50–62.

Alan S. Blinder. *Hard Heads Soft Hearts* (Reading, Mass.: Addison Wesley, 1987).

Norman Bowie. *Business Ethics* (Englewood Cliffs, N.J.: Prentice Hall Inc., 1982).

Norman Bowie with Ronald Duska. *Business Ethics.* 2nd ed. (Englewood Cliffs, N.J.: Prentice Hall Inc., 1990).

Norman Bowie. "The Firm as a Moral Community," in Richard M. Coughlin, ed., *Perspectives on Socio-Economics* (White Plains, N.Y.: M.E. Sharpe, Inc., 1991; forthcoming).

Albert Carr. "Is Business Bluffing Ethical?" *Harvard Business Review.* January–February 1968, pp. 143–146.

Thomas Donaldson. *The Ethics of International Business* (New York: Oxford University Press, 1989).

William E. Evan and R. Edward Freeman. "A Stakeholder Theory of the Modern Corporation: Kantian Capitalism," in Tom L. Beauchamp and Norman E. Bowie, eds., *Ethical Theory and Business.* 3rd ed. (Englewood Cliffs, N.J.: Prentice Hall, 1988).

Robert Frank, *Passions Within Reason* (New York: W.W. Norton & Co., 1988).

R. Edward Freeman. *Strategic Management: A Stakeholder Approach* (Marshfield, Mass.: Pitman, 1984).

Milton Friedman. *Capitalism & Freedom* (Chicago: University of Chicago Press, 1962).

Milton Friedman, "The Social Responsibility of Business Is to Increase Its Profits," *New York Times Magazine.* September 13, 1970, pp. 32–34, 122–126.

Immanuel Kant, *Foundations of the Metaphysics of Morals* (Lewis White Beck, trans.) (Indianapolis: Bobbs Merrill, 1969).

Theodore Levitt, "The Dangers of Social Responsibility," *Harvard Business Review,* September–October 1958, pp. 41–50.

Theodore Levitt. "The Morality(?) of Advertising," *Harvard Business Review,* July–August 1970, pp. 84–92.

John Rawls, *A Theory of Justice* (Cambridge, Mass.: Harvard University Press, 1971).

Alicia Swasy, "For Consumers, Ecology Comes Second," *Wall Street Journal,* August 23, 1988, p. B1.

QUESTIONS FOR DISCUSSION

1. Hoffman and Newton detail a number of steps a corporation can take to develop an ethical corporate culture. Can you think of any additional steps that might be needed? Do firms serving different areas of the economy, for example, bio-tech firms and automobile manufacturers, need to develop ethical cultures in different ways, or have different components in their codes of ethics?
2. In your judgment, can corporations be too ethical? If there is a conflict between ethics and profits, what should be done?
3. Bowie argues that corporations should no longer take profit as their main goal. What does he propose to substitute in its place? Explain why you agree or disagree with his answer. If Bowie's proposals were implemented, what sort of changes do you think would occur in the business world over the next five years? The next twenty years? Would such changes make the United States more prosperous or less so? Would the United States be a better or worse place to live?

The Future Corporate Ethos

At Hughes Aircraft: A Hotline for All Seasons

Andrew W. Singer
Editor and Publisher, *Ethikos*

When Hughes Aircraft Company established its ethics hotline system in 1987, it was widely viewed as a way to stem corporate waste, fraud, and abuse. There was nothing particularly unusual in this. Hughes, a major government contractor, was a signatory to the Defense Industry Initiative (DII), which encouraged such initiatives as hotlines.

Since that time, however, the hotline system has evolved to fill another key purpose. It has become an important communication link to employees, particularly during the wrenching "restructuring" that Hughes, like other California defense contractors, is now going through.

From *Ethikos,* Vol. 6, No. 3 (November–December 1992). Reprinted by permission of the publisher.

BEYOND COMPLIANCE ISSUES

Layoffs have helped keep the hotline phones busy, notes Allan MacAller, Manager, Corporate Ethics Programs. Many of the calls are queries about matters like employee benefits.

"It gets an awful lot of traffic, beyond compliance and beyond ethics."

The company is not displeased that the hotlines are being used in this way. Every other week in fact, it publishes internally the names and numbers of its hotline administrators. There are 19 ethics administrators.

When the hotlines were first set up in 1987, about 60 percent of calls were "allegations," i.e., incriminations, finger pointing, reports of wrongdoing.

The company made a conscious effort to turn this around. At present, about 60 percent of calls are employees simply asking for advice, reports MacAller.

ENGULFED IN PERSONNEL MATTERS?

Is the company concerned that it may become engulfed by these sorts of personnel matters—which often have little to do with waste, fraud, and abuse?

"No," answers MacAller, "It reflects the credibility of the program." The ethics program was established "to reflect the value system of the company, not just the rules and regulations. As a result, a lot of what comes across in the hotline deals with human resources."

When the company undertook its restructuring, it was perhaps a "natural follow-on" that the hotline would absorb much of the anxiety that accompanies such a circumstance.

"We get a lot of calls about business conflicts, e.g., what am I permitted to do without damaging my relationship with the company." Those sorts of calls have increased in recent months. "Some people think about branching out, developing their own businesses." They often query the hotline about the propriety of doing this.

QUESTIONS OF TRUST

Hotlines in general don't always enjoy the full trust of corporate employees. In some companies workers suspect that hotline complaints will incite retribution from angry managers. MacAller has heard his colleagues at DII meetings report that employees are often scared to use hotlines, for reasons valid or not. Stories abound of employees who used the hotline, only to find themselves being monitored by corporate security.

Is this a problem at Hughes? MacAller believes that the numbers speak for themselves. In 1991, Hughes ethics administrators received calls from about 4.3 percent of the company's population. (Hughes has 60,000 employees.) This year, he estimates that number will increase by at least 10 percent. If employees were scared of the hotline, he reasons, would they be using it in such droves?

Allegations of wrongdoing comprise about 35 percent of the hotline calls, "but only 15 to 16 percent of the allegations are substantial. We always call them back," to let them know how an investigation is proceeding, says MacAller.

Hughes, like other firms, will accommodate anonymous hotline calls. In that case "we give them a code number" so they can call back and get an update on their cases.

The highest proportion of "allegations" deal with time card violations.

The ethics administrators are usually more senior people with human resources experience, such as contracts managers and human resource directors. "Not all are full-time jobs," says MacAller. The company has, in fact, only five full-time ethics administrators.

Asked about the selection process for the ethics administrators, MacAller answers that they are generally high-level people conversant with the company's policies and practices who have a high degree of integrity. (MacAller himself was formerly a corporate labor manager who specialized in negotiating labor contracts.)

The ethics administrators report to a senior ethics administrator within each "sector" (i.e., division, such as radar systems), who in turn reports to the sector's president. (The ethics administrators also report to MacAller's corporate ethics office.) "Most sectors also have ethics committees," which establish guidelines about how to conduct an ethics investigation, and other matters.

ETHICS TRAINING

Training plays a key part in Hughes' ethics program. New hires get a one-hour ethics briefing during their orientation period. They are issued a copy of the company's code of conduct, are shown an ethics film, and sign off on the rules and regulations, indicating that to the best of their knowledge they don't have a conflict of interest, for instance.

Three or four weeks later they're invited to a longer session run by the ethics administrator. Here they watch the Ethics Resource Center's ethics video "Tough Decisions." The ethics administrator and the employees go through exercises that accompany this video program, which Hughes Aircraft helped sponsor. This session takes two to four hours.

MacAller's group also conducts training programs for supervisors, puts on management development workshops, and performs other specialized training. All materiel people, for instance, go through regular training to certify that they are free of any conflicts of interest. (Hughes uses the Ethics Resource Center's "Buying Trouble" video here.) "We use similar programs for marketing people." (Overall, he speaks well of the ERC, which has conducted sessions for Hughes' higher level executives, as well as its ethics trainers.)

Overall, the principal aim of the ethics training is "to ensure that the best interests of the taxpayers are being served." But "a second benefit is that the ethics program is often able to uncover practices that may not be up to snuff in terms of 1990 and beyond."

ETHICS AND TQM

Ethics is a useful component of the company's Total Quality Management (TQM) effort, called "Continuous Measured Improvement," or CMI. "The ethics program is a resource for CMI that's unique."

Practically speaking, how can ethics contribute to productivity? Take time-card reporting. "If you don't report properly, you will have to give that money back, and that comes out of profits."

The ethics hotline has resulted in productivity gains in other areas, such as the inspection of parts. Someone calls up and says: "It's not being done right." An investigation typically sets it right.

The ethics program "permits us to more properly explain to an employee what is expected. It reduces that 'fog index.' "

The company, unlike some defense contractors, has extended its ethics program to the commercial side of the business. MacAller admits "that there's a big difference in the relationship with customers" when dealing with commercial customers compared with the government. One develops an "arm's length" relationship with government people. "With commercial people, you often want to get closer to them."

But even this has its limits. Hughes and parent General Motors both have a tough code for dealing with customers and vendors, he says.

KEEP HOTLINES OUT OF LAW DEPARTMENT

Asked about the dos and don'ts of running an ethics program, MacAller opines: "I don't think the hotline should be in the legal department," as is the case in a number of companies. Employees should have the opportunity to speak with someone to whom they can open up, he says.

Many companies evidently fear that they might hear some horrific things from employees, which is why they often prefer to have a lawyer on the other line. But this may be something of an over-reaction.

The ethics administrator should be a listener, one who listens with "the utmost deference and makes the caller feel welcome," says MacAller.

He agrees with those who say the corporate ethics function must go beyond mere work rules. "We do a tremendous amount of ethics awareness: we try to provide a compass where the employee doesn't have one. Ethics awareness provides tools."

It is true, however, that compliance training (as opposed to ethics training) absorbs more time. But that is because "employees are liable under the law and the company feels morally responsible" to do all that it can to prevent them from going astray. "I'm not embarrassed that we tell people: 'Here's the catechism.' "

A 'TOUGH PROGRAM'

As for sanctions: "Ethics is a tough program. We've fired a lot of people here." About 50 cases go "upstairs" each year, i.e., result in sanctions. Initially, dismissal was the most common sanction, occurring about 50 percent of the time, but that percentage has since dropped. Other common sanctions are suspensions and reprimands.

Conduct that has resulted in discharge includes contract mischarging, faulty expense reporting, and conflicts of interest.

"Our most frequent cause of discharge is time card falsification," which is technically a kind of fraud, albeit usually a minor one.

Not everyone is fired for time card violations. The company believes that matters should be dealt with on a case-by-case basis. The company wouldn't fire a 15-year veteran with no previous problems, for instance, for a 15-minute time-card falsification. On the other hand, a worker of one-year's standing who intentionally and repeatedly falsifies his card would likely be discharged.

From April 1987 to June 1992, sanctions were lodged against 467 employees, of whom 36 percent were discharged. "Sanctions have to be tough if they're to be taken seriously," says MacAller.

About 30 percent of those sanctioned are managers. The company has fired vice-presidents and group vice-presidents for these sorts of abuses, according to MacAller.

When Hughes and other companies signed the DII, they suddenly took plant rules that had applied to the rank and file and applied them to white-collar workers. That came as a mild shock to some managers.

The company first "briefed the heck out of everyone," recalls MacAller, but it was soon made clear that if a manager didn't comply he or she could be fired.

Investigations are not usually conducted by ethics administrators, but by corporate attorneys, security managers, and other appropriate parties.

BEGINNING WITH PURCHASING

The Hughes Aircraft ethics program began in 1984, when the company suspected that a few people in its materiel group (which encompasses the purchasing function) were accepting gratuities.

That year the company began "a strenuous program to acquaint all employees of the proper relationship to the vending community." Hughes developed a film in which the president and vice president of materiel discussed ethical dilemmas. The company developed a code of conduct to deal with "ethics and buying," and shared that with new hires and existing employees.

The program continued until 1986, when Hughes met with the Packard Commission, out of which grew the Defense Industry Initiative (DII), the voluntary guidelines developed by the nation's largest defense contractors to promote ethical business conduct. The company was one of the early signatories of the DII. Since those first days, the ethics program has been expanded significantly, and today encompasses such areas as political relations and company benefits.

IMPACT FROM NEW SENTENCING GUIDELINES?

MacAller has not had to modify the company's ethics program as a result of the new U.S. Corporate Sentencing Guidelines. "I've lined up our requirements against those that appear to be required. I'm hopeful that the design of our program will meet the test of the current guidelines, although as legal cases are developed under the guidelines, that could change. I'm not so sure about the future, although I'm satisfied for the time being."

Can he assess the program? "I think it's had a positive impact on employees."

It has opened up lines of communication. When Hughes established its ethics initiative, people called up to say: "We're glad that you're doing this." Today, the company promotes the program when it is recruiting at colleges. "We go to lengths to tell people that we're a company that's interested in protecting the taxpayers."

Split Personality at Stride Rite

Joseph Pereira
Staff Reporter, *The Wall Street Journal*

At the gleaming headquarters building of Stride Rite Corp. in bustling Kendall Square here, plaques on the walls honor the shoe company for its good deeds.

In the past three years alone, Stride Rite has re-

---

ceived 14 public-service awards, including ones from the National Women's Political Caucus, Northeastern University, the Northeast Human Resources Association and Harvard University, which praised it for "improving the quality of life" in its community and the nation.

While doing good, Stride Rite also has done well. It has posted a profit, usually a record, for the past 32 quarters. This year, its sales are expected to top $625 million, more than double the 1986 level. Its stock has increased sixfold since then, making it a favorite on the New York Stock Exchange and among socially conscious investors.

A VERY DIFFERENT SIGHT

But just a few miles away, in Boston's rough inner-city Roxbury neighborhood, stands another Stride Rite building: a weather-beaten, red-brick structure surrounded by empty lots, crumbling roads and chain-link fences. It once housed corporate headquarters and employed 2,500 people making the company's Keds sneakers and Sperry Top-Sider shoes.

Today, the building is just a distribution center employing only 175 workers. Next year, even they will be gone. Stride Rite plans to close the warehouse—and another one in New Bedford, Mass.—and move the operations to Kentucky.

In Roxbury, so close to corporate headquarters but yet so far, Stride Rite's citations for corporate citizenship ring hollow. With the local unemployment rate estimated at nearly 30%, the soon-to-be-jobless workers see a bleak future.

"Where are you supposed to go?" wonders Miguel Brandao, a 46-year-old Cape Verdean immigrant who has worked at the plant 11 years. "There is no place to go."

BITTERNESS IN NEW BEDFORD

In New Bedford, where unemployment runs about 14% of the labor force, Stride Rite's plan to leave stirs bitterness. Since the company's announcement earlier this year, two suspicious fires have caused plant damage estimated at more than $750,000, and three workers are under investigation.

And last June, Stride Rite closed another plant, in Tipton, Mo., and laid off 280 workers. The unemployment rate is grim there, too. Three other shoe companies also closed nearby factories at about the same time, idling 1,400 workers. Angie and Stanley Shewmaker, who both worked for Stride Rite in Tipton, are still unemployed. They have been in job training—and in counseling for a marriage strained by money worries. "I'm all nerves," Mrs. Shewmaker says. "I'm on tranquilizers. I can't sleep at night. It's been hard. I'm fighting depression all the time."

In the past decade, Stride Rite has prospered partly by closing 15 factories, mostly in the Northeast and several in depressed areas, and moving most of its production to various low-cost Asian countries. The company still employes 2,500 workers in the U.S., but that is down from a peak of about 6,000.

DIFFICULT QUESTIONS

So yet-another departure from yet-another inner-city neighborhood such as Roxbury is hardly surprising. Neither is the transfer of work to the Far East. But when the company behind the moves is a Stride Rite, one that has received so many accolades, it raises difficult questions: What makes a company socially responsible? And how far can social responsibility be expected to go?

Is it sufficient to do good deeds, as everyone agrees Stride Rite has done? It has contributed 5% of its pretax profit to a foundation, sent 100,000 pairs of sneakers to strife-torn Mozambique, paid Harvard graduate students to work in a Cambodian refugee camp, given scholarships to inner-city youths, permitted employees to tutor disadvantaged children on company time and been a pioneer in setting up on-site day-care and elder-care facilities.

Or is something more basic needed, such as providing jobs in depressed areas even at the expense of profits? To many who have watched much of corporate America leave inner cities, the answer is clear. "The most socially responsible thing a company can do is to give a person a job," argues Donald Gillis, executive director of Boston's Economic

Development and Industrial Corp., which tried to persuade Stride Rite to stay.

Adds Gilda Haas, an economic and urban-planning lecturer at the University of California at Los Angeles: "It strikes me as strange that we're having this conversation about inner-city jobs only a year after the civil unrest in South Central Los Angeles. What exactly did the corporate sector mean when they spoke of the need for inner-city jobs last year as Los Angeles burned?"

Stride Rite contends that it has been socially responsible but nevertheless has to balance the demands of two masters—shareholders and society. If a company doesn't stay competitive, its executives contend, it can't grow, it would provide even fewer jobs, it would earn too little to afford its community programs, and, at worst, it might jeopardize its survival. "Putting jobs into places where it doesn't make economic sense," Chairman Ervin Shames says, "is a dilution of corporate and community wealth."

So, even while Stride Rite was nurturing social programs, it slowly and reluctantly began closing plants in Maine and New Hampshire in the late 1960s and shifting production overseas. And as the quality and efficiency of foreign workers improved, Stride Rite, and its competitors, started to export jobs more rapidly. Higher-priced American workers simply weren't competitive; even Stride Rite's efforts to run small, cost-efficient factories in rural New England failed.

Nike Inc., too, briefly tried running a factory in Maine in the late 1970s, but gave up after losing more than $5 million a year. "Athletic shoes are best made in parts of the world other than the U.S.," a Nike spokesman says. "If the Air Jordan shoe were to be made in the U.S. today, it could retail for $280 to $310 a pair." The Taiwan-made shoe costs about $100.

By the early 1980s, only half of Stride Rite's shoes were U.S.-made. "You could stay in the U.S. if you were doing high-end shoes," a niche Stride Rite wasn't in, says Myles Slosberg, a director and former executive vice president. "Otherwise, it was going to be pretty darn difficult."

One of the company's biggest layoffs, of 2,500 people, came in 1984. Stride Rite closed three plants, including its children's shoe factory in Roxbury, and moved the jobs overseas. It had to, it says, to survive. That year, its net income plummeted 68% to $5.4 million from $16.8 million in 1983—the first drop in 13 years. In 1986, the company closed two more Massachusetts plants, in Brockton and Lawrence. It still operates two factories in Missouri, but it now makes only 10% of its shoes in the U.S. It doesn't own the overseas factories or directly employ the workers; instead, it contracts with local companies.

The labor savings are huge. Andy Li, a Taiwan contractor who has found subcontractors to work for Stride Rite, says skilled workers in China earn $100 to $150 a month, working 50 to 65 hours a week. Unskilled workers—packers and sorters—get $50 to $70 a month. By comparison, Stride Rite's U.S. workers average $1,200 to $1,400 per month in wages alone, plus modest fringe benefits.

"It has become virtually impossible to manufacture sneakers in the U.S. and still be in the competition," says Carl Steidtmann, chief economist at Price Waterhouse's merchandise-consulting division. The obvious consequence in Missouri: Shoemaking jobs dwindled to 8,250 last year from a peak of 25,000 in 1968.

Even overseas, Stride Rite continues its quest for labor bargains. In recent years, it has switched from factories in South Korea as pay rose there to lower-wage Indonesia and China. "It has become sort of Holy Grail for us," Mr. Slosberg says.

Stride Rite also contends it has little choice but to pull its distribution centers out of Roxbury and New Bedford. "It was a difficult decision," Mr. Shames says. "Our hearts said, 'Stay,' but our heads said, 'Move.' " Stride Rite will save millions of dollars, he adds, by going to the Midwest. When the company profiled its retailers, he says, "the average customer tended to be in the Midwestern or Southern part of the nation."

Moreover, the central location will make shipping generally more efficient. Now, most Stride Rite shoes are shipped from the Far East to Los Angeles and Seattle and then trucked to Boston and New Bedford, where they are sorted and labeled and then dispatched to retailers nationwide. The new distribution center in Louisville will eliminate

800 to 1,200 miles on some truck routes, speeding delivery by 2 1/2 to four days. "After the numbers were added up, it wasn't even a close decision," says Mr. Slosberg, who is now a Massachusetts assistant attorney general.

Within Stride Rite's top management, however, the decision has caused soul-searching. Arnold Hiatt, a former chairman who retired last year but remains a director, says, "I objected to that decision as much as I could. I was overruled." He passionately espoused a "Jeffersonian vision" linking corporate and social responsibility. When Stride Rite joined 54 other companies to form Businesses for Social Responsibility last year, he said, "If you're pro-business, you also have to be concerned about things like jobs in the inner city and the 38 million Americans living below the poverty line."

But Mr. Hiatt concedes that the issue is complicated. For three months, officials reviewed offers in connection with the warehouse from Indiana, Ohio, Massachusetts and Kentucky. Kentucky won mainly because of a $24 million tax break over 10 years, vs. a $3 million offer from Massachusetts. Lower wage rates also played a role.

Mr. Hiatt acknowledges that he himself moved many jobs out of Roxbury in his 24 years as a top officer. "To the extent that you can stay in the city, I think you have to," he says. But "if it's at the expense of your business, I think you can't forget that your primary responsibility is to your stockholders."

It was under Mr. Hiatt, a staunch liberal who served as treasurer for Sen. Eugene McCarthy's 1968 presidential campaign, that Stride Rite became known for progressive policies. In 1971, he opened a day-care center at the Roxbury plant, a move that cost some money but more than paid off in goodwill. In 1988, another day-care center, at the Cambridge headquarters, was expanded to become a widely praised "intergenerational center," caring for the aged as well.

Stride Rite also contributes heavily to charity. In 1991, its board decided to allot 5% of pretax profits—or about $5 million last year—to the Stride Rite Charitable Foundation. Part of that money helps 40 inner-city students attend Harvard; in return for the $5,000-a-year scholarships, the students serve as mentors to other inner-city youths, helping them with school work and spending summers in housing projects. After graduation, the scholarship recipients can continue their public service for a year under a fellowship offering a $15,000 stipend. One student who last year was headed for a Wall Street job chose instead to work in a New York hospital that serves many AIDS patients.

Stride Rite has won admirers among many business critics. The company "is a case study of giving something back to the community," says Peggy Charren, a Cambridge resident who founded Action for Children's Television, which lobbies for better TV programming for kids.

For a long time, the Roxbury site, then the company headquarters, was relatively unscathed despite the sharply deteriorating neighborhood. Then, in 1981, came a stunning blow: Stride Rite moved its offices to Cambridge. "We held out as long as we could," Mr. Hiatt says, "but it became clear that people that had the more skilled jobs at Stride Rite were coming from other parts of the city and were increasingly reluctant to go into Roxbury." One day, a bullet smashed through his window, he says, "and I knew it was time to go."

To soften the impact on Roxbury, Stride Rite moved in distribution centers from Atlanta and Salem, N.H. But the respite was brief. In 1984, it closed the factory.

Now, the departure of the warehouse compounds Roxbury's problems. Ames Department Stores Inc. closed its Roxbury store in March and Digital Equipment Corp. shut its factory in the neighborhood this month.

"It is very devastating," says Roderick Dowdell, a worker at the nearby Common Bostonian restaurant. "It is like back-to-back grand slams by the opposing team." A few doors from Stride Rite in Roxbury, Edward Williams says his Hair Salon is struggling. "We did 150 clients a week; now, I'm lucky to do 25," he says.

In the wake of the closings, community leaders called a huddle, seeking ways to stimulate new businesses and hold onto existing ones. But one ray of hope, a proposed biotechnology center that will create 150 jobs, is little consolation to Stride Rite employees; many speak little or no English and lack the skills that even entry-level jobs at the center will require. Stride Rite employees need "$3,000 worth of education" to have hope of getting in the door, says Sue Swartz, director of the Boston Workers Assistance Center. But her project allows for only half that.

"How can I hope to find a job?" wonders Alberto Andrade, a 60-year-old native of Cape Verde whose eight years at Stride Rite don't qualify him for a pension.

The talk of schooling draws looks of amusement from a few workers. With eight children, Mr. Brandao, a sorter at the warehouse, says he must work an average of 14 hours overtime a week to make ends meet. "Who will feed my children?" he asks in thickly accented English.

The approximately 500 employees at the Roxbury and New Bedford facilities could request transfers to Kentucky but would compete with local applicants for the 275 positions. Many probably won't even try. "Why would we want to go there?" says Carol Pitta, an inventory controller at New Bedford. "There won't be a union, the pay will be less and what happens if in two months they don't want you? Who'll pay my way home?"

Realizing that about 250 co-workers will soon flood an already-tight job market, Tom Camara, a shop steward in New Bedford, is already pounding the pavement. He was unemployed more than a year before landing a job at Stride Rite two years ago. What will life be like after Stride Rite? "Don't know," he shrugs. "One thing's for sure: It's going to be tough."

Mr. Camara won't get much disagreement from people in Tipton, even though the federal government offered them retraining because the jobs lost in Missouri went abroad. Not all the unemployed could take advantage of the programs.

"It costs $80 a week for a baby sitter, and I'm getting $175 a week in unemployment assistance," explains Anita Bracht, a former Stride Rite employee in Tipton who has four children. Her husband, Donny, worked at Stride Rite, too, and also is unemployed. "He's tried everything," Mrs. Bracht says. "The union tells him there are 500 people on the waiting list" for jobs contracted by the union. With their unemployment benefits nearing an end, she adds, "I'm about ready to panic."

Among the many lessons learned from the closings, one has struck especially close to home for Mr. Brandao in Roxbury. A 70-year-old Irish immigrant, who rented a room from him, died recently, leaving behind a 32-year-old mentally disabled son. "I don't have the heart to ask him to leave," he says with the help of a translator. "If I did, I would be doing to him what my company is doing to me."

The Case of the Environmental Impasse

Alissa J. Stern
Former Ford Fellow in International Law, Harvard Law School

Environmentalists of every stripe disliked the Vermilion Paper Company. Even in an industry notorious for pumping rivers full of noxious waste and clear-cutting woodlands in county-sized chunks, Vermilion had a reputation for insensitivity. At one time or another, almost every jurisdiction in which it owned forests or mills had taken legal action against it for violating some environmental statute. In the 1970s, one of its own major stockholders sued the company for polluting a river the man liked to fish in.

Recently, however, Vermilion management had begun to see the green writing on the wall. The retirement of several executives who had begun their careers at a time when many people accepted pollution as a condition of progress had made way for fresh ideas and a more "socially responsible" manufacturing and marketing strategy. Moreover, consumers still associated the Vermilion name with good paper products at a good price and knew little or nothing of the company's shabby environmental record, so it was not too late to change course.

On the other hand, it was none too soon. Over the past five years, several international environmental groups had organized a campaign called Vermilion Action to inform the public about Vermilion's record and bring pressure to bear on the company to clean up its act. If environmentalists continued to target Vermilion as a public enemy, sooner or later the image would begin to stick.

In the mid-1980s, the company launched a campaign to change its image. Essentially a marketing effort, the campaign was built around the slogan "Green Vermilion" and consisted primarily of television ads and bright green labels on every bright red package of tissue and paper towels proclaiming environmentally friendly products and policies. For example, the company made much of the fact that it did not cut virgin forest, though in fact it had not cut any virgin forest in the United States since the mid-1940s, when it ran out of virgin forest to cut and went to tree farms. The green labels also declared in large type that the product inside was biodegradable, as if biodegradable paper were Vermilion's own scientific breakthrough. Still, the company actually did take steps to cut pollution at its paper mills even beyond state and federal air and water standards. It purchased the best new equipment and initiated research into new production methods that would reduce the amount of sulfites and chlorine used to make and bleach its paper.

So the new strategy was timely, disingenuous, and nevertheless real. Most executives cared more about the company's profits and image than about its environmental impact, but many saw the two as closely related and thought it ought to be possible to clean up operations enough to satisfy conscience and preserve Vermilion's good name in the marketplace without hurting dividends. There were even a few who believed that ways could be found to make paper profitably without polluting rivers or destroying ecologically valuable forests—and that it was the paper industry's responsibility to find them.

One of these was Peter Ostenson, director of offshore production, and it was offshore, especially in the Third World, that a genuine environmental policy would have its greatest impact. Vermilion expected its own pulp needs to grow some two million tons a year by the turn of the century, and tropical forests would inevitably provide much of the increase. The tropics were new to Vermilion, and Ostenson wanted to get off on the right foot. He was convinced that the environmental agenda and the business agenda had to come together to the benefit of both. Otherwise, they would collide to the detriment of both.

He had his work cut out for him selling this idea to top management. Oliver Hibbing, the president and CEO of Vermilion Paper, actively supported the so-called environmental strategy, but he made it clear to Ostenson that his first responsibility was to the stockholders.

"I'm a company man, Peter. So if you tell me we have to learn new ways of doing business because that's what our customers want, that's what we'll do. If I didn't buy that argument, I certainly wouldn't be spending all this money. But let somebody else run the environment. I'm with you on strategy—what more do you want?"

Ostenson always responded the same way. "It's a false distinction, Oliver. The company is *part* of the environment."

With rain forests nearly as vast as those of Brazil or Indonesia, the nation of Equitania has a quarter of its 210 million acres of land in some type of forestry production. The country produces nearly 20% of the world's tropical hardwoods and supplies the wood for about two million tons of paper pulp annually. All told, forestry contributes some $2 billion annually in foreign exchange and is Equitania's second highest export earner. Japanese companies hold about half the foreign forestry concessions, the other half belongs to companies from South Korea, Malaysia, Thailand, Singapore, Hong Kong, and the Philippines.

In the mid-1980s, Vermilion Paper began exploring the possibility of starting a eucalyptus plantation in Equitania to help meet the company's growing pulp and paper needs. Ostenson and Hibbing calculated that by 1993, the venture would need to produce the raw material for about 500,000 tons of pulp per year at an estimated startup cost of roughly $350 million, plus $180 million for expansion of an existing pulp-and-paper mill in Indonesia to process Equitanian eucalyptus as it arrived by sea. On Ostenson's recommendation, they chose Wendell Buyck to set up an office in Palakra, the Equitanian capital, identify a site, and pursue Equitanian government approval.

Buyck had no foreign experience to speak of. What he did have, in addition to seven years' experience in Vermilion middle management and an undergraduate degree in forestry, was energy, intelligence, and determination. Even more important, he shared Ostenson's views about incorporating sound environmental principles into Vermilion's business agenda.

On setting up shop in Palakra, Buyck found a bewildering array of government agencies and regulations. He quickly saw that many of the regulations were absurd and some of the agencies dishonest, but with little knowledge of the country and no capacity for bribery, he realized that all he could do was play by the rules.

An official at the Ministry of Forests encouraged him. "Many of us would rather deal with Americans because they try to comply with the law. Most Asian companies do not even make the attempt," he said. "On the other hand, that is probably why Americans do poorly here."

With this ambiguous advice to go on, Buyck decided to seek full, formal government authorization for the project at every step rather than run the risk of government sanctions at a later date. Although government authorization would not prevent officials from invoking additional regulations—or demanding payoffs—in the future, it would improve his odds of building a viable project.

As a first step, Buyck complied with foreign-investment regulations by forming a joint venture between Vermilion and Ankora Corporation, an Equitanian conglomerate dealing mostly in minerals and construction. As president of the joint venture, called Veranko, Buyck applied to the government for permission to create a eucalyptus plantation. In hopes that his application would move faster and more smoothly if he made friends and contacts at the ministries, Buyck met personally with dozens of key officials.

After months of delays, the government granted Veranko a 35-year, 398,000-acre concession in the Keewa Tinang province. Almost half of the land had recently been lumbered for hardwoods, and the foreign timber company involved had leveled the forest. This clear-cutting was an asset for Veranko. Buyck's plan to farm eucalpytus required open land, and Buyck had been looking for a recently logged parcel, partly so Veranko wouldn't have to cut any rain forest, partly for the satisfaction of reclaiming—and being seen to reclaim—deforested, despoiled land.

Government permit in hand, Buyck then turned his attention to nongovernmental bodies with stakes in the forest industry. The most powerful of these was Equitrass, the Equitanian Trade Association, a kind of self-appointed but quasi-official regulatory agency that enforced the rules of a dozen ministries—generously for member companies, harshly for others. While membership dues were modest, Equitrass also assessed large mandatory fees for its "production fund." Refusing to pay was tantamount to refusing to join, and refusing to join meant certain failure. Veranko chose to join and to make the production fund payments.

Buyck's next move was suggested by the experience of foreign companies in several nearby countries. In Indonesia, for example, the residents of one town ransacked and forced the closure of a Dutch-owned rubber plantation because the company had operated without community approval. In Malaysia, villagers revolted against logging in the rain forest even though the timber company had struck a deal with provincial leaders.

Suspecting that a concession from the government was not enough, Buyck decided that Veranko should seek approval directly from the local residents. Locating the plantation in Keewa Tinang increased the potential for problems because the Keewatinians resented the economic and political domination of the central government at Palakra, which they saw as little better than a colonialist power. They were also concerned about losing ultimate ownership rights to a foreign corporation and about the fate of their villages, lakes, and sacred tribal sites.

Buyck agreed to lease the land directly from the Keewatinians for a term of 35 years at a specified fee, in addition to the rent negotiated with the government in Palakra. He further assured local and provincial officials that he would keep the plantation away from villages, watersheds, lakes, and religious sites and that he would set aside the remaining rain forest in the concession as a nature preserve. Buyck also agreed to employ local people and to provide the province with a hospital, a school, and 100 kilometers of roads.

"He met our demands," recalls one community leader. "Other companies just come in and do whatever they want. Buyck was willing to listen."

Wendell Buyck had now spent nearly two years in Equitania. To Hibbing and the directors back in Michigan, progress seemed painfully slow. At this rate, the paper mill would come on line years behind the market opportunity. And now this man Buyck was agreeing to build schools and hospitals. Preserving virgin rain forest had the right sound to it, but schools and hospitals? Vermilion Paper was not a general contractor and certainly not a social service organization. These commitments might have some public relations value, but what about all those millions of paper towels that wouldn't be sold while Vermilion saved the world?

Peter Ostenson had to remind his superiors that Buyck was not trying to save the world, only Vermilion Paper. He took every opportunity to resell the environmental strategy to Hibbing, who still did not entirely buy Ostenson's contention that the time and money spent on this one project could pay a tenfold return in Third World goodwill, marketplace approval, and the increasingly well-publicized scorekeeping of environmentalists.

Ostenson himself began to wish that Buyck could move faster. But Buyck could smell victory on his own terms and was making no compromises. His next move was to conduct a six-month pilot study in the concession area to find a fast-growing species of eucalpytus. Of 109 varieties, Buyck chose one that would permit harvesting every five years, instead of the usual six to eight, which meant Veranko could grow more trees in less space.

The pilot study impressed the Equitanian government. "We would be in great shape if all companies were as thorough as Vermilion Paper," one official at the Ministry of Forests told Buyck.

Finally, Buyck began to address the concerns of Equitanian environmental groups, an unprecedented step for any foreign corporation. He asked the leaders of PELLONA, a consortium of more than 100 Equitanian environmental and community groups, for their advice on the Veranko project. Initially, PELLONA was unwilling to talk to Buyck because it feared alienating its own constituency. At the time, PELLONA was aligned with the international Vermilion Action campaign.

"Buyck was different, or at least he sounded different," recalls Maria Biwapik, PELLONA's director. "But we found it hard to believe that Vermilion had really changed its stripes. In fact, Buyck was a little too good to be true. Because he worked for Vermilion, we drew the obvious conclusion: he *wasn't* true. He was just Vermilion's way of getting its hands on that concession. Once it co-opted all the potential opposition, it would revert to business as usual—cutting rain forest, draining wetlands, ignoring the natives."

Buyck was undaunted by PELLONA's refusal to listen. He turned to the minister of environmental affairs—by now a friend—and asked him to set up a discussion between Veranko and PELLONA. After much urging and arm-twisting, PELLONA finally agreed to a meeting, but only after an internal struggle between PELLONA leadership and a group of dissenting member organizations led by MYP, a small, militant organization that opposed all further forest exploitation in Equitania. Since a closed meeting with Buyck would conjure up the awful specter of PELLONA getting into bed with the enemy, the meeting was to include delegates from at least a dozen PELLONA constituents, MYP among them. No one in PELLONA was taking any chances. In a meeting with deforesters, there had to be witnesses, concensus, and daylight.

Buyck opened the meeting by reading a statement picturing Veranko as a friend of the environment, supporting the concept of environmentally responsible development, and asking for a common effort to make such a strategy work—in effect a quid pro quo between business and environmental interests. Hackles rose. The MYP representative attacked Vermilion at length. Buyck backpedaled.

He said he was sorry if he had offended anyone and told them he needed their help. He then spoke passionately of his personal convictions. He told them how carefully and conscientiously he had satisfied the demands of government ministries. He described his negotiations with the tribal elders in Keewa Tinang, emphasizing the school and hospital. He made much of the pilot project. He underlined the fact that Veranko would plant only on land already cleared and would cut no new rain forest. He avoided any mention of resistance within his own company.

He did not succeed in allaying suspicions—dislike of Vermilion was too intense for that—but Maria Biwapik, for one, began to sense an opportunity If Buyck meant even half of what he said, why not hold him to his word, seize him by his outstretched hand, and not let go? And why not use the opportunity to give PELLONA some valuable limelight?

She asked Buyck if he would sign a binding agreement limiting the size of the tree farm and guaranteeing the rain forest now within the concession as a permanent preserve. She also asked him to give PELLONA a permanent right of access and oversight. She rejected the idea of a quid pro quo but pointed out that PELLONA could hardly raise comprehensive objections to a plantation operated according to a plan that PELLONA itself had helped create and had the right to monitor.

Buyck blanched. He knew that Vermilion could not possibly yield anything approaching even token control of its operations to environmentalists, even if they had been a lot more friendly than PELLONA. He proposed a compromise. Veranko would hire PELLONA as a consultant to the project. He offered a fee of $20,000.

The MYP delegate called it blood money. Biwapik and the others wanted to know what guarantee they had that Veranko would follow their recommendations. "None," Buyck said. But what guarantee did they have now? He needed their advice, he said. His record demonstrated an honest desire to do right by the rain forest, by Equitania, and by the Keewatinians. He reminded them that he had asked for this meeting. He assured them that enlightened Vermilion leadership had come to believe—as this project made clear—that the paper industry could live in harmony with the environment.

It wasn't much, but it was more than Biwapik had expected. She actually found herself believing in Buyck's sincerity. The following day, the PELLONA steering committee held a long, heated meeting. No single delegate or member organization believed Vermilion could be trusted, but, like Biwapik, most instinctively trusted Buyck. Only the MYP delegate and one or two others held fast to the too-good-to-be-true theory and thought Buyck was actually lying.

In the end, the steering committee voted to accept the consulting assignment, refuse the fee, and take a position of guarded "nondisapproval" of the Veranko project. What that meant in practice, Maria later explained to Buyck on the phone, was that for the time being, PELLONA would refrain from condemning Veranko but would keep its options open. "That's all I ask," Buyck said. "But what about MYP?" Though she had her doubts, Maria assured him that MYP would consent.

In fact, MYP had voted loudly against any form of cooperation with Vermilion. But MYP was chronically short of money, and if it wanted to remain inside PELLONA and use PELLONA's resources, it would have to go along with the majority—or so Maria reasoned. Of course MYP had a point: Vermilion certainly wasn't to be trusted and had to be watched closely. But this could be the chance PELLONA had been waiting for to bring pressure to bear on other foreign companies and convince the government and Equitrass that a strict environmental policy could work. And if PELLONA could take some of the credit for a success in Keewa Tinang, which Buyck's arrangement would let it do, so much the better. She wasn't about to let MYP sabotage such a rich opportunity.

For his part, Buyck was immensely pleased and relieved. He knew Hibbing was close to abandoning the whole project out of sheer impatience. Now Ostenson could tell him the project had passed its last great hurdle. Detailed planning and construction could now proceed with the blessings of the Equitanian government, the trade association, the Keewatinian community, and, however guardedly, some of the very environmental groups that had been supporting the Vermilion Action campaign. Reason had won a victory over both greed and passion. The environmental strategy was going to be a success. Buyck and Ostenson were vindicated.

Six weeks later, the Forest Defense Legion—a militant U.S. environmental group with close, informal ties to the Equitanian MYP—ran in four major U.S. dailies a full-page ad condemning Vermilion.

The Forest Defense Legion held a press conference later the same day to announce that unless Vermilion cancelled its project in Keewa Tinang within 30 days, the FDL would organize a worldwide boycott of Vermilion products.

The following day, meetings were held in Equitania and Michigan. In Equitania, Maria Biwapik and the other members of the PELLONA steering committee considered ways of limiting the damage. If Vermilion canceled the project, that was the end of PELLONA's golden opportunity to play in a bigger league and convert its convictions into practice. But if PELLONA defended Vermilion Paper and urged it to stay, it risked the utter loss of its credibility with other environmentalists.

Maria and many of the others were furious with MYP. "Why in God's name did you have to pick Vermilion?" she demanded. "There are a dozen worse companies doing business in this country and a thousand worse projects. What were you thinking of?"

"Don't climb on that high horse with me," the man from MYP responded angrily. "Are you trying to tell me that once our backs are turned, they won't cut rain forest to raise their yield? You're naive. They're all run for profit, these companies, and we attack them where we can. Most of the others have no retail customers we can appeal to. Vermilion does. It's as simple as that."

"I'm afraid you're the one who's naive," Maria said. "Please tell me what other company is even going to make the effort to work with us after this? Not only have you thrown away our chance to influence this project and every other forest project still to come, now we're going to have the government and Equitrass on our backs as well."

She paused. "This could set back the cause of the rain forest by ten years," she said. "And it could ruin PELLONA."

In Michigan, the choices were equally stark. Ostenson wanted to fight. The sheer injustice of the accusations made him dizzy. Who were these people? Did they really mean to make it impossible to change?

"If we don't fight this," he argued, "we lose not only the concession but also the strategy. Aside from the fact that it's so damned unfair, it's a business mistake to cut and run."

But Hibbing was not interested. "Peter, I don't know what you and Buyck think you've been up to these past three years, but it sure as hell hasn't been a business agenda. How is it *possible* you didn't see this coming? You weren't born yesterday. Buyck's been playing footsy with every bleeding heart in the Far East, and now the whole thing's exploded in his hands. What did he expect?"

"No one could have predicted that this one little group would go nuclear on us. Buyck made a superhuman effort to work with those people, and I still think he was right. We have to stand behind him and Veranko or give up the presence of having any strategy or vision beyond our own bottom line. We're on trial here. Canceling is an admission of guilt—and we're not guilty."

Hibbing was icily patient. "Millions and millions of people haven't seen these ads," he said. "And if we write off this fairly small investment, they never will. If we fight it, we're inviting a worldwide boycott that will make Vermilion Action look pale by comparison. We're only on trial if we choose to be. Justice, Peter, has no net present value."

"Okay, you're right. This is not a question of justice," Ostenson said. "But it's not a question of image either. It's a question of strategy, tactics, and politics. To protect this company over the long haul, we simply can't lose sight of the bigger issues."

Hibbing gave Ostenson a long, cold look. "Well, then, how about this for a bigger issue. If we fight this thing, the stockholders would be fully justified in getting rid of both of us. And then having us committed. Boycotts are a kind of lunacy, Peter, and—maybe you're right—a kind of politics. But I'm a businessman. What are you?"

SHOULD VERMILION FIGHT OR FOLD?

Four experts in environmental strategy discuss the options.

PIETER WINSEMIUS *is director of the Amsterdam office of McKinsey & Company and leads its worldwide environmental practice. He was the Netherlands' minister of environment from 1982 to 1986.*

Vermilion should face this challenge openly. It has a good record in Equitania; why not emphasize it?

Much like individuals, organizations react to challenge in predictable ways. First comes denial of the problem; then anger; and finally, the search for a solution. Oliver Hibbing and Peter Ostenson should take heed. Even though Wendell Buyck would be justified in reacting this way, it would be counterproductive for him to do so. Vermilion executives may be hurt, but they must swallow their pride and refrain from calling "foul." They have to deal pragmatically with the problem at hand.

First and foremost, Ostenson must convince Hibbing to buy into his views on the environment. In doing so, Ostenson should abide by three principles:

Be Responsive. Vermilion should organize a response that stresses accountability. Hibbing, as chief executive officer, should take responsibility for Vermilion's actions. He must be open with the press and the public; outsiders have an uncanny instinct for detecting half-truths or escapism. A straightforward response will demonstrate that Vermilion takes the concerns of consumers and environmentalists seriously.

Vermilion has a pretty good record in Equitania; why not emphasize it? Hibbing could publicly offer, and confirm in large-scale advertisements, to conduct an environmental impact assessment—or even more appropriately in this case, a societal impact assessment. Hibbing can present this to PELLONA, the Forest Defense Legion, or any other group for scrutiny. Most important, he can eliminate many doubts with regard to self-serving sweetheart statements by asking a group of world-class experts to give a second opinion, again publicly. Given the amount of homework already done, this should be relatively easy and should deflate much of the challenge from the FDL and the MYP.

Learn from Experience. Clearly, Vermilion must review its internal procedures and take measures to prevent falling into this trap again. At the minimum, it should reassess its own personnel policies. People in pivotal positions must have both the will and the skill to deal with such crises. It is unfair and a waste of good resources to send an inexperienced young talent like Buyck on such an important and complicated mission. Considering the mistakes he made—offering payment to environmental groups for consulting services and trying to gain sympathy by distancing himself from his company—I find it amazing that Buyck survived as long as he did. Vermilion would have fared far better if Buyck were backed by strong nations or, ideally, if Vermilion had educated and trained Equitanians to run this project.

This points to a weakness often found among even the largest multinationals: a lack of international management expertise amplified by an alarming degree of environmental naivete. Many companies are shocked when they encounter protests from activists who rarely forgive environmental "mishaps," especially ones caused by "foreigners." Vermilion should form an advisory board of international outside experts who will meet several times a year and will help keep the company on its toes. Vermilion should also consider appointing someone with a strong environmental background to its board of directors.

Finally, Vermilion should launch a full-scale investigation of the safety and environmental risks of all activities at all sites. Though costly, this is a doable exercise that provides a solid framework for creating action programs that reduce the risks associated with products, processes, and facilities. It enhances the organizational ability to deal with any remaining risks through environmental skill building, installing appropriate safety devices and information systems, and developing the expertise and procedures necessary for emergency management.

This operational assessment can be supported by an additional strategic focus attained through a policy impact assessment, which provides structured insight into the potential impact of new environmental policies in different countries. Contrary to popular belief, environmental policy tends to be quite predictable once one understands the underlying logic and the cultures of the players involved. By providing a window on the future, such an assessment can be a powerful tool in planning corporate strategic development.

Don't Back Down. Above all, Vermilion should not retreat from the progress it has made toward a sounder environmental policy. As Peter Ostenson points out, that would be a business mistake. It would also send a negative signal to all Vermilion employees that could erode much of the environmental groundwork the company has laid in the last five years. And it would provide further "evidence" for the environmentalists' Vermilion Action campaign and would do little good for the company's own Green Vermilion campaign.

In the long run, Vermilion will need to find new sources for its pulp supply. Forest management in the Third World can benefit both the company and its host countries. The pulp and paper industry, with its vast consumption of natural resources and its highly visible presence in consumer products and household waste, must expect increasing environmental scrutiny from the public, from policymakers—even from employees, who want to be proud of the company they work for. The environment is no longer a side issue for only governments and environmentalists to worry about. No company can permit itself to live in disharmony with the environment.

ANTHONY L. ANDERSEN *is president and CEO of H. B. Fuller, a chemical products company headquarterd in Saint Paul, Minnesota.*

Vermilion should not try to outtalk the Forest Defense Legion but should humbly build on the coalitions it has already established.

Vermilion should move forward with its plans in Equitania. As a global company with a growing need for pulp from outside the United States, it should be committed to making this test case a success. If it can't find the pulp in Equitania, it will have to find it elsewhere. And no matter where it goes, it will find conditions like those in Equitania.

Moreover, Vermilion's bad reputation will precede it. The Forest Defense Legion will see to that. Vermilion's marketing campaign to convince the public of its environmental soundness didn't cut the mustard with anybody for one simple reason: you can't just talk about doing something; you have to do it—and do it well over time.

For these reasons, Vermilion should not undertake a campaign against the FDL. The company cannot outtalk the group. Instead, it should humbly and strongly build the coalitions it has already begun. Vermilion should recognize this not as a short-term event but as part of a long-term strategic plan: the company needs pulp today and will need it tomorrow. It should move forward with these seven steps:

1. *Obtain an option to roll over the lease of the property beyond 35 years.* Go for 50 years. Go for 70, 100. The whole purpose of concern for the environment is long-term existence and balance. If Vermilion doesn't send a clear message of long-term commitment, it is not being honest with shareholders, environmental groups, or governments.

2. *Formalize the agreements with the federal government of Equitania and the provincial government of Keewa Tinang.* Establish that the terms are for the full length of the lease—that there will be no changing the rules without mutual consent. This is not an inappropriate request: Weyerhauser and other paper companies that grow their own trees have 100-year plans for the use of resources.

3. *Convince Oliver Hibbing to "make his stand."* Hibbing is going to have to make a public stand on this issue or be booed out of office by investors or the board of directors. First, he needs to acknowledge that environmentalists have an important role to play in Vermilion's long-term strategy. Until he does this, the company will always be under pressure. Furthermore, Hibbing's involvement up front, both internally and externally, could make him a hero. He could come out of this posi-

tively received by all constituencies. In that sense, this confrontation represents an opportunity for Vermilion to make progress: dramatic situations call for dramatic actions. Hibbing must commit his full support or drop the whole initiative.

4. *Encourage the FDL to meet with and join PELLONA*. This will bring U.S. environmental groups into the process of monitoring Vermilion's operations in Equitania. This will also force the FDL to put up or shut up. It is going to be either part of the problem or part of the solution; this way, the FDL is part of the solution.

5. *Hold off on any board decision until the MYP and FDL are part of the project*. In other words, be vulnerable. Vermilion should open itself up and say that it won't make a decision until these groups are part of the process. Then if the MYP and FDL drag their feet, local governmental organizations will have a stake in this issue, will worry about the loss of jobs, and so might actually pressure the groups to join the project. Moreover, Vermilion directors should be given the time to visit, observe, and make an informed decision. I would schedule the board meeting at least six months in advance so that the board perceives a real opportunity to make the right decision.

6. *Continue to build on the relationship with Maria Biwapik*. Credit her publicly for anything positive that comes along, and make it clear that Vermilion genuinely appreciates her efforts. Biwapik is taking quite a risk, and risk takers have to be encouraged.

7. *Take no action against the FDL for its newspaper ad*. Let the attack go unchallenged—no retaliatory ads or lawsuits. Don't inflame the conflict in the media: that's an impossible battle to win. Play it cool and defuse the emotion. If Vermilion challenges the FDL's claims, its past will come back to haunt the company.

Vermilion will have to get along with the environmental groups for the length of the lease. If it starts the project in a confrontational way, some people might react emotionally and make it their objective never to give Vermilion any peace.

JACQUELINE ALOISI DE LARDEREL *is director of the industry and environment office at the United Nations Environment Program in Paris. The views expressed here do not necessarily represent the policy statement of UNEP.*

Vermilion needs to start thinking about the environment as an issue that won't go away.

The public meltdown over the Equitanian project will force Vermilion to take at least one positive step: confront the fact that it has no overall environmental policy. Vermilion must stop reacting to external pressure on an ad hoc basis and begin to incorporate the environmental dimension in its long-term strategy. Until Vermilion does this, these crises will inevitably occur.

Vermilion's top management merely pays lip service to environmental concerns. Indeed, Oliver Hibbing's speeches show that the company does not value them at all. For all its hype, Vermilion has not incorporated environmental values into its decision-making process. It lacks even the most basic procedures or mechanisms to deal with environmental issues. It did not, for instance, subject the Veranko project to an environmental impact assessment—a tool that since the mid-1980s has been an effective way to assess potential environmental impacts and identify possible remedies. Nor does Vermilion value the ability to deal with environmental issues and related problems as a criterion in choosing its managers. The company provides no incentive to develop cleaner processes, while those who do take action—such as Wendell Buyck—are left without support.

Buyck's results are not as negative as they sound. He has initiated a successful dialogue with many of the partners, including the environmental groups. Yet despite his good and genuine intentions, Buyck was bound to fail without any true management support. He was unable to defend his statements picturing Vermilion as a friend of the environment because he had no credibility. He lacked the data to show both the environmental performance of Vermilion's operations in other parts of the world and the environmental impact of his project.

Buyck also failed because he doesn't have the proper skills and experience. He could have pushed the Equitrass negotiations as an opportunity to incorporate environmental principles into Vermilion's agenda. He never discussed a replantation or reforestation plan with the community, nor did he suggest organizing the training of local people in forestry. Finally, he contacted the environmental groups too late in the process.

Vermilion must start to follow through on its environmental claims. It cannot use marketing to address the environment—as it did when it launched an advertising campaign to tout the environmental investments it made only when activists began to apply pressure! As Sigvard Hoggren, a vice president of Volvo, has said, the most dangerous thing you can do is to look at your environmental ethics as a PR exercise: this won't work. The point is that it is the action that counts—not the hype. And not action merely in one plant but in the whole company.

Vermilion needs to start thinking about the environment as an issue that won't go away. It needs to assess the environmental impact of the company's products, processes, and facilities. And it needs to translate its environmental values into practice—from training employees to deciding whether to use recycled or virgin pulp.

The Veranko joint venture should not be abandoned but be rethought in the framework of this new global policy. The Veranko case can be used to show Vermilion's willingness to change its policy. I would keep Buyck in the project: he has opened the dialogue, he has a good local image, and he believes in what he is doing. What he needs is backup. Vermilion should provide someone with experience who will help Buyck take advantage of the valuable work he has already done and the solid relationships he has already built. Above all, the company should continue the important dialogues Buyck has established—even with the Forest Defense Legion.

Vermilion should not shut down the project but continue moving forward at a slower pace. This is a long-term process that requires flexibility as the company learns how to implement its policy goals. The more immediate action Vermilion needs to take is the one it should have taken at the beginning of the process: to think through just how its overall environmental policy fits within its global company strategy and then design steps to make the policy work.

JAY D. HAIR *is president of the National Wildlife Federation, a private, nonprofit conservation organization based in Washington, D.C.*

> Environmental advocates have the responsibility both to criticize negligent companies and to support exemplary ones.

Vermilion has no option but to press on with its plans. The cost of forgoing this venture goes far beyond a negative return on investment: Peter Ostenson and Wendell Buyck have provided a rare and valuable blueprint for other corporations to follow in developing environmentally sound business strategies. If this experiment fails, the corporate and environmental communities will both be worse off for it.

Vermilion's problem is one of trust. Its reputation is a result of years of insensitivity to environmental concerns and will not be easy to change. The environmental community has learned from dealing with Vermilion that caution, wariness, and a healthy dose of skepticism are good qualities to have. So how can Vermilion change its image and gain the acceptance and cooperation of environmental groups? There are four strategic steps the company can take to build on the trust established by Ostenson and Buyck:

Avoid Quick Fixes Green cheerleading without substance invites a backlash that will negate whatever environmental goodwill a company has shown. For Vermilion and other companies, justice may have no net present value, but corporate greenwash promises an equally dismal rate of return.

Implement Progressive Environmental Protection Programs Going above and beyond the call of regulatory duty is a sure way to gain the attention and respect of environmentalists. Companies will find them more willing to listen if environmental improvements are driven by culture rather than compliance.

Don't Cut Corners Buyck's meticulous efforts to involve all interest groups in the planning and development process have been instrumental in his successes so far. Community involvement and respect for cultural diversity are essential for any development game plan.

Recognize the Expanded Role of Corporations in Achieving Sustainable Economic Development Environmental protection is the tip of the social policy iceberg. Buyck was right on target in trying to involve the company in local health and education improvement programs. Sustainable development involves more than just environmental protection. If Vermilion ignores other critical social needs, the whole development effort is in danger of collapsing.

Overall, Vermilion should avoid two mistaken conclusions from this experience. First, the company may be tempted to pursue a divide-and-conquer strategy and take advantage of what it perceives to be a fragmented environmental front. This would be disastrous. There is diversity within the environmental community, just as there is diversity in any industrial trade group. But as every biologist knows, diversity is a sign of health, vitality, and strength. Environmental groups have proven their effectiveness in working together and make a formidable team. Corporations electing to manage their environmental affairs by playing interest groups off each other are destined to fail.

The other, equally erroneous conclusion would be that the effort was a waste of time and that an anticorporate bias will eventually doom any proactive measures Vermilion decides to pursue. The bottom line is that environmental groups do have responsibilities regarding their involvement with corporations. As environmental advocates, we have a responsibility to criticize companies that have been negligent in their environmental stewardship and to draw public attention to them. We also have an obligation to promote and support exemplary corporate environmental accomplishments. That means identifying positive actions a company may take to improve environmental quality and offering alternative solutions to problems when we believe the proposed options are not enough.

These principles are particularly relevant to Vermilion. The environmental community can be an important touchstone for industry in identifying issues of public concern and in establishing the trust and communication necessary for beneficial environmental practices. Nevertheless, there will always be some inherent conflict. Even if Vermilion sheds its old habits and follows a strategy of always "doing the right thing," it may face opposition from environmentalists in the future. Why? Because there will be occasions when the long-term ecological values at stake are so great that the best mitigation and contingency plans will not sufficiently address environmentalists' concerns.

Equitania, however, is not one of those situations. The clock is ticking. Oliver Hibbing should increase his visibility, take the offensive, and bring in the environmental, governmental, and public opinion leaders to participate in the development plan. He must demonstrate his personal and lasting commitment to Buyck's efforts. If the plan is as good as advertised, he will find a very receptive and helpful audience.

Bibliography

Action, H.B. *The Morals of Markets: An Ethical Exploration.* London: Longman Group Limited, 1971.

Arthur, John, and William H. Shaw, eds. *Justice and Economic Distribution.* Englewood Cliffs, N.J.: Prentice-Hall, 1978.

Attfield, Robin. *The Ethics of Environmental Concern.* New York: Columbia University Press, 1983.

Barry, Vincent, ed. *Moral Issues in Business.* Belmont, Calif.: Wadsworth Publishing Company, 1979, 1983, 1986.

Beauchamp, Tom, and Norman Bowie, eds. *Ethical Theory and Business.* Englewood Cliffs, N.J.: Prentice-Hall, 1979, 1983, 1988, 1993.

Becker, Lawrence C. and Charlotte B. Becker, eds. *Encyclopedia of Ethics.* vols. 1–2. New York & London: Garland Publishing, Inc., 1992.

Blackstone, William T., ed. *Philosophy and the Environmental Crisis.* Athens, Ga.,: University of Georgia Press, 1974.

Blackstone, William T., and Robert D. Heslep, eds. *Social Justice and Preferential Treatment.* Athens: University of Georgia Press, 1977.

Blanchard, Kenneth, and Norman Vincent Peale. *The Power of Ethical Management.* New York: William Morrow and Company, 1988.

Boatright, John R. *Ethics and the Conduct of Business.* Englewood Cliffs, N.J.: Prentice-Hall, 1993.

Bok, Sissela. *Secrets.* New York: Pantheon Books, 1983.

Bond, Kenneth M. *Bibliography of Business Ethics and Business Moral Values,* 4th ed., April, 1992. Published by Humboldt State University, Arcata, Calif. and also distributed by the Center for Business Ethics, Bentley College, Waltham, Mass.

Buchanan, Allen E. *Ethics, Efficiency and the Market.* Totowa, N.J.: Rowman & Allenheld, 1985.

Buchholz, Rogene A. *Essentials of Public Policy for Management.* Englewood Cliffs, N.J.: Prentice-Hall, 1985.

Buchholz, Rogene A. *Principles of Environmental Management: The Greening of Business.* Englewood Cliffs, N.J.: Prentice-Hall, 1993.

Buchholz, Rogene, A. *Fundamental Concepts and Problems in Business Ethics.* Englewood Cliffs, N.J.: Prentice-Hall, 1989.

Buono, Anthony F., and Larry Nichols. *Corporate Policy, Values and Social Responsibility.* New York: Praeger, 1985.

Cairncross, Frances. *Costing the Earth.* Boston, Mass.: Harvard Business School Press, 1992, 1993.

Cavanagh, Gerald F. *American Business Values,* 2d ed. Englewood Cliffs, N.J.: Prentice-Hall, 1984.

———, and Arthur F. McGovern. *Ethical Dilemmas in the Modern Corporation.* Englewood Cliffs, N.J.: Prentice-Hall, 1988.

Cohen, Marshall, Thomas Nagel, and Thomas Scanlon, eds. *Equality and Preferential Treatment.* Princeton, N.J.: Princeton University Press, 1977.

Commons, Dorman L. *Tender Offer: The Sneak Attack in Corporate Takeovers.* University of California Press, 1985.

Corporate Ethics. New York: The Conference Board. Research Report No. 900, 1987.

Corporate Ethics: A Prime Business Asset. A Report on Policy and Practice in Company Conduct. New York: The Business Roundtable, 1988.

Daniels, Norman, ed. *Reading Rawls: Critical Studies of a Theory of Justice.* New York Basic Books, 1976.

De George, Richard T. *Business Ethics.* New York: Macmillan, 1982, 1986.

De George, Richard T. *Competing with Integrity in International Business.* New York: Oxford University Press, 1993.

Des Jardins, Joseph R., and John J. McCall, *Contemporary Issues in Business.* Belmont, Calif.: Wadsworth, 1985.

Des Jardins, Joseph R. *Environmental Ethics: an Introduction to Environmental Philosophy.* Belmont, Calif.: Wadsworth, 1993.

Dickie, Robert B., and Leroy S. Rouner, eds. *Corporations and the Common Good.* Notre Dame, Ind.: University of Notre Dame Press, 1986.

Donaldson, Thomas. *Corporations and Morality.* Englewood Cliffs, N.J.: Prentice-Hall, 1982.

———, ed. *Case Studies in Business Ethics.* Englewood Cliffs, N.J.: Prentice-Hall, 1984.

———, and Patricia H. Werhane, eds. *Ethical Issues in Business: A Philosophical Approach.* Englewood Cliffs, N.J.: Prentice-Hall, 1979, 1983, 1988.

Donaldson, Thomas. *The Ethics of International Business.* New York: Oxford University Press, 1989.

Dworkin, Gerald, Gordon Bermanto, and Peter G. Brown, eds. *Markets and Morals.* Washington, D.C.: Hemisphere Publishing, 1977.

Elliot, Robert, and Arran Gare, eds. *Environmental Philosophy.* University Park, Penn.: The Pennsylvania State University Press, 1983.

Elliston, Frederick, et al. *Whistleblowing: Managing Dissent in the Workplace.* New York: Praeger, 1985.

Ezorsky, Gertrude. *Moral Rights in the Workplace.* Albany: SUNY Press, 1987.

Fairfield, Roy P., ed. *Humanizing the Workplace.* New York: Prometheus Books, 1974.

Freeman, R. Edward. *Strategic Management: A Stakeholder Approach.* Boston: Pitman, 1984.

Freeman, R. Edward, and Daniel R. Gilbert, Jr. *Corporate Strategy and the Search for Ethics.* Englewood Cliffs, N.J.: Prentice-Hall, 1988.

French, Peter. *Collective and Corporate Responsibility.* New York: Columbia University Press, 1984.

Friedman, Milton. *Capitalism and Freedom.* Chicago: University of Chicago Press, 1962.

Fullinwider, Robert K. *The Reverse Discrimination Controversy.* Totowa, N.J.: Rowman and Littlefield, 1980.

———, and Claudia Mills, eds. *The Moral Foundations of Civil Rights.* Totowa, N.J.: Rowman and Littlefield, 1986.

Galbraith, John Kenneth. *The Affluent Society.* Boston: Houghton Mifflin, 1958.

Gauthier, David. *Morals By Agreement.* New York: Oxford University Press, 1986.

Gert, Bernard. *Morality: A New Justification of the Moral Rules.* New York: Oxford University Press, 1966, 1967, 1970, 1973, 1988.

Goodpaster, K.E., and K. M. Sayre. *Ethics and Problems of the 21st Century.* Notre Dame, Ind.: University of Notre Dame, 1979.

Gross, Barry R., ed. *Reverse Discrimination.* Buffalo, N.Y.: Prometheus Books, 1977.

Hayek, F.A. *Law, Legislation and Liberty,* vols. 1–3. Chicago, Ill.: University of Chicago Press, 1976.

Held, Virginia. *Property, Profits and Economic Justice.* Belmont, Calif.: Wadsworth Publishing, 1980.

Hoffman, W. Michael, et al., eds. *Corporate Governance and Institutionalizing Ethics.* Lexington, Mass.: Lexington Books, 1983.

Hoffman, W. Michael, et al., eds. *Business Ethics and the Environment: The Public Policy Debate.* New York: Quorum Books, 1990.

Hoffman, W. Michael, et al., eds. *The Corporation, Ethics and the Environment.* New York: Quorum Books, 1990.

Jackall, Robert. *Moral Mazes.* New York: Random House, 1986.

Jones, Donald G., ed. *Doing Ethics in Business.* Cambridge, Mass.: Oelgeschlager, Gunn & Hain, 1982.

Kipnis, Kenneth, and Diana T. Meyers. *Economic Justice.* Totowa, N.J.: Rowman & Allenheld, 1985.

Ladd, John. "Morality and the Ideal of Rationality in Formal Organizations." *Monist,* vol. 54, 1970, pp. 489–499.

Levitt, Theodore. "The Dangers of Corporate Social Responsibility." *Harvard Business Review,* September–October, 1958, pp. 41–50.

Linowes, David F. *The Corporate Conscience.* New York: Hawthorne Books, 1974.

Lodge, George C. *The New American Ideology.* New York: Alfred A. Knopf, 1979.

Lowrance, William W. *Of Acceptable Risk.* Los Altos, Calif.: William Kaufman, Inc. 1976.

MacIntyre, Alasdair. *After Virtue: A Study in Moral Theory.* Notre Dame, Ind.: University of Notre Dame Press, 1981.

May, Larry. *The Morality of Groups.* Notre Dame, Ind.: University of Notre Dame Press, 1987.

Mishan, E.J. *The Economic Growth Debate.* London: George Allen & Unwin, 1977.

Nader, Ralph, Mark Green, and Joel Seligman. *Taming the Giant Corporation.* New York: W.W. Norton, 1976.

Nelkin, Dorothy, and Michael S. Brown. *Workers at Risk: Voices from the Workplace.* Chicago: University of Chicago Press, 1984.

Novak, Michael. *The Spirit of Democratic Capitalism.* New York: Simon & Schuster, 1982.

Nozick, Robert. *Anarchy, State and Utopia.* New York: Basic Books, 1974.

Pastin, Mark. *The Hard Problems of Management: Gaining the Ethics Edge.* San Francisco: Jossey-Bass, 1986.

Paul, Jeffrey, ed. *Reading Nozick: Essays on Anarchy, State and Utopia.* Totowa, N.J.: Rowman & Allenheld, 1981.

Peters, Thomas J., and Robert H. Waterman, Jr. *In Search of Excellence: Lessons from America's Best-Run Companies.* New York: Harper and Row, 1982.

Phelps, E.S. *Altruism, Morality and Economic Theory.* New York: Russell Sage, 1975.

Posner, Richard A. *The Economics of Justice,* 2d ed. Cambridge, Mass.: Harvard University Press, 1983.

Preston, Ivan L. *The Great American Blow-Up: Puffery in Advertising and Selling.* Madison, Wisc.: The University of Wisconsin Press, 1975.

Rachels, James. *The Elements of Moral Philosophy.* New York: McGraw-Hill, 1986.

Rawls, John. *A Theory of Justice.* New York: Bobbs-Merrill, 1966.

Regan, Tom, ed. *Earthbound: New Introductory Essays in Environmental Ethics.* New York: Random House, 1984.

Sagoff, Mark. *The Economy of the Earth.* London: Cambridge University Press, 1988.

Scherer, Donald, and Thomas Attig, eds. *Ethics and the Environment.* Englewood Cliffs, N.J.: Prentice-Hall, 1983.

Schudson, Michael. *Advertising, the Uneasy Persuasion.* New York: Basic Books, 1984.

Schwartz, Barry. *The Battle for Human Nature.* New York: W.W. Norton & Company, 1986.

Singer, Peter, ed. *A Companion to Ethics.* London: Blackwell, 1991.

Stone, Christopher D. *Should Trees Have Standing?* Los Altos, Calif.: William Kaufman, Inc., 1972.

Stone, Christopher D. *Where the Law Ends: The Social Control of Corporate Behavior.* New York: Harper & Row, 1975.

Tavis, Lee, ed. *Multinational Managers and Poverty in the Third World.* Notre Dame, Ind.: Notre Dame University Press, 1982.

Terkel, Studs. *Working.* New York: Pantheon Books, 1974.

Tuleja, Tad. *Beyond the Bottom Line.* New York: Penguin Books, 1985.

VanDeVeer, Donald, and Christine Pierce, eds. *People, Penguins, and Plastic Trees: Basic Issues in Environmental Ethics.* Belmont, Calif.: Wadsworth, 1986.

Walzer, Michael. *Spheres of Justice: A Defense of Pluralism and Equality.* New York: Basic Books, 1983.

Weidenbaum, Murray. *Strengthening the Corporate Board.* St. Louis: Washington University, Center for Study of American Business, 1985.

White, Thomas I. *Business Ethics.* New York: Macmillan, 1993.

Zimmerman, Michael E., et al., eds. *Environmental Philosophy: From Animal Rights to Radical Ecology.* Englewood Cliffs, N.J.: Prentice-Hall, 1993.